The Cambridge Handbook of Multimedia Learning

During the past 10 years, the field of multimedia learning has emerged as a coherent discipline with an accumulated research base that has never been synthesized and organized in a handbook. *The Cambridge Handbook of Multimedia Learning* constitutes the world's first handbook devoted to comprehensive coverage of research and theory in the field of multimedia learning. Multimedia learning is defined as learning from words (e.g., spoken or printed text) and pictures (e.g., illustrations, photos, maps, graphs, animation, or video). The focus of this handbook is on how people learn from words and pictures in computer-based environments. Multimedia environments include online instructional presentations, interactive lessons, e-courses, simulation games, virtual reality, and computer-supported in-class presentations. *The Cambridge Handbook of Multimedia Learning* seeks to establish what works (i.e., to determine which features of a multimedia lesson affect learning), to explain how it works (i.e., to ground research in cognitive theory), and to consider when and where it works (i.e., to explore the implications of research for practice).

Richard E. Mayer is Professor of Psychology at the University of California, Santa Barbara, where he has served since 1975. In 2000, he received the E. L. Thorndike Award for career achievement in educational psychology. He is the author or editor of 20 books and more than 250 articles and chapters, including *Multimedia Learning* (2001), *e-Learning and the Science of Instruction* (2003) with Ruth Clark, and *Learning and Instruction* (2003).

The Cambridge Handbook of Multimedia Learning

Edited by

Richard E. Mayer

University of California, Santa Barbara

CAMBRIDGE UNIVERSITY PRESS
Cambridge, New York, Melbourne, Madrid, Cape Town, Singapore, São Paulo

Cambridge University Press
40 West 20th Street, New York, NY 10011-4211, USA

www.cambridge.org
Information on this title: www.cambridge.org/9780521838733

First published 2005

Printed in the United States of America

A catalog record for this publication is available from the British Library.

Library of Congress Cataloging in Publication Data

The Cambridge handbook of multimedia learning / edited by Richard E. Mayer.
　　p.　cm.
Includes bibliographical references and index.
ISBN 0-521-83873-8 (hardback) – ISBN 0-521-54751-2 (pbk.)
1. Computer-assisted instruction – Handbooks, manuals, etc.　2. Audio-visual
education – Handbooks, manuals, etc.　3. Interactive multimedia – Handbooks,
manuals, etc.　I. Mayer, Richard E., 1947–　II. Title.
LB1028.5.C283　2005
371.33′4 – dc22　　　　　　　　　　　　　　　　　　　2005001322

ISBN-13　978-0-521-83873-3 hardback
ISBN-10　0-521-83873-8 hardback

ISBN-13　978-0-521-54751-2 paperback
ISBN-10　0-521-54751-2 paperback

Contents

PART IV

MULTIMEDIA LEARNING IN CONTENT AREAS

Preface

During the past 10 years, the field of multimedia learning has emerged as a coherent discipline with an accumulated research base that has never been synthesized and organized in a handbook. *The Cambridge Handbook of Multimedia Learning* constitutes the world's first handbook devoted to comprehensive coverage of research and theory in the field of multimedia learning. For purposes of the *Handbook*, multimedia learning is defined as learning from words (e.g., spoken or printed text) and pictures (e.g., illustrations, photos, maps, graphs, animation, or video). The focus of the *Handbook* is on how people learn from words and pictures in computer-based environments. Multimedia environments include online instructional presentations, interactive lessons, e-courses, simulation games, virtual reality, and computer-supported in-class presentations. Overall, the *Handbook* seeks to establish what works (i.e., to determine which features of a multimedia lesson affect learning), to explain how it works (i.e., to ground research in cognitive theory), and to consider when and where it works (i.e., to explore the implications of research for practice).

What distinguishes this book from edited books on distance learning or Web-based instruction is our commitment to taking a scientific, evidence-based approach. My goal as editor is to provide a comprehensive and focused overview of the state of scientific research on multimedia learning. Each chapter is based on empirical research and grounded in cognitive theory, rather than offering unsubstantiated recommendations, describing best practices, or summarizing software development accomplishments. As the first comprehensive research-based handbook on multimedia learning, *The Cambridge Handbook of Multimedia Learning* is intended to define and shape the field for years to come.

There are many books providing advice on how to design multimedia-learning environments, but these books are largely based on the practical experience and wisdom of the authors. Similarly, there are books reporting on the development of online instructional programs and Web sites, but these reports of development efforts are generally based on best practices and informal case studies. Until recently, the lack of scientific research evidence in many multimedia-learning books could be justi-fied on the grounds that a solid research base did not yet exist. However, the quantity and quality of scientific research – conducted by researchers around the world – has reached a level warranting the field's first comprehensive research-based handbook of multimedia learning.

As editor, I asked the world's leading multimedia researchers to author chapters in areas in which they have contributed to the empirical research base. In particular, I sought authors who are leading researchers in the field of multimedia learning – that is, those with the strongest records of research publication. Because the field is largely international, the chapter authors for the *Handbook* span the globe. Each chapter author had a specific charge – that is, directions to review a well-defined subarea such as the role of online worked-out examples or the role of speech versus on-screen text. The chapters in each section follow the same general structure: describing the major research issue or question, providing examples of the research issue or question, summarizing research in which measures of learning are the central focus, critiquing the research, and discussing implications for theory and practice.

The *Handbook* consists of 35 chapters organized into five parts. Each chapter focuses on a particular theory of multimedia learning (part 1), a basic principle of multimedia learning (part 2), an advanced principle of multimedia learning (part 3), multimedia learning in a content area (part 4), or multimedia learning within an advanced computer-based context (part 5). In order to provide a common structure among the chapters of the *Handbook*, I asked authors to organize their chapters around a common set of issues. In particular, I asked the authors of the theory chapters in part 1 to provide a concise description of the theory or model with concrete examples, to summarize the theory's contributions to cognitive theory (i.e., to specify predictions that have been tested), to summarize the theory's contributions to instructional design (i.e., to specify recommendations for instruction), to

describe any limitations of the theory, and to suggest future directions for research. I asked the authors of each of the other chapters to provide a clear definition and example of the central principle or topic of the chapter, to review the relevant published research literature in sufficient detail, to assess the limitations of the research base, to summarize the implications for cognitive theory and instructional design, and to suggest directions for future research.

I solicited chapters that were concise (i.e., containing no more than 25 double-spaced pages), focused (i.e., reviewing the research on a specified topic), well-referenced (i.e., containing a rich set of relevant references), evidence-based (i.e., providing an up-to-date review of the best empirical evidence), theory-based (i.e., relating the findings to testable predictions of theories when appropriate), and educationally relevant (i.e., drawing implications for educational practice when appropriate). In order to minimize confusion, I asked authors to clearly define jargon terms in the text as well as in a glossary at the end of the chapter. Each chapter was reviewed and revised.

The intended audience includes anyone interested in how people learn from words and pictures in computer-based environments. Although this handbook summarizes the research base in multimedia learning, it is intended to be accessible to a general audience. On one hand, this handbook is designed to support readers with practical interests in how to design or select multimedia learning environments that promote learning. On the other hand, this handbook is designed to support readers who have academic interests in conducting or evaluating research in multimedia learning. The *Handbook* would be appropriate for courses related to cognitive science, educational psychology, instructional design, human factors, multimedia arts and technology, professional training, and interface design. It also would be useful for instructors interested in designing or improving multimedia lessons in school settings, job training contexts, and informal environments. In short, *The Cambridge Handbook of Multimedia Learning* belongs on the bookshelf of anyone who is interested in an evidence-based approach to Web-based learning, e-learning, hypermedia, multimedia, Web site design, distance learning, instructional technology, human–computer interaction, virtual environments, or applied cognitive psychology.

As editor, I have tried to ensure that this handbook reflects the values that I think are important for our field. In particular, I sought to produce a handbook that is:

research based – The Handbook is intended to summarize the empirical research on multimedia learning, rather than describe untested best practices or software development projects. Although I have much respect for the craft knowledge of practitioners and designers, it is important to know if recommendations are supported by scientific evidence and under what conditions they are supported. Thus, I value a focus on scientific evidence as the key to progress in our field.

theory grounded – The Handbook is intended to relate empirical research to cognitive theories of how people learn. My overriding premise is that multimedia learning environments should be designed in ways that are consistent with what is known about how people learn.

educationally relevant – The Handbook focuses on issues that are relevant to education, that is, to helping people learn. Thus, I sought chapters that offer research-based implications for instructional design.

comprehensive – The Handbook offers a broad view of the field, including contributions from multimedia researchers around the world. I value the perspectives of researchers who have devoted so much of their energy to understanding multimedia learning.

timely – The Handbook offers an up-to-date overview of the field. I value timeliness because the scientific study of multimedia learning is maturing at a rapid pace, and so are the practical demands for building multimedia learning environments – ranging from e-courses to in-class simulations.

readable – In my role as editor I have tried to ensure that the chapters are clear and concise, with key terms defined and concrete examples provided. In a multidisciplinary field such as this one, it is important that the chapters communicate what is known in a way that general readers can appreciate.

In short, my values have motivated me to seek chapters that are based on empirical research and grounded in cognitive theory rather than chapters that mainly describe development efforts or best practices.

Editing this book has been a treat for me, because I could commission chapters from the best researchers in the field and be the first to learn what they had to say. I am pleased to share the fruits of this enterprise with you in a timely fashion. My hope is that you enjoy reading this handbook as much as I have enjoyed editing it. I will consider this handbook to be a success if it helps you to understand what is known about how people learn from words and pictures; gives you useful help in building or selecting effective multimedia learning environments; or encourages you to produce or investigate research that contributes to cognitive theory and educational practice. I hope that you will feel free to contact me at mayer@psych.ucsb.edu to share your comments about The Cambridge Handbook of Multimedia Learning.

Acknowledgments

Although my name is listed as the editor, this handbook depended on the contributions of many people. In particular, I thank the authors for producing excellent chapters, for keeping this project on schedule, and for responding so well to the reviewer's comments. I thank the members of the handbook's editorial board – John Sweller, Jeroen van Merriënboer, and

Wolfgang Schnotz – for their useful service to this project. I also wish to thank Philip Laughlin and the staff of Cambridge University Press for their many contributions to making this book a success. I am grateful to my many research collaborators who have worked with me over the years in the study of multimedia learning, including Richard B. Anderson, Robert Atkinson, Julie Campbell, Paul Chandler, Dorothy Chun, Gayle Dow, Joan Gallini, Shannon Harp, Julie Heiser, James Lester, Steven Lonn, Patricia Mautone, Sarah Mayer, Roxana Moreno, Harold O'Neil, Jr., Jan Plass, Hiller Spires, and Valerie Sims. I appreciate my home institution – the University of California, Santa Barbara – and numerous funding agencies – including the National Science Foundation, the Office of Naval Research, and the Andrew Mellon Foundation – that have supported my research on multimedia learning. Finally, my deepest appreciation goes to my wife, Beverly; my children, Ken, David, and Sarah; and to the memory of my parents, James and Bernis Mayer.

Richard E. Mayer
Santa Barbara, California

Contributors

Editor

RICHARD E. MAYER
Department of Psychology
University of California
Santa Barbara, CA 93106-9660
USA
mayer@psych.ucsb.edu

Editorial Board

JEROEN J. G. VAN MERRIËNBOER
Educational Psychology Expertise
  Center
Open University of the Netherlands
P.O. Box 2960
NL-6401 DL Heerlen
The Netherlands
Jeroen.vanMerrienboer@ou.nl

WOLFGANG SCHNOTZ
Faculty of Psychology
University of Koblenz-Landau
Thomas-Nast-Str. 44
D-76829 Landau
Germany
schnotz@uni-landau.de

JOHN SWELLER
School of Education
University of New South Wales
Sydney, NSW 2052
Australia
j.sweller@unsw.edu.au

Chapter Contributors

IVAN K. ASH
Department of Psychology
1007 W. Harrison Street
University of Illinois at Chicago
Chicago, IL 60607
USA
iash1@uic.edu

ROBERT K. ATKINSON
Psychology in Education
Arizona State University
Tempe, AZ 85287
USA
Robert.Atkinson@asu.edu

PAUL AYRES
School of Education
University of New South Wales
Sydney, NSW 2052
Australia
p.ayres@unsw.edu.au

MIREILLE BETRANCOURT
TECFA
Department of Psychology and Education
University of Geneva
CH 1211 Geneve 4
Switzerland
Mireille.Betrancourt@tecfa.unige.ch

MICHELENE T. H. CHI
Learning Research and Development Center
3939 O'Hara Street
University of Pittsburgh
Pittsburgh, PA 15260
USA
chi@pitt.edu

RICHARD E. CLARK
Rossier School of Education
University of Southern California
WPH 601C
Los Angeles, CA 90089-0031
USA
clark@usc.edu

RUTH COLVIN CLARK
Ruth Clark Training and Consulting
1423 E. Main Street #193
Cortez, CO 81321
USA
Ruth@Clarktraining.com

SUE COBB
Virtual Reality Applications Research Team
University of Nottingham
University Park
Nottingham, NG7 2RD
United Kingdom
sue.cobb@nottingham.ac.uk

ANDREW DILLON
School of Information
SZB 564
1 University Station, D700
University of Texas
Austin, TX 78712
USA
adillon@ischool.utexas.edu

DAVID F. FELDON
Graduate School of Education and Information
    Sciences
University of California, Los Angeles
Los Angeles, CA 90095-1521
USA
feldon@gseis.ucla.edu

J. D. FLETCHER
Institute for Defense Analysis
4850 Mark Center Drive
Alexandria, VA 22311
USA
fletcher@ida.org

DANAË STANTON FRASER
Department of Psychology
University of Bath
Bath, BA2 7AY
United Kingdom
D.StantonFraser@bath.ac.uk

MARY HEGARTY
Department of Psychology
University of California
Santa Barbara, CA 93106-9660
USA
hegarty@psych.ucsb.edu

JENNIFER JOBST
School of Information
SZB 564
1 University Station, D700
University of Texas
Austin, TX 78712
USA
jenj@mail.utexas.edu

DAVID H. JONASSEN
School of Information Science and Learning
    Technologies
221C Townsend Hall
University of Missouri
Columbia, MO 65211
USA
jonassen@missouri.edu

LINDA C. JONES
University of Arkansas
Department of Foreign Languages
Kimpel Hall 425
Fayetteville, AR 72701
USA
lcxjones@uark.edu

TON DE JONG
Faculty of Behavioral Sciences
University of Twente
P.O. Box 217
7500 AE Enschede
The Netherlands
jong@edte.utwente.nl

SLAVA KALYUGA
Educational Assessment Australia
University of New South Wales
12-22 Rothschild Avenue
Rosebery 2018
Australia
S.Kalyuga@eaa.unsw.edu.au

LIESBETH KESTER
Educational Technology Expertise Center
Open University of the Netherlands
P.O. Box 2960
NL-6401 DL Heerlen
The Netherlands
Liesbeth.Kester@ou.nl

ROBERT KOZMA
Center for Technology in Learning
SRI International
333 Ravenswood Avenue
Menlo Park, CA 94025
USA
robertkozma@sri.com

JAMES LAFFEY
School of Information Science and Learning
    Technologies
221L Townsend Hall
University of Missouri
Columbia, MO 65211
USA
laffeyj@missouri.edu

SUSANNE P. LAJOIE
Department of Educational and Counseling
    Psychology
McGill University
3700 McTavish Street
Montreal, Quebec
Canada H3A IT2
Susanne.lajoie@mcgill.ca

CHWEE BENG LEE
School of Information Science and Learning
    Technologies
111 London Hall
University of Missouri
Columbia, MO 65211
USA
cuimin@signet.com.sg

RENAE LOW
School of Education
University of New South Wales
Sydney, NSW 2052
Australia
r.low@unsw.edu.au

RICHARD K. LOWE
Department of Education
Curtin University of Technology
G.P.O. Box U1987
Perth, Western Australia 6845
Australia
r.k.lowe@curtin.edu.au

RICHARD E. MAYER
Department of Psychology
University of California
Santa Barbara, CA 93106-9660
USA
mayer@psych.ucsb.edu

ROXANA MORENO
Educational Psychology Program
Simpson Hall, Room 123
University of New Mexico
Albuquerque, NM 87131-1246
USA
moreno@unm.edu

CARLOS NAKAMURA
Department of Educational and Counseling
    Psychology
McGill University
3700 McTavish Street
Montreal, Quebec
Canada H34 IT2
Carlos.nakamura@mail.mcgill.ac

FRED PAAS
Educational Psychology Expertise
    Center
Open University of the Netherlands
P. O. Box 2960
6401 DL Heerlen
Heerlen
The Netherlands
Fred.Paas@ou.nl

JAN PLASS
The Steinhart School of Education
New York University
East Building, 239 Greene Street, #308
New York, NY 10003
USA
jan.plass@nyu.edu

HERVÉ POTELLE
University of Poitiers
Laboratoire Langage et Cognition FRE
    CNRS 2725
99 Avenue du Recteur Pineau
86022 Poitiers
France
herve.potelle@univ-pointiers.fr

DAVID REINKING
Eugene T. Moore School of Education
Clemson University
418 Tillman Hall
Clemson, SC 29634
USA
reinking@clemson.edu

ALEXANDER RENKL
University of Freiburg
Psychological Institute
Educational Psychology
Engelbergerstr. 41
D-79085 Freiburg
Germany
renkl@psychologie.uni-freiburg.de

LLOYD P. RIEBER
Department of Educational Psychology and
    Instructional Technology
603C Aderhold Hall
University of Georgia
Athens, GA 30602-7144
USA
lrieber@coe.uga.edu

JEAN-FRANCOIS ROUET
University of Poitiers
Laboratoire Langage et Cognition FRE
    CNRS 2725
99 Avenue du Recteur Pineau
86022 Poitiers
France
jean-francois.rouet@univ-poitiers.fr

MARGUERITE ROY
Learning Research and Development Center
3939 O'Hara Street
University of Pittsburgh
Pittsburgh, PA 15260
USA
mar982@pitt.edu

JOEL RUSSELL
Department of Chemistry
Oakland University
Rochester, MI 48309
USA
russell@oakland.edu

WOLFGANG SCHNOTZ
Faculty of Psychology
University of Koblenz-Landau
Thomas-Nast-Str. 44
D-76829 Landau
Germany
schnotz@uni-landau.de

AMY M. SHAPIRO
Department of Psychology
285 Old Westport Road
University of Massachusetts, Dartmouth
N. Dartmouth, MA 02747
USA
ashapiro@umassd.edu

JOHN SWELLER
School of Education
University of New South Wales
Sydney, NSW 2052
Australia
j.sweller@unsw.edu.au

HUIB K. TABBERS
Institute of Psychology
Erasmus University, Rotterdam
P. O. Box 1738
3000 DR Rotterdam
The Netherlands
tabbers@fsw.eur.nl

SIGMUND TOBIAS
Teachers College
Columbia University
New York, NY 10027-6696
USA
Stobi@aol.com

PASCAL W. M. VAN GERVEN
Faculty of Psychology
Department of Neurocognition
Maastricht University
P. O. Box 616
6200 MD Maastricht
The Netherlands
p.vangerven@psychology.unimaas.nl

JEROEN J. G. VAN MERRIËNBOER
Educational Psychology Expertise Center
Open University of the Netherlands
P.O. Box 2960
NL-6401 DL Heerlen
The Netherlands
Jeroen.vanMerrienboer@ou.nl

JENNIFER WILEY
Department of Psychology
1007 W. Harrison Street
University of Illinois at Chicago
Chicago, IL 60607
USA
jwiley@uic.edu

CHIA-CHI YANG
School of Information Science and Learning
    Technologies
111 London Hall
University of Missouri
Columbia, MO 65211
USA
cymp8@mizzou.edu

CHAPTER 1

Introduction to Multimedia Learning

Richard E. Mayer

University of California, Santa Barbara

Abstract

People can learn more deeply from words and pictures than from words alone. This seemingly simple proposition – which can be called the multimedia learning hypothesis – is the main focus of *The Cambridge Handbook of Multimedia Learning*[1]. Each of the 35 chapters in this handbook examines an aspect of the multimedia learning hypothesis. In particular, multimedia researchers are interested in how people learn from words and pictures, and in how to design multimedia learning environments that promote learning. In this chapter, I provide a definition of multimedia learning, offer a rationale for multimedia learning, outline the research base for multimedia learning, and draw distinctions between two approaches to multimedia design, three metaphors of multimedia learning, three kinds of multimedia learning outcomes, and two kinds of active learning.

What Is Multimedia Learning?

Table 1.1 summarizes definitions of multimedia, multimedia learning, and multimedia instruction.

Multimedia

The term *multimedia* conjures up a variety of meanings. You might think of sitting in a room where images are presented on one or more screens and music or other sounds are presented using speakers – that is, multimedia as a "live" performance. Alternatively, you might think of sitting in front of a computer screen that presents graphics on the screen along with spoken words from the computer's speakers – that is, multimedia as an online lesson. Other possibilities include watching a video on a television screen while listening to the corresponding words, music, and sounds, or watching a PowerPoint

Table 1.1. Definitions

Term	Definition
Multimedia	Presenting words (such as printed text or spoken text) and pictures (such as illustrations, photos, animation, or video)
Multimedia learning	Building mental representations from words and pictures
Multimedia instruction	Presenting words and pictures that are intended to promote learning

presentation along with listening to the speaker's corresponding commentary. Low-tech examples of multimedia include a "chalk-and-talk" presentation where a speaker draws or writes on a blackboard (or uses an overhead projector) while presenting a lecture, or a textbook lesson consisting of printed text and illustrations.

I define *multimedia* as presenting both words (such as spoken text or printed text) and pictures (such as illustrations, photos, animation, or video). By words, I mean that the material is presented in *verbal form*, such as using printed text or spoken text. By pictures, I mean that the material is presented in *pictorial form*, such as using static graphics, including illustrations, graphs, diagrams, maps, or photos, or using dynamic graphics, including animation or video. This definition is broad enough to include all of the scenarios I described in the previous paragraph – ranging from multimedia encyclopedias to online educational games to textbooks. For example, in a multimedia encyclopedia, words may be presented as narration, and pictures may be presented as animation. In a textbook, words may be presented as printed text and pictures may be presented as illustrations.

If multimedia involves presenting material in two or more forms, then an important issue concerns how to characterize a form of presentation. Three solutions to this problem are the delivery media view, the presentation modes view, and the sensory modalities view. According to the delivery media

view, multimedia requires two or more delivery devices, such as computer screen and amplified speakers or a projector and a lecturer's voice. According to the presentation modes view, multimedia requires verbal and pictorial representations, such as on-screen text and animation or printed text and illustrations. According to the sensory modalities view, multimedia requires auditory and visual senses, such as narration and animation or lecture and slides.

I reject the delivery media view because it focuses on the technology rather than on the learner. Instead, I opt for the presentation modes view, and to some extent the sensory modalities view. The presentation modes view allows for a clear definition of multimedia – presenting material in verbal and pictorial form – and is commonly used by multimedia researchers (Mayer, 2001a). The presentation modes view is also the basis for Paivio's (1986) dual-code theory as well theories of multimedia learning presented in this handbook (Mayer, chapter 3; Schnotz, chapter 4; Sweller, chapter 2; van Merriënboer & Kester, chapter 5). The sensory modalities view is also relevant because words can be presented as printed text (initially processed visually) or as spoken text (initially processed auditorily), whereas pictures are processed visually. In conclusion, as shown in Table 1.1, multimedia refers to using words and pictures.

Multimedia Learning

Multimedia learning occurs when people build mental representations from words (such as spoken text or printed text) and pictures (such as illustrations, photos, animation, or video). As you can see in this definition, *multimedia* refers to the presentation of words and pictures, whereas *learning* refers to the learner's construction of knowledge. The process by which people build mental representations from words and pictures is the focus of Mayer's cognitive theory of multimedia learning (Mayer, chapter 3), Sweller's cognitive load theory (Sweller, chapter 2), and Schnotz's integrative model of text and picture comprehension (Schnotz, chapter 4).

Multimedia Instruction

Multimedia instruction (or a multimedia learning environment) involves presenting words and pictures that are intended to promote learning. In short, multimedia instruction refers to designing multimedia presentations in ways that help people build mental representations. The instructional design principles described in parts 2 and 3 of this handbook suggest ways of creating multimedia presentations intended to promote multimedia learning.

What Is the Rationale for Multimedia Learning?

What is the value of adding pictures to words? Do students learn more deeply from words and pictures than from words alone? These questions are essential to the study of multimedia learning. For example, suppose I asked you to listen to a short explanation of how a bicycle tire pump works: "When the handle is pulled up, the piston moves up, the inlet valve opens, the outlet valve closes, and air enters the lower part of the cylinder. When the handle is pushed down, the piston moves down, the inlet valve closes, the outlet valve opens, and air moves out through the hose." Then, I ask you to write down an explanation of how a bicycle tire pump works (i.e., retention test) and to write answers to problem-solving questions such as "Suppose you push down and pull up the handle of a pump several times but no air comes out. What could have gone wrong?" (i.e., transfer test). If you are like most of the students in our research studies (Mayer & Anderson, 1991, 1992), you remembered some of the words in the presentation (i.e., you did moderately well on retention) but you had difficulty in using the material to answer problem-solving questions (i.e., you did poorly on transfer).

In contrast, suppose I showed you an animation of a bicycle tire pump that depicts the actions in the pump as the handle is pulled up and then as the handle is pushed down. Frames from the animation are shown in Figure 1.1. If you are like most students in our research studies (Mayer & Anderson, 1991, 1992), you would not do well on a retention test or on a transfer test.

Finally, consider the narrated animation summarized in Figure 1.2. In this situation, you hear the steps described in words and see the steps depicted in the animation. When words and pictures are presented together as in a narrated animation, students perform well both on retention and transfer tests (Mayer & Anderson, 1991, 1992). In particular, when we focus on tests of problem-solving transfer – which are designed to measure the student's understanding of the presented material – students perform much better with words and pictures than from words alone. My colleagues and I found this pattern in nine out of nine studies, yielding a median effect size of 1.50 (Mayer, 2001a). I refer to this finding as the *multimedia principle* and it is examined in detail by Fletcher and Tobias in chapter 7.

The multimedia principle epitomizes the rationale for studying multimedia learning. There is reason to believe that – under certain circumstances – people learn more deeply from words and pictures than from words alone. For hundreds of years, the major format for instruction has been words – including lectures and books. In general, verbal modes of presentation have dominated the way we convey ideas to one another and verbal learning has dominated education. Similarly, verbal learning has been the major focus of educational research.

With the recent advent in powerful computer graphics and visualization technologies, instructors have the ability to supplement verbal modes of instruction with pictorial modes of instruction. Advances in computer technology have enabled an explosion in the availability of visual ways of presenting material, including large libraries of static images as well as compelling dynamic images in the form of animations and video. In light of the power of computer graphics, it may be useful to ask whether

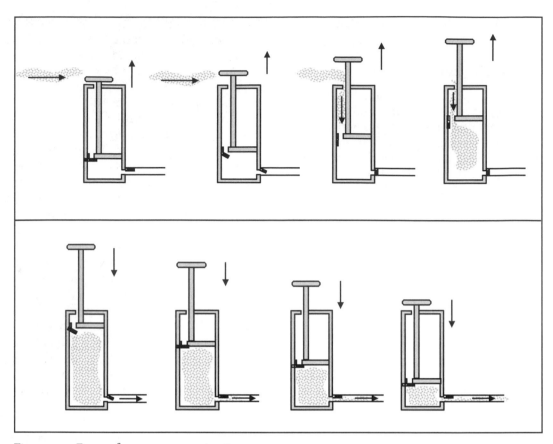

Figure 1.1. Frames from a pumps animation.

it is time to expand instructional messages beyond the purely verbal. What are the consequences of adding pictures to words? What happens when instructional messages involve both verbal and visual modes of learning? What affects the way that people learn from words and pictures? In short, how can multimedia presentations foster meaningful learning? These are the kinds of questions addressed in this handbook.

The case for multimedia is based on the idea that instructional messages should be designed in light of how the human mind works. Let's assume that humans have two information-processing systems – one for verbal material and one for visual material, as described more fully in part 1 of this handbook. Let's also acknowledge that the major format for presenting instructional material is verbal. The rationale for multimedia presentations – that is, presenting material in words and pictures – is that it takes advan-

tage of the full capacity of humans for processing information. When we present material only in the verbal mode, we are ignoring the potential contribution of our capacity to also process material in the visual mode.

Why might two channels be better than one? Two possible explanations are the quantitative rationale and the qualitative rationale. The quantitative rationale is that more material can be presented on two channels than on one channel – just like more traffic can travel over two lanes than one lane. In the case of explaining how a bicycle tire pump works, for example, the steps in the process can be presented in words or can be depicted in illustrations. Presenting both is like presenting the material twice – giving the learner twice as much exposure to the explanation. While the quantitative rationale makes sense as far as it goes, I reject it mainly because it is incomplete. In particular, I am concerned about the assumption

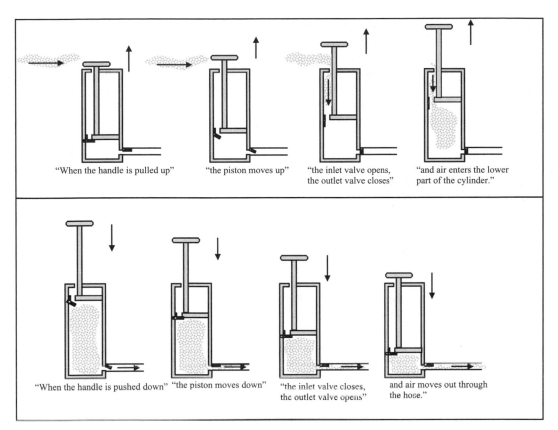

Figure 1.2. Frames from a pumps animation with corresponding narration.

that the verbal and visual channels are equivalent, that is, that words and pictures are simply two equivalent ways for presenting the same material.

In contrast, the qualitative rationale is that words and pictures, while qualitatively different, can complement one another and that human understanding is enhanced when learners are able to mentally integrate visual and verbal representations. As you can see, the qualitative rationale assumes that the two channels are not equivalent. Words are useful for presenting certain kinds of material – perhaps representations that are more abstract and require more effort to translate, whereas pictures are more useful for presenting other kinds of material – perhaps more intuitive, more natural representations. In short, one picture is not necessarily equivalent to 1,000 words (or any number of words).

The most intriguing aspect of the qualitative rationale is that understanding occurs when learners are able to build meaningful connections between visual and verbal representations – such as being able to see how the words "the inlet valve opens" relate to the forward motion of the inlet valve in the cylinder of the pump. In the process of trying to build connections between words and pictures, learners are able to create a deeper understanding than from words or pictures alone. This idea is at the heart of the theories of multimedia learning described in part 1 of this handbook.

In summary, the rationale for the study of multimedia learning is that students may learn more deeply from words and pictures than from words alone. Thus, the motivation for this handbook is to explore the proposal that adding pictures to words may be a way of helping people understand better than by simply presenting words alone. However, not all pictures are equally effective. It is important to understand how best to incorporate pictures with words.

Just because technologies are available that allow for state-of-the-art visualizations, this does not mean that instructors are well advised to use them. What is needed is a research-based understanding of how people learn from words and pictures and how to design multimedia instruction that promotes learning.

What Is the Research Base for Multimedia Learning?

Although research on verbal learning has a long and fruitful history in psychology and education, corresponding research on multimedia learning is just beginning to flourish. The *Cambridge Handbook of Multimedia Learning* is the world's first comprehensive summary of research on multimedia learning. In an attempt to organize the research base in multimedia learning, this handbook is divided into five parts.

Part 1: Theoretical Foundations contains chapters that describe the theories of multimedia learning that have had the greatest impact on research: Sweller's cognitive load theory (CLT) (chapter 2), Mayer's cognitive theory of multimedia learning (CTML) (chapter 3), Schnotz's integrative model of text and picture comprehension (chapter 4), and van Merriënboer and Kester's four-component instructional design (4C-ID) model for multimedia learning (chapter 5).

Part 2: Basic Principles of Multimedia Learning begins with a chapter documenting mistaken principles of multimedia learning, that is, principles that are commonly accepted but for which supporting evidence is lacking (Clark & Feldon, chapter 6) The remaining chapters explore the research evidence concerning basic principles for how to design multimedia learning environments:

multimedia principle – People learn better from words and pictures than from words alone (Fletcher & Tobias, chapter 7).

split-attention principle – People learn better when words and pictures are phys-

ically and temporally integrated (Ayres & Sweller, chapter 8). This is similar to Mayer's (chapter 12) spatial contiguity and temporal contiguity principles.

modality principle – People learn better from graphics and narration than graphics and printed text (Low & Sweller, chapter 9). This is similar to Mayer's modality principle (chapter 11).

redundancy principle – People learn better when the same information is not presented in more than one format (Sweller, chapter 10). This is similar to Mayer's redundancy principle (chapter 12).

segmenting, pretraining, and modality principles – People learn better when a multimedia message is presented in learned-paced segments rather than as a continuous unit, people learn better from a multimedia message when they know the names and characteristics of the main concepts, and people learn better from a multimedia message when the words are spoken rather than written (Mayer, chapter 11).

coherence, signaling, spatial contiguity, temporal contiguity, and redundancy principles – People learn better when extraneous material is excluded rather than included, when cues are added that highlight the organization of the essential material, when corresponding words and pictures are presented near rather than far from each other on the screen or page or in time, and people learn better from graphics and narration than from graphics, narration, and on-screen text (Mayer, chapter 12).

personalization, voice, and image principles – People learn better when the words of a multimedia presentation are in conversational style rather than formal style and when the words are spoken in a standard-accented human voice rather than a machine voice or foreign-accented human voice; but people do not necessarily learn better when the speaker's image is on the screen (Mayer, chapter 13).

Part 3: Advanced Principles of Multimedia Learning contains chapters that explore the research evidence for advanced principles of multimedia learning:

guided-discovery principle – People learn better when guidance is incorporated into discovery-based multimedia environments (de Jong, chapter 14).

worked-out example principle – People learn better when they receive worked-out examples in initial skill learning (Renkl, chapter 15).

collaboration principle – People can learn better with collaborative online learning activities (Jonassen, Lee, Yang, & Laffey, chapter 16).

self-explanation principle – People learn better when they are encouraged to generate self-explanations during learning (Roy & Chi, chapter 17).

animation and interactivity principles – People do not necessarily learn better from animation than from static diagrams (Betrancourt, chapter 18).

navigation principles – People learn better in hypertext environments when appropriate navigation aids are provided (Rouet & Pottelle, chapter 19).

site map principle – People can learn better in an online environment when the interface includes a map showing where the learner is in the lesson (Shapiro, chapter 20).

prior knowledge principle – Instructional design principles that enhance multimedia learning for novices may hinder multimedia learning for more expert learners (Kalyuga, chapter 21).

cognitive aging principle – Instructional design principles that effectively expand working memory capacity are especially helpful for older learners (Paas, van Gerven & Tabbers, chapter 22).

Part 4: Multimedia Learning in Content Areas takes a somewhat different cut by ex-amining research on how to design multimedia learning environments in various content areas. The chapters summarize research on multimedia learning in content areas that have generated the most research on multimedia learning including reading (Reinking, chapter 23), history (Wiley & Ash, chapter 24), mathematics (Atkinson, chapter 25), chemistry (Kozma & Russell, chapter 26), meteorology (Lowe, chapter 27), complex physical systems (Hegarty, chapter 28), second language learning (Plass & Jones, chapter 29), and cognitive skills (Lajoie & Nakamura, chapter 30).

Finally, in *Part 5: Multimedia Learning in Advanced Computer-Based Contexts*, the chapters examine multimedia learning research involving emerging new technologies. The chapters summarize research on multimedia learning with advanced technologies that have generated the most research, such as animated pedagogical agents (Moreno, chapter 31); virtual reality (Cobb & Fraser, chapter 32); games, simulations, and microworlds (Rieber, chapter 33); hypermedia (Dillon & Jobst, chapter 34); and e-courses (Clark, chapter 35).

In each of the chapters the focus is on empirical research evidence, including implications of research for theory and practice. Overall, each chapter in this handbook is intended to showcase the research base in a subarea of multimedia learning, note its limitations, and offer suggestions for future research.

Two Approaches to Multimedia Learning: Technology Centered Versus Learner Centered

Multimedia represents a potentially powerful learning technology – that is, a system for enhancing human learning. A practical goal of research on multimedia is to devise design principles for multimedia presentations. In addressing this goal, it is useful to distinguish between two approaches to multimedia design – a technology-centered approach and a learner-centered approach.

Technology-Centered Approaches

The most straightforward approach to multimedia design is technology centered. Technology-centered approaches begin with the functional capabilities of multimedia and ask, "How can we use these capabilities in designing multimedia presentations?" The focus is generally on cutting-edge advances in multimedia technology, so technology-centered designers might focus on how to incorporate multimedia into emerging communications technologies such as wireless access to the World Wide Web or the construction of interactive multimedia representations in virtual reality. The kinds of research issues often involve media research (i.e., determining which technology is most effective in presenting information). For example, a media research issue is whether students learn as well from an online lecture – in which the student can see a lecturer in a window on the computer screen – as they can from a live lecture – in which the student is actually sitting in a classroom.

What's wrong with technology-centered approaches? A review of educational technologies of the twentieth century shows that the technology-centered approach generally fails to lead to lasting improvements in education (Cuban, 1986). For example, when the motion picture was invented in the early 20th century hopes were high that this visual technology would improve education. In 1922, the famous inventor Thomas Edison predicted that "the motion picture is destined to revolutionize our educational system and that in a few years it will supplant largely, if not entirely, the use of textbooks" (cited in Cuban, 1986, p. 9). Like current claims for the power of visual media, Edison proclaimed that "it is possible to teach every branch of human knowledge with the motion picture" (cited in Cuban, 1986, p. 11). In spite of the grand predictions, a review of educational technology reveals that "most teachers used films infrequently in their classrooms" (Cuban, 1986, p. 17). From our vantage point beyond the close the 20th century it is clear that the predicted educational revolution in which movies would replace books has failed to materialize.

Consider another disappointing example that may remind you of current claims for the educational potential of the World Wide Web. In 1932, Benjamin Darrow, founder of the Ohio School of the Air, proclaimed that radio could "bring the world to the classroom, to make universally available the services of the finest teachers, the inspiration of the greatest leaders..." (cited in Cuban, 1986, p. 19). His colleague, William Levenson, the director of the Ohio School of the Air predicted in 1945 that a "radio receiver will be as common in the classroom as the blackboard" and "radio instruction will be integrated into school life" (cited in Cuban, 1986, p. 19). As we rush to wire our schools and homes for access to the educational content of the Internet, it is humbling to recognize what happened to a similarly motivated movement for radio: "Radio has not been accepted as a full-fledged member of the educational community" (Cuban, 1986, p. 24).

Third, consider the sad history of educational television – a technology that combined the visual power of the motion picture with the worldwide coverage of radio. By the 1950s, educational television was touted as a way to create a "continental classroom" that would provide access to "richer education at less cost" (Cuban, 1986, p. 33). Yet, a review shows that teachers used television infrequently, if at all (Cuban, 1986).

Finally, consider the most widely acclaimed technological accomplishment of the 20th century – computers. The technology that supports computers is different from film, radio, and television, but the grand promises to revolutionize education are the same. Like current claims for the mind-enhancing power of computer technology, during the 1960s computer tutoring machines were predicted to eventually replace teachers. The first large-scale implementation occurred under the banner of computer-assisted instruction (CAI) in which computers presented short frames, solicited a response from the learner, and provided feedback to the learner. In spite of a large financial investment to support

CAI, sound evaluations showed that the two largest computer-based systems in the 1970s – PLATO and TICCIT – failed to produce better learning than traditional teacher-lead instruction (Cognition and Technology Group at Vanderbilt, 1996).

What can we learn from the humbling history of the 20th century's great educational technologies? Although different technologies underlie film, radio, television, and computer-assisted instruction, they all produced the same cycle. First, they began with grand promises about how the technology would revolutionize education. Second, there was an initial rush to implement the cutting-edge technology in schools. Third, from the perspective of a few decades later it became clear that the hopes and expectations were largely unmet.

What went wrong with these technologies that seemed poised to tap the potential of visual and worldwide learning? I attribute the disappointing results to the technology-centered approach taken by the promoters. Instead of adapting technology to fit the needs of human learners, humans were forced to adapt to the demands of cutting-edge technologies. The driving force behind the implementations was the power of the technology rather than an interest in promoting human cognition. The focus was on giving people access to the latest technology rather than helping people to learn through the aid of technology.

Are we about to replicate the cycle of high expectations, large-scale implementation, and disappointing results in the realm of multimedia technology? In my opinion, the answer to that question depends on whether or not we continue to take a technology-centered approach. When we ask, "What can we do with multimedia?" and when our goal is to "provide access to technology," we are taking a technology-centered approach with a 100-year history of failure.

Learner-Centered Approaches

Learner-centered approaches offer an important alternative to technology-centered approaches. Learner-centered approaches

begin with an understanding of how the human mind works and ask, "How can we adapt multimedia to enhance human learning?" The focus is on using multimedia technology as an aid to human cognition. Research questions focus on the relation between design features and the human information processing system, such as, comparing multimedia designs that place light or heavy loads on the learner's visual information processing channel. The premise underlying the learner-centered approach is that multimedia designs that are consistent with the way the human mind works are more effective in fostering learning than those that are not. This premise is the central theme of part 1 of this handbook, which lays out theories of multimedia learning.

Norman (1993, p. xi) eloquently makes the case for a learner-centered approach to technology design, which he refers to as *human-centered technology*: "Today we serve technology. We need to reverse the machine-centered point of view and turn it into a person-centered point of view: Technology should serve us." Consistent with the learner-centered approach, Norman (1993, p. 3) shows how "technology can make us smart" – that is, technology can expand our cognitive capabilities. Norman (1993, p. 5) refers to tools that aid the mind as *cognitive artifacts*: "anything invented by humans for the purpose of improving thought or action counts as an artifact." Examples include mental tools such as language and arithmetic as well as physical tools such as paper and pencils. As the 20th century's most important new cognitive artifact, computer technology represents a landmark invention that has the potential to assist human cognition in ways that were previously not possible.

Norman's (1993, p. 9) assessment is that "much of science and technology takes a machine-centered view of the design of machines" so that "the technology that is intended to aid human cognition...more often interferes and confuses." In contrast, Norman's (1993, p. 12) vision of a learner-centered approach to technology design is that "technology...should complement human abilities, aid those activities for which

Table 1.2. Two Approaches to the Design of Multimedia Instruction

Design Approach	Starting Point	Goal	Issues
Technology centered	Capabilities of multimedia technology	Provide access to information	How can we use cutting-edge technology in designing multimedia instruction?
Learner centered	How the human mind works	Aid human cognition	How can we adapt multimedia technology to aid human cognition?

we are poorly suited, and enhance and help develop those for which we are ideally suited." The design of multimedia technology to promote human cognition represents one exemplary component in the larger task of creating what Norman (1993, p. xi) calls "things that make us smart."

In his review of computer technology, Landauer (1995, p. 3) proclaims that "the computer and information revolution is widely predicted to be as consequential as the industrial revolution of the previous two centuries." Further, he describes two major phases in the use of computer technology – *automation* and *augmentation*. In the automation phase, computers are used to replace humans on certain tasks ranging from robots in manufacturing to imaging devices (e.g., CAT scans and MRIs) in medicine to computer-based switching in telecommunications. However, Landauer (1995, p. 6) observes that the automation phase "is running out of steam" because almost all of the easy to automate tasks have been computerized.

The second phase of computer application – augmentation – involves the use of computers to enhance human performance on various cognitively complex tasks. Augmentation involves designing computer systems "to act as assistants, aids, and power tools" (Landauer, 1995, p. 7). However, Landauer (1995, p. 7) is disappointed with progress in the augmentation phase: "It is here . . . that we have failed." A major challenge in making the augmentation phase work involves the learner-centered design of computer-based technologies: "They are still too hard to use" (Landauer, 1995, p. 7). The design of multimedia learning environments that promote meaningful human learning is an example of using computers to augment

or aid human cognition – and thus one element in Landauer's augmentation phase.

The differences between the technology-centered and learner-centered approaches to multimedia design are summarized in Table 1.2.

Three Metaphors of Multimedia Learning: Response Strengthening, Information Acquisition, and Knowledge Construction

In making decisions about how to design or select a multimedia learning environment, you may be influenced by your underlying conception of learning. Table 1.3 compares three views of multimedia learning – *multimedia learning as response strengthening, multimedia learning as information acquisition* and *multimedia learning as knowledge construction*. If you view multimedia learning as response strengthening, then multimedia is a feedback delivery system. If you view multimedia learning as information acquisition, then multimedia is an information delivery system. If you view multimedia learning as knowledge construction, then multimedia is a cognitive aid.

Multimedia Learning as Response Strengthening

According to the response strengthening view, learning involves increasing or decreasing the connection between a stimulus and a response. The underlying principle is that the connection is strengthened if a response is followed by reward and is weakened if the response is followed by punishment. This

Table 1.3. Three Metaphors of Multimedia Learning

Metaphor	Definition	Content	Learner	Teacher	Goal of multimedia
Response strengthening	Strengthening and weakening connections	Connections	Passive receiver of rewards and punishments	Dispenser of rewards and punishments	Exercise system
Information acquisition	Adding information to memory	Information	Passive receiver of information	Dispenser of information	Delivery system
Knowledge construction	Building a coherent mental structure	Knowledge	Active sense maker	Cognitive guide	Cognitive guidance system

view entails assumptions about the nature of what is learned, the nature of the learner, the nature of the teacher, and the goals of multimedia presentations. First, learning is based on building connections, so "what is learned" is that a certain response is connected to a certain situation. Second, the learner's job is to make a response and receive feedback on the response; thus, the learner is a passive recipient of rewards and punishments. Third, the teacher's job – or, in some cases, the instructional designer's job – is to dispense rewards and punishments. Overall, the teacher controls the instructional episode by providing a prompt or question – such as, "What is the definition of multimedia learning?" – and then providing feedback on the answer given by the learner – such as, "Yes, that's correct" or "No, you left out _____." Finally, the goal of multimedia instruction is to provide practice in exercising skills, that is, to act as a trainer. The underlying metaphor is that multimedia is an exercise system, that is, a system for practicing skills with feedback.

The response strengthening view reflects the first major theory of learning proposed by educational psychologists in the early 1900s – the law of effect (Thorndike, 1913). According to Thorndike's law of effect, if a response is followed by a satisfying state of affairs it will be more likely to occur under the same circumstances, and if a response is followed by a unsatisfying state of affairs it will be less likely to occur under the same circumstances. This straightforward principle has been a pillar of psychology and ed-

ucation for more than 100 years (Mayer, 2001b), dominating the field through the 1950s. The law of effect was the guiding principle for many early instructional programs delivered by teaching machines in the 1960s. This view of learning still can be seen in multimedia environments that emphasize drill and practice such as an online game that teaches arithmetic computation by giving the learner points for each correctly answered arithmetic problem.

What is wrong with the response strengthening view (or more accurately, the response strengthening and weakening view)? My main objection is not that it is incorrect but rather that it is incomplete. Although certain cognitive skills (and motor skills, for that matter) can best be learned through drill and practice, the teaching of other kinds of knowledge – such as concepts and strategies – may best be taught with other methods of instruction based on other views of learning. For example, when the goal of instruction is to foster meaningful learning reflected in the ability to solve transfer problems, drill and practice aimed at response strengthening may be too limited. Thus, the response strengthening view is appropriate for guiding the design of multimedia learning environments mainly when the goal of instruction is to help people learn specific skills. However, when the goal of instruction is to help people learn concepts and strategies that can be applied to new situations, the response strengthening view is not adequate.

Multimedia Learning as Information Acquisition

According to the information acquisition view, learning involves adding information to one's memory. As with the other views, the information acquisition view entails assumptions about the nature of what is learned, the nature of the learner, the nature of the teacher, and the goals of multimedia presentations. First, learning is based on information – an objective item that can be moved from place to place (such as from the computer screen to the human mind). Second, the learner's job is to receive information; thus, the learner is a passive being who takes in information from the outside and stores it in memory. Third, the teacher's job – or, the multimedia designer's job – is to present information. Fourth, the goal of multimedia presentations is to deliver information as efficiently as possible. The underlying metaphor is that of multimedia as a delivery system. According to this metaphor, multimedia is a vehicle for efficiently delivering information to the learner.

The information acquisition view is sometimes called the *empty vessel* view because the learner's mind is seen as an empty container that needs to be filled by the teacher pouring in some information. Similarly, this is sometimes called the *transmission* view because the teacher transmits information to be received by the learner. Finally, this is sometimes called the *commodity* view because information is seen as a commodity that can be moved from one place to another.

What's wrong with the information acquisition view? If your goal is to help people learn isolated fragments of information, then I suppose nothing is wrong with the information acquisition view. However, when your goal is to promote understanding of the presented material, the information acquisition view is not very helpful. Even worse, it conflicts with the research base on how people learn complex material (Bransford, Brown, & Cocking, 1999). When people are trying to understand presented material – such as

a lesson on how a bicycle tire pump works – they are not tape recorders who carefully store each word. Rather, humans focus on the meaning of presented material and interpret it in light of their prior knowledge.

Multimedia Learning as Knowledge Construction

In contrast to the information acquisition view, according to the knowledge construction view multimedia learning is a sense-making activity in which the learner seeks to build a coherent mental representation from the presented material. Unlike information – which is an objective commodity that can be moved from one mind to another – knowledge is personally constructed by the learner and cannot be delivered in exact form from one mind to another. This is why two learners can be presented with the same multimedia message and come away with different learning outcomes. Second, according to the knowledge construction view, the learner's job is to make sense of the presented material; thus, the learner is an active sense maker who experiences a multimedia presentation and tries to integrate the presented material into a coherent mental representation. Third, the teacher's job is to assist the learner in this sense-making process; thus, the teacher is a cognitive guide who provides needed guidance to support the learner's cognitive processing. Fourth, the goal of multimedia presentations is not only to present information, but also to provide guidance for how to process the presented information – that is, for determining what to pay attention to, how to mentally organize it, and how to relate it to prior knowledge. Finally, the guiding metaphor is that of multimedia as a helpful communicator. According to this metaphor, multimedia is a sense-making guide, that is, an aid to knowledge construction.

Overall, I favor a knowledge construction view because it is more consistent with the research base on how people learn and because it is more consistent with my goal of promoting understanding of presented

Table 1.4. Two Goals of Multimedia Instruction

Goal	Definition	Test	Example Test Item
Remembering	Ability to reproduce or recognize presented material	Retention	Write down all you can remember from the presentation you just studied.
Understanding	Ability to use presented material in novel situations	Transfer	List some ways to improve the reliability of the device you just read about.

material. Rather than seeing the goal of multimedia presentations as exposing learners to vast quantities of information or exercising correct responses, my goal for multimedia is to help people develop an understanding of important aspects of the presented material. For example, Bransford et al. (1999, p. xi) note that "in the last 30 years... views of how effective learning proceeds have shifted from the benefits of diligent drill and practice to focus on students' understanding and application of knowledge." In short, the knowledge construction view offers a more useful conception of learning when the goal is to help people to understand and to be able to use what they learned.

Three Kinds of Multimedia Learning Outcomes: No Learning, Rote Learning, and Meaningful Learning

There are two major kinds of goals of learning: remembering and understanding. Remembering is the ability to reproduce or recognize the presented material, and is assessed by retention tests. The most common retention tests are recall – in which learners are asked to reproduce what was presented

(such as writing down all they can remember for a lesson they read) – and recognition – in which learners are asked to select what was presented (as in a multiple choice question) or judge whether a given item was presented (as in a true–false question). Thus, the major issue in retention tests involves quantity of learning – that is, how much was remembered.

Understanding is the ability to construct a coherent mental representation from the presented material. It is reflected in the ability to use the presented material in novel situations, and is assessed by transfer tests. In a transfer test, learners must solve problems that were not explicitly given in the presented material – that is, they must apply what they learned to a new situation. An example is an essay question that asks learners to generate solutions to a problem, which requires going beyond the presented material. The major issue in transfer tests involves the quality of learning – that is, how well can someone use what they have learned. The distinction between remembering and understanding is summarized in Table 1.4. A major goal of the research presented in this handbook is to promote understanding as well as retention.

Table 1.5 summarizes three kinds of learning outcomes: no learning, rote learning,

Table 1.5. Three Kinds of Multimedia Learning Outcomes

Learning Outcome	Cognitive Description	Test Performance	
		Retention	Transfer
No learning	No knowledge	Poor	Poor
Rote learning	Fragmented knowledge	Good	Poor
Meaningful learning	Integrated knowledge	Good	Good

and meaningful learning. The distinguishing feature of no learning is poor performance on retention and transfer. In this case, the learner lacks knowledge. The distinguishing pattern for rote learning outcomes is good retention and poor transfer. In this case, the learner has what can be called *fragmented knowledge* or *inert knowledge*, knowledge that can be remembered but cannot be used in new situations. In short, the learner has acquired a collection of *factoids* – isolated bits of information. Finally, meaningful learning is distinguished by good transfer performance as well as good retention performance. In this case, the learner's knowledge is organized into an integrated representation. Overall, the chapters in this handbook examine design features of multimedia that foster meaningful learning, that is, ways of integrating words and pictures that foster meaningful learning.

Two Kinds of Active Learning: Behavioral Activity versus Cognitive Activity

What's the best way to promote meaningful learning outcomes? The answer rests in *active learning* – meaningful learning outcomes occur as a result of the learner's activity during learning. However, does active learning refer to what is going on with the learner's physical behavior – such as the degree of hands-on activity – or to what is going on in the learner's mind – such as the degree of integrative cognitive processing? In short, if the goal is to foster meaningful learning outcomes, should multimedia presentations be designed mainly to prime behavioral activity or cognitive activity?

Consider the following situation. Alan is preparing for an upcoming test in meteorology. He sits in front of a computer and clicks on an interactive tutorial on lightning. The tutorial provides hands-on exercises in which he must fill in blanks by writing words. For example, on the screen appears the sentence: "Each year approximately ____ Americans are killed by lightning." He types in an answer, and the computer then provides the correct answer. In this case, Alan is behaviorally active in that he is typing answers on the keyboard, but he may not be cognitively active in that he is not encouraged to make sense of the presented material.

In contrast, consider the case of Brian, who is also preparing for the same upcoming meteorology test. Like Alan, he sits in front of a computer and clicks on a tutorial about lightning. However, Brian's tutorial is a short narrated animation explaining the steps in the lightning formation. As he watches and listens, Brian tries to focus on the essential steps in lightning formation and to organize them into a cause-and-effect chain. Wherever the multimedia presentation is unclear about why one step leads to another, Brian uses his prior knowledge to help create an explanation for himself – which Chi, Bassok, Lewis, Reimann, and Glaser (1989) call a *self-explanation* (see also Roy & Chi, chapter 17). For example, when the narration says that positively charged particles come to the surface of the earth, Brian mentally creates the explanation that opposite charges attract. In this scenario, Brian is behaviorally inactive because he simply sits in front of the computer. However, he is cognitively active because he is actively trying to make sense of the presentation.

Which type of active learning promotes meaningful learning? Research on learning shows that meaningful learning depends on the learner's cognitive activity during learning rather than on the learner's behavioral activity during learning. You might suppose that the best way to promote meaningful learning is through hands-on activity, such as a highly interactive multimedia program. However, behavioral activity per se does not guarantee cognitively active learning. It is possible to engage in hands-on activities that do not promote active cognitive processing – such as in the case of Alan or many highly interactive computer games. You might suppose that presenting material to a learner is not a good way to promote active learning because the learner appears to sit passively. In some situations, your intuitions would be right – presenting a long, incoherent, and boring lecture or textbook chapter is unlikely to foster meaningful learning. However, in other situations, such as in the case of Brian, learners can achieve meaningful learning in a behaviorally inactive environment such as a multimedia instructional message. My point is that well-designed multimedia instructional messages can promote active cognitive processing in learners, even when learners seem to be behaviorally inactive.

Summary

In summary, the definition of multimedia learning is learning from words and pictures, the rationale for studying multimedia learning is to understand how to design multimedia learning environments that promote meaningful learning, and the research base concerning multimedia learning is reflected in the 35 chapters of this handbook. The approach taken in this handbook is learner centered rather than technology centered, views learning as a constructive process rather than solely as a processes of adding new information to memory or strengthening associations, seeks to foster meaningful learning rather than rote learning, and favors appropriate cognitive activity during learning rather than behavioral activity per se.

Glossary

Learner-centered approach: An approach to instructional design that focuses on using multimedia technology as an aid to human cognition, based on the premise that multimedia designs that are consistent with the way the human mind works are more effective in fostering learning than those that are not.

Meaningful learning: Occurs when a learner builds organized and integrated knowl-

edge, resulting in good performance on tests of retention and transfer.

Multimedia: Presenting both words (such as spoken text or printed text) and pictures (such as illustrations, photos, animation, or video).

Multimedia instruction: Presenting words (such as spoken text or printed text) and pictures (such as illustrations, photos, animation, or video) that are intended to promote learning.

Multimedia learning: Occurs when people build mental representations from words (such as spoken text or printed text) and pictures (such as illustrations, photos, animation or video).

Multimedia principle: People learn better from words and pictures than from words alone.

Rote learning: Occurs when a learner builds fragmented knowledge (or inert knowledge), resulting in good retention performance and poor transfer performance.

Technology-centered approach: An approach to instructional design that focuses on how to incorporate emerging technologies into instruction and on which technology is most effective in presenting information.

Note

This chapter is based on "Chapter 1: The Promise of Multimedia Learning" in Mayer (2001a).

Footnote

1. There may be some conditions in which words or pictures alone are better than words and pictures combined, such as the redundancy effect described by Sweller in chapter 10 or the expertise reversal effect described by Kalyuga in chapter 21.

References

Bransford, J. D., Brown, A. L., & Cocking, R. R. (1999). *How people learn.* Washington, DC: National Academy Press.

Chi, M. T. H., Bassok, M., Lewis, M. W., Reimann, P., & Glaser, R. (1989). Self-explanations: How students study and use examples in learning to solve problems. *Cognitive Science, 13,* 145–182.

Cognition and Technology Group at Vanderbilt (1996). Looking at technology in context: A framework for understanding technology in education. In D. Berliner & R. C. Calfee (Eds.), *Handbook of educational psychology* (pp. 807–840). New York: Macmillan.

Cuban, L. (1986). *Teachers and machines: The classroom use of technology since 1920.* New York: Teachers College Press.

Landauer, T. K. (1995). *The trouble with computers.* Cambridge, MA: MIT Press.

Mayer, R. E. (2001a). *Multimedia learning.* New York: Cambridge University Press.

Mayer, R. E. (2001b). Changing conceptions of learning: A century of progress in the scientific study of education. In L. Corno (Ed.), *Education across a century: The centennial volume. One hundredth yearbook of the National Society for the Study of Education* (pp. 34–75). Chicago: University of Chicago Press.

Mayer, R. E., & Anderson, R. B. (1991). Animations need narrations: An experimental test of a dual-coding hypothesis. *Journal of Educational Psychology, 83,* 484–490.

Mayer, R. E., & Anderson, R. B. (1992). The instructive animation: Helping students build connections between words and pictures in multimedia learning. *Journal of Educational Psychology, 84,* 444–452.

Norman, D. A. (1993). *Things that make us smart.* Reading, MA: Addison-Wesley.

Paivio, A. (1986). *Mental representations: A dual coding approach.* Oxford, England: Oxford University Press.

Thorndike, E. L. (1913). *Educational psychology.* New York: Columbia University Press.

Part I

THEORETICAL FOUNDATIONS

CHAPTER 2

Implications of Cognitive Load Theory for Multimedia Learning

John Sweller

University of New South Wales

Abstract

Humans have evolved with a working memory that has no logical central executive available when required to organise novel information. Consequently, failing instruction, we must randomly propose organisational combinations and test them for effectiveness. This procedure is only possible with a very limited number of elements and as a consequence, working memory is severely limited when dealing with novel information. In contrast, familiar, organised information previously stored in long-term memory can act as a central executive and eliminate the need for working memory limitations. These structures are central to cognitive load theory. They suggest that instruction should act as substitute for the missing central executive when dealing with novel information and that factor, in turn, determines multimedia instructional principles.

Introduction

Good instructional design is driven by our knowledge of human cognitive structures and the manner in which those structures are organised into a cognitive architecture. Without knowledge of relevant aspects of human cognitive architecture such as the characteristics of and intricate relations between working memory and long-term memory, the effectiveness of instructional design is likely to be random. Cognitive load theory has been one of the theories used to integrate our knowledge of human cognitive structures and instructional design principles. This chapter is concerned with the elements of that theory and its general implications for multimedia learning, specifically, words presented in spoken or written form along with pictures or diagrams.

I will begin with some aspects of human cognitive architecture relevant to instruction. Along the way I will suggest that the processes and structures of human cognition are closely analogous to the processes and structures associated with evolution by natural selection and that accordingly, evolutionary theory, which is much older and better developed than cognitive theory, can be used as a guide to assess which instructional procedures may or may not be effective.

Long-Term Memory

Long-term memory has the same central role in human cognition as a genetic code has in biology (Sweller, 2003). Just as a genetic code heavily determines a biological life, so long-term memory heavily determines our cognitive lives. All the information in a genetic code has been determined by adaptation to an environment (evolution by natural selection) and similarly, everything in long-term memory has been learned in order to cognitively adapt to an environment. On this analogy between a genetic code and long-term memory, almost all human cognitive activity is determined by information held in long-term memory. This information must be learned over time just as the information held in a genetic code is acquired over time. Learning is defined as an alteration in long-term memory. If nothing has altered in long-term memory nothing has been learned. Accordingly, appropriate alterations to long-term memory should be the primary aim of instruction.

The suggestion that information in long-term memory is analogous to a genetic code, that most human cognitive activity is driven by information held in long-term memory, and that the aim of instruction should be to alter long-term memory, imply that the long-term memory store is very large. The evidence for a very large long-term memory is now overwhelming. The origin of this discovery is unusual: the game of chess.

De Groot (1965) studied the factors that permitted chess grand masters to almost invariably defeat less able players. The only factor he could find that distinguished between more able and less able chess players was in memory for board configurations taken from real games. If shown a board configuration taken from a real game for a few seconds and then asked to reproduce that configuration, chess grand masters could replace most of the pieces correctly. Less able players could correctly replace few of the pieces. Chase and Simon (1973) replicated this result but found it could not be replicated using random board configurations.

The result only was obtainable using board configurations taken from real games.

In the late 1970s and 1980s, a similar result was obtained many times in a variety of fields by several investigators (e.g., Egan & Schwartz, 1979; Jeffries, Turner, Polson, & Atwood, 1981; Sweller & Cooper, 1985). Experts have a vastly superior memory to novices for problem states in their field of expertise. For example, Simon and Gilmartin (1973) have estimated that chess grand masters have memorised up to 100,000 board configurations. It is this store of information in long-term memory that constitutes expertise. As a consequence, problem-solving skill is critically determined by information in long-term memory concerning problem states and the best move associated with each state. Such knowledge held in long-term memory allows an expert to immediately recognise most of the situations faced and the actions required by that situation. That large body of knowledge permits the fluency shown by experts in their own area. A major function of instructional design is to assist learners to acquire a similar fluency. Fluent procedures imply that the necessary knowledge that underpins skilled performance in any substantive area has been acquired.

The Structure of Knowledge in Long-Term Memory

Emphasising the importance of accumulating knowledge in long-term memory as the primary goal of instruction is sometimes misinterpreted as an emphasis on rote learning. In fact, both rote learning and learning with understanding result in changes in long-term memory. Rote learning occurs when some connections between elements occur but other, essential connections, are omitted. If a student learns to recite the letters of the alphabet but not how they can be used to produce written language, or learns to recite a multiplication table but not that multiplication is a shorthand procedure for repeated addition, there are changes in long-term memory due to the rote learned material. If the student begins to learn to read or learns to use multiplication instead of repeated addition to determine the cost of three pencils, as well as the changes in long-term memory due to rote learning, there are further changes due to the increased level of understanding. Understanding can be largely described by the additional changes in long-term memory (along with the effect of those changes on working memory to be discussed in the following text). Without changes in long-term memory, nothing has been understood.

What is the nature of changes in long-term memory as material is learned? The process probably can best be described in terms of schema construction. Schemas are cognitive constructs that allow multiple elements of information to be categorised as a single element. (For examples and theory associated with problem-solving schemas, see Chi, Glaser, & Rees, 1982; Larkin, McDermott, Simon, & Simon, 1980.) An intuitive feel for the power of schemas and indeed, an intuitive feel for the power of information held in long-term memory, may be gleaned by considering the cognitive processes required to read this page. Objectively, writing is an almost indescribably complex series of squiggles. A person can read because schemas for individual letters permit an infinite number of shapes to be recognised (hence the ability to read handwriting), schemas for combinations of letters that form words and combinations of words to form phrases permit extremely complex combinations of squiggles to be recognised. Further, additional schemas connect these squiggles to objects, events, and procedures permitting meaning to be derived. These schemas are acquired over very long periods of time and are all stored in long-term memory. In character and function, there is every reason to believe that schemas for reading are identical to the schemas acquired by chess grand masters for chessboard configurations. All skilled performance in complex domains requires the acquisition of countless numbers of schemas held in long-term memory.

From a multimedia perspective, knowledge is held in a schematic form in long-term memory whether it is pictorial or verbal, written, or spoken. Recognising chessboard configurations or written text is largely visual and requires visual schemas. Recognising where words begin and end in the continuous sound that constitutes speech requires auditory schemas. In all cases, that ability to appropriately categorise information requires immense numbers of schemas held in long-term memory.

While schema acquisition is a major form of learning it is not the only one. Material held in long-term memory can be processed either consciously or automatically (Kotovsky, Hayes, & Simon, 1985; Schneider & Shiffrin, 1977; Shiffrin & Schneider, 1977). Once a schema has been acquired, further practice over long periods of time can permit it to be processed automatically without conscious control. Once the letters of the alphabet and their combination into words and phrases has occurred, further learning allows one to read without consciously considering those letters or even considering individual words and some combinations of words. Such processes have become automated and other activities can be engaged in such as attending to meaning. Again, automated schemas are held in long-term memory and can be either pictorial or verbal, spoken or written.

Working Memory

What does it mean to say some material can be processed consciously or automatically, or that some material has been learned with understanding or is not yet understood? Working memory and its interactions with long-term memory provide an explanation. When dealing with novel information, working memory has two severe limitations. Miller (1956) indicated that working memory is only able to hold about seven elements of information. It can probably process in the sense of combine, contrast, or manipulate no more than about 2–4 elements. On these numbers, the capacity of working memory when dealing with new information is severely constrained. The duration of working memory is also constrained. Peterson and Peterson (1959) found that without rehearsal, almost all the contents of working memory are lost within about 20 seconds.

What are the instructional design consequences of these working memory limitations? All instruction requiring learners to deal with novel information must be processed by a structure that is minute in capacity and that retains the new information for no more than a few seconds. These limitations should be a central consideration of instructional design. While the aim of instruction should be the acquisition of automated schemas, the execution of this aim requires a constant monitoring of the working memory consequences of any recommended procedure. Instructional designs that ignore working memory limitations are likely to be random in their effectiveness.

Many instructional design recommendations do ignore working memory limitations. As an example, any inquiry-based instructional design inevitably places a heavy load on working memory. For this reason, it is important to place human working memory limitations into a theoretical framework to facilitate a full understanding of the reasons for a limited working memory. Working memory limitations when dealing with novel information are not accidental. They are an essential concomitant of human cognitive architecture. Without those limitations, our cognitive mechanisms could not function. They are there for a purpose and that purpose directly impacts instructional design considerations.

Why Working Memory Is Limited

Consider a student learning a new task such as how to navigate the Web. The student is faced with a screen page containing many buttons each likely to represent a link to other pages and functions that also contain many more links and functions. The amount of information is massive, consisting of a large number of interacting elements. The student needs to learn how those elements interact. What is the consequence of clicking on one button as opposed to another?

Faced with such a complex task that imposes a heavy working memory load, it is natural to assume that if humans had evolved with a much larger working memory, we would be better able to deal with natural complexity. That assumption may be incorrect.

Consider the process by which the student has to learn which buttons on the screen to press in order to successfully navigate. It is a new task and so the student has no knowledge informing him or her of the procedures to be followed. Assuming there is no one present to provide direct guidance, the student must engage in problem solving to determine an appropriate procedure. Failing knowledge (either one's own or someone else's knowledge), a problem-solving search can only function by randomly proposing a step and then testing that step for effectiveness. That random component is quite unavoidable when dealing with novel material that necessitates problem solving. It has profound implications both for how our cognitive architecture is organised and for instructional design.

Consider a working memory such as our own that is severely limited in that it can only combine about four elements at any given time. There are many ways those elements could be combined but let us assume they are being combined using the logic of permutations. With four elements, there are $4! = 24$ permutations. It may be difficult to determine which of 24 permutations is best but it is likely to be possible. In contrast, assume a somewhat larger working memory that can handle 10, rather than 4, elements. With 10 elements, there are $10! = 3,628,800$ permutations. A cognitive architecture structured to test the relative effectiveness of millions of possibilities is likely to be unworkable. As a consequence, and paradoxically, a somewhat smaller working memory is likely to be more efficient than a larger one. We may have evolved with a limited working memory because a slightly larger, or worse, unlimited working memory may be counterproductive.

As was the case with long-term memory, these processes are directly analogous to those used by evolution by natural selection. A species faced with a changing environment may evolve to handle the new circumstances. The manner in which it evolves is not predetermined. It is heavily dependent on the variations to be found between members of the species. All variations between species and between individual members of species can ultimately be sourced to random mutations. In effect, whenever a mutation occurs, it is checked for effectiveness with effective mutations leaving more offspring and ineffective mutations leaving fewer or even no offspring. From an information-processing perspective, this process is indistinguishable from human problem solving, which also depends on random generation followed by tests of effectiveness. The underlying logic of both systems is identical.

General Instructional Implications of Working Memory Characteristics

Instructional implications flow from the suggestion that a student learning something new must use the same information-processing system as a species learning to adapt to an environment. Left to his or her own devices without assistance, a student learning, for example, how to navigate the Web, has no choice but to randomly try procedures and test them for effectiveness. Where knowledge is available, either from another person or source, or from long-term memory, it is likely to be used. Where it is not available, random generation followed by effectiveness testing is the only alternative. In its essence, all inquiry-based learning depends on a random generation followed by effectiveness testing procedure. It is likely to be a long, slow, and ineffective procedure for acquiring knowledge.

Once we understand that working memory capacity is small and why it must necessarily be small when dealing with novel information, we can begin to understand that a major function of instruction is to overcome the inevitable limitations of working memory. Having students learn in the same way as species evolve is fine if there is no alternative. Frequently, there are alternatives and a major function of instructional design is to find those alternatives. Many of those alternatives are discussed in subsequent chapters of this handbook.

Multimedia and Working Memory Limitations

Early work on working memory treated it as a single entity. Current theories, either explicitly or implicitly, assume that working memory consists of multiple streams, channels, or processors. Baddeley's (1992) working memory model is probably the most influential. It consists of a coordinating central executive and two subsystems: a visuo/spatial sketchpad for dealing with two- and three-dimensional objects and a phonological loop for dealing with verbal material. Generally speaking, the visuo/spatial sketchpad deals with vision while the phonological loop deals with auditory material such as speech. At present, while there is strong evidence, as discussed in the following text, for the two partially independent, subsystems, there is less evidence for the coordinating role of the central executive.

There are instructional consequences that follow from this division of working memory. Penney (1989), in a review, provided evidence that appropriate use of both subsystems can increase working memory capacity. While the increase is not additive in the sense that all of the information being processed by auditory working memory can be added to all of the material processed by visual working memory, there is a lesser but demonstrable increase and that increase supports the hypothesis of partially separate processors. The increase also can be used for instructional purposes. If instruction is designed to make use of multiple processors, learning can be facilitated (Mayer, 2001).

Relations Between Long-Term and Working Memory

Human cognitive architecture has evolved with an ingenious set of relations between long-term and working memory. The nature of those relations provides the centre-piece of human cognitive functioning and is critical to any theory of instructional design. The intellectual heights that humans have reached and to which they aspire are made possible by the manner in which information in long-term memory alters the characteristics of working memory.

The limitations of working memory were discussed previously. It must be emphasised that those limitations apply only to novel information fed to working memory through the sensory system (known as sensory memory). Information that has already been organised into schemas in long-term memory can also be fed into working memory. Neither the duration nor capacity limitations attached to novel information received from sensory memory applies to information from long-term memory. That information has no measurable limitations of either duration or capacity. It can be indefinite in size and duration. In effect, information in long-term memory vastly expands working memory. That expansion trivialises any biological differences between humans in the capacity of working memory. Basic differences between people in working memory capacity are likely to be irrelevant given the huge alterations in this processor that occur when it is dealing with organised information taken from long-term memory.

Historically, the influence of long-term memory on working memory dates back to the initial research on working memory. Miller's (1956) concept of chunking suggested that people could learn to "chunk" together elements of information that could be processed in working memory as a single element. While the concept of chunks was not explicitly connected with long-term memory because the distinction between working and long-term memory was articulated later, using current knowledge, chunking cannot occur without long-term memory. Chunks either reside in long-term memory or are formed using information held in long-term memory.

Atkinson and Shiffrin (1968) provided a model that delineated sensory, working, and long-term memory stores. That model is central to most subsequent treatments with information moving between the stores. In that model, we begin to see the influence of long-term memory on working memory although the major influence, the alteration of the characteristics of working memory by information in long-term memory, was not made explicitly.

Another major advance came from Ericsson and Kintsch (1995) with their concept of long-term working memory. They suggested that because the characteristics of working memory when processing information from long-term memory are so dramatically different to its characteristics when processing information from sensory memory, it is appropriate to assume a separate processor – long-term working memory.

In the current treatment, rather than assuming a separate processor that processes information in a qualitatively different manner depending on whether the information comes from sensory or long-term memory, the same working memory processor will be assumed irrespective of whether information comes from sensory or long-term memory, with its characteristics gradually altering as the novelty or familiarity of information alters (Sweller, 2003). At one end of a continuum, when dealing with unfamiliar information, working memory limitations are critical. They become successively less critical as familiarity increases, in other words, as more and more information from long-term memory is used. At the other extreme, when dealing with information incorporated in well-entrenched, automated schemas, working memory limitations become irrelevant. Thus, the extent to which working memory limitations matter depends on the extent to which the information being dealt with has been organised in long-term memory. The characteristics of working memory and the manner in which working memory functions is critically dependent on what has been stored in long-term memory.

Relations between working memory and long-term memory can also be used to explain understanding (Marcus, Cooper, & Sweller, 1996). Understanding occurs when all relevant elements of information can be processed simultaneously in working memory. Because of the limitation of working memory when dealing with novel information, if faced with new material that must be learned, there may be too many elements to simultaneously process in working memory. If the elements are essential, understanding can't occur until it becomes possible to process them. While studying the material, elements are organised and combined into schemas held in long-term memory. When schema construction and automation have progressed to the point where all of the elements essential to understanding the topic can be processed in working memory, understanding has occurred. Based on these interactions, understanding can be defined as the ability to simultaneously process required elements in working memory. On this definition, the relations and interplay between working and long-term memory are central to understanding.

As was the case when individually considering long-term and working memory, it is appropriate to consider the relations between the processors within an evolutionary framework. In the case of both evolution and human cognition, large amounts of information can only be dealt with after they have been appropriately organised. Prior to being organised, the amount of information that can be dealt with is necessarily very small. In the case of genetic information, huge amounts of organised information can be dealt with and transmitted from generation to generation but alterations to a genome are not and cannot be organised. Random alterations followed by effectiveness testing are unavoidable and so any viable alterations will be relatively minuscule. Similarly, a huge amount of schematically organised information held in long-term memory can and is used repeatedly but failing direct guidance through instruction, changes to long-term memory cannot be organised. Random proposals followed by effectiveness testing must be used and this procedure cannot result in rapid, massive, effective changes to long-term memory. Alterations must be small and a small working memory when dealing with new information is a consequence.

Schemas as a Central Executive for Working Memory

The relations between working and long-term memory go beyond long-term memory altering the characteristics of working memory. Schemas in long-term memory act as a central executive for working memory. They indicate what should be done, when it should be done and how it should be done. In other words, organised information in long-term memory directs the manner in which information is processed in working memory. It is ideally placed to do so precisely because it is organised. Thus, in this sense also, information in long-term memory alters the characteristics of working memory.

Not only do schemas act as a central executive, they are the only conceivable central executive. If schemas are not available, as occurs when dealing with new information, there is no alternative central executive to call upon. As previously indicated, when relevant information in long-term memory is not available, random generation followed by effectiveness testing is the only remaining alternative. Contrary to theories such as that of Baddeley (1992), there is no logical manner in which a central executive other than a learned central executive, can function (Sweller, 2003). Just as no central executive function can direct evolution by natural selection, similarly no unlearned central executive can direct information in working memory. In both cases, if previously acquired information is not available, decision making can only occur by random generation followed by effectiveness testing.

Instructional Consequences: Cognitive Load Theory

It was stated previously that schemas held in long-term memory constitute the only conceivable central executive for organising information. In one sense, that is not entirely true. Information provided by others can also act as a central executive. If there is no schema available, rather than randomly organising information and then testing for effectiveness, schemas held by someone else can be used to organise the information. In other words, other people's knowledge, imparted in either spoken or written form, can act as a central executive if one's own schema-based central executive is unavailable. Of course, other people's knowledge can only act as a central executive if it is available in a suitable form. Many instructional procedures explicitly recommend techniques that place a primary emphasis on random generation followed by testing. All inquiry-based recommendations fall in this category and are unlikely to act as a suitable central executive.

The alternative is direct, instructional guidance that provides a substitute for the missing schemas and allows learners to develop their own schemas without engaging in the difficult, time-consuming process of almost limitless random generation followed by testing. There is nothing in our cognitive architecture that suggests that a random generation and testing procedure should be superior to direct instructional guidance. Furthermore, how that direct instructional guidance is organised should also depend on the structures and characteristics of human cognitive architecture. Instruction that does not have as its primary aim the accumulation of knowledge in long-term memory through schema construction and automation and that does not consider working memory characteristics, is likely to be less than optimal. Instructors need to keep in mind that before learners faced with novel material can organise and incorporate it in long-term memory, they must process it using a limited working memory that includes

partially independent channels for auditory and visual information. These characteristics of human cognitive architecture have implications for the design of instruction, especially multimedia instruction.

Cognitive load theory (Paas, Renkl, & Sweller, 2003, 2004, Sweller, 1999; 2003; Sweller, Van Merriënboer, & Paas, 1998) and the instructional principles it has generated are all based on these assumptions concerning human cognitive architecture. There are three categories of cognitive load discussed by the theory: extraneous, intrinsic, and germane cognitive load.

Extraneous cognitive load is caused by inappropriate instructional designs that ignore working memory limits and fail to focus working memory resources on schema construction and automation. There is a wide range of instructional design principles that are based on cognitive load theory. Each principle takes a commonly used instructional procedure, analyses it from the perspective of relevant aspects of human cognition, and then redesigns the instruction to reduce working memory load and increase schema construction and automation. The worked example (chapter 15 in this volume), split-attention (chapter 8), modality (chapter 9), redundancy (chapter 10), and expertise-reversal effects (chapter 21) are directly relevant to multimedia learning and because they are discussed in some of the following chapters will only be summarised briefly here. (A summary of other cognitive load effects may be found in Sweller, 2003.)

The worked example effect (e.g., Cooper and Sweller, 1987) is demonstrated when learners studying worked examples that provide a solution to a problem learn more than learners who are required to solve the equivalent problem. Searching for a solution during problem solving places heavy demands on working memory and those demands interfere with schema construction. A worked example, by reducing or eliminating search, reduces extraneous cognitive load and so facilitates learning.

The split-attention effect (e.g., Sweller, Chandler, Tierney, & Cooper, 1990) occurs when attention must be split between multiple sources of visual information that are all essential for understanding. A geometric diagram and its associated statements provide an example. The multiple sources must be mentally integrated before the instruction can be understood and the material learned. Mental integration imposes a heavy extraneous cognitive load that is reduced by physically integrating the multiple sources of information.

The modality effect (e.g., Tindall-Ford, Chandler, & Sweller, 1997) also occurs under conditions where multiple sources of information are essential for understanding and learning and where the visual information requires learners to split their attention. In the case of the modality effect, the extraneous cognitive load is reduced, not by physically integrating the sources of information but by presenting verbal material in spoken rather than written form. Cognitive load is reduced because the use of dual modality increases effective working memory capacity (as noted previously).

The redundancy effect (e.g., Chandler & Sweller, 1991) differs from the split-attention and modality effects in that it does not deal with multiple sources of information, all of which are essential for understanding and learning. Rather, it deals with multiple sources of information in which one source is sufficient to allow understanding and learning while the other sources merely reiterate the information of the first source in a different form. They are redundant. A diagram plus a statement that redescribes the diagram in words provide an example. Extraneous cognitive load is reduced and learning is facilitated, not by eliminating split-attention or using dual modality presentation but instead, by eliminating the redundant information.

The expertise reversal effect (Kalyuga, Ayres, Chandler, & Sweller, 2003) occurs when instructional procedures such as physically integrating multiple sources of information or presenting instruction in dual mode format first lose their advantage with increasing learner expertise and then become disadvantageous compared to split-source visual presentation. The effect oc-

curs because information that is essential for novices becomes redundant for more expert learners. (There are other conditions under which the expertise reversal effect occurs, discussed in chapter 21.)

Intrinsic cognitive load is the cognitive load due to the natural complexity of the information that must be processed. It is determined by levels of element interactivity. For example, if someone is learning to translate some of the nouns of a foreign language, each translation can be learned independently of every other translation. One can learn to translate the word *cat* without learning to translate the word *dog*. In this example, element interactivity is low and so working memory load is low. In contrast, the elements that constitute other material may interact in the sense that one cannot meaningfully learn one element without simultaneously learning many other elements. For example, if learning the appropriate word order in English for the words *when learning a language*, one cannot attend to individual words to determine that *a language learning when* is inappropriate. One must consider all of the words and the relations among them because they interact. Element interactivity is high resulting in a high intrinsic cognitive load. While there are other reasons why learning can be difficult such as the material including a very large number of elements irrespective of whether they interact, understanding and learning high element interactivity material are difficult for a specific and important reason: Because high element interactivity material imposes a high working memory load.

Lastly, germane cognitive load (Paas & Van Merriënboer, 1994) is "effective" cognitive load. It is the cognitive load caused by effortful learning resulting in schema construction and automation. Providing learners with a variety of examples demonstrating a point increases cognitive load but the increase is germane in that it is likely to assist schema construction.

Extraneous, intrinsic, and germane cognitive load are additive. The aim of instruction should be to reduce extraneous cognitive load caused by inappropriate instructional procedures. Reducing extraneous cognitive load frees working memory capacity and so may permit an increase in germane cognitive load. Nevertheless, if intrinsic cognitive load is low, increases in germane cognitive load may be possible even with high levels of extraneous cognitive load because a low intrinsic cognitive load results in a relatively low total cognitive load. In other words, how one designs instruction may not be particularly important when dealing with simple material that can be easily understood. Even with poor instructional designs, working memory capacity may not be exceeded. Instructional design may only be critical when dealing with complex material that imposes a heavy working memory load due to its intrinsic nature. Adding a heavy extraneous cognitive load to a heavy intrinsic cognitive load may exceed working memory capacity whereas adding a heavy extraneous cognitive load to a light intrinsic cognitive load may not exceed capacity. As a consequence, the cognitive load effects due to extraneous cognitive load and summarised previously can only be demonstrated using material that is high in element interactivity (Sweller & Chandler, 1994; Tindall-Ford, et al., 1997). If element interactivity is low, material can frequently be understood and learned even if extraneous cognitive load is high. This effect is the element interactivity effect.

Conclusions

Instructional design that proceeds without reference to human cognition is likely to be random in its effectiveness. Until relatively recently, that lamentable state of affairs was unavoidable because our knowledge of human cognitive architecture was too sparse to effectively apply to instruction. The immense expansion of that knowledge, including suggestions concerning the evolutionary origins of human cognitive architecture, has altered the instructional design landscape. The limitations of working memory when dealing with novel information, the elimination of those limitations when dealing

with well-known information, and the consequences of partially separate auditory and visual working memory channels all have profound implications for instructional design in general and multimedia instruction in particular. Those implications have changed and are likely to continue to change instructional procedures.

Glossary

Auditory working memory (or auditory processor): That component of working memory that deals with speech and other auditory information.

Automation (or automaticity): A process by which schemata held in long-term memory become sufficiently well-practiced to enable them to bypass, or to be processed without conscious use of, working memory. Automated schemata impose a minimal strain on working memory.

Cognitive architecture: The manner in which the cognitive structures used to learn, think, and solve problems are organised.

Cognitive load: The load imposed on working memory by information being presented.

Cognitive load theory: An instructional theory based on our knowledge of human cognitive architecture that specifically addresses the limitations of working memory.

Direct instructional guidance: Instruction in which procedures are directly demonstrated to learners. Can be contrasted with inquiry-based learning.

Dual-modality instruction: The use of both auditory and visual information under split-attention conditions. Can be contrasted with single modality instruction, normally presented in visual only mode.

Element interactivity: The extent to which elements of information that must be processed interact. If material that must be learned has high element inter-activity, elements cannot be processed individually in working memory and so that material will be seen as complex and difficult to understand (see *intrinsic cognitive load*).

Inquiry-based learning: Instruction in which learners, rather than having a procedure demonstrated, are required to discover it themselves. Can be contrasted with direct instructional guidance.

Integrated instructions: Instructions in which multiple sources of information are physically integrated so that working memory resources do not need to be used for mental integration. Can be contrasted with split-attention instructions.

Intrinsic cognitive load: The cognitive load that is imposed by multiple, interacting elements (see *element interactivity*) that, because they interact, must be processed simultaneously rather than successively in working memory resulting in a heavy load.

Learning: Any change in long-term memory involving an accumulation of information.

Long-term memory: The cognitive structure that stores our knowledge base. We are only conscious of those contents of long-term memory that are transferred to working memory.

Redundant instructions: Instructions presenting the same information in different forms.

Schema: A cognitive construct that schematically organises information for storage in long-term memory. When brought into working memory from long-term memory, a schema allows us to treat multiple elements of information as a single element classified according to the way in which it will be used.

Sensory memory: The cognitive structure that permits us to perceive new information.

Split-attention instructions: Instructions in which multiple sources of information are not physically integrated so that working memory resources need to be used for mental integration. Can be contrasted with integrated instructions.

Visual working memory or visual processor: That component of working memory that deals visually with two- or three-dimensional objects.

Working memory: The cognitive structure in which we consciously process information. Notable for its severe capacity and duration limits when dealing with new information.

References

Atkinson, R., & Shiffrin, R. (1968). Human memory: A proposed system and its control processes. In K. Spence & J. Spence (Eds.), *The psychology of learning and motivation* (Vol. 2, pp. 89–195). New York: Academic Press.

Baddeley, A. (1992). Working memory. *Science*, 255, 556–559.

Chandler, P., & Sweller, J. (1991). Cognitive load theory and the format of instruction. *Cognition and Instruction*, 8, 293–332.

Chase, W. G., & Simon, H. A. (1973). Perception in chess. *Cognitive Psychology*, 4, 55–81.

Chi, M., Glaser, R., & Rees, E. (1982). Expertise in problem solving. In R. Sternberg (Ed.), *Advances in the psychology of human intelligence* (pp. 7–75). Hillsdale, NJ: Erlbaum.

Cooper, G., & Sweller, J. (1987). The effects of schema acquisition and rule automation on mathematical problem-solving transfer. *Journal of Educational Psychology*, 79, 347–362.

De Groot, A. (1965). *Thought and choice in chess*. The Hague, Netherlands: Mouton. (Original work published 1946.)

Ericsson, K. A., & Kintsch, W. (1995). Long-term working memory. *Psychological Review*, 102, 211–245.

Egan, D. E., & Schwartz B. J. (1979). Chunking in recall of symbolic drawings. *Memory and Cognition*, 7, 149–158.

Jeffries, R., Turner, A., Polson, P., & Atwood, M. (1981). Processes involved in designing software. In J. R. Anderson (Ed.), *Cognitive skills and their acquisition* (pp. 255–283). Hillsdale, NJ: Erlbaum.

Kalyuga, S., Ayres, P., Chandler, P., & Sweller, J. (2003). Expertise reversal effect. *Educational Psychologist, 38*, 23–33.

Kotovsky, K., Hayes, J. R., & Simon, H. A. (1985). Why are some problems hard? Evidence from Tower of Hanoi. *Cognitive Psychology, 17*, 248–294.

Larkin, J., McDermott, J., Simon, D., & Simon, H. (1980). Models of competence in solving physics problems. *Cognitive Science, 4*, 317–348.

Marcus, N., Cooper, M., & Sweller, J. (1996). Understanding instructions. *Journal of Educational Psychology, 88*, 49–63.

Mayer, R. E. (2001). *Multimedia Learning.* New York: Cambridge University Press.

Miller, G. A. (1956). The magical number seven, plus or minus two: Some limits on our capacity for processing information. *Psychological Review, 63*, 81–97.

Paas, F., Renkl, A., & Sweller, J. (2003). Cognitive load theory and instructional design. *Educational Psychologist, 38*, 1–4.

Paas, F., Renkl, A., & Sweller, J. (2004). Cognitive load theory: Instructional implications of the interaction between information structures and cognitive architecture. *Instructional Science, 32*, 1–8.

Paas, F., & Van Mërrienboer, J. (1994). Variability of worked examples and transfer of geometrical problem solving skills: A cognitive-load approach. *Journal of Educational Psychology, 86*, 122–133.

Penney, C. G. (1989). Modality effects and the structure of short-term verbal memory. *Memory and Cognition, 17*, 398–422.

Peterson, L., & Peterson, M. (1959). Short-term retention of individual verbal items. *Journal of Experimental Psychology, 58*, 193–198.

Schneider, W., & Shiffrin, R. (1977). Controlled and automatic human information processing: I. Detection, search and attention. *Psychological Review, 84*, 1–66.

Shiffrin, R., & Schneider, W. (1977). Controlled and automatic human information processing: II. Perceptual learning, automatic attending, and a general theory. *Psychological Review, 84*, 127–190.

Simon, H., & Gilmartin, K. (1973). A simulation of memory for chess positions. *Cognitive Psychology, 5*, 29–46.

Sweller, J. (1999). *Instructional design in technical areas.* Melbourne, Australia: ACER Press.

Sweller, J. (2003). Evolution of human cognitive architecture. In B. Ross (Ed.), *The Psychology of Learning and Motivation* (Vol. 43, pp. 215–266). San Diego, CA: Academic Press.

Sweller, J., & Chandler, P. (1994). Why some material is difficult to learn. *Cognition and Instruction, 12*, 185–233.

Sweller, J., Chandler, P., Tierney, P., & Cooper, M. (1990). Cognitive load and selective attention as factors in the structuring of technical material. *Journal of Experimental Psychology: General, 119*, 176–192.

Sweller, J., & Cooper, G. A. (1985). The use of worked examples as a substitute for problem solving in learning algebra. *Cognition and Instruction, 2*, 59–89.

Sweller, J., van Merriënboer, J., & Paas, F. (1998). Cognitive architecture and instructional design. *Educational Psychology Review, 10*, 251–296.

Tindall-Ford, S., Chandler, P., & Sweller, J. (1997). When two sensory modes are better than one. *Journal of Experimental Psychology: Applied, 3*, 257–287.

CHAPTER 3

Cognitive Theory of Multimedia Learning

Richard E. Mayer

University of California, Santa Barbara

Abstract

A fundamental hypothesis underlying research on multimedia learning is that multimedia instructional messages that are designed in light of how the human mind works are more likely to lead to meaningful learning than those that are not. The cognitive theory of multimedia learning (CTML) is based on three cognitive science principles of learning: the human information processing system includes dual channels for visual/pictorial and auditory/verbal processing (i.e., dual-channels assumption); each channel has limited capacity for processing (i.e., limited capacity assumption); and active learning entails carrying out a coordinated set of cognitive processes during learning (i.e., active processing assumption). The cognitive theory of multimedia learning specifies five cognitive processes in multimedia learning: selecting relevant words from the presented text or narration, selecting relevant images from the presented illustrations, organizing the selected words into a coherent verbal representation, organizing selected images into a coherent pictorial representation, and integrating the pictorial and verbal representations and prior knowledge. Multimedia instructional messages should be designed to prime these processes.

The Case for Multimedia Learning

What is the rationale for a theory of multimedia learning? People learn more deeply from words and pictures than from words alone. This assertion – which can be called the *multimedia principle* – underlies much of the interest in multimedia learning. For thousands of years, words have been the major format for instruction – including spoken words, and within the last few hundred years, printed words. Today, thanks to further technological advances, pictorial forms of instruction are becoming widely available, including dazzling computer-based graphics. However, simply adding pictures to words does not guarantee an improvement in learning – that is, all multimedia presentations are not equally effective. In this chapter I explore a theory aimed at understanding how to use words and pictures to improve human learning.

A fundamental hypothesis underlying research on multimedia learning is that multimedia instructional messages that are designed in light of how the human mind works are more likely to lead to meaningful learning than those that are not. For the past 15 years my colleagues and I at the University of California, Santa Barbara have been engaged in a sustained effort to construct an evidenced-based theory of multimedia learning that can guide the design of effective multimedia instructional messages (Mayer 2001, 2002, 2003a; Mayer & Moreno, 2003).

What is a multimedia instructional message? A multimedia instructional message is a communication containing words and pictures intended to foster learning. The communication can be delivered using any medium, including paper (i.e., book-based communications) or computers (i.e., computer-based communications). Words can include printed words (such as you are now reading) or spoken words (such as in a narration); pictures can include static graphics – such as illustrations or photos – or dynamic graphics – such as animation or video clips. This definition is broad enough to include textbook chapters, online lessons containing animation and narration, and interactive simulation games. For example, Figure 3.1 presents frames from a narrated animation on lightning formation, which we have studied in numerous experiments (Mayer, 2001).

Learning can be measured by tests of retention (i.e., remembering the presented information) and transfer (i.e., being able to use the information to solve new problems). Our focus is on transfer because we are mainly interested in how words and pictures can be used to promote understanding. In short, transfer tests can help tell us how well people understand what they have learned. We are particularly interested in the cognitive processes by which people construct meaningful learning outcomes from words and pictures.

What is the role of a theory of learning in multimedia design? Much of the work presented in this handbook is based on the premise that the design of multimedia instructional messages should be compatible with how people learn. In short, the design of multimedia instructional messages should be sensitive to what we know about how people process information. The cognitive theory of multimedia learning represents an attempt to help accomplish this goal by describing how people learn from words and pictures, based on consistent empirical research evidence (e.g., Mayer, 2001, 2002, 2003a; Mayer & Moreno, 2003) and on consensus principles in cognitive science (e.g., Bransford, Brown, & Cocking, 1999; Lambert & McCombs, 1998; Mayer, 2003b).

In building the cognitive theory of multimedia learning my colleagues and I were guided by four criteria: *theoretical plausibility* – the theory is consistent with cognitive science principles of learning; *testability* – the theory yields predictions that can be tested in scientific research; *empirical plausibility* – the theory is consistent with empirical research evidence on multimedia learning; and *applicability* – the theory is relevant to educational needs for improving the design of multimedia instructional messages. In this chapter, I describe the cognitive theory of multimedia learning, which is intended to meet these criteria. In particular, I summarize three underlying assumptions of the theory derived from cognitive science; describe three memory stores, five cognitive processes, and five forms of representation in the theory; and then provide examples and a conclusion.

Three Assumptions of the Cognitive Theory of Multimedia Learning

Decisions about how to design a multimedia message always reflect an underlying conception of how people learn – even when the underlying theory of learning is not stated. In short, the design of multimedia messages

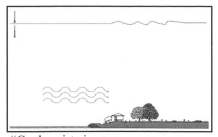

"Cool moist air moves over a warmer surface and becomes heated."

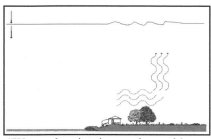

"Warmed moist air near the earth's surface rises rapidly."

"As the air in this updraft cools, water vapor condenses into water droplets and forms a cloud."

Figure 3.1. Selected frames from a narrated animation on lightning formation.

is influenced by the designer's conception of how the human mind works. For example, when a multimedia presentation consists of a screen overflowing with multicolored words and images – flashing and moving about – this reflects the designer's conception of human learning. The designer's underlying conception is that human learners possess a single-channel, unlimited capacity, and passive-processing system. First, by not taking advantage of auditory modes of presentation, this design is based on a single-channel assumption – all information enters the cognitive system in the same way regardless of its modality. It follows that it does not matter which modality is used to present information – such as presenting words as sounds or text – just as long as the information is presented. Second, by presenting so much information, this design is based on an unlimited capacity assumption – humans can handle an unlimited amount of material. It follows that the designer's job is to present information to the learner. Third, by presenting many isolated pieces of information, this design is based on a passive processing assumption – humans act as tape recorders who add as much information to their memories as possible. It follows that learners do not need any guidance in organizing and making sense of the presented information.

What's wrong with this vision of learners as possessing a single-channel, unlimited capacity, and passive processing system? Current research in cognitive psychology paints a quite different view of how the human mind works (Bransford et al., 1999; Lambert & McCombs, 1998; Mayer, 2003b). Thus, a difficulty with this commonsense conception of learning is that it conflicts with what is known about how people learn. In this section, I explore three assumptions underlying the cognitive theory of multimedia learning – *dual channels*, *limited capacity*, and *active processing*. These assumptions are summarized in Table 3.1.

Dual-Channel Assumption

The dual-channel assumption is that humans possess separate information processing channels for visually represented material and auditorily represented material. The dual-channel assumption is incorporated into the cognitive theory of multimedia learning by proposing that the human information-processing system contains an auditory/verbal channel and a visual/pictorial channel. When information is presented to the eyes (such as illustrations, animations, video, or on-screen text), humans begin by processing that information

Table 3.1. Three Assumptions of a Cognitive Theory of Multimedia Learning

Assumption	Description	Related citations
Dual channels	Humans possess separate channels for processing visual and auditory information	Paivio (1986), Baddeley (1986, 1999)
Limited capacity	Humans are limited in the amount of information that can be processed in each channel at one time	Baddeley (1986, 1999), Chandler & Sweller (1991)
Active processing	Humans engage in active learning by attending to relevant incoming information, organizing selected information into coherent mental representations, and integrating mental representations with other knowledge	Mayer (2001), Wittrock (1989)

in the visual channel; when information is presented to the ears (such as narration or nonverbal sounds), humans begin by processing that information in the auditory channel. The concept of separate information processing channels has a long history in cognitive psychology and currently is most closely associated with Paivio's dual-coding theory (Clark & Paivio, 1991; Paivio, 1986) and Baddeley's model of working memory (Baddeley, 1986, 1999).

WHAT IS PROCESSED IN EACH CHANNEL?

There are two ways of conceptualizing the differences between the two channels – one based on *presentation modes* and the other based on *sensory modalities*. The presentation-mode approach focuses on whether the presented stimulus is verbal (such as spoken or printed words) or nonverbal (such as pictures, video, animation, or background sounds). According to the presentation-mode approach, one channel processes verbal material and the other channel processes pictorial material and nonverbal sounds. This conceptualization is most consistent with Paivio's (1986) distinction between verbal and nonverbal systems.

In contrast, the sensory-modality approach focuses on whether learners initially process the presented materials through their eyes (e.g., for pictures, video, animation, or printed words) or ears (e.g., for spoken words or background sounds). According to the sensory-modality approach, one channel processes visually represented ma-

terial and the other channel processes auditorily represented material. This conceptualization is most consistent with Baddeley's (1986, 1999) distinction between the visuospatial sketchpad and the phonological (or articulatory) loop.

Whereas the presentation-mode approach focuses on the format of the stimulus-as-presented (i.e., verbal or nonverbal), the sensory-modality approach focuses on the stimulus-as-represented in working memory (i.e., auditory or visual). The major difference concerning multimedia learning rests in the processing of printed words (i.e., on-screen text) and background sounds. On-screen text is initially processed in the verbal channel in the presentation-mode approach but in the visual channel in the sensory-modality approach. Background sounds, including nonverbal music, are initially processed in the nonverbal channel in the presentation-mode approach but in the auditory channel in the sensory-mode approach.

For purposes of the cognitive theory of multimedia learning, I have opted for a compromise in which I use the sensory-modality approach to distinguish between visually presented material (e.g., pictures, animations, video, and on-screen text) and auditorily presented material (e.g., narration and background sounds) as well as a presentation-mode approach to distinguish between the construction of pictorially based and verbally based models in working memory. However, additional research is needed to clarify the nature of the differences between the two channels.

Although information enters the human information system through one channel, learners may also be able to convert the representation for processing in the other channel. When learners are able to devote adequate cognitive resources to the task, it is possible for information originally presented to one channel to also be represented in the other channel. For example, on-screen text may initially be processed in the visual channel because it is presented to the eyes, but an experienced reader may be able to mentally convert images into sounds, which are processed through the auditory channel. Similarly, an illustration of an object or event such as a cloud rising above the freezing level may initially be processed in the visual channel, but the learner may also be able to mentally construct the corresponding verbal description in the auditory channel. Conversely, a narration describing some event such as "the cloud rises above the freezing level" may initially be processed in the auditory channel because it is presented to the ears, but the learner may also form a corresponding mental image that is processed in the visual channel. Cross-channel representations of the same stimulus play an important role in Paivio's (1986) dual-coding theory.

Limited Capacity Assumption

The second assumption is that humans are limited in the amount of information that can be processed in each channel at one time. When an illustration or animation is presented, the learner is able to hold only a few images in working memory at any one time, reflecting portions of the presented material rather than an exact copy of the presented material. For example, if an illustration or animation of a tire pump is presented, the learner may be able to focus on building mental images of the handle going down, the inlet valve opening, and air moving into the cylinder. When a narration is presented,

the learner is able to hold only a few words in working memory at any one time, reflecting portions of the presented text rather than a verbatim recording. For example, if the spoken text is "When the handle is pushed down, the piston moves down, the inlet valve opens, the outlet valve closes, and air enters the bottom of cylinder," the learner may be able to hold the following verbal representations in auditory working memory: "handle goes up," "inlet valve opens," and "air enters cylinder." The conception of limited capacity in consciousness has a long history in psychology, and some modern examples are Baddeley's (1986, 1999) theory of working memory and Chandler and Sweller's (1991; Sweller, 1999) cognitive load theory.

If we assume that each channel has limited processing capacity, it is important to know just how much information can be processed in each channel. The classic way to measure someone's cognitive capacity is to give a memory span test (Miller, 1956; Simon, 1980). For example, in a digit span test, I can read a list of digits at the rate of one digit per second (e.g., 8-7-5-3-9-6-4) and ask you to repeat them back in order. The longest list that you can recite without making an error is your memory span for digits (or digit span). Alternatively, I can show you a series of line drawings of simple objects at the rate of one per second (e.g., moon-pencil-comb-apple-chair book-pig) and ask you to repeat them back in order. Again, the longest list you can recite without making an error is your memory span for pictures. Although there are individual differences, on average memory span is fairly small – approximately five to seven chunks.

With practice, of course, people can learn techniques for chunking the elements in the list, such as grouping the seven digits 8-7-5-3-9-6-4 into three chunks 875-39-64 (e.g., "eight seven five" pause "three nine" pause "six four"). In this way, the cognitive capacity remains the same (e.g., five to seven chunks) but more elements can be remembered within each chunk. Researchers have developed more refined measures of verbal and visual working memory capacity, but continue to show that human processing capacity is severely limited (Miyake & Shah, 1999).

The constraints on our processing capacity force us to make decisions about which pieces of incoming information to pay attention to, the degree to which we should build connections among the selected pieces of information, and the degree to which we should build connections between selected pieces of information and our existing knowledge. *Metacognitive strategies* are techniques for allocating, monitoring, coordinating, and adjusting these limited cognitive resources. These strategies are at the heart of what Baddeley (1986, 1999) calls the *central executive* – the system that controls the allocation of cognitive resources – and play a central role in modern theories of intelligence (Sternberg, 1990).

Active Processing Assumption

The third assumption is that humans actively engage in cognitive processing in order to construct a coherent mental representation of their experiences. These active cognitive processes include paying attention, organizing incoming information, and integrating incoming information with other knowledge. In short, humans are active processors who seek to make sense of multimedia presentations. This view of humans as active processors conflicts with a common view of humans as passive processors who seek to add as much information as possible to memory, that is, as tape recorders who file copies of their experiences in memory to be retrieved later.

Active learning occurs when a learner applies cognitive processes to incoming material – processes that are intended to help the learner make sense of the material. The outcome of active cognitive processing is the construction of a coherent mental representation, so active learning can be viewed as a process of model building. A *mental model (or knowledge structure)* represents the key parts of the presented material and their relations. For example, in a multimedia presentation of how lightning storms develop, the learner may attempt to build a cause-and-effect system in which a change in one part of the system causes a change in another part. In a lesson comparing and contrasting two theories, construction of a mental model involves building a sort of matrix structure that compares the two theories along several dimensions.

If the outcome of active learning is the construction of a coherent mental representation, it is useful to explore some of the typical ways that knowledge can be structured. Some basic knowledge structures include *process, comparison, generalization, enumeration,* and *classification* (Chambliss & Calfee, 1998; Cook & Mayer, 1988). Process structures can be represented as cause-and-effect chains and consist of explanations of how some system works. An example is an explanation of how the human ear works. Comparison structures can be represented as matrices and consist of comparisons among two or more elements along several dimensions. An example is a comparison between how two competing theories of learning view the role of the learner, the role of the teacher, and useful types of instructional methods. Generalization structures can be represented as a branching tree and consist of a main idea with subordinate supporting details. An example is a chapter outline for a chapter explaining the major causes for the American Civil War. Enumeration structures can be represented as lists and consist of a collection of items. An example is the names of principles of multimedia learning listed in this handbook. Classification structures can be represented as hierarchies and consist of sets and subsets. An example is a biological classification system for sea animals.

Understanding a multimedia message often involves constructing one of these kinds

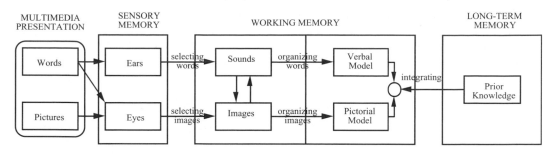

Figure 3.2. Cognitive theory of multimedia learning.

of knowledge structures. This assumption suggests two important implications for multimedia design: (1) the presented material should have a coherent structure and (2) the message should provide guidance to the learner for how to build the structure. If the material lacks a coherent structure – such as being a collection of isolated facts – the learner's model-building efforts will be fruitless. If the message lacks guidance for how to structure the presented material, the learner's model-building efforts may be overwhelmed. Multimedia design can be conceptualized as an attempt to assist learners in their model-building efforts.

WHAT ARE THE COGNITIVE PROCESSES INVOLVED IN ACTIVE LEARNING?

Three processes that are essential for active learning are selecting relevant material, organizing selected material, and integrating selected material with existing knowledge (Mayer, 1996, 2001; Wittrock, 1989). Selecting relevant material occurs when a learner pays attention to appropriate words and images in the presented material. This process involves bringing material from the outside into the working memory component of the cognitive system. Organizing selected material involves building structural relations among the elements – such as one of the five kinds of structures described in the preceding text. This process takes place within the working memory component of the cognitive system. Integrating selected material with existing knowledge involves building connections between incoming material and relevant portions of prior knowledge. This process involves activating knowl-

edge in long-term memory and bringing it into working memory. For example, in a multimedia message on the cause of lightning, learners must pay attention to certain words and images, arrange them into a cause-and-effect chain, and relate the steps to prior knowledge such as the principle that hot air rises.

In sum, the implicit theory of learning underlying some multimedia messages is that learning is a single-channel, unlimited-capacity, passive-processing activity. In contrast, I offer a cognitive theory of multimedia learning that is based on three basic assumptions about how the human mind works – namely, that the human mind is a dual-channel, limited-capacity, active-processing system.

Three Memory Stores in Multimedia Learning

Figure 3.2 presents a cognitive model of multimedia learning intended to represent the human information-processing system. The boxes represent memory stores, including sensory memory, working memory, and long-term memory. Pictures and words come in from the outside world as a multimedia presentation (indicated at the left side of the figure) and enter sensory memory through the eyes and ears (indicated in the sensory memory box). Sensory memory allows for pictures and printed text to be held as exact visual images for a very brief time period in a visual sensory memory (at the top) and for spoken words and other sounds to be held as exact auditory images for a very brief time period in an auditory sensory memory (at the bottom). The arrow from pictures to eyes corresponds to a picture being registered in the eyes, the arrow from words to ears corresponds to spoken text being registered in the ears, and the arrow from words to eyes corresponds to printed text being registered in the eyes.

The central work of multimedia learning takes place in working memory so let's focus there. Working memory is used for temporally holding and manipulating knowledge in active consciousness. For example, in reading this sentence you may be able to actively concentrate on only some of the words at one time, or in looking at Figure 3.2 you may be able to hold the images of only some of the boxes and arrows in your mind at one time. This kind of processing – that is, processing that involves conscious awareness – takes place in working memory. The left side of working memory represents the raw material that comes into working memory – visual images of pictures and sound images of words – so it is based on the two sensory modalities that I call visual and auditory. In contrast, the right side of working memory represents the knowledge constructed in working memory – pictorial and verbal models and links between them – so it is based on the two representation modes that I call pictorial and verbal. I use the term *pictorial model* to include spatial representations. The arrow from sounds to images represents the mental conversion of a sound (such as the spoken word *cat*) into a visual image (such as an image of a cat) – that is, when you hear the word "cat" you might also form a mental image of a cat. The arrow from images to sounds represents the mental conversion of a visual image (e.g., a mental picture of a cat) into a sound (e.g., the sound of the word "cat") – that is, you mentally hear the word *cat* when you see a picture of one. The major cognitive processing required for multimedia learning is represented by the arrows labeled *selecting images, selecting words, organizing images, organizing words*, and *integrating*, which are described in the next section.

Finally, the box on the right is labeled *long-term memory* and corresponds to the learner's storehouse of knowledge. Unlike working memory, long-term memory can hold large amounts of knowledge over long periods of time, but to actively think about material in long-term memory it must be brought into working memory (as indicated by the arrow from long-term memory to working memory).

Five Processes in the Cognitive Theory of Multimedia Learning

For meaningful learning to occur in a multimedia environment, the learner must engage in five cognitive processes: (1) selecting relevant words for processing in verbal working memory, (2) selecting relevant images for processing in visual working memory, (3) organizing selected words into a verbal model, (4) organizing selected images into a pictorial model, and (5) integrating the verbal and pictorial representations with each other and with prior knowledge. Although I present these processes as a list, they do not necessarily occur in linear order, so a learner might move from process to process in many different ways. Successful multimedia learning requires that the learner coordinate and monitor these five processes.

Selecting Relevant Words

The first labeled step listed in Figure 3.2 involves a change in knowledge representation from the external presentation of spoken words (e.g., computer-generated narration) to a sensory representation of sounds to an internal working memory representation of word sounds (e.g., some of the words in the narration). The input for this step is a spoken verbal message – that is, the spoken words in the presented portion of the multimedia message. The output for this step is a word sound base (called *sounds* in Figure 3.2) – that is, a mental representation in the learner's verbal working memory of selected words or phrases.

The cognitive process mediating this change is called *selecting relevant words* and involves paying attention to some of the words that are presented in the multimedia message as they pass through auditory sensory memory. If the words are presented as speech, this process begins in the auditory channel (as indicated by the arrows from *words* to *ears* to *sounds*). However, if the words are presented as on-screen text or printed text, this process begins in the visual channel (as indicated by the arrow from *words* to *eyes*) and later may move to the auditory channel if the learner mentally articulates the printed words (as indicated by the arrow from *images* to *sounds* in the left portion of working memory). The need for selecting only part of the presented message occurs because of capacity limitations in each channel of the cognitive system. If the capacity were unlimited, there would be no need to focus attention on only part of the verbal message. Finally, the selection of words is not arbitrary. The learner must determine which words are most relevant – an activity that is consistent with the view of the learner as an active sense maker.

For example, in the lightning lesson, one segment of the multimedia presentation contains the words, "Cool moist air moves over a warmer surface and becomes heated," the next segment contains the words, "Warmed moist air near the earth's surface rises rapidly," and the next segment has the words, "As the air in this updraft cools, water vapor condenses into water droplets and forms a cloud." When a learner engages in the selection process, the result may be that some of the words are represented in verbal working memory – such as, "Cool air becomes heated, rises, forms a cloud."

Selecting Relevant Images

The second step involves a change in knowledge representation from the external presentation of pictures (e.g., an animation segment or an illustration) to a sensory representation of unanalyzed visual images to an internal representation in working memory (e.g., a visual image of part of the animation or illustration). The input for this step is a pictorial portion of a multimedia message that is held briefly in visual sensory memory. The output for this step is a visual image base (called *images* in Figure 3.2) – a mental representation in the learner's working memory of selected images.

The cognitive process underlying this change – *selecting relevant images* – involves paying attention to part of the animation or illustrations presented in the multimedia message. This process begins in the visual channel, but it is possible to convert part of it to the auditory channel (e.g., by mentally narrating an ongoing animation). The need to select only part of the presented pictorial material arises from the limited processing capacity of the cognitive system. It is not possible to process all parts of a complex illustration or animation so learners must focus on only part of the incoming pictorial material. Finally, the selection process for images – like the selection process for words – is not arbitrary because the learner must judge which images are most relevant for making sense out of the multimedia presentation.

In the lightning lesson, for example, one segment of the animation shows blue-colored arrows – representing cool air – moving over a heated land surface that contains a house and trees; another segment shows the arrows turning red and traveling upward above a tree; and a third segment shows the arrows changing into a cloud with lots of dots inside. In selecting relevant images, the learner may compress all this into images of a blue arrow pointing rightward, a red arrow pointing upward, and a cloud. Details such as the house and tree on the surface, the wavy form of the arrows, and the dots in the cloud are lost.

Organizing Selected Words

Once the learner has formed a word sound base from the incoming words of a segment of the multimedia message, the next step is to organize the words into a coherent representation – a knowledge structure that I call a *verbal model*. The input for this step is the word sound base – the word sounds selected from the incoming verbal message. The output for this step is a verbal model – a coherent (or structured) representation in the learner's working memory of the selected words or phrases.

The cognitive process involved in this change is *organizing selected words* in which the learner builds connections among pieces of verbal knowledge. This process is most likely to occur in the auditory channel and is subject to the same capacity limitations that affect the selection process. Learners do not have unlimited capacity to build all possible connections so they must focus on building a simple structure. The organizing process is not arbitrary, but rather reflects an effort at sense making – such as the construction of a cause-and-effect chain.

For example, in the lightning lesson, the learner may build causal connections between the selected verbal components: "First: cool air is heated; second: it rises; third: it forms a cloud." In mentally building a causal chain, the learner is organizing the selected words.

Organizing Selected Images

The process for organizing images parallels that for selecting words. Once the learner has formed an image base from the incoming pictures of a segment of the multimedia message, the next step is to organize the images into a coherent representation – a knowledge structure that I call a *pictorial model*. The input for this step is the visual image base – the images selected from the incoming pictorial message. The output for this step is a pictorial model – a coherent (or structured) representation in the learner's working memory of the selected images.

This change from images to pictorial model requires the application of a cognitive process that I call *organizing selected images*. In this process, the learner builds connections among pieces of pictorial knowledge. This process occurs in the visual channel, which is subject to the same capacity limitations that affect the selection process. Learners lack the capacity to build all possi-ble connections among images in their working memory, but rather must focus on building a simple set of connections. As in the process of organizing words, the process of organizing images is not arbitrary. Rather, it reflects an effort to build a simple structure that makes sense to the learner – such as a cause-and-effect chain.

For example, in the lightning lesson, the learner may build causal connections between the selected images: The rightward-moving blue arrow turns into a rising red arrow, which turns into a cloud. In short, the learner builds causal links in which the first event leads to the second and so on.

Integrating Word-Based and Image-Based Representations

Perhaps the most crucial step in multimedia learning involves making connections between word-based and image-based representations. This step involves a change from having two separate representations – a pictorial model and a verbal model – to having an integrated representation in which corresponding elements and relations from one model are mapped onto the other. The input for this step is the pictorial model and the verbal model that the learner has constructed so far, and the output is an integrated model, which is based on connecting the two representations. In addition, the integrated model includes connections with prior knowledge.

I refer to this cognitive process as *integrating words and images* because it involves building connections between corresponding portions of the pictorial and verbal models as well as knowledge from long-term memory. This process occurs in visual and verbal working memory, and involves the coordination between them. This is an extremely demanding process that requires the efficient use of cognitive capacity. The process reflects the epitome of sense making because the learner must focus on the underlying structure of the visual and verbal representations. The learner can use prior knowledge to help coordinate the integration process, as indicated by the arrow from long-term memory to working memory.

Table 3.2. Five Cognitive Processes in the Cognitive Theory of Multimedia Learning

Process	Description
Selecting words	Learner pays attention to relevant words in a multimedia message to create sounds in working memory
Selecting images	Learner pays attention to relevant pictures in a multimedia message to create images in working memory
Organizing words	Learner builds connections among selected words to create a coherent verbal model in working memory
Organizing images	Learner builds connections among selected images to create a coherent pictorial model in working memory
Integrating	Learner builds connections between verbal and pictorial models and with prior knowledge

For example, in the lightning lesson, the learner must see the connection between the verbal chain – "First, cool air is heated; second, it rises; third, it forms a cloud" – and the pictorial chain – the blue arrow followed by the red arrow followed by the cloud shape. In addition, prior knowledge can be applied to the transition from the first to the second event by remembering that hot air rises.

The five cognitive processes in multimedia learning are summarized in Table 3.2. Each of the five processes in multimedia learning is likely to occur many times throughout a multimedia presentation. The processes are applied segment by segment rather than to the entire message as a whole. For example, in processing the lightning lesson, learners do not first select all relevant words and images from the entire passage, then organize them into verbal and pictorial models of the entire passage, and then connect the completed models with one another at the very end. Rather, learners carry out this procedure on small segments: they select relevant words and images from the first sentence of the narration and the first few seconds of the animation; they organize and integrate them; and then this set of processes is repeated for the next segment, and so on.

Five Forms of Representation

As you can see in Figure 3.2, there are five forms of representation for words and pic-
tures, reflecting their stage of processing. To the far left, we begin with *words and pictures in the multimedia presentation*, that is, the stimuli that are presented to the learner. In the case of the lightning message shown in Figure 3.1, the words are the spoken words presented through the computer's speakers and the pictures are the frames of the animation presented on the computer's screen. Second, as the presented words and pictures impinge on the learner's ears and eyes, the next form of representation is *acoustic representations (or sounds) and iconic representations (or images) in sensory memory*. The sensory representations fade rapidly, unless the learner pays attention to them. Third, when the learner selects some of the words and images for further processing in working memory, the next form of representation is *sounds and images in working memory*. These are the building blocks for knowledge construction – including key phrases such as, "warmed air rises," and key images such as red arrows moving upward. The fourth form of representation results from the learner's construction of a *verbal model and pictorial model in working memory*. Here the learner has organized the material into coherent verbal and pictorial representations, and also has mentally integrated them. Finally, the fifth form of representation is *knowledge in long-term memory*, which the learner uses for guiding the process of knowledge construction in working memory. Sweller (1999, and chapter 2, this volume) refers to this knowledge as *schemas*. After new knowledge is constructed in working memory, it is stored

Table 3.3. Five Forms of Representation in the Cognitive Theory of Multimedia Learning

Type of knowledge	Location	Example
Words and pictures	Multimedia presentation	Sound waves from computer speaker: "Warmed moist air. . . ."
Acoustic and iconic representations	Sensory memory	Received sounds in learner's ears: "Warmed moist air. . . ."
Sounds and images	Working memory	Selected sounds: "warmed air rises"
Verbal and pictorial models	Working memory	Mental model of cloud formation
Prior knowledge	Long-term memory	Schema for differences in air pressure

in long-term memory as prior knowledge to be used in supporting new learning. The five forms of representation are summarized in Table 3.3.

Examples of How Three Kinds of Presented Materials Are Processed

Let's take a closer look at how three kinds of presented materials are processed from start to finish according to the model of multimedia learning summarized in Figure 3.2: pictures, spoken words, and printed words. For example, suppose that a student clicks on an entry for lightning in a multimedia encyclopedia and is presented with a static picture of a lightning storm with a paragraph of on-screen text about the number of injuries and deaths caused by lightning each year. Similarly, suppose the student then clicks on the entry for lightning in another multimedia encyclopedia and is presented with a short animation along with narration describing the steps in lightning formation. In these examples, the first presentation contains static pictures and printed words whereas the second presentation contains dynamic pictures and spoken words.

Processing of Pictures

The top frame in Figure 3.3 shows the path for processing of pictures – indicated by thick arrows and darkened boxes. The first event – represented by the "pictures" box under "multimedia presentation" at the left side of Figure 3.3 – is the presentation of

the lightning photograph from the first encyclopedia (i.e., a static picture) or the lighting animation from the second encyclopedia (i.e., a dynamic picture). The second event – represented by the "eyes" box under "sensory memory" – is that the pictures impinge on the eyes, resulting in a brief sensory image – that is for a brief time the student's eye beholds the photograph or the animation frames.

These first two events happen without much effort on the part of the learner, but next, the active cognitive processing begins – the processing over which the learner has some conscious control. If the student pays attention to the fleeting images coming from the eyes, parts of the images will become represented in working memory. This attentional processing corresponds to the arrow labeled "selecting images" and the resulting mental representation is labeled "images" under "working memory." Once working memory is full of image pieces, the next active cognitive processing involves organizing those pieces into a coherent structure – a process indicated by the "organizing images" arrow. The resulting knowledge representation is a *pictorial model*, that is, the student builds an organized visual representation of the main parts of a lightning bolt (from the first encyclopedia) or an organized set of images representing the cause-and-effect steps in lightning formation (from the second encyclopedia).

Finally, active cognitive processing is required to connect the new representation with other knowledge – a process indicated by the "integrating" arrow. For example, the

Processing of Pictures

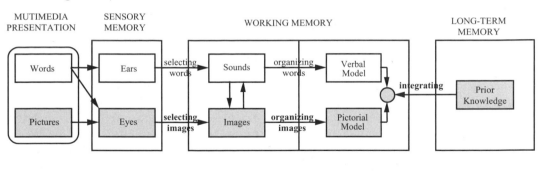

Processing of Spoken Words

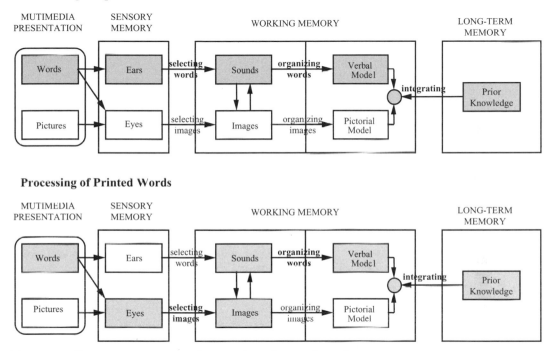

Processing of Printed Words

Figure 3.3. Processing pictures, spoken words, and printed words.

student may use prior knowledge about electricity to help include moving positive and negative charges in the mental representation of the lightning bolt or may use prior knowledge of electricity to help explain why the negative and positive charges are attracted to one another. In addition, if the learners have also produced a verbal model, they may try to connect it to the pictorial model – such as looking for how a phrase in the text corresponds to a part of the image. This processing results in an integrated learning outcome indicated by the circle under "working memory."

Processing of Spoken Words

The middle frame in Figure 3.3 shows the path for processing of spoken words – indicated by thick arrows and darkened boxes. When the computer produces narration (as indicated by the "words" box under "multimedia presentation") the sounds are picked up by the student's ears (as indicated by the "ears" box under "sensory memory"). For example, when the computer says, "The negatively charged particles fall to the bottom of the cloud, and most of the positively charged particles rise to the top," these words are picked up by the student's ears and held temporarily in auditory sensory memory. Next, active cognitive processing can take place. If the student pays attention to the sounds coming into the ears (as indicated by the arrow labeled "selecting words"), some of the incoming sounds will be selected for inclusion in the word sound base (indicated by the "sounds" box under "working memory"). For example, the resulting collection of words in working memory might include "positive top, negative bottom." The words in the word base are disorganized fragments, so the next step – indicated by the "organizing words" arrow – is to build them into a coherent mental structure – indicated by the "verbal model" box. In this process, the words change from being represented based on sound to being represented based on word meaning. The result could be a cause-effect chain for the steps in lightning formation. Lastly, the student may use prior knowledge to help explain the transition from one step to another and may connect words with pictures – such as connecting "positive top, negative bottom" with an image of positive particles in the top of a cloud and negative charges in the bottom. This process is labeled "integrating" and the resulting integrated learning outcome is indicated by the circle under "working memory."

Processing of Printed Words

So far, cognitive processing of pictures takes place mainly in the bottom channel of Figure 3.2 – that is the visual/pictorial channel – whereas the cognitive processing of spoken words takes place mainly in the top channel – that is, the auditory/verbal channel. However, the arrow from "images" to the "sounds" in working memory indicates that the learner can mentally create sounds corresponding to the visual image – such as thinking the word *wind* upon seeing wavy arrows in the animation. Similarly, the arrow from "sounds" to "images" in working memory indicates that the learner can mentally create images corresponding to the words – such as visualizing a plus sign when the narration says "positively charged particle."

The presentation of printed text in multimedia messages creates an information-processing challenge for the dual-channel system portrayed in Figure 3.2. For example, consider the case of a student who must read text and view an illustration. The words are presented visually so they must initially be processed through the eyes – as indicated by the arrow from "words" to "eyes." Then, the student may attend to some of the incoming words (as indicated by the "selecting images" arrow) and bring them into working memory as part of the images. Then, by mentally pronouncing the images of the printed words the student can get the words into the auditory/verbal channel – as indicated by the arrow from the images to the sounds. Once the words are represented in the auditory/verbal channel they are processed like the spoken words, as described previously. This path is presented in the bottom frame of Figure 3.3. As you can see, when verbal material must enter through the visual channel, the words must take a complex route through the system, and must also compete for attention with the illustration that the student is also processing through the visual channel. The consequences of this problem are addressed in chapters 9 and 11 on the modality principle.

Conclusion

Historical Overview

The cognitive theory of multimedia learning has evolved within the body of research papers produced by my colleagues and me at the University of California, Santa Barbara (UCSB) over the past 15 years. Although the name has changed over the years, the underlying elements of the theory – that is, dual channels, limited capacity, and active processing – have remained constant. Some names used early in the research program – such as "model of meaningful learning" (Mayer, 1989) and "cognitive conditions for effective illustrations" (Mayer & Gallini, 1990) – emphasized the active processing element. Other names used later – such as "dual-coding model" (Mayer & Anderson, 1991, 1992) and "dual-processing model of multimedia learning" (Mayer & Moreno, 1998; Mayer, Moreno, Boire, & Vagge, 1999) – emphasized the dual-channels element. Yet other names – such as "generative theory" (Mayer, Steinhoff, Bower, & Mars, 1995) and "generative theory of multimedia learning" (Mayer, 1997; Plass, Chun, Mayer, & Leutner, 1998) – emphasized all three elements. The current name, "cognitive theory of multimedia learning," was used in Mayer, Bove, Bryman, Mars, and Tapangco (1996), Moreno and Mayer (2000), and Mayer, Heiser, and Lonn (2001), and was selected for use in major reviews (Mayer, 2001, 2002, 2003a; Mayer & Moreno, 2003).

An early predecessor to the flowchart representation shown in Figure 3.2 in this chapter was a dual-coding model shown in Mayer and Sims (1994, Figure 1) which contained the same two channels and three of the same five cognitive processes, but lacked two of the cognitive processes and sensory memory. Mayer, Steinhoff, Bower, and Mars (1995, Figure 1) and Mayer (1997, Figure 3) presented an intermediate version that is almost identical to the flowchart shown in Figure 3.2 except that it lacked long-term memory and sensory memory. Finally, the current version of the flowchart appeared in Mayer, Heiser, and Lonn (2001), and was reproduced in subsequent reviews (Mayer, 2001, Figure 2; Mayer, 2002, Figure 7; Mayer, 2003a, Figure 2; Mayer & Moreno, 2003, Figure 1). Thus, the model has developed by adding components – both cognitive processes and mental representations – and clarifying their role. The result is the cognitive theory of multimedia learning that is represented in the flowchart in Figure 3.2 of this chapter.

Comparison With Related Theories

As can be seen in Figure 3.2, the cognitive theory of multimedia learning involves (a) two channels (i.e., visual and verbal), (b) limited processing capacity, (c) three kinds of memory stores, and (d) five cognitive processes (selecting words, selecting images, or-

ganizing words, organizing images, and integrating), and (e) five kinds of representations (i.e., presented words and pictures; sounds and images in sensory memory; selected sounds and images in working memory; verbal and pictorial models in working memory; and knowledge in long-term memory). The theory incorporates elements from classic information-processing models, such as *two channels* from Paivio's (1986) dual-coding theory, *limited processing* capacity from Baddeley's (1986, 1999) model of working memory, and a flowchart representation of *memory stores* and *cognitive processes* from Atkinson and Shiffrin (1968).

Key components of the cognitive theory of multimedia learning are consistent with other multimedia instructional design theories such as Sweller's (1999, 2003, chapter 2) cognitive load theory, and Schnotz and Bannert's (2003; Schnotz, chapter 4) integrated model of text and picture comprehension.

First, consider Sweller's (1999, 2003, chapter 2) cognitive load theory. Like the cognitive theory of multimedia learning, Sweller's (1999) cognitive load theory acknowledges "separate channels for dealing with auditory and visual material" (p. 138) and emphasizes that "we can hold few elements in working memory" (p. 4). Like the cognitive theory of multimedia learning, the architecture of the human information processing allows for several kinds of representations: elements in the presented material correspond to words and pictures in the multimedia presentation, elements in working memory correspond to verbal and pictorial models in working memory, and schemas in long-term memory correspond to knowledge in long-term memory. Cognitive load theory elaborates on the implications of limited working memory capacity for instructional design, and focuses on ways in which instruction imposes cognitive load on learners. However, it does not focus on the kinds of information processes involved in multimedia learning.

Second, consider Schnotz and Bannert's integrated model of text and picture comprehension as summarized in Figure 3.2 of

Schnotz and Bannert (2003). Like the cognitive theory of multimedia learning, Schnotz and Bannert's model emphasizes two channels, but unlike the cognitive theory of multimedia learning it does not emphasize limited capacity. All five cognitive processes are represented although with some differences in conceptualization: subsemantic processing corresponds to selecting words, perception corresponds to selecting images, semantic processing corresponds to organizing words, thematic selection corresponds to organizing images, and model construction/inspection corresponds to integrating. Four of the five representations are included although, again, with some differences in conceptualization: text and picture/diagram corresponds to words and pictures in the multimedia presentation; text surface representation and visual image correspond to sounds and images in working memory; propositional representation and mental model correspond to verbal model and pictorial model; and conceptual organization corresponds to knowledge in long-term memory.

In summary, the cognitive theory of multimedia learning is compatible and somewhat similar to other multimedia design theories. Sweller's (1999, 2003, chapter 2) cognitive load theory offers further elaborations on the role of limited capacity in instructional design for multimedia learning, and Schnotz and Bannert's (2003, Schnotz, chapter 4) offers further elaborations on the nature of mental representations in multimedia learning.

Future Directions

Although we have made progress in creating a cognitive theory of multimedia learning, much remains to done, particularly (a) in fleshing out the details of the mechanisms underlying the five cognitive processes and the five forms of representation, (b) in integrating the various theories of multimedia learning, and (c) in building a credible research base. First, more work is needed to understand and measure the basic constructs in theories of multimedia learning, such as determining how to measure cognitive load during learning, determining the optimal size of a chunk of presented information, or determining the way that a mental model is represented in the learner's memory. Second, there is a need to find consensus among theorists, such as reconciliation among cognitive load theory (Sweller, chapter 2), and the cognitive theory of multimedia learning (this chapter), the integrative model of text and picture comprehension, (Schnoz, chapter 4), the four-component instructional design model (Merriënboer & Kester, chapter 5), and related theories. Third, we have a continuing need to generate testable predictions from theories of multimedia learning and to test these predictions in rigorous scientific experiments. The best way to insure the usefulness of theories of multimedia learning is to have coherent research literature on which to base them.

Summary

In summary, multimedia learning takes place within the learner's information system – a system that contains separate channels for visual and verbal processing, a system with serious limitations on the capacity of each channel, and a system that requires coordinated cognitive processing in each channel for active learning to occur. In particular, multimedia learning is a demanding process that requires selecting relevant words and images; organizing them into coherent verbal and pictorial representations; and integrating the verbal and pictorial representations with each other and with prior knowledge. In the process of multimedia learning, material is represented in five forms: as words and pictures in a multimedia presentation; acoustic and iconic representations in sensory memory; sounds and images in working memory; verbal and pictorial models in working memory; and knowledge in long-term memory. The theme of this chapter is that multimedia messages should be designed to facilitate multimedia learning processes. Multimedia messages that are designed in light of how the human mind works are more likely to lead to meaningful learning than those that are not. This proposition is tested empirically in the chapters of this handbook.

Glossary

Cognitive theory of multimedia learning: A theory of how people learn from words and pictures, based on the idea that people possess separate channels for processing verbal and visual material (dual-channels assumption), each channel can process only a small amount of material at a time (limited-capacity assumption), and meaningful learning involves engaging in appropriate cognitive processing during learning (active-processing assumption).

Long-term memory: A memory store that holds large amounts of knowledge over long periods of time.

Multimedia instructional message: A communication containing words and pictures intended to foster learning.

Multimedia principle: People learn more deeply from words and pictures than from words alone.

Sensory memory: A memory store that holds pictures and printed text impinging on the eyes as exact visual images for a very brief period and that holds spoken words and other sounds impinging on the ears as exact auditory images for a very brief period.

Working memory: A limited-capacity memory store for holding and manipulating sounds and images in active consciousness.

Note

This chapter is based on chapter 3, "A Cognitive Theory of Multimedia Learning," in *Multimedia Learning* (Mayer, 2001). I appreciate the helpful comments of Jeroen van Merrienböer, Wolfgang Schnotz, and John Sweller.

References

Atkinson, R. C., & Shiffrin, R. M. (1968). Human memory: A proposed system and its control processes. In K. W. Spence (Ed.), *The psychology of learning and motivation* (pp. 89–195). New York: Academic Press.

Baddeley, A. D. (1986). *Working memory*. Oxford, England: Oxford University Press.

Baddeley, A. D. (1999). *Human memory*. Boston: Allyn & Bacon.

Bransford, J. D., Brown, A. L., & Cocking, R. R. (1999). *How people learn*. Washington, DC: National Academy Press.

Chambliss, M. J., & Calfee, R. C. (1998). *Textbooks for learning*. Oxford, England: Blackwell.

Chandler, P., & Sweller, J. (1991). Cognitive load theory and the format of instruction. *Cognition and Instruction, 8*, 293–332.

Clark, R. E., & Paivio, A. (1991). Dual coding theory and education. *Educational Psychology Review, 3*, 149–210.

Cook, L. K., & Mayer, R. E. (1988). Teaching readers about the structure of scientific text. *Journal of Educational Psychology, 80*, 448–456.

Lambert, N. M., & McCombs, B. L. (1998). *How students learn*. Washington, DC: American Psychological Association.

Mayer, R. E. (1989). Systematic thinking fostered by illustrations in scientific text. *Journal of Educational Psychology, 81*, 240–246.

Mayer, R. E. (1996). Learning strategies for making sense out of expository text: The SOI model for guiding three cognitive processes in knowledge construction. *Educational Psychology Review, 8*, 357–371.

Mayer, R. E. (1997). Multimedia learning: Are we asking the right questions? *Educational Psychologist, 32*, 1–19.

Mayer, R. E. (2001). *Multimedia learning*. New York: Cambridge University Press.

Mayer, R. E. (2002). Multimedia learning. In B. H. Ross (Ed.), *The psychology of learning and motivation: Volume 41* (pp. 85–139). San Diego, CA: Academic Press.

Mayer, R. E. (2003a). The promise of multimedia learning: Using the same instructional design methods across different media. *Learning and Instruction, 12*, 125–141.

Mayer, R. E. (2003b). *Learning and instruction*. Upper Saddle River, NJ: Merrill Prentice Hall.

Mayer, R. E., & Anderson, R. B. (1991). Animations need narrations: An experimental test of the dual-coding hypothesis. *Journal of Educational Psychology, 83*, 484–490.

Mayer, R. E., & Anderson, R. B. (1992). The instructive animation: Helping students build connections between words and pictures in multimedia learning. *Journal of Educational Psychology, 84*, 444–452.

Mayer, R. E., Bove, W., Bryman, A., Mars, R., & Tapangco, L. (1996). When less is more: Meaningful learning from visual and verbal summaries of science textbook lessons. *Journal of Educational Psychology, 88*, 64–73.

Mayer, R. E., & Gallini, J. K. (1990). When is an illustration worth ten thousand words? *Journal of Educational Psychology, 82*, 715–726.

Mayer, R. E., Heiser, J., & Lonn, S. (2001). Cognitive constraints on multimedia learning: When presenting more material results in less understanding. *Journal of Educational Psychology, 93*, 187–198.

Mayer, R. E., & Moreno, R. (1998). A split-attention effect in multimedia learning: Evidence for dual processing systems in working memory. *Journal of Educational Psychology, 90*, 312–320.

Mayer, R. E., & Moreno, R. (2003). Nine ways to reduce cognitive load in multimedia learning. *Educational Psychologist, 38*, 43–52.

Mayer, R. E., Moreno, R., Boire, M., & Vagge, S. (1999). Maximizing constructivist learning from multimedia communications by minimizing cognitive load. *Journal of Educational Psychology, 91*, 638–643.

Mayer, R. E., & Sims, V. K., (1994). For whom is a picture worth a thousand words? Extensions of a dual-coding theory of multimedia learning. *Journal of Educational Psychology, 86*, 389–401.

Mayer, R. E., Steinhoff, K., Bower, G., & Mars, R. (1995). A generative theory of textbook design: Using annotated illustrations to foster meaningful learning of science text. *Educational Technology Research & Development, 43*, 31–43.

Miller, G. A. (1956). The magic number seven, plus or minus two: Some limits on our capacity for processing information. *Psychological Review, 63*, 81–97.

Miyake, A., & Shah, P. (Eds.). (1999). *Models of working memory*. New York: Cambridge University Press.

Moreno, R., & Mayer, R. E. (2000). A coherence effect in multimedia learning: The case for minimizing irrelevant sounds in the design of multimedia instructional messages. *Journal of Educational Psychology, 92*, 117–125.

Paivio, A. (1986). *Mental representations: A dual coding approach*. New York: Oxford University Press.

Plass, J. L., Chun, D. M., Mayer, R. E., & Leutner, D. (1998). Supporting visual and verbal learning preferences in a second-language multimedia learning environment. *Journal of Educational Psychology, 90*, 25–36.

Schnotz, W., & Bannert, M. (2003). Construction and interference in learning from multiple representation. *Learning and Instruction, 13*, 141–156.

Simon, H. A., (1974). How big is a chunk? *Science, 183*, 482–488.

Sternberg, R. J. (1990). *Metaphors of mind: Conceptions of the nature of intelligence*. New York: Cambridge University Press.

Sweller, J. (1999). *Instructional design in technical areas*. Camberwell, Australia: ACER Press.

Sweller, J. (2003). Evolution of human cognitive architecture. In B. Ross (Ed.), *The psychology of learning and motivation* (Vol. 43, pp. 215–216). San Diego, CA: Academic Press.

Wittrock, M. C. (1989). Generative processes of comprehension. *Educational Psychologist, 24*, 345–376.

CHAPTER 4

An Integrated Model of Text and Picture Comprehension

Wolfgang Schnotz
University of Koblenz-Landau, Germany

Abstract

This chapter presents an integrated model of text and picture comprehension that takes into account that learners can use multiple sensory modalities. The model encompasses reading comprehension, listening comprehension, visual picture comprehension, and sound comprehension (i.e., auditory picture comprehension). The model's cognitive architecture consists of sensory registers, working memory, and long-term memory. It furthermore includes a cognitive level and a perceptual level. The cognitive level is characterized by two representational channels: a verbal channel and a pictorial channel. The perceptual level is characterized by multiple sensory channels. After presenting the model, the chapter derives predictions, which can be empirically tested. It reports research findings that can be explained by the model, and it derives practical suggestions for instructional design. Finally, the chapter discusses limitations of the model and points out directions for further research.

Introduction

The term *multimedia* means different things on different levels. On the level of technology, it means the use of multiple delivery media such as computers, screens, and loudspeakers. On the level of presentation formats, it means the use of different forms of representation such as texts and pictures. On the level of sensory modalities, it means the use of multiple senses such as the eye and the ear. The level of technology is of course very important in practice, but it is not of high interest from a psychological point of view, because comprehension is not fundamentally different when a text passage is delivered either by a computer screen or by a printed book, or if a picture is presented by a poster or by a slide. Comprehension is highly dependent on what kind of information is presented and how it is presented. The psychology of multimedia learning focuses therefore on the level of presentation formats and on the level of sensory modalities.

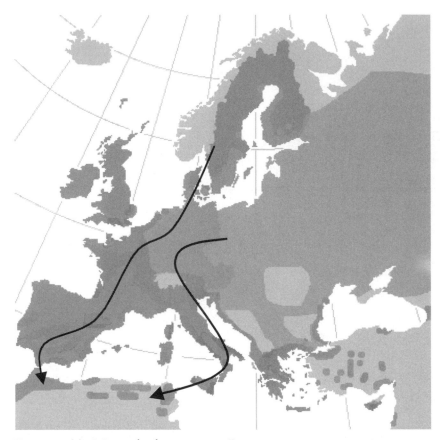

Figure 4.1 (a). Map on bird migration in Europe.

What is multimedia learning? The core of multimedia learning from the viewpoint of psychology is the combined comprehension of text and pictures (Mayer, 1997). This does not necessarily require high technology. Multimedia learning is also possible with printed books or blackboards instead of computer screens and simply with the human voice instead of loudspeakers. Multimedia learning is therefore not a modern phenomenon. It has a long tradition, which goes back to Comenius (1999) who emphasized in his pioneer work *Orbis sensualium pictus* (published first in 1658) the importance of adding pictures to texts. Multimedia learning can occur in different forms. A learner can listen to a lecture accompanied by pictures; this is lecture-based multimedia learning. He or she can read a book with pictures; this is book-based multimedia learning. He or she can read an illustrated text from the Internet on a computer screen or listen to a text accompanied by pictures from a loudspeaker; this is Web-based multimedia learning (Mayer, 2001).

Individuals usually combine these different kinds of multimedia learning in a flexible way. Consider the following example. A teacher explains to her class of eighth-graders the migration of birds in Europe. She presents a map of the continent (shown in Figure 4.1a), which indicates where some birds live in summer and where they stay in winter. While pointing on the map, she gives oral explanations like the following:

(a) *"Many birds breed in Middle and Northern Europe in summer, but do not stay there during winter. Instead, they fly in September to warmer areas in the Mediterranean area. These birds are called 'migrant'."*

At the end of the lesson, Daniel, one of her students, has to learn as a homework task

Figure 4.1 (b). Drawing of a marsh harrier.

about a specific bird, the marsh harrier, and to give a report to his classmates the next day. Daniel walks into a library and looks up in a printed encyclopedia of biology, where he finds a drawing of the marsh harrier (shown in Figure 4.1b) and the following text:

> *(b) "The marsh harrier is a bird of prey with an average wingspan of 47" and a face similar to owls. The drawing shows the typical gliding position of the bird. The marsh harrier is usually found in wetlands, especially in marshes, swamps, and lagoons. It feeds mostly on small birds or mammals (like rodents or rabbits), and on reptiles. The marsh harrier is migrant."*

As the encyclopedia does not contain further information about the bird's migration, Daniel decides to search the Internet, where he finds a Web site including a bar graph (shown in Figure 4.1c) and the following text:

> *(c) "The marsh harrier is found all year round in Spain, France, and around the Mediterranean. In other areas of Europe the bird is migrant, breeding in Middle and Northern Europe while wintering in tropical marshes and swamps in North Africa. The bar graph shows a typical frequency pattern of marsh harriers in a Middle European habitat."*

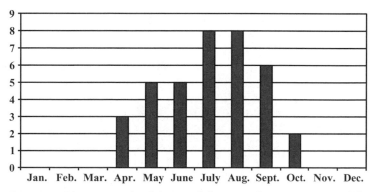

Figure 4.1 (c). Bar graph of the marsh harrier's frequency in a Middle European habitat.

Furthermore, the Web site offers a sound button. After clicking on it, Daniel hears the typical call of the bird near its breeding place.

Altogether, Daniel has practiced three kinds of multimedia learning using various external sources of information. At school, he has performed lecture-based multimedia learning, using the map and the teacher's oral text as information sources. In the library, he has performed book-based multimedia learning, using the drawing of the bird and the printed text as information sources. With the Internet, he has performed Web-based multimedia learning, using the bar graph, the on-screen text, and the sound pattern as information sources. In each case, information was presented to him in different formats such as visual texts, visual pictures (i.e., a map, a drawing, a bar graph) and sound, and he has processed this information through different sensory modalities: the visual modality (written text and pictures) and the auditory modality (oral text and sounds).

As the example demonstrates, multimedia learning environments can be rather complex and they can involve a variety of external representations of a learning content. These representations can take different forms such as spoken text, written text, maps, drawings, graphs, and sound. Multimedia learning occurs when an individual understands what is presented, that is, when he or she uses the external representations as information sources in order to construct in working memory internal (mental) representations of the learning content and he or she stores these representations in long-term memory. In the first part of this chapter, a distinction between two different forms of representations is made and applied to both external and internal representations. As multimedia comprehension and learning is constrained by the functioning of different memory systems, these constraints are analyzed in the second part. In the third part, the theoretical concepts introduced before will be combined into an integrated model of text and picture comprehension, which involves reading comprehension, listening comprehension, visual picture comprehension, and auditory picture compre-

hension (i.e., sound comprehension). The fourth part presents empirical evidence for the integrated model, whereas the fifth part explains what kind of instructional consequences can be derived from the integrated model. Finally, the sixth part points out various limitations of the model and suggests directions of future research in the area.

External and Internal Representations

Forms of Representation

How many basic forms of representation do exist? Despite numerous variants of representations, one can distinguish only two basic forms of representations: descriptions and depictions. Texts are the most common kind of descriptions. However, there are also other kinds of descriptive representations. Mathematical expressions such as $V = s^3$ (describing the relation between a cube's size and its volume) or the formula $F = m * a$ in physics (describing the relation between force, mass and acceleration according to Newton's Second Law) are also descriptive representations. Descriptive representations consist of symbols. Symbols are signs that have no similarity with their referent (Peirce, 1931–1958). The word *bird* for example, has no similarity with a real bird. It is a symbol, and its meaning is based on a convention. In texts, we use nouns (such as *bird* and *breeding*) as symbols for objects and events. We use verbs and prepositions (such as *feed* and *on*) as symbols for relations, and we use adjectives (such as *small* and *migrant*) as symbols for attributes. Of course, there are also other kinds of symbols.

Pictures such as photographs, drawings, paintings, and maps are depictive representations. However, they are not the only kind of depictive representations. A miniature model of a building, a line graph, or the swing of a pointer are also depictive representations. Depictive representations consist of icons. Icons are signs that are associated with their referent by similarity or by another structural commonality. A map such as the one in Figure 4.1a or the drawing of a bird as shown in Figure 4.1b are graphical objects that have some similarity with the corresponding referent (i.e., the European continent or the marsh harrier). A graph has a more abstract structural commonality with its referent. The meaning of the bar graph shown in Figure 4.1c, for example, is based on an analogy: The height of the bars corresponds to the number of marsh harriers in a habitat during the corresponding month, and the sequence of bars corresponds to the sequence of months during the year.

Descriptive representations and depictive representations have different uses for different purposes. Descriptive representations are more powerful in expressing abstract knowledge. For example, it is no problem to say a sentence like *"The Marsh Harrier feeds on mammals or reptiles,"* which connects abstract concepts (e.g., *mammals, reptiles*) by a disjunctive *or*. In a depictive representation it is only possible to show a specific mammal (e.g., a mouse) or a specific reptile (e.g., a lizard). The disjunctive *or* cannot be represented by only one picture. It requires a series of pictures (e.g., one picture showing the bird eating a mouse and another picture showing the bird eating a lizard). On the other hand, descriptive representations have the advantage of being informationally complete. A map, for example, includes all geometric information of the depicted geographical area, and a picture of a marsh harrier eating a mouse includes not only information about the shape of the bird and the shape of a mouse, but necessarily also about their size, their orientation in space, how it holds its pray, and so forth. Depictive representations are therefore more useful to draw inferences, because the new information can be read off directly from the representation (Kosslyn, 1994).

Mental Representations

Does the distinction between descriptive and depictive representations apply also to internal (i.e., mental) representations? In text and picture comprehension, an individual generally constructs multiple mental representations. When a learner reads a text or listens to a text, he or she constructs three kinds of mental representations (Graesser, Millis, & Zwaan, 1997; van Dijk & Kintsch, 1983). For example, when he or she reads a sentence like *"Some migrant birds fly to the South of Europe for wintering,"* he or she forms a mental representation of the text-surface structure. This text-surface representation is not yet understanding, but it allows repeating of what has been read. Based on this surface representation, the reader then constructs a propositional representation. This representation includes the ideas expressed in the text on a conceptual level, which is independent from the specific wording and syntax of the sentence. In the previous example, this would include the idea that migrant birds in Europe fly to the South in September, represented by the proposition "FLY(agent: MIGRANT BIRDS, location: EUROPE, aim: SOUTH, time: SEPTEMBER)." Finally the reader constructs a mental model of the text content. In the previous example, this could be a mental map of Europe including a movement from the North to the South.

When a learner understands a picture, he or she also constructs multiple mental representations (Kosslyn, 1994; Lowe, 1996). The learner creates a perceptual representation (i.e., a visual image) of the picture and he or she then constructs a mental model of the picture's content. For example, when a learner understands the bar graph shown in Figure 4.1c, he or she perceives vertical bars on a horizontal line and creates a corresponding visual image. Based on this visual image, he or she constructs a mental model of a Middle European habitat that includes different numbers of marsh harriers during the course of the year. The mental model can be used then for reading off specific information, for example, that the birds stay in this habitat in summer. The read-off information is encoded as a proposition such as "STAY(agent: BIRDS, location: HABITAT, time: SUMMER)."

The distinction between descriptive and depictive representations applies also to these mental representations. A text-surface representation and a propositional representation are descriptive representations, as they use symbols to describe the subject matter. A visual image and a mental model, on the contrary, are depictive representations, as they are assumed to have an inherent structure that corresponds to the structure of the subject matter (Johnson-Laird, 1983; Kosslyn, 1994). A visual image is sensory specific, because it is linked to the visual modality. A mental model is not sensory specific because it is able to integrate information from different sensory modalities. A mental model of a spatial configuration, for example, can be constructed with visual, auditory, and touch information. It is therefore more abstract than a visual image. In picture comprehension, mental models and visual images differ also with respect to their information content. On the one hand, irrelevant details of the picture, which are included in the visual image, may be ignored in the mental model. On the other hand, the mental model contains additional information from prior knowledge that is not included in the visual image. In understanding bird migration, for example, a mental model of the European continent might include snowfall in Northern areas during winter, although no snow is indicated in the map.

Based on the distinction between descriptive and depictive representations, Schnotz and Bannert (2003) have proposed a theoretical framework for analyzing text and picture comprehension that is shown in Figure 4.2. The model includes a verbal (i.e., descriptive) channel and a pictorial (i.e., depictive) channel for the storage and processing of information. The verbal channel involves the external text, the mental text-surface representation, and the mental propositional representation. Information is processed in this channel by symbol processing. The pictorial channel involves the external picture, the visual image of the picture and the mental model of the subject matter. Information is processed in this channel by structure mapping. This framework corresponds to the dual-coding concept of Paivio (1986), who assumes a verbal system and an image system in the human mind with different forms of mental codes. Contrary to the traditional dual-coding theory, however, the

framework assumes that multiple representations are formed both in text comprehension and in picture comprehension.

Multiple Memory Systems

When learners understand texts and pictures, they construct multiple mental representations in a cognitive system, which has a specific architecture. Research in cognitive psychology suggests that the human cognitive architecture includes multiple memory systems: working memory, sensory registers, and long-term memory (Atkinson & Shiffrin, 1971). These memory systems have different functions, and they constrain processes of text and picture comprehension.

Working Memory

The descriptive channel and the depictive channel are constrained by the limited capacity of working memory. According to Baddeley (1986), working memory consists of a central executive and different subsystems for the storage of information. Two of these subsystems have received much attention in research: auditory working memory and visual working memory. Auditory working memory is conceived as an articulatory-phonological loop. Visual working memory is conceived as a visuo-spatial sketchpad. The articulatory-phonological loop specializes in verbal material presented in auditory modality. It has limited capacity corresponding on the average to what can be articulated within about two seconds. The visuo-spatial sketchpad specializes in spatial information presented in the visual modality. It has a limited capacity of about five units on the average. However, as people with a highly reduced articulatory-phonological loop are nevertheless capable of normal language comprehension, there might be also other subsystems involved in text comprehension (Baddeley, 2000; Vallar & Shallice, 1990).

Working memory plays an important role on higher levels of text comprehension (Daneman & Carpenter, 1983). One can therefore assume also a propositional

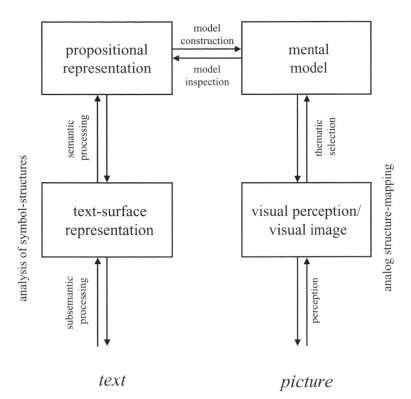

Figure 4.2. Two representational channels in text and picture comprehension.

subsystem that allows the individual to hold a limited number of propositions simultaneously in working memory (Kintsch & van Dijk, 1978). Research findings also suggest that there is a subsystem for mental model construction in working memory. Mental model construction is more influenced by the capacity of the visuospatial sketchpad than by the capacity of the articulatory-phonological loop (Friedman & Miyake, 2000). More specifically, it is highly related to spatial cognitive processing (Sims & Hegarty, 1997). Research of Knauff and Johnson-Laird (2002) indicates that visual imagery and spatial reasoning are based on different cognitive subsystems. This suggests distinguishing between a visual working memory (or sketchpad) for visual images and a spatial working memory for mental model construction.

Sensory Registers

Information enters working memory from the outside world through sensory channels.

Written text is usually visual language read with the eyes, but can sometimes also be read with the fingers (e.g., in the case of blind people reading Braille). Similarly, pictures are usually seen with the eyes, but can sometimes also be perceived by touch (e.g., maps for blind people). Spoken text is usually perceived by the ear, but deaf people can sometimes also read lips and touch the vibration of the larynx. Sound patterns (e.g., the call of a bird), which can be conceived as sound images, are also perceived by the ear. Accordingly, there is no a priori connection between representational formats and sensory modalities. Instead, both verbal and pictorial information can enter working memory through different sensory channels. There are multiple sensory channels according to the multiple sensory modalities between the outside world and working memory. In the following, however, only two sensory channels will be considered: the visual channel, which conveys information from the eye to visual working memory, and the auditory channel, which conveys information from the ear to auditory working memory.

Visual information that meets the eye is stored very briefly (i.e., less than 1 second) in a visual register. If attention is directed to information in the visual register, the information gets transmitted to visual working memory through the visual channel for further cognitive processing. Auditory information that meets the ear is stored briefly (i.e., less then 3 seconds) in an auditory register. If attention is directed to information in the auditory register, the information gets transmitted to auditory working memory through the auditory channel for further cognitive processing.

Long-Term Memory

Text and picture comprehension require prior knowledge that is stored in long-term memory. In text comprehension, prior knowledge about the graphic pattern of written words, about the sound pattern of spoken words, and about possible syntax structures is needed for the mental text-surface representation. In picture comprehension, prior knowledge is needed for the perception of the picture. Prior knowledge influences how easily pictorial information is categorized. Objects can be recognized faster and more easily, when they are presented from a typical perspective (such as the bird shown in Figure 4.1b) than when they are presented from an unusual perspective (Palmer, Rosch, & Chase, 1981). Conceptual knowledge about the domain (e.g., about the breeding of birds and the meteorological conditions at different seasons) is needed both for the construction of a propositional representation and the construction of a mental model (e.g., of bird migration) in text comprehension as well as in picture comprehension.

Text and picture comprehension are therefore not only based on external sources of information (i.e., the text and the picture), but also on prior knowledge as an internal source of information. Prior knowledge can partially compensate for a lack of external information, for lower working memory capacity (Adams, Bell, & Perfetti, 1995; Miller & Stine-Morrow, 1998), and for deficits of the propositional representation (Dutke, 1996; McNamara, Kintsch, Songer, & Kintsch, 1996; Soederberg Miller, 2001). There seems to be a trade-off between the use of external and internal information sources: Pictures are analyzed more intensively if the content is difficult and the learners' prior knowledge is low (Carney & Levin, 2002).

Integrated Comprehension of Text and Pictures

The idea of two representational channels and of multiple sensory channels of limited capacity and the idea of a cognitive architecture including multiple memory systems will in the following be combined into an integrative model of text and picture comprehension. More specifically, the model integrates the concepts of multiple memory systems (Atkinson & Shiffrin, 1971), working memory (Baddeley, 1986, 2000), and dual coding (Paivio, 1986). It furthermore integrates the idea of multiple mental representations in text comprehension and in picture comprehension (Kosslyn, 1994; van Dijk & Kintsch, 1983). It also integrates ideas from the cognitive theory of multimedia learning (CTML) of Mayer (1997, 2001) and from the model of text and picture comprehension of Schnotz and Bannert (2003). The model, which is schematically shown in Figure 4.3, refers to the single or combined comprehension of written text, spoken text, visual pictures, and auditory pictures (i.e., sound images). It is based on the following assumptions:

- Text and picture comprehension take place in cognitive architecture including a working memory of limited capacity, modality-specific sensory registers as information input systems, and a long-term memory.
- Verbal information (i.e., information from written texts or spoken texts) and pictorial information (i.e., information

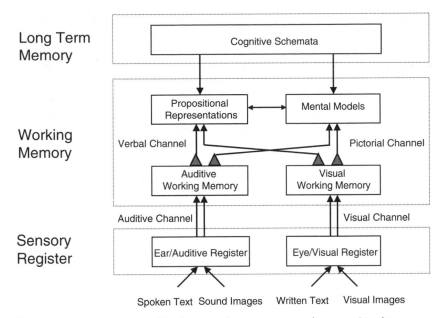

Figure 4.3. Integrative model of text and picture comprehension. [Auditive refers to auditory.]

from visual pictures and from auditory pictures, or from sounds, respectively) is transmitted to working memory through the visual channel and the auditory channel. The channels have limited capacity to process and store information.

- Further information processing in working memory takes place in two different representational channels: the verbal channel and the pictorial channel. Information from written or spoken text is processed in the verbal channel. Information from visual pictures or from sounds is processed in the pictorial channel. The channels have limited capacity to process and store information.

- Text and picture comprehension are active processes of coherence formation. In comprehension, individuals engage in building coherent knowledge structures from the available external verbal and pictorial information and from their prior knowledge.

A perceptual level and a cognitive level of processing can be distinguished within the model. The perceptual level refers to the information transfer between the external environment and working memory. This level is characterized by the functioning of the sensory channels. The cognitive level refers to the information processing within working memory and the exchange of information between long-term and working memory. This level is characterized by the functioning of the verbal channel and the pictorial channel.

READING COMPREHENSION

If a written text is understood, visual verbal information enters the visual register through the eye and is then forwarded through the visual channel to visual working memory. The resulting information pattern in visual working memory corresponds to the text-surface representation in reading comprehison. A verbal filter (filters are symbolized in Figure 4.3 by triangles) selects the verbal information from visual working memory and forwards it through the verbal channel to propositional working memory, where it triggers the formation of propositions, which in turn triggers the construction or elaboration of a mental model. In a text on bird migration, for example, the graphic pattern of the word *bird* is forwarded through the visual channel to visual working memory, selected from there by a verbal filter, and forwarded through the verbal channel to propositional working memory. The concept BIRD is activated in propositional working memory and included into a propositional representation, which finally triggers the construction of a mental model of bird migration.

LISTENING COMPREHENSION

If a spoken text is understood, auditory verbal information enters the auditory register through the ear and is then forwarded through the auditory channel to auditory working memory. The information pattern in auditory working memory corresponds to the text-surface representation in listening comprehension. A verbal filter selects the verbal information from auditory working memory. Further processing is assumed to be the same as in reading comprehension: The information is passed through the verbal channel to propositional working memory, leads to a propositional representation, and finally triggers the construction or elaboration of a mental model. In the example of a text on bird migration, the auditory pattern of the spoken word *bird* is forwarded through the auditory channel into auditory working memory, selected by a verbal filter, and processed through the verbal channel to propositional working memory, where the concept BIRD is included into a propositional representation. This representation finally triggers the construction of a mental model of bird migration.

VISUAL PICTURE COMPREHENSION

If a visual picture is understood, visual pictorial information enters the visual register through the eye and is then forwarded through the visual channel to visual working memory, where it results in a visual perceptual representation of the picture. A visual pictorial filter selects pictorial information from visual working memory and forwards it through the pictorial channel, where it leads to the construction or elaboration of a mental model. The mental model can be used

to read off new information and to encode it in propositional working memory. For example, if a map about bird migration in Europe such as in Figure 4.1b is understood, the visual pattern of the map is forwarded through the visual channel and creates a visual image of the map in visual working memory. Selected pictorial information is then processed in the pictorial channel, which results in the construction or elaboration of a mental model of bird migration in Europe. The individual can read off then further information from the model (such as the fact that migrant birds fly from Northern Europe to the Mediterranean area in fall).

AUDITORY PICTURE COMPREHENSION (SOUND COMPREHENSION)

If a sound is understood, auditory pictorial information enters the auditory register through the ear and is then forwarded through the auditory channel to auditory working memory, where it results in an auditory perceptual representation of the sound. An auditory pictorial filter selects pictorial information from auditory working memory and forwards it through the pictorial channel where it leads to the construction or elaboration of a mental model. The model can then be used to read off new information. For example, if the call of a marsh harrier (as bird of prey) and a call of a small bird (as its possible prey) are heard, the acoustic patterns are forwarded through the auditory channel and lead to the auditory perception in auditory working memory. If an individual has sufficient knowledge about different birds, the selected information can be further processed in the pictorial channel and lead to the construction or elaboration of the mental model of a predator–prey scenario. The individual can then read off information from the mental model (e.g., that a small bird is in danger of falling prey to a marsh harrier).

Which cognitive processes lead to meaningful learning? Meaningful learning from text and pictures requires a coordinated set of cognitive processes including selection of information, organization of information, activation of prior knowledge, and active coherence formation by integration of information from different sources. In comprehension of written or spoken texts, the learner selects relevant verbal information from words, sentences, and paragraphs as an external source of information. He or she organizes this information, activates related prior knowledge as an internal source of information, and constructs both a coherent propositional representation and a coherent mental model. In comprehension of visual pictures, the learner selects relevant pictorial information from a drawing, map, or graph as an external source of information; organizes this information; activates related prior knowledge as a further source of information; and constructs a coherent mental model complemented by a propositional representation. In comprehension of auditory pictures (i.e., sound comprehension), the learner selects relevant acoustic information, organizes this information, activates related prior knowledge as an internal source of information, and constructs a coherent mental model complemented by a propositional representation.

In the rest of this chapter, the integrated text and picture comprehension model described is called the *ITPC model* or simply the *integrated model*. The model has various assumptions in common with the cognitive theory of multimedia learning (CTML) proposed by Mayer (2001), but it also differs from CTML under important aspects. Both models assume a cognitive architecture including multiple memory systems with a working memory system of limited capacity, and they assume different channels for processing and storage of information according to the concept of dual coding. The models differ in the following respect: In the model of Mayer, sensory modality and representational format are merged by the assumption of an auditory–verbal channel and a visual–pictorial channel. The integrated model, on the contrary, assumes that verbal information is not necessarily associated with the auditory modality, but can also be conveyed by other sensory modalities. In CTML verbal information can therefore enter through the visual–pictorial channel (from printed text) or through the auditory–verbal channel

(from spoken text), as shown in Figure 3.2 of chapter 3. The integrated model further assumes that pictorial information is not necessarily associated with the visual modality, but can also be conveyed by other sensory modalities (e.g., sound images).

The integrated model therefore distinguishes sensory channels (visual, auditory, touch, and others) on the perceptual level from representational channels (verbal and pictorial) on the cognitive level. The distinction between a perceptual level and a cognitive level is also part of CTML, where sounds and images correspond to the perceptual level whereas verbal and pictorial models correspond to the cognitive level, as shown in Figure 3.2 of chapter 3. Accordingly, different kinds of text and picture comprehension use different combinations of sensory and representational channels. Reading comprehension of texts combines the visual and the verbal channel, whereas listening comprehension of texts combines the auditory and the verbal channel. Visual picture comprehension combines the visual and the pictorial channel, whereas auditory picture comprehension (sound comprehension) combines the auditory and the pictorial channel. A further difference between the two theoretical approaches is that Mayer assumes the construction of a verbal mental model and a pictorial mental model that then have to be integrated. The integrated model on the contrary assumes that only one mental model is constructed that integrates information from different sources from the beginning. However, the models are consistent with one another in that both assume that pictorial and verbal material are integrated in working memory.

The ITPC model offers a framework for the analysis of text and picture comprehension that allows explanation of a broad variety of empirical findings. However, it can also be used as a framework for the analysis of writing texts and of creating pictures. For example, if an author writes a text, he or she starts with a mental model of a subject matter, then constructs a propositional representation and a text-surface representation, which is then transformed into a written text. Similarly, a graphic designer starts with a mental model of a subject matter, then maps it onto a visual image, which is then transformed into a corresponding picture. The model also allows the learner to analyze combinations of comprehension and production of text and pictures. For example, a learner can read a text, construct a mental model of the text content, and then create his or her own visualization of the content. Similarly, a learner can observe a picture, construct a mental model of its content, and then write his or her own text about the content.

To summarize, the ITPC model incorporates concepts from semiotics, from research on text processing, from research on picture processing, and from memory research, as well as ideas on the human cognitive architecture. Furthermore, it takes the active and constructive nature of comprehension and learning into account. Insofar, the model is embedded into a broader framework of human cognition.

Empirical Evidence

How much support does the integrated model get from empirical research? In order to demonstrate validity, the model should be able to predict under which conditions a combination of text and pictures will be beneficial for learning. However, the model should also be able to predict under which conditions such a combination will have detrimental effects. This part of the chapter analyzes how far the ITPC model is able to successfully predict or explain positive and negative effects of using texts and pictures instead of using texts alone or pictures alone.

Positive Effects of Combining Texts and Pictures

Numerous studies have shown that students learn generally better from words and pictures than from words alone (Levie & Lentz, 1982; Levin, Anglin, & Carney, 1987). This is what Mayer (1997) has called the mul-

timedia effect (see chapter 7). He and his coworkers have shown that the multimedia effect cannot be found under all conditions. Instead, the effect is bound to specific external and internal requirements.

COHERENCE AND CONTIGUITY

Students learn better from words and pictures than from words alone, if the words and pictures are semantically related to each other (the coherence condition) and if they are presented closely together in space or in time (the contiguity condition). These findings (see chapter 12) are explained by the integrated model in a similar way as by Mayer's CTML (2001). The integrated model assumes that a text and a picture can only contribute to the joint construction of the same mental model if the text and the picture are semantically related. This corresponds to the *coherence* condition. The model further assumes, that the text and picture can only contribute to a joint mental model construction, if corresponding text information and picture information are simultaneously available in working memory. As information decays quickly from working memory, this requires a combined presentation of words and pictures as far as possible, which corresponds to the *contiguity* condition.

If a picture is combined with a spoken text, simultaneous availability of related pictorial and verbal information in working memory is enhanced by simultaneous presentation of the picture and semantically related part of the text (i.e., *temporal contiguity*), because pictorial information can be forwarded through the visual channel at the same time as verbal information is forwarded through the auditory channel (see chapter 12). If a picture is combined with written text, all information has to enter working memory through the visual channel. Thus, only one kind of information can be processed through the visual channel at the same time, because the eye has to switch between pictures and words. This so-called split of visual attention implies that unproductive visual search processes from the picture to the text and vice versa have to take place. If pictures and related written words are presented closely to each other (i.e., *spatial contiguity*), visual search processes are reduced. Therefore, high spatial contiguity of pictures and written words enhances simultaneous availability of pictorial and verbal information in working memory.

MODALITY

Various studies have shown that students learn better when pictures are presented with spoken text instead of written text. This is what Mayer and his colleagues have called the *modality effect* (see chapters 9 and 11). According to the integrated model, one part of the modality effect results from avoiding split-attention (see chapter 8). If a picture is combined with written text, information processing has to be highly selective: The eye has to focus either on the picture or on the text and, thus, information from only one source can be conveyed at a specific moment. Because all information has to be processed through the visual channel, which has a limited capacity to convey information, the overall information input into working memory within a limited amount of time is lower than if both the visual and the auditory channels are used. Thus, split-attention, which is essentially the use of one information channel for different sources of information, results in a reduced amount of information that is put into working memory within a specific amount of time. This is clearly different from a situation when both the visual and the auditory channels are used and when the visual channel is devoted only to the picture and the auditory channel is devoted only to the text. The negative effects of split-attention on learning are especially pronounced when animated pictures are used instead of static pictures due to the fleeting nature of animations (Mayer, 2001).

However, the modality effect is more than just a result of avoiding a split of visual attention. Another part is how much working memory capacity is involved in further information processing. Moreno and Mayer (1999) presented text and pictures to learners in a consecutive way and, thus, avoided split-attention. Nevertheless, spoken text with pictures resulted in better learning than written text with pictures. How can this result be explained? As was mentioned previously, the construction of propositions and of mental models requires simultaneous availability of corresponding text information and picture information in working memory. Working memory has high decay rates. According to the integrated model, simultaneous availability of text information and picture information in working memory is easier to attain if more rather than less working memory capacity is involved in storage and further processing of information. Thus, it is beneficial for text and picture comprehension, if both visual and working memory are involved, even if the two systems get their input only in a consecutive manner. To summarize, the ITPC model assumes that the modality effect results both from differences in the amount of information that is processed through sensory channels and from differences in the amount of working memory capacity that is involved in further cognitive processing.

SEQUENCING

Sometimes a picture is too large and too complex to be presented simultaneously with a corresponding text and therefore does not allow temporal contiguity. Instead, the picture has to be presented either before or after the text. Various studies have shown that it is better to present a picture before a corresponding text than after the text (Kulhavy, Stock, & Caterino, 1994). The integrated model explains this sequence effect by the fact that every description leaves a margin for variation due to some indeterminacy. A text never describes a subject matter with enough detail to fit just one single picture or one single mental model. Instead, it allows some variation for pictures and for mental model construction. If a mental model is constructed only from a text, the model will therefore differ in some respects from the picture that illustrates the subject matter. If the picture is presented after the text, the picture will therefore most likely interfere with the picture. Such interferences are avoided when the picture is presented before the text. This is called the *picture–text sequencing effect*.

READING ABILITY AND PRIOR KNOWLEDGE

The ITPC model assumes that text comprehension and picture comprehension correspond to different routes of constructing mental models and propositional representations. It further assumes that the construction process uses texts, pictures, and prior knowledge as different information sources. If one source provides only little information or if one route does not work well, the other sources and routes become more important. When learners are poor readers, the combination of the visual channel with the verbal channel does not operate efficiently. In this case, picture comprehension (i.e., the combination of the visual channel and the pictorial channel) becomes more important. Thus, the integrated model predicts that poor readers profit more from illustrations in written texts than good readers. This prediction corresponds to various empirical findings reported by Cooney and Swanson (1987), Levie and Lentz (1982), and Mastropieri and Scruggs (1989).

When learners have low prior knowledge, they possess a poor internal source of information. Under this condition, mental model construction only from written text can become too difficult. Under this condition, adding a picture as another source of information can considerably enhance comprehension, because it offers an additional route for mental model construction. When learners have high prior knowledge, on the contrary, they are able to construct a mental model also without external support from a picture. The integrated model therefore predicts that learners with low prior knowledge profit more from pictures in texts than learners with high prior knowledge. This corresponds to the results of various studies that found that pictures in texts are more beneficial for students with low prior knowledge than for those with high prior knowledge (Mayer, 2001; see also chapter 21).

Negative Effects of Combining Texts and Pictures

REDUNDANCY (SPECIFIC)

Multimedia designers frequently try to adapt to the needs of individual learners who are assumed to prefer either spoken text or written text. They therefore present pictures simultaneously with both written text and spoken text. Learners are in this way supposed to choose their preferred sensory modality: Those who prefer to listen can focus on the spoken text, and those who prefer to read can focus on the written text. However, the integrated model predicts that individuals do not learn better from pictures accompanied by spoken and written text, but that they learn better from pictures combined with only spoken text. The prediction is derived from the assumption that even if the same text is presented in an auditory manner, it is difficult for learners to ignore a simultaneously presented written text. Thus, the presentation of a picture combined with a written text results in a split of visual attention despite of the simultaneous auditory presentation of the same text. Another possible reason for the negative effect of presenting pictures with spoken and redundant written text might be a problem of synchronization between listening and reading. Skilled readers are often able to read a text faster than the auditory text is spoken. Such differences can lead to interference between reading and listening. Various studies of Mayer and his coworkers have demonstrated that individuals show lower performance if they learn from pictures accompanied by spoken and written text than from pictures and only spoken text (Mayer, 2001). This is called, in this chapter, the *specific redundancy effect* (see chapter 12), because it is distinct from a more general redundancy effect, which is described in the next section.

REDUNDANCY (GENERAL)

Contrary to the dual-coding theory, which assumes that adding pictures to texts leads always to better learning, because two codes in memory are better than one, the integrated model predicts that the combination of texts and pictures can have also detrimental effects under specific conditions. One of the negative effects is what is called, in this chapter, the *general redundancy effect* (Chandler & Sweller, 1996; Sweller, van Merriënboer, & Paas, 1998; see also chapter 10). If learners have high prior knowledge, they frequently do not need both text and pictures as information sources, because one source provides all the information required for mental model construction. In this case, adding a picture to a written text or adding a written text to a picture means adding redundant, unneeded information. Although one of the two information sources is not needed, the eye wanders between the two sources, which implies split-attention. Thus, the learner loses time and mental effort with the search for redundant information. The general redundancy effect has a negative impact on learning, because the additional source of information occupies working memory capacity for processing information that does not lead to better comprehension. A combination of text and pictures that has a positive effect on mental model construction when learners have low prior knowledge may therefore have a negative effect on learning when prior knowledge is high. The integrated model therefore predicts that experts perform better with only one information source (i.e., text or picture) instead of two information sources (i.e., text and pictures). Corresponding findings have been reported by Kalyuga, Chandler, and Sweller (2000), who have named this the *expertise reversal effect* (see chapter 21).

STRUCTURE MAPPING

One and the same subject matter can often be visualized in different ways. Contrary to the dual-coding theory (Paivio, 1986), the ITPC model takes different possibilities of visualization into account and predicts that pictures are beneficial for learning only if task-appropriate forms of visualization are used, whereas they are harmful in the case of task-inappropriate forms of visualization.

This prediction derives from the assumption that during picture comprehension information processing is performed in the pictorial channel by structure mapping. This implies that the form of visualization affects the structure of the mental model. Accordingly, the ITPC model predicts that the efficiency of a mental model for a specific task corresponds to the picture's efficiency for this task (Larkin & Simon, 1987). In this chapter, this will be called the *structure-mapping effect*. Corresponding empirical findings were reported by Schnotz and Bannert (2003), who studied learning from text combined with different pictures, when the pictures were informationally equivalent but used different forms of visualization. The authors found that pictures enhance comprehension only if the learning content is visualized in a task-appropriate way. If the learning content is visualized in a task-inappropriate way, the pictures interfere with the construction of a task-appropriate mental model. Thus, well-designed pictures are not only important for low prior knowledge learners who need pictorial support for mental model construction. They are also important for high prior knowledge learners, because mental model construction can interfere with inappropriate forms of visualization.

DEEP VERSUS SUPERFICIAL PROCESSING

As the integrated model assumes that text comprehension and picture comprehension correspond to different routes for constructing mental representations it also takes into account the possibility that one route replaces the other one to some extent: Pictures can be used instead of a text and a text can be used instead of pictures. The model therefore predicts that if a picture is added to a text and if the same amount of mental effort is invested into learning, text information becomes less important due to the additional picture information. The text will therefore be processed less deeply, resulting in lower memory for text information than if the text had been processed without pictures. Corresponding findings have been reported by Mayer and Gallini (1990).

MEMORY FOR INFORMATION SOURCES

The cognitive theory of multimedia learning supposes that learners construct both a verbal mental model and a pictorial mental model when they understand a text combined with pictures (Mayer 2001). On the contrary, the integrated model assumes that only one joint mental model is constructed from an illustrated text. However, both theories share the idea that learners integrate verbal and pictorial representations in working memory, although they use the term *mental model* somewhat differently. Previous research has found that after long retention intervals text information can usually be retrieved more easily from a mental model than from a propositional representation (Graesser et al., 1997). Based on the assumption that a mental model can be held in long-term memory for a longer time than a propositional representation, the integrated model predicts that after longer retention intervals learners can no longer remember correctly whether specific information was presented in the text or in the picture. This is supported by the research results of Peeck (1989). He found that individuals who were learning from text and pictures frequently showed good comprehension of the content some time after learning, but could not remember correctly whether information was presented verbally or pictorially. If one further assumes that mental models are more closely associated with pictures than with texts, whereas propositional representations are more associated with texts than with pictures, and if one assumes that mental models can be stored more easily in memory than propositional representations, the ITPC model predicts that text information will be more likely associated falsely with the picture than picture information will be falsely associated with the text. Corresponding findings were also reported by Peeck (1989).

COGNITIVE ECONOMY

The ITPC model finally provides a framework for considerations of cognitive economy in learning from multiple external representations, especially from texts and pictures. Multiple external representations support comprehension, because each representation both constrains and elaborates the interpretation of other representations. However, understanding of each representation also creates cognitive costs. In the case of understanding multiple texts and pictures, the benefits and the costs of processing an information source depend on the ease or difficulty of using the corresponding sensory and representational channels. When more and more representations about one topic are processed, it is possible that the additional benefit for comprehension is not worth the additional cognitive costs. If the benefits from processing an additional information source are lower than the required costs, the learner will follow the principle of cognitive economy, and he or she will not engage in further cognitive processing. Instead, the learner will consider only some representations and ignore the other ones. This could explain why individuals in self-directed learning frequently ignore information sources. This finding has been reported repeatedly in research on learning from multiple representations (Ainsworth, 1999; Sweller et al., 1998).

Instructional Implications

What does the integrated model contribute to instructional design? The integrated model suggests various principles for instructional design that focus on the use of text and pictures in multimedia learning environments. Some principles correspond to those derived from CTML (Mayer, 2001). Other principles go beyond the suggestions of CTML, and some further principles contradict the latter suggestions. A basic commonality between the integrated model and CTML is that they reject the idea that simple rules of thumb such as the suggestion to use multiple forms of representations and the suggestion to use multiple sensory channels can be a useful guide to effective multimedia learning. Instead, both views agree that multimedia learning can only be successful to the extent that its use is guided by sufficient understanding of human perception and human cognitive processing based on careful empirical research. Accordingly, both the integrated model and CTML make the following suggestions for instructional design:

- *Multimedia principle.* Use text combined with content-related pictures, when learners have low prior knowledge, but sufficient cognitive abilities to process both the text and the pictures.
- *Spatial contiguity principle.* If written text is used, present it in close spatial proximity to the picture.
- *Temporal contiguity principle.* If spoken text is used, present it in close temporal proximity to the picture.
- *Modality principle.* If animation is used, use spoken text instead of written text.
- *Specific redundancy principle.* Do not add written text that duplicates spoken text combined with pictures.
- *Coherence principle.* Do not use extraneous words and pictures. Do not add unnecessary sound or music.

The overall message of these suggestions is that designers of instructional material should resist the temptation to add irrelevant bells and whistles to multimedia learning environments. Simply speaking: Less can be more.

The integrated model makes also some further suggestions that go beyond those of the cognitive theory of multimedia learning:

- *Picture–text sequencing principle.* If a written text and a picture cannot be presented simultaneously, present the picture before the text rather than the other way round.
- *Structure-mapping principle.* If a subject matter can be visualized by different pictures in different ways that are informationally equivalent, use a picture with the form of visualization that is most appropriate for solving future tasks.
- *General redundancy principle.* Do not combine text and pictures if learners have sufficient prior knowledge and cognitive

ability to construct a mental model from one source of information.

The modality effect seems to suggest that pictures should be combined always with spoken text instead of written text in order to avoid split-attention and in order to benefit from higher working memory capacity. However, the integrated model does not accept this as a general suggestion because split-attention becomes less important if static pictures are used and if learning time is not limited. The same points are made by Mayer (see chapter 12) and Sweller (see chapter 8). The integrated model considers the modality effect as only one aspect. Another aspect is how much control the learner has on the pace of processing. Written text is usually stable, whereas spoken text is fleeting. Accordingly, written text provides more control of cognitive processing, because it allows leaping backward to reread difficult passages, which is not possible with spoken text. This advantage of written over spoken text is called, in this chapter, the *control-of-processing principle*. Control of cognitive processing by the learner is especially important if a text is difficult to understand. The integrated model therefore also suggests:

- *Control-of-processing principle*: If a static picture is combined with text, if the text is difficult to understand, and if learning time is not limited, use written text rather than spoken text.

Limitations of the Integrated Model and Directions for Future Research

Despite its relative complexity, the integrated model still simplifies things considerably and therefore needs further elaboration. For example, there might exist multiple levels of propositional representations within the verbal channel instead of only one level. The different levels might range from the micropropositions expressed in the text to various levels of macropropositions constructed by the learner (van Dijk & Kintsch, 1983). Similarly, there might exist multiple levels of mental models in the pictorial channel ranging from coarse-grained overview models to detailed models with high granularity. Furthermore, the interaction between the verbal channel and the pictorial channel might occur not only between a propositional representation and a mental model as shown in Figure 4.3. Mental models can sometimes be constructed directly from the text-surface representation without a propositional representation (Perfetti & Britt, 1995). Similarly, it is possible to create a propositional representation directly from a perceptual representation of a picture without a mental model.

Another aspect not included in the ITPC model is that learning from text and pictures requires us not only to understand the verbal and pictorial information, but also to know where which kind of information can be found. In multimedia environments, texts and pictures are frequently distributed across a complex nonlinear hyperspace. In this case, the learner has to construct not only a mental model of the learning content, but also a mental model of the hyperspace.

The integrated model assumes that text and picture comprehension is a process of constructing multiple mental representations through multiple information channels on different levels of processing, in which the channels are constrained by the capacity of working memory. Future research should also investigate whether the structure of the model needs further elaboration. For example, in written text comprehension the integrated model assumes that verbal information is conveyed through the visual channel to visual working memory (i.e., the visual sketchpad) before it is further processed through the verbal channel. Letter and word recognition might need the visual sketchpad with beginning readers. If these processes are highly automatized with skilled readers, however, it might be possible that these processes do not use the visual sketchpad any more. Visual letter and word information could instead be forwarded through a special channel that bypasses the visual sketchpad. If this conjecture is correct, the model needs to be elaborated (cf. Ellis & Young, 1996).

Further research is also needed to predict more precisely under which conditions the combination of text and pictures is beneficial and under which circumstances it is harmful for learning. Further specification is needed with regard to the relative strengths of the different effects under different conditions. The positive or negative effects of combining text and pictures can be considered as a result of different efficiencies of the involved sensory and representational channels under specific external and internal conditions of processing. External conditions include, for example, the structure and content of the written or spoken text, text–picture coherence, text–picture redundancy, contiguity of text–picture presentation, time constraints, and learning objectives. Internal conditions include, for example, prior knowledge, cognitive abilities, and individual preferences. Corresponding studies should estimate the relative size of the various effects also for different types of texts and for different forms of visualization in different domains.

Future elaborations of the model should address also the learners' strategies of selecting relevant verbal or pictorial information and of giving special emphasis to specific mental representations according to the aims of learning. As far as learners follow the principle of cognitive economy in knowledge acquisition, the efficiency of the different paths for constructing mental representations is a central concept for the analysis of strategic self-directed learning. Further research should investigate to what extent individuals follow this principle in learning from text and pictures. Individuals may prefer one information channel more than another channel. With regard to the representational channel, for example, the so-called verbalizers prefer the verbal channel, whereas the so-called visualizers prefer the pictorial channel (Kirby, Moore, & Schofield, 1988; Plass, Chun, Mayer, & Leutner, 1998). Future research should also analyze, whether there are preferences with regard to the visual or the auditory channel in learning from multiple representations.

The ITPC model of text and picture comprehension provides a framework for the analysis of learning from multiple representations including spoken or written text, visual pictures, and sound pictures. It is embedded into a broader framework of human cognition and incorporates concepts from various disciplines of cognitive science. The model aims at contributing to a deeper understanding of learning from text and pictures presented using different sensory modalities (i.e., learning from multiple representations) and to enable better-informed decisions in instructional design. Future research will clarify to what extent the model will reach this goal.

Glossary

Cognitive economy: A principle of cognitive processing that tries to reach cognitive aims with a minimum of cognitive effort.

Coherence condition: A condition for the multimedia effect, which corresponds to high semantic relatedness between text and picture.

Contiguity condition: A condition for the multimedia effect, which corresponds to high proximity of text and picture in space or time.

Depictive representation: A form of representation that uses iconic signs (such as visual pictures) to show characteristics of a subject matter.

Descriptive representation: A form of representation that uses symbols (such as natural language) to describe characteristics of a subject matter.

Integrated model of text and picture comprehension (ITPC model): A model of how individuals understand text and pictures presented in different sensory modalities, based on the assumption that the human perceptual system includes multiple sensory channels, whereas the cognitive system includes two representational channels: a verbal (descriptive) channel and a pictorial (depictive) channel and that these channels have limited capacity for information processing and active coherence formation.

Listening comprehension: The construction of propositional representations and mental models based on spoken text.

Mental model: A mental representation of a subject matter by an internal structure that is analogous to the subject matter.

Modality effect: Students learn better from text and pictures if the text is presented as spoken rather than as written text, because of avoidance of visual split attention and because of a higher working memory capacity involved in the comprehension process.

Multimedia effect: Students learn better from text and pictures than from text alone, if specific conditions are met.

Picture–text sequencing principle: If a written text and a picture cannot be presented simultaneously, present the picture before the text instead of after the text.

Propositional representation: A mental representation of ideas expressed in a text or in a picture without reference to a specific words and phrases.

Reading comprehension: The construction of propositional representations and mental models based on written text.

Redundancy (general): The combination of multiple information sources if learners have sufficient prior knowledge and cognitive ability to construct a mental model also from one source.

Redundancy (specific): The use of written text that duplicates spoken text combined with pictures.

Sensory register: A memory store that holds information from a specific sensory modality (e.g., the eye or the ear) for a very short time as a basis for further information processing.

Sound comprehension (auditory picture comprehension): The construction of mental models and propositional representations based on sounds (as auditory pictures).

Split-attention: The use of one information channel for different sources of information.

Structure mapping: The transfer of a structure consisting of elements and relations between the elements onto another structure with different elements, but the same relations.

Text-surface representation: A mental representation of a text including exact wording and syntax structure.

Visual picture comprehension: The construction of mental models and propositional representations based on visual pictures (e.g., drawings, maps, or graphs).

Working memory: A memory store that holds and manipulates information that is in the individual's focus of attention, including a visual store, an auditory store, a propositional store, and a spatial mental model store.

References

Adams, B. C., Bell, L., & Perfetti, C. (1995). A trading relationship between reading skill and domain knowledge in children's text comprehension. *Discourse Processes, 20*, 307–323.

Ainsworth, S. (1999). The functions of multiple representations. *Computers & Education, 33*, 131–152.

Atkinson, C., & Shiffrin, R. M. (1971). The control of short-term memory. *Scientific American, 225*, 82–90.

Baddeley, A. D. (1986). *Working memory*. Oxford, England: Clarendon Press.

Baddeley, A. (2000). The episodic buffer: a new component of working memory? *Trends in Cognitive Science, 4*, 417–423.

Carney, R. N., & Levin, J. R. (2002). Pictorial illustrations still improve students' learning from text. *Educational Psychology Review, 14*, 5–26.

Chandler, P., & Sweller, J. (1996). Cognitive load while learning to use a computer program. *Applied Cognitive Psychology, 10*, 151–170.

Comenius, J. A. (1999). *Orbis pictus (Facsimile of the 1887 edition)*. Whitefish, MT: Kessinger Publishing.

Cooney, J. B., & Swanson, H. L. (1987). Memory and learning disabilities: An overview. In H. L. Swanson (Ed.), *Memory and learning disabilities: Advances in learning and behavioral disabilities* (pp. 1–40). Greenwich, CT: JAI.

Daneman, M., & Carpenter, P. A. (1983). Individual differences in integrating information between and within sentences. *Journal of Experimental Psychology: Learning, Memory, and Cognition, 9*, 561–583.

Dutke, S. (1996). Generic and generative knowledge: Memory schemata in the construction of mental models. In W. Battmann & S. Dutke (Eds.), *Processes of the molar regulation of behavior* (pp. 35–54). Lengerich, Germany: Pabst Science Publishers.

Ellis, A. W., & Young, A. W. (1996). *Human cognitive neuropsychology*. London: Taylor & Francis.

Friedman, N. P., & Miyake, A. (2000). Differential roles for visuospatial and verbal working memory in situation model construction. *Journal of Experimental Psychology: General, 129*, 61–83.

Graesser, A. C., Millis, K. K., & Zwaan, R. A. (1997). Discourse comprehension. *Annual Review of Psychology, 48*, 163–189.

Johnson-Laird, P. N. (1983). *Mental models*. Cambridge: Cambridge University Press.

Kalyuga, S., Chandler, P., & Sweller, J. (2000). Incorporating learner experience into the design of multimedia instruction. *Journal of Educational Psychology, 92*, 126–136.

Kintsch, W., & van Dijk, T. A. (1978). Toward a model of text comprehension and production. *Psychological Review, 85*, 363–394.

Kirby, J. R., Moore, P. J., & Schofield, N. J. (1988). Verbal and visual learning styles. *Contemporary Educational Psychology, 13*, 169–184.

Knauff, M., & Johnson-Laird, P. (2002). Visual imagery can impede reasoning. *Memory and Cognition, 30*, 363–371.

Kosslyn, S. M. (1994). *Image and brain*. Cambridge, MA: MIT Press.

Kulhavy, R. W., Stock, W. A., & Caterino, L. C. (1994). Reference maps as a framework for remembering text. In W. Schnotz & R. W. Kulhavy (Eds.), *Comprehension of graphics* (pp. 153–162). Amsterdam: Elsevier Science B. V.

Larkin, J. H., & Simon, H. A. (1987). Why a diagram is (sometimes) worth ten thousand words. *Cognitive Science, 11*, 65–99.

Levie, H. W., & Lentz, R. (1982). Effects of text illustrations: A review of research. *Educational Communication and Technology Journal*, 30, 195–232.

Levin, J. R., Anglin, G. J., & Carney, R. N. (1987). On empirically validating functions of pictures in prose. In D. M. Willows & H. A. Houghton, (Eds.), *The psychology of illustration. Vol. 1* (pp. 51–86). New York: Springer.

Lowe, R. K. (1996). Background knowledge and the construction of a situational representation from a diagram. *European Journal of Psychology of Education*, 11, 377–397.

Mastropieri, M. A., & Scruggs, T. E., (1989). Constructing more meaningful relationships: Mnemonic instruction for special populations. *Educational Psychology Review*, 1, 83–111.

Mayer, R. E. (1997). Multimedia learning: Are we asking the right questions? *Educational Psychologist*, 32, 1–19.

Mayer, R. E. (2001). *Multimedia learning*. New York: Cambridge University Press.

Mayer, R. E., & Gallini, J. K. (1990). When is an illustration worth ten thousand words? *Journal of Educational Psychology*, 82, 715–726.

McNamara, D. S., Kintsch, E., Songer, N. B., & Kintsch, W. (1996). Are good texts always better? Interactions of text coherence, background knowledge, and levels of understanding in learning from text. *Cognition and Instruction*, 14, 1–43.

Miller, L. M. S., & Stine-Morrow, E. A. L. (1998). Aging and the effects of knowledge on on-line reading strategies. *Journal of Gerontology: Psychology Sciences*, 53B, 223–233.

Moreno, R., & Mayer, R. E. (1999). Cognitive principles of multimedia learning: The role of modality and contiguity. *Journal of Educational Psychology*, 91, 358–368.

Paivio, A. (1986). *Mental representations: A dual coding approach*. Oxford, UK: Oxford University Press.

Palmer, S. E., Rosch, E., & Chase, P. (1981). Canonical perspective and the perception of objects. In J. Long & A. Baddeley (Eds.), *Attention and performance. Vol. 9* (p. 135–151). Hillsdale, NJ: Erlbaum.

Peeck, J. (1989). Trends in the delayed use of information from an illustrated text. In H. Mandl & J. R. Levin (Eds.), *Knowledge acquisition from text and pictures* (pp. 263–277). Amsterdam: North Holland.

Peirce, C. S. (1931–1958). *Collected Writings (Vols. 1–8)*. (Eds. C. Hartshorne, P. Weiss, & A. W Burks). Cambridge, MA: Harvard University Press.

Perfetti, C. A., & Britt, M. A. (1995). Where do propositions come from? In C. A. Weaver III, S. Mannes, & C. R. Fletcher (Eds.), *Discourse comprehension. Essays in honor of Walter Kintsch* (pp. 11–34). Hillsdale, NJ: Erlbaum

Plass, J. L., Chun, D. M., Mayer, R. E., & Leutner, D. (1998). Supporting visual and verbal learning preferences in a second-language multimedia learning environment. *Journal of Educational Psychology*, 90, 25–36.

Schnotz, W., & Bannert, M. (2003). Construction and interference in learning from multiple representations. *Learning and Instruction*, 13, 141–156.

Sims, V. K., & Hegarty, M. (1997). Mental animation in the visuospatial sketchpad: Evidence from dual-tasks studies. *Memory and Cognition*, 25, 321–332.

Soederberg Miller, L. M. (2001). The effects of real-world knowledge on text processing among older adults. *Aging, Neuropsychology, and Cognition*, 8, 137–148.

Sweller, J., van Merriënboer, J. G., & Paas, F. G. W. C. (1998). Cognitive architecture and instructional design. *Educational Psychological Review*, 10, 251–296.

Vallar, G., & Shallice, T. (Eds.) (1990). *Neuropsychological impairments of short-term memory*. Cambridge: Cambridge University Press.

van Dijk, T. A., & Kintsch, W. (1983). *Strategies of discourse comprehension*. New York: Academic Press.

CHAPTER 5

The Four-Component Instructional Design Model: Multimedia Principles in Environments for Complex Learning

Jeroen J. G. van Merriënboer
Liesbeth Kester
Open University of the Netherlands

Abstract

The Four-Component Instructional Design (4C-ID) model claims that four components are necessary to realize complex learning: (1) learning tasks, (2) supportive information, (3) procedural information, and (4) part-task practice. This chapter discusses the use of the model to design multimedia learning environments and relates 14 multimedia principles to each of the four components. Students may work on learning tasks in simulated task environments, where relevant multimedia principles primarily facilitate a process of inductive learning. They may study supportive information in hypermedia systems, where principles facilitate a process of elaboration and mindful abstraction. They may consult procedural information in Electronic Performance Support Systems (EPSSs), where principles facilitate a process of knowledge compilation. Finally, they may be involved in part-task practice with drill and practice Computer-Based Training (CBT) programs, where principles facilitate a process of psychological strengthening. Research implications and limitations of the presented framework are discussed.

Introduction

Theories about learning with multimedia can be positioned at different levels. At a basic level, psychological theories describe memory systems and cognitive processes that explain how people process different types of information and how they learn with different senses. Examples of such theories are Paivio's dual-coding theory (1986; Clark & Paivio, 1991) and Baddeley's working memory model with a central executive and two slave systems, the visuo-spatial sketchpad and the phonological loop (1992; 1997). At a higher level, theories for instructional message design identify multimedia principles and provide guidelines for devising multimedia messages consisting of, for instance, written text and pictures, spoken text and animations, or explanatory video with a mix of moving images with spoken and written text. Examples of such theories are Mayer's generative theory of multimedia learning (2001) and Sweller's cognitive load theory (2004; Sweller, van Merriënboer, & Paas, 1998). At an even higher level, theories and models for course and curriculum design prescribe how to develop educational programs, which contain a mix of educational media including texts, images, speech, manipulative materials, and networked systems. Well-designed educational programs take both human cognitive architecture and multimedia principles into account to ensure that learners will work in an environment that is goal-effective, efficient, and appealing.

The main goal of this chapter is to present a theory that is positioned at the third level, namely, the 4C/ID-model (van Merriënboer, 1997; van Merriënboer, Clark, & de Croock, 2002; van Merriënboer, Jelsma, & Paas, 1992; van Merriënboer, Kirschner, & Kester, 2003), and to discuss how this theory is used to design multimedia learning environments for complex learning. Such complex learning explicitly aims at the integration of knowledge, skills and attitudes; the ability to coordinate qualitatively different constituent skills; and the transfer of what is learned to daily life or work settings. The 4C/ID-model views authentic learning tasks that are based on real-life tasks as the driving force for learning and thus the first component in a well-designed environment for complex learning – a view that is shared with several other recent instructional theories (for an overview, see Merrill, 2002). The three remaining components are supportive information, procedural information, and part-task practice.

While the 4C/ID-model is not specifically developed for the design of multimedia environments for learning, it has important implications for the selection of a mix of suitable educational media as well as the presentation of information and arrangement of practice and feedback through these media. This chapter will first present a general description of how people learn complex skills in an environment that is built from the four blueprint components. Second, the relationship between the four components and the assumed cognitive architecture is explained, focusing on the role of a limited working memory and a virtually unlimited long-term memory for schema construction and schema automation – processes

that lay the foundation for meaningful learning. Third, educational media and 14 multimedia principles are related to each of the four components. The chapter ends with a discussion that reviews the contributions of the 4C/ID-model to cognitive theory and instructional design, indicates the limitations of the model, and sketches directions for future research.

How Do People Learn Complex Skills?

The basic message of the 4C/ID-model is that well-designed environments for complex learning can always be described in terms of four interrelated blueprint components:

1. *Learning tasks.* Meaningful whole-task experiences that are based on real-life tasks. Ideally, the learning tasks ask the learners to integrate and coordinate many if not all aspects of real-life task performance, including problem-solving aspects and reasoning aspects that are different across tasks and routine aspects that are consistent across tasks.

2. *Supportive information.* Information that is supportive to the learning and performance of problem-solving and reasoning aspects of learning tasks. It describes how the task domain is organized and how problems in this domain can best be approached. It builds a bridge between what learners already know and what may be helpful to know in order to fruitfully work on the learning tasks.

3. *Procedural information.* Information that is prerequisite to the learning and performance of routine aspects of learning tasks. This information provides an algorithmic specification of how to perform those routine aspects. It is best organized in small information units and presented to learners precisely when they need it during their work on the learning tasks.

4. *Part-task practice.* Additional exercises for routine aspects of learning tasks for which

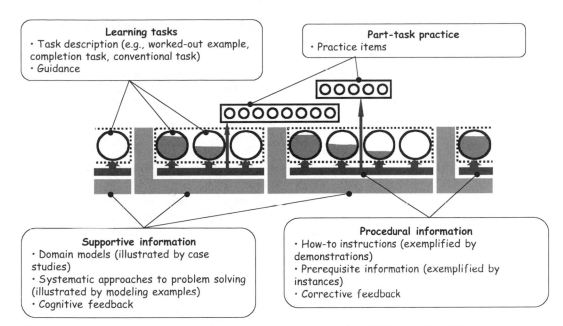

Figure 5.1. A schematic overview of the four components in the 4C/ID-model and their main elements.

a very high level of automaticity is required after the instruction. Part-task practice is only necessary if the learning tasks do not provide enough repetition for a particular routine aspect to reach the required high level of automaticity.

Figure 5.1 provides a schematic overview of the four components. The learning tasks are represented as circles; a sequence of tasks serves as the backbone of the course or curriculum. Equivalent learning tasks belong to the same *task class* (in Figure 5.1, the dotted rectangles around a set of learning tasks). Learning tasks within the same task class are equivalent to each other in the sense that they can be performed on the basis of the same body of knowledge – but they are different on the dimensions that also vary in the real world such as the context in which the task is performed, the way the task is presented, the saliency of defining characteristics, and so forth. Each new task class is more difficult than the previous task classes. Students receive much support and guidance for their work on the first learning task in a class (in Figure 5.1, this is indicated by the filling of the circles), but support

smoothly decreases in a process of scaffolding as learners acquire more expertise. One type of support – product-oriented – is embraced in the *task description*. For instance, worked examples provide maximum support because they present both a problem and an acceptable solution that must only be studied or evaluated by the learners; completion tasks provide medium support because they present a problem and a partial solution that must be completed by the learners; and conventional tasks provide no support at all because they present a problem that must be solved independently by the learners. Another type of support – process-oriented – has the form of *guidance*. This is information in the form of process worksheets or guidelines that lead the learner through the problem-solving process. In general, students work without any support on the final learning tasks in a task class. These conventional tasks without guidance may also be used as test tasks for the assessment of students' performance.

The supportive information is linked to task classes, because this information is relevant to all learning tasks within the same class (see the L-shaped, light gray shapes in

Figure 5.1). For each subsequent task class, the supportive information is an addition to or an embellishment of the previously presented information, allowing learners to do things that they could not do before. It is the information that teachers typically call "the theory" and consists of three parts. First, it describes *domain models*, answering questions like "what is this?" (conceptual models), "how is this organized?" (structural models), and "how does this work" (causal models). These models are typically illustrated with case studies. Second, supportive information describes *Systematic Approaches to Problem solving* (SAPs) that specify the successive phases in a problem-solving process and the rules of thumb that may be helpful to successfully complete each phase. SAPs may be exemplified by modeling examples, which show an expert who is performing a task and simultaneously explaining why she or he is doing what she or he is doing. Third, supportive information pertains to the *cognitive feedback* that is given on the quality of the learner's task performance. Because there is no simple correct or incorrect behavior for the problem-solving and reasoning aspects of performance, cognitive feedback will often invite students to critically compare their own solutions with expert solutions or solutions of their peers.

The procedural information is represented in Figure 5.1 by dark gray rectangles with upward-pointing arrows, indicating that information units are explicitly coupled to separate learning tasks. This information is preferably presented exactly when learners need it to perform particular routine aspects of learning tasks. This removes the need for memorization beforehand. Procedural information primarily consists of *how-to instructions*, rules that algorithmically prescribe the correct performance of the routine aspects of learning tasks. They are formulated at the level of the lowest-ability learner, so that all students can correctly perform them. How-to instructions may be exemplified by demonstrations that are preferably given in the context of the whole, meaningful task. Second, procedural information may pertain to *prerequisite information*, that

is, information that learners must know to correctly perform the how-to instructions. This information may be exemplified by "instances." For example, a how-to instruction may state that "You now connect the digital device to one of the USB ports." Related prerequisite information for carrying out this instruction may give a definition of what a USB port is, and an instance may show a photograph of the USB ports of a personal computer. Finally, *corrective feedback* may be given on the quality of performance of routine aspects. Such feedback indicates that there is an error, explains why there is an error, and gives hints that may help the learner to get back on the right track. If learners start to master the routine aspects, the presentation of the procedural information quickly fades away in a process of fading.

Part-task practice is indicated in Figure 5.1 by the small series of circles, representing *practice items*. Often, the learning tasks provide sufficient practice for routine aspects of performance to obtain the desired level of automaticity. But for routine aspects that are very basic or that are critical in terms of safety, additional part-task practice may be necessary, such as musicians practicing musical scales, children drilling multiplication tables, or air-traffic controllers practicing the recognition of dangerous air-traffic situations from a radar screen. Part-task practice for a selected routine aspect never starts before this aspect has been introduced in a whole, meaningful learning task, so that there is an appropriate cognitive context. It is preferably intermixed with learning tasks, so that there is distributed or spaced practice of routines. Drill and practice on a vast set of practice items is an effective instructional method to obtain a very high level of automaticity.

Complex learning requires that students work on whole, meaningful learning tasks. The tasks may have different descriptions (e.g., worked examples, completion tasks, conventional tasks) and different levels of guidance. To be able to perform the problem-solving and reasoning aspects of those tasks and to learn from them, students consult and study domain models and SAPs and receive cognitive feedback on the quality of their performance. During task performance, how-to instructions specify how to perform the routine aspects of the task. Prerequisite information ensures that learners can carry out those instructions and corrective feedback is given if errors are made. Finally, part-task practice may offer a large set of practice items for the additional training of routine aspects.

From this description, it should be clear that people learn from words, pictures, and other representations (realia, smell, touch, etc.) in many different ways. On the one hand, each of the four components may require that learners combine representations. Learning tasks may ask learners to simultaneously read displays, process spoken text, and operate controls; supportive information may include a video recording of an expert modeling a problem-solving process and explaining why she or he is doing what she or he is doing; procedural information may include a quick reference guide with written instructions for operating a complex device as well as pictures of this device; and part-task practice may include operating a software program with texts and icons. Furthermore, procedural information is typically presented to learners while they are working on learning tasks or performing part-task practice, yielding two sources of information (how-to information and a task for which this information is relevant) that must be mentally integrated by the learner in order to successfully complete the task. For each situation, another set of multimedia principles applies because there are different learning processes involved. This will be further explained in the next section.

Cognitive Architecture and Meaningful Learning

The 4C/ID-model assumes that all human knowledge is stored in cognitive schemata. It further supposes a cognitive architecture that is broadly accepted in the psychological literature and for which ample empirical support is available. This architecture distinguishes a working memory with a very limited capacity when dealing with novel information as well as an effectively unlimited long-term memory, holding cognitive schemata that vary in their degree of richness (i.e., number of elements and interconnections between those elements) and their level of automation. Learning processes are either related to the construction of schemata, including the formation of new schemata and the embellishment of existing schemata, or to the automation of schemata.

Memory Systems

To begin with, all novel information must be processed in working memory to construct cognitive schemata in long-term memory. This processing is heavily limited by the fact that only a few elements can be simultaneously active in working memory: about seven distinct elements that need to be stored or about two to four elements and their interactions if the elements need to be interrelated to each other. Furthermore, it is assumed that working memory can be subdivided into partially independent channels or processes (Baddeley, 1992). One channel consists of a phonological loop to deal with verbal material based on an auditory working memory; another channel consists of a visual-spatial sketch pad to deal with diagrammatic or pictorial information based on a visual working memory. Using both the visual and auditory channels rather than either one channel alone increases the effective working memory capacity (Penney, 1989). Long-term memory alters the characteristics of working memory by reducing or even eliminating its limitations. Human expertise is the result of the availability of rich and automated cognitive schemata, *not* from an ability to engage in reasoning with many elements that yet need to be organized in long-term memory. Human working memory simply does not support this type of many-elements processing.

Expertise develops through two complementary processes, namely, schema construction and schema automation. Schema construction refers to the – often conscious and mindful – formation of increasing numbers of ever more complex schemata, by combining elements consisting of lower-level schemata into higher-level schemata. These schemata organize and store knowledge, but also heavily reduce working memory load because even highly complex schemata can be dealt with as *one* element in working memory. Thus, a large number of elements for one person may be a single element for another, more experienced person, who already has a cognitive schema available that incorporates the elements. As a result, novel information may be easy to understand by someone with relevant experience, and very hard to understand by someone without this experience.

Schema automation occurs if a task performer repeatedly and successfully applies a particular cognitive schema. As is the case for schema construction, automation can free working memory capacity for other activities because an automated schema directly steers the routine aspects of behavior, without the need to be processed in working memory. As a direct consequence, instructional designs for complex learning should not only encourage the construction of problem-solving and reasoning schemata, but also the automation of schemata for those aspects of a complex skill that are consistent across problems or tasks. In a learning environment that is developed according to the 4C/ID-model, learners' work on learning tasks and study of supportive information helps them to *construct* cognitive schemata. Their consultation of procedural information, repeated performance of routine aspects of learning tasks, and drill on part-task practice helps them to *automate* schemata. Thus, meaningful learning is the result of both schema construction and schema automation.

Cognitive Processes That Lead to Meaningful Learning

The 4C/ID-model makes a further division in learning processes that are directly coupled to the four components of the model. With regard to schema construction, a distinction is made between induction through experiential learning, which refers to the construction of schemata by – often mindfully – abstracting away from concrete learning tasks (component 1), and elaboration, which refers to the construction of schemata by relating already existing knowledge in long-term memory to new supportive information (component 2). *Induction* is at the heart of complex learning and refers both to the generalization and discrimination of cognitive schemata (see Holland, Holyoak, Nisbett, & Thagard, 1989). When learners generalize or abstract away from well-designed learning tasks, they construct schemata that leave out the details so that they apply to a wider range of events or to events that are less tangible. Discrimination is just the opposite of generalization. A more specific schema may be constructed if a set of failed solutions is available for a class of related tasks. Then, particular conditions may be added to the schema and restrict its range of use. Induction is typically a strategic and controlled cognitive process, which requires conscious processing from the learners (also called *mindful abstraction*) (Perkins & Salomon, 1989).

The *elaboration* of new supportive information refers to those cognitive activities that integrate new information with cognitive schemata already available in memory (see Willoughby, Wood, Desmarais, Sims, & Kalra, 1997). When learners elaborate new supportive information, they first search their memory for general cognitive schemata that may provide a cognitive structure for understanding the information in general terms, and for concrete schemata or cases that may provide a useful analogy. These schemata are connected to the new information, and elements from the retrieved schemata that are not part of the new information are now related to it. Thus, learners use what they already know about a topic to help them structure and understand the new information.

With regard to schema automation, a distinction is made between knowledge compilation, which refers to the preliminary automation of schemata on the basis of procedural information (component 3), and strengthening, which refers to the development of very high levels of automaticity through part-task practice (component 4). *Knowledge compilation* refers to the process by which procedural information is embedded in automated schemata that directly steer behavior, that is, evoke particular actions under particular conditions. Newly acquired schemata or worked examples may be used to yield an initial solution, and compilation is the process that creates highly specific schemata from this solution (Anderson, 1993; Anderson & Lebiere, 1998). After the knowledge is compiled, the solution is generated by directly coupling the actions to the conditions in the specific schema. This greatly speeds up performance.

Finally, *strengthening* makes it possible for learners to perform a routine aspect of a complex skill, after it has been separately trained in a process of part-task practice, at a very high level of automaticity. It is usually assumed that an automated schema has a strength associated with it, determining the chance that it applies under the specified conditions as well as how rapidly it then applies. While knowledge compilation leads to highly specific schemata, which are assumed to underlie accurate performance of the skill, they still have a weak strength. Strengthening is a straightforward learning mechanism. It is simply assumed that automated schemata accumulate strength each time they are successfully applied. The improvement that results from strengthening requires long periods of "overtraining" (Palmeri, 1999).

Meaningful Multimedia Learning According to the 4C/ID-Model

As discussed in the previous section, the four components (learning tasks, supportive information, procedural information, and part-task practice) aim at the facilitation of different learning processes, with clear implications for the selection of suitable educational media and relevant multimedia prin-

ciples. These media and principles are discussed in the next sections.

Learning Tasks and Learning in Simulated Task Environments

Learning tasks primarily aim at schema construction through inductive learning. The educational medium must allow learners to work on those tasks and typically takes the form of a real or simulated task environment. One may think of a project room, a simulated office, a physical simulator, or an internship in a real company. In multimedia learning, the heart of the learning environment will typically consist of a computer-simulated task environment. For many complex skills, such as holding a plea in court, conducting psychological experiments, or troubleshooting a chemical factory, current multimedia technology does not yet offer the possibilities that are needed for high fidelity simulation (i.e., missing input-output facilities, lack of simulation models that can run in the background, etc.). The opportunities will be better in the near future thanks to virtual reality, broadband technology, and new input and output devices such as virtual-reality helmets and data gloves. Although the necessary multimedia technology to implement optimal instructional methods is not always available, many multimedia applications already offer the opportunity to perform learning tasks that are somehow based on real-life tasks. Table 5.1 summarizes the main multimedia principles (1–6) that should be taken into account in simulated task environments and provides for each principle an example of how it could be applied.

SEQUENCING PRINCIPLE

The sequencing principle indicates that it is often better to sequence learning tasks or complex pieces of information from simple to complex, than to present them in their full complexity at once. Mayer and Moreno (2003) refer to this as a "pretraining" effect, when they review studies showing better transfer test performance when students must first study which components make

Table 5.1. Examples of Prominent Multimedia Principles for Each of the Four Components of the 4C/ID-Model.

Multimedia principle	Example
Learning Tasks and Learning in Simulated Task Environments	
1. Sequencing principle	For physics students who learn to troubleshoot electrical circuits, start with circuits with only very few elements (e.g., a lamp, battery, and switch) and continue with circuits with increasingly more elements.
2. Fidelity principle	For medical students who learn to diagnose patients, start with textual case descriptions, continue with computer-simulated patients or patients played by peers, go on with simulated patients played by actors, and end with real patients in an internship in hospital.
3. Variability principle	For law students who learn to prepare pleas to be held in court, make sure that learning tasks ask them to prepare pleas for different fields of law (civil law, criminal law), different clients (guilty, not guilty), different courts (police court, law court, supreme court), and so on.
4. Individualization principle	For computer science students who learn to write computer programs, continuously assess with which programming constructs they have difficulties and select new learning tasks that offer optimal opportunities to remedy their misconceptions.
5. Training-wheels principle	For accountancy students who learn to make budgets with a spreadsheet program, first block all toolbars and menu options that are not strictly necessary to perform the task, but only add these when they become necessary because students progress to making more complex budgeting tasks.
6. Completion-strategy principle	For students in architecture who learn to design constructional blueprints, first let them evaluate the qualities of blueprints of existing buildings, then let them redesign blueprints for the renovation of buildings, and finally let them design blueprints for new buildings.
Supportive Information and Learning from Hypermedia	
7. Redundancy principle	For students in econometrics who learn to explain periods of economic growth, first present a qualitative model (allows them to predict if there will be any growth) and only then present a more encompassing quantitative model (laws that may help them to compute the amount of growth) – but *without* repeating the qualitative information as such.
8. Self-explanation principle	For medical students who learn to diagnose malfunctions in the human cardiovascular system, present an animation of how the heart works and provide prompts that provoke them to explain the underyling mechanisms to themselves or to their peers.
9. Self-pacing principle	For students in psychotherapy who learn to conduct intake conversations with depressed clients, show video examples of real-life intake conversations and give them the opportunity to stop/replay the recording after each segment in order to reflect on this particular segment.
Procedural Information and Electronic Performance Support Systems	
10. Temporal split-attention principle	For students in Web design who learn to develop Web pages in a new software environment, tell them how to use the different functions of the software environment precisely when they need them to implement a particular aspect of their design – instead of discussing all available functions beforehand.

Multimedia principle	Example
11. Spatial split-attention principle	For social science students who learn to conduct statistical analyses on their data files with SPSS®, present procedural information describing how to conduct a particular analysis also on the computer screen and not in a separate manual.
12. Signaling principle	For students in car engineering who learn to disassemble an engine block, animate the disassembling process in a step-by-step fashion and always put a spotlight on those parts that are loosened and removed.
13. Modality principle	For students in instructional design who learn to develop training blueprints by studying a sequence of more and more detailed blueprints, explain the blueprints with narration or spoken text instead of visual (on-screen) text.
Part-Task Practice and Drill and Practice CBT Programs	
14. Component-fluency principle	For students in air-traffic control who learn to direct incoming aircraft, provide additional and extensive part-task practice on immediately recognizing potentially dangerous air-traffic situations from the radar screen.

up a system (i.e., a conceptual model) and only then how the system works (i.e., a causal or functional model) (Mayer, Matthias, & Wetzell, 2002). These results are consistent with the findings of Pollock, Chandler, and Sweller (2002), who found that first presenting isolated elements and then interrelated elements is better than presenting all elements simultaneously. For low-expertise learners the results of Clarke, Ayres, and Sweller (in press) show it is important to present and practice enabling, technological skills (i.e., using spreadsheets) before practicing the ultimate skills the training is aiming at (i.e., mathematical skills). Kester, Kirschner, and van Merriënboer (in press a; in press b) studied the sequencing principle in the context of the 4C/ID-model. In the domain of electronics troubleshooting, they found that presenting high element interactivity supportive information either before or after low element interactivity procedural information, led to better transfer test performance. The 4C/ID-model primarily uses task classes to accommodate the sequencing principle. Task classes and their related supportive information range from simple to complex, while the learning tasks within the same task class are equally difficult. The basic guideline of the 4C/ID-model is to start with a task class where the learning tasks can be solved on the basis of a simple domain model or SAP, and to continue with task classes where the supportive information pertains to increasingly more complex and elaborated domain models or SAPs (i.e., mental model progression) (van Merriënboer et al., 2003).

FIDELITY PRINCIPLE

Learning tasks are performed in some kind of task environment. While the learning tasks are based on real-life tasks, they can yet be performed in an environment that is very close to the real task environment (i.e., high fidelity) or in an environment that merely offers the opportunity to perform the tasks, with no attempts to mimic the real task environment (i.e., low fidelity). The fidelity principle indicates that for novice learners, a high-fidelity task environment often contains irrelevant details that may deteriorate learning. This principle is in agreement with the finding that there is better transfer when interesting but irrelevant materials, such as background music and nonessential video clips, are excluded from a training program. Students perform better on transfer tests after receiving a concise narrated animation instead of an embellished narrated animation

(Mayer, Heiser, & Lonn, 2001; Moreno & Mayer, 2000). For a Web-based course, Gulikers, Bastiaens, and Martens (in press) found that novices perform better in a low-fidelity, text-based environment than in a high-fidelity environment where multimedia features are used to mimic the real task environment. Harp and Mayer (1998) also report that "seductive details" that are not directly relevant for learning deteriorate performance. According to the 4C/ID-model, training should best start with task classes in which the learning tasks are performed in a low-fidelity environment, which only represents those aspects of the real environment that are necessary to perform the task. There is a high *psychological* fidelity because the learning task is representative for a real-life task, but there is no or little physical correspondence with the real environment. Only in later task classes and with more advanced learners, it becomes necessary to perform the learning tasks in a high fidelity or real environment (see also Maran & Glavin, 2003).

VARIABILITY PRINCIPLE

The variability principle indicates that learning tasks must be sufficiently different from each other to allow for the construction of general, abstract schemata that make transfer of learning possible. Ideally, learning tasks should differ on all dimensions that also vary in the real world, such as the conditions under which the task is performed, the way of presenting the task, or the saliency of defining characteristics. Several studies showed that a high variability across learning tasks yields superior transfer test performance (e.g., Paas & van Merriënboer, 1994; Quilici & Mayer, 1996). Van Merriënboer, Schuurman, de Croock, and Paas (2002) and de Croock, van Merriënboer, and Paas (1998) studied contextual interference, which is a special type of variability referring to the way in which differences between tasks are divided across acquisition tasks. Suppose that students learn to diagnose three types of errors: A, B, and C. Low contextual interference may then be produced by a blocked

practice schedule, in which the skills necessary for diagnosing one type of error are practised before continuing to another type of error (e.g., AAA, BBB, CCC). High contextual interference may be produced by a random practice schedule, in which different errors are sequenced in a random order (e.g., CABBCABAC). High contextual interference prohibits a quick and smooth mastery of the skills being trained, but yields higher transfer test performance because learners are promoted to construct general cognitive schemata. The 4C/ID-model takes the variability principle into account and suggests including in *each* task class, learning tasks that exhibit high variability and high contextual interference. Recent research of Gerjets, Scheiter, and Catrambone (2004), however, seems to imply that optimal transfer does not always require a high variability of learning tasks within each task class, as long as the variability is sufficiently high for the learning tasks in the *whole set* of task classes (i.e., in the whole training program).

INDIVIDUALIZATION PRINCIPLE

Recent studies show that adaptive training systems, which dynamically select learning tasks based on the characteristics of the individual learner, yield higher transfer than nonadaptive training systems, which present a fixed sequence of tasks that is identical for all learners (Salden, Paas, & van Merriënboer, in press). In these adaptive systems the dynamic selection of the next learning task is typically based on performance (i.e., accuracy and/or speed), but it can also be based on the amount of mental effort invested in performing the previous task(s), on a combination of performance and mental effort (e.g., see Camp, Paas, Rikers, & van Merriënboer, 2001; Kalyuga & Sweller, in press; Salden, Paas, Broers, & van Merriënboer, 2004), or on a qualitative student model (e.g., van Merriënboer & Luursema, 1996). The individualization principle typically takes differences between learners into account by selecting learning tasks in such a way that the task difficulty and/or the available level of support is adjusted to the learner. This fits in very well with the 4C/ID-model. For each learning task, performance needs to be assessed in order to give cognitive feedback to the learners (Straetmans, Sluijsmans, Bolhuis, & van Merriënboer, 2003). This assessment information can also be used to select a new task. If performance is low, an equivalent task with a higher level of support will be selected from the same task class or, in the worst case, an easier task will be selected from a previous task class. If performance is high, an equivalent task with a lower level of support will be selected from the same task class, or, if all performance criteria have been reached, the learner is allowed to move on to the next task class from which a more difficult task with a high level of support is selected.

TRAINING-WHEELS PRINCIPLE

Even performing relatively easy learning tasks in a low-fidelity environment is difficult for novice learners, because they are still "whole" tasks that require the coordination of many different constituent skills. One way to help learners is to provide either process-oriented worked examples that show an expert who is performing the task (van Gog, Paas, & van Merriënboer, 2004) or to give process worksheets that ask leading questions that guide the learners step-by-step through the problem-solving or reasoning process (e.g., Nadolski, Kirschner, & van Merriënboer, 2001). However, a potential drawback of these methods is that learners must divide their attention between the task and the support, which may negatively affect learning (van Merriënboer et al., 2003). An additional way to support learners is to *constrain* their performance, that is, to make sure that they cannot perform actions that are not necessary to reach the performance goals. A metaphor for these performance constraints is provided by the training wheels on children's bikes, which prevent them from falling over (Carroll, 2000). Dufresne, Gerace, Thibodeau-Hardiman, and Mestre (1992) studied the training-wheels principle for a problem-solving task in physics. Students' performance was constrained in

such a way that they had to mimic an expert's approach to problem solving, which had positive effects on their transfer test performance. In another study, Leutner (2000) also found positive effects of training wheels on test performance, but his study also indicated that both too many constraints and too little constraints might produce suboptimal effects on learning. In the 4C/ID-model, the training-wheels principle is included as one way to decrease guidance for learning tasks within one task class. While the learning tasks in the same task class are equally difficult, they start with high guidance and guidance decreases until none as expertise increases.

COMPLETION-STRATEGY PRINCIPLE

In contrast to the training-wheels principle, which primarily concerns guidance or *process support*, the completion-strategy principle concerns support that is implied by the task description. The completion strategy (van Merriënboer, 1990; van Merriënboer & de Croock, 1992) starts with worked examples that must be studied by the learners, continues with completion tasks that present partial solutions that must be completed by the learners, and ends with conventional tasks for which the learners must independently generate whole solutions. Many studies indicate that novice learners learn more from studying worked examples (for an overview, see Atkinson, Derry, Renkl, & Wortham, 2000) or from performing completion tasks that require them to complete partial solutions (for an overview, see Sweller et al., 1998) than from solving the equivalent conventional problems. In addition, Kalyuga, Chandler, Tuovinen, and Sweller (2001) and Tuovinen and Sweller (1999) found that this effect reverses for more experienced learners, which is an example of the *expertise reversal effect* (Kalyuga, Ayres, & Chandler, 2003). Thus, novices benefit more from studying worked examples, but experienced learners profit more from solving the equivalent conventional problems. The completion strategy accommodates the findings on the expertise reversal effect and proved to be very effective in facilitating transfer of learning (Renkl & Atkinson, 2003; Renkl, Atkinson, & Grosse, 2004). In the 4C/ID-model, the completion-strategy principle is included as one way to decrease support for learning tasks within one task class. In the beginning of a task class, high support may be provided by the use of worked examples. Then, increasingly lesser support may be provided by completion tasks for which the learners have to generate larger and larger parts of the solution. Finally, conventional tasks provide no support at all.

Supportive Information and Learning From Hypermedia

Supportive information mainly aims at schema construction through elaboration, that is, connecting new information to knowledge that is already available in long-term memory. Traditional media for supportive information are textbooks, teachers, and realia. Textbooks contain a description of the "theory," that is, the domain models that characterize a field of study and, alas, often in a lesser degree the SAPs that may help to solve problems and perform nontrivial tasks in the domain. Teachers typically discuss the highlights in the theory (lectures), demonstrate or provide expert models of SAPs, and provide cognitive feedback on learners' performances. Realia or descriptions of real entities (case studies) are used to illustrate the theory. Hypermedia and hypertext systems may take over part of those functions. They may present theoretical models and concrete cases that illustrate those models in a highly interactive way, and they may explain problem-solving approaches and illustrate those approaches by showing, for example, expert models on video. As indicated before, it is critical that students elaborate and deeply process this information. On the one hand, hypermedia may well help to reach this goal, because their structure reflects the way that human knowledge is organized in elements (called *nodes*) and nonarbitrary relationships between those elements (called

links). But on the other hand, it is of utmost importance to provoke deep processing through asking questions, stimulating reflection, and promoting discussion. Principles 7–9 in Table 5.1 summarize the main multimedia principles that should be taken into account in hypermedia systems and provide illustrations of their application.

REDUNDANCY PRINCIPLE

This principle indicates that the presentation of redundant information typically has a negative impact on learning (for an overview of studies, see Sweller et al., 1998). It is a counterintuitive principle, because most people think that the presentation of the same information, in a somewhat different way, will have a neutral or even positive effect on learning. However, learners have to find out that the information from different sources is actually redundant, which is a cognitively demanding process that does not contribute to meaningful learning. In recent studies, Mayer, Heiser et al. (2001), Moreno and Mayer (2002), and Leahy et al. (2003) presented visual information to learners (e.g., an animation) and a concurrent narration that explained this visual information. Negative effects on learning were found when the concurrent narration was duplicated by a redundant on-screen text. Kalyuga, Chandler, and Sweller (2000) related the redundancy principle to the expertise reversal effect. They found that information that is helpful for novice learners is detrimental to more experienced learners, because it is redundant with what they already know. The 4C/ID-model relates the finding that the presentation of redundant information may seriously hamper learning primarily to the distribution of supportive information over task classes. The supportive information for each new task class is always an addition to, or embellishment of, the information that has been presented for previous task classes. While the conceptual link between the new information and the previous information should be pointed out to the learners, it is important *not* to repeat the information from previous task classes in order to prevent negative effects of redundancy.

SELF-EXPLANATION PRINCIPLE

Salomon (1998) discusses the "butterfly defect" in hypermedia and Web-based learning: "...touch, but don't touch, and just move on to make something out of it." Multimedia may act as an affordance to relax (e.g., watching television), but for meaningful learning to occur they should be associated with deep processing and invite learners to "self-explain" information. Renkl (1999) introduced the self-explanation principle in the context of learning from worked examples. The degree to which learners explain the solution steps in worked examples to themselves is a good predictor for learning outcomes, and direct elicitation of self-explanation by prompting the learners had some beneficial effects on transfer. Stronger evidence for the facilitation of transfer by self-explanation was found in a study with the completion strategy (Atkinson, Renkl, & Merrill, 2003). In this study, prompts were designed to encourage learners to identify the underlying principles illustrated in worked-out solution steps, and these prompts had beneficial effects on transfer test performance. Similar results were found in a study by Mayer, Dow, and Mayer (2003), who found positive effects on learning by using prequestions to guide self-explanation; by Aleven and Koedinger (2002), who found better transfer by using a cognitive tutor to guide self-explanation in a classroom setting; and by Moreno and Valdez (in press), who found positive effects on transfer of postponing feedback so that learners had to evaluate their own actions. For the presentation of supportive information, the 4C/ID-model stresses the importance of instructional methods that promote elaboration and schema construction. Prompting for self-explanation of domain models and SAPs, as well as illustrations of them by case studies and modeling examples, is one particularly important instructional method to reach this.

SELF-PACING PRINCIPLE

The self-pacing principle indicates that giving learners control over the pace of the instruction may facilitate elaboration and deep processing of information. Elaboration is an effortful, time-consuming process and especially "streaming" or transient information (video, dynamic animation, etc.) may leave learners insufficient time for this type of processing. Mayer and Moreno (2003) report higher transfer test performance if information is presented in learner-controlled segments rather than as one continuous unit, an example of the self-pacing principle they called the *segmentation effect*. In an experiment by Mayer and Chandler (2001), learners who were allowed to exercise control over the pace of a narrated animation performed better on transfer tasks compared with learners who received the same narrated animation at normal speed without any learner control. Tabbers (2002) found the same result for visual text accompanying diagrams. Self-paced presentation of the instructional texts led to higher transfer test performance than system-paced instructional texts. In the 4C/ID-model, streaming information will often refer to case studies (e.g., an animation illustrating a particular dynamic domain model) and modeling examples (e.g., a video of an expert modeling a particular problem-solving process or SAP). For this type of multimedia information presentation, it is important to give learners control over the pace at which the information is presented to them. The self-pacing principle allows them to pause and better reflect on the new information in order to couple it to already existing cognitive structures.

Procedural Information and Electronic Performance Support Systems

Procedural information primarily aims at schema automation through knowledge compilation. The traditional media for procedural information are the teacher and all kinds of job and learning aids. The teacher's role is to walk through the classroom, laboratory, or workplace and to watch over his learners' shoulder (the teacher's name is Aloys – the Assistant Looking Over Your Shoulder), and to give directions for performing the routine aspects of learning tasks (e.g., "No, you should hold that instrument like this. . . ."; "Watch, you should now select this option. . . ."). Job aids may be the posters with frequently used software commands that are stuck on the wall of a computer class, quick reference guides next to a piece of machinery, or booklets with safety instructions for interns in industry. In multimedia learning environments, these functions are mainly taken over by EPSSs such as online job aids and help systems, wizards, and (intelligent) pedagogical agents (Bastiaens, Nijhof, Streumer, & Abma, 1997). Such systems provide procedural information on request of the learner (e.g., on-demand help) or on their own initiative (e.g., pedagogical agent), preferably precisely when students need it for their work on the learning tasks. Table 5.1 summarizes the main multimedia principles (10–13) that should be taken into account in EPSSs and provides some examples of how they can be applied.

TEMPORAL SPLIT-ATTENTION PRINCIPLE

The temporal split-attention principle originally indicates that learning from mutually referring information sources is facilitated if these sources are not separated from each other in time, that is, if they are presented simultaneously. Mayer and Moreno (2003) refer to the principle as the "temporal contiguity effect" and review several studies that report higher transfer test performance for the simultaneous presentation of mutually referring pictures and text than for their consecutive presentation. The same is true for the concurrent presentation of animation and corresponding narration, which yields better transfer than their successive presentation (Mayer & Anderson, 1991, 1992; Mayer & Sims, 1994; Mayer, Moreno, Boire, & Vagge, 1999). In the context of the 4C/ID-model, the temporal split-attention principle is particularly important for the presentation of procedural information, which refers to how-to instructions for performing the routine aspects of the learning task the learner is working on. If this infor-

mation is presented *just in time*, precisely when the learner needs its, all elements necessary for knowledge compilation to occur are available in working memory at the time the skill is practiced. Kester, Kirschner, and van Merriënboer (2003; see also Kester et al., in press) compared the just-in-time presentation of procedural information with a split-attention format (i.e., first present the information and then practice the task) and found beneficial effects on transfer test performance of the simultaneous presentation.

SPATIAL SPLIT-ATTENTION PRINCIPLE

The spatial split-attention principle, which is also called the *spatial contiguity effect* (Mayer & Moreno, 2003), refers to the finding that higher transfer test performance is reached when mutually referring information sources are physically integrated with each other in space. Extensive research has been carried out showing the beneficial effects of integrating pictures with explanatory text. The text that refers to the picture is typically split up in smaller segments so that the text segment that refers to a particular part of the figure can be linked to this particular part or be included in the picture (e.g., Chandler & Sweller, 1991, 1992; Kalyuga, Chandler, & Sweller, 1999). In the context of the 4C/ID-model, Kester et al. (in press) studied the integration of procedural information in the task environment, in such a way that it was physically integrated with the learning tasks students were working on. Specifically, they integrated the procedural information in electronic circuits students had to troubleshoot. This also resulted in higher transfer test performance, a finding that is in agreement with Cerpa, Chandler, and Sweller (1996), who demonstrated that students learning a computer application learned better if all of the material was placed on the computer screen, as opposed to having a manual and computer on which to work. Combining both information sources prevents spatial split-attention between the task environment (i.e., the computer screen) and the procedural information in the manual (see also Chandler &

Sweller, 1996; Sweller & Chandler, 1994). In general, procedural information should thus be presented in such a way that it is optimally integrated with the learning tasks and the task environment.

SIGNALING PRINCIPLE

The signaling or attention-focusing principle indicates that learning may be improved if the learner's attention is focused on the critical aspects of the learning task or the presented information. It reduces the need for visual search and so frees up cognitive resources that may then be devoted to schema construction and automation, with positive effects on transfer test performance. Jeung, Chandler, and Sweller (1997) and Tabbers, Martens, and van Merriënboer (in press) found beneficial effects on learning from the synchronous use of explanatory spoken text and cues in complex pictures, that is, the moment a particular part of the complex picture was explained it was highlighted or color coded. Kalyuga, Chandler, and Sweller (1999) found similar positive effects of signaling with visual-only instructions. Furthermore, Mautone and Mayer (2001) found positive effects of signaling on transfer test performance when it was used in printed text, spoken text, as well as spoken text with corresponding animation. In the 4C/ID-model, signaling is particularly important if procedural information is related to routine aspects of task performance. For instance, if a teacher instructs a learner how to operate a piece of machinery it is useful to point a finger at those parts that must be controlled, and if a video-based example is used to demonstrate particular routine aspects of performance it is helpful to focus the learners' attention through signaling (e.g., by spotlighting hand movements) on precisely those aspects.

MODALITY PRINCIPLE

The modality principle indicates that dual-mode presentation techniques that use auditory text or narration to explain visual diagrams, animations, or demonstrations, result in better learning than equivalent, single-mode presentations that only use visual information. Moreno and Mayer (1999) and Tindall-Ford, Chandler, and Sweller (1997) present results that provide empirical support for the modality principle. The positive effect of dual-mode presentation is typically attributed to an expansion of effective working memory capacity, because for dual-mode presentations both the auditory and visual subsystems of working memory can be used rather than either one subsystem alone. This hypothesis was confirmed by Tabbers, Martens, and van Merriënboer (2001), who found that students who studied complex diagrams explained by spoken text reported lower perceived mental effort than students who studied the same diagrams with visual text. With regard to the 4C/ID-model, procedural information that just-in-time presentation specifies how to perform routine aspects of learning tasks can thus better be spoken by a teacher or other pedagogical agent than be visually presented.

Part-Task Practice and Drill and Practice Computer-Based Training

With regard to the fourth component, part-task practice aims at schema automation through strengthening. Especially for this component, the computer has proved its worth in the last decades. Drill and practice CBT is without doubt the most successful type of educational software. The computer is sometimes abused for its use of drill, but most critiques seem to miss the point. They contrast drill and practice CBT with educational software that focuses on rich, authentic learning tasks. But according to the 4C/ID-model drill and practice will never replace meaningful whole-task practice; it merely complements the learners' work on rich learning tasks and is applied *only* when the learning tasks cannot provide enough practice to reach the desired level of automaticity for selected routine aspects. If such part-task practice is necessary, the computer is probably the most suitable medium because it can make drill effective and appealing through giving procedural support; compressing simulated time so that more exercises can be done than in real time; giving knowledge of results and immediate feedback on errors; and using multiple representations, gaming elements, sound effects, and so forth. Table 5.1 gives an example of the application of the component fluency principle (14), that is, the most important multimedia principle in drill and practice CBT programs.

COMPONENT-FLUENCY PRINCIPLE

The component-fluency principle indicates that drill and practice on one or more routine aspects of a task may have positive effects on learning and performing the whole task. Strengthening may produce a very high level of automaticity for routine aspects, which frees up cognitive capacity because these automated aspects no longer require resources for conscious processing. As a result, all available cognitive capacity can be allocated to the nonroutine, problem-solving and reasoning aspects of whole-task performance. Carlson, Sullivan, and Schneider (1989) and Carlson, Khoo, and Elliot (1990) found evidence for the component fluency principle, but *only* when part-task practice took place after the learners were introduced to the whole task, that is, when it was provided in an appropriate "cognitive context." For this reason, the 4C/ID-model is reserved with the application of part-task practice and, if it is used at all, suggests starting part-task practice for particular routine aspects only *after* the learners have been introduced to these aspects in the context of whole learning tasks. Only then, the learners are able to identify the activities that are required to integrate the routines in the whole task.

Discussion

The 4C/ID-model provides guidelines for the design of environments in which complex learning takes place, that is, learning directed toward the integration of knowledge, skills, and attitudes; the ability to coordinate qualitatively different constituent skills; and the transfer of what is learned to real-life situations. This model was elaborated for the design of multimedia learning environments. Such applications are typically built around a simulated task environment that offers the opportunity to perform learning tasks (component 1). They may further contain hypermedia that allow learners to actively study supportive information (component 2), EPSSs with procedural information specifying how to perform routine aspects of complex tasks (component 3), and, finally, drill and practice CBT programs that provide opportunities for overlearning selected routine aspects that need to be performed at a very high level of automaticity after the training (component 4). Each of these four components relates to another set of prominent multimedia principles.

In the introduction to this chapter, theories about learning with multimedia were positioned at three different levels: The psychological level, the message design level, and the course design level. As a theory at the level of course and curriculum design, the 4C/ID-model yields no direct contributions to cognitive theory in the sense that it provides a new perspective on human cognitive architecture or uncovers new cognitive processes. We believe, however, that it indirectly contributes to cognitive theory by synthesizing many different findings and showing the importance of the psychological study of real-life complex task performance. Learning processes such as inductive learning, elaboration, knowledge compilation, and strengthening have each been thoroughly studied in many experimental studies, often using relatively straightforward laboratory tasks. No doubt, this is vital research but in addition it is becoming more and more important to study different types of learning processes in connection with each other. The 4C/ID-model tries to do so, and our results clearly indicate that complex learning on the basis of real-life tasks can only be described in terms of qualitatively different learning processes that often simultaneously occur.

With regard to instructional design and, in particular, theories at the level of message design, the contributions of the 4C/ID-model are more straightforward. Traditional design models analyze a learning domain in terms of distinct learning objectives. A common premise is that different objectives can best be reached by the application of particular instructional principles (the "conditions of learning," Gagné, 1985). The optimal principles are chosen to design the message for each objective; the objectives are taught one-by-one; and the general educational goal is believed to be met after all messages have been conveyed. In the early 1990s, authors in the field of instructional design started to question the value of this approach because it yields instruction that is fragmented and piecemeal (e.g., Gagné & Merrill, 1990). For real-life tasks, there are many interactions between the different aspects of task performance and their related objectives. Integrated objectives should not only aim at the ability to effectively perform each aspect of a complex task in isolation, but also pay attention to the ability to *coordinate* these different aspects in real-life task performance. An important contribution of the 4C/ID-model is that it provides a whole-task methodology to deal with such integrated objectives. At the same time, the four components provide an organizing framework for instructional methods, including multimedia principles (cf. Table 5.1). At least, the 4C/ID-model points out to designers under which conditions, and for which components of a learning environment, particular multimedia principles should be considered.

The framework discussed in this chapter has several limitations. First, the 4C/ID-model may well be used to design multimedia learning environments, but if this is actually desirable in a particular situation is yet another question. Many factors determine the selection of media in instructional design, including *constraints* (e.g., manpower, equipment, time, money), *task requirements* (e.g., media attributes necessary for performing learning tasks and required response options for learners), and *target group characteristics* (size of the group, computer literacy, handicaps). The 4C/ID-model does not pro-

vide guidelines for this process of media selection. Second, when positioned in the general Analysis, Design, Development, Implementation, and Evaluation (ADDIE), model the 4C/ID-model clearly focuses on analysis and design activities, and does neither provide specific guidelines for the development, production, and construction of multimedia materials nor for their implementation and evaluation. And third, while we focused our discussion on the most prominent multimedia principles for each of the four blueprint components, this does not imply that particular principles cannot be important for other blueprint components.

For instance, the fidelity principle is particularly important to sequence learning tasks from working in low-fidelity to working in high-fidelity environments, but it may also be relevant to all the other three components that, after all, also determine aspects of the learning environment. Likewise, the training-wheels principle and the individualization principle are not exclusively useful for the design of learning tasks, but may also be applied to gradually relax performance constraints and to control a learner's progress during part-task practice. The self-pacing principle is particularly important to the design of supportive information, but may also be useful for the presentation of procedural information (e.g., giving students control over the pace of a demonstration, so that they can view it step-by-step, is more effective then presenting the demonstration as one uninterrupted streaming video). And finally, split-attention, signaling, and modality principles are particularly important for the presentation of procedural information, because this is typically presented while the learners work on their learning tasks, but the same principles may also be relevant to the design of complex pieces of supportive information.

To conclude, psychological knowledge about how people learn with multimedia is rapidly increasing and many findings from cognitive theory have been incorporated in instructional theories that yield useful guidelines for the design of instructional messages. Less is known about how to apply those guidelines in environments for complex learning that try to reach integrated learning goals by using a mix of traditional and new educational media. Future research must identify the real-life conditions under which particular principles do and do not work and, especially, develop higher-level principles that help designers to stretch multimedia design from the message design level to the course design level, where simulated task environments, hypermedia, EPSSs, drill and practice CBT programs, and other (traditional) media should seamlessly link up with each other. Future research should also acknowledge that advanced networked multimedia systems enable people to learn in ways that were inconceivable in the past. In order to make scientific progress in the field of multimedia learning, we should both study how good old-fashioned learning principles inform the design of artifacts and how implicit design principles in advanced technological artifacts affect the way in which people learn.

Glossary

Completion-strategy principle: Sequencing learning tasks from worked examples that students must study, using completion tasks with incomplete solutions that must be finished, to conventional problems that must be solved has a positive effect on inductive learning and transfer.

Component-fluency principle: Training routine aspects, or, consistent components of a task up to a very high level of automaticity, in addition to training the whole task, has a positive effect on learning (in particular, strengthening) and transfer of the whole task.

Elaboration: A category of learning processes by which learners connect new information to knowledge that they already have available in memory. It is a form of schema construction that is especially important for learning supportive information using, for instance, hypermedia.

Fidelity principle: Sequencing learning tasks in such a way that they are first performed in an environment that does not try to mimic the real task environment (i.e., low fidelity) and later performed in environments that more and more resemble the real environment (i.e., increasing fidelity) has a positive effect on inductive learning and transfer.

Individualization principle: Adapting the difficulty and the amount of available support of learning tasks to the level of expertise of individual learners has a positive effect on inductive learning and transfer.

Induction: A category of learning processes, including generalization and discrimination, by which learners mindfully abstract away from their concrete experiences. It is a form of schema construction that is especially important for learning from learning tasks in real or simulated task environments.

Knowledge compilation: A category of learning processes by which learners embed new information in highly domain-specific schemata that directly steer behavior. It is a form of schema automation that is especially important for learning procedural information from, for instance, EPSSs.

Learning task: A meaningful whole-task experience that is typically based on a real-life task and promotes inductive learning. Learning tasks are performed in a real or simulated task environment.

Modality principle: Replacing a written explanatory text and another source of visual information such as a diagram (unimodal) with a spoken explanatory text and a visual source of information (multimodal) has a positive effect on knowledge compilation and transfer.

Part-task practice: Additional exercises to train a particular routine aspect up to a very high level of automation through strengthening. Drill and practice CBT is a suitable medium for part-task practice.

Procedural information: Information that is relevant for learning the routine aspects of learning tasks through knowledge compilation. This information is typically presented during task performance by EPSSs.

Redundancy principle: Replacing multiple sources of information that are self-contained (i.e., they can be understood on their own) with one source of information has a positive effect on elaborative learning and transfer.

Self-explanation principle: Prompting learners to self-explain new information by asking them, for instance, to identify underlying principles has a positive effect on elaborative learning and transfer.

Self-pacing principle: Giving learners control over the pace of instruction, which may have the form of transient information (e.g., animation, video), has a positive effect on elaborative learning and transfer.

Sequencing principle: Sequencing learning tasks from simple to complex, instead of presenting them in their full complexity at once, has a positive effect on inductive learning and transfer.

Signaling principle: Focusing learners' attention on the critical aspects of learning tasks or presented information reduces visual search and has a positive effect on knowledge compilation and transfer.

Spatial split-attention principle: Replacing multiple sources of information (frequently pictures and accompanying text) with a single, integrated source of information has a positive effect on knowledge compilation and transfer.

Strengthening: A category of learning processes responsible for the fact that domain-specific schemata accumulate strength each time they are successfully applied. It is a form of advanced schema automation that is especially important for (over)learning on the basis of part-task practice with, for instance, drill and practice CBT.

Supportive information: Information that is relevant for learning the problem-solving and reasoning aspects of learning tasks through elaboration and understanding. This information is typically presented before learners start to work on the learning tasks by hypermedia that stress relations between pieces of knowledge.

Temporal split-attention principle: Presenting multiple sources of information (e.g., mutually referring pictures and text) at the same time, instead of one by one, has a positive effect on knowledge compilation and transfer.

Training-wheels principle: Sequencing learning tasks in such a way that learners' performance is first constrained (i.e., unproductive actions are blocked), and then slowly loosening the constraints until none has a positive effect on inductive learning and transfer.

Variability principle: Organizing learning tasks in such a way that they differ from each other on dimensions that also differ in the real world has a positive effect on inductive learning and transfer.

References

Aleven, V. A. W. M. M., & Koedinger, K. R. (2002). An effective metacognitive strategy: Learning by doing and explaining with a computer-based cognitive tutor. *Cognitive Science, 26,* 147–179.

Anderson, J. R. (1993). *Rules of the mind.* Hillsdale, NJ: Lawrence Erlbaum.

Anderson, J. R., & Lebiere, C. (1998). *The atomic components of thought.* Mahwah, NJ: Lawrence Erlbaum.

Atkinson, R. K., Derry, S. J., Renkl, A., & Wortham, D. (2000). Learning from examples: Instructional principles from the worked examples research. *Review of Educational Research, 70*, 181–214.

Atkinson, R. K., Renkl, A., & Merrill, M. M. (2003). Transitioning from studying examples to solving problems: Effects of self-explanation prompts and fading worked-out steps. *Journal of Educational Psychology, 95*, 774–783.

Baddeley, A. D. (1992). Working memory. *Science, 255*, 556–559.

Baddeley, A. D. (1997). *Human memory: Theory and practice* (Rev. ed.). Hove, UK: Psychology Press.

Bastiaens, Th., Nijhof, W. J., Streumer, J. N., & Abma, H. J. (1997). Working and learning with electronic performance support systems: An effectiveness study. *Training for Quality, 5*(1), 10–18.

Camp, G., Paas, F., Rikers, R., & van Merriënboer, J. J. G. (2001). Dynamic problem selection in air traffic control training: A comparison between performance, mental effort and mental efficiency. *Computers in Human Behavior, 17*, 575–595.

Carlson, R. A., Khoo, H., & Elliot, R. G. (1990). Component practice and exposure to a problem-solving context. *Human Factors, 32*, 267–286.

Carlson, R. A., Sullivan, M. A., & Schneider, W. (1989). Component fluency in a problem solving context. *Human Factors, 31*, 489–502.

Carroll, J. M. (2000). *Making use: Scenario-based design of human-computer interactions.* Cambridge, MA: MIT Press.

Cerpa, N., Chandler, P., & Sweller, J. (1996). Some conditions under which integrated computer-based training software can facilitate learning. *Journal of Educational Computing Research, 15*, 345–367.

Chandler, P., & Sweller, J. (1991). Cognitive load theory and the format of instruction. *Cognition and Instruction, 8*, 293–332.

Chandler, P., & Sweller, J. (1992). The split attention effect as a factor in the design of instruction. *British Journal of Educational Psychology, 62*, 233–246.

Chandler, P., & Sweller, J. (1996). Cognitive load while learning to use a computer program. *Applied Cognitive Psychology, 10*, 151–170.

Clark, J. M., & Paivio, A. (1991). Dual coding theory and education. *Educational Psychology Review, 3*, 149–210.

Clarke, T., Ayres, P., & Sweller, J. (in press). The impact of sequencing and prior knowledge on learning mathematics through spreadsheet applications. *Educational Technology, Research and Development.*

De Croock, M. B. M., van Merriënboer, J. J. G., & Paas, F. (1998). High versus low contextual interference in simulation-based training of troubleshooting skills: Effects on transfer performance and invested mental effort. *Computers in Human Behavior, 14*, 249–267.

Dufresne, R. J., Gerace, W. J., Thibodeau-Hardiman, P., & Mestre, J. P. (1992). Constraining novices to perform expertlike problem analyses: Effects on schema acquisition. *The Journal of the Learning Sciences, 2*, 307–331.

Gagné, R. M. (1985). *The conditions of learning* (4th ed.). New York: Holt, Rinehart and Winston.

Gagné, R. M., & Merrill, M. D. (1990). Integrative goals for instructional design. *Educational Technology, Research and Development, 38*, 23–30.

Gerjets, P., Scheiter, K., & Catrambone, R. (2004). Designing instructional examples to reduce intrinsic cognitive load: Molar versus modular presentation of solution procedures. *Instructional Science, 32*, 33–58.

Gulikers, J. T. M., Bastiaens, Th. J., & Martens, R. L. (in press). The surplus value of an authentic learning environment. *Computers in Human Behavior.*

Harp, S. F., & Mayer, R. E. (1998). How seductive details do their damage: A theory of cognitive interest in science learning. *Journal of Educational Psychology, 90*, 414–434.

Holland, J. H., Holyoak, K. J., Nisbett, R. E., & Thagard, P. R. (Eds.) (1989). *Induction: Processes of inference, learning, and discovery.* Cambridge, MA: MIT Press.

Jeung, H., Chandler, P., & Sweller, J. (1997). The role of visual indicators in dual sensory mode instruction. *Educational Psychology, 17*, 329–343.

Kalyuga, S., Ayres, P., & Chandler, P. (2003). The expertise reversal effect. *Educational Psychologist, 38*, 23–31.

Kalyuga, S., Chandler, P., & Sweller, J. (1999). Managing split-attention and redundancy in multimedia instruction. *Applied Cognitive Psychology, 13*, 351–371.

Kalyuga, S., Chandler, P., & Sweller, J. (2000). Incorporating learner experience into the design of multimedia instruction. *Journal of Educational Psychology, 92*, 126–136.

Kalyuga, S., Chandler, P., Tuovinen, J., & Sweller, J. (2001). When problem solving is superior to studying worked examples. *Journal of Educational Psychology*, 93, 579–588.

Kalyuga, S., & Sweller, J. (in press). Rapid dynamic assessment of expertise to improve the efficiency of adaptive e-learning. *Educational Technology, Research and Development*.

Kester, L., Kirschner, P. A., & van Merriënboer, J. J. G. (2003). Information presentation and troubleshooting in electrical circuits. *International Journal of Science Education*, 26, 239–256.

Kester, L., Kirschner, P. A., & van Merriënboer, J. J. G. (in press-a). Timing of information presentation in learning statistics. *Instructional Science*.

Kester, L., Kirschner, P. A., & van Merriënboer, J. J. G. (in press-b). The management of cognitive load during complex cognitive skill acquisition by means of computer simulated problem solving. *British Journal of Educational Psychology*.

Leahy, W., Chandler, P., & Sweller, J. (2003). When auditory presentations should and should not be a component of multimedia instruction. *Applied Cognitive Psychology*, 17, 401–418.

Leutner, D. (2000). Double-fading support – a training approach to complex software systems. *Journal of Computer Assisted Learning*, 16, 347–357.

Maran, N. J., & Glavin, R. J. (2003). Low- to high-fidelity simulation: A continuum of medical education? *Medical Education*, 37(1), 22–28.

Mautone, P. D., & Mayer, R. E. (2001). Signaling as a cognitive guide in multimedia learning. *Journal of Educational Psychology*, 93, 377–389.

Mayer, R. E. (2001). *Multimedia learning*. New York: Cambridge University Press.

Mayer, R. E., & Anderson, R. B. (1991). Animations need narrations: An experimental test of a dual-coding hypothesis. *Journal of Educational Psychology*, 83, 484–490.

Mayer, R. E., & Anderson, R. B. (1992). The instructive animation: Helping students build connections between words and pictures in multimedia learning. *Journal of Educational Psychology*, 84, 444–452.

Mayer, R. E., & Chandler, P. (2001). When learning is just a click away: Does simple user interaction foster deeper understanding of multimedia messages? *Journal of Educational Psychology*, 93, 390–397.

Mayer, R. E., Dow, G. T., & Mayer, S. (2003). Multimedia learning in an interactive self-explaining environment: What works in the design of agent-based microworlds? *Journal of Educational Psychology*, 95, 806–812.

Mayer, R. E., Heiser, J., & Lonn, S. (2001). Cognitive constraints on multimedia learning: When presenting more material results in less understanding. *Journal of Experimental Psychology*, 93, 187–198.

Mayer, R. E., Matthias, A., & Wetzell, K. (2002). Fostering understanding of multimedia messages through pre-training: Evidence for a two-stage theory of mental model construction. *Journal of Experimental Psychology: Applied*, 8, 147–154.

Mayer, R. E., & Moreno, R. (2003). Nine ways to reduce cognitive load in multimedia learning. *Educational Psychologist*, 38, 43–52.

Mayer, R. E., Moreno, R., Boire, M., & Vagge, S. (1999). Maximizing constructivist learning from multimedia communications by minimizing cognitive load. *Journal of Educational Psychology*, 91, 638–643.

Mayer, R. E., & Sims, V. K. (1994). For whom is a picture worth a thousand words? Extensions of a dual-coding theory of multimedia learning. *Journal of Educational Psychology*, 86, 389–401.

Merrill, M. D. (2002). First principles of instruction. *Educational Technology, Research and Development*, 50, 43–59.

Moreno, R., & Mayer, R. E. (1999). Cognitive principles of multimedia learning: The role of modality and contiguity. *Journal of Educational Psychology*, 91, 358–368.

Moreno, R., & Mayer, R. E. (2000). A coherence effect in multimedia learning: The case for minimizing irrelevant sounds in the design of multimedia instructional messages. *Journal of Experimental Psychology*, 94, 117–125.

Moreno, R., & Mayer, R. E. (2002). Verbal redundancy in multimedia learning: When reading helps listening. *Journal of Educational Psychology*, 94, 156–163.

Moreno, R., & Valdez, F. (in press). Cognitive load and learning effects of having students organize pictures and words in multimedia environments: The role of student interactivity and feedback. *Educational Technology, Research and Development*.

Nadolski, R. J., Kirschner, P. A., & van Merriënboer, J. J. G. (2001). A model for optimizing step size of learning tasks in competency-based multimedia practicals. *Educational Technology, Research and Development*, 49, 87–103.

Paas, F., & van Merriënboer, J. J. G. (1994). Variability of worked examples and transfer of geometrical problem-solving skills: A cognitive-load approach. *Journal of Educational Psychology*, 86, 122–133.

Paivio, A. (1986). *Mental representation: A dual coding approach*. New York: Oxford University Press.

Palmeri, T. J. (1999). Theories of automaticity and the power law of practice. *Journal of Experimental Psychology: Learning, Memory, and Cognition*, 25, 543–551.

Penney, C. (1989). Modality effects and the structure of short-term working memory. *Memory and Cognition*, 17, 398–422.

Perkins, D. N., & Salomon, G. (1989). Are cognitive skills context-bound? *Educational Researcher*, 18, 16–25.

Pollock, E., Chandler, P., & Sweller, J. (2002). Assimilating complex information. *Learning and Instruction*, 12, 61–86.

Quilici, J. L., & Mayer, R. E. (1996). Role of examples in how students learn to categorize statistics word problems. *Journal of Educational Psychology*, 88, 144–161.

Renkl, A. (1999). Learning mathematics from worked-out examples: Analyzing and fostering self-explanations. *European Journal of Psychology of Education*, 14, 477–488.

Renkl, A., & Atkinson, R. K. (2003). Structuring the transition from example study to problem solving in cognitive skill acquisition: A cognitive load perspective. *Educational Psychologist*, 38, 15–22.

Renkl, A., Atkinson, R. K., & Grosse, C. S. (2004). How fading worked solution steps works – A cognitive load perspective. *Instructional Science*, 32, 59–82.

Salden, R. J. C. M., Paas, F., Broers, N. J., & van Merriënboer, J. J. G. (2004). Mental effort and performance as determinants for the dynamic selection of learning tasks in air traffic control training. *Instructional Science*, 32, 153–172.

Salden, R. J. C. M., Paas, F., & van Merriënboer, J. J. G. (in press). A comparison of approaches to learning task selection in the training of complex cognitive skills. *Computers in Human Behavior*.

Salomon, G. (1998). Novel constructivist learning environments and novel technologies: Some issues to be concerned with. *Research Dialogue in Learning and Instruction*, 1 (1), 3–12.

Straetmans, G., Sluijsmans, D. M. A., Bolhuis, B., & van Merriënboer, J. J. G. (2003). Integratie van instructie en assessment in competentiegericht onderwijs [Integration of instruction and assessment in competence based education]. *Tijdschrift voor Hoger Onderwijs*, 21, 171–197.

Sweller, J. (2004). Instructional design consequences of an analogy between evolution by natural selection and human cognitive architecture. *Instructional Science*, 32, 9–31.

Sweller, J., & Chandler, P. (1994). Why some material is difficult to learn. *Cognition and Instruction*, 12, 185–233.

Sweller, J., van Merriënboer, J. J. G., & Paas, F. (1998). Cognitive architecture and instructional design. *Educational Psychology Review*, 10, 251–296.

Tabbers, H. K. (2002). *The modality of text in multimedia instructions. Refining the design guidelines*. Unpublished doctoral dissertation, Open University of the Netherlands, Heerlen, The Netherlands.

Tabbers, H. K., Martens, R. L., & van Merriënboer, J. J. G. (2001). The modality effect in multimedia instructions. In J. D. Moore & K. Stennings (Eds.), *Proceedings of the twenty-third annual conference of the Cognitive Science Society* (pp. 1024–1029). Mahwah, NJ: Lawrence Erlbaum.

Tabbers, H. K., Martens, R. L., & van Merriënboer, J. J. G. (in press). Multimedia instructions and cognitive load theory: Effects of modality and cueing. *British Journal of Educational Psychology*.

Tindall-Ford, S., Chandler, P., & Sweller, J. (1997). When two sensory modes are better than one. *Journal of Experimental Psychology: Applied*, 3, 257–287.

Tuovinen, J., & Sweller, J. (1999). A comparison of cognitive load associated with discovery learning and worked examples. *Journal of Educational Psychology*, 91, 334–341.

Van Gog, T., Paas, F., & van Merriënboer, J. J. G. (2004). Process-oriented worked examples: Improving transfer performance through enhanced understanding. *Instructional Science*, 32, 83–98.

Van Merriënboer, J. J. G. (1990). Strategies for programming instruction in high school: Program completion vs. program generation. *Journal of Educational Computing Research, 6,* 265–285.

Van Merriënboer, J. J. G. (1997). *Training complex cognitive skills.* Englewood Cliffs, NJ: Educational Technology Publications.

Van Merriënboer, J. J. G., Clark, R. E., & de Crosck, M. B. M. (2002). Blueprints for complex learning: The 4C/ID-model. *Educational Technology Research and Development, 50,* 39–64.

Van Merriënboer, J. J. G., & de Croock, M. B. M. (1992). Strategies for computer-based programming instruction: Program completion vs. program generation. *Journal of Educational Computing Research, 8,* 365–394.

Van Merriënboer, J. J. G., Jelsma, O., & Paas, F. (1992). Training for reflective expertise: A four-component instructional design model for complex cognitive skills. *Educational Technology Research and Development, 40,* 23–43.

Van Merriënboer, J. J. G., Kirschner, P. A., & Kester, L. (2003). Taking the load of a learners' mind: Instructional design for complex learning. *Educational Psychologist, 38,* 5–13.

Van Merriënboer, J. J. G., & Luursema, J. J. (1996). Implementing instructional models in computer-based learning environments: A case study in problem selection. In T. T. Liao (Ed.), *Advanced educational technology: Research issues and future potential* (pp. 184–206). Berlin, Germany: Springer Verlag.

Van Merriënboer, J. J. G., Schuurman, J. G., de Croock, M. B. M., & Paas, F. (2002). Redirecting learners' attention during training: Effects on cognitive load, transfer test performance and training efficiency. *Learning and Instruction, 12,* 11–37.

Willoughby, T., Wood, E., Desmarais, S., Sims, S., & Kalra, M. (1997). Mechanisms that facilitate the effectiveness of elaboration strategies. *Journal of Educational Psychology, 89,* 682–685.

Part II

BASIC PRINCIPLES OF MULTIMEDIA LEARNING

CHAPTER 6

Five Common but Questionable Principles of Multimedia Learning

Richard E. Clark

University of Southern California

David F. Feldon

University of California at Los Angeles

Principle: *A basic generalization that is accepted as true and that can be used as a basis for reasoning or conduct.*

OneLook.com Dictionary

Abstract

This chapter describes five commonly held principles about multimedia learning that are not supported by research and suggests alternative generalizations that are more firmly based on existing studies.[1] The questionable beliefs include the expectations that multimedia instruction: (1) yields more learning than live instruction or older media; (2) is more motivating than other instructional delivery options; (3) provides animated pedagogical agents that aid learning; (4) accommodates different learning styles and so maximizes learning for more students; and (5) facilitates student-managed constructivist and discovery approaches that are beneficial to learning.

Introduction

Multimedia instruction is one of the current examples of a new area of instructional research and practice that has generated a considerable amount of excitement. Like other new areas, its early advocates begin with a set of assumptions about the learning and access problems it will solve and the opportunities it affords (see, e.g., a report by the American Society for Training and Development, 2001). The goal of this chapter is to examine the early expectations about multimedia benefits that seem so intuitively correct that advocates may not have carefully examined research evidence for them. If these implicit assumptions are incorrect we may unintentionally be using them as the basis for designing multimedia instruction that does not support learning or enhance motivation. Even when easily available research findings contradict widely shared beliefs about benefits, it is tempting to ignore the research by assuming, without careful analysis,

97

that the multimedia instruction has been poorly designed.

Definition of Multimedia

So many different definitions of multimedia have been offered (see, e.g., Clark, 2001) that it is important at the start of this discussion to clearly specify what is being discussed. *Instructional media* generally refers to any vehicle for presenting or delivering instruction. Examples of these vehicles usually refer to computers, books, television, radio, newspapers, and people. *Multimedia* usually refers to the capacity of computers to provide real-time representations of nearly all existing media and sensory modes of instruction. Sensory modes are distinguished from media because they relate to the sensory format of information so that it is compatible with one of the five senses. Visual and aural forms of information can be provided by a variety of media whereas taste, smell, and texture representations in media are very limited. Multimedia instruction is most often offered at a "distance" from live teachers and so is occasionally referred to as *distance education*. One of the issues raised in this chapter is that the impressive breadth of multimedia formats for instruction and learning may invite a confounding of the specific factors that influence (or fail to influence) learning and motivation for different people and different learning tasks.

Chapter Goals

This chapter examines the research evidence for five of the implicit assumptions one finds in much of the current literature on multimedia instruction. Each of these assumptions seem to be so widely shared, that they have taken on the mantle of "principles" that guide the design of instruction and research on multimedia instruction. Yet each of these beliefs has been examined by a body of well-designed research and found either to be incorrect or only to apply in a very limited set of circumstances. The goal of this chapter is to provide a brief survey of some of the research and related analysis that challenge each of the five mistaken principles. In each

case, the discussion will provide an alternative generalization that seems warranted, given the current research. The discussion begins with the most dominant and perhaps the most erroneous multimedia assumption, that learning benefits are greater from multimedia than from other instructional media.

Principle 1: Multimedia Instruction Produces More Learning than "Live" Instruction or Older Media

There is no credible evidence of learning benefits from any medium or combination of media that cannot be explained by other, nonmultimedia factors (Clark, 2001; Clark & Salomon, 1986; Mielke, 1968; Salomon, 1984; Schramm, 1977). Even the critics of this conclusion, for example, Robert Kozma (1994), have acknowledged that no evidence exists to support the argument that media has influenced learning in past research. Critics of the "no learning from media" view who are familiar with the research, hope that multimedia will provide unique forms of influence on learning in the future. Yet it appears that this optimistic hope is swimming upstream against a considerable body of evidence to the contrary extending back over 75 years (Clark, 2001; Mielke, 1968).

The capacity of multimedia is broad and inclusive. It even permits us to provide presentations by human instructors that have been "recorded" on video and presented on a computer screen as well as all instructional methods, including interactivity between instruction and learner (e.g., feedback to the learner on their progress or answering questions posed by learners as they progress through instruction), the providing of examples in the form of simulations or models, and other methods of teaching that have been found to influence learning. In order to fully understand the impact of multimedia on learning and motivation, it is important to separate it from the instructional methods multimedia can present and the sensory modality (visual, aural, olfactory, tactile, and taste information) chosen to represent instructional methods. Research and evaluation studies that provide evidence for more learning from multimedia than from live instruction or other media have been challenged because of their failure to separate media from method and sensory mode. A number of reviews have argued that when experiments or evaluation studies report learning advantages for multimedia when compared with other media, the learning benefits attributed to multimedia are more plausibly due to the uncontrolled effects of instructional methods and/or sensory mode influences (not media) and/or different test-relevant information being given to different groups (Clark & Salomon, 1986; Mielke, 1968; Morrison, 1994; Salomon, 1984; Schramm, 1977). Clark (2001) has argued that all instructional methods, sensory modes, and information components of instruction can be presented in a variety of media with equal learning outcomes but with very different costs and access outcomes.

Method Confounding

The most promising approach to learning is to assume that it is influenced by instructional methods (Cronbach & Snow, 1977) that can be embedded in instruction and presented by a variety of media and not only by multimedia per se. Instructional methods are defined as "... any way to shape information that compensates for or supplants the cognitive processes necessary for achievement or motivation. For example, learners often need an example to connect new information in a learning task with information in their prior experience. If students cannot (or will not) give themselves an adequate example, an instructional (method) must provide it for them" (Clark, 2001, p. 208). Variations in interactivity can be provided to learners by a number of media, including live instructors. If studies provide a necessary method of instruction in a multimedia condition and do not provide an equivalent form of the method in a compared instructional treatment, the results will appear to favor multimedia when in fact, the method influenced the learning. The key issue is whether any

instructional method can be presented in more than one medium. Clark (2001) has argued that all instructional methods that are necessary for any kind of learning can be presented in a variety of media. He claims therefore, that the benefits of media are economic or are to be found in the increased access to instruction by disadvantaged groups in society, but that learning benefits due to multimedia alone have not been found and cannot be claimed.

Sensory Mode and Learning

Multimedia instructional designers are tempted toward instructional presentations that, besides agents, include very active animation, motion video, colorful graphic displays, background sounds, music, and other multisensory depictions of course concepts, voice-over narration, and other visually and aurally exciting displays. While many learners seem to welcome the visual and aural entertainment, the best evidence suggests that learners are often overloaded by seductive but irrelevant distractions or the effort of processing redundant information so their learning is reduced (Mayer, 2001; Moreno & Mayer, 2000; see also chapter 12). Mayer (2001) has described a systematic program of research designed to tease out the benefits of multimedia-supported integrations of visual and aural depictions of processes that are being learned. He reports evidence that multimedia lessons where both visual and text-based explanations of processes are spatially or temporarily separated, and/or are heavily text laden seem to overload the working memory of many students and decrease their learning. He also reports instances where the presentation of spatially and temporally integrated visual and aural descriptions of the same process can enhance learning (Mayer, 2001). He suggests that providing both a visual and a narrative description of a process being learned will increase the amount of time information about the process can be held and processed in working memory. This finding suggests that formatting process information in two sensory modes results in better learning than presenting the same information in either visual or auditory form alone. Multimedia, computer-based instruction is a very efficient vehicle for presenting integrated visual and auditory information yet other media (including live instructors using silent motion films or television) could provide the same instruction. Because a number of different media will present visual and aural sensory mode information, this instructional method is not considered to be a potential learning benefit that is exclusive to multimedia.

Meta-analytic Studies of Multimedia

The most recent summary of instructional media research has been provided in an extensive meta-analysis conducted by Bernard et al. (in press) who examined over 650 empirical studies comparing live and multimedia distance learning to locate 167 studies that met their criteria for design. Their comprehensive analysis concluded that a very weak learning advantage for multimedia in empirical studies was attributable to uncontrolled instructional methods. They also reviewed four previous meta-analyses of earlier and different multimedia issues and suggested that the evidence in all of them pointed to "no differences" as the most reasonable conclusion.

A Recent Example of Methods and Multimedia

An interesting example of the difference between multimedia and instructional method can be found in a series of experiments by Corbett (2001) that focused on the impact of a variety of instructional methods used to teach Lisp programming based on Anderson's Lisp tutor (see Anderson & Gluck, 2001). Corbett describes an approximate 1.5 sigma effect size increase in learning over standard mastery learning methods due instructional methods called *model tracing* and *cognitive mastery*. The addition of scaffolding (providing more tracing and cognitive mas-

tery support for novice students then withdrawing it slowly as they gain expertise) increased the effect size impact another 0.42. This means that Corbett's methods produce a learning benefit of approximately 60% over instruction that gave all necessary information to students but did not use the experimental methods.

Time to Learn

Equally interesting is that when the new methods were compared with mastery methods (Bloom, 1984) they produced a 40% increase in learning. The methods described were derived not from a study of multimedia but instead from recent research on cognitive architecture and its influence on the learning of complex knowledge (Anderson & Gluck, 2001). All methods were delivered by a computer but all could have been provided by human tutors although with much less efficiency. The latter point is emphasized by Corbett's (2001) finding that the computer-delivered version of the powerful methods resulted in a 40% decrease in the time required to learn when compared with human tutors.

If Not "Learning Benefits," What Are the Advantages of Multimedia Instruction?

Clark (2000) has described a number of strategies for evaluating multimedia instructional programs that separate the benefits of the media from the benefits of the instructional methods used. Multimedia benefits, he suggests, are to be found in the cost of instruction, including time savings for students and instructors (when the investment in instructional design and development are amortized across increasing numbers of students) and increased access to quality instruction by disadvantaged or rural groups of students. Evidence for cost and time savings can be found in the work of Corbett (2001) described previously and cost-benefit and cost-effectiveness studies conducted by Levin and his colleagues (Levin, Glass, & Meister, 1987; Levin & McEwan, 2001).

Evidence for access benefits is more difficult to locate and it is possible that this is a less explored area. One example is a government report of increased access to instruction by people whose educational alternatives are severely limited by geography or other handicapping conditions such as economic, physical, or social barriers (Office of Technology Assessment, 1988).

In addition to learning benefits, advocates often implicitly and explicitly (e.g., Abrahamson, 1998) claim that multimedia results in increased motivation to learn when compared with more traditional instructional media. The discussion turns next to this issue.

Principle 2: Multimedia Instruction Is More Motivating Than Traditional Instructional Media or Live Instructors

Abrahamson (1998) may represent the majority of multimedia advocates when he states that "a primary function of the use of television, computers, and telecommunications in distance learning is to motivate students rather than just to provide information to them" (p. 2). However, evidence for the motivational qualities of multimedia instruction has been elusive at best. The best conclusion at this point is that overall, multimedia courses may be more attractive to students and so they tend to choose them when offered options, but student interest does not result in more learning and overall it appears to actually result in significantly less learning than would have occurred in "instructor-led" courses (Bernard et al., in press). In order to explain this ironic twist in empirical research, the discussion turns first to a definition of motivation.

What Is Motivation?

Pintrich and Schunk (2002) in their review of research on motivation to learn suggest that the existing research focuses on one or more of three "indexes" or outcomes of motivation: (1) active choice (actively starting to do something that one formerly "intended" to do but had not started), (2) persistence (continuing to work toward a goal, despite distractions or competing goals), and (3) mental effort, defined by Salomon (1984) as "the number of nonautomatic elaborations invested in learning" (p. 647).

Each of these indices play a different role in the learning process and some may not be related to learning. On one hand it is possible that active choice (e.g., the choice to engage in multimedia learning by choosing to start a multimedia lesson or to select a multimedia course alternative over a more traditional option) may be facilitated by attractive multimedia features such as ease of access, flexibility of scheduling, and the personal control students are often able to exercise when starting, pausing, or moving between different sections of a course of instruction (often called *navigation control*). Yet initially attractive features of a multimedia course might work against students when they engage in learning.

Do Motivated Students Learn Less in Multimedia Instruction?

In their comprehensive meta-analysis of 232 empirical studies reporting nearly 600 comparisons conducted between 1985 and 2002, Bernard et al. (in press) concluded that courses reporting high levels of student interest also tended to report lower levels of achievement. They also concluded that end-of-course measures of interest tended to be negatively correlated with end-of-course achievement. Thus, as achievement increased in multimedia distance studies, student interest and satisfaction decreased. They conclude that "interest satisfaction may not indicate success but the opposite, since students may spend less effort learning, especially when they choose between [multimedia distance education] and regular courses for convenience purposes (i.e., happy to have a choice and satisfied but because they wish to make less of an effort to learn . . .)" (words in brackets inserted to replace acronym, p. 43). Salomon (1984) presented compelling evidence that may explain the negative relationship between interest and satisfaction with multimedia courses and significantly lower learning by students who express a preference for multimedia. He hypothesized that student interest in newer media is based on an expectation that it will be a less demanding way to learn. This expectation results in the investment of lower levels of mental effort, and consequent lower achievement levels, when compared to instructional conditions that are perceived as more demanding. He presented compelling evidence to support his hypothesis. This finding has been replicated a number of times with different media (see, e.g., the discussion of related studies in Clark, 2001). Salomon's theory is the most compelling explanation for Bernard et al's. (in press) meta-analytic finding of an inverse relationship between interest and achievement.

Mental Effort

Apart from the Salomon (1984) studies, not much is known about the direct impact of multimedia instructional formats on mental effort but recent research is not promising. Studies by John Sweller and others (e.g., Mousavi, Low, & Sweller, 1995; Sweller & Chandler, 1994) indicate that many instructional strategies and complex screen displays risk overloading working memory and causing "automated" cognitive defaults (Clark, 2001) where mental effort is both reduced and directed to nonlearning goals. Complicating this finding is strong evidence that learners are not aware when they become overloaded and enter a default state (Gimino, 2000). Because all methods used to measure mental effort involve self report (e.g., Bandura, 1997), this finding is very distressing. Pintrich and Schunk (2002) suggest the use of various measures for ongoing assessment of motivation including self-efficacy (Bandura, 1997), value for learning goals (Eccles & Wigfield, 2000), mood or emotionality, and dual-task mea-

sures for mental effort (Gimino, 2000). In general, it seems that mental effort may be influenced in large part by the amount of perceived difficulty in a multimedia course. It is possible that when moderately challenging learning goals and tasks are presented, mental effort increases. When learning tasks are too easy or impossibly difficult, mental effort decreases radically. Students seem to be able to accurately report the amount of mental effort they are investing in easy to moderately difficult tasks. Yet there is disturbing evidence that they seem unaware when they stop investing mental effort as learning tasks become extremely difficult or impossible. Designers must exercise caution not to overwhelm multimedia students with extremely complex tasks or screen design features that overload working memory. Meanwhile, researchers should continue to study how specific tasks and design features impact mental effort.

Separating Motivation to Choose Multimedia Courses and Motivation to Learn

Many of the currently measured motivation variables in multimedia studies seem to reflect interest and enjoyment factors that influence access to instruction or choice of instructional media rather than learning. Students appear to choose multimedia courses based on expected flexibility and ease of learning, but those expectations may cause them to reduce their effort and learn less. This is Bernard et al.'s (in press) conclusion in their review of empirical work. On the other hand, persistence and mental effort seem to be very important learning-related motivation indexes for multimedia because the added control computers allow students may make it more possible for them to become distracted and avoid instruction. Imagine a scenario where students stop a multimedia lesson when they are tired or bored, intending to restart soon, and yet become distracted and allow a great deal of time pass before restarting the lesson. These gaps in time may make recall of previously learned material more difficult and/or push students so close to course or lesson completion deadlines that they must rush to finish on time. While multimedia lessons do not have to permit this kind of flexibility because it is possible to program required "milestone" completion schedules, the attractiveness of flexibility may increase the probability that students will take multimedia courses if they have choices. Thus, increases access while at the same time placing considerable stress on motivational processes that support persistence over time.

Persistence in Multimedia Courses

Multimedia courses may be chosen over other forms of instruction because students expect that they will receive more individualized instructor contact. While there appears to be no empirical work on this issue, in Kennedy's (2000) survey of a group of online students, 68% of the 40 respondents said they enrolled online rather than self-study because they wanted instructor feedback and guidance through the course. Most students also believe that the heightened instructor contact enhanced their learning in the course. The State University of New York students who reported the highest levels of instructor interaction also reported the highest levels of value for the course (Fredericksen, Pickett, Shea, Pelz, & Swan, 2000). The University of California Los Angeles has also reduced drop out with a system, in which course managers contact "missing" students to prod them into persisting (Frankola, 2001). Thus, although it seems clear that multimedia instruction *can* include (or be perceived to include) more instructor-student contact, and that this increased interaction may enhance the value of the course and student persistence, to the extent that such increased interaction is missing, motivation to persist may be lacking as well. Additional studies concerning the factors and strategies that would further enhance student persistence in multimedia courses would be useful.

One issue that has been examined for a number of years is the extent to which

multimedia allows designers to accommodate learning styles and therefore enhance the learning of a broader range of students.

Principle 3: Multimedia Shapes Instruction for Different Learning Styles

Quite understandably, individual differences between people that may impact the efficacy of instruction have been a major focus of research for decades. If we were to understand all of the factors that contributed to instructional outcome differences, it could be expected that we would be able to optimally align pedagogical approaches with learner profiles, thereby narrowing achievement gaps. While this goal is an important one for the future of instructional research and multimedia design, to date researchers in this area have found no evidence that tailoring multimedia instruction to different learning styles results in learning benefits. This section briefly reviews the research on a variety of individual differences investigated in the research literature (learning preferences, cognitive styles, motivation, intelligence, and prior knowledge) and identifies those that have consistently been found to be relevant factors in the success of learning outcomes in most instructional environments, including multimedia courses, and those that have not.

Cognitive Styles and Learning Preferences

Cognitive styles and learning preferences have been advocated by some researchers for a number of years as traits that contribute to differential success in learning tasks on the basis of learners' innate approaches to learning or solving problems. By understanding these proclivities, it is argued, multimedia instruction can be optimally matched to the learner in order to maximize achievement. Unfortunately, these constructs have proven notoriously difficult to validate for both the stable assessment of learner characteristics and the customization of instruction to improve student outcomes (e.g., Duff & Duffy, 2002; Henson & Hwang, 2002; Kavale & Forness, 1987; Loo, 1997; Richardson, 2000; Stahl, 1999). In general, cognitive style theories posit one or more linear scales on which learners can score closer to one extreme or another. These descriptors typically have a global, integrative, contextualized reasoning pattern at one extreme and a highly focused, isolative, decontextualized pattern at the other (e.g., Cassidy, 2004). In similarly structured dichotomies, some theories also include a visualizer/verbalizer differentiation for sensory, rather than logical, cognition or other descriptive dimensions (e.g., Riding & Cheema, 1991).

Classifying learners in these systems entails requiring each learner to complete a self-report instrument that usually asks questions about their preferred learning modalities and typical approaches to solving problems. However, in addition to persistent problems achieving intraindividual score reliability over time and across domains, attempts to validate these styles have also failed to yield consistent differentiation between cognitive style and measures of intelligence (Richardson & Turner, 2000).

An additional problem with cognitive and learning styles lies in the self-report method of identification wherein learners are asked to report their preferences for approaches to learning and solving problems. Mayer and Massa (2003) tested 95 undergraduates using measures of visual and verbal reasoning ability and found no significant relationship between subjects' self-reported measures of style and their performance on the reasoning tests. This finding is consistent with other investigations of learners' abilities to adequately select effective learning approaches. Clark (1982) found in an extensive meta-analysis of studies that utilized learner preference or enjoyment for particular instructional media or techniques that learner enjoyment was typically uncorrelated or negatively correlated to performance outcomes. That is, subjects who reported preferring a particular instructional technique typically did not derive any instructional benefit from experiencing it. Salomon (1984) found similar results in an experimental study of sixth-grade learner preferences for learning from television or print: The subjects who learned more of the material presented in instruction were those who did not receive instruction through their preferred medium. More recently, these results were replicated with adult distance learners by Li, O'Neil, and Feldon (in press).

Motivation/Goal Orientation

Another individual difference known to impact achievement in instructional settings is goal orientation. Goal orientation refers to the source of an individual's motivation for learning. Those who are classified as having mastery goal orientations pursue the acquisition of new knowledge for their own satisfaction and are not motivated by the comparison of their performance to that of others. In contrast, performance-oriented learners invest effort in learning primarily for the purpose of attaining public or comparative recognition for their accomplishments (Pintrich & Schunk, 2002). Because mastery-oriented students engage with the material for the purpose of understanding, they have been consistently found to be more likely to expend effort to learn the concepts presented and engage with the material more strategically and at a deeper level. However, their internal focus may sometimes prove maladaptive in the context of an evaluated course, because their focus may not have been on the learning objectives on which they would be assessed (Barron & Harackiewicz, 2001). Likewise, performance-oriented learners can manifest both adaptive and maladaptive behaviors. Successful behaviors are referred to as "approach" strategies, because they entail a proactive attempt to gain recognition for success by self-regulating and scaffolding learning opportunities to ensure success. In contrast, "avoidance" behaviors are those by which performance-oriented learners seek to dissociate their performance in the learning environment from negative evaluations of their abilities through self-handicapping behaviors that prevent their best efforts from being demonstrated (Eccles & Wigfield, 2002).

Intelligence

One of the first traits found to account for stable differences between learners is intelligence. Fluid reasoning ability has been found to reliably predict performance on novel problem-solving tasks (Cattell, 1987). However, as instruction familiarizes learners with a given set of skills and problems over time, such advantages diminish when criterion-referenced performance is evaluated (e.g., Ackerman, 1987, 1988, 1990, 1992). Indeed, studies of experts in a variety of fields have found no correlation between fluid ability and performance (e.g., Ceci & Liker, 1986; Doll & Mayr, 1987; Ericsson & Lehmann, 1996; Hulin, Henry, & Noon, 1990; Masunaga & Horn, 2001), precisely because the high levels of deliberate practice that are necessary to excel in a domain entail the development of skills that are applied to problems whose qualities are known. Although individuals can acquire new knowledge and problem-solving strategies and apply them to improve their performance within a particular domain, there is not yet any evidence that such improvements can impact the general problem-solving skills associated with fluid ability (Perkins & Grotzer, 1997).

Prior Knowledge

Learners' acquired knowledge prior to participating in a course can also account for significant individual differences in academic outcomes. Not only do discrete pieces of knowledge relevant to the course material provide a relative advantage to those learners who possess them, but having such knowledge can directly affect the efficacy of certain pedagogical strategies. When novices acquire knowledge in a domain, the learning process is slow and effortful. The requisite effort to process relevant information decreases as schemas are constructed and skills are practiced. As a result, learners with low levels of prior knowledge require more extensive instructional support

to minimize the level of unnecessary cognitive load imposed by the material presented. By reducing the amount of effort required of novice learners, more attentional capacity is available for the accurate encoding of material. If excessive or unstructured information is presented to the novice learner, he will become overloaded and subsequent performance will suffer (van Merriënboer, Kirschner, & Kester, 2003). Conversely, learners with higher levels of prior knowledge in the domain benefit from less-structured instruction. Whereas the novice requires scaffolding to properly organize the information presented without overwhelming limited working memory, for a more knowledgeable learner, superfluous instructional support likely will interfere with existing schemas and consequently impose unnecessary cognitive load, resulting in performance decrements (Kalyuga, Ayres, Chandler, & Sweller, 2003).

Conclusions About Accommodating Learning Styles

Whereas cognitive and learning styles have not proven to be robust foundations on which to customize instruction to accommodate individual differences, intelligence, motivational goal orientations, and prior knowledge have demonstrated significant effects. Although there seems to be little that can be done to modify intelligence and goal orientation, the assessment of prior knowledge for the customization of multimedia instruction offers great promise. Past studies have demonstrated significant relative improvements in instruction when learner support was faded out as learners acquired more knowledge (Kalyuga, Chandler, Tuovinen, & Sweller, 2001), and new research suggests that rapid assessments of learners' knowledge states can dynamically shape the course of computer-based instruction to effectively improve overall achievement (Kalyuga & Sweller, in press-a, in press-b).

The multimedia pedagogical support used to scaffold learning for less experienced students is often provided by animated instructional figures or "agents." This chapter turns next to a review of the research on the learning impact of multimedia agents.

Principle 4: Multimedia Instruction Can Provide Active Pedagogical Agents That Increase Motivation and Aid Learning

Animated pedagogical agents are defined by Craig, Gholson, and Driscoll (2002) as "a computerized character (either humanlike or otherwise) designed to facilitate learning" (p. 428). Many multimedia instructional programs directed to both children and adults seem to provide instructional support in the form of animated agents. Atkinson (2002) suggests that agents ". . . reside in the learning environment by appearing as animated 'humanlike' characters, which allows them to exploit . . . communication typically reserved for human-human interaction . . . [and] can focus a learner's attention by moving around the screen, using gaze and gesture, providing . . . feedback and conveying emotions" (p. 416–417). Agents are a product of recent technological advances in multimedia computer animation and user interface design. Advocates suggest that they have great potential for aiding human learning (e.g., Sampson, Karagiannidis, & Kinshuk, 2002). The use of agents is a recent, welcome, and visible attempt to insert pedagogical support into multimedia instruction yet initial empirical studies suggest that they may distract and interfere with learning more than aid it.

Agent Research Results Are Mixed

In some studies, agent-based instruction results in more learning and/or more positive attitudes toward lessons (e.g., Bosseler & Massaro, 2003; Mitrovic & Suraweera, 2000; Moundridou & Virvou, 2002; Ryokai, Vaucelle, & Cassell, 2003), whereas in others agents produce no learning or motivational benefits (e.g., André, Rist, & Müller, 1999; Baylor, 2002; Craig, Driscoll, & Gholson,

2004; Mayer, Dow, & Mayer, 2002). However, in other experiments, results are mixed and somewhat confusing (e.g., Atkinson, 2002; Moreno, Mayer, Spires, & Lester, 2001) and many studies that demonstrate learning benefits from agents have been criticized for design errors (Choi & Clark, 2004). Our review of these studies suggests that positive learning results most often come from studies where the method being used by the agent to "teach" are not compared with conditions where the method is provided to students without the agent.

Design Problems

Very few agent studies control for the type of hypothesized learning and/or motivational support the agent is providing in a balanced, alternative condition where the same type of learning support is provided by a lower technology, nonagent condition. If the agent is providing a specific type of instructional support, study designs should include a "low technology" alternative method of providing the same type of support to a comparison or control group. Any pedagogical support provided by an agent can also be provided in a "lean" format. Dehn & van Mulken (2000) explain that without this type of design control, ". . . differences between the two conditions cannot be attributed exclusively to [the agent]" (p. 18). An adequate test requires that the nonagent or control condition provide all of the learning and motivational support available from the agent condition, otherwise a comparison will be potentially confounded by the uncontrolled effects of the instructional methods the agent provides and by the agent itself.

Confusion About the Source of Measured Benefits

For example, Atkinson (2002) compared a "voice plus agent" group with "voice only" and "text only" groups (Experiment 2). In the voice-plus-agent group, participants listened to the agent's verbal explanations and saw the agent highlighting relevant information on the screen simultaneously by using pointing gestures. Alternatively, participants in the voice-only and text-only conditions only received explanations delivered either in voice or text, respectively. In other words, participants in the voice-only and text-only groups did not have the benefit of a visual, highlighting indicator for important information, which might have forced the participants to use their scarce cognitive resources to connect verbal explanation with related visual information on the screen. Therefore, although the voice-plus-agent group outperformed the other two groups in far-transfer performance, it is problematic to attribute the obtained learning benefit exclusively to the presence of the agent. The critical learning support provided by the agent – directing learner's attention to the key information in the screen display, was not available to the two comparison groups. A leaner version of the agent's pointing gesture would be to simply use an animated arrow and/or to underline the same information selected by the agent in the comparison conditions. Other studies that also failed to control the types of instructional and motivation supports provided in agent and alternative conditions include Moundridou & Virvou (2002) and Ryokai, et al. (2002).

Adequately Designed Studies Provide Consistent Results

André and colleagues (1999) conducted a well-controlled study that avoided this design pitfall. To find empirical support for the affective and cognitive benefits of their "PPP Persona" agent, they exposed participants to two different memory tasks – a technical description (the operation of pulley systems) and an informational presentation that included the names, pictures, and office locations of fictitious employees. Both experiment and control versions provided the same treatments except that the control groups did not have the PPP Persona agent. The control group heard a voice conveying the same explanations that the

agent provided to the experimental group. The agent's pointing gesture was replaced with an arrow that pointed to important information in the control condition. Following the presentations, participants' affective reactions to the agent and control condition were measured through a questionnaire whereas the cognitive impact was measured by comprehension and recall questions. The results showed significant differences only in the affective measures. Participants interacting with the PPP Persona agent for the technical description found the presentation less difficult and more entertaining. The positive effects, however, disappeared for the informational presentation about the fictitious employees. Participants reported that the PPP Persona agent was less appropriate for employee information and less helpful as an attention direction aid. No significant achievement differences were found between the experimental and control groups for either the technical description or information presentation tasks on comprehension or recall measures. Thus, in this well-designed study, the agent did not provide learning or motivational benefits that translated to greater learning. Yet, because of the adequate design, there is the serendipitous finding that learners may believe that agents are more appropriate and likeable in some learning tasks but not in others.

Craig, et al. (2002) also employed an adequate design where participants learned the process by which lightning occurs presented through an agent and through alternative multimedia (i.e., picture, narration, or animation). An animated agent that pointed to important instructional elements on a computer screen was contrasted with a sudden onset of highlighting (i.e., color singleton or electronic flashing) and animation of the same information (without the agent) for comparison groups. The narrative information was synchronized simultaneously with the agent's pointing gestures, separated and provided prior to the agent's pointing, or in a third condition, with a sudden onset of highlighting and animation of relevant parts of an instructional picture. Craig, et al.'s results indicated that the agent made no difference in learners' performance both in cognitive load assessment and performance tests (i.e., retention, matching, and transfer). Rather, they reported a significant benefit from both a sudden onset of and animation of parts of the pictures for focusing learners' attention. This may be an example of an effect that van Merrienboer (1997) calls "just in time" learning support.

Conclusion – Animated Agents Do Not Increase Learning

These results provide evidence that in multimedia studies of agents, measured differences in student learning may not be due to the agent by itself or any increased motivation or attention caused by the agent, but rather due to the pedagogical method provided by the agent. Thus we should ask a question: Is the animated pedagogical agent the only way to deliver these types of instructional methods in a multimedia learning environment? If alternative ways can deliver the same instruction with the same learning and motivation, but with less cost, shouldn't we choose the least expensive option?

Erickson (1997) argued that the adaptive functionality of an instructional system is often enough for learners to perform a task and achieve the same outcome without the guidance of an agent. He further suggested that when including an agent, instructional designers should think about what benefits and costs the agent would bring, and far more research should be conducted on how people experience agents. Furthermore, Nass and Steuer (1993) found that simply using a human voice without the image of an agent was sufficient to induce learners to use social rules when interacting with a computer. Moreno and colleagues (2001) also noted that learners may form a social relationship with a computer without the help of an agent and thus, the image of an agent might not be necessary to invoke a social agency metaphor in a computer-based learning environment. Baylor (2002), Craig, et al. (2004), and Mayer, et al. (2003) found no

effect of agent image on learning outcomes. This research is also reviewed in chapter 13 of this volume.

Principle 5: Multimedia Instruction Provides Learner Control and Discovery Pedagogy To Enhance Learning

There is a persistent belief among some segments of the education and training communities that the most effective learning experiences are those in which learners navigate unstructured multimedia learning environments or solve novel problems presented without instructional supports (Land & Hannafin, 1996). However, this assumption about pure discovery learning has been tested repeatedly over 40 years of research and found to lack empirical validation when its efficacy, efficiency, and impact on successful transfer of skills have been compared to well-structured, guided instruction (Mayer, 2004). Several factors have been found to play key roles in enactive learning environments that have significant impacts on student success, specifically cognitive load, instructional supports, and prior knowledge.

Cognitive Load Theory

Developed by John Sweller and his colleagues, cognitive load theory reliably predicts instructional learning outcomes by analyzing the pedagogical materials and features of the learning environment to determine the amounts of relevant and irrelevant load placed on working memory (Sweller, 1988, 1989, 1999; Sweller, van Merriënboer, & Paas, 1998; chapter 2). Because working memory capacity is limited, unnecessary features function as artificial constraints on the amount of mental resources that can be directed toward the necessary semantic elements for new knowledge to be successfully acquired. As novice learners develop skills and organizational schemas within the domain of instruction, the information occupies significantly less "space," which allows for the processing of more advanced (i.e., higher load) elements and complex problem solving. Because adaptive organizational schemas are difficult to acquire, resources that could otherwise be dedicated to conceptual understanding must be dedicated to imposing meaningful structure on the material presented if external supports and carefully controlled presentation of material is not utilized. If these supports are not used, fewer cognitive resources are available to be focused on the mastery of conceptual content (Chandler & Sweller, 1991; Sweller, Chandler, Tierney, & Cooper, 1990).

Instructional Support

As learners gain mastery of basic knowledge and organizational structures, their need for external supports to optimize their learning efforts decreases. Because the schemas organize the information presented effectively, it becomes redundant for those frameworks to be provided externally within the learning environment. Thus, providing more structure than is appropriate to the level of the learner can impose extraneous cognitive load and redirect working memory resources away from the target material. Known as the expertise reversal effect, it has been demonstrated that optimal instruction utilizes instructional supports that fade in proportion to the learner's level of expertise for a particular skill or concept (Kalyuga, et al., 2003).

These findings present a complex picture for the appropriate use of discovery learning environments. Because by definition, pure discovery learning does not use instructional supports, it imposes large amounts of extraneous cognitive load on novice and intermediate learners, thereby increasing the amount of time and mental effort expended on learning while decreasing postlearning performance relative to more structured approaches (Tuovinen & Sweller, 1999). However, learners with high levels of expertise in the material presented have been found to perform better after learning in unstructured environments that do not impose unnecessary scaffolding. As such, pure discovery learning is maximally beneficial only to those learners who require additional training least.

Types of Support

The specific nature of the instructional supports that have been used to guide discovery learning processes also plays a major role in the efficacy of the instruction (see also chapter 14). De Jong and van Joolingen (1998) reviewed a variety of tools that were used in computer-based discovery learning environments and concluded that providing enhanced task structure for learners consistently improved learner outcomes. For example, a number of studies found that up to four times as many students were able to grasp concepts central to a simulation-based discovery program when instructions specifying how to proceed in solving the problem were provided when compared with subjects who experienced the pure discovery mode (e.g., Gruber, Graf, Mandl, Renkl, & Stark, 1995; Linn & Songer, 1991). Even when overall results did not indicate a significant difference in subsequent student performance between guided and pure discovery learning environments, deeper analyses indicated that students with lower levels of ability in the target domain who received guidance did attain posttest scores significantly higher than their unguided counterparts, providing a replication of the expertise reversal effect discussed previously (Veenman & Elshout, 1995). Further, several studies demonstrated high correlations between intelligence and success in discovery learning environments across a number of domains, suggesting that such forms of instruction are less able to generate strong results for all learners (Veenman, 1993). Indeed, Funke (1991) reported that correlations between intelligence and achievement linked to discovery learning simulations increase as the level of guidance offered by the environment falls. Similarly, Shute and Glaser (1990) found that embedding guidance tools into the learning environment resulted in only a very low correlation between achievement and intelligence.

Thrashing

One of the problems that learners frequently encounter in pure discovery learning environments is that of "thrashing" (Lewis, Bishay, & McArthur, 1993) or "floundering" (Goodyear, Njoo, Hijne, & van Berkum, 1991), in which learners lack an effective and/or systematic approach to interacting with the learning environment and consequently are unable to draw valid or helpful inferences from simulation outcomes or events. In Lewis, et al.'s study, students were directed to engage in discovery learning tasks using a geometry software tool to identify formulas describing mathematical relationships between geometric figures. When they reached an impasse and no scaffolding or assistance was available, students generally persisted in their attempts to use a strategy that had been previously effective. After multiple attempts at using the maladaptive strategy, students were then observed to progressively attempt less and less appropriate solution strategies until they eventually quit the program or selected a new, unrelated goal to pursue. Such thrashing in pursuit of a solution did not yield a successful solution for any of the study participants but occupied as much as 25% of their total instructional time. Similarly, Goodyear, et al. found that when students engaged in this kind of behavior, they were unable to identify the causal relationships that existed between their actions and resulting events within the learning environment. The lack of a systematic approach prevented them from adequately tracking their own actions, and learners were thus unable to extract functional principles from the interactions.

Even when goals and processes are relatively clear, discovery learning environments can produce impediments to learning through uncontrolled sequencing of material. Kester, Kirschner, van Merrienboer, & Baumer (2001) found in an exploratory study that the timeliness of information presentation predicts performance in learning tasks designed to facilitate complex skill acquisition. Their just-in-time instructional model holds that abstract "supportive" information (e.g., mental model explanation) must be presented prior to learner attempts to solve authentic complex tasks, whereas prerequisite information (e.g., facts relevant to a specific problem scenario) should be presented to the learner during the execution of the tasks. Further, in a recent study, Clarke, Ayres, and Sweller (in press) found that when students were given a learning task to master mathematics concepts through the manipulation of a spreadsheet, those students who were not provided with specific instructions for using the spreadsheet program prior to attempting to learn the mathematics material performed at a much lower level than those who had acquired spreadsheet knowledge prior to attempting the learning task.

Similarly, many of the studies reviewed by de Jong and van Joolingen (1998) that required students to discover scientific principles within simulated environments found that only those students who acquired strong scientific inquiry skills prior to attempting identification of the science concepts were able to achieve at high levels. Although many such environments provided related procedural support if requested by the learner during the discovery task, meta-analyses of students' self-assessments with regard to their learning needs have found consistent evidence that students – especially novices – do not accurately determine which pedagogical formats and tools will be most beneficial for them (Clark, 1982, 1989).

General Conclusion

Multimedia instruction offers extraordinary benefits to education including a wide range of instructional options and, with adequate instructional design, considerable reductions in the time required to learn, the time required of expert teachers, and when large numbers of students are involved, the cost of learning (Clark, 2001). Like all new and exciting educational innovations it also suffers from mistaken beliefs about its potential and achievements. This chapter reviewed five commonly held beliefs about multimedia that have not been supported by research. For example, multimedia does not increase student learning beyond any other media including live teachers.

It also appears that studies examining the motivational benefits of multimedia instruction provide good news and bad news. While multimedia may be a more attractive option for instructions by students than older media, the bad news is that their interest most often seems to lead them to reduce their effort to learn. Meta-analytic evidence from many studies suggests that as student interest in multimedia courses increases, learning tends to decrease because students may feel that learning in these courses requires less work.

If multimedia does not produce more learning than other options, and if motivation to choose multimedia courses produces an ironic reduction in course achievement, the solution seems to require increasing the focus on pedagogical support in multimedia courses. A pedagogical approach that seems very common in multimedia courses is an attempt to tailor instructional sequences for learners with different learning styles. The flexibility of multimedia permits the tailoring of instruction to a variety of learning styles by providing different versions of the same lesson to accommodate different styles. However, attempts to validate this assumption over the past 30 years have generally failed. New efforts, such as those initiated by Mayer and Massa (2003), may meet with success in the future. However given the data currently available, it appears that the two most promising individual differences that can be used to shape adaptive instructional programs are the prior knowledge and learning goal orientation of students, and nothing inherent to these factors seems to require use of multimedia for tailored accommodation.

Attempts to insert socially engaging learning support into multimedia courses with animated pedagogical agents also seem not to increase learning and sometimes appear to diminish instructional effectiveness, because agents often produce cognitive overload for students. Evidence from well-designed studies suggests that agents may be expensive and unnecessary, because appropriately designed narration and instructional methods embedded into instruction can achieve similar learning outcomes at less cost.

Finally, multimedia advocates have often embraced constructivist-based discovery and problem-based learning pedagogy. The flexibility of multimedia technology permits the design of courses where students can control not only the (beneficial) pacing of instruction, but also students' navigations between and within lessons. The latter type of control combined with unguided or minimally guided instruction seems most often to harm learning for students with less prior knowledge of course subject matter. In another ironic twist, strong instructional guidance and scaffolding seems to interfere with the learning of more advanced students. Thus, tailoring instruction to student prior knowledge does seem to be beneficial, but it does not require most of the features of multimedia instruction.

The main concern addressed in this chapter is the need to check research evidence for the presumed benefits of all instructional media and related pedagogies. Research sometimes provides counterintuitive evidence and so prevents us from unintentionally causing damage or investing scarce resources in instruction that does not support learning. It can also point in directions that can lead to dramatically increases in achievement such as Corbett's (2001) 2 sigma gain in learning accompanied by a 40% reduction in learning time.

Footnotes

1. Parts of the discussion in this chapter have been summarized from two previous manuscripts including: Choi, S. & Clark, R. E. (April 2004). Five suggestions for the design of

experiments on the effects of animated pedagogical agents. Symposium paper presented at the American Educational Research Association Annual Convention in San Diego California; and Clark, R. E. (2003). Research on web-based learning: A half-full glass. In R., Bruning, C. A., Horn, & L. M. Pytlik Zillig (Eds.), *Web-based learning: What do we know? Where do we go?* (pp. 1–22). Greenwich, CT: Information Age Publishers.

References

Abrahamson, C. E. (1998). Issues in interactive communication in distance education. *College Student Journal*, 32 (1), 33–42.

Ackerman, P. L. (1987). Individual differences in skill learning: An integration of psychometric and information processing perspectives. *Psychological Bulletin*, 102, 3–27.

Ackerman, P. L. (1988). Determinants of individual differences during skill acquisition: Cognitive abilities and information processing. *Journal of Experimental Psychology: General*, 117, 288–318.

Ackerman, P. L. (1990). A correlational analysis of skill specificity: Learning, abilities, and individual differences. *Journal of Experimental Psychology: Learning, Memory, and Cognition*, 16, 883–901.

Ackerman, P. L. (1992). Predicting individual differences in complex skill acquisition: Dynamics of ability determinants. *Journal of Applied Psychology*, 77, 598–614.

American Society for Training and Development (2001). *E-Learning: If you build it, will they come?* Alexandria, VA: ASTD.

Anderson, J. R., & Gluck, K. (2001). What role do cognitive architectures play in intelligent tutoring systems. In D. Klahr & S. Carver (Eds.), *Cognition and instruction: 25 years of progress* (pp. 227–262). Mahwah, NJ: Lawrence Erlbaum.

André, E., Rist, T., & Müller, J. (1999). Employing AI methods to control the behavior of animated interface agents. *Applied Artificial Intelligence*, 13, 415–448.

Atkinson, R. K. (2002). Optimizing learning from examples using animated pedagogical agents. *Journal of Educational Psychology*, 94 (2), 416–427.

Bandura, A. (1997). *Self-efficacy: The exercise of control.* New York: Freeman.

Barron, K. E., & Harackiewicz, J. M. (2001). Achievement goals and optimal motivation: Testing multiple goal models. *Journal of Personality and Social Psychology*, 80 (5), 706–722.

Baylor, A. L. (2002). Expanding preservice teachers' metacognitive awareness of instructional planning through pedagogical agents. *Educational Technology Research and Development*, 50 (2), 5–22.

Bernard, R., Abrami, P., Lou, Y., Borokhovski, E., Wade, A., Wozney, L. et al. (in press). How does distance education compare to classroom instruction? A meta-analysis of the empirical literature. *Review of Educational Research.*

Bloom, B. (1984) The 2-sigma problem: The search for methods of group instruction as effective as one-to-one tutoring. *Educational Researcher*, 13, 4–16.

Bosseler, A., & Massaro, D. (2003). Development and evaluation of a computer-animated tutor for vocabulary and language learning in children with autism. *Journal of Autism and Developmental Disorders*, 33 (6), 653–672.

Cassidy, S. (2004). Learning styles: An overview of theories, models, and measures. *Educational Psychology*, 24 (4), 419–444.

Cattell, R. B. (1987). *Intelligence: Its structure, growth and action.* Amsterdam: North Holland.

Ceci, S. J., & Liker, J. K. (1986). A day at the races: A study of IQ, expertise, and cognitive complexity. *Journal of Experimental Psychology*, 115, 255–266.

Chandler, P. & Sweller, J. (1991). Cognitive load theory and the format of instruction. *Cognition and Instruction*, 8, 293–332.

Choi, S., & Clark, R. E. (2004). Five suggestions for the design of experiments on the effects of animated pedagogical agents. Symposium paper presented at the Annual Meeting of the American Educational Research Association, San Diego, CA.

Clark, R. E. (1982). Antagonism between achievement and enjoyment in ATI studies. *Educational Psychologist*, 17 (2), 92–101.

Clark, R. E. (1989). When teaching kills learning: Research on mathemathantics. In H. N. Mandl, N. Bennett, E. de Corte, and H. F. Freidrich (Eds.). *Learning and instruction. European research in an international context. Volume II.* London: Pergamon Press Ltd.

Clark, R. E. (2000). Evaluating distance education: Strategies and cautions. *The Quarterly Journal of Distance Education*, 1 (1), 5–18.

Clark, R. E. (Ed.). (2001). *Learning from media: Arguments, analysis and evidence*. Greenwich, CT: Information Age Publishers.

Clark, R. E., & Salomon, G. (1986). Media in teaching. In M. Wittrock (Ed.), *Handbook of research on teaching* (3rd ed.). New York: Macmillan.

Clarke, T., Ayres, P., & Sweller, J. (in press). The impact of sequencing and prior knowledge on learning mathematics through spreadsheet applications. *Educational Technology Research and Development*.

Corbett, A. (2001). Cognitive computer tutors: Solving the two-sigma problem. In M. Bauer, P. Gmytrasiewicz, & J. Vassileva (Eds.), *User Modeling 2001: Proceedings of the 8th International Conference, UM 2001* (pp. 137–146). New York: Springer.

Craig, S., Driscoll, D. M., & Gholson, B. (2004). Constructing knowledge from dialog in an intelligent tutoring system: Interactive learning, vicarious learning, and pedagogical agents. *Journal of Educational Multimedia and Hypermedia, 13*(12), 163–183.

Craig, S. D., Gholson, B., & Driscoll, D. M. (2002). Animated pedagogical agents in multimedia educational environments: Effects of agent properties, picture features and redundancy. *Journal of Educational Psychology, 94*(2), 428–434.

Cronbach, L., & Snow, R. E. (1977). *Aptitudes and instructional methods*. New York: Irvington.

Dehn, D. M. & van Mulken, S. (2000). The impact of animated interface agents: A review of empirical research. *International Journal of Human-Computer Studies, 52*, 1–22.

de Jong, T., & van Joolingen, W. R. (1998). Scientific discovery learning with computer simulations of conceptual domains. *Review of Educational Research, 68*(2), 179–201.

Doll, J., & Mayr, U. (1987). Intelligenz und schachleistung – eine untersuchung an schachexperten. [Intelligence and achievement in chess – a study of chess masters.] *Psychologische Beiträge, 29*, 270–289.

Duff, A., & Duffy, T. (2002). Psychometric properties of Honey and Mumford's learning styles questionnaire. *Learning and Individual Differences, 33*, 147–163.

Eccles, J. S., & Wigfield, A. (2000). Schooling's influences on motivation and achievement. In S. Danziger and J. Waldfogel (Eds.), *Securing the future: Investing in children from birth to college* (pp. 153–181). New York: Russell Sage Foundation.

Eccles, J. S., & Wigfield, A. (2002). Motivational beliefs, values, and goals. *Annual Review of Psychology, 53*, 109–132.

Erickson, T. (1997). Designing agents as if people mattered. In J. M. Bradshaw (Ed.), *Software agents* (pp. 79–96). Menlo Park, CA: MIT Press.

Ericsson, K. A., & Lehmann, A. C. (1996). Expert and exceptional performance: Maximal adaptation to task constraints. *Annual Review of Psychology, 47*, 273–305.

Frankola, K. (2001). Why online learners drop out. *Workforce, 80*(10), 52–60.

Fredericksen, E., Pickett, A., Shea, P., Pelz, W., & Swan, K. (2000). *Student satisfaction and perceived learning with on-line courses: Principles and examples from the SUNY learning network*. Retrieved June 30, 2002, from http://www.aln.org/alnweb/journal/Vol4_issue2/le/Fredericksen/LE-fredericksen.htm

Funke, J. (1991). Solving complex problems: exploration and control of complex systems. In R. J. Sternberg & P. A. Frensch (Eds.), *Complex problem solving: Principles and mechanisms* (pp. 185–223). Hillsdale, NJ: Erlbaum.

Gimino, A. (2000). *Factors that influence students' investment of mental effort in academic tasks: A validation and exploratory study*. Unpublished doctoral dissertation, University of Southern California, Los Angeles, CA.

Goodyear, P., Njoo, M., Hijne, H., & van Berkum, J. J. A. (1991). Learning processes, learner attributes and simulations. *Education and Computing, 6*, 263–304.

Gruber, H., Graf, M., Mandl, H., Renkl, & Stark, R. (1995). Fostering applicable knowledge by multiple perspectives and guided problem solving. Proceedings of the *Annual Conference of the European Association for Research on Learning and Instruction*, Nijmegen, The Netherlands.

Henson, R. K., & Hwang, D. (2002). Variability and prediction of measurement error in Kolb's learning style inventory scores: A reliability generalization study. *Educational and Psychological Measurement, 62*(4), 712–727.

Hulin, C. L., Henry, R. A., & Noon, S. L. (1990). Adding a dimension: Time as a factor in the generalizability of predictive relationships. *Psychological Bulletin, 107*, 328–340.

Kalyuga, S., Ayres, P., Chandler, P., & Sweller, J. (2003). Expertise reversal effect. *Educational Psychologist*, 38, 23–31.

Kalyuga, S., Chandler, P., Tuovinen, J., & Sweller, J. (2001). When problem solving is superior to studying worked examples. *Journal of Educational Psychology*, 93, 579–588.

Kalyuga, S., & Sweller, J. (in press-a). Measuring knowledge to optimize cognitive load factors during instruction. *Journal of Educational Psychology*.

Kalyuga, S., & Sweller, J. (in press-b). Rapid dynamic assessment of expertise to improve the efficiency of adaptive E-learning. *Educational Technology: Research and Development*.

Kavale, K. A., & Forness, S. R. (1987). Substance over style: Assessing the efficacy of modality testing and teaching. *Exceptional Children*, 54(3), 228–239.

Kennedy, C. (2000). *Quick online survey summary*. Retrieved June 30, 2002, from http://www.smccd.net/kennedyc/rsch/qcksrv.htm

Kester, L., Kirschner, P., van Merrienboer, J., & Baumer, A. (2001). Just-in-time information presentation and the acquisition of complex cognitive skills. *Computers in Human Behavior*, 17, 373–391.

Kozma, R. B. (1994). Will media influence learning? Reframing the debate. *Educational Technology Research and Development*, 42(2), 7–19.

Kozma, R. (2000). Reflections on the state of educational technology. *Educational Technology, Research and Development*, 48, 5–15.

Land, S., & Hannafin, M. J. (1996). A conceptual framework for the development of theories in action with open learning environments. *Educational Technology Research and Development*, 44(3), 37–53.

Levin, H. M, Glass, G., & Meister, G. R. (1987). Cost-effectiveness of computer assisted instruction. *Evaluation Review*, 11(1), 50–72.

Levin, H. M., & McEwan, P. J. (2001). *Cost-effectiveness analysis: Methods and applications* (2nd ed.). Thousand Oaks, CA: Sage.

Lewis, M., Bishay, M., & McArthur, D. (1993). The macrostructure and microstructure of inquiry activities: Evidence from students using a microworld for mathematical discovery. *Proceedings of the World Conference on Artificial Intelligence and Education*, Edinburgh, Scotland.

Li, L., O'Neil, H. F., & Feldon, D. F. (in press). The effects of effort and worry on distance learning with text and video. *The American Journal of Distance Education*.

Linn, M. C., & Songer, N. B. (1991). Teaching thermodynamics to middle school students: What are appropriate cognitive demands? *Journal of Research in Science Teaching*, 28, 885–918.

Loo, R. (1997). Evaluating change and stability in learning styles: A methodological concern. *Educational Psychology*, 17, 95–100.

Masunaga, H., & Horn, J. (2001). Expertise and age-related changes in components of intelligence. *Psychology and Aging*, 16(2), 293–311.

Mayer, R. E. (2001). *Multimedia learning*. New York: Cambridge University Press.

Mayer, R. E. (2004). Should there be a three-strikes rule against pure discovery learning? *American Psychologist*, 59(1), 14–19.

Mayer, R. E., Dow, G. T., & Mayer, S. (2002). Multimedia learning in an interactive self-explaining environment: What works in the design of agent-based microworlds? *Journal of Educational Psychology*, 95(4), 806–813

Mayer, R. E., & Massa, L. J. (2003). Three facets of visual and verbal learners: Cognitive ability, cognitive style, and learning preference. *Journal of Educational Psychology*, 95(4), 833–846.

Mayer, R. E., Sobko, K., & Mautone, P. D. (2003). Social cues in multimedia learning: Role of speaker's voice. *Journal of Educational Psychology*, 94, 419–425.

Mielke, K. W. (1968). Questioning the questions of ETV research. *Educational Broadcasting*, 2, 6–15.

Mitrovic, A., & Suraweera, P. (2000). Evaluating an animated pedagogical agent. *Lecture Notes in Computer Science, No. 1839*, 73–82.

Moreno, R., & Mayer, R. (2000). A learner centered approach to multimedia explanations: Deriving instructional design principles from cognitive theory. Retrieved from http://imej.wfu.edu/articles/2000/2/05/printver.asp

Moreno, R., Mayer, R. E., Spires, H. A., & Lester, J. C. (2001). The case for social agency in computer-based teaching: Do students learn more deeply when they interact with animated pedagogical agents? *Cognition and Instruction*, 19(2), 177–213.

Morrison, G. R. (1994). The media effects question: "Unresolvable" or asking the right question. *Educational Technology Research and Development, 42* (2), 41–44.

Moundridou, M., & Virvou, M. (2002). Evaluating the persona effect of an interface agent in a tutoring system. *Journal of Computer Assisted Learning, 18* (3), 253–261

Mousavi, S. Y., Low, R., & Sweller, J. (1995). Reducing cognitive load by mixing auditory and visual presentation modes. *Journal of Educational Psychology, 87,* 319–334.

Nass, C., & Steuer, J. (1993). Anthropomorphism, agency, and ethopoeia: Computers as social actors. *Human Communication Research, 19* (4), 504–527.

Office of Technology Assessment. (1988, September). *Power on: New tools for teaching and learning* Retrieved June 30, 2002, from http://www.wws.princeton.edu/~ota/disk2/1988/8831_n.html

Perkins, D. N., & Grotzer, T. A. (1997). Teaching intelligence. *American Psychologist, 52* (10), 1125–1133.

Pintrich, P. R., & Schunk, D. H. (2002). *Motivation in education: Theory, research, and applications (2nd ed.).* Englewood Cliffs, NJ: Prentice Hall.

Richardson, J. A., & Turner, T. E. (2000). Field dependence revisited I: Intelligence. *Educational Psychology, 20* (3), 255–270.

Richardson, J. T. (2000). *Researching students' learning: Approaches to studying in campus-based and distance learning.* Buckingham, UK: Society for Research into Higher Education and Open University Press.

Riding, R. J., & Cheema, I. (1991). Cognitive styles: An overview and integration. *Educational Psychology, 11,* 193–215.

Ryokai, R., Vaucelle, C., & Cassell, J. (2003). Virtual peers as partners in storytelling and literacy learning. *Journal of Computer Assisted Learning, 19,* 195–208.

Salomon, G. (1984). Television is "easy" and print is "tough": The differential investment of mental effort in learning as a function of perceptions and attributions. *Journal of Educational Psychology, 76* (4), 647–658.

Sampson, D., Karagiannidis, C., & Kinshuk. (2002). Personalised learning: Educational, technological and standardisation perspective. *Interactive Educational Multimedia, 4,* 24–39.

Schramm, W. (1977). *Big media, little media.* Beverly Hills, CA: Sage.

Shute, V. J., & Glaser, R. (1990). A large-scale evaluation of an intelligent discovery world: Smithtown. *Interactive Learning Environments, 1,* 51–77.

Stahl, S. A. (1999). Different strokes for different folks? A critique of learning styles. *American Educator, 23* (3), 27–31.

Sweller, J. (1988). Cognitive load during problem solving: Effects on learning. *Cognitive Science, 12,* 257–285.

Sweller, J. (1989). Cognitive technology: Some procedures for facilitating learning and problem solving in mathematics and science. *Journal of Cognitive Psychology, 81* (4), 457–466.

Sweller, J. (1999). *Instruction design in technical areas.* Camberwell, Australia: ACER.

Sweller, J., & Chandler, P. (1994). Why some material is difficult to learn. *Cognition and Instruction, 12,* 185–233.

Sweller, J., Chandler, P., Tierney, P., & Cooper, M. (1990). Cognitive load as a factor in the structuring of technical material. *Journal of Experimental Psychology: General, 119* (2), 176–192.

Sweller, J., van Merriënboer, J. G., & Paas, F. G. (1998). Cognitive architecture and instructional design. *Educational Psychology Review, 10,* 251–296.

Tuovinen, J. E., & Sweller, J. (1999). A comparison of cognitive load associated with discovery learning and worked examples. *Journal of Educational Psychology, 91* (2), 334–341.

van Merriënboer, J. J. G., Kirschner, P. A., & Kester, L. (2003). Taking the load off a learner's mind: Instructional design for complex learning. *Educational Psychologist, 38* (1), 5–13.

van Merriënboer, J. J. G. (1997). *Training complex cognitive skills: A four-component instructional design model for technical training.* Englewood Cliffs, NJ: Educational Technology Publications.

Veenman, M. V. J. (1993). *Intellectual ability and metacognitive skill: Determinants of discovery learning in computerized learning environments.* Unpublished doctoral dissertation. University of Amsterdam.

Veenman, M. V. J., & Elshout, J. J. (1995). Differential effects of instructional support on learning in simulation environments. *Instructional Science, 22,* 363–383.

CHAPTER 7

The Multimedia Principle

J. D. Fletcher

Institute for Defense Analysis

Sigmund Tobias

Teachers College, Columbia University

Abstract

The *multimedia principle* states that people learn better from words and pictures than from words alone. It is supported by empirically derived theory suggesting that words and images evoke different conceptual processes and that perception and learning are active, constructive processes. It is further supported by research studies that have found superior retention and transfer of learning from words augmented by pictures compared to words presented alone and superior transfer when narration is accompanied by animation compared to narration or animation presented alone. Research has also found that the effectiveness of combining imagery with text varies with the content to be learned, the conditions under which performance is measured, and individual differences in spatial ability, prior knowledge, and general learning ability. Cognitive theory derived from these findings posits interactions between three stages of memory – sensory, working, and long term – that are connected by cooperative, additive channels used to process information arriving from different sensory modalities.

The Multimedia Principle

It is commonly assumed that adding pictures to words, rather than presenting text alone, makes it easier for people to understand and learn. The proverb that a picture is worth a thousand words attests to the popularity and acceptance of this assumption. The assumption leads to what may be called the *multimedia principle*. This principle, as stated by Mayer (2001), is that people learn better from words and pictures than from words alone, or, more specifically, that people learn more or more deeply when appropriate pictures are added to text (Mayer, in press).

This chapter addresses these possibilities with findings drawn from empirical research. It reviews their foundations in both cognitive theory and empirical research and their practical application to instructional design. It also identifies gaps in the research and suggests efforts that might help to fill them.

Of course adding pictures to text is not equally useful for all situations or all people. For instance, the profusion of pictures in children's books decreases markedly as the age of the readers rises toward adulthood.

To some extent this decrease may reflect the notion that pictures are most useful for individuals, such as children, with little prior knowledge. It complements the hypothesis (Tobias, 1976, 1982, 1989) that adding support such as graphics and pictures to instruction is especially beneficial for students with limited prior knowledge of the domain they are learning. Tobias's instructional support hypothesis also predicts that adding graphics is of little benefit to students with substantial prior knowledge. Among other matters, this chapter examines whether pictures may be differentially beneficial for students varying in prior familiarity with the subject they are about to learn.

While publishers have augmented text with pictures or graphics for a long time, enhanced interest in this topic arises from the instructional success and popularity of computer-based presentations (Fletcher, 1991, 2004), which allow ready access to a full range of multimedia and which may be used standing alone or over the Internet. In such materials, graphics, still and animated pictures, video, voice, music, and sound effects may accompany text. Mayer (2001, p. 3) defines *multimedia learning* as "learning from words and pictures," and the term will be so used in this chapter.

This chapter, then, focuses on visual imagery used to enhance learning materials that would otherwise be presented solely as text. This emphasis responds to available research findings and the cognitive theories discussed in this chapter. Other media such as voice, music, and sound effects might also be used to enhance learning from text presentations and may reasonably be included in later discussions of the multimedia principle as research on them progresses. Tactile and haptic capabilities are additional multimedia possibilities (e.g., Youngblut, 2003), but these are not discussed here, again reflecting the current state of empirical findings.

Finally, this chapter attempts to avoid the issues that arise from comparisons involving the instructional effectiveness of different media. Media comparisons have been the subject of considerable and often inconclusive research (Clark, 1983, 2001; Russell, 1999; Sugrue & Clark, 2000; Wetzel, Radtke, & Stern, 1994). Often it is not possible to disentangle the effects of instructional method and media, nor is it clear that different media ever present exactly the same instructional material (Fletcher, 2003). Clark and others have argued that media alone have little effect on instructional outcomes unless different media engage alternative cognitive processes that control learning.

This position is similar to one articulated by Tobias (1982) who pointed out that varying instructional methods – media based or otherwise – can lead to different outcomes only if they engage different cognitive processes, or if one method leads to more intensive processing than another. Mayer (1997) reanalyzed nine studies that compared instructional material presented using text and graphics on the one hand and computer animation and narration on the other and found only minor differences between the media. These findings suggest simply that it is not the media that matter, but how they are used.

The basic question examined in this chapter, then, is whether augmenting text with graphic presentations, or vice versa, leads to improved learning. Such augmentations are presumed to lead to more intense or improved cognitive processing of instructional material, which, in turn, will enhance instructional effectiveness.

Theoretical Foundations

Why should we expect the multimedia principle to work? Like most ideas, psychological theory included, this expectation has its basis in philosophy. The 18th-century philosophy of Bishop George Berkeley may have been seminal in this case. Berkeley believed that nothing exists or has meaning unless it is perceived by some mind.[1] Words and images are important because they give both existence and meaning to matter. But Berkeley pointed out that words are abstract and generic while images are concrete and specific. The word *tree* will bring different meanings to different minds and also, as we might say today, different associations. An image of a specific tree will suggest more specifically and strongly the meaning, the reality, that someone using the word tree has in mind.

This basic observation led Berkeley to considerably more profound philosophical ruminations than we will discuss here, but they also lead to at least two notions that are important for this discussion. The first of these is that at some level, words and images evoke different conceptual processes. The second is that perception and learning are active, constructive processes involving more than the simple transmission and reception of whole entities. The first notion has been studied extensively (but not exclusively) by Paivio (e.g., 1986; 1991) and his colleagues. The second is at the core of what today we describe as cognitive psychology. Both notions have been brought together, extended, and applied to instructional psychology and multimedia learning by a variety of researchers. They have been specifically used by both Sweller and Mayer in formulating the multimedia principle.

In an extensive and productive program of research, Paivio and his colleagues developed and examined what they called the coding redundancy hypothesis and dual-coding theory. Much of this work is summarized in two books (Paivio, 1986, 1991). The coding redundancy hypothesis posits that imagery acts as an additional memory code to facilitate the recall of concrete nouns. Dual-coding theory is more general and based on a large body of research concerning cognitive processing of observational (concrete) and theoretical (abstract) items. This research found that imagery contributed to the successful recall of individual items. On the basis of these findings, Paivio suggested that the coding of words and images involved processes that are to a significant degree both independent (involving separate cognitive mechanisms) and additive (capable of complementing, corroborating, and elaborating each other), and that because of their concreteness, images are superior to words in promoting recall –

suggestions that form the basis for dual-coding theory.

In cognitive psychology, a substantial body of empirical findings from research into human learning, memory, perception, and cognition has led to the view that cognitive processes are constructive and regenerative. These processes involve an "analysis by synthesis" activity in which the information received by our sensory receptors (e.g., eyes and ears) is filtered and reassembled as cues that are used to construct an executable simulation of "reality" – the world as we perceive it. Instruction, then, does not involve the transmission of intact "chunks" of information from teachers to students, but rather the transmission of cues that students use to construct, verify, and modify their models of the world (Fletcher, 1982). Cognitive notions have caused general theories of perception and learning to evolve from the logical positivism of behavioral psychology, which emphasized the study of directly observable and directly measurable actions, to greater consideration of the internal, less observable processes that are assumed to mediate and enable human perception, memory, and learning.

The keynote of these conceptions of cognition – and much contemporary cognitive psychology – was articulated by Ulric Neisser, who stated, "The central assertion is that seeing, hearing, and remembering are all acts of *construction*, which may make more or less use of stimulus information depending on circumstances" (1967, p. 10). Although they have had moments both in and out of fashion, these ideas have been part of the fabric of scientific psychology since its inception. For instance, William James gave as the general law of perception: "Whilst part of what we perceive comes through our senses from the object before us, another part (and it may be the larger part) always comes out of our mind" (1890/1950, p. 747).

Mayer and his colleagues have sustained an extensive and productive program of research on the multimedia principle for more than 20 years. Although the program is continuing, Mayer (2001) summarized many of its findings in his book on multimedia learning. In this book (and elsewhere) he has unified and extended the notions of dual-coding theory and constructive, cognitive psychology, among others, into a cognitive theory of multimedia learning (CTML). The theory is based on three fundamental assumptions that echo earlier research findings: First, humans possess separate channels for processing visual and auditory information; second the channels are limited in the amount of information each can process at one time; and third, learning is an active and constructive activity consisting of filtering, organizing, and integrating information through these channels.

Figure 3.2 in chapter 3 summarizes Mayer's cognitive theory of multimedia learning. The theory posits dual channels of limited capacity for processing visual and auditory input. As in other models of this sort (e.g., Craik & Lockhart, 1972; Wickens & Flach, 1988), three types of memory are assumed: sensory memory, working memory, and long-term memory. Dual (separate) channels are maintained in both sensory and working memory, but not in long-term memory, which consists of integrated prior knowledge. The limited capacity of working memory can be enhanced to an appreciable degree by the independent operation and additive effects of the channels operating in working memory. Individuals actively attend to incoming information, selecting, organizing, and integrating data from alternate channels into coherent internal representations. They then relate the information to relevant prior knowledge stored in long-term memory.

Mayer's theory is well supported by a program of research on cognitive load theory conducted by Sweller and his colleagues (Paas, Renkl, & Sweller, 2003; Sweller, 1994; Sweller, in press). Briefly, the theory holds that instruction can best facilitate the acquisition of knowledge by reducing heavy loads on the limited capacity of working memory. It is similar to Mayer's hypothesis in that it assumes that visual and auditory information combine to reduce cognitive load, thus increasing the efficiency of processing in working memory. It also resembles both

Tobias's (1989) and Mayer's positions in assuming that cognitive load is reduced by expertise, learned patterns, and prior knowledge, which are held in long-term memory. Cognitive load theory assumes that sensory inputs can be matched to prior knowledge and patterns (evoked as appropriate from long-term memory) and bundled together, thereby reducing the processing load on working memory (Sweller, in press).

Taking a more pragmatic than theoretic point of view, Hannafin, Hannafin, Hooper, Rieber, and Kini (1996) list three benefits found in research on the instructional use of illustrations. First, it provides advanced organization, clarifying the structure of the information to be learned. Second, it highlights important concepts making it more likely to be recalled. Third, it helps learners integrate lesson content. These benefits, while based on other aspects of cognitive theory and research, also support the multimedia principle.

In sum, there are theories, well based in experimental psychology, that lead us to expect that the multimedia principle will enhance learning. In contrast to instructional techniques that do not apply the multimedia principle, instructional techniques that do should make more complete use of available cognitive processing capabilities, reduce the cognitive effort needed to augment long-term memory storage, and thereby increase the amount of information stored in long-term memory per time spent in instruction. It may now be time to look at the data.

Empirical Foundations

Mayer's 2001 book and his chapter currently in press summarize many of the empirical assessments of the multimedia principle. Through this research, Mayer and his colleagues investigated whether it was "better to present words and pictures rather than words alone" (p. 72) by examining retention (amount of information retained at the end of instruction) and transfer (ability to apply what was learned to new problems).

Instructional Effectiveness

In nine studies summarized by Mayer (2001), student participants received instruction consisting of either words alone or words augmented by pictures. Mayer and his colleagues generally measured retention by asking students to write down everything in 5–6 minutes that they could remember about how the system presented in the instruction works. Retention scores consisted of the number of main ideas each student mentioned in the explanation. Transfer was measured by asking students to solve problems using information presented in the instruction. They were given about 2.5 minutes for their responses. Transfer scores depended on the number of creative solutions they generated. Six of the nine studies indicated better recall for the multiple representation groups, with a median retention gain of 23% and a median effect size of 0.67. When it came to transfer problems, the word and picture groups performed better in all nine studies with a median gain of 89% and a median effect size of 1.50 (Mayer, 2001). Elsewhere, with a slightly different set of experimental studies, Mayer reported a median effect size for transfer under the multimedia principle of 1.67 (Mayer, in press).

Mayer (in press) discusses nine other research-based principles of multimedia learning in addition to the multimedia principle. All of these are discussed in later sections of this handbook, but two seem particularly relevant to instruction that seeks to observe the multimedia principle.

First, the *contiguity principle* suggests that verbal and pictorial information should be coordinated (see chapter 12). That is to say that words and pictures should be presented together in time (i.e., temporal contiguity principle) and space (i.e., spatial contiguity principle) rather than successively. Mayer (in press) reports that eight comparisons of these two approaches showed a median effect size of 1.30 in favor of simultaneous presentation of narration and animation on transfer task performance. Findings for spatial contiguity may be explained by Hegarty,

Carpenter, and Just (1996) who studied the eye movements of participants while reading text and illustrations. They found that students would proceed through a selection by alternately reading short text segments and then inspecting the parts of the illustration described by the text. Evidently, presenting the text and illustrations in close proximity facilitates this processing and results in improved learning. Sweller and his colleagues (Chandler and Sweller, 1992; Sweller, 1994; Sweller, in press) reported similar findings and referred to the advantage of spatial contiguity as overcoming the effects of *split-attention*.

Mayer and Anderson (1991) investigated temporal contiguity of narration and animations. They found, in accord with their predictions, that groups receiving narration presented together with animation compared to groups who received narration followed later by animation demonstrated about the same amount of retention, measured by a test of verbal recall, but significantly greater (about 50%) transfer. Their prediction was based on the notion (and Mayer's theory) that when narration and animation are presented separately, only one channel is called into play at a time and no additive effect can occur. Both groups then have an equal opportunity to construct and extract from long-term memory a verbal response to a retention question. Their result for transfer test performance is consistent with Mayer's (and Paivio's) expectation of an additive effect arising from the complementary functioning of the visual and aural channels, thereby facilitating the construction of referential connections. When narration and animation are presented together, this additive effect can, and evidently does support performance of transfer tasks, which require cognitive manipulation of information from long-term memory.

Second, the *coherence principle* concerns the inclusion or exclusion of extraneous material, such as irrelevant words and pictures, in multimedia instruction. Summarizing findings from six studies, Mayer (2001) reported a median effect size of 2.37 in retention and an effect size of 1.66 in transfer task performance, both favoring the exclusion of interesting but irrelevant material from multimedia instruction. Similarly, Moreno and Mayer (2000) found that adding background music and sounds to narration interfered with learning yielding an effect size of 1.11 for retention scores in two studies. Mayer explains this finding as a result of competition in the auditory channel between speech sounds and the added background music and sounds.

There is another point to be made about the coherence principle. It touches on issues that concern both the multimedia principle itself and the research examining it. The perfectly reasonable focus in this research is on effectiveness measured by retention and transfer administered immediately (or at least very soon) after the instruction is finished. However, instructional objectives may be keyed to much longer term retention of instruction and transfer capabilities. Conditions that are optimal for acquisition may well differ from those that are ideal for long-term retention and/or transfer (Hesketh, 1997; Schmidt & Bjork, 1992).

For instance overlearning is a common technique to ensure long-term retention, but it clearly adds to the time and effort needed to reach instructional objectives (Hagman & Rose, 1983; Wisher, Sabol, & Ellis, 1999). Long-term retention and transfer may also be enhanced by techniques such as increasing interference and confusion (Schneider, Healy, & Bourne, 1998), adding in secondary task components (Healy & Bourne, 1995), and providing multiple contexts and perspectives (Healy, Wohldmann, & Bourne, in press). All these techniques may reduce the effectiveness and efficiency of initial learning – and they affect the type and quality of multimedia presentations provided. Instructional material that uses any of these techniques will be less efficient, that is, it will be able to present less new material in the time available for instruction. This situation suggests that a trade-off exists between what can be achieved in initial learning and what must be retained or sustained over the long run. It also suggests research that is needed to determine more specifically what these trade-offs may be.

In general, research findings concerning these two additional principles suggest that augmenting text with pictures does not facilitate learning uniformly and that the multimedia principle is not enough by itself to ensure receiving full benefit from the use of pictorial information. The principle is more likely to be effective if it is combined with other good multimedia practices than if it is not.

Animation and Video

In addition to the research reported earlier in this chapter, Mayer and Anderson (1991, 1992) went on to compare performance following instruction using either narration with animation, animation alone, narration alone, and no instruction (as a control). In one set of studies, Mayer and Anderson (1991), found that retention in the narration with animation group did not differ significantly from the narration-only group, but the retention performance for each was significantly superior to that of the animation-only group and (as expected) the control group. In measures of transfer, the performance of the narration with animation group was significantly superior to all three other groups.

In the studies they reported in 1992, Mayer and Anderson used the same treatment groups, and found that the three experimental groups showed significantly more retention than the control group but, in accord with their predictions, did not differ significantly from one another. They found, again in accord with their predictions, that the narration with animation group significantly outperformed the three groups on the transfer tasks.

The Mayer and Anderson results for retention differ somewhat from those reported by Al-Seghayer (2001) whose criterion measures in teaching second-language vocabulary were similar to Mayer and Anderson's retention test. Al-Seghayer compared the effects of video with printed text, still pictures with text, and text alone on vocabulary acquisition using multiple-choice items to assess students' recognition of targeted vocabulary and their ability to write word definitions to assess their recall of word meanings. He found that video with text presentations produced results that were significantly superior to those from still picture with text presentations, which, in turn, produced significantly superior results than did text alone. His findings concerning text alone are in accord with those of both theory and other experiments concerning the multimedia principle.

The superiority of video over still pictures has been found elsewhere by Hanley, Herron, and Cole (1995). This effect may require more theoretical development. It seems reasonable to expect such superiority, but explanations of the cognitive mechanisms involved should result in more effective and efficient instructional design. It may be that the video provides more information, or more meaning in Bishop Berkeley's terms, for the visual channel to use. Interviews with Al-Seghayer's students suggested that the video clips did help them understand more precisely the meaning of the target vocabulary words. Presumably, the video clips were providing additional information. If they were simply repeating information already available from text and still pictures, their impact should have been small. In any case, more research may be needed on video presentations to resolve the theoretical issues they raise.

Student Characteristics

Mayer (2001) also discussed the effects of student characteristics on multimedia learning. Mayer and Gallini (1990) found that a well-designed presentation using both text and illustrations, compared to a poorly designed presentation using only text, resulted in better transfer performance for students with low prior knowledge of the domain, whereas there was much less difference between the two presentations for students with high prior knowledge. Across several experiments, they found that although both low and high prior knowledge students benefited from materials using both text and illustrations rather than materials using only text, low prior knowledge students benefited about 0.80 standard deviations more than did high prior knowledge students from the better designed materials.

Similar results were reported by Kalyuga, Chandler, and Sweller (1998) who found that students with limited prior knowledge learned most from an integrated presentation including text and diagrams whereas knowledgeable students profited most from a diagram-only format. In a further study Kalyuga, Chandler, and Sweller (2000) also found that low prior knowledge participants benefited most from a diagram with audio-text presentation. Once students were trained that effect disappeared and those receiving only diagrams improved more than any other group. In a second study reported in the 2000 paper, Kalyuga et al. found that for high prior knowledge students a diagram-only group learned more than a group receiving diagrams with audio text. Because prior knowledge was experimentally manipulated by training in this study, the results are particularly persuasive with respect to its importance.

These results are consistent with earlier studies such as those indicating that learner control requires prior knowledge to be used successfully in instruction (Gay, 1986) and reviews of interactive multimedia suggesting that more instructional guidance is needed when students know less about the device, effect, or situation being simulated (Fletcher, 1991). These findings substantially support Tobias's hypothesis (1976, 1989) that instructional support in general improves the learning of students with limited prior domain knowledge, but has much less impact on students with higher knowledge. That hypothesis is echoed by the findings of Kalyuga, Ayres, Chandler, and Sweller (2003) who summarized a number of studies in different fields demonstrating the "expertise reversal effect" that indicates that high levels of instructional support are needed for novice learners but have little effect on experts and may actually interfere with their learning (see chapter 21).

Finally, it may be worth noting that student characteristics other than the amount of prior knowledge they possess may deserve attention in applying the multimedia principle to the design of instruction. For instance, Mayer and Sims (1994) report two experiments resembling those reported by Mayer and Anderson (1991, 1992) in which narration and animation were presented either concurrently (narration with animation) or successively (narration followed by animation).

Overall Mayer and Sims replicated the Mayer and Anderson finding of significantly superior transfer task performance when narration and animations were presented concurrently. However, they then compared the transfer task performance of their high spatial ability students with that of their low spatial ability students. They found that high spatial ability students who received concurrent instructional presentations provided 50% more transfer solutions than did those who received successive presentations. However, low spatial ability students who received concurrent presentations provided no more transfer solutions than did low spatial ability students who received successive presentations. This result appears to support Mayer's cognitive theory. High spatial ability students may have more cognitive resources to provide Paivio's (and Mayer's) additive coding effect and thereby may benefit more from concurrently presented animations than do low spatial ability students who profit less from material arriving simultaneously from both the aural and visual channels.

In sum, it appears that individual differences in spatial ability and prior knowledge matter. Mayer's dual-coding theory of multimedia learning both predicts and is supported by findings arising from empirical research on the effects of these student characteristics.

Implications for Instructional Design

The evidence is clear that simply augmenting text with illustrations to spruce up the text does not necessarily improve learning unless the illustrative material serves a relevant instructional purpose (Mayer, 2001). Despite this evidence, many textbooks include irrelevant material. Mayer (2001, p. 76) found "In an analysis of how space was used in sixth grade science text books...that about half of the page space was devoted to illustrations and about half was devoted to words...the overwhelming majority of illustrations served no important instructional purpose." In a similar analysis of fifth-grade mathematics textbooks, Mayer found that "30% of the space was used for illustrations, but again, the majority of the illustrations were irrelevant to the goal of the lesson" (p. 77). Similar findings regarding the failure of illustrations in texts to improve comprehension were reported by Britton, Woodward, and Binkley (1993).

In the area of animation, Rieber also noted the need for relevance. In a comprehensive review, Rieber (1994) found a paucity of research on animation, but concluded from the available evidence that for animation to be effective there should be instructional objectives requiring external visualization of change in some object over time and/or in a certain direction or trajectory. He also emphasized the value of allowing students to interactively and systematically manipulate animations, which would support both memory coding and active hypothesis testing while providing feedback for the learner.

Despite the intuitive notion of using multimedia materials to increase motivation, it appears that adding material to an instructional presentation just to enhance interest may neither improve learners' motivation nor improve learning. Studies dealing with adding seductive details to multimedia presentations indicate that such practices may actually interfere with instructional aims (Kalyuga, Chandler, & Sweller, 1999; Mayer, Heiser, & Lonn, 2001). If instructional designers want to make a presentation more interesting, the materials added must be directly relevant to the purpose of the instruction. Trying to spice up the interest by adding extraneous material appears to interfere with learning and performance, rather than enhance it.

Graphic detail is also an issue for consideration. Adding visual information to text can rarely be done for free. For instance, Garris et al. (1990) reviewed requirements for job performance aids covering a single control system in an M-1 tank and found that they required production of 500 graphics. Garris et al. found that it would require 37.5 staff-weeks of effort to produce full-detail renditions of these graphics. However, they also found that it would require only 2.1 staff-weeks to produce graphics at the lowest level of detail needed for the performance aids and 12.5 staff-weeks to produce these graphics at a more complete but moderate level of detail. The number of production staff-weeks (and costs) needed appears to fall almost linearly with the percentage of details that might be omitted from the graphics.

With these costs in mind, some investigators have studied the level of detail needed for graphics presentations. For instance, Ricci, Garris, Mulligan, and McCallum (1990) studied the amount of graphics detail needed to train and perform a 13-step oscilloscope set-up procedure. They investigated 100%, 15%, and 10% levels of detail. They found no differences in training time, but the 100% condition produced significantly faster initial task performance time and fewer inital errors overall. They concluded that by identifying specific, critical cues to include in graphics, levels of detail substantially less than 100% could support procedural training. More research is needed to develop methods that suggest optimal trade-offs between the costs of providing graphics detail and requirements for detail in instruction and performance aiding. Such research should produce substantial practical payoff.

In summary, instruction should capitalize on availability of the different input channels that are available for cognitive processing. Using the same modality for all of the material being presented, even if it is redundant material, may lead to channel overload and reduce learning. Further, to maximize the effectiveness of human cognition with its separate, additive channels, material intended for different channels should be in close temporal and spatial proximity, rather than separated. When animations or graphic presentations are combined with verbal presentations, it is more effective to have the verbal material presented using an aural channel, rather than overloading the visual channel by adding text.

Implications for Cognitive Theory

The large gains on transfer tasks attributable to multimedia presentation are particularly impressive aspects of Mayer's (2001) findings. Transfer is a crucial and frequently neglected dependent measure in research on learning in multimedia contexts as well as in others. Transfer is a critically important outcome because people must often apply school learning in settings that are very different from the ones in which the learning occurred. Evidence of transfer in multimedia settings suggests that the learning is relatively "deep" (Craik & Lockhart, 1972) leading to the substantial transfer effects reported by Mayer. Mayer's findings emphasize transfer and reflect his observation that "transfer is often cited as the major goal of education, and the concept is at the heart of the science of instruction" (2004, p. 717).

Mayer's findings regarding the effect of various factors on the retention of multimedia learning may need elaboration, particularly in the area of long-term retention of both knowledge and skill. Wisher et al. (1999) reviewed the literature on retention and found that forgetting was a function of the type of content, the thoroughness of learning, the conditions under which recall was required, and student characteristics. That is, Wisher et al. found that forgetting varied not only with the type of learning, for example procedural or declarative knowledge, but also with such factors as the presence of feedback, availability of performance aids, and extent of overlearning. Variations in long-term retention were even found among different procedural tasks depending upon the number of steps in the procedure, whether the steps had to be performed sequentially, and whether the procedure required recognition or recall memory. Furthermore, retention was found to be a function of students' learning ability. Therefore, it seems likely that findings dealing with the multimedia principle may have to be qualified by the content to be learned, student characteristics, and the conditions under which performance is measured.

It is generally agreed (Mayer, 2001; Sweller, in press) that some cognitive integration between visual and auditory channels is needed to coordinate the information arriving from them. The internal representation of both channels implies that they are held in working memory simultaneously while students figure out the relationships between them and code them for transfer to long-term memory. Furthermore, some search of long-term memory must also occur to integrate the new information with a relevant schema held in long-term store. Holding the two input streams in working memory, integrating the two channels, searching long-term memory for relevant schemas, transferring the new material to the long-term store, and integrating the learning with existing schemas, must absorb some portion of working memory. Research is needed to form a clearer picture of how this integration occurs and how much working memory is saved using two channels rather than one.

Sweller (in press) specifically rejects a coordinating central executive process to manage and coordinate the integration. His theory assumes that the executive function is keyed to the structure of prior knowledge in long-term memory. The processes by which the coordination of channels occurs prior to their storage in long-term memory and how the load on working memory is reduced by using two channels both need clarification.

Working Memory

Mayer (2001), Sweller (in press), and their associates discuss enhancements in learning through reductions in cognitive load, but more reliable and valid measures of cognitive load are needed to support their the-

oretical assumptions and to guide instructional designers. Paas et al. (2003) found that self-reports on rating scales have been the most frequently used measures of cognitive load. Brünken, Plass, and Leutner (2003) found that reaction time in performing a relatively easy alternate task may be a reliable indicator of cognitive load. Paas, Tuovinen, Tabbers, and Van Gerven (2003) describe preliminary work attempting to assess cognitive load by measuring brain and eye activity. Brünken et al. describe some neuroimaging techniques to get at cognitive load more directly.

A research program conducted at the now disbanded Air Force Armstrong Laboratory Test Development Center in San Antonio, Texas, examined correlates of working memory (Kyllonen, 1996). Kyllonen found a close relationship between Spearman's "g" and working memory capacity. Kyllonen (in press) reported correlations between 6 measures of working memory capacity and 15 reasoning measures that range from 0.80 to 0.88, and a 0.99 correlation between 9 measures of working memory and the 10-test Armed Forces Vocational Ability Battery. Similar findings were reported by Süß, Oberauer, Wittman, Wilhelm, and Schultze (1996), as well as by Wittman and Süß (1999).

These results have several implications for researchers who are investigating multimedia learning and cognitive load theory. First, the measures of working memory they use may be directly adopted by others seeking additional ways to assess working memory. Second, it may be appropriate to think of working memory as general learning ability, or general intelligence. These findings make a good deal of sense when working memory is considered as a proxy for general intelligence. Third, the working memory capacity construct appears to be important for research on multimedia and cognition. In view of the interactions between presentation modes and student characteristics discussed briefly in a later section, the multimedia principle may be of greater importance for students with smaller working memory capacity, or general learning ability, than their higher capacity peers. Such research would add to the body of knowledge concerning multimedia learning, in addition to providing benchmarks for instructional designers interested in tailoring instruction to their students' needs.

Motivation and Metacognition

Currently, measures of cognitive load can realistically be obtained only for small samples of students working on a particular instructional segment. Measuring working memory is usually too intrusive to be assessed continuously while individuals work on a course lasting several hours, days, or weeks. Students' work at any educational level is likely to be a function not only of their working memory capacity, but also of their willingness to deploy their cognitive resources for the length of time it takes to complete a course.

The impact of interest (Renninger, Hidi, & Krapp 1992) and motivational goal orientation (a vigorous field of research summarized by Maehr & Meyer, 1997) remain active areas of research in instructional psychology. Research is also beginning to explore the effect of motivation on metacognition (Tobias, in press). As noted previously, these constructs need to be included in models of multimedia learning and cognitive load to make them more relevant to learning in real-life contexts, whether in school or over the Internet. When students expend the effort to complete a course in everyday instructional contexts, they are either interested in the material, motivated to attain some goal of importance to them, or both. These variables need to be incorporated into multimedia and cognitive load theories if they are to benefit real-world learning that requires course length commitment of time and cognitive resources.

It may also be worthwhile to study the effects of metacognition on multimedia learning. For example, research on metacognitive knowledge monitoring (Seignon & Tobias, 1996; Tobias & Everson, 2000) found that explicit feedback was less needed by students who could accurately monitor this metacognitive knowledge than by their peers who could not. It seems likely that the other principles of multimedia learning described earlier may vary for students with different metacognitive characteristics. Such research will clarify issues in multimedia learning, metacognition, and the general area of adapting instruction to student characteristics.

Aptitude-Treatment Interaction Research

As indicated, some forms of instructional support are effective for students with limited domain knowledge, but have little effect, and may even interfere, with the learning of those with substantial prior experience. While multimedia evidence for this effect remains limited, it coincides with findings reported in reviews of research on the interactions between student characteristics and instructional treatments. These interactions have been observed across a variety of instructional areas (Corno & Snow, 1986; Gustaffson & Undheim, 1996; Tobias, 1989), thereby enhancing both the plausibility and generality of interactions between student characteristics and instructional treatments. Because instructional materials without augmentations are usually less costly, requiring less effort to prepare them and less student time to peruse them, an ideal strategy would be to assign students to the most efficient treatment in terms of cost effectiveness, rather than assigning all students to one presentation mode.

Aptitude-Treatment Interaction (ATI) research is concerned with the interactions of any student characteristic, not just cognitive ones, with instructional treatments. ATI work was quite popular in the 1960s and 1970s (Cronbach & Snow, 1977) but fell into disfavor when interactions were difficult to verify and replicate (Cronbach & Snow, 1977; Tobias, 1989). Findings are beginning to accumulate (Kalyuga, et al., 2003; Kalyuga Chandler, & Sweller, 1998, 2000; Mayer 2001; Renkl & Atkinson, 2003; van Merriënboer, Kirschner, & Kester, 2003) that multimedia presentations are differentially effective for different students. Such interactions were much sought by ATI researchers, but rarely found and even more rarely replicated (Cronbach & Snow, 1977). The multimedia findings provide clear evidence of ATIs because they indicate interactions between the multimedia principle and student characteristics.

One of the critical problems faced by prior ATI research was that it was difficult to specify the cognitive processes required by different instructional methods and to determine if those processes were differentially available to students (Tobias, 1989). The cognitive and constructivist research paradigms dominating research on human learning in the last three decades, and the work on multimedia learning have clarified many of these processes. We may be at a time when ATI research can realize its original promise not only in multimedia learning, but in all areas of instruction. ATI research results should lead to a series of replicated interactions between student characteristics and instructional treatments that would enable instructional designers to create presentations ideally suited to learners with different characteristics.

Kyllonen's findings (in press) suggest that studying interactions between general learning ability and the multimedia principle would be productive. However, an advantage of examining interactions with prior knowledge (Tobias, 1989) rather than with general ability is that even though prior knowledge is highly related to ability, it can be more easily assessed, using a straightforward pretest, than can general ability. Furthermore, unlike general ability, prior knowledge may also be readily manipulated by pretraining students, as was demonstrated in Kalyuga, Chandler, et al. (2000) research. The domain specificity of prior knowledge, compared to learning ability, is also an important advantage. It is possible that students may have substantial prior knowledge in some domain as a result of intensive interest and prior experience, yet have only average general learning ability. Thus, ATIs between instructional methods and prior knowledge may generate more interpretable results because they

can be indexed to specific domains. Finally, using prior knowledge provides guidelines for instructional designers to use in devising specific pretraining for students who need to augment low levels of prior knowledge. If ATI findings continue to be fruitful, their practical consequences in multimedia contexts, as well as in others, need to be considered.

An interesting question may arise about whether the instructional designer should mandate options, or if students should be given some degree of choice in selecting them. Research on students' prior reading (Tobias, 1987) indicated that for those who were unfamiliar with a domain, mandated review was superior to voluntary review, whereas for knowledgeable students voluntary review was superior. These results, coupled with Sugrue and Clark's (2000) observation that students do not necessarily select the instructional method that is optimal for them, suggest that permitting some student choice might be best for those with substantial prior knowledge of the domain, but that alternate options had best be prescribed by the instructional system for those with more limited knowledge.

Summary and Next Steps

The multimedia principle, which suggests that learning and understanding are enhanced by adding pictures to text rather than by presenting text alone, appears to be well supported by findings from empirical research. Cognitive theory derived from these findings posits three stages of memory – sensory, working, and long term – and their interactions with independent but cooperating (additive) channels for inputting auditory/verbal and visual/pictorial information. In addition to being well supported by existing findings, predictions based on this theory have been made and empirically verified.

Of course more remains to be done and learned through research. Mayer's extensive and systematic program of research on multimedia learning provides an important empirical foundation for the multimedia principle. But his measures of transfer emphasize students' abilities to access learned material for problem solving more than their abilities to apply what was learned to a new task. Also, his retention measures emphasize recall soon after learning, rather than retention of learned material over extended periods of time. Further research on multimedia learning and cognitive load theory might usefully include measures of short- and long-term recall, and the measures of transfer employed might also require applications of the learned material to new tasks.

In very practical (cost and effectiveness) terms, graphic detail must be relevant to instructional objectives, but a better understanding of the trade-offs between the costs of detail and instructional effectiveness is needed. Similar understanding is needed to determine practicable trade-offs between the need to maximize instructional effectiveness in the short run and increase retention and transfer of knowledge and skills over the long run.

In the theoretical arena, clarification of the coordinating mechanisms between auditory and visual channels, as well as between those channels and long-term memory is needed to provide a clearer understanding of the facilitating effects of multimedia learning. Such clarification may provide guidelines for instructional designers in preparing multimedia courseware. Similarly, it seems important to broaden multimedia research by including motivational goal orientation, interest, and metacognitive variables to extend the relevance of multimedia research to everyday learning in school and work environments. Research is also needed to provide a clearer understanding of how multimedia presentations reduce load on working memory or learning ability. Useful techniques for assessing working memory are emerging from research dealing in general with intelligence and memory. These techniques may be of particular value in investigating the effects of multimedia presentations on cognitive load and learning. They should be reviewed by multimedia researchers and adopted as appropriate.

Student characteristics such as prior knowledge and spatial ability have been shown to interact with the multimedia principle, but, as in other areas of instructional design, work is needed to take more complete account of individual student characteristics and individual differences. For instance, prior knowledge, a construct of both theoretical and practical significance, has been shown to be one of the best predictors of future learning (Dochy, 1992). The multimedia research reviewed here has noted the importance of prior knowledge in identifying optimal instructional methods for multimedia contexts, among others. More generally, it appears that a significant beginning has been made in both theoretical and practical directions regarding the interaction between student characteristics and alternate instructional treatments in multimedia contexts, but more remains to be done if we are to take full advantage of the tools technology has placed in our hands.

Extending research on multimedia presentations and prior knowledge will broaden our understanding of learning from instruction in general and from multimedia presentations in particular. In addition such research can provide guidelines to instructional designers for the development of alternate multimedia presentation modes or, if needed, prefamiliarization with the content for those students needing it (see chapter 11). In a variety of ways, enhanced understanding of the multimedia principle will help to clarify our knowledge of learning and instruction across many contexts.

Glossary

Additive coding: The ability of different cognitive processing channels (such as those for pictures and words) to reinforce each other, reduce cognitive processing requirements, and increase the likelihood that information will be transmitted to long-term memory.

Aptitude-treatment interaction: The concept that instructional strategies (treatments) are more effective when they are adapted to the specific abilities and/or attributes of individuals.

Cognitive load theory: A theory that posits a short-term working memory interacting with relatively permanent elements in long-term memory to process sensory input and organize it in accord with patterns (schemas) in order to perform cognitive tasks and effect changes in long-term memory. Cognitive load is defined in terms of the amount of working memory processing capacity that is being used.

Dual-coding theory: The theory that there are two independent, but complementary cognitive subsystems, one used for processing imagery and the other used for processing verbal information, operating in an additive fashion.

Long-term memory: A relatively permanent memory store of general world knowledge including patterns and associative links.

Multimedia principle: The observation, abstracted from numerous research findings, that people learn better from words and pictures presented together than from words presented alone.

Sensory memory: The ability to retain impressions of sensory information – especially sights (iconic memory) and sounds (echoic memory) – after the original, physical stimulus sensation has ended.

Working memory: An active capability that temporarily stores and processes information from both sensory and long-term memory in order to perform cognitive tasks.

Footnote

1. God's mind is included, so the physical world did not, for Berkeley, depend for its existence on human minds.

References

Al-Seghayer, K. (2001). The effect of multimedia annotation modes on L2 vocabulary acquisition: A comparative study. *Language Learning and Technology, 5*, 202–232.

Britton, B. K., Woodward. A., & Binkley, M. (Eds.). (1993). *Learning from textbooks: Theory and practice*. Hillsdale, NJ: Lawrence Erlbaum Associates.

Brünken, R., Plass, J. L., & Leutner, D. (2003). Direct measurement of cognitive load in multimedia learning. *Educational Psychologist, 38*, 53–61.

Chandler, P., & Sweller, J. (1992). The split-attention effect as a factor in the design of instruction. *British Journal of Educational Psychology, 62*, 233–246.

Clark, R. E. (1983). Reconsidering research on learning from media. *Review of Educational Research, 53*, 445–459.

Clark, R. E. (Ed.). (2001). *Learning from media: Arguments, analysis, and evidence*. Greenwich, CT: Information Age Publishing.

Corno, L., & Snow, R. E. (1986). Adapting teaching to individual differences among learners. In M. C. Wittrock (Ed.), *Handbook of research on teaching* (3rd ed., pp. 605–629). New York: Macmillan.

Craik, E. I. M., & Lockhart, R. S. (1972). Levels of processing: A framework for memory research. *Journal of Verbal Learning and Verbal Behavior, 11*, 671–684.

Cronbach, L. J., & Snow, R. E. (1977). *Aptitudes and instructional methods*. New York: Irvington.

Dochy, F. J. R. C. (1992). *Assessment of prior knowledge as a determinant for future learning*. Utrecht/London: Lemma B. V./Jessica Kingsley Publishers.

Fletcher, J. D. (1982) Training technology: An ecological point of view. In R. A. Kasschau, R. Lachman, & K. R. Laughery (Eds.), *Psychology and society: Information technology in the 1980s* (pp. 166–191). New York: Holt, Reinhart, and Winston.

Fletcher, J. D. (1991). Effectiveness and cost of interactive videodisc instruction. *Machine Mediated Learning, 3*, 361–385.

Fletcher, J. D. (2003) Evidence for learning from technology-assisted instruction. In H. F. O'Neil Jr. & R. Perez (Eds.), *Technology applications in education: A learning view* (pp. 79–99). Hillsdale, NJ: Lawrence Erlbaum Associates.

Fletcher, J. D. (2004). Technology, the columbus effect, and the third revolution in learning. In M. Rabinowitz, F. C. Blumberg, & H. Everson (Eds.), *The design of instruction and evaluation: Affordances of using media and technology* (pp. 139–157). Mahwah, NJ: Lawrence Erlbaum Associates.

Garris, R. D., Mulligan, C. P., Ricci, K. E., Dwyer, D. J., McCallum, G. A., Moskal, P. J. (1990). *Effects of graphics detail on locator task performance for computer-based training.* (NTSC Tech Rep 87-034). Orlando, FL: Naval Training Systems Center.

Gay, G. (1986). Interaction of learner control and prior understanding in computer-assisted video instruction. *Journal of Educational Psychology,* 78, 225–227.

Gustafsson, J. E., & Undheim, J. O. 1996. Individual differences in cognitive functions. In D. C. Berliner & R. C. Calfee (Eds.), *Handbook of educational psychology* (pp. 186–242). New York: Simon & Schuster Macmillan.

Hagman, J. D., & Rose, A. M. (1983). Retention of military tasks: A review. *Human Factors,* 25(2), 199–213.

Hanley, J., Herron, C., & Cole, S. (1995). Using video as advance organizer to a written passage in the FLES classroom. *The Modern Language Journal,* 79, 57–66.

Hannafin, M. J., Hannafin, K. M., Hooper, S. R., Rieber, L. P., & Kini, A. S. (1996). Research on and research with emerging technologies. In D. H. Jonassen (Ed.), *Handbook of research for education communications and technology* (pp. 378–402). New York: Macmillan Reference USA.

Healy, A. F., & Bourne, L. E., Jr. (1995). *Learning and memory of knowledge and skills: Durability and specificity.* Thousand Oaks, CA: Sage.

Healy, A. F., Wohldmann, E., & Bourne, L. E., Jr. (in press). The procedural reinstatement framework: Studies on training, retention, and transfer. In A. F. Healy (Ed.), *Experimental cognitive psychology and its applications: Festschrift in honor of Lyle Bourne, Walter Kintsch, and Thomas Landauer.* Washington, DC: American Psychological Association.

Hegarty, M., Carpenter, P. A., & Just, M. A. (1996). Diagrams in the comprehension of scientific texts. In R. Barr, M. L. Kamil, P. Mosenthal, & P. D. Pearson (Eds.), *Handbook of reading research. Volume II* (pp. 641–668). Mahwah, NJ: Erlbaum.

Hesketh, B. (1997). Dilemmas for training transfer and retention. *Applied Psychology: An International Review,* 46, 317–386.

James, W. (1890/1950). *Principles of psychology: Volume I.* New York: Dover Press.

Kalyuga, S., Ayres, P., Chandler, P., & Sweller, J. (2003). The expertise reversal effect. *Educational Psychologist,* 38, 23–31.

Kalyuga, S., Chandler, P., & Sweller, J. (1998). Levels of experise and instructional design. *Human Factors,* 40, 1–17.

Kalyuga, S., Chandler, P., & Sweller, J. (1999). Managing split-attention and redundancy in multimedia instruction. *Applied Cognitive Psychology,* 13, 351–371.

Kalyuga, S., Chandler, P., & Sweller, J. (2000). Incorporating learner experience into the design of multimedia instruction. *Journal of Educational Psychology,* 92, 126–136.

Kyllonen, P. C. (1996). Is working-memory capacity Spearman's g? In I. Dennis & P. Tapsfield (Eds.), *Human abilities: Their nature and measurement* (pp. 49–76). Mahwah, NJ: Lawrence Erlbaum Associates.

Kyllonen, P.C. (in press). 'g': Knowledge, speed, strategies, or working-memory capacity? A systems perspective. In R. J. Sternberg & E. L. Grigorenko (Eds.), *The general factor of intelligence: How general is it?* Mahwah, NJ: Lawrence Erlbaum Associates.

Maehr, M. L., & Meyer, H. A. (1997). Understanding motivation and schooling: Where we've been, where we are, and where we need to go. *Educational Psychology Review,* 9, 371–409.

Mayer, R. E. (1997). Multimedia learning: Are we asking the right questions? *Educational Psychologist,* 32, 1–19.

Mayer, R. E. (2001). *Multimedia learning.* New York: Cambridge University Press.

Mayer, R. E. (in press). Ten research-based principles of multimedia learning. In H. F. O'Neil, Jr. & Perez, R. S. (Eds.), *Web-based learning: Theory, research and practice.* Mahwah, NJ: Lawrence Erlbaum Associates.

Mayer, R. E., & Anderson, R. B. (1991). Animations need narrations: An experimental test of a dual-coding hypothesis. *Journal of Educational Psychology,* 83, 484–490.

Mayer, R. E., & Anderson, R. B. (1992). The instructive animation: Helping students build connections between words and pictures in multimedia learning. *Journal of Educational Psychology,* 84, 444–452.

Mayer, R. E., & Gallini, J. (1990). When is an illustration worth ten thousand words? *Journal of Educational Psychology,* 82, 715–726.

Mayer, R. E., Heiser, J., & Lonn, S. (2001). Cognitive constraints on multimedia learning:

When presenting more material results in less understanding. *Journal of Educational Psychology, 93,* 187–198.

Mayer, R. E., & Sims, V. K. (1994). For whom is a picture worth a thousand words? Extensions of a dual-coding theory of multimedia learning. *Journal of Educational Psychology, 84,* 389–401.

Moreno, R., & Mayer, R. (2000). A coherence effect in multimedia learning: The case for minimizing irrelevant sounds in the design of multimedia instruction. *Journal of Educational Psychology, 92,* 117–125.

Neisser, U. (1967). *Cognitive psychology.* New York: Appleton, Century, Crofts.

Paas, F., Renkl, A., & Sweller, J. (2003). Cognitive load theory and instructional design: Recent developments. *Educational Psychologist, 38,* 1–4.

Paas, F., Tuovinen, J. E., Tabbers, H., & Van Gerven, P. W. M. (2003). Cognitive load measurement as a means to advance cognitive load theory. *Educational Psychologist, 38,* 63–71.

Paivio, A. (1986). *Mental representations: A dual-coding approach.* New York: Oxford University Press.

Paivio, A. (1991). *Images in mind: The evolution of a theory.* Hempstead, Herfordshire, UK: Harvester Wheatshaft.

Renkl, A., & Atkinson, R. K. (2003). Structuring the transition from example study to problem solving in cognitive skill acquisition: A cognitive load perspective. *Educational Psychologist, 38,* 15–22.

Renninger, K. A., Hidi, S., & Krapp, A. (1992). *The role of interest in learning and development.* Hillsdale, NJ: Erlbaum.

Ricci, K. E., Garris, R. D., Mulligan, C. F., & McCallum, G. A. (1990). *Effects of graphics detail parameters on procedural task performance for computer-based training.* (NTSC Tech Rep 89-023). Orlando, FL: Naval Training Systems Center. (DTIC AD-B154 814).

Rieber, L. P. (1994). *Computers, graphics, and learning.* Dubuque, IA: Brown & Benchmark.

Russell, T. L. (1999). *The no significant differences phenomenon.* Chapel Hill, NC: Office of Instructional Telecommunications, North Carolina State University.

Schmidt, R. A., & Bjork, R. A. (1992). New conceptualizations of practice: Common principles in three paradigms suggest new concepts for training. *Psychological Science, 3,* 207–217.

Schneider, V. I., Healy, A. F., & Bourne, L. E., Jr. (1998). Contextual interference effects in foreign language vocabulary acquisition and retention. In A. F. Healy & L. E. Bourne, Jr. (Eds.), *Foreign language learning: Psycholinguistic studies on training and retention* (pp. 77–90). Mahwah, NJ: Erlbaum.

Seignon, N., & Tobias, S. (1996, April). *Metacognitive knowledge monitoring and need for feedback.* Paper presented at the annual meeting of the American Educational Research Association, New York.

Sugrue, B., & Clark, R. (2000). Media selection for training. In S. Tobias & J. D. Fletcher (Eds.), *Training and retraining: A handbook for business, industry, government, and the military* (pp. 208–234). New York: Macmillan Reference USA.

Süß, H-M., Oberauer, K., Wittman, W. W., Wilhelm, O., & Schultze, R. (1996). *Working memory capacity and intelligence: An integrative report based on Brunswik symmetry* (Research Report No. 8). Mannheim, Germany: University of Mannheim.

Sweller, J. (1994). Cognitive load theory, learning difficulty, and instructional design. *Learning and Instruction, 4,* 295–312.

Sweller, J. (in press). Why understanding instructional design principles requires an understanding of the evolution of human cognitive architecture. In H. F. O'Neil, Jr. & R. S. Perez (Eds.), *Web-based learning: Theory, research, and practice.* Mahwah, NJ: Lawrence Erlbaum Associates.

Tobias, S. (1976). Achievement treatment interactions. *Review of Educational Research, 46,* 61–74.

Tobias, S. (1982). When do instructional methods make a difference? *Educational Researcher, 11* (4), 4–9.

Tobias, S. (1987). Mandatory text review and interaction with student characteristics. *Journal of Educational Psychology, 79,* 154–161.

Tobias, S. (1989). Another look at research on the adaptation of instruction to student characteristics. *Educational Psychologist, 24,* 213–227.

Tobias, S. (in press). The importance of motivation, metacognition, and help seeking in web based learning. In H. F. O'Neil, Jr. & Perez, R. S. (Eds.), *Web-based learning: Theory, research and practice.* Mahwah, NJ: Lawrence Erlbaum Associates.

Tobias, S., & Everson, H. T. (2000). Assessing metacognitive knowledge monitoring. In

G. Schraw & J. C. Impara (Eds.), *Issues in the measurement of metacognition* (pp. 147–222). Lincoln, NE: Buros Institute of Mental Measurements.

van Merriënboer, J. J. G., Kirschner, P. A., & Kester, L. (2003). Taking the load of a learner's mind: Instructional design for complex learning. *Educational Psychologist, 38*, 5–13.

Wetzel, C. D., Radtke, P. H., & Stern, H. W. (1994). *Instructional effectiveness of video media.* Hillsdale, NJ: Erlbaum.

Wickens, C. D., & Flach, J. M. (1988). Information processing. In E. L. Wiener & D. C. Nagel (Eds.), *Human factors in aviation* (pp. 111–155). San Diego, CA: Academic Press.

Wisher, R. A., Sabol, M. A., & Ellis, J. A. (1999). *Staying sharp: Retention of military knowledge and skills* (ARI Special Report 39). Alexandria, VA: U.S. Army Research Institute for the Behavioral and Social Sciences. Retrieved June 30, 2004, from http://www.ari.army.mil

Wittman, W. W, & Süß, H-M. (1999). Investigating the paths between working memory, intelligence, knowledge, and complex problem-solving performances via Brunswik Symmetry. In P. L. Ackerman, P. C. Kyllonen, & R. D. Roberts (Eds.), *Learning and individual differences: Process, trait, and content determinants.* Washington, DC: American Psychological Association.

Youngblut, C. (2003). *Experience of presence in virtual environments* (IDA Document D-2960). Alexandria, VA: Institute for Defense Analysis.

CHAPTER 8

The Split-Attention Principle in Multimedia Learning

Paul Ayres
John Sweller
University of New South Wales

Abstract

The split-attention principle states that when designing instruction, including multimedia instruction, it is important to avoid formats that require learners to split their attention between, and mentally integrate, multiple sources of information. Instead, materials should be formatted so that disparate sources of information are physically and temporally integrated thus obviating the need for learners to engage in mental integration. By eliminating the need to mentally integrate multiple sources of information, extraneous working memory load is reduced, freeing resources for learning. This chapter provides the theoretical rationale, based on cognitive load theory, for the split-attention principle, describes the major experiments that establish the validity of the principle, and indicates the instructional design implications when dealing with multimedia materials.

Definition of Split-Attention

Instructional split-attention occurs when learners are required to split their attention between and mentally integrate several sources of physically or temporally disparate information, where each source of information is essential for understanding the material. Cognitive load is increased by the need to mentally integrate the multiple sources of information. This increase in extraneous cognitive load (see chapter 2) is likely to have a negative impact on learning compared to conditions where the information has been restructured to eliminate the need to split attention. Restructuring occurs by physically or temporally integrating disparate sources of information to eliminate the need for mental integration. The split-attention effect occurs when learners studying integrated information outperform learners studying the same information

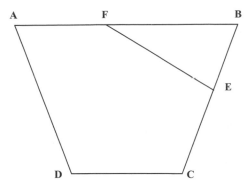

Task: In the above diagram find the value of angle BFE when

line AB is parallel to line DC

Angle BCD = 110°

Angle BEF = 50°

Solution:

Angle FBE = 180 – 110 = 70° (Co-interior angles between parallel lines sum to 180°)

Angle BFE = 180 – 50 – 70 (Angles in a triangle sum to 180)

= 60°.

Figure 8.1. Split-attention in a geometry worked example.

presented in split-attention format. The split-attention principle flows from the split-attention effect. It states that when presenting disparate sources of information that must be mentally integrated in order for the information to be understood, those sources of information should be presented in integrated format.

Examples of the Split-Attention Effect

The different sources of information that cause split-attention vary. For example, the sources can be text and text, or text and mathematical equations, or different forms of multimedia. Using Mayer's definition of multimedia as "the presentation of materials using both words and pictures" (Mayer 2001, p. 1) it can be seen that split-attention will frequently occur using multimedia as there will always be at least two sources of information involved.

Figure 8.1 demonstrates an example of materials that include a requirement to split attention in the mathematical domain of geometry. In Figure 8.1 the diagram is separated from the solution that explains how the task (find Angle BFE) is completed. Neither source of information makes sense without the other. The diagram provides no solution information and the solution information is unintelligible without the diagram. To understand this worked example, a learner will be forced to integrate many pieces of information. Initially, learners will have to locate the given information (the parallel lines and the two angles) on the diagram. If the learner can write this information on the diagram then split-attention only occurs once at this stage. However, to follow the two steps to solution, learners have to mentally integrate these steps with specific angles and geometrical configurations in the diagram. This requirement to split attention between the diagram and text followed by mental integration is a classic example of split-attention. If the learner is a novice, possessing few developed schemas in this domain, it might be expected that substantial cognitive resources will need to be devoted to splitting attention between the disparate sources of information and mentally integrating them.

To avoid split-attention, researchers have successfully employed the strategy of physically integrating the various sources of information. Figure 8.2 demonstrates how the two parts (diagram and text) of the worked example in Figure 8.1 have been integrated. First, the given information on angles and parallel lines are drawn on the diagram. Parallel lines are represented by the universal symbol of the two arrows, and the two angles 110° and 50° are marked. Second, the two steps to solution are written on the diagram at the precise location where the values for the angles are calculated thus eliminating the need for the learner to keep refocusing attention from diagram to text and vice versa. Searching for referents in multi-

ple sources of information is likely to be a major source of extraneous cognitive load. The order in which the solution steps are calculated, are also marked on the diagram and indicated by the numbers 1 and 2. As a consequence of this physical integration, the need for mental integration is reduced and extraneous cognitive load is kept to a minimum.

Basic Research Into the Split-Attention Effect

The initial research into the split-attention effect was conducted by Tarmizi and Sweller (1988) who investigated the effectiveness of worked examples on learning geometry. Prior to this study, worked examples (see chapter 15) had proven to be highly effective for learning algebra (Cooper & Sweller, 1987; Sweller & Cooper, 1985) and in other mathematical domains (Zhu & Simon, 1987). However, in their initial experiments, Tarmizi and Sweller found that neither worked examples nor guided solutions (highly directed but not a full worked example) enhanced performance compared with conventional problem-solving strategies.

The failure of worked examples in geometry was initially perplexing. However Tarmizi and Sweller reasoned that the format of the worked examples, a diagram followed by the solution steps (Figure 8.1 provides an example), must increase

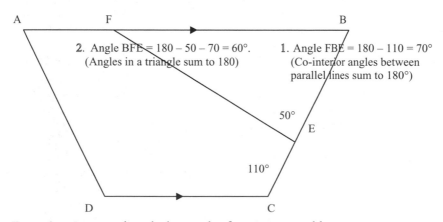

Figure 8.2. Integrated worked example of a geometry problem.

cognitive load. In particular, they argued that the source of increased cognitive load was the requirement for learners to mentally integrate the two sources of information (diagram and textual solutions) that had split their attention. They further hypothesised that if diagrams and texts were integrated, then split-attention would be avoided leading to effective worked examples. In the final two experiments of this study, Tarmizi and Sweller successfully showed that learners who studied integrated worked examples performed at a superior level (fewer errors and quicker solution times) compared to learners who followed a conventional problem-solving strategy during acquisition.

Researchers sought to test these findings in other domains following the identification of the split-attention effect and the success of integrated material in the geometry domain. Sweller, Chandler, Tierney, and Cooper (1990) reproduced the Tarmizi and Sweller findings using coordinate geometry materials. Again, traditionally structured worked examples in this domain have used a diagram associated with solution steps next to or under the diagram. Using this format, as indicated previously, learners are forced to search for the location of referents in either the diagram or the text and that search process requires working memory resources. Sweller et al. (1990) found that learners studied worked examples formatted in the traditional way performed no better than learners required to solve a conventional problem. In contrast, learners who studied an integrated worked example format where steps to the solution were written on the diagram at locations designed to reduce unnecessary search, performed significantly better than learners studying conventionally structured worked examples or solving problems. Furthermore, as might be expected, these results were not restricted to instruction using worked examples. In further experiments, Sweller et al. found that initial instructions presented in an integrated format were superior to the same instructions presented in a split-attention format.

Additional evidence of the split-attention effect and how it could be avoided was provided by Ward and Sweller (1990) in the area of physics. Using mechanics problems based on the formulae associated with constant acceleration, Ward and Sweller found that worked examples compared poorly with a problem-solving strategy. Following on from the earlier research of Tarmizi and Sweller, Ward and Sweller reasoned that the worked examples were structured using a format that promoted split-attention. Figure 8.3a depicts a worked example in dynamics following the traditional textbook format. The problem statement and the initial given states are presented first followed by the appropriate formulae and the solution steps. Using this structure, the learner has to mentally integrate the problem statement, the initial givens, the formula, and the solution steps at various points. In contrast Figure 8.3b demonstrates how this information can be integrated physically to reduce split-attention. The key to this integration is to place the algebraic variables (e.g., v) immediately next to their numeric values to reduce search for the appropriate referents and to complete the algebraic manipulation and substitution before the question is stated to reduce the problem-solving search associated with a problem goal. Employing this integration strategy, Ward and Sweller successfully showed that integrated worked examples were superior to both a problem-solving strategy and to studying conventionally structured worked examples.

The three studies described all contained problems that required mathematical solutions. However, during this early period of research into the split-attention effect, evidence was also collected in nonmathematical domains. Chandler and Sweller (1991) found that instructional materials designed for electrical apprentices contained many cases of split-attention. For example, in learning about the installation of electrical wiring, instructions invariably included diagrams of electrical circuits separated from written explanations on how the circuits worked. By integrating texts and diagrams, Chandler and Sweller demonstrated that the

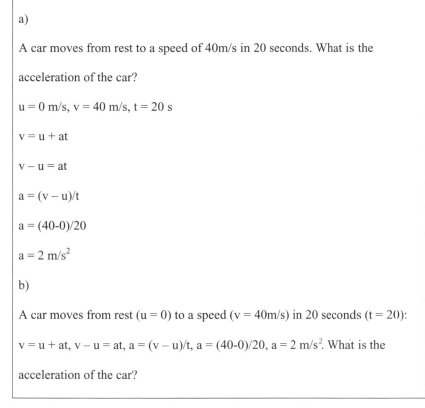

a)

A car moves from rest to a speed of 40m/s in 20 seconds. What is the

acceleration of the car?

u = 0 m/s, v = 40 m/s, t = 20 s

v = u + at

v − u = at

a = (v − u)/t

a = (40-0)/20

a = 2 m/s^2

b)

A car moves from rest (u = 0) to a speed (v = 40m/s) in 20 seconds (t = 20):

v = u + at, v − u = at, a = (v − u)/t, a = (40-0)/20, a = 2 m/s^2. What is the

acceleration of the car?

Figure 8.3. Split-attention and integrated dynamics problem.

split-attention effect could be avoided, resulting in superior performance by the integrated design group.

As part of this study, Chandler and
Sweller also conducted an experiment using
a topic in biology. Students were required to
learn how blood flowed through the heart
and lungs. In this experiment instructions
that integrated both diagrams and text were
not found to be superior to instructions that
kept diagrams and text separate. In this experiment, a third group that received their
instructions in the form of a diagram only,
learned the most. In this case, information on
the diagram and in the text relayed the same
information, although presented in a different form. Consequently, information was redundant in one form or the other – both
were not needed to understand the materials. *Redundancy* is discussed in detail in chapters 10 and 12. The diagram-only treatment
used in the biology experiment by Chandler

and Sweller (1991) was superior to the integrated format because redundant material
was excluded.

It must be strongly emphasised that the
logical relation between sources of information is critical for the split-attention effect.
The effect can only be obtained when multiple sources of information are essential for
understanding and so cannot be understood
in isolation. If multiple sources of information provide the same information in different forms and so are redundant, integrating
them is not beneficial (see chapter 10).

Substantial work on multimedia associated with the split-attention principle has
been carried out by Richard E. Mayer. Although Mayer has focused more generally
on how illustrations and animations facilitate learning, his research has also extended
the knowledge base on split-attention and
other cognitive load theory phenomena particularly in the computer domain.

Early work by Mayer (1989) indicated that including illustrations in expository scientific text has clear advantages. In two experiments, Mayer demonstrated that labelled illustrations during instruction were particularly effective. Mayer found that providing pictures without labels or labels without pictures were inferior to providing both together. Mayer concluded: ". . . without a coherent diagram that integrated the information, students performed relatively poorly on problem solving" (p. 244). It is notable in this study that Mayer identified the importance of integrated information. While this work was not directly concerned with the split-attention effect, inspection of Mayer's diagrams clearly shows that both the labels and the text are presented in a fashion so as to avoid split-attention.

Although Mayer (1989) did not compare integrated with nonintegrated information directly, a later study did. In developing a generative theory of textbook design, Mayer, Steinhoff, Bower, and Mars (1995) argued that an important step for meaningful learning to occur was to build connections between pictorial and verbal representations. Furthermore they argued that this was more likely to occur when text and illustrations were presented *contiguously* (p. 33) on the page rather than separately. To test this hypothesis, a series of experiments was designed around instruction on how lightning worked. In this study, undergraduates with varying knowledge about lightning were randomly assigned to either an integrated group or a separated group. Students in the integrated group received a 600-word text on one page and five illustrations about how lightning worked on a facing page in the same booklet. Each illustration, which also contained labels and a caption, was placed next to the corresponding paragraph that described it. In contrast, the separated group received the same 600-word text and illustrations (without labels and captions) in separate booklets. The results from this study showed that students who received the integrated materials performed at a higher level on problem-solving tasks than students who received separated materials. However, this difference was only observed using students with a low knowledge base prior to commencing the trial. For students with a greater understanding of meteorology, no difference was found between the two groups.

Cognitive load theory can explain the Mayer et al. (1995) results in terms of the split-attention effect. All students in the separated group were forced to integrate information from two physically separated sources, which was cognitively demanding. Students with little knowledge in the domain were unable to access schemas that could help reduce these demands, resulting in a poorer performance than students who followed the less demanding format (information already integrated). However, students with more knowledge, had readily available schemas that reduced the demands made by split-attention.

Further evidence of the beneficial effects of presenting verbal and visual materials in an integrated format came from Moreno and Mayer (1999). In a computer-based environment using meteorological tasks, Mayer and Moreno showed that the separation of text and diagram didn't have to be on different pages or substantially removed from each other to produce a split-attention effect. Differences could be quite subtle. On tests of verbal recall and transfer, an integrated format group outperformed a separated format group. Although the text was short and the diagrams were straightforward, the separated group was forced to expend more cognitive resources than the integrated group to assimilate the information. A further finding in this study was that students who received illustrations with no written text at all, but with a concurrent narration, performed at a higher level than the other two groups. This is an example of the modality effect (discussed in chapters 9 and 11).

Over a number of studies, Mayer and his colleagues have collected evidence that integrating words and pictures leads to superior learning compared with a more spatially remote multimedia design. These findings have led Mayer (2001) to formulate the *spatial contiguity principle*: "Students learn better when corresponding words and pictures are presented near rather than far from each other on the page or screen" (p. 81). This principle is one of seven that constitutes Mayer's cognitive theory of multimedia learning (for more detail see Mayer, 2001, p. 184). The results found by Mayer are also in accord with cognitive load theory. If learners are forced to engage in a search for referents because words are separated from pictures or diagrams in a book or on a page or screen, then cognitive resources may be diverted from learning. Search processes will increase extraneous cognitive load. The need to search is reduced by integrating words and pictures, thus decreasing load and increasing learning.

E-Learning and the Split-Attention Effect

The basic research into the split-attention effect identified many learning environments where integrated rather than split-source information should be used. Potentially, any instructional material that contained more than one source of information was a candidate for integrating split-source information. However, the initial research focused on materials that were presented solely using paper-based media. When researchers turned their attention to learning in a computer environment (e-learning) the research base was significantly expanded.

In the initial days of the computer revolution, learning how to use computer and/or computer applications relied heavily on an accompanying computer manual. Such manuals are still common although largely for economic reasons, screen-based information is now increasingly popular. Typically, computer manuals contain instructions that the reader must follow while attending to information on the computer screen while using a keyboard and mouse. In these situations, split-attention between the manual, computer, and keyboard seems inevitable.

The first to demonstrate the split-attention effect caused by the simultane-

ous use of both manual and computer-based information were Sweller and Chandler (1994) and Chandler and Sweller (1996). In the 1994 study, Sweller and Chandler tested a conventional method of learning a computer application against an integrated approach designed to reduce split-attention. For the conventional method, students were required to learn a computer-aided design/computer-aided manufacture (CAD/CAM) package using both a manual and a computer. This conventional procedure required a number of mental integrations among the instructions in the manual, use of the keyboard, and displays on the computer. To reduce split-attention, the integrated group received all their instructions in a modified manual. No computers or their keyboards were used, instead, the screen and keyboard were replaced by diagrams in the manual. Furthermore, to reduce split-attention within this medium, text and diagrams were fully integrated, requiring students to follow a number of ordered steps. In a direct comparison based on a postacquisition test that included use of the hardware, the group following the integrated approach using no hardware was found to be superior to the conventional group, suggesting that the simultaneous use of a manual and computer created a split-attention effect. That effect resulted in students who had had practice using the hardware demonstrating less proficiency in hardware use than students who had learned without direct access to the relevant equipment.

In a second study Chandler and Sweller (1996) reproduced this result, again demonstrating that fully integrated instructions on a computer application presented on paper alone were superior to simultaneously using a computer. Practice using the computer was far less important than properly formatted instructions presented on paper. Over the two studies, Chandler and Sweller demonstrated the effect using a number of different materials. However, these studies also identified the critical importance played by element interactivity (see chapter 2). Element interactivity refers to the number of elements that must be simultaneously processed in working memory in order to understand the information. Materials low in element interactivity are easy to learn because they keep working memory demands to a minimum. In contrast, materials high in element interactivity are more complex and place more demanding loads on working memory. Element interactivity affects intrinsic cognitive load, whereas the split-attention effect is considered extraneous cognitive load because it is created by the format of the instructional materials (chapter 2).

In two studies, Chandler and Sweller found that the split-attention effect only occurred when the materials were high in element interactivity. Secondary tasks were used to measure cognitive load where a secondary task consists of, for example, responding to a sound while engaged in the primary task, in this case learning the computer application. A high cognitive load on a primary task should depress performance on a secondary task (e.g., see Brünken, Plass, & Leutner, 2003). Measures of cognitive load using secondary tasks clearly indicated that the split-attention effect was first, caused by cognitive load effects and second, only obtainable under conditions of high intrinsic cognitive load caused by high levels of element interactivity. Clearly, in these computer environments, the interaction between intrinsic and extraneous cognitive load is extremely important. For very simple tasks, such as adding data to a spreadsheet cell using the computer and manual simultaneously, split-attention may have little effect because of low element interactivity. An inadequate instructional format may not overload working memory if the intrinsic cognitive load associated with the task is low. For tasks high in element interactivity, such as completing a complicated spreadsheet formula, a split-attention format will have a negative impact on learning. The addition of a heavy working memory load due to high element interactivity and due to split-attention may be overwhelming.

The Chandler and Sweller results described so far may appear controversial or counterintuitive, as they appear to suggest that the best way to learn about computers is not to use one. However, as these authors argued, the integrated noncomputer approach was best suited to learning computer skills at the very early stages. Obviously, we need to use computers at some stage and indeed, Chandler and Sweller (1996) made the following point about the strategy: "It can be suggested that, under some circumstances, the removal of computing equipment during critical phases of learning may provide considerable benefit" (p. 168).

Following the success of the integrated manual approach, Cerpa, Chandler, and Sweller (1996) reasoned that its effectiveness could plausibly be caused by differences in the media rather than split-attention; that is, paper-based material enhances learning compared with electronic versions, although there were no theoretical grounds for this explanation. Consequently, Cerpa et al. devised a study to test this possibility. Instead of integrating the materials on paper, a fully integrated package was constructed on the computer. Working in the domain of spreadsheet learning, students were required to acquire a number of skills ranging from selecting cells, rows, and columns to using functions and entering formulae. An integrated design was constructed by inserting all the instructions into the software at the appropriate points, thus reducing the effects of split-attention. One group of students received instructions in this integrated mode and were compared with a second group who received a traditional instructional package of manual and computer.

On test questions following the instructions, the integrated (computer-only) group significantly outperformed the split-attention group (computer plus manual). However, this difference was only found on test questions tapping knowledge that was high in element interactivity, such as creating a formula. On low element interactivity tasks such as selecting a row, no differences were found between groups. The results from this study eliminated the possibility that print media were superior to an electronic medium, and provided further evidence to support the split-attention effect and the role played by element interactivity. The study also demonstrated that computers could be used effectively provided the split-attention effect was avoided. It is also worth noting at this point that Cerpa et al. employed a third group in the study that received both a computer-based instructional package and a manual. This group also proved to be inferior to the computer-based-only group because of redundancy (see chapter 10).

Temporal Versions of the Split-Attention Principle

The split-attention examples described all have one thing in common: The various sources are physically separate. Regardless whether the cause of split-attention is text and a diagram, or computers and a manual, the two different sources of information are physically separate in a manner that requires search in order to locate relevant referents. It is that act of search that imposes an extraneous cognitive load.

Physical separation is not the only form of separation generating unnecessary search. Multiple sources of information that must be integrated before they can be understood can also be separated in time, resulting in temporal separation. It is reasonable to suppose that temporal separation also generates an extraneous cognitive load for exactly the same reasons as physical separation. Learners must unnecessarily find referents between separated sources of information, in this case temporal separation, and that requirement to mentally coordinate multiple sources of information requires working memory resources. Temporal integration, that is, simultaneously presenting multiple sources of information that must otherwise be mentally integrated before they can be understood, should reduce the need for mental integration and so reduce extraneous cognitive load. A comparison of temporally separate and integrated instruction should yield evidence of superior learning under integrated conditions yielding a temporal version of the split-attention effect. As indicated previously, Mayer and his colleagues have researched the phenomena associated with presenting diagrams and text together during instruction but in addition, have considered the consequences of temporal rather than spatial versions of the split-attention effect.

Mayer (2001) called this principle the *temporal contiguity principle*: "Students learn better when corresponding words and pictures are presented simultaneously rather than successively" (p. 96). So far, all instructional materials reported in this chapter, have engaged the learner in the visual medium only. However, the temporal contiguity principle extends the split-attention theory to include sound. Since the invention of the modern cinema, pictures and the spoken word have been presented together to provide instruction on a film screen, a television screen, and more recently, on a computer screen (although we must not forget that teachers have been reading to their students, while simultaneously presenting pictures or demonstrating skills for considerably longer). Consequently, how sounds and pictures should be presented is also an important consideration.

Mayer (2001) argued that because of the limitations of working memory, words and pictures should not be separated temporally. For example, consider the case of a computer-based multimedia presentation where a narration episode is followed by an animation episode, which depicts the content of the narration. To understand fully what both episodes mean, the learner must hold some or all of the narration in working memory and then integrate this narration with the animation. Furthermore, if the narration is long, then information may be lost without constant rehearsal, or even be too large to assimilate in the first instance.

Mayer developed the temporal contiguity principle based on the results of a number of studies conducted using animation in a computer-based environment. An initial influence was a study by Baggett (1984). Baggett designed an experiment in which a film was shown to college students where the visual and auditory components (voice-over) were presented in seven different conditions. Three conditions presented the visual material either 7, 14, or 21 seconds before the auditory component, and three conditions presented the visual material either 7, 14, or 21 seconds after the auditory components. The final condition presented both the visual and auditory materials simultaneously. On recall tests students who received the concurrent mode or the visuals 7 seconds before the voice-over performed at a superior level to the other five groups. This experiment demonstrated the importance of presenting both media together in close proximity.

Initial research by Mayer and Anderson (1991) compared the effect of receiving instruction that presented words before pictures with instructions that presented both words and pictures simultaneously. In the first experiment of this study, students studied an animation that showed how a bicycle tyre pump worked. A words-before-picture group received a narrative description of how the pump worked before the animation (silent) was presented. The words-with-pictures-together group received both sound and pictures simultaneously. The group that received the simultaneous presentation scored higher on problem-solving tasks.

In a second study, Mayer and Anderson (1992) extended this research. The number of presentations was increased, and the impact of varying the order of narration and animation was examined. On problem-solving tasks, a concurrent group outperformed all other groups and notably, groups who received narration before animation, or vice versa, performed at the same level as a control group with no instruction.

Mayer and Sims (1994) also found evidence that a concurrent presentation of narration and animation was superior to a sequential presentation of either narration followed by animation or animation followed by narration on problem-solving tasks. The study domains were the human respiratory system and bicycle pumps. In addition, this study also examined the influence of spatial ability on these presentation modes.

For high spatial-ability learners there was a significant temporal contiguity effect. However, for low spatial-ability learners the concurrent group performed at the same level as the sequential group. Mayer and Sims explained this finding by arguing that students with low spatial ability had to devote relatively more cognitive resources to connecting the two sources of information compared with students with high spatial abilities. In particular high spatial awareness was particularly advantageous in building visual representations.

The preceding studies demonstrated that students who received information simultaneously (integrated narration and animation) outperformed students who received nonintegrated instructions (narration and animation separated temporally). These differences were found consistently on transfer (problem-solving) tests and less frequently on retention tests. The results support Mayer's temporal contiguity principle (Mayer, 2001).

Further research by Moreno and Mayer (1999) into temporal contiguity investigated the impact of using smaller segments in computer-based episodes of narration and animation. In this study, the large instructional episodes on the formation of lightning used in previously described experiments were divided into 16 smaller segments. Groups of students were presented with either 16 successive alternations of mini narrations and animation in that order, or vice-versa. These groups were compared with students who received the whole episode in an integrated fashion described previously. As few differences were found between groups on retention and transfer tests (results marginally favoured the integrated whole episode approach), Moreno and Mayer (see also Mayer, 2001) concluded that students who received the smaller segment episodes were not subjected to high working memory loads because successive presentations were very short (one or two lines at a time). Consequently, learners were able to successfully integrate the two sources of information themselves and performed at a level comparable to the fully integrated approach.

Implications for Instructional Design

The split-attention effect is a robust, easily demonstrated effect leading to the split-attention principle: Where instruction includes multiple sources of information that must be mentally integrated in order to be intelligible, those sources of information should be both physically and temporally integrated in order to reduce unnecessary search for referents and to reduce extraneous cognitive load. Now there are many studies demonstrating that substantial learning gains can be achieved by physically integrating disparate sources of information rather than requiring learners to use mental resources in mentally integrating the same information. Those studies use a wide variety of materials and participants under many conditions.

Notwithstanding the strength of the split-attention effect, considerable care must be taken when physically integrating disparate sources of information. Simply placing, for example, all text onto a diagram, is no substitute for an understanding of the split-attention principle. There are many conditions under which the principle does not apply or worse, where attempts to apply the principle will have negative rather than positive effects on learning. We would like to emphasise the following points:

1. The principle only applies when multiple sources of information are unintelligible in isolation. For example, physically integrating a diagram with statements that merely redescribe the diagram has negative, not positive effects on learning due to the redundancy effect (see chapter 10). If all sources of information are intelligible in isolation and redundant, elimination of redundancy rather than physical integration should be pursued. Thus, analysing the relation between multiple sources of information prior to physical integration is critical.
2. The split-attention principle only applies to high element interactivity material. If intrinsic cognitive load is not high, whether or not an extraneous cognitive load is added due to split-attention is likely to be irrelevant (see chapter 2). A

diagram and related text that have few interacting elements and so are easily understood are unlikely to be rendered more intelligible by physically integrating them. They can be easily learned even when presented in split-source format.

3. Whether sources of information are intelligible in isolation and whether the information is high in element interactivity not only depends on the instructional material, it also depends on learner characteristics. Material that is unintelligible in isolation and high in element interactivity for low knowledge learners may be intelligible in isolation and low in element interactivity for learners with more knowledge. For high knowledge individuals, physical integration may be deleterious, resulting in the expertise reversal effect (see chapter 21). Alternative instructional techniques are required under such circumstances with the elimination of redundant information being the most common technique.

These limitations under which the split-attention effect can be observed strengthen its scientific validity in that they clearly indicate the experimental conditions that lead to the effect. Nevertheless, from an instructional perspective, they require instructional designers to take many factors into account. A simple recommendation such as "eliminate split-attention between diagrams and text" is not sufficient. To adequately understand the split-attention effect, instructional designers may require considerably more training in cognitive theory and its instructional implications than is currently the norm.

Conclusions

Split-attention is pervasive. The format of much instruction is determined by tradition, economic factors, or the whim of the instructor. Cognitive factors are rarely considered resulting in instructional designs in which split-attention is common. Cognitive load theory, which gave rise to the split-attention principle and which is based on an understanding of human cognitive architecture, especially the relations between working and long-term memory, is able to provide theory-based and experimentally tested instructional guidelines. Those guidelines that are associated with the split-attention effect and that have been discussed in this chapter have the potential to substantially improve multimedia instruction.

Glossary

Integrated instructions. Instructions in which multiple sources of information are physically integrated so that working memory resources do not need to be used for mental integration. Can be contrasted with split-attention instructions.

Split-attention instructions. Instructions in which multiple sources of information are not physically or temporally integrated so that working memory resources need to be used for mental integration. Can be contrasted with integrated instructions.

References

Baggett, P. (1984). Role of temporal overlap of visual and auditory material in forming dual media associations. *Journal of Educational Psychology, 76*, 408–417.

Brünken, R., Plass, J. L., and Leutner, D. (2003). Direct measurement of cognitive load in multimedia learning. *Educational Psychologist, 38*, 53–62.

Cerpa, N., Chandler, P., & Sweller, J. (1996). Some conditions under which integrated computer-based training software can facilitate learning. *Journal of Educational Computing Research, 15*, 345–367.

Chandler, P., & Sweller, J. (1991). Cognitive load theory and the format of instruction. *Cognition and Instruction, 8*, 293–332.

Chandler, P., & Sweller, J. (1996). Cognitive load while learning to use a computer program. *Applied Cognitive Psychology, 10*, 151–170.

Cooper, G., & Sweller, J. (1987). The effects of schema acquisition and rule automation on mathematical problem-solving transfer. *Journal of Educational Psychology, 79*, 347–362.

Mayer, R. E. (1989). Systematic thinking fostered by illustrations in scientific text. *Journal of Educational Psychology, 81*, 240–246.

Mayer, R. E. (2001). *Multimedia learning.* New York: Cambridge University Press.

Mayer, R., & Anderson, R. (1991). Animations need narrations: An experimental test of a dual-coding hypothesis. *Journal of Educational Psychology, 83*, 484–490.

Mayer, R., & Anderson, R. (1992). The instructive animation: Helping students build connections between words and pictures in multimedia learning. *Journal of Educational Psychology, 84*, 444–452.

Mayer, R. E., & Sims, V. K. (1994). For whom is a picture worth a thousand words? Extensions of a dual-coding theory of multimedia learning. *Journal of Educational Psychology, 86*, 389–401.

Mayer, R. E., Steinhoff, K., Bower, G., & Mars, R. (1995). A generative theory of textbook design: Using annotated illustrations to foster meaningful learning of science text. *Educational Technology Research and Development, 43*, 31–43.

Moreno, R., & Mayer, R. E. (1999). Cognitive principles of multimedia learning: The role of modality and contiguity. *Journal of Educational Psychology, 91*, 358–368.

Sweller, J., & Chandler, P. (1994). Why some material is difficult to learn. *Cognition and Instruction, 12*, 185–233.

Sweller, J., Chandler, P., Tierney, P., & Cooper, M. (1990). Cognitive load and selective attention as factors in the structuring of technical material. *Journal of Experimental Psychology: General, 119*, 176–192.

Sweller, J., & Cooper, G. A. (1985). The use of worked examples as a substitute for problem solving in learning algebra. *Cognition and Instruction, 2*, 59–89.

Tarmizi, R., & Sweller, J. (1988). Guidance during mathematical problem solving. *Journal of Educational Psychology, 80*, 424–436.

Ward, M., & Sweller, J. (1990). Structuring effective worked examples. *Cognition and Instruction, 7*, 1–39.

Zhu, X., & Simon, H., (1987). Learning mathematics from examples and by doing. *Cognition and Instruction, 4*, 137–166.

CHAPTER 9

The Modality Principle in Multimedia Learning

Renae Low
John Sweller
University of New South Wales

Abstract

The capacity limitations of working memory are a major impediment when students are required to learn new material. Furthermore, those limitations are relatively inflexible. Nevertheless, in this chapter we explore one technique that can effectively expand working memory capacity. Under certain, well-defined conditions, presenting some information in visual mode and other information in auditory mode can expand effective working memory capacity and so reduce the effects of an excessive cognitive load. This effect is called the *modality effect* or *modality principle*. It is an instructional principle that can substantially increase learning. This chapter discusses the theory and data that underpin the principle and the instructional implications that flow from the principle.

Introduction

There is evidence to indicate that the manner in which information is presented will affect how well it is learned and remembered (e.g., Mayer, Bove, Bryman, Mars, & Tapangco, 1996). This chapter deals with evidence documenting the importance of presentation modes, specifically the modality effect that occurs when information presented in a mixed mode (partly visual and partly auditory) is more effective than when the same information is presented in a single mode (either visual or auditory alone). The instructional version of the modality effect derives from the split-attention effect (see chapter 8), a phenomenon explicable by cognitive load theory (see chapter 2). It occurs when multiple sources of information that must be mentally integrated before they can be understood have written (and therefore visual) information presented in spoken (and therefore auditory) form. For example, consider a geometry problem consisting of a diagram and associated statements. Although the diagram has to be presented visually, the associated statements can be presented visually or orally. According to the modality principle, students learn better when the associated statements are narrated rather than presented visually.

As is the case with the split-attention effect, the logical relation between two sources of visual information is critical. Neither effect is obtainable unless the two sources of information are unintelligible in isolation and so must be mentally integrated in order to be understood. Thus, in the preceding example, neither the diagram nor the statements are likely to be intelligible in isolation and so are candidates for the split-attention or modality effects. In the case of the split-attention effect, the two sources of information are still presented visually but in physically integrated form. In the case of the modality effect, written statements are converted to spoken statements. It should be further noted that if both sources of information are intelligible in isolation, they may be candidates for the redundancy effect (see chapters 10 and 12).

We begin with a brief outline of those aspects of cognitive load theory relevant to the modality effect, particularly the division of working memory into multiple processors. Next, the empirical evidence for the multiprocessor hypothesis and the manner in which that evidence is related to the suggestion that mixed mode presentations of information can enhance information processing (the modality effect) are discussed. Lastly, we discuss the data that have been presented suggesting that instructional designs that make use of multimodal presentations are superior to unimodal presentations, including the various conditions required for the effect.

Cognitive Load Theory and the Modality Effect

According to cognitive load theory, many instructional materials and techniques may be ineffective because they ignore the limitations of human working memory and impose a heavy cognitive load. This type of load is referred to as extraneous cognitive load and has been the main concern of cognitive theorists whose focus has been on devising alternatives to those conventional instructional designs and procedures that were developed without taking into consideration the structure of human memory. Theoretically, there are two ways in which extraneous cognitive load can be manipulated. First, instructional procedures can alleviate extraneous cognitive load by formatting instructional material in such a way that minimises cognitive activities that are unnecessary to learning so that cognitive resources can be freed to concentrate on essential activities. Indeed, initial research generated from cognitive load theory aimed to minimise extraneous cognitive load, resulting in a range of effects such as the worked examples (see chapter 15), completion, and split-attention effects (see chapter 8).

The consequences of extraneous cognitive load can also be alleviated by increasing effective working memory capacity. Working memory was initially considered a unitary structure. More recent research has indicated that working memory may consist of multiple processors rather than a single processor (Baddeley, 1992; Schneider & Detweiler, 1987). These multiple stores, processors, channels, or streams (the terminology varies among researchers) are frequently associated with the separate processing of visual-spatial and language-based material. For example, Baddeley's model of working memory (Baddeley, 1986, 1992, 1999) divides working memory into a visual-spatial scratch pad that processes visually based information such as diagrams and pictures, and a phonological loop that processes auditory information.

There is considerable evidence to suggest that the visual-spatial scratch pad and the phonological loop process different types of information independently, at least to some extent. If the two systems are relatively independent, the total amount of information that can be processed by working memory may be determined by the mode (auditory or visual) of presentation. It may be possible to increase effective working memory capacity by presenting information in a mixed visual and auditory mode rather than a single mode.

Research Evidence for Independent Processors

There is a considerable body of research evidence that supports the notion of relatively independent processing systems in working memory for visual and auditory materials. The following is a brief account of a selection of the research studies contributing to this body of evidence (see Penney, 1989, for a detailed review of this earlier work).

Murdock (1971) presented participants with four words simultaneously, two in a visual mode and the other two in an auditory mode. The visual words were presented in capital or lowercase type and the auditory words were presented in a male or female voice. Each set of four words contained one pair of highly associated words such as *cat-dog, day-night, good-bad*. One word of each pair was presented auditorially and the other visually. Participants were required to report the four words, and to report the target word when the experimenter gave the attribute (male or female voice, capital or lowercase type). For example, a "capital" attribute required the participants to report the word that had been presented in capital letters. Results showed that the order of words reported was organised by mode of presentation, even when highly associated words were split across modes. Furthermore, providing a visual probe interfered with the recall of a visual target word but had no effect on recall of an auditory target word, and vice versa. These findings indicate the possibility of separate auditory and visual systems in working memory.

Margrain (1967) also examined the extent to which visual and auditory memory systems were separate. Different visual and auditory digits were presented in a mode-by-mode order. Participants were required to recall the digits either orally or by writing their responses. Results showed that delayed recall of auditory lists was superior to delayed recall of visual lists regardless of whether the required recall was oral or in a written form. This finding suggests that under some conditions auditory retention may be superior to visual retention in working memory. Further, recall of visual digits was inferior when the recall was in a written form compared to when the recall was oral. In contrast, recall of auditory digits was better under the written than under the oral condition. These results showed that written recall lowered retention of visual digits while oral recall interfered with memory of auditory digits indicating that retention of digits was better if recall was in a modality different from that of presentation. According to Margrain (1967), the data from the research provided evidence for two working memory systems, one processing visual material and the other processing auditory materials.

Penney (1980) suggested that if visual and auditory information are processed separately in working memory, then when presented with a mixture of audio and visual information, one would prefer to recall information by mode of presentation rather than order of presentation. University students were presented with lists of 10 digits in a sequence where the presentation mode changed after every second digit resulting in four patterns of presentation: AAVV..., VVAA..., AVVA..., and VAAV. Some students were instructed to report the digits in their correct order within each modality while others were required to recall the digits in the order of presentation, ignoring the presentation mode. Recall of digits was better when students were required to report by modality rather than by the order of presentation. Based on these results, Penney (1980) suggested that processing items in working memory might be organised in terms of modality rather than order of presentation.

In a further study using a probe recall task similar to that used by Murdock (1971), Penney and Butt (1986) required subjects to study lists of 10 digits in which presentation modality changed after every second digit. At the end of each list, one digit was repeated as a probe. There were two recall conditions. In one condition, subjects were required to report the next item after the probe. For example, if the list was in the order of

AAVVAAVVAA and the probe was the fourth visual digit, the target digit would be the auditory digit in the fifth position. The probe and target could have been presented in the same modality or different modality. In the second condition, the correct response to the probe was the next digit in the same mode of the presentation as the probe. In the preceding example, the target digit would be the next visual digit, which was the seventh digit. Under this condition, it was possible that two digits in the other mode intervened between the probe and the target. The data showed that recall of the target digit was higher when the probe was in the same modality. This result was maintained even when the probe was separated from the target by two digits in a different modality. Together, the results indicated the importance of presentation modality.

The research discussed in the preceding text provides evidence to support the notion that working memory can be subdivided into partially independent processors consisting of an auditory working memory system to deal with verbal material and a visual working memory system to deal with diagrammatical/pictorial information. Because the two processors deal with appropriate information independently to some extent, it is plausible that a mixed mode of presentation can increase the amount of information processed in working memory. In a detailed review of the experimental literature, Penney (1989) provided two different lines of evidence demonstrating an appreciable increase in effective working memory capacity by employing both visual and auditory, rather than any single, processor. One line of evidence shows improved ability to perform two concurrent tasks when information was presented in a partly audio, partly visual format, rather than in either single format. The other line of evidence demonstrates improved memory when information was presented to two sensory modalities rather than one. As indicated in the introduction, the occurrence of increased working memory capacity due to the employment of a dual, rather than a single mode of presentation, is termed the modality effect. A discussion of

research demonstrating the modality effect is presented next.

Evidence for the Modality Effect

Allport, Antonis, and Reynolds (1972) reported two experiments that demonstrated that effective memory capacity was increased when a dual, rather than a single modality was used. The results indicated that participants could repeat continuous speech while concurrently processing unrelated visual items. In one experiment, participants were required to repeat an auditory prose passage (a task known as *shadowing*) while simultaneously committing to memory verbal or nonverbal material. There were three sets of test items that required memorisation: a list of 15 words presented orally, 15 words presented in a written form, and 15 photographs. Results from the memorisation task showed that, in the absence of shadowing, there was no significant difference in the memorisation of orally presented words, visually presented words, or the photographs. In contrast, when participations were required to shadow the auditory passage, memorisation of the orally presented words declined significantly, while memorisation of the visually presented words or photographs was not significantly affected. Apparently, concurrent performance of two tasks is more impaired when the tasks are performed in the same modality than when they are performed in different modalities. This result suggests the independence of auditory and visual working memory so that concurrent tasks performed in differing sensory modalities do not interfere with each other. Similar results were obtained by Rollins and Thibadeau (1973) who found that the requirement to shadow reduced the retention of auditory words to a greater extent than that of visual words.

The modality effect has also been found in research where the task performed concurrently with shadowing does not involve memory. For example, Shaffer (1975) tested a skilled typist on typing a prose message while shadowing a different prose message.

Relative to the no-shadowing condition, the skilled typist could type a visually presented prose passage and simultaneously shadow a different auditorially presented prose message without a decrement in typing accuracy. In contrast, when the prose message to be typed was auditory rather than visual, both typing and shadowing performance declined significantly.

Dennis (1977) obtained a similar finding in a study that required participants to shadow or to listen silently to an auditory prose passage while simultaneously monitoring an auditory or a visual list for specific target words. When the word list was presented auditorially, there were more shadowing errors and more missed on the detection of target words compared to when the list of words was presented visually. Similar research by Spelke, Hirst, and Neisser (1976) demonstrated that participants could successfully read and comprehend a prose message while simultaneously writing auditory words.

In a series of three experiments, Rollins and Hendricks (1980) required participants to monitor lists of auditory or visual words for targets while at the same time processing an auditory message. In all three experiments, detection of auditory targets was much lower than the detection of visual targets and shadowing performance while monitoring visual words was better than that while monitoring auditory words.

In one experiment, Treisman and Davies (1973) required participants to monitor words simultaneously while either looking or listening for a target word. There were three conditions: both lists presented visually, both lists presented auditorially, or one list presented auditorially and the other visually. Each list consisted of 16 pairs of words of which one word was the target. Participants were asked to look at or listen to each pair of words and to press a key if they saw or heard the target. Target words differed in terms of modality of presentation (visual or auditory), physical property (e.g., words containing the letters "END" or the sound "end" as in *lender* and *pretend*), or semantic property (animal names, e.g., *bee*, *ape*). For both physically and semantically defined targets, detection was superior when the lists were presented in different modalities. The participants were better able to divide their attention between two inputs from different modalities than divide their attention between inputs in the same modality.

The literature on concurrent tasks performance shows clearly that a dual mode of presentation can result in increased performance on both memory tasks and monitoring tasks. It seems that there are modality-specific processing resources such that attention can be more effectively managed between messages presented in two modalities than between messages presented in a single modality.

The assumption of modality-specific processing resources is consistent with the model of separate processors in working memory. If there are separate processors for visual and auditory information, it should be possible to show that retention is greater if information is presented to two modalities than when only one mode is used. An early study (Brooks, 1967) involving visualisation (constructing a mental image from information presented) demonstrated this effect. Brooks (1967) postulated that the process of visualisation would improve if instructions were presented in an auditory mode rather than audiovisual mode (audio form accompanied by written instructions). According to Brooks, the process of visualisation and reading would compete for the same cognitive resources. In contrast, listening would not interfere with the visualisation process. In one experiment, Brooks presented participants with a series of messages, which described spatial relations of matrices. In order to understand the messages, visualisation was required. Some of these messages were presented orally. Others were spoken at the same speed but were accompanied by a typewritten copy. Participants were required to repeat each message verbatim. Results showed that repetition of the message was superior when participants were presented the message in an auditory mode compared to the dual mode. It appeared that inclusion of the written message interfered with the visualisation process. Because both visualising and reading are visual tasks, it is possible that performing both tasks resulted in the overload of the visual memory store. Eliminating one visual task, reading, by presenting the material in an auditory mode enabled processing to occur in the two separate stores. The use of the two stores increased effective working memory capacity and enhanced recall.

In a later study, Levin and Divine-Hawkins (1974) again demonstrated that improvement in performance occurs when a dual modality, rather than a single mode is used. The study involved primary aged children who either listened to, or read a story. Half of the students from each group were asked to visualise the prose passage while reading or listening. Students were then tested on the material they had read or listened to. Results from the test indicated that visualisation enhanced performance of students who listened to the story. When students read the story, visualisation was not as successful. It appears that reading and visualising require the same cognitive resources from the visual store in working memory so that when students were asked to read and visualise simultaneously, there was a conflict. This conflict was averted when students were asked to listen to the story, as listening and visualising involve different stores in working memory.

Frick (1984) demonstrated increased digit span by using both auditory and visual working memory stores. In one experiment, the participants were first given a test of digit span using auditory presentation to provide a baseline measurement. The participants were then tested with an all-auditory, all-visual, or a mixed presentation. In the mixed presentation, four visual digits were presented followed by four auditory digits. In all three presentation modes, visual items were presented simultaneously while auditory digits were presented sequentially. Frick found that when the participants were required to report the auditory digits before the visual, the number of items correctly recalled was higher in the mixed presenta-

tion condition than in either the auditory-alone or the visual-alone condition. However, the improvement did not extend to the condition in which the visual digits were reported first.

It should be noted that while Frick's (1984) work demonstrates that short-term retention can be improved by a dual rather than a single-mode presentation, recall levels under dual mode conditions are not equal to the sum of single-mode recall levels. There is no evidence to suggest the additivity of the visual and auditory capacities.

The preceding experimental work unambiguously established that performance could be enhanced by using dual-mode presentation techniques. Cognitive load theory, in conjunction with this work, was used to suggest that an instructional version of the modality effect could be obtained. It was suggested that an instructional modality effect could be obtained under conditions where the split-attention effect occurs. Those conditions are discussed next.

Split-Attention Effect

Split-attention occurs when two or more sources of visual information must be processed simultaneously in order to derive meaning from material (see chapter 8). The working memory load imposed by the need to mentally integrate the disparate sources of information interferes with learning. Consider a conventionally structured geometry worked example consisting of a diagram and its associated solution statements, as described at the beginning of this chapter. The diagram alone does not communicate the solution to the problem. The statements, in turn, are incomprehensible until they have been integrated with the diagram. Learners must mentally integrate the two sources of information (the diagram and the statements) in order to understand them. This process can be cognitively demanding thus imposing a cognitive load that is extraneous simply because of the particular format. An alternative to the split-attention format is an integrated format in which the diagram and text are physically integrated obviating the need to search for relations between them (see chapter 8 for split-attention and integrated geometry worked examples). Instead of having to use limited working memory resources to mentally integrate the two visual sources of information, physical integration is used so that there is no need for mental integration. Training conditions comparing split-attention and integrated formats are expected to yield results demonstrating the superiority of the integrated format. This result is known as the *split-attention effect*.

If effective working memory can be increased by using dual-modality presentation techniques, then this procedure may be just as effective in facilitating learning as physically integrating two sources of visually presented information. The instructional version of the modality effect derives from the split-attention effect in that both effects rely on two sources of visually separated information (e.g., written text and diagrams) that are unintelligible in isolation and so must be mentally integrated in order to derive meaning. To obtain the split-attention effect, the two visually separated sources of information are physically integrated to reduce the need for mental integration. To obtain the modality effect, verbal material is presented in spoken rather than written form. The instructional modality effect is obtained when such dual-mode presentation is superior to a visual-only, split-attention presentation.

Modality Effect and Instructional Design

The instructional predictions that flow from the experimental work on the modality effect are straightforward. Assume instruction that includes a diagram and text that are unintelligible unless they are mentally integrated. A geometry diagram and associated text provide one of many examples. From a cognitive load theory perspective, the modality effect can be explained by ascribing memory load to each of the treatment conditions, the diagram (or picture) with text presentation induces a higher load in the visual working memory because both sources of information are processed in this system. In contrast, the diagram and narration version induces a lower load in visual working memory because auditory and visual information are each processed in their respective system. Therefore, the total load induced by this version is spread between the visual and the auditory components in the working memory system. In other words, integration of the audio and visual information may not overload working memory if its capacity is effectively expanded by using a dual-mode presentation.

Using the cognitive load framework as a theoretical base, Mousavi, Low, and Sweller (1995) tested for the modality effect using split-attention geometry material consisting of a diagram and its associated statements (see chapter 8). It is obvious that a geometry diagram must be presented in visual form. However, the textual information could be presented in either visual (written) or auditory form. A visually presented diagram and auditorially presented text may increase effective working memory and so facilitate learning over conditions where visual working memory alone must be used to process all of the information. In a series of experiments, Mousavi et al. obtained this result. Audio-visual instructions were consistently superior to visual-visual instructions, demonstrating the modality effect. Furthermore, strong evidence was obtained indicating that the effect was due to working memory considerations, not merely due to the physical fact that auditory and visual signals can be received simultaneously while two visual signals (e.g., from a diagram and separate text) cannot be perceived simultaneously but must be attended to successively. The effect was retained even when the geometric diagram and its associated text were presented successively rather than simultaneously in both the audio-visual and visual-visual conditions. Remembering and using a previously presented statement while looking at a diagram is easier when the statement is spoken rather than written.

Tindall-Ford, Chandler, and Sweller (1997) replicated the basic, modality effect finding in another series of experiments with electrical engineering instructional materials. In addition, these experiments differentiated between materials that were low or high in element interactivity where element interactivity refers to the number of elements that must be simultaneously processed in working memory because they interact (see chapter 2). Low element interactivity material consists of elements that can be processed individually because they do not interact. Because the elements can be processed individually, they impose a low load on working memory and such material is described as having a low intrinsic cognitive load. In contrast, the elements of high element interactivity material, because they interact, must be processed simultaneously in working memory if the material is to be understood. Such material has a high intrinsic cognitive load.

Tindall-Ford et al. predicted that low element interactivity material with its low intrinsic cognitive load would not demonstrate the modality effect because increasing effective working memory would be irrelevant under conditions where the information that had to be processed did not strain working memory capacity. The modality effect was obtained with high but not low element interactive materials. In addition, assessment of comparative cognitive load using subjective ratings (see Paas and Van Merriënboer, 1993) indicated that cognitive load was higher under visual-visual then under audio-visual conditions, but only when the instructional material was high in element interactivity. Jeung, Chandler, and Sweller (1997) found that the modality effect was enhanced when visual indicators were used to indicate to learners which parts of complex information were being referred to by the spoken text. Leahy, Chandler, and Sweller (2003) demonstrated the modality principle but also found that the modality effect could only be obtained under split-attention conditions where the information of both modalities was essential for understanding. The effect was not obtained under redundancy conditions (see chapter 10) where one modality could be understood in isolation and the other was redundant in that it presented the same information in a different form.

The importance of split-attention conditions (i.e., both sources of information essential for understanding) rather than redundancy conditions (both sources of information independently intelligible) for the modality effect can be seen from the work on the expertise reversal effect (see chapter 21). Expertise reversal occurs when instructional techniques that are highly effective with inexperienced learners lose their effectiveness and may even have negative consequences when used with more experienced learners. Information in a dual-mode presentation may become redundant when presented to more experienced learners. Kalyuga, Chandler, and Sweller (2000) demonstrated that if experienced learners attend to redundant auditory explanations, learning might be inhibited. In a set of experiments with instructions on using industrial manufacturing machinery, inexperienced learners in a domain clearly benefited most from studying a visually presented diagram combined with simultaneously presented auditory explanations. After additional training, the relative advantage of the narration disappeared whereas the effectiveness of the diagram-only condition increased. When the same students became even more experienced after further intensive training in the subject area, the diagram-only condition was far superior to the diagram with narration condition, reversing the advantage of the dual-mode presentation previously obtained.

The importance of the logic of the relations between auditory and visual information to the modality principle cannot be overemphasised. The modality effect will only be obtained when both the spoken and written information are essential to understanding. If one or other source of information is redundant, the modality principle will not apply. (For examples of dual-mode re-dundancy, see Craig, Gholson & Driscoll, 2002; Kalyuga et al., 1999, 2000, in press; Mayer, Heiser & Lonn, 2001; Moreno & Mayer, 2002.)

The modality effect is especially impor-tant in the context of multimedia learning because the instructional medium involves different presentation modes and sensory modalities. Multimedia instruction is be-coming increasingly popular and findings as-sociated with the modality effect that can be interpreted within a cognitive load frame-work can provide a coherent theoretical base for multimedia investigations and applica-tions. Indeed, in a number of Web-based in-structional studies, Mayer and his colleagues have demonstrated that students performed better on tests of problem-solving trans-fer when scientific explanations were pre-sented as pictures and narration rather than as pictures and on-screen text (Mayer & Moreno, 1998; Moreno & Mayer, 1999; Moreno, Mayer, Spires, & Lester, 2001). Ac-cording to the researchers, such results are consistent with dual information-processing theory. When pictures and words are both presented visually, the visual processor can become overloaded but the auditory pro-cessor is unused. When words are narrated, they can be dealt with in the auditory pro-cessor, thereby leaving the visual processor to deal with the pictures only. Thus, the use of narrated animation reassigns some of the essential processing from the overloaded visual processor to the underloaded audi-tory processor. Unlike the earlier research that used book-based materials, the work of Mayer, Moreno, and their colleagues used on-screen materials.

More recently, Brünken, Steinbacher, Plass, and Leutner (2002) replicated the modality effect in two different multimedia learning environments while using a dual-task approach to measure cognitive load. Learners' performance on a visual secondary reaction time task was taken as a direct mea-sure of the cognitive load induced by mul-timedia instruction. Brünken et al. found evidence that the differences in learning outcome demonstrated by the modality ef-fect are related to different levels of cog-nitive load induced by the different pre-sentation formats of the learning material. Specifically, they found that an emphasis on visual presentation of material resulted in a decrement on a visual secondary task, indi-cating an overload of the visual processor. In further work, Brünken, Plass, and Leutner (2004) again reproduced the modality ef-fect while measuring cognitive load using a dual-task methodology. In this work, the sec-ondary task was auditory instead of visual and there was a decrement in performance on the auditory secondary task when the pri-mary task placed an emphasis on the audi-tory processor.

Conclusions

The modality effect has both theoretical and practical implications. From a theoretical perspective, the results provide further ev-idence that to some extent, effective work-ing memory capacity may be increased and this increase can be used to reduce cognitive load and facilitate learning. From a practi-cal perspective, the results provide a new in-structional procedure. Under split-attention conditions, rather than physically integrat-ing disparate sources of information, learn-ing may be facilitated by presenting a writ-ten source of information in auditory mode. While care must be taken to ensure the au-ditory material is essential and not redun-dant and that the instructional material is sufficiently complex to warrant the use of a cognitive load reducing technique, under appropriate circumstances, the instructional gains can be large.

Until relatively recently, the advantages of multimodality presentation techniques were more theoretical than practical because of the practical difficulties of presenting visual and auditory material. The development of e-learning technologies has altered the prac-tical equation. The modality principle dis-cussed in this chapter provides a cognitive base leading to practical applications for e-learning and multimedia presentations.

Glossary

Auditory working memory or auditory processor: That component of working memory that deals with speech and other auditory information.

Dual-modality instruction: The use of both auditory and visual information under split-attention conditions. Can be contrasted with single modality instruction, normally presented in visual only mode.

Element interactivity: The extent to which elements of information that must be processed interact. If material that must be learned has high element interactivity, elements cannot be processed individually in working memory and so that material will be seen as complex and difficult to understand. (See *intrinsic cognitive load*.)

Integrated instructions: Instructions in which multiple sources of information are physically integrated so that working memory resources do not need to be used for mental integration. Can be contrasted with split-attention instructions.

Intrinsic cognitive load: The cognitive load that is imposed by multiple, interacting elements (see *element interactivity*) that, because they interact, must be processed simultaneously rather than successively in working memory resulting in a heavy load.

Schema: A cognitive construct that schematically organises information for storage in long-term memory. When brought into working memory from long-term memory, a schema allows us to treat multiple elements of information as a single element classified according to the way in which it will be used.

Split-attention instructions: Instructions in which multiple sources of information are not physically integrated so that working memory resources need to be used for mental integration.

Can be contrasted with integrated instructions.

Visual working memory or visual processor: That component of working memory that deals visually with two- or three-dimensional objects.

References

Allport, D. A., Antonis, B., & Reynolds, P. (1972). On the division of attention: A disproof of the single channel hypothesis. *Quarterly Journal of Experimental Psychology, 24*, 225–235.

Baddeley, A. D. (1986). *Working memory*. Oxford, England: Oxford University Press.

Baddeley, A. D. (1992). Working memory. *Science, 255*, 556–559.

Baddeley, A. D. (1999). *Human memory*. Boston: Allyn & Bacon.

Brooks, L. (1967). The suppression of visualization by reading. *Quarterly Journal of Experimental Psychology, 19*, 289–299.

Brünken, R., Plass, J. L., Leutner, D. (2004). Assessment of cognitive load in multimedia learning with dual task methodology: Auditory load and modality effects. *Instructional Science 32*, 115–132.

Brünken, R., Steinbacher, S., Plass, J. L., & Leutner, D. (2002). Assessment of cognitive load in multimedia learning using dual-task methodology. *Experimental Psychology, 49*, 109–119.

Craig, S., Gholson, B., & Driscoll, D. (2002). Animated pedagogical agents in multimedia educational environments: Effects of agent properties, picture features, and redundancy. *Journal of Educational Psychology, 94*, 428–434.

Dennis, I. (1977). Component problems in dichotic listening. *Quarterly Journal of Experimental Psychology, 29*, 437–450.

Frick, R. (1984). Using both an auditory and a visual short-term store to increase digit span. *Memory and Cognition, 12*, 507–514.

Jeung, H., Chandler, P., & Sweller, J. (1997). The role of visual indicators in dual sensory mode instruction. *Educational Psychology, 17*, 329–343.

Kalyuga, S., Chandler, P., & Sweller, J. (1999). Managing split-attention and redundancy in multimedia instruction. *Applied Cognitive Psychology, 13*, 351–371.

Kalyuga, S., Chandler, P., & Sweller, J. (2000). Incorporating learner experience into the design of multimedia instruction. *Journal of Educational Psychology*, 92, 126–136.

Kalyuga, S., Chandler, P., & Sweller, J. (in press). When redundant on-screen text in multimedia technical instruction can interfere with learning. *Human Factors*.

Kolers, P. A. (1979). A pattern-analyzing basis of recognition. In L. S. Cermak & F. I. M. Craiks (Eds.), *Levels of processing in human memory*. Hillsdale, NJ: Lawrence Erlbaum Associates.

Leahy, W., Chandler, P., & Sweller, J. (2003). When auditory presentations should and should not be a component of multimedia instruction. *Applied Cognitive Psychology*, 17, 401–418.

Levin, J., & Divine-Hawkins, P. (1974). Visual imagery as a prose-learning process. *Journal of Reading Behaviour*, 6, 23–30.

Margrain, S. (1967). Short-term memory as a function of input modality. Quarterly *Journal of Experimental Psychology*, 19, 109–114.

Mayer, R. E., Bove, W., Bryman, A., Mars, R., & Tapangco, L. (1996). When less is more: Meaningful learning from visual and verbal summaries of science textbook lessons. *Journal of Educational Psychology*, 88, 64–73.

Mayer, R. E., Heiser, J., & Lonn, S. (2001). Cognitive contraints on multimedia learning: When presenting more material results in less understanding. *Journal of Educational Psychology*, 93, 187–198.

Mayer, R. E., & Moreno, R. (1998). A split-attention effect in multi-media learning: Evidence for dual processing systems in working memory. *Journal of Educational Psychology*, 90, 312–320.

Miller, G. A. (1956). The magical number seven, plus or minus two: Some limits on our capacity for processing information. *Psychological Review*, 63, 81–97.

Moreno, R., & Mayer, R. E. (1999). Cognitive principles of multimedia learning: The role of modality and contiguity. *Journal of Educational Psychology*, 91, 358–368.

Moreno, R., & Mayer, R. E. (2002). Learning science in virtual reality multimedia environments: Role of methods and media. *Journal of Educational Psychology*, 94, 598–610.

Moreno, R., Mayer, R. E., Spires, H. A., & Lester, J. C. (2001). The case for social agency in computer-based multimedia learning: Do students learn more deeply when they interact with animated pedagogical agents? *Cognition and Instruction*, 19, 177–214.

Mousavi, S., Low, R., & Sweller, J. (1995). Reducing cognitive load by mixing auditory and visual presentation modes. *Journal of Educational Psychology*, 87, 319–334.

Murdock, B. B., Jr. (1971). Four-channel effects in short-term memory. *Psychonomic Science*, 24, 197–198.

Mwangi, W., & Sweller, J. (1998). Learning to solve compare word problems: The effect of example format and generating self-explanations. *Cognition and Instruction*, 16, 173–199.

Paas, F., Renkl, A., & Sweller, J. (2003). Cognitive load theory and instructional design: Recent developments. *Educational Psychologist*, 38, 1–4.

Paas, F., & Van Merriënboer, J. (1993). The efficiency of instructional conditions: An approach to combine mental-effort and performance measures. *Human Factors*, 35, 737–743.

Penney, C. (1980). Order of report in bisensory verbal short-term memory. *Canadian Journal of Psychology*, 34, 190–195.

Penney, C. (1989). Modality effects and the structure of short-term verbal memory. *Memory and Cognition*, 17, 398–422.

Penney, C., & Butt, A. (1986). Within- and between-modality associations in probed recall: A test of the separate streams hypothesis. *Canadian Journal of Psychology*, 40, 1–11.

Rollins, H. A., & Hendricks, R. (1980). Processing of words presented simultaneously to eye and ear. *Journal of Experimental Psychology: Human Perception and Performance*, 6, 99–109.

Rollins, H. A., & Thibadeau, R. (1973). The effects of auditory shadowing on recognition of information received visually. *Memory and Cognition*, 1, 164–168.

Schneider, W., & Detweiler, M. (1987). A connectionist/control architecture for working memory. In G. H. Bower (Ed.), *The psychology of learning and motivation*. (Vol. 21, pp. 53–119). New York: Academic Press.

Shaffer, L. H. (1975). Multiple attention in continuous verbal tasks. In P. M. A. Rabbitt & S. Dornic (Eds.), *Attention and performance V* (pp. 157–167). London: Academic Press.

Spelke, E., Hirst, W., & Neisser, U. (1976). Skills of divided attention. *Cognition*, 4, 215–230.

Sweller, J., Chandler, P., Tierney, P., & Cooper, M. (1990). Cognitive load as a factor in the structuring of technical material. *Journal of Experimental Psychology: General, 119*, 176–192.

Sweller, J., van Merriënboer, J., & Paas, F. (1998). Cognitive architecture and instructional design. *Educational Psychology Review, 10*, 251–296.

Tarmizi, R., & Sweller, J. (1988). Guidance during mathematical problem solving. *Journal of Educational Psychology, 80*, 424–436.

Tindall-Ford, S., Chandler, P., & Sweller, J. (1997). When two sensory modes are better than one. *Journal of Experimental Psychology: Applied, 3*, 257–287.

Treisman, A. M., & Davies, A. (1973). Divided attention to ear and eye. In S. Kornblum (Ed.), *Attention and performance IV* (pp. 101–117). New York: Academic Press.

Ward, M., & Sweller, J. (1990). Structuring effective worked examples. *Cognition and Instruction, 7*, 1–39.

CHAPTER 10

The Redundancy Principle in Multimedia Learning

John Sweller

University of New South Wales

Abstract

The *redundancy principle* suggests that redundant material interferes with rather than facilitates learning. Redundancy occurs when the same information is presented in multiple forms or is unnecessarily elaborated. In this chapter, the long, but until recently unknown, history of the principle is traced. In addition, an explanation of the principle using cognitive load theory is provided. The theory suggests that coordinating redundant information with essential information increases working memory load, which interferes with the transfer of information to long-term memory. Eliminating redundant information eliminates the requirement to coordinate multiple sources of information. Accordingly, instructional designs that eliminate redundant material can be superior to those that include redundancy.

Introduction

The history of the redundancy effect or principle is a history of academic amnesia.

The effect has been discovered, forgotten, and rediscovered many times over many decades. This unusual history probably has two related causes: first, the effect is seen as counterintuitive by many researchers and practitioners and second, until recently, there has not been a clear theoretical explanation to place it into context. As a consequence of these two factors, demonstrations of the effect have tended to be treated as isolated peculiarities unconnected to any mainstream work. Memories of each demonstration have faded with the passage of time until the next demonstration has appeared. Worse, each demonstration has tended to be unconnected to the previous one. Hopefully, current explanations of the effect can alter this lamentable state of affairs.

What Is the Redundancy Principle?

The redundancy effect occurs when additional information presented to learners results in learning decrements compared to the presentation of less information. The additional information, rather than having positive effects on learning has negative effects and in that sense, is redundant. There are two variations of the effect: (1) Identical information may be presented to learners in two or more different forms or media, such as pictures and words or words in both auditory and written form. If one of these forms or media is redundant then the elimination of that form may result in enhanced learning resulting in the redundancy effect. (It should be noted that Mayer, 2001, uses the term *redundancy effect* in a more limited sense to refer only to situations in which graphics with spoken text result in better learning than graphics with spoken text and printed text.) (2) In an attempt to enhance or elaborate information, additional information may be presented. A full text may be compared with a reduced or summarised text, for example. If the additional explanations or elaborations are redundant then the exclusion of that additional information may enhance learning providing another example of the effect. (Note that Mayer, 2001, uses the term *coherence effect* to refer to this situation.)

It should be noted that there is considerable overlap between these two categories in that the same information presented in a different medium may be essentially an elaboration. Nevertheless, the distinction is real in that some elaborations use the same medium while others use different media. In either case, the effect is identical: redundant information can interfere with learning.

Cognitive load theory (chapter 2) has been used to explain the effect. Because a failure to provide a coherent theoretical explanation of the effect permitting it to be related to other instructional design phenomena may have been a major reason for its spasmodic appearance and disappearance in the literature, an explanation of the effect in cognitive load theory terms will be presented next.

Cognitive Load Theory and the Redundancy Principle

As indicated in chapter 2, cognitive load theory assumes that the function of instruction is to alter the contents of long-term memory but the limitations of working memory when dealing with novel information can interfere with or prevent the realisation of this goal. Instruction should be designed to take into account the basic characteristics of human cognitive architecture and failure to consider these characteristics will result in ineffective or randomly effective instructional designs. The well-known characteristics of working memory are central to cognitive load theory. When dealing with novel information, working memory is severely limited with respect to both capacity and duration. Only a few items of novel information can be processed in working memory at any given time and novel information can be held in working memory for no more than a few seconds unless it is refreshed by rehearsal. These characteristics of working memory only apply to novel information. Established information held in long-term memory has no known capacity nor duration limits when brought into working memory.

It follows from these characteristics of human cognitive architecture that novel information should be presented in a manner that reduces an unnecessary working memory load. Redundancy in instruction provides an example of the violation of this principle. Consider the following example. Assume learners are presented with some textual material. Assume further that it is being presented in a multimedia format and so identical text is presented in both written and spoken form. Based on cognitive load theory, the following processes can be expected to occur. If learners are attending to both the written and spoken text, they must ensure that both forms are closely coordinated because if learners' reading of the text is out of phase with the speaker, the information will become disjointed and probably unintelligible. Working memory resources will be required to coordinate the two sources of information and those resources will not be available for learning. In contrast, if either spoken or written text only is provided, the requirement to coordinate both sources is eliminated freeing cognitive resources for learning. The effect should be improved learning performance for a written or spoken presentation alone rather than a simultaneous presentation of both.

As discussed in the following text, precisely this effect has been obtained on several occasions in several laboratories. For present purposes, the general theoretical reasons need to be considered. The example given falls into the first category of redundancy provided in the preceding text in which identical information is presented in multiple forms. The cognitive load theory explanation can be applied in general terms to all forms of redundancy including other examples of identical information presented in multiple forms and to redundancy consisting of additional, explanatory information. Any redundant information, whatever its form, must be coordinated with essential information. The act of processing redundant information always requires working memory resources and those resources are accordingly, unavailable for learning. A history of the redundancy effect will be presented in the following sections. That history will provide examples of how commonly used instructional procedures frequently incorporate redundancy. The relevant experiments demonstrate the negative consequences of that redundancy.

Experimental Evidence for the Redundancy Principle

Experimental evidence for the redundancy effect is obtained when the elimination of information from instructional material results in improved learning. A typical experiment might consist of two conditions. One condition includes all of the material that experimental participants are required to learn while the other condition consists of a reduced set of the material that a different group of participants must learn. If learners presented the reduced set perform at a higher level on a subsequent test than learners presented the full set, then the redundancy effect has been obtained.

Miller (1937) may have been the first to use this experimental design to demonstrate the redundancy effect. (It should be noted that the term *redundancy effect* was not used until Chandler & Sweller, 1991.) Miller studied young children learning how to read. In the redundant condition she used the procedure, still commonly used, of presenting the children with a written noun accompanied by an appropriate picture. Thus, the word *cow* was presented with a picture of a cow. The word *cow* was simultaneously spoken. The reduced, nonredundant condition was identical except that the picture of the cow was eliminated. Performance on the subsequent reading test was better for the condition without the pictures.

Why are pictures redundant when learning how to read? A major task when learning to read is to identify the combination of letters that go to make up the relevant word. Those letters and their combinations are complex for novice readers and are likely to impose a working memory strain. Any additional load may easily overburden working memory. Pictures are very likely to capture attentional (or working memory) resources. The more the children look at a picture, the fewer resources are available for looking at and learning the elements that go to make up the written word. Learning the elements that constitute the written word is the sole point of the exercise. Processing the picture requires resources that otherwise could be used to learn to read the word. The picture is redundant because it interferes with what needs to be learned.

Since Miller's (1937) demonstration, the picture/word effect has been replicated frequently (e.g., Solman, Singh, & Kehoe, 1992). Nevertheless, because it is counterintuitive, it is probably true to say that most reading texts used by teachers still employ pictures.

Reder and Anderson (1980, 1982) provided another demonstration of the redundancy effect. In a series of 10 experiments, under one of the conditions, they presented participants with chapters taken from commonly used texts in a variety of areas such as geography, linguistics, economics, or history.

In the other condition, the texts were summarised with summaries typically being about 20% of the length of the original texts. Over all experiments, the summaries were consistently superior over a variety of test questions including direct questions on the text, questions requiring inferences, and transfer questions. Furthermore, the superiority was maintained for periods up to 12 months. As the authors indicated (Reder & Anderson, 1982, p. 97) "To our surprise, all...experiments indicated that subjects learn information better when they read an abridged or summarized version of the original text than when they read the original chapter." While counterintuitive, the redundancy effect can be very robust.

Reder and Anderson did not interpret their findings as an example of the redundancy effect (it had not been described as an effect in the early 1980s) nor explain their results in terms of working memory limitations. A cognitive load theory explanation of their results assumes that if an appropriately written text provides all of the points that a learner requires, any elaboration of those points requires additional processing in working memory. A main point and its elaboration need to be related and coordinated. If the main point is intelligible to begin with, the act of coordinating it with its elaboration has no function. It requires cognitive resources that consequently are unavailable for learning. Unnecessary elaborations do not have a neutral or positive effect, they have a negative effect.

The next example of the redundancy effect came from Carroll and his co-workers (Carroll, 1990; Carroll, Smith-Kerker, Ford, & Mazur-Rimetz, 1987; see also Lazonder & Van der Meij, 1993) who were working on what they termed the *minimal manual*. They were concerned with constructing manuals for computer applications. Over several experiments, identical results to those of Reder and Anderson were obtained. Computer manuals that minimised the explanatory text proved superior to more conventional manuals.

Mayer, Bove, Bryman, Mars, and Tapangco (1996) obtained additional evidence for summary/full-text redundancy.

They gave students information concerning lightning formation and found that a summary with illustrations and captions was superior to a full-text version. Elimination of the illustrations and captions or the addition of text to the summary reduced or eliminated its effectiveness.

When Paul Chandler and I began our work on the redundancy effect in the early 1990s (Chandler & Sweller, 1991), we were oblivious to all of the earlier work. It had not been systematised and the various research streams were not related to each other. Despite the previously discussed work, the general assumption of the field was that the presentation of the same information in multiple formats would at worst, have neutral effects but would never have negative effects.

The impetus for Chandler and Sweller's (1991) work was not the more closely related work discussed previously but rather, the split-attention effect (see chapter 8). The split-attention effect occurs when multiple sources of information that must be integrated in order to be intelligible, are presented as separate entities. When learners must split their attention between those entities, working memory load is increased compared to a presentation in which they are integrated into a single entity resulting in reduced learning.

Most of the work on the split-attention effect had been conducted using diagrams and their associated text. A geometry worked example consisting of a diagram and its associated statements provides a common example, but there are many others. It was assumed that the common split-attention effect findings of superior learning following the integration of text into the relevant diagram was universal but we were faced with a sudden conundrum. Using some categories of instructional material, the normal, very strong split-attention effect was obtained with integrated materials far superior to their split-attention counterparts. Using other types of material, we obtained no effect, with the split-attention format proving no worse than the integrated format. There seemed no obvious reason for the failure to find a split-attention effect.

The solution to the contradiction could be found in the logical relation between the diagram and text. Consider a geometry worked example consisting of a diagram and its text. The diagram does not provide a solution to the problem. The text does provide a solution but is unintelligible without the diagram. (A statement such as "Angle ABC = Angle XYZ cannot be interpreted without reference to an appropriate diagram.") Both the diagram and text are essential for understanding. In contrast, consider instruction on the flow of blood in the heart, lungs, and body. Frequently, it will consist of a diagram of the heart, lungs, and body with arrows indicating the direction of blood flow in the veins and arteries. In addition, textual material may consist of statements such as, "The blood entering the aorta is pumped back into the body" or, "Blood from the lungs flows into the left atrium." In contrast to the geometry example, the diagram is self-contained and intelligible. It may show, through arrows and labelling, that blood entering the aorta is pumped back into the body and that blood from the lungs flows into the left atrium. The text merely repeats the same information in a different form. It is redundant.

Assume that such redundant text is integrated with the diagram by being placed at appropriate locations on the diagram. The text is now not only redundant, it is also very difficult to avoid. Anyone looking at the diagram is very likely to read the text as well. In contrast, if the text is below or next to the diagram rather than integrated with the diagram, it is much easier to ignore. Because the best strategy when faced with redundant material is to ignore it, we might expect that learners presented integrated diagrams and text will perform no better than learners presented the same materials in nonintegrated form. That result of no difference between split-attention and integrated material was obtained by Chandler and Sweller (1991) when presenting learners with instructional material on the flow of blood in the heart, lungs, and body. In fact, the best condition was one in which the textual material, rather than being integrated with the diagram, was eliminated entirely. Redundant instructional material should be eliminated.

At the time of writing Chandler and Sweller (1991), we thought we had discovered the redundancy effect. A few months later (see Sweller & Chandler, 1991) we discovered some of its history. Because the effect can be obtained so easily, it is likely that there are other cases prior to 1991 that have not, as yet, been identified as examples of the redundancy effect.

Since 1991 the effect has been demonstrated in a variety of contexts. It is not just diagrams and redundant text that can be used to demonstrate the redundancy effect. While diagrams are frequently more intelligible than the equivalent text (e.g., Larkin and Simon, 1987) rendering the text redundant, any one of diagrams, the presence of equipment, or auditory input, as well as text, may be redundant. What is redundant depends on what is being taught. These forms of redundancy will be discussed in the following text.

Bobis, Sweller, and Cooper (1993) demonstrated textual redundancy teaching elementary school children basic geometry using a paper-folding task. They found that textual explanations added to diagrammatic depictions of the task resulted in decrements rather than increments in test performance. The text was redundant. In addition, in another experiment, they found that adding additional diagrams also had a negative effect. Instead of providing a single set of diagrams of the paper-folding task, multiple sets providing different perspectives of the same task were provided. In order to process the multiple sets, they needed to be mentally coordinated. The additional diagrammatic information, rather than being useful, was cognitively demanding and redundant. The task could be understood without the additional diagrams. On subsequent tests, the results indicated better performance under the nonredundant condition.

Sweller and Chandler (1994) and Chandler and Sweller (1996) tested the hypothesis that when learning to use a computer application, the presence of the computer and the act of working on the computer would interfere with the intellectual activities required to use the application. In other words, it was suggested that the computer and the work done on the computer were redundant. Under one condition, learners were presented a computer manual that included text integrated with diagrams of the keyboard and screen but did not have access to a computer to physically attempt the procedures described. Under the other condition, both the manual and computer were available. It was hypothesised that physically working the machinery was largely irrelevant to the task of understanding and learning how to use the program but would require working memory resources that consequently would be unavailable for the real task – assimilating the appropriate procedures into long-term memory. The results supported the hypothesis. Over several experiments, learners who had learned with the assistance of the computer performed more poorly on subsequent tests than learners who had never practiced using the computer. The tests were practical tests of ability to use the computer application. It should also be noted that these results were only obtainable for high element interactivity material that imposed a high intrinsic cognitive load (see chapter 2) and that Chandler and Sweller (1996) used secondary task analyses to confirm that the results were due to cognitive load rather than other factors.

Kalyuga, Chandler, and Sweller (1999) provided evidence of written/spoken text redundancy. They demonstrated the modality effect (see chapter 9) by finding that a diagram and written text, under split-attention conditions, was worse than the same diagram and spoken text. The advantage disappeared using a diagram and written text plus spoken text. Having identical written and spoken text was redundant and interfered with learning. This result has now been obtained on many occasions. Kalyuga et al. (2000) again demonstrated that the replacement of written text associated with a diagram by auditory text resulted in superior learning but the addition of auditory text eliminated any advantage. This finding was only obtained with novices. More expert learners learned best with a diagram alone demonstrating the expertise reversal effect (see chapter 21 and the following text).

Kalyuga et al. (in press) demonstrated that nonconcurrent presentation of identical spoken and written text was superior to concurrent presentation. Nonconcurrent presentation is essentially revision and should not impose a working memory load. Concurrent presentation requires redundant coordination between the two modalities, which overloads working memory.

Mayer and his associates have conducted a substantial series of studies on written/spoken redundancy. Mayer, Heiser, and Lonn (2001) had learners view an animation while listening to concurrent spoken text. They found that additional, concurrent written text that either summarised or duplicated the spoken text, interfered with learning. The animation required visual-processing resources and adding written text both overloaded the visual processor and was redundant. Moreno and Mayer (2002a) compared spoken text, written text, and concurrent spoken and written text in a virtual reality environment. They found written text inferior to both spoken text and a combination of written and spoken text on both retention and transfer items but there was no difference between spoken and combined spoken/written texts. Thus while written text in a spoken/written combination was redundant compared to spoken text alone, written text in the spoken/written combination was not redundant compared to spoken text alone. Moreno and Mayer attributed this failure to find redundancy to the virtual reality environment. They suggested that students are unlikely to read an unnecessary text box when encompassed by such an environment, eliminating any difference between spoken and combined spoken/written conditions. A similar result under similar conditions was obtained by Craig, Gholson, and Driscoll (2002) providing strong replicative evidence for this finding. Nevertheless, it needs to be noted that Moreno and Mayer (2002b) obtained a reverse redundancy effect with concurrent spoken and written text superior to spoken text alone. This finding seems to be the only example of a reverse redundancy effect under instructional conditions. It may be due to the nature of the materials used by Moreno and Mayer. Those materials included no graphical material and may have been readily understood by learners resulting in a reduced intrinsic cognitive load associated with the visual channel. If intrinsic cognitive load is low, extraneous cognitive load tends to be irrelevant.

The Centrality of the Redundancy Effect to the Expertise Reversal Effect

The expertise reversal effect (chapter 21) occurs when an instructional technique that is relatively effective compared to an alternative when dealing with novices, loses its advantage and may even become less effective than the alternative when levels of expertise increase. For example, explanatory text is better presented integrated with a diagram rather than in split-attention format (chapter 8) but this advantage may disappear or reverse as expertise increases. Similarly, it may be advantageous for novices to learn with many worked examples rather than attempting to learn by solving the equivalent problems (chapter 15) but as levels of expertise increase, this advantage too may disappear or reverse with problem solving proving superior to studying worked examples.

The redundancy effect provides a direct cause of most (though not all) reversals in the effectiveness of instructional techniques. For novices, explanatory material may be essential. Such explanatory material may consist of, for example, textual material added to a diagram or demonstrations of the solution to a problem in the case of a worked example. In isolation, without additional explanatory material, the diagram may be unintelligible or the problem insoluble unless a worked example is provided. As levels of expertise increase, these additional explanations are likely to become unnecessary and so redundant. Textual additions to diagrams, essential for novices to understand the diagram and so best presented in integrated rather than split-attention format, become redundant for more advanced study and so interfere with rather than facilitate learning. The diagrams may be best presented in isolation rather than with attendant text. When presented to more knowledgeable learners, worked examples demonstrating problem solutions may take longer to process and require more cognitive resources than solving a problem oneself. Thus, material that may be essential for novices may become redundant as expertise increases resulting in the expertise reversal effect. In this sense, the redundancy effect is a precursor of and so essential to an understanding of many examples of the expertise reversal effect.

Instructional Implications of the Redundancy Principle

In one sense, the instructional implications that flow from the redundancy principle are straightforward: eliminate all redundant materials presented to learners and all redundant activity that instruction may encourage learners to engage in. In another sense, while this principle answers questions that otherwise would be unanswerable and, indeed, remained unanswerable for decades, it also raises its own questions. While we now know why certain instructional procedures such as removing seemingly innocuous material can facilitate learning, the redundancy principle alone does not indicate precisely what material may or may not be redundant. Information that is redundant under one set of circumstances is essential under another, information that is redundant for one person may be essential for another. We cannot look at a set of instructional materials and irrespective of context, indicate whether they do or do not contain redundant information. In other words, the redundancy principle does not lead to a simple, universally applicable rule.

If the redundancy principle does not lead to a simple rule, how can it be applied? The answer lies in cognitive load theory. The redundancy principle can be explained by cognitive load theory and should always be considered in conjunction with the theory. Cognitive load theory can be used readily to indicate when and how the principle should be applied. It can be used to provide guidance on what material is likely to be redundant and the conditions that determine redundancy.

For example, when determining whether text should be added to a diagram, an instructional designer needs to consider several factors. Is the diagram intelligible in isolation? If so, the text may be redundant. Does the text add essential information? If so it is not redundant and should be retained. Is the text complex in the sense that to understand one element one must simultaneously consider many other elements (high element interactivity)? If so, it almost certainly should not be presented with the diagram unless it is quite unavoidable. If the diagram is high in element interactivity, contains all required information, and so is potentially intelligible in isolation, no additional text should be added whether high or low in element interactivity. For such information, any additional material runs the risk of overloading working memory. Lastly, all decisions on whether information is intelligible in its own right and is high in element interactivity must be made from the learner's point of view. Information that is intelligible in its own right for more expert learners who do not require additional explanatory material may be anything but intelligible to novices who do require additional material. Similarly, information that is high in element interactivity for novices and so has cognitive load implications may be low in element interactivity for more expert learners who have schemas incorporating the interacting elements within them. Those schemas will ensure the material does not overload working memory. Thus, whether or not additional material is redundant can be determined by considering the cognitive load implications of that material.

There is one other point that needs to be made concerning the conditions under which instructional information may or may not be redundant. Because, as indicated previously, the presentation of the same material in a different form is frequently redundant, it is sometimes assumed that an advocate of the elimination of redundant material subscribes to the view that revising newly learned material is unnecessary. Revision is not a redundant activity. Furthermore, presenting the same material in multiple forms that require coordination, is not revision. Most learners must revise newly learned, complex information. Unless the original presentation of the material was badly flawed, there is no need to alter the format of the material for revision. Gratuitous format alterations are merely likely to increase extraneous cognitive load as learners unnecessarily attempt to relate the multiple formats. The only justification for such format changes is if learners need to become familiar with multiple formats because in the area of interest, they are likely to encounter the same information presented in several different, but standard forms. Under those conditions, teaching learners how to deal with multiple forms of the same material becomes important.

Conclusions

The redundancy principle is often seen as counterintuitive. It is easy to assume that presenting the same information in multiple forms or presenting additional explanatory information could be advantageous and at worst, will be neutral. Such an assumption ignores what we now know of human cognitive architecture. Information must be processed by working memory and when dealing with novel information, working memory is extremely limited. Requiring learners to unnecessarily coordinate and relate multiple forms of the same information or process unnecessary explanatory information imposes an extraneous cognitive load that interferes with learning.

There is now overwhelming evidence stretching over decades from a very large number of controlled experiments that redundant information is not neutral. Those experiments demonstrate in a wide variety of fields and under a wide variety of conditions that learning is facilitated by the removal of redundant information. The instructional implications are clear-cut: Unless learners need to be taught to recognise particular information in multiple forms, information should be presented in a single form only, i.e., with all other versions and all unnecessary explanation eliminated. Multiple versions of the same information or unnecessary explanations do not compensate for an inadequate instructional design. Rather, they compound design problems.

Glossary

> *Redundancy principle*: Instructions that present the same information in different forms or with unnecessary explanatory material increase extraneous cognitive load that interferes with learning.

References

Bobis, J., Sweller, J., & Cooper, M. (1993). Cognitive load effects in a primary school geometry task. *Learning and Instruction, 3*, 1–21.

Carroll, J. M. (1990). *The Nurnberg funnel: Designing minimalist instruction for practical computer skill.* Cambridge, MA: MIT Press.

Carroll, J. M., Smith-Kerker, P., Ford, J., & Mazur-Rimetz, S. (1987). The minimal manual. *Human-Computer Interaction, 3*, 123–153.

Chandler, P., & Sweller, J. (1991). Cognitive load theory and the format of instruction. *Cognition and Instruction, 8*, 293–332.

Chandler, P., & Sweller, J. (1996). Cognitive load while learning to use a computer program. *Applied Cognitive Psychology, 10*, 151–170.

Craig, S., Gholson, B., & Driscoll, D. (2002). Animated pedagogical agents in multimedia educational environments: Effects of agent properties, picture features, and redundancy. *Journal of Educational Psychology, 94*, 428–434.

Kalyuga, S., Chandler, P., & Sweller, J. (1999). Managing split-attention and redundancy in multimedia instruction. *Applied Cognitive Psychology, 13*, 351–371.

Kalyuga, S., Chandler, P., & Sweller, J. (2000). Incorporating learner experience into the design of multimedia instruction. *Journal of Educational Psychology, 92*, 126–136.

Kalyuga, S., Chandler, P., & Sweller, J. (in press). When redundant on-screen text in multimedia technical instruction can interfere with learning. *Human Factors.*

Larkin, J., & Simon, H. (1987). Why a diagram is (sometimes) worth a thousand words. *Cognitive Science, 11*, 65–69.

Lazonder, A., & Van der Meij, H. (1993). The minimal manual: Is less really more? *International Journal of Man-Machine Studies, 39*, 729–752.

Mayer, R. E. (2001). *Multimedia learning.* New York: Cambridge University Press.

Mayer, R., Bove, W., Bryman, A., Mars, R., & Tapangco, L. (1996). When less is more: Meaningful learning from visual and verbal summaries of science textbook lessons. *Journal of Educational Psychology, 88*, 64–73.

Mayer, R., Heiser, J., & Lonn, S. (2001). Cognitive constraints on multimedia learning: When presenting more material results in less understanding. *Journal of Educational Psychology, 93*, 187–198.

Miller, W. (1937). The picture crutch in reading. *Elementary English Review, 14*, 263–264.

Moreno, R., & Mayer, R. (2002a). Learning science in virtual reality multimedia environments: Role of methods and media. *Journal of Educational Psychology, 94*, 598–610.

Moreno, R., & Mayer, R. (2002b). Verbal redundancy in multimedia learning: When reading helps listening. *Journal of Educational Psychology, 94*, 156–163.

Reder, L., & Anderson, J. R. (1980). A comparison of texts and their summaries: Memorial consequences. *Journal of Verbal Learning and Verbal Behavior, 19*, 121–134.

Reder, L., & Anderson, J. R. (1982). Effects of spacing and embellishment on memory for main points of a text. *Memory and Cognition, 10*, 97–102.

Solman, R., Singh, N., & Kehoe, E. J. (1992). Pictures block the learning of sight words. *Educational Psychology, 12*, 143–153.

Sweller, J., & Chandler, P. (1991). Evidence for cognitive load theory. *Cognition and Instruction, 8*, 351–362.

Sweller, J., & Chandler, P. (1994) Why some material is difficult to learn. *Cognition and Instruction, 12*, 185–233.

CHAPTER 11

Principles for Managing Essential Processing in Multimedia Learning: Segmenting, Pretraining, and Modality Principles

Richard E. Mayer

University of California, Santa Barbara

Abstract

When a concise narrated animation containing complicated material is presented at a fast rate, the result can be a form of cognitive overload called *essential overload*. *Essential overload* occurs when the amount of essential cognitive processing (similar to intrinsic cognitive load) required to understand the multimedia instructional message exceeds the learner's cognitive capacity. Three multimedia design methods intended to minimize essential overload are the segmenting, pretraining, and modality principles. The segmenting principle is that people learn more deeply when a multimedia message is presented in learner-paced segments rather than as a continuous unit. This principle was supported in three out of three experimental tests, yielding a median effect size of 0.98. The pretraining principle is that people learn more deeply from a multimedia message when they know the names and characteristics of the main concepts. This principle was supported in seven out of seven experimental tests, yielding a median effect size of 0.92. The modality principle is that peo-ple learn more deeply from a multimedia message when the words are spoken rather than printed. This principle was supported in 21 out of 21 experimental tests, yielding a median effect size of 0.97.

What Are the Segmenting, Pretraining, and Modality Principles?

Definitions

Consider a multimedia learning situation in which too much essential information is presented at too fast a rate for you to adequately process. A *concise narrated animation* contains *essential material* – needed for understanding the lesson – but does not contain *extraneous material* – material not needed for understanding the lesson. For example, when a concise narrated animation containing complicated material is presented at a fast rate, the result can be a form of cognitive overload called *essential overload*. *Essential overload* occurs when the amount of essential cognitive processing required by the multimedia instructional message exceeds the learner's cognitive capacity. *Essential processing* (similar to Sweller's (1999) *intrinsic cognitive load*) refers to cognitive processing – such as selecting relevant words and images, and initial organizing and integrating of selected words and images (as described in chapter 3) – required to make sense out of the essential material.[1] *Cognitive capacity* refers to the total amount of processing that can be supported by both the auditory and visual channels of the learner's working memory at any one time. *Essential material* refers to the words and pictures needed to achieve the instructional objective, such as understanding how a lightning storm develops.

The goal of this chapter is to examine the research evidence concerning three principles for multimedia design aimed at minimizing the effects of essential overload – segmenting, pretraining, and modality principles. The segmenting principle is that people learn more deeply when a multimedia message is presented in user-paced segments rather than as a continuous unit. The pretraining principle is that people learn more deeply from a multimedia message when they know the names and characteristics of the main concepts. The modality principle is that people learn more deeply from a multimedia message when the words are spoken rather than printed.

Theory

A major challenge for instructional designers is to create instructional messages that are sensitive to the characteristics of the human information-processing system. In particular, the cognitive theory of multimedia learning summarized in Figure 3.2 of chapter 3 shows that much of the cognitive processing for meaningful learning occurs within working memory. According to the cognitive theory of multimedia learning (CTML), the visual/pictorial and auditory/verbal channels in working memory are extremely limited so that only a few items can be held or manipulated in each channel at any one time.

When an instructional message – such as a narrated animation – contains a lot of essential material presented at a rapid rate, the cognitive capacity of the information-processing system is easily overloaded – a situation we call *essential overload*. Carrying out cognitive processing takes time, but a fast-paced presentation that requires a lot of mental model building may not allow enough time. As a result, the learner may not be able to engage in all of the cognitive processing needed for making sense of the presented material, so full understanding may not be achieved (Mayer, 2001; Mayer & Moreno, 2003).

Table 11.1 presents two overload scenarios, each involving a form of essential overload (Mayer & Moreno, 2003). In the first scenario (called *type 1 essential overload*), both channels are overloaded by essential processing demands (or intrinsic cognitive load). This overload scenario can occur when a narrated animation concerning a complex topic is presented at a fast pace. Two load-reducing methods are *segmenting* and *pretraining*, both of which are explored in this chapter. The theoretical rationale for segmenting is that it slows the pace of presentation, thereby enabling the learner to carry out essential processing. The theoretical rationale for pretraining is that it equips the learner with prior knowledge (similar to Sweller's (1999) *schemas*) that the learner can use to process the subsequent narrated animation with less cognitive effort. Thus, segmenting gives the learners the time they need to carry out essential processing whereas pretraining reduces the amount of essential processing that is required.

In the second overload scenario (called *type 2 essential overload*), the visual channel is overloaded by essential processing demands.[2] This overload scenario can occur when a lesson with animation and concurrent on-screen text (or with static diagrams and printed text) is presented at a fast pace. A load-reducing method is to off-load the verbal processing from the visual channel to the auditory channel by presenting the

Table 11.1. Load-Reduction Methods for Two Overload Scenarios

---

Type 1 essential overload: Essential processing (in both channels) > cognitive capacity

---

Definition: Both channels are overloaded by essential processing demands (or intrinsic cognitive load). For example, a narrated animation on a complex topic is presented at a fast pace.
Load-reducing methods:
  Segmenting: Allow time between successive bite-size segments. For example, present narrated animation in learner-controlled segments rather than as a continuous unit.
  Pretraining: Provide pretraining in the names and characteristics of components. For example, present narrated animation after pretraining in the names and characteristics of components rather than without pretraining.

Type 2 essential overload: Essential processing in visual channel > cognitive capacity

---

Definition: Visual channel is overloaded by essential processing demands (or intrinsic cognitive load). For example, animation with concurrent on-screen text is presented at a fast pace.
Load-reducing method:
  Modality: Off-load some essential processing from the visual channel to the auditory channel. For example, present words as narration rather than animation.

---

words as narration rather than as on-screen text. This approach is also examined in chapter 8 on the modality principle, and only briefly reviewed in this chapter.[3]

What Are Examples of the Segmenting, Pretraining, and Modality Principles?

How can we create multimedia instructional messages – particularly narrated animations – so that they do not create essential overload? In other words, what can we do to a multimedia instructional message to reduce the amount of essential cognitive processing that is required to take place at any one time? In this chapter, I explore three techniques for reducing essential overload – segmenting techniques, pretraining techniques, and modality techniques.

Segmenting Techniques

Let's begin with a narrated animation such as a 140-second narrated animation explaining the steps in the formation of lightning. Frames from the narrated animation are shown in Figure 3.1 of chapter 3. The explanation is complex, consisting of more

than a dozen steps and including more than a dozen interacting elements. Students must focus on the key words and images (such as moist cool air coming into contact with a warm surface), must note how a state change in one element causes another change (such as noting that the air rises when it becomes heated), and must relate the events to prior knowledge (such as knowing that heat causes a gas to expand and thereby become relatively lighter). Many students–particularly those with low prior knowledge – may have difficulty keeping up with the pace of the presentation so they are not able to engage in all of the needed processing.

One solution to this essential overload problem is to allow the learner to control the pace of presentation. For example, we can break the 140-second narrated animation on lightning into 16 segments, each lasting about 10 seconds and consisting of a sentence or two. Table 11.2 shows how we can break the script of the lightning lesson into 16 segments. Further, we can put a *Continue* button in the lower right corner of the screen that appears at the end of each segment. Figure 11.1 shows how we can add a *Continue* button in the lower-right portion of the screen at the end of an animation segment. The learner can use the mouse

Table 11.2. *How to Break the Lightning Script into 16 Segments*

1. Cool moist air moves over a warmer surface and becomes heated.
2. Warmed moist air near the earth's surface rises rapidly.
3. As the air in this updraft cools, water vapor condenses into water droplets and forms a cloud.
4. The cloud's top extends above the freezing level, so the upper portion of the cloud is composed of tiny ice crystals.
5. Eventually, the water droplets and ice crystals become too large to be suspended by updrafts.
6. As raindrops and ice crystals fall through the cloud, they drag some of the air in the cloud downward, producing downdrafts.
7. When downdrafts strike the ground, they spread out in all directions, producing the gusts of cool wind people feel just before the start of the rain.
8. Within the cloud the rising and falling air currents cause electrical charges to build.
9. The charge results from the collision of the cloud's rising water droplets against heavier, falling pieces of ice.
10. The negatively charged particles fall to the bottom of the cloud, and most of the positively charged particles rise to the top.
11. A stepped leader of negative charges moves downward in a series of steps. It nears the ground.
12. A positively charged leader travels up from objects such as trees and buildings.
13. The two leaders generally meet about 165 feet above the ground.
14. Negatively charged particles then rush from the cloud to the ground along the path created by the leaders. It is not very bright.
15. As the leader stroke nears the ground, it induces an opposite charge, so positively charged particles from the ground rush upward along the same path.
16. The upward motion of the current is the return stroke. It produces the bright light that people notice as a flash of lightning.

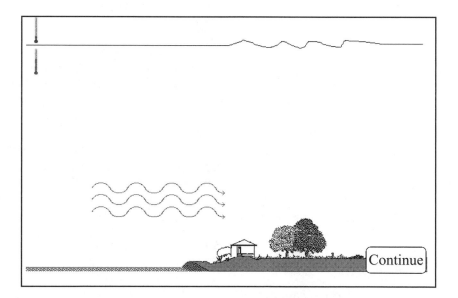

"Cool moist air moves over a warmer surface and becomes heated."

Figure 11.1. A frame from the lightning lesson with a Continue button in the lower right corner.

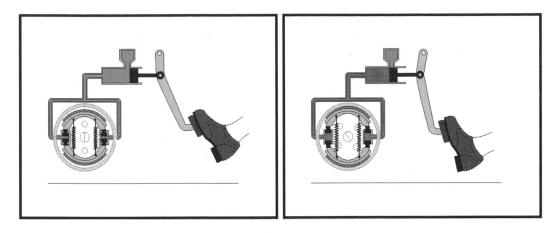

When the driver steps on the car's brake pedal, a piston moves forward inside the master cylinder.
The piston forces brake fluid out of the master cylinder and through the tubes to the wheel cylinders.
In the wheel cylinders, the increase in fluid pressure makes a smaller set of pistons move.
These smaller pistons activate the brake shoes.
When the brake shoes press against the drum, both the drum and the wheel stop or slow down.

Figure 11.2. Some selected frames and script for the brakes lesson.

to click on *Continue* whenever the learner is ready to go on to the next segment. When the learner has digested one segment – that is, when the learner has engaged in the five cognitive processes shown in Figure 3.2 of chapter 3 – then, the learner can move on to the next segment. In this way, the learner has some modest control over the pace of presentation of the narrated animation, and thus a way of avoiding the problem of not having enough time to carry out the required cognitive processing.

As a second example, consider a narrated animation that explains how an electric motor works. The motor consists of many unfamiliar parts – such as a wire loop, commutator, magnet, battery, and wires – and many causal links. For an inexperienced learner, the pace of presentation may not allow for the complete cognitive processing needed to build a meaningful mental model. To reduce this problem, we can put a list of questions in the upper right corner of the screen such as, "What happens when the motor is in the start position?"; "What happens when the motor has rotated a quarter turn?"; "What happens when the motor has rotated a half turn?"; "What happens when the motor has rotated three quarters of a turn?"; and "What

happens when the motor has rotated a full turn?" The learner can click on any of the elements in the electric motor – such as the magnet, wire loop, commutator, wires, or battery – and then click on any of the questions. A short segment of narrated animation appears addressing this question. In this way, the learner sees exactly the same narrated animation as in the continuous presentation, but can control the pace and order of the presentation.

Pretraining Techniques

Another solution to the essential overload problem is to equip the learner with knowledge that will make it easier to process a narrated animation. For example, suppose we present a narrated animation explaining how a car's braking system works. The script for the lesson and some selected frames are shown in Figure 11.2. Mayer, Mathias, and Wetzell (2002) proposed a two-stage learning process in which learners first build component models for each major part in the system, and second build a causal model. Building component models consists of learning the name and behavior of each component, such as knowing that the piston in the master cylinder can move forward or backward, the brake fluid in the tube can be compressed or not compressed, and so on. Building a causal model consists of learning the causal chain, such as stepping on the car's brake pedal causes a piston to move forward in the master cylinder, which in turn causes brake fluid in the tube to compress, and so on.

The pace of presentation may be so fast that by the time learners are able to build component models, there is no time left to build a causal model. To overcome this overload problem, we can provide pretraining to the learners concerning the names and characteristics of each component. For example, Figure 11.3 shows frames from a pretraining episode in which learners can click on any part in a diagram of the braking system – such as the piston in the master cylinder – and then be given the name for that part and shown the states the part can be in. After the learner has clicked on each part, the learner can be shown the narrated animation. However, because the learner already knows the name and characteristics of each part, the learner can engage in cognitive processes for building a causal model of the system, leading to better understanding. In this way, the pretraining provides prior knowledge that reduces the amount of processing needed to understand the narrated animation.

Modality Techniques

Finally, suppose you are given an animation explaining lightning formation, along with captions (i.e., one or two sentences in length) at the bottom of the screen that describe the events rendered in the animation. In this situation, the words in the multimedia message are presented as on-screen text. This situation may overload the visual channel because the learner must look at both the animation and the on-screen text at the same time. In order to off-load some of the visual processing, we can present the words as concurrent narration. In this way, learners can watch the lightning animation with their eyes and listen to the verbal explanation of lightning formation with their ears.

What Do We Know About the Segmenting, Pretraining, and Modality Principles?

During the past few years, a small but consistent research base has developed concerning the segmenting, pretraining, and modality principles. In this review, I consider articles published in archival journals in which (a) the task is an instructional lesson involving words and pictures; (b) the independent variable involves whether or not the presentation was segmented (i.e., continuous versus segmented), whether or not pretraining was provided on elements in the presentation (pretraining versus no pretraining), or whether or not the words were in spoken or printed form (spoken text versus printed text); (c) the dependent measure is performance on a problem-solving transfer test; and (d) reported statistics include the mean and standard deviation of each group. When the participants were broken down by prior experience, I included comparisons for low-experience students but not high-experience students, because high-experience students may be less susceptible to essential overload. I computed effect size for each comparison by subtracting the mean problem-solving transfer score of the control group from the mean problem-solving transfer score of the experimental group (e.g., segmented group – continuous group, pretraining group – no pretraining group, or spoken-text group–printed-text group) and dividing by the pooled standard deviation (Cortina & Nouri, 2000). Following Cohen (1988), I consider an effect size of 0.2 to be small, 0.5 to be medium, and 0.8 to be large.

Research on the Segmenting Principle

Do students learn more deeply when a narrated animation is presented in learner-paced segments rather than as a continuous unit? Table 11.3 summarizes three comparisons between a group that received a narrated animation broken into segments with the pace controlled by the learner (i.e., segmented group) and a group that received the same narrated animation as a single

Table 11.3. Evidence Concerning the Segmentating Principle

Source	Content	Effect size
Mayer & Chandler (2001, Expt. 2)	Lightning	1.13
Mayer, Dow, & Mayer (2003, Expt. 2a)	Electric motor	0.82
Mayer, Dow, & Mayer (2003, Expt. 2b)	Electric motor	0.98
Median		0.98

continuous presentation (i.e., continuous group). The left side of the table lists the experiment that is the source of the data, the middle portion of the table lists the content of the lesson, and the right side of the table lists the effect size. Overall, in three

of three comparisons, there was a large positive effect size, with a median effect size of 0.98.

In the first study listed in Table 11.3, Mayer and Chandler (2001) compared the learning outcomes of students who viewed a 140-second narrated animation on lightning formation as a continuous presentation (i.e., continuous group) to the learning outcomes of students who viewed the same presentation in 16 segments (i.e., segmented group). Each segment lasted about 10 seconds and contained about a sentence of narration (as shown in Table 11.2). After the narrated animation segment was complete, a *Continue* button appeared on the screen (as shown in Figure 11.1). When the learner clicked on the button, the next segment appeared.

Frame 1

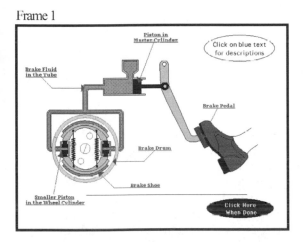

Frame 2

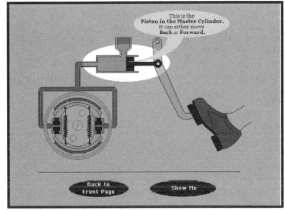

Frame 3

Frame 4

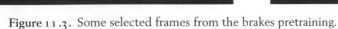

Figure 11.3. Some selected frames from the brakes pretraining.

Table 11.4. Evidence Concerning the Pretraining Principle

Source	Content	Effect size
Pollock, Chandler, & Sweller (2002, Expt. 1)	Electrical engineering	1.22
Pollock, Chandler, & Sweller (2002, Expt. 3)	Electrical engineering	1.15
Mayer, Mathias, & Wetzell (2002, Expt. 1)	Brakes	0.79
Mayer, Mathias, & Wetzell (2002, Expt. 2)	Brakes	0.92
Mayer, Mathias, & Wetzell (2002, Expt. 3)	Tire pump	1.00
Mayer, Mautone, & Prothero (2002, Expt. 2)	Geology simulation game	0.57
Mayer, Mautone, & Prothero (2002, Expt. 3)	Geology simulation game	0.85
Median		0.92

This procedure was repeated so the learner saw the continuous presentation twice or the segmented presentation twice. The top line of Table 11.3 shows that the segmented group performed better than the continuous group on a problem-solving transfer test, yielding a large effect size.

In a second set of studies, Mayer, Dow, and Mayer (2003) compared the learning outcomes of students who learned about electric motors from a simulation game in which they interacted with an on-screen agent named Dr. Phyz. In the continuous version, when the student clicked on the electric motor, Dr. Phyz narrated a continuous animation showing how the electric motor works. In the segmented version, a list of questions appeared corresponding to segments of the narrated animation. When the student clicked on a question, Dr. Phyz narrated an animation concerning a segment of the presentation. When the segment was completed, the student could click on another question to see another segment of the narrated animation. As shown in lines 2 and 3 of Table 11.3, the segmented group produced much better transfer test performance than the continuous group, yielding large effect sizes in both cases. Overall, there is preliminary evidence for the *segmenting principle*: People learn more deeply when a multimedia message is presented in learner-paced segments rather than as a continuous unit.

Research on the Pretraining Principle

Does it help student understanding of a multimedia lesson if you provide pretraining concerning the names and characteristics of the major elements in the lesson? Table 11.4 lists seven tests of the pretraining principle. In the first set of studies (Pollock, Chandler, & Sweller, 2002), apprentices took a course in electrical engineering that included a two-phase multimedia lesson on conducting safety tests for electrical appliances. For some learners (pretraining group), the first phase focused on how each component worked and the second phase focused on how all the components worked together within the electrical system. For other learners (no pretraining group), both phases focused on how all the components worked together within the electrical system. On a subsequent problem-solving transfer test concerning how the elements worked together within the electrical system, learners in the pretraining group performed better than students in the no-pretraining group, yielding large effect sizes in both cases as shown in the first two lines of Table 11.4. Importantly, these results were for low-experience learners, whereas high-experience learners did not show strong positive effects, indicating that high-experience learners were less likely to encounter essential overload.

In the second set of studies (Mayer, Mathias, & Wetzell, 2002), students received a narrated animation explaining the workings of a car's braking system or a bicycle tire pump and then took problem-solving transfer tests. Before the brakes lesson, some students (pretraining group) received pretraining in which they learned the name and possible states of each component in the brake system – for example, the piston in

Table 11.5. Evidence Concerning the Modality Principle

Source	Content	Effect size
Jeung, Chandler, & Sweller (1997, Expt. 1)	Math problems	0.87
Jeung, Chandler, & Sweller (1997, Expt. 2)	Math problems	0.33
Jeung, Chandler, & Sweller (1997, Expt. 3)	Math problems	1.01
Mayer & Moreno (1998, Expt. 1)	Lightning	1.49
Mayer & Moreno (1998, Expt. 2)	Brakes	0.78
Kalyuga, Chandler, & Sweller (1999, Expt. 1)	Electrical engineering	0.85
Moreno & Mayer (1999b, Expt. 1)	Lightning	1.02
Moreno & Mayer (1999b, Expt. 2)	Lightning	1.09
Kalyuga, Chandler, & Sweller (2000, Expt. 1)	Electrical engineering	0.79
O'Neil et al. (2000, Expt. 1)	Aircraft simulation	1.00
Moreno et al. (2001, Expt. 4a)	Environmental science game	0.60
Moreno et al., (2001, Expt. 4b)	Environmental science game	1.58
Moreno et al. (2001, Expt. 5a)	Environmental science game	1.41
Moreno et al. (2001, Expt. 5b)	Environmental science game	1.71
Craig, Gholson, & Driscoll (2002, Expt. 2)	Lightning	0.97
Moreno & Mayer (2002, Expt. 1a)	Environmental science game	0.93
Moreno & Mayer (2002, Expt. 1b)	Environmental science game	0.62
Moreno & Mayer (2002, Expt. 1c)	Environmental science game	2.79
Moreno & Mayer (2002, Expt. 2a)	Environmental science game	0.74
Moreno & Mayer (2002, Expt. 2b)	Environmental science game	2.24
Mayer, Dow, & Mayer (2003, Expt. 1)	Electric motor	0.79
Median		0.97

master cylinder could be forward or back, the fluid in the brake tube could be compressed or not compressed, and so on. Before the tire pump lesson, some students (pretraining group) received pretraining with a clear plastic model in which they were asked to pull up and push down on the handle several times. On a subsequent test of problem-solving transfer, students in the pretraining group performed better than students in the no-pretraining group across all three experiments. The third through fifth lines of Table 11.4 show that the effect sizes were large.

Finally, in a third set of two studies (Mayer, Mautone, & Prothero, 2002), students learned about geology in a simulation game called the Profile Game. The goal of the game was to determine which geological feature was on a certain portion of the earth's surface, represented as a window on the computer screen. Students could use a mouse to draw lines and were shown the depth or height at each point along the line. Some students (pretraining group) were shown illustrations of the major geological

features – such as a ridge or a trench – before the lesson, whereas others (no-pretraining group) were not. As you can see in lines 6 and 7 of Table 11.4, the pretraining group performed better on a subsequent test of problem-solving transfer than did the no-pretraining group, yielding medium to large effect sizes.

Overall, Table 11.4 shows consistent, mostly large effect sizes favoring the pretraining group, with a median effect size of 0.92. These findings are consistent with the *pretraining principle*: People learn more deeply from a multimedia message when they know the names and characteristics of the main concepts.

Research on the Modality Principle

The modality principle has been the focus of more than two dozen studies, beginning with a classic set of studies by Mousavi, Low, and Sweller (1995). In keeping with the other studies reported in this chapter, I focus on modality studies in which the material is presented using a computer. Table 11.5

summarizes research on modality by listing the source of the study, the instructional content, and the effect size comparing the transfer test performance of students who received graphics and printed text with the transfer test performance of students who received graphics and narration. Across the studies, the graphics were presented as diagrams (Jeung, Chandler, & Sweller, 1997; Kalyuga, Chandler, & Sweller, 1999, 2000), as animation (Craig, Gholson, & Driscoll, 2002; Mayer, Dow et al., 2003; Mayer & Moreno, 1998; Moreno & Mayer, 2002, Expts. 1a and 1b; Moreno et al., 2001), or using a head-mounted display as virtual reality (O'Neil, et al., 2000; Moreno & Mayer, 1999; Moreno & Mayer, 2002). The studies cover a wide variety of instructional topics including math problems mainly for high school students (Jeung et al., 1997), electrical engineering procedures mainly for industrial trainees (Kalyuga et al., 1999, 2000), an environmental science simulation game mainly for high school and college students (Moreno et al., 2001; Moreno & Mayer, 2002); an aircraft simulation for working adults (O'Neil et al., 2000); and narrated animations concerning lightning formation (Craig et al., 2002; Mayer & Moreno, 1998; Moreno & Mayer, 1999b), how brakes work (Mayer & Moreno, 1998), or how electric motors work (Mayer, Dow et al., 2003) mainly for college students. In all studies in this review, I focused on the dependent measure that best assessed transfer such as generating creative solutions to written problems (e.g., Mayer & Moreno, 1998), troubleshooting electrical problems (e.g., Kalyuga et al., 1999), or time to solve transfer problems (e.g., Jeung et al., 1997). In some studies involving multiple versions of treatments, I selected the treatment groups that most closely corresponded to graphics-and-printed-words and graphics-and-spoken-words, such as using a graphics-and-narration treatment in which elements of a diagram were highlighted as they were discussed by the narrator (Jeung et al., 1997). In instances where the learners were broken into low and high experience, I focused only on the low experience learners (e.g., Kalyuga et al., 2000).

Overall, across a wide variety of learning situations, there was strong and consistent support for the modality principle, with a median effect size of 0.97. In all 21 comparisons reported in Table 11.5, people scored better on transfer tests after learning with graphics and narration rather than graphics and printed text. These findings strongly support the modality principle: People learn more deeply from multimedia messages when the words are presented as spoken text rather than printed text. Although all of the studies reported in Table 11.5 involved computer-based environments, similar results have been obtained in paper-based environments comparing diagrams containing printed text with diagrams paired with tape-recorded speech (Mousavi et al., 1995; Tinsdall-Ford, Chandler, & Sweller, 1997). The modality principle is explored in more detail in chapter 8.

What Are the Implications of Research for Cognitive Theory?

The research results summarized in Tables 11.3, 11.4, and 11.5 provide support for the predictions of the cognitive theory of multimedia learning as summarized in Figure 3.2 of chapter 3. When learners do not have enough time to engage in active cognitive processing of the essential material, their learning outcomes suffer – as indicated by tests of problem-solving transfer. According to the cognitive theory of multimedia learning, three ways to handle an essential overload situation are to allow the learner to slow down the pace of presentation (i.e., segmenting principle), provide the learner with knowledge that reduces the need for cognitive processing of the presentation (i.e., pretraining principle), or off-load some of the visual information onto the auditory channel (i.e., modality principle). Thus, each of these principles has theoretical plausibility because it was derived from the cognitive theory of multimedia learning – particularly, concerning the limited capacity for processing information in working memory. The empirical evidence in support of each of these principles provides empirical plausibility as well as support for the predictions of the cognitive theory of multimedia learning.

What Are the Implications of Research for Instructional Design?

The research reviewed in this chapter shows that instructional designers should be sensitive to working memory constraints when presenting a concise narrated animation. If the concise narrated animation contains a lot of interacting concepts and is presented at a fast pace, the demand for cognitive processing can exceed the learner's cognitive capacity. Even if extraneous material has been eliminated from the presentation, the remaining essential material may be presented at a rate that exceeds the learner's capacity. The segmenting, pretraining, and modality principles are particularly relevant to the design of narrated animations that contain a lot of interacting concepts presented at a fast pace. Based on the segmenting principle, it would be useful to break a narrated animation into meaningful segments and to allow the learner to control the onset of each segment, such as by clicking on a *Continue* button. Based on the pretraining principle, it would be useful to sequence the instruction to begin with descriptions of the key concepts or elements, before describing how they interact. Based on the modality principle, it would be useful to use narrated animation rather than animation with onscreen text. Furthermore, the designer should take learner characteristics into account and be aware that well-designed multimedia instruction may be most effective for low-experience learners.

What Are the Limitations of Current Research and What Are Some Productive Directions for Future Research?

The principles described in this chapter are subject to limitations in the nature of the task and in the dependent measures. Concerning the nature of the task, most of the research studies involved short narrated animations presented in a controlled laboratory environment. Research is needed in which the principles are tested within more ecologically valid environments, such as with students within their classrooms. Concerning the dependent measures, I have focused on measures of problem-solving transfer because I am most interested in improving learners' understanding. However, a central assumption underlying the principles described in this chapter is that they work because they effectively reduce cognitive load. Thus, it would be useful to include direct measures of cognitive load in future research (Brunken, Plass, & Leutner, 2003; Paas, Tuovinen, Tabbers, and van Gerven, 2003).

Further research work is also needed to better understand the conditions under which each of the principles is most effective. Concerning the segmenting principle, some of the studies focused solely on allowing the learner to control the pace of presentation whereas others focused on allowing the learner to control both the pace and order of presentation. Research is needed to determine the relative effects of learner control of presentation pace and learner control of presentation order, and whether such effects depend on the characteristics of the learner and on the characteristics of the learning task. For example, inexperienced learners may lack the metacognitive skills to make effective decisions about the order of presentation whereas experienced learners may be able to make such decisions effectively. The role of the learner's prior knowledge is examined in detail by Kalyuga in chapter 21 on the prior knowledge principle.

Also concerning segmenting, research is needed to determine the most effective size of a segment and whether optimal segment size depends on the characteristics of the learner and the learning task. In the studies reported in this chapter, the segments were fairly short – approximately 10 seconds of animation along with a few sentences of narration – and the segments described meaningful steps in a process. Having small segments may distract and irritate some learners, whereas having large segments may result in cognitive overload.

Concerning pretraining, research is needed to extend the principle beyond cause-and-effect systems. In the studies reported in this chapter, the learning goal was to understand how some mechanical or physical system works. In such situations, it was useful to know the names and behaviors of each component before learning about the causal model. Further research is needed to determine whether similar benefits for pretraining occur for different kinds of lessons, such as an explanation of how to solve a mathematics problem or an analysis of a historical controversy.

Concerning modality, there may be situations in which on-screen text would be helpful such as for complex technical terms or with learners who are nonnative speakers. Further research is needed to determine the conditions for the modality principle.

Glossary

Cognitive capacity: The total amount of processing that can be supported by the learner's working memory at any one time.

Concise narrated animation: A narrated animation that contains *essential material* – material needed for understanding the lesson – but does not contain *extraneous material* – material not needed for understanding the lesson.

Essential material: Words and pictures needed to achieve the instructional objective, such as understanding how a mechanical system works.

Essential overload: When the amount of essential cognitive processing required to understand the multimedia instructional message exceeds the learner's cognitive capacity.

Essential processing: Cognitive processing (such as selecting relevant words and images, organizing selected words and images, and integrating) required to make sense out of the essential

material; similar to Sweller's (1999) *intrinsic cognitive load*.

Pretraining principle: People learn more deeply from a multimedia message when they know the names and characteristics of the main concepts.

Segmenting principle: People learn more deeply when a multimedia message is presented in user-paced segments rather than as a continuous unit.

Note

Preparation of this chapter was supported by Grant No. N000140410553 from the Office of Naval Research, titled "Role of Cognitive Style in Learning from Multimedia Training." I appreciate the helpful comments of Jeroen van Merriënboer, Wolfgang Schnotz, and John Sweller.

Footnotes

1. Throughout this chapter, I use the term *essential cognitive processing* to refer to largely the same concept as Sweller's (chapter 2, 1999) *intrinsic cognitive load*.

2. Sweller (chapter 2, 1999) considers type 1 essential overload to involve intrinsic cognitive load and type 2 essential overload to involve extraneous cognitive load. Intrinsic cognitive load is caused by the inherent complexity of the material, which is not under the instructor's control, whereas extraneous cognitive load is caused by the way the material is presented, which is under the instructor's control. According to this definition, the modality effect involves extraneous cognitive load because the instructor can change the presentation format of the words from printed text to spoken text. The taxonomy of five overload scenarios that I provide in Table 11.1 of this chapter and Table 12.1 of the following chapter is consistent with Sweller's distinction between intrinsic and extraneous cognitive load, but my taxonomy breaks cognitive load into five types. The first one (type 1 essential overload) involves Sweller's intrinsic cognitive load whereas each of the others involves Sweller's extraneous cognitive load. I agree with Sweller that the modality effect (i.e., type 2 essential

overload) represents a different type of cognitive overload than type 1 essential overload. However, I have included modality in this chapter because type 2 essential overload involves a scenario in which one channel (i.e., the visual/pictorial channel) is overloaded with essential processing. Thus, both type 1 and type 2 essential overload occur when too much essential material is presented at a fast pace – either to both channels (type 1 essential overload) or to the visual/pictorial channel (type 2 essential overload). Thus, my taxonomy of five scenarios is compatible with Sweller's distinction between intrinsic and extraneous cognitive load.

3. Sweller considers the modality effect to be related to the split-attention effect in that both require two or more sources of information that cannot be understood in isolation and so must be mentally or physically integrated. Split-attention effects include spatial contiguity and temporal contiguity, which I examine in the next chapter on extraneous overload. I agree that modality effects and split-attention effects derive from the same problem. In particular, modality effects can occur when the learner must focus on two kinds of visual information presented at the same time (printed words and animation), which may overload the learner's visual channel. I have chosen to include modality in this chapter because it corresponds to a form of essential overload (according to the taxonomy in Table 11.1 in this chapter) – having too much material presented at one time to the visual system. I have placed split-attention effects in the next chapter because I attribute them to confusing layout (a form of extraneous overload according to Table 12.1 in chapter 12). Thus, there is no major disagreement between Sweller's analysis of the modality principle and mine.

References

Brunken, R., Plass, J. L., & Leutner, D. (2003). Direct measurement of cognitive load in multimedia learning. *Educational Psychologist*, 38, 53–62.

Cohen, J. (1988). *Statistical power analysis for the behavioral sciences* (2nd ed.). Hillsdale, NJ: Lawrence Erlbaum Associates.

Cortina, J. M., & Nouri, H. (2000). *Effect size for ANOVA designs*. Thousand Oaks, CA: Sage.

Craig, S. D., Gholson, B., & Driscoll, D. M. (2002). Animated pedagogical agents in multimedia educational environments: Effects of agent properties, picture features, and redundancy. *Journal of Educational Psychology*, 94, 428–434.

Jeung, H., Chandler, P., & Sweller, J. (1997). The role of visual indicators in dual sensory mode instruction. *Educational Psychology*, 17, 329–343.

Kalyuga, S., Chandler, P., & Sweller, J. (1999). Managing split-attention and redundancy in multimedia instruction. *Applied Cognitive Psychology*, 13, 351–371.

Kalyuga, S., Chandler, P., & Sweller, J. (2000). Incorporating learner experience into the design of multimedia instruction. *Journal of Educational Psychology*, 92, 126–136.

Mayer, R. E. (2001). *Multimedia learning*. New York: Cambridge University Press.

Mayer, R. E., & Chandler, P. (2001). When learning is just a click away: Does simple user interaction foster deeper understanding of multimedia messages? *Journal of Educational Psychology*, 93, 390–397.

Mayer, R. E., Dow, G., & Mayer, S. (2003). Multimedia learning in an interactive self-explaining environment: What works in the design of agent-based microworlds? *Journal of Educational Psychology*, 95, 806–813.

Mayer, R. E., Mathias, A., & Wetzell, K. (2002). Fostering understanding of multimedia messages through pre-training: Evidence for a two-stage theory of mental model construction. *Journal of Experimental Psychology: Applied*, 8, 147–154.

Mayer, R. E., Mautone, P., & Prothero, W. (2002). Pictorial aids for learning by doing in a multimedia geology simulation game. *Journal of Educational Psychology*, 94, 171–185.

Mayer, R. E., & Moreno, R. (1998). A split-attention effect in multimedia learning: Evidence for dual processing systems in working memory. *Journal of Educational Psychology*, 90, 312–320.

Mayer, R. E., & Moreno, R. (2003). Nine ways to reduce cognitive load in multimedia learning. *Educational Psychologist*, 38, 43–52.

Moreno, R., & Mayer, R. E. (1999). Cognitive principles of multimedia learning: The role of modality and contiguity. *Journal of Educational Psychology*, 91, 358–368.

Moreno, R., & Mayer, R. E. (2002). Learning science in virtual reality multimedia environments: Role of methods and media. *Journal of Educational Psychology*, 94, 598–610.

Moreno, R., Mayer R. E., Spires, H., & Lester, J. (2001). The case for social agency in computer-based teaching: Do students learn more deeply when they interact with animated pedagogical agents? *Cognition and Instruction, 19*, 177–214.

Mousavi, S. Y., Low, R., & Sweller, J. (1995). Reducing cognitive load by mixing auditory and visual presentation modes. *Journal of Educational Psychology, 87*, 319–334.

O'Neil, H. F., Mayer, R. E., Herl, H. E., Niemi, C., Olin, K., & Thurman, R. A. (2000). Instructional strategies for virtual aviation training environments. In H. F. O'Neil & D. H. Andrews (Eds.), *Aircrew training and assessment* (pp. 105–130). Mahwah, NJ: Erlbaum.

Paas, F., Tuovinen, J. E., Tabbers, H., & van Gerven, P. W. M. (2003). Cognitive load measurement as a means to advance cognitive load theory. *Educational Psychologist, 38*, 63–72.

Pollock, E., Chandler, P., & Sweller, J. (2002). Assimilating complex information. *Learning and Instruction, 12*, 61–86.

Sweller, J. (1999). *Instructional design in technical areas.* Camberwell, Australia: ACER Press.

Tinsdall-Ford, S., Chandler, P., & Sweller, J. (1997). When two sensory modes are better than one. *Journal of Experimental Psychology: Applied, 3*, 257–287.

CHAPTER 12

Principles for Reducing Extraneous Processing in Multimedia Learning: Coherence, Signaling, Redundancy, Spatial Contiguity, and Temporal Contiguity Principles

Richard E. Mayer

University of California, Santa Barbara

Abstract

Extraneous overload occurs when essential cognitive processing (required to understand the essential material in a multimedia message) and extraneous cognitive processing (required to process extraneous material or to overcome confusing layout in a multimedia message) exceeds the learner's cognitive capacity. Five multimedia design methods intended to minimize extraneous overload are the coherence, signaling, redundancy, spatial contiguity, and temporal contiguity principles. The coherence principle is that people learn more deeply from a multimedia message when extraneous material is excluded rather than included. This principle was supported in 10 out of 11 experimental tests, yielding a median effect size of 1.32. The signaling principle is that people learn more deeply from a multimedia message when cues are added that highlight the organization of the essential material. This principle was supported in three out of three experimental tests, yielding a median effect size of 0.60. The redundancy principle is that people learn more deeply from graphics and narration than from graphics, narration, and on-screen text. This principle was supported in 10 out of 10 experimental tests, yielding a median effect size of 0.69. The spatial contiguity principle is that people learn more deeply from a multimedia message when corresponding words and pictures are presented near rather than far from each other on the page or screen. This principle was supported in eight out of eight experimental tests, yielding a median effect size of 1.11. The temporal contiguity principle is that people learn more deeply from a multimedia message when corresponding animation and narration are presented simultaneously rather than successively. This principle was supported in eight out of eight experimental tests, yielding a median effect size of 1.31.

What Are the Coherence, Signaling, Redundancy, Spatial Contiguity, and Temporal Contiguity Principles?

Definitions

Consider a multimedia learning situation in which so much extraneous material is included – such as extraneous words and graphics – or the layout is so confusing that the learner is not able to adequately process the essential material. This situation creates a cognitive processing challenge that can be called *extraneous overload*. *Extraneous overload* occurs when essential cognitive processing (required to understand the essential material in a multimedia message) and extraneous cognitive processing (required to process extraneous material or to overcome confusing layout in a multimedia message) exceeds the learner's cognitive capacity. *Essential material* refers to words and pictures needed to achieve the instructional objective, such as understanding how a mechanical system works, and requires processing similar to Sweller's (1999) *intrinsic cognitive load*. *Extraneous material* refers to words and pictures that are not relevant to achieving the instructional objective, such as interesting stories or pictures, and requires processing similar to Sweller's (1999) *extrinsic cognitive load*. *Cognitive capacity* refers to the total amount of processing that can be supported by the learner's working memory at any one time.

The purpose of this chapter is to explore research evidence for five theory-based instructional design techniques intended to reduce extraneous overload – the *coherence, signaling, redundancy, spatial contiguity, and temporal contiguity principles*. The *coherence principle* is that people learn more deeply from a multimedia message when extraneous material is excluded rather than included. The *signaling principle* is that people learn more deeply from a multimedia message when cues are added that highlight the organization of the essential material. The *redundancy principle* is that people learn more deeply from graphics and narration

than from graphics, narration, and on-screen text. The *spatial contiguity principle* is that people learn more deeply from a multimedia message when corresponding words and pictures are presented near rather than far from each other on the page or screen. The *temporal contiguity principle* is that people learn more deeply from a multimedia message when corresponding animation and narration are presented simultaneously rather than successively.

Theory

Principles for reducing extraneous cognitive load are based on the cognitive theory of multimedia learning summarized in Figure 3.2 of chapter 3. In particular, according to the cognitive theory of multimedia learning (CTML), much of the cognitive processing required for building a meaningful learning outcome – such as selecting, organizing, and integrating – occurs in working memory. Three important features of working memory are (a) dual channels – that is, separate channels for pictorial and verbal processing, (b) limited capacity – that is, severe limits on the amount of processing that can occur in each channel at any one time, and (c) active processing – that is, meaningful learning requires engaging in cognitive processing such as selecting, organizing, and integrating (as described in chapter 3). A major challenge for instructional designers is to create instructional messages that are sensitive to the characteristics of the human information-processing system, so that the amount of processing required in each channel of working memory does not exceed the learner's cognitive capacity.

When an instructional message contains a lot of essential material and a lot of extraneous material, the cognitive capacity of the information-processing system is easily overloaded – a situation we call *extraneous overload*. Carrying out cognitive processing takes time and effort – both of which are limited. If the learner is required to engage in extraneous processing – that is, processing of extraneous material – the learner may not be able

Table 12.1. Load-Reduction Methods for Three Overload Scenarios

---

Type 1 **extraneous overload:** *Essential processing + extraneous processing (caused by extraneous material) > cognitive capacity*

Definition: One or both channels are overloaded by essential processing and extraneous processing (attributable to extraneous material). For example, a multimedia lesson contains extraneous words and/or pictures.

Load-reducing methods:

Coherence: Eliminate extraneous material to reduce processing of extraneous material. For example, exclude interesting but irrelevant statements or graphics.

Signaling: Provide cues for how to process the lesson to reduce processing of extraneous material. For example, add signals that show the learner what to attend to and how to organize it.

Redundancy: Avoid presenting identical streams of printed and spoken words concurrently with corresponding animation. For example, present words as narration rather than as narration and on-screen text.

Type 2 **extraneous overload:** *Essential processing + extraneous processing (caused by confusing layout) > cognitive capacity*

Definition: One or both channels are overloaded by essential processing and extraneous processing (attributable to a confusing layout). For example, a multimedia lesson presents essential words and/or pictures in a confusing layout.

Load-reducing method:

Spatial contiguity: Place printed words near corresponding parts of graphics to reduce the need for visual scanning. For example, put printed words near rather than far from corresponding parts of an illustration (on paper) or animation (on a screen).

Type 3 **extraneous overload:** *Essential processing + representational holding (caused by confusing layout) > cognitive capacity*

Definition: One or both channels are overloaded by essential processing and representational holding. For example, an animation is presented before or after a corresponding narration.

Load-reducing method:

Temporal contiguity: Present corresponding narration and animation at the same time to minimize the need to hold representations in memory. For example, present corresponding narration and animation simultaneously rather than successively.

---

to engage in essential processing – that is, the cognitive processing needed for making sense of the essential material. As a result, full understanding may not be achieved (Mayer, 2001; Mayer & Moreno, 2003).

Table 12.1 presents three overload scenarios, each involving a form of extraneous overload (Mayer & Moreno, 2003), in which essential processing demands (or intrinsic cognitive load) and extraneous processing demands (or extraneous cognitive load) exceed the learner's cognitive capacity. In the first scenario (i.e., *type 1 extraneous overload*), one or both channels are overloaded by the need to process essential material and the need to process extraneous mate-

rial. This overload scenario can occur when a multimedia instructional message contains too much detail, embellishment, or gratuitous information or when the layout of material is confusing. Two load-reducing methods for combating this scenario are *coherence* and *signaling*, both of which are explored in this chapter. The theoretical rationale for coherence is that it weeds out irrelevant material, thereby enabling the learner to use all available cognitive capacity for essential processing. The theoretical rationale for signaling is that it directs the learner's attention toward essential material, thereby enabling the learner to ignore extraneous material and use all available cognitive capacity to process essential material. In short, coherence techniques eliminate extraneous material – and thus extraneous processing – whereas signaling techniques guide the learner's attention toward essential material – thus eliminating the need for processing of extraneous material.

Alternatively, this overload scenario can occur with animation (or illustrations) and narration when redundant on-screen text is added. A load-reducing technique for addressing this situation is redundancy – eliminating the redundant on-screen text. The theoretical rationale for redundancy is that it reduces extraneous processing such as trying to reconcile the auditory and printed stream of words, and it eliminates the problem of having to process both animation (or illustration) and printed words in the visual channel (as discussed in the modality principle in chapter 11). Thus, redundant printed text can be seen as a special case of extraneous material. Redundancy techniques eliminate this extraneous material altogether.

In the second overload scenario (*type 2 extraneous overload*), one or both channels are overloaded by essential processing (attributed to understanding the essential material) and extraneous processing (attributed to dealing with a confusing layout). This overload scenario can occur with text and graphics when corresponding printed text and graphics are far from each other on the page or screen. A load-reducing technique is spatial contiguity, that is, placing printed words near rather than far from corresponding parts of an illustration or animation. The theoretical rationale for spatial contiguity is that it reduces the effort required to scan back and forth between the text and the graphic. Eye-movement studies by Hegarty, Carpenter, and Just (1996) have shown that students tend to read a portion of text and then look for the corresponding portion of the graphic, then read the next portion of text and look for the corresponding portion of the graphic, and so on. Spatial contiguity techniques can reduce the effort involved in visually scanning the screen or page – a form of extraneous processing. Thus, spatial con-

Table 12.2. Portion of Added Text from Embellished Lessons on Lightning

Inserted in the First Paragraph
When flying through updrafts, an airplane ride can become bumpy. Metal airplanes conduct lightning very well, but they sustain little damage because the bolt, meeting no resistance, passes right through.

Inserted in the Second Paragraph
When lightning strikes the ground, fulgurites may form, as the heat from the lightning fuses sand into the shape of the electricity's path.

Inserted in the Third Paragraph
In trying to understand these processes, scientists sometimes create lightning by launching tiny rockets into overhead clouds.

Inserted in the Fourth Paragraph
Golfers are prime targets of lightning strikes because they tend to stand in open grassy fields, or huddle under trees.

Inserted in the Fifth Paragraph
Approximately 10,000 Americans are injured by lightning every year. Eyewitnesses in Burtonsville, Maryland, watched as a bolt of lightning tore a hole in the helmet of a high school football player during practice. The bolt burned his jersey and blew his shoes off. More than a year later, the young man still won't talk about his near death experience.

tiguity techniques provide cues that direct the learner's attention.

In the third overload scenario (*type 3 extraneous overload*), both channels are overloaded by essential processing and representational holding (i.e., maintaining a mental representation in working memory). This overload scenario can occur when an animation explaining a topic is presented before or after a corresponding narration explaining the same topic. A load-reducing method is temporal contiguity, which also is explored in this chapter. The theoretical rationale for temporal contiguity is that it insures corresponding words and pictures are in working memory at the same time, thereby eliminating the need to hold a representation in working memory for an extended period of time.

What Are Examples of the Coherence, Signaling, Redundancy, Spatial Continuity, and Temporal Contiguity Principles?

How can we modify multimedia instructional messages so that they do not create extraneous overload? In other words, what can we do to a multimedia instructional message to reduce the amount of extraneous cognitive processing that is required of learners? In this chapter, I explore five techniques for reducing extraneous overload – coherence, signaling, redundancy, spatial contiguity, and temporal contiguity. In each case, the cognitive theory of multimedia learning predicts that reducing extraneous processing will increase the quality of the learning outcome as manifested in improved performance on problem-solving transfer tests.

Coherence Techniques

Sometimes a multimedia message contains words and/or pictures that are not relevant to the instructional goal. For example, consider a book-based lesson that explains the steps in lightning formation using printed words and illustrations, including the words shown in Figure 12.1. We could spice up the lesson by inserting additional sentences in each paragraph describing interesting stories about lightning, such as an incident in which a high school student was struck by lightning while playing football, as shown in Table 12.2. Alternatively, consider a computer-based lesson that explains lightning formation using narration and animation, as exemplified in Figure 3.1 of chapter 3. To spice up the lesson we could add short video clips of lightning storms along with interesting facts about lightning, or we could include background music and environmental sounds.

A straightforward solution to this extraneous overload problem is to eliminate words, pictures, and sounds that are not relevant to the instructional goal. For example, we could eliminate the extraneous printed words and illustrations from the book-based lesson on lightning (i.e., not using the words

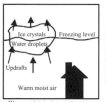

When the surface of the earth is warm, moist air near the earth's surface becomes heated and rises rapidly, producing an updraft. As the air in these updrafts cools, water vapor condenses into water droplets and forms a cloud. The cloud's top extends above the freezing level. At this altitude, the air temperature is well below freezing, so the upper portion of the cloud is composed of tiny ice crystals.

Warm moist air rises, water vapor condenses and forms a cloud.

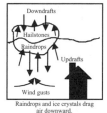

Eventually, the water droplets and ice crystals in the cloud become too large to be suspended by updrafts. As raindrops and ice crystals fall through the cloud, they drag some of the air from the cloud downward, producing downdrafts. The rising and falling air currents within the cloud may cause hailstones to form. When downdrafts strike the ground, they spread out in all directions, producing gusts of cool wind people feel just before the start of the rain.

Raindrops and ice crystals drag air downward.

Within the cloud, the moving air causes electrical charges to build, although scientists do not fully understand how it occurs. Most believe that the charge results from the collision of the cloud's light, rising water droplets and tiny pieces of ice against hail and other heavier, falling particles. The negatively charged particles fall to the bottom of the cloud, and most of the positively charged particles rise to the top.

Negatively charged particles fall to the bottom of the cloud.

The first stroke of a cloud-to-ground lightning flash is started by a stepped leader. Many scientists believe that it is triggered by a spark between the areas of positive and negative charges within the cloud. A stepped leader moves downward in a series of steps, each of which is about 50-yards long, and lasts for about 1 millionth of a second. It pauses between steps for about 50 millionths of a second. As the stepped leader nears the ground, positively charged upward-moving leaders travel up from such objects as trees and buildings, to meet the negative charges. Usually, the upward-moving leader from the tallest object is the first to meet the stepped leader and complete a path between the cloud and earth. The two leaders generally meet about 165 feet above the ground. Negatively charged particles then rush from the cloud to the ground along the path created by the leaders. It is not very bright and usually has many branches.

Two leaders meet, negatively charged particles rush from the cloud to the ground.

As the stepped leader nears the ground, it induces an opposite charge, so positively charged particles from the ground rush upward along the same path. This upward motion of the current is the return stoke and it reaches the cloud in about 70 microseconds. The return stoke produces the bright light that people notice in a flash of lightning, but the current moves so quickly that its upward motion cannot be perceived. The lightning flash usually consists of an electrical potential of hundreds of millions of volts. The air along the lightning channel is heated briefly to a very high temperature. Such intense heating causes the air to expand explosively, producing a sound wave we call thunder.

Positively charged particles from the ground rush upward along the same path.

Figure 12.1. Book-based integrated presentation on lightning.

in Table 12.2), or we could eliminate the extraneous video or music from the computer-based lesson.

Signaling Techniques

Another solution to the problem of having too much extraneous material in a multimedia lesson is to insert cues that direct

Table 12.3. Portion of Script for Lessons on Airplane Lift (Signaling Consists of Added Outline and Headings Indicated by Underlining and Spoken Emphasis Indicated by Bolding)

What is needed to cause an aircraft, which is heavier than air, to climb into the air and stay there? An aerodynamic principle formulated by Daniel Bernouille in 1738 helps explain it. Bernouille's Principle explains how upward forces, called lift, act upon the plane when it moves through the air. To understand how lift works, you need to focus on differences between the top and bottom of the airplane's wing. First, how the top of the wing is **shaped** differently than the bottom; second, how quickly **air flows** across the top surface, compared to across the bottom surface; and third, how the **air pressure** on the top of the wing compares to that on the bottom of the wing.

Wing shape: Curved upper surface is longer. A cross section of a bird's wing, a boomerang, and a Stealth bomber all share a shape similar to that of an airplane wing. The upper surface of the wing is curved more than the bottom surface. The surface on the **top** of the wing is **longer** than on the **bottom**. This is called an airfoil.

Air flow: Air moves faster across top of wing. In order to achieve lift, air must flow over the wing. The wingspan of a 747 is more than 200 feet; that's taller than a 15-story building. When the airplane moves forward, its wings cut through the air. As the air moves across the wing, it will push against in all directions, perpendicular to the surface of the wing.

When an airplane is in flight, air hitting the front of the wing separates. Some air flows over the wing and some flows under the wing. The air meets up again at the back of the wing. The air flowing over the top of the wing has a longer distance to travel in the same amount of time. Air traveling over the curved **top** of the wing **flows faster** than air that flows under the **bottom** of the wing.

Air pressure: Pressure on the top is less. When air moves faster, its pressure decreases. You have probably noticed that when you turn on the water in the shower, the curtain moves in. The running water makes the air in the shower move faster and since it exerts less pressure against the curtain than the still air outside the curtain does, the curtain is pushed in. A similar principle is at work on airplane wings.

Since the air over the top of the wing is moving faster, it gets more spread out and therefore pressure on the top part of the wing decreases. The **top** surface of the wing now has **less pressure** exerted against it than the **bottom** surface of the wing. The downward force of the faster moving air on the top of the wing is not as great as the upward force of the slower moving air under the wing and, as a result, there is a net upward force on the wing – a lift.

the learner's attention toward the essential material. For example, suppose we present a narrated animation explaining how an airplane achieves lift, using the script shown in Table 12.3 (without the underlined sentences and without emphasizing the bolded words). This script contains some material that is not essential to understanding the process of lift, so we can direct the learner's attention by using signals such as an outlining sentence that lists the main steps (indicated by the underlined sentences inserted at the end of the first paragraph in Table 12.3), headings for each step (as shown in the underlined phrases before the second, third, and fifth paragraphs in Table 12.3), and spoken emphasis on key words (indicated by the words in bold font in Table 12.3). As you can see, the signals do not add any new in-

formation but rather highlight the essential material in the lesson.

Redundancy Techniques

Suppose you are viewing a narrated animation on lightning formation as exemplified in the left side of Figure 12.2. I refer to this as a nonredundant multimedia presentation because the words are presented in spoken form only. It might be tempting to add concurrent on-screen text that mirrors the narration, in an attempt to accommodate various learning styles, as exemplified in the right side of Figure 12.2. In this case, the narrator speaks the words at the same time as the words are printed on the bottom of the screen. I refer to this as a redundant multimedia presentation because the same words

Nonredundant   **Redundant**

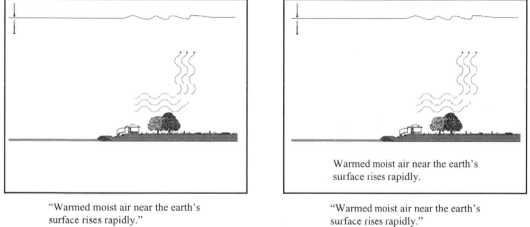

Figure 12.2. Some selected frames from nonredundant and redundant presentation of lightning.

are presented in both spoken and printed form. A shortcoming of redundant presentations is that they may induce extraneous processing, such as trying to reconcile the flow of spoken and printed words. According to the redundancy principle, students will learn more deeply from the nonredundant presentation than the redundant presentation because the redundant presentation requires more extraneous processing.

Spatial Contiguity Techniques

Next, consider a situation in which a learner reads a booklet explaining lightning formation consisting of text on one page and il-

lustrations on another page as shown in Figure 12.3. This layout is an example of what I call separated presentation because corresponding words and pictures are far from each other. In contrast, we can reduce the need to scan back and forth between the words and pictures by creating an integrated presentation as shown in Figure 12.1. In this layout, each illustration is placed next to the paragraph that describes it, and words from the paragraph have been inserted into the illustration, creating spatial contiguity. In this way, the learner has cues for combining corresponding words and pictures and does not have to waste cognitive processing by scanning around the page.

Temporal Contiguity Techniques

Next, consider a situation in which a learner views an animation depicting the steps in lightning formation before (or after) listening to a narration describing the same steps. In this situation, the learner has to hold all of the relevant images in working memory until the narration is presented (or must hold all of the relevant words in working memory until the animation is presented). The task of holding all relevant words or images in working memory – which we call *representational holding* – is likely to overload the learner's cognitive capacity, resulting in the loss of essential information. A useful way to eliminate the need for representational holding is to present corresponding words and pictures at the same time – a technique that can be called *temporal contiguity*.

What Do We Know About the Coherence, Signaling, Redundancy, Spatial Contiguity, and Temporal Contiguity Principles?

In this review, I consider articles published in archival journals in which (a) the task is an instructional lesson involving words and pictures; (b) the independent variable involves whether or not the presentation was coherent (i.e., concise versus embellished), whether or not signals were provided (i.e., signaled versus nonsignaled), whether or not the words were in spoken form or spoken and printed form (i.e., nonredundant versus redundant) whether or not corresponding words and pictures were placed near each other on the page or screen (i.e., integrated versus separated) whether the narration and animation were presented at the same time or after one another (i.e., simultaneous versus successive); (c) the dependent measure is performance on a problem-solving transfer test; and (d) reported statistics include the mean and standard deviation of each group. When the participants were broken down by prior experience, I included comparisons for low-experience students but not

high-experience students. When the participants were broken down by spatial ability, I included comparisons for high-spatial students but not low-spatial students, because low-spatial students may have difficulty taking advantage of well-designed multimedia material. I computed effect size for each comparison by subtracting the mean problem-solving transfer score of the control group from the mean problem-solving transfer score of the experimental group (e.g., the concise group – the embellished group, the signaled group – nonsignaled group, the nonredundant group – the redundant group, the integrated group – separated group, or the successive group – the simultaneous group) and dividing by the pooled standard deviation (Cortina & Nouri, 2000). Following Cohen (1988) I consider an effect size of 0.2 to be small, 0.5 to medium, and 0.8 to be large.

Research on the Coherence Principle

Do people learn more deeply when extraneous words, sounds, and pictures are excluded? Table 12.4 summarizes 11 comparisons between a group that received a concise multimedia presentation (i.e., concise group) and a group that received the multimedia presentation with added material that is not relevant to the goal of the lesson (i.e., embellished group). The left side of the table lists the experiment that is the source of the data, the middle portion of the table lists the content of the lesson, and the right side of the table lists the effect size. Overall, in 10 of 11 comparisons, there was a large positive effect size favoring the concise group, with a median effect size of 1.32.

In the first set of three comparisons listed in Table 12.4 (Mayer, Bove, Bryman, Mars, & Tapangco, 1996), students read a booklet explaining lightning formation and then took a transfer test. The concise booklet was a summary of the main steps in lightning formation, in the form of a series of annotated illustrations. The embellished booklet contained the same printed words and illustrations along with additional text providing details about lightning. As you can see, in the

Figure 12.3. Portion of book-based separated presentation on lightning. (Next page has same words as in Figure 12.1)

first three lines of Table 12.4, students performed better on transfer tests after reading the summary than after reading the longer lesson in two out of three tests.

In a second set of five studies (Harp & Mayer, 1997, 1998), students also read a booklet about lightning formation and then took a transfer test. The concise booklet included several paragraphs and several corre- sponding illustrations explaining the process of lightning formation, whereas the embellished booklet contained identical words and illustrations along with several interspersed illustrations and sentences concerning interesting stories about lightning. As in the first set of studies, students performed better on a subsequent transfer test after reading the concise rather than the embellished booklet, yielding effect sizes above 1 in all five comparisons.

The remaining three comparisons listed in Table 12.4 are based on computer-based presentations consisting of animation and narration. In one set of studies on lightning and how brakes work (Moreno & Mayer, 2000), adding background music and environmental sounds resulted in poorer transfer test performance than not having the added music and sounds (as shown in the ninth and tenth lines of Table 12.4). In a study on lightning (Mayer, Heiser, & Lonn, 2001), interspersing short video clips showing lightning storms – along with short narration about interesting lightning facts – resulted in poorer transfer test performance than not having the added clips (as shown in the last line of Table 12.4). These results show that coherence is important both in paper-based and computer-based presentations.

Overall, there is strong and consistent evidence for the *coherence principle*: People learn more deeply from a multimedia message when extraneous material is excluded rather than included.

Table 12.4. Evidence Concerning the Coherence Principle

Source	Content	Effect size
Mayer et al. (1996, Expt. 1)	Lightning	−0.17
Mayer et al. (1996, Expt. 2)	Lightning	0.70
Mayer et al. (1996, Expt. 3)	Lightning	0.98
Harp & Mayer (1997, Expt. 1)	Lightning	1.33
Harp & Mayer (1998, Expt. 1)	Lightning	1.68
Harp & Mayer (1998, Expt. 2)	Lightning	1.45
Harp & Mayer (1998, Expt. 3)	Lightning	1.27
Harp & Mayer (1998, Expt. 4)	Lightning	1.58
Moreno & Mayer (2000, Expt. 1)	Lightning	1.49
Moreno & Mayer(2000, Expt. 2)	Brakes	0.51
Mayer, Heiser, & Lonn (2001, Expt. 3)	Lightning	0.70
Median		1.32

Table 12.5. Evidence Concerning the Signaling Principle

Source	Content	Effect size
Harp & Mayer (1998, Expt. 3a)	Lightning	0.34
Mautone & Mayer (2001, Expt. 3a)	Airplane	0.60
Mautone & Mayer (2001, Expt. 3b)	Airplane	0.70
Median		0.60

Research on the Signaling Principle

Another technique for reducing extraneous processing is to provide signals to the learner, showing what to attend to. Table 12.5 lists three tests of the signaling principle. In the first study (Harp & Mayer, 1998), some students (nonsignaled group) read a paper-based lesson on lightning such as described in the previous section and then took a transfer test. For other students (signaled group), the text was modified by adding an organizational sentence listing the seven main steps, and then inserting numbers such as "(1)" to correspond to each step as it was described in the lesson. As shown in the first line of Table 12.5, this form of signaling produced a small effect size.

In the second set of two studies (Mautone & Mayer, 2001), some students (nonsignaled group) received a narrated animation explaining how an airplane achieves lift and then took a transfer test. Other students (signaled group) received the same instruction and test, except that the narration was signaled – that is, the narrator began by listing the three steps, and the narrator inserted a heading sentence before each section. Signaling benefited the students, yielding medium effect sizes as shown in the last two lines of Table 12.5.

Overall, Table 12.5 shows preliminary support for the *signaling principle*: People learn more deeply from a multimedia message when the text is signaled rather than nonsignaled. The signaling principle was supported in three out of three tests, yielding a median effect size of 0.60. Given that the effects are not strong and are based on only three tests, support for the signaling principle should be considered promising but preliminary.

Research on the Redundancy Principle

Finally, another way to reduce extraneous cognitive load for narrated animations (or narrated graphics) is to refrain from adding redundant on-screen text. Table 12.6 summarizes 10 experimental tests of the redundancy principle. The first two lines are based on studies by Mousavi, Low, and Sweller (1995) in which secondary school students learned to solve geometry proof problems through worked examples. Some students (redundant group) received worked examples in the form of a sheet with printed diagrams and printed words as well as an audio message with spoken words that were identical to the printed words. Other students (nonredundant group) received worked examples in the form of a sheet with printed diagrams and an audio message with spoken words. On a subsequent test of solving a transfer problem, the nonredundant group outperformed the redundant group, yielding effect sizes in the medium range.

The next two lines of Table 12.6 are based on studies by Kalyuga, Chandler, and Sweller (1999, 2000) in which trainees learned electrical engineering topics. Some students were given a computer presentation containing a printed diagram on the screen and an audio message with spoken words (nonredundant group) or a computer presentation containing a printed diagram and printed text on the screen along with an audio message with spoken words that were identical to the printed words (redundant group). On a subsequent problem-solving transfer test, the nonredundant group outperformed the redundant group, yielding high effect sizes. In the second study, shown on the fourth line of Table 12.6, the results were obtained for low-experience learners only. High-experience learners may have so much free processing capacity that they did not suffer from processing redundant materials.

Table 12.6. Evidence Concerning the Redundancy Principle

Source	Content	Effect size
Mousavi, Low, & Sweller (1995, Expt. 1)	Math problems	0.65
Mousavi, Low, & Sweller (1995, Expt. 2)	Math problems	0.49
Kalyuga, Chandler, & Sweller (1999, Expt. 1)	Electrical engineering	1.38
Kalyuga, Chandler, & Sweller (2000, Expt. 1)	Electrical engineering	0.86
Craig, Gholson, & Driscoll (2002, Expt. 2)	Lightning	0.67
Mayer, Heiser, & Lonn (2001, Expt. 1)	Lightning	0.88
Mayer, Heiser, & Lonn (2001, Expt. 2)	Lightning	1.21
Moreno & Mayer (2002b, Expt. 2)	Lightning	0.72
Moreno & Mayer (2002a, Expt. 2a)	Environmental science game	0.19
Moreno & Mayer (2002a, Expt. 2b)	Environmental science game	0.25
Median		0.69

The next four lines of Table 12.6 summarize studies (Craig, Gholson, & Driscoll, 2002; Mayer, Heiser et al., 2001; Moreno & Mayer, 2002b) in which students viewed a narrated animation on lightning formation (nonredundant group) or the same narrated animation along with redundant on-screen text (redundant group). In each comparison, the nonredundant group performed better than the redundant group on a problem-solving transfer test, with effect sizes in the medium and large range.

Finally, the last two lines of Table 12.6 summarize studies by Moreno and Mayer (2002a) involving an environmental science game in which the game was presented on a desktop computer (i.e., 9th line) or using a head-mounted display in virtual reality (i.e., 10th line). As part of the game, some students viewed animations and heard concurrent explanations (nonredundant group) whereas others viewed animations, heard concurrent explanations, and also saw on-screen text that was identical to the spoken explanations (redundant group). The nonredundant group performed better than the redundant group but the effect sizes were small.

Overall, there is consistent support for the redundancy principle: People learn more deeply from graphics and narration than from graphics, narration, and on-screen text. In all 10 tests, the nonredundant group outperformed the redundant group on tests of problem-solving transfer, yielding a median effect size of 0.69. The redundancy princi-

ple described in this chapter involves a specific situation in which the narration (i.e., the spoken words) and the on-screen text (i.e., the printed words) are identical. The redundancy principle described in this chapter represents a subset of Sweller's redundancy principle as described in chapter 10. In chapter 10, Sweller defines redundancy as occurring when "the same information is presented in multiple forms or is unnecessarily elaborated." This definition includes what I call redundancy (this chapter) and coherence (this chapter) as well as situations in which words and graphics convey the same information (which I do not address).

Research on the Spatial Contiguity Principle

Another way to reduce extraneous processing is to guide the learner's cognitive processing by placing printed words near the graphics they describe. Table 12.7 summarizes the results of eight tests of the spatial contiguity principle. In the first study listed in Table 12.7 (Mayer, 1989), students read a paper-based lesson on how brakes work and then took a transfer test. For some students (integrated group), the words describing an action – such as the piston moving forward in the master cylinder – were placed next to the corresponding part of an illustration – such as the master cylinder. For other students (separated group), each picture was at the top of a page and the corresponding words were in a paragraph at the bottom of

Table 12.7. Evidence for the Spatial Contiguity Principle

Source	Content	Effect size
Mayer (1989, Expt. 2)	Brakes	1.36
Sweller et al. (1990, Expt. 1)	Mathematics problems	0.71
Chandler & Sweller (1991, Expt. 1)	Electrical engineering	2.20
Mayer et al. (1995, Expt. 1)	Lightning	1.09
Mayer et al. (1995, Expt. 2)	Lightning	1.35
Mayer et al. (1995, Expt. 3)	Lightning	1.12
Tindall-Ford et al. (1997, Expt. 1)	Electrical engineering	1.08
Moreno & Mayer (1999, Expt. 1)	Lightning	0.82
Median		1.11

the page. The integrated group performed much better than the separated group on a transfer test, yielding an effect size above 1.

The second line in Table 12.7 summarizes a study by Sweller, Chandler, Tierney, and Cooper (1990) in which students learned to solve geometry problems by examining worked examples. In the integrated booklet, the text and symbols describing each step were placed next to the corresponding part of the geometry diagram, whereas in the separated booklet, the text and symbols describing each step were placed below the geometry diagram. The time to solve a transfer problem was less for students who learned with the integrated rather than the separated booklet, yielding a medium-to-high effect size. Although Sweller et al. found similar results in other experiments as well, these experiments are not included in Table 12.7 because means and standard deviations were not reported.

The third line in Table 12.7 summarizes a study in which trainees learned about topics in electrical engineering from an integrated or separated booklet, and later were asked to solve practical problems (Chandler & Sweller, 1991). In the integrated booklet, text describing each step in a procedure was placed next to the corresponding element in a diagram, whereas in the separated booklet the words were on the top of the sheet and the diagram was on the bottom. As in the previous study, the integrated group outperformed the separated group, yielding an effect size greater than 1. Chandler and Sweller also reported several other experiments in which students learned faster and

remembered more from integrated booklets than from separated booklets, but these experiments were not included in Table 12.7 because they did not report means and standard deviations for transfer test performance. Sweller and Chandler (1994) found similar results with a booklet on computer programming, but these results were not included in Table 12.7 because the separated treatment required information provided on a computer screen as well as information in a booklet.

Lines 4 through 6 of Table 12.7 show three comparisons in which students read an integrated or separated booklet on lightning formation and then took a transfer test (Mayer, Steinhoff, Bower, & Mars, 1995). For the integrated booklet, each illustration was placed next to the paragraph that described it and each illustration had a summary caption that contained words selected from the corresponding paragraph. For the separated booklet, the printed words were on a different page than the illustrations. In each of three comparisons, students performed better on the transfer test if they had read the integrated booklet rather than the segregated booklet, with effect sizes greater than 1 in each case.

In a follow-up study involving a computer-based animation with on-screen text (Moreno & Mayer, 1999), the on-screen text was either placed near the corresponding element in the animation (i.e., integrated group) or at the bottom of the screen (i.e., separated group). As shown in the eighth line of Table 12.7, students performed better on the transfer test if they had received the integrated presentation rather than the segregated presentation, with an effect size greater than 0.80.

Tindall-Ford, Chandler, and Sweller (1997) asked apprentices to read a booklet on topics in electrical engineering and then solve some practical problems. Some apprentices read an integrated booklet in which text describing each step in a procedure was placed next to the corresponding part of a diagram; others read a separated booklet in which the text was presented below the corresponding diagram. As shown in the seventh line of Table 12.7, the integrated group performed better on solving practical problems than did the separated group, yielding an effect size greater than 1.

In most cases the effect sizes favoring integrated presentation were large, yielding a median effect size of 1.11. Thus, there is strong and consistent support for the spatial contiguity principle: People learn more deeply from a multimedia message when corresponding text and pictures are presented near rather than far from each other on the page or screen. The spatial contiguity principle represents a subset of Ayres and Sweller's (chapter 8) split-attention principle. The split-attention principle refers to "avoiding formats that require learners to split their attention between, and mentally integrate, multiple sources of information" and includes what I refer to as spatial contiguity and temporal contiguity (described in this chapter), and situations in which students must use different multiple delivery systems such as both a computer-based lesson and a paper-based lesson (which I do not cover).

Research on the Temporal Contiguity Principle

Does presenting corresponding words and pictures at the same time foster deeper understanding than presenting them successively? Table 12.8 summarizes the results of eight tests of the temporal contiguity principle. The first set of two studies in Table 12.8 involves learning from a narrated animation explaining how a tire pump works (Mayer & Anderson, 1991). For some learners (simultaneous group), the words of the narration were synchronized with the events depicted in the animation, so that, for example when the narrator said "the inlet valve opens" the animation showed the inlet valve opening. For other learners (successive group), the entire narration was presented either before or after the entire animation. On subsequent tests of problem-solving transfer, the simultaneous group outperformed the successive group. Similar results were obtained with narrated animations concerning tire pumps and brakes (Mayer & Anderson, 1992), tire pumps and the human respiratory system (Mayer & Sims, 1994), and lightning and brakes (Mayer, Moreno, Boire, & Vagge, 1999). Importantly, the results reported by Mayer and Sims hold for high-spatial learners, but not for low-spatial learners, suggesting that low-spatial learners are less able to take advantage of improvements in temporal contiguity. In all eight cases the effect sizes were large, yielding a median effect size of 1.31. Thus, there is strong and consistent support for the temporal contiguity principle: People learn more deeply from a multimedia message when corresponding animation and narration are presented simultaneously rather than successively. Some research on temporal contiguity is also reviewed by Ayres and Sweller in chapter 8 on the Split Attention Principle. Split-attention refers to the need to integrate material from disparate sources, which is a broader concept than temporal contiguity.

What Are the Implications of Research for Cognitive Theory?

The research results summarized in Tables 12.4, 12.5, 12.6, 12.7, and 12.8 provide support for the predictions of the cognitive theory of multimedia learning as summarized in Figure 3.2 of chapter 3. When learners have to waste some of their precious

Table 12.8. Evidence Concerning the Temporal Contiguity Principle

Source	Content	Effect size
Mayer & Anderson (1991, Expt. 1)	Tire pump	0.92
Mayer & Anderson (1991, Expt. 2a)	Tire pump	1.14
Mayer & Anderson (1992, Expt. 1)	Tire pump	1.66
Mayer & Anderson (1992, Expt. 2)	Brakes	1.39
Mayer & Sims (1994)	Tire pump	0.91
Mayer & Sims (1994)	Lungs	1.22
Mayer et al. (1999, Expt. 1)	Lightning	2.22
Mayer et al. (1999, Expt. 2)	Brakes	1.40
Median		1.31

cognitive resources on processing of extraneous material, they allocate less cognitive processing to making sense of the essential material, and thus may not be able to build meaningful learning outcomes. In short, when they are prevented from active cognitive processing of the essential material, their learning outcomes suffer – as indicated by tests of problem-solving transfer.

According to the cognitive theory of multimedia learning, five ways to handle an extraneous overload situation are to eliminate extraneous material (coherence principle), insert signals emphasizing the essential material (signaling principle), eliminate redundant printed text (redundancy principle), place printed text next to corresponding parts of graphics (spatial contiguity principle), and eliminate the need to hold essential material in working memory for long periods of time (temporal contiguity principle). In each case, the guiding premise is that "less is more," that is, learners benefit when they can focus on processing the essential material rather than processing both essential and extraneous material. With the coherence and redundancy principles, the extraneous material is eliminated; with the signaling and spatial contiguity principles, typographic and linguistic cues draw learners' attention to the essential material; with temporal contiguity, the need for holding material in working memory for extended periods is eliminated. Thus, each of these principles has theoretical plausibility because they were derived from the cognitive theory of multimedia learning – particularly, concerning the limited capacity for processing information in working memory. The empirical evidence in support of each of these principles provides empirical plausibility as well as support for the predictions of the cognitive theory of multimedia learning.

What Are the Implications of Research for Instructional Design?

The research reviewed in this chapter shows that instructional designers should be sensitive to the limitations of working memory by being careful about the amount and layout of information that is presented to learners. That is, instructional designers should work hard to minimize the amount of unneeded and confusing detail in the graphical and textual material in multimedia messages. Extraneous material should be ruthlessly weeded out whenever possible so that the core of essential material is salient to the learner. Alternatively, cues should be included to direct the learner's cognitive processing of the essential material. The coherence and redundancy principles recommend minimizing the amount and detail of information presented, whereas the signaling and spatial contiguity principles recommend directing the learner's attention toward the essential material. Based on the coherence principle, multimedia messages should not include words, pictures, and sounds that are not directly relevant to the goal of instruction. Based on the signaling principle, the multimedia message should contain cues that emphasize the core essential material, such as an outline and headings. Based on the redundancy principle, when a multimedia message consists of animation (or illustrations) and narration, it is important to avoid the temptation to add redundant on-screen text that mirrors the narration. Based on the spatial contiguity principle, when a multimedia message consists of graphics and printed words, the printed words should be placed near the part of the graphic they refer to. When a multimedia message says, "see Figure 12.1," there is a good chance that the spatial contiguity principle has been violated. Finally, based on the temporal contiguity principle, it is important to present corresponding animation and narration at the same time. Furthermore, the designer should take learner characteristics into account and be aware that well-designed multimedia instruction may be most effective for low-experience learners and high-spatial learners.

What Are the Limitations of Current Research and What Are Some Productive Directions for Future Research?

The principles described in this chapter are subject to limitations in the nature of the task and in the dependent measures. Concerning the nature of the task, research is needed in which the principles are tested within ecologically valid environments. Some positive examples include research in secondary school classrooms (e.g., Mousavi et al., 1995; Sweller et al., 1990) and in industrial training programs (e.g., Chandler & Sweller, 1991; Kalyuga et al., 1999, 2000). Concerning the dependent measures, given that the goal of the five methods presented in this chapter is to reduce cognitive load, it would be useful to include direct measures of cognitive load in future research (Brunken, Plass, & Leutner, 2003; Paas, Tuovinen, Tabbers, & van Gerven, 2003).

Further research work is also needed to better understand the conditions under which each of the principles is most effective. Concerning the coherence principle, minimizing detail in graphics and verbal explanations may be a good approach for novices, but more experienced learners may require a greater amount of detail. For example, according to the expertise reversal effect (described in chapter 21) techniques that are helpful for novices may have the opposite effect for experts. Research is needed to calibrate the amount of detail that is appropriate for learners with different levels of prior knowledge.

Concerning the signaling principle, the preliminary results reported in this chapter are promising but much more work is needed to determine the strength and robustness of the effect. Although signaling has been found to improve learning from printed text (Loman & Mayer, 1983; Lorch, 1989), further research is needed to determine if signaling has the same effects in a multimedia environment.

Concerning redundancy, there may be situations in which presenting redundant spoken and printed words is warranted. For example, redundant multimedia messages may be more effective for special populations such as nonnative speakers of the language or learners with hearing disabilities. Redundant multimedia messages may be more effective when the verbal material includes technical terms. Finally, when there are no graphics, redundant spoken and printed words can boost learning (Moreno & Mayer, 2002a), so additional research is needed concerning the conditions under which redundancy is helpful.

Concerning spatial contiguity, most of the studies have involved a small amount of material, such as a few pages. An important issue concerns whether it makes sense to revamp textbooks so that the layout of each page is designed to integrate words and graphics. Similar issues concern the design of online e-courses and the design of PowerPoint slides. Thus, there is a need for research that broadens the learning context beyond a few pages of integrated text and pictures.

Concerning temporal contiguity, it would be useful to determine the temporal limits of the principle. For example, do the words and pictures need to be presented at exactly the same time, or can they be separated by a few seconds? Based on research by Baggett and Ehrenfeucht (1983) and Baggett (1984), it appears that learners experience difficulty even when corresponding words and pictures are separated by a few seconds. Further research is needed to determine the timing limitations for coordinating narration and animation in multimedia messages.

Glossary

Cognitive capacity: The total amount of processing that can be supported by the learner's working memory at any one time.

Coherence principle: People learn more deeply from a multimedia message when extraneous material is excluded rather than included.

Essential material: Words and pictures needed to achieve the instructional objective, such as understanding how a mechanical system works.

Essential processing: Cognitive processing – such as selecting relevant words and images, organizing selected words and images, and integrating – required to make sense out of the essential material; similar to Sweller's (1999) *intrinsic cognitive load*.

Extraneous material: Words and pictures that are not relevant to achieving the instructional objective, such as interesting stories or pictures.

Extraneous overload: When the amount of cognitive processing required by the essential and extraneous material in a multimedia instructional message exceeds the learner's cognitive capacity.

Extraneous processing: Cognitive processing required when an instructional message contains too much detail, embellishment, or gratuitous information, or when the layout of the material is confusing; similar to Sweller's (1999) *extraneous cognitive load*.

Redundancy principle: People learn more deeply from graphics and narration than from graphics, narration, and on-screen text.

Representational holding: Holding a representation of words or images in working memory.

Signaling principle: People learn more deeply from a multimedia message when cues are added that highlight the organization of the essential material.

Spatial contiguity principle: People learn more deeply from a multimedia message when corresponding words and pictures are presented near rather than far from each other on the page or screen.

Temporal contiguity principle: People learn more deeply from a multimedia message when corresponding animation and narration are presented simultaneously rather than successively.

Note

Preparation of this chapter was supported by Grant No. N000140410553 from the Office of Naval Research, titled "Role of Cognitive Style in Learning from Multimedia Training." I appreciate the helpful comments of Jeroen van Merriënboer, Wolfgang Schnotz, and John Sweller.

References

Baggett, P. (1984). Role of temporal overlap of visual and auditory material in forming dual media associations. *Journal of Educational Psychology*, 76, 408–417.

Baggett, P., & Ehrenfeucht, A. (1983). Encoding and retaining information in the visuals and verbals of an educational movie. *Educational Communications and Technology Journal*, 31, 23–32.

Brunken, R., Plass, J. L., & Leutner, D. (2003). Direct measurement of cognitive load in multimedia learning. *Educational Psychologist*, 38, 53–62.

Cohen, J. (1988). *Statistical power analysis for the behavioral sciences* (2nd ed.). Hillsdale, NJ: Lawrence Erlbaum Associates.

Cortina, J. M., & Nouri, H. (2000). *Effect size for ANOVA designs.* Thousand Oaks, CA: Sage.

Chandler, P., & Sweller, J. (1991). Cognitive load theory and the format of instruction. *Cognition and Instruction, 8,* 293–332.

Craig, S. D., Gholson, B., & Driscoll, D. M. (2002). Animated pedagogical agents in multimedia educational environments: Effects of agent properties, picture features, and redundancy. *Journal of Educational Psychology, 94,* 428–434.

Harp, S. F., & Mayer, R. E. (1997). The role of interest in learning from scientific text and illustrations: On the distinction between emotional interest and cognitive interest. *Journal of Educational Psychology, 89,* 92–102.

Harp, S. F., & Mayer, R. E. (1998). How seductive details do their damage: A theory of cognitive interest in science learning. *Journal of Educational Psychology, 90,* 414–434.

Hegarty, M., Carpenter, P. A., & Just, M. A. (1996). Diagrams in the comprehension of scientific texts. In T. Barr, M. L. Kamil, P. Mosenthal, & P. D. Pearson (Eds.), *Handbook of reading research, Volume II* (pp. 641–668). Mahwah, NJ: Erlbaum.

Kalyuga, S., Chandler, P., & Sweller, J. (1999). Managing split-attention and redundancy in multimedia instruction. *Applied Cognitive Psychology, 13,* 351–371.

Kalyuga, S., Chandler, P., & Sweller, J. (2000). Incorporating learner experience into the design of multimedia instruction. *Journal of Educational Psychology, 92,* 126–136.

Loman, N. L., & Mayer, R. E. (1983). Signaling techniques that increase the understandability of expository prose. *Journal of Educational Psychology, 75,* 402–412.

Lorch, R. F., Jr. (1989). Text signaling devices and their effects on reading and memory processes. *Educational Psychology Review, 1,* 209–234.

Mautone, P. D., & Mayer, R. E. (2001). Signaling as a cognitive guide in multimedia learning. *Journal of Educational Psychology, 93,* 377–389.

Mayer, R. E. (1989). Systematic thinking fostered by illustrations in scientific text. *Journal of Educational Psychology, 81,* 240–246.

Mayer, R. E. (2001). *Multimedia learning.* New York: Cambridge University Press.

Mayer, R. E., & Anderson, R. B. (1991). Animations need narrations: An experimental test of a dual-coding hypothesis. *Journal of Educational Psychology, 83,* 484–490.

Mayer, R. E., & Anderson, R. B. (1992). The instructive animation: Helping students build connections between words and pictures in multimedia learning. *Journal of Educational Psychology, 84,* 444–452.

Mayer, R. E., Bove, W., Bryman, A., Mars, R., & Tapangco, L. (1996). When less is more: Meaningful learning from visual and verbal summaries of science textbook lessons. *Journal of Educational Psychology, 88,* 64–73.

Mayer, R. E., Heiser, H., & Lonn, S. (2001). Cognitive constraints on multimedia learning: When presenting more material results in less understanding. *Journal of Educational Psychology, 93,* 187–198.

Mayer, R. E., & Moreno, R. (2003). Nine ways to reduce cognitive load in multimedia learning. *Educational Psychologist, 38,* 43–52.

Mayer, R. E., Moreno, R., Boire, M., & Vagge, S. (1999). Maximizing constructivist learning from multimedia communications by minimizing cognitive load. *Journal of Educational Psychology, 91,* 638–643.

Mayer, R. E., & Sims, V. K. (1994). For whom is a picture worth a thousand words? Extensions of a dual-coding theory of multimedia learning? *Journal of Educational Psychology, 86,* 389–401.

Mayer, R. E., Steinhoff, K., Bower, G., & Mars, R. (1995). A generative theory of textbook design: Using annotated illustrations to foster meaningful learning of science text. *Educational Technology Research and Development, 43,* 31–43.

Mousavi, S. Y., Low, R., & Sweller, J. (1995). Reducing cognitive load by mixing auditory and visual presentation modes. *Journal of Educational Psychology, 87,* 319–334.

Moreno, R., & Mayer, R. E. (1999). Cognitive principles of multimedia learning: The role of modality and contiguity. *Journal of Educational Psychology, 91,* 358–368.

Moreno, R., & Mayer, R. E. (2000). A coherence effect in multimedia learning: The case for minimizing irrelevant sounds in the design of multimedia messages. *Journal of Educational Psychology, 92,* 117–125.

Moreno, R., & Mayer, R. E. (2002a). Verbal redundancy in multimedia learning: When reading helps listening. *Journal of Educational Psychology, 94,* 156–163.

Moreno, R., & Mayer, R. E. (2002b). Learning science in virtual reality multimedia environments: Role of methods and media. *Journal of Educational Psychology, 94,* 598–610.

Paas, F., Tuovinen, J. E., Tabbers, H., & van Gerven, P. W. M. (2003). Cognitive load measurement as a means to advance cognitive load theory. *Educational Psychologist, 38,* 63–72.

Sweller, J. (1999). *Instructional design in technical areas.* Camberwell, Australia: ACER Press.

Sweller, J., & Chandler, P. (1994). Why some material is difficult to learn. *Cognition and Instruction, 12,* 185–233.

Sweller, J., Chandler, P., Tierney, P., & Cooper, M. (1990). Cognitive load and selective attention as factors in the structuring of technical material. *Journal of Experimental Psychology: General, 119,* 176–192.

Tindall-Ford, S., Chandler, P., & Sweller, J. (1997). When two sensory modalities are better than one. *Journal of Experimental Psychology: Applied, 3,* 257–287.

CHAPTER 13

Principles of Multimedia Learning Based on Social Cues: Personalization, Voice, and Image Principles

Richard E. Mayer

University of California, Santa Barbara

Abstract

Social cues may prime social responses in learners that lead to deeper cognitive processing during learning and hence better test performance. The *personalization principle* is that people learn more deeply when the words in a multimedia presentation are in conversational style rather than formal style. This principle was supported in 10 out of 10 experimental tests, yielding a median effect size of 1.3. The *voice principle* is that people learn more deeply when the words in a multimedia message are spoken in a standard-accented human voice rather than in a machine voice or foreign-accented human voice. This principle was supported in four out of four experimental comparisons, with a median effect size of 0.8. The *image principle* is that people do not necessarily learn more deeply from a multimedia presentation when the speaker's image is on the screen rather than not on the screen. This principle was based on nine experimental tests with mixed results, yielding a median effect size of 0.2.

What Are the Personalization, Voice, and Image Principles?

Definitions

The goal of this chapter is to examine the research evidence concerning three principles for multimedia design that are based on social cues – personalization, voice, and image principles. The *personalization principle* is that people learn more deeply when the words in a multimedia presentation are in conversational style rather than formal style. The *voice principle* is that people learn more deeply when the words in a multimedia message are spoken in a standard-accented human voice rather than in a machine voice or foreign-accented human voice. The *image principle* is that people do not necessarily learn more deeply from a multimedia presentation when the speaker's image is on the screen rather than not on the screen.

Rationale

Mayer, Fennell, Farmer, and Campbell (2004) have argued that there are two paths for fostering meaningful learning in multimedia learning environments: (1) designing multimedia instructional messages in ways that reduce the learner's cognitive load thus freeing the learner to engage in active cognitive processing, and (2) designing multimedia messages in ways that increase the learner's motivational commitment to active cognitive processing. Although cognitive considerations have received the most attention in research on multimedia learning (Mayer, 2001; Mayer & Moreno, 2003; Paas, Renkl, & Sweller, 2003; Sweller, 1999), progress in designing computer-based learning environments also can be made by attending to social considerations that affect the learner's motivation to engage in cognitive processing (Lepper, Woolverton, Mumme, & Gurtner, 1993; Mayer et al., 2004; Mayer, Sobko, & Mautone, 2003).

Theory

How do social cues affect multimedia learning? The top portion of Figure 13.1 lays out a framework in which social cues in a multimedia instructional message – such as the nature of the speaker's voice or conversational style – prime the activation of a social response in the learner – such as the commitment to try to make sense out of what the speaker is saying. This social response causes increases in active cognitive processing by the learner – as the learner works harder to select, organize, and integrate incoming information – which in turn leads to a learning outcome that is better able to support problem-solving transfer performance. The bottom portion of Figure 13.1 summarizes the scenario when multimedia instructional messages lack social cues, in which a social response is not activated, the learner does not work harder to process the incoming information, and the learning outcome is not improved.

Concerning the arrow from the first box to the second box, Reeves and Nass (1996) have shown that people are easily induced into accepting computers as social partners. This line of research suggests that subtle cues such as a speaker's voice or conversation style can encourage learners to respond socially to an online tutor. Concerning the arrow from the second box to the third box, Grice (1975) has shown that in human-to-human communication, people assume the speaker is trying to make sense by being informative, accurate, relevant, and concise. Based on what Grice calls the *cooperation principle*, the listener works hard to understand the speaker because the listener and speaker have an implicit agreement to do so. Concerning the arrow from the third box to the fourth box, the cognitive theory of multimedia learning proposes that increases in active processing, such as the five processes shown in Figure 3.2 of chapter 3, lead to higher quality learning outcomes that better support problem-solving transfer (Mayer, 2001; also chapters 11 and 12 in this volume). We use the term *social agency theory* to refer to the theoretical framework summarized in the top of Figure 13.1, that is, the idea that social cues in multimedia instructional messages can prime a social response in learners that leads to deeper cognitive processing and better learning outcomes. Social agency theory can be seen as an enhancement or addition to the cognitive theory of multimedia learning.

What Are Examples of the Personalization, Voice, and Image Principles?

How can we modify multimedia instructional messages so that they activate appropriate social responses in learners? In other words, what can we do to a multimedia instructional message to increase the learner's feeling of social presence, that is, to make the learner feel a stronger personal

How Social Cues Prime Deeper Learning

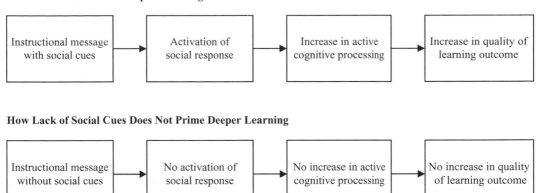

Figure 13.1. How the presence or absence of social cues affects learning.

relationship with the instructor? In this chapter, I explore three kinds of social cues that are intended to activate social presence in the learner – personalization cues, voice cues, and image cues.

Personalization Cues

Personalization involves taking the words in a multimedia lesson and converting them from formal style to conversational style. Two major techniques for creating conversational style are (1) to use *you* and *I* rather than relying solely on third-person constructions, and (2) to add sentences in which the instructor makes direct comments to the learner. For example, suppose a learner clicks on *lightning* in a multimedia encyclopedia and a 140-second narrated animation appears explaining the steps in lightning formation. The words are in formal style, such as shown in Table 13.1. Then, to help personalize the script, (1) in eight locations you change some words such as "the" to "your" or "people" to "you", and (2) in six locations you add a sentence that speaks directly to the learner, such as, "Brr! I'm feeling cold just thinking about it." In Table 13.1, the added material is indicated by the brackets and the deleted words are in italics. In converting the lightning script from formal to conversational style, however, the instructional content remains the same – that is, the explanation of the steps in lightning formation is not altered.

As another example, suppose you are a learner playing a science simulation game concerning how to design plants to survive in an alien environment. An on-screen agent named Herman-the-Bug interacts with you, giving you suggestions, feedback, and basic explanations for how plants grow. In the nonpersonalized version of the program, Herman speaks in a formal style, without using *I* or *you* and without making direct comments to you. Portions of this nonpersonalized script are shown in Table 13.2. In order to personalize the script, we can reword sentences to use conversational style, such as exemplified in the personalized portions of script shown in Table 13.2. As with the lightning script, the personalized and nonpersonalized versions contain the same instructional content.

Finally, consider a 60-second narrated animation explaining how the respiratory system works. The nonpersonalized version of the script is shown in Table 13.3. To personalize the script, we can simply change *the* to *your* in 12 places, as shown by the brackets in Table 13.3. Although the changes are modest, the goal is to create a conversational style, while not altering the instructional content of the lesson.

Table 13.1. Nonpersonalized and Personalized Versions of the Script for the Lightning Lesson (with Personalized Additions Indicated in Brackets and Deletions Indicated by Italics)

[Let me tell you what happens when lightning forms. Suppose you are standing outside, feeling the warm rays of the sun heating up the earth's surface around you.] Cool moist air moves over a warmer surface and becomes heated. The warmed moist air near the earth's surface rises rapidly. As the air in this updraft cools, water vapor condenses into water droplets and forms a cloud. [Congratulations! You have just witnessed the birth of your own cloud.]

[As you watch, you tilt your head skyward. Your] *The* cloud's top extends above the freezing level, so the upper portion of [your] *the* cloud is composed of tiny ice crystals. [Brr! I'm feeling cold just thinking about it!] Eventually, the water droplets and ice crystals become too large to be suspended by updrafts. As raindrops and ice crystals fall through [your] *the* cloud, they drag some of the air in [your] *the* cloud downward, producing downdrafts. When downdrafts strike the ground, they spread out in all directions, producing the gusts of cool wind [you] *people* feel just before the start of the rain. [If you could look inside your cloud, you would see a neat pattern:] *Within the cloud* the rising and falling air currents cause electrical charges to build. The charge results from the collision of [your] *the* cloud's rising water droplets against heavier, falling pieces of ice. The negatively charged particles fall to the bottom of the cloud, and most of the positively charged particles rise to the top.

[Now that your cloud is charged up, I can tell you the rest of the story:] A stepped leader of negative charges moves downward in a series of steps. It nears the ground. A positively charged leader travels up from objects [around you] such as trees and buildings. The two leaders generally meet about 165 feet above the ground. Negatively charged particles then rush from [your] *the* cloud to the ground along the path created by the leaders. It is not very bright. As the leader stroke nears the ground, it induces an opposite charge, so positively charged particles from the ground rush upward along the same path. The upward motion of the current is the return stroke. It produces the bright light that [you] *people* notice as a flash of lightning.

Voice Cues

Another possible way to affect the learner's social response to a multimedia instructional message is to alter the voice in the narration. For example, suppose that the words in the nonpersonalized lightning script shown in Table 13.1 are spoken by a native English speaker with a standard accent. A human voice, speaking with a standard accent conveys a sense of social presence – that is, it conveys the idea that someone is speaking directly to you. In contrast, we could run the same script through a speech synthesizer such as *Bruce (high quality)* provided in the voice folder of Macintosh G4 computers (Mayer, Sobko, & Mautone, 2003). A machine-synthesized voice – although perceptually discernable – may convey less of a sense of social presence – that is, it may not strongly convey the idea that someone is speaking directly to you. A human voice with a foreign accent – such as a Russian accent – may also diminish the learner's social response to the message. Thus, voice cues may affect the degree to which a learner feels a social response to the instructional message.

Image Cues

A seemingly straightforward way to increase the learner's sense of social presence is to add an on-screen character who delivers the script. For example, an animated pedagogical agent is a on-screen character who appears to interact with the learner. For example, in a narrated animation of lightning formation, we could add an on-screen character in the form of a man who points to the events in the narration as he describes them (Craig, Gholson, & Driscoll, 2002). In an environmental science simulation game, we could add an on-screen cartoon-like character named Herman-the-Bug who gestures as he speaks the words in the script in Table 13.2 (Moreno, Mayer, Spires, & Lester, 2001). Alternatively, in a lesson that explains worked-out examples of how to solve arithmetic word problems, we can add an

Table 13.2. Portion of Text of Nonpersonalized and Personalized Versions for an Environmental Science Simulation Game

---

Nonpersonalized Version of the Game's Introduction
This program is about what type of plant survives on different planets. For each planet, a plant will be designed. The goal is to learn what type of roots, stem, and leaves allow plants to survive in each environment. Some hints are provided throughout the program.

Personalized Version of the Game's Introduction
You are about to start on a journey where you will be visiting different planets. For each planet, you will need to design a plant. Your mission is to learn what type of roots, stem, and leaves will allow your plant to survive in each environment. I will be guiding you through by giving out some hints.

Nonpersonalized Introduction to First Environment
The goal is to design a plant that will survive, maybe even flourish, in an environment of heavy rain. It is perfect for any root and stem, but the leaves need to be flexible so they won't be damaged by the heavy rain.

Personalized Introduction to First Environment
Your only goal here is to design a plant that will survive, maybe even flourish, in this environment of heavy rain. It is perfect for any of the roots and stems, but your leaves need to be flexible so they won't be damaged by the heavy rain.

Nonpersonalized Explanation Concerning Rainy Environments
In very rainy environments, plant leaves have to flexible so they are not damaged by the rainfall. What really matters for the rain is the choice between thick and thin leaves.

Personalized Explanation Concerning Rainy Environments
This is a very rainy environment and the leaves of your plant have to be flexible so they're not damaged by the rainfall. What really matters for the rain is your choice between thick leaves and thin leaves.

---

on-screen character – Peedy the parrot – who points to steps in the solution as he describes them (Atkinson, 2002), or in a simulation game explaining the operation of electric motors we can add an on-screen character named Dr. Phyz who flies around the relevant portions of the screen as he gives his explanation (Mayer, Dow, & Mayer, 2003). In each case, the animated pedagogical agent uses exactly the same words as in the lesson that did not have an on-screen agent.

What Do We Know About the Personalization, Voice, and Image Principles?

During the past few years, a small but consistent research base has developed concerning the personalization, voice, and image principles. In this review, I consider articles published in archival journals in which (a) the task is an instructional lesson involving words and pictures; (b) the independent

Table 13.3. Nonpersonalized and Personalized Versions for the Lungs Script (with Personalized Additions Indicated in Brackets and Deletions Indicated by Italics)

There are three phases in respiration: inhaling, exchanging, and exhaling. During inhaling, *the* [your] diaphragm moves down creating more space for *the* [your] lungs, air enters through *the* [your] nose or mouth, moves down through *the* [your] throat and bronchial tubes to tiny air sacs in *the* [your] lungs. During exchange, oxygen moves from *the* [your] air sacs to the bloodstream running nearby, and carbon dioxide moves from the bloodstream to *the* [your] air sacs. During exhaling, *the* [your] diaphragm moves up creating less room for *the* [your] lungs, air travels through *the* [your] bronchial tubes and throat to *the* [your] nose and mouth where it leaves *the* [your] body.

Table 13.4. Personalization Effect: Summary of Results

Source	Content	Effect Size
Moreno & Mayer (2000, Expt. 1)	Lightning (voice)	1.05
Moreno & Mayer (2000, Expt. 2)	Lightning (text)	1.61
Moreno & Mayer (2000, Expt. 3)	Environmental science simulation game (voice)	1.92
Moreno & Mayer (2000, Expt. 4)	Environmental science simulation game (text)	1.49
Moreno & Mayer (2000, Expt. 5)	Environmental science simulation game (voice)	1.11
Moreno & Mayer (2004, Expt. 1a)	Environmental science simulation game (voice)	1.58
Moreno & Mayer (2004, Expt. 1b)	Environmental science simulation game (voice, virtual reality)	1.93
Mayer et al. (2004, Expt. 1)	Lungs (voice)	0.52
Mayer et al. (2004, Expt. 2)	Lungs (voice)	1.00
Mayer et al. (2004, Expt. 3)	Lungs (voice)	0.79
Median		1.30

variable involves degree of personalization of the speaker's speech (i.e., personalized versus nonpersonalized), the type of voice (machine versus human, or foreign accented versus standard accented), or the presence of the speaker's visual image (image present or no image present); (c) the dependent measure is performance on a problem-solving transfer test; and (d) reported statistics include the mean and standard deviation of each group. I focused on problem-solving transfer scores because I am most interested in how to promote understanding of the presented material. I computed effect size for each comparison by subtracting the mean problem-solving transfer score of the control group from the mean problem-solving transfer score of the experimental group (e.g., the personalized group – the nonpersonalized group, the human voice group – the machine voice group, or the image-present – no image-present group) and dividing by the pooled standard deviation (Cortina & Nouri, 2000). Following Cohen (1988), I consider an effect size of 0.2 to be small, 0.5 to medium, and 0.8 to be large.

Research on the Personalization Principle

Do students learn more deeply when the words in a multimedia lesson are changed from formal style to conversational style? Table 13.4 summarizes 10 comparisons between a group that received instruction with the words presented in conversational style (i.e., personalized group) and a group that received the words presented in formal style (i.e., nonpersonalized group). The left side of the table lists the experiment that is the source of the data, the middle portion of the table lists the content of the lesson, and the right side of the table lists the effect size. Overall, in each of 10 comparisons, there is a strong positive effect size, with a median effect size of 1.29.

In one set of studies, Moreno and Mayer (2000) compared the learning outcomes of students who viewed a 140-second narrated animation on lightning formation in which the speaker used conventional style (i.e., personalized group) or the speaker used formal style (i.e., nonpersonalized group). In the version with conversational style, the speaker used first person (i.e., *I*) and second person (i.e., *you*) and made comments directly to the learner; in the version with formal style the speaker did not use *I* or *you* and did not directly comment to the learner. However, both versions contained the same description of the steps in lightning formation – the core of the lesson. For example, Table 13.1 presents the words used in the

Table 13.5. Voice Effect: Summary of Results

Source	Content	Effect Size
Mayer, Sobko, & Mautone (2003, Expt. 1)	Lightning (foreign accent)	0.90
Mayer, Sobko, & Mautone (2003, Expt. 2)	Lightning (machine voice)	0.79
Atkinson, Mayer, & Merrill (in press, Expt. 1)	Mathematics word problems (machine voice)	0.69
Atkinson, Mayer, & Merrill (in press, Expt. 1)	Mathematics word problems (machine voice)	0.78
Median		0.79

personalized and nonpersonalized versions. The top line of Table 13.4 shows that the personalized group performed better than the nonpersonalized group on a problem-solving transfer test in which the learner had to use what was learned to solve new problems about lightning. Similarly, the same pattern was found when the words were presented as on screen text in personalized or nonpersonalized style (as shown in the second line of Table 13.4). In both comparisons the effect size was large, which can be defined as greater than 0.8.

In a second set of studies, Moreno and Mayer (2000, 2004) compared the learning outcomes of students who learned from an environmental science simulation game in which they interacted with an onscreen agent named Herman-the-Bug. In the personalized version, Herman spoke (or produced on-screen text) that was in conversational style and in the nonpersonalized version Herman spoke (or produced on-screen text) that was in formal style. Table 13.2 lists some of the script for the personalized and nonpersonalized versions. The instructional content of both versions was identical, that is, both provided the same descriptions of how plants grow. As shown in lines 3 through 7 of Table 13.4, the personalized group produced much better transfer test performance than the nonpersonalized group, yielding large effect sizes (i.e., greater than 0.8) in all cases. Even when the lesson was presented in virtual reality (Moreno & Mayer, 2004), using a head-mounted display rather than on a desktop computer, the personalization effect was strong (as shown in the seventh line of Table 13.4).

Finally, in a third set of studies, Mayer et al. (2004) examined a much more modest form of personalization in a 60-second narrated animation explaining how the human respiratory system works. As shown in Table 13.3, in the nonpersonalized version the article *the* was used, whereas in the personalized version, *the* was changed to *your* in 12 places. Even this seemingly minor change created medium-to-large effect sizes favoring the personalization group across three separate experiments, as shown in lines 8 through 10 of Table 13.4.

Overall, there is strong and consistent evidence for the *personalization principle*: People learn more deeply when words are presented in conversational style rather than formal style.

Research on the Voice Principle

Does it hurt student understanding of a multimedia lesson to change the spoken words from a human voice with standard accent to a machine voice or human voice with foreign accent? Table 13.5 lists four tests of the voice principle. In the first set of studies (Mayer, Sobko, & Mautone, 2003), students received a 140-second narrated animation on lightning formation in nonpersonalized style in which the words were spoken with a Russian accent or a standard accent (Experiment 1) or with a machine-synthesized voice or a human voice with a standard accent (Experiment 2). Although both the foreign-accented voice and the machine-synthesized voice were clearly discernable, they resulted in much worse performance on a subsequent problem-solving transfer

Table 13.6. Image Effect: Summary of Results

Source	Content	Effect Size
Moreno et al. (2001, Expt. 4a)	Environmental science simulation game (cartoon image, voice)	−0.50
Moreno et al. (2001, Expt. 4b)	Environmental science simulation game (cartoon image, text)	0.22
Moreno et al. (2001, Expt. 5a)	Environmental science simulation game (video image, voice)	0.22
Moreno et al. (2001, Expt. 5b)	Environmental science simulation game (video image, voice)	0.35
Craig, Gholson, Driscoll (2002, Expt. 1)	Lightning (cartoon image, voice)	0.26
Atkinson (2002, Expt. 1a)	Mathematics word problems (cartoon image, voice)	0.26
Atkinson (2002, Expt. 1b)	Mathematics word problems (cartoon image, text)	−0.22
Atkinson (2002, Expt. 2)	Mathematics word problems (cartoon image, voice)	0.58
Mayer, Dow, & Mayer (2003, Expt. 4)	Electric motor (cartoon image, voice)	0.19
Median		0.22

test as compared with the standard-accented human voice.

In the second set of studies (Atkinson, Mayer, & Merrill, in press), students studied worked examples of arithmetic word problems that were explained by an on-screen cartoon-like character named Peedy that spoke with a machine voice or a human voice. On a subsequent test of problem-solving transfer to dissimilar problems, students in the machine-voice group performed worse than those in the human-voice group across two separate experiments.

Overall, Table 13.5 shows consistent, medium-to-large effect sizes favoring the human voice over the machine voice, yielding a median effect size of 0.79. These findings are consistent with the *voice principle*: People learn more deeply when narration in a multimedia lesson is spoken in a standard-accented human voice rather than in a machine voice or foreign-accented human voice.

Research on the Image Principle

Does adding an image of the speaker on the screen – such as a cartoon-like character – help students learn more deeply from a multimedia lesson? Table 13.6 summarizes

the results of nine separate tests of the image principle.

The first set of four studies in Table 13.6 involves learning about environmental science in a simulation game (Moreno et al., 2001), with the help of an on-screen animated pedagogical agent named Herman-the-Bug. In the first experiment (shown in the first line of Table 13.6), students who had Herman's image on the screen as he spoke performed worse on a subsequent problem-solving transfer test than did students who heard only his voice. In a second experiment (shown in the second line of Table 13.6), students who had Herman's image on the screen as his comments appeared as on-screen text performed slightly better than students who saw only the on-screen text. In two follow-up studies (shown in lines 3 and 4 of Table 13.6), students who saw a window with video of a human talking head performed slightly better on a subsequent transfer test than did students who only heard the human voice.

The next study in Table 13.6 (shown in line 5) involves a narrated animation explaining how lightning forms (Craig et al., 2002). Some students received a narrated animation that included a cartoon-like character that pointed to relevant aspects of the animation as he spoke, whereas others received the narrated animation without an on-screen character. The image-present group performed slightly better than the no-image-present group on a subsequent problem-solving transfer test.

The third set of studies in Table 13.6 (shown in lines 6 through 8) involves a lesson in which students learn to solve mathematics problems from worked examples (Atkinson, 2002). Some students received an on-screen cartoon-like character, named Peedy, who spoke to them (or generated on-screen text) as he pointed to relevant parts of the example, whereas others received the identical words but without an on-screen character. Across three comparisons, respectively, the image-present group performed slightly worse, slightly better, and moderately better than the no-image-present group.

Finally, the bottom line in Table 13.6 is based on an interactive lesson on how electric motors work (Mayer et al., 2003). When the learner clicked on a question, a narrated animation appeared on the screen. For some learners, the explanation was accompanied by an on-screen character named Dr. Phyz, whereas for others Dr. Phyz did not appear on the screen. Students in the image-present group performed slightly better than those in the no-image-present group.

Overall, there are negative or negligible effect sizes in three studies, small effect sizes in five studies, and a medium effect in one study, yielding a median effect size of 0.22. Thus, there is not strong support for adding the speaker's image on the screen. Based on these findings, the current state of the image principle is: People do not necessarily learn more deeply from a multimedia lesson when the speaker's image is added to the screen.

What Are the Implications of Research for Cognitive Theory?

The research results summarized in Tables 13.4, 13.5, and 13.6 provide support for the social agency theory as summarized in Figure 13.1. Social cues such as the conversational style of the speaker or the accent of the speaker's voice can have substantial effects on how well learners understand the material in a multimedia presentation. Table 13.4 shows that there is strong and consistent evidence for the personalization principle in which conversational style serves as a social cue; and Table 13.5 shows that there is solid preliminary support evidence for the voice principle in which the voice's accent serves as a social cue. Interestingly, Table 13.6 shows that the physical presence of a character on the screen may not be an important social cue that affects the learner's motivation to work hard to understand the presented material. However, on-screen characters may serve as cognitive aids by directing the learner's attention through pointing or gesturing.

What Are the Implications of Research for Instructional Design?

The research reviewed in this chapter shows that instructional designers should be sensitive to social considerations as well as cognitive considerations when they create multimedia instructional messages. Based on the personalization principle, multimedia instructional messages should be presented in conversation style rather than formal style. However, too much emphasis on extraneous conversational tactics might create a *seductive detail* that distracts the learner (Harp & Mayer, 1998). Based on the voice principle, the spoken words in multimedia instructional messages should come from a standard-accented human voice. However, it is possible that over time learners could become accustomed to a machine voice or a foreign-accented human voice or that certain learners might prefer certain types of machine or accented voices. Finally, based on the image principle, it does not appear necessary to create on-screen agents as a way to promote social engagement; however, in some cases on-screen agents may serve a cognitive role by directing the learner's attention. These recommendations are particularly relevant for the design of animated pedagogical agents – computer-based characters that help students learn – as described by Moreno (chapter 31) as well as by Cassell, Sullivan, Prevost, and Churchill (2000).

What Are the Limitations of Current Research and What Are Some Productive Directions for Future Research?

Although the research summarized in Tables 13.4, 13.5, and 13.6 provides somewhat consistent support for the personalization, voice, and image principles, respectively, the existing research base is limited in terms of the task environment, dependent measures, and independent variables.

First, concerning the task environment, many of the reported studies involve short narrated animations presented to college students in laboratory settings with immediate tests. Further studies are needed that are conducted within a more realistic, ecologically valid environment, while still maintaining rigorous experimental control.

Second, concerning dependent measures, all of the effects reported in Tables 13.4, 13.5, and 13.6 are based on measures of problem-solving transfer because I am particularly interested in how to promote understanding. Studies that focus only on measures of retention do not adequately inform the issue of learner understanding, so future research should continue to use measures of transfer. In addition, social agency theory is based on the idea that social cues prime social responses in learners such as responding to the computer as a social partner. For example, in some studies, the authors included surveys in which the learner's rated their affect for the instructor (e.g., Atkinson, 2002; Mayer et al., 2004). Although such measures represent a useful first step that should be continued, more systematic and direct measures of social responses are needed. The current research base lacks direct evidence concerning whether or not social cues activate social responses in learners, so direct measures of social responses should be included in future research.

Third, concerning the independent variables, I am concerned with the fidelity and consistency of the treatments across studies as well as possible confounding variables. For example, there are no firm guidelines for how to add personalization to a script, and for how much personalization to add. Research is needed to calibrate how much personalization and what kind of personalization is most effective and under what conditions. Concerning the voice principle, although machine voices and Russian-accented voices may impair learning for U.S. students, more research is needed to determine whether certain foreign accents (such as a British accent) foster different affective responses and learning outcomes in learners; whether learners prefer and learn better from a speaker who has their kind of accent; and whether voice effects are eliminated as learners spend more time with a particular speaker. Similarly, concerning the image principle, it would be useful to tease apart the effects of having a character's image on the screen and having the character make gestures, such as pointing, that help guide the learner's attention. For example, Craig et al. (2002) found that students learned at about the same level from an agent that gestured as from an agent that did not gesture. More research is needed to determine the independent contribution of an agent's on-screen image and an agent's pointing to relevant aspects of the display.

Finally, although social cues are intended to prime deeper processing in learning, a potential confounding factor is the role of cognitive load. Adding certain kinds of personalization – such as extraneous sentences – may create extraneous cognitive load (Sweller, 1999); machine voice or foreign-accented voice may also create additional cognitive load because the learner has to work harder to decipher the words; and the agent's image on the screen may serve as a seductive detail that distracts the learner (Harp & Mayer, 1998). Possible increases in cognitive load may offset or reduce the advantages of some social cues. Future research should investigate this possibility by incorporating measures of cognitive load (Brunken, Plass, & Leutner, 2003; Paas, Tuovinen, Tabbers, & van Gerven, 2003).

Glossary

Animated pedagogical agents: On-screen characters who communicate with learners by providing feedback, guidance, and encouragement.

Image principle: People do not necessarily learn more deeply from a multimedia presentation when the speaker's image is on the screen rather than not on the screen.

Personalization principle: People learn more deeply when the words in a multimedia presentation are in conversational style rather than formal style.

Social cues: Aspects of multimedia instructional messages that encourage the learner to view the tutor as a social partner, such as conversational style and human voice.

Voice principle: People learn more deeply when the words in a multimedia message are spoken in a standard-accented human voice rather than in a machine voice or foreign-accented human voice.

Note

Preparation of this chapter was supported by Grant No. 0121330 from the National Science Foundation, titled "Social Intelligence in Interfaces in Educational Software." I appreciate the helpful comments of Robert Atkinson and John Sweller.

References

Atkinson, R. K. (2002). Optimizing learning from examples using animated pedagogical agents. *Journal of Educational Psychology, 94,* 416–427.

Atkinson, R. K., Mayer, R. E., & Merrill, M. M. (in press). Fostering social agency in multimedia learning: Examining the impact of an animated agent's voice. *Contemporary Educational Psychology.*

Brunken, R., Plass, J., & Leutner, D. (2003). Direct measurement of cognitive load in multimedia learning. *Educational Psychologist, 38,* 53–62.

Cassell, J., Sullivan, J., Prevost, S., & Churchill, E. (Eds.). (2000). *Embodied conversational agents.* Cambridge, MA: MIT Press.

Cohen, J. (1988). *Statistical power analysis for the behavioral sciences* (2nd ed.). Hillsdale, NJ: Lawrence Erlbaum Associates.

Cortina, J. M., & Nouri, H. (2000). *Effect size for ANOVA designs.* Thousand Oaks, CA: Sage.

Craig, S. D., Gholson, B., & Driscoll, D. M. (2002). Animated pedagogical agent in multimedia educational environments: Effects of agent properties, picture features, and redundancy. *Journal of Educational Psychology, 94,* 428–434.

Grice, H. P. (1975). Logic and conversation. In P. Cole & J. Morgan (Eds.), *Syntax and semantics* (Vol. 3, pp. 41–58). New York: Academic Press.

Harp, S. F., & Mayer, R. E. (1998). How seductive details do their damage: A theory of cognitive interest in science learning. *Journal of Educational Psychology, 90,* 414–434.

Lepper, M. R., Woolverton, M., Mumme, D., & Gurtner, J. (1993). Motivational techniques of expert human tutors: Lessons for the design of computer-based tutors. In S. P. Lajoie & S. J. Derry (Eds.), *Computers as cognitive tools* (pp. 75–105). Hillsdale, NJ: Erlbaum.

Mayer, R. E. (2001). *Multimedia learning.* New York: Cambridge University Press.

Mayer, R. E., Dow, G., & Mayer, S. (2003). Multimedia learning in an interactive self-explaining environment: What works in the design of agent-based microworlds? *Journal of Educational Psychology, 95,* 806–813.

Mayer, R. E., Fennell, S., Farmer, L., & Campbell, J. (2004). A personalization effect in multimedia learning: Students learn better when words are in conversational style rather than formal style. *Journal of Educational Psychology, 96,* 389–395.

Mayer, R. E., & Moreno, R. (2003). Nine ways to reduce cognitive load in multimedia learning. *Educational Psychologist, 38,* 43–52.

Mayer, R. E., Sobko, K., & Mautone, P. D. (2003). Social cues in multimedia learning: Role of speaker's voice. *Journal of Educational Psychology*, 95, 419–425.

Moreno, R., & Mayer, R. E. (2000). Engaging students in active learning: The case for personalized multimedia messages. *Journal of Educational Psychology*, 92, 724–733.

Moreno, R., & Mayer, R. E. (2004). Personalized messages that promote science learning in virtual environments. *Journal of Educational Psychology*, 96, 165–173.

Moreno, R., Mayer, R. E., Spires, H. A., & Lester, J. C. (2001). The case for social agency in computer-based teaching: Do students learn more deeply when they interact with animated pedagogical agents? *Cognition and Instruction*, 19, 177–213.

Paas, F., Renkl, A., & Sweller, J. (2003). Cognitive load theory and instructional design: Recent developments. *Educational Psychologist*, 38, 1–4.

Paas, F., Tuovinen, J. E., Tabbers, H., & van Gerven, P. W. M. (2003). Cognitive load measurement as a means to advance cognitive load theory. *Educational Psychologist*, 38, 63–72.

Reeves, B., and Nass, C. (1996). *The media equation*. New York: Cambridge University Press.

Sweller, J. (1999). *Instructional design in technical areas*. Camberwell, Australia: ACER Press.

Part III

ADVANCED PRINCIPLES OF MULTIMEDIA LEARNING

CHAPTER 14

The Guided Discovery Principle in Multimedia Learning

Ton de Jong
University of Twente

Abstract

Inquiry or scientific discovery learning environments are environments in which a domain is not directly offered to learners but in which learners have to induce the domain from experiences or examples. Because this is a difficult task the discovery process needs to be combined with guidance for the learner. The most effective way to provide this guidance is to integrate it in the learning environment. Guidance may be directed at one or more of the discovery learning processes, for example, hypothesis generation or monitoring, or at structuring the overall process. With adequate guidance discovery learning can be an effective learning approach in which mainly "intuitive" or "deep" conceptual knowledge can be acquired. Inquiry learning now finds new directions in collaborative inquiry and modeling environments.

Guided Discovery Learning

In the design of learning environments the emphasis in the learning process is often placed on the learning material or the teacher. In this way instruction that explains principles and rules in a domain to a learner is created. This *instructive mode* of teaching and learning can be contrasted with an *inductive learning mode* in which the emphasis in the learning process is with the learner. This scientific discovery (or inquiry) learning is characterized by the induction of principles from experiences and/or examples (Swaak & de Jong, 1996). The learner's knowledge acquisition process progresses by stating rules or hypotheses on the basis of concrete situations and by subsequently testing these hypotheses in new situations.

In scientific discovery learning learners more or less take the role of scientists who want to design theory based on empirical observations. Scientific discovery learning, therefore, is a complex learning method that consists of a number of specific learning processes based on an empirical cycle (de Groot, 1969). Many, quite similar, classifications of scientific discovery processes exist. Friedler, Nachmias, and Linn (1990), for example, distinguish the following processes: "(a) define a scientific problem; (b) state a hypothesis; (c) design an experiment; (d) observe, collect, analyze, and interpret data; (e) apply the results; and (f) make predictions on the basis of the results" (p. 173). De Jong and Njoo (1992) made a main distinction between *transformative processes* (processes that directly yield knowledge) and *regulative processes* (processes that are necessary to manage the discovery process). The transformative processes are similar to the ones distinguished by Friedler et al. (1990). The regulative processes include *planning, verifying*, and *monitoring*. Planning can take place at the level of the complete discovery process, or at the level of one of the transformative processes previously indicated. Verifying is checking the correctness of actions and results at a conceptual level. Finally, learners observe and keep track of all the actions they have done and the conclusions drawn by monitoring.

In a review of research de Jong and van Joolingen (1998) conclude that learners may have serious problems with all of the previously mentioned discovery learning processes. In general, learners may have trouble stating hypotheses, designing experiments, and interpreting data. They often do not engage in overall planning and do not adequately monitor what they have been doing (de Jong & van Joolingen, 1998). These inquiry process problems may be associated with wrong mental models of systems in general (Kanari & Millar, in press; Kuhn, Black, Keselman, & Kaplan, 2000) and it may lead to the alteration or negation of experimental outcomes from the experiments that were performed in the inquiry (Chinn & Brewer, 1993). On this basis and also based on overall research in discovery learning many researchers, therefore, conclude that learners need guidance in the discovery process (Mayer, 2004).

Guided Discovery Learning: An Example

One of the most relevant types of multimedia environments for scientific discovery learning is computer simulation. *Computer simulations* are programs that contain a model of a real system. The learner's basic actions are changing values of input variables and observing the resulting changes in values of output variables (de Jong, 1991). Simulations may cover many topics such as physics, chemistry, medicine, or economics and the interface of a simulation can be very simple but can also have sophisticated and realistic input devices and output facilities, such as dynamic graphs, animations, and so forth. (Alessi, 2000b). From manipulating values of input variables and observing values of output variables the learner can induce the properties of the model that drives the simulation. This simulation interface can be extended with cognitive tools that give the learner guidance in the scientific discovery process. SimQuest is an authoring environment for the creation of simulation-based learning environments that include learner guidance (van Joolingen & de Jong, 2003). An example of such an extended learner interface is depicted in Figure 14.1.

In Figure 14.1 the learning environment concerns the physics topic of "torque" (van der Meij & de Jong, 2004). In the simulation students explore the physics concept of torque in several situations. The learning environment has three progression levels. In progression level one, learners explore torque caused by force and length by investigating the behavior of torque on a bolt caused by a force on an open-end spanner. They do this in a qualitative way guided by seven assignments. In progression level two, learners explore the same simulation in a quantitative way and two graphs (moment-force and moment-arm) are introduced. In addition, a second force is introduced. Level two contains 16 assignments. In progression level three, learners explore torque caused by force, length, and height by investigating torque on a hoisting crane caused by a load, again accompanied by a torque-force graph and a torque-height graph. Students can change the position of the load by moving it up, down, left, or right and they can change the weight of the load (by changing the force caused by the load). Level three

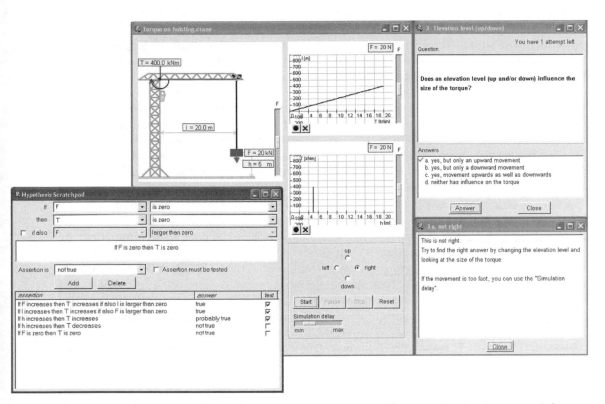

Figure 14.1. An example of a SimQuest learning environment. Shown are the simulation (top left), an assignment (top right), the feedback to the assignment (bottom right), and a hypothesis scratchpad (bottom left).

contains seven assignments. An excerpt from this model progression level is depicted in Figure 14.1. In this example, learners are guided in several ways. There is model progression (White & Frederiksen, 1990) that helps learners by starting at a more simple level and gradually increasing the complexity. In this way learners are supported in their planning processes and also potential cognitive overload (Moreno, 2004) can be avoided. Another type of guidance in this environment comes from the assignments. The assignments are integrated with the simulation, which means that an assignment may set the simulation in a certain state. In this way assignments in SimQuest may point learners to specific issues in the domain and if presented in a certain sequence may help them in their planning. Figure 14.1 also contains an example of a hypothesis scratchpad, a tool that intends to help learners state testable hypotheses (van

Joolingen & de Jong, 1991). The hypothesis scratchpad offers the learner a set of predefined variables, relations, and conditions to compose hypotheses.

Types of Guidance

The guidance (scaffolding or cognitive tools) that is given to learners during discovery learning can take many different forms. De Jong and Njoo (1992) make a distinction between directive and nondirective support. Directive support is support that steers the learner in a certain direction. Examples are assignments, like the one depicted in Figure 14.1, that advise the learner to perform certain actions, or hints that are suggested to learners in the context of a planning tool (van Joolingen, de Jong, Lazonder, Savelsbergh, & Manlove, submitted). An example of nondirective support is the hypothesis scratchpad as presented in Figure 14.1. This is an open tool in which learners can state any hypothesis they wish. Another example is the so-called monitoring tool as introduced by Veermans, de Jong, and van Joolingen (2000). In a monitoring tool learners can save, reorganize, and replay experiments that they have been doing. Both the hypothesis scratchpad and the monitoring tool do not give the learner suggestions on what hypothesis to state or what experiments to save and they are therefore nondirective.

Reid, Zhang, and Chen (2003) following a typology of learning processes distinguish _interpretative support,_ this is support that helps in the structuring of their knowledge of the domain; _experimental support_, this is support that helps students in setting up and interpreting experiments; and _reflective support_, which is support that assists learners in reflections on the learning process and the knowledge acquired. An example of interpretative support is the activation of prior knowledge (Reid et al., 2003), a modeling tool (Penner, 2001) or a concept-mapping tool (Slotta, 2004) that helps to make a representation of the domain, or feedback that presents learners interpretations of their findings (Moreno, 2004). Experimental support may consist of experimentation hints such as "vary one variable at a time" (Chen & Klahr, 1999), or of guiding questions that help students to find the relevant data in the set of data or on feedback on experiments (Reiser et al., 2001). Veermans et al. (2000), for example, created a system that analyzed learners' experimentation behavior in relation to the hypothesis that was under investigation and provided learners with feedback on the correctness of their conclusions from the experiment. Reflective support may consist of tools that help students write and reflect over their discovery process (van Joolingen et al., submitted).

As became clear from the analysis of discovery learning processes by de Jong and Njoo (1992), presented in the preceding text, besides transformative processes also regulative processes are a principal component of discovery learning. Discovery learning is a self-directed way of learning in which the planning and monitoring of the learning process are in the hands of the learner. This also concerns the overall approach in discovery. Learners can be trained in this discovery approach prior to the engagement in the discovery learning environment. For example, Friedler et al. (1990) provided learners with a training on two discovery skills: observation and prediction. Learners indeed gained proficiency in the discovery skills that were trained but only to a limited extent. In a recent study, Keselman (2003) found positive effects of an instruction in making predictions in a domain with outcomes that are dependent on a multitude of interacting variables. In both studies, however, the authors conclude that despite the improvement the inquiry skills remained poor. Partly based on the relative ineffectiveness of general training programs for discovery skills (Roth and Roychoudhury, 1993), many learning environments include the training or scaffolding of scientific discovery skills as an integral part of the scientific discovery learning process and in the context of a specific domain. An early example is Smithtown (Shute & Glaser, 1990) a simulation environment in which discovery skills were taught in the domain of economics. In the work by Njoo and de Jong (1993) students were provided with a "discovery scheme" in which a structured overview of the discovery learning process was presented. This proved to be an effective way of supporting students. Nowadays, many of the more comprehensive discovery learning environments have some sort of structured process overview often combined with hints in each of the distinguished processes. For example, in BGuILE, a learning environment for scientific inquiry in biology, a structure of the inquiry task is presented to learners together with a set of specific tools for specific processes (Reiser, 2002; Reiser et al., 2001). In the Knowledge Integration Environment (KIE), Computer as Learning Partner (CLP) environment, and Web-Based Inquiry Science Environment (WISE) (Linn, Davis, & Bell, 2004) sequences of inquiry phases together with specific tools are used to scaffold learners.

Co-Lab is an environment in which collaboration, modeling, and inquiry in a simulation and remote laboratories context are combined. In Co-Lab students can use a "process coordinator" that helps them in the inquiry process (van Joolingen et al., submitted).

Fidelity

The internal representation of a real system in a model and the way that this representation is presented to a learner determine the *fidelity* of the simulation. Next to the guidance given to a learner, the fidelity of a simulation determines the learning effectiveness of a simulation-based learning environment. Hays and Singer (1989) make a distinction between *physical* (the "look and feel" of the simulation) and *functional* (what can be done in the simulation) fidelity. Levin and Waugh (1988) make a further distinction of physical fidelity into *perceptual fidelity* (what does the simulation look and sound like) and *manipulative fidelity* (can the learner act in a similar way as in reality).

A reason for striving for a high level of fidelity is that transfer of knowledge acquired in the training situation to the "real world" should be enhanced when differences between training and the real situation are minimized (Alessi, 1988). A second reason is that high fidelity may raise motivation (De Hoog, De Jong, & De Vries, 1991). A third reason is that high fidelity, for example in the form of animations, supports the visualization processes, and thus understanding, of learners (Rieber, 1991).

There are also, however, reasons for making the training situation different from the real situation. First, it may be necessary to add specific features that are needed for training (Lewis, Stern, & Linn, 1993), and, second, it sometimes may be useful to remove features from the real situation in order to simplify the training situation in initial stages of learning (Cunningham, 1984). Another reason for not introducing full fidelity is that fidelity generally costs money, and if a reduced fidelity does not hamper transfer

too seriously, using such a reduced fidelity would mean more cost-effective training.

Hays and Singer (1989) report a large number of empirical studies that compared the effectiveness of training with simulations of different levels of fidelity, mostly for operational simulations. The overall results were inconclusive. Some studies favored high fidelity; others showed that a low fidelity may be sufficient. For troubleshooting training, for example, Hays and Singer (1989) concluded that functional fidelity is more important than physical fidelity. Miller and Leroux-Demers (1992) conclude on the basis of studies into business simulations that there is some optimum level of fidelity that is needed to make the simulation realistic and challenging enough, but beyond which complexity gets so high that it might hamper learning. Alessi (2000c) makes a plea for introducing what he calls "dynamic fidelity," which is starting with low fidelity (to promote initial learning) and ending with high fidelity (to promote transfer).

Effectiveness of Simulation-Based Discovery Learning

It is hard to state firm conclusions on the effectiveness of simulation-based discovery learning compared to other types of instruction. The first reason is that there are relatively few well-controlled studies in this area. It seems to be as Robinson (1992) stated that "... proponents of simulations and games felt that the priority was their invention rather than their evaluation" (p. 309). The second reason is that overview studies provide us with a very mixed results. In an overview study on business simulations, Miller and Leroux-Demers (1992) conclude that management simulation games are generally more effective in teaching cognitive skills than the use of cases. Randel, Morris, Wetzel, and Whitehill (1992) reviewing 67 studies over 28 years, found that 22 studies favor simulation games over conventional instruction, 3 studies show advantages for conventional instruction, and 38 show no difference. Randel et al.'s study seems impressive in the number of studies used but their sources are unclear because they do not list all the studies that were reviewed.

In any case an overall conclusion, as also stated previously, is that unguided scientific discovery generally is not a very effective and efficient way of learning (Bangert-Drowns, Kulik, & Kulik, 1985; Mayer, 2004; Rieber & Parmley, 1995), certainly not for students with little prior knowledge (Touvinen & Sweller, 1999). In a recent study Klahr and Nigam (2004), again, found that carefully designed directive instruction may be much more effective than pure discovery where students are left alone without any form of support. When guidance is taken into account, however, Mayer (1987) summarizes the results of comparative studies and concludes that guided discovery leads to better long-term retention and transfer than expository means of instruction. The situation, however, is not always that straightforward. Swaak, de Jong, and van Joolingen (2004), for example, compared two learning environments in the domain of physics (i.e., collisions). Both environments were comparable concerning content, presentation, and student guidance. Student guidance consisted of model progression (gradually increasing the complexity of the model), assignments, and just-in-time explanations. The difference was that in one of the environments students could perform experiments themselves with a simulation, and in the other environment the information was presented through a hypertext system. In both environments there were considerable learning gains and overall there were larger gains for the hypertext environment as compared to the simulation environments. An analysis of interaction processes indicated that the differences between both environments in their actual usage were less distinctive than expected. In the simulation group many students followed the assignments given and did not engage in self-guided discovery. Because the assignments were rather directive this resulted in discovery behavior that focused on generating outcomes; outcomes

that were also, and more directly presented in the hypertext environment. This study shows that guidance for learners can become counterproductive.

De Jong and van Joolingen (1998) presented an overview of studies in which different types of guidance were compared. Their overall conclusions were the following: providing direct access to domain information, such as explanations, appears to be effective. This information should be presented just-in-time in the learning environment itself and not be trained as prior knowledge. Also assignments (e.g., questions or exercises) have a positive effect on learning outcomes. Model progression encourages better learning outcomes but only when the final model is sufficiently complex. Structuring the environment may lead to more effective learning, but studies of these kinds of environments (e.g., BGuILE, WISE, and Co-Lab) never study the structuring in phases in separation, but always in combination with more fine-grained scaffolding within the phases, which prevents direct conclusions on the structuring per se.

Later studies overall confirm these conclusions. Providing *domain knowledge* indeed works, if delivered in conjunction with the simulation. Rieber, Tzeng, and Tribble (in press) in a study on learning with a simulation in the physics domain of motion, found that learners who received explanations of motion principles that were embedded in the simulation outperformed learners who did not receive those explanations. Reid et al. (2003) reported similar effects of what they call *interpretative support* in a study with a simulation on the topic of "floating and sinking." This support included permanent access during experimentation to a reference book with relevant domain information. Moreno (2004) found that students who had to "design a plant" in a botany simulation profited from receiving domain information in relation to the choices that they made.

Reid et al. (2003) also evaluated the influence of providing learners with *online experimentation hints*, but found no effect. In a later study (Zhang, Chen, Sun, & Reid,

2004) these authors combined experimentation hints with concrete examples that resulted in a stronger effect. This is in line with results by Hulshof and de Jong (submitted). In a study with a simulation in the physics domain of optics they gave part of their subjects embedded experimentation hints. These hints were made concrete with examples from the domain involved (optics). Students who received the experimentation hints outperformed the group of students that received no hints. Zhang et al. (2004) also found, however, that the effect of the experimentation hints was only present for students with low reasoning ability skills, thus indicating that the influence of the scaffolding may be mediated by individual characteristics. Again, as was the case with providing domain knowledge, when the training (or modeling) of experimentation strategies takes place *before* the experimentation and is not integrated with the experiments it does not seem to be effective. Mayer, Mautone, and Prothero (2002) found no effect of a specific (verbal) modeling strategy that took place before students worked with a simulation in the domain of geology. In their study Mayer et al. (2002) found an effect of a pictorial aid that helped students make an interpretation of the (visual) data of their experiments and that could be used alongside the simulation.

Mayer et al.'s (2002) study also emphasized the importance of the representational code used in the simulation. In this context, Rieber et al. (in press) found that presenting results from a simulation in a graphical way was far more effective than presenting the outcomes of the experiments as numerical data. Clark and Jorde (2004) worked with a simulation on heat and temperature. In this simulation students could see rate of heat flow and temperature change as arrows and numerical figures. Clark and Jorde (2004) found that students provided with an additional opportunity to click objects and see by means of a picture and text, and hear through a voice the temperature of an object gave significant better performances on understanding of thermal equilibrium as compared with a group that did not receive this

more extensive interface. Van der Meij and de Jong (2004) found that integrating different representations is beneficial for learning. Though these results indicate that the representation influences learning, an overall conclusion is not evident (Ainsworth & van Labeke, in press). Ainsworth and van Labeke (in press) present an overview of characteristics of (multiple) representations of simulations that may help to better order results and that may lead to a general framework for classifying external representations.

Though the conclusions that are stated here are presented as general conclusions it is clear that the actual impact of specific types of guidance depend on quite some factors: the complexity and characteristics of the domain; the prior knowledge level and other characteristics of students; the learning goals; the context of learning; and the design of the learning environment (de Jong et al., in press).

Limitations of Research

Though research on discovery learning with simulations is progressing, the studies presented clearly show three shortcomings in the design and study of simulation environments. First, guidance as presented to learners is only to a certain extent adaptive to the learner's knowledge, skills, and actions. Second, the analysis of the discovery processes from online registered learner data is troublesome. Third, many studies do not use adequate knowledge measures.

Adaptivity of Guidance

Guidance should in principle be adapted to (a) the actual behavior of the learner, (b) the learner's prior knowledge, and (c) the learner's scientific discovery skills. Quite often guidance is presented based on learner's actions, but these actions are quite superficial and the guidance is predefined and does not really incorporate the learner's interaction with the system. Making the guidance adaptable to the learner's individual knowledge and experimentation skills is hardly ever seen, despite the fact that these are seen as important determinants of discovery learning (de Jong et al., in press). For example, Huppert, Lomask, and Lazarowitz (2002) found that the stage of development of a learner (concrete or transition operational) was related to the learner's achievement in a simulation-based learning environment. Veermans et al. (2000) created a system in which a deep analysis of the learners' experimentation strategies was made and genuine adaptive guidance was given by explaining why conclusions drawn by learners over specific hypotheses were correct or not based on the experiments that were done. Veermans et al. (2000) found that providing learners with the adaptive feedback triggered a learning process that focused on the interpretation of experiments whereas in the control group with fixed feedback there was an emphasis on acquiring definitional knowledge.

Assessment of the Discovery Learning Process

Assessing learners' discovery strategies from online process data is a difficult issue. Often in studies all learners' actions are logged and these logfiles are used for later inspection (Hulshof, in press). Also, regularly, these process data are related to performance data. In this way measures of overall activity (e.g., the number of experiments done) and statistics on the use of guidance measures are correlated with scores on knowledge tests. The overall picture that emerges from this is not very clear. For example, overall activity (e.g., number of experiments done) of learners is sometimes related to performance (e.g., de Jong, de Hoog, & de Vries, 1993) and sometimes not (e.g., Reid et al., 2003). Also, the relation between the use of guidance and performance level can be a complicated one. Veermans et al. (2000), for example, found that in one condition the number of assignments done in a simulation correlated with performance on a post-test and in another condition the way the assignments were done (e.g., the number of unique experiments done). There is a clear need for a

more encompassing framework on how specific learning processes can be operationalized in actual learning behavior.

Assessment of the Outcome of Discovery Learning

Large-scale evaluations of simulation-based classes compared to traditional classes have shown that the assessment of learning outcomes is of great importance for valuing the learning environments (Hickey, Kindfield, Horwitz, & Christie, 2003). The experiential way of learning that is characteristic of discovery learning is not a way of learning that leads to traditional explicit knowledge. The classic experiment by Berry and Broadbent (1984) showed that there can be a separation between action knowledge (that is knowing how to handle skillfully) and explicit knowledge of the underlying principle. Swaak and de Jong (1996) developed for this purpose the "what-if" test for intuitive knowledge. In this test learners are asked to make predictions in situations that are close to the ones that they have experienced. In simulation-based discovery learning several studies (Reid et al., 2003; Rieber et al., in press) have shown the usefulness of tests of "implicit" or "intuitive" knowledge, but many studies still use traditional types of tests for measuring the outcomes of discovery learning. In relation to this it can be stated that scientific discovery learning is not the most suited for the acquisition of more superficial or procedural types of tasks (Touvinen & Sweller, 1999).

Theoretical Considerations

Two more general theories that are often applied in the context of discovery learning with simulations are dual-coding theory and cognitive load theory. Dual-coding theory (Paivio, 1986), in short, asserts that information that is coded in both the visual and verbal system is better retrieved than information that is coded only once. In multimedia discovery environments information is often presented in different representational codes

(Ardac & Akaygun, 2004; van der Meij & de Jong, 2004) that will lead to better encoding (Rieber et al., in press). Cognitive load theory (Sweller, 1994; Touvinen & Sweller, 1999) assumes that the complexity of multimedia simulation learning environments per se may be so high that this consumes too many of the cognitive resources of a learner, leaving too few resources for learning. Adequate design and learner guidance may help to reduce the cognitive load for the learner (Mayer et al., 2002; Moreno, 2004). Both theories may explain to a certain extent why discovery learning may fail or may be successful but neither gives full justice to the specific characteristics of scientific discovery learning.

The more specific theoretical approaches to discovery learning either focus on the scientific discovery processes, as outlined previously (de Jong & Njoo, 1992), or on the developing knowledge states of the learner. The main representative for the latter line of work is embodied in Klahr and Dunbar's (1988) Scientific Discovery as Dual Search (SDDS) model. The SDDS model describes discovery learning as a search process through two spaces: the hypothesis space and the experiment space. The hypothesis space is the search space that contains all rules describing the phenomena that can be observed within the domain. The experiment space consists of all experiments that can be performed within the domain. Following Klahr and Dunbar's theory, discovery learning is determined by the prior knowledge (i.e., the configuration of hypothesis and experiment space) and skills (i.e., discovery processes) of an individual. To portray discovery learning in complex domains Van Joolingen and De Jong (1997) extended the SDDS model. They introduced different regions in the hypothesis space and designed a taxonomy to describe different search operations. This taxonomy makes a distinction between operations that change variables (e.g., generalization of a variable), operations that change relations (e.g., specialization or adding conditions), and operations that affect the set of hypothesis (e.g., splitting a hypothesis). De Jong et al. (in press) give a more detailed overview of the specific characteristics of processes and moves in hypothesis space that are related to successful scientific discovery learning.

Future Directions

Scientific discovery learning recently has seen developments in two directions. The first one is that discovery learning is seen as a collaborative enterprise in which part of the guidance can come from the fellow learner. The second one is that there is a gradual shift from learning from models in simulations to construction of those models by the learners.

Collaborative Discovery

Real scientific work also has a strong collaborative aspect (Dunbar, 2001). Also in learning situations collaboration and discovery can be good companions. By collaborating in scientific discovery learning, learners may divide the task among them and support each other in the discovery aspects. Moreover, externalizing ideas to each other helps the receiving learners, but also helps the learners who externalize their thoughts (Kaartinen & Kumpulainen, 2002; Okada & Simon, 1997). Collaborative discovery is a situation in which cognitive conflicts (de Vries, Lund, & Baker, 2002; Limón, 2001) can be experienced in a sensible context (Vahey, Enyedy, & Gifford, 2000). Gijlers and de Jong (in press) found that pairs of students with a larger difference in prior knowledge had more dialogue on hypotheses in a simulation environment than pairs where the difference was not that large. As a follow-up they created an environment in which two learners separately gave their view on a long list of propositions in a domain and when two learners started to work together their lists were coupled and they could easily inspect on which the propositions they agreed and disagreed. Gijlers and de Jong (submitted) found that this list presenting cognitive conflicts led to higher learning gains than a tool that enabled students to collaboratively build propositions.

Modeling

In inquiry learning with simulations learners are basically asked to discover the model that is running the simulation. One step further would be to ask learners to build such models themselves (Löhner, van Joolingen, & Savelsbergh, 2003). Alessi (2000a) describes a whole range of modeling languages that can be used by learners and he lists a number of conditions under which building simulations would be recommended. The first condition has to do with the domain. Alessi states that building a model can be beneficial when the model is rather simple. For example, he mentions an upper limit of 20 variables that determine the main variance in the system. A second condition is when expert models are not widely accepted as being true (e.g., a model of climate change), so that it would be misleading to present learners with an existing model. The third condition, according to Alessi, for building instead of using simulations is when the primary goal is to solve a problem in the system rather than to understand it. His fourth condition is an obvious one, modeling may be preferred when the goal is more general thinking or problem solving. Fifth, modeling, being a complex process, can only be successful if learners have ample time. And, finally, some modeling may precede the use of a simulation when, for example, diagnosis of relatively simple systems is at stake. Of course modeling can also be combined with simulation in systems where learners can model a system and compare the behavior of their model with the behavior of a simulation or a real laboratory setup (van Joolingen et al., submitted).

Conclusions

Finding out which types of guidance are effective in scientific discovery learning is the main research question for the coming years. Quintana et al. (2004) list a large number of "scaffolds" of inquiry learning environments, including simulations. Most of the guidelines that they present, however, have not as yet been systematically tested. Finding out under which circumstances (i.e., characteristics of the learner and the learning environment) these scaffolds prove effective is a major challenge. A further item on the research agenda is to find new ways of scaffolding that are more sensitive to these changing characteristics of the environment and the learner. In the area of learning how to solve programming problems, Merrill, Reiser, Merrill, and Landes (1995) analyzed the behavior of a tutor and found that expert tutoring consisted of a careful monitoring of the problem-solving process, letting the learner do as much as possible, and only giving guidance when the problem-solving process was going astray. Even in a situation as the one studied by Merrill et al. (1995) in which the problem-solving process knows a theoretically best route, the tutoring process requires a skillful and expert tutor. In more open hypermedia learning environments positive effects of scaffolding by a human tutor are found (Azevedo, Cromley, & Seibert, 2004). Scientific discovery learning environments are even more open than hypermedia learning environments; it is not possible to define one "optimal solution path." This not only presents a challenge to human tutors but certainly also to the designers of these learning environments. New developments that enable programs to make deeper interpretations of the discovery learning process (Veermans, van Joolingen, & de Jong, submitted), and blended forms of learning combining the power of the software and control by the learner or teacher are promising roads to more adaptive and effective guidance for learning in discovery settings.

Glossary

Cognitive tools: Software instruments that support learners in a specific learning process, either by taking over specific parts of the process (scaffolding) or by providing learners with sufficient information to carry out the learning process themselves.

Computer simulation: Computer programs that contain a model of a real system. Generally, values of input variables can be changed and resulting changes in values of output variables can be observed.

Scientific discovery learning: A way of learning in which knowledge acquisition is based on the induction of domain rules through structured experimentation.

References

Ainsworth, S., & van Labeke, N. (in press). Multiple forms of dynamic representation. *Learning and Instruction*.

Alessi, S. M. (1988). Fidelity in the design of instructional simulations. *Journal of Computer-Based Instruction*, 15, 40–47.

Alessi, S. M. (2000a). Building versus using simulations. In J. M. Spector & T. M. Anderson (Eds.), *Integrated and holistic perspectives on learning, instruction and technology* (pp. 175–196). Dordrecht, The Netherlands: Kluwer Academic Publishers.

Alessi, S. M. (2000b). Designing educational support in system-dynamic-based interactive learning environments. *Simulation and Gaming*, 31, 178–196.

Alessi, S. M. (2000c). Simulation design for training and assessment. In J. H. F. O'Neil & D. H. Andrews (Eds.), *Aircrew training and assessment* (pp. 197–222). Mahwah, NJ: Lawrence Erlbaum Associates.

Ardac, D., & Akaygun, S. (2004). Effectiveness of multimedia-based instruction that emphasizes molecular representations on students' understanding of chemical change. *Journal of Research in Science Teaching*, 41, 317–338.

Azevedo, R., Cromley, J. G., & Seibert, D. (2004). Does adaptive scaffolding facilitate students' ability to regulate their learning with hypermedia? *Contemporary Educational Psychology*, 29, 344–370.

Bangert-Drowns, R., Kulik, J., & Kulik, C. (1985). Effectiveness of computer-based education in secondary schools. *Journal of Computer Based Instruction*, 12, 59–68.

Berry, D. C., & Broadbent, D. E. (1984). On the relationship between task performance and associated verbalizable knowledge. *The Quarterly Journal of Experimental Psychology*, 36A, 209–231.

Chen, Z., & Klahr, D. (1999). All other things being equal: Acquisition and transfer of the control of variables strategy. *Child Development*, 70, 1098–1120.

Chinn, C. A., & Brewer, W. F. (1993). The role of anomalous data in knowledge acquisition: A theoretical framework and implications for science instruction. *Review of Educational Research*, 63, 1–51.

Clark, D., & Jorde, D. (2004). Helping students revise disruptive experientially supported ideas about thermodynamics: Computer visualisations and tactile models. *Journal of Research in Science Teaching*, 41, 1–23.

Cunningham, J. B. (1984). Assumptions underlying the use of different types of simulations. *Simulations & Games*, 15, 213–234.

de Groot, A. D. (1969). *Methodology, foundations of inference and research in the behavioural sciences*. The Hague, The Netherlands: Mouton.

de Hoog, R., de Jong, T., & de Vries, F. (1991). Interfaces for instructional use of simulations. *Education and Computing*, 6, 359–385.

de Jong, T. (1991). Learning and instruction with computer simulations. *Education and Computing*, 6, 217–229.

de Jong, T., Beishuizen, J., Hulshof, C. D., Prins, F., van Rijn, H., van Someren, M., et al. (in press). Determinants of discovery learning. In P. Gärdenfors, U. Riis, & P. Johansson (Eds.), *Cognition, education and communication technology*. Mahwah, NJ: Lawrence Erlbaum Associates.

de Jong, T., de Hoog, R., & de Vries, F. (1993). Coping with complex environments: The effects of overviews and a transparent interface on learning with a computer simulation. *International Journal of Man-Machine Studies*, 39, 621–639.

de Jong, T., & Njoo, M. (1992). Learning and instruction with computer simulations: Learning processes involved. In E. de Corte, M. Linn, H. Mandl, & L. Verschaffel (Eds.), *Computer-based learning environments and problem solving* (pp. 411–429). Berlin, Germany: Springer-Verlag.

de Jong, T., & van Joolingen, W. R. (1998). Scientific discovery learning with computer simulations of conceptual domains. *Review of Educational Research*, 68, 179–202.

de Vries, E., Lund, K., & Baker, M. (2002). Computer-mediated epistemic dialogue: Explanation and argumentation as vehicles for understanding scientific notions. *The Journal of the Learning Sciences, 11*, 63–103.

Dunbar, K. (2001). What scientific thinking reveals about the nature of cognition. In K. Crowley, C. D. Schunn, & T. Okada (Eds.), *Designing for science: Implications from everyday, classroom, and professional settings* (pp. 115–140). Mahwah, NJ: Lawrence Erlbaum Associates.

Friedler, Y., Nachmias, R., & Linn, M. C. (1990). Learning scientific reasoning skills in microcomputer-based laboratories. *Journal of Research in Science Teaching, 27*, 173–191.

Gijlers, H., & de Jong, T. (in press). The relation between prior knowledge and students' collaborative discovery learning processes. *Journal of Research in Science Teaching*.

Gijlers, H., & de Jong, T. (submitted). Sharing and confronting propositions in collaborative scientific discovery learning.

Hays, R. T., & Singer, M. J. (1989). *Simulation fidelity in training system design*. New York: Springer-Verlag.

Hickey, D. T., Kindfield, A. C. H., Horwitz, P., & Christie, M. A. T. (2003). Integrating curriculum, instruction, assessment, and evaluation in a technology-supported genetics learning environment. *American Educational Research Journal, 40*, 495–538.

Hulshof, C. D. (in press). Log file analysis. In K. Kempf-Leonard (Ed.), *Encyclopedia of social measurement*. San Diego, CA: Academic Press.

Hulshof, C. D., & de Jong, T. (submitted). Using just-in-time information to support discovery learning about geometrical optics in a computer-based simulation.

Huppert, J., Lomask, S. M., & Lazarowitz, R. (2002). Computer simulations in the high school: Students' cognitive stages, science process skills and academic achievement in microbiology. *International Journal of Science Education, 24*, 803–821.

Kaartinen, S., & Kumpulainen, K. (2002). Collaborative inquiry and the construction of explanations in the learning of science. *Learning and Instruction, 12*, 189–213.

Kanari, Z., & Millar, R. (in press). Reasoning from data: How students collect and interpret data in science investigations. *Journal of Research in Science Teaching*.

Keselman, A. (2003). Supporting inquiry learning by promoting normative understanding of multivariable causality. *Journal of Research in Science Teaching, 40*, 898–921.

Klahr, D., & Dunbar, K. (1988). Dual space search during scientific reasoning. *Cognitive Science, 12*, 1–48.

Klahr, D., & Nigam, M. (2004). The equivalence of learning paths in early science instruction: Effects of direct instruction and discovery learning. *Psychological Science, 15*, 661–668.

Kuhn, D., Black, J., Keselman, A., & Kaplan, D. (2000). The development of cognitive skills to support inquiry learning. *Cognition and Instruction, 18*, 495–523.

Levin, J. A., & Waugh, M. (1988). Educational simulations, tools, games, and microworlds: Computer-based environments for learning. *International Journal of Educational Research, 12*, 71–79.

Lewis, E. L., Stern, J. L., & Linn, M. C. (1993). The effect of computer simulations on introductory thermodynamics understanding. *Educational Technology, 33*, 45–58.

Limón, M. (2001). On the cognitive conflict as an instructional strategy for conceptual change: A critical appraisal. *Learning and Instruction, 11*, 357–380.

Linn, M. C., Davis, E. A., & Bell, P. (2004). Inquiry and technology. In M. Linn, E. A. Davis, & P. Bell (Eds.), *Internet environments for science education* (pp. 3–28). Mahwah, NJ: Lawrence Erlbaum Associates.

Löhner, S., van Joolingen, W. R., & Savelsbergh, E. R. (2003). The effect of external representation on constructing computer models of complex phenomena. *Instructional Science, 31*, 395–418.

Mayer, R. E. (1987). *Educational psychology, a cognitive approach*. Boston: Little, Brown and Company.

Mayer, R. E. (2004). Should there be a three-strikes rule against pure discovery learning? *American Psychologist, 59*, 14–19.

Mayer, R. E., Mautone, P., & Prothero, W. (2002). Pictorial aids for learning by doing in a multimedia geology simulation game. *Journal of Educational Psychology, 94*, 171–185.

Merrill, D. C., Reiser, B., J, Merrill, S. K., & Landes, S. (1995). Tutoring: Guided learning by doing. *Cognition and Instruction, 13*, 315–372.

Miller, R., & Leroux-Demers, T. (1992). Business simulations: Validity and effectiveness. *Simulation/Games for Learning*, 22, 261–285.

Moreno, R. (2004). Decreasing cognitive load for novice students: Effects of explanatory versus corrective feedback in discovery-based multimedia. *Instructional Science*, 32, 99–113.

Njoo, M., & de Jong, T. (1993). Exploratory learning with a computer simulation for control theory: Learning processes and instructional support. *Journal of Research in Science Teaching*, 30, 821–844.

Okada, T., & Simon, H. A. (1997). Collaborative discovery in a scientific domain. *Cognitive Science*, 21, 109–146.

Paivio, A. (1986). *Mental representation: A dual coding approach*. New York: Oxford University Press.

Penner, D. E. (2001). Cognition, computers, and synthetic science: Building knowledge and meaning through modelling. *Review of Research in Education*, 25, 1–37.

Quintana, C., Reiser, B. J., Davis, E. A., Krajcik, J., Fretz, E., Duncan, R. G., et al. (2004). A scaffolding design framework for software to support science inquiry. *The Journal of the Learning Sciences*, 13, 337–387.

Randel, J. M., Morris, B. A., Wetzel, C. D., & Whitehill, B. V. (1992). The effectiveness of games for educational purposes: A review of recent research. *Simulation and Gaming*, 23, 261–276.

Reid, D. J., Zhang, J., & Chen, Q. (2003). Supporting scientific discovery learning in a simulation environment. *Journal of Computer Assisted Learning*, 19, 9–20.

Reiser, B. J. (2002). Why scaffolding should sometimes make tasks more difficult for learners. In G. Stahl (Ed.), *Computer support for collaborative learning foundations for a CSCL community* (pp. 255–264). Hillsdale, NJ: Lawrence Erlbaum Associates.

Reiser, B. J., Tabak, I., Sandoval, W. A., Smith, B., Steinmuller, F., & Leone, T. J. (2001). BGuILE: Strategic and conceptual scaffolds for scientific inquiry in biology classrooms. In S. M. Carver & D. Klahr (Eds.), *Cognition and instruction: Twenty five years of progress* (pp. 263–305). Mahwah, NJ: Lawrence Erlbaum Associates.

Rieber, L. P. (1991). Animation, incidental learning, and continuing motivation. *Journal of Educational Psychology*, 83, 318–328.

Rieber, L. P., & Parmley, M. W. (1995). To teach or not to teach? Comparing the use of computer-based simulations in deductive versus inductive approaches to learning with adults in science. *Journal of Educational Computing Research*, 14, 359–374.

Rieber, L. P., Tzeng, S., & Tribble, K. (in press). Discovery learning, representations, and explanation within a computer-based simulation: finding the right mix. *Learning and Instruction*.

Robinson, N. (1992). Evaluating simulations and games: An economist's view. *Simulations/Games for Learning*, 22, 308–325.

Roth, W., & Roychoudhury, A. (1993). The development of science process skills in authentic contexts. *Journal of Research in Science Teaching*, 30, 127–152.

Shute, V. J., & Glaser, R. (1990). A large-scale evaluation of an intelligent discovery world: Smithtown. *Interactive Learning Environments*, 1, 51–77.

Slotta, J. (2004). The web-based inquiry science environment (WISE): Scaffolding knowledge integration in the science classroom. In M. Linn, E. A. Davis, & P. Bell (Eds.), *Internet environments for science education* (pp. 203–233). Mahwah, NJ: Lawrence Erlbaum Associates.

Swaak, J., & de Jong, T. (1996). Measuring intuitive knowledge in science: The development of the what-if test. *Studies in Educational Evaluation*, 22, 341–362.

Swaak, J., de Jong, T., & van Joolingen, W. R. (2004). The effects of discovery learning and expository instruction on the acquisition of definitional and intuitive knowledge. *Journal of Computer Assisted Learning*, 20, 225–234.

Sweller, J. (1994). Cognitive load theory, learning difficulty, and instructional design. *Learning and Instruction*, 4, 295–312.

Touvinen, J. E., & Sweller, J. (1999). A comparison of cognitive load associated with discovery learning and worked examples. *Journal of Educational Psychology*, 91, 334–341.

Vahey, P., Enyedy, N., & Gifford, B. (2000). Learning probability through the use of a collaborative, inquiry-based simulation environment. *Journal of Interactive Learning Research*, 11, 51–84.

van der Meij, J., & de Jong, T. (2004). *Learning with multiple representations: Supporting students' translation between representations in a simulation-based learning environment*. Paper presented at the American Educational Research Association, San Diego, CA.

van Joolingen, W. R., & de Jong, T. (1991). Supporting hypothesis generation by learners exploring an interactive computer simulation. *Instructional Science, 20*, 389–404.

van Joolingen, W. R., & de Jong, T. (1997). An extended dual search space model of learning with computer simulations. *Instructional Science, 25*, 307–346.

van Joolingen, W. R., & de Jong, T. (2003). SimQuest: Authoring educational simulations. In T. Murray, S. Blessing, & S. Ainsworth (Eds.), *Authoring tools for advanced technology educational software: Toward cost-effective production of adaptive, interactive, and intelligent educational software* (pp. 1–31). Dordrecht, The Netherlands: Kluwer Academic Publishers.

van Joolingen, W. R., de Jong, T., Lazonder, A. W., Savelsbergh, E., & Manlove, S. (submitted). Co-Lab: Research and development of an online learning environment for collaborative scientific discovery learning. *Computers in Human Behavior*.

Veermans, K. H., de Jong, T., & van Joolingen, W. R. (2000). Promoting self directed learning in simulation based discovery learning environments through intelligent support. *Interactive Learning Environments, 8*, 229–255.

Veermans, K. H., van Joolingen, W. R., & de Jong, T. (submitted). Using heuristics to facilitate discovery learning in a simulation learning environment in a physics domain.

White, B. Y., & Frederiksen, J. R. (1990). Causal model progressions as a foundation for intelligent learning environments. *Artificial Intelligence, 42*, 99–157.

Zhang, J., Chen, Q., Sun, Y., & Reid, D. J. (2004). Triple scheme of learning support design for scientific discovery learning based on computer simulation: Experimental research. *Journal of Computer Assisted Learning, 20*, 269–282.

CHAPTER 15

The Worked-Out Examples Principle in Multimedia Learning

Alexander Renkl
University of Freiburg

Abstract

People gain a deep understanding when they receive worked-out examples in initial cognitive skill acquisition. This is, however, only true when the following guidelines are considered: prompt or train self-explaining examples (guideline of self-explanation elicitation); provide principle-based, minimalist, and example-related instructional explanations as help (help guideline); design examples so that the relations between different representations can be easily detected (easy-mapping guideline); make salient the examples' structural features that are relevant for selecting the correct solution procedure (structure-emphasizing guideline); and facilitate the isolation of meaningful building blocks in worked-out procedures (meaningful building-blocks guideline). Furthermore, series of examples with successively faded worked-out steps should be employed in order to structure the transition from example study to problem solving in later phases of skill acquisition.

Introduction

Learning by doing and *learning by solving complex problems* are methods of learning that are *en vogue* and frequently propagated in the literature on learning and instruction in general as well as on multimedia learning. However, often learners have a very restricted understanding of the domain when they try to solve the first problems. In this case, they typically rely on general, domain-*unspecific* problem-solving heuristics such as means-ends analysis. This actually leads to the correct answer in many cases. However, does such *striving for the right answer* lead to a profound understanding of the domain? Would it not be better for the students to begin solving problems after they have already gained some significant understanding of the domain? In the latter case they could engage not only in general heuristics but also in domain-specific reasoning, which in turn can deepen their understanding. The basic argument of this chapter is that providing worked-out examples is an effective method when we want students to be prepared for productive problem solving by first acquiring a basic understanding of the domain. Thus, the worked-out-examples principle in multimedia learning states that people gain a deep understanding of a skill domain when they receive worked-out examples in the beginning of cognitive skill acquisition.

What Is Learning From Worked-Out Examples?

Worked-out examples consist of a problem formulation, solution steps, and the final solution. They are typically employed in instructional materials in the domains of mathematics or physics in the following fashion: (1) a principle (or a rule or theorem) is introduced; (2) a worked-out example is provided; and (3) one or more to-be-solved problems are supplied. Worked-out examples are, thus, designed to support initial acquisition of cognitive skills. Many studies, however, have shown that the potential of learning from worked-out examples is not fully exploited by this traditional procedure in which just one worked-out example is presented. It is more effective to use a series of worked-out examples or worked-out example-problem pairs as in the classical studies of Sweller and colleagues (e.g., Sweller & Cooper, 1985). When we refer to the term *learning from worked-out examples* or *example-based learning* (both terms are used as synonyms) we always mean that more than just a single example is used.

Figure 15.1 shows the type of examples that we employed in a series of experiments on example-based learning from multiple representations in the domain of probability (Große & Renkl, 2003). The solution to a problem is shown in two representational formats: a solution in the form of a tree diagram and an arithmetical solution. The multiplication rule is applied. Usually this rule is acquired by the learners, but they rarely understand *why* the fractions have to

be multiplied. This can be understood by looking at the ramifications of the tree (e.g., for the denominator there are five times four branches). The learners are supported in integrating the information from the tree (e.g., the ramifications) with the respective arithmetical information (e.g., the multiplication signs). This is accomplished by simultaneously flashing the corresponding information from the different representations – information pair after information pair (see also chapter 12 on signaling).

What is the Worked-Out Example Principle?

One advantage of worked-out examples is that they are an information source that is preferred by learners (LeFevre & Dixon, 1986). This aspect is of major importance in multimedia learning because it is often employed in computer-based environments whose use (or at least the duration of its use) is determined by the learner. Hence, the environments have to be accepted by the learners. The preference of examples is nicely illustrated by Recker and Pirolli (1994) who presented a hypertext environment about programming to their learners. At points in the environment in which the learners could choose between textual information and examples, they looked at the examples in 77% of the cases. Gerjets and colleagues (e.g., Gerjets & Scheiter, 2003) who employed a hypertext environment on combinatorics showed that there are individual differences in the preference of worked-out examples that are also related to learning outcomes. Studying many examples in this hypertext leads to better learning.

In addition, there are numerous experiments that have shown that learning from worked-out examples leads to superior learning outcomes as compared to the traditional method of problem solving after one single example (for an overview see Atkinson, Derry, Renkl, & Wortham, 2000). This superiority of example-based learning can be explained by cognitive load

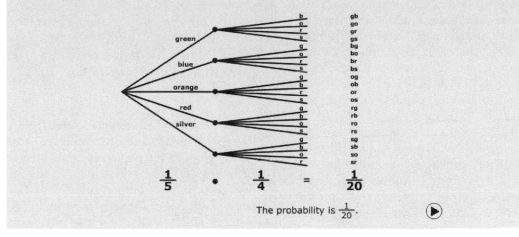

Figure 15.1. A multimedia worked-out example from the domain of probability.

theory (Paas, Renkl, & Sweller, 2003; Renkl & Atkinson, 2003; Sweller, van Merriënboer, & Paas, 1998; see also chapter 2 on cognitive load theory). In the beginning of a learning process, the low level of a learner's prior knowledge has two consequences: (1) the learner is unable to apply domain- or task-specific solution procedures so, instead, general problem-solving strategies must be employed; and (2) the learner cannot build bigger, meaningful information chunks, so that the representation of a problem with many information units leads to high load in working memory (i.e., *intrinsic load*). In such situations, learners usually adopt a means-ends-analysis strategy that requires a substantial portion of working memory capacity. The learners have to maintain the following aspects of the problem in their mind: current problem state, goal state, differences between these states, operators that reduce the differences between the goal state and the present state, and subgoals. Although means-ends-analysis can be an effective problem-solving strategy, it unfortunately does not directly foster understanding because the learners focus on the details of

a concrete problem's solution, but not on the principles behind it. Hence, this strategy imposes an unproductive load (i.e., *extraneous load*) and, as a consequence, there is little or no room left for processes that deepen understanding such as generating self-explanations (i.e., *germane load*). In contrast, when studying worked-out examples, the learners are freed from performance demands and they can concentrate on gaining understanding. Renkl, Gruber, Weber, Lerche, and Schweizer (2003) tested and confirmed this cognitive load explanation by employing a dual-task paradigm.

However, it is important to note that studying worked-out examples loses its effectiveness with increasing expertise. It is hardly possible to become a proficient programmer just by studying worked-out programming code. In later stages of skill acquisition, emphasis is on increasing speed and accuracy of performance, and skills, or at least subcomponents of them, should become automated (Renkl & Atkinson, 2003). This can be best accomplished by actual problem solving. This argument is underlined by Kalyuga, Chandler, Tuovinen, and

Sweller (2001) who analyzed mechanical trade apprentices' learning about relay circuits and their programming in different stages of skill acquisition. Whereas in the initial phase of cognitive skill acquisition, learning from worked-out examples was superior, this advantage faded over time. In fact, the authors found that when learners had ample experience in this domain, learning by solving problems proved to be superior to studying examples. Hence, there was a reversal of the worked-example effect across the phases of skill acquisition (for details of the expertise-reversal effect see Kalyuga, Ayres, Chandler, & Sweller, 2003).

In the context of multimedia learning the experiments of Tarmizi and Sweller (1988) on the effectiveness of examples are of special interest. These authors presented conventional problems from the domain of geometry to be solved in one group and worked-out examples in the other group. They found no difference between groups with respect to learning. Does this mean that there is no *example effect* in multimedia learning? Definitely not! Tarmizi and Sweller (1988) explained this finding by the fact that in geometry there are typically two sources of information: a graphical representation (e.g., a depicted triangle) and an arithmetical representation (e.g., computation of an angle). Typically, these sources are not integrated and the learners have to devote many cognitive resources in order to relate these information sources to each other, creating a *split-attention effect*. Thereby, the *resource-saving* effect of example study is countermanded. In order to foster the positive example effect, Tarmizi and Sweller integrated the arithmetical and graphical information into each other so that it was easy to see the relation between these representations (see Figure 15.2 for an example in a split-attention format and an integrated format). Actually, it was shown in two further experiments (Experiments 4 and 5) that such integrated multimedia examples were superior to the conventional problem-solving procedure (see also chapter 12 on the contiguity principle). These findings imply that the worked-out-examples principle

can be formulated more precisely: People gain a deep understanding of a skill domain when they receive worked-out examples in the beginning of cognitive skill acquisition, however, only if the example-based learning is *well-designed*. What does *well-designed* exactly mean in this context? The next section clarifies this issue.

What Factors Moderate the Effectiveness of Worked-Out Examples?

As illustrated by Tarmizi and Sweller (1988), learning from worked-out examples is not effective per se, but only when implemented according to specific guidelines. In the following sections we outline guidelines for directly fostering example processing by the learners, and guidelines for example design in order to indirectly foster example processing (Renkl & Atkinson, 2002).

Guidelines for Fostering Example Processing

The classical studies of Sweller and Cooper (1985; Cooper & Sweller, 1987) have shown that it is sufficient to employ worked-out examples in order to heighten learning outcomes in comparison to the traditional problem-solving procedure. However, the positive effects were typically restricted to similar problems with the same solution procedure (i.e., same underlying structure). Transfer to novel problems where a modified solution procedure had to be found (i.e., different structure) was usually not influenced. As shown in the following, supporting the processing of worked-out examples further enhances learning outcomes and is especially important for fostering transfer to novel problems that require deep understanding.

THE GUIDELINE OF SELF-EXPLANATION ELICITATION

In a classical study, Chi, Bassok, Lewis, Reimann, and Glaser (1989) analyzed individual differences with respect to how

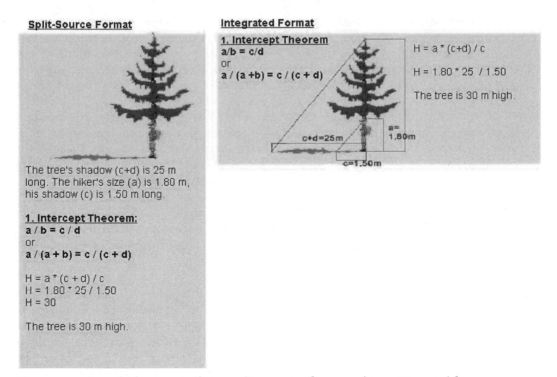

Figure 15.2. A worked-out example in a split-attention format and in an integrated format.

intensively learners self-explained the solution steps of multimedia worked-out examples from the domain of physics. They found that successful learners studied the examples for longer periods and explained them more actively to themselves, that is, they tried to figure out the rationale of the solution procedure. Renkl (1997) showed that even when the example study time was held constant, self-explanation activity is related to learning outcomes.

Central self-explanation activities are the following (Chi et al., 1989; Renkl, 1997):

(1) *Principle-based explanations.* A learner assigns meaning to operators by identifying the underlying domain principles (e.g., in a probability example the multiplication rule is elaborated: "In this step, the probabilities are multiplied because the events occur together and are independent"). This activity fosters a principle-based understanding of solution procedures.

(2) *Explication of goal-operator combinations.* A learner assigns meaning to operators by identifying the subgoals achieved by these operators (e.g., in a probability example: "By subtracting the probability of x from 1, we get the probability of non-x"). This activity fosters the representation of the goal structure of certain problem types and of knowledge about operators for achieving the (sub-) goals.

(3) *Example comparisons.* A learner notices similarities or differences between different examples. When structurally identical examples are compared, the construction of schemas are fostered that allows for (a) abstracting from surface features that are not relevant for selecting the correct solution path (i.e., persons, objects, and numbers in a problem's cover story) and (b) focusing on relevant structural features. When structurally different examples from a content domain are compared, additionally the differentiation of different problem types can be learned so that the selection of solution procedures is not misguided by irrelevant surface features.

(4) *Anticipative reasoning.* The learner tries to anticipate the next solution step and then confirms her/his prediction by looking it up. This activity serves two important goals: (a) to construct first mental rules for problem solving and (b) to check understanding, so that in cases of unsuccessful anticipations actions toward "repairing" knowledge gaps can be undertaken.

Renkl (1997), however, found that most learners were passive and superficial self-explainers. This finding is of special relevance because self-explaining is particularly relevant for fostering transfer to problems with a novel structure. Against this background, the learners should be guided to actively self-explain worked-out examples.

Renkl, Stark, Gruber, and Mandl (1998) analyzed the effects of a short self-explanation training (10–15 min) focusing on principle-based self-explanations and explication of goal-operator combinations. This intervention included the following components: (a) information on the importance of self-explanations (i.e., *informed training*), (b) modeling self-explanations (i.e., one worked-out example), and (c) coached practice (i.e., another worked-out example). Half of the participants received such a training and the other half (control group) a thinking-aloud training. After these interventions, all participants independently learned from a set of worked-out examples in the domain of compound interest and real interest calculation. The explicit-training intervention had a strong effect on self-explanation activities and on learning outcomes as assessed by performance on similar problems and on novel problems.

Atkinson, Renkl, and Merrill (2003) showed that prompting principle-based self-explanations in a computer-based learning environment providing worked-out examples led to very favorable learning outcomes in terms of performance on similar problems and novel problems in the domain of probability. They requested the learners to select the principle underlying a solution step from a list at each worked-out step. After selecting

a principle, the correct one was displayed so that the learners received feedback. Further evidence for the positive effects of self-explanation prompting when learning from computer-based multimedia examples were provided by Conati and Van Lehn (2000) and by Schworm and Renkl (2002, 2004).

The guideline of self-explanation elicitation is regarded as central because the processing of the examples corresponds to the central knowledge-building activities in example-based learning. The guidelines presented in the following are primarily meant to support and facilitate learner's knowledge construction from examples by self-explaining.

THE HELP GUIDELINE

Why were self-explanations emphasized in the last section? Is it not more effective and efficient to provide instructional explanations that are always correct and do not depend on the learners' abilities and willingness to engage in self-explanation? There is a larger number of studies that have shown that the effects of instructional explanations are typically disappointing (e.g., Atkinson, Catrambone, & Merrill, 2003; Brown & Kane, 1988; Chi, 1996; Gerjets, Scheiter, & Catrambone, 2003; Schworm & Renkl, 2002). It is often more effective to prompt self-explanations than to offer instructional explanations. On the other hand, relying solely on self-explanations is associated with several disadvantages. For instance, it is very likely that at times learners will not be able to self-explain a specific solution step or their given self-explanations will be incorrect. Therefore, it can be sensible to support self-explanation activity by help in the form of instructional explanations.

One way to make such help in computer-supported learning environments effective was developed by Renkl (2002). He postulated a set of instructional principles for providing instructional explanations. The central principles related to the design of instructional explanations were the following: (1) *Provision on learner demand.* Instructional explanations should be presented on learner demand. This should ensure that the instructional explanations are appropriately timed and are actually used in the ongoing knowledge-construction activities of the learners. (2) *Minimalism*. In order to facilitate their processing, instructional explanations should be minimalist. Explanations that are integrated in help systems of computer-based learning programs are often not used because they are too long, too redundant, and too labor-intensive to process. (3) *Focus on principles*. With respect to the content of instructional explanations, their focus should be on the underlying principles of the respective domain. This claim is supported by the special significance of principle-based explanations when studying worked-out examples. Renkl (2002) demonstrated that learners having the possibility to demand instructional explanations designed according to these principles outperformed their counterparts not having this possibility on performance on novel problems in the domain of probability.

Atkinson and Renkl (2004; Renkl & Atkinson, 2002) experimentally investigated similar help in the form of instructional explanations as used by Renkl (2002) in the domain of probability. The results supplemented Renkl's findings in the following ways: (1) It is equally effective to provide instructional explanations on learner demand or in reaction to a learner's error when filling in a *blank* in a worked-out example. (2) It is especially important to help the learners to relate the explanation to the example at hand, by integrating the explanations into the example and to make the connection between the example and the explanation obvious. In summary, help in form of instructional explanations should be focused on principles, be minimalist and integrated, related to the example at hand, and provided on learner demand or in reaction to a learner's error.

Another way of delivering effective help in the form of instructional explanations was developed by Atkinson (2002). He showed that an animated agent delivering aural explanations, and thereby using gaze and gestures to direct the attention of the learners to relevant parts of the examples, is also effective (see chapters 9 and 12 on the modality and signaling principles).

In summary, instructional explanations are typically of very restricted use in example-based learning. However, when designed properly, they can sensibly supplement self-explanation activities and thereby foster learning outcomes.

Guidelines for Example Design

THE EASY-MAPPING GUIDELINE

As previously outlined, Tarmizi and Sweller (1988) showed that the advantage of worked-out examples from geometry gets lost when substantial cognitive resources have to be devoted in order to integrate different representations. The visual search processes require so much cognitive capacity that productive self-explanations were hindered. Integrating, that is, making the mapping between representations easier, makes cognitive resources available for productive learning processes such as self-explanations and, thereby, renders examples effective again. These findings were replicated by Ward and Sweller (1990) for physics worked-out examples and by Mwangi and Sweller (1998) for worked-out examples of mathematical word problems. Mayer and colleagues obtained analogous results in their research program (Mayer & Moreno, 2003; see chapter 12 on the contiguity principle).

Another way to facilitate the mapping between two representations is to combine aural and visual presentation modality. According to cognitive models of memory and information processing (e.g., Baddeley, 1986; Mayer & Moreno, 2003), the capacity to process information is distributed over several subsystems. Hence, cognitive resources can be more effectively used by providing some information in an aural and some information in a visual modality. Mousavi, Low, and Sweller (1995) showed that a partly auditory and partly visual mode of presentation for geometry worked-out examples fostered learning (see chapter 9 on the modality principle). However, the results of Jeung, Chandler, and Sweller (1997) qualified these findings. In three experiments, in which the difficulty of mapping between representations was varied, they showed that for visually complex, unfamiliar material, the superiority of aural explanations on visually presented examples disappeared. It only reappeared when electronic flashing was additionally used showing to which part of the diagram the spoken text was referring (see chapter 12 on signaling). The previously mentioned experiment by Atkinson (2002) also showed that having an animated agent that uses gaze and gestures to direct attention to relevant parts of worked-out examples, in addition to a dual-mode presentation, fosters learning.

An open question is when to integrate and when to use dual mode and signaling. There is no definitive empirical answer to this question. A pragmatic answer is to use an integrated format in the cases when an aural presentation is not, or hardly possible, due to technical restrictions and to use dual mode and signaling (e.g., flashing) when elements in one representation do not correspond to certain, well-circumscribed parts in the other representation. For instance, in the worked-out example displayed in Figure 15.1 the 20 in the denominator of the resulting probability corresponds to the 20 branches of the tree-like structure. In this context a "classical" integrated format in the sense of Sweller is hardly possible.

In summary, in order to make self-explanation processes during example study possible, it is necessary to foster the mapping between representations in multimedia learning. This can be best accomplished by graphically integrating different representations or by providing textual representations in an aural mode together with signaling (e.g., by electronic flashing or the gestures of an agent).

THE STRUCTURE-EMPHASIZING GUIDELINE

A characteristic of expert-like problem solving is to perceive problems not in terms of their surface features (e.g., cover stories, numbers, objects) but in terms of their structural features that are relevant with respect to the selection of the correct solution procedure. Therefore, learners should acquire the ability to detect, for example, that a certain solution step in physics is related to a specific Newton Law or that a certain step in probability is related to a certain probability rule such as the multiplication principle.

When the goal is learning to detect the structure of one problem type, multiple isomorphic examples (i.e., problems with the same structure) can be employed. Thereby, the learners can compare the examples and, in the optimal case, detect that not example-specific surface characteristics (e.g., objects and numbers) but the common structural features are relevant for selecting the correct solution procedure. In addition, the learners acquire the ability to detect the structural features when they encounter a problem with new surface features. However, Catrambone and Holyoak (1989) found that providing multiple examples is not sufficient. The learners have to be explicitly instructed to compare the examples with respect to similarities and differences (i.e., prompting for self-explanations related to example comparisons).

When the goal is learning to differentiate between different problem types in a domain that can be easily mixed up, a *structure-emphasizing example set* can be employed. Quilici and Mayer (1996) investigated this approach by developing two example sets for teaching statistical concepts, one that emphasized surface features, and one that emphasized structure. In the set that emphasized surface, very similar surface stories were used for all examples of a given type; in the example set that emphasized structure, a different surface story was used for all problems of a given type. The structure was emphasized by arranging examples so that (a) each problem type is exemplified by a set of different cover stories and (b) the same set of cover stories is used across the problems. Thereby, it is shown that cover stories and structure types do not covary and relying on surface features does not lead to correct solutions. In two experiments, learners in the structure-emphasizing condition outperformed their counterparts with respect to sorting problems according to their structure and solving problems similar to the ones presented for learning. Recent results of Scheiter, Gerjets, and Schuh (2003) have, however, shown that even in the case of a structure-emphasizing example set, it is important to instruct the learners to compare the examples with respect to similarities and differences; without such instructions, Scheiter et al. failed to detect positive effects of a structure-emphasizing example set.

To sum up, learners can be guided to perceive examples and problems in terms of their solution-relevant structure when multiple examples are employed. When problem types are to be differentiated, *structure-emphasizing example sets* can be recommended. However, in order to assure the indented effects, learners should be asked to self-explain the differences and commonalities of the presented examples.

THE MEANINGFUL BUILDING-BLOCKS GUIDELINE

When solving problems in a domain, learners encounter novel transfer problems that they cannot solve by already known solution procedures. A modified solution procedure has to be found. Often this can be accomplished by assembling building blocks (solutions steps) of known procedures in a new way. The basic assumption of the research program of Catrambone (e.g., 1995, 1996, 1998) is that the ability to assemble new procedures can be fostered by making subgoals in worked-out solution procedures salient, either by visually isolating them (e.g., making circles around them) or by assigning a label. This counteracts the tendency of learners to learn a solution procedure as a fixed chain of steps that has to be applied as a whole when a certain problem type is encountered. Especially when novel problems with new structures are encountered, it is important that the learners have understood the single building blocks of solutions, that is, they know which (sub-) goals were achieved by which operators. Catrambone (e.g., 1995, 1996) replicated the positive effects of making (sub-) goals salient on learning in a series of experiments. It also was shown that salient subgoals lead to self-explanations about what these steps accomplished (Catrambone, 1998). As a result, learning outcomes were enhanced.

Another possibility to make (sub-) goals salient is to use a step-by-step presentation of worked-out examples. For example,

Renkl (1997) showed the problem specification and the solution steps of each example on four screen pages. On the first page, the problem givens were displayed. The learner could read them and then go to the next page, on which the first solution step was presented in addition to the problem formulation. After inspecting this solution step on the second page, the participants proceeded to the following page where the next solution step was added, and so on. After the entire solution of a problem was presented, the learner could move to the next page where the cycle began all over again with the first page of a new example being presented. This procedure demarcates very clearly the single (sub-) goals. In addition, the fact that the next solution step was not immediately visible – as is the case with usual paper-pencil presentation of a worked-out example – was intended to serve as a situational *incentive* to anticipate the next solution step (i.e., *anticipative reasoning*). As previously mentioned, some of the learners in the Renkl (1997) study extensively anticipated solution steps and thereby achieved favorable learning outcomes.

Atkinson and Derry (2000) experimentally examined the effectiveness of a subgoal-oriented step-by-step presentation in comparison to a simultaneous provision of the solution steps in a computer-based multimedia environment. They found that learners who received a step-by-step presentation outperformed learners who studied simultaneously presented steps on problem-solving transfer.

Recently, researchers have shown that it is not only effective to make the (sub-) goals of given worked-out solution procedures salient and thereby render their building blocks meaningful, but also to transform solution procedures so that meaningful building blocks can be determined at all by the learners. In domains such as statistics or probability, there are frequently used solution procedures that are computationally efficient but very hard to understand. For example, the problem displayed in Figure 15.1 could have also been solved by the general formula, $1/(n!/[n-k]!)$ where n is the number of possible events and k is the number of selections. This formula is typically presented in statistics text books. However, it is very hard to understand why this *molar* solution is as it is. Therefore, the worked-out solution shown in Figure 15.1 shows another procedure that is *modular*: The probabilities of the single selections are determined and multiplied. Particularly when integrating this information with the tree-like diagram, one can figure out with relative ease why this solution works. Gerjets, Scheiter, and Catrambone (2004) reported several experiments in which molar and modular worked-out solution procedures from probability were compared. They found that the computationally not-so-efficient modular solution procedures led to better performance on isomorphic as well as novel problems. Atkinson, Catrambone et al. (2003) obtained similar results in the domain of statistics. What Gerjets et al. (2004) have called *modular solutions* was called *conceptually oriented equations* by Atkinson et al. It was also shown that transfer to novel problems is better fostered by conceptually oriented equations than by solution procedures designed for efficient computation.

In summary, worked-out examples should include conceptually oriented (modular) solution procedures and the single (sub-) goals should be made salient by visually isolating them, by assigning a label, or by a subgoal-oriented step-by-step presentation. Thereby the learners can identify meaningful building blocks of solution procedures that they can rearrange in order to solve novel problems.

Worked-Out Examples for Initial Skill Acquisition: How to Proceed?

Right from the beginning of skill acquisition, combining example study with problem-solving elements fosters learning (e.g., Mwangi & Sweller, 1998; Stark, Gruber, Renkl, & Mandl, 2000; Sweller & Cooper, 1985). For example, Stark (1999) compared a group of learners studying incomplete examples after a set of complete examples,

while the other group learned from complete examples only in the domain of probability. In the *incomplete group*, the learners were asked to supplement missing solution steps and thereby *forced* to employ the self-explanation activity of *anticipative reasoning*. After doing that, or at least making the attempt, the complete step was presented so that learners received feedback. Incomplete examples led to more elaborated self-explanations and to better learning outcomes based on performance on similar and novel problems.

Sweller and his colleagues (e.g., Mwangi & Sweller, 1998; Sweller & Cooper, 1985) have usually employed pairs of one worked-out example and one similar problem to-be-solved in their research on example-based learning. The control group learned just from solving problems. Trafton and Reiser (1993) showed that example-problem pairs are indeed more effective than a *blocked* series of examples that are followed by problems to-be-solved.

Although the studies mentioned demonstrated that integrating example study and problem solving is effective, they do not provide a satisfying answer to the question of how to structure the transition between example study in the earlier stages of skill acquisition to problem solving in the later stages. In response, Renkl, Atkinson, Maier, and Staley (2002; Renkl & Atkinson, 2003) proposed the following transition procedure: First, a complete example is presented. Second, a structurally identical incomplete example is presented in which one single step is omitted; after trying to supplement the faded step, the learner receives feedback about the correct solution. Third, in the following isomorphic examples, the number of blanks is increased step-by-step until just the problem formulation is left, that is, a problem to-be-solved. For instance, for an example/problem type with *three* solution steps, the following instructional procedure is proposed: (1) problem formulation (pf) – worked step – worked step – worked step; (2) pf – worked step – worked step – faded step; (3) pf – worked step – faded step – faded step; (4) pf – faded step – faded step – faded step. In this way, a smooth transition from example study to working on incomplete examples to problem solving is implemented. By gradually increasing problem-solving demands, the learners should retain sufficient cognitive capacity to successfully cope with these demands and, thereby, to focus on gaining understanding.

Renkl et al. (2002) have documented the effectiveness of such a fading procedure – in comparison to the tried-and-tested procedure of using example-problem pairs – in a field study in the domain of physics and two laboratory experiments in the domain of probability. Replications were provided by Atkinson, Renkl et al. (2003) and by Renkl, Atkinson, and Große (2004). In addition, Atkinson, Renkl et al. found that prompts of principle-based self-explanations at the worked-out steps further enhanced the effectiveness of faded examples.

To sum up, the transition from example study in earlier stages of skill acquisition to problem solving in later stages can be productively structured by faded examples. This fading procedure can be enriched by prompting self-explanations.

What Are the Implications for Instructional Design?

It is not hard to derive implications for the instructional design of example-based learning environments from the preceding sections. They can be summarized by the following main recommendations:

(1) Use sequences of faded examples for certain problem types in order to foster understanding in skill acquisition.
(2) Foster self-explanations by prompting or training.
(3) Provide a well-designed help system to support self-explanation activity.
(4) Design the provided examples so that self-explanations are facilitated. This can be accomplished by attending to the following principles: the easy-mapping guideline, the structure-emphasizing guideline, and the meaningful building-blocks guideline.

What are the implications of the research for cognitive theory on learning and instruction?

Three major implications for cognitive theories on learning and instruction can be derived from the research reported in this chapter:

(1) *Problem solving and learning are not (always) two sides of a coin.* Some approaches of learning and instruction that emphasize the productivity of problem solving (e.g., Schank, Berman, & Macpherson, 1999) hardly distinguish between processes of problem solving and learning, and seem to assume that learning is accomplished by solving problems. Research on worked-out examples has convincingly shown that problem solving and learning do not necessarily go hand in hand. Instead, it is important to distinguish between these processes and to acknowledge that, particularly in the beginning of skill acquisition, problem-solving demands may hinder learning.

(2) *Emphasizing the importance of guided constructive activity.* Presently, the notion of *constructivist learning*, with its emphasis on student activity, leads many people to view example-based learning as a traditional, *nonconstructivist* learning method with too much emphasis on presenting contents instead of active problem solving, communicating, and social knowledge construction activities. However, very open and ill-structured learning environments that rely heavily on the self-regulation capabilities of learners often fail to show improved learning outcomes. The more complex learning tasks are the more important guidance is in order to assure efficient and effective learning (see chapter 14 for the guided discovery principle). The case of learning by self-explaining worked-out examples is a very good instance that supports the notion that effective learning needs a well-balanced mixture of provided structure and information (e.g., worked-out steps, prompts) and room for active

knowledge construction (e.g., self-explanations). Putting primary focus on either side – structure/guidance or self-regulation – impairs the quality of the learning outcomes.

(3) *Cognitive load is an important aspect to be considered in learning.* Many constructivist approaches emphasize learning from complex, ill-defined, and authentic problems. As the results of research on example-based learning show, learners can be easily overwhelmed by such complex learning tasks. Mentally representing a complex learning task and simultaneously performing the required complex problem-solving processes impose, in many cases, too much cognitive load on working memory. This aspect is often neglected in problem-based approaches. Research on worked-out examples implies that it is important for theories of learning and instruction that recommend the employment of authentic problems to deal with the danger of cognitive overload. An example of an instructional approach that tries to balance load and complexity is the Four-Component Instructional Design model (4C/ID-model) of van Merriënboer (see chapter 5). In addition to presenting authentic tasks, van Merriënboer recommends worked-out examples and the simplifying assumptions approach in which learning starts from the simplest version of an authentic task that experts encounter in the real world (see also the similar *simplifying conditions method* of Reigeluth, 1999). By using examples and simple versions of authentic problems initial cognitive overload can be avoided.

Worked-Out Examples Approach: Limitations, Recent Developments, and Need for Further Research

Although research on learning by self-explaining worked-out examples has provided a well-founded knowledge base, four main restrictions can be stated:

(1) *Focusing on only one solution.* Traditional worked-out examples show just one solution procedure, although in many cases multiple solutions are possible. This is a disadvantage against the background that, for example, mathematics educators nowadays regard the inclusion of multiple solution methods as a feature of good teaching. This assumption is derived from findings concerning Japanese mathematics instruction that seems to be very successful (Stigler, Gallimore, & Hiebert, 2000). Furthermore, it can be argued that examples with one solution method affirm the dysfunctional belief about mathematics that problems have just a single correct solution (e.g., Schoenfeld, 1988). In order to address this restriction of traditional examples, Große and Renkl (2003) tested the effects of worked-out examples with multiple solution methods. Half of the subjects studied an arithmetical and a graphical method as shown in Figure 15.1 for certain problem types so that they could compare these solution methods (i.e., *multiple condition*). In the uniform condition, the same number of problems and of arithmetical and graphical solutions was studied but each problem type was just solved by the best-fitting method. The *multiple group* outperformed the *uniform group* on a posttest requiring the solution of similar problems, the evaluation of solution procedures, and argumentation about the coherence of different solution methods along with the advantages and disadvantages of certain methods. Hence, there is first evidence that the worked-out examples method can be productively combined with a multiple-solution approach. However, it is still an open question to what extent the findings of Große and Renkl (2003) can be generalized (e.g., to other domains and to mono-representational multiple solutions).

(2) *No exploitation of error-triggered learning.* Traditional worked-out examples provide only correct solution methods. This might be seen as a deficit because several prominent models of cognitive skill acquisition such as VanLehn's (e.g., 1999) cascade emphasize that errors are triggers for reflection that deepen understanding. In addition, many classroom researchers emphasize that effective instruction should take up errors as opportunities for in-depth discussions in order to deepen understanding. Against

this background, Große and Renkl (2004) analyzed the effects of presenting worked-out examples with errors after some correctly worked-out examples in the domain of probability. Three groups were compared: (1) only correctly worked-out examples, (2) correct and faulty examples with the error to be found by the learner, and (3) correct and faulty examples with errors highlighted. The main finding was that for learners with a low level of prior mathematical domain knowledge, both types of faulty examples impede learning, and for learners with a high level of domain knowledge faulty examples fostered learning as indicated by problem solving on novel problems (see chapter 21 on the expertise principle). Thus, Große and Renkl (2004) showed that faulty examples can be productive, but only under certain circumstances. Surely further research is needed in order to specify the exact context condition that renders learning from faulty examples effective.

(3) *Relevant only to a limited range of domains.* Worked-out examples include not only the final solution but also the steps toward reaching the solution. However, a manageable set of solution steps that directly lead to a final answer can only be provided in skill domains where algorithms can be applied, as, for example, in mathematics, physics, or programming. However, for skills such as writing a text, interpreting poems, drawing a picture, cooperating in a productive way, designing effective learning materials, scientific argumentation, and many other skills, solutions steps are more difficult to describe.

With respect to three previously mentioned types of skills (cooperating in a productive way, designing effective learning materials, and scientific argumentation), recent studies have shown that it is possible to extend the worked-out examples approach to nonalgorithmic domains. For these domains, an example provides just the problem and a solution (no steps); we call such examples *solved example problems.* Rummel and Spada (in press), for instance, provided video-based solved example problems of a successful computer-mediated collaboration in interdisciplinary problem solving on a psychiatric case. In the example condition, the participants learned from a dialogue between an advanced medical student and an advanced psychology student working productively on a joint case. Afterward the participants had to work together on a diagnosis and therapy plan for a new case. Compared to a second instructional condition, in which learning with a trial case was structured by a script prescribing the different phases of the participants' collaborative work, example-based learning lead to a better joint diagnosis. Collaborations in both instructional conditions (i.e., example-based and scripted) resulted in better therapy plans than in the control conditions (i.e., trial case without instructional support and no trial case). In a recent series of experiments, Renkl and colleagues employed solved example problems for the skill domains of designing learning materials in school mathematics and physics (Hilbert, Schworm, & Renkl, 2004; Schworm & Renkl, 2002) and in scientific argumentation (Schworm & Renkl, 2004). The focus of these studies was on the effects of prompting self-explanations when studying such solved example problems. It has been shown that prompting self-explanations is also of major importance when studying solved example problems, especially when the prompts focus on the underlying principles, eliciting principle-based explanations. Taken together, although it is a significant restriction of research on example-based learning that it focuses on algorithmic skill domains, research on example-based learning has at least begun to broaden the range of skill domains that are considered.

(4) *Evidence primarily from experimental settings of limited ecological validity.* Most of the studies on worked-out examples, particularly when multimedia examples were employed, were conducted in well-controlled laboratory settings and within learning environments of a limited range with respect to both the content covered and the time span for the development of a complex cognitive skill. In order to test whether the research findings on example-based learning hold true for comprehensive multimedia computer-based learning environments, it would be fruitful to analyze the effects of

multimedia environments (a) that cover a broader topic (e.g., statistics for social science), (b) in which the *state-of-the-art* of structuring example-based learning is implemented in a consequent way (cf. the guideline previously outlined), and (c) in which the proposed transition from fully worked-out examples to faded examples to problems to be solved is realized in several circles for the single subskills of a complex domain. Although there have been first attempts to design complex example-based environments covering larger amounts of content (e.g., Stark & Mandl, in press), there is presently no comprehensive environment that implements at least most of the design principles that have been identified previously. The design of such a state-of-the-art multimedia environment and an evaluation of its effects would be an important contribution examining the usefulness of an example-based approach in *real-world* learning environments.

In summary, the classical approach of learning from worked-out examples has several restrictions, such as focusing on one *single correct* solution and on *algorithmic* skill domains. These deficits substantially narrow the applicability of this learning method. In addition, research evidence comes primarily from laboratory studies. There are, however, first approaches that address these issues. As research on example-based learning in multimedia environments is a very active research field, it can be expected that the restrictions previously mentioned will be successfully addressed in the near future.

Glossary

Extraneous load: Refers to the working memory resources that are bound by demands of learning tasks or settings that do not contribute to knowledge construction (e.g., visual search processes for information during learning).

Germane load: Refers to the working memory resources that are bound by information processing that directly leads to knowledge construction (e.g., self-explaining when studying examples).

Intrinsic load: Refers to the working memory resources that are bound by the demand to represent the learning task/content. It is a function of the relation between the complexity of the learning task/content (number of elements and their interactions) on the one hand and on the learner's prior knowledge on the other hand (what is complex for a beginner is simple for an expert).

Prompts: Requests directed to learners. They require the learners to process the to-be-learned contents in specific ways.

Self-explanations: Explanations provided by learners and mainly directed to themselves. They contain information that is not directly given in the learning materials and that refer to solution steps and the reasons for them. They can also refer to structural and surface features of problems or problem types.

Solved example problems: Consist of a problem formulation and a solution (no solution steps).

Structure (of problems): Refers to problem features that determine which algorithm or solution procedure leads to the solution.

Surface features (of problems): Refer to problem characteristics that are not relevant for the selection of a solution algorithm or procedure (e.g., cover stories of mathematical word problems).

Worked-out examples: Consist of a problem formulation, solution steps, and the final solution.

References

Atkinson, R. K. (2002). Optimizing learning from examples using animated pedagogical agents. *Journal of Educational Psychology, 94*, 416–427.

Atkinson, R. K., Catrambone, R., & Merrill, M. M. (2003). Aiding transfer in statistics. Examining the use of conceptually oriented equations and elaborations during subgoal learning. *Journal of Educational Psychology, 95*, 762–773.

Atkinson, R. K., & Derry, S. J. (2000). Computer-based examples designed to encourage optimal example processing: A study examining the impact of sequentially presented, subgoal-oriented worked examples. In B. Fishman & S. F. O'Connor-Divelbiss (Eds.), *Proceedings of the Fourth International Conference of Learning Sciences* (pp. 132–133). Hillsdale, NJ: Erlbaum.

Atkinson, R. K., Derry, S. J., Renkl, A., & Wortham, D. W. (2000). Learning from examples: Instructional principles from the worked examples research. *Review of Educational Research, 70*, 181–214.

Atkinson, R. K., & Renkl, A. (2004). *The effects of help provision in a computer-based learning environment.* Manuscript submitted for publication.

Atkinson, R. K., Renkl, A., & Merrill, M. M. (2003). Transitioning from studying examples to solving problems: Combining fading with prompting fosters learning. *Journal of Educational Psychology, 95*, 774–783.

Baddeley, A. D. (1986). *Working memory.* New York: Oxford University Press.

Brown, A. L., & Kane, M. J. (1988). Preschool children can learn to transfer: Learning to learn and learning from examples. *Cognitive Psychology, 20*, 493–523.

Catrambone, R. (1995). Aiding subgoal learning: Effects on transfer. *Journal of Educational Psychology, 87*, 5–17.

Catrambone, R. (1996). Generalizing solution procedures learned from examples. *Journal of Experimental Psychology: Learning, Memory, and Cognition, 22*, 1020–1031.

Catrambone, R. (1998). The subgoal learning model: Creating better examples so that students can solve novel problems. *Journal of Experimental Psychology: General, 127*, 355–376.

Catrambone, R., & Holyoak, K. J. (1989). Overcoming contextual limitations on problem-solving transfer. *Journal of Experimental Psychology: Learning, Memory, and Cognition, 15*, 1147–1156.

Chi, M. T. H. (1996). Constructing self-explanations and scaffolded explanations in tutoring. *Applied Cognitive Psychology, 10*, S33–S49.

Chi, M. T., H., Bassok, M., Lewis, M. W., Reimann, P., & Glaser, R. (1989). Self-explanations: How students study and use examples in learning to solve problems. *Cognitive Science, 13*, 145–182.

Conati, C., & Van Lehn, K. (2000). Toward computer-based support of meta-cognitive skills: A computational framework to coach self-explanation. *International Journal of Artificial Intelligence in Education, 11*, 398–415.

Cooper, G., & Sweller, J. (1987). Effects of schema acquisition and rule automation on mathematical problem-solving transfer. *Journal of Educational Psychology, 79*, 347–362.

Gerjets, P., & Scheiter, K. (2003). Goal configurations and processing strategies as moderators between instructional design and cognitive load: Evidence from hypertext-based instruction. *Educational Psychologist, 38*, 33–41.

Gerjets, P., Scheiter, K., & Catrambone, R. (2003). Reducing cognitive load and fostering cognitive skill acquisition: Benefits of category-avoiding examples. In F. Schmalhofer, R. Young, & G. Katz (Eds.), *Proceedings of EuroCogSci 03. The European Cognitive Science Conference 2003* (pp. 133–139). Mahwah, NJ: Erlbaum.

Gerjets, P., Scheiter, K., & Catrambone, R. (2004). Designing instructional examples to reduce intrinsic cognitive load: Molar versus modular presentation of solution procedures. *Instructional Science, 32*, 33–58

Große, C. S., & Renkl, A. (2003). Example-based learning with multiple solution methods fosters understanding. In F. Schmalhofer, R. Young, & G. Katz (Eds.), *Proceedings of EuroCogSci 03. The European Cognitive Science Conference 2003* (pp. 163–168). Mahwah, NJ: Erlbaum.

Große, C. S., & Renkl, A. (2004). Learning from worked examples: What happens if errors are included? In P. Gerjets, J. Elen, R. Joiner, & P. Kirschner (Eds.), *Instructional design for effective and enjoyable computer-supported learning* (pp. 356–364). Tübingen, Germany: Knowledge Media Research Center.

Hilbert, T., Schworm, S., & Renkl, A. (2004). Learning from worked-out examples: The transition from instructional explanations to self-explanation prompts. In P. Gerjets, J. Elen, R. Joiner, & P. Kirschner (Eds.), *Instructional design for effective and enjoyable computer-supported learning* (pp. 184–192). Tübingen, Germany: Knowledge Media Research Center.

Jeung, H., Chandler, P., & Sweller, J. (1997). The role of visual indicators in dual sensory mode instruction. *Educational Psychology*, *17*, 329–433.

Kalyuga, S., Ayres, P., Chandler, P., & Sweller, J. (2003). The expertise reversal effect. *Educational Psychologist*, *38*, 23–31.

Kalyuga, S., Chandler, P., Tuovinen, J., & Sweller, J. (2001). When problem solving is superior to studying worked examples. *Journal of Educational Psychology*, *93*, 579–588.

LeFevre, J.-A., & Dixon, P. (1986). Do written instructions need examples? *Cognition and Instruction*, *3*, 1–30.

Mayer, R. E., & Moreno, R. (2003). Nine ways to reduce cognitive load in multimedia learning. *Educational Psychologist*, *38*, 43–52.

Mousavi, S. Y., Low, R., & Sweller, J. (1995). Reducing cognitive load by mixing auditory and visual presentation modes. *Journal of Educational Psychology*, *87*, 319–334.

Mwangi, W., & Sweller, J. (1998). Learning to solve compare word problems: The effect of example format and generating self-explanations. *Cognition and Instruction*, *16*, 173–199.

Paas, F., Renkl, A., & Sweller, J. (2003). Cognitive load theory and instructional design: Recent developments. *Educational Psychologist*, *38*, 1–4.

Quilici, J. L., & Mayer, R. E. (1996). Role of examples in how students learn to categorize statistics word problems. *Journal of Educational Psychology*, *88*, 144–161.

Recker, M., & Pirolli, P. (1994). Modeling individual differences in students' learning strategies. *The Journal of the Learning Sciences*, *4*, 1–38.

Reigeluth, C. M. (1999). The elaboration theory: Guidance for scope and sequence decisions. In C. M. Reigeluth, (Ed.), *Instructional design theories and models* (Vol. II, pp. 425–453). Mahwah, NJ: Erlbaum.

Renkl, A. (1997). Learning from worked-out examples: A study on individual differences. *Cognitive Science*, *21*, 1–29.

Renkl, A. (2002). Learning from worked-out examples: Instructional explanations supplement self-explanations. *Learning and Instruction*, *12*, 529–556.

Renkl, A., & Atkinson, R. K. (2002). Learning from examples: Fostering self-explanations in computer-based learning environments. *Interactive Learning Environments*, *10*, 105–119.

Renkl, A., & Atkinson, R. K. (2003). Structuring the transition from example study to problem solving in cognitive skills acquisition: A cognitive load perspective. *Educational Psychologist*, *38*, 15–22.

Renkl, A., Atkinson, R. K., & Große, C. S. (2004) How fading worked solution steps works – a cognitive load perspective. *Instructional Science*, *32*, 59–82.

Renkl, A., Atkinson, R. K., Maier, U. H., & Staley, R. (2002). From example study to problem solving: Smooth transitions help learning. *Journal of Experimental Education*, *70*, 293–315.

Renkl, A., Gruber, H., Weber, S., Lerche, T., & Schweizer, K. (2003). Cognitive Load beim Lernen aus Lösungsbeispielen [Cognitive load during learning from worked-out examples]. *Zeitschrift für Pädagogische Psychologie*, *17*, 93–101.

Renkl, A., Stark, R., Gruber, H., & Mandl, H. (1998). Learning from worked-out examples: The effects of example variability and elicited self-explanations. *Contemporary Educational Psychology*, *23*, 90–108.

Rummel, N., & Spada, H. (in press). Learning to collaborate: An instructional approach to promoting collaborative problem-solving in computer-mediated settings. *The Journal of the Learning Sciences*.

Schank, R., Berman, T. R., & Macpherson, K. A. (1999). Learning by doing. In C. M. Reigeluth, (Ed.), *Instructional design theories and models* (Vol. II, pp. 161–181). Mahwah, NJ: Erlbaum.

Scheiter, K., Gerjets, P., & Schuh, J. (2003). Are multiple examples necessary for schema induction? In F. Schmalhofer, R. Young, & G. Katz (Eds.), *Proceedings of EuroCogSci 03. The European Cognitive Science Conference 2003* (pp. 283–288). Mahwah, NJ: Erlbaum.

Schoenfeld, A. H. (1988). When good teaching leads to bad results: The disaster of "well-taught" mathematics courses. *Educational Psychologist*, *23*, 145–166.

Schworm, S., & Renkl, A. (2002). Learning by solved example problems: Instructional explanations reduce self-explanation activity. In W. D. Gray & C. D. Schunn (Eds.), *Proceedings of the 24th Annual Conference of the Cognitive Science Society* (pp. 816–821). Mahwah, NJ: Erlbaum.

Schworm, S., & Renkl, A. (2004). *Learning with video-based models: Self-explanation prompts for the acquisition of cognitive skills? Their quality is the deciding factor!* Manuscript submitted for publication.

Stark, R. (1999). *Lernen mit Lösungsbeispielen. Der Einfluß unvollständiger Lösungsschritte auf Beispielelaboration, Motivation und Lernerfolg* [Learning by worked-out examples. The impact of incomplete solution steps on example elaboration, motivation, and learning outcomes]. Bern, Switzerland: Huber.

Stark, R., Gruber, H., Renkl, A., & Mandl, H. (2000). Instruktionale Effekte einer kombinierten Lernmethode: Zahlt sich die Kombination von Lösungsbeispielen und Problemlöseaufgaben aus? [Instructional effects of a combined learning method: Does the combination of worked-out examples and problems to-be-solved pay off?]. *Zeitschrift für Pädagogische Psychologie, 14*, 206–218.

Stark, R., & Mandl, H. (in press). Web-based learning in the field of empirical research methods. *Computers & Education.*

Stigler, J. W., Gallimore, R., & Hiebert, J. (2000). Using video surveys to compare classrooms and teaching across cultures: Examples and lessons from the TIMSS video studies. *Educational Psychologist, 35*, 87–100.

Sweller, J., & Cooper, G. A. (1985). The use of worked examples as a substitute for problem solving in learning algebra. *Cognition and Instruction, 2*, 59–89.

Sweller, J., van Merriënboer, J. J. G., & Paas, F. G. (1998). Cognitive architecture and instructional design. *Educational Psychology Review, 10*, 251–296.

Tarmizi, R. A., & Sweller, J. (1988). Guidance during mathematical problem solving. *Journal of Educational Psychology, 80*, 424–436.

Trafton, J. G., & Reiser, B. J. (1993). The contributions of studying examples and solving problems to skill acquisition. In M. Polson (Ed.), *Proceedings of the Fifteenth Annual Conference of the Cognitive Science Society* (pp. 1017–1022). Hillsdale, NJ: Lawrence Erlbaum Associates.

VanLehn, K. (1999). Rule-learning events in the acquisition of a complex skill: An evaluation of CASCADE. *The Journal of the Learning Sciences, 8*, 71–125.

Ward, M., & Sweller, J. (1990). Structuring effective worked examples. *Cognition and Instruction, 7*, 1–39.

CHAPTER 16

The Collaboration Principle
in Multimedia Learning

David H. Jonassen
Chwee Beng Lee
Chia-Chi Yang
James Laffey
University of Missouri

Abstract

Based on sociocultural and social cognitive theory, computer support for collaborative learning (CSCL) has emerged as a new research and development subdiscipline of computer-mediated communication. The emphasis of CSCL is on supporting collaborative learning activities in online multimedia environments. In this chapter, we review research on the nature of the technology used, how the learning groups are comprised (e.g., group size, learner characteristics), the learning outcome engaged by the task, the role of the tutor, the effects of community-building activities, the nature of the learning or communication assessment, and the effects of scaffolds or discussion constraints on learning. Based on this research, we make a variety of recommendations for the design and implementation of learning environments.

Introduction to the Collaboration Principle

In the past decade, the study of learning has been influenced increasingly by constructivism and social theories. Not only have the epistemological and ontological assumptions about the nature of learning changed as a result of constructivist influences, but the nature of instructional and learning activities has changed dramatically. At the risk of oversimplification, the most obvious effect of this influence has been a shift from emphasis on instructional communication systems to an emphasis on practice-based, collaborative learning systems. The goal of instructional systems, informed by objectivist assumptions, was to effectively design messages to support the efficient transmission of knowledge about the world. The current goal of learning sciences, informed by constructivist assumptions, is the immersion of learners in simulated practice fields or more authentic fields of practice (Barab & Duffy, 2000). These practice fields not only engage students in more authentic, complex, and ill-structured problem-solving tasks, but they also necessitate, engage, and support socially mediated forms of learning such as collaboration.

Supporting collaborative learning in educational practice fields is examined in the relatively new field of study, computer-supported collaborative learning (CSCL). Supporting group work and workplace learning through a shared workspace for groups to work in practice communities has been examined by the field, computer-supported collaborative work (CSCW). While both fields of academic discourse are important and burgeoning, this chapter focuses on CSCL research and its implications for designing multimedia learning environments.

CSCL systems support formal and informal student learning in collaborative groups by mediating and scaffolding group processes and group dynamics in discourse communities, communities of learners, and communities of practice. Groups may consist of learners working at the same workstation but most often on separate machines connected by networks. CSCL systems enable learners to communicate ideas interactively, access information, and engage in collaborative problem-solving activities.

Theoretical Assumptions of Computer Support for Collaborative Learning

First and foremost, collaborative learning assumes that learners must cooperate, that is, knowingly and willingly participate in some joint activity. True cooperation requires that the members are positively interdependent (i.e., in yoked performance), individually responsible and accountable, supportive of the efforts of all members to complete tasks, and reflective of the achievements of the group processing (Johnson & Johnson, 2004). Collaborative groups are usually assigned by teachers. However, members of these assigned groups are not usually sensitive of each other's commitment, so positive interdependence may be a problem requiring teacher encouragement (Johnson & Johnson, 2004).

As stated before, the practice of CSCL has ridden the theoretical wave of constructivism that has washed over the field of learning in the past decade or so. Con-

structivism provides an epistemological and ontological foundation for theorizing about the nature of reality, knowledge, the mind, thought, and meaning. Constructivists think about learning in at least two separate ways. Cognitive constructivists focus on the internal meaning making and conceptual change processes of individual learners. Chief among these theories is genetic epistemology (Piaget, 1970), which describes the ontogenesis of knowledge and its psychological origins and operations. Piaget described how we adapt to our environment by constantly constructing and equilibrating knowledge structures.

CSCL, however, is based on more socially oriented theories of knowledge construction and meaning making. Chief among these is Vygotsky's sociocultural theory of learning that avers that human intelligence originates in our society or culture, and individual cognition results from interpersonal interaction with our social environment (Vygotsky, 1978). Cognition is constrained by the learner's "zone of proximal development" that describes the nature of activity that is possible with the help of more capable peers, adults, or social artifacts. Highly related are theories of socially shared cognition that claim that cognition is distributed among such important elements as the participants, the artifacts they use, and the social institutions within which they are housed (Brown & Cole, 2000). Like most of these social theories, social cognition emphasizes joint mediated activity of people in a context and assumes that cognition is coconstructed and distributed among individuals. An assumption of CSCL and most social theories of meaning making is that cognition is distributed among individuals and artifacts, that is, that cognition exists in the world – in the social relationships, in the artifacts, and in the discourse among individuals (Jonassen & Henning, 1999). Cognitions are situated and distributed in nature (Salomon, 1995).

Finally, CSCL systems draw on assumptions of activity theory, which avers that consciousness and activity coexist and are mutually supportive. Activity theory is a form of sociocultural and sociohistorical analysis that examines human activity embedded in a social matrix of people and artifacts (Docq, 2001; Nardi, 1996). Activity systems contain interacting components, such as subject, tools, object, division of labor, community, and rules (Engeström, 1987). Knowledge construction is mediated by human activities in the context of different activity systems focused by the interaction of minds in the world, socially constructing and sharing meaning (Holt & Morris, 1993).

An analysis of these theoretical foundations could comprise the entire chapter. One of the most important reasons why CSCL represents a new paradigm of learning is that it is based on socially mediated theories of learning rather than individual cognitive theories. Learning results not only from the accretion and reorganization of individual knowledge structures but also from the conversations and collaborations that groups of learners conduct. The social nature of CSCL has resulted in decidedly different research issues than from individual theories of learning. These issues and recommendations for the design of multimedia learning environments are presented next.

Online collaboration can take many forms. Students in knowledge-building activities using Web Forum collaborate to construct a knowledge base. Students may also collaborate to design new products or systems, or they may work together to solve vexing scientific problems. Students may also assume different roles in a social studies environment focusing on political processes. Collaboration occurs when students knowingly seek to achieve a common goal.

Research-Based Principles for Collaboration

As a result of the process of identifying and analyzing the research literature on CSCL, we have identified seven different issues related to CSCL systems, including the nature of the technology used to support CSCL; the nature of the group composition; the nature of the task engaging learners; the role of the students and instructors in CSCL systems; the process of community building during CSCL sessions; the nature of the learning and communication assessment; and finally the effects of different communication scaffolds on group performance. We anticipate that the variety and sensitivity of research issues related to CSCL will increase dramatically in the next decade.

Nature of Technology

It is axiomatic that CSCL and other computer-mediated communication (CMC) systems include technology. However, educators have choices among technological systems, each with features and affordances for different pedagogies, participants, and task requirements. Additionally, technological advances are providing new capabilities and becoming more accessible and affordable. Principles of CSCL will be more robust to the extent that they incorporate how the aspects of the technology mediate communication and collaboration.

Researchers have examined how technological systems support or constrain collaborative learning. They have examined the use of simple tools, such as e-mail, discussion forums, and chat, as well as integrated systems of tools. The most common integrated systems are general purpose courseware systems, such as the commercially available Blackboard and WebCT systems, but there are also custom-built systems that serve unique conditions or goals. The iExpeditions system (Wang, Laffey, & Poole, 2001) designed to meet the special requirements of a program to teach problem solving and leadership for children of Motorola employees is an example of a custom application.

RESEARCH FINDINGS

A key question for many educators and researchers has been how does using technology to support collaborative learning differ from face-to-face learning or how may it enhance traditional classroom approaches. In general, responses to the use of asynchronous tools are viewed positively by students (Ocker & Yaverbaum, 2001; Shaw & Pieter, 2000), support substantial collaborative activity (Curtis & Lawson, 2001), and show no significant differences for student outcomes (Arbaugh, 2000; Russell, 1997; Schrader et al., 2003). However, the processes and characteristics of CSCL implementation may differ substantially from face-to-face classes. Smith, Ferguson, and Caris (2001) interviewed college instructors who had taught in both formats and report that Web-based classes have a profoundly different communication style than face-to-face classes. Communication in online classes shows greater equality between students and instructors, greater explicitness of written instructions required, greater workloads for instructors, and deeper thinking manifested in discussions. They also note a paradox of initial feelings of anonymity and isolation giving way to emerging online identities and community. Thus because of the fewer channels of communication online courses are at risk for early student drop out, but for those students who persist, the potential for a sense of community is at least as great as for face-to-face classes. Meyer (2003) noted that there are advantages to holding discussion in either format, but reported that students spend more time in online discussions and exhibit higher order thinking through exploratory and integrative comments. Researchers have noted that students who work full time (Biscaglia & Monk-Turner, 2001) and have learning preferences that fit online modes (Meyer, 2003) have the most favorable attitudes toward online instruction. Researchers (Arbaugh, 2000; Ocker & Yaverbaum, 2001; Rovai, 2001) have also found gender-based differences in participation and satisfaction that favor female students in online instruction. In contrast to the generally positive acceptance and benefits shown by users of CSCL, De Simone, Schmid, and McEwen (2001) found that students engaged in building group-based electronic concept maps did not use the asynchronous tools available to them. The reasons for not using the communication tools were frustrations with delays in exchanging information and difficulty in understanding the contributions of others without face-to-face discussion.

Using synchronous tools, such as chat, or asynchronous tools such as discussion boards, is a primary choice point for educators. Researchers have examined the relative benefits of supporting collaboration with synchronous or asynchronous tools. Bhattachyra (1999) compared the use of synchronous chat and asynchronous bulletin boards and found that users preferred the discussion boards because they felt less hurried and had time for analysis, reflection, and composition. Similarly, Veerman and Veldhuis-Diermanse (2001) showed that technology was effective in supporting collaborative learning in academic education and found advantages for asynchronous media because it provides student groups with more options to think and reflect on information, to organize and keep track of discussions, and to engage in large-group discussions when compared to synchronous media. Sotillo (2000) showed the advantage of having both formats of communication in a language-learning context in that synchronous discussions were similar to the types of interactional modifications found in face-to-face conversations that are deemed necessary for second-language acquisition, and the delayed nature of asynchronous discussions gives learners more opportunities to produce syntactically complex language. Sotillo concludes that asynchronous and synchronous CMC have different discourse features that may be exploited for different pedagogical purposes. Pairs of medical and psychology students were required to develop a plan of therapy for a psychiatric case study (Herman, Rummel, & Spada, 2001). Dyads using simpler-email/audio/text editor systems were better able to coordinate their collaboration (an essential part of the problem-solving process), than dyads using video conferencing with a text editor. However, the synchronous video helped participants work more collaboratively. Similarly, Shotsberger (1999) compared online chat transcripts with asynchronous communication and found the synchronous tools beneficial because they encouraged simultaneity and debate. These findings highlight that there are strengths and limitations to each form of technology, and that benefits accrue to those who fit the technology well to the tasks at hand.

For the most part researchers have documented successful use of CSCL, but some researchers have noted limitations in how these systems support collaborative activity and learning objectives. Marttunen and Laurinen (2001) found that most of the messages (78%) that the students wrote during a course were interactive in nature, but that most (60%) of these interactive messages were dialogue messages consisting of interaction between only two students, failing to meet the instructor's goal of encouraging active collaborative argumentation. Biesenbach-Lucas (2003) used online discussions to effectively extend course-related discussions outside the regular face-to-face class meetings, but that students perceived the asynchronous discussions to be forced and unnatural and found it difficult to make connections to prior postings. After studying higher education students in an online course, McLoughlin and Luca (2001) conclude that students need orientation and support to help them engage in critical analysis of their own views and revision of concepts when confronted with multiple viewpoints and disconfirming evidence in online discussions. Similarly, Thomas (2002) studied learner outcomes and patterns of interaction within an online discussion forum and concluded that the typical nonlinear branching structure of online discussion may be insufficient for the realization of truly conversational modes of learning.

In serving pedagogical goals in CSCL systems, technologies may be appropriated or resisted by members of a course or learning group. Several researchers (Fishman and Gomez, 1997; Ku & Lohr, 2001; Lahti, Seitamaa-Hakkarainen, & Hakkarainen, 2001; Scanlon, O'Shea, Smith, & Li, 1997; Wang et al. 2001) have documented that different students appropriate technology in different ways. The differences may be based on cultural background, language skills, teachers attitudes toward tools, and types of support available. Anderson and Kanuka (1997) used Roger's criterion for adoption of innovations (Rogers, 1995) to study the use of online forums for professional development and found that from some users' perspectives online learning had little relative advantage over face-to-face sessions. They speculated that the technology may have greater relative advantage for moderators, sponsors, and employers of the forum, and that attention to whom the technology provides advantage may prove useful for studies of the use of online learning. These findings highlight that the usability of the technology and the context within which technology is used are critical to explaining the usage and outcomes of technology implementation for collaborative learning.

LIMITATIONS OF RESEARCH

One should approach the findings reported in this section cautiously. For the most part the reports are not advancing a general theory of how technology supports collaboration, but rather are describing small sample studies of how technology shapes collaboration practices and learning outcomes in a local context. These studies present insights about practice that have merit for considering how to implement technology for online learning. Readers, however, are cautioned to pay close attention to the conditions under which the implementations take place.

IMPLICATIONS AND RECOMMENDATIONS

The findings of this section show that technology can augment regular classrooms by supporting collaborative learning or in some cases actually replace the classroom and still provide an effective workplace for collaborative learning. Implementers of CSCL are advised to select technology that matches the pedagogy of the instruction, design instructional practices that take advantage of the technological tools, and identify student attributes that may interact with using technology for collaborative learning. A challenge as well as opportunity for educators and researchers advancing CSCL is an ever-changing landscape of technological tools available to support online collaborative learning. For example Constantiono-Gonzalez, Suthers, and Santos (2003) demonstrated an intelligent agent that could be used to augment and automate some aspects of collaboration in online learning. Similarly, the use of wireless personal digital assistants (PDAs) and Web-enabled cell phones portend ubiquitous access to online learning activities and groups in ways that may substantially change the nature of instruction from learning about subject matter to being supported during authentic practice. Additionally new formats of online communication are evolving. Weblogs and wikis are just a few examples of asynchronous tools for shared knowledge construction with the potential to augment CSCL.

Nature of Group Composition

Educational success is dependent upon having appropriate instruction for each learner. Socially oriented theories of knowledge construction explain and situate learning and individual cognitive development in the interpersonal interactions of the social context and the class or learning group provides much of the social context. Thus, a key challenge of education is to provide an appropriate educational experience for each student within the context of a class or learning group. Additionally learning in groups is mediated to a substantial extent by group dynamics, group membership, and the attributes and perspectives that the members bring to the group work. Online collaborative learning environments provide new opportunities to compose different and more varied groups and these differences may contribute to the richness and interactivity of the learning. For example, Orly, Avigail, and David (2001) showed how educationally oriented MOOs (Multi-User Dimension Object-Oriented environments) were creating informal opportunities for educators, students, and technologists to interact and learn from one another. Using online systems

for collaboration among members may also create new or unforeseen problems. For example, Scanlon et al. (1997) reported that when group size rose above four that group performance diminished for participants using an audio and video synchronous collaboration tool. Researchers of online collaborative learning environments are challenged to understand how the composition and attributes of learning groups and the design and implementation of online systems influence group activity and individual performance and learning.

RESEARCH FINDINGS

Researchers of online collaborative environments have investigated how gender, group size, and learner characteristics (including language, culture, and professional orientation) influence group activity and learning online.

Gender. How males and females may differentially participate and benefit from online collaborative learning is a frequent topic of research. In reviewing literature on participation in distance education Bisciaglia and Monk-Turner (2001) point out that the majority of those enrolled in distance education are females. This finding contrasts with Orly et al. (2001), who reported that the majority of users of informal online educational systems are males. Some researchers have found that females benefit from the use of online systems. Rovai (2001) examined the dynamics of classroom community during a five-week graduate-level course taught entirely at a distance using a commercial e-learning system. In this study females manifested a stronger sense of community than their male counterparts both at the start and end of the course. Additionally, female students exhibited a mostly connected communication pattern while the communication pattern of males was mostly independent. Ocker and Yverbaum (2001) compared female and male students' experiences of collaborative activity in face-to-face and in asynchronous online environments while taking a business course. The results show that the females were less satisfied than men with the face-to-face collaborative work, but more satisfied with the online collaborative work. The researchers speculate that the asynchronous environment created an opportunity for more equal participation. Marttunen and Laurinen (2001) examined how Finnish students practiced argumentation in two e-mail study groups as part of an academic debating course. In this study female students showed agreement more often than men, while counterattacking and elaborative neutrality were more common among men. In contrast to the studies showing females exhibiting more positive collaborative activity in online learning, Kirkley, Savery, and Grabner-Hagen (1998) reported males contributed more messages than females in two advanced higher education courses.

Group Size. The next most popular group composition feature is group size. The work of Scanlon et al. (1997) mentioned previously suggest that an optimal size may be dependent on tasks and technology. Nonetheless, many researchers have compared working online in a group with working alone. In a laboratory experiment Jessup, Egbert, and Connolly (1995) studied the effects of group member interaction frequency during an idea-generation task using an automated brainstorming system. The controlled study found that frequently interacting groups of students were more productive than individuals or than groups who were allowed to interact less frequently. However, the students in the frequently interacting groups also felt more interrupted and more hurried. Participant comments revealed that frequently interacting groups tended to make more supportive and critical remarks and arguments; ask more questions about problems and solutions; make more comments about the group and about ancillary issues; and ask more questions overall than did individuals and the pooled and infrequently interacting groups. Uribe, Klein, and Sullivan (2003) investigated the effect of computer-mediated collaboration on solving ill-defined problems. Results indicated that participants who worked in computer-mediated collaborative dyads spent more time on tasks and performed significantly better than did participants who worked alone. In general, participants benefited and indicated a preference for working collaboratively.

Learner Characteristics. Various cultural, social, and cognitive characteristics of group membership have also been investigated to help explain participation and outcomes with online learning. Kirkley et al. (1998) studied electronic dialogue in higher education courses and found that U.S. students sent more messages than Asian students by ratios of 2:1 in one class and 4:1 in another. The differences of participation in the face-to-face class sessions was in the same direction but not as great. An opposite finding is reported by Pilkington and Walker (2003) who reported that in the use of a virtual learning environment (VLE) nonnative speakers made more use of the communication tools than native speakers. Expertise is an important issue in any learning research. Oshima and Oshima (2002) compared expert learners (graduate students) with novices (sophomores in college) and found that the experts were far more able to use a collaborative knowledge-building system for improving their knowledge-building activities than were the novices. They conclude that the success of the experts was based on their ability to recognize the value of the technology for overcoming communication problems and their ability to find ways to coordinate the various communication channels. The novices were less able to use the system because they were not able to work in a *culture of learning* and their discourse was mainly *telling*.

Tapola et al. (2001) found that elementary school students who were characterized by a high learning orientation (i.e., motivation) in regular class sessions engaged at high levels in a CSCL environment relative to students characterized by low learning orientations. In other words, the high learning-oriented students, and most girls, engaged in rather intensive processes of inquiry within the CSCL. The low learning-oriented students, in contrast, produced fewer comments or pieces of knowledge during the projects examined. Other studies of learning orientation in elementary school students by the same authors indicated that CSCL may be engaging for pupils with low learning orientations toward traditional school tasks (Hakkarainen, Jarvela, & Byman, 2001; Lipponen & Hakkarainen, 1997).

LIMITATIONS OF RESEARCH

The research reported here has competing and inconclusive findings. Most of the reports present data collected during natural course delivery and so there are varying and uncontrolled conditions that may influence the findings. The subjects span elementary school through graduate education and include synchronous and asynchronous technologies that are used in some situations to mediate the entire experience of the course while in others to supplement face-to-face sessions. These findings confirm that group composition plays a role in online learning, but are inconclusive about the level of influence and in some cases even the direction of influence.

IMPLICATIONS AND RECOMMENDATIONS

Much is still to be learned about the effects of group composition on online collaboration and learning outcomes. The ability of individuals to collaborate in groups is a function of motivation, abilities to complete the required tasks, adequate support and resources available in the social context, and cohesiveness of the group in pursuing goals. Most research has examined subsets of this broad picture. More research and attention to social theories of learning and cognition are needed to understand how these group composition attributes influence participation and outcomes in online learning. Practitioners seeking to implement CSCL should consider how the attributes of the group work that are under their control can be managed toward supporting collaboration and performance. For example, following Jonassen and Grabowski (1993), one can find best matches between cognitive requirements of tasks and individual differences related to the tasks and make assignments accordingly. One can extend this guidance by analyzing the social roles and factors inherent in the collaborative work and assign members to groups based upon the roles that they can best fulfill. O'Malley (1995) concluded that constructive collaboration can occur only if members assume appropriate roles.

Activity theory and distributed cognitions theory (Hutchins, 1995; Jonassen, 2000; Salomon, 1995; Wertsch, 1998) also provide a framework for making sense of how activity (including online group activity) is mediated by tools, sign systems, divisions of labor, and cultural customs. Selecting CSCL systems with appropriate affordances and constraints for the tasks and the group composition and roles is recommended to support collaboration and facilitate learning.

Nature of Task

After intelligence or specific cognitive abilities, learning is most affected by the nature of the task that engages learners. Learner awareness and acceptance of the learning task impels their thinking processes more than any instructional intervention (Jonassen & Wang, 1993). Therefore, from a design perspective, it is important to select or design activities that capitalize on the affordances of online collaboration. Too many studies have examined the effects of collaboration on individual recall tasks without preparing learners to collaborate or even examining the nature of the collaboration that occurs. We next compare and contrast a number of CSCL studies that have engaged learners in different tasks that engage collaboration, including case studies. Most of the research has examined the effects of online collaboration by engaging learners in topic-based discussions.

RESEARCH FINDINGS

The overwhelming majority of studies have focused on the effects of online discussion of course-related topics and issues (e.g., Arbaugh, 2000; Curtis & Lawson, 2001; Hara, Bonk, & Angeli, 2000; Marttunen, 1998; Murphy, 1998; Picciano, 2002; Sotillo,

2000). However, those topics and their required comprehension processes are too diverse to yield any conclusions. A smaller body of research has focused on the effects of online collaboration on specific, higher-order kinds of tasks, such as case studies, debates, and problem solving. We briefly review this research next.

Case Studies. A few studies have examined online collaboration while engaged in case studies. Benbunan-Fich and Hiltz (1999) found that collaborative groups produced lengthier reports and better solutions to ethical case studies than individuals, and that online students produced lengthier reports and better solutions than offline students. Angeli, Valanides, and Bonk (2003) used an online conferencing system to engage preservice teachers in analyzing teaching cases from their field experiences. Rather than supporting their analyses with any significant reasoning (reflections, explanations, task restructuring, etc.), these preservice teachers relied almost exclusively on personal experiences to provide social acknowledgement, advice, or suggestions to each other. These results were consistent with Jonassen and Remidez (2005), where students in a scaffolded conference supported their conjectures almost exclusively with personal beliefs and experiences. In at least one study, negative effects of online participation were found. Online electronic groups in a business policy and strategy class answering questions about case studies reported a significantly lower quality of communication, spent less time communicating, and were more likely to be dominated by one or two members than in conventional face-to-face groups (Scifers, Gundersen, & Behara, 1998).

Rather than studying existing cases, Järvelä and Häkkinen (2002) examined the effects of online conferencing on preservice teachers' creations of case descriptions (successes and failures) related to student motivation and multicultural education. Most of the discussions engaged joint knowledge building and lower-level comment and opinions with less than one fourth of the discussions being theory-based. They also ex-

amined perspective taking because of its importance to social interaction and found that most of the higher-level case discussions engaged mutual and reciprocal perspective taking.

Debates. In order to engage learners more interactively, some researchers have employed debates as the focus of collaboration. Debates engage students in argumentation. Argumentation is an essential kind of informal reasoning that is central to the intellectual ability involved in solving problems, making judgments and decisions, and formulating ideas and beliefs (Kuhn, 1991). Argumentation is a process of making claims (drawing conclusions) and providing justification (premises) for the claims using evidence (Toulmin, 1958) as well as counterarguments against other positions.

A few studies have engaged students in debates. For example, in a study by Bernard and Lundgren-Cayrol (2001), students debated for and against the use of technology in formal learning situations, requiring them to develop initial positions, critically evaluate others' opinions, and develop counterarguments. However, the nature of the activity was not one of the variables manipulated or assessed. Gunawardena, Lowe, and Anderson (1997) examined the interactions in a global online debate and found that the debate inhibited the coconstruction of knowledge. Participants were committed to exploring common ground despite the moderators' attempts to continue the debate. That is, the debate format prevented participants from moving toward synthesis. Similar results arose when Finnish students practicing argumentation provided only neutral elaborations and support for each others' positions (Marttunen & Laurinen, 2002). Students actually provided more disagreement and attacked more during role-playing activities than during debates leading the researchers to conclude that role playing is more effective for engaging higher-level argumentative discussion. However, when students were trained to play different roles (e.g., inquiry, task management, encouraging, positive and negative feedback, and content building) in online debates, the effects did not transfer to follow-up online discussions (Pilkington & Walker, 2003).

Problem Solving. Problem solving is the most intentional, meaningful, and engaging task that people undertake in both formal and informal settings (Jonassen, 2004). A number of studies have focused on the effects of various forms of online collaboration on problem solving, especially when solving ill-structured problems. When students were engaged in conducting expeditions solving real-life problems, their knowledge construction activities were focused by the expedition activities (Wang et al., 2001). Uribe et al. (2003) found that collaborative dyads worked harder and better solved ill-defined problems. Jonassen and Kwon (2001) found that communication patterns of online groups solving Harvard Business Cases more closely resembled the general problem-solving process of problem definition, orientation, and solution development as group interaction progressed, while the face-to-face group interactions tended to follow a linear sequence of interactions. Finally, Cho and Jonassen (2002) compared the effects of argumentation scaffolds on college students solving well-structured and ill-structured problems. Ill-structured problems produced more extensive arguments because of the importance of generating and supporting alternative solutions. The effects of argument generation transferred to individual follow-up problems. Similarly, college students learning to program in collaborative groups significantly outperformed individual learners on a transfer programming activity, although no differences were found between distributed and face-to-face collaborative groups (Jehng, 1997). Veerman and Veldhuis-Diermanse required learners to engage in discourse about four different kinds of problems, including analysis of a theoretical model, design of a computer program, evaluation of predefined claims, and role playing. They concluded that open-ended tasks in which information can be discussed from multiple perspectives and problems can be solved in many different ways are preferable in online collaboration.

Younger students have shown more difficulties with solving ill-structured problems. Sixth graders made ineffective use of evidence from the Kids as Global Scientist data while helping others to forecast weather (Lee & Songer, 2001). Elementary students building flying objects in another study created two primary kinds of e-mail messages: just-in-time messages seeking information (i.e., stacking) and compound messages relating to old lessons and newer ones (van der Meij & Boersma, 2002), however, the messages were not really interactive. Additionally, teachers had to construct mixed groups of skilled and nonskilled e-mailers in order to scaffold the task.

Problem solving often requires more than communication; it requires a task environment. Problem solvers need to jointly manipulate some problem space. Scanlon et al. (1997) provided access to shared simulations in physics and statistics and communication through audio or video. The video channel encouraged more interaction about the problem and altered the pattern of interaction, with the audio-only condition requiring more negotiation about the task. In a game show simulation, Scanlon et al. (1997) asked learners to make predictions based on observations. The use of the simulation evinced a number of misconceptions about probability.

Solution generation, an essential component of ill-structured problems, is facilitated by online collaboration. When asked to use an online brainstorming tool to generate and evaluate possible solutions to the university's parking problems, pooled groups (three individuals working independently) and interacting groups (three individuals working, one group interacting frequently and another less frequently) outproduced individuals, with groups in the frequently interacting condition producing the highest number of suggestions (Jessup et al., 1995).

LIMITATIONS OF RESEARCH

As discussed previously, one of the most important determinants of learning is the nature of the task that students willingly and intentionally engage in. While there are many interactive and constructive activities that can effectively engage learners in problem solving, such as case studies, debates, and problems, the vast majority of research on online collaboration is limited by traditional conceptions of learning activities. CSCL has not been conclusively effective, we believe, because the nature of the tasks it supports is not productive of meaningful learning. When is communication most important? When does it make the greatest difference to learning? The little bit of research that we have reviewed suggests that online collaboration will not change the nature of learning in classrooms until the nature of the task necessitates online collaboration.

Another limitation of the potential for research is the culture of most formal classrooms (K–16), which inhibits student disagreements, especially during discussions. This unwillingness to critique other's positions reduces the potential efficacy of debates. Although academic argumentation is contrary to most classroom cultures, academic argumentation is essential to meaning making and problem solving. Thus, students must be better prepared to critically argue.

IMPLICATIONS AND RECOMMENDATIONS

Meaningful collaboration necessitates a meaningful task. Individual memorization or knowledge acquisition will not likely result in meaningful collaboration because there is no interdependence. The more difficult and complex the task, the more likely it is that group members will meaningfully collaborate. Problem-solving tasks, especially ill-structured problems such as policy analysis and design problems are the most authentic and complex and therefore the most in need of collaborative efforts (Jonassen, 2004). Therefore, our primary recommendation is to use online collaboration to support more complex, authentic, and meaningful learning tasks, such as problem solving. Because students are ill-prepared to engage in problem solving and other higher order tasks, online collaboration systems should provide

scaffolds to support the kind of required reasoning or thinking. If complex tasks, such as problem solving are impossible to require, then the nature of the task needs to be articulated to students. We recommend that the moderator of any collaboration provide rubrics that describe intellectual expectations of the task.

Role of Tutor

An assumption of CSCL is that educational communications and collaboration should be supported by a tutor (e.g., teacher or professor). The role of online moderation is complex. In addition to technical skills (knowing how to use all features of the software), Salmon (2000) identifies numerous required communication skills, including writing personable messages, interacting with and engaging with people online, and being courteous and respectful. In addition to content expertise, online moderators must establish their own online identity, adapt to new teaching roles, and create online learning communities. Because of the primary reliance on verbal messages and the absence of visual and other nonverbal cues, online moderators must be especially sensitive to the needs of their students in their communications.

RESEARCH FINDINGS

Research has not yet confirmed the importance of all of the roles that Salmon (2000) recommended, however, some of the competencies have been validated. Tutors can play numerous roles in support of online learning, just as classroom teachers also play numerous roles. Most educators agree that students need guidance and feedback in online environments. Veerman and Veldhuis-Diermanse (2001) showed that students in guided discussions sent more messages than in nonguided discussions, and that when guidance was aimed at stimulating critical argumentation, students' contributions to discussion were more critical. Student teachers preferred more active tutors who explained ideas and facilitated discussions (Admiraal, Lockhorst, Wubbels, Korhagen, & Veen,

1998). One study contradicts these results. Bernard and Lundgren-Cayrol (2001) found that low tutor intervention resulted in higher exam scores and idea units generated when groups were randomly assigned.

What kinds of interventions are especially important? Providing models of the kinds of messages that students should write (i.e., a blend of procedural and conceptual scaffolding) and providing feedback on messages improved the quality of the scientific discourse and helped students understand the tasks and tools they were using (Lee & Songer, 2001). Students with higher levels of prior knowledge received more conceptual scaffolding that resulted in more sophisticated understanding. As with face-to-face classes, students with motivational problems need more structured instruction and encouragement during computer-supported study projects and even students with strong learning orientation need guidance in their inquiry practices (Tapola et al., 2001).

What are the characteristics of a good tutor? The most important tutor competencies are knowledge of instructional design, planning skills, and content knowledge (Murphy, 1998) while the most important factors in stimulating students' participation in online discussions are the enthusiasm and expertise of the tutor (Oliver & Shaw, 2003). Chou (2001) observed that providing continuous guidance and support to students, one-on-one coaching, concern for students' progress, accessibility, immediate feedback, and clear explanation of grading policies facilitated online learning. The instructor's attitude played the most important role in encouraging student participation.

LIMITATIONS OF RESEARCH

The role of the tutor in online discussion has been examined very rarely in research. Therefore, the proper role of tutors remains unvalidated, except for generic advice based on face-to-face teaching. Is collaborative learning enhanced more from information presented by the tutor, feedback on performance provided by the tutor, probing and critical questions generated by the tutor, general encouragement to participate provided by the tutor, or mentoring provided by the tutor? Hopefully studies comparing the various tutor roles in different contexts will be conducted.

IMPLICATIONS AND RECOMMENDATIONS

Research has shown that tutors need to be empathetic, enthusiastic, and friendly in their communication. Empathy, enthusiasm, and friendliness are more important in online environments because students need more support. Tutors must also be consistent in their instructions, directions, and advice. Students appear to have lower tolerances for ambiguity and inconsistency, so the tutor must carefully and consistently administer the online activities. Changing requirements in most online courses is unacceptable. Tutors must provide timely feedback and instructions to students. Students' tolerance for delays in online discussions appears to be very low.

The nature of the intervention or guidance provided by the tutor should be supportive of the task. Coaching (e.g., providing feedback about communication performance, content issues, or prompting certain kinds of responses) is one of the most important roles, probably more important than information dissemination. Previously, we described a study by Jonassen and Remidez (2005) that found that students, when unconstrained, primarily provided personal opinions and personal experiences as evidence to support warrant in a conversation. The tutor should definitely intervene here and point out that arguments need a variety of evidentiary support in order to be cogent. Feedback needs to be consistent and timely.

Community Building

Education is a social activity and the members, values, practices, and resources that constitute the community of learners provide both opportunities and constraints for what and how students learn. In traditional face-to-face learning the social context is often taken for granted as fixed by the four walls of the classroom and roles of instructor and students. Kumpulainen and Wray (2002) reviewed research on how face-to-face classroom interactions contributed to learning and concluded that simply participating in social interaction does not necessarily lead to meaningful learning. They argue for attention to how the patterns, content, and context of interactions support or challenge learning. They highlight how learning arises both from guided participation by a more capable other and, incidentally, through collective peer activity. Wenger (1998) formulated a social theory of learning to articulate the implications of situated practice and social context for designing learning experiences. He focuses upon learning as social participation. Participating in a social unit provides meaning to activity in the world, and provides shared perspectives and resources for sustaining engagement in activity.

Online learning creates new opportunities for changing membership and interactions to make courses more closely fit the goal of practice fields for authentic activity. However, online learning is often criticized as lacking the vitality and spontaneity of face-to-face classrooms. In this section we review how the community context influences how students interact and learn online and in turn how those interactions build community. There have been relatively few studies of how online interactions contribute to community building and learning, and these studies have primarily examined postsecondary or adult education. Two areas have attracted the most interest of researchers: (1) how the conditions of the online community support social interaction, and (2) how the nature of the interactions influence learning and community-building outcomes.

RESEARCH FINDINGS

Social Interaction. One area of investigation has been in how well the online technology supports social interaction in online learning. Rourke and Anderson (2002) found that when the content of online discussions included social messages that students experienced asynchronous conferencing on discussion boards as friendly, warm, and trusting. They argue that the pervasive notion that asynchronous, text-based communications technologies are unable to support social interaction is becoming untenable in the light of mounting evidence to the contrary. Indeed they make the case that much of student dissatisfaction with computer communication is because they are too social relative to the support they provide for task accomplishment. Results show that addressing others by name, complimenting, expressing appreciation, posting messages using the reply feature, expressing emotions, using humor, and using salutations were positively related to the students experiencing the computer conferencing as a social environment. Orly et al. (2001) investigated the social and educational potential of MOOs (Multi User Dimension Object Oriented environments) used voluntarily by teachers, students, and programmers. They found that the respondents characterized their MOO as both social (80.7%) and educational (86.4%). They argue that when MOOs and other voluntary computer-mediated environments are viewed as learning environments they have potential for developing professional communities based on communal interests and work. Sotillo (2000) examined discourse functions and syntactic complexity in synchronous and asynchronous online communication for English-as-a-second-language learners (ESL). The results showed that the quantity and types of discourse functions present in synchronous discussions were similar to those found in face-to-face conversations that lead to second-language acquisition. She found the discourse functions in asynchronous discussions were more constrained than those found in synchronous discussions but similar to the question-response-evaluation sequence of the traditional language classroom. She also found that the delayed nature of the online asynchronous environment gave learners more opportunities to produce syntactically complex language. Poole (2000) found that Web-based delivery of courses contributed to the formation of a cohesive group. Students referred to each other in their bulletin board posts, indicating an effort to maintain the dialogue as conversation rather than as distinct and unconnected messages. Similarly, students' written responses were such that class members could interpret meaning, emotion, and sarcasm. Researchers, who are investigating online communication, are finding that under some circumstances that these environments are highly social and provide mediums for appropriate social interaction.

Learning and Community. The second area of investigation has focused on how the social attributes of online learning influence learning or community. Stacey and Rice (2002) showed that high teacher interaction encouraged high student response. However, when students were organized into small groups there was less need for teacher leadership. Students in this study described the online group communication as providing motivation for learning and that the sharing of resources contributed to a sense of community. Poole (2000) found that having students take the role of moderator for online discussions led to longer and more frequent posts. Having a shared and more elaborated role may have also contributed to students feeling a greater sense of community. Picciano (2002) studied interaction, presence, and performance in a graduate course in educational administration and found that the feeling of social presence correlated positively and significantly (0.547) with performance on a written assignment that required replicating the type of work done on the class discussion board, but was inversely correlated (−0.375) with scores on a multiple choice format final exam that was explicitly asocial and impersonal. Picciano concludes that how interaction affects learning outcomes and what are the relationships between the two are complex pedagogical phenomena in need of further study. Häkkinen et al. (2001) showed how a pedagogical model explicitly designed to build a cognitive common ground among participants led to higher levels of knowledge construction. The authors conclude that the pedagogy of online learning needs to account for social context and support shared understanding. Their results show that knowledge construction on the part of students is not simply inherent in the technological environment nor in the tasks of writing, but must be understood in its social context. In this study pedagogical approaches that fostered perspective sharing and negotiation of meaning led to reciprocal understanding, joint goals, and socially constructed meaning.

LIMITATIONS OF RESEARCH

As noted previously, there have been relatively few studies that examine how the social aspects of online interactions contribute to community building and learning. These studies have typically been done with postsecondary students and with small sample sizes. For the most part these studies are descriptive and exploratory. Some constructs, such as social presence, are beginning to emerge but efforts to explicate these social constructs in online environments are needed. Similarly, the factors that lead to or the implications of constructs like social presence may be different in asynchronous versus synchronous environments or in environments that are solely online versus those that combine face-to-face and online modalities. Additionally improved or more commonly used methods of examining online interaction are needed. For example, Drayton and Falk (2003) suggest that greater use of discourse analytic techniques can lead to better understandings of the quality and nature of online interaction. Techniques such as examining the linguistic and thematic cohesiveness of messages can provide evidence of attentiveness and mutuality.

IMPLICATIONS AND RECOMMENDATIONS

Education is a social endeavor and using online environments does not change the fundamental importance of social context. The studies reviewed in this section suggest that online learning is influenced by the quality of social interaction and that educators have many resources for shaping the conditions and climate of social interaction. Social interaction and participation are fostered by encouraging the use of social content in messages, by instructor interaction, by creating small groups, by providing students with roles such as moderators, and by implementing pedagogical structures that support shared understanding. Research also suggests that the way online environments support social interaction shapes learning outcomes and the sense of community. The research cited in this section must be considered as explanatory rather than confirmatory. However, the research does suggest that online learning may be substantially different than stand-alone multimedia learning because of the social interactions and community context. More research is needed to build constructs and develop methodology for understanding the social nature of online learning. Additionally, more studies are needed of the social nature of online learning in K–12 and communities of practice.

Nature of Assessment

Assessment of learning, especially meaningful learning, is the Achilles heel of formal education. No one doubts that learning in formal settings is, to a large degree, assessment driven. However, constructing assessments of meaningful learning is a skill absent in most formal educators. Why? Few formal educators have ever consistently reflected on the cognitive and epistemological requirements of their goals. Educators tacitly assume that because they are skilled, if they convey what they know, students will become skilled as well. However, articulating their skills requires epistemic cognition of their knowledge and skills (Kitchner, 1983). Additionally, educators generally have been unable to devote the time and intellectual energy to construct meaningful evaluations. As a result, there is consistent incongruity between educators' goals and their assessment methodologies.

RESEARCH FINDINGS

Historically, a substantial portion of the research studies on CSCL have analyzed only the discourse and other collaborative processes and student perceptions of the experiences. The most common forms of assessment have been student participation in and perceptions of the online collaborative experience, usually assessed through a survey of student satisfaction (e.g., Bisciglia & Monk-Turner, 2001; Hewitt, 2001; Meyer, 2003; O'Reilly & Newton, 2002; Rourke & Anderson, 2002) and quality of discourse among students (e.g., Angeli et al., 2003; Hara et al., 2000; Meyer, 2003; Smith et al., 2001; Stacey & Rice, 2002). Recently, researchers have been assessing learning outcomes in addition to discourse processes and perceptions. We briefly review research involving different instruments in the following text.

Essays. A few researchers have used essays to assess learning outcomes, because of the similarity of essays to student discourse. Suthers and Hundhausen (2003a, 2003b) required their participants to write a short essay describing research hypotheses that groups generated and the evidence supporting those hypotheses as well as the hypotheses that were best supported by data they were given in order to test the effects of three different treatments. The essays failed to support the structure of the interactions while engaged in online collaboration. In another study, essays were unable to discern between online versus face-to-face learners or native from nonnative speakers (Pilkington & Walker, 2003). The weakness of essays may be due to the lack of authentic activity required by the writing. When Cho and Jonassen (2002) required students to write essays about how they would solve problems, their results confirmed the effects of discourse scaffolds used during the online conference.

Concept Mapping. Another method of assessment that is gaining widespread popularity in both online and residential instruction is concept mapping. Concept maps consist of nodes and labeled links between them that depict their knowledge structures. De Simone et al. (2001) found through interviews that concept mapping helped students learn because of its graphic form of representation. Students preferred to share their concept maps synchronously where continuous dialog and feedback can be maintained. In another study of online learning, however, concept maps were unable to discern learning effects of three different case study treatments (Schrader et al., 2003). Too much assessment power has been ascribed to concept maps, which can provide important confirmatory assessment but should probably not be used as the sole form of assessment of any kind of meaningful learning (Jonassen, Reeves, Hong, Dyer, & Peters, 1997).

Examinations. Picciano (2002) used examinations to intentionally move beyond student perceptions. Jehng (1997) showed that collaboration improved students performance on a posttest when compared with individuals learning alone. Shaw and Pieter (2000) showed that students who contributed more frequently to a class news group scored significantly better on the final examination. Not surprisingly, the use of a final exam was much more strongly predicted by individual prior achievement than group assignment in collaboration groups (Bernard & Lundgren-Cayrol, 2001).

LIMITATIONS OF RESEARCH

The majority of CSCL research has focused on the nature of discourse and collaboration in a variety of collaborative environments without relating those results to learning outcomes. From a research perspective, assessing communication and collaboration is important. However, without examining the effects of that communication or collaboration on learning outcomes, the implications of computer-supported collaborative *learning* may never be established. Social cognitive theory argues that discourse entails considerable learning. Although this belief is widely accepted, CSCL researchers have an opportunity to validate the nature of the learning that different forms of discourse engage.

IMPLICATIONS AND RECOMMENDATIONS

There is no single form of assessment that is adequate for assessing meaningful learning such as problem solving (Jonassen, 2004). The more complex the learning outcome, the more forms of assessment are required

to meaningfully assess that outcome. This is problematic because of the difficulty of constructing and evaluating different forms of assessment. If CSCL is to fulfill its promise, researchers must embed multiple forms of assessment in their research in order to validate the richly complex social and cognitive outcomes of collaboration.

Assessing the effects and processes of online collaboration is just as difficult as assessing meaningful learning outcomes. The CSCL field has advanced from early efforts that counted messages. However, skill in analyzing collaborative discourse is still needed. Among the most promising of methods is Computer-Mediated Discourse Analysis (CMDA; Herring, 2004).

Scaffolding Collaboration and Knowledge Construction

Communication and collaboration on meaningful tasks (which are the goals of CSCL systems) presume that students are competent communicators and collaborators. Additionally, students are required to communicate in modes quite different from their social chatter and written assignments. Therefore, some CSCL systems attempt to scaffold different forms of communication and reasoning in the design of their environments that constrain the kinds of comments that students can post to a discussion. The most common kind of scaffold is argumentative, that is, support for student construction of online arguments. A number of systems that scaffold arguments have been developed. For example, the Collaboratory Notebook is a collaborative hypermedia composition system designed to support scientific conjecturing (O'Neill & Gomez, 1994). During a project, the teacher or any student can pose a question or a conjecture to which learners can only "provide evidence" or "develop a plan" to support that conjecture. Belvedere provides a framework for organizing, displaying, and recording the argumentation process, so that the students can easily develop their argument toward solving a problem as they work with group members. Specifically, Belvedere (Suthers, 1998) provides four predefined conversation nodes ("hypothesis," "data," "principles," and "unspecified") and three links ("for," "against," and "and"). Constraints in this system are determined by the types of nodes and the links between them. Users are required to link their comments to an already existing comment using one of the four message types. For example, data and principles are meant to modify hypotheses. Students use these predefined boxes and links to develop their arguments during a problem-solving session. When responding to a message, the student must specify the kind of response it is (a question, comment, rebuttal, or an alternative). Convince Me is a domain-independent "reasoner's workbench" program that supports argument development and revision and provides feedback about how coherent arguments are based on the theory of explanatory coherence (Ranney & Schank, 1998). Convince Me incorporates tools for diagramming an argument's structure and modifying one's arguments and belief ratings. Using Convince Me, individuals can (a) articulate their beliefs about a controversy, (b) categorize each belief as either evidential or hypothetical, (c) connect their beliefs in order to support or reject a thesis, (d) provide ratings to indicate the believability of each statement, and (e) run a connectionist simulation that provides feedback about the coherence of their arguments. This feedback makes Convince Me among the most powerful argumentation tools available.

RESEARCH FINDINGS

Suthers and Hundhausen (2003a) compared the effects of two different scaffolds on solving public health and science problems. The graphic node-link version provided by the Belvedere environment (Suthers, 1998) represented hypotheses and evidence in a concept map format and the matrix representation presented hypotheses and evidence in a spreadsheet format. Using both versions, students elaborated their arguments more than with the text version. Matrix users added and revisited more evidentiary relations, while the graph users produced better essays.

This contradicts Cho and Jonassen (2002) who found that graphical representation increased production of arguments. Providing a constraint-based argumentation scaffold during group problem-solving activities increased the generation of coherent arguments and also resulted in significantly more problem-solving actions during collaborative group discussions. The effects of the argument scaffold consistently transferred to the production of arguments in individual problem-solving essays.

Rather than manipulating the task, Constantino-Gonzalez (2003) described the use of intelligent agents to recommend different interactions to students in a collaborative Web-based environment for solving entity-relation problems. The agent analyzes the nature of the collaboration and provides coaching based on an expert model.

LIMITATIONS OF RESEARCH

The primary limitation of this kind of research is its paucity. Because meaningful discourse is the essence of CSCL, the ability to scaffold different kinds of discourse that engage different forms of productive reasoning appears potentially powerful.

IMPLICATIONS AND RECOMMENDATIONS

When designing CSCL systems, determine the nature of the reasoning that will best support the activities about which students are discoursing. Use that model to impose constraints on the discussions that students have. For example, solution proposals can be responded to with warrants, such as reason to support, reason to rebut, or modify proposal. Warrants can be responded to only with evidence, such as research results, personal experience, or theoretical reasons. The structure of the constraints should resemble the rhetorical structure of the discussion the instructor hopes to engage.

Future Directions for Research

CSCL is an emerging learning and research paradigm. Like most research paradigms, more is unknown about the practice than is known. Because of the ubiquity of online learning and e-learning, CSCL will constitute one of the pivotal research issues of the next decade. Based on our review of the research, we present some of the issues and questions that need to be researched.

Which technologies will provide the affordances for the most meaningful communication and collaboration? In addition to the synchronous/asynchronous issue, how can multimedia resources be integrated into collaborative workspaces and communication media? How can we use multimedia resources to foster social presence in CSCL environments?

We must learn more about the nature of collaboration. What kinds of collaborative groups are most effective in multimedia environments? What kinds of strategies (e.g., collaborative strategies, self-regulated strategies, social interpersonal skills) do learners need to use in a CSCL environment? Are similar groups of learners most effective, or should some learners supplant the deficient skills of other learners? How can we support the development of these strategies and skills? Research suggests that building in performance scaffolds will probably work better than direct instruction.

Which tasks most effectively engaged collaboration? A primary reason that effects of collaboration have not transferred is that the tasks do not really require collaboration. Our hypothesis is that the more ill-structured and complex the task, the more likely it is that collaboration will support the activity. Additionally, we propose that the problems of community building are closely associated with the task. When learners willfully engage in a meaningful task, community building becomes much less of a problem.

How different are the roles of online tutors from face-to-face tutors. Salmon (2000) suggests numerous differences. The efficacy of those differences need to be validated.

How should the communication processes and learning outcome in online environments most effectively be assessed? Too much of the early CSCL used meaningless metrics for assessing the effects of online collaboration, such as the number of messages. Current research is more consistently analyzing the content of discussions. Research needs to validate different analysis methods, such as interaction analysis for examining social construction of knowledge in computer conferencing, (Gunawardena et al., 1997) or computer-mediated discourse analysis (Herring, 2004).

These are but a few of the questions that need to be answered before we are able to design the most effective CSCL environments. By the time the second edition of this book is published, we should have the answers to many of these questions that we can apply to the design of newer multimedia learning environments.

Glossary

Activity theory: Activity theory is an organizing structure for analyzing the mediational roles of tools and artifacts within a cultural-historical context.

Asynchronous communication tools: Asynchronous tools enable communication and collaboration over a period of time through a "different time/different place" mode. These tools allow people to connect together at each person's own convenience and own schedule. Asynchronous tools are useful for sustaining dialogue and collaboration over a period of time and providing people with resources and information that are accessible, day or night. Asynchronous tools possess the advantage of being able to involve people from multiple time zones. In addition, asynchronous tools are helpful in capturing the history of the interactions of a group, allowing for collective knowledge to be more easily shared and distributed.

Computer-mediated discourse: Computer-mediated discourse is the communication produced when human beings interact with one another by transmitting messages using networked computers. The study of computer-mediated discourse is a specialization within the broader interdisciplinary study of computer-mediated communication, distinguished by its focus on *language and language use* in computer networked environments, and by its use of *methods of discourse analysis* to address that focus.

Constructivism: Constructivism is an underlying philosophy or way of seeing the world. Constructivists view reality and meaning as personally rather than universally defined. It focuses on an individual's own construction of meaning. Learning is an active process in which learners construct new ideas or concepts based on their existing knowledge and by reflecting on their experiences.

Discourse scaffolds: Some CSCL systems attempt to scaffold different forms of communication and reasoning in the design of their environments that constrain the kinds of comments that students can post to a discussion. The most common kind of scaffold is argumentative, that is, support for student construction of online arguments. Scaffolds are determined by identifying the nature of the reasoning that will best support the activities about which students are discoursing. Models and structures are then developed to constrain the way students discuss the topic.

Distributed cognitions theory: Distributed cognition emphasizes the interaction and reciprocal process among individual, environmental and cultural artefacts. In effect, the cognition is distributed over the person and the person's social and physical environment.

Ill-structured problem: The kinds of problems that are most often encountered in everyday and professional practice. Also known as *wicked problems*, these problems do not necessarily conform to the content domains being studied, so their solutions are neither predictable nor convergent. Ill-structured problems are interdisciplinary, that is they usually cannot be solved by only applying concepts and principles from a single domain.

Intelligent agent: Software that can make decisions based on what it knows about the user and the task.

Multi-User Dimension Object-Oriented environment (MOO): A MOO has traditionally been a text-based virtual reality environment that provides synchronous communication between individuals and enables participants to contribute to building the virtual spaces. Recent implementations of MOOs incorporate Web-based features so that MOOs are no longer only limited to text-based interaction.

Online collaboration: Through the use of computer networks, learners in different geographical locations interact with each other and collaboratively build knowledge either in synchronous (concurrent) or asynchronous (occurring at different times) mode.

Simulations: Simulations model phenomena. The context of the simulation may be a business plan, a laboratory experiment, or an animation of the working of a chemical plant. Simulations usually are implemented with interactive graphics and give the learner the ability to visualize a process as well as explore the effect of changing parameters on the operation of the system.

Social cognitive theory: This theory accords a central role to cognitive, vicarious, self-regulatory, and self-reflective processes in human adaptation and change. Social cognitive theory is rooted in an agentic perspective. In this view, people are self-organizing, proactive, self-reflecting, and self-regulating, not just reactive organisms shaped and shepherded by environmental forces or driven by concealed inner impulses. Human functioning is the product of a dynamic interplay of personal, behavioral, and environmental influences.

Social participation: The social theory of learning, describes learning as a process of social participation. Social participation includes participating in the practices of social groups and influences how participants perceive themselves and understand what they are doing. Participating in a social unit provides meaning to activity in the world, and provides shared perspectives and resources for sustaining engagement in activity.

Social presence: Social presence is the "degree of salience of the other person in the (mediated) interaction and the consequent salience of the interpersonal relationships" (Short, Williams, & Christie, 1976). Social presence is seen as both an attribute of the communication medium and users' perceptions of media.

Synchronous communication tools: Synchronous tools (e.g., chat) enable real-time communication and collaboration in a "same time-different place" mode. These tools allow people to communicate at a single point in time, at the same time.

References

Admiraal, W. F., Lockhorst, D., Wubbels, T., Korthagen F. A. J., & Veen, W. (1998). Computer-mediated communication environments in teacher education: Computer conferencing and the supervision of student teachers. *Learning Environments Research 1* (1), 59–74.

Anderson, T., & Kanuka, H. (1997). On-line forums: New platforms for professional development and group collaboration. *Journal of Computer-Mediated Communication, 3* (3). Retrieved January 30, 2004, from http://www.ascusc.org/jcmc/vol3/issue3/anderson.html

Angeli, C., Valanides, N., & Bonk, C. J. (2003). Communication in a web-based conferencing system: The quality of computer-mediated interactions. *British Journal of Educational Technology, 34* (1), 31–43.

Arbaugh, A. B. (2000). Virtual classroom versus physical classroom: An exploratory study of class discussion patterns and student learning in an asynchronous internet-based MBA course. *Journal of Management Education, 24*, 213–233.

Aviv, R., Erlich, Z., Ravid, G., & Geva, A. (2003). Network analysis of knowledge construction in asynchronous learning networks. *Journal of Asynchronous Learning Networks, 7*, 1–23.

Barab, S. A., & Duffy, T. M. (2000). From practice fields to communities of practice. In D. H. Jonassen & S. L. Land (Eds.), *Theoretical foundations of learning environments* (pp. 25–55). Mahwah, NJ: Lawrence Erlbaum Associates.

Benbunan-Fich, R., & Hiltz, S. R. (1999). Educational applications of CMCS: Solving case studies through asynchronous learning networks. *Journal of Computer-Mediated Communication, 4* (3). Retrieved January 30, 2004, from http://www.ascusc.org/jcmc/vol4/issue3/benbunan-fich.html

Bernard, R. M., & Lundgren-Cayrol, K. (2001). Computer conferencing: An environment for collaborative project-based learning in distance education. *Educational Research and Evaluation, 7* (2/3), 241–261.

Bhattachary, M. (1999). A study of asynchronous and synchronous discussion on cognitive maps in a distributed learning environment. In P. De Bra, & Legget, J. J. (Ed.), *WebNet Conference on the WWW and Internet* (Vol. 1, pp. 100–105). Charlottesville, VA: AACE.

Biesenbach-Lucas, S. (2003). Asynchronous discussion groups in teacher training classes: Perceptions of native and non-native students. *Journal of Asynchornous Learning Networks, 7*, 24–46.

Biscaglia, M. G., & Monk-Turner, E. (2001). Differences in attitudes between on site and distance site students in group teleconference course. *The American Journal of Distance Education, 16*, 37–52.

Brown, K., & Cole, M. (2000). Socially-shared cognition: System design and the organization of collaborative research. In D. H. Jonassen & S. L. Land (Eds.), *Theoretical foundations of learning environments* (pp. 197–214). Mahwah, NJ: Lawrence Erlbaum Associates.

Cho, K.-L., & Jonnasen, D. H. (2002). The effects of argumentation scaffolds on argumentation and problem solving. *Educational Technology Research and Development, 50* (3), 5–22.

Chou, C. (2001). Formative evaluation of synchronous CMC systems for learner-centered online course. *Journal of Interactive Learning Research, 12*, 173–192.

Constantino-Gonzalez, M. D. L. A., Suthers, D. D., & Santos, J G. E. D. L. (2003). Coaching web-based collaborative learning based on problem based solution differences and participation. *International Journal of Artificial Intelligence in Education*, 13, 156–169.

Curtis, D. C., & Lawson, M. J. (2001). Exploring collaborative online learning. *Journal of Asynchrounous Learning Networks*, 13, 21–34.

De Simone, C., Schmid, R. F., & McEwen, L. A. (2001). Supporting the learning process with collaborative concept mapping using computer-based communication tools and processes. *Educational Research and Evaluation*, 7(2/3), 263–283.

Docq, F., & Daele, A. (2001, March). *Uses of ICT tools for CSCL: How do students make as their own the designed environment?* Paper presented at Euro CSCL 2001, Maastricht, The Netherlands.

Drayton, B., & Falk, J. (2003). Discourse analysis of Web texts: Initial results from a telementoring project for middle school girls. *Education, Communication and Information*, 3(1), 71–104.

Engeström, Y. (1987). *Learning by expanding: An activity theoretical approach to developmental research*. Helsinki, Finland: Orienta-Konsultit Oy.

Fishman, B. J., & Gomez, L. M. (1997, December). *How activities foster CMC tool use in classroom*. Paper presented at CSCL 1997, Toronto, Canada.

Gunawardena, C. N., Lowe, C. A., & Anderson, T. (1997). Analysis of a global online debate and the development of an interaction analysis model for examining social construction of knowledge in computer conferencing. *Journal of Educational Computing Research*, 17(4), 397–431.

Häkkarainen, K., Lipponen, L., & Järvelä, S. (2002). Epistemology of inquiry and computer-supported collaborative learning. In T. Koschmann, R. Hall., & N. Miyake (Eds.), *CSCL2: Carrying forward the conversation*. Mahwah, NJ: Lawrence Erlbaum Associates.

Häkkinen, P., Järvelä, S., & Byman, A. (2001, March). *Sharing and making perspectives in web-based conferencing*. Paper presented at Euro CSCL 2001, Mastricht, The Netherlands.

Hara, N., Bonk, C. J., & Angeli, C. (2000). Content analysis of online discussion in an applied educational psychology course. *Instructional Science*, 28(2), 115–152.

Hermann, H., Rummel, N., & Spada, H. (2001, March). *Solving the case together: The challenge of net-based interdisciplinary collaboration*. Paper presented at Euro CSCL 2001, Maastricht, The Netherlands.

Herring, S. C. (2004). Computer-mediated discourse analysis: An approach to researching online behavior. In S. Barab, R. Kling, & J. H. Gray (Eds.), *Designing for virtual communities in the service of learning*. New York: Cambridge University Press.

Hewitt, J. (2001). Beyond threaded discourse. *International Journal of Educational Telecommunications*, 7(3), 207–221.

Holt, G. R., & Morris, A. W. (1993). Activity theory and the analysis of organization. *Human Organization*, 52(1), 97–109.

Hutchins, E. (1995). *Cognition in the wild*. Cambridge: MIT Press.

Issroff, K., Scanlon, E., & Jones, A. (1997, December). *Two empirical studies of CSCL in science: Methodological and affective implications*. Paper presented at CSCL 1997, Toronto, Canada.

Järvelä, S., & Häkkinen, P. (2002). Web-based cases in teaching and learning – the quality of discussions and a stage of perspective taking in asynchronous communication. *Interactive Learning Environments*, 10(1), 1–22.

Jehng, J.-C. J. (1997). The psycho-social processes and cognitive effects of peer-based collaborative interactions with computers. *Journal Educational Computing Research*, 17(1), 19–46.

Jessup, L. M., Egbert, J. L., & Connolly, T. (1995). Understanding computer-supported group work: The effects of interaction frequency on group process and outcome. *Journal of Research on Computing in Education*, 28, 190–208.

Johnson, D. W., & Johnson, R. T. (2004). Cooperation and the use of technology. In D. H. Jonassen (Ed.), *Handbook of research on educational communications and technology* (pp. 785–811). Mahwah, NJ: Lawrence Erlbaum Associates.

Jonassen, D. H. (2000). Revisiting activity theory as a framework for designing student-centered learning environments. In D. H. Jonassen & S. L. Land (Eds.)., *Theoretical foundations of learning environments* (pp. 197–214). Mahwah, NJ: Lawrence Erlbaum Associates.

Jonassen, D. H. (2004). *Learning to solve problems: An instructional design guide*. San Francisco: Pfeiffer/Jossey-Bass.

Jonassen, D. H., & Grabowski, B. G. (1993). *Handbook of individual differences, learning, and instruction.* Hillsdale, NJ: Lawrence Erlbaum Associates.

Jonassen, D. H., & Henning, P. (1999). Mental models: Knowledge in the head and knowledge in the world. *Educational Technology,* 39(3), 37–42.

Jonassen, D. H., & Kwon, H. I. (2001). Communication patterns in computer-mediated vs. face-to-face group problem solving. *Educational Technology, Research and Development,* 49(10), 35–52.

Jonassen, D. H., Reeves, T. C., Hong, N., Dyer, D., & Peters, K. M. (1997). Concept mapping as cognitive learning and assessment tools. *Journal of Interactive Learning Research,* 8(3/4), 289–308.

Jonassen, D. H., & Remidez, H. (2005). Mapping alternative discourse structures onto computer conferences. *International Journal of Knowledge and Learning,* 1(1), 113–129.

Jonassen, D. H., & Wang, S. (1993). Acquiring structural knowledge from semantically structured hypertext. *Journal of Computer-based Instruction,* 20(1), 1–8.

Kirkley, S. E., Savery, J. R., & Grabner-Hagen, M. M. (1998). Electronic teaching: Extending classroom dialogue and assistance through e-mail communication. In C. J. Bonk and K. S. King (Eds.), *Electronic collaborators: Learner-centered technologies for literacy, apprenticeship, and discourse* (pp. 209–232). Mahwah, NJ: Lawrence Erlbaum Associates.

Kitchner, K. S. (1983). Cognition, metacognition, and epistemic cognition: A three-level model of cognitive processing. *Human Development,* 26, 222–232.

Ku, H. K. & Lohr, L. (2001). A case study of Chinese students' attitudes toward their first online learning experience. *Educational Technology Research and Development,* 50, 94–102.

Kuhn, D. (1991). *The skills of argument.* Cambridge, UK: Cambridge University Press.

Kumpulainen, K., & Wray, D. (Eds.). (2002). Classroom interaction and social learning. From theory to practice. London: Routledge Falmer.

Lahti, H., Seitamaa-Hakkarainen, P., & Hakkarainen, K. (2001, March). *The nature of collaboration in computer supported designing.* Paper presented at Euro CSCL 2001, Maastricht, The Netherlands.

Lee, S.-Y., & Songer, B. B. (2001, April). *To what extent does classroom discourse synergistically support electronic discourse?* A study of the kids as global scientists message board. Paper presented at the annual meeting of the American Educational Research Association, Seattle, WA.

Lipponen, L., & Hakkarainen, K. (1997). Developing culture of inquiry in computer-supported collaborative learning. In R. Hall, N. Miyake, & N. Enyedy (Ed.), *Proceedings of CSCL '97: The Second International Conference on Computer Support for Collaborative Learning* (pp. 164–168). Mahwah, NJ: Lawrence Erlbaum Associates.

Marttunen, M. (1998). Electronic mail as a forum for argumentative Interaction in higher education studies. *Journal of Educational Computing Research,* 18(4), 387–408.

Marttunen, M., & Laurinen, L. (2001). Quality of students' argumentation by e-mail. *Learning Environments Research,* 5(1), 99–123.

McLoughlin, C., & Luca, J. (2001). Investigating processes of social knowledge construction in online environments. *World Conference on Educational Multimedia, Hypermedia and Telecommunications,* 2001(1), 1287–1292.

Meij, H. V. D., & Boersma, K. (2002). Email use in elementary school: An analysis of exchange patterns and content. *British Journal of Educational Technology,* 22, 189–200.

Meyer, K. A. (2003). Face-to-face versus threaded discussions: The role of time and higher-order thinking. *Journal of Asynchronous Learning Networks,* 7, 55–65.

Murphy, K. L. (1998). A constructivist look at interaction and collaboration via computer conferencing. *International Journal of Educational Telecommunications,* 4(2/3), 237–261.

Nardi, B. A. (1996). Studying context: A comparison of activity theory, situated action models, and distributed cognition. In B. A Nardi (Ed.), *Context and consciousness: Activity theory and human-computer interaction.* Cambridge, MA: MIT Press.

Ocker, R. J., & Yaverbaum, G. J. (2001). Collaborative learning environments: Exploring student attitudes and satisfaction in face-to-face and asynchronous computer conferencing settings. *Journal of Interactive Learning Research,* 12, 427–449.

Oliver, M., & Shaw, G. P. (2003). Asynchronous discussion in support of medical education.

Journal of Asynchornous Learning Networks, 7, 57–67.

O'Malley, C. (1995). *Computer supported collaborative learning.* New York: Springer-Verlag.

O'Neil, D. K., & Gomez, C. M. (1994). The Collaboratory Notebook: A distributed knowledge building environment for project-based learning. *Proceedings of EDMEDIA 94.* Vancouver, BC.

O'Reilly, M., & Newton, D. (2002). Interaction online: Above and beyond requirements of assessment. *Australian Journal of Educational Technology, 18*(1), 57–70.

Orly, Y., Avigail, O., & David. M. (2001). The educational MOO-user profile. *International Journal of Educational Telecommunications, 7*, 271–293.

Oshima, J., & Oshima, R. (2002). Coordination of asynchronous and synchronous communication: Differences in qualities of knowledge advancement discourse between experts and novices. In T. Koshmann, R. Hall., & N. Miyake (Eds.), *CSCL2: Carrying forward the conversation.* Mahwah, NJ: Lawrence Erlbaum Associates.

Piaget, J. (1970). *Genetic epistemology.* New York: Columbia University Press.

Picciano, A. G. (2002). Beyond student perceptions: Issues of interaction, presence, and performance in an online course. *Journal of Asynchronous Learning Networks, 6*(1), 21–40.

Pilkington, R. M., & Walker, S. A. (2003). Facilitating debate in networked learning: Reflecting on online synchronous discussion in higher education. *Instructional Science, 31*, 41–63.

Poole, D. M. (2000). Student participation in a discussion-oriented online case: A case study. *Journal of Research on Computing in Education, 33*, 167–177.

Ranney, M., & Schank, P. (1998). Modeling, observing, and promoting the explanatory coherence of social reasoning. In S. Read & L. Miller (Eds.), *Connectionist and PDP models of social reasoning.* Hillsdale, NJ: Lawrence Erlbaum associates.

Rogers, E. M. (1995). *Diffusion of innovations.* New York: Free Press.

Rourke, L., & Anderson, T. (2002). Exploring social communication in computer conferencing. *Journal of Interactive Learning Research, 13*, 259–276.

Rovai, A. P. (2001). Building classroom community at a distance: A case study. *Educational Technology Research and Development, 49*, 33–48.

Salmon, G. (2000) *E-moderating: The key to teaching and earning online.* London: Kogan Page.

Salomon, G. (1995). *Distributed cognitions: Psychological and educational considerations.* Cambridge, UK: Cambridge University Press.

Scanlon, E., O'Shea, T., Smith, R. B., & Li, Y. (1997, December). *Supporting the distributed synchronous learning of probability: Learning from an experiment.* Paper presented at CSCL 1997, Toronto, Ontario, Canada.

Schrader, P. G., Leu, D. J. J., Ataya, R., Kinzer, C. K., Cammack, D., Teale, W. H., et al. (2003). Using internet delivered video cases, to support pre-service teachers' understanding of effective early literacy instruction: An exploratory study. *Instructional Science, 31*, 317–340.

Scifers, E. L., Gunderson, D. E., & Behara, R. S. (1998). An empirical investigation of electronic groups in the classroom. *Journal of Education for Business, 73*, 247–250.

Shaw, G. P., & Pieter, W. (2000). The use of asynchronous learning networks in nutrition education: Student attitude, experiences and performance. *Journal of Asynchronous Learning Networks, 4*, 40–51.

Short, J., Williams, E., & Christie, B. (1976). *The social psychology of telecommunications.* London: John Wiley and Sons.

Shotsberger, P. G. (1999). *Forms of synchronous dialogue resulting from web-based professional development.* Society for Information Technology and Teacher Education International Conference, 1999, 1777–1782.

Smith, G. G., Ferguson, D., & Caris, M. (2001). Teaching on-line versus face-to-face. *Journal of Educational Technology, 30*, 337–364.

Sorensen, E. K., & Takle, E. S. (2002). Collaborative knowledge building in web-based learning: Assessing the quality of dialogue. *International Journal on E-learning, 1*, 28–34.

Sotillo, S. M. (2000). Discourse functions and syntactic complexity in synchronous and asynchronous communication. *Language Learning and Technology, 14*, 82–119.

Stacey, E., & Rice, M. (2002). Evaluating an online learning environment. *Australian Journal of Educational Technology, 18*(3), 323–340.

Suthers, D. D. (1998, April). *Representations for scaffolding collaborative inquiry on ill-structured problems*. Paper presented at the Annual Meeting of the American Educational Research Association, San Diego, CA.

Suthers, D. D., & Hundhausen, C. D. (2003). An experimental study of the effects of representational guidance on collaborative learning processes. *The Journal of the Learning Sciences, 12*, 183–218.

Suthers, D. D., & Hundhausen, C. (2003). Deictic roles of external representations in face-to-face and online collaborations. In B. Wasson, S. Ludvigsen, & U. Hoppe (Eds.), *Computer Support for Collaborative Learning*, (pp. 173–182). Dordrecht, The Netherlands: Kluwer Academic Publications.

Tapola, A., Niemivirta, M., Hakkaranien, K., Syri, J., Lipponen, L., & Palonen, T. (2001, March). *Motivation and participation in inquiry learning within a networked learning environment*. Paper presented at Euro CSCL 2001, Maastricht, The Netherlands.

Thomas, M. J. W. (2002). Learning within incoherent structures: The space of online discussion forums. *Journal of Computer Assisted Learning, 18*(3), 351–366

Toulmin, S. (1958). *The uses of argument*. Cambridge, England: Cambridge University Press.

Uribe, D., Klein, J. K., & Sullivan, H. (2003). The effect of computer-mediated collaborative learning on solving ill-defined problems. *Educational Technology Research and Development, 51* (1), 5–19.

Veerman, A., & Veldhuis-Diermanse, D. (2001, March). *Collaborative learning through computer mediated communication in academic education*. Paper presented at Euro CSCL 2001, Maastricht, The Netherlands.

Vygotsky, L. (1978). *Mind in society: The development of higher psychological processes*. Cambridge, MA: Harvard University Press.

Wang, M., Laffey, J., & Poole, M. J. (2001). The construction of shared knowledge in an Internet-based shared environment for *Expeditions (iExpeditions)*. *International Journal of Educational Technology, 2* (2). Retrieved January 30, 2004 from http://www.outreach.uiuc.edu/ijet/v2n2/v2n2feature.html

Wertsch, J. (1998). *Mind as action*. New York: Oxford University Press.

Wenger, E. (1998). Communities of Practice – Learning, Meaning, and Identity. New York: Cambridge University Press.

CHAPTER 17

The Self-Explanation Principle in Multimedia Learning

Marguerite Roy
Michelene T. H. Chi
University of Pittsburgh

Abstract

Learning in multimedia environments is hard because it requires learners to actively comprehend and integrate information across diverse sources and modalities. Self-explanation is an effective learning strategy that helps learners develop deep understanding of complex phenomena and could be used to support learning from multimedia. Researchers have established the benefits of self-explaining across many domains for a range of ages and learning contexts (including multimedia situations). This research demonstrates that some learners are natural self-explainers and also indicates that learners can be trained to self-explain. However, even when trained, there remain large individual differences in effective self-explaining. Additional support, which may be afforded by multimedia environments, appears to be needed for engaging some learners in this activity. This chapter reviews related literature and explores the relationship between multimedia learning and self-explaining.

Introduction

Multimedia learning environments have the potential to substantially improve student learning compared to single media (Mayer & Moreno, 2002; Najjar, 1996). Controlled studies that compare multimedia (e.g, combinations of text and illustrations or narration and animation) with single media resources have found that students learn better from a combination of media, provided that the materials are well-designed (Goldman, 2003; Mayer, 1993; Mayer & Anderson, 1991; Mayer & Gallini, 1990; Mayer, Heiser, & Lonn, 2001).

Two distinct advantages of multimedia resources over single media are that different modes and types of external representations can provide both unique perspectives and tailored descriptions. For example, text and narrations present information in a verbally encoded linear sequence whereas illustrations or pictures present information simultaneously. In addition, text may be a more effective means for describing abstract and general information whereas illustrations and animations are particularly effective at conveying spatial configuration or dynamic information. These complementarities of information, tailored to a suitable modality (oral or visual) and/or format (text or illustrations), may explain the advantage of learning from multimedia over a single media.

However, in order to benefit from multimedia descriptions, the learner must actively construct a conceptual knowledge representation that relates and integrates different kinds of information from diverse sources and modalities into a coherent structure (Schnotz & Bannert, 2003). Using eye-movement data of students' online processing of multimedia materials describing a functional system, Hegarty and Just (1993) have shown that in order to form a complete mental model of the device, readers need to process both media (i.e., text and diagrams). Readers do this by gradually integrating information across media from a local representation of several subparts of the system to a more global representation of the entire system. Other studies have confirmed this general need to integrate information across representations in order to construct a deep understanding (Ainsworth, Bibby, & Wood, 2002; Chandler & Sweller, 1991; Glenberg & Langston, 1992; Hegarty & Just, 1993).

However, merely exposing learners to rich multimedia descriptions does not automatically result in deep comprehension and learning (Kozma, 1994). For example, some learners may be passive in the way they process multimedia (Guri-Rozenblit, 1989; Reinking, Hayes, & McEneaney, 1988). The processes of selecting, organizing, translating, coordinating, and integrating information across modalities and formats that are necessary to learning in a multimedia context may be difficult for learners (Ainsworth, 1999).

In short, learning in multimedia environments is potentially very effective, but only if learners engage in the demanding behaviors of constructing, integrating, and monitoring knowledge in an ongoing manner.

Thus, to benefit from the advantages of multimedia resources, one challenge is to engage learners in the active knowledge construction and monitoring processes necessary for learning. However, this challenge may be mitigated by the possibility that multimedia environments, especially well-designed ones, might actually be more natural environments for supporting constructive activity, as compared to a single media environment. In this chapter, we explore the hypothesis that one affordance that multimedia environments provide is to naturally support a student's ability to engage in knowledge construction and monitoring activities. We investigate this hypothesis in the context of one constructive activity that has been shown to be effective in learning – self-explaining.

We begin with a brief review of self-explaining, followed by an example of how self-explaining can mediate learning in a multimedia context. We then provide a brief analysis of why multimedia environments might be particularly suitable context for self-explaining, along with a presentation of data across several studies showing that multimedia environments seem to serve as a more effective context for supporting a student's ability to generate self-explanations than a single media. We end with some ideas to consider about the characteristics of a well-designed multimedia environment.

Self-Explaining

Self-explanation is a domain-general constructive activity that engages students in active learning and insures that learners attend to the material in a meaningful way while effectively monitoring their evolving understanding. Several key cognitive mechanisms are involved in this process including, generating inferences to fill in missing information, integrating information within the study materials, integrating new information with prior knowledge, and monitoring and repairing faulty knowledge. Thus, self-explaining is a cognitively demanding but deeply constructive activity.

The Effectiveness of Self-Explanation

Self-explaining was originally postulated as a potential learning activity in trying to understand how students are able to learn successfully from text materials that are incomplete. Learning materials often include informational gaps or omissions both in the text passages (Chi, de Leeuw, Chiu, & LaVancher, 1994) as well as in descriptions of the steps involved in worked-out problem examples (Chi, Bassok, Lewis, Reimann, & Glaser, 1989).

The general procedure used in studies of self-explanation is to have a group of learners spontaneously explain the meaning of each sentence of a passage as they study some target domain. The learners' explanation protocols are then coded into several statement types. The coding schemes typically include categories for "low-quality" statements such as those that involve simply rereading or paraphrasing and categories for "high-quality" statements such as those involving tacit knowledge that links pieces of explicitly stated text, or inferences that fill information gaps, and so on (Chi, 2000). In some cases the explanations are knowledge-monitoring statements. Throughout this chapter, we use the term *high-quality self-explanations* to refer to statements that demonstrate the generation of inferences, integrating statements, and various comments that reflect deep analyses of the resources, and *low-quality self-explanations* to refer to paraphrases and rereading statements.

Once the protocols have been coded, learning gains are correlated with the frequency and quality of self-explanations demonstrated. Such studies find high-quality self-explanation to be positively related to learning gains across a wide variety of domains and tasks, including solving problems in physics (Chi & Bassok, 1989), Lisp programming (Pirolli & Recker, 1994; Recker & Pirolli, 1995), and logic (Neuman, Leibowitz, & Schwarz, 2000). In the following text, we review several key studies in more detail to highlight some of the important findings regarding the use and benefits of engaging in spontaneous self-explaining.

In the original self-explanation study, Chi et al. (1989) had students talk aloud as they studied worked-out physics examples involving a mix of text and diagrams prior to solving problems. Students were classified as "good" or "poor" learners based on their post problem-solving scores. An analysis of the worked-out examples suggested that several important reasoning steps were missing from the study materials. When the protocols of more-effective learners were compared to those of the less-effective learners, it was found that students who spontaneously generated a larger number of high-quality self-explanations while studying the incomplete worked examples scored twice as high on a posttest than students who generated fewer high-quality self-explanations. Good learners generated more inferences that linked new text material to examples and to their prior knowledge, and generated more task-related ideas that made more references to central domain principles. The poor students, on the other hand, generated low-quality self-explanation behaviors such as generating paraphrases and rereading the materials without generating any inferences. Furthermore, the good students demonstrated more frequent and accurate monitoring of their understanding, whereas the poorer students tended to overestimate their understanding. Thus, worked examples that omitted several reasoning steps were not detrimental to learning provided that the learners actively explained the examples to themselves.

A similar pattern of results were obtained by Fergusson-Hessler and de Jong (1990) who investigated the study behaviors of "good" and "poor" achieving students assigned to learn physics by studying a textbook (again using a mix of text and diagrams). They found that while both "good" and "poor" students engaged in an equal number of study processes, the good students tended to use deeper strategies (including integrating information, making relationships explicit, and imposing structure) whereas poor students were more likely to use behaviors that resulted in superficial processing (e.g., rereading).

Again, using worked examples of probability problems involving a text and formulae, Renkl (1997) found a significant learning benefit associated with generating self-explanations, even after the effects of time on task was controlled. He distinguished two separate styles of successful self-explanation and two unsuccessful styles. The most successful gainers (*principle-based explainers*) tended to employ explanations relating operators to domain principles, while the second cluster of successful learners (*anticipative reasoners*) tended to have more prior knowledge and to anticipate computations before viewing them. Unfortunately, most learners were either *passive* or *superficial* explainers and were less successful solvers.

This line of research shows two robust findings. First, it validates the effectiveness of self-explaining as a constructive activity in the context of learning. The depth to which learners engage in this activity is a significant predictor of the learner's ability to develop deep meaningful understanding of the material studied. Second, it demonstrates that learners differ in the degree to which they spontaneously self-explain while studying worked examples or reading text.

Because many of the studies reviewed are correlational in nature, they potentially confound the tendency to engage in high-quality self-explanation with other important learner variables such as prior knowledge, motivation, or ability. That is, students who spontaneously demonstrate a high degree of quality self-explaining may simply be better learners who are able to engage in this activity regardless of the informational context. Additionally, the quantity and quality of self-explanation and learning across various instructional formats is not directly addressed by such studies. Thus, we cannot tell directly whether the utility of self-explaining varies with learning context (i.e., learning from single versus multimedia). In the next section we review research that explores the utility of encouraging or training students to use self-explaining strategies. This approach allows researchers to go beyond correlational analyses and provides some insights into the problem of how to design learning environments that support self-explaining.

Self-Explanation as a Trainable Learning Strategy

Experimental studies that involve the use of random assignment to a prompted or trained group versus a control group address many of the problems described previously. A number of such studies have been conducted in order to assess the effectiveness of designing instructional means to foster effective self-explanations. In general, these studies indicate that self-explanation can be successfully prompted or trained rather than spontaneously generated with similar learning benefits.

Chi et al. (1994) experimentally compared a prompted to an unprompted group of learners reading a text on human circulatory system. The prompts were designed to encourage students to analyze the text, to attempt to explain it to themselves, and to encourage learners to monitor their comprehension of the material. The prompted group demonstrated significantly greater learning improvements relative to the control group, particularly for the most difficult questions (those requiring deep domain knowledge). Thus, this study demonstrates that self-explaining can be beneficial even when it is explicitly elicited.

Training can also benefit a middle school student's ability to generate high-quality self-explanations and thereby improve their learning. Wong, Lawson, and Keeves (2002) trained middle school students to use self-explanation strategies and compared this group to a control group of students who used their usual studying techniques in a subsequent transfer session in which they studied a new geometry theorem involving text and diagrams. Both groups attained equal mastery on a domain-specific knowledge test following completion of training.

However, the self-explanation group demonstrated a positive and sustained advantage on problem-solving performance, particularly for solving the most difficult problems. The self-explanation training facilitated the student's ability to later access and use knowledge and to self-monitor during study of new geometry theorem, and this in turn affected subsequent problem-solving performance for near and far transfer items.

A variety of training procedures have been used across several domains and learning contexts. They range from simple prompting in learning from text in the domain of biology (Chi et al., 1994), learning engineering in a Web-based course (Chung, Severance, & Chung, 2003), and learning to solve statistics word problems (Renkl, Stark, Gruber, & Mandl, 1998) and geometry problems (Aleven & Koedinger, 2002), to giving a prequestion to guide learners' self-explanations in multimedia environments (Mayer, Dow, & Mayer, 2003), directly training students how to engage in high-quality self-explanation and self-regulation strategies in the domain of programming (Bielaczyc, Pirolli, & Brown, 1995), to very elaborate training and practice in self-explaining and strategy identification for learning from science text (McNamara, in press). These studies show unambiguously that learners can be trained to self-explain.

Individual Differences in Self-Explaining

Although self-explaining has been shown to be an overall effective strategy that promotes learning, there are robust learner differences in terms of either the amount or quality of self-explanations generated. Such individual differences hold whether students are free to spontaneously generate self-explanations or whether they are prompted or trained to self-explain.

In the studies reviewed previously, we have already discussed the fact that more successful learners tend to generate more and better quality self-explanations. For example, even within the prompted group in the Chi et al., study (1994), some students generated many more self-explanation inferences (the high self-explainers) than other students (the low self-explainers), and on a posttest the high explainers were able to answer more complex questions correctly and were better able to induce the correct mental model of the circulatory system. Similarly, when Conati and Van Lehn (2000) implemented a self-explanation coach to scaffold students' attempts to generate explanations as they learned physics problems, the level of assistance necessary for generating self-explanations varied with the student's prior knowledge. Novice students benefited from highly structured help for self-explaining whereas experts needed less support. In agreement with this finding, McNamara (in press) reported that an elaborate training procedure in self-explaining and reading strategy use significantly helped low prior-knowledge readers to generate quality self-explanations and to comprehend a transfer text, but did not significantly alter the performance of high prior-knowledge readers compared to untrained controls. Thus, individuals may require different amounts of situational support in order to engage in a cognitively demanding constructive activity such as self-explaining.

Such support must go beyond simple methods such as merely encouraging learners to talk aloud which does not in itself lead learners to generate effective self-explanations. For example, Teasley (1995) compared children's performances on a scientific reasoning task for those working alone to those in dyads, and who were instructed to either talk as they worked or not. She found that the type of talk rather than amount was significantly related to improved performance. Specifically children who worked in dyads and demonstrated more interpretive forms of talk that related to the deep structure of problems were the ones who demonstrated the greatest improvements. Thus, effective situational supports for self-explaining must encourage learners to engage in appropriate constructive activity.

it's the lens actually does the rest of the work. I thought it was all the cornea or all the lens cause I thought it was the same thing. Okay, I'm actually learning something."

There are several points of interest to be noted in this example. First, this learner demonstrates evidence of metacognitive knowledge monitoring in several utterances (e.g., "I'm wondering what's the other 30%?," "now I understand," "now I realize," and "I'm actually learning"). In addition, he demonstrates evidence of accessing prior knowledge and comparing his flawed understanding to new information in the learning materials (e.g., "I always thought that there's just the lens and that the cornea and the lens were the same thing," and "I thought it was all the cornea or all the lens cause I thought it was the same thing"). This series of events in turn gives him an opportunity to revise and repair his incorrect mental model (i.e., failing to distinguish between the cornea and the lens). Finally, the learner makes the correct inference that "the lens does the *rest of the work*" (i.e., of refracting light energy) resulting in new knowledge. Interestingly, this inference was made by integrating information across media. Specifically, it is based in part on his understanding of the text description that was previously read ("The shape of the cornea is responsible for about 70% of the eye's focusing power") in conjunction with his understanding of an illustration identifying the cornea and lens as scparate structures and showing how the shape and trajectory of light energy changes as it passes through these structures. Although this process is actually described later in the text, this particular learner has not yet seen or read that section – but he has accurately predicted it.

The preceding example demonstrates that multimedia learning situations can provide a rich context for stimulating and supporting the different psychological mechanisms that have been proposed to underlie the self-explanation principle: the generation of learner-initiated inferences and the monitoring and repair of knowledge. In fact, we have already pointed out that in order to learn effectively from multimedia descriptions, learners must engage in knowledge construction activities. Self-explaining seems to be an ideal candidate.

Evidence of Self-Explanations in Multimedia Resources

Do multimedia environments lend themselves to the use of self-explanation more readily than single-media resources? While there are no existing studies that directly compare self-explaining in multimedia to single-media learning contexts, many of the studies reviewed previously actually involve learning from multiple media (e.g., Aleven & Koedinger, 2002; Chi et al., 1989; Fergusson-Hessler & de Jong, 1990; Mayer et al., 2003; Renkl, 1997; Wong et al., 2002). Thus, there is evidence that learning in multimedia environments does benefit from self-explaining.

Moreover, there are a few studies that show more directly that self-explaining can help learners to integrate information across media, one of the aspects of learning from multimedia that may be difficult for learners. For example, Neuman and Schwartz (2000) performed a case study of six students solving multiple algebra problems while thinking aloud. The problems require that the student translate a text description (word problem) into a tabular array of relevant variables and quantities, then translate this representation into an appropriate algebraic form to be solved. Their analysis of learner protocols revealed that a particular type of self-explanation (categorical explanations) was associated with successful translation between the text and tabular representations.

A study by Aleven and Koedinger (2002) showed that prompting learners to generate self-explanations specifically helped students develop declarative knowledge that integrated verbal and visual information. In two classroom studies comparing the performance of a prompted self-explanation group (in which students were asked to explain in their own words the principle involved in each solution step used) to the performance of an unprompted group in a computer-based tutoring environment for learning geometry, they found that the prompted group was more successful on transfer problems and was better able to explain solution steps. The pattern of group differences on transfer problems correlated with different mathematical models of hypothesized internal knowledge constituents, thus suggesting that the best fitting model was a declarative knowledge model that integrated verbal and visual knowledge.

Finally, using Palinscar and Brown's (1984) reciprocal teaching technique, a technique that supports many of the same processes as self-explaining, Scevak, Moore, and Kirby (1993) also found positive learning effects when the students were encouraged to more deeply process and relate text and map information. Thus, these three studies, taken together, provide some evidence that self-explaining can help learners integrate cross-modal information in multimedia situations. However, again, we cannot confidently conclude that self-explaining is in fact more effective in a multimedia versus a single-media context.

Is there any evidence to suggest that self-explaining is even more necessary and useful in different media contexts? Some have claimed that diagrams can be effective at encouraging high-level processing such as self-explanation (Brna, Cox, & Good 2001; Cox, 1999; Winn, 1991) because diagrams may provide computational offloading – freeing up cognitive resources for engaging in high-level cognitive operations such as generating verbal self-explanations. It is also asserted that the low expressivity of graphics (when compared to text) may assist learners to more accurately reflect on their understanding and constrain their self-explaining to fit within a specific explicit context. In addition, we offer a contrasting hypothesis, that instead of constraining learners' interpretation's, the low expressivity of graphics and diagrams may actually necessitate more

self-explaining in order to fill in and elaborate the information that is absent from such illustrations.

A recent study comparing the self-explanation effect across two different single-media situations – text and diagrams – has provided the first direct evidence that diagrams are better than text at eliciting more and better quality self-explanations from learners (Ainsworth & Loizou, 2003). These researchers compared the self-explanation effect in a text-only condition with an informationally matched diagrams-only condition in the domain of biology. They found that students given diagrams performed significantly better on posttest, independently of the effects of time on task, pretest score, and amount of talk generated. Furthermore, the diagram students generated more self-explanations, particularly goal-driven explanations in which they described the purpose of an action. Finally, they found that the benefits of self-explanation were greater in the diagram condition, that is, the correlation between self-explanations and knowledge gains was only significant within this group.

The results of Ainsworth and Loizou clearly indicate that the medium of instructional material can influence the amount of quality self-explanations and associated gains among learners. However, while the researchers offer a variety of reasons as to why this might be the case, it is not clear as to which of these possibilities is supported. Furthermore, the question of what the combined effects of such media (e.g., text and diagrams) would be on self-explanation remains an open one.

Comparing Results Across Information Formats

Do multimedia environments lend themselves to the use of self-explanation more readily than single media-resources? If so, we would expect to see more frequent use of high-quality self-explaining and larger associated learning gains for self-explanation studies that use multimedia rather than

Table 17.1. Percent of Self-Explanation for Different Learning Contexts

Study	Text	Multimedia	Diagrams
Ainsworth & Loizou (2003)	57.69%		91.61%
Chi et al. (1989)		63.00%	
Chi et al. (1994)	58.00%		
Hausmann & Chi (2002)	8.45%		
Fergusson-Hessler & de Jong (1990)		72.00%	
McNamara (in press)	19.43%		
Wong et al. (2002)		69.80%	
Average Estimate	35.89%	68.26%	91.61%
	45.04%*		

Note: *Excludes the results of Hausmann & Chi (2002), which may seriously underestimate the amount of orally generated self-explanations supported in text learning environments.

single-media learning materials. Table 17.1 presents a summary of data reporting the amount of quality self-explanations for learning contexts with different information formats (i.e., multimedia, text only, and diagrams only).

A brief explanation of how the presented numbers were calculated is in order. Obviously, only studies that report data on the frequencies of their codings of verbal protocols could be included. Second, all codes that fall under the description of inferencing, prior knowledge access and/or use, self-monitoring, and metacognition were pooled together as estimates of the frequency of self-explanation. Third, the pooled frequencies estimates have been converted to percentages (i.e., self-explanation statements relative to total statements that include other types of statements such as paraphrases) to enable fair comparison across studies. Finally, the amounts for studies that report separate numbers for high versus low explainers (Chi et al., 1994), high versus low learners (Chi et al., 1989; Fergusson-Hessler & de Jong, 1990), prompted versus unprompted explainers (Hausmann & Chi, 2002), or trained versus untrained explainers (McNamara, in press; Wong et al., 2002) were pooled across their comparison categories to yield average estimates. Average estimates are reported for each learning context. Also, the average estimate for the text-only context is reported both with and without the data from Hausmann and

Chi (2002). That study required learners to type their self-explanations, which appears to have seriously hampered the frequency of self-explanations generated.

The resulting percentages indicate that the frequency of self-explanation is lowest in text-only situations and substantially higher in multimedia situations, as predicted. This pattern provides some support for the hypothesis that multimedia situations are better at stimulating and supporting self-explaining than text-only learning situations. Not surprisingly, the amount of self-explanation was highest for the diagrams-only condition. This supports our hypothesis that the low expressivity and sketchiness of illustrations and diagrams may necessitate a greater amount of self-explaining in order for the learners to construct a coherent understanding.

In addition to comparing the percentage of self-explaining activity across different learning contexts, we were also interested in comparing associated learning outcomes. If multimedia environments are better at supporting the generation of quality self-explanations than single media, we should see an associated difference in the size of learning gains observed. That is, pre- to post-test gains should be higher in multimedia contexts. Table 17.2 presents estimates of learning gains from pretest to posttest for self-explanation studies across different learning contexts. The results of Table 17.2 indicate that the overall average

Table 17.2. Learning Gains for Self-Explanations in Different Learning Contexts

Study	Text	Multimedia	Diagrams
Ainsworth & Loizou (2003)			
Unprompted self-explaining			
Text/illustration-based questions (gain)	18.00%		45.00%
Diagram of blood path (gain)	11.11%		42.22%
Chi et al. (1994)			
Verbatim and inference questions (gain)			
Prompted self-explaining (gain)	32.00%		
Unprompted self-explaining (gain)	22.00%		
Hausmann & Chi (2002)			
Vocabulary			
Unprompted self-explaining (gain)	24.8%		
Control (gain)	23.4%		
Renkl (1997)			
Unprompted self-explaining			
Total problem solving (gain)		47.33%	
Wong et al. (2002)			
Total problem-solving (gain)			
Trained (gain)		13.68%	
Control (gain)		−00.09%	
Average Overall Gains (pooled across groups)	21.86%	20.37%	43.16%

gain in learning is roughly equal for text and multimedia learning context but that the gain for diagrams-only context is substantially higher. However, the gain (21.86%) of the text-only condition may be overestimated, because the learning measures in the text-only studies reported previously tend to be or include shallow measures of learning (e.g., vocabulary, verbatim questions, text-based questions), whereas the multimedia studies in Table 17.2 report deep learning gains (e.g., problem-solving performance). In particular, the results of the Wong et al. (2002) study includes far transfer problem-solving items.

Because many studies do not use pre-posttest designs or report additional performance data at posttest only (e.g., transfer data), in order to get a larger sample, Table 17.3 presents observed post performance outcomes for the different groups within each study (e.g., "high" versus "low" learners, "prompted" versus "unprompted" explainers, and "trained" versus "untrained" explainers) for the different types of learning context. As predicted, the overall average performance (i.e., pooled across groups) was

larger for explainers in the multimedia situation compared to the text-only situation. Again, this difference is probably somewhat conservative in that several of the text-only studies reported in Table 17.3 include shallow indices of performance of learning (e.g., vocabulary, verbatim questions, text-based questions), whereas the multimedia studies report deep learning performance (e.g., transfer). The trend of a greater learning from text to multimedia to diagrams, corresponds to the increasing trend of a greater amount of self-explaining from text to multimedia to diagram.

Similar to the data regarding the frequency of self-explaining, we see that the diagrams-only condition produced even higher gains than the multimedia condition. This outcome is consistent with our hypothesis suggesting that the diagrams-only condition is even less constraining than learning in a multimedia environment and is therefore a more effective context for eliciting self-explaining. That is, because there is typically more information for learners to fill in or generate in learning from diagrams, learners are more active and simply generate more

Table 17.3. Post Performance for Self-Explanation in Different Learning Contexts

Study	Text	Multimedia	Diagrams
Ainsworth & Loizou (2003)			
Unprompted self-explaining (post)			
Implicit questions	49.17%		61.67%
Knowledge inference	46.67%		78.33%
Chi et al. (1989)			
Near transfer			
High learners (post)		96.00%	
Low learners (post)		62.00%	
Far transfer			
High learners (post)		68.00%	
Low learners (post)		30.00%	
Hausmann & Chi (2002)			
Verbatim questions	61.7%		
Unprompted self-explaining (post)	60.0%		
Control (post)	1.70%		
Integration questions			
Unprompted self-explaining (post)	31.2%		
Control (post)	38.4%		
McNamara (in press)			
Text-based questions			
Trained (post)	56.75%		
Control group performance (post)	43.95%		
Bridging questions			
Trained performance	31.95%		
Control group performance	25.35%		
Wong et al. (2002)			
Near transfer			
Trained (post)		86.06%	
Control (post)		78.23%	
Far Transfer			
Trained (post)		59.84%	
Control (post)		42.28%	
Average Overall (pooled across groups)	44.51%	52.54%	70.00%

self-explanations resulting in deeper learning. While further research is required to substantiate this pattern, these data do suggest that multimedia environments are more effective then text at stimulating and supporting quality self-explaining.

Taken together the results of Tables 17.1, 17.2, and 17.3 indicate that self-explaining is more prevalent in multimedia than in text environments, and that the associated benefits for those who tend to self-explain a great deal is larger in multimedia environments than in text-only situations. This pattern of results indicates that engaging in deep constructive activity such as self-explanation is even more necessary for effectively learning in multimedia than single-media contexts.

Instructional Design Implications

How should multimedia environments be designed so that they effectively encourage and support the generation of quality self-explanations? As we noted previously, many studies demonstrate that students learn better from a combination of media providing that the materials are designed with some important properties of the human cognitive system in mind.

It is clear that the use of self-explanation strategies takes up substantial cognitive resources. In fact, it has been suggested by various researchers that if the learning material imposes a heavy cognitive load then learners may not be able to engage in such resource-demanding activity (Chandler & Sweller, 1991; Mayer, 1997; Mayer et al., 2003; Mayer et al. 2001). One explanation for poor learning outcomes in such environments is that the learner's opportunity to engage in self-explanation is hampered. Thus, when designing multimedia environments that will support self-explanation, one ought to try and minimize placing undue cognitive load on the learner by presenting related text and diagrams closely, by minimizing the use of unrelated information, and by avoiding the duplication of messages across two different modalities that use the same information processing channel (e.g., text and narration).

The environment should assist learners to think inwardly and reflectively. Specifically, it should encourage learners to bring their prior knowledge to bear on the interpretation of materials and allow them to monitor and test their evolving understanding. Presenting the target domain in multiple related external representational formats should increase the probability of activating relevant prior knowledge from the learners leading to increased opportunities to relate new information to prior knowledge.

A good multimedia learning environment should encourage the generation of new inferences in which the learner relates information within and between media and to relate this to prior knowledge. As argued at the outset of this chapter, multimedia learning situations can provide a rich context for eliciting and supporting quality inferences by providing complementary information. Such resources have the potential to be more structured and constraining than single-media contexts. For example, illustra-

tions, being an external model of the discourse situation, can serve as a particular context in which to interpret and reason about the text (i.e., to self-explain about the text content and how that may relate to the content depicted in one or more illustration(s) as well as to what learners already know). As such, the presence of illustrations in the context of text should constrain what information the learner integrates within the text, between text and illustrations, and between the newly derived knowledge with the learner's prior knowledge. Such constraints might facilitate the generation of more relevant and deeper self-explanations.

Another instructional design concern has to do with the mode of expressing self-explanations. Hausmann and Chi (2002) found that the amount of self-explanation that learners generated in a computer environment was suppressed by having learners type rather than verbalize their thoughts. Thus, modality of expression matters. Supporting alternative and multiple media to express self-explanations may generate more sensitive measures of what learners understand and are able to make sense of (Crowder, 1996; Koschmann & LeBaron, 2002). It is possible that generating diagrams as a part of verbal self-explanation may be useful. By restricting learners to adopt a linguistic modality some inadequacy of their current interpretations of materials may be concealed or go unnoticed. It may well be that constructing an external representation in an alternative modality may have a significant effect on learning (Cox, 1999). Indeed, Chi et al. (1994) found that students who were high self-explainers also drew more diagrams.

Furthermore, it is possible that prompting students to explain their self-generated diagrams would be beneficial. This position is supported by a study carried out by Van Meter (2001) examining the use of drawing as a learning strategy for fifth and sixth graders reading a science text. She found that students who were prompted to compare their own drawings to a provided illustration (similar to prompted self-explanation) learned more effectively than unprompted students, students who were simply encouraged to create drawings, or a no drawing control group. Furthermore, all drawing groups learned more than the control group and engaged in significantly more self-monitoring while reading.

Finally, multimedia environments could be designed to scaffold self-explanations for learners at different levels of skill acquisition (e.g., Conati & VanLehn, 2000) or who are very young or novice (e.g., Siegler, 2002) thereby supporting a greater variety of learners.

Discussion

Meaningful learning in multimedia environments requires learners to construct coherent integrated representations. The existing self-explanation literature supports the assertion that learning from multimedia environments is substantially improved when learners engage in deep knowledge construction and integration activities, like those involved in self-explaining.

It is also true, however, that deep understanding does not come easy. The activity of self-explaining is cognitively demanding and there is consistent evidence that many learners have difficulty engaging in generating a sustained level of quality explanations. We have reviewed the self-explanation literature with an eye for suggesting that many learners would benefit from self-explanation training or prompting within multimedia environments. Essentially, we have argued that because they are informationally rich, multimedia environments afford the generation of many opportunities for explaining encoded information and accessing and relating prior knowledge. Furthermore, because there are additional relationships between media, multimedia situations are somewhat more constrained (certainly more constrained than diagrams or illustrations), and should facilitate the integration of information and the generation of certain infer-

ences, particularly for low prior-knowledge learners. Again, the self-explanation literature appears to support this assertion.

While we found only one study that focuses directly on the effects of diagrams on self-explaining and learning, there seems to be a trend in the literature indicating that self-explanation effects are smallest in text context, greatest in diagram context, and intermediate in multimedia context. This pattern seems to suggest that the more information learners must (and can) fill in to make sense of the materials, the greater the effect of self-explanation.

Acknowledgments

The authors would like to thank Rod Roscoe, Robert G. M. Hausmann, and Nancy Lavigne for their helpful feedback and advice on this chapter.

Glossary

Self-explanation principle: The self-explanation principle refers to the finding that people learn more deeply when they spontaneously engage in or are prompted to provide explanations during learning.

Note

The authors are grateful for the support provided in part by NSF Grant 0205506 and in part by NSF ITR Grant No. 0325054 for the preparation of this paper.

References

Ainsworth, S. (1999). The function of multiple representations. *Computers and Education*, 33, 131–152.

Ainsworth, S., Bibby, P., & Wood, D. (2002). Examining the effects of different multiple representational systems in learning primary mathematics. *The Journal of the Learning Sciences*, 11, 25–61.

Ainsworth, S., & Loizou, A. (2003). The effects of self-explaining when learning with text or diagrams. *Cognitive Science, 27*, 669–681.

Aleven, V., & Koedinger, K. (2002). An effective metacognitive strategy: Learning by doing and explaining with a computer-based cognitive tutor. *Cognitive Science, 26*, 147–179.

Bielaczyc, K., Pirolli, P. L., & Brown, A. L. (1995). Training in self-explanation and self-regulation strategies: Investigating the effects of knowledge acquisition activities on problem solving. *Cognition and Instruction, 13*, 221–252.

Brna, P., Cox, R., & Good, J. (2001). Learning to think and communicate with diagrams: 14 questions to consider. *Artificial Intelligence Review, 15*, 115–134.

Chandler, P., & Sweller, J. (1991). Cognitive load theory and the format of instruction. *Cognition and Instruction, 8*, 293–332.

Chi, M. T. H. (2000). Self-explaining expository texts: The dual processes of generating inferences and repairing mental models. In R. Glaser (Ed.), *Advances in instructional psychology* (pp. 161–238). Mahwah, NJ: Lawrence Erbaum Associates.

Chi, M. T. H., & Bassok, M. (1989). Learning from examples via self-explanations. In L. B. Resnick (Ed.), *Knowing, learning, and instruction: Essays in honor of Robert Glaser* (pp. 251–282). Hillsdale, NJ: Lawrence Erlbaum Associates.

Chi, M. T. H., Bassok, M., Lewis, M., Reimann, P., & Glaser, R. (1989). Self-explanations: How students study and use examples in learning to solve problems. *Cognitive Science, 13*, 145–182.

Chi, M. T. H., de Leeuw, N., Chiu, M. H., & Lavancher, C. (1994). Eliciting self-explanations improves understanding. *Cognitive Science, 18*, 439–477.

Chung, S., Severance, C., & Chung, M. (2003). Design of support tools for knowledge building in a virtual university course. *Interactive Learning Environments, 11* (10), 41–57.

Conati, C., & Van Lehn, K. (2000). Toward computer-based support of metacognitive skills: A computational framework to coach self-explanation. *International Journal of Artificial Intelligence in Education, 11*, 389–415.

Cox, R. (1999). Representation constructing, externalized cognition and individual differences. *Learning and Instruction, 9*, 343–363.

Crowder, E. M. (1996). Gestures at work in sense-making: Science talk. *The Journal of the Learning Sciences, 5*, 173–208.

Fergusson-Hessler, M., & de Jong, T. (1990). Studying physics texts: Differences in study processes between good and poor performers. *Cognition and Instruction, 7*, 41–54.

Glenberg, A., & Langston, W. E. (1992). Comprehension of illustrated text: Pictures help to build mental models. *Journal of Memory and Language, 31*, 129–151.

Goldman, S. R. (2003). Learning in complex domains: When and why do multiple representations help? *Learning and Instruction, 13*, 239–244.

Guri-Rosenblit, S. (1989). Effects of tree diagrams on students' comprehension of main ideas in multi-thematic expository text. *Reading Research Quarterly, 24*, 236–247.

Hausmann, R. G. M., & Chi, M. T. H. (2002). Can a computer interface support self-explaining? *International Journal of Cognitive Technology, 7*, 4–14.

Hegarty, M., & Just, M. A. (1993). Constructing mental models of machines from text and diagrams. *Journal of Memory and Language, 32*, 717–742.

Koschmann, T., & LeBaron, C. (2002). Learner articulation as interactional achievement: Studying the conversation of gesture. *Cognition and Instruction, 20*, 249–282.

Kozma, R. B. (1994). Will media influence learning? Reframing the debate. *Educational Technology Research and Development, 42*, 7–19.

Mayer, R. E. (1993). Illustrations that instruct. In R. Glaser (Ed.), *Advances in instructional psychology (Vol. 4)*, (pp. 253–284). Hillsdale, NJ: Lawrence Erlbaum Associates.

Mayer, R. E. (1997). Multimedia learning: Are we asking the right questions? *Educational Psychologist, 32*, 1–19.

Mayer, R. E. (2003). The promise of multimedia learning: Using the same instructional design methods across different media. *Learning and Instruction, 13*, 125–139.

Mayer, R. E., & Anderson, R. B. (1991). Animations need narration: An experimental test of a dual-coding hypothesis. *Journal of Educational Psychology, 83*, 484–490.

Mayer, R. E., Dow, G. T., & Mayer, S. (2003). Multimedia leaning in an interactive self-explaining environment: What works in the design of agent-based microworlds? *Journal of Educational Psychology, 95*, 806–813.

Mayer, R. E., & Gallini, J. K. (1990). When is an illustration worth ten thousand words? *Journal of Educational Psychology, 82*, 715–726.

Mayer, R. E., Heiser, J., & Lonn, S. (2001). Cognitive constraints on multimedia learning: When presenting more material results in less understanding. *Journal of Educational Psychology, 93*, 187–198.

Mayer, R. E., & Moreno, R. (2002). Aids to computer-based multimedia leaning. *Learning and Instruction, 12*, 107–119.

McNamara, D. S. (in press). SERT: Self-explanation reading training. *Discourse Processes*.

Mwangi, W., & Sweller, J. (1998). Learning to solve compare word problems: The effect of example format and generating self-explanations. *Cognition and Instruction, 16*, 173–199.

Najjar, L. J. (1996). Multimedia information and learning. *Journal of Educational Multimedia and Hypermedia, 5*, 129–150.

Neuman, Y., Leibowitz, L., & Schwarz, B. (2000). Patterns of verbal mediation during problem solving: A sequential analysis of self-explanation. *Journal of Experimental Education, 68*, 197–213.

Neuman, Y., & Schwarz, B. (2000). Substituting one mystery for another: The role of self-explanations in solving algebra word-problems. *Learning and Instruction, 10*, 203–220.

O'Reilly, T., Symons, S., & MacLatchy-Gaudet, H. (1998). A comparison of self-explanation and elaborative interrogation. *Contemporary Educational Psychology, 23*, 434–445.

Palinscar, A. S., & Brown, A. L. (1984). Reciprocal teaching of comprehension-fostering and monitoring activities. *Cognition and Instruction, 1*, 117–175.

Pirolli, P., & Recker, M. M. (1994). Learning strategies and transfer in the domain of programming. *Cognition and Instruction, 12*, 235–275.

Recker, M. M., & Pirolli, P. (1995). Modeling individual differences in students' learning strategies. *The Journal of the Learning Sciences, 4*, 1–38.

Reinking, D., Hayes, D. A., & McEneaney, J. E. (1988). Good and poor readers use of explicitly cued graphic aids. *Journal of Reading Behavior, 20*, 229–247.

Renkl, A. (1997). Learning from worked-out examples: A study on individual differences. *Cognitive Science, 21*, 1–29.

Renkl, A., Stark, R., Gruber, H., & Mandl, H. (1998). Learning from worked-out examples: The effects of example variability and elicited self-explanations. *Contemporary Educational Psychology, 23*, 90–108.

Roscoe, R. D., & Chi, M. T. H. (2003). *Learning from self-directed and other-directed explaining.* Paper presented at the 84th Annual Meeting of the American Education Research Association, Chicago, IL.

Scevak, J. J., Moore, P. J., & Kirby, J. R. (1993). Training students to use maps to increase text recall. *Contemporary Eductional Psychology, 18*, 401–413.

Schnotz, W., & Bannert, M. (2003). Construction and interference in learning from multiple representation. *Learning and Instruction, 13*, 141–156.

Siegler, R. S. (2002). Microgenetic studies of self-explanation. In N. Granott & J. Parziale (Eds.), *Microdevelopment: Transition processes in development and learning* (pp. 31–58). New York: Cambridge University Press.

Teasley, S. D. (1995). The role of talk in children's peer collaborations. *Developmental Psychology, 31*, 207–220.

Van Meter, P. (2001). Drawing construction as a strategy for learning from text. *Journal of Educational Psychology, 93*, 129–140.

Winn, W. (1991). Learning from maps and diagrams. *Educational Psychology Review, 3*, 211–247.

Wong, R. M. F., Lawson, M. J., & Keeves, J. (2002). The effects of self-explanation training on students' problem solving in high school mathematics. *Learning and Instruction, 12*, 233–262.

CHAPTER 18

The Animation and Interactivity Principles in Multimedia Learning

Mireille Betrancourt
Geneva University

Abstract

Computer animation has tremendous potential to provide visualizations of dynamic phenomena that involve change over time (e.g., biological processes, physical phenomena, mechanical devices, and historical development). However, the research reviewed in this chapter showed that learners did not systematically take advantage of animated graphics in terms of comprehension of the underlying causal or functional model. This chapter reviewed the literature about the interface and content features that affect the potential benefits of animation over static graphics. Finally, I proposed some guidelines that designers should consider when designing multimedia instruction including animation.

What Are the Animation Principle and the Interactivity Principle?

In the last decade, with the rapid progression of computing capacities and the progress of graphic design technologies, multimedia learning environments have evolved from sequential static text and picture frames to increasing sophisticated visualizations. Two characteristics appear to be popular among instruction designers and practitioners: the use of animated graphics as soon as depiction of dynamic system is involved, and the capability for learners to interact with the instructional material.

Conceptions of Animation

Despite its extensive use in instructional material, computer animation still is not well understood. Baek and Layne (1988) defined animation as "the process of generating a series of frames containing an object or objects so that each frame appears as an alteration of the previous frame in order to show motion" (p. 132). Gonzales (1996) proposed a broader definition of animation as "a series of varying images presented dynamically according to user action in ways that help the user to perceive a continuous change over time and develop a more appropriate mental model of the task" (p. 27). This definition however contained the idea that the user interacts with the display (even minimally by hitting any key). In this chapter we do not restrict animation to interactive graphics, and choose Betrancourt and Tversky's (2000) definition: "computer animation refers to any application which generates a series of frames, so that each frame appears as an alteration of the previous one, and where the sequence of frames is determined either by the designer or the user" (p. 313). This definition is broader by design than either of the preceding definitions. It does not stipulate what the animation is supposed to convey, and it separates the issue of animation from the issue of interaction.

According to Schnotz and Lowe (2003), the concept of animation can be characterized using three different levels of analysis: technical, semiotic, and psychological. First, the technical level refers to the technical devices used as the producers and carriers of dynamic signs. With the evolution of the computer graphics industry, distinguishing between events captured by way of a camera or events completely generated by computer is becoming harder and irrelevant to learning issues. Second, there is a semiotic level, which refers to the type of sign, that is the kind of dynamics that is conveyed in the representation. This includes concerns about what is changing in the animation and how (e.g., motion, transformation, or changing of points of view). Third, there is a psychological level, which refers to the perceptual and cognitive processes involved when animations are observed and understood by learners. Discussions about the design of animation often focus on technical or surface characteristics. From a learning perspective, issues regarding realism, three-dimensionality, or abstraction are important only insofar as they change the way the content to be learned is going to be perceived and comprehended by the learners.

Conceptions of Interactivity

First of all, a clear distinction should be made between two kinds of interactivity: control and interactive behavior. In this chapter we do not consider that control and interactive behavior are different degrees on the same scale but rather are two different dimensions. Whereas control is the capacity of the learner to act upon the pace and direction of the succession of frames (e.g., pause-play, rewind, forward, fast forward, fast rewind, step by step, and direct access to the desired frame), interactivity is defined as the capability to act on what will appear on the next frame by action on parameters. In this case animation becomes a simulation of a dynamic system in which some rules have been implemented. Simulations are not the focus of this chapter and are mentioned as a specific feature of animation (for more details on simulation, see chapter 33). For purposes of this chapter, interactivity is meant as control over the pace of animation (see also chapter 11).

Examples of Scenario Using Animation and Interactivity

The main concern for instructional designers and educational practitioners can be summarized by the simple question: When and how should animation be used to improve learning? Three main uses of animation in learning situations can be distinguished.

Supporting the Visualization and the Mental Representation Process

The first situation is not substantially different from the situations in which graphics are used. Animation provides a visualization of a dynamic phenomenon, when it is not easily observable in real space and time scales (e.g., plate tectonics, circulatory system, or weather maps), when the real phenomenon is practically impossible to realize in a learning situation (e,g., too dangerous or too costly), or when it is not inherently visual (e.g., electrical circuit, expansion of writing over times, or representation of forces). In this perspective, animation is not opposed to static graphics but to the observation of the real phenomenon.

For example, we used an animation to explain an astronomic phenomenon (i.e., the transit of Venus) and particularly why it occurs irregularly (Rebetez, Sangin, Betrancourt, & Dillenbourg, 2004). This animation was designed following Narayanan and Hegarty's (2002) principles. The instruction first depicted the three objects involved (i.e., Earth, Venus, and the sun) and their relative motion. In order to understand the phenomenon, two frames of reference alternate: a galactic view (the planets are seen from outside the solar system) and an earth view (in order to see Venus's trajectory on the sun as seen from the earth). The animation was segmented in 16 frames, the sequence of which was under the learner's control. An aural commentary synchronized with the animation was provided.

Producing a Cognitive Conflict

Animation can be used to visualize phenomena that are not spontaneously conceived the way they are in the scientific domain. For example, there are many situations in physics in which naïve conceptions dominate over the scientific conceptions (e.g., the fact that objects of same volume and different weights fall at the same speed, or the trajectory of falling objects from moving objects). In this case an instructional scenario can provide several animations of the same phenomenon and ask the learner to pick up the correct situation. Kaiser, Proffitt, Whelan, and Hecht (1992) used such situations, but although learners recognized the correct animation, they were still unable to produce in a drawing the correct trajectory afterward. A scenario that includes groups of learners viewing and discussing the animations could improve learning in encouraging learners to make their conceptions explicit.

Enabling Learners to Explore a Phenomenon

In this third use, the learner actively explores the animation in order to understand and memorize the phenomenon. Here interactivity is a key factor. It can be a simple VCR control on the pace and direction of the animation with a suitable learning activity. But it can include a high degree of interactivity with a learning task that encourages learners to generate hypotheses and test them by manipulating the parameters. In this case the animation becomes a simulation that is used in a discovery-learning approach.

Whatever the function animation serves, it can include several levels of interactivity from the simple "resume" function, to complete learner control over the pace and direction of the animation. Roughly speaking, complete control should benefit advanced learners more than beginners, because it supposes that learners have the capability to monitor their inspection of the animation. Another feature of interactivity that can be incorporated into an animation is the possibility to change the viewpoint. Changing the viewpoint enables learners to explore the phenomenon from different perspectives, similar to those that would be available to an active, moving observer. Although this feature is not difficult to implement, it is hardly used in multimedia instructions, but is extensively used in video games.

Review of Research on Animation and Interactivity

It seems reasonable to assume that providing a visualization of what "really" happens in a dynamic system will facilitate learners' comprehension of the functioning of the system. Space in graphics is used to convey spatial and functional relations between objects, which are directly perceived by learners whereas they must be inferred from verbal information. Similarly temporal changes in animations make temporal information directly perceivable by learners whereas they must be inferred from static graphics. However, as with the research on the effect of pictures in text, the research on animation yields mixed and contradictory results, with actual effects of animation ranging from highly beneficial to detrimental to learning. The question whether animation is more effective than static graphics can not been answered in the general case. Rather the question should be: *when* and *why* is animation more effective than static graphics?

In many cases, animation does not add any benefit compared with static graphics, even when the content involved changes over time (Betrancourt & Tversky, 2000; Tversky, Bauer-Morrison, & Betrancourt, 2002). For example, Narayanan and Hegarty (2002) report studies on learning in the domain of mechanics in which animation could be expected to improve understanding of novices, because the behavior of the system is not predictable from naïve conceptions. In one experiment, they compared two hypermedia and two printed versions of instruction about the functioning of a flushing cistern. The first hypermedia instruction was designed following guidelines deriving from a cognitive model of multimedia comprehension (Hegarty, Quilici, Narayanan, Holmquist, & Moreno, 1999). The second hypermedia instruction was a commercially available product. The two hypermedia instructions were compared to printed versions of either the cognitively designed hypermedia material or the commercial product. Both hypermedia instructions included animated and interactive graphics. Participants spent their time studying one of the four presentations. Then they were asked to write a causal description of how the device works and two answer-comprehension questions about the functioning of the system. The results showed that participants studying with the cognitively designed material outperformed participants studying with the commercial product on all comprehension measures. However, there was no difference in comprehension between the cognitively designed hypermedia and its printed version. In other words, animated and interactive graphics did not improve comprehension compared with their static equivalents. Moreover, students in the hypermedia conditions did not rate the material as more interesting than students in the paper conditions. We may think that the benefits of animation would appear more clearly when the domain is abstract in nature, such as computer algorithms or a physics concept. In a lesson designed for elementary school students explaining Newton's laws of motion, animation did not lead to better comprehension scores although motion is an essentially dynamic concept (Rieber, 1989; Rieber and Hannafin, 1988). Using an instructional material explaining computer algorithms, that are known to be difficult for students to comprehend, Catrambone and Fleming Seay (2002) found that animation had a positive impact on performances in difficult transfer problems, but that the benefits of animation disappeared when the accompanying text was carefully designed to provide all the critical information.

When animation provides benefits over static graphics, it may be due to interactivity in the animated graphics, with the system reacting according to learner's input (what I define here as a *simulation*). In this case, the animation leads the learner to make predictions about the behavior of the system, which can in itself improve deep understanding. Using instructional material on computer algorithms, Byrne, Catrambone, and Stasko (1999) found that the benefits of using animation were equivalent to the benefits of prompting learners to make predictions, and that the two effects were not cumulative. The same results were obtained with mechanical systems (Hegarty, Kriz, & Cate, 2003; Hegarty, Narayanan, & Freitas, 2002): Participants who studied the animation with oral commentary did not get better comprehension scores than those who studied equivalent static graphics with written text, but those who were asked questions that induced them to predict the behavior of the system had better understanding of the device than those who were not asked prediction questions.

Two main explanations related to the way humans perceive and conceive of dynamic information may account for the failure of animation to be beneficial to learning. First, human perceptual equipment is not very efficacious regarding processing of temporally changing animation. Although we track motion quite automatically, we are very poor in mentally simulating real trajectories (Kaiser et al. 1992). Second, even when actual

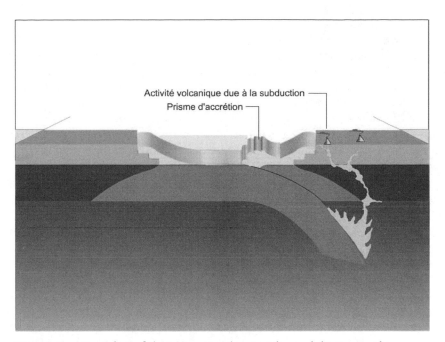

Figure 18.1. Snapshot of the instructional material on subduction used in Rebetez et al. (2004). In picture captions: "Subduction inducted volcanic activities"; "Accretionary wedge."

motion is smooth and continuous, people may conceive of it as composed of discrete steps (Hegarty, 1992; Zacks, Tversky & Iyer, 2001). For example, the functioning of the four-stroke engine is represented by a static picture of each of the four steps in most mechanical handbooks. If dynamic systems are conceived of a series of discrete steps, giving an animation will not make comprehension easier than a series of static graphics. In learning how a flushing cistern works, Hegarty et al. (2003) found that an animation did not lead to better understanding than a series of three static diagrams representing phases of the system, both conditions being more beneficial than one static diagram of the system. However, animation is the only way to represent transitions between the discrete steps in a dynamic system and remains necessary for learners who are not able to mentally simulate the functioning of the system from static graphics (which Schnotz [2002] called the enabling function of animation). Rebetez et al. (2004) showed that a continuous (but learner controllable) animation led to better comprehension performance than a succession of static snapshots for instructional ma-

terials explaining geological and astronomic phenomena when learners were in pairs (Figure 18.1).

Interactivity may overcome these perceptual and conceptual obstacles. Control over pace and direction could be considered as a simple surface feature at the interface level, which would hardly affect learners' motivation. Research showed, however, that learners in control of the pace of the animation not only find the material more enjoyable but also perform better on tests of deep learning than learners who have no control of animation. This gain has been found even when control was minimal such as deciding when to run the next sequence (Mayer & Chandler, 2001). Control can thus overcome perceptual limitations, because the presence of pauses in the animation enables learners to process the continuous flow of information without perceptual and conceptual overload. New information can be processed and integrated progressively in the mental model (Mayer & Chandler, 2001). Moreover, learners who have complete control over the pace and direction of the animation can monitor the cognitive resources (e.g., attention and processing) they allocate to each part of the animation. Schwan and his colleagues (Schwan, Garsoffky, & Hesse, 2000; Schwan & Riempp, 2004) showed that users who were in control of the pace and direction of a video spent more time on difficult parts of the video.

Another concern is the need to provide segmentation in order to help learners conceptualize the functioning of the system. A direct way to convey segmentation in the animation is to insert a pause after each main phase. According to this conception, learners should benefit more from computer-paced than user-paced control device. The research shows that users who had partial or full control over the animation performed better on a posttest than users who had no control (Mayer & Chandler, 2001), but results are scarce and inconsistent regarding the gain of having full control. Preliminary research showed that in most cases novice learners do not have the knowledge to identify the most relevant parts of the animation and do not monitor the control very effectively (Kettanurak, Ramamurthy, & Haseman, 2001; Lowe, 2003).

What Are the Limitations of Research on Animation and Interactivity?

The effect of using animated displays with or without interactivity has mostly been investigated in laboratory experiments with the traditional mental model paradigm, involving studying the material and then answering explicit and transfer questions on a posttest with little or no delay. The effect of animation over longer retention intervals has hardly been investigated, primarily for practical reasons (e.g., engaging participants to come back one or several weeks later, or ensuring that they did not study the material in the meantime). Similarly, studies on animation in real learning settings and using rigorous experimental methods are scarce. Although such studies could provide interesting and ecological results, it should be made sure that the animated and nonan-

imated situations are equivalent with all other respects, especially the attitude of the teacher or trainer and the learning activities.

Research carried out from a cognitive perspective has not shown much consideration for the kind of learning material. Designing an animation, such as designing graphics, requires decisions on the way objects, motion, and other nonvisual features (force, speed, etc.) are represented. Animation involves in most cases a mixture of representational features, which bear a resemblance to the real object, of domain-specific or common conventional signs and symbols (e.g. arrows), and, of primary importance, of verbal information. As some format factors have multimedia instructional value, the semiotic information conveyed by representational, symbolic, and verbal information and their relationships probably affect the way learners process the material. At least designers should ensure contiguity between verbal and graphic information, use signaling to reinforce important information and logical links, and provide commentary in the aural modality (see chapter 12).

Other determinants of the effectiveness of animation that seem of primary importance but are scarcely investigated are individual differences in expertise in the domain and visuo-spatial abilities. Generally, benefits due to the instructional format are greater for novices than experts (e.g., Mayer & Sims, 1994). Experts, who have already formed mental models in the domain, can rely on long-term memory processes to learn about complex phenomena. In some cases, providing animation to learners who are able to mentally animate the system is detrimental to learning because it induces a shallow processing of the material (Schnotz, Boeckheler, and Gzrondziel, 1999; Schnotz & Lowe, 2003). Conversely, animation indices a complex visual processing and may be beneficial only to learners with high visuo-spatial abilities (Mayer & Sims, 1994). Studies are needed to confirm these results in a large variety of learning tasks and objectives, which could help designers adapt the instructional material to the targeted learners.

Finally, the research has mostly covered the effect of animation on off-line learning outcomes, but little is known about the way people explore and process animation, although it can have direct implications for design. Lowe (2003; chapter 27) showed that novices focused their attention on perceptually salient rather than thematically relevant features of the animation. To lower this tendency the design of the animation should include devices that guide learners' attention to important features of the animation such as arrows or visual highlighting.

Implications for Cognitive Theory

As Schnotz (2003) stated, three functions can be attributed to animations with regard to the elaboration of a mental model of a dynamic system: *enabling, facilitating, or inhibiting functions*. When learners are novices or have poor imagery capabilities, animations enable learners to visualize the system that otherwise they would not be able to mentally simulate. Even when learners are capable of mentally simulating a dynamic system, providing animation can lower the cognitive cost of mental simulation thus saving cognitive resources for learning. The formation of a "runnable" mental model of the system (Mayer, 1989) is then facilitated. However, as animation saves learners from mentally simulating the functioning of the system, it may induce a shallow processing of the animated content, and consequently leads to what can be called the *illusion of understanding*. Then the elaboration of a mental model is inhibited by animation. This obstacle can be avoided by carefully designing the instructional situation, in which learners are engaged in active processing while viewing the animated document.

Animation appears as a paradigm to investigate what a runnable mental model is. Is it a succession of steps that may be hierarchically organized (Hegarty, 1992; Zacks et al. 2001) or a kind of mental simulation of the system? To generate inferences from the mental model, do learners base their reasoning on static states of the system and the combination of rules, or do they mentally run the system and inspect it? In the latter case, animation would help the formation of the model, but in the first case, static representation of essential steps and knowledge of rules would suit better. A promising research track involves studying online processing of animation through qualitative data (self-confrontation methods in ecological situations) in relation to more classical measures of learning performance (Lowe, 2003, 2004).

Implications for Instructional Design

Animations are attractive and intrinsically motivating for learners. However, they are hard to perceive and conceive, their processing requires a heavy cognitive load, and there is a chance that learners do not get any benefit from studying the animation compared with static graphics. In this context, and given the cost of designing animated graphics compared to static ones, the first question an instructional designer should ask is "Do I really need to use animation?" According to the research on animation, animation should be used only when needed, that is when it is quite clear that learners will benefit from an animation. There are two conditions: (1) When the concept or phenomenon depicted in the animation involves change over time and it can be assumed that learners would not be able to infer the transitions between static depictions of the steps. If animation is used when it is not really needed from a cognitive point of view, learners will process material that is complex but not directly useful for understanding how the phenomenon works. Mayer, Heiser, and Lonn (2001) have shown that learning is impaired when non-relevant material is added (see also the *coherence principle* in chapter 12). (2) When learners are novices of the domain, so they cannot form a mental model of the phenomenon (i.e, *enabling function*) or are faced with a very high cognitive load (i.e., *facilitating function*). If learners are able to mentally simulate the phenomenon given a reasonable mental effort, providing them with an animation will prevent them from performing the mental simulation of the system, thus leading to a shallow processing of the graphic matter. In this case animation is not beneficial and even can impair learning (i.e., *inhibiting function* mentioned in Schnotz, 2002).

The effect of using animated displays is often investigated in laboratory experiments, in which learners study the material and then answer explicit and transfer questions. From a designer or practitioner point of view, some reflection is needed on pedagogical uses of animation. As described in the introduction, three main uses of animation in learning situations can be distinguished: (a) to support the visualization and the mental representation process, (b) to produce a cognitive conflict, or (c) to have learners explore a phenomenon.

Design Principles of Instructional Animation

Given that the content is appropriate, five design principles can be derived from the research, besides the contiguity principle, modality principle, and signaling principle described in chapters 9, 11, and 12.

Apprehension Principle (Tversky et al., 2002): The external characteristics should be directly perceived and apprehended by learners. In other words, the graphic design of objects depicted in the animation follow the conventional graphic representation in the domain. This principle also recommends that any additional cosmetic feature that is not directly useful for understanding should be banished from animation. For example, three-dimensional graphics should be avoided as should bidimensional motion or change in the display. Similarly, realism is not necessary when the point is to understand the functioning of a system or to distinguish its parts.

Congruence Principle: Changes in the animation should map changes in the conceptual model rather than changes in the behavior of the phenomenon. In other words, the realism of the depicted phenomenon can be distorted if it helps understanding the cause-effect

relationships between events in the system. For example, in mechanics, events that occur simultaneously can be successive in the chain of causality (e.g., a valve opens and the water flows in). In this case, it would be better to represent the two events successively in the animation, so that the learners can build a functional mental model of the display.

Interactivity Principle: The information depicted in the animation is better comprehended if the device gives learners the control over the pace of the animation. This can be a simple "Resume" function in a presegmented animation, which has be shown to improve learning (Mayer & Chandler, 2001). Not only does this simple control give learners time to integrate information before proceeding to the next frame, but it also segments the animation into relevant chunks. The addition of a higher degree of control (traditional functions of a VCR) should be used when it can be assumed that learners have the capabilities of monitoring the cognitive resources they should allocate to each phase of the animation. In Schwan et al.'s (2000) study, learners could evaluate their needs because they could mimic the procedure of tying the knot. Conversely, Lowe (2003) showed that learners were not able to evaluate the most conceptually relevant parts of animation but rather that they focused on perceptually salient features.

Attention-Guiding Principle: As animation is fleeting by nature, often involving several simultaneous changes in the display, it is very important to guide learners in their processing of the animation so that they do not miss the change. Moreover, Lowe (2003) showed that learners' attention is driven by perceptually salient features rather than thematically relevant changes, simply because novice learners are not able to distinguish between relevant and irrelevant features (see also chapter 27). To direct learners' attention to specific parts of the display, designers can use signaling in the verbal commentary and graphic devices (e.g., arrows or highlights) that appear close to the element under focus (see also chapter 12).

Flexibility Principle: As it is not often possible to know in advance the actual level of knowledge of learners, multimedia instructional material should include some options to activate the animation. Then information provided in the animation should be clearly described to avoid redundancy between the static and animated visual material.

Animation has tremendous potential to improve understanding of dynamic information such as trajectories, transformations, or relative motions, both in physical domains (e.g., biology, mechanics, geology) and abstract domains (e.g., electric or magnetic forces, computer algorithms). However, the research rarely found benefit from having animation compared with traditional and low-cost instructions. In this chapter I mentioned the available guidelines both on the content and design levels that designers should keep in mind when planning to use animation. Further research is needed to fully understand when animation should be used and how it should be designed to promote learning.

Glossary

Animation: Animation refers to any application that generates a series of frames, so that each frame appears as an alteration of the previous one, and in which the sequence of frames is determined either by the designer or the user.

Dynamic information: Information that involves a change over time, such as translations (trajectories, motions), transformation (deformation, relative positions, and actions) and progression (adjunction or subtraction of elements).

Interactivity: The possibility for the learner to act upon what will appear on the next frame by action on parameters (e.g., by clicking directly on sensitive areas or by scaling up and down cursors) in a multimedia presentation.

Learner control: The possibility for the learner to act upon the pace and/or the direction of the succession of frames in a multimedia presentation.

References

Baek, Y. K., & Layne, B. H. (1988). Color, graphics, and animation in a computer-assisted learning tutorial lesson. *Journal of Computer-Based Instruction*, 15, 131–135.

Betrancourt M., & Tversky, B. (2000). Effect of computer animation on users' performance: A review. *Le travail Humain*, 63, 311–330.

Byrne, M. D., Catrambone, R., & Stasko, J. T. (1999). Evaluating animations as student aids in learning computer algorithms. *Computers and Education*, 33, 253–278.

Catrambone, R., & Fleming Seay, A. (2002). Using animation to help students learn computer algorithms. *Human Factors*, 44, 495–511.

Gonzales, C. (1996). Does animation in user interfaces improve decision making? R. Bilger, S. Guest, & M. J. Trauber (Eds.), *Proceedings of Computer Human Interaction*, CHI'96, pp. 27–34. Vancouver, British Columbia, Canada: ACM Press.

Hegarty, M. (1992). Mental animation: Inferring motion from static displays of mechanical systems. *Journal of Experimental Psychology: Learning, Memory and Cognition*, 18(5), 1084–1102.

Hegarty M., Kriz S., & Cate C. (2003). The roles of mental animations and external animations in understanding mechanical systems. *Cognition and Instruction*, 2, 325–360.

Hegarty, M., Narayanan, N. H., & Freitas, P. (2002). Understanding machines from multimedia and hypermedia presentations. In J. Otero, J. A. Leon, & A. Graesser, (Eds.), *The Psychology of Science Text Comprehension* (pp. 357–384). Hillsdale, NJ: Lawrence Erlbaum associates.

Hegarty, M., Quilici, J., Narayanan, N. H., Holmquist, S., & Moreno, R. (1999). Designing multimedia manuals that explain how machines work: Lessons from evaluation of a theory-based design. *Journal of Educational Multimedia and Hypermedia*, 8, 119–150.

Kaiser, M. K., Proffitt, D. R., Whelan, S. M., & Hecht, H. (1992). Influence of animation on dynamical judgments. *Journal of Experimental Psychology: Human Perception and Performance*, 18, 669–690.

Kettanurak, V. N., Ramamurthy, K., & Haseman, D. (2001). User attitude as a mediator of learning performance improvement in an interactive multimedia environment: An empirical investigation of the degree of interactivity and learning styles. *International Journal of Human-Computer Studies*, 54, 541–583.

Lowe, R. K. (2003). Animation and learning: Selective processing of information in dynamic graphics. *Learning and Instruction*, 13, 247–262.

Lowe, R. K. (2004). Interrogation of a dynamic visualization during learning. *Learning and Instruction*, 14, 257–274.

Mayer, R. E., & Chandler, P. (2001). When learning is just a click away: Does simple interaction foster deeper understanding of multimedia messages? *Journal of Educational Psychology*, 93, 390–397.

Mayer, R. E., Heiser, J., & Lonn, S. (2001). Cognitive constraints on Multimedia learning: When presenting more material results in less understanding. *Journal of Educational Psychology*, 93, 187–198.

Mayer, R. E., & Sims, K. (1994). For whom is a picture worth a thousand words? Extensions of a dual-coding theory of multi-media learning. *Journal of Educational Psychology*, 86, 389–401.

Narayanan, N. H., & Hegarty, M. (2002). Multimedia design for communication of dynamic information. *International Journal of Human-Computer Studies*, 57, 279–315.

Rebetez, C., Sangin, M., Betrancourt, M., & Dillenbourg, P. (2004). Effects of collaboration in the context of learning from animations. In *Proceedings of EARLI SIG Meeting on Comprehension of Text and Graphics: Basic and Applied Issues*, September, 9–11, Universitat de Valencia: Valencia Spain, 187–192.

Rieber, L. P. (1989). The effects of computer animated elaboration strategies and practice on factual and application learning in an elementary science lesson. *Journal of Educational Computing Research*, 5, 431–444.

Rieber, L. P., & Hannafin, M. J. (1988). Effects of textual and animated orienting activities and practice on learning from computer-based instruction. *Computers in the Schools*, 5, 77–89.

Schnotz, W. (2002, July). *Enabling, facilitating, and inhibiting effects in learning from animated pictures*. Paper presented at the Dynamic Visualizations workshop, Knowledge Media Research Centre, Tübingen, Germany.

Schnotz, W., Boeckheler, J., & Grzondziel, H. (1999). Individual and co-operative learning with interactive animated pictures. *European Journal of Psychology of Education*, 14, 245–265.

Schnotz, W., & Lowe, R. K. (2003). External and internal representations in multimedia learning. *Learning and Instruction*, 13, 117–123.

Schwan, S., Garsoffky, B., & Hesse, F. W. (2000). Do film cuts facilitate the perceptual and cognitive organization of activity sequences? *Memory and Cognition*, 28, 214–223.

Schwan, S., & Riempp, R. (2004). The cognitive benefits of interactive videos: Learning to tie nautical knots. *Learning and Instruction*, 14, 293–305.

Tversky, B., Bauer-Morrison, J., & Betrancourt, M. (2002) Animation: Can it facilitate? *International Journal of Human-Computer Studies*, 57, 247–262.

Zacks, J., Tversky, B., & Iyer, G. (2001). Perceiving, remembering, and communicating structure in events. *Journal of Experimental Psychology: General*, 130, 29–58.

CHAPTER 19

Navigational Principles in Multimedia Learning

Jean-Francois Rouet
Hervé Potelle
CNRS and University of Poitiers

Abstract

This chapter discusses the role of navigational aids in the comprehension and use of complex hypermedia documents. Navigational aids constitute a broad category of verbal and graphical devices ranging from local cues, (e.g., headings, introductions and connectors) to global content representations (e.g., tables, outlines and concept maps). Text-processing research has demonstrated that the principled use of cues and content representations improves learners' comprehension and memory for text. Navigational aids are also helpful in hypertext-based learning, provided that the aids are considerate to the users' needs. We review relevant research studies indicating that the benefits of various types of content representations vary as a function of the reader's expertise and purpose. We offer an explanation in terms of conceptual activation in memory, based on behavioral and computational evidence. Research results suggest that any attempt to optimize the design of instructional hypermedia systems should consider readers' prior knowledge, the contents to be presented, and how the contents will be used.

Introduction to Navigational Principles

Information resources, whether in print or online, play an increasing role in learning communities. Students in secondary and higher education are now commonly asked to learn by interacting with vast repositories of documents, in the context of more or less specific study assignments. For example, students may be asked to gather information about the causes of the 19th-century Irish potato famine, or to find out how the sea otter catches her food. Such tasks involve not just reading, but also searching and navigating multiple sources of information. Designing information systems that support such learning tasks raises new challenges for information systems designers. Effective instructional information systems must include devices that help learners make their way through complex information (i.e., navigational aids). Navigational aids constitute a broad category of verbal and graphical devices ranging from local cues (e.g., headings, introductions, and connectors) to global content representations (e.g., tables, outlines, and concept maps). Traditional navigational aids are used both in print and computer-based information systems. Computerized multimedia systems, however, may include innovative navigational aids, such as hierarchical menus, hyperlinks, and interactive concept maps.

The purpose of this chapter is to present a review of the research on the effects of navigational aids on learning from complex texts presented in print or through computerized interfaces. We use the phrase *complex text* to designate any coherent set of verbal materials, represented either in print or in electronic media. Textbook chapters, hypertexts, and multimedia documents are examples of complex texts. In the first section of the paper, we briefly review the role of content representations in printed text comprehension. Research on printed text is highly relevant to new media, because most of the signaling devices used in printed text will be largely reused in online information systems. In the second and third parts of the chapter, we examine innovative content representation devices typical of the electronic media (e.g., hyperlinks, interactive menus, and content maps). We review the available evidence concerning the processing of these devices and the effects of different design strategies on hypertext comprehension and use.

The Role of Content Representations in Text Processing

Psychological theories of comprehension offer an appropriate framework to understand the effects of navigational aids. For the past three decades, research on text processing has investigated the psychological processes that underlie the comprehension and memorization of information from simple texts. According to a widespread view, comprehension requires the building of mental representations at several levels: a surface representation, a propositional text base, and a situation model (Kintsch, 1998;

Kintsch & van Dijk, 1978). The surface representation consists in encoding the explicit form of the message: visual features, letters, words, and sentences. During the reading process, the surface representation is quickly subsumed by a propositional representation, in which content words are connected into micro- and macropropositions. Finally, propositions from the text are integrated with the reader's prior knowledge in order to form the situation model. Similarly, the mental model theory by Johnson-Laird (1983) assumes that readers form internal representations that share analogical properties with the objects and events described in the text.

Text-processing research has pointed out the prominent role played by the structural properties of texts in the comprehension of texts. Texts are easier to understand if they are organized according to standard rhetorical schemata (Kintsch & Yarbrough, 1982; Meyer, 1985). In authentic texts, structure is usually represented in the text, but also through the use of various devices called *textual organizers*, *signaling devices*, or *content representations*. Content representations are verbal expressions that convey the topic or core content of a text. Headings, outlines, and introductory sentences are examples of verbal content representations. Text comprehension researchers have extensively studied the effects of headings on readers' comprehension and memory for text (for reviews see Goldman & Rakestraw, 2000; Hartley & Davies 1976; Lorch, 1989). Early studies demonstrated that, in rather extreme cases, headings are absolutely necessary for the reader to make sense of the text (Bransford & Johnson, 1972; Dooling & Lachman, 1971). In more common cases, headings, introductions, and connecting statements improve comprehension and memory for text. Headings may even artificially focus the reader's attention on detail information (Kozminsky, 1977). Headings, however, will not be effective if their wording is unfamiliar to the reader (Spyridakis & Standal, 1987).

Several interpretations have been proposed to explain the facilitative effects of content representations. A popular interpretation, based on Kintsch's propositional analysis of text meaning, states that readers use initial information as a foundation for building a propositional text base (Kieras, 1980; Kintsch & van Dijk, 1978; Schwartz & Flammer, 1981). Incoming propositions are connected to the initial proposition set through referential and coherence links. Thus, the qualitative organization of the text base varies as a function of the information contained in the title or initial sentence (Kieras, 1980; Kozminsky, 1977). Other authors have proposed that headings may improve text comprehension by facilitating word identification. For example, Wiley and Rayner (2000) found that headings decreased the frequency of regressive eye fixations and the duration of "wrap up" pauses during text comprehension. Further experiments indicated that headings speed up the activation of word meanings from memory, suggesting a clearly bottom-up influence. Van den Broek and his colleagues (Gaddy, van den Broek, & Sung, 2001) have proposed a similar interpretation of the role of text organizers in text comprehension, through a set of neo-connectionist activation rules.

Other comprehension theorists have called upon a strategic view of comprehension to interpret the effects of headings. According to this view, the inclusion of content representations in the materials would lead readers to use a structure-building strategy (i.e., to actively search for the conceptual structure that connects ideas together) (Loman & Mayer, 1983; Lorch & Lorch, 1996). Thanks to textual organizers, the visual structure of a text would act as a system of "processing instructions" telling the readers how the materials should be connected (Goldman & Rakestraw, 2000). Evidence comes from tasks in which readers are invited to express their macrostructural representation of the text (e.g., in a summary). Lorch, Lorch, Ritchey, McBovein, and Coleman (2001) found that providing heading for all paragraphs in an expository text improved the inclusion of topic information in summaries. Moreover, including headings for half the paragraphs increased the inclusion of signaled topics, and decreased the inclusion of nonsignaled topics in the summary. Thus, readers of signaled expository texts would use headings to activate preexisting cognitive structures as a building framework (Bock, 1980) or a default conceptual schema (Smith & Swinney, 1992).

The bottom-up and the strategy-shift interpretations of signal effects are not mutually exclusive. Signals may well act both through propositional construction and memory activation mechanisms, on the one hand, and through higher-level, strategic mechanisms, on the other hand. In any case, there is ample evidence that textual organizers can actually improve comprehension, provided that they are labeled and placed in accordance with the actual conceptual structure presented in the text (Spyridakis & Standal, 1987).

So far, the scientific literature is much less informative as regards the effect of more global content representations (e.g., tables of contents, concept maps, and flowcharts) on the comprehension of text. Such a lack of evidence is striking considering that these devices are extremely common in real-life expository materials, such as textbooks, manuals, or encyclopedias. As mentioned previously, however, experimental research has tended to focus on simple, paragraph-long texts, in which global content representations are perhaps less essential. Most research studies conducted until now also used very basic task settings, for example, asking participants to read or order to memorize or to prepare for a comprehension test. Such tasks call for rather linear, coherence-based reading strategies. This is to be compared to the way texts are normally organized and used in naturally occurring printed materials. Readers of textbooks, manuals, or encyclopedias most often have to make their way through dozens of pages before they can access and read relevant materials. And these materials often take the form of a collection of texts, often accompanied by pictures and diagrams, and structured through various types of content representations. In such situations, text-processing strategies strongly rely on the readers' purposes and on their ability to make use of global content representations. Readers' purposes are often determined by a preexisting context or task, which determines which information source will be relevant or useful, and how the information should be used. Readers' knowledge of the rhetorical properties of various types of texts is essential in this process (see Rouet, Favart, Britt, & Perfetti, 1997). Whenever the task requires readers to address complex texts, or collections of texts, the role of global content representations becomes essential.

Some evidence suggests that global content representations are also essential in helping readers make sense of complex texts. For instance, Glenberg and Langston (1992) found that a flowchart diagram helped readers construct a mental model of a procedure described in a text (e.g., how to write a scientific paper). Mannes (1994) found that an outline introducing a lengthy expository text, but with a slightly discrepant structure, promoted deep comprehension of the materials, as evidenced in a diagram drawing task and in a relatedness judgment task. Rouet, Vidal-Abarca, Bert-Erboul, and Millogo (2001) observed that the inclusion of an explicit table of contents at the top of a lengthy scientific text presented online increased text review and facilitated the location of key information while searching. Dreher and Guthrie (1990) found that efficient searchers tend to spend more time studying top-level content representations before they make a selection among topics presented in a textbook chapter. Thus, whether in comprehension or in search tasks, global content representations facilitate the processing of complex texts. They are especially useful when the reader has to design a relevance-based comprehension strategy, for example, in order to decide which parts of a complex document are relevant to his or her task.

In the next section, we turn to an examination of global content representations in hypermedia documents. We first examine the role of text-based content representations (e.g., hyperlinks and menus). Then we review evidence concerning the impact of graphical content representations such as diagrams or concept maps.

Verbal Content Representations in Hypertext Systems

Hypertext may be broadly defined as a database of textual units (or pages) connected through semantic links (Conklin, 1987). Hypertext is usually characterized as a nonlinear networked information structure with no predefined reading path. In hypertext, it is up to readers to "navigate" information pages by making selections among the links available, as a function of their needs or interests. In order to be functional, a hypertext database must be made accessible through a user interface in which the content units and the links are clearly signaled to the user. Assisting navigation seems even more crucial in hypertext than it is in traditional printed documents. In fact, early hypertext studies found that users often experience disorientation and cognitive overhead while navigating hypertext (Wright, 1991). Whether used for the purpose of knowledge exploration, or for specific search tasks, hypertext systems often proved disappointingly inefficient compared to more traditional print-based technologies (see Chen & Rada, 1996; Dillon & Gabbard, 1998; Rouet & Levonen, 1996 for reviews). As evidence accumulated, it became clear that the lack of an explicit structure was a frequent problem (Charney, 1994). Thus, readers seem to experience the same need for global coherence in hypertext as they do in traditional text (Foltz, 1996; Lee & Tedder, 2003).

Research on navigational aids in hypertext has revolved around several core issues: Should links that allow navigation from page to page be embedded in the text or displayed as explicit menus? Should menus be broad (i.e., with many options per page and few levels of choice) or deep (i.e., with few options per level and more levels)? Are graphical content representations such as concept maps more apt to convey the structure of nonlinear information than traditional,

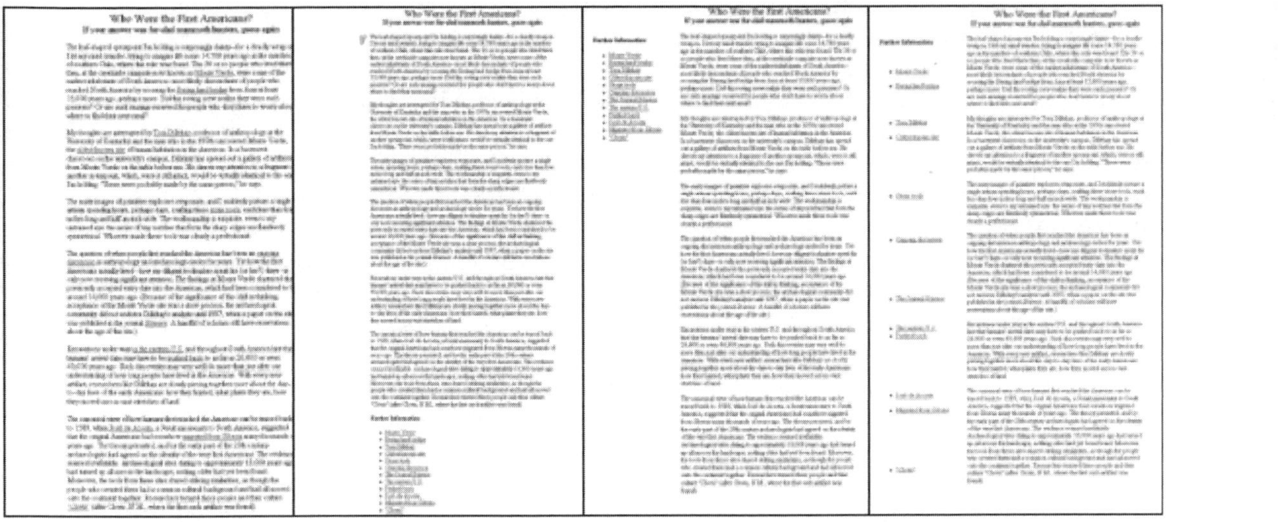

Figure 19.1. Four types of hyperlink presentations studied in the study by Bernard, Hull & Drake (2001). From left to right: embedded links, explicit menu at bottom, explicit menu at top left, and explicit menu to the left, leveled with textual context.

list-based menus? If so, does the graphical layout of a concept map influence readers' comprehension processes? We review the state of the art on each of these issues.

Embedded versus Explicit Linking of Information Pages

Designers of hypertext systems may either present links in lists separated from the actual page contents, or embed links within content information. In the latter case, expressions used as links are signaled by using a different color and/or underlining. Koved and Shneiderman (1986) argued that embedded menus are preferable because they save screen space, and they preserve the semantic context in which the link appears. Koved and Shneiderman listed several applications of embedded menus in online databases, catalogs, spelling checkers, and programming editors. They briefly reviewed experiments showing mixed, but rather positive evidence in favor of embedded links. Since then, other studies have found positive evidence in favor of embedded links. Bernard, Hull, and Drake (2001) examined whether the location of links on a Web page influence readers' abilities to locate information, as well as their subjective evaluation of document quality. They used four two-level hypertext articles borrowed from *Scientific American* online. General information was included at level 1, and hypertext links allowed the reader to access complementary information in specific topics (level 2). As shown in Figure 19.1, each hypertext was redesigned in four versions: links embedded within the contents of page 1 (version 1); links at the bottom of page 1 (version 2); links at the top left of page 1 (version 3); and links in the left margin, close to corresponding content information (version 4).

Twenty volunteer students performed 10 search tasks with each version (content and presentation order were counterbalanced). There was no difference in search accuracy, time, or economy across versions. However, embedded links (version 1) raised higher ratings in ease of navigation and ability to recognize key information, while bottom links had the lowest ratings in comprehensibility and ability to follow the main idea. Overall, embedded links were preferred most often, while bottom links were never preferred. Thus, it seems that embedded links facilitate the retrieval of specific information in unfamiliar science reports. It should be noted, however, that performance at a retrieval task does not necessarily mean better comprehension. As Foltz (1996) noted, in comprehension tasks hypertext readers are usually more conservative, following links in the order suggested by the top-level structure of the document (see also Tung, Debreceny, Chan, & Le, 2003).

Even though the effectiveness of embedded links has been demonstrated, they should be considered a complement rather than an alternative to content representation pages. In hypertexts containing more than a few pages, the use of cover pages, indexes, or other forms of content representations is necessary. In the absence of such devices, hypertext readers will often wonder "what's behind the door" (Gordon, Gustavel, Moorie, & Hankey, 1988). Compared to readers of a printed version, readers of a hypertext science report get less out of documents that do not pertain to the cover page (Macedo-Rouet, Rouet, Epstein, & Fayard, 2003). In the next section, we discuss relevant dimensions in the design of hypertext menus and the impact of design options on users' navigation.

The Breadth-Depth Trade-Off in Hypertext Menus

Most Web portals and other online services use menu structures as access devices. In some portals, menus provide access to hundreds of categories in potentially all areas of interest to the general public. Menu design varies a great deal from one portal to another. Some portals offer deep menus with only a few options available at each level, while others offer broad menus with many categories available at each level. In some cases, the items are listed alphabetically, while in other cases the items are grouped by semantic categories (e.g., finance, travel, etc.).

Menu structures and their effects on users' abilities to retrieve information have been the object of a large number of studies (Norman, 1991). Miller (1981) asked students to locate a target word among 64 words or expressions presented as lists on a computer screen. The lists were structured along dimensions of breadth and depth. In the broader version, all 64 items were presented on a single page. In the deeper version, only two items appeared on each page. Selecting an item resulted in a new screen with two items, and so forth until the target item was located, thus resulting in six embedded layers of information. In the latter case, items in intermediate levels were category names (e.g., culture > geography > countries > Europe > Western Europe > Spain). Intermediate versions contained two levels of choice with eight items per level, and three levels of choice with four items per level. Miller found that selection time was shorter in the intermediate menu structures. The breadth-depth trade-off effect has been replicated in numerous experiments using either artificial tree structures (Snowberry, Parkinson, & Sisson, 1983) or more realistic applications such as navigation maps (Chiu & Wang, 2000). In a study involving 19 volunteer students, Larson and Czerwinski (1998) manipulated the structure of menus in an electronic encyclopedia. They found that two-level menus (e.g., 16×32 items or 32×16 items) resulted in faster location of targets, and a lesser feeling of disorientation, compared to a three-level menu ($8 \times 8 \times 8$ items). The 32×16 items was the menu most often preferred by the participants. Thus, menu depth seems to increase a user's feeling of complexity, as if the user was trying to memorize the route followed in the hierarchy. Deeper menus might also make it more difficult for a user to design an alternate route in case of a mistaken selection. Two-level menus give a sense of "shallowness" that reduces feelings of disorientation and improves selection performance (Tung et al., 2003).

Semantic Grouping and Expandable Menus

When designing large hypertext databases, designers often have to present menus including several dozen items. Research has found that, in order for the user to locate information rapidly, items should be grouped into explicit semantic categories.

Snowberry et al. (1983), using the same materials as Miller (1981), found that in the broadest menu condition (i.e., 64 items on a single page) selection performance improved when items were grouped semantically. Giroux, Bergeron, and Lamarche (1987) conducted a similar experiment in French and obtained the same pattern of results. Grouping items according to semantic categories probably prompts a top-down search strategy in which readers first browse the higher-level items, select the most relevant one, and examine the subordinate items more closely.

With the advent of graphical interfaces, menu designers have proposed alternatives to traditional static menus. For instance, many Web sites propose pull-down menus in which the user may examine the contents of a subcategory without losing the subordinate menu structure. The effects of these alternatives in terms of effectiveness and user preference have not been clearly established. Yu and Roh (2002) examined the effects of pull-down menus versus traditional menus on university students' search performances and evaluations of a virtual shopping mall. They found that a pull-down menu that maximized the visibility of intermediate categories was the most effective in terms of searching speed for both specific and more global search tasks. Students' estimates of design quality and disorientation, however, did not vary across menu types. Another study by Zaphiris, Shneiderman, and Norman (2002) showed rather conflicting results. They found that search was generally faster with a traditional hierarchical menu than with an expandable menu, especially with a deep menu structure. The participants (21 university students) did not show any clear-cut preference for one type of menu. However, when the structure was deeper, they preferred the sequential menu over the expandable one. Zaphiris et al. concluded that expandable menus are acceptable only for shallow menu structures.

In conclusion, despite the fast technological advances in the field, research studies have contributed some principles for the design of usable nonlinear hypertexts. Embedded links may be used as a complement to explicit menus. In large hypertexts, explicit menus should be structured so as to balance depth (number of selection levels) and breadth (number of items per level). In broad menus, semantic grouping may be preferred to alphabetic or random listing. Finally, pull-down menus that preserve a visual representation of the top-down path may be used, at least for so-called "shallow" hierarchies.

Concept Maps and Other Graphical Representations

Menus, concept maps, and other types of content representations play an essential role in hypermedia usability (Nielsen, 1999). There is no agreement, however, as to which type of representation is to be preferred, depending on the application, the user, and the task at hand. It may be that alphabetical lists rather than concept maps are efficient for different types of tasks, for instance browsing the contents for comprehension rather than locating specific facts in a hypertext. In this section, we first review research on hypertext comprehension. Then we turn to studies of information search in hypertext.

Concept Maps in Hypertext Comprehension

Cover pages, tables of contents, and concept maps play the role of advance organizers, that is, they help the reader build a representation of the contents and organization of the materials. Such a representation is useful in order to activate relevant knowledge, to encode the relations between topics, and to make informed decisions while searching for specific items. One might expect, therefore, that the coherence of a top-level representation is critical in readers' abilities to navigate a hypertext structure. Indeed, experiments have found that variations in the content page may deeply affect reader navigation and comprehension. Britt, Rouet, and Perfetti (1996) examined the effects of different presentation modes of a multidocument hypertext on college students' comprehension of the history of the Panama

Canal. They manipulated the organization of the table of contents, by listing documents either in an order consistent with the story and document types, or in a scrambled order. Even though individual documents in their hypertext systems were self-contained, the structured table of contents seemed beneficial to most students, especially in the hypertext condition. Users of the structured table of contents made more use of hyperlinks and spent more time on the documents. They also had a better understanding of intertextual relationships (see also Rouet et al., 2001).

Concept maps have been proposed as alternatives to verbal content representations in hypertext systems. Nilsson and Mayer (2002) defined concept maps as:

> a graphic representation of a hypertext document, in which the pages of the document are represented by visual objects (whether simply the title of a page or an icon representing a page) and the links between pages are represented by lines or arrows connecting the visual objects. (p. 2)

In a concept map, each node represents the contents of a text passage by a thematic phrase. Links represent different kinds of relationships between concepts (Stanton, Taylor, & Tweedie, 1992). Several studies have tried to assess the benefits of concept maps as navigation and comprehension aids in hypertext. McDonald and Stevenson (1998) showed that navigation aids facilitate low prior-knowledge readers' comprehension. Psychology students read a hypertext on the topic of discourse production. The text was presented either with a navigational aid (i.e., a network concept map or a simple list), or without such an aid (i.e., only as a set of hypertext nodes and links). Both types of aids lead to better comprehension, but only in low prior-knowledge students. Moreover, the time needed to answer questions was shorter when using a concept map than a list. Shapiro (1999) asked undergraduate students with low prior knowledge on ecosystems and high prior knowledge on animal families to read a hypertext on these topics, with either the goal to learn specifically

about animal relationships to their ecosystem (goal A) or about similarities and differences between animal families (goal B). The participants had to read the hypertext either using a hierarchical interactive map showing the categorical organization of species, or read the hypertext without such a map. The hierarchical map led to better answers to inferential comprehension questions, but only for the low prior-knowledge participants. Trumpower and Goldsmith (2004) showed similar results with networked maps. They found that college students with no previous computer-programming experience get to transfer and to use their knowledge in programming tasks when working with a network map rather than an alphabetic list of domain concepts.

In other studies, however, the most elaborate content representations were not always the better. Hofman and van Oostendorp (1999) tried to assess the effects of content representations on several representation levels as a function of a reader's prior knowledge. Undergraduate students with high versus low prior topic knowledge were asked to study a science text on sun radiation and health. The text was presented either through a network concept map showing various types of relationships between ultraviolet radiation and skin cancer, or through an alphabetic topic list (i.e., without explicit high-level relations). Structural levels of text information (i.e., microstructure vs. macrostructure questions) as well as representation levels of text (i.e., text base versus situation model questions) were manipulated so as to produce four types of comprehension questions. Hofman and van Oostendorp found that the concept map hindered the low knowledge students' construction of a situation model. They concluded that the concept map had diverted readers' attention from more appropriate levels of processing. For readers with little prior knowledge, simpler representations, for example, content lists or hierarchical maps, may be more productive than complex network representations.

In fact the benefits of concept maps seems to be a function of how they are designed, that is, the amount and type of links

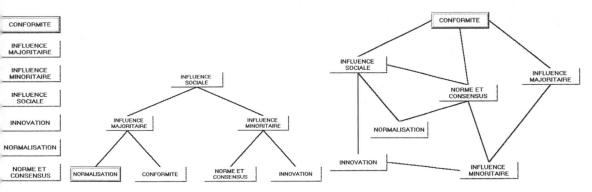

Figure 19.2. The three content representations used in the study by Potelle and Rouet (2003): alghabetic list (left), hierarchical map (center), and network map (right).

they display. Potelle and Rouet (2003) suggested that maps showing hierarchical representations may help low knowledge students, whereas network representations may be more beneficial to high knowledge students. Hierarchical maps may facilitate the construction of the hypertext macrostructure in low knowledge students (Dec-Lucas & Larkin, 1995; Shapiro, 1999) because they display basic global relationships among the topics dealt with in the text (Lorch & Lorch, 1996). Reading a hierarchical map may help the low knowledge students to build a mental representation organized with categorical/thematic links. On the other hand, a network map could hinder low knowledge students' construction of the macrostructure because of its too complex semantic links (Hofman & van Oostendorp, 1999). As shown in Figure 19.2, Potelle and Rouet (2003) designed a simple hypertext made of seven content cards on the topic of social influence. They designed three content representations of the hypertext: a *hierarchical map*, a *network map*, and an *alphabetic list*.

Potelle and Rouet hypothesized that the hierarchical map would function as a structural cue for all the readers, which would improve comprehension, especially at a macrostructural level. The relations depicted in the network map, however, were more complex and could be detrimental to novice readers. Forty-seven students, categorized either as novices or as specialists based on a pretest, studied the hypertext for a period of 20 minutes, with an explicit com-

prehension objective. Comprehension was assessed through a 16-item multiple choice questionnaire and a summary task. The participants were also asked to draw a map of the hypertext from memory. Low knowledge students had better scores when using the hierarchical map than with the other two formats. For the more expert students, the type of content representation had no significant impact. Low knowledge students also included more thematic ideas in their summaries when reading from a hierarchical map. Finally, they drew more accurate maps of the hierarchical hypertext than of the other two systems.

Thus, the effects of a global content representation on comprehension depend in part on the reader's prior knowledge. To be effective, a content representation should be easy to understand. Readers must be able to recognize and use the symbols presented in the map. If the map is ambiguous, or uses unfamiliar symbols, then the result will be an added burden on the reader, with dubious effects on comprehension and recall. When designing hypertext systems, care should be taken to adjust the level and type of structural information to the capabilities and needs of the user (see also Carmel, Crawford, & Chen, 1992; Stanton et al., 1992).

The Role of Content Representations in Hypertext Search Tasks

Searching for information is a fairly specific mental activity. Searching occurs as part of everyday activities (e.g., traveling, cooking, or setting up devices). Searching is also a prevalent reading mode in occupational activities (Guthrie & Kirsch, 1987) and, of course, in learning. There is evidence that reading for comprehension and reading in order to locate information are two rather distinct activities (Guthrie, 1988; Rouet & Vidal-Abarca, 2002). Searching requires the student to form an objective, or search goal. During search, information found in documents is not processed according to textual importance or coherence. Instead, the fate of the information depends on its relevance with respect to the person's goal. Compared to reading comprehension, search is also a more demanding activity, because the reader must retain and update her/his representation of the goal as he or she selects, reads, evaluates, and integrates content information. How does the organization or information affect searching? More specifically, do graphical concept maps facilitate or hinder the search process?

Early studies of hypertext search found that hierarchical structures were generally more effective than simple list or networked structures for information search. Edwards and Hardman (1989) compared three ways of structuring a 50-page hypertext about the City of Edinburgh. Twenty-seven college students (9 in each condition) used either a hierarchical menu, an index, or a combination of both devices to answer 20 questions. The index was more economical in terms of pages visited per search, but the performance tended to improve more with the hierarchical index. Furthermore, the hierarchical presentation led to a better incidental learning of the hypertext, as evidenced in a post-test. Mohageg (1992) studied the effects of different menu structures on the usability of a hypertext geographical database. The database was intrinsically hierarchical, that is, information about each country was organized into topics (e.g., economy, demography) and subtopics (e.g., language, family structure). The database was presented according to four presentation formats: The *linear version* presented topics in a sequence coherent with hierar-

chical relations; in the *hierarchical version*, each country card contained links to topics, which in turn contained links to subtopics; in the *network version*, each card contained links to semantically related topics (e.g., the economy card for a country might be connected to the language card if it dealt with language issues); and the *mixed version* had both hierarchical and semantic links. Sixty-four adult paid volunteers were assigned to one of the four presentation formats. The subjects were asked to use the database to answer questions requiring the study of two, four, or six nodes. The main finding was a benefit of the hierarchical and mixed formats over the networked database. Furthermore, participants showed interesting orientation-preserving strategies. For instance, when backtracking to the top level in the hierarchical database, many subjects retraced their steps, level by level, instead of using the faster "home" key.

Given that hierarchies are found more effective than menu lists, it is likely that the use of graphical metaphors (e.g., concept maps) may facilitate the retrieval of information from hypertexts. Nilsson and Mayer (2002) discussed the effects of concept maps in light of current theories of learning. They pointed out that concept maps may have paradoxical effects in terms of task difficulty and learning effectiveness. On the one hand, maps would decrease the cognitive cost of searching by providing an external representation of the structure. On the other hand, using a map may reduce the amount of elaborative processes brought to bear by the learner while studying the document. This, in turn, may lead to a lesser learning of the hypertext contents. Nilsson and Mayer tested those predictions using a 150-page hypertext encyclopedia about aquatic animals. Pages in the encyclopedia were linked according to categorical and semantic relationships. In one version, the system included a map showing the individual cards and their connections. In the first experiment, 53 undergraduate students used either the map or the no-map version to answer 30 factual questions divided in two consecutive blocks: a learning block and a test block. Participants in the map condition searched fewer pages per trial, but the students' performances in the no-map versions improved more dramatically from the first to the second block. As a result, search in the no-map group was slightly more efficient in the second block. The authors also found that participants in the map condition seemed less involved in analyzing the demands of each task. In the second experiment, they replaced the "passive" content maps by a list of path-type expressions that showed the location of the animal currently displayed within each of the three hierarchies (e.g., Habitats < Marine < Open waters < Mediterranean open waters). The user could click on any of the component phrases to go directly to the corresponding group page. The implicit version of the system did not include any organizer. Fifty-one students were asked to answer the same questions as in experiment 1. In the test phase, the group in the explicit organizer condition was significantly faster than the control group. Nilsson and Mayer concluded that the simple view that any organizer would facilitate hypertext navigation is inaccurate. They recommended that maps be used in systems aimed at one-time or occasional users, with no ambition of learning the system. The pathlike organizer, on the other hand, seemed useful as a learning device, but only after a training period. Thus, different types of users may need different types of content representations.

Whether or not they make use of graphical metaphors, content representations provided in support of search activities should be designed with care. This implies, for instance, that the status of each unit in the system be clearly signaled, that links are unambiguous to the reader, and that the representation looks consistent overall. Dallal, Quibble, and Wyatt (2000) found that the application of these and other design guidelines improved the effectiveness of content representations, both verbal (i.e., menus) and graphical (i.e., maps) in a Web-based hypertext. The guideline-compliant versions lead to better comprehension (retrieval) performance, faster performance, and higher subjective estimates of comprehension. In-

terestingly, there was no difference between the graphical and verbal versions (i.e., content maps did not lead to faster or better performance than content lists). Danielson (2002) demonstrated the benefits of having the content map constantly visible on the screen. In his study, 20 adult subjects performed search tasks in one of five existing Web sites dealing with different topics (e.g., recreation, law, leisure activities). The sites were presented either with a map on the top-level page, or with a constantly visible map presented to the left. Participants using the constant map attained target pages more directly, and gave up on fewer trials. They also spent more time in pages deep in the hierarchy, and made more distant jumps within the Web site.

Research on hypertext structuring and content representations has to take into account the rapid progress of technology. As new content representation devices are created, new questions emerge as to their effectiveness and impact on learning. So far, however, the evidence favors clear hierarchical structuring at least for nonexpert users in the context of search tasks. Content maps help users build a representation of the system, and make their way through it when searching for specific information. They may, however, encourage a passive-viewing approach that may hinder the memorization of the hypertext contents. Thus the decision to include graphical content representation should take into account the purposes and the type of public the system is intended to serve.

Conclusions

Hypermedia and other online information systems are more and more widely used as learning resources. Whether at school, at the workplace, or at home, people can easily access huge repositories of multimedia information through the Web. Providing guidance to the user is an overarching challenge for designers of hypermedia systems. Because of the flexibility inherent to digital information, hypermedia systems can be structured in many different ways, allowing for a diversity of interaction modes, but also many sources of confusion and disorientation. Thus, the quality of content representations and user guidance devices is a critical prerequisite to the usability and learning effectiveness of hypermedia systems.

Despite their innovative features, hypermedia systems rely heavily on traditional rhetorical forms such as chapters, pages, texts, and illustrations. Therefore, comprehension and learning from such systems calls upon the same set of cognitive and language processes as traditional text processing (Charney, 1994; Dee-Lucas & Larkin, 1995; Rouet & Levonen, 1996). This means that textual organizers and signaling devices that are known to facilitate text comprehension should also be effective in hypermedia systems. Research on text comprehension has demonstrated that thematic cues such as headings and introduction generally facilitate a reader's construction of consistent mental representations of the contents. Headings, in particular, help readers recruit relevant knowledge, identify semantic links across textual concepts, and adopt a structure-building strategy that fosters their comprehension and memory. Consequently, Web pages, especially ones with a pedagogical intent, should feature a clear page layout, titles, headings, and paragraph structures.

Global content representations, such as tables, diagrams, and indexes, are also widely used to convey the gist of the organization of large bodies of textual information, especially when the information is expository or technical. This means, of course, that experienced readers rely heavily on such devices in naturalistic reading situations. In turn, the prevalent use of global content representations in mundane reading tasks points to the fact that reading is often selective and based on a preexisting objective or task (Guthrie & Kirsch, 1987). Curiously, though, research on text comprehension has tended to focus on simple, short texts and on tasks that hardly require any prior selection or evaluation of text materials. Before the generalization of computer-based information systems, the amount of published literature on global content representations

was very small compared to, for instance, research studies on the role of headings. It is interesting to note that the advent of hypertext and Web sites has contributed to refocusing the research effort on global content representations, an area hardly investigated in earlier text-processing research.

Research conducted so far clearly suggests that any information system comprising several pages should include a clear top-level content representation. Users of online materials are just as much in need of coherence and visibility as users of printed materials. Coherence may be provided by representing contents in the form of explicit lists in which items are grouped according to semantic categories. Furthermore, the grouping of items on electronic menus should keep the breadth and depth dimensions in balance. Embedded links are thought to be an efficient way to augment readers' perceptions of the semantic organization of nonlinear materials, even though they may not replace, but rather complement explicit content representations.

Hypertext also allows the design of concept maps, which integrate both verbal and iconic symbols as representations of the semantic organization of the materials. In many studies, such devices have proven beneficial to the readers, because readers do seem to model their mental representation of the contents after what they perceive from those devices. It is not the case, however, that "anything goes" as regards the design of content maps. The size, shape, and the types of symbols used are all critical in determining a map's readability. Simple, unambiguous maps are preferable in materials aimed at nonexpert readers. Sophisticated representations, for instance those that include several types of graphical metaphors for representing semantic relations, may be fit only to the more experienced content specialist. In addition, graphical content representations may sometimes give readers an "illusion of knowing" that may prevent them from actually processing the materials in depth (Nilsson & Mayer, 2002). Therefore, when designing instructional materials, designers should be aware of the need to include content representations that will help without being – literally – "the tree that hides the forest."

Reading and using text plays an ever-increasing role in information-based societies. Technological advances have a lot to offer, but they also pose new challenges to designers, educators, and text-processing researchers. Future research on text processing will have to cope with the increased complexity that results from the growing variability of text forms (i.e., printed, electronic, linear, or networked) and of reading contexts (i.e., reading for comprehension, search, or other purposes) that characterize readers' environments in the information age.

Glossary

Concept map: A concept map is a graphic representation of the conceptual organization of a document or an area of knowledge. Concept maps can be structured hierarchically or as networks.

Content representation: Any information in a verbal or graphical form aimed at representing the contents of a complex document.

Hyperlink: A verbal expression (usually a word) in a hypertext page that can be selected to display another related page. Hyperlinks can be arranged into explicit menus or embedded in the page content.

Hypertext: A hypertext is a complex electronic document made of a network of pages connected through hyperlinks. A hypertext page can be connected to any number of pages located within the hypertext or in other hypertexts.

Macrostructure: In Kintsch and van Dijk's (1978) theory, a macrostructure is a set of concepts and semantic propositions that represent the gist meaning of a text.

Navigation: In the context of information technology, the term *navigation* is used to describe the series of selections made by users as they go through a complex document.

Situation model: A situation model is a memory representation that incorporates information read from a text and the reader's own prior knowledge.

Text base: In Kintsch and van Dijk's (1978) theory, a text base is the set of semantic propositions that make up the literal meaning of a text.

References

Bernard, M., Hull, S., & Drake, D. (2001). Where should you put the links? A comparison of four locations. *Usability News, 3.2.* Retrieved May 10, 2004, from http://psychology.wichita.edu/surl/usabilitynews/3S/links.htm

Bock, M. (1980). Some effects of titles on building and recalling text structures. *Discourse Processes, 3,* 301–311.

Brandsford, J. D., & Johnson, M. K. (1972). Contextual prerequisites for understanding: Some investigations in comprehension and recall. *Journal of Verbal Learning and Verbal Behavior, 11,* 717–726.

Britt, M. A., Rouet, J.-F., & Perfetti, C. A. (1996). Using hypertext to study and reason about historical evidence. In J.-F. Rouet, J. J. Levonen, A. P. Dillon, and R. J. Spiro (Eds.), *Hypertext and cognition* (pp. 43–72). Mahwah, NJ: Lawrence Erlbaum Associates.

Carmel, E., Crawford, S., & Chen, H. (1992). Browsing in hypertext: A cognitive study. *IEEE Transactions on Systems, Man, and Cybernetics, 22,* 865–884.

Charney, D. (1994). The impact of hypertext on processes of reading and writing. In S. J. Hilligoss & C. L. Selfe (Eds.), *Literacy and computers: The complications of teaching and learning with technology* (pp. 238–263). New York: Modern Language Association.

Chen, C., & Rada, R. (1996). Interacting with hypertext: A meta-analysis of experimental studies. *Human-Computer Interaction, 11,* 125–156.

Chiu, C.-H., & Wang, F.-M. (2000). The influence of navigation map scope on disorientation of elementary students in learning a web-based hypermedia course. *Journal of Educational Computing Research, 22,* 135–144.

Conklin, J. (1987). Hypertext: An introduction and survey. *Computer, 20,* 17–41.

Dallal, N. P., Quibble, Z., & Wyatt, C. (2000). Cognitive design of home pages: An experimental study of comprehension on the World Wide Web. *Information Processing and Management, 36*, 607–621.

Danielson, D. R. (2002). Web navigation and the behavioral effects of constantly visible site maps. *Interacting with Computers, 14*, 601–618.

Dee-Lucas, D., & Larkin, J. H. (1995). Learning from electronic texts: Effects of interactive overviews for information access. *Cognition and Instruction, 13*, 431–468.

Dillon, A., & Gabbard, R. (1998). Hypermedia as an educational technology: A review of the quantitative research literature on learner comprehension, control and style. *Review of Educational Research, 68*, 322–349.

Dooling, D. J., & Lachman, R. (1971). Effects of retention on the comprehension of prose. *Journal of Experimental Psychology, 88*, 216–222.

Dreher, M. J., & Guthrie, J. T. (1990). Cognitive processes in textbook chapter search tasks. *Reading Research Quarterly, 25*, 323–339.

Edwards, D., & Hardman, L. (1989). "Lost in hyperspace": Cognitive mapping and navigation in a hypertext environment. In R. McAleese (Ed.), *Hypertext: Theory into practice* (pp. 105–125). Oxford, England: Intellect.

Foltz, P. W. (1996). Comprehension, coherence and strategies in hypertext and linear text. In J.-F. Rouet, J. J. Levonen, A. P. Dillon, and R. J. Spiro (Eds.), *Hypertext and cognition* (pp. 109–136). Mahwah, NJ: Lawrence Erlbaum Associates.

Gaddy, M. L., van den Broek, P., & Sung, Y.-C. (2001). The influence of text cues on the allocation of attention during reading. In T. Sanders, J. Schilperoord, & W. Spooren (Eds.), *Cognitive approaches to text coherence* (pp. 89–110). Amsterdam/Philadelphia: Benjamins.

Giroux, L., Bergeron, G., & Lamarche, J.-P. (1987). Organisation sémantique des menus dans les banques de données [semantic organization of menus in databases], *Le Travail Humain, 50*, 97–107.

Glenberg, A. M., & Langston, W. E. (1992). Comprehension of illustrated text: Pictures help build mental models. *Journal of Memory and Language, 31*, 129–151.

Goldman, S. R., & Rakestraw, J. A. Jr. (2000). Structural aspects of constructing meaning from text. In M. L. Kamil, P. B. Mosenthal, P. D. Pearson, and R. Barr (Eds.), *Handbook of reading research. Volume III* (pp. 311–335). Mahwah, NJ: Lawrence Erlbaum Associates.

Gordon, S., Gustavel, J., Moore, J., & Hankey, J. (1988). The effect of hypertext on reader knowledge representation. *Proceedings of the 32nd Annual Meeting of the Human Factors Society* (pp. 296–300). Santa Monica, CA: Human Factors Society.

Guthrie, J. T. (1988). Locating information in documents: Examination of a cognitive model. *Reading Research Quarterly, 23*, 178–199.

Guthrie, J. T., & Kirsch, I. (1987). Distinctions between reading comprehension and locating information in text. *Journal of Educational Psychology, 79*, 210–228.

Hartley, J., & Davies, I. K. (1976). Preinstructional strategies: The role of pretests, behavioral objectives, overviews and advance organizers. *Review of Educational Research, 46*, 239–265.

Hofman, R., & van Oostendorp, H. (1999). Cognitive effects of a structural overview in a hypertext. *British Journal of Educational Technology, 30*, 129–140.

Johnson-Laird, P. N. (1983). *Mental models*. Cambridge, UK: Cambridge University Press.

Kieras, D. E. (1980). Initial mention as a signal to thematic content in technical passages. *Memory and Cognition, 8*, 345–353.

Kintsch, W. (1988). The role of knowledge in discourse comprehension: A construction-integration model. *Psychological Review, 95*, 163–182.

Kintsch, W., & van Dijk, T. A. (1978). Toward a model of text comprehension and production. *Psychological Review, 85*, 363–394.

Kintsch, W., & Yarbrough, J. C. (1982). Role of rhetorical structure in text comprehension. *Journal of Educational Psychology, 74*, 828–834.

Koved, L., & Shneiderman, B. (1986). Embedded menus: Selecting items in context. *Communications of the ACM, 29*, 312–318.

Kozminsky, E. (1977). Altering comprehension: The effect of biasing title on text comprehension. *Memory and Cognition, 5*, 482–490.

Larson, K., & Czerwinski, M. (1998). Web page design: Implications of memory, structure and scent for information retrieval. *Proceedings of CHI'98 Conference* (pp. 25–32). New York: ACM Press.

Lee, M. J., & Tedder, M. L. (2003). The effects of three different computer texts on readers' recall: Based on working memory capacity. *Computers in Human Behavior, 19*, 767–783.

Loman, N. L., & Mayer, R. E. (1983). Signalling techniques to increase the understandability of expository prose. *Journal of Educational Psychology, 75*, 402–412.

Lorch, R. F. (1989). Text-signaling devices and their effects on reading and memory processes. *Educational Psychology Review, 1*, 209–234.

Lorch, R. F., & Lorch, E. P. (1996). Effects of organizational signals on free recall of expository text. *Journal of Educational Psychology, 88*, 38–48.

Lorch, R. F., Jr., Lorch, E. P., Ritchey, K., McGovern, L., & Coleman, D. (2001). Effects of headings on text sumarization. *Contemporary Educational Psychology, 26*, 171–191.

Macedo-Rouet, M., Rouet, J.-F., Epstein, I., & Fayard, P. (2003). Reading and understanding a science report through paper and hypertext – an experimental study. *Science Communication, 25*, 99–128.

Mannes, S. (1994). Strategic processing of text. *Journal of Educational Psychology, 88*, 577–588.

McDonald, S., & Stevenson, R. J. (1998). An evaluation of the effects of navigational tools and subject matter expertise on browsing and information retrieval in hypertext. *Interacting with Computers, 10*, 129–142.

Meyer, B. J. F. (1985). Prose analysis: Purposes, procedures, and problems. In B. K. Britton & J. B. Black (Eds.), *Understanding expository text* (pp. 11–64). Hillsdale, NJ: Lawrence Erlbaum Associates.

Miller, D. P. (1981). The depth/breadth tradeoff in hierarchical computer menus. *Proceedings of the Human Factors Society*, 296–300.

Mohageg, M. F. (1992). The influence of hypertext linking structures on the efficiency of information retrieval. *Human Factors, 34*, 351–367.

Nielsen, J. (1999). *Designing Web Usability: The Practice of Simplicity*. Indianapolis: New Riders.

Nilsson, R. M., & Mayer, R. E. (2002). The effects of graphical organizers giving cues to the structure of a hypertext document on users' navigation strategies and performance. *International Journal of Human-Computer Studies, 57*, 1–26.

Norman, K. (Ed.). (1991). *The psychology of menu selection*. Norwood, NJ: Ablex Publishing Co.

Potelle, H., & Rouet, J.-F. (2003). Effects of content representation and readers' prior knowledge on the comprehension of hypertext. *International Journal of Human-Computer Studies, 58*, 327–345.

Rouet, J.-F., Favart, M., Britt, M. A., & Perfetti, C. A. (1997). Studying and using multiple documents in history: Effects of discipline expertise. *Cognition and Instruction, 15*, 85–106.

Rouet, J.-F., & Levonen, J. J. (1996). Studying and learning with nonlinear documents: Empirical studies and their implications. In J.-F. Rouet, J. J. Levonen, A. P. Dillon, and R. J. Spiro (Eds.). *Hypertext and cognition* (pp. 9–24). Mahwah, NJ: Lawrence Erlbaum Associates.

Rouet, J.-F., & Vidal-Abarca, E. (2002). "Mining for meaning": A cognitive examination of inserted questions in learning from scientific text. In J. Otero, J. A. Leon, & A. C. Graesser (Eds.), *The psychology of science text comprehension* (pp. 417–436). Mahwah, NJ: Lawrence Erlbaum Associates.

Rouet, J.-F., Vidal-Abarca, E., Bert-Erboul, A., & Millogo, V. (2001). Effects of information search tasks on the comprehension of instructional text. *Discourse Processes, 31*, 163–186.

Schwartz, M. N. K., & Flammer, A. (1981). Text structure and title-effect on comprehension and recall. *Journal of Verbal Learning and Verbal Behavior, 20*, 61–66.

Shapiro, A. M. (1999). The relationship between prior knowledge and interactive overviews during hypermedia-aided learning. *Journal of Educational Computing Research, 20*, 143–163.

Smith, E. E., & Swinney, D. A. (1992). The role of schemas in reading text: A real-time examination. *Discourse Processes, 15*, 303–316.

Snowberry, C., Parkinson, S., & Sisson, N. (1983). Computer display menus. *Ergonomics, 26*, 699–712.

Spyridakis, J. H., & Standal, T. C. (1987). Signals in expository prose: Effects on reading. *Reading Research Quarterly, 22*, 285–298.

Stanton, N. A., Taylor, R. G., & Tweedie, L. A. (1992). Maps as navigational aids in hypertext environments: An empirical evaluation. *Journal of Educational Multimedia and Hypermedia, 1*, 431–444.

Tung, L. L., Debreceny, R., Chan Y. G., Chan A. T., & Le, S. E. (2003). Interacting with hypertext: An experimental investigation of navigation tools. *Electronic Commerce Research and Applications, 2*, 61–72.

Trumpower, D. L., & Goldsmith, T. E. (2004). Structural enhancement of learning. *Contemporary Educational Psychology*, 29, 426–446.

Wiley, J., & Rayner, K. (2000). Effects of titles on the processing of text and lexically ambiguous words: Evidence from eye movements. *Memory and Cognition*, 28, 1011–1021.

Wright, P. (1991). Cognitive overheads and prostheses: Some issues in evaluating hypertexts. In R. Furuta & D. Stotts (Eds.), *Proceedings of the Third ACM Conference on Hypertext* (pp. 1–12). New York: ACM Press.

Yu, B.-M., & Roh, S.-Z. (2002). The effects of menu-design on information seeking performance and users' attitude on the World Wide Web. *Journal of the American Society for Information Science and Technology*, 53, 923–933.

Zaphiris, P., Shneiderman, B., & Norman, K. L. (2002). Expandable indexes versus sequential menus for searching hierarchies on the World Wide Web. *Behaviour and Information Technology*, 21, 201–207. Retrieved May 17, 2004 from *http://www.cs.umd.edu/hcil/pubs/tech-reports.shtml#1999*

Zhang, H., & Hoosain, R. (2001). The influence of narrative text characteristics on thematic inference during reading. *Journal of Research in Reading*, 24, 173–186.

CHAPTER 20

The Site Map Principle in Multimedia Learning

Amy M. Shapiro

University of Massachusetts Dartmouth

Abstract

Site maps provide learners with a bird's eye view of a hypertext's content. The *site map principle* proposes that learners can benefit from appropriately structured site maps. Site maps can reduce cognitive load and orient learners in a hypertext. While their ability to augment learning for advanced learners in a domain has not been demonstrated (perhaps due to lack of study), there is evidence that they can be effective learning tools for domain newcomers. Laboratory work has also shown that other user variables such as learning goals mediate the process of learning with site maps. How these variables interact with each other or with specific map traits to affect learning is a question requiring further research. Nonetheless, it is recommended that developers and researchers consider characteristics of the intended users when designing site maps for educational hypertext.

What Is the Site Map Principle?

Site maps offer a bird's eye view of a hypermedia site, allowing users to get a sense of the site's content and structure. They can appear in different forms and levels of detail. In its simplest form, a site map may appear as a traditional table of contents that provides a "manifest" of a site's topics. A site map may be much more detailed, however, as it may provide a graphical representation of the site's documents and even the network of links connecting them. In this way, a site map may appear as a graphical web. Regardless of the level of detail provided by site maps, they may function either as static overviews or, more commonly, as interactive tools in which the entries serve as live links to the pages they represent. Some sites provide site maps as part of the home page, while others allow them to be accessed through a site map link or as a help menu option.

The purpose of a site map is to keep learners from "getting lost in hyperspace" while simultaneously supporting their learning goals. The site map principle proposes that beginning students learn better in hypertext environments when they receive appropriate site maps. If the devil is in the details, the demon to be wrestled here is the definition of *appropriate*. A clear and complete site map that accurately represents the hypertext will provide the best possible mechanism for keeping learners oriented. Even the clearest organization, however, can actually impede users' learning if it does not complement their learning goals. Thus, the best site maps for the purpose of learning are those that support learners' goals while accurately representing the hypertext content.

What Is an Example of the Site Map Principle?

This section will provide two examples of site maps with the intention of providing readers with a sense of how they work and may be used. Specifically, it will discuss the Web site published by The National Zoo in Washington DC (http://natzoo.si.edu). This site provides two different site maps designed to help users of different levels of sophistication use the site.

The bottom of each page on the National Zoo site contains a link to its site map. Following that link takes the user to a hierarchically structured overview of the site. The major headings of the hierarchy list the nine major sections of the site (Visit, Animals, About Us, Activities and Events, Conservation and Science, Education, Publications, Join FONZ, and Support the Zoo). The headers also serve as active links to the major subsections of the site. Under each heading appears a short paragraph that explains the general contents of that portion of the site. Embedded in each paragraph are links to pages on the site's subtopics.

The site map provides visitors with a sense of the site's structure and contents at a glance. A visitor interested in finding information about educational programs, specific animals, or the zoo's staff can narrow his or her search by browsing the bulleted listing of the site's major topics and clicking on subheadings to access the area of interest. In this way, the site map allows users to bypass irrelevant information in the site and isolate the information of greatest interest. It can also expand users' interest, however, by exposing visitors to a listing of topics about which they were unaware but may find useful.

While the site map just described is meant for general use, the home page of the National Zoo site also displays an abbreviated, iconic map targeted at children. It is simple to find, as it is the first thing one sees when entering the site. Reading skills are not necessary, as the map is comprised of a 4×4 grid of animal pictures. Each picture represents an animal family in residence at the zoo (e.g., a tiger for the great cats exhibits, an iguana for the reptiles and amphibians exhibits, etc.). Each picture doubles as an active link that takes the user to a page that provides more pictures, facts about the animals, conservation efforts, information about the exhibits, and so forth. This site map only provides links to a portion of the site, but it directs users to the topics most likely to be of interest to younger explorers.

A child interested in learning about the great apes, for example, might visit the National Zoo site as a logical place to find relevant information. Upon entering, the student is presented with the grid of images, one of which depicts a baby gorilla. Clicking on the gorilla will take the learner to the portion of the site that discusses the great apes and other primates. Once there, he or she will find links to facts about these animals in the wild and in captivity. Students can even watch the "Gorilla Cam" and observe the gorillas at the zoo in real time. Simple site maps such as this are very useful to younger learners, as they provide clear direction to specific pieces of information and require minimal cognitive effort.

The two site maps on this single web site serve as a good example of the nature of site maps, and the possible variability in their style and content. The graphical map located on the home page is directed at the least sophisticated or knowledgeable visitors to the site. Specifically, this map is directed at young learners, who may have limited reading skills. The graphical style is interesting, inviting, and easy to use. Because this group is not likely to be interested in ways to donate to the zoo or obtain zoo press packs, such information is not included in this site map. In this way, the simple map keeps children from getting lost amid information they are unlikely to need. Because young visitors are likely to be most interested in the animals, this map serves the simple purpose of listing the major animal families represented at the zoo and providing a straightforward way of navigating to those pages. In this way, the goal of learning about animals in residence at the zoo is supported by the site map.

The more comprehensive, linguistic site map is directed at users with greater sophistication. It provides much more information about the site's content than the graphical map. This site map is typical in its hierarchical structure of topics and subtopics. It is somewhat unusual in that it provides a bit of narrative about the site's content. A more typical site map generally provides a listing of topics to pages on the site without providing any context. The contextualizing paragraphs create a more "chatty," friendly feel to this site map. It also allows users to rely less on their prior knowledge, intuition, or inferences to determine where to go in order to meet their goals. The topic listings and bits of prose about each of the major sections inform visitors unfamiliar with the zoo, its programs, and the web site about these topics and direct them to sections of the site appropriate to their needs. In this sense, this site map keeps visitors oriented in the site and supports a wider array of possible learning goals than the graphical map.

What Do We Know About the Site Map Principle?

Most people have had the experience of being on a World Wide Web site and finding themselves confused about how they got where they are, how to get back to a page they visited several clicks ago, or where they are in the site. That feeling of disorientation is commonly known as being "lost in hyperspace." Getting lost in this way is detrimental to learning because it requires the learner to expend precious cognitive re-

sources on finding one's way that could otherwise be spent on learning. The goal of keeping learners oriented in a hypertext is effectively attained by providing site maps. Site maps provide learners with a bird's eye view of where they are and where they want to go, much like the familiar "you are here" maps at museums and shopping malls. As such, they can be effective tools for "finding one's way" in a hypertext (Hammond and Allinson, 1989). In their review of studies exploring the effectiveness and efficiency of hypertext-assisted learning, Chen and Rada conclude that site maps "appear to be necessary for users dealing with large and complex information structures and to be useful to resolve the problems of disorientation and high cognitive overhead" (1996, p. 149).

How or whether site maps actually improve learning is more difficult to assess, as the research findings are mixed. While detailed, clear site maps are often helpful for keeping learners oriented, several reports have cast doubt on their effectiveness as educational tools. In one such study, Wenger and Payne (1994) tested subjects' abilities to learn from hypertexts that either provided or did not provide site maps. They found that including a site map had no effect on recall or comprehension of the system's content, nor did it alter recall of text structure. The only effect of the site map was to increase the number of pages visited by users and to make their navigation more efficient. Another study reported by Niederhauser, Reynolds, Salmen, and Skolmoski (2000) also explored the effect of using site maps on learning. Niederhauser et al. presented subjects with a hypertext on learning theory and monitored the extent and quality of participants' site map use. While they found a statistically significant effect of site maps on subjects' performances on multiple choice and essay posttests, the regression analysis revealed that the effect was minimal.

Other work has produced more positive results about the educational value of site maps. The first reports of this nature appeared prior to the widespread use of hypertext. That is, researchers expended a great deal of effort understanding the role of *advance organizers* in traditional text-based learning. Advance organizers are overviews of text-based print media. The decades of research of advance organizers eventually served as a jumping off point for researchers who were interested in exploring their electronic cousins, site maps, for educational hypertext. In sum, a large body of evidence indicates the effectiveness of advance organizers in augmenting the learning outcome with traditional text (Glover & Krug, 1988; Kraiger, Salas, & Cannon-Bowers, 1995; Snapp & Glover, 1990; Townsend & Clarihew, 1989). Indeed, Mayer's (1979) analysis of the research on advance organizers concluded that advance organizers effectively promote text-based learning. His results indicated that they work by providing cues to relevant memory structures within which to embed new information.

In cases where a learner has insufficient prior knowledge to draw from, advance organizers can still be useful. Specifically, they can provide support for attaining a first understanding in a domain. For example, Townsend and Clarihew (1989) were able to show that 7-year-old through 10-year-old novices who viewed an advance organizer containing pictures outperformed others who did not see the organizer on tests of comprehension. Likewise, Mannes and Kintsch (1987) presented novice subjects with a text and one of two advance organizers. Subjects were randomly assigned to compatible and incompatible groups. The compatible group was exposed to an organizer that was structured in a similar way to the text. Those in the incompatible group, however, saw an organizer that was structured differently from the text. Mannes and Kintsch found that subjects in the consistent condition performed better on tests of recall and recognition. They interpret the results to mean that when the advance organizer and text were compatible, the organizer acted as an aid for organizing and creating an understanding of the text's content. It should also be noted, however, that those in the inconsistent condition did better on tests of problem solving. While the inconsistent organizer offered poor support for learning large portions of the text's content, it did promote the integration of some text content with prior knowledge, thus increasing problem-solving ability.

Some of the research on advance organizers has transferred nicely to learning from site maps. Indeed, it has been shown that low knowledge learners can benefit from the structure provided by a site map. For example, Potelle and Rouet (2003) provided learners with high or low prior knowledge of social psychology and presented them with hypertexts containing one of three site maps. The *hierarchical* map was a hierarchical depiction of the relationships between the documents in the hypertext. In the hierarchical map, each hypertext page was represented by a labeled box. The relationships between topics were denoted by lines connecting superordinate boxes with subordinate boxes. The *network* map presented the same nodes but used lines to represent all of the links that were actually in the hypertext. The hierarchical relationship between topics was obscured by this representation. The *alphabetical* map simply presented an alphabetical list of the seven pages contained in the hypertext.

Potelle and Rouet found that high knowledge subjects learned equivalently regardless of which site map they used. Low knowledge subjects learned significantly better with the hierarchical site map. What advantage did the hierarchical map offer? Although the network map more accurately depicted the richness of the information, it contained more links and ambiguated the topic's overall structure. As such, this representation required greater effort by the learner to use and understand. The hierarchical map may have worked better for novices because it organized and simplified the material.

Shapiro (2000) also tested the effects of site map structure on learning. In that study, subjects were presented with a hypertext that presented information about a fictional world of animals. Further, each system provided a site map structured around either animal families or ecosystems. Both systems presented the same documents about specific animals and a site map that embedded links to each animal in a hierarchy. The ecosystems condition, however, structured the site map by ecosystems (e.g., mountains, forests) while the animal families condition structured its hierarchy by animal families (e.g., birds, reptiles).

Subjects were assigned the goal of learning about either animal families or ecosystems, with the goal and site map factors fully crossed. After the learning phase, subjects were administered cued-association and card-sorting posttests as measures of conceptual structure. Strong main effects of site map structure were found on both measures, as subjects' recall and sorting patterns largely reflected the site map to which they were exposed. The learners' goals had only a small effect on the shape of conceptual structure and there were no significant interactions between goal and site map structure on any measure. These results demonstrate that the influence of a site map can be powerful enough not only to guide the structure of a learner's internal representations, but also to overshadow the effect of the learning goal during that process.

Like Potelle and Rouet (2003), Shapiro (1998) was also able to show that the effects of a site map's structure on learning is related to prior knowledge. She pretested subjects for knowledge of animal family resemblances and interspecies relationships within ecosystems. Only those tested as having poor background knowledge of ecosystems (e.g., symbiosis, predator-prey relationships, etc.) but moderate to high knowledge of animal family relationships (e.g., adaptations of and similarities between members of a given family) were included. As in Shapiro (2000), subjects were assigned to one of two goal conditions and one of two interactive site map conditions.

All groups performed equivalently on posttest items that probed knowledge of animal families. These results indicate that, even when subjects were not explicitly told about the relationships between animals in a common family, they were able to understand how each related to the others. In other words, they were able to use prior knowledge to create a coherent representation of each animal family, even when those relationships were obscured by the site map's overt structure.

The posttest of ecosystem knowledge, however, revealed the importance of site map structure when a learner's prior knowledge is sparse. Subjects who did not see the ecosystems site map performed poorly on the ecosystems posttest items. This was true even for those assigned to the ecosystems goal condition. The ecosystem site map, however, aided learners in learning about each ecosystem. The effect was strong enough to produce incidental learning effects, as subjects who were not assigned to the ecosystems goal condition also learned more about ecosystems than those who were asked to learn about ecosystems but were shown the animal families site map. Thus, learners with low prior knowledge of ecosystems were better able to learn about ecosystems when the site map was structured so as to make that information explicit. There is evidence, then, that the effectiveness of a site map may hinge on an interaction between site map structure, a learner's level of domain expertise, and his or her learning goals. When learners have sufficient prior knowledge, they require less help to create an integrated understanding of a hypertext's content. The explicit pointers provided by site maps to the relationships between documents or ideas, however, may aid those with less knowledge. If the learning goal is to understand a new aspect of a topic, the organization of a site map can either help or hinder that effort.

The importance of matching a site map to learners' goals has been demonstrated in other studies. Dee-Lucas and Larkin (1995) gave learners hypertexts equipped with either structured (hierarchical) or unstructured (alphabetical index) site maps. A third group read the same information as the hypertext groups but read it in traditional text format. That group received no site map for the text. All subjects were asked to learn the content but were provided with no well-defined learning goal. Dee-Lucas and Larkin found that the traditional text group was outperformed by both hypertext groups on a post-test of learning. Despite the differences in their site maps, there was no difference between the two hypertext groups. In a second experiment, however, learners were given the explicit goal of summarizing the material they read. In all other ways this experiment was identical to the first. Subjects using the structured site map in experiment 2 outperformed those using the unstructured site map.

It is reasonable to hypothesize that the goal acted as a motivator, as it put subjects on notice that they would be tested. The goal also provided direction to learners, giving them a better idea of what aspects of the material to focus on. This explanation is consistent with the notion of *encoding specificity*, which suggests that memory is encoded differently depending upon how the learner believes it will be used in the future (Leonard & Whitten, 1983). Because of encoding specificity, a defined goal can have an enormous effect on the nature of memory for a hypertext. Recognizing main topics and how they relate to one another is important if one is to be called upon to summarize the material. While an index merely lists the main topics, a hierarchy organizes information in a way that highlights main ideas and makes their relationships very clear. The hierarchical site map, then, provided a structure that was compatible with the goal of summarizing the hypertext. It would seem that such compatibility is important to learning from site maps. This result is similar to that of Shapiro (2000), who also found that novice subjects' abilities to meet their learning goals was enhanced when the site map was structured to match those goals.

What Are the Limitations of Research on the Site Map Principle?

As described in the previous section, there appears to be some degree of contradiction within the literature that explores the effectiveness of site maps on learning. Some found little or no effect of site maps while others found significant effects for certain users. What underlies these seeming contradictions? One reason may be differences in the control conditions against which site maps are compared across studies. Some studies have compared the learning of subjects using site maps with others who are given no site map. Other studies have compared groups using a graphical site map with another using linguistic site maps. Some experimental site maps have been structured while others provide only alphabetical indexes. In short, whether site maps have shown to be effective depends, in part, on what they are compared to.

The differences between studies exploring graphical versus linguistic site maps has been discussed by Chen and Rada (1996) in their review of hypertext learning research. They compiled the results of seven studies that compared the effectiveness of graphical and textual site maps (Leidig, 1992; Monk, Walsh, & Dix, 1988; Nosek & Roth, 1990; Simpson, 1990; Simpson & McKnight, 1990; Vicente & Williges, 1988; Wey, 1992). They concluded that whether a site map is graphical or textual appears to influence its effectiveness. Specifically, they found that the graphical maps were more effective in all studies, with a medium-to-large combined effect size ($r = .38$). They conclude that "a graphical map is a very important factor that can improve the effectiveness and efficiency of interacting with a hypertext system" (1996, p. 149). It is important to note, however, that Wenger and Payne (1994), who found no effect of their site map on learning, used a graphical site map. It is clear, then, that the question of whether site maps improve learning does not hinge *solely* on the simple question of whether a site map is graphic or linguistic.

Another reason for the seemingly contradictory findings of site map studies may be the role of factors mediating their use. Studies discussed in the previous section demonstrate that learners' goals and prior knowledge are relevant to the effectiveness of a site map. It is likely that learners' metacognitive ability is also important. Although I know of no studies conducted specifically to test that premise, metacognition has proven to be important in a wide array of learning outcomes studies (Azevedo, Guthrie, Wang, & Mulhern, 2002; Azevedo, Seibert et al., 2002; Brown, 1987; Kauffman, 2002). Because of such consistent findings, the role of metacognition in the process of learning from site maps is a reasonable place to search for answers. When evaluating research on site maps, then, it is important to consider that learners' goals and prior knowledge (and perhaps their metacognitive ability) mediate the process of learning with site maps to determine (a) whether a site map will facilitate learning and (b) what sort of site map will facilitate learning.

Finally, another drawback of the literature on site maps is the lack of reported fieldwork. Because of the strong evidence suggesting that learners' goals are relevant to their hypertext use and learning, studying site map use in real contexts is vital. How are site maps really used by students of various ages and expertise levels? How does the nature of their learning goals affect site map use? Without sufficient data on how students use site maps in naturalistic settings and how that use affects learning, the literature is incomplete.

In sum, while the site map principle specifies that appropriate site maps may augment learning for domain novices, much more research is needed to determine what an appropriate site map is. The answer to that question is likely to change depending on the characteristics of the hypertext in question and the nature of a learner's goals, knowledge, and abilities.

What Are the Implications of the Research for Cognitive Theory?

A number of cognitive theories have been used to explain the results obtained in empirical studies of site maps' educational values. Among these is the construction-integration model (Kintsch, 1988), which proposes that learned information is incorporated or stored in macrostructures. Macrostructures are comprised of information units or propositions that are linked by virtue of their association. As such, macrostructures store and organize knowledge. When new information is learned, each proposition from a text or hypertext is stored and connected with related propositions.

Macrostructures may be formed from the content of a text or hypertext alone. Such structures are called *text bases*. Their structure mirrors that of the original source and contains no information from outside that source. When the learner's prior knowledge becomes incorporated with the text base, a larger macrostructure called a *situation model* is formed. Because prior knowledge enhances the content of the knowledge stored in a textbase, the situation model is representative of a learner's deeper understanding.

Other theories have also relied on the notion of combining old information with new information to arrive at deeper understanding. For example, Ausubel's (1968, 1969, 1977) assimilation theory also incorporates the notion of prior knowledge as the foundation for learning. Specifically, it proposes that meaningful learning requires the activation of existing structures during or after study.

The construction-integration model predicts the results of studies that have demonstrated the interaction between learners' prior knowledge and the effectiveness of site maps. For example, Potelle and Rouet (2003) found that the structure of a site map did not effect learning for high knowledge subjects. For those with low knowledge of the domain, however, use of a hierarchical map enhanced learning about macrostructural content (i.e., the content of the hypertext as a whole, as opposed to propositions contained on specific pages, or the microstructural content) over that of a more complicated network or index. The construction-integration model can account for this finding by explaining that the hierarchical map promoted the construction of a text base for the novices. Because a hierarchy clarifies and organizes the relationships between ideas, subjects were able to construct mental representations (text bases) that accurately reflected the material in question. For more knowledgeable learners, a well-organized site map is unnecessary because they already have a knowledge base to draw from as they attempt to organize and understand the hypertext.

The construction-integration model can also account for observations made by Shapiro (2000). In that study, learners with some knowledge of animal families but little knowledge of ecosystems were shown site maps structured either by animal families or ecosystems. All subjects learned about animal families yet only those who saw the ecosystem map learned about ecosystems. The construction-integration model would explain that the existing knowledge of animal families provided these subjects with a macrostructure into which information about animal families from the hypertext could be incorporated. As such, they did not need the map to provide a structure. Because the subjects had little knowledge of ecosystems, only those who saw the ecosystem map were able to create a structured representation for the ecosystem information and learn about that topic.

Cognitive flexibility theory was proposed in an attempt to explain the flexible nature of knowledge and may also explain much of the experimental results reviewed in this chapter (Spiro, Coulson, Feltovitch, & Anderson, 1988; Spiro, Feltovitch, Jacobson, & Coulson, 1992; Spiro & Jehng, 1990; Spiro, Vispoel, Schmitz, Samarapungavan, & Boerger, 1987). In developing this theory, Spiro and his colleagues noted that those who know a lot about a domain generally have the ability to apply their knowledge to new problems, generate new knowledge, or understand new information more fully. According to cognitive flexibility theory, they are able to do so because they actively reconstruct their knowledge of a domain each time it is invoked. In other words, the nature and structure of knowledge is not static, but changes each time it is used. As Spiro et al. explain, "The reconstruction of knowledge requires that it first be deconstructed – flexibility in applying knowledge depends both on schemata (theories) and cases first being disassembled so that they may later be adaptively reassembled" (1988, p. 186). The implication of this theory is that advanced learning takes place not only as a consequence of active learning and prior knowledge use, but also as a consequence of constructing knowledge anew for each novel problem.

Spiro and colleagues have proposed that the nature of hypertext offers the opportunity to learn a domain in such a way as to promote expertlike flexibility of knowledge. They use the metaphor of "criss-crossing a landscape" to explain their theory. Because hypertext is nonlinear, they propose that it can expose learners to a topic from multiple perspectives. They propose that the kind of understanding gleaned from such activity is deeper and more flexible than that obtained from a linear presentation, offered from a single perspective.

The results of Shapiro (2000) are also predicted by cognitive flexibility theory. Because learners in that experiment already possessed knowledge about the nature of animal families, those who saw the site map organized by ecosystems were offered a new perspective on the topic. Those who saw the animal families site map were presented with the material from a familiar perspective. The animal families site map group learned about animal families but not ecosystems, while those who saw the ecosystems map learned about both subtopics. Cognitive flexibility theory would explain that seeing information from an unfamiliar perspective allowed the ecosystems site map group to gain a fuller understanding of the hypertext's content.

In sum, studies of learning with site maps do not serve to support either of these theories over the other. Much of the laboratory evidence, however, may be explained quite satisfactorily by both.

What Are the Implications of the Research for Instructional Design?

This chapter notes a number of limitations of the site map research that constrain their interpretation. The next section of this chapter will propose some productive areas for future research based on the issues raised previously. Until those issues are fully addressed the use of site maps in instructional systems must be approached cautiously. With this caveat in mind, the research does suggest some guidelines for profitable site map use.

First, site maps are likely to be useful in very large systems where the possibility of becoming lost or disoriented is high. Keeping learners oriented may indirectly enhance learning, as it allows learners to focus their efforts on learning rather than finding their way.

The question of how to craft site maps to best support learning directly is less clear. The data do suggest, however, that it is important to keep users' individual characteristics in mind. For example, there is little or no evidence that advanced learners in a domain will reap any benefit from site maps beyond that obtained by staying oriented in hyperspace. Novices are most likely to profit directly from site maps. Simple maps that show the content and structure of a hypertext in a clear, unambiguous way (such as a hierarchy) are most effective. A site map's structure can determine how they will organize the material and what aspect of it will become most salient to them. For intermediate learners, a site map may augment learning by providing a new perspective on existing knowledge, thereby enhancing their understanding of a domain.

Finally, it is also suggested that site maps should be structured to support the goals of a learner. Because learners using a given system in an educational context are likely to vary significantly in their knowledge and learning goals, it may prove beneficial for educators to create multiple versions of a site map and supply students with the one most appropriate for an assigned learning goal.

What Are Some Productive Future Directions for Research?

The most pressing area for future research is in disentangling the contradictory research on learning with site maps. As noted previously, some studies have shown a positive effect of site maps on learning while others have not. The real effect of site maps on learning will only be disambiguated by gaining a full understanding of the interplay between the site map and learner characteristics that are relevant to hypertext-based learning. The research discussed here suggests that the relevant variables are the user's prior knowledge and goals, the structure of the site map, and the graphical versus linguistic nature of the map. Other important variables are likely to be learners' metacognitive ability, the level of detail contained in the map, and the size of the hypertext. Tergan (1997) has noted the hypertext size variable as a confounding factor in the comparison of hypertext-based learning research in general. Controlling for hypertext size has not been done in any site map studies of which I am aware.

Creating a robust, cohesive understanding of a hypertext's global content is not a simple task. For novices, a well-designed site map can provide an initial structure for the domain in question and augment learning. Work reported by Potelle and Rouet (2003) and Shapiro (1998) have demonstrated that simple hierarchical site maps can be effective in this way. Little work has focused on site map use among more advanced learners, however. Perhaps due to this oversight, little laboratory evidence has been found to suggest that high knowledge learners benefit much from site maps. Nonetheless, both the construction-integration model (Kintsch, 1988) and cognitive flexibility theory (Spiro et al., 1988; 1990; 1992) predict that high knowledge learners will learn more when presented with materials that encourage the use of prior knowledge. With this in mind, studying characteristics of site maps that may encourage prior knowledge use could be a productive area of inquiry. Patterns of successful site map use among advanced learners would also be informative to educators, designers, and theorists.

It would also be interesting to see whether incidental learning is boosted through the use of site maps. Wenger and Payne (1994) found that site maps increased the amount of a hypertext read by their subjects. While their posttests found that the increase did not parlay into increased learning, there is reason to pursue this line of inquiry. Specifically, it would be interesting to see whether site map use is related to enhanced incidental learning for users who are given a broadly defined learning goal in a large hypertext. Within such a context, it is reasonable to hypothesize that the increase in information access observed by Wenger and Payne could translate into greater incidental learning.

As mentioned previously, metacognition is likely to be important to learning from site maps. In spite of metacognition's consistent appearance as a relevant variable in learning across a variety of contexts, little or no work has been done specifically to explore how it may affect learning from site maps. This gap in the literature is important, in part, because metacognition and prior knowledge are highly correlated. Because prior knowledge has been shown to be important to the effectiveness of site maps, it is important to isolate these variables' respective effects.

While it is important to determine the degree to which metacognition affects learning with site maps, it is also important to determine if site maps can improve metacognition. Wenger and Payne (1994) found that their subjects visited more of the site and used better navigation strategies when they were allowed to see a site map. This finding suggests that the site map enabled learners to recognize what information they were missing and to take action to remedy that state. Because such actions are a hallmark of metacognition, it is reasonable to explore that relationship further.

In the more distant future, the study of adaptive site maps should be a profitable area of research, as well. That is, once a fuller understanding of how the interplay between site map structure and user characteristics affects learning is gained, the field will be ready to explore adaptive site maps. Adaptive site maps could be constructed to fit the profile of a given learner and his or her learning goal. Theoretically, the relevant information could be entered into an intelligent module that would generate a site map tailored for each user. Once the relevant parameters have been identified, research on such adaptive modules should be very productive.

Glossary

Advance organizer: A linguistic or graphical representation of the organization of main ideas in a text.

Hypertext: A collection of electronic text documents containing links that move users to related documents. The addition of sound or visual resources transforms hypertext into hypermedia.

Metacognition: The ability to question one's own knowledge state, recognize its strengths and weaknesses, and take steps to remedy errors or fill in missing pieces.

Site map: A graphical or linguistic representation of the organization of a hypertext.

Situation model: The mental representation of one's deep understanding of a domain that may integrate information from a variety of sources.

Text base: The mental representation of information contained in a single text.

References

Ausubel, D. P. (1968). *Educational psychology: A cognitive view.* New York: Holt, Rinehart and Winston.

Ausubel, D. P. (1969). A cognitive theory of school learning. *Psychology in the Schools,* 6(4), 331–335.

Ausubel, D. P. (1977). The facilitation of meaningful verbal learning in the classroom. *Educational Psychologist,* 12(2), 162–178.

Azevedo, R, Guthrie, J., Wang, H-Y., & Mulhern, J. (2001, April). *Do different instructional interventions facilitate students' ability to shift to more sophisticated mental models of complex systems?* Paper presented at the annual meeting of the American Educational Research Association, Seattle, WA.

Azevedo, R, Seibert, D, Guthrie, J., Cromley, J., Wang, H.-Y., & Tron, M. (2002, April). *How do students regulate their learning of complex systems with hypermedia?* Paper presented at the annual meeting of the American Educational Research Association, New Orleans, LA.

Balajthy, E. (1990). Hypertext, hypermedia, and metacognition: Research and instructional implications for disabled readers. *Journal of Reading, Writing, and Learning Disabilities International*, 6(2), 183–202.

Brown, A. (1987). Metacognition, executive control, self-regulation, and other more mysterious mechanisms. In F. E. Weinert and R. H. Kluwe (Eds.), *Metacognition, motivation, and understanding* (pp. 60–108). Hillsdale, NJ: Lawrence Erlbaum Associates.

Chen, C., & Rada, R. (1996). Interacting with hypertext: A meta-analysis of experimental studies. *Human-Computer Interaction*, 11, 125–156.

Clark, R. C., & Mayer, R. E. (2003). *E-Learning and the science of instruction: Proven guidelines for consumers and designers of multimedia learning*. San Francisco: Jossey-Bass/Pfeiffer.

Dee-Lucas, D., & Larkin, J. H. (1995). Learning from electronic texts: Effects of interactive overviews for information access. *Cognition and Instruction*, 13(3) 431–468.

Glover, J., & Krug, D. (1988). Detecting false statements in text: The role of outlines and inserted headings. *British Journal of Educational Psychology*, 58(3), 301–306.

Hammond, N., & Allinson, L. (1989). Extending hypertext for learning: An investigation of access and guidance tools. In K. Bice & C. H. Lewis (Eds.), *Proceedings of the ACM CHI 80 Human Factors in Computing Systems Conference*. New York: ACM Press.

Kauffman, D. (2002, April). *Self-regulated learning in web-based environments: Instructional tools designed to facilitate cognitive strategy use, metacognitive processing, and motivational beliefs*. Paper presented at the annual meeting of the American Educational Research Association, New Orleans, LA.

Kintsch, W. (1988). The use of knowledge in discourse processing: A construction integration model. *Psychological Review*, 95, 163–182.

Kraiger, K., Salas, E., & Cannon-Bowers, J. (1995). Measuring knowledge organization as a method for assessing learning during training. *Human Factors*, 37(4), 804–816.

Leidig, P. (1992). *The relationship between cognitive styles and mental maps in hypertext-assisted learning*. Dissertation abstracts International, Vol. 53(5-A), p. 1372.

Leonard, J. M., & Whitten, W. B. (1983). Information stored when expecting recall or recognition. *Journal of Experimental Psychology: Learning, Memory, and Cognition*, 9, 440–455.

Mayer, R. E. (1979). Twenty years of research on advance organizers: Assimilation theory is still the best predictor of results. *Instructional Science*, 8, 133–167.

Mannes, B., & Kintsch, W. (1987). Knowledge organization and text organization. *Cognition and Instruction*, 4, 91–115.

Monk, A., Walsh, P., & Dix, A. (1988). A comparison of hypertext, scrolling, and folding as mechanisms for program browsing. In D. M. Jones & R. Winder (Eds.), *People and computers IV*, pp. 421–435. Cambridge, UK: Cambridge University Press.

Niederhauser, D. S., Reynolds, R. E., Salmen, D. J., & Skolmoski, P. (2000). The influence of cognitive load on learning from hypertext. *Journal of Educational Computing Research*, 23(3), 237–255.

Nosek, J., & Roth. I. (1990). A comparison of formal knowledge representation schemes as communication tools: Predicate logic vs. semantic network. *International Journal of Man-Machine Studies*, 33, 227–239.

Potelle, H., & Rouet, J.-F. (2003). Effects of content representation and readers' prior knowledge on the comprehension of hypertext. *International Journal of Human-Computer Studies*, 58, 327–345.

Shapiro, A. M. (1998). The relationship between prior knowledge and interactive organizers during hypermedia-aided learning. *Journal of Educational Computing Research*, 20(2), 143–163.

Shapiro, A. M. (2000). The effect of interactive overviews on the development of conceptual structure in novices learning from electronic texts. *Journal of Educational Multimedia and Hypermedia*, 9(1), pp. 57–78.

Simpson, A. (1990). The interface to a hypertext journal. In D. Diaper, D. Gilmore, G. Cockton, & B. Shackel (Eds.), *Human-Computer Interaction-INTERACT'90* (pp. 869–874). Amsterdam: North-Holland.

Simpson, A., & McKnight, C. (1990). Navigation in hypertext: Structural cues and mental maps. In R. McAleese and C. Green (Eds.), *Hypertext: state of the art*. Oxford, England: Intellect.

Snapp, J., & Glover, J. (1990). Advance organizers and study questions. *Journal of Educational Research*, 83(5), 266–271.

Spiro, R, Coulson, R., Feltovitch, P., & Anderson, D. (1988). Cognitive flexibility theory: Advanced knowledge acquisition in ill-structured domains. In *Proceedings of the Tenth Annual Conference of the Cognitive Science Society* (pp. 375–383). Hillsdale, NJ: Lawrence Erlbaum Associates.

Spiro, R., Feltovitch, P., Jacobson, M., & Coulson, R. (1992). Cognitive flexibility, constructivism, and hypertext: Random access instruction for advanced knowledge acquisition in ill-structured domains. In T. Duffy & D. Jonassen (Eds.), *Constructivism and the technology of instruction: A conversation* (pp. 57–75). Hillsdale, NJ: Lawrence Erlbaum Associates.

Spiro, R. J., & Jehng, J. C. (1990). Cognitive flexibility and hypertext: Theory and technology for the nonlinear and multidimensional traversal of complex subject matter. In D. Nix & R. Spiro (Eds.), *Cognition, education, and multimedia: Exploring ideas in high technology* (pp. 163–205). Hillsdale, NJ: Lawrence Erlbaum Associates.

Spiro, R., Vispoel, W., Schmitz, J., Samarapungavan, A., & Boerger, A. (1987). Knowledge acquisition for application: Cognitive flexibility and transfer in complex content domains. In B. Britton & S. Glynn (Eds.), *Executive control processes in reading* (pp. 177–199). Hillsdale, NJ: Lawrence Erlbaum Associates.

Tergan, S. (1997). Conceptual and methodological shortcomings in hypertext/hypermedia design and research. *Journal of Educational Computing Research*, 16(3), 209–235.

Townsend, M., & Clarihew, A. (1989). Facilitating children's comprehension through the use of advance organizers. *Journal of Reading Behavior*, 21(1) 15–35.

Vicente, K. J., & Williges, R. C. (1988). Accommodating individual differences in searching a hierarchical file system. *International Journal of Man-Machine Studies*, 29, 647–668.

Wenger, M. J., & Payne, D. G. (1994). Effects of a graphical browser on readers' efficiency in reading hypertext. *Technical Communication: Journal of the Society for Technical Communication*, 41, pp. 224–233.

Wey, P. S. (1992). *The effects of different interface presentation modes and users' individual differences on users' hypertext information access performance.* Unpublished doctoral dissertation, University of Illinois at Urbana Champagne (University Microfilms No. 93-05730).

CHAPTER 21

Prior Knowledge Principle in Multimedia Learning

Slava Kalyuga
University of New South Wales

Abstract

This chapter summarizes research and theory concerned with the effects of learner prior knowledge on multimedia learning principles. In many situations, design principles that help low-knowledge learners may not help or even hinder high-knowledge learners. The main theoretical issue associated with the prior knowledge principle concerns the integration in working memory of instructional information with information held in long-term memory. The major implication for instructional design is the need to tailor instructional formats and procedures to changing levels of expertise. Essential future research directions include identifying instructional procedures that are optimal for different levels of expertise and developing viable instruments of cognitive diagnosis of schematic knowledge structures suitable for real-time online evaluation of learner progress.

What Is the Prior Knowledge Principle?

Design principles for multimedia learning environments depend on the prior knowledge of the learner: design principles that help low-knowledge learners may not help or even hinder high-knowledge learners. Many multimedia design recommendations do not explicitly refer to learner knowledge levels, although most of them have only been tested in experiments with learners who had limited experience in the relevant domain. Could the same recommendation be applied to more experienced learners? Experienced or high-knowledge learners are considered learners who have substantial previously acquired knowledge in a specific domain and who are involved in learning relatively new, more advanced information in this domain. The evidence suggests that multimedia design recommendations for such learners

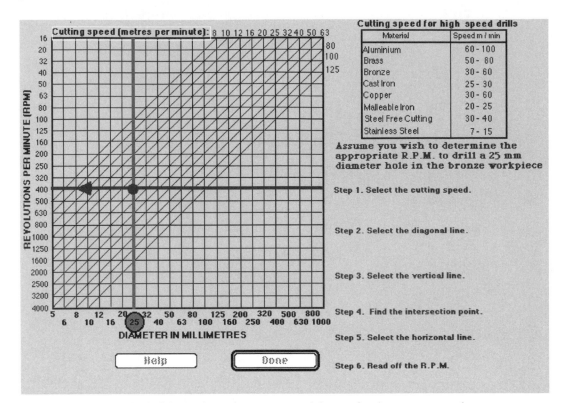

Figure 21.1. A snapshot of the multimedia instructional format for the cutting speed nomogram. Adapted from Kalyuga, Chandler, & Sweller (2000). Copyright © 2000 by the American Psychological Association, Inc.

should be different, sometimes contrary to recommendations for novice learners.

What Is an Example of the Prior Knowledge Principle?

Figure 21.1 shows a snapshot of a multimedia instructional presentation on how to use the depicted diagram (which is called the cutting speed nomogram) to determine the appropriate number of revolutions-per-minute needed to drill a hole of a given size in the given material. When a learner clicks on any of the displayed headings of sequential steps, corresponding auditory explanations are provided simultaneously with screen-based animations and selected highlights of the appropriate elements of the nomogram (e.g., lines, intersection points, material names, moving flashing arrows). This instruction was designed according to established multimedia design principles. It involves learning both from words and pictures rather than from words alone or pictures alone (multimedia principle), and uses animation and narration rather than animation and on-screen text (modality principle). Corresponding words and visual images (highlighted elements of the nomogram) are synchronized in time (contiguity principle). The learner's attention is directed by highlighting and flashing appropriate elements of the diagram (signalling principle). Learners can control the order and pace of presentation by clicking on corresponding headings (interactivity principle). Learners start learning with fully worked-out examples that provide guidance in how to use the nomogram rather than engage in unguided exploration of procedures or problem solving (worked-out examples principle). According to the multimedia design principles, this instructional presentation should be an effective learning procedure.

Figure 21.2 represents an alternative format of the same instructional episode. This diagram-only format contains the nomogram without any textual (visual or auditory) explanations. Instead, learners can explore the nomogram by constructing their own tasks and trying to solve them. To provide assistance in locating intersection points and tracing corresponding numbers on the axes, the computer display may allow learners to highlight any line by clicking on it (a repeated click would eliminate the highlight). Nevertheless, this exploratory-like instructional format violates most of the previously mentioned multimedia design principles and therefore might be expected to be ineffective.

When materials similar to these were used in actual training sessions (Kalyuga, Chandler, & Sweller, 2000) with learners who were novices in the domain and had never used nomograms before, the previously mentioned predictions about the effectiveness of the instructional formats were confirmed. The multimedia format was a very effective learning tool, and the diagram-only format was much less helpful for most of the students. However, when the same students gradually (over several training sessions) acquired more experience in using similar nomograms with some variations, and later were required to learn how to use yet another variation, the best format was a diagram-only format. Surprisingly, using diagram-only formats to instruct experienced trainees in using new types of nomograms produced better performance outcomes than using fully explained and well-detailed multimedia instructions.

Thus, as levels of learner knowledge in a domain changed, relative effectiveness of different instructional formats reversed. Design principles that helped low-knowledge learners did not help, but hindered, high-knowledge learners. Such a reversal in the relative effectiveness of instructional procedures is referred to as the *expertise reversal effect* (Kalyuga, Ayres, Chandler, & Sweller, 2003). The effect generally occurs when high-information instruction is

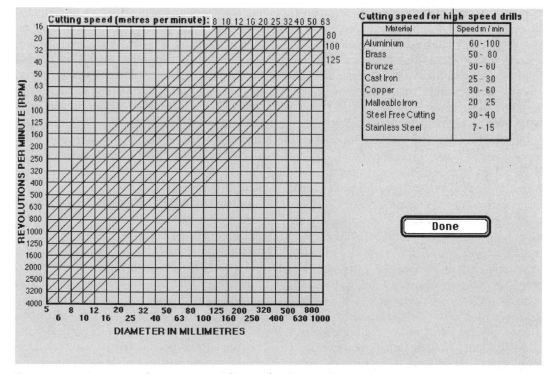

Figure 21.2. Diagram-only instructional format for the cutting speed nomogram.

beneficial for novices when compared with the performance of novices who receive a low-information format, but is disadvantageous for more expert learners when compared with the performance of experts who receive a low-information format. It should be noted that experts do not necessarily perform worse in absolute terms compared to novices. Rather, experts' performances are worse in relative terms, when compared to other experts who learn the new material using an alternative format.

What Do We Know About the Prior Knowledge Principle?

The need for instructional designers to consider levels of learners' knowledge in a domain has been well recognised as an example of an aptitude-treatment interaction between learner characteristics and instructional treatment (e.g., Cronbach & Snow, 1977; Lohman, 1986; Mayer, Stiehl, & Greeno, 1975; Snow & Lohman, 1984). Some early studies in multimedia instruction indicated that multimedia learning was effective only for low-knowledge learners. For example, reviews of earlier research in learning from text and graphics revealed that using graphics in text usually improved the learning of students with low prerequisite-knowledge levels, but had little effect on those with high prior-knowledge levels (Kozma, 1991; Levie & Lentz, 1982).

Studies of multimedia learning by Richard Mayer and his associates demonstrated that well-designed multimedia instructional presentations better support the cognitive processes of low knowledge than high-knowledge learners (Mayer, 1999; 2001). Mayer and Gallini (1990) compared text-only instruction with different formats of text-and-illustrations instruction. Low-knowledge learners who studied texts accompanied by fully explanatory illustrations labelling parts and operating stages of a device (e.g., brakes, pump, or generator) significantly improved their retention and problem-solving transfer-test performances

in comparison with text-only instruction. Mayer, Steinhoff, Bower, and Mars (1995) compared a separate text and illustration format with integrated text and illustrations explaining the mechanism of lightning development. An expected split-attention effect (see chapter 8) on the transfer test was obtained only for low-knowledge learners, but not for high-knowledge learners. Although a full expertise reversal was not observed in those studies, elimination of beneficial effects of multimedia presentations was obtained with increases in expertise providing considerable evidence for the prior knowledge principle. Mayer (2001) computed an effect size difference for each of those experiments by subtracting the effect size for the high-knowledge learners from the effect size for the low-knowledge learners. Median effect size differences were 0.60 for retention questions and 0.80 for transfer. The multimedia effect was 0.60 and 0.80 standard deviations stronger for low-knowledge learners than for high-knowledge learners. The effect was called the "individual differences principle" (Mayer, 2001, p. 161) and explained by high-knowledge learners' use of their knowledge to compensate for a lack of instructional guidance.

Ollerenshaw, Aidman, and Kidd (1997) compared the effects of several formats of instruction explaining the operation of technical objects (pumps). Text-only, text with diagrams labelling parts, text with diagrams depicting major stages of operation, and text with a computer-based animated simulation of the objects' operation labelling parts and operating stages were used. They found that students with low prior knowledge clearly benefited most from the multimedia computer-simulated diagrams. Effect size differences computed by subtracting the effect sizes for the high-knowledge learners from the effect sizes for the low-knowledge learners using higher standard deviation values (conservative estimations of effect sizes) based on Ollerenshaw et al. (1997) data tables are represented in Table 21.1. The beneficial effects of the multimedia format for low-knowledge students were substantially

Table 21.1. Prior Knowledge Effect: Summary of Results

Source	Instructional Formats	Effect Size Difference	Percent Gain Difference
Mayer (2001) Medians for a series of studies	Text and illustrations vs. text only		
	Retention questions	0.60	157
	Transfer questions	0.80	61
Ollerenshaw et al. (1997)	Multimedia vs. text only	0.62	100
	Multimedia vs. text with diagram labelling parts	0.51	55
	Multimedia vs. text with diagram labelling operating stages	−0.23	−33
Pollock et al. (2002)	Isolated-interacting vs. interacting-interacting elements		
Experiments 1 and 2	Low-element interactivity test	0.57	90
	High-element interactivity test	0.75	87
	Test of the practical application	0.87	123
Experiments 3 and 4	Low-element interactivity test	0.84	131
	High-element interactivity test	1.69	150
Cooper et al. (2001)	Studying vs. imagining procedure		
Experiments 2 and 3		2.23	180
Experiment 4		1.66	221
Kalyuga et al. (1998)	Diagram + embedded text vs. diagram-only		
	Operation and troubleshooting test	2.11	135
	Fault-finding test	2.77	131
Kalyuga et al. (2000)	Animated diagram with narrated text vs. diagram-only	1.80	153
Kalyuga, Chandler, Tuovinen, and Sweller (2001)	Worked examples vs. problem solving		
Experiment 1	Writing programs for relay circuits	0.67	74
Experiment 2	Writing switching equations for circuits	0.49	65
Kalyuga, Chandler, and Sweller (2001), Experiment 2	Worked examples vs. exploratory learning	1.02	148

reduced when that format was used for high-knowledge students (i.e., a small effect size increase was still obtained for multimedia instruction in comparison with text and diagram labelling operating stages).

Hegarty, Quilici, Narayanan, Holmquist, and Moreno (1999) did not obtain the expected benefits from using hypermedia-based instructional materials on the operation of machines using animation coupled with narration compared to static paper-based text-and-diagram presentations. A suggested possible explanation for the failure was that students' prior knowledge and familiarity with the machines had not been taken into account. Knowledgeable participants were able to understand the operation of the machines from static diagrams only and mentally animate those diagrams rendering redundant any additional explicit textual explanations.

Pollock, Chandler, and Sweller (2002) developed an isolated elements instructional technique to improve learning of complex technical devices by initially presenting complex material as a set of isolated elements of information that could be processed serially, rather than simultaneously, in working memory. The material used was high in element interactivity (see chapter 2) where element interactivity refers to the number of elements that need to be processed simultaneously in working memory in order to understand the material. Learners saw only brief headings of sequential steps (isolated elements) without detailed explanations of each step and relations between them. This technique could reduce possible cognitive overload and assist learners in acquiring some partial basic schemas that, in turn, could be expected to reduce working memory load during subsequent learning from the fully explained complex material. Thus, the initial learning with limited understanding could result in better understanding at the following stages of instruction. Pollock et al. (2002) demonstrated that the isolated elements instruction followed by the fully interacting elements instruction (explaining the application and operation of complex devices using diagrams and text) was a more effective instructional procedure for novice learners in comparison with the traditional approach that used complex materials during both stages. However, there were no differences between the methods for learners who possessed some relevant prior knowledge in the domain. Estimations of effect size differences between the low-knowledge and high-knowledge learners associated with learning from the isolated-interacting elements instructions on conducting the insulation resistance test and operation of an electrical circuit used to power an industrial oven in comparison with the interacting-interacting elements instruction, based on Pollock et al. (2002) data tables are represented in Table 21.1. The isolated-interacting elements instructions clearly benefited only low-knowledge learners providing evidence for the prior knowledge principle.

Another example of an interaction between levels of learner expertise and formats of multimedia instruction was provided by Cooper, Tindall-Ford, Chandler, and Sweller (2001) who investigated the imagination effect in instruction. This effect occurs when imagining procedures and concepts produces better instructional outcomes than simple studying of examples. Learners were asked to imagine the procedures described in a computer-based instructional presentation on how to use a spreadsheet application (a set of diagrams with embedded textual explanations of sequential steps) rather than simply study the material. In this study, high-knowledge students who had appropriate prerequisite schemas to incorporate the interacting elements and support constructing and running corresponding mental representations, found the imagining technique more beneficial for learning compared to the simple study of the material. Low-knowledge students, on the other hand, had to process all components of instruction as individual elements in limited working memory. The imagining procedure had a negative effect for these students compared to studying.

Estimated effect size differences (Table 21.1) based on Cooper et al.'s (2001) data tables indicated that the positive effect of the imagining worked-examples instruction for higher-knowledge students was substantially increased. The effect reversed depending on the learners' knowledge level, providing a clear example of the prior knowledge principle. When studying worked examples, low-knowledge learners constructed new schemas of complex procedures that contained many interacting elements. More knowledgeable learners already had such schemas and studying the worked examples was a redundant activity for these learners. Imagining corresponding procedures provided additional practice for these learners leading to a higher degree of schema automation.

Kalyuga, Chandler, and Sweller (1998, 2000, 2001) conducted a series of studies that were specifically designed to investigate interactions between multimedia instructional formats and levels of learner expertise (the expertise reversal effect; see Kalyuga, Ayres, Chandler, & Sweller, 2003 for an overview) and demonstrated that the effectiveness of different multimedia design principles might drastically depend on levels of learner expertise in a domain. Instructional techniques that were very effective with low-knowledge learners became ineffective and eventually had negative consequences when used with more knowledgeable learners.

Kalyuga, Chandler, and Sweller (1998, Experiment 1) found that novice industrial trainees benefited significantly from detailed visual textual explanations embedded into the diagrams of wiring diagrams compared to trainees who were presented with a diagram-alone format. As levels of the trainees' expertise in the domain increased (Experiment 2), the relative improvement in performance of the trainees who learned from the diagram-only instructions was superior to those who studied the integrated diagram-and-text instructions resulting in similar levels of performance. Much more experienced trainees (Experiment 3) learned new circuits significantly more efficiently with wiring diagrams-only instructions compared to trainees who studied the detailed explanations format. In addition, the high-knowledge trainees reported increased mental effort (measured by subjective ratings of learning difficulty) associated with studying the integrated text-and-diagram format. Estimated effect size differences between the initial and final stages of this longitudinal study are represented in Table 21.1. Instruction designed according to multimedia and split-attention principles (chapters 7 and 8) was effective for novices but ineffective for more knowledgeable learners, thus demonstrating an expertise reversal effect.

According to the modality principle (chapter 9), learners can integrate textual explanations and pictures more effectively when the text is narrated rather than presented in an on-screen form. However, for high-knowledge learners narrated explanations may become redundant and reduce learning effectiveness. Kalyuga et al. (2000) demonstrated that for inexperienced industrial trainees (Experiment 1, Stage 1), an on-screen animated diagram combined with simultaneously narrated detailed explana-

tions (Figure 21.1) was the most effective instructional format (test questions required application of learned procedural steps in different new task situations). However, when the trainees became more experienced in the domain after several intensive training sessions that were identical for all participants (Experiment 1, Stage 2) the relative advantage of a narrated text format (used with a different modification of the nomogram) vanished while the corresponding diagram-alone condition became more effective. Finally, when the trainees further increased their knowledge in the domain after additional intensive training (Experiment 2), the animated diagram-alone format group significantly outperformed the diagram with narrated text group, effectively reversing the results of the first stage (Table 21.1). A cognitive load explanation of the results was supported by subjective ratings of learning difficulty collected at each stage of the experiment.

According to the worked-out-example principle (chapter 15), properly designed worked-out examples providing full instructional guidance are often more effective than instructional procedures with none or limited guidance such as problem-solving or exploratory (discovery) learning. In a longitudinal study conducted by Kalyuga, Chandler, Tuovinen, and Sweller (2001), inexperienced mechanical trainees benefited from computer-based worked-out examples of procedures for writing programs for relay circuits (in programmable logic controllers) more than from problem-solving practice. The worked-out examples group performed better (test questions required trainees to write programs for circuits with different numbers of components) with lower ratings of learning difficulty. However, as the participants were gradually trained to become more experienced in the domain, the comparative effectiveness of conditions became indistinguishable. Although a full reversal effect was not observed in this experiment, a substantial effect size reduction was obtained (Table 21.1). Experiment 2 used a similar experimental design with different materials (writing Boolean switching equations for relay circuits) in the domain that was more familiar to the trainees at that stage. Initially there was no difference between conditions but eventually, after additional intensive training in the domain, the learning of new materials was better supported by problem solving than by worked-out examples (the effect size difference is represented in Table 21.1).

Tuovinen and Sweller (1999) compared worked-out examples with an exploratory-based instructional approach to learning how to use a database program. Low-knowledge students benefited more from worked-out examples, while there were no differences between instructional procedures for higher-knowledge students. Kalyuga, Chandler, and Sweller (2001, Experiment 2) compared a series of computer-based worked-out examples of how to construct switching equations for relay circuits with an exploratory learning environment in which learners were invited to construct their own circuits (using an interactive screen-based template) and then write switching equations for those circuits. Initially, the worked-out examples group performed better (test questions required trainees to select the correct switching equations for circuits with a different number of components). As the knowledge level of trainees was raised as a consequence of the training sessions, the exploratory group demonstrated better results than the worked-out examples group (Table 21.1). In this study, two levels of task were investigated: simple tasks with a very limited problem space and a small number of possible options to explore, and complex tasks with a larger problem space and numerous options to explore. The previously described effect-reversal pattern was obtained only for the complex tasks. There were no differences between the procedures for the simple tasks.

What Are the Limitations of Research on the Prior Knowledge Principle?

In the reviewed studies, a full reversal effect was obtained only in strictly controlled ex-perimental conditions in longitudinal studies where the same learners were gradually trained in relatively narrow domains from a novice to a relatively expert state. Accordingly, the level of complexity of learned materials was also gradually increased, so that experts always learned relatively new and more complex information in the same domain. Selecting appropriate instructional materials was a time-consuming and challenging part of the experimental planning in those studies. On the one hand, an instructional domain should be narrow enough to allow increases in the level of expertise in a reasonable amount of time (weeks or months). On the other hand, it should be expandable to allow gradual increases in the complexity of tasks. Technical areas with many wiring diagrams, switching circuits, and nomograms were used in the experiments because their levels of complexity could be easily manipulated by changing the numbers of elements involved, while retaining the same set of general operating principles.

The research on the prior knowledge principle is a logical extension of the aptitude-treatment interactions (ATI) approach. However, although the need for instructional designers to consider levels of learners' knowledge in a domain has been well recognised as part of that approach and notwithstanding thirty years of ATI research, few instructional design research studies and their recommendations show explicitly how to use the ATI approach in practice. It is important not just to demonstrate an expertise reversal effect (or other examples of an ATI), but to investigate new instructional procedures and techniques that will deal with it. A major limitation of the research on the prior knowledge principle is the limited number of studies of new techniques and procedures for optimization of instructional presentations at different levels of learner expertise.

An important part of the optimization problem is the availability of appropriate measures of levels of expertise in a domain. Questionnaires and rating scales of familiarity with specific knowledge areas that were used in most of the reviewed studies are very coarse-grained measures lacking sufficient diagnostic potential. They are hardly suitable for the evaluation of different levels of acquisition of schematic knowledge structures that is necessary for an appropriate tailoring of instructional procedures to levels of learner expertise. Schema-based methods of cognitive diagnosis are required as an essential means of optimizing instructional presentations.

What Are the Implications of the Research for Cognitive Theory?

Prior knowledge has been considered as one of the factors contributing to individual differences in the effect of instruction for a long time, together with visual, spatial, and other cognitive abilities, learning skills, and learning styles (Schnotz, 2002). Based on the analysis of functions of pictorial illustrations in text, Carney and Levin (2002) concluded that the supportive effect of visual displays was evident mostly for individuals with low prior-knowledge learning complex subject matter. Investigating students' learning from maps and texts, Verdi and Kulhavy (2002) noted prior knowledge as an essential factor that influenced their model of learning. Prior knowledge determines how students process information, and provides them with a framework for orienting the material and linking it to what they already know. Schnotz, Picard, and Hron (1993) demonstrated that successful learners used graphic information in a time zone map in a different way than unsuccessful learners did. The successful learners (university students) used graphics more intensively and concentrated on information that was relevant to the construction of a mental model (without calling upon textual information). Similar individual differences in strategies used to comprehend weather maps by experienced meteorologists and nonmeteorologists were observed by Lowe (1993). The meteorologists used their high-level knowledge structures to process the material and construct rich mental models, while novices concentrated on surface spatial features of the maps.

Commenting on those studies, Mayer (1993) highlighted the need for deeper understanding of individual differences in integrating text and graphics in order to improve the instructional use of graphics.

Studies of expert–novice differences have demonstrated that the schematic knowledge base held in long-term memory is the most critical characteristic of competent performance in any subject area (e.g., Chi, Feltovich, & Glaser, 1981; Chi & Glaser, 1985; Chi, Glaser, & Farr, 1988; Ericsson & Smith, 1991; Reimann & Chi, 1989; Sternberg & Frensch, 1991). Domain-specific knowledge structures held in long-term memory, when activated and brought into working memory, allow high-knowledge learners to treat many elements of related information in working memory as a single higher-level element, thus reducing the total cognitive load. However, instructional designs do not always allow high-knowledge learners to take advantage of their knowledge base. Mayer (1989) noted that the prior knowledge that a learner brings to the learning situation is a major factor influencing construction of a conceptual model for the to-be-learned material: more knowledgeable learners already have and spontaneously use their sophisticated models that may conflict with models presented in instructional materials. The cognitive conflict between available and presented cognitive constructs and the need to reconcile them might be a major cause of cognitive overload resulting in the expertise reversal effect.

The main theoretical issue associated with the prior knowledge principle concerns the integration in working memory of instructional information with information held in long-term memory. Presenting detailed instructional explanations to knowledgeable learners may interfere with retrieval and application of available schemas, especially if the learners cannot ignore or otherwise avoid processing the explanations. According to the general model of multimedia learning (chapter 3), these schemas must be integrated in working memory with instructional explanations, and this integration requires an appropriate share of working memory capacity. When an instructional message forces knowledgeable learners into activities that support construction of schemas that they have already acquired in addition to schema retrieval and application, the redundant activities may overload working memory capacity resulting in reduced learning outcomes.

The expertise reversal effect might be incorporated into a more general framework that considers cognitive processes along with the instructional procedures directed to a specific level of learner knowledge. As learners gradually move from being novices to experts in a domain, their dominant cognitive activities gradually change (Sweller, 2003). For novices, construction of new schemas represents the prevailing activity that needs to be appropriately supported by instructional materials. Providing detailed textual (visual or auditory) explanations together with animated pictures in proper formats (e.g., worked examples) might be optimal for these learners. At this stage, the learners do not have many relevant, preacquired cognitive structures available for retrieval from long-term memory, so minimal instruction (e.g., problem statements alone or diagrams alone) would not constitute appropriate instructional formats.

As learners progress toward intermediate levels of knowledge, the importance of such limited instruction increases. Some lower-level or partial schemas have been already acquired at this stage. The learners can retrieve and use these schemas. Instructional procedures supporting construction of such schemas become redundant. They unnecessarily consume scarce cognitive resources, distracting learners from more appropriate activities of constructing new, unavailable schemas. The more expert a learner is, the more irrelevant (nonoptimal) such instructional messages become. Diagrams alone, problem statements alone, and so forth, associated with previously acquired cognitive structures become more appropriate and cognitively efficient. Thus, the simultaneous presence of knowledge-based and rich instruction-based cognitive constructs when processing the same information may substantially increase cognitive load and

have negative consequences for more knowledgeable learners.

What Are the Implications of the Research for Instructional Design?

The prior knowledge principle has been supported by a large number of studies using a range of instructional materials and participants, and involving most of the previously described multimedia learning principles. This chapter reviewed empirical studies supporting the prior knowledge principle and showed that this principle has a plausible theoretical explanation within a cognitive load framework. The need of high-knowledge learners to integrate and cross-reference redundant instructional explanations with their available knowledge structures may place an excessive load on limited working memory resources. A minimal instructional format without redundant guidance would allow more experienced learners to use their available schema-based knowledge structures held in long-term memory in the most efficient way. The most important implication of this principle for instructional design is that, to be effective, instructional design should be tailored to changing levels of learner expertise.

The general strategy for tailoring instructions to levels of learner expertise is to gradually replace high-structured instructional procedures and formats with low-structured instructions as knowledge levels increase. This strategy can be related to the instructional design principle of scaffolding (van Merriënboer, Kirschner, & Kester, 2003), which requires providing novice learners with considerable information in the form of worked-out examples but gradually reducing worked-out example support as levels of expertise increase. A possible approach is to use a series of worked-out examples, completion assignments, and conventional problems combined in a completion strategy (van Merriënboer, 1990). This strategy incorporates a variety of instructional procedures from fully worked-out examples with complete task solutions to conventional problems. Studies have demonstrated the instructional effectiveness of completion tasks that present a problem statement and a partial solution to learners who then must complete the solution (van Merriënboer & de Croock, 1992; van Merriënboer & Paas, 1989). Renkl (1997), Renkl and Atkinson (2003), and Renkl, Atkinson, and Maier (2000) suggested that, with increased levels of learner knowledge in a domain, detailed well-guided worked-out examples should be gradually faded out and replaced with problem-solving steps (the faded worked-out example technique). Renkl, Atkinson, Maier, and Staley (2002) demonstrated that a fading out procedure is superior to a sudden switch to problems (the guidance fading effect).

The isolated-interacting elements instructional technique that artificially removes complex interactions between elements (Pollock et al., 2002) could also be used to reduce cognitive overload and assist novices at the initial stages of learning complex materials, before being replaced with fully interactive elements as learners acquire some partial basic schemas in the domain. Initially permitting novice learners to control the speed of an animation in multimedia presentations could assist these learners in obtaining familiarity with isolated elements within specific animation "frames" and benefit them more than using a fully system-controlled high-element interactivity animation (Mayer & Chandler, 2001). As levels of learner expertise in a domain increase, more low-structured instructional environments such as system-paced presentations with minimal or no textual explanations, exploratory (discovery) learning environments, or problem-solving exercises could be used to assist high-knowledge individuals in learning advanced complex materials in their area of expertise (Kalyuga et al., 2001).

What Are Some Productive Future Directions for Research?

If multimedia instructional formats need to change significantly with alterations in learners' knowledge levels, learner-adapted instructional procedures optimized according to learner levels of expertise are needed. An essential future research direction is identifying instructional designs and procedures that are optimal for different levels of expertise. Also, the development of user-adapted instructional systems requires simple instruments that would allow rapid and accurate measures of learner levels of expertise. Such cognitive diagnostic tools should be suitable for real-time online evaluation of learner progress and adaptation of instructional procedures to changing levels of expertise. However, at present, no such cognitively oriented assessment procedures are available to be used in conjunction with the new instructional design principles.

When dealing with high-level cognitive activities in complex domains, long-term memory structures associated with components of working memory create long-term working memory structures with characteristics that are different from those of working memory in knowledge-lean situations (Ericsson & Kintsch, 1995). A possible approach to rapid evaluation of a learner's level of expertise in a domain could be based on the assessment of the content of her/his long-term working memory when the learner approaches tasks in the domain, and the extent to which working memory load has been reduced by schematic knowledge structures retrieved from long-term memory.

Glossary

Experienced learners (also *expert, advanced learners, high-knowledge learners*): Learners who have previously acquired substantial knowledge in a specific domain and are involved in learning relatively new, more advanced information in this domain.

Expertise reversal effect: Reversal in the relative effectiveness of instructional formats or procedures as levels of learner knowledge in a domain change. Represents a strong form of the prior knowledge principle when

CHAPTER 22

The Cognitive Aging Principle in Multimedia Learning

Fred Paas

Open University of the Netherlands

Pascal W. M. Van Gerven

Maastricht University

Huib K. Tabbers

Tilburg University

Abstract

We show that age-related cognitive changes necessitate considerations for the design of multimedia learning environments. These considerations mainly relate to the *cognitive aging principle*, which states that limited working memory may be effectively expanded by using more than one sensory modality, and some instructional materials with dual-mode presentation may be more efficient than equivalent single-modality formats, especially for older adults. The principle is based on the *modality effect* and *multimedia effect* that have been researched extensively in the context of Sweller's (1999) *cognitive load theory* (CLT) and Mayer's (2001) *cognitive theory of multimedia learning* (CTML). The research on cognitive aging in relation to multimedia processing is reviewed to explore current understanding of age-related design principles for multimedia learning environments. The potential implications of age-related cognitive changes for the design of multimedia learning environments are highlighted and complemented with important future directions in multimedia learning. The role of CLT and CTML as versatile frameworks for the design of multimedia learning environments for the elderly is discussed.

The Cognitive Aging Principle in the Design of Multimedia Learning

Demographic and technological developments will lead to a growing proportion of independent, active, and eager-to-learn elderly adults who in their everyday lives are more and more confronted with multimedia applications, such as learning environments. Generally, these learning environments consist of many relevant and irrelevant information elements, which are presented together at a fast pace and through different sensory modalities. Consequently, for meaningful understanding to commence, people have to deal with high cognitive load, efficiently increase activation of relevant information, suppress activation of irrelevant information, and integrate the information across the auditory and visual channels. This makes multimedia understanding a difficult goal to achieve for people at all ages but, due to cognitive changes across the life span, especially for older people.

In multimedia learning people typically have to deal with information from several sources. However, combining different sources of information is only advantageous to learning if it supplies information about the learning task that is unavailable from any single source. If the different information sources are relevant to each other and need to be coordinated, a correspondence has to be established between them. If these sources are not relevant or redundant to each other, interference may be experienced across modalities and only the information that is necessary for ongoing processes needs to be processed and the information that is not necessary needs to be suppressed. The ability to integrate different sources of information is not only considered an essential process in the understanding of multimedia learning material, but also in many of today's everyday activities, such as the processing of information from television, which involves the integration of information across the auditory and visual channels. So, an important question is to what extent the elderly learner is capable of the integrative processing required by multimodal presentation.

In this chapter we argue that the juxtaposition of increased longevity and growing dependence on technology poses interesting challenges for instructional designers. We show that age-related cognitive changes necessitate considerations for the design of multimedia learning environments. Multimedia learning environments that support the cognitive functions involved in the processing of multimedia, might be expected to be particularly helpful for older adults and to make multimedia learning not only a necessary, but also an enjoyable experience. The structure of this chapter is as follows. First, the central findings of cognitive

aging research that are relevant to multimedia understanding are discussed. It will be argued that to exploit the benefits of multimedia learning environments for older people, it is important to understand the cognitive changes that occur in older adults. Second, a multitheoretical approach drawing on dual-coding theory, cognitive load theory, and the cognitive theory of multimedia learning is presented as a promising basis for the design of powerful multimedia-based learning environments. By providing a theoretical framework for the age-related cognitive changes, educational designers are able to identify older adults' special instructional needs regarding multimedia learning and to create instructional design solutions that accommodate age-related cognitive declines. Third, the cognitive aging principle, its associated research, and its implications for instructional design are presented. Fourth, guidelines for instructional design are derived from other potentially relevant effects regarding age-related cognitive changes with implications for multimedia processing. Finally, the general guidelines that follow from these lines of research are discussed.

Cognitive Aging

The aging brain is characterized by widespread decreases in neural and metabolic efficiency, which compromise the computational capacity needed for high cognitive performance (Reuter-Lorenz, Stanczak, & Miller, 1999). Not surprisingly, one of the central findings in cognitive aging research is that the efficiency of working memory operations declines with age in adults. A major focus of recent cognitive aging research has been on various explanations proposed to account for this decline. The most popular explanations are based on reduced working-memory capacity, slowed processing speed, difficulties inhibiting selected-against or irrelevant information, and deficits in integrative or coordinative aspects of working memory.

The *reduced working memory capacity view* suggests that an age-related loss of available capacity impairs the ability to engage in demanding operations. Indeed, there is a substantial body of evidence to support the hypothesis that age-related declines in cognitive performance are most likely to occur in complex cognitive tasks requiring effortful processing (e.g., Gilinski & Judd, 1994; Salthouse, Mitchell, Skovronek, & Babcock, 1989; Wingfield, Stine, Lahar, & Aberdeen, 1988). Because these tasks are highly dependent upon the availability of sufficient cognitive resources for their successful completion, these tasks are disproportionately compromised by age-related declines in cognitive capacity. Older adults appear to be slower than younger adults especially when tasks become more complex or require large amounts of mental processing. With regard to the *reduced processing speed view*, variations in speed have often been argued to be at the center of observed age differences in performance (Fisk & Warr, 1996; Salthouse, 1994, 1996).

According to several recent theories that propose an active suppression or inhibition process that operates directly on unselected or distracting information, efficient selection is achieved not only by enhancing availability of selected information, but also by suppressing responses to irrelevant information (e.g., Hartman & Hasher, 1991; Hasher & Zacks, 1988; Stolzfus, Hasher, Zacks, Ulivi, & Goldstein, 1993; Zacks & Hasher, 1997). Older people, however, cannot inhibit selected-against or irrelevant information to the same extent as younger adults (Adam et al., 1998; Spieler, Balota, & Faust, 1996; Stolzfus et al., 1993). Consequently, irrelevant or extraneous information imposes more load on the cognitive system of older adults than younger adults according to this *reduced inhibition view*.

The *reduced integration or coordination view* has received empirical support from various studies. With regard to deductive reasoning, Light, Zelinski, and Moore (1982) found that older adults were not able to integrate information across several premises even when these premises could be accurately recognized. Much of the macrospatial research comparing memory for routes of young and old adults has found that mem-

ory for both novel and familiar environments decreases with age (e.g., Kirasic, Allen, & Haggerty, 1992; Lipman & Caplan, 1992). Older individuals' memory for landmarks is relatively unimpaired, but they have difficulty with more integrative aspects involved in layout memory (Lipman & Caplan, 1992). Using figural transformation tasks, Mayr and collaborators (Mayr & Kliegl, 1993; Mayr, Kliegl, & Krampe, 1996) were able to show that age-related slowing is larger in coordinative complexity than in sequential complexity conditions. According to Mayr and Kliegl, sequential complexity refers to any task manipulation that leads to a variation in the number of independent processing steps but does not increase the amount of information exchange between single steps. Coordinative complexity refers to the amount of coordinative processing required to regulate and monitor the flow of information between interrelated processing steps.

With the various explanations for the age-related declines in the efficiency of working memory operations in mind, it is clear that to make electronic learning environments accessible to seniors, instruction needs to compensate for their reduced processing capacity, cognitive slowing, and lack of inhibition. However, it should be noted that for instructional manipulations to become effective, instructional designers have to deal with sensory deficits in the form of age-related changes in vision and hearing. These deficits necessitate special attention to the presentation of visual and auditory information. Especially, older adults' auditory processing problems may hamper their understanding in multimedia learning environments. Therefore, special attention should be given to the audio component in multimedia learning materials. Based on our knowledge about age-related declines in the efficiency of working memory operations, we argue that a multitheoretical approach drawing on dual-coding theory, cognitive load theory, and the cognitive theory of multimedia learning can be considered a promising framework for the design of powerful electronic learning environments for older adults.

THE COGNITIVE AGING PRINCIPLE

Although multimedia learning in older adults seems to establish an inevitable paradox, research on the proper design of electronic learning environments has defined new dimensions in the lifelong learning debate. Existing theories on instructional design and the integration of verbal and pictorial learning material have appeared to be of direct relevance to older learners. In this section, we will focus on three of the most important theories in this field: Paivio's (1986) classical dual-coding theory, Sweller's (1999; Paas, Renkl, & Sweller, 2003, 2004) cognitive load theory, and Mayer's (2001) cognitive theory of multimedia learning. We will describe the potential benefits of these theories for elderly learners and present some recent empirical findings. First of all, however, we will briefly describe the cognitive architecture on which these theories are based.

The Cognitive Architecture of Learning

Basically, there are three levels at which audiovisual information is processed by the cognitive system. First, there is the sensory level, which can be defined as the initial registration of visual and auditory information in the iconic and echoic stores. Second, there is the level of working memory, which according to Baddeley (1992, 2003) consists of two modality-specific slave systems. These slave systems – a phonological loop and a visuospatial sketchpad – hold information for a limited amount of time. In this period, information can be manipulated by a central executive and in some cases information is transferred to the long-term store. The long-term store establishes a third level of processing: the representational level. The representational level is not so much a final stage, in which information is fixed into a permanent form, but rather a dynamic network of interconnected elements, which is almost constantly altered by a frequent inflow of fresh information.[1]

This cognitive architecture bears an important constraint. Where the long-term store is theoretically unlimited with respect to its storage capacity, working memory is particularly limited in the amount of information it can handle. Because working memory serves as a gate to long-term memory, this has considerable consequences for the learning process. The limited processing capacity of working memory can be compensated in at least two ways, however. First, new information can be connected to prior knowledge in the long-term store, which accelerates the transfer of information to long-term memory (Ericsson & Kintsch, 1995). Often, however, prior knowledge is not available. Therefore, a second strategy is to present information such that it is absorbed in a highly efficient manner. This is exactly the aim of most theories of instructional and multimedia design.

Theories of Multimedia Design

Instructional interventions are primarily directed at the working memory level and indirectly at the representational level. That is, working memory plays a key role in transferring knowledge to the long-term store, but is the only cognitive level which can be directly addressed using the sensory level. Instructional interventions can optimize both the quality and the quantity of knowledge transfer. According to *dual coding theory* (Paivio, 1986), the quality of knowledge acquisition can be enhanced by encoding information both verbally and nonverbally. It is assumed that long-term memory incorporates separate stores for verbal and nonverbal information. However, associated elements are interconnected. Essentially, dual coding theory states that verbal and nonverbal representations have equal valence, but that a combination of verbal and nonverbal encoding enhances retrieval of knowledge from the long-term store. The philosophy of dual coding theory is considered to be of great importance to education (Clark & Paivio, 1991) and was adopted by subsequent theories on instructional and multimedia design. However, these theories do not so much stress the importance of dual coding on the representational level, but rather on the level of working memory.

The first instructional theory adopting the dual-coding principle is CLT (Paas et al., 2003, 2004; Sweller, 1999; Sweller, Van Merriënboer, & Paas, 1998). CLT acknowledges the limited capacity of the modality-specific stores in working memory by advocating the use of dual stores to prevent either one of these stores from getting overloaded. At the same time, it considers the educational practice of presenting graphical, nonverbal information visually and related textual, verbal information through the auditory channel as a way to effectively expand the capacity of working memory for learning. Most importantly, the cross-modal presentation of verbal and nonverbal information stimulates the process of dual coding and integration. This has proven to be a successful learning strategy (e.g., Kalyuga, Chandler, & Sweller, 1999; Leahy, Chandler, & Sweller, 2003; Mousavi, Low, & Sweller, 1995; Tindall-Ford, Chandler, & Sweller, 1997). Another reason for adopting a bimodal dual-coding approach is that it prevents the learner from extraneous visual search between printed text and corresponding parts of a diagram. That is, if diagrams are accompanied by narrated explanations, the learner does not need to split his or her attention between interdependent textual and pictorial information sources. However, if the complexity of the diagram is too high, visual cues are needed to prevent visual search and direct the learner's gaze to the relevant parts of the picture (Jeung, Chandler, & Sweller, 1997).

The principles of dual coding were further refined in Mayer's (2001) *cognitive theory of multimedia learning* (CTML). This theory stresses integration of audiovisual information at the working memory level. A number of concrete recommendations have been formulated to optimize this integration process (for a recent overview, see Mayer & Moreno, 2003). Apart from the modality effect, the most important recommendations of CTML are based on the following five effects, which all yield enhanced learning. The *coherence effect* is obtained if interesting, but redundant information, such as background music, is stripped out as much as possible (Mayer, Heiser, & Lonn, 2001; Moreno & Mayer, 1999). The *signaling effect* occurs if parts of the pictorial material are highlighted at moments that they are referred to in the narration (Mautone & Mayer, 2001). The *redundancy effect* is obtained if visual material is accompanied by auditory commentary instead of both auditory and visually presented commentary (Mayer, Heiser, & Lonn, 2001). Finally, there are two "contiguity effects." The *spatial contiguity effect* is found if text is printed near the corresponding parts of a diagram, so that visual search is minimized (e.g., Moreno & Mayer, 1999; Sweller & Chandler, 1994). The *temporal contiguity effect* is obtained if narration and diagrams are presented simultaneously rather than successively (e.g., Chandler & Sweller, 1992; Mayer, Moreno, Boire, & Vagge, 1999).

Given the interplay between the findings from cognitive aging research and these theories, we describe a framework for multimedia instructional design for the elderly. Beneficial learning effects of multimedia learning environments based on the preceeding theories have already been obtained in young adults. As we will see in the next section, the principles of these learning environments happen to be particularly helpful to seniors. It is peculiar, therefore, that research interests have only recently shifted toward older learners.

Mapping Multimedia Design on the Needs of Older Learners

Recall that apart from sensory deficits, elderly learners have to cope with at least four cognitive declines: (1) reduced working memory capacity (e.g., Wingfield et al., 1988), (2) reduced cognitive speed (e.g., Salthouse, 1996), (3) reduced inhibition (e.g., Hasher & Zacks, 1988), and (4) reduced integration (e.g., Mayr et al. 1996). These declines mark a general reduction of cognitive efficiency. The good news is that cognitive efficiency is exactly what the aforementioned theoretical approaches are aimed at. With respect to CLT, this idea was theoretically elaborated by Van Gerven, Paas, van Merriënboer, and Schmidt

Table 22.1. Cognitive Aging Declines and Possible Compensatory Multimedia Strategies

Cognitive Decline	Compensatory Multimedia Strategy	Corresponding Effect(s)
Reduced working memory capacity	Bimodal (audiovisual) presentation	Modality effect
Reduced cognitive speed	Bimodal (audiovisual) presentation	Modality effect
	Enhanced timing	Temporal contiguity effect
	Omitting redundant information	Coherence effect
		Redundancy effect
Reduced inhibition	Omitting redundant information	Coherence effect
		Redundancy effect
	Attention scaffolding	Signaling effect
		Spatial contiguity
Reduced integration	Bimodal (audiovisual) presentation	Modality effect
	Enhanced timing	Temporal contiguity effect
	Enhanced layout	Spatial contiguity effect
	Omitting redundant information	Coherence effect
		Redundancy effect

(2000). Van Gerven et al. state that because the "total cognitive capacity" of elderly learners is smaller than that of young learners, the potential gain from enhanced instruction is proportionally greater. This was empirically established by Paas, Camp, and Rikers (2001), who showed that instruction designed according to CLT can compensate for age-related cognitive declines. They studied the differential effects of goal specificity on maze learning among 40 young and 40 old adults. The hypotheses that the presence or absence of a specific goal would disproportionately compromise or enhance, respectively, the elderly's performance were confirmed. Although young adults outperformed old participants in all conditions, these differences were much smaller in the nonspecific goal conditions. Although this study has no multimedia component, it suggests that attempts to engineer the instructional control of cognitive load by using the modality effect might also be effective in compensating for age-related cognitive declines. It seems that for older learners efficient learning strategies are likely to be a matter of "all or nothing." More specifically,

in the elderly these strategies may determine the difference between no comprehension on the one hand and at least minimal comprehension on the other hand. Most importantly, however, all the aforementioned deficits can theoretically be tackled with well-designed multimedia instructions (see Table 22.1 for an overview).

Let us first consider reduced working memory capacity. As we have seen, the visual and auditory components of working memory have a limited capacity. Because this seems even more the case in the elderly, addressing both the visual and the auditory working memory components might be especially beneficial to older learners. In the context of CLT, this idea was first explored by Van Gerven, Paas, van Merriënboer, Hendriks, and Schmidt (2003). They found training with audiovisually presented worked examples to be more efficient than training with purely visually presented worked examples in that lower levels of experienced cognitive load led to comparable performance levels on a transfer test. Comparable results were found in a subsequent study by Van Gerven, Paas, van

Merriënboer, and Schmidt (2004a). Although in neither of these studies was found a proportionally greater modality effect in the elderly, the results are promising. Unfortunately very little research has been done on the modality effect in elderly learners. Among the few, Constantinidou and Baker's (2002) research suggests that especially the visual modality plays a beneficial role in verbal learning by older adults.

The second important decline to be tackled is reduced cognitive speed. The most important problem with reduced cognitive speed is the "simultaneity mechanism" (Salthouse, 1996; see also Salthouse & Babcock, 1991), which is the failure to integrate interdependent information elements in working memory, because the activation of one element has dissipated by the time a later element is activated. There are multiple strategies to deal with this problem. First, a bimodal presentation of learning material would be of great help, because it enables parallel processing. The simultaneity mechanism is less likely to occur if the lag between visual and auditory material is as short as possible, that is if audiovisual information is processed in parrallel rather than in serial. An optimal timing of visual and auditory information is crucial, of course. Temporal contiguity – that is, simultaneous rather than successive presentation of auditory and visual material – is the best possible strategy in this respect. Another strategy is to avoid the processing of irrelevant information. This can preclude an unnecessary delay between two mutually dependent information elements entering working memory and thus prevent the simultaneity mechanism.

The third problem to cope with is reduced inhibition. This deficit concerns both the failure to suppress irrelevant information originating from long-term memory (e.g., Hasher & Zacks, 1988) and the failure to ignore distracting stimuli in the visual field (e.g., Hasher, Stolzfus, Zacks, & Rypma, 1991). The most straightforward strategy to tackle this problem is to prevent irrelevant information from entering working memory by omitting redundant information as much as possible (cf. the coherence and redun-

dancy effect). A second strategy is to scaffold visual attention. Basically attention should be focused on information that is relevant on a certain moment and not on information that is irrelevant at that moment (but may become relevant in the future). This can be achieved by simply highlighting those parts of the visual field that are important at a given time (cf. the signaling effect). A second technique is to minimize the perceptual distance between interdependent information elements (e.g., text and figures; cf. the spatial contiguity effect). This would reduce the chance of attending to irrelevant information.

The fourth and final important problem that needs to be instructionally controlled is the difficulties that older people experience with the coordinative processing required to regulate and monitor the flow of information between interrelated processing steps, and the integration of the information (Mayr & Kliegl, 1993). The instructional actions that can be taken to support these cognitive processes closely resemble those related to reduced cognitive speed. In particular, an optimal timing in the form of temporal contiguity of visual and auditory information is considered important. Additionally, for older people it is particularly important to use a combination of visual and auditory sources of information only if it supplies information about the learning task that is unavailable from any single source. To prevent interference across modalities, redundancy of information should be prevented at all times.

Future Directions in Multimedia Learning

Two approaches to the design of multimedia learning environments that have only recently been investigated might be especially beneficial for older learners. First of all, although the beneficial effects of adding learner control to instructional materials are not totally undisputed (see Williams, 1996, for a discussion), some promising results have been reported in the field of multimedia learning (Mayer & Chandler, 2001; Mayer, Dow, & Mayer, 2003; Tabbers,

Martens, & van Merriënboer, 2001, 2004). Secondly, presenting multimedia material in a part-whole sequence has been shown to result in better and more efficient learning as well (Mayer & Chandler; Mayer, Mathias, & Wetzell, 2002; Pollock, Chandler, & Sweller, 2002). Both ways of dealing with the cognitive load of the instructions will be discussed here in relation to the cognitive aging effect.

The issue of adding learner control to multimedia instructions has been put forward by Tversky, Morrison, and Bétrancourt (2002), who report the disappointing results of earlier research comparing instructive animations with static pictures. Tversky et al. conclude that most animations cannot be perceived accurately as a result of cognitive constraints on the learner's side. According to their *apprehension principle*, instructive animations should be designed with these constraints in mind. One major way of achieving this goal is by giving the learner control over the instruction in such a way that the learner can adapt the instructional material to his or her cognitive system. One major control option is allowing learners to set the pace of the instruction. Studies by Mayer and Chandler (2001) and by Mayer et al. (2003) showed beneficial effects of giving learners control over the pacing of their multimedia instructions in terms of learning results. Moreover, in studies by Tabbers et al. (2001, 2004), learning pacing seemed to undo the negative cognitive effects of learners having to split their attention between visual text and graphics.

The implications of these results for older learners are evident. Because age-related slowing is larger in coordinative complexity than in sequential complexity and older people may differ substantially in processing speed, it is very important to design multimedia learning environments with learner-controlled rather than system-controlled pacing. Moreover, supplying the learners with more elaborate interactive tools that help them navigate through the learning materials, zoom in and out of an animation, and change viewing perspective, might have the potential of being especially helpful for the older learner. On the other hand, these interactive tools require coordination and proper handling, and therefore impose an extra load on the learner's mind that might be detrimental to older learners. Further research will have to reveal the potential benefits and pitfalls of adding tools for user interaction to multimedia learning environments, especially for older learners.

A second approach that might help taking the load off the older learner's mind in multimedia learning is the part-whole approach. With multimedia instruction, the learner has to process a great amount of information in a short period of time and working memory is easily overloaded. One way of dealing with this information overload is presenting some parts of the information *before* presenting the whole instruction. This way, the information can get stored in long-term memory and subsequently be processed with less cognitive effort. For example, Mayer and Chandler (2001) showed that presenting their multimedia learning material in parts before presenting it as a whole yielded better learning results than first presenting the whole animation and then the parts.

A similar problem arises when instructional materials describe machines or systems that contain a lot of smaller elements. Although the instruction might be on the functioning of the total system, the learner is overwhelmed by all the new elements that have to be taken into account. Again, a good strategy to reduce cognitive load is presenting the separate components *before* presenting the whole system. According to the *two-stage theory of mental model construction* introduced by Mayer et al. (2002), the learner first constructs several component models of the elements, and only then constructs a causal model of the system. In their experiments, Mayer et al. obtained results that supported the theory and that showed that pretraining led to better learning results with instructional animations than no pretraining or training after the animation. Pollock et al. (2002) found similar results using paper-and-pencil instructions about electrical systems.

The part-whole strategy seems to be very suitable for designing multimedia instruction for the elderly. Especially because older people are less able to inhibit information about parts that are not relevant at a given moment and have more trouble coordinating and integrating the different elements in an instruction, learning the separate elements before turning to the causal functioning of the system seems to be the most effective and efficient way of learning. However, this has yet to be shown empirically.

In sum, both learner control and the part-whole strategy seem to be very promising ways of dealing with the effects of cognitive aging. A further issue that researchers in the field could focus on is a combination of the two strategies. Presenting information about the parts of a system or animation in an interactive manner, so that the learner can control whether and when information is shown, might lead to a cognitively optimal situation of just-in-time information presentation (see Kester, 2003; Kester, Kirschner, van Merriënboer, & Baumer, 2001). At the same time, however, care should be taken not to overload the cognitive system with too many interactive tools, which might have just the opposite effect on learning.

Discussion

In this chapter we argued that age-related cognitive impairments in the efficiency of working memory operations necessitate considerations for the design of multimedia learning environments. The nature of these impairments mainly relates to declines in cognitive capacity, processing speed, inhibition of irrelevant information, and the integration of different sources of information. Cognitive load theory and the cognitive theory of multimedia learning were identified as versatile frameworks to deal with the declines in multimedia learning environments. To enable instructional designers to compensate for age-related cognitive declines, both theories were used to formulate instructional design guidelines. In addition, we presented two promising instructional approaches relating to learner control

and part-whole sequencing of training problems, which might be beneficial for older learners. Future research is necessary to investigate the impact of both approaches on learning performance of older people in multimedia environments.

Although, the preliminary findings regarding the cognitive aging principle (e.g., Paas et al. 2001; Van Gerven et al., 2003) are promising in terms of lifelong learning, it is clear that the principle needs further experimental confirmation with more realistic tasks under different experimental task conditions. Because the instructional control of cognitive load is considered of major importance for meaningful understanding of multimedia learning materials to commence, measurements of cognitive load are necessary in these experiments. Cognitive load research has convincingly shown that such measurements can inform instructional designers about how to optimize and tailor cognitive load for individual learners, whether they be novices or experts, young or old (for an overview see, Paas, Tuovinen, Tabbers, & Van Gerven, 2003). The studies by Van Gerven et al. (2003, 2004b) suggest that with older people, ratings of the perceived amount of invested mental effort are superior to physiological measurements based on the learner's pupil dilation.

Another factor that needs to be considered in future research is the learners' experience. Experience has been found to mediate the relationship between age and performance in such a way that age differences in performance can be eliminated, probably because of the development of compensatory skills (Czaja & Sharit, 1993). Often the amount of experience with a task might be a better predictor of performance than age. However, it is clear that not all age-related declines can be prevented by intensive prolonged practice. Therefore, learners' experience with, or expertise in a task needs to be considered as an important mediating variable. On the other side of the spectrum, inexperienced older computer users have to get acquainted with basic computer skills (e.g., Czaja, 1996; Morrell & Echt, 1996), before they can actually receive the benefits of multimedia learning environments.

Finally, it is important to note that although multimedia techniques might represent an important tool for enhanced learning in the elderly, they should not be a goal on their own. In fact, there are instructional strategies that do not necessarily rely on multimedia techniques, such as the application of worked-out examples rather than conventional practice problems (Van Gerven, Paas, Van Merriënboer, & Schmidt, 2002) and the manipulation of training variability (Jamieson & Rogers, 2000; Van Gerven et al., 2004a). It may have become clear that extensive research is needed to establish the actual benefits of multimedia for senior learners.

Glossary

Apprehension principle: Guideline for the design of effective graphics, as formulated by Tversky et al. (2002), stating that the structure and content of an external representation (e.g., an instructional animation) should be readily and accurately perceived and comprehended.

Cognitive aging: Normal, age-related cognitive decline, typically associated with a diminished working memory performance.

Cognitive load theory (*CLT*): Theory of instructional design developed by John Sweller and coworkers. Incorporates three types of cognitive load: intrinsic, task-inherent cognitive load; extraneous (irrelevant), instruction-based cognitive load; and germane (relevant), instruction-based cognitive load. CLT is primarily aimed at the acquisition of complex skills, which imposes a high intrinsic cognitive load on the learner. Furthermore, it acknowledges the limited capacity of working memory as a gateway to long-term memory. In this context, the basic philosophy of CLT is to develop instructions that (a) impose a minimal level of extraneous cognitive load, and (b) an optimal level of germane cognitive load. This philosophy should lead to an optimal learning result.

Inhibition: The ability to suppress irrelevant information in working memory. (See also *reduced inhibition view*.)

Integration or coordination: The ability to relate and integrate different, mutually dependent sources of information.

Just-in-time information presentation: Presenting information in instructional materials just when a learner needs it for effective learning to take place. For example, providing general information about the context *before* a task, and task-related information such as rules or formulas *during* a task.

Parts-whole sequencing of training problems: Presenting separate components of a task before presenting the whole task, in order to prevent cognitive overload.

Processing speed: General cognitive speed, including activation speed, memory scanning speed, perceptual speed, and so forth (See also *reduced processing speed view*.)

Reduced inhibition view: View of cognitive aging that assumes a decline of the ability to inhibit irrelevant information in working memory. This view is considered as an alternative to the reduced working memory capacity view. (See also *inhibition, reduced working memory capacity view*.)

Reduced integration or coordination view: View of cognitive aging that assumes a decline of the ability to integrate and coordinate different sources of information.

Reduced processing speed view: View of cognitive aging that assumes a general decline of cognitive processing speed. Reduced processing speed can lead to comprehension problems if mutually dependent information elements are not activated simultaneously. (See also *processing speed*.)

Reduced working memory capacity view: View of cognitive aging that assumes a reduction of the processing capacity of working memory.

Training variability: Variability in the sequencing of training problems. If training variability is low, training problems are clustered according to certain categories (e.g., addition problems, subtraction problems, multiplication problems, etc.). If training variability is high, training problems are randomly sequenced. The latter method is assumed to lead to deeper processing of individual training problems than the former method.

Two-stage theory of mental model construction: Theory about how people construct mental models of complex systems. According to Mayer et al. (2002), learners construct models of separate components first, and only then construct a causal model of the system.

Working memory capacity: The capacity of working memory to store and manipulate information.

Footnote

1. The term *information* is used here in the broad sense in that it not only entails declarative knowledge, but also procedural knowledge, which forms the basis for cognitive skills.

References

Adam, J. J., Paas, F., Teeken, J. C., Van Loon, E. M., Van Boxtel, M. P. J., Houx, P. J., & Jolles, J. (1998). Effects of age on performance in a finger-precuing task. *Journal of Experimental Psychology: Human Perception and Performance, 24*, 870–883.

Baddeley, A. (1992). Working memory. *Science, 255*, 556–559.

Baddeley, A. (2003). Working memory: Looking back and looking forward. *Nature Reviews Neuroscience, 4*, 829–839.

Chandler, P., & Sweller, J. (1992). The split-attention effect as a factor in the design of instruction. *British Journal of Educational Psychology, 62*, 233–246.

Clark, J. M., & Paivio, A. (1991). Dual coding theory and education. *Educational Psychology Review, 3*, 149–210.

Constantinidou, F., & Baker, S. (2002). Stimulus modality and verbal learning performance in normal aging. *Brain and Language, 82*, 296–311.

Czaja, S. J. (1996). Aging and the acquisition of computer skills. In W. A. Rogers, A. D. Fisk, & N. Walker (Eds.), *Aging and skilled performance: Advances in theory and applications* (pp. 201–220). Mahwah, NJ: Erlbaum.

Czaja, S. J., & Sharit, J. (1993). Age differences in the performance of computer-based work. *Psychology and Aging, 8*, 59–67.

Ericsson, K. A., & Kintsch, W. (1995). Long-term working memory. *Psychological Review, 102*, 211–245.

Fisk, J. E., & Warr, P. (1996). Age and working memory: The role of perceptual speed, the central executive, and the phonological loop. *Psychology and Aging, 11*, 316–323.

Gilinski, A. S., & Judd, B. B. (1994). Working memory and bias in reasoning across the life span. *Psychology and Aging, 9*, 356–371.

Hartman, M., & Hasher, L. (1991). Aging and suppression: Memory for previously relevant information. *Psychology and Aging, 6*, 587–594.

Hasher, L., Stoltzfus, E. R., Zacks, R. T., & Rypma, B. (1991). Age and inhibition. *Journal of Experimental Psychology: Learning, Memory, and Cognition, 17*, 163–169.

Hasher, L., & Zacks, R. T. (1988). Working memory, comprehension, and aging: A review and a new view. In G. G. Bower (Ed.), *The psychology of learning and motivation* (Vol. 22, pp. 193–225). San Diego, CA: Academic Press.

Jamieson, B. A., & Rogers, W. A. (2000). Age-related effects of blocked and random practice schedules on learning a new technology. *Journal of Gerontology: Psychological Sciences, 55B*, P343–P353.

Jeung, H., Chandler, P., & Sweller, J. (1997). The role of visual indicators in dual sensory mode instruction. *Educational Psychology, 17*, 329–343.

Kalyuga, S., Chandler, P., & Sweller, J. (1999). Managing split-attention and redundancy in multimedia instruction. *Applied Cognitive Psychology, 1 3 , 351–371.*

Kester, L. (2003). *Timing of information presentation and the acquisition of complex skills.* Unpublished doctoral dissertation, Open University of the Netherlands, Heerlen, the Netherlands.

Kester, L., Kirschner, P. A., van Merriënboer, J. J. G., & Baumer, A. (2001). Just-in-time information presentation and the acquisition of complex cognitive skills. *Computers in Human Behavior, 1 7 , 373–391.*

Kirasic, K. C., Allen, G. L., & Haggerty, D. (1992). Age-related differences in adults' macrospatial processes. *Experimental Aging Research, 1 8 , 33–40.*

Leahy, W., Chandler, P., & Sweller, J. (2003). When auditory presentations should and should not be a component of multimedia instructions. *Applied Cognitive Psychology, 1 7 , 401–418.*

Light, L. L., Zelinski, E. M., & Moore, M. G. (1982). Adult age differences in inferential reasoning from new information. *Journal of Experimental Psychology: Learning, Memory, and Cognition, 8 , 435–447.*

Lipman, P. D., & Caplan, L. J. (1992). Adult age differences in memory for routes: Effects of instruction and spatial diagram. *Psychology and Aging, 7 , 435–441.*

Mautone, P. D., & Mayer, R. E. (2001). Signaling as a cognitive guide in multimedia learning. *Journal of Educational Psychology, 93 , 377–389.*

Mayer, R. E. (2001). *Multimedia learning.* Cambridge, UK: Cambridge University Press.

Mayer, R. E., & Chandler, P. (2001). When learning is just a click away: Does simple user interaction foster deeper understanding of multimedia messages? *Journal of Educational Psychology, 93 , 390–397.*

Mayer, R. E., Dow, G. T., & Mayer, S. (2003). Multimedia learning in an interactive self-explaining environment: What works in the design of agent-based microworlds? *Journal of Educational Psychology, 95 , 806–813.*

Mayer, R. E., Heiser, J., & Lonn, S. (2001). Cognitive constraints on multimedia learning: When presenting more material results in less understanding. *Journal of Educational Psychology, 93 , 187–198.*

Mayer, R. E., Mathias, A., & Wetzell, K. (2002). Fostering understanding of multimedia messages through pre-training: Evidence for a two-stage theory of mental model construction. *Journal of Experimental Psychology: Applied, 8 , 147–154.*

Mayer, R. E., & Moreno, R. (2003). Nine ways to reduce cognitive load in multimedia learning. *Educational Psychologist, 38 , 43–52.*

Mayer, R. E., Moreno, R., Boire, M., & Vagge, S. (1999). Maximizing constructivist learning from multimedia communications by minimizing cognitive load. *Journal of Educational Psychology, 91 , 638–643.*

Mayr, U., & Kliegl, R. (1993). Sequential and coordinative complexity: Age-based processing limitations in figural transformations. *Journal of Experimental Psychology: Learning, Memory, and Cognition, 1 9 , 1297–1320.*

Mayr, U., Kliegl, R., & Krampe, R. T. (1996). Sequential and coordinative processing dynamics in figural transformations across the life span. *Cognition, 59 , 61–90.*

Moreno, R., & Mayer, R. E. (1999). Cognitive principles of multimedia learning: The role of modality and contiguity. *Journal of Educational Psychology, 91 , 358–368.*

Morrell, R. W., & Echt, K. V. (1996). Instructional design for older computer users: The influence of cognitive factors. In W. A. Rogers, A. D. Fisk, & N. Walker (Eds.), *Aging and skilled performance: Advances in theory and applications* (pp. 241–265). Mahwah, NJ: Lawrence Erlbaum Associates.

Mousavi, S. Y., Low, R., & Sweller, J. (1995). Reducing cognitive load by mixing auditory and visual presentation modes. *Journal of Educational Psychology, 87 , 319–334.*

Paas, F., Camp, G., & Rikers, R. (2001). Instructional compensation for age-related cognitive declines: Effects of goal specificity in maze learning. *Journal of Educational Psychology, 93 , 181–186.*

Paas, F., Renkl, A., & Sweller, J. (2003). Cognitive load theory and instructional design: Recent developments. *Educational Psychologist, 38 , 1–4.*

Paas, F., Renkl, A., & Sweller, J. (2004). Cognitive load theory: Instructional implications of the interaction between information structures and cognitive architecture. *Instructional Science, 32 , 1–8.*

Paas, F., Tuovinen, J., Tabbers, H., & Van Gerven, P. W. M. (2003). Cognitive load measurement as a means to advance cognitive load theory. *Educational Psychologist, 38 , 63–71.*

Paivio, A. (1986). *Mental representations: A dual coding approach.* New York: Oxford University Press.

Pollock, E., Chandler, P., & Sweller, J. (2002). Assimilating complex information. *Learning and Instruction, 12*, 61–86.

Reuter-Lorenz, P. A., Stanczak, L., & Miller, A. C. (1999). Neural recruitment and cognitive aging: Two hemispheres are better than one, especially as you age. *Psychological Science, 10*, 494–500.

Salthouse, T. A. (1994). Aging associations: Influence of speed on adult age differences in associative learning. *Journal of Experimental Psychology: Learning, Memory, and Cognition, 20*, 1486–1503.

Salthouse, T. A. (1996). The processing-speed theory of adult age differences in cognition. *Psychological Review, 103*, 403–428.

Salthouse, T. A., & Babcock, R. L. (1991). Decomposing adult age differences in working memory. *Developmental Psychology, 27*, 763–776.

Salthouse, T. A., Mitchell, D. R. D., Skovronek, E., & Babcock, R. L. (1989). Effects of adult age and working memory on reasoning and spatial abilities. *Journal of Experimental Psychology: Learning, Memory, and Cognition, 15*, 507–516.

Spieler, D. H., Balota, D. A., & Faust, M. E. (1996). Stroop performance in healthy younger and older adults and in individuals with dementia of the Alzheimer's type. *Journal of Experimental Psychology: Human Perception and Performance, 22*, 461–479.

Stolzfus, E. R., Hasher, L., Zacks, R. T., Ulivi, M. S., & Goldstein, D. (1993). Investigations of inhibition and interference in younger and older adults. *Journal of Gerontology: Psychological Sciences, 48*, 179–188.

Sweller, J. (1999). *Instructional design in technical areas.* Camberwell, Australia: ACER Press.

Sweller, J., & Chandler, P. (1994). Why some material is difficult to learn. *Cognition and Instruction, 12*, 185–233.

Sweller, J., van Merriënboer, J. J. G., & Paas, F. (1998). Cognitive architecture and instructional design. *Educational Psychology Review, 10*, 251–296.

Tabbers, H. K., Martens, R. L., & van Merriënboer, J. J. G. (2001). The modality effect in multimedia instructions. In J. D. Moore & K. Stenning (Eds.), *Proceedings of the Twenty-Third Annual Conference of the Cognitive Science Society* (pp. 1024–1029). Mahwah, NJ: Lawrence Erlbaum Associates.

Tabbers, H. K., Martens, R. L., & van Merriënboer, J. J. G. (2004). Multimedia instructions and cognitive load theory: Effects of modality and cueing. *British Journal of Educational Psychology, 74*, 71–81.

Tindall-Ford, S., Chandler, P., & Sweller, J. (1997). When two sensory modes are better than one. *Journal of Experimental Psychology: Applied, 3*, 257–287.

Tversky, B., Morrison, J. B., & Bétrancourt, M. (2002). Animation: Can it facilitate? *International Journal of Human-Computer Studies, 57*, 247–262.

Van Gerven, P. W. M., Paas, F., van Merriënboer, J. J. G., Hendriks, M., & Schmidt, H. G. (2003). The efficiency of multimedia learning into old age. *British Journal of Educational Psychology, 73*, 489–505.

Van Gerven, P. W. M., Paas, F., van Merriënboer, J. J. G., & Schmidt, H. G. (2000). Cognitive load theory and the acquisition of complex cognitive skills in the elderly: Towards an integrative framework. *Educational Gerontology, 26*, 503–521.

Van Gerven, P. W. M., Paas, F., van Merriënboer, J. J. G., & Schmidt, H. G. (2002). Cognitive load theory and aging: Effects of worked examples on training efficiency. *Learning and Instruction, 38*, 87–107.

Van Gerven, P. W. M., Paas, F., van Merriënboer, J. J. G., & Schmidt, H. G. (2004a). Modality and variability as factors in training the elderly. Manuscript submitted for publication.

Van Gerven, P. W. M., Paas, F., van Merriënboer, J. J. G., & Schmidt, H. G. (2004b). Memory load and the cognitive pupillary response in aging. *Psychophysiology, 41*, 167–174.

Williams, M. D. (1996). Learner-control and instructional techniques. In D. H. Jonassen (Ed.), *Handbook of research for educational communications and technology* (pp. 957–983). New York: MacMillan.

Wingfield, A., Stine, E. A., Lahar, C. J., & Aberdeen, J. S. (1988). Does the capacity of working memory change with age? *Experimental Aging Research, 14*, 103–107.

Zacks R., & Hasher, L. (1997). Cognitive gerontology and attentional inhibition: A reply to Burke and McDowd. *Journal of Gerontology: Psychological Sciences, 52B*, P274–P283.

Part IV

MULTIMEDIA LEARNING IN CONTENT AREAS

CHAPTER 23

Multimedia Learning of Reading

David Reinking

Clemson University

Abstract

Addressing how multimedia learning intersects with teaching reading and learning to read entails unique challenges when compared to other school subjects. Those challenges spring from the prominent place that reading instruction occupies in the school curriculum and in daily life. As the first of the three Rs, learning to read is foundational to all school subjects. Further, the ability to read and comprehend textual information is integral to all schooling and indeed to living a productive and fulfilling life in developed areas of the world (Brandt, 2001).

Introduction

In part because the stakes are high and in part because reading is an intriguingly complex cognitive activity, the teaching and learning of reading have historically attracted attention from diverse disciplines. The literature pertaining to reading is an interdisciplinary amalgam including not only main-stream scholars of reading pedagogy, but also educational researchers in other curricular areas, psychologists of every stripe, sociologists, historians, philosophers, and even those in the medical field such as ophthalmologists. The appearance of multimedia forms of communication made possible by computer technology has reinforced and extended the interdisciplinary mix to include scholars in fields such as journalism and mass media, library science, instructional design, and computer science.

Further, because a citizenry's collective reading achievement is perceived to have important economic and political consequences, reading pedagogy and the scholarly work that informs it are almost daily in the public eye. Multimedia forms of communication have likewise attracted interest in the pedagogical and political dimensions of how best to prepare children to be more broadly literate in digital, multimedia environments (e.g., Flood, Heath, & Lapp, 1997; Leu & Kinzer, 2000), and to compete in a global economy (Wagner & Kozma, 2003).

The content of reading instruction is likewise diverse and sometimes controversial often raising issues about the appropriate and most effective ways to teach beginning reading (e.g., the debate over whole-language and phonics often termed the *Reading Wars*); the causes of reading difficulties and how to ameliorate them; how to assess reading; how reading and writing interact; and so forth. Digital, multimedia forms of communication have complicated these issues while raising interesting possibilities for enhancing instruction. Although a diversity of computer-based multimedia materials and activities for teaching reading have been widely available since the earliest days of instructional computing (e.g., the Stanford Project; see Atkinson & Hansen, 1966–67) and there has been much interest in their use, they have not had a notable effect on instruction (International Reading Association, 2001; Leu, 2000; Reinking, Labbo, & McKenna, 2000). Many educators and researchers who are invested in conventional print and the instruction based on it have done little to accommodate or assimilate new digital forms into their work and sometimes greet digital forms as interlopers of marginal importance to mainstream reading pedagogy and research (Reinking, 1995, 1998).

Limitations and Caveats

The preceding brief summary provides the background for several limitations and caveats to a review of multimedia and learning to read. First, the relevant literature is broad, but shallow. It is broad in the sense that it cuts across a wide range of disciplinary, theoretical, topical, and methodological terrain. That it is shallow is evidenced in part by the relatively few studies investigating issues of digital literacy in the mainstream journals publishing research about learning to read (see Kamil, Kim, & Intrator, 2000; Kamil & Lane, 1998). Further, previously published reviews of the literature pertaining to reading and digital technologies (Blok, Oostdam, Otter, and Overmaat, 2002; Labbo & Reinking, 2003; Leu, 2000; Leu & Reinking, 1996; Reinking

& Bridwell-Bowles, 1991; Reinking, Labbo, & McKenna, 1997) do not attend predominantly to multimedia as a dimension of learning to read and make broad generalizations rather than specific recommendations. Thus, the present review focusing on multimedia and what recommendations might be derived from the available literature seems warranted.

Another caveat is that much of the available research related to digital technologies and learning to read has been judged to be methodologically weak. For example, in an early review of the research on computers and reading Reinking and Bridwell-Bowles (1991) pointed out that many of the available studies were atheoretical, horserace-like comparisons of reading with and without a computer. More recently, computer technology and reading instruction was one of a few key topics investigated by the National Reading Panel (2000) charged by the U.S. Congress to draw conclusions about reading instruction based on scientific evidence. Scientific evidence was defined narrowly as experimental studies (supplemented secondarily by correlation studies) that met certain standards of methodological rigor with the aim of conducting meta-analyses across studies. However, a comprehensive search of the literature on technology and reading between 1986 and 1999 produced only 21 studies that met the panel's criteria, which was deemed an insufficient number for conducting a meta-analysis. Further in a meta-analysis of 42 studies published since 1990 and investigating computer-assisted instruction in beginning reading instruction, Blok, Oostdam, Otter, and Overmaat (2002) indicated that the relatively low overall effect size ($d = 0.2$) should be interpreted with caution, in part because many of the studies were of poor quality.

Another caveat is that approaching the topic of multimedia and reading pedagogy depends to some extent upon one's theoretical and pedagogical orientation to reading and reading instruction. If reading is viewed as a bottom-up process (e.g., Gough, 1984) in which decoding letters and words are foundational to comprehension, beginning reading instruction is likely to be conceived as a hierarchy of subskills. If reading is viewed as a top-down process (e.g., Goodman, 1976) where existing knowledge allows predictions that aid and direct decoding, beginning reading instruction is likely to be conceived as a more holistic, less linear endeavor. These alternative views affect how multimedia materials and texts might be conceptualized, developed, and researched in relation to learning to read, particularly in the early stages of learning to read (Miller & Olson, 1998).

Further, much of the research literature pertaining to multimedia and reading is targeted toward increasing the comprehension of particular textual content or studying the processes by which readers come to understand textual content presented in multimedia formats. Many of the other chapters in this volume present work in this area. That research is relevant and important to reading instruction, particularly as it pertains to comprehension and learning in other subject areas and in determining how best to prepare students for new reading environments. However, given the scope of this chapter and the fact that many other chapters in this volume address those issues, in this chapter I will focus my review on multimedia materials aimed specifically at learning to read as a subject in the elementary and middle school where instruction in reading is more often a distinct curricular area. However, first I define multimedia in relation to teaching and learning to read.

Defining Multimedia in Relation to Texts and Learning to Read

The term *multimedia* has different meanings and these different meanings vary by context and by discipline (Mayer, 2001). In relation to teaching and learning subjects in schools, *multimedia* is frequently used to modify words such as *program*, *materials*, *presentation*, *learning*, and so forth. In that usage, *multimedia* typically refers to computer-based presentations of instructional content and activities that blend prose (written or verbal), sound effects, and dynamic rather than static graphical information (i.e., animations and video clips, as opposed to still pictures or illustrations). To teachers and educational researchers *multimedia* usually means more than words and pictures conjoined in conventional printed texts, and more than simply employing an array of independent audio-visual technologies to teach in a classroom, the latter of which has a long history in teaching reading (e.g., Dale, 1946). Instead, it means using the capability of a computer to combine in interactive formats the capabilities of previously independent, stand-alone technologies for presenting audio and visual information.

However, the term *multimedia* as used in such contexts is problematic from a theoretical point of view (Reinking, 2001). First, general, nonspecific uses of the term provide no clear basis for distinguishing the acquisition of information from written texts in general and printed texts in particular and from other sources of information, and thus leaves unanswered what reading really is in relation to listening and viewing. This ambiguity is reflected to some extent in calls for expanded definitions of literacy to include listening and viewing (e.g., Flood et al., 1997; Cognition and Technology Group at Vanderbilt University, 1994), which essentially begs the issue of why that might be advisable other than that there are now more multimedia forms of communication. Second, it provides no basis for conceptualizing, predicting, or assessing what digital technologies might contribute instructionally to learning to read in a conventional sense nor what the dimensions of reading might be in digital, multimedia environments.

These issues remain to be sorted out precisely. However, several theoretical positions are relevant. In relation to the first issue, for example, Birkerts (1994) is an often-cited apologist for the benefits of reading conventional printed texts over digital, multimedia texts, although his argument is more romantic and literary than theoretical. Bolter (1991), on the other hand, has suggested that the essence of reading is that it establishes a space for reflection not naturally afforded by multimedia forms that provide less mediated experience (virtual reality being an extreme form). However, he has also introduced the concept of *remediation*, which argues that there is a natural tendency to use one medium to mimic the characteristics of other media (e.g., paintings that look like photographs and vice versa), but that vestiges of established media typically survive in new media forms (e.g., the "electronic book" or "e-book"). However, the development and use of various media are always shaped by a press to reach an ideal of unmediated experience (Bolter, 2001). Lanham (1993) has argued a complementary perspective postulating that digital texts, because they create options that subordinate alphanumeric text (see also Reinking & Chanlin, 1994), are naturally more visual than printed texts and thus more rhetorical and less philosophical. That idea is captured by his distinction between printed texts, which fundamentally encourage readers to look *through* the text to find meaning, and digital texts, which more fundamentally encourage readers to find meaning by looking *at* the text.

There is also theoretical work related to how the dynamic, audio-visual capabilities of computer-based materials might contribute to learning to read or to defining more clearly what new directions in teaching reading might be warranted. For example, Salomon's (1979) seminal work outlining the characteristics that distinguish one medium from another suggests that printed and digital texts may be distinctly different media with different cognitive requirements and with different opportunities to effect cognitive processing. That is, the technologies supporting digital texts make available new symbol systems (an open-ended technology that can flexibly use diverse symbol systems, which arguably is a more precise definition of multimedia; see Reinking, 2001) as well as new situations (e.g., Internet usage) and contents (e.g., easy juxtapositions of diverse information). In his theory, two consequences of different media are particularly important from an instructional standpoint: (a) media vary in the cog-

nitive skills necessary to extract information from them and thus what skills become well practiced in using a medium; and (b) media vary in the extent to which their symbol systems and technologies can model or supplant requisite cognitive skills. In an example directly related to the focus of this chapter, he and his colleagues demonstrated that digital texts specifically designed to scaffold novice readers' understanding of texts in ways not possible in conventional printed materials increased metacognitive awareness and comprehension (Salomon, Globerson, & Guterman, 1989).

Using Salomon's theoretical perspective Reinking (1992, 1997) has argued that five differences distinguish reading printed and digital texts, which justifies thinking of them as different media, but which also suggests differences that might guide the teaching and learning of reading. In this scheme, the unique characteristics of digital texts are that they: (a) create literal (as opposed to a metaphorical) interactions between texts and readers (e.g., dynamic texts capable of responding and adapting to an individual reader's needs); (b) enable information to be organized and accessed in nonlinear formats (i.e., hypertexts); (c) use a broader range of symbolic elements to carry meaning (e.g., ranging from the easier use of colored, stylized fonts to the use of audio, animation, and video); (d) broaden the boundaries of freedom and control available for accessing information during reading (e.g., hotlinks in Web-based documents on the freedom side and making access to subsequent text contingent on demonstrated mastery of essential concepts on the control side); and (e) change the conventions or pragmatics of written communication (e.g., e-mail and listservs have emerging acceptable and unacceptable uses and behaviors for users).

In summary, *multimedia* is a term that has been used in the education literature to refer to the use of a computer to present instructional content and activities in flexible, interactive formats employing a variety of audio and visual effects. In this usage *multimedia* refers to audio-visual capabilities that were previously unavailable to print-based learning. However, in a theoretical sense the term *multimedia* may mean something more specific and less consistent with the etymological roots of the term (literally "many media"). That is, it refers to fundamental differences between print-based and digital texts that make them separate media and that suggest new content and avenues for teaching and learning, particularly in relation to textual materials. Although it is debatable from the standpoint of learning content whether alternative media (e.g., print or digital texts) make a difference in learning (see Jonassen & Reeves, 1996), it seems less debatable that learning how to extract information from various media has implications for developing competence in a cognitive skill such as reading. Although understandings of multimedia at a theoretical level are at least implicit in the review that follows, the field has not yet produced a comprehensive theory.

Multimedia Applications in Learning to Read: Examples, Research, and Theory

Teaching reading as a school subject can be roughly divided into three areas, each of which has an extensive theoretical, empirical, and pedagogical base in the literature of reading education: (a) decoding (identifying words automatically for the sake of developing reading fluency); (b) comprehending (building capacity and strategies to understand and think critically about texts); and (c) building interest in reading (instilling an enjoyment of reading as a pleasant and fulfilling activity). In this section I provide examples of multimedia materials that have been developed and used instructionally in each of these areas, and I summarize and evaluate the status of theory and research supporting their use.

Decoding

The capability to incorporate audio-visual presentations into learning to read has had the most direct and obvious influence in the area of decoding. That influence can be understood by considering the nature of decoding and how it fits into reading instruction. At the decoding stage of learning to read, the emphasis is on breaking the alphabetic code, typically by teaching sound-symbol correspondences, although the extent and focus of that emphasis as well as how it should be dealt with instructionally has long been controversial. Nonetheless, there is a fair degree of consensus that an important goal of beginning reading instruction is to develop fluent readers (i.e., automatic decoders) whose attention and cognitive resources can be devoted to comprehension rather than to decoding. Thus, any technology facilitating the ability to highlight sound-symbol correspondences toward helping students become fluent, automatic decoders fits well into conventional conceptions of beginning reading instruction and is likely to be favorably accepted even by educators and researchers invested in printed forms.

Unlike printed materials, a computer can provide individualized, on-demand access to pronunciations and allows instructional designers to set contingencies that provide different types or levels of access to pronunciations. For example, certain readers under certain conditions may benefit from the availability of audio that provides pronunciations at the level of a syllable, a word, a phrase, a sentence, or a connected text. These contingencies have been investigated extensively, at least more extensively than most other applications that might be referred to as multimedia, and they have been more often guided by theories relevant to the pedagogy of reading.

The intuitive appeal of using computer for multimedia applications related to decoding surfaced early in the era of instructional computing long before synthesized and digitized speech became more feasible and commonplace as it is today. For example, in early work in this area McConkie and Zola (1987) used specially designed equipment interfaced with a computer to allow marginally literate adults in prison to read high-interest content on a touch-sensitive computer screen, which allowed them to access the pronunciation of unfamiliar words. The growth in reading ability for the adults in this essentially free-reading condition compared favorably to more conventional instruction.

However, most of the research and development in this area has focused on young children or on children in the elementary grades experiencing difficulties in learning to read. Clearly, the most prominent researchers in this area are Richard Olson and Barbara Wise, whose incremental, ongoing, collaborative work began in the mid 1980s. Several useful findings have emerged from their work. For example, in preliminary studies they established that synthetic speech could equally support children's recognition of targeted words when compared to actual spoken language (Olson, Foltz, & Wise, 1986a) and that providing feedback for difficult words in stories promoted more learning of those words than simply reading stories (Olson et al., 1986b). Later they investigated providing children with alternative segmentation patterns of audio feedback when encountering unfamiliar words (whole word, e.g., *pencil*; syllable, e.g., *pen-cil*; and onset-rime, e.g., *p-en/c-il*) finding that segmentation pattern made little difference. However, they found that the computer-based feedback did accelerate the progress of participants when compared to a control group (Wise et al., 1989) and that children who had established phonemic awareness (the ability to hear the smallest units of sounds in a language) benefited more than those who did not (Olson & Wise, 1992). Their subsequent work varied conditions of training and implementation and examined transfer to more distal measures (e.g., Wise, Ring, & Olson, 1999, 2000). In a more recent paper (Olson & Wise, 2004) they have provided a notably candid evaluation of the limitations of their research and findings, future directions for research, and a critique of research on commercial programs employing computer-based speech for reading development, which unfortunately has often been conducted by researchers who

have a financial interest in the success of those programs.

Other researchers have investigated similar approaches to using the computer to develop decoding skills, but with different populations. These include, for example, Reitsma and Wesseling (1998) with emergent readers; Barron, Lovett, and McCabe (1998) with neurologically impaired readers; Lundberg (1995) with special education students; Segers and Verhoeven (2004) with children diagnosed with speech and language problems; and Ho and Ma (1999) with Chinese children labeled as dyslexic. Reitsma and Wesseling's (1998) study, which demonstrated positive effects for using the computer to develop phonological awareness, is noteworthy because it was a methodologically strong longitudinal study that took into account multiple factors including various student characteristics and the school and home environments.

McKenna, Reinking, and Bradley (2003) have also investigated providing various conditions of digitized speech to children in regular kindergarten and first-grade classrooms in conjunction with reading online versions of popular children's books. In one condition they provided digitized oral phonics analogies when children clicked on a word. That is, when children clicked on the word *fix*, they would hear a female voice compare the word *fix* to *six*, a more familiar and analogous word that was also displayed on the screen. They were interested in determining whether various conditions might effect improvements not only in the identification of target words, but new, analogous words, as well as sight words (i.e., high frequency, but often irregularly spelled words, decoded as units by sight; such as *have*, *was*, *done*, and *of*). In a two-part experiment, children who had not reached the alphabetic stage of development (i.e., some awareness of sound-symbol correspondence) exhibited no statistically significant benefits in decoding development. However, in a second experiment, children who had reached that stage exhibited an increase in sight word development, thus supporting a theoretically hypothesized relation between phonological development and sight word recognition (Ehri, 1992).

Comprehension

Comprehension is the ultimate goal of reading instruction, but unlike decoding, it entails ill-defined, open-ended, and complex cognitive processes (Paris, in press). Consequently, it is less clear how it might be developed as a general cognitive ability through teaching activities. Traditionally, classroom reading instruction aimed explicitly at developing comprehension ability has been shown to be sparse. Typically it has included engaging children in activities requiring them to do little more than demonstrate that comprehension had occurred such as finding the main ideas of text, separating fact from opinion, or interpreting tables and graphs (Durkin, 1978–79). More recently, there has been an emphasis on improving comprehension through activities aimed at helping students become more engaged and strategic readers (Pressley, 2000) and heightened interest in instructional activities aimed at externalizing the internal process of comprehension. Expanding students' meaning vocabulary has also traditionally been considered to be part of comprehension instruction, although this area too has benefited from more innovative teaching strategies and activities, many of which proceeded from theoretical advances in cognitive psychology.

Computer applications, employing multimedia, have played a role in comprehension instruction, but those applications, although often more innovative in their conception when compared to decoding applications, have nonetheless been more diverse and less well researched. They have also often been embedded in the context of learning subjects such as social studies and science. Excluding applications aimed at increasing comprehension of a particular text, there are several lines of research and development in the literature. These include investigating (a) how digital forms of reading might enhance strategic reading and engagement with texts, including how new

forms such as hypertexts may uniquely develop conventional skills and new comprehension skills associated with reading digital texts; (b) whether multimedia elements may distract readers, therefore undermining comprehension; and (c) whether multimedia may play a role in developing a more evaluative or critical stance toward texts. Subsequently, I provide examples in each of these areas.

Interestingly, perhaps the earliest example of using a multimedia application involving computers in the area of reading comprehension was developed and investigated by the famed psychologist George Miller and reported in *Scientific American* (Miller & Gildea, 1987). Based on his work demonstrating that children's use of dictionary definitions alone in seeking meanings of unfamiliar words led to sometimes humorous misuses of those words, he explored how a computer interfaced with a video player might remedy this phenomenon. For example, after viewing a video of the film *Raiders of the Lost Ark*, children were shown a text describing the scene in which targeted vocabulary words had been highlighted. Fifth-grade children could then select to see a definition of the word, the word used appropriately in a sentence, and a video clip illustrating the words meaning, the latter option being particularly useful with words such as *jovial*, in which the video could show someone who was projecting that emotional state. He found that children using this application recognized more meanings of targeted words and used them more appropriately in a sentence. Complementing these findings is the work of Reinking and Rickman (1990) who found that upper-elementary school children who had immediate access to technical terms while reading a science text on a computer screen were more likely to investigate the words' meanings, choose their correct meanings on a postexperimental vocabulary measure, and to comprehend the text in which the terms appeared. However, students in their study were provided written definitions without audio or video support.

Another relatively early example of a multimedia application aimed at increasing comprehension ability is the Young Sherlock Project, one of several projects developed by the Learning Technology Center at Vanderbilt University (Kinzer & Risko, 1988). Based on a theoretical orientation referred to as anchored instruction, the overall aim of these projects was to (a) increase students' abilities to solve problems and to learn independently; (b) teach general literacy skills involving reading and writing; and (c) build background knowledge including vocabulary, story grammars, and historical information (Sharp et al., 1992). The Young Sherlock project engaged children in a variety of online and offline activities centered on an interactive exploration of the popular film *Young Sherlock Holmes* within the context of learning about the Victorian era. A study of fifth-grade, at-risk, and average-ability students revealed that they outperformed a control group in their spontaneous use of targeted vocabulary, in the number of story elements and links to characters in writing about the movie, and in the use of historical information to make inferences (Risko et al., 1989).

In another study, also focusing on historical content, Stahl, Hynd, Britton, McNish, & Bosquet (1996) investigated the potential of using hypertext to engage high school students in critically evaluating textual information more like historians. The computer application allowed students to easily access and compare different accounts and explanations of the Gulf of Tonkin incident, a controversial event used to justify American's entry into the Vietnam War. Specifically, they were interested in investigating the extent to which hyptertextual presentations of historical events would enrich students' mental models, how students would approach the historical information, whether students would integrate information across texts, and whether students would engage in corroborating, sourcing, and contextualizing, three activities found to characterize the way historians approach textual information (Wineburg, 1991). They found that students' mental models were more consis-

tent after reading at least two source documents, but the overall results were disappointing to the extent that students tended to gravitate toward the textbook explanations of events rather than to form opinions based on comparisons across original source documents. They concluded that hypertextual access to multiple texts presenting conflicting information may not benefit students without specific instruction in relevant strategies and orientations.

This finding is consistent with other studies suggesting that simply exposing students to unique reading experiences on the computer does not produce immediate, profound improvements or changes in general comprehension ability (cf. Hynd, Jacobson, & Reinking, 1999; Rouet, Levonen, Dillon, & Spiro, 1996). Nonetheless, Spiro and his colleagues (Spiro, Feltovitch, Jacobson, & Coulson, 1992) reported that presenting information as hypertexts to more mature and capable learners such as medical students resulted in increased ability to apply that information to a diagnosis, but decreased recall of factual information when compared to students reading conventional texts. The theory guiding their research was cognitive flexibility theory, which postulates that learning content in ill-structured domains such as performing a medical diagnosis or making decisions about teaching children will be enhanced when knowledge is deconstructed and then reconstructed flexibly in relation to specific cases. Presenting information in hypertextual formats has been considered to be a logical means for instantiating this theoretical orientation (Shapiro & Niederhauser, 2004) and perhaps in creating more active comprehension and learning (cf. Niederhauser, Reynolds, Salmen, & Skolmoski, 2000; Shapiro, 1998).

Some work has indicated that computer-based reading might affect readers' comprehension strategies, at least in the short term, although that work has not focused specifically on using the audio-visual capabilities of computer-based texts. For example, Tobias (1987, 1988) inserted questions in online texts that required review of previously presented material when readers answered a question incorrectly. That is, the computer made access to texts contingent on readers demonstrating that they had comprehended the text presented previously, thus illustrating the unique capabilities of digital forms of reading to manage and perhaps shape comprehension processes. However, he found that mandatory review, while increasing learning of information targeted by the inserted questions, decreased learning of other potentially important information, which reflected a phenomenon evidenced in the literature investigating the effects of inserting questions in conventional printed texts. He speculated that under conditions of mandatory review, readers focus their review on quickly finding portions of the text that allow them to answer the question correctly, thus increasing recall of that information at the expense of other information. Extending his work, Reinking, Pickle, and Tao (1996) investigated the possibility of overcoming this limitation by providing high school readers with the same or a different question after mandatory review. They found that indeed readers devoted more time to reviewing paragraphs containing information relevant to an inserted question when they received the same question, but that they more equally distributed their review time across several paragraphs when they received a different question after mandatory review.

In a similar vein, Hegarty, Carpenter, and Just's (1991) work illustrates how digital texts employing animation might compensate for readers lacking requisite cognitive skills for comprehending textual information. They reported one study (Carpenter, Just, & Fallside, 1988) in which they measured eye movements and comprehension of participants who read a text explaining the operation of a machine and viewed an accompaning diagram of the machine. In one condition a printed text presented a conventional static diagram on a page. In another condition, the text was presented on a computer screen and the accompanying diagram was animated to show the movement of the machine. All readers attended to the animated graphical representation longer, but

the comprehension of readers assessed to be of low mechanical ability, and presumably less adept at imaging the machine's operation, increased significantly when reading the online animated version. However, these examples of altering or supplanting cognitive processing, because they involve short-term interventions, illustrate mainly the potential effects *of* a medium, in this case computer-based reading, to alter or supplant strategic aspects of acquiring information as opposed to more long-term effects *with* media that might generalize to other texts and contexts for reading (see Salomon, Perkins, & Globerson, 1991).

A different line of research has investigated reading comprehension among young children interacting with digital versions of popular children's stories that include a variety of audio-visual effects not possible in the printed versions of these stories. "Talking Books," or "CD-ROM stories" have been extensively researched although the scope of that research extends into the area of decoding described in the previous section (i.e., stories that include the pronunciation of unfamiliar words; e.g., see Chera & Wood, 2003; McKenna, Reinking, & Bradley, 2003) and the area of building interest and motivation as described in the subsequent section of this chapter. An obvious benefit of these stories is that young children with little or no independent reading ability can interact with them without the assistance of an adult or more competent reader.

The relation between pictures and story content in printed texts has been a topic of research for many years. For example, Beck and McKeown (2001) found that pictures inconsistent with the story led children to misunderstand stories. However, digital stories complicate this issue. For example, many online stories include sound effects and animations, many of which are incongruent with the story line. Further, many of these stories implicitly or explicitly encourage children to access story events in an order not consistent with the original printed version. Do such multimedia versions of the stories interfere with story recall? Do they compare less favorably with adult-assisted reading of printed versions? Do they generate more interest and motivation in reading by encouraging more playful explorations of story content? These are the type of questions that have been researched.

Research thus far does not provide a clear answer to these questions, although some clarifications of contradictory findings are beginning to emerge. It is clear across the available studies that children become engaged in playful interactions with these stories, which are likely to be motivating (e.g., Cordova & Lepper, 1996; DeJong & Bus, 2003). What is not clear is the extent to which these playful explorations enhance or inhibit story understanding particularly when compared to conventional printed stories that adults read to children. For example Ricci and Beal (2002) found that comprehension was not affected by animations unrelated to the story. Likewise Cordova and Lepper (1996) concluded that animations may increase motivation and interest and therefore may increase comprehension. On the other hand, James (1999) found that children didn't navigate through an entire story, seemed distracted by pictorial details, and became engrossed in less relevant and entertaining animations after an initial pass through the story. Similarly, DeJong and Bus (2002) found that children in their study did not recall the structure of electronic stories as well as children who listened to adults read the same story to them. Further children reading electronic stories explored the story in a seemingly random order focusing more on appealing animations.

A few studies suggest some explanations for these inconsistent or contradictory findings. For example, Labbo and Kuhn (2000) applied the concept of considerate and inconsiderate texts (considerate in relation to being sensitive to readers' attempts to understand) to evaluating the effects of talking books. That is, they distinguished between electronic stories that provided audio-visual effects that were congruent or incongruent to the plot of the stories they accompanied. They found that texts they deemed to be considerate (i.e., with special effects congruent with the story) supported understanding as determined by story retellings, which

they attributed to a weaving of affective responses, cognitive processes, and metacognitive activity. In a more recent study, DeJong and Bus (2004) found evidence suggesting that the effects of talking books may be related to a child's level of cognitive development. That is, kindergarten children who had reached a stage of development where they had a distinct sense of story beyond attending to pictures were not distracted from story comprehension even when, using Labbo and Kuhn's terminology, there were many effects incongruent to the story.

Comprehension instruction in schools also includes developing the ability to critically evaluate textual information, although this aspect of reading instruction typically receives short shrift in classrooms, at least beyond skill work such as distinguishing between fact and opinion or beyond discussing propaganda techniques. That conclusion can be confirmed by a quick scan of leading textbooks aimed at preparing reading teachers, which include little, if any, attention to this area of comprehension. Computer-based activities have played some role in expanding attention to this neglected area. For example, the ready juxtaposition in digital environments of historical texts representing differing viewpoints in the work of Stahl et al. (1996) cited previously in this section illustrates some of the possibilities.

One example of the possibilities for using multimedia in developing a critical stance toward textual information is illustrated by the work of Myers, Hammett, and McKillop (1998). They engaged students in developing multimedia documents comparing and contrasting images of Pocahantas in various media ranging from the Disney animated version to Elizabethan paintings. Students' work, which presumably involved much reading and viewing of textual materials and visual images, also explored related themes pertaining to spiritual images related to Native American and Christian religions and environmental themes. Myers et al. (1998), writing from the perspective of critical pedagogy, concluded that children who were engaged in these activities exhibited more "resistant" processing of information consistent with a critical pedagogy, which includes an examination of societal distribution of power and reading the world critically.

Building Interest in Reading

Reading educators and researchers have always considered building interest in reading and creating conditions that promote a enjoyment of reading to be an important aspect of reading instruction. However, this aspect of reading instruction moved closer to the mainstream of the curriculum when Stanovich (1986) introduced the theoretical point of view he termed *Matthew Effects* after the biblical gospel that includes the line "the rich get richer and the poor get poorer." He argued that much of the widening discrepancy across the school years between children of low and high achievement in reading could be accounted for by the fact that children who initially perform poorly in reading are less motivated (or expected) to read and thus read less, thus compounding their lack of achievement. Children who, on the other hand, experience initial success are likely to read more and thus become better by virtue of their increased practice, background knowledge, and so forth.

Relatively few applications and even fewer studies have explored the possibilities of using computer-based multimedia formats to increase motivation to read and the amount of reading that children do, thus, presumably, in light of the Matthew Effects, addressing the gap in achievement between good and poor readers. Labbo's (1996) work is at least indirectly related to this area of instruction, because her work focused on the audio-visual aspects of young children's playful interactions with computer-based texts. Using a semiotic framework, she analyzed the way children constructed and used texts created with a commercial program that combined drawing and illustrating tools with word processing functions, which is consistent with the now widely accepted view that drawing is a precursor to playful writing and more advanced forms of literacy. Based on her analysis of children's experimentation with and interaction about these texts, she introduced an overarching construct she termed *screenland*, which en-

tailed several cognitive metaphors for the way children engaged with this multimedia environment: screen as landscape, playground, stage, canvas, and paper. However, an important element of the activity was the promotion of personally meaningful self-expression and presumably interest and motivation, which the computer-based multimedia activities seemed to promote. Also relevant to the overall focus of the present chapter, Labbo raised the question of the extent to which such early experiences with multiple symbol systems might lay a foundation for subsequent literacy development that accommodates a broader range of symbolic elements. She asked, "Is it possible that having opportunities to use depictive or transformative symbolism to represent ideas allow children to make associations with typographic and linguistic forms of meaning making?" (p. 381).

Another study addresses more directly the issue of how multimedia might transform conventional instructional activities toward increasing elementary students' independent reading. Reinking and Watkins (2000) investigated engaging teachers and students in developing multimedia book reviews as an alternative to the conventional book report that is a pervasive, but largely ineffective, approach that many teachers employ to inspire more reading in elementary and middle schools. Using Hypercard, a tool that allows for the flexible integration of pictorial and audio information in menu-driven and nonlinear formats, children developed a template that allowed them to develop personal and creative responses to the books they had read. Further, these multimedia book reviews were compiled into a searchable database that other students, teachers, and parents might choose to investigate. Using mixed methods within the methodology of a formative experiment they found that, across two years, in nine fourth- or fifth-grade classrooms in three schools effects varied considerably depending on contextual factors (e.g., administrative and professional climate of the school). Further, increased reading was mediated in unexpected ways such as students' interacting about books incidentally in the context of helping each other use the technological options available to create multimedia texts. Overall, the amount of reading increased and attitudes toward in-school and out-of-school reading remained constant. The latter finding was noteworthy because attitudes toward reading are known to decline steadily during the elementary grades (McKenna, Kear, & Ellsworth, 1995).

One relevant, but untested, theoretical perspective related to multimedia is directly relevant to this area of increasing engagement in reading and motivation to read. Reinking (2001) has argued that reading in multimedia environments is inherently more engaging than reading in print environments. Based fundamentally on the argument that printed and digital texts are theoretically distinct and separate media, he presented four theses in support of that conclusion: Multimedia texts are inherently (a) interactive, thus passive reading is less likely; (b) less difficult because they make various types of assistance available to readers, and they may be designed to determine if a reader is having difficulty and to respond accordingly; (c) tend to be less serious and philosophical and more playful, rhetorical and concrete; and (d) meet a wider range of social needs (e.g., chat rooms on the Internet). This theory suggests a variety of testable hypotheses. For example, do multimedia reading environments that possess all or various configurations of these qualities lead to more extensive reading, more persistence in reading difficult content, greater comprehension, heightened interest in textual topics (e.g., more off-line reading), more strategic reading, more communication with others about one's reading, and so forth when compared to conventional printed texts?

Implications and Future Directions for Research, Theory, Instruction, and Instructional Design

The focus of this chapter has been on research and theory pertaining to the use of computer-based multimedia materials and activities that might apply to teaching reading in the elementary school and middle school where reading is an identifiable component of the language arts curriculum. The relevant research base is broad yet shallow with relatively few studies conducted by mainstream literacy researchers interested in teaching reading in schools (Kamil et al., 2000; Kamil & Lane, 1998). Whereas the literature is replete with articles addressing the importance of technology to literacy instruction and lamenting the shortage of research, there is a paucity of research studies to guide the field in this area. Disturbingly, many of the calls for more research come from writers in the field of literacy who have themselves published little relevant empirical research. Consequently, much of the research relevant to using digital technologies in reading have been conducted by educational psychologists and instructional designers who are typically focused more on how readers process multimedia texts, how comprehension and learning of specific texts might be enhanced, or how screens might be designed to increase ease of use (e.g., Walker & Reynolds, 2000). They typically conduct studies of mature readers, mainly college students (see Lawless, Mills, & Brown, 2003 for an exception). Although informative, findings and implications from these studies are not directly applicable to younger children and classroom teaching.

Thus, one clear implication of the existing literature is that there is much room for more research that focuses on how computer-based, multimedia materials and activities might enhance the teaching and learning of reading in the elementary school and middle school. Among literacy researchers, there is a need to focus more attention on conducting rigorous empirical investigations published in mainstream, peer-reviewed journals. Among educational psychologists and other researchers, there is an opportunity to focus more attention on how multimedia might contribute to teaching reading and learning to read in schools. Although research is logistically more difficult to conduct in school settings, the benefits of knowing how developing readers process multimedia materials and how those materials might contribute to enhancing reading achievement and comprehension are likely to be greater theoretically and practically than knowing how to effect improvements in reading and learning among readers at a later stage of development. One way to address these challenges to researchers inside and outside the community of literacy researchers would be to form interdisciplinary research teams that include researchers who are well grounded in the pedagogy of reading and intimately familiar with the environments of classrooms and schools.

On the other hand, the current research base related to multimedia and learning to read is theoretically rich – much richer now, that is, than it was characterized in earlier reviews focusing on computer applications to reading and writing, which judged many studies to be atheoretical, horserace-like comparisons. For example, the current literature makes use of general theories such as the cognitive flexibility theory (Spiro et al., 1992); dual-coding theory (Sadoski & Paivio, 2001); semiotics (Labbo, 1996); theories of media, multimedia, and instructional design (e.g., Mayer, 2001; Salomon, 1979), and anchored instruction (Cognition and Technology Group at Vanderbilt University, 1994). It also includes more specific theories pertaining to reading pedagogy (e.g., the role of phonological development, e.g., see Wise & Olson, 1995), theories of how digital media comprise a new medium of reading and writing (Reinking, 1992, 1997), and theories about integrating technology into instructional contexts (e.g., Bruce & Rubin, 1993; Labbo & Reinking, 1999; Karchmer, 2001). That theoretical diversity reflects the many, sometimes competing, goals that literacy instruction entails and the many factors and variables that figure into designing instructional experiences to achieve those goals. Theoretical diversity, however, makes it sometimes difficult to synthesize strong recommendations for developing and implementing multimedia instructional interventions and activities that might enhance reading development. Nonetheless, a few at least tentative conclusions and recommendations emerge from the existing literature.

Currently, the deepest research base pertaining to multimedia and learning to read involves using synthesized or digitized speech to assist young readers acquire basic decoding skills. Using the capability of a computer to provide beginning readers assistance in the form of audio pronunciations of words and word parts under various conditions clearly seems to benefit decoding skills at least as much as adult-led activities using conventional printed materials. Further, young children do not seem to have difficulty recognizing and understanding high-quality pronunciations synthesized by the computer (Olson et al., 1986a). These conclusions are important given that computers may expand opportunities to children reading independently when an adult or other knowledgeable reader is unavailable to provide individual assistance with any word in a text.

However, the research is less clear on what the optimal conditions are for providing such assistance and what category of beginning readers might most benefit. There is some evidence that for such multimedia materials to be effective, children must have attained a stage of reading development where they have achieved a basic understanding that letters represent sounds (e.g., McKenna et al., 2003; Olson & Wise, 1992). However, the majority of research in this area has focused on children experiencing difficulty in learning to read. Despite gaps in the research, there seems to be no reason for designers of multimedia materials for young children to be cautious about making available the pronunciations of particular words in the text. Ideally perhaps, from a pedagogical point of view and consistent with the empirical uncertainty of the research, such applications would provide a teacher with various options for tailoring what words are available for pronunciation, what additional feedback might be included (e.g., phonics analogies), along with a tracking of children's selections.

The research base pertaining to how multimedia materials and activities might contribute to developing general comprehension ability (as opposed to enhancing comprehension of specific texts) and interest in reading is more diverse and typically less well developed, although the research in these areas showcases some interesting and innovative possibilities. Paralleling the findings related to decoding words, there is consistent evidence that providing readers of online texts with immediate access to the meanings of unfamiliar words enhances readers' meaning vocabularies and perhaps also readers' comprehension and their propensity to investigate words' meanings (Reinking & Rickman, 1990). Further, explanations that include video may be particularly helpful with some concepts (Kinzer & Risko, 1988; Miller & Gildea, 1987). However, this line of research has been dormant for many years, perhaps because it is relatively easy to conceptualize and implement such assistance and the demonstrated benefits seem logical and intuitive. Designers of instructional materials would seem well advised to include assistance with potentially difficult vocabulary employing the full range of media effects at their disposal (e.g., the written definition of an unfamiliar musical instrument might be accompanied by a sample of its sound, or a video clip showing someone playing it). In fact, organizations such as the Center for Applied Special Technology (http://www.cast.org/) have spearheaded the development of such types of textual assistance for online learning materials and lobbied for its use to assist students with a variety of disabilities.

Nonetheless, the research investigating young children's explorations of digital stories suggests caution in providing too much multimedia assistance if the goal is to promote story understanding. That caution seems particularly warranted for multimedia effects not directly related to the plot (Labbo & Kuhn, 2000) and for young readers who do not have a well-developed sense of story (DeJong & Bus, in press). Online versions of stories supplemented with multimedia effects do, however, seem to be motivating (Cordova & Lepper, 1996; DeJong & Bus, 2003), although it is unclear to what extent

young children may benefit from interacting with an adult during story reading or how online children's stories might be presented to duplicate the positive benefits of adult–child interactions during conventional storybook reading. Another possibility, yet to be investigated, is the extent to which engaging online multimedia reading materials might stimulate more interest and engagement in reading in general, including conventional printed materials.

Other important areas of teaching reading and learning to read are less well researched. Specifically, there have been few computer applications developed and researched aimed at helping readers to become more strategic in their approach to reading and to assume a more critical stance toward what they read, perhaps because using multimedia in service of these goals requires more complex theoretical perspectives and more divergent thinking and innovation to develop computer-based applications. Further, measuring fundamental changes in these aspects of reading is difficult requiring perhaps a commitment to long-term and longitudinal studies. The research suggests, for example, that students' familiarity with conventional printed texts and how they are typically used as authoritative sources of information across years of schooling may supercede the potential effects of a more critical and evaluative stance (e.g., Stahl et al., 1996). However, the few studies reviewed in the previous section of this chapter suggest some promising directions for designers and researchers, particularly those willing to make a long-term commitment to pursuing the possibilities afforded by multimedia formats and juxtaposing diverse texts in digital environments.

Likewise, little research has investigated how multimedia might generate more interest in and motivation to read. However, a few studies suggest that computer applications employing diverse media may contribute to teachers' attempts to address this goal in classrooms (Labbo, 1996; Reinking & Watkins, 2000). One theoretical point of view has been offered to argue that multimedia environments for reading are inherently more engaging than reading in print-based environments (Reinking, 2001), but this theory has yet to be investigated empirically.

Several issues are important for the future of research on how multimedia applications affect teaching reading and learning to read. First, more researchers and educators need to expand their conceptions of literacy to include multimedia forms of reading and writing and to accept that these forms have implications for virtually every aspect of teaching reading and learning to read. Although there have been continual calls to do so (e.g., Lemke, 1998; Leu & Reinking, 2004; Reinking, 1995), the field has been slow to respond. It seems difficult for literacy researchers and educators to abandon conventional print-based ideas and topics centered in the alphabetic code. For example, the concept of textual difficulty in terms of decoding and comprehension is central to long-standing conceptions of reading pedagogy (e.g., matching readers to texts in terms of difficulty). However, what makes a text difficult when readers have the option of hearing the pronunciation of a word they cannot decode or seeing a video that explains the meaning of an unfamiliar word?

A second and related issue is determining what skills and orientations reading teachers might teach to develop students' abilities to read multimedia texts, particularly on the Internet, which is increasingly a mainstream context for reading. What strategies are students using and what strategies are useful in processing multimedia information on the Internet? What criteria might be used to evaluate the reliability of such information? These and similar questions for the most part await empirical investigation among elementary and middle school students. Preliminary work has attempted to provide a theoretical orientation within which these questions might be framed in relation to developing literacy in schools (Leu, Kinzer, Coiro, & Commack, 2004).

A third issue revolves around the following question: How might promising instructional activities related to multimedia forms of reading be integrated into the language arts curriculum and instruction?

This question is critical given the investment of many educators in traditional models of schooling and conventional print-based literacy, the consequent slow pace of technology integration in teaching reading (see the International Reading Association, 2001), and the potentially radical changes in curriculum and instruction implied by digital access to multimedia sources of information (see standards established by the International Society for Technology in Education, 2002).

Research has established convincingly that simply making available new applications and activities involving computer-based technologies does not alone insure that they will be integrated effectively into instruction or that they will be used to promote new visions of language arts instruction. For example, Bruce and Rubin (1993) found that teachers used a computer-based application designed specifically to promote reading and writing for authentic purposes but they used it in a way that addressed their commitment to more conventional instructional goals and that was contrary to its intended purposes. Likewise, research has consistently shown that effective integration of new technologies in schools is related to teachers' beliefs about technology and about instruction and to a host of contextual factors that affect teaching and learning in schools (Ertmer, Addison, Lane, Ross, & Woods, 1999; McGee, 2000; Windschitl & Sahl, 2002; Zhao, Pugh, Sheldon, & Byers, 2002). One framework has been proposed for facilitating integration among literacy educators who as a whole are likely to be invested in printed materials (Reinking et al., 2000). Another dimension to facilitating integration of multimedia materials and activities into literacy instruction is to engage preservice teachers in exploring possibilities in programs of teacher education.

In the final analysis, knowing how multimedia might affect learning to read is not enough to insure that it will. We need research and methodologies that allow us not only to understand the implications and possibilities that multimedia forms of communication suggest for learning to read, but that also allow us to understand how we can effectively use that knowledge to effect positive changes in how it is taught in schools. Formative experiments contextualized in authentic school settings have been shown to be well suited for studying how technology can transform instruction (e.g., Reinking & Watkins, 2000). In the end, because learning to read takes place in schools, knowing how multimedia interacts with learning to read is as much about understanding schools as it is about understanding how multimedia changes texts and how students read them.

References

Atkinson, R., & Hansen, D. (1966–67). Computer-assisted instruction in initial reading: The Stanford project. *Reading Research Quarterly, 2*, 5–26.

Barron, R., Lovett, M., & McCabe, R. (1998). Using talking computers to remediate reading and spelling disabilities: The critical role of the print-to-sound unit. *Behavior Research Methods, Instruments and Computers, 30*(4), 610–616.

Beck, I. L., & McKeown, M. G. (2001). Text Talk: Capturing the benefits of read-aloud experiences for young children. *The Reading Teacher, 55*, 10–20.

Birkerts, S. (1994). *The Gutenberg elegies: The fate of reading in an electronic age.* Boston: Faber and Faber.

Blok, H., Oostdam, R., Otter, M. E., & Overmaat, M. (2002). Computer-assisted instruction in support of beginning reading instruction: A Review. *Review of Educational Research, 72*, 101–130.

Bolter, J. D. (1991). *Writing space: The computer, hypertext, and the history of writing.* Mahwah, NJ: Lawrence Erlbaum Associates.

Bolter, J. D. (2001). *Writing space: Computers, hypertext, and the remediation of print.* Mahwah, NJ: Lawrence Erlbaum Associates.

Bolter, J. D., & Grusin, R. (2000). *Remediation: Understanding new media.* Cambridge, MA: MIT Press.

Brandt, D. (2001). *Literacy in American lives.* New York: Cambridge University Press.

Bruce, B. C., & Rubin, A. (1993). *Electronic quills: A situated evaluation of using computers for writing in classrooms.* Hillsdale, NJ: Lawrence Erlbaum Associates.

Carpenter, P. A., Just, M. A., & Fallside, D. C. (1988). *The role of animation in understanding descriptions of kinematics.* Pittsburgh, PA: Carnegie Mellon University.

Chera, P., & Wood, C. (2003). Animated multimedia "talking books" can promote phonological awareness in children beginning to read. *Learning and Instruction, 13*(1), 33–52.

Cognition and Technology Group at Vanderbilt University. (1994). Multimedia environments for developing literacy in at-risk students. In B. Means (Ed.), *Technology and education reform: The reality behind the promise* (pp. 23–56). San Francisco: Jossey-Bass.

Cordova, D. I., & Lepper, M. R. (1996). Intrinsic motivation and the process of learning: Beneficial effects of contextualization, personalization, and choice. *Journal of Educational Psychology, 88*, 715–730.

Dale, E. 1946. *Audiovisual methods in teaching.* New York: Holt, Rinehart, and Winston.

DeJong, M. T., & Bus, A. G. (2002). Quality of book-reading matters for emergent readers: An experiment with the same book in a regular or electronic format. *Journal of Educational Psychology, 94*, 145–208.

DeJong, M. T., & Bus, A. G. (2003). How well suited are electronic books to supporting literacy? *Journal of Early Childhood Literacy, 3*, 147–164.

DeJong, M. T., & Bus, A. G. (2004). The efficacy of electronic books in fostering kindergarten children's emergent story understanding. *Reading Research Quarterly 39*, 378–393.

Durkin, D. (1978–79). What classroom observations reveal about reading comprehension instruction. *Reading Research Quarterly, 15*, 483–533.

Ehri, L. C. (1992). Reconceptualizing the development of sight word reading and its relationship to decoding. In P. B. Gought, L. C. Ehri, & R. Trieman (Eds.), *Reading acquisition* (pp. 107–143). Hillsdale, NJ: Lawrence Erlbaum Associates.

Ertmer, P. A., Addison, P., Lane, M., Ross, E., & Woods, D. (1999). Examining teachers' beliefs about the role of technology in the elementary classroom. *Journal of Research on Computing in Education, 32*, 54–72.

Flood, J., Heath, S. B., & Lapp, D. (Eds.). (1997). *Handbook of research on teaching literacy through the communicative and visual arts*. New York: McMillan.

Goodman, K. (1976). Reading: A psycholinguistic guessing game. In H. Singer, & R. Ruddell (Eds.), *Theoretical models and processes of reading* (pp. 497–508). Newark, DE: International Reading Association.

Gough, P. B. (1984). Word recognition. In P. D. Pearson (Ed.), *Handbook of reading research*, (Vol. 1, pp. 225–253). New York: Longman.

Hegarty, M., Carpenter, P. A., & Just, M. A. (1991). Diagrams in comprehension of scientific texts. In R. Barr, M. L. Kamil, P. Mosenthal, & P. D. Pearson (Eds.), *Handbook of reading research* (Vol. 2, pp. 641–648). New York: Longman.

Ho, C., & Ma, R. (1999). Training phonological strategies improves Chinese dyslexic children's character reading skills. *Journal of Research in Reading*, 22(2), 131–142.

Hynd, C. R., Jacobson, M., & Reinking, D. (1999, April). *Students' understanding of history using multiple texts: Development of disciplinary knowledge in a hypertext environment*. Paper presented at the annual meeting of the American Educational Research Association, Montreal, Quebec, Canada.

International Reading Association (2001). *Integrating literacy and technology into the curriculum: A position statement of the International Reading Association*. Retrieved August 2, 2004 from http://www.reading.org/focus/techn.html.

International Society for Technology in Education (2002). The National Educational Technology Standards (NETS) Project. Retrieved August 2, 2004 from http://cnets.este.org.

James, R. (1999). Navigating CD-ROMs: An exploration of children reading interactive narratives. *Children's Literature in Education*, 30, 47–63.

Jonassen, D. H., & Reeves, T. C. (1996). Learning with technology: Using computers as cognitive tools. In D. H. Jonassen (Ed.), *Handbook of research for educational communication and technology* (pp. 693–719). New York: Mcmillan.

Kamil, M. L., Kim, H., & Intrator, S. (2000). Effects of other technologies on literacy and literacy learning. In M. L. Kamil, P. B. Mosenthal, P. D. Pearson, R. Barr (Eds.), *Handbook of reading research. Vol. 3*, pp. 773–791. Mahwah, NJ: Lawrence Erlbaum Associates.

Kamil, M. L., & Lane, D. M. (1998). Researching the relation between technology and literacy: An agenda for the 21st century. In D. Reinking, M. C. McKenna, L. D. Labbo, & R. D. Kieffer (Eds.), *Handbook of literacy and technology: Transformations in a post-typographic world* (pp. 323–342). Mahwah, NJ: Lawrence Erlbaum Associates.

Karchmer, R. A. (2001). The journey ahead: Thirteen teachers report how the Internet influences literacy and literacy instruction in their K–12 classrooms. *Reading Research Quarterly*, 36, 442–466.

Kayany, J. M., & Yelsma, P. (2000). Displacement effects of online media in the socio-technical contexts of households. *Journal of Broadcasting Media*, 44, 215–229.

Kinzer, C. K., & Risko, V. J. (1988). *Macrocontexts to facilitate learning*. Paper presented at the 33rd Annual Conference of the International Reading Association, Toronto, Ontario, Canada.

Kress, G. (1996). *Reading images: The grammar of visual design*. London: Routledge.

Labbo, L. D. (1996). A semiotic analysis of young children's symbol making in a classroom computer center. *Reading Research Quarterly*, 31, 356–385.

Labbo, L. D., & Kuhn, M. R. (2000). Weaving chains of affect and cognition: A young child's understanding of CD-ROM talking books. *Journal of Literacy Research*, 32, 187–210.

Labbo, L. D., & Reinking, D. (1999). Negotiating the multiple realities of technology in literacy research and instruction. *Reading Research Quarterly*, 34, 478–492.

Labbo, L. & Reinking, D. (2003). Computers and early literacy education. In N. Hall, J. Larson, & J. Marsh (Eds.), *Handbook of early childhood literacy* (pp. 338–354). London, UK: Sage.

Lanham, R. A. (1993). *The electronic word: Democracy, technology, and the arts*. Chicago, IL: University of Chicago Press.

Lawless, K. A., Mills, R., & Brown, S. W. (2003). Children's hypertext navigation strategies. *Journal of Research on Technology in Education*, 34, 274–284.

Lemke, J. L. (1998). Metamedia literacy: Transforming meanings and media. In D. Reinking, M. C. McKenna, L. D. Labbo, & R. D. Kieffer (Eds.), *Handbook of literacy and technology: Transformations in a post-typographic world* (pp. 283–302). Mahwah, NJ: Lawrence Erlbaum Associates.

Leu, D. J. (2000). Literacy and technology: Deictic consequences for literacy education in an information age. In M. L. Kamil, P. B. Mosenthal, P. D. Pearson, & R. Barr (Eds.), *Handbook of reading research: Volume III* (pp. 743–770). Mahwah, NJ: Lawrence Erlbaum Associates.

Leu, D. J., & Kinzer, C. K. (2000). The convergence of literacy instruction with networked technologies for information, communication, and education. *Reading Research Quarterly, 35*, 108–127.

Leu, D. J., Kinzer, C. K., Coiro, J. L., & Commack, D. W. (2004). Toward a theory of new literacies emerging from the Internet and other information and communication technologies. In R. B. Ruddell & N. J. Unrau (Eds.), *Theoretical models and processes of reading* (5th ed.) (pp. 1570–1613). Newark, DE: International Reading Association.

Leu, D. J., & Reinking, D. (1996). Bringing insights from reading research to research on electronic learning environments. In H. van Oostendorp (Ed.), *Cognitive aspects of electronic text processing* (pp. 43–75). Norwood, NJ: Ablex.

Lundberg, I. (1995). The computer as a tool of remediation in the education of students with reading disabilities: A theory-based approach. *Learning Disability Quarterly, 18*(2), 89–99.

Mayer, R. E. (2001). *Multimedia learning*. Cambridge, UK: Cambridge Press.

McConkie, G. W., & Zola, D. (1987). Two examples of computer-based research on reading: Eye movement monitoring and computer-aided reading. In D. Reinking (Ed.), *Reading and computers: Issues for theory and practice* (97–108). New York: Teachers College Press.

McGee, P. (2000). Persistence and motivation: A new teacher's path to technology infusion. *Computers in the Schools, 16*, 197–211.

McKenna, M. C. Kear, J. J., & Ellsworth, R. A. (1995). Children's attitudes toward reading: A national survey. *Reading Research Quarterly, 30*, 934–957.

McKenna, M. C., Reinking, D., & Bradley, B. A. (2003). The effects of electronic trade books on the decoding growth of beginning readers. In R. M. Joshi, C. K. Leong, & B. L. J. Kaczmarek (Eds.), *Literacy acquisition: The role of phonology, morphology, and orthography* (pp. 193–202). Amsterdam: IOS Press.

Miller, G. A., & Gildea, P. M. (1987). How children learn words. *Scientific American, 257*(3), 94–99.

Miller, L., & Olson, J. (1998). Literacy research oriented toward features of technology and classrooms. In D. Reinking, M. C. McKenna, L. D. Labbo, & R. D. Kieffer (Eds.), *Handbook of literacy and technology: Transformations in a post-typographic world* (pp. 343–360). Mahwah, NJ: Lawrence Erlbaum Associates.

Myers, J., & Beach, R. (2001). Hypermedia authoring as critical literacy. *Journal of Adolescent and Adult Literacy, 44*, 538–545.

Myers, J., Hammett, R., & McKillop, A. M. (1998). Opportunities for critical literacy and pedagogy in student-authored hypermedia. In D. Reinking, M. C. McKenna, L. D. Labbo, & R. D. Kieffer (Eds.), *Handbook of literacy and technology: Transformations in a post-typographic world* (pp. 63–78). Mahwah, NJ: Lawrence Erlbaum Associates.

National Reading Panel (2000). *Teaching Children to Read: Summary Report*. Retrieved January 7, 2004, from http//www.nationalreadingpanel.org/.

Niederhauser, D. S., Reynolds, R. E., Salmen, D. J., & Skolmoski, P. (2000). The influence of cognitive load on learning from hypertext. *Journal of Eduational Computing Research, 23*, 237–255.

Olson, K. & Johnston, J. (1989). *The use of the computer as a writing tool in a kindergarten and first grade classroom* (CIEL Pilot Year Final Report, Part 2). Ann Arbor, MI: Ann Arbor School of Education.

Olson, R. K., Foltz, G., & Wise, B. W. (1986a). Reading instruction and remediation using voice synthesis in computer interaction. *Proceeding of the Human Factors Society, 2*, 1336–1339.

Olson, R. K., Foltz, G., & Wise, B. W. (1986b). Reading instruction and remediation with the aid of computer speech. *Behavior Research Methods, Instruments, and Computer, 18*, 93–99.

Olson, R. K., & Wise, B. W. (1992). Reading on the computer with orthographic and speech feedback: An overview of the Colorado Remedial Reading Project. *Reading and Writing: An Interdisciplinary Journal, 4*, 107–144.

Olson, R. K., & Wise, B. W. (2004, January). *Computer-based remediation for reading and related phonological disabilities in 2nd to 5th grade children, and the importance of appropriate controls in research*. Paper presented at the

International Workshop on Computer-Based Reading Instructional Programs, Paris, France.

Olson, R. K., Wise, B., Ring, J., & Johnson, M. (1997). Computer-based remedial training in phoneme awareness and phonological decoding: Effects on the post training development of word recognition. *Scientific Studies in Reading, 1*, 235–253.

Paris, S. (in press). Re-interpreting the development of reading skills. *Reading Research Quarterly.*

Pressley, M. (2000). What should comprehension instruction be the instruction of? In M. L. Kamil, P. B. Mosenthal, P. D. Pearson, & R. Barr (Eds.), *Handbook of reading research: Volume III* (pp. 545–561). Mahwah, NJ: Lawrence Erlbaum Associates.

Reinking, D. (1992). Differences between electronic and printed texts: An agenda for research. *Journal of Educational Multimedia and Hypermedia 1* (1), 11–24.

Reinking, D. (1995). Reading and writing with computers: Literacy research in a post-typographic world. In K. A. Hinchman, D. J. Leu, & C. K. Kinzer (Eds.), *Perspectives in literacy research and practice* (pp. 17–34). Forty-fourth Yearbook of the National Reading Conference. Chicago, IL: National Reading Conference.

Reinking, D. (1997). Me and my hypertext: A multiple digression analysis of technology and literacy (sic). *The Reading Teacher, 50*, 626–643.

Reinking, D. (1998). Synthesizing technological transformations of literacy in a post typographic world. In D. Reinking, M. McKenna, L. D. Labbo, & R. Kieffer (Eds.), *Handbook of literacy and technology* (pp. xi–xxx). Mahwah, NJ: Lawrence Erlbaum Associates.

Reinking, D. (2001). Multimedia and engaged reading in a digital world. In L. Verhoeven & C. Snow (Eds.), *Literacy and motivation: Reading engagement in individuals and groups* (pp. 195–221). Mahwah, NJ: Lawrence Erlbaum Associates.

Reinking, D., & Bridwell-Bowles, L. (1991). Computers in reading and writing research. In R. Barr, M. L. Kamil, P. Mosenthal, & P. D. Pearson (Eds.), *Handbook of reading research: Vol. 2* (pp. 310–340). New York: Longman.

Reinking, D., & Chanlin, L. J. (1994). Graphic aids in electronic texts. *Reading Research and Instruction, 33*, 207–232.

Reinking, D., Labbo, L. D., & McKenna, M. (1997). Navigating the changing landscape of literacy: Current theory and research in computer-based reading and writing. In J. Flood, S. B. Heath, and D. Lapp (Eds.), *Handbook of research on teaching literacy through the communicative and visual arts* (pp. 77–92). New York: Macmillan.

Reinking, D., Labbo, L. D., & McKenna, M. C. (2000). From assimilation to accommodation: A developmental framework for integrating digital technologies into literacy research and instruction. *Journal of Research in Reading 23* (2), 110–122.

Reinking, D., Pickle, M., & Tao, L. (1996). *The effects of inserted questions and mandatory review in computer-mediated texts* (Reading Research Report #50). Athens, GA: National Reading Research Center.

Reinking, D., & Rickman, S. S. (1990). The effects of computer-mediated texts on the vocabularly learning and comprehensions of intermediate-grade readers. *Journal of Reading Behavior, 22*, 395–411.

Reinking, D., & Watkins, J. (2000). A formative experiment investigating the use of multimedia book reviews to increase elementary students' independent reading. *Reading Research Quarterly, 35*, 384–489.

Reistma, P. (1988). Reading practice for beginners: Effects of guided reading, reading while-listening, and independent reading with computer-based speech feedback. *Reading Research Quarterly, 23*, 219–235.

Reitsma, P., & Wesseling, R. (1998) Effects of computer-asisted training of blending skills in kindergarten. *Scientific Studies of Reading, 2* (4), 301–320.

Ricci, C. M., & Beal, C. R. (2002). The effect of interactive media on children's story memory. *Journal of Educational Psychology, 94*, 138–144.

Risko, V. J., Kinzer, C. K., Goodman, J., McLarity, K., Dupree, A., & Martin, H. (1989). *Effects of macrocontexts on reading comprehension, composition of stories, and vocabulary development.* Paper presented at the meeting of the American Education Research Association, San Francisco, CA.

Rouet, J. F., Levonen, J. J., Dillon, A., & Spiro, R. J. (1996). *Hypertext and cognition.* Mahwah, NJ: Lawrence Erlbaum Associates.

Sadoski, M., & Paivio, A. (2001). *Imagery and text: A dual coding theory of reading and writing.* Mahwah, NJ: Lawrence Erlbaum Associates.

Salomon, G. (1979). *Interaction of media, cognition, and learning.* San Francisco: Jossey-Bass

Salomon, G., Globerson, T., & Guterman, E. (1989). The computer as a zone of proximal development: Internalizing reading-related metacognitions from a reading partner. *Journal of Educational Psychology, 81*, 620–627.

Salomon, G., Perkins, D. N., & Globerson, T. (1991). Partners in cognition: Extending human intelligence with intelligent technologies. *Educational Researcher, 20*(3), 2–9.

Segers, E., & Verhoeven, L. (2004). Computer-supported phonological awareness intervention for kindergarten children with specific language impairment. *Language, Speech, and Hearing Services in Schools, 35*, 229–239.

Shapiro, A. M. (1998). Promoting active learning: The role of system structure in learning from hypertext. *Human-Computer Interaction, 13*, 1–35.

Shapiro, A., & Niederhauser, D. (2004). Learning from hypertext: Research issues and findings. In D. Jonassen (Ed.), *Handook of research for educational communications and technology* (pp. 605–620). Mahwah, NJ: Lawrence Erlbaum Associates.

Sharp, D. L. M., Bransford, J. D., Vye, N. J., Goldman, S. R., Kinzer, C., & Soraci, Jr., S. (1992). Literacy in an age of integrated media. In M. J. Dreher & W. H. Slater (Eds.) *Elementary school literacy: Critical issues* (pp. 183–210). Norwood, MA: Christopher Gordon.

Spiro, R., Feltovitch, P., Jacobson, M., & Coulson, R. (1992). Cognitive flexibility, constructivism, and hypertext: Random access for advanced knowledge acquisition in ill-structured domains. In T. Duffy & D. Jonassen (Eds.), *Constructivism and the technology of instruction* (pp. 57–75). Hillsdale, NJ: Lawrence Erlbaum Associates.

Stahl, S. A., Hynd, C. R., Britton, B. K., McNish, M. M., & Bosquet, D. (1996). What happens when students read multiple source documents in history? *Reading Research Quarterly, 31*, 430–436.

Stanovich, K. E. (1986). Matthew effects in reading: Some consequences of individual differences in the acquisition of literacy. *Reading Research Quarterly, 21*, 360–407.

Tobias, S. (1987). Mandatory text review and interaction with stuent characteristics. *Journal of Educational Psychology, 79*, 154–161.

Tobias, S. (1988). Teaching strategic text review by computer and interaction with student characteristics. *Computers in Human Behavior, 4*, 299–310.

Wagner, D., & Kozma, R. (2003). *New technologies for literacy and adult education: A global perspective.* Retrieved August 2, 2004, from http://www.literacyonline.org/ICTconf/

Walker, S., & Reynolds, L. (2000). Screen design for children's reading: Some key issues. *Journal of Research in Reading, 23*, 224–234.

Windschitl, M, & Sahl, K. (2002). Tracing teachers' use of technology in a laptop computer school: The interplay of teacher beliefs, social dynamics and institutional culture. *American Educational Research Journal, 39*, 165–205.

Wineburg, S. S. (1991). Historical problem solving: A study of the cognitive processes used in the evaluation of documentary and pictorial evidence. *Journal of Educational Psychology, 83*, 73–77.

Wise, B., & Olson, R. (1995). Computer-based phonological awareness and reading instruction. *Annals of Dyslexia, 45*, 99–122.

Wise, B., Olson, R., Anstett, M., Andrews, L., Terjak, M., Schnider, V., & Kostuch, J. (1989). Implementing a long-term computerized remedial reading program with synthetic speech feedback: Hardware, software, and real-world issues. *Behavior Research Methods, Instruments, and Computers, 21*, 173–180.

Wise, B. W., Ring, J., & Olson, R. K. (1999). Training phonological awareness with and without attention to articulation. *Journal of Experimental Child Psychology, 72*, 271–304.

Wise, B. W., Ring, J., & Olson, R. K. (2000). Individual differences in gains from computer-assisted remedial reading with more emphasis on phonological analysis or accurate reading in context. *Journal of Experimental Child Psychology, 77*, 197–235.

Zammit, K., & Callow, J. (2000). Ideology and technology: A visual and textual analysis of two popular CD-ROM programs. *Linguistics in Education, 10*, 89–105.

Zhao, Y., Pugh, K., Sheldon, S., & Byers, J. L. (2002). Conditions for classroom technology innovations. *Teachers College Record, 104*, 482–515.

CHAPTER 24

Multimedia Learning of History

Jennifer Wiley
Ivan K. Ash
University of Illinois at Chicago

Abstract

This chapter discusses how multimedia learning environments have been used in history instruction and when learning with multimedia is effective. For the purposes of this chapter, multimedia learning is defined as acquiring knowledge in a domain through interacting with an educational environment that presents information using multiple sources. Media here are defined as channels by which information is accessed that differ based on the document, source (e.g., newspaper, biography, political speech, textbook), or mode of communication (e.g., texts, sounds, pictures, video, animation, maps, charts, graphs). Multimedia learning environments are used in history instruction for two main purposes: (1) multiple-source environments attempt to make history learning more like the activities of real historians, and (2) graphics or archives are often used to make the context of the time under question more engaging, vivid, or personally relevant for the learner.

Introduction

Multimedia learning usually refers to computer-based learning tools such as CD-ROMs or the Internet in which text, pictures, animation, sounds, movies, and other media can be combined in the presentation of information. However, this is a somewhat narrower interpretation of multimedia than is appropriate in the case of learning about history. The usual history textbook combines texts of historical narratives with maps, charts, timelines, pictures, diagrams, and paintings to convey the historical facts or events. Furthermore, history teachers often supplement reading assignments and lectures with films or documentaries based on historical events. Therefore, even traditional textbook or classroom instruction in history can be considered multimedia. Likewise, the sense of multimedia needs to be broadened when we consider the various information sources that historians use as they attempt to study history by searching out, considering, and interpreting different types of historical artifacts or evidence. In reconstructing a historical event, a historian may look to original source documents such as diaries, government documents, logs, photographs, and physical artifacts, or secondary documents such as newspaper reports, magazine articles, biographies, or other historians' evidence and interpretations. Therefore, the study of history, as the historian knows it, is essentially a multimedia experience as the historian compares and contrasts information across multiple sources, even when all sources might be of the same medium. Considering the information available in multiple artifacts requires integration across the different sources of information. Therefore, in a broad sense, learning from multiple sources, as it represents a form of multiple-channel learning, can also be considered as multimedia learning.

This chapter discusses the available evidence on how features of multimedia learning environments affect history learning and when learning with multimedia is effective. For the purposes of this chapter, multimedia learning is defined as acquiring knowledge in a domain through interacting with an educational environment that presents information using multiple sources. Media here is defined as channels by which information is accessed that differ based on the document, source (e.g., newspaper, biography, political speech, textbook), or mode of communication (e.g., texts, sounds, pictures, video, animation, maps, charts, graphs). Under this definition, educational activities that present a topic using multiple sources and/or multiple modes of communication are considered multimedia learning environments. Conversely, any topic that is introduced solely through one source or mode (text or otherwise) would be considered single-media learning.

Multimedia learning environments appear to be used in history instruction for two main purposes: (1) multiple-source environments attempt to make history learning more like the activities of real historians, and (2) graphics or archives are often used to make the context of the time under question more engaging, vivid, or personally relevant for the learner.

Enhancing Collective Memory versus Disciplinary Knowledge

The goal of learning in history is subject to multiple interpretations by educators (e.g., Quinlan, 1999). Seixas (2000) discussed two of the potential goals of history education as either "enhancing collective memory" or the "disciplinary approach." Enhancing collective memory is the traditional view of history education, which proposes that the goal of history instruction is to provide learners with a base of historical knowledge that is deemed important by authority figures who guide educational policy. Under this goal of history education, students' primary task is the memorization of events, names, dates, and locations preferably in the order in which they occurred (Spoehr & Spoehr, 1994).

The second approach to history instruction is based on teaching the skills of inquiry used by historians, and is consistent with constructivist theories of learning. The constructivist perspective proposes that learning that is done as a form of inquiry leads to better understanding of the subject matter than learning that is transmitted through lecture or memorization. In a history classroom with this approach, rather than being simply told to believe a single story or learn what is in the textbook, students are presented with information from a variety of sources and perspectives, and taught the standards of historical inquiry, investigation, and debate. Specifically, students learn by generating their own historical accounts and by evaluating the claims of other historical interpretations. In this "disciplinary approach" (Seixas, 2000), students come to understand what makes a valid historical account, the relation between evidence and interpretation, and the importance of comparison among alternative accounts.

The goal behind such a constructivist approach is to advance learning in history beyond the simple accumulation in memory of isolated historical facts. It could be argued that the content domain of history could span all of the seminal events in human existence. Therefore, exhaustive teaching of all historical domain knowledge would seem to be an impossible exercise. Hence, teaching the skills necessary to assimilate, judge, and apply historical information may be a more appropriate goal of history education. An additional argument for this approach is that historical thinking skills of engaging in historical inquiry and writing in the historical genre are now part of the National Standards for History (National Center for History in the Schools, 1996). Similarly, the Advanced Placement (AP) tests in history include document-based questions, which usually provide both textual and graphic documents (e.g., editorial cartoons, charts, or maps) and require students to write short essay answers that require the integration and interpretation of the evidence provided in the documents. These reasons may explain why most research in multimedia instruction in history has been based in a "disciplinary approach" to history instruction.

Research on Multimedia Learning of History

Two exemplary studies mark the beginning of cognitive approaches to multimedia history instruction. An influential monograph by Thomas Holt, a professional historian and college educator, sparked serious interest in teaching students relatively authentic historical inquiry skills (Holt, 1990). His monograph discusses providing students with primary sources in order to learn about Reconstruction efforts in the U.S. South following the Civil War. To learn about these people and this time, students were given several primary sources including a letter from freed slaves of Edisto Island, South Carolina, eloquently arguing for their right to own land they were given by the government, and that was subsequently taken from them and returned to the former (white)

owners. The students' use of multiple primary sources was supported by the teacher through a specific inquiry question. The students then were left to reason through the available evidence and confront the task of interpretation for themselves. Holt reported that students who engaged in this sort of history lesson started to see history as much more than learning names, dates, or "someone else's" facts about historical events. History is more than ordering events into established chronologies. Instead, authentic materials such as letters and diary entries prompt thinking, questioning, and interpretation. Students gain an understanding of history as an inquiry process. They construct their own understanding of both the subject matter and the discipline. Holt further reccommends this method of instruction at both college and high school levels, based on his interviews with high school students. His intuitions as a history teacher fall very close to a constructivist learning approach that is currently favored by many cognitively oriented researchers.

Around the same time as the Holt monograph, Wineburg published his own empirical investigation of the differences between the ways historians and students approach source documents and historical problem solving (Wineburg, 1991). Again, his study involved presenting people with multiple sources, in this case related to the Battle of Lexington during the American Revolutionary War. Participants were presented with several kinds of documents, including diary entries, a letter, a newspaper report, three paintings, and excerpts from an autobiography, a formal deposition, a historical novel, and a high school textbook. Then they were asked to think aloud as they constructed historical accounts of the battle. Wineburg documented several striking differences between novices and expert historians in the way they approached the documents. First, historians were more likely to identify the source of the information, comment on it, and use it as they interpreted the content. Wineburg refers to this as a *sourcing heuristic*. Second, historians attempted to place the events noted in the sources in a temporal

Irish Potato Famine from either the Sourcer's Apprentice environment or a textbook-like chapter. Students were presented with either eight "sources" about the potato famine, or a single chapter containing the same exact information. Additionally, there was a manipulation of the writing task that students were given. All students were told that "Historian's work from sources including newspaper articles, autobiographies, and government documents like census reports to create histories.... Your task is to take the role of historian and develop a historical account about what produced the significant changes in Ireland's population between 1846 and 1850." Students were either asked to write an argument or a narrative by replacing the underlined phrase with "a narrative" or "an argument." No further instruction was given on what either type of essay would require. Students relied on their own intuitions about these essay types. Several measures of learning showed that students given the argument writing instruction and a multiple source environment, learned better than students in the single text and narrative instruction conditions. Follow-up studies found that the ability to look at multiple sources at once (Wiley, 2001) was also critical and allowed students to engage in more comparison and integration across sources. The important results that have been replicated across several studies (Voss & Wiley, 1997, 2000; Wiley, 2001; Wiley & Voss, 1996, 1999) are that learning tasks that seem to prompt the integration of information across sources, such as writing an argument, lead to the best learning from multiple sources. Presenting multiple sources alone does not lead to better learning. The interaction of the task and the presentation of information is significant, and both need to be present for students to engage in active learning and construct their own understanding of the topic to be explained. The importance of using a writing task that prompts integration or explanation has also been studied by other researchers. For instance, Stahl and his colleagues (Stahl, Hynd, Britton, McNish, & Bosquet, 1996) have examined differences

in learning when students write opinion versus descriptive essays. This work is also consistent with Greene (1994), who has found that writing tasks that prompt interpretation are best for developing historical thinking.

A final related study on the benefits of learning from multiple sources in history comes from O'Neill and colleagues (O'Neill & Sohbat, 2004; O'Neill, Sohbat, Martin, Asgari, Lort, & Sha, 2003) who designed a Web-based mentorship program to complement inquiry learning at the high school level. This program, called Tracking Canada's Past (TCP), is a 10-week history unit on the construction of the Canadian Pacific Railway (CPR). Instruction began with a two-week unit in which students were instructed on the traditional "textbook" history of the CPR. Then, they began group projects on issues about the CPR that were not presented in the textbook such as economic issues, labor issues, legal issues, and how the construction affected the native peoples.

What is interesting about this project is that the nature and content of the multimedia materials used by the students in their investigations was not controlled by the researchers (in contrast to all of the studies listed previously that preselected information for students), and due to this the content varied greatly between the different schools that participated. For example, some of the schools had limited access to the Internet while others had ample access, and some were able to use the public archives in their towns, while other towns discouraged the use of public archives by school groups (O'Neill et al., 2003). Instead of controlling or tracking the sources and modes of information accessed by students, this project used an online discussion board called the Knowledge Forum, (Scardamalia & Bereiter, 1994), where each student group communicated with an expert mentor. These mentors were either history graduate students or individuals from area historical societies who were familiar with the topic. The volunteer mentors communicated back and forth with students by posting messages on the discussion board, which were accessible to all members of a group. The mentors worked with the students to help them decide how and where to look for evidence, how to judge and interpret the evidence, and how to report their findings. In their original design study, O'Neill et al. (2003) found that although there was great variability in the use of the discussion board between and within groups, the majority of students actively posted messages to the board and the vast majority of postings were project related. In a follow-up to their original design study, O'Neill and Sohbat (2004) attempted to assess students' levels of thinking about historical evidence and methodology before and after the program using an assessment based on Shemilt's (1987) categories of understanding of history. They found that 48% of the 112 tenth-graders that participated in the program showed signs of more advanced understanding of history as compared to pre-program measures. These results are promising because they show that multimedia-based inquiry projects may influence students' understanding of history as a discipline.

This project used learning activities with a complex set of features: extensive initial instruction in the content area, working in groups, the assignment of specific inquiry tasks, access to original source information, interaction with knowledgeable mentors to guide the multimedia inquiry, and the presentation of the results of the inquiry projects to the class. All of the features of the environment may have had an influence on how the students learned to talk about historical evidence. It has been noted that one of the primary differences between the expert and students in Wineburg's (1991) seminal study was their sense of audience in their presentation of arguments as evidence (see also Greene, 1994; Seixas, 1994a). Professional historians' writings were presented as if intended for a large audience engaged in an ongoing discourse on a controversy, while students discussed their writing as if it was intended for a single authority who would judge the "correctness" of their argument. The students in the TCP program may have achieved a more ex-

pert sense of audience through both their interactions with their expert mentors, as well as through having to present their findings to their peers. More study is needed to ferret out which set of this program's activities is responsible for improvements in students' historical thinking, but it is especially interesting to determine if providing students with expert and peer audiences for their thinking helps them to understand the nature of history better.

The preceding studies have all highlighted how multimedia environments can be used for inquiry tasks, in which the student emulates the authentic process of historical inquiry. A second main class of use of multimedia in the history classroom is the use of graphics, videos, or other artifacts to make the context of the time under question more engaging, vivid, or personally relevant for the learner.

In terms of generating interest, video-based media seems among the most compelling. Films have a huge impact on our sense of history. Starting as young children we glean our first images of heroes and historical events from films. Among fourth and fifth graders, Barton (1995) found that the most commonly reported sources of historical knowledge were from relatives and then from popular media, especially television and movies. But films, as informal sources of historical knowledge, perhaps remain the largest source of historical information for many. Both Wineburg and Seixas have noted the influence of films on people's understanding of history. Wineburg (2000) noted that both students and their parents make references to movies such as *Forrest Gump* and *Schindler's List* to support claims in their arguments about historical events. Seixas (1994b) found students were unable to appreciate that the film *Dances with Wolves* did not accurately depict that time.

In terms of use of film media in formal (classroom) instruction, some positive learning effects have been documented. For example, Swan (1994, 1996–1997) has investigated the use of a commercial hypermedia application called *Set on Freedom* to teach students about the civil rights movement.

Several studies have found advantages when students learned from chapters with video than from chapters without. Further, Swan has found that including videos as part of a hypermedia environment helps students to see relationships between historical events and people, places and ideas.

Another interesting use of graphics in interactive multimedia has been to teach young children a sense of historical time (Masterman & Rogers, 2002). Elementary school children often have great difficulty thinking about the past as continuous and connected to the present. Instead children's sense of the past has been described as an undifferentiated time when their parents or other people were young, and there were wars, dinosaurs, kings, and sometimes Jesus (Barton & Levstik, 1996; Lynn, 1993). Young children develop a number of heuristics for reasoning about historical time, such as the past being "colorless" (Masterman & Rogers, 2002) explaining why black and white photographs are of older times than those in color. The past happens before the child's life, and young children's only sense of chronology is through what they have experienced. Thus, their understanding of past time is often disconnected from the present and lumped together as one time before they were born. However, an understanding of chronology across both present and past is essential for historical understanding, and is a critical precursor to the skill of contextualization where the reader needs to place new information on events in their historical time and context. The understanding of historical time and chronology is often still incomplete even by the time students enter secondary school (Masterman & Rogers, 2002).

Using the metaphor of time travel, Masterman and Rogers (2002) developed a multimedia system that provided a road map timeline along which students found photographs, video, text, and audio clips about personalities and events in British history. In addition to mapping out a timeline, the program integrated some learning activities that involved sequencing tasks such as unscrambling diary pages and spotting anachronisms. Students navigated the road map with tasks such as figuring out what happened during the Fire of London and finding out how the days of the week got their names. Students reported their findings in a logbook. Five pairs of British school children aged six and seven all showed some ability to reason about time using this system. All pairs were able to put the events of the Fire of London in sequence. Most pairs showed lively debate when asked to spot anachronisms. These observations suggest that sequencing activities such as these may facilitate the development of an understanding of historical time, but further evaluation needs to be done.

Several other researchers have used activities with photographs and graphics to help students develop a sense of historical time. In a series of studies, Barton and Levstik have also examined young children's abilities to sequence historical photos, and other ways of incorporating photographs into the history classroom (Barton & Levstik, 1996; Levstik & Barton, 1996). Based on his research, Barton (2001) has suggested that using historical pictures in the classroom is one way to engage students in historical inquiry activities. Barton proposes that instead of using pictures as mere visual aids or examples, historical pictures can be the content of the lesson, with students being explicitly taught how to analyze the photographs. In one activity, Barton suggests teachers could present students with historic pictures from different times at a single location, and ask probing questions to help the students think about what the differences are between sets of historical images, or differences between the historical images and what they see today. Smith and Blankinship (1999) created a multimedia activity very close to this suggestion in which students used digital cameras to take pictures of buildings and locations around their communities. Back at school, the students download the picture and location information into an interactive computer interface. Using Global Positioning System information, this system then searches a database for any pictures of that building or location from a large online database of historic photographs. This interface also gives students tools to use to identify objects in the historic photos and make notes on differences and similarities between different eras. Both activities are intended to improve historical reasoning and analysis skills through the compelling and personally involving medium of photographs. However, because there has been no research done on these activities measuring learning outcomes, the effectiveness of using historic photographs in these ways in the classroom is still unknown.

Finally, one of the most powerful sources of information for historians are data archives, such as census data. In keeping with the trend toward authentic or discipline-based instruction, attempts have been made to use these tools in the classroom as well (Radinsky, 2004). For example, Radinsky and colleagues have developed a unit that uses census data as well as texts and maps, to teach students about the Great Migration of African Americans to the urban north of the United States in the early 20th century. This instructional unit was developed and tested on college students preparing to be history teachers. By design, the unit had four phases: (1) students read and discuss a secondary text and primary sources, and develop research questions, (2) students gather data from online documents, (3) students develop a historical argument and prepare a presentation, and (4) students present the results of their inquiry to the class.

The Great Migration unit has embedded in it several supports that seem important for effective learning. Embedded in the first phase was explicit instruction in the conventions of working from primary sources: making explicit observations from artifacts and discriminating observation from interpretation or inference. Students are also supported in this phase by the development of a concept map on the blackboard. All proposed inquiry questions are also recorded. For the second phase, students are given a preselected page of Web resources that can be used as starting points for their online inquiry. They are also scaffolded in their investigation through the use of a worksheet that prompts them to consider the nature of the source, and the claims and evidence it

offers (and conveniently, the program links the information entered on the worksheet to the original source). Students can also generate and add original text. Finally, students are prompted to give a theme label to each note they create. This helps them to reflect on which inquiry questions might be most answerable given the information they found, and theme labels often shift as inquiry progresses. Students are supported in creating an argument through a template Web page (basically a five-paragraph essay). Arguments consist of a main page with an introduction, outline of points, and conclusion, and are linked to three-point pages in which students must provide specific claims and evidence. Again the links to the original data sources are included.

The intended outcome, in addition to developing Web searching and authoring skills, is that students will gain a better understanding of what it is to "do history," that is improvement in the skills of developing arguments from evidence and developing relevant and answerable research questions. Although no evaluation yet is available on this project, it incorporates several design principles that have been successful in supporting argument–evidence coordination in other subject matter areas (Loh et al., 2001) and several elements of this instructional unit are similar to those that have been used successfully in history instruction in the past (Britt & Aglinskas, 2002; Spoehr & Spoehr, 1994; Wiley & Voss, 1999). The use of census data and population maps is an interesting addition to the multimedia and primary sources that have been previously included in instruction and it will be interesting to see whether it can be leveraged into better student learning.

Limitations of Research on Multimedia Learning of History

At the beginning of this chapter, we proposed that the process of authentic historical inquiry is by definition a multimedia experience. A growing number of researchers are examining how instruction in the knowledge and skills of history as a discipline can be accomplished through specific-inquiry learning tasks and multimedia environments. A few studies have shown, on the basis of controlled experiments, that such multimedia learning can be effective (Britt & Aglinskas, 2002; Spoehr & Spoehr, 1994; Wiley & Voss, 1999). In addition to these important pieces of evidence about when multimedia learning in history can be effective, there have been many more investigations that have looked at other new and innovative ways to incorporate multimedia and technology into the classroom. One limitation of the remainder of this research is that the investigations tend to consist of "design studies" instead of controlled experiments. The data reported for many of these studies are observations about the pragmatic constraints of the technology and reports of the students' acceptance of or abilities to use the educational tools. While the systems or tools developed in this type of research are often strikingly creative, research that focuses on the usability of the technology should be viewed as research on multimedia design or use, and not as research on multimedia learning of history. The main difference is while the former avenue of research attempts to engineer multimedia technologies and courses for the classroom, the later attempts to uncover how multimedia learning environments affect the quality and type of domain knowledge students acquire.

There may be several reasons behind the lack of well-designed studies that systematically investigate the effects of the content and design of multimedia environments on history learning. First, because of the nature of history as a discipline, the need for and advantages of multimedia learning may often be taken for granted. A second reason may be that while rote memorization learning lends itself to easy assessment of learning outcomes, assessing improvement in historical disciplinary knowledge is less intuitive and straightforward.

Some studies on multimedia instruction in history do report pre-post gains in learning and this is a good start. However, pre-post designs cannot address whether the multimedia environment is better than learning from a textbook or lectures. This is a critical question because the costs of multimedia instruction are typically higher than those that involve textbooks. The limitation of the literature on multimedia instruction in history is that only a small portion of studies have seen their way through to controlled experiments that can help us to understand which alternatives produce the best learning outcomes.

Implications of Research on Multimedia Learning in History

Multimedia learning environments seem to be well suited for history instruction, especially when the goal of the instruction is to promote disciplinary knowledge in students. Historical thinking and reasoning skills can be acquired through inquiry-based learning tasks that require students to assess historical evidence and materials from across a number of sources. Students need to learn to compare and contrast differing accounts of historical events based on evidence from primary sources and historical artifacts. In multimedia inquiry tasks, students construct their knowledge of a historical topic, as opposed to being presented with information in one "true" narrative format. Because of the constructivist nature of these tasks, they are also consistent with cognitive theories of learning that predict that active inquiry tasks should be the most effective methods of promoting content knowledge. This prediction has been supported by some of the studies reviewed in this chapter (Britt and Aglinskas, 2002; Wiley & Voss, 1996, 1999). Therefore, the use of inquiry tasks in multimedia learning environments seems to be an effective way for learners to acquire both disciplinary knowledge and topic content knowledge.

However, as Wineburg (1991) showed in his expert/novice study of historical reasoning, these disciplinary skills of historical inquiry do not come naturally to students. Therefore, simply giving students access to multiple sources or multimedia learning environments will not guarantee any meaningful learning. This type of knowledge needs to be acquired through participation in highly structured, guided activities with a clear problem-solving or inquiry goal. All the research studies in which significant learning gains were obtained in multimedia environments put students in these types of guided learning contexts. Furthermore, the research suggests that there are benefits to active instruction or guidance in the skills of historical inquiry (O'Neill & Sohbat, 2004) and that this type of instruction is appropriate in the earliest stages of education (Barton, 2002). Hence, at every level of history education students may benefit from direct instruction in the way historians use, judge, and interpret historical sources and evidence. This interaction between the educational task and the nature or structure of the multimedia environment is of primary importance in planning curriculum, designing multimedia technology, and researching the effectiveness of multimedia instruction.

Future Directions for Research on Multimedia Learning in History

Although there are many possible future directions for this research, we will focus on three that seem most striking: (1) the need to develop new ways of assessing historical understanding, (2) the need for investigations of individual differences and how they may effect learning from multimedia, and (3) the need for controlled studies investigating the effects of multimedia instruction on student learning and understanding.

In terms of the first future direction, to the extent that instruction continues using the disciplinary approach to teach historical thinking skills, then it is an important question as to how historical reasoning skill may be best assessed. Wineburg (2000), among others, has noted the difficulty of

attempting to measure historical understanding using traditional methods such as multiple-choice tests. Simple fact-based tests will likely not be good measures of improvements in historical thinking skills or understanding (Alonso-Tapia & Villa, 1999). It is clear that authentic training approaches warrant authentic, discipline-based assessments, or at least assessments that focus on the acquisition of conceptual understanding, the development of a model of events that is able to explain cause-effect relations (Downey & Levstik, 1991; Leinhardt, Stainton, & Virji, 1994), or the development of a causal mental model (Wiley & Voss, 1999).

Several alternative measures have been used in recent studies as indicators of historical understanding. These include the use of concept maps (Spoehr, 1992), analyses of student's written reports, multimedia projects, arguments (Britt & Aglinskas, 2002: Spoehr, 1992, Spoehr & Spoehr, 1994; Wiley & Voss, 1999), post-tests based on whether or not students can correctly identify inferences that follow from presented information (Wiley & Voss, 1999), and reasoning about analogical or hypothetical events (Alonso-Tapia & Villa, 1999; Wiley & Voss, 1999).

A second important area that needs more attention in the future is the investigation of individual differences in prior content knowledge and cognitive ability, and whether learners of different ages or abilities can gain the same benefits from the disciplinary approach to instruction and inquiry-based multimedia learning activities. Individual differences in prior content knowledge could be a factor in the benefit a student gains from interaction with multimedia environments or activities. For the most part, the multimedia sources used in these studies have been preselected for students or students are provided with support through direct mentoring or introductory lectures on the inquiry topics. These aspects of the successful instructional approaches discussed in this chapter may be critical for novices (i.e., students with low prior knowledge) to approach expertlike reasoning as they engage in multimedia inquiry tasks. It would make sense that some prior knowledge of either the topic or the task, or both, needs to be put in place in order for students to benefit from inquiry learning. But, whether this is the case, and how the background instruction and inquiry activities should be integrated into classroom instruction are important open questions that need to be directly researched.

Individual differences in students' cognitive abilities could also mediate the effectiveness of multimedia learning environments. Several studies by Ferretti, MacArthur, and Okolo have investigated multimedia-based learning activities with learning-disabled students and have generally found that these students benefit from multimedia inquiry tasks. In one study (Ferretti, MacArthur, & Okolo, 2001) students participated in an eight-week project-based, technology-supported investigation about westward expansion in the United States. Both learning disabled and non-learning disabled groups of students showed pre-post gains knowledge and understanding of historical content, as well as increases in their self-efficacy as learners and their understanding of historical inquiry. Other projects have investigated learning through the design of multimedia presentations about controversial topics such as immigration policy (Okolo & Feretti, 1998) and through debates about these topics (MacArthur, Ferretti, & Okolo, 2002) where students work collaboratively to represent and defend one side of a controversy. Although none of their studies has involved comparison groups, pre-post measures generally indicate that these activities led to learning gains as well as increases in engagement by learning disabled students, suggesting multimedia learning activities such as these may be effective for lower-ability students as well as more able students.

Finally, in terms of age appropriateness of multimedia learning in history, Booth (1994) has suggested that historical reasoning skills are more a function of instruction than they seem to be of developmental stages. Several studies (Ashby & Lee, 1987; Booth, 1980, 1983; Dickinson & Lee, 1984) have shown that students of a wide range of ages and abilities can engage in realistic historical analysis and reasoning from sources.

As mentioned in the limitations section, there is a clear need for controlled experimental designs that measure the effects of multimedia instruction on learning outcomes. This is a third important direction for future research. More studies need to systematically investigate the effects of the content and design of multimedia environments on history learning. Design studies and studies with pre-post learning measures are initial steps in a larger research agenda that seeks to understand how and why multimedia instruction in history can lead to better understanding of both subject matter and the discipline. At present, many multimedia instructional activities have not been assessed in terms of their effectiveness in comparison to normal classroom instruction. Nor is there much research on which aspects of multimedia inquiry tasks are responsible for better learning outcomes. These are critical questions that need to be addressed in order for us to engage in a cost/benefits analysis when we consider whether multimedia is "worth it." Finally, it is only through studies that manipulate multimedia presentation and measure learning that we can come to understand what elements of learning environments affect the quality and type of domain knowledge students acquire. Findings such as these will then be central toward advancing theories of cognition as well as instruction.

Glossary

Concept-mapping tasks: Tasks that are designed to evaluate students understanding of the relationships between concepts in a subject domain, usually in node and link format. For example, Spoehr (1992) asked students to list all of the aspects (people, events, locations) of a topic and their causal relations to each other. This type of measure taps not only students' memories for the important facts in a topic, but also their deeper understanding of the underlying relationships among these facts.

Constructivism: A philosophy or theory of learning that proposes that individuals actively construct their understanding of the world. Based on prior experience, individuals generate mental representations of situations, which they use to make sense of their environment. Therefore, learning is the process of adapting one's mental representations to accommodate new information and experiences.

Contextualization heuristic: Term used by Wineburg (1991) to describe a strategy used by expert historians to draw conclusions based on historical documents. When trying to construct accounts of historical events from sources, expert historians often explicitly consider *when* and *where* this event took place. This allows them to incorporate previously known information or look for new information about the social, political, chronological, and geographic aspects of the event to aid in their description and explanation.

Controlled experiments: In educational research, these are studies that are designed to systematically manipulate an educational treatment in order to investigate its effect on learning outcomes. Most importantly, in controlled experiments only single aspects of a learning environment are manipulated between treatment groups, thereby allowing any change in a learning outcome to be attributed to that aspect of the learning environment.

Corpus: A large collection of writings of a specific kind or on a specific subject.

Corroboration heuristic: Term used by Wineburg (1991) to describe a strategy used by expert historians to draw conclusions based on historical documents. When considering new information presented in a document, experts often seek out independent sources on the same topic to see if they support or confirm this information.

Design studies: In educational research, these types of studies investigate the feasibility, cost, and practical constraints of introducing new curricula or educational technology into the classroom. Although these studies sometimes include learning outcomes, they often do not examine alternative instructional conditions.

Heuristics: An informal and usually simple "rule-of-thumb" procedure or strategy used in problem-solving situations to help save time and effort.

Hypermedia: A computer-based information retrieval system that enables a user to gain or provide access to texts, audio and video recordings, photographs, and computer graphics related to a particular subject.

Hypertext: A computer-based system that enables a user to access to related Web pages or other electronic documents by clicking on highlighted or underlined words in the text of a document.

Inquiry learning: The acquisition of information or knowledge through actively seeking to answer a question or solve a proposed problem. Often contrasted with rote or memorization learning where individuals acquire information through simple repeated exposure to information or concepts.

Learning outcomes: Measures of knowledge acquisition or change as a result of some environmental event or educational experience. The key aspect of learning outcome measures is that an individual's knowledge is measured on multiple occasions (e.g., before completing an educational activity, then again after). Only measures of changes in knowledge are considered learning outcome measures.

Simply testing knowledge after an activity is a memory outcome, because it does not distinguish between prior and newly obtained knowledge.

Mental model: The internal representation of a system, situation, event, story, and so forth, that an individual constructs in the process of understanding incoming information. These models are thought to be formed based on prior experience or memory schemas and are important in the comprehension of new concepts and in problem solving.

Multiple-channel learning: Knowledge or concept acquisition that requires a learner to integrate across information presented using different sensory modalities (e.g., visual and auditory), types of media, and/or sources.

Primary sources: Original documents used in historical research such as diaries, government documents, logs, photographs, and physical artifacts. Can be contrasted with secondary sources such as newspaper reports, magazine articles, and biographies that are based on other authors' evidence and interpretations.

Scaffolding: Designing educational curricula or materials to provide a meaningful structure that aids in the students' development of an appropriate mental model or representation of the concept or topic.

Sequencing tasks: Educational tasks that ask students to place information, people, and events into chronological order, or spot information that is inconsistent with the chronological order of historical events. These tasks can be used as either inquiry learning activities, or as learning outcome measures.

Sourcing heuristic: Term used by Wineburg (1991) to describe a strategy used by expert historians to draw conclusions based on historical documents. When experts read a document, they often seek out information about the author (e.g., name, credentials, affiliations, relationship to information they are writing about) and the document (e.g., where it was published, document type) in order to draw conclusions about the credibility of the information.

Vertical links: Navigational links in a hypermedia environment that direct the student to information within the same content domain. For example, in a unit on the Civil War, accessing a vertical Gettysburg link could direct the student from an overview of the war to information on the Gettysburg battlefield. In contrast, a *horizontal link* for Gettysburg could lead to more information in another content domain, such as "tourist attractions in Pennsylvania."

Note

This work was supported by grants from the Office of Naval Research (Grant No. N000140110339) and the National Science Foundation (Grant No. 0126265) to the first author. Any opinions, findings, and conclusions or recommendations expressed in this material are those of the author(s) and do not necessarily reflect the views of either organization. We thank Melinda Jensen for her invaluable assistance in the preparation of this chapter.

References

Alonso-Tapia, J., & Villa, J. L. (1999). How can historical understanding best be assessed? Use of prediction tasks to assess how students understand the role of causal factors that produce historical events. *European Journal of the Psychology of Education*, 14(3), 339–358.

Ashby, R., & Lee, P. (1987). Discussing the evidence. *Teaching History*, 48, 13–17.

Barton, K. C. (1995). *"My mom taught me": The situated nature of historical understanding.* Paper presented at the annual meeting of the American Educational Research Association, San Francisco, CA.

Barton, K. C. (2001). A picture's worth: Analyzing historical photographs in the elementary grades. *Social Education, 65*(5), 278–283.

Barton, K. C. (2002). "Oh, that's a tricky piece!": Children, mediated action, and the tools of historical time. *The Elementary School Journal, 103*(2), 161–185.

Barton, K. C., & Levstik, L. S. (1996). "Back when God was around and everything": The development of children's understanding of historical time. *American Educational Research Journal, 33*, 419–454.

Booth, M. B. (1980). A modern world history course and the thinking of adolescent pupil. *Educational Review, 32*, 245–257.

Booth M. B. (1983). Students' historical thinking and the History National Curriculum in England. *Theory and Research in Social Education, 21*, 105–127.

Booth, M. (1994). Cognition in history: A British perspective. *Educational Psychologist, 29*(2), 61–69.

Britt, M. A., & Aglinskas C. (2002). Improving students' ability to identify and use source information. *Cognition and Instruction, 20*(4), 485–522.

Britt, M. A., & Gabrys G. (2002). Implications of document-level literacy skills for Web site design. *Behavior Research Methods, Instruments, and Computers, 34*(2), 170–176.

Britt, M. A., Perfetti, C. A., Van Dyke, J., & Gabrys, G. (2000). The Sourcer's Apprentice: A Tool for Document-Supported History Instruction. In P. Stearns, P. Seixas, & S. Wineburg (Eds.), *Knowing, teaching and learning history: National and international perspectives.* New York: NYU Press.

Brush T., & Saye J. (2000). Implementation and evaluation of a student-centered learning unit: A case study. *Educational Research and Development, 48*(3), 79–100.

Dickinson, A. K., & Lee, P. J. (1984). Making sense of history. In A. K. Dickinson & P. J. Lee (Eds.), *Learning history.* London: Heinemann Educational.

Downey, M. T., & Levstik, L. S. (1991). Teaching and learning history. In J. P. Shaver (Ed.), *Handbook of research on social studies teaching and learning.* New York: Macmillan.

Ferretti, R. P., MacArthur, C. D., & Okolo, C. M. (2001). Teaching for historical understanding in inclusive classrooms. *Learning Disability Quarterly 24*(1), 59–71.

Greene, S. (1994). The problems of learning to think like a historian: Writing history in the culture of the classroom. *Educational Psychologist, 29*(2), 89–96.

Holt, T. (1990). Thinking historically: Narrative, imagination, and understanding. *The Thinking Series.* New York: College Board.

Leinhardt, G., Stainton, C., & Virji, S. M. (1994). A sense of history. *Educational Psychologist, 29*(2), 79–88.

Leinhardt, G., & Young, K. M. (1996). Two texts, three readers: Issues of distance and expertise. *Cognition and Instruction, 14*(4), 441–486.

Levstik, L. S., & Barton, K. C. (1996). "They still use some of their past": Historical saliences in children's chronological thinking. *Journal of Curriculum Studies, 28*, 531–576.

Loh, B., Reiser, B. J., Radinsky, J., Edelson, D. C., Gomez, L. M., & Marshall, S. (2001). Developing reflective inquiry practices: A case study of software, the teacher, and students. In K. Crowley, C. Schunn, & T. Okada (Eds.), *Designing for science: Implications from everyday, classroom, and professional settings.* Mahwah, NJ: Erlbaum.

Lynn, S. (1993). Children reading pictures: History visuals at key states 1 and 2. *Education 3–13, 21*(3), 23–30.

MacArthur, C. A., Ferretti, R. P., & Okolo, C. M. (2002). On defending controversial viewpoints: Debates of sixth graders about the desirability of early 20th-century American immigration. *Learning Disabilities: Research and Practice 17*(3), 160–172.

Masterman, E., & Rogers, Y. (2002). A framework for designing interactive multimedia to scaffold young children's understanding of historical chronology. *Instructional Science, 30*, 221–241.

National Assessment of Educational Progress. (1996). *NAEP 1994 U.S. history report card: Findings from the National Assessment of Educational Progress.* Princeton, NJ: Educational Testing Service.

National Center for History in the Schools, (1996). *National standards for United States history: Exploring the American experience.* Los Angeles: University of California.

Okolo, C. M., & Ferretti, R. P. (1998). Multimedia design projects in an inclusive social studies classroom: "Sometimes people argue with words instead of fists." *TEACHING Exceptional Children, 31*(2), 50–57.

O'Neill, D. K., & Sohbat, E. (2004). *How high schoolers account for different accounts: Developing a practical classroom measure of thinking about historical evidence and methodology*. Paper presented at the annual meeting of the American Educational Research Association, San Diego, CA.

O'Neill, D. K., Sohbat, E., Martin, A., Asgari, M., Lort, M., & Sha., L. (2003). *Sharing accountability through sharing our accounts: Piloting an on-line community for high school history learning*. Paper presented at the annual meeting of the American Educational Research Association, Chicago, IL.

Perfetti, C. A., Britt, M. A., & Georgi, M. C. (1995). *Text-based learning and reasoning: Studies in history*. Hillsdale, NJ: Lawrence Erlbaum Associates.

Perfetti, C. A., Britt, M. A., Rouet, J.-F., Georgi, M. C., & Mason, R. A. (1994). How students use texts to learn and reason about historical uncertainty. In M. Carretero & J. F. Voss (Eds.), *Cognitive and instructional processes in history and the social sciences* (pp. 257–283). Hillsdale, NJ: Lawrence Erlbaum Associates.

Quinlan, K. M. (1999). Commonalities and controversy in context: A study of academic historians' educational beliefs. *Teaching and Teacher Education, 15*, 447–463.

Radinsky, J. (2004). *Teaching the teaching of history with digital resources: Possibilities and limitations of an on-line inquiry project in a methods course*. Paper presented at the International Conference of the Learning Sciences, Santa Monica, CA.

Rouet, J.-F., Britt, M. A., Mason, R. A., & Perfetti, C. A. (1996). Using multiple sources of evidence to reason about history. *Journal of Educational Psychology, 88*, 478–493.

Saye, J. W., & Brush, T. (2002). Scaffolding critical reasoning about history and social issues in multimedia-supported learning environments. *Educational Technology Research and Development, 50*(3), 77–96.

Scardamalia, M., & Bereiter, C. (1994). Computer support for knowledge-building communities. *Journal of the Learning Sciences, 3*(3), 265–283.

Seixas, P. (1994a). When psychologists discuss historical thinking: A historian's Perspective. *Educational Psychologist, 29*(3), 107–109.

Seixas, P. (1994b). Confronting the moral frames of popular film: Young people respond to historical revisionism. *American Journal of Education, 102*, 261–285.

Seixas, P. (2000). Schweigen! die Kinder! Or, does postmodern history have a place in the schools? In P. N. Sterns, P. Seixas, & S. Wineburg (Eds.), *Knowing, teaching, and learning history: National and international perspectives*. New York: New York University Press.

Shemilt, D. (1987). Adolescent ideas about evidence and methodology in history. In C. Portal (Ed.), *The history curriculum for teachers*. London, England: The Falmer Press.

Smith, B. K., & Blankinship, E. (1999). *Imagery as data: Structures for visual model building*. In Proceedings of the Computer Support for Collaborative Learning, Palo Alto, California.

Spoehr, K. T. (1992). *Using hypermedia to clarify conceptual structures: Illustrations from history and literature*. Paper presented at the meeting of the American Educational Research Association, San Francisco, CA.

Spoehr K. T., & Spoehr, L. W. (1994). Learning to think historically. *Educational Psychologist, 29*(2), 71–77.

Stahl, S. A., Hynd, C. R., Britton, B. K., McNish, M. M., & Bosquet, D. (1996). What happens when students read multiple source documents in history? *Reading Research Quarterly, 31*(4), 430–456.

Swan, K. (1994). History, hypermedia, and crisscrossed conceptual landscapes. *Journal of Educational Multimedia and Hypermedia, 3*(2), 120–139.

Swan, K. (1996–97). Exploring the Role of Video in Enhancing Learning from Hypermedia. *Journal of Educational Technology Systems, 25*(2), 179–188.

Voss, J. F., & Wiley, J. (1997). Developing understanding while writing essays in history. *International Journal of Educational Research, 27*, 255–265.

Voss, J. F., & Wiley, J. (2000). A case study of developing historical understanding via instruction: The importance of integrating text components and constructing arguments. In P. Stearns, S. Wineburg, & P. Seixas (Eds.), *Knowing, teaching, and learning in history* (pp. 375–389). New York: New York University Press.

Wiley, J. (2001). Supporting understanding through task and browser design. *Proceedings of the 23rd Annual Conference of the Cognitive Science Society.* Hillsdale, NJ: Erlbaum.

Wiley, J., & Voss, J. F. (1996). The effects of "playing historian" on learning in history. *Applied Cognitive Psychology, 1 0,* 63–72.

Wiley, J., & Voss, J. F. (1999). Constructing arguments from multiple sources: Tasks that promote understanding and not just memory for text. *Journal of Educational Psychology, 91* (2), 301–311.

Wineburg, S. S. (1991). Historical problem solving: A study of the cognitive processes used in the evaluation of documentary and pictorial evidence. *Journal of Educational Psychology, 83*(1), 73–87.

Wineburg, S. (2000). Making historical sense. In P. N. Sterns, P. Seixas, & S. Wineburg (Eds.), *Knowing, teaching, and learning history: National and international perspectives.* New York: New York University Press.

CHAPTER 25

Multimedia Learning of Mathematics

Robert K. Atkinson

Arizona State University

Abstract

Multimedia learning of mathematics encompasses learning from instructional material – both paper- and computer-based – that combine words and pictures in the domain of mathematics. This chapter explores our current state of knowledge about this topic and is based solely on research utilizing rigorous, evidence-based methods. It also outlines several limitations associated with the research conducted to date as well as the implications of this research for cognitive theory and instructional design. Finally, the chapter concludes by proposing several productive avenues for future research.

What Is Multimedia Learning of Mathematics?

In general, multimedia learning entails learning from words and pictures (Mayer, 2001). More specifically, multimedia learning occurs when learners build coherent mental representations from instructional material containing words and pictures. According to this paradigm, words – or the verbal form of the instructional material – can be either *printed* or *spoken*, while pictures – or the pictorial form of instructional material – can encompass *static* graphics, such as illustrations, graphs, photos, maps, or *dynamic* graphics, such as animation or video.

Clearly, multimedia learning is applicable across a wide range of domains. Of particular interest is the burgeoning area of the research literature that examines multimedia learning in the domain of mathematics. Specifically, the focus of the chapter is on multimedia learning of mathematics, which entails learning in the domain mathematics from both pencil/paper and computer-based instructional material leveraging both words and pictures.

What Is an Example of Multimedia Learning of Mathematics?

Consider the following learning scenario. Suppose a learner is asked to study a worked

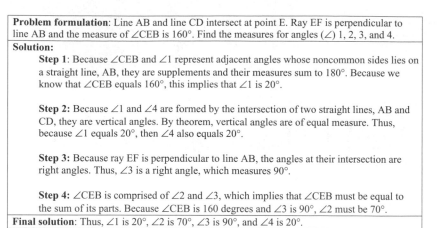

Problem formulation: Line AB and line CD intersect at point E. Ray EF is perpendicular to line AB and the measure of ∠CEB is 160°. Find the measures for angles (∠) 1, 2, 3, and 4.

Solution:

 Step 1: Because ∠CEB and ∠1 represent adjacent angles whose noncommon sides lies on a straight line, AB, they are supplements and their measures sum to 180°. Because we know that ∠CEB equals 160°, this implies that ∠1 is 20°.

 Step 2: Because ∠1 and ∠4 are formed by the intersection of two straight lines, AB and CD, they are vertical angles. By theorem, vertical angles are of equal measure. Thus, because ∠1 equals 20°, then ∠4 also equals 20°.

 Step 3: Because ray EF is perpendicular to line AB, the angles at their intersection are right angles. Thus, ∠3 is a right angle, which measures 90°.

 Step 4: ∠CEB is comprised of ∠2 and ∠3, which implies that ∠CEB must be equal to the sum of its parts. Because ∠CEB is 160 degrees and ∠3 is 90°, ∠2 must be 70°.

Final solution: Thus, ∠1 is 20°, ∠2 is 70°, ∠3 is 90°, and ∠4 is 20°.

Figure 25.1. Worked example involving perpendicularity.

example that consists of a problem formulation, solution steps, and the final solution (see Figure 25.1). In this case, the worked example is designed to illustrate perpendicularity, a fundamental concept in geometry. As illustrated in Figure 25.1, the example consists solely of written text describing a perpendicularity problem involving two lines and a ray, as well as the angles that are formed by the intersection of these elements. It illustrates how to use information from the problem formulation in combination with general knowledge about lines, angles, and perpendicular lines to determine the measurement associated with four angles. It is conceivable that this particular example would enable a learner to select relevant words and build internal connections among selected words to form a coherent verbal model. However, without the benefit of a diagram, the learner is likely to experience difficulty forming a coherent mental representation of the problem because there is no readily available pictorial model with which to integrate the verbal model. For instance, it is difficult to image how a learner would form a coherent mental presentation of Step 1 of the solution without consulting a diagram ("Because ∠CEB and ∠1 represent adjacent angles whose noncommon sides lies on a straight line, AB, they are supplements and their measures sum to 180° . . . ").

In contrast, suppose that the learning scenario is revised to include a static diagram that conveys a visual representation of the problem (see Figure 25.2). As with the initial learning scenario, the learner is still able to select relevant words and build internal connections among selected words to form a coherent verbal model from the text. But in this revised scenario, the learner is now able to leverage the diagram to select the relevant parts of the images and build internal connections among the images, which represent two important activities that help foster a coherent pictorial model of the problem. In order to integrate the verbal and pictorial models, the learner must split his or her attention between these two instructional elements and mentally integrate them. For instance, in order to understand the final solution step ("∠CEB is comprised of ∠2 and ∠3, which implies that ∠CEB must

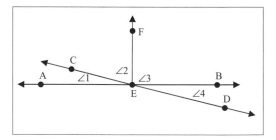

Figure 25.2. Diagram for perpendicularity worked example.

Frame	Animation	Narration
7	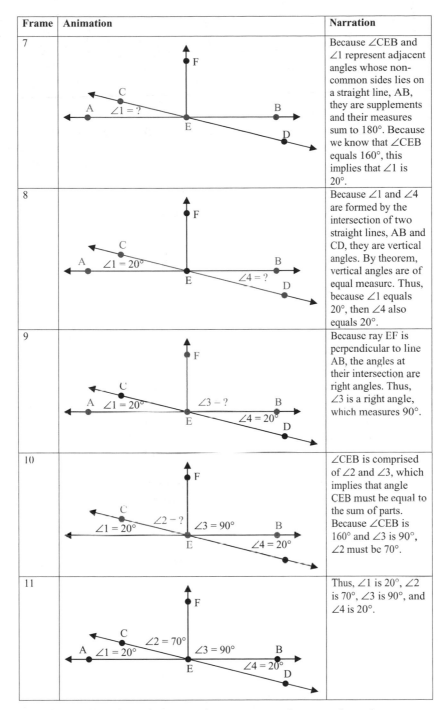	Because ∠CEB and ∠1 represent adjacent angles whose non-common sides lies on a straight line, AB, they are supplements and their measures sum to 180°. Because we know that ∠CEB equals 160°, this implies that ∠1 is 20°.
8		Because ∠1 and ∠4 are formed by the intersection of two straight lines, AB and CD, they are vertical angles. By theorem, vertical angles are of equal measure. Thus, because ∠1 equals 20°, then ∠4 also equals 20°.
9		Because ray EF is perpendicular to line AB, the angles at their intersection are right angles. Thus, ∠3 is a right angle, which measures 90°.
10		∠CEB is comprised of ∠2 and ∠3, which implies that angle CEB must be equal to the sum of parts. Because ∠CEB is 160° and ∠3 is 90°, ∠2 must be 70°.
11		Thus, ∠1 is 20°, ∠2 is 70°, ∠3 is 90°, and ∠4 is 20°.

Figure 25.3. A multimedia approach to presenting the example's solution steps.

be equal to the sum of its parts ... "), the learner must locate ∠2 and ∠3 in the diagram, identify their relationship to ∠CEB using the diagram, either recall from memory or consult the text of the worked example to determine that ∠3 = 90°, and then mentally follow the arithmetic formulation that 160° − 90° = 70°. The problem is that the combination of all of these activities may exhaust the learner's mental resources, leaving no room for the learner to build connections between the verbal and pictorial models not to mention trying to incorporate prior knowledge into the process. Although this revised learning scenario captures a learning situation that combines text and pictures, it represents a less than optimal way of accomplishing the task.

Now consider an alternative learning scenario that leverages the affordances associated with a multimedia learning approach to mathematics instruction. Although the content of the worked example remains the same, in this instance the example is presented in a computer-based learning environment using animation and narration. Unlike examples that simultaneously display all of the solution components, an animated example appears initially unsolved. The learning environment is structured to enable the learner to watch a sequential presentation of solution steps, where steps are successively added over a series of pages until the final page in the series presented the solution in its entirety. Coupled with the visual presentation of each solution step, instructional explanations (i.e., narration) designed to underscore what is occurring in that step are delivered aurally. Moreover, through highlighting, flashing, or some other type of signal, the learner is guided to the section of the visual material being referenced by the auditory material. Ideally, this enables a learner to generate connections between corresponding image-based and word-based representations, thereby creating a more coherent mental representation of the concept illustrated by the worked example.

For instance, Figure 25.3 illustrates one way of presenting the problem solution from the perpendicularity worked example using an optimal multimedia approach. In the figure, the left-hand column indicates the frame number, the middle column depicts the image that appears in that particular frame of the animation, and the right-hand column captures the accompanying narration. Looking across the frames, it should

quickly become apparent that instead of presenting the solution it is entirety, the animation depicts how the solution is constructed incrementally over time. Specifically, the measurements for each angle appear only after they are determined. Also notice that within each frame, the relevant section of the image is highlighted when the associated statement is delivered aurally. For example, in the initial frame, where the narration is discussing $\angle CEB$ and $\angle 1$, the relevant aspects of the diagram are highlighted in an effort to guide the learner to the section of the visual material being described by the auditory material. This same principle applies to each subsequent frame of the animation until finally, in frame 6, the entire solution is presented.[1]

Clearly, this last scenario best epitomizes a multimedia learning approach to mathematics. Although the second scenario illustrated a case in which instruction contains words and pictures, the manner in which the instruction was designed appears poorly suited to encourage meaningful learning. Unfortunately, this scenario is not uncommon among today's mathematics textbooks. Given that ill-conceived multimedia designs can easily overload the human information-processing system, such as those that force the learner to process information only in one channel, the question becomes "how can we adapt multimedia to enhance learning" (Mayer, 2001, p. 10). The last scenario illustrates a way of adapting a multimedia environment to create a more learner-centered approach. According to Mayer (2001), "the premise underlying the learner-centered approach is that multimedia designs that are consistent with the way the human mind works are more effective in fostering learning than those that are not" (p. 10). In the latter scenario, it is much easier to see how the learning environment aids the learner in forming a verbal model, a pictorial model, and integrating the two into a coherent mental representation of the problem. Furthermore, the learning scenario was informed by the research literature, which offers some helpful insights into how to design multimedia instruction to foster meaningful learning. This literature base is described in the next section.

What Do We Know About Multimedia Learning of Mathematics?

As previously implied, an overview of the research literature pertaining to multimedia learning of mathematics can be framed in terms of two dimensions. The first dimension is the nature of the pictorial form of instructional material, whether it consists of static or dynamic graphics. The second dimension is the verbal form of the instructional material, whether it consists of written or spoken text. When considered together, these two dimensions permit one to segment the literature into four different sections (static graphics and written text, static graphics and spoken text, dynamic graphics and written text, and dynamic graphics and spoken text), which are each described in turn in the following text.

Static Graphics and Written Text

In an effort to explore what constituted appropriate instructional guidance during mathematical problem solving, Tarmizi and Sweller (1988) conducted an experimental study that examined the use of static graphs and written text. They focused their efforts on examining guidance during geometry instruction, specifically Euclidean geometry that involves theorems of circles, on the plane or in three dimensions. Although they report the results of five experiments, only two of the experiments are relevant to this discussion.

In Experiment 3, they compared two conditions, namely conventional problem solving and worked example. In the conventional condition, participants were provided with six pairs of problems that they were expected to solve in a timely fashion. The problems involved applying one of two theorems to determine the measurements of a set of angles. The learners were provided a sheet containing the theorems and the relevant diagrams. The worked-example condition, on the other hand, was identical to the conventional group with one notable exception: the first problem in each pair was a worked example. The examples consisted of a diagram and a sequential set of equations referring to the relations between elements of the diagram. It is worth noting that this latter condition is essentially equivalent to the second of the three learning scenarios proposed in the previous section. The authors found that there were no significant differences between the two conditions across a set of dependent measures, including time to solution and number of problem-solving errors. Tarmizi and Sweller noted that this outcome was unexpected given the established finding in the literature that pairing worked examples with practice items fostered learning better than problem solving only (e.g., Cooper & Sweller, 1987; Sweller & Copper, 1985). They suggested that this unanticipated result might occur because worked-example participants were forced to mentally integrate the solution steps with the information from the diagram, which quickly exhausted their cognitive capacity and counteracted the learning gains associated with worked examples.

To examine this supposition, in Experiment 4 Tarmizi and Sweller compared the impact of presenting high school students with an instructional lesson involving either conventional problem solving, conventionally formatted worked examples, or modified worked examples. The first two conditions were identical to the ones used in the previous experiment. In contrast, in the modified examples, the diagrams and sequential set of equations referring to the relations between elements of the diagram were integrated. As with the previous experiment, they found that providing learners with conventionally formatted examples resulted in no learning advantage over problem solving only. However, consistent with their prediction, they found that the participants assigned to the modified example condition processed significantly more problems during the study phase, solved the practice items more efficiently, and required significantly less time to solve the test problems than the other two conventionally formatted conditions. Additionally, analysis of verbal protocols collected during the test phase indicated that the learners in the modified example condition were significantly more likely to use an effective strategy to solve the test problems than their peers in the conventional example condition. In sum, Tarmizi and Sweller established that modifying conventionally formatted worked examples such that the diagram and the set of equations referring to the relations between elements of the diagram are integrated fosters learning. By not requiring learners to integrate multiple sources of information in the instructional material, the authors found that this integrated format reduced the cognitive load imposed by the instructional material, which consequently freed up cognitive resources needed to promote learning.

Sweller, Chandler, Tierney, and Cooper (1990) conducted a series of six experiments (two of which are relevant to this chapter) in an effort to examine whether Tarmizi and Sweller's (1988) findings would generalize beyond Euclidean geometry to coordinate geometry, where the plane is typically defined by two axes, the horizontal x-axis and the vertical y-axis, located at right angles to each other. As with the Euclidean geometry, coordinate geometry requires learners to mentally integrate a diagram and a set of equation. Similar to Experiment 4 of Tarmizi and Sweller's study, participants in Sweller et al.'s (1990) initial experiment were provided with an instructional lesson involving either conventional problem solving, conventionally formatted worked examples, or modified worked examples. Once again the conventionally formatted examples required learners to mentally integrate a diagram and set of equations whereas these elements were physically integrated in the modified examples. The results mirrored those of Tarmizi and Sweller (1988). Specifically, Sweller et al. (1990) found that the participants presented with integrated ex-

amples illustrating how to solve problems involving coordinate geometry required significantly less time to solve the post-test items and solved the items more accurately.

Often times, instructional overviews are provided to learners prior to the presentation of instructional items such as worked examples and practice problems. These overviews, which are provided prior to asking learners to engage in problem solving, typically provide an initial introduction to new material and often contain diagrams and textual material. In Experiment 2, Sweller et al. (1990) examined whether integrating diagrams and related textual information in instructional overviews, irrespective of whether any instructional items actually accompanied them, fostered learning more than nonintegrated instructional overviews. To examine this issue, they provided learners with either integrated diagrammatic and textual material or nonintegrated introductory material. In both instances, the overviews were without accompanying examples and practice problems. The learners were then asked to solve three test problems. Sweller and his colleagues found that their results clearly supported the integrated instructional format. Based on these findings, the authors concluded that "when material could be combined into a unitary source of information not requiring attention splitting, performance was substantially enhanced" (Sweller et al., 1990, p. 188).

Static Graphics and Spoken Text

Based in some measure on several studies by Mayer and Anderson (1991, 1992) involving the use of narrations coupled with graphics in nonmathematical domains, Mousavi, Low, and Sweller (1995) conducted a series of experiments that collectively explored the effects of manipulating the presentation modality of the text that accompanies static graphics in the context of geometry instruction. In Experiments 1 and 2, participants were assigned to one of three groups. Although each of the groups was presented with a set of worked examples that consisted of a diagram coupled with associated problem and proof statements, what varied across the groups were the presentation modality of these statements. In the visual–visual condition, the participants were provided a sheet of paper containing the statements. In the visual–auditory condition, the participants were provided an audiotape of the statements. In the simultaneous condition, the participants were provided with both a sheet of paper with the statements and an audiotape containing the identical information. The authors found that the participants in the visual–auditory – or dual-mode – condition required less time to solve a set of test problems than their counterparts assigned to the visual–visual – or single-mode – simultaneous condition. Thus, presenting spoken text with static diagrams was superior to static diagrams accompanied by written text. Moreover, presenting redundant written and spoken text was detrimental to learning.

In an effort to rule out an alternative explanation for their initial findings, Experiments 3 and 4 examined the possibility that the superiority of the visual–auditory condition was an artifact of the simultaneous presentation of the auditory statements with the diagram. In contrast, the visual–visual condition required the learners to maintain the written statements in memory while redirecting attention from the textual statements to the diagram. To address this issue, Mousavi et al. conducted several experiments based on a 2 × 2 factorial design with presentation (simultaneous or sequential) and mode (visual–audio or visual–visual) as factors. The simultaneous presentation mode presented learners with the diagram and its associated statements at the same time while the sequential presentation mode presented learners with the statements and the diagram sequentially. Across both experiments, results suggested that presenting learners with a diagram accompanied by spoken problem and proof statements fosters learning more than written statements even when learners are forced to remember the information conveyed in the statements and maintain

it in their working memory prior to viewing the diagram (i.e., sequential presentation mode). Mousavi et al. concluded that "when students must split their attention between multiple sources of information that require mental integration, cognitive resources available for learning can be increased by presenting some of the verbal material in auditory rather than written form" (p. 333).

Jeung, Chandler, and Sweller (1997) conducted a study examining the impact of incorporating visual cues or indicators in a multimedia learning environment involving elementary geometry measurement. Specifically, they conducted three experiments in which they examined the use of visual indicators to direct learners' visual search under three basic conditions: (1) visual–visual, where the diagrams and associated statements were presented visually; (2) audio–visual, where the diagrams were presented visually and the associated statements were presented aurally; and (3) audio–visual-flashing, which was identical to the audio-visual condition with the exception that the relevant section of the diagram flashed when the associated statements were delivered aurally.

In their first experiment, Jeung et al. (1997) examined the learning effects associated with these three conditions under low and high visual-search conditions. The high visual-search condition required learners to engage in a more extensive search of the visual information in order to determine which elements were being referenced by the coordinated auditory information. When high visual-search material was used, they found that the learning gain attributed to the learners assigned to the audio–visual-flashing condition was significantly larger than those of the learners in the visual–visual condition and, more interestingly, than those assigned to the condition with aurally delivered statements but no flashing (i.e., audio–visual condition). In contrast, when low visual-search material was used, the learners assigned to the two mixed-mode conditions (audio–visual-flashing and audio–visual conditions) did not outperform their peers in the visual–visual condition, an outcome that conflicted with the results of the Mousavi et al. (1995) study.

The second and third experiments probed these initial findings. In the second experiment, Jeung and Chandler (1997) sought to replicate the advantage associated with the audio–visual-flashing condition over the audio–visual and visual–visual conditions using diagrammatic material that was markedly higher in visual-search complexity than the material from the initial experiment. Holding constant the new set of high visual-search material, the three basic conditions were once again examined for their relative effects on learning. Their findings replicated the results from Experiment 1. That is, the participants assigned to the audio–visual-flashing condition once again outperformed their counterparts in the audio–visual and visual–visual conditions on a variety of learning processes and learning outcome measures. The final experiment returned to the issue raised in Experiment 1, namely the lack of a modality effect between the audio–visual and visual–visual conditions. The authors replaced the low search material from Experiment 1 with material that was considered noticeably lower in visual-search complexity and then once again compared the three conditions. This time, across several dependent measures, the audio–visual-flashing and audio–visual conditions were associated with better indicators of learning than the visual–visual condition, thus replicating a modality effect. Under these extremely low visual-search conditions, however, there was no advantage found for the presence of flashing. Based on the findings, Jeung et al. suggest that "...if visual search is likely to be high, then the inclusion of visual indicators such as flashing, color change, or simple animation is essential for audio-visual instruction to be an effective instructional teach technique [whereas] if visual search is low then such indicators are less necessary and standard mixed mode presentations are likely to be superior to equivalent visual instructional formats" (p. 337).

Dynamic Graphics and Written Text

Beyond static graphics, dynamic graphics are potentially powerful aids to multimedia learning (Mayer & Moreno, 2002). One form of dynamic graphics is animation, which can be defined as a visual representation consisting of "a series of frames, each showing incremental changes in the position of the subject images which when shown in sequence, at high speed, give the illusion of movement" (Roncarrelli, 1989, p. 8). Presenting problem states sequentially, like other forms of dynamic media, can bolster mathematical thinking in general by emphasizing variation over time. As Kaput (1992) posits, "one very important aspect of mathematical thinking is the abstraction of invariance....[B]ut, of course, to recognize invariance – to see what stays the same – one must have variation" (p. 526). He also suggests that in "static media, the states of notational objects cannot change as a function of time, whereas in dynamic media they can. Hence, time can become an information-carrying dimension" (p. 526).

Nathan, Kintsch, and Young (1992) conducted a pioneering study that examined the use of animations to facilitate learning of mathematics, specifically to help learners to comprehend and solve algebra word problems. The authors created ANIMATE, which they describe as "an interactive tutor that facilitates comprehension of word problems by helping the student to construct a formal problem network, which is then used to run a simple animation of the problem" (p. 346). Essentially, a learner used the learning environments to create a formal, graphical representation for each distance/rate/time problem presented in the learning environment, which it then used to generate an animation. The learner could then view the animation to consider whether his or her initial formal problem representation was accurate. Additionally, the interactive learning environment relied on written text to deliver feedback to the learner when they entered solutions to a set of practice problems contained in the environment.

In an experiment designed to evaluate the environments effectiveness, Nathan et al. (1992) tested the full version of ANIMATE with tutors containing incrementally less functionality. Basically, there were three features inherent in the ANIMATE tutor, including the ability to: (1) construct a formal network, (2) set up a problem situation, and (3) run the equation-driven animation. Of the four conditions used in their study, ANIMATE was the only learning environment that permitted learners to employ the animations. The authors employed two nonanimation tutors, a stopping condition with two features of the tutor-enabled (construct a formal network and set up a problem situation), and a network-only condition with only one feature enabled (construct a formal network), in addition to a no tutor control in their design. With just 30 minutes of treatment, Nathan and his colleagues found that learners who used the ANIMATE tutor demonstrated a larger pre-to-post-test learning gain than their peers with access to the nonanimation tutors or those in the control group that did not use any tutor. They also determined that during training, ANIMATE tutor learners solved the practice problems more accurately than their counterparts assigned to the nonanimation tutors or the control. Overall, these results show that animations may bolster mathematical thinking.

Another study that explored the efficacy of creating computer-based environments comprised of animations and written text was conducted by Moreno and Mayer (1999). Their learning environment, which was designed to teach elementary school students addition and subtraction of signed whole numbers, was tested across two experiments. In Experiment 1, two conditions were compared: A control group, where learners were provided access to symbolic number sentences for each problem, and a treatment group, where learners had access to the same symbolic number sentences in addition to animations. The animations depicted an animated bunny's movements along a number line designed to help ground the formal computational procedures of addition and subtraction of signed whole numbers in their existing conceptual knowledge. Essentially, interaction in the control group consisted of written text whereas the treatment group consisted of written text plus animation. Examining the pre-to-post-test learning gains, the authors found that the participants in the animation condition gained significantly more than their control counterparts on difficult items, albeit on easier items there was no statistically significant difference. Moreover, Moreno and Mayer determined that high-achieving students assigned to the animation condition gained significantly more across both easy and difficult items than their high-achieving peers in the control condition but that this difference did not extend to low-achieving students.

In a subsequent experiment, Moreno and Mayer compared the effects of presenting low and high spatial-ability learners with their animation-based learning environment. As predicted, they found that high spatial-ability students who interacted with the environment produced significantly larger pre-to-post-test learning gains than their low spatial-ability counterparts. Across the two experiments, the authors found that animation (a) provided a supportive environment for students in general when learning challenging mathematical concepts, (b) benefited high-achieving students more than low-achieving students, and (c) helped high spatial-ability students more than low spatial-ability students. More generally, this study suggests that students engaged in mathematical thinking can benefit on a conceptual level by interacting with learning environments consisting of written-text narrations coupled with animations.

Dynamic Graphics and Spoken Text

According to the cognitive theory of multimedia learning (CTML), combining spoken text (e.g., narration) with dynamic graphics (e.g., animation) should promote learning with understanding. Atkinson (2002) conducted a study that empirically examined the use of animation and narration in the context of mathematics instruction. Specifically, the computer-based learning environment used in the study was designed to foster a learner's understanding of how to solve multistep, proportion word problems with a set of worked examples paired with practice problems. The worked examples were structured to consist of a sequential presentation of problem states or animation. Unlike examples that simultaneously display all of the solution components (i.e., static examples), the animated examples used in Atkinson's study appeared initially unsolved. The learning environment permitted a learner to proceed through each example and watch as problem states were successively added over a series of pages until the final page in the series presented the solution in its entirety. Each animated solution step was coordinated with explanations designed to underscore what was occurring in that step (e.g., "First, we need to set up a proportional relationship to determine the production rate") that were delivered – depending on condition – as either written text or as spoken text.

Although there were several foci of the initial experiment, one question concerned the relative effectiveness of single-mode versus dual-mode animated examples. The single-mode examples consisted of animated solutions coupled with written instructional explanations whereas the dual-mode examples consisted of the same solutions coupled with instructional explanations spoken by a female tutor. Atkinson found that the learners presented with explanations delivered as spoken text reported that they perceived the worked examples as less difficult during instruction and subsequently produced conceptually more accurate solutions on the posttest than their counterparts presented with explanations delivered in written form.

A second experiment was conducted that compared three conditions including two conditions with spoken text and animation and one with written text and animation. When the two spoken-voice conditions were combined and compared to

the written-text condition, Atkinson found that the participants in the voice conditions reported less perceived example difficulty, produced more conceptually accurate solutions on practice problems and near-transfer items, and reported a higher average affective score. Atkinson concluded that his study "provides additional empirical support for the proposal that example processing and problem-solving performance can be improved by incorporating the use of a dual mode of presentation in example-based instruction . . . and, more generally, that the use of a dual mode of presentation enhances learning outcomes in multimedia learning environments" (Atkinson, 2002, p. 426).

Atkinson, Mayer, and Merrill (2005) conducted another study that examined the use of dynamic graphics and spoken text. However, instead of comparing written text versus spoken text, the authors explored the effects associated with the characteristics of the spoken text. Across two experiments, participants received a narrated set of animated worked examples involving proportional reasoning word problems. The participants were randomly assigned in equal proportions to one of two conditions: the human voice condition, where they listened to narration by a female native-English speaker, or the machine voice condition, where they listened to the narration by a female machine-synthesized voice. It is important to note that the human voice condition was identical to the dual-mode condition described by Atkinson (2002). Experiment 1 involved college undergraduates working in a university-based computer laboratory whereas Experiment 2 involved high school students working in situ in a computer classroom. Across both experiments, the authors collected learning process measures (i.e., perceived example understanding and difficulty, and performance on practice problems) as well as learning outcome measures (i.e., a post-test containing near- and far-transfer items, and a speaker-rating questionnaire).

Across both experiments, Atkinson et al. (2005) determined that learners produced more conceptually accurate solutions on measures of transfer when the animated examples were narrated by human voice instead of a machine-synthesized voice. Moreover, based on the questionnaire sensitive to the social characteristics of speakers, learners attributed more positive social characteristics to the human voice rather than a machine-synthesized voice. Based on the results from these two experiments, the authors postulated a *voice principle*, which suggests that "designers of multimedia learning environments should create life-like on-screen agents that speak in a human voice rather than a machine-synthesized voice."

Finally, an experiment by Merrill (2003) directly tested the effects of combining narration with either static visual representations or dynamic visual representations (i.e., animation). Merrill adapted the computer-based learning environment employed by Atkinson (2002) and Atkinson et al. (2005), which was designed to foster a learner's understanding of how to solve multistep, proportion word problems. The participants in this experiment were randomly assigned in equal proportions to one of six conditions, as defined by the cells of a 2 × 3 factorial design. Of relevance to this discussion is the two-level factor that captured the visual representation of each worked example's solution steps.[2] In the static condition, the worked examples simultaneously displayed all of the solution components in their entirety. The dynamic condition corresponded to the dual-mode animated examples condition used by Atkinson (2002) and the human-voice narrated condition described by Atkinson et al. (2005).

Although there was no statistically significant main effect for type of visual representations accompanying narration on the learning process measures, Merrill (2003) found that the participants assigned to the dynamic visual environment outperformed their peers in the static visual environment in terms of near-transfer test performance. Moreover, this same difference appeared on the far-transfer items as well. Specifically, learners that viewed an animated worked example accompanied by narration (i.e., dynamic visual environment) produced conceptually more accurate solutions on far-transfer items than their counterparts presented with a static image of the solution accompanied by the same human voice narrating the example's solution steps (i.e., static visual environment). Based on this finding, the author postulated a *dynamic principle:* When designing a multimedia learning environment consisting of a pictorial representation and narration, present the pictorial representation as a dynamic graphic (i.e., animation) rather than a static graphic.

What Are the Limitations of Research on Multimedia Learning of Mathematics?

Although there is a considerable amount of published research that focuses on multimedia learning of science (for a review, see Mayer & Moreno, 2002), the literature focusing on issues related to multimedia learning of mathematics is relatively small in comparison. While the educational literature is filled with many examples of articles describing "best practices," there is an extremely modest amount of sound, empirically based research.

Another limitation associated with this area of the literature emerges from the research focusing on combining words – both written and spoken – with static graphics. To date, the research in this area has worked exclusively with geometry instruction. Naturally, this is an ideal mathematical subdomain to explore the efficacy of multimedia learning given that words and graphics are so prevalent during instruction. However, it is critical that the empirically derived instructional principles be generalized to additional mathematical subdomains.

The nature of the research participants is also a limitation. For instance, while several studies involved school-age children as participants (e.g., Moreno & Mayer, 1999; Tarmizi & Sweller, 1988), a number relied instead on college-age students (e.g., Atkinson, 2002; Nathan et al., 1992). It would be helpful to determine whether the aforementioned results generalize across learners of different ages and grade levels. Moreover, given that Moreno and Mayer (1999) established that both achievement and spatial ability play a role in how well a multimedia learning environment advances student understanding and learning in mathematics, it would be prudent for future studies to incorporate these variables into their designs.

Finally, some might argue that the manner in which evidence of learning and transfer was measured across the various studies is a shortcoming of this area of the literature. To date, these studies have relied on a single transfer test administered immediately after the treatment. In contrast, the Committee on Development in the Science of Learning suggests that "learning and transfer not be evaluated by 'one-shot' tests of transfer" (Bransford, Brown, & Cocking, 2000, p. 236). Instead, they advocate that researchers take into consideration "how learning affects subsequent learning, such as increased speed of learning in a domain" (p. 236). It appears worthwhile for researchers to move beyond the standard one-shot approach to assessing transfer by including a delayed transfer test.

What Are the Implications of the Research for Cognitive Theory?

The research described in this chapter supports the cognitive theory of multimedia in several ways. Specifically, the research provides support for each of theory's three assumptions: limited capacity, dual channel, and active processing (Mayer, 2001). First, consistent with the limited-capacity assumption, requiring learners to mentally integrate disparate sources of mutually referring information, such as a diagram and a set of equations referring to the relations between elements of the diagram, quickly exhausts their cognitive capacity and impairs learning. Across several experiments, Sweller and his colleagues documented that nonintegrated material was detrimental to

learning, presumably because this format required learners to retain the equations in their working memory as they attempted to locate the relevant elements in the diagram (Sweller et al., 1990; Tarmizi & Sweller, 1988). On the other hand, they found that an integrated format facilitated learning.

Second, corresponding to the dual-channel assumption, the research supports the notion that a learners' working memory capacity is optimized under dual mode. According to Mayer (2001), the "dual-channel assumption [suggests] that humans possess separate information channels for visually represented material and auditorily represented material" (p. 46). In particular, a number of researchers (Jeung et al., 1997; Mousavi et al., 1995) established that relying on both channels, by presenting a static diagram visually while simultaneously presenting the relevant statements aurally, facilitated learning more than relying on a single channel (i.e., visual–pictorial channel). Moreover, this assumption proved tenable in the context of animations as well (Atkinson, 2002).

Third, congruent with the active-processing assumption, creating multimedia presentations that encourage learners to build coherent mental representations enhances learning. Specifically, properly designed multimedia presentations can guide learners as they attempt to construct their mental model of the situation represented in the instruction. For instance, incorporating signaling in multimedia presentations, such as simple flashing, can successfully guide learners as they attempt to make sense of the presented material (Jeung et al., 1997). This is particularly true of situations with high visual-search complexity. Essentially, using signals to help learners discriminate relevant from irrelevant information can help them effectively integrate their verbal and visual representations. Similarly, the active-processing assumption is supported by research showing that dynamic animations coupled with either written text (Moreno & Mayer, 1999; Nathan et al., 1992) or spoken text (Merrill, 2003) facilitate learning.

What Are the Implications of the Research for Instructional Design?

The research literature described in this chapter provides results with direct implications for the design of instruction. Specifically, the research provides us with a set of empirically based principles that can guide the design of multimedia learning environments involving mathematics. These empirically based principles are categorized according to the aforementioned dimensions involving the pictorial form (static or dynamic graphics) and the verbal form (written or spoken text) of the instructional material.

Static Graphics and Written Text

Research in this segment of the literature suggests the following instructional design guideline for multimedia learning environments involving mathematics: When using static graphics coupled with written text it is advisable to integrate the text directly into the graphic. Two of the experiments described in this chapter support the idea that diagrams and their associated text should be integrated (Sweller et al., 1990; Tarmizi & Sweller, 1988) while another experiment supports the notion that this integration should also occur with instructional overviews (Sweller et al., 1990). This guideline is consistent with Mayer's (2001) *spatial contiguity principle*, which states that "presenting corresponding words and pictures near each other on the page or screen results in better learning than presenting them far from each other" (p. 93).

Static Graphics and Spoken Text

The results of several experiments in this segment of the literature support several instructional design guidelines for multimedia learning environments involving mathematics: (a) when feasible, combine static graphics with spoken text, (b) when combining graphics with spoken text, do not provide equivalent written text, and (c) for visually complex diagrammatic material, use signals with spoken text to direct learners'

visual search. The first principle is empirically supported by the work of Mousavi et al. (1995), which established that combining static graphics with narration fostered learning. This guideline corresponds with Mayer's (2001) *modality principle*, which recommends that "substituting on-screen text for narration detracts from multimedia learning" (p. 144). The second principle also follows from Mousavi et al.'s (1995) research where they found that it was detrimental to learning when learners were provided static graphics coupled with written text that was identical to the simultaneously presented spoken text. This is compatible with Mayer's (2001) *redundancy principle*, which posits that "when making a multimedia presentation consisting of a concise narrated animation, do not add on-screen text that duplicates words that are already in the narration" (p. 159). The third principle, which does not correspond to any of Mayer's multimedia design principles, is derived from the research by Jeung et al. (1997). It is not, however, necessary to signal under low visual-search conditions.

Dynamic Graphics and Written Text

If an instructional designer intends to use dynamic graphics (e.g., animations), there are several principles that should be kept in mind. Research in this segment of the literature suggests the following instructional design guidelines for multimedia learning environments involving mathematics: (a) animation plus narration is better than narration alone, and (b) animations may be more beneficial for high-achieving and high spatial-ability learners. The first principle follows from Nathan et al.'s (1992) work with the equation-driven animations in ANIMATE and Moreno and Mayer's (1999) research. This principle correlates with Mayer's (2001) *multimedia principle*, which suggests that we "present words and pictures rather than words alone" (p. 79). The second principle follows from Moreno and Mayer's (1999) study where whey found that high-achieving and high spatial-ability students were more likely to benefit from dynamic graphics and written text than low-achieving and low spatial-ability students. This guideline is partially compatible with Mayer's (2001) *individual differences principle*, which proposes that "when working with low-experience and high spatial-learners, be particularly careful to employ relevant principles of multimedia design" (p. 181). Although Moreno and Mayer's (1999) research suggests that animation helps high spatial-ability learners, they found that high-achieving learners – instead of low-achieving or low-experience ones – profited the most from animations.

Dynamic Graphics and Spoken Text

Research in this segment of the literature suggests the following instructional design guidelines for multimedia learning environments involving mathematics: (a) when feasible, combine dynamic graphics with spoken text, and (b) use a human voice not a machine-generated voice with animations. These guidelines emerge from research by Atkinson and his colleagues (2002; Atkinson et al., in press) and Merrill (2003) involving computer-based multimedia learning environments. As Atkinson (2002) points out, computers "provide a more favorable environment in which to implement some forms of effective instruction, such as the coordination of the visual presentation of sequential problem states with an auditory description of each of those states" (p. 426). The second principle, which does not correspond to any of Mayer's (2001) original multimedia design principles, is referred to as the *voice principle*: Designers of multimedia learning environments of mathematics should use a human voice rather than a machine-synthesized voice in conjunction with animations.

What Are Some Productive Future Directions for Research?

Clearly, there needs to be significantly more research conducted on this topic in the future. While there are dozens of articles dedicated to exploring multimedia learning in science and other nonmathematical domains, there are only a modest number focusing on mathematics. For instance, in a recent review article focusing on animation as an aid to multimedia learning, seven principles with instructional implications were outlined (Mayer & Moreno, 2002). Out of the 31 experiments cited as the sources of these seven principles, only one experiment – Experiment 1 from Moreno and Mayer (1999) – involved mathematics. Simply put: More research is needed to explore how to advance student understanding and learning in mathematics using multimedia learning environments.

Although to a large extent Mayer's (2001) multimedia message design principles were based on research involving nonmathematical domains, this chapter documents strong empirical support for these principle from within the domain of mathematics. Specifically, the research in this chapter supports at least four of these principles including: the multimedia principle, the spatial contiguity principle, the modality principle, and (to some degree) the individual differences principle. Because there are some diverging results on the individual differences principle, future research should attempt to determine what role achievement plays in the effectiveness of animations. Additionally, a productive line of research would involve exploring the applicability of the remaining design principles in the context of mathematics instruction, including the temporal contiguity principle, the coherence principle, the redundancy principle, and the personalization principle.

Another productive line of research that follows from this review of the literature is a closer examination of how animation can be used to promote learner understanding in mathematics. Given that computer-based learning environments offer many affordances that can be leveraged to improve learning, we clearly need to better understand how to design learning environments with animation and narration such that they advance student understanding and learning in mathematics. This is particularly important in light of research that suggests that adding bells and whistles (Moneno & Mayer, 2000) or conceptually irrelevant video clips (Mayer, Heiser, & Lonn, 2001) to multimedia environments in domains other than mathematics impedes learning. Also, because our cognitive architecture prevents us from simultaneously processing all parts of a complex picture or a particular segment of an animation, we should consider addressing the issue of how to focus the learners' attention on the relevant aspects of the complex image or animation.

Finally, to return to several ideas introduced in this chapter, one avenue for future research is a consideration of delayed transfer tasks and transfer tests that measure efficiency of learning in new domains. One-shot transfer tests provide an incomplete picture of how these multimedia learning environments foster transfer. The literature needs additional evidence that multimedia learning environments foster understanding of mathematics on a long-term basis. Also, subsequent research should attempt to replicate and extend the research described in this chapter, particularly for the research involving static graphics. It is important to examine whether we can generalize these findings beyond geometry instruction to other subdomains of mathematics.

Glossary

Dynamic graphics: Animation or video.

Near-transfer items: Items that are structurally identical to problems presented during instruction but using different surface or cover stories.

Far-transfer items: Items that are not structurally identical to any of the problems presented during instruction.

Multimedia learning of mathematics: Learning in the domain of mathematics from both pencil/paper and computer-based instructional material leveraging both words and pictures.

Static graphics: Illustrations, graphs, photos, or maps.

Footnotes

1. Note that in the interest of space, these animation frames are actually at a rather coarse grain size. It is conceivable that each of these frames could be approached at a finer grain size by dividing each one into three or four frames, resulting in an animation that easily consist of 20 or more frames.

2. The second factor was the type of animated pedagogical agent present in the learning environment (fully embodied agent, minimally embodied agent, or voice only).

References

Atkinson, R. K. (2002). Optimizing learning from examples using animated pedagogical agents. *Journal of Educational Psychology, 94*, 416–427.

Atkinson, R. K., Mayer, R. E., & Merrill, M. M. (2005). Fostering social agency in multimedia learning: Examining the impact of an animated agent's voice. *Contemporary Educational Psychology, 30*, 117–139.

Bransford, J. D., Brown, A. L., & Cocking, R. R. (2000). *How people learn: Brain, mind, experience, and school.* Washington, DC: National Academy Press.

Cooper, G., & Sweller, J. (1987). The effect of schema acquisition and rule automation on mathematical problem-solving transfer. *Journal of Educational Psychology, 79*, 347–362.

Jeung, H., Chandler, P., & Sweller, J. (1997). The role of visual indicators in dual sensory mode instruction. *Educational Psychology, 17*, 329 433.

Kaput, J. (1992). Technology and mathematics education. In D. A. Grouws (Ed.), *Handbook of research on mathematics and learning: A project of the National Council of Teachers in Mathematics* (pp. 515–556). New York: Macmillian.

Mayer, R. E. (2001). *Multimedia learning.* New York: Cambridge University Press.

Mayer, R. E. (2003). The promise of multimedia learning: Using the same instructional design methods across different media. *Learning and Instruction, 13*, 125–139.

Mayer, R. E., & Anderson, R. (1991). Animations need narrations: An experimental test of a dual-coding hypothesis. *Journal of Educational Psychology, 83*, 484–490.

Mayer, R. E., & Anderson, R. (1992). The instructive animation: Helping students build connections between words and pictures in multimedia learning. *Journal of Educational Psychology,* 93, 444–452.

Mayer, R. E., & Moreno, R. (2002). Animation as an aid to multimedia learning. *Educational Psychology Review, 14,* 87–99.

Mayer R. E., Heiser, J., & Lonn, S. (2001). Cognitive constraints on multimedia learning: When processing more material results in less understanding. *Journal of Educational Psychology,* 93, 187–198.

Merrill, M. M. (2003). *The role of animated pedagogical agents in multimedia learning environments.* Paper presented at the annual meeting of the Mid-South Educational Research Association, Biloxi, MS.

Moreno, R., & Mayer, R. E. (1999). Multimedia-supported metaphors for meaning making in mathematics. *Cognition and Instruction, 17,* 215–248.

Moreno, R., & Mayer, R. E. (2000). A coherence effect in multimedia learning: The case for minimizing irrelevant sounds in the design of multimedia instructional messages. *Journal of Educational Psychology,* 92, 117–125.

Mousavi, S. Y., Low, R., & Sweller, J. (1995). Reducing cognitive load by mixing auditory and visual presentation modes. *Journal of Educational Psychology,* 87, 319–334.

Nathan, M. J., Kintsch, W., & Young, E. Y. (1992). A theory of algebra-word-problem comprehension and its implications for the design of learning environments. *Cognition and Instruction,* 9, 329–389.

Roncarrelli, R. (1989). *The computer animation dictionary.* New York: Springer-Verlag.

Sweller, J., & Cooper, G. (1985). The use of worked examples as a substitute for problem solving in learning algebra. *Cognition and Instruction,* 2, 59–89.

Sweller, J., Chandler, P., Tierney, P., & Cooper, M. (1990). Cognitive load as a factor in the structuring of technical material. *Journal of Experimental Psychology: General,* 119, 176–192.

Tarmizi, R., & Sweller, J. (1988). Guidance during mathematical problem solving. *Journal of Educational Psychology,* 80, 424–436.

CHAPTER 26

Multimedia Learning of Chemistry

Robert Kozma

Center for Technology in Learning, SRI International

Joel Russell

Oakland University

Abstract

This chapter proposes the use of a "situative" theory to complement the cognitive theory of multimedia learning (CTML) of chemistry. The chapter applies situative theory to examine the practices of chemists and to derive implications for the use of various kinds of representations in chemistry education. The two theories have implications for different but complementary educational goals – cognitive theory focusing on the learning of scientific concepts and situative theory focusing on learning science as an investigative process. We go on to present and contrast several examples of multimedia in chemistry that address each goal. We critically review the current state of research on multimedia in chemistry and derive implications for theory development, instructional design and classroom practice, and future research in the area.

What Is the Multimedia Learning of Chemistry?

Multimedia to Support Cognition

Richard Mayer (chapter 3; 2001; 2002, 2003), and others (Schnotz, chapter 4; Sweller, chapter 2) describe an information-processing, cognitive theory of learning. There are three tenets at the base of this theory: dual-channel input, limited-memory capacity, and active processing. Mayer draws on this theory to develop a series of design principles for multimedia presentations that use both auditory–verbal and visual–pictorial channels; address limited cognitive capacity for storing and processing information from these channels; and support students' active selection, organization, and integration of information from both auditory and visual inputs. These authors present compelling research in support of the finding that the implementation of these principles results in deeper learning – that is, understanding of difficult concepts and principles that can then be used to solve novel problems. Among the principles most relevant to chemistry learning are the:

- *Multimedia principle*: Learning from words and pictures results in deeper learning than learning from words alone.
- *Contiguity principle*: People learn more deeply when corresponding words and pictures are presented near rather than far from one another in space or time.
- *Modality principle*: People learn more deeply from animation and narration rather than animation and on-screen text.
- *Signaling principle*: People learn more deeply when guidance is provided for directing the learner's attention.
- *Interactivity principle*: People learn more deeply when they can control the order and pace of presentation.

The application of these principles to instructional presentations could make important contributions to the learning of students who have significant difficulties understanding key chemistry concepts and principles (Gable, 1998; Gable & Bunce, 1994; Nakhleh, 1992). For example, the multimedia and modality principles would suggest that designers of multimedia chemistry software that illustrates a difficult concept, such as equilibrium, provide narrated molecular animations in which chemical species are presented in different colors and the concentrations of these species shift over time until the point of equilibrium is reacted. The signaling principle suggests that narration of the animation could point out that the concentrations of each species are changing; it could identify the point at which the system has reached equilibrium; and it could mention that at equilibrium, the forward and backward reactions continue at the same rate. The interactivity principle could allow the students to manipulate temperature or pressure and look at the impact this has on the equilibrium of the system. In-

deed, we found that such software results in increased student understanding of this difficult concept (Kozma, Russell, Jones, Marx, & Davis, 1996), as described in detail in the following section.

Multimedia to Support Practice

However, in the field of chemistry as well as other sciences, various external representations such as diagrams, equations, formulae, and graphs serve a more profound role in the understanding and practice of scientists than that implied by the use of pictures, diagrams, or animations in multimedia instructional presentations. The daily practice of chemists depends heavily on the use of various representations to shape and understand the products of chemical investigations. For example, in our study of professional chemists in an academic and a pharmaceutical chemistry laboratory (Kozma, Chin, Russell, & Marx, 2000), we found that chemists used multiple representations together to construct an understanding of the chemical phenomena they investigated in their experiments. Chemists used structural diagrams to describe the composition and geometry of the compounds that they were trying to synthesize. They used diagrams and chemical equations to reason about the reaction mechanisms needed to transform reagents into products and the physical processes that would support these transformations. Chemists analyzed various instrumental displays and printouts to verify the composition and structure of the compounds that they were trying to synthesize. As they worked together to understand the results of their investigations, chemists made references to specific features of the printouts (e.g., peaks on nuclear magnetic resonance (NMR) or mass spectra) as warrants for claims that the desired products were obtained.

The ways these representations are used by chemists has important implications for the use of multimedia in chemical education, if the educational goal is to develop students' practice of chemistry as an investigative scientific process. National science standards emphasize the learning of science as both a body of significant concepts and as a process of investigation. For example, the National Science Education Standards (National Research Council, 1996) state that this new vision of science standards "requires that students combine processes and scientific knowledge as they use scientific reasoning and critical thinking to develop their understanding of science. . . . Science as inquiry is basic to science education and a controlling principle in the ultimate organization and selection of students' activities" (p. 103). These complementary goals are both addressed in this chapter.

However, the goal of learning as a process of ongoing investigation requires a different theoretical base; one focused on knowledge as practice, as well as on the acquisition of concepts and principles. Greeno (1998), Roth (1998, 2001; Roth & McGinn, 1998), and others (Brown, Collins, & Duguid, 1989; Lave & Wenger, 1991) describe a *situative theory* of learning and understanding in which the practices of a community are influenced by the physical and social characteristics of a specific setting and, in turn, the characteristics of the setting are influenced by the community of practice. In these settings, characteristics of physical objects and social resources enable or constrain the way people can talk, think, understand, and so forth. For example, discussions about the color, viscosity, smell, and so forth of solutions are enabled by the physical characteristics of chemical reagents in the laboratory. Beyond physical objects, *representations* play a particularly important role within situative theory because the use of representations enables the consideration and discussion of objects and processes that are not present or otherwise apparent in a specific situation, as it did for the chemists in our observational study who used representations to discuss the molecular structure of their reagents (Kozma et al., 2000). Through the use of structural diagrams, equations, and instrumental printouts chemists are able to visualize, discuss, and understand the molecules and chemical processes that account for the more perceivable substances and phenomena they observe in the laboratory.

Greeno (1998) characterizes classrooms that are oriented toward situative theory as ones that encourage students to participate in activities that include the formulation and evaluation of conjectures, examples, applications, hypotheses, evidence, conclusions, and arguments. Conceptual understanding occurs in the context of these participatory activities. In these participation-oriented classrooms, discussions are organized not only to foster students' learning of subject-matter concepts and principles, but also their learning to participate in authentic practices – in the case of chemistry, scientific investigation. From this perspective, multiple representations are used by students not only to express their understanding of key concepts in the domain, but also support students' engagement in authentic science practices, such as asking research questions; designing investigations and planning experiments; constructing apparatus and carrying out procedures; analyzing data and drawing conclusions; and presenting findings (Krajcik et al., 1998).

The use of representations to support chemistry practice is illustrated by an observational study one of us conducted in a university organic chemistry course in which we examined pairs of students as they interacted with each other while synthesizing a compound in the wet lab (Kozma, 2000a). We observed that unlike chemists, chemistry students in this study rarely used representations in the laboratory and, as a consequence, their practices and discussions were focused exclusively on the physical aspects of their experiments. The primary interaction among student lab partners was focused on setting up equipment, trouble shooting procedural problems, and interacting with the physical properties of the reagents they were using (e.g., was their crystalline product washed enough or dry enough?). We observed very little discussion among students about the molecular properties of the compounds they were synthesizing or the reaction mechanism that might be taking place during their experiments. However in a subsequent session, these same students worked together while using a *molecular modeling* software program that allowed them to build, examine, and manipulate representations of the same compound that they synthesized in the previous wet lab session. During the computer laboratory session, student discourse – much like the discourse we observed among professional chemists (Kozma et al., 2000) – was filled with references to the molecular properties and processes that underlie the chemical synthesis that they previously performed in the wet lab.

A number of principles for the design of learning experiences and multimedia resources can be derived from situative theory (Kozma et al., 2000). For example, teachers could engage students in the generation of visualizations as a way to pose their research questions, make predictions, or state the goals of their investigations. When designing their investigations, students could be prompted to think about the representational form of the data they will collect, how it would be displayed, and why a particular display might work better for their purposes than another. When constructing their apparatus, they could describe the relationship between the physical changes they expect to observe and the data that are generated by instruments. The representations generated by these instruments could support students' discussions of physical changes in terms of the features built into these displays (e.g., axes labeled "pH" and "Concentration"), features that correspond to both physical observations and underlying chemistry. In presenting their findings, students could use these displays along with other representations to explain their findings and argue for their conclusions. In this regard, it could be particularly effective to use the features of multiple representations together (such as student-generated structural diagrams and instrument-generated printouts) to explain the results and serve as the warrants for conclusions about findings. Indeed, we found that students increased their use of representations in this way when provided with a representational environment to support their laboratory investigations, as detailed in the next section.

In the remainder of this chapter, we extend our consideration of both cognitive and situative theories to examine their relevance to multimedia learning of chemistry. We examine and contrast applications of these theories to two examples of multimedia chemistry environments developed in our laboratories, as well as those developed elsewhere in the United States. We consider the results and the limitations of research on multimedia in chemistry, along with their implications for learning theory, instructional design and classroom practice, and further research needed in this area.

Examples of Multimedia Learning of Chemistry

Multimedia to Support the Learning of Concepts and Principles

Several examples of multimedia learning of chemistry illustrate the contrasting and complementary nature of the cognitive and situative perspective. Our first example, *SMV:Chem* (*Synchronized Multiple Representations in Chemistry*) and its prototype predecessor, *4M:Chem* (*MultiMedia and Mental Models in Chemistry*), illustrates the application of cognitive theory. *SMV:Chem* (Russell, Kozma, Becker, & Susskind, 2000) is a multimedia chemical software program designed to show experiments illustrating key chemistry concepts using molecular-scale animations, graphs, molecular models, and equations. *4M:Chem* (Russell & Kozma, 1994; see also Kozma et al., 1996; Russell et al., 1997) was a prototype used to develop the technology and test some of the underlying theoretical principles. These packages were designed for use both by the instructor in the classroom during lecture and by students outside the classroom as part of homework exercises. Both programs used a screen design that displayed videos of experiments in the upper-left quadrant, *nanoscale* animations in the upper-right quadrant, graphic

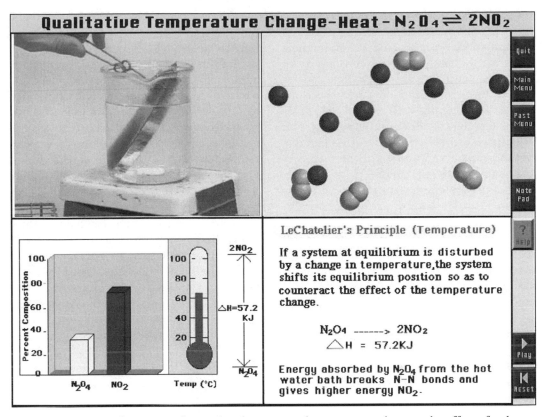

Figure 26.1. *SMV:Chem* screen for LeChatelier's principle experiment showing the effect of a change in temperature on the equilibrium compositions of the sample.

representations in the lower left, and other representations such as chemical equations, text, data collection sheets, and molecular models in the lower-right quadrant (see Figure 26.1).

The screens in Figure 26.1 show on the right tool bar the navigation controls for a specific experiment. Each of these four windows can be independently activated such that users can view a single window or any combination of windows. There is an audio track for the video window describing the experiment. There are separate audio tracks for the other three windows that can be activated when a window is viewed by itself.

Figure 26.1 illustrates LeChatelier's principle for a gas phase equilibrium, $N_2O_4(g) \leftrightarrow 2NO_2(g)$, subject to a change in temperature. The concept of equilibrium is very difficult to understand, as documented by numerous studies of student misconceptions of this topic (Banerjee, 1995; Camacho &

Good, 1989; Gorodetsky & Gussarsky, 1986; Kozma, Russell, Johnston, & Dershimer, 1990; Thomas & Schwenz, 1998).

As the experiment proceeds, the video window shows a change in equilibrium composition that produces more N_2O_4 resulting from increasing the temperature (Figure 26.1). The experiment starts with two tubes containing equilibrium mixtures of these two gases. One tube is placed in a boiling water bath. Students are able to observe that after this change in temperature the color of the gas in the heated tube is darker than the color of the gas in the room temperature tube because the composition has shifted to produce more red-brown NO_2 (a monomer) leaving less colorless N_2O_4 (a dimer). The animation window shows initially equal numbers of red-brown spheres and coupled gray spheres all in constant motion. Prior to increasing the temperature, the distribution of species is seen to fluctuate with at times two more red-brown monomers and one less gray dimer as the dimers decompose and the monomers dimerize showing the dynamic property of a chemical equilibrium. After the temperature change the animation shows the composition fluctuating with either one or two dimers present and the rest monomers. The graph window shows the relative increase in the percent composition of the species as the temperature is increased, with the percent of NO_2 increasing more. Class discussion or homework questions ask students to consider what is shown in the animation that is not visible in the video of the experiment, which properties of a chemical equilibrium are correctly and which incorrectly shown by the animation, and how LeChatelier's principle could be used to explain the observed and portrayed shift in composition.

The features of *SMV:Chem* are an example of how the multimedia, modality, signaling, and interactivity design principles described by Mayer can be implemented in multimedia chemistry software. Our research on students' use of this software illustrates its effectiveness. Research on the *4M:Chem* prototype (Kozma et al., 1996) showed a significant increase in college students' understanding of concepts related to equilibrium after a lecture using a unit of *4M:Chem* similar to the *SMV:Chem* unit illustrated in Figure 26.1. There was also a significant reduction in common equilibrium misconceptions. A more recent study (Russell, 2004) using *SMV:Chem* over the course of a semester showed significantly higher scores for students who attended lectures supplemented by *SMV:Chem* demonstrations and who used the software to do homework assignments than for students who were not exposed to the software or those who saw the software used in lecture but did not use it for homework.

A small study by Kozma (2000b) using the *4M:Chem* unit on gas-phase equilibrium indicates that specific features of the medium play a particularly important role in these results. In this study, students used a worksheet to guide their interactions with the software. One group had access only to the animation window; another group used only the video window; a third group used only the graph window; and a fourth group used all three windows. Each group had an audio narration customized to the visual features in that presentation. The group that received all three presentations had a narration that coordinated features across all of the representations. The animation group scored higher than the other groups on test items having to do with the dynamic nature of gas-phase equilibrium. The graph group scored highest on items dealing with relative pressures. The group that received all three media and the group that received video only did not outscore the other groups on any of the items, indicating that video may not have provided students with information they needed to understand the concept and multiple representations may have exceeded students' capacities to process all of them simultaneously.

Connected Chemistry is another example of a multimedia project that also targets the learning of difficult chemistry concepts (Stieff & Wilensky, 2003; http://ccl.northwestern.edu/netlogo/models/). The software is a collection of computer-based *simulations* of closed chemical systems that students can interact with in several ways. Each simulation focuses on a chemical concept such as factors effecting rates of reaction or LeChatelier's principle. Unlike *SMV:Chem*, which uses "canned" animations, *Connected Chemistry* is written in NetLogo, a multiagent modeling language and it actually generates the graphics on the fly in response to student input. The interface window of *Connected Chemistry* for the "Simple Kinetic 3" module is shown in Figure 26.2. The interface consists of three fundamental components: a graphics window for a nanoscale representation of the system, a plotting window for graphs of macroscopic properties of the system, and an area for setting system parameters and starting, pausing, restarting, and resetting the simulation. It does not display videos of the actual experiment, as does *SMV:Chem*, nor does it provide an audio narration of the various graphic representations it

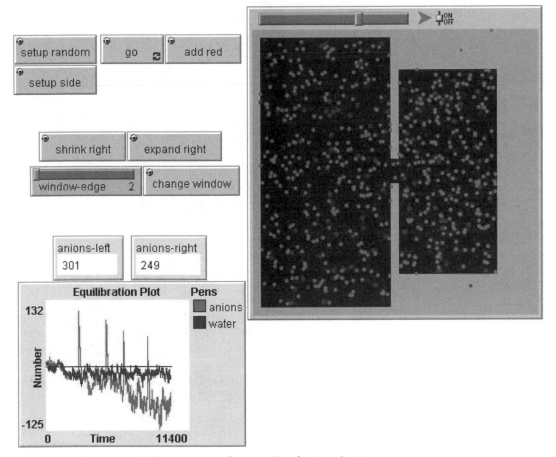

Figure 26.2. Connected Chemistry interface window for Simple Kinetics 3.

provides. The module in Figure 26.2 simulates the equilibrium distributions of a solute species and water molecules between two connected volumes as various parameters are adjusted. The graphics window displays visualizations for solute molecules shown as red circles (majority species) and water molecules shown as blue circles (minority species). As the simulation runs, all molecules in the graphics window are in rapid motion. The plotting window shows the difference in numbers of solute molecules in the right and left sides. Figure 26.2 shows five changes to a system that initially had equal left and right volumes and numbers of solute and water molecules on each side – first a decrease in volume of the right side followed by four additions each of 125 extra solute molecules to the right side. The excess of water on the left side

(negative numbers in graph) is influenced only by the volume change. After each addition of solute species the equilibrium distribution changes to give a larger excess of solute species on the left side.

Yet another multimedia software package designed to support the learning of difficult concepts in chemistry is *Molecular Workbench* (http://workbench.concord. org/modeler/index.html). *Molecular Workbench* also uses advanced computational techniques to provide a variety of real-time, interactive simulations of chemical phenomena by adding sets of rules describing chemical reactions to a molecular dynamics modeling system (Xie & Tinker, in press). All simulations display a two-dimensional molecular dynamics model with graphs of potential energy. The software has the flexibility to allow users to set

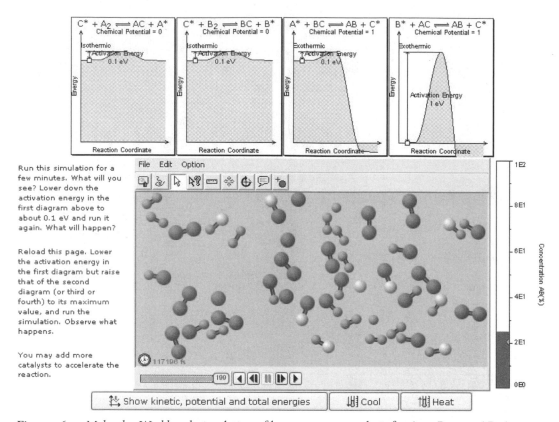

Figure 26.3. *Molecular Workbench* simulation of homogeneous catalysis for $A_2 + B_2 \rightarrow 2\,AB$. A variety of topics are available at http://workbench.concord.org/modeler/index.html.

most initial parameters including the atoms, their positions, velocities, and bonds as well as all potential energies parameters. As an example of one *Molecular Workbench* simulation, Figure 26.3 shows a snapshot of the computer screen as the simulation progresses for a homogeneous catalysis. As with *Connected Chemistry* and unlike *SMV:Chem*, *Molecular Workbench* does not provide narration or a video of the experiment as it appears on the lab bench.

Multimedia to Support Laboratory Investigation

While *SMV:Chem* and other environments described in the preceding text are applications of cognitive theory to support student learning of chemical concepts and principles, *ChemSense* is an application of situative theory designed to support student inquiry in the wet lab (http://chemsense.org). With *SMV:Chem*, students *manipulate* and *observe* multiple representations of prespecified chemical experiments. On the other hand, the *ChemSense* environment offers students an ensemble of tools with which they can *create and analyze* representations of their own experiments (Schank & Kozma, 2002). An essential component of the *ChemSense* design is that the tools are used within social (i.e., students working collaboratively) and physical (i.e., working in the wet lab) contexts to investigate, analyze, and discuss chemical phenomena. Within these contexts, students jointly conduct wet lab experiments and use multiple representations to analyze, discuss, and understand their goals, results, and conclusions.

Figure 26.4 shows the basic layout of *ChemSense*. The environment contains a set of tools – drawing, animation, graphing, and text tools – for creating and viewing representations, and a commenting feature for peer review. A Web interface, called the *ChemSense Gallery*, is also available for viewing and commenting on work, and managing groups and accounts. Several examples of student-generated items can be seen in Figure 26.4. At the top of the window are two animations that students created to show the process of a gas – specifically, carbon dioxide – dissolving in water. To create these animations, students constructed individual frames that stepped through the breaking of bonds between the carbon, oxygen, and hydrogen, and the subsequent formation of carbonic acid, H_2CO_3 (aq). Below and to the right of the animations is a display of a dynamic graph that shows student-collected data from an experiment on the change in pH of the solution as carbon dioxide is dissolved over time. This data was collected at the lab bench through the use of probeware

(developed by Pasco Inc., Roseville, CA) and imported into *ChemSense*. Below the graph is a comment area where other students can submit and view comments and questions. Every item in the workspace has its own personal comment area. To the left of the graph is a student-constructed description of the lab purpose, procedure, and findings.

As an application of situative theory, *ChemSense* is designed to shape the way students think and talk about representations, physical phenomena, and underlying chemical entities and processes. For example, in considering the dissolving of carbon dioxide into water, students can use the animation tool to build a representation of this dynamic process. As they create their animation they are confronted with a set of decisions about how to represent their understanding of the dissolving process: What

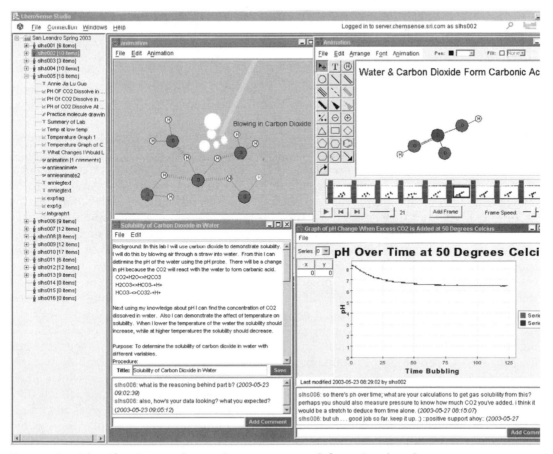

Figure 26.4. The *ChemSense* tool set with navigation tree (left pane) and workspace containing sample high school student work on the process of carbon dioxide dissolving in water.

does a water molecule look like? What is the structure of carbon dioxide? What happens to the water and carbon dioxide structures as they meet? Which atoms are involved? How many are there of each kind? The *ChemSense* environment also gives students the means to coordinate these representations with observable phenomena using probeware. For example, students collect wet-lab data such as temperature or pH and import the data into *ChemSense*. They then can create and run two representations – a nanoscopic-level representation showing the underlying process and a tool-generated representation (i.e., the graph) showing the change in observable properties. The purpose of using two representations that show parallel changes at the nanoscopic and physical levels is to support student discussions about what is happening at the nanoscale that determines the emergent properties of what they see on the lab bench.

ChemSense is used with curriculum units specially designed to support investigative activities and to scaffold student use of interconnected representations in order to ask questions, describe, explain, and argue about the chemical experiments they are conducting on the lab bench. In addition, the environment allows students to peer review each other's work by way of interlaced discussion and commentary. For example, a teacher may include an activity that asks students to review the work of other lab groups and ask questions related to the chemistry in their representations. As part of their assignment, each lab group is responsible for providing critical feedback on other students' work. Used appropriately, this function further supports the possibility for students to collectively arrive at new understandings of scientific concepts by asking students to probe other students' thinking (Brown & Campione, 1996; Scardamalia & Bereiter, 1994).

In a study (Schank & Kozma, 2002) of high school students using a *ChemSense*-based, three-week unit on solubility, we found that students who created more drawings and animations in *ChemSense* developed greater skill in using representations (i.e.,

representational competence) and deeper understanding of geometry-related aspects of chemical phenomena in their animations. Analysis of videotapes of two high school groups working in the ChemSense environment showed that use of the tools prompts students to think more carefully about specific aspects of chemical phenomena to which they might not otherwise attend, such as the number of molecules involved in a reaction, the particular bonds created in the reaction, the bond angles, or the sequence of steps in a reaction. Throughout these collaborative sessions, students used the representations to both develop and reveal their understandings of chemical phenomena.

Another example of multimedia chemistry software that supports investigation is *ChemDiscovery* (formerly called *ChemQuest*). *ChemDiscovery* provides a technology-based inquiry-oriented learning environment (Agapova et al., 2002). Rather than using lectures and worksheets as the primary instructional vehicles, *ChemDiscovery* features interactive Web pages linked to activities, databases, and design studios and coordinates them with hands-on laboratory activities. Students work in pairs or small cooperative learning teams with instructors functioning as coordinators and facilitators.

ChemDiscovery consists of eight projects or "quests" that can be used individually to supplement a traditional classroom or as a set to replace most of the traditional curriculum. Each project includes design activities such as those shown in Figure 26.5. In this example students can increase or decrease the relative concentration of one of the species involved in the equilibrium between hydrogen, iodine, and hydrogen iodide using the arrows on the bar for the selected species. Prior to making the change students are asked to predict if the equilibrium composition will shift and if so in which direction. After running this simulation students then predict the direction of change for a number of reactions that are represented both by symbols and by molecular representations. A typical *ChemDiscovery* classroom would have student teams working

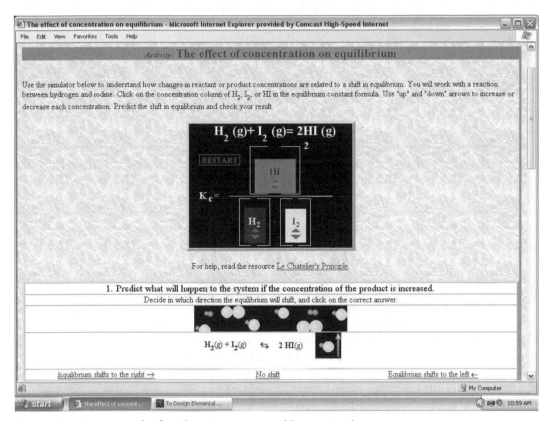

Figure 26.5. Design studio for ChemDiscovery equilibrium simulator.

simultaneously on a range of activities that allow students to benefit from the actions of their team as well as the actions of others in the class.

What We Know About Multimedia Learning of Chemistry

As described in the preceding text, recent years have seen a significant amount of development work in chemistry using the most advanced multimedia technologies, such as multiagent-generated real-time animations of molecular systems. However, most of the research studies on multimedia in chemistry have been with older technologies, such as still pictures and simple, canned animations. Nonetheless, these studies shed light on the effectiveness of multimedia learning of chemistry.

A study by Noh & Scharmann (1997) examined the impact of molecular-level pic-tures on the acquisition of chemistry concepts and problem-solving skills. Groups of Korean high school chemistry students were randomly assigned to treatment and control groups and, over a 13-week period, were given 21 hours of chemistry instruction on concepts related to chemical equations, gases, liquids and solids, and solutions. As each concept was introduced, students in the treatment group received a series of still pictures of chemical phenomena, a total of 25 sets of materials over the period of the treatment. The pictures were a combination of macrolevel representations (e.g., iconic drawings of containers under different amounts of pressure) and nanoscopic representations (e.g., cutaways of the containers showing different densities of molecules, as represented by two-dimensional balls, moving about, as represented by trailing lines). Teachers used these pictures as part of their verbal explanations of concepts. Students in the control group received traditional expository instruction. Students were tested using two standard chemistry tests, the *Chemistry Conceptions Test* and the *Chemistry Problem-Solving Test*. Both tests used items that employed molecular-level pictures of chemical systems as well as items that involved text or numerical responses. Students who received the pictorial treatment scored higher on the concept posttest than did students in the treatment group, while there were no significant differences between the two groups on the problem-solving test. Differences in mean scores between the groups did not hold across the entire concept test but were due to significant differences on the Diffusion and Dissolution subtests, not on the Particle and State subtests.

In a study involving high school teachers from 12 different schools, Bunce and Gabel (2002) examined the impact of static nanoscopic, or "particulate," representations used in three, two-week modules on tests of chemistry concepts, including states of matter, solutions and bonding, and stoichiometry. The treatment group received instruction using three representations of matter: macroscopic (e.g., demonstrations of observable chemical phenomena), particulate (e.g., still pictures of chemical systems with molecules represented by two-dimensional structures composed of dots or circles representing elements), and symbolic (e.g., using chemical or mathematical symbols and equations). The control group used the same curriculum materials but received instruction using only the macroscopic and symbolic representations. The treatment group out performed the control group across the three modules on common teacher-made tests, consisting of items using each of the representational forms. However, the results were due primarily to significant differences on the first module, States of Matter, and to items on the test that used particulate representations. The study found differences that favored males over females in the control group but females did as well as males in the treatment group.

Ardac and Akaygun (2004) conducted a similar experiment with eighth-grade science students in Turkey. Students in the experimental group interacted with a multimedia software program, *Chemical Change*, that allowed students to view simultaneous presentations at the macroscopic (i.e., video of experiments), symbolic (i.e., chemical equations), and molecular (i.e., molecular drawings and simple animations) levels. The study spanned 10 classes over a two-week period and included topics such as physical and chemical changes, chemical reactions, conservation of mass, as so forth. Each student worked individually at a computer and their interaction was guided by a worksheet that asked them to explore a particular topic, interconnect the multiple representations, and respond to questions. Students in the control group received lectures on the same topics accompanied by equations and molecular drawings on the chalkboard. Students were tested with true and false and multiple choice items. Some items used molecular-level representations; others just used text and equations. Students in the experimental group scored higher on the posttest items that used molecular representations. Students in the experimental group also displayed more particulate-level representations and showed more conceptual accuracy in a posttest interview than did control group students.

The effects of molecular-level animations were explicitly examined in several studies. Williamson and Abraham (1995) used such animations (i.e., molecules represented by dots bouncing around and interacting) with students in one of two sections of a university general chemistry course. Both sections received the same series of 10 lectures on concepts related to gases, liquids, solids, and solution reactions. The instructor used static pictures and chalk diagrams with both lecture sections. In the treatment section, the lectures were supplemented by a series of animations illustrating the concepts at a molecular level. A subset of students in the treatment group was also allowed to see the animations, multiple times if desired, and respond to worksheets in the computer lab during their discussion section meetings. There were no differences between the three groups on the course exam. However, there were differences between the control group and the treatment groups on tests specifically designed to assess students' understanding of the concepts using molecular-level diagrams. Students in both treatment groups scored higher than students in the control group but there were no significant differences between the two treatment groups.

Sanger and Greenbowe (2000) examined the impact of animations and conceptual change strategies on students' conceptions of current flow in electrolyte solutions. In this 2×2 design, university students in one group received a lecture along with an animation accompanied by lecturer's narration showing the electrochemical processes occurring in a galvanic cell at the nanoscopic level with a focus on the chemical half-reactions occurring at each electrode and the transfer of ions through a salt bridge. Students in the other lecture section saw only static chalkboard drawings of the process. Half the students in these groups also received a conceptual change strategy that confronted typical misconceptions while the other half did not. Students were tested using algorithmic, visual, and verbal test items on both an immediate and a delayed post-test. There were no significant differences between any of the treatment and control groups on the algorithmic or visual test items. There was, however, a main effect in favor of the conceptual change strategy (but not one for the use of animations) on the verbal items on both the immediate and delayed posttests. There was also an interaction between the animation and conceptual change treatments for these items on the immediate posttest such that students who did not receive the conceptual change strategies scored higher with the animations than those students who received the conceptual change strategies but not the animations.

In a study by Yang, Andre, and Greenbowe (2004), university students who received a lecture on chemical reactions that occur inside a battery also received animations accompanied by lecture narrations. Students in another section received the lecture only accompanied by static diagrams. On a test of topic knowledge, students in the animation group outperformed the students receiving the static diagrams. However on a test of transfer, there was an interaction such that students with higher spatial ability who received animations performed better than students with low spatial ability or those that did not receive the animations.

In an experiment by Sanger, Phelps, and Fienhold (2000), students in the treatment group viewed an animation accompanied by narration that showed representations at both macroscopic (i.e., a can being heated, sealed, and crushed upon cooling) and nanoscopic levels (i.e., numbers of two-dimensional balls representing molecules moving around both inside and outside the can, more quickly or slowly) three times. Students in both the treatment group and the control group received a lecture on gas behavior and observed a physical demonstration of the can-crushing experiment. Students in the treatment group scored significantly higher on measures related to understanding a similar demonstration. In another experimental study (Sanger & Badger, 2001), students in the treatment group received instruction on and demonstrations of miscibility of polar, nonpolar, and ionic compounds supplemented by both molecular-level animations of intermolecular attractions, as well as shaded two-dimensional pictures of electron density plots ("eplots") that used color to show the polar (i.e., charged) regions of various molecules. Students in the control group received only instruction and demonstrations. Students in the treatment group scored significantly higher on an experimenter-constructed test in which students were asked to identify polar molecules not discussed in the instruction, make predictions about the miscibility of compounds, and explain their answers.

There is a new technology – *interactive molecular modeling graphics* – that is increasingly being used by professional chemists (although we did not happen to observe this technology being used in our study of practicing chemists [Kozma et al., 2000]). Molecular models are computer constructions of three-dimensional molecular structures projected on a two-dimensional computer screen that consist of space-filling, ball-and-stick, or wire-frame representations of a single, sometimes very complex, molecule of a species (Francoeur, 2002). With this technology, the user can construct a model, rotate it through three-dimensional space, examine energies, and measure angles and the lengths of bonds. This technology is starting to be used rather widely in chemistry education at the university level (Bragin, 1996; Jones, 2001; Kantardjieff, Hardinger, & Van Willis, 1999; Martin, 1998; Montgomery, 2001) and occasionally even at the high school level.

A few studies have been conducted on the effect of this new technology on learning. Dori and her colleagues (Barnea & Dori, 1999; Dori & Barak, 2001) have used computer models with high school students in Israel as part of a chemistry program to improve students' understanding concepts of molecular bonding and structure, their spatial ability, and their perceptions of the concept of a model. In the first study, students in the experimental group worked in pairs to conduct a series of investigations using a workbook and molecular modeling program. Under the guidance of the workbook, students selected different molecules from a library of models, displayed them in different representational modes, rotated the models in three-dimensional space, and measured the bond lengths and angles. As part of their investigations, students had to decide on what geometric shape of the models to use, along with other structural properties. Students in the control group studied the same topics in the traditional way using plastic models rather than computer models. Students in the experimental group scored higher than those in the control group on measures of their understanding of structure and bonding. Students in both groups scored higher from pre- to post-tests on standard measures of spatial ability, the experimental group significantly more so. Experimental group students also scored higher on measures of the concept of a model (i.e., "model perception") in which students were asked to describe models and how they are used. Experimental group females improved their model perception more than control group females in understanding ways to create models and in the role of models as mental structures and prediction tools. In the second, parallel study students in the experimental group scored higher than the control group on tests that measured students' understanding of isomers in organic compounds. They scored higher on all types of test items, those that involved graphics, text, and a combination of graphics and text. As with the previous study, experimental group students scored higher than control group students on measures of the concept of model.

The Limitations of Research on Multimedia Learning of Chemistry

In general, the findings from the research studies that we have reviewed support the use of multimedia to teach concepts and principles in chemistry. With one exception (Sanger & Greenbowe, 2000) multimedia was more effective than the alternative; the use of still pictures and animations of molecular systems, and interactive models and electron density plots of single molecules all proved to be effective. However, there are some important limitations in this research.

Unlike the experiments done in Mayer's cognitive laboratory, all of these studies were done within regular chemistry classroom settings. Classroom research is an important way to establish external validity of findings when using multimedia. At the same time, these studies typically lack the kind of experimental control that is needed to specifically support one design principle or another. For example, there were problems with treatment fidelity in several studies. In the Sanger and Badger study (2001) dynamic animations were used along with static eplots in the treatment group making it difficult to attribute the effect to one or the other treatment. Observations of lectures in the Noh and Scharmann (1997) study of static pictures versus traditional instruction found that control-group lecturers were using chalkboard diagrams as part of their instruction. Similarly, control group students in the Ardac and Akaygun (2004) study received molecular-level drawings during lecture. There are other general problems related to experimental control, such as the failure to control the specific verbal content across lectures or the specific timing and function of verbal content, relative to the presentation of visual content. While these problems are inherent with classroom research it means that conclusions cannot sort out the extent to which the effects due to application of a specific principle, such as the multimedia principle or the signaling principle.

In several studies the findings favoring multimedia were limited to specific kinds of topics, such as results favoring static pictures for units on states of matter, but not bonding or stoichiometry (Bunce & Gabel, 2002) and for diffusion and dissolution, but not particulate matter or states of matter (Noh & Scharmann, 1997). Most of the studies used tests that were specially designed to include molecular-level diagrams. In the Bunce and Gabel (2002) and the Ardac and Akaygun (2004) studies, differences between the experimental and control groups were limited to those test items that used molecular-level diagrams. The findings of all these studies, and their limitations, have implications for cognitive theory, instructional design and classroom practice, and future research.

Implications of the Research for Cognitive Theory

Even with their limitations, the findings of these studies generally support the cognitive theory of Mayer and others as it applies to chemistry learning. However, they also raise additional questions that should be pursued in future research, questions that if answered might help us better understand how multimedia supports the learning of concepts and principles. For example within the visual channel, are there differences among different kinds of visual symbol systems (e.g., graphs, animations) in their support of learning? Do different representations support the learning of different kinds of concepts and principles? The Kozma (2000b) study of 4M:Chem found that students who used the animations did better on test items related to the dynamic nature of gas-phase equilibrium and students who used graphs of relative pressures over time did better on items related to partial pressures. Are there differences between the features of these visual symbol systems that support one concept over the other? Noh and Scharmann (1997) found that even static pictures of dynamic systems did better on portions of the test related to dynamics (i.e., diffusion and dissolution) but they did not help on less dynamic concepts (i.e., particle and state). We need to further refine our cognitive theories about how the surface features or properties of specific representations (such as motion, color, shape) and their syntax (i.e., rules for putting these features together in certain ways) can support learning of concepts with certain underlying characteristics related to geometrics, dynamics, rate, and so on. These refinements of cognitive theory require further research (see following text).

By intent, theory and research have a symbiotic relationship. Sometimes research results allow us to refine or modify our theories; sometimes theory influences the type of research that is done. Cognitive theory has had a strong influence on the kind of research done on multimedia learning of chemistry. Almost all of the studies we reviewed focused on the use of multimedia to support the learning of chemical concepts and principles. Few studies focused on the use of representations to support the goal of learning chemistry as a process of investigation. The exceptions to this situation are the Kozma (2000a) study of university inorganic chemistry students working with modeling software in their laboratory course and the Schank and Kozma (2002) study of high school students using ChemSense to support their laboratory investigations. If we are going to expand our research base to include studies focused on the outcome goal of learning science as a process of investigation, we need to expand our theoretical base for multimedia learning to include situative theory that focuses on the use of representations to support investigative practices.

Implications of the Research for Instructional Design and Classroom Practice

In general, the results of the research that we reviewed justify use of multimedia in chemistry instruction, when the goal is to teach concepts and principles. Multimedia seemed to be effective for lower secondary, upper secondary, and college chemistry students. We identified instances in which the use of still pictures of molecular systems to supplement lectures was successful in teaching concepts related to states of matter, diffusion, and dissolution. We found studies in which animations accompanied by narrations were successful in teaching concepts related to equilibrium, reaction chemistry, electrochemistry, and miscibility. We found studies in which the use of molecular models supported students' understanding of structure and bonding. Several significant multimedia development projects, such as *SMV:Chem*, *Connected Chemistry*, and *Molecular Workbench*, are providing instructors and instructional designers with new technological resources to bring multimedia into the chemistry classroom in support of conceptual understanding. However we are not able to say, given the state of research, for which topics or students it is best to use animations versus still pictures or models. Nor can we say how these various media can be used together and when it is best to do so. For the time being, all of these practical issues are left up to the art and judgment of instructors and instructional designers.

If the goal is to teach chemistry as a process of investigation, we can say even less, based on research done to date. Situative theory would argue for the use of various representations in the context of laboratory investigations, using them to ask questions, plan experiments, carry out procedures, analyze data, and present findings. New software systems, such as *ChemSense* and *ChemDiscovery*, provide instructors with powerful tools to support students' investigations. But there is little research so far that helps guide instructors and instructional designers on how to effectively integrate these tools into classroom and laboratory activities.

There are, however, many studies that have implications for student assessment. Almost all of the studies that we reviewed used specially designed tests that measured students' understanding in new ways and measured new goals for chemistry learning, such as increasing students' abilities to use appropriately diverse forms of representations in problem solving, as they are used by experts. Indeed, multimedia applications had the greatest effect on test items of this sort. These findings argue for the integration of still pictures, animations, models, and other multimedia into the tests and examinations of chemistry courses and the widespread availability of new technologies makes the use of these new tests more feasible.

Implications for Research

As cited previously, there is an urgent need for more research in the area of multimedia learning in chemistry. There is a need for carefully controlled cognitive experiments that supplement classroom studies. These experiments could carefully analyze the effects of static pictures versus animation versus molecular models on the learning of various types of chemical concepts and principles. They could examine for which concepts it would be most effective to use models of single molecules, animations of a single molecular reaction, or simulations of entire systems. They could examine a broader range of symbol systems that include chemical formulae and equations, graphs, and instrument printouts and displays as they might influence the learning of one type of concept or another. And there is a need for research that looks at the effectiveness of using these various symbol systems together.

A number of studies that we examined identified aptitude by treatment interactions (ATIs). Bunce and Gabel (2002) found an ATI favoring females when using stills and Barnea and Dori (1999) found one favoring females when using molecular modeling software. Yang, Andre, and Greenbowe (2003) found an ATI that favored high spatial-ability students when using animations. There was also a treatment by treatment interaction (Sanger & Greenbowe, 2000) and numerous treatment by measurement interactions (Bunce & Gabel, 2002; Noh & Scharmann, 1977; Sanger & Greenbowe, 2000; Williamson & Abraham, 1995; Yang, Andre, & Greenbowe, 2003). While ATIs were not systematically examined across studies and no consistent patterns were established, the number of ATIs that emerged argues for including gender, spatial ability, and measurement variables as regular features in the design of future multimedia studies in chemistry.

There is also a significant need for research that focuses on the process of laboratory investigation and how it is that the use of various symbol systems and multimedia environments facilitates investigative practices. There is a need to extend research beyond the lecture hall or computer lab into the chemistry laboratory. New assessments must be designed and used that measure investigation practices and related skills, such as representational competence (Kozma & Russell, 1997; Kozma & Russell, 1997, in press). In order to integrate cognitive and situative perspectives, research studies must examine the relationship between learning investigative practices and the development of chemical understanding.

Finally, there is a need to systematically evaluate large multimedia projects, such as *SMV:Chem, Connected Chemistry, Molecular Workbench, ChemSense,* and *ChemDiscovery*. Significant investments have been made in these projects (typically by the National Science Foundation) and more research is needed as these projects are scaled beyond their use by the initial faculty members and teachers affiliated with the development projects.

Glossary

Molecular models or *interactive molecular modeling graphics*: Computer software programs that display the arrangement and bonding of atoms within a molecule. These programs typically allow users to construct molecules (or view molecules constructed by others) and operate on these structures by rotating them in three-dimensional space, measuring bond length and angles, and viewing them in different forms (e.g., space filling or wire tube).

Nanoscopic: Term used to refer to structures measured in nanometers (usually 0.1–100 nm) and of a size below that which can be seen with the aided eye.

Representation: In this context, the word refers to *external* symbols or symbolic structures that refer to other objects or events. These external representations are distinguished from internal, or mental, representations and are sometimes referred to as *inscriptions* (see Roth & McGinn, 1998). In chemistry, representations often refer to entities or processes that can not be observed directly (e.g., atoms, molecules and reactions) and can take a variety of forms (e.g., structural diagrams, equations).

Representational competence: A set of skills and practices that allow a person to use a variety of representations, singly and together, to think about, communicate, and act on aperceptual physical entities and processes, such as molecules and their reactions (see Kozma et al., 2000; Kozma & Russell, in press).

Simulation: In this context, the word refers to computational environments that represent a chemical system composed of large numbers of molecules – usually by a number of clustered balls or dots (representing molecules) that

Russell, J., & Kozma, R. (1994). 4M:Chem – Multimedia and Mental Models in Chemistry. *Journal of Chemical Education, 71* (669–670).

Russell, J., Kozma, R., Becker, D., & Susskind, T. (2000). SMV:Chem – Synchronized Multiple Visualizations in Chemistry [Computer software]. New York: John Wiley.

Russell, J., Kozma, R., Jones, T., Wykoff, J., Marx, N., & Davis, J. (1997). Use of simultaneous-synchronized macroscopic, microscopic, and symbolic representations to enhance the teaching and learning of chemical concepts. *Journal of Chemical Education, 74*(3), 330–334.

Sanger, M., & Badger, S. (2001). Using computer-based visualization strategies to improve students' understanding of molecular polarity and miscibility. *Journal of Chemical Education, 78*(10), 1412–1416.

Sanger, M., & Greenbowe, T. (2000). Addressing student misconceptions concerning electron flow in aqueous solutions with instruction including computer animiations and conceptual change strategies. *International Journal of Science Education, 22*(5), 521–537.

Sanger, M., Phelps, A., & Fienhold, J. (2000). Using a computer animation to improve students' conceptual understanding of a con-crushing demonstration. *Journal of Chemical Education, 77*(11), 1517–1520.

Scardamalia, M., & Bereiter, C. (1994). Computer support for knowledge-building communities. *Journal of the Learning Sciences, 3*(3), 265–283.

Schank, P., & Kozma, R. (2002). Learning chemistry through the use of a representation-based knowledge-building environment. *Journal of Computers in Mathematics and Science Teaching, 21*(3), 253–279.

Stieff, M., & Wilensky, U. (2003). Connected Chemistry: Incoporating interactive simulations into the chemistry curriculum. *Journal of Science Education and Technology, 12*(3), 285–302.

Thomas, P., & Schwenz, R. (1998). College physical chemistry students' conceptions of equilibrium and fundamental thermodynamics. *Journal of Research in Science Teaching, 35*(10), 1151–1160.

Williamson, V., & Abraham, M. (1995). The effects of computer animation on the particulate mental models of college chemistry students. *Journal of Research in Science Teaching, 32*(5), 521–534.

Xie, Q., & Tinker, R. (in press). Molecular dynamics simulations of chemical reactions for use in education. *Journal of Chemical Education.*

Yang, E.-M., Andre, T., & Greenbowe, T. (2003). Spatialability and the impact of visualization/animation on learning electrochemistry. *International Journal of Science Education, 25*(3), 329–349.

CHAPTER 27

Multimedia Learning of Meteorology

Richard K. Lowe

Curtin University

Abstract

Meteorology increasingly relies on visualizations but the particular contributions that multimedia's visual components make to learning are relatively unexplored. This chapter examines the basis for comprehending weather maps and how learners extract information from static and animated depictions. Meteorological knowledge deficiencies hamper learners' processing. Information extracted is superficial and fragmentary with key information in the animation neglected despite being explicitly depicted and flexibly available via user control. Inadequate processing stems from the display's perceptual characteristics. For such specialized visualizations to be effective in multimedia learning materials, they may need to be given extensive support. Implications for multimedia learning theory and instructional design practice are discussed.

What Is Multimedia Learning of Meteorology?

Multimedia approaches to the learning of meteorology are well established within the field and widely accepted internationally. This acceptance is reflected in the large-scale instructional initiatives in both the United States (the COMET Program; http://www.comet.ucar.edu/) and Europe (the EUMETCAL Program; http://eumetcal.meteo.fr/) that for some years have provided computer-based professional education and training in this domain. The multimedia materials produced under these programs combine a diverse range of visual and verbal components (including written text, narrations, static pictures, animations, and video). In recent years, technological advances in delivery systems such as Web casting have led to an increasing emphasis on dynamic and interactive forms of presentation in these materials.

While meteorology educators have shown great enthusiasm for using multimedia approaches, empirical research evidence is lacking regarding how to maximize their educational effectiveness. Designers and developers of multimedia resources for learning meteorology tend to rely on generic instructional design guidelines rather than research findings that are specific to this domain. For example, Parrish (1999) has shown how broad recommendations about designing instructional illustrations can be applied to the types of diagrams that are used to teach meteorology, particularly in multimedia learning contexts. Although the advice given by Parrish is useful in a general sense, it does not tackle specific instructional challenges that arise from the distinctive nature of meteorological subject matter. However, Parrish's emphasis on pictorial representations does serve to highlight just how crucial visualizations are in the multimedia learning of meteorology.

The focus in this chapter is upon this visual aspect of multimedia learning, something that has received relatively little attention in its own right. A prevailing view among practicing instructional designers is that the visuals used in multimedia learning materials function to support the accompanying verbal information. While research has addressed various questions concerning the best ways of presenting and arranging verbal–visual combinations, there has been less questioning of the role of visuals *per se* in these materials. Multimedia developers too often treat visuals as unproblematic adjuncts that clarify the verbal explanation ("a picture is worth ten thousand words"). However, with some types of visuals the situation may be less straightforward. Weather maps appear to be one such example.

In most domains that have adopted multimedia approaches to learning, verbal information (either written or spoken) plays the central role in presenting content to the learner. The visualisations (e.g., pictures, diagrams, etc.) that accompany this text are typically accorded a supportive role. For example, they provide a more concrete representation of the situation being addressed in the text and facilitate its verbal explanation. In contrast, the visualisations used in meteorology themselves constitute a key part of the domain's content. They cannot be treated merely as instructional adjuncts for supporting other forms of representation.

Practising meteorologists rely on various types of information in their daily work. Verbal, numerical, and pictorial representations each contribute their own particular perspective to a meteorological analysis. Meteorology is a domain that is intrinsically "multimedia" in nature. However, the work of today's meteorologists is increasingly reliant on pictorial representations. Since the middle of the last century, advances in measurement and imaging technologies have considerably broadened the range and sophistication of visualizations that meteorologists must be able to understand and use. The multimedia nature of meteorology, therefore, comes not only from its integration of different media, but also from the multiple types of visualization it involves. Meteorologists are required to interpret these visualizations, both individually and in combination, then decide on their implications for the weather. Mean Sea Level synoptic charts (i.e., traditional "weather maps") were one of the first types of visual representation devised to assist professional meteorologists' work and are still a fundamental tool for activities such as forecasting.

A key requirement in using both traditional and more recent types of meteorological visualization is the capacity to generate appropriate predictions of how their appearance will change over a specific time scale. For example, when given a weather map for the current day, a forecaster needs to be able to generate a prognosis map showing what the meteorological pattern will look like the following day. This visual prediction in turn helps the meteorologist to infer likely characteristics of the following day's weather (that typically will be expressed in both verbal and numerical form). Predictive tasks of this type are primarily concerned with the solving of complex ill-defined problems and in the case of generating future weather map patterns, require sophisticated capacities for visual inference. While well-designed meteorological displays may contribute to forecasting effectiveness (Hoffman, 1991), predictive success ultimately depends on the cognitive processes forecasters use to construct and manipulate mental models based on the externally displayed information (Bally, Boneh, Nicholson, & Korb, in press). A major challenge for those teaching meteorology is to provide learning experiences that will help develop the perceptual and cognitive capacities necessary to support the building of high-quality mental models.

Research into factors likely to influence multimedia learning of meteorology has tended to focus on visual rather than verbal representations. This is partly because visualisations are so fundamentally important in meteorology but also because of the complex, abstract nature of these depictions. The visual material alone poses considerable challenges for learners even without its being incorporated into a multimedia combination along with other forms of representation.

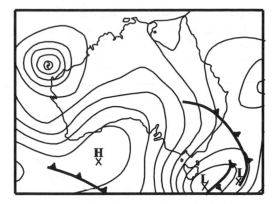

Figure 27.1. Australian weather map showing pictorial information referred to in verbal forecast information.

What Is an Example of Multimedia Learning of Meteorology?

To set the scene, I will describe an approach intended to help students learn meteorology that I observed being used in an introductory university course. The students' task was to study the visual and verbal information provided with daily weather maps in order to suggest changes likely to occur in the next 24 hours. By means of this activity, students were expected to learn some fundamentals about how weather maps change over time and use the understandings so gained to develop their capacity for predicting future weather map patterns. The exercise was seen as a way in which the students could combine the meteorological theory they learned using their lecture notes with its visual exemplification in daily weather maps and the real-life consequences for the weather. Unfortunately, these ambitious expectations

were rarely realised in practice and most students performed poorly on this exercise. A fundamental but unstated assumption underlying this activity was that students were capable of "reading" the provided weather maps appropriately. However, this assumption remained essentially untested. The following example suggests that the task set for these students was in fact extremely demanding with many of its demands arising from the hidden conceptual complexity of weather map displays.

We will consider a verbal weather forecast and an associated standard weather map. This particular combination has been selected partly because of its familiarity and apparent simplicity. However, it has also been chosen because much of the empirical research carried out on multimedia learning in this domain has been based upon learning about weather maps similar to those described in the following text. Nevertheless, it should be emphasized that multimedia approaches are currently used to support the learning of a wide range of topics in meteorology. The available learning resources are by no means restricted to traditional aspects such as weather maps and general forecasts, but extend to the latest developments in imaging techniques and abstract process models.

The following extract is the kind of general forecast that could be produced by a professional meteorologist to accompany the weather map shown in Figure 27.1.

A ridge of high pressure extends south of Western Australia, with a weak high in the Australian Bight. Further south, a weak cold front is moving into the southern ocean. A broad trough is located off the west coast, and is gradually deepening. Strong easterly winds are expected tomorrow over the southern half of Western Australia, resulting in higher maximum temperatures. Further north, tropical cyclone "Rebecca" is located off the Pilbara coast, and a tropical cyclone warning is current for communities between Coral Bay and Port Hedland. The tropical cyclone is expected to intensify over the next 24 hours, and is likely to cross the coast just to the east of Karratha, bringing destructive winds, heavy rain, widespread flooding, and possible storm surge.

This forecast and its associated weather map exemplifies the multimedia nature of meteorological information. The verbal forecast component is a high-level summary that both complements the pictorial component and singles out certain meteorological features of the map that are particularly relevant to the weather situation. To the experienced professional meteorologist, these two components form a complex and tightly integrated set of information that has a rich hierarchical structure. At a fundamental level within this structure, there are verbal and pictorial representations of the overall region to which the forecast refers (i.e., "Western Australia") and particular locations of significance within that region (i.e., "south," "Australian Bight," etc.). These representations correspond in a simple, direct way to fixed concrete referents (part of an actual landmass, or specific physical areas within it).

Superimposed on this geographic framework are various basic meteorological features (mostly pressure cells such as highs, lows, and cyclones, but also a cold front; these are referred to as *primary* features). The verbal labels for these features correspond to particular configurations of graphic markings on the weather map. In contrast to the geographic components just mentioned, these markings do not have direct concrete referents. Instead, they represent mathematical and conceptual abstractions

that meteorologists have devised to help them characterize meteorologically important properties of the atmosphere across a region. Each of the pressure cells is essentially composed of a localized group of lines (i.e., isobars) generated by interpolating between places having the same atmospheric pressure. These pressure cells are mathematical constructions rather than physical entities and are accorded various properties such as their relative magnitude (e.g., "a weak high"). When entire pressure cells are depicted on a weather map, they can be recognized from the distinctive concentric graphic patterns among their component isobars. Another group of markings represent frontal features that embody the concept of a sharp temperature discontinuity. The symbol for a front indicates the leading edge of a large mass of air that is moving through a region with a different temperature. Thus, a cold front marking (shown as a line containing a set of barbs) specifies the location and extent of a cooler mass of air moving into a warmer region. In terms of their referents, frontal symbols represent entities that are less concrete than map outlines but more concrete than isobars and pressure cells.

Pressure cells are not distributed across a weather map at random but tend to occur in particular conjunctions that are conceptualized in terms of higher order meteorological structures (e.g., the "ridge" mentioned in the preceding example). These structures also occur in the area between well-defined pressure cells where they can be recognized as regularities in the patterning of intervening isobars (e.g., the "trough"). Entities that belong to this overarching level of the meteorological hierarchy are referred to as *secondary* features. The different levels of structure within a weather map are mutually constraining so the component markings are always tightly coordinated. However, both primary and secondary meteorological features are highly changeable. They can undergo extensive alteration in form as time passes (e.g., "deepening") with these changes occurring at differing rates (e.g., "gradually"). They also change position relative to the map's fixed geographic framework (e.g., "cyclone...likely to cross the coast") and with respect to each other. The dynamic nature of the entities depicted on a weather map and the interactions between various meteorological factors result in changes that have direct effects on the weather we experience (e.g., "higher maximum temperatures," "destructive winds"). Forecasters use their understanding of changes in the atmosphere as represented by verbal concepts and pictorial displays to predict pending meteorological patterns. From these they infer the weather conditions likely to result, and determine specific values for characteristics such as pressure or temperature expected at a particular location.

It can be seen from the preceding discussion that the superficial graphic simplicity of weather maps is misleading. They are in fact a highly sophisticated and multilayered form of depiction in which the constituent pictorial elements vary in the specific relationships they have to their referents. While the geographic framework provided by the map's landmass outlines is a fixed feature of the depiction, the other markings on a weather map are not. They provide a conceptual snapshot representing only an instantaneous state of a system that is actually in continual flux with no permanent components. It is illuminating to compare the weather map with other types of visual components used in studies relevant to multimedia learning. Many of these depict a mechanical or quasimechanical system such as a pulley set (Hegarty & Just, 1993), an automobile brake (Mayer & Gallini, 1990), a tire pump (Mayer & Anderson, 1991, 1992), or a flushing toilet cistern (Narayanan & Hegarty, 2002). Other depictions have been used that represent less concrete subject matter such as computer program routines (Narayanan & Hegarty, 1998), time-zone differences (Schnotz & Bannert, 2003), chemical reactions (Kozma, 2003), and gravitational lensing of light (Lewalter, 2003). While visuals of the type used in this latter group are more abstract, the behavior of entities involved in the phenomena they depict are governed by comparable sets of well-defined

cause–effect rules. The learner's main task in understanding such systems is to construct a mental model that accurately represents the key steps in the causal chains involved. This requirement is exemplified in the studies by Mayer and Moreno (Mayer & Moreno, 1998; Moreno & Mayer, 1999) where the effects of various multimedia alternatives for learning about how lightning is formed were investigated. Although this topic fits into the general domain of meteorology, the processes involved in lightning formation are much more straightforward, bounded, and linear than those involved in weather map dynamics. In these lightning studies, explanation of the phenomenon was presented to learners as a well-defined eight-step causal chain involving clearly nominated entities such as "cool moist air," "a warmer surface," and so forth.

Weather maps differ from most types of depictions used for multimedia learning research in a number of important respects. They are fundamentally different in terms of the nature of the referent subject matter and how it is depicted. Because meteorology is concerned with the Earth's atmosphere, meteorological representations deal with states and behaviors of a specific segment of a global mass of gaseous fluid. The depictions used in this domain do not represent some assemblage of discrete concrete objects, each of which has a set of distinctive ongoing properties. Rather, the system they represent is essentially a continuous whole in which localized variations of properties (e.g., pressure, temperature, moisture level, etc.) occur over time but where a measure of structural cohesion is nevertheless maintained overall. While the daily weather gives us direct everyday experience of the end result of these variations, most of the mechanisms by which such variation occurs are not accessible to our senses. As well as being largely invisible and intangible, these processes occur on a scale that is too vast for us to experience in our normal everyday activities. As a result, those of us who are not professional meteorologists have little background knowledge that is directly relevant to the entities, properties, and relations involved in these processes. In addition, meteorological events cannot be characterised in terms of straightforward cause–effect relations because of the complex, mutually influencing interactions involved. Rather, constellations of associated meteorological features at various levels take part in patterns of events that tend to occur in particular sequences. Contrast this to the situation regarding our background knowledge of the entities, properties, and relations that are required to understand the clearcut causal linkages in a mechanical system such as a tire pump. This device is made up of a small set of finite components whose properties and behaviour we can readily see, feel, and hence explore. These general types of active components and the causal chains involved are also extremely familiar to us as a result of everyday interactions with our physical world. Much of this real world knowledge is directly applicable to systems such as the tire pump and can be called upon as a basis for comprehension.

What Do We Know About Multimedia Learning of Meteorology?

Basis for Comprehending Weather Maps

Because visualizations play such a crucial role in meteorology, special attention needs to be paid to the visual components of multimedia learning materials for this domain. Particular consideration should therefore be given to how learners may process these components. The investigations discussed here were prompted by the difficulties students of meteorology experienced in learning about this domain using the weather map prediction exercises described in the preceding text. The way a learner mentally represents the array of graphic elements constituting a weather map will shape the type of perceptual and cognitive activity that occurs during the learning process. Accordingly, this section is fundamentally concerned with the mental representations that underlie learners' interpretations of weather maps. Do these mental represen-

tations provide beginning students of meteorology with a suitable basis for using these visualizations as effective resources for learning? One indication of a mental representation's suitability is its consistency with the way experts conceptualize the field.

Two complementary investigations were carried out to gauge the extent to which nonmeteorologists' existing mental representations of weather maps were consistent with those of professional meteorologists. In the first study (Lowe, 1993), information about these mental representations was gathered by investigating how meteorologists and nonmeteorologists copied and then recalled a given weather map. During the copying task, participants took successive glances at the given weather map and from these gradually built up a drawing of that map's meteorological markings by copying them onto a blank map. For each participant, the order in which the map's component markings were copied was recorded as was the duration of pauses between each drawing action. The given map and its copy were then removed and the participant provided with a new blank map upon which to produce drawn recall of the original map. Using the copy-drawing data from individual participants, overall sequence trends for the production of the map's meteorological markings were determined for the meteorologist and nonmeteorologist groups. Differences in the pause lengths separating the drawing of each of the markings were used to produce a hierarchical clustering reflecting the extent of their association. A similar treatment was applied to data from the recall task and the map's markings were evaluated for the quality of recall.

The results indicated that the nonmeteorologists' mental representations of the weather map were very different from those of the meteorologists. In particular, the nonmeteorologists appeared to have divided up the meteorological pattern in a superficial way that reflected the figural similarity of the meteorological markings and their proximity. This suggests that they relied largely on domain-general visuo-spatial knowledge to process the display. Their copying and recall was performed on the basis of low-level graphic characteristics and it seems that they did not process the markings in terms of the visualization's meteorological meaning. In contrast, the meteorologists' clustering of markings was consistent with the meteorological significance of these graphic entities, indicating that their mental representation of the weather map was in terms of the referent situation it depicted. Their recall was superior to that of the nonmeteorologists suggesting that they were able to build higher quality mental models from the given information.

In a further study (Lowe, 1996), reasons for the fundamental differences in how meteorologists and nonmeteorologists dealt with the previous copy-recall task were explored. Of particular interest was the basis for the markings clusters that emerged, that is, the nature of the relationships linking the clustered markings together. Meteorologists and nonmeteorologists performed a three-stage hierarchical card sorting activity in which they classified all the markings comprising a particular weather map and explained the basis for their classifications. Cluster analysis of data obtained from the groupings established during the classification process revealed overall patterns in the organization of markings similar to those found in the previous copy-recall study. However, additional detail also emerged from this card sorting investigation indicating a richness in the information structures produced by the meteorologists that was not present with the nonmeteorologists. For the meteorologists, these structures appeared to include large-scale meteorological patterns that extended beyond the given weather map's boundaries. There was no corresponding high-level structuring or suggestions of broader contextualization of the map for the nonmeteorologists. Participants' explanations for their groupings confirmed that the nonmeteorologists represented weather map markings on a very localized basis only and related them primarily in terms of their superficial appearance and proximity. This contrasted with meteorologists' explanations that were based on the broad atmospheric situation indicated by the map's pattern of meteorological markings and the underlying domain-specific relationships existing between the meteorological features depicted by these graphic entities.

Findings from the studies summarized in the preceding text hinted that meteorologists situated a given weather map within a broader meteorological context. In contrast, there was no indication of any such contextualization with the nonmeteorologists. A capacity to infer the nature of meteorological features present over a wider area than that depicted in the limited scope of a regional weather map should facilitate prediction of features likely to enter or leave the map area. It should also provide high-level organizational structures to assist with the proper arrangement of meteorological markings when making a prediction. Meteorologists' and nonmeteorologists' mental representations of this broader meteorological context were explored using a map extension study (Lowe, 1994b). The participants' task was to draw the meteorological markings they expected would exist beyond the borders of a given weather map that showed a typical summer weather pattern. Their markings were to be added in an extended area surrounding the given map that contained only outlines of the landmasses present in that region. The nonmeteorologists drew significantly fewer markings in the extended area. Those they did draw appeared to be the result of highly localized domain-general extrapolations and interpolations that were closely based upon the preexisting weather map markings. Widely spaced entities that were in fact parts of the same meteorological macrostructures were incorrectly treated as if they were essentially independent of each other. However, the meteorologists' extensions did not reflect the nonmeteorologists' mechanical reliance on low-level visuospatial characteristics of the given markings. Instead, their added markings were used to introduce completely new meteorological features outside of the original map boundary and to generate meteorological macrostructures that integrated the original map into a wider context.

The investigations reviewed so far indicate that beginning students of meteorology can be expected to have mental representations of weather maps that differ in a number of fundamental respects from those of meteorologists. They appear likely to be based on superficial visuo-spatial characteristics rather than underlying meteorological structures and to be far more limited in scope. Such differences could be accounted for in terms of specialized background knowledge about the domain of meteorology. Given the nature of these differences, the students' basis for interpreting the visual components of multimedia resources that rely on weather maps is possibly quite inappropriate and prejudicial to learning. An inappropriate mental representation of weather maps could have serious consequences for key aspects of learning meteorology, such as making predictions. The capacity to construct a high-quality, "runnable" mental model can be assumed as a precondition for generating a satisfactory prediction from a given weather map. It seems from the research discussed previously that beginning students of meteorology would be poorly equipped to take advantage of weather maps included in introductory multimedia learning materials. Weather maps are unlikely simply to function as conventional visual adjuncts to multimedia's verbal components.

Comprehension for Prediction

Being able to comprehend the markings of a weather map in terms of their meteorological significance is a prerequisite for generating effective predictions. If nonmeteorologists mentally represent weather map patterns in largely visuo-spatial terms, their prediction would be expected to reflect this characterization. A prediction task was used to explore the effects of a lack of domain-specific background knowledge on the type of mental model learners are able to construct from a static weather map (Lowe, 1999a). University students with no formal training in meteorology were asked to draw predictions of how they would expect the meteorological markings on a given map to look 24 hours later. The same task was also performed by a group of professional meteorologists.

The nonmeteorologists' predicted markings appeared to be based largely on information already provided in the original map. Changes they made to the original markings were simplistic and overgeneralised. It seemed that to produce their predictions, groups of markings in the middle section of the given map were merely translated further to the east *en masse*, while those originally at the map's western and eastern borders were either stretched or squeezed to fit in with this general easterly movement of features. Thus, within the confines of the map borders, meteorological features neither appeared nor disappeared (as some should have).

In contrast, the professional meteorologists' predictions were not slavishly tied to the original markings. They introduced new markings, removed original ones, and were far more discriminating in the changes they made to the various features that were retained. Individual features differed in the extent to which their positions were shifted and the types of form changes they underwent. Further, whereas the nonmeteorologists appeared to have treated the meteorological features as if they approximated discrete objects with quasi-solid characteristics, the changes made by the meteorologists were smoothed across the map as a whole, consistent with the atmosphere's true nature as a continuous gaseous fluid. The results of this investigation suggest that beginning students of meteorology are poorly equipped to make an appropriate reading of a static weather map, let alone use such a map as a basis for constructing a satisfactory dynamic mental model of the situation it represents.

Making Meteorological Dynamics Explicit

The investigations discussed in the preceding text indicated that the mental models constructed by nonmeteorologists from static weather maps were seriously flawed with respect to implicit spatial and temporal information. Their predictions suggested an inability to go beyond the information given explicitly in the weather map upon which their forecast was to be based and a highly simplistic, undifferentiated approach to modification of the original map's markings. These weaknesses were attributed to nonmeteorologists' lack of domain-specific knowledge, particularly with respect to the broader meteorological context of a weather map and the types of daily changes that meteorological features undergo.

One possible way to address these deficiencies in the mental models that nonmeteorologists construct is with an instructional intervention designed to improve the fundamental background-knowledge structures upon which construction of those models is based. The approach taken in the research described in the following text was to provide learners with *explicit* information about meteorological dynamics using a sequence showing highly typical patterns of change in a weather map. A seven-day animated weather map sequence was produced with videolike controls that gave the user great freedom to vary the speed, direction, and continuity of the 28-frame animation's presentation. Users were thus able to explore the animation as they wished and so confront their existing conceptions about meteorological dynamics in a manner that was personally appropriate. The intention was to give them the opportunity to both revise and enrich their existing knowledge structures by way of a succession of interim mental models formed during their interrogation (see Lowe, 1999a; 2001).

Predictions produced by beginning meteorology students who used this animation were in some respects superior to those generated without such support (Lowe, 1995). In particular, their predic-tions showed greater differentiation among the various types of primary meteorological features (e.g., highs, lows, fronts) in terms of their dynamic character. However, this success at the level of individual markings was not reflected on a broader scale. The secondary features that should provide a framework for higher level of structuring of markings were lacking. While the predictions had localized "islands" of structure that constituted the primary features, these fragments were not bound together to form a larger whole. Although the requisite dynamic information for building a well-integrated mental model was available to these learners, key aspects of it were apparently not being taken up by them. Because the animation provided an explicit depiction of the information necessary to produce better predictions, its limited success must be related to what happened when it was used by learners. Two possibilities are that learners extracted only part of the relevant information from the animation or that they did not incorporate all relevant information into the mental models they constructed as the basis for their predictions. The next study collected data on the amount and type of information that learners obtained from the animation by specifically asking them to interrogate it in order to generate prediction guidelines.

A field investigation using the previously described weather map animation required beginning students of meteorology to study the animation in order to compile a set of notes on how weather maps change over time (Lowe, 1999b). Their purpose in this activity was to end up with key information that would be helpful in improving their weather map prediction performance (specifically, to be better able to draw the pattern of meteorological markings expected 24 hours later than those shown on a given static weather map). Analysis of the notes suggested a perceptual dominance effect in which participants focused their observations on primary features, particularly those that had conspicuous visuo-spatial or temporal characteristics (such as a rapidly moving well-formed high-cell feature and a distinctively shaped cold front feature). In comparison, there was very little evidence of secondary features in the learners' notes. It seemed that what participants noticed about a feature depended to some extent on its relative mobility. With fast-moving features, the trajectory was noted; whereas for slow-moving features, intrinsic aspects such as changes of size and shape were more likely to be recorded. In addition, information about causality was rarely recorded in learners' notes. When it was recorded, causal attributions were made on an everyday rather than a domain-appropriate basis. These attributions were limited to short causal chains in which the meteorological entities involved were characterized as concrete objects interacting as they would in a simple mechanical device.

Extracting Dynamic Information

While the previous study provided some indirect indications of how learners were extracting information from the animation, these had to be inferred from the products generated. To provide more direct evidence of what was occurring as learners interacted with the animation, process-oriented investigations were carried out. In one study (Lowe, 2003), university students who had not studied meteorology were provided with a printed copy of a weather map (the "original") and the user-controllable weather map animation described previously. Their task was to draw on a blank map a prediction of the pattern of meteorological markings they expected would be present one day later than the original. They were to construct this prediction on the basis of information obtained from their concurrent interrogation of the animation.

Analysis of video records of participants' drawing activities supported indications from the previous study that the type of information extracted from the animation was strongly influenced by the perceptual characteristics of the display. With respect to the intrinsic characteristics of the displayed markings (e.g., size, shape, orientation), it seemed that the learners preferentially attended to material that was perceptually conspicuous, irrespective of its degree of meteorological relevance. This could help to explain why secondary features, subtle aspects of a weather map pattern that have low visual salience, were largely absent from predictions. With regard to the extrinsic characteristics of markings (i.e., their movement relative to the map border), the distribution of learner attention seemed to be influenced by dynamic contrast. In this case, learner attention appeared to be directed toward markings (or groups) whose movement was very different from that of the surrounding meteorological pattern. This was interpreted as a dynamic field-ground effect that could perhaps be considered as an analogue of the well-known field-ground perceptual phenomenon found with static depictions. Information indicated as being most readily extracted from the animation would be of limited value in building high-quality mental models because of its incomplete and fragmentary nature.

A further investigation using a similar task placed more focus on the strategies used by learners while interrogating the animated weather map and related these to the nature of the predictions made (Lowe, 2004). Verbal and gestural data were collected on video as individual participants carried out the task while thinking aloud. Overall, participants appeared to confine themselves to one or two highly localized spatial and temporal strategies for interrogating the animation. These main strategies had the effect of severely limiting the proportions of the total display area and total display period searched. For example, most of the interrogation activity was allocated to the well-defined primary meteorological features of the pattern and tended to be restricted to short segments of animation sequence considered most directly informative about these features. It was inferred that participants adopted such approaches in order to control demands on their processing resources in an effort to ensure the learning task remained manageable. More processing-intensive global search strategies that could have revealed overarching spatial or temporal patterns were very rare or absent. Participants completed drawing the primary features one by one and only after finishing these went on to add isobars to the space in between. The verbal and gestural data indicated that participants considered these intervening isobars to be relatively unimportant aspects of the meteorological pattern and they received correspondingly scant attention. However, these are the very regions that frequently contain the subtle alignments of isobars signifying a secondary feature such as a trough or ridge is present. The predictions drawn by participants as a result of this interrogation contained inaccuracies and exhibited a lack of cohesion. These flaws are both consistent with the learners' neglect of the strong overarching structural framework that is provided by the weather map's grid of secondary features.

All the investigations summarized in the preceding text concentrate on the visual component of multimedia learning in meteorology. This concentration is justified because of the special role of visualizations in this domain and the severe processing demands learners can face due to the sophistication of these depictions. Taken together, the findings suggest that weather maps are unlikely to be processed effectively by beginning students of meteorology unless considerable structured support is provided. Much of the challenge that students face in dealing with these displays can be related to their lack of domain-specific background knowledge. For this reason, adopting the standard approaches to the less specialized types of visual components found in most multimedia resources would probably be unsuitable in this case.

When beginning students of meteorology process a weather map, they are likely to do this on the basis of quite inappropriate mental representations. These representations characterize its component markings in terms of their low-level graphic characteristics rather than their overarching meteorological significance. Because there is a lack of scope, structure, and richness in their knowledge of weather maps in general, students are ill-equipped to generate a high-quality mental model from a specific weather map. When faced with weather map tasks requiring domain-specific inference, they are overly reliant on pre-existing markings because of the meteorological poverty of their mental representations. As a consequence, they simply modify the given markings by invoking inappropriate domain-general visual-inference strategies. Lacking knowledge of the wider meteorological context implied by the map's markings, the mental models they construct are inadequate for problem-solving tasks such as prediction. Because their mental models do not contain detailed information about meteorological dynamics and context, the predictions generated are little more than simplistic geometric distortions of the original weather map pattern. The treatment of meteorological features as discrete entities that behave according to straightforward cause–effect principles is more appropriate for a simple mechanical system than for the complex events occurring in a continuous gaseous fluid.

Using animation to explicitly depict the fluid-like behaviour of meteorological patterns and details of their highly differentiated dynamics was only partially successful in improving predictions. Despite learners having a high degree of user control over the animation, the predictions they generated consisted essentially of a patchwork of isolated primary features that were not meaningfully connected into larger-scale meteorological structures. This lack of cohesion seemed to originate in how learners came to selectively extract information about primary features from the animation. Because their attention was directed toward these perceptually conspicuous aspects of the display, its visually subtle but structurally crucial secondary features were neglected. Explicit depiction of the dynamic character of the meteorological pattern appeared to exacerbate rather than ameliorate this unbalanced extraction of information, possibly due to a dynamic field-ground effect. The bias toward markings that comprised primary features was consistent with learners' choices of highly localized spatial and temporal exploration strategies. These strategies were interpreted as an approach that learners adopted for managing the processing challenges they faced in dealing with such a complex display.

What Are the Limitations of Research on Multimedia Learning of Meteorology?

Because of the complexity of meteorological subject matter, research relevant to multimedia learning in this domain tends to have been limited in its focus. The studies summarized in the preceding text targeted meteorological visuals, specifically weather maps. This limitation was justified in terms of the pervasive nature of images in meteorology and the richness of the information they represent. However, there is certainly a need for more attention to verbal and numerical interpretation of the visual displays that are also a vital part of meteorological practice. Important contributions in this area have recently been made by Trafton and colleagues' (e.g., Trafton, Marshall, Mintz, & Trickett, 2002) investigations of how professional meteorologists mentally represent and process meteorological information.

Fundamental to the effective use of meteorological visualisations is the extraction of both explicit information (e.g., reading off the numerical pressure value from a given isobar) and implicit information (e.g., determining the pressure at a location that does not have an isobar running directly through it). Trafton et al. (2002) used eye tracking to examine meteorologists' performances of the latter task and suggested they use spatial or imagerial reasoning processes to infer the pressure value for locations between isobars. In determining this implicit pressure information, the forecasters made extensive use of "bridging" glances back and forth between the two pressure lines bounding the location for which the inference had to be made. Dealing with the highly implicit nature of much of the visual information used

in meteorology seems to require that students first learn how to interact with those visualisations in specialised ways. At present, most research into multimedia learning neglects domain-specific visual-processing capacities and so principled guidance about how such specialised capacities could be fostered is lacking.

Bogacz and Trafton (2002) investigated how experienced professional forecasters generated verbal information from the diverse range of information sources available to them on computer-based forecasting workstations. Their task was to produce a written forecast of the weather situation likely to apply across a specific region over the next 12 hours. Of particular interest in this process-oriented study was the meteorologists' relative use of the static, set, and dynamic visualisations available on the workstations (i.e., a single visual, a series of related static visuals, or an animated pictorial display). Data were collected on the type of visualisation being studied and the comments made by forecasters indicating the nature of the information they extracted from the visualisations (i.e., static or dynamic). Contrary to expectations, most of the dynamic information forecasters generated was produced when they were working with static visualisations rather than with dynamic visualisations or sets of images. The authors suggest that this was because they were able to build dynamic, qualitative mental models from static images. Being able to construct a "runnable" dynamic mental model from a static visualisation appears to be fundamental in making meteorological forecasts. However, the studies by Lowe referred to previously indicate the difficulties of learning to generate such mental models, even when the necessary dynamic information is explicitly provided. At present there is no research evidence about acquisition of the capacity to mentally animate a static meteorological visualization in a domain-appropriate fashion.

Learning meteorology also involves learning how to deal effectively with the multiplicity of visual displays that forecasters use. Trafton, Trickett, and Mintz (in press) found that forecasters make extensive use of comparisons and contrasts during their work. These mental operations were carried out either between two different visualisations or between the forecaster's mental model and a visualisation. To date, research into multimedia learning has tended to be more interested in comparisons between multimedia's verbal and visual components than in comparisons of either multiple visual components or of a visual component and its mental representation. Both latter types of comparison pose some formidable methodological challenges so it is perhaps not surprising that they are yet to be addressed. Indications in studies presented previously in this chapter were that nonmeteorologists also tend to treat a weather map's constituent features in isolation rather than comparing meteorological markings across the map. While this is possibly a result of efforts to manage processing load, no direct evidence has been collected on why their approach is restricted to isolated fragments. Learning to make extensive use of comparison and contrast seems to be fundamental to developing meteorological expertise. Such processes would favour the generation of weather maps in which features are tightly integrated so that the display as a whole has high level coherence.

A major area of multimedia learning of meteorology that remains unexplored is the effect of combining verbal information with specialized meteorological visualizations of the type described here. Given that the processing demands of dealing with these visualizations alone are already very high, it may be that adding verbal explanations of even moderate complexity would be quite prejudicial to learning. Alternatively, the capacity to articulate meteorological principles is no guarantee that they will be applied effectively when generating inferences from a weather map (Hegarty, 2003). However, perhaps verbal information could be given a somewhat different purpose so that it serves a supportive function rather than being a primary carrier of information. This would fit with the current trends toward giving pictures far more responsibility for presenting to-be-learned content than has traditionally been the case in educational materials. Another important limitation of research on multimedia learning of meteorology is related to the reality of meteorologists' current working environments. They are reliant on a range of visualizations that are available to them simultaneously and in various combinations. Research should address this reality by investigating how students of meteorology can learn to handle this complex visual environment effectively and efficiently. The forecasting environment's natural "multimedia ecology" provides many opportunities for such research.

What Are the Implications of the Research for Cognitive Theory?

Current theories of multimedia learning tend to emphasise cognitive aspects of processing involved in the combining of verbal and visual components of multimedia resources in order to produce a coherent mental representation of the referent situation. However, research in the visually dominated field of meteorology suggests that the visual dimensions of these theories could well be further developed. At present, our understanding of how the visual components of multimedia resources are processed does not begin to approach the sophisticated understanding we have of how verbal information is processed. Perhaps concepts such as depth of processing and information search strategies, notions that are well established with respect to the learning of complex verbal information, could usefully be applied to the visual components of multimedia resources. It also seems that certain aspects of *perceptual* processing play a particularly important role in learning from static and dynamic visual components and these may warrant rather more attention than they receive amid the current concern with constraints on *cognitive* processing.

Considerable elaboration of current theories of multimedia learning is needed in order to take account of the very different structural characteristics of verbal and visual information. For example, there are various notions such as split-attention that are presently used only when considering media combinations. However, with highly complex visuals, it is possible that split-attention effects could occur solely within the visual components due to competition for attention between a visual's different constituent graphic entities and their configurations. Research on learners' processing of weather maps suggests that they face considerable challenges in selecting appropriate aspects of these visual images. On one hand, they can neglect key components of the weather map display and on the other they can fail to make appropriate connections between those aspects that do capture their attention. This could be a major impediment for the multimedia learning of meteorology because building a satisfactory mental model of the subject matter is fundamentally dependent on the effectiveness of the early selection stage of processing and the capacity to form appropriate connections.

While the contribution of background knowledge is acknowledged in present cognitive theories of multimedia learning, it is an aspect of these theories that remains relatively underdeveloped. The research related to learning in meteorology discussed in this chapter suggests that background knowledge can be of crucial importance for the effective processing of visual components of multimedia. Decomposing a visual display into thematically relevant graphic entities, assigning appropriate properties to those entities, and detecting important relationships among those entities can rely heavily on the possession of domain-specific background knowledge. This is particularly likely when the entities, properties, and relationships that characterize the presented subject matter have little in common with those familiar to us in our everyday surroundings. Because multimedia approaches to learning are often recommended for topics that are abstract, unfamiliar, and difficult for students, the issue of background knowledge deserves more theoretical consideration.

What Are the Implications of the Research for Instructional Design?

Prevailing instructional design approaches tend to lack sophistication in how they deal with the visual components of multimedia learning materials. Pictures and diagrams are too often treated as unproblematic resources that make an unambiguously positive contribution to learning. However, the preceding discussion of weather maps suggests that it is not only the verbal component of multimedia systems that may challenge learners with its complex multilevel information structure. Some visual representations can also be very demanding in this respect and these demands are compounded because visuals lack text's highly conventionalized structural characteristics for guiding learners' reading processes. An unsupported depiction offers the learner virtually infinite possibilities in terms of the processing paths that could be taken. Learners lacking background knowledge of the depicted domain can be largely at the mercy of the visualization's perceptual characteristics. Their everyday domain-general background knowledge is likely to be of little help and may even be harmful to learning. The superficial appearance of the visual components and their arrangement can direct learner attention in specific ways, but as we have seen with weather maps, the perceptual salience of graphic entities does not necessarily correspond with their thematic relevance. Further, the intrinsic perceptual cues within a visualization may give misleading indications of how the depicted entities are actually related to each other.

Given the increasing reliance on visuals in multimedia learning materials, it seems appropriate for instructional design to adopt a less laissez-faire approach to their use. Far more sophisticated approaches are warranted for visuals, particularly those depicting complex and abstract subject matter that is beyond the realm of everyday experience. These visualizations need to be subjected to the same level of rigorous and detailed analysis that instructional designers routinely apply to difficult verbal material. Outcomes of these more sophisticated approaches could in many cases be better-designed visual components. To some extent, it is possible to manipulate a depiction's graphic characteristics so that information of particular relevance to the learning task is made more conspicuous. This can be done by giving visual emphasis to high-relevance information and by de-emphasizing or entirely removing other information. One common way of removing this other information is to limit the scope of a depiction to the area of immediate interest (as is done in a weather map). Unfortunately, this also decontextualizes the depiction which, as we saw with the weather map example, can be particularly problematic when it comes to high-level learning involving inference. A possible implication here for instructional designers is that multimedia learning resources should endeavor to set visualizations in their broader spatial and temporal contexts. Fortunately, today's multimedia technology makes it relatively easy to provide such contextualisation.

In some cases, as with a weather map, the design of the visualization to be incorporated in multimedia learning materials is already absolutely fixed as a result of many years of professional practice. With these "established" visuals, instructional designers could provide a much greater level of support for learners in dealing with a visualization's entrenched but unhelpful visual design characteristics. Learners need to be guided in both how best to segment a whole visual display into domain-relevant components and how to group the graphic elements comprising the display into meaningful clusters. In addition, instructional designers should help learners to locate features of the display that have low perceptual salience but high thematic relevance so these are not overlooked. While such guidance is needed for both static and dynamic graphics, the latter type poses particular challenges for instructional designers. This is because of the additional perceptual effects (including dynamic contrast) that would complicate decisions about which aspects of the display learners are likely to attend to at any point in time.

With visuals that depict specialized content outside of the learner's everyday experience, it seems unlikely that mere provision of explicit information about the system's dynamics will lead to the building of satisfactory runnable mental models. Without background knowledge about the distinctive properties of the entities depicted, it is difficult for learners to differentiate between them and really understand the particularities of their individual and collective behaviours. It could also be argued that simply giving learners total freedom to explore animated depictions of complex situational dynamics may do more harm than good because they lack a domain-appropriate basis upon which to manage the excessive processing demands. Instead, it would seem wiser to constrain learners' interrogation of the animation so that exploration of the presented information can be guided along productive pathways.

It often appears that the visualizations used in multimedia learning materials are implicitly assumed to "speak for themselves" regarding how they should be processed. The user-controllable animations that are increasingly provided in multimedia learning resources are an extreme example. There seems to be an expectation that exploratory freedom will allow learners to match the demands and style of the presentation regime to fit their individual processing capacities and preferences. However, the preceding discussion indicates that this is certainly not the case for highly specialised visualizations and guidance appears essential to facilitate effective processing. Given the complexity of these depictions, the question arises as to what form such guidance should take. At first sight, visual guidance seems be a reasonable choice. Unfortunately, visual cueing also has the potential to make the situation worse by further increasing the visual complexity of the display and interfering with the interpretation of the original display. An interesting alternative would be to use a verbal approach in which spoken cues are given to direct the learner's attention to specific regions within the depiction, to relevant entities, to crucial relationships between components, and (for animations) to significant changes in the display. This approach casts the verbal component of multimedia learning in a role that is very different from that it is usually expected to play. Rather than being a central means of providing content information and explanation, the verbal component is allocated a support role similar to that typically accorded to multimedia's visual components.

What Are Some Productive Future Directions for Research?

Well-designed visualizations can undoubtedly make a substantial contribution to the effectiveness of multimedia learning in general by supporting verbal explanations. However, in some domains (e.g., meteorology), visualizations are a central part of the to-be-learned content. In these cases, it is crucial that learners develop high-quality mental models as a result of their interaction with a multimedia resource's visual components. This suggests two major directions for future research, both of which address possible ways of helping this interaction to be more effective. The first of these concerns design factors that are likely to influence what information learners extract from visualizations. We have seen that perceptual characteristics can have a dominant effect on which aspects of a display capture a learner's attention and so become the locus of subsequent processing activity; this applies for both static and animated visualizations. There is a need for systematic investigation of the effects on learning of manipulating the way subject matter is depicted. A particularly challenging but important aspect of such investigation would be cases in which there is a clear contradiction between the perceptual salience of some features of

the graphic representation and its thematic relevance.

The second suggestion for future research would be particularly applicable to visualizations that are not amenable to design manipulations but could also be used in association with redesigned visual components. This research would focus upon the various types of external processing support that could be provided to make the processing of visualizations more effective. As mentioned previously, one possibility is to recast the multimedia's verbal component in the role of a support resource. Exploration of the effectiveness of using verbal instructions to direct the learner's attention to thematically relevant aspects of a depiction has the potential to raise important questions about current theories of multimedia learning. In particular, research in this area may challenge the way we conceptualize the contributions that visual and verbal information make to multimedia learning.

Glossary

Cyclone: In Australia, a tropical cyclone is a tropical low-pressure system of sufficient intensity to produce sustained gale-force winds. Severe tropical cyclones correspond to the hurricanes or typhoons of other parts of the world.

Ridge: An elongated area of relatively high atmospheric pressure.

Synoptic chart: A weather chart reflecting the state of the atmosphere over a large area at a given moment.

Trough: An elongated area of relatively low atmospheric pressure.

References

Bally, J., Boneh, T., Nicholson, A. E., & Korb, K. B. (in press). Developing an ontology for the meteorological forecasting process. *Proceedings of the 2004 International Federation for Information*

Processing (IFIP) International Conference on Decision Support Systems (DSS2004), Prato, Italy.

Bogacz, S., & Trafton, J. G. (2002). Understanding static and dynamic visualisations: In H. Narayanan (Ed.), Diagrammatic representation and inference (pp. 247–249). Berlin: Springer-Verlag.

Hegarty, M. (2003, June). The role of knowledge and display characteristics in interpretation of weather maps. Paper presented at the ONR Workshop on Attention, Perception and Modeling for Complex Displays, Rensselaer Polytechnic Institute, Troy, NY.

Hegarty, M., & Just, M. A. (1993). Constructing mental models of machines from text and diagrams. Journal of Memory and Language, 32, 717–742.

Hoffman, R. R. (1991). Human factors psychology in the support of forecasting: The design of advanced meteorological workstations. Weather and Forecasting, 6, 98–110.

Kozma, R. (2003). The material features of multiple representations and their cognitive and social affordances for science understanding. Learning and Instruction, 13, 205–226.

Lewalter, D. (2003). Cognitive strategies for learning from static and dynamic visuals. Learning and Instruction, 13, 177–189.

Lowe, R. K. (1993). Constructing a mental representation from an abstract technical diagram. Learning and Instruction, 3, 157–179.

Lowe, R. K. (1994a). Diagram prediction and higher order structures in mental representation. Research in Science Education, 24, 208–216.

Lowe, R. K. (1994b). Selectivity in diagrams: Reading beyond the lines. Educational Psychology, 14, 467–491.

Lowe, R. K. (1995, August). Interactive animated diagrams for learning high level meteorological chart structures. Paper presented at the 6th European Conference for Research on Learning and Instruction, Nijmegen, Netherlands.

Lowe, R. K. (1996). Background knowledge and the construction of a situational representation from a diagram. European Journal of Psychology of Education, 11, 377–397.

Lowe, R. K. (1999a). Domain-specific constraints on conceptual change in knowledge acquisition from diagrams. In W. Schnotz, S. Vosniadou, & M. Carretero (Eds.), New perspectives on conceptual change. (pp. 223–245) Amsterdam: Elsevier.

Lowe, R. K. (1999b). Extracting information from an animation during complex visual learning. European Journal of Psychology of Education, 14, 225–244.

Lowe, R. K. (2001). Understanding information presented by complex animated diagrams. In J-F. Rouet, J. J. Levonen, & A. Biardeau (Eds.), Multimedia learning: Cognitive and instructional issues (pp. 65–74). London: Pergamon.

Lowe, R. K. (2003). Animation and learning: Selective processing of information in dynamic graphics. Learning and Instruction, 13, 247–262.

Lowe, R. K. (2004). Interrogation of a dynamic visualization during learning. Learning and Instruction, 14, 257–274.

Mayer, R. E., & Anderson, R. B. (1991). Animations need narrations: An experimental test of a dual-coding hypothesis. Journal of Educational Psychology, 83, 484–490.

Mayer, R. E., & Anderson, R. B. (1992). The instructive animation: Helping students build connections between words and pictures in multimedia learning. Journal of Educational Psychology, 84, 444–452.

Mayer, R. E., & Gallini, J. K. (1990). When is an illustration worth ten thousand words? Journal of Educational Psychology, 82, 715–726.

Mayer, R. E., & Moreno, R. (1998). A split-attention effect in multimedia learning: Evidence for dual processing systems in working memory. Journal of Educational Psychology, 90, 312–320.

Moreno, R., & Mayer, R. E. (1999). Cognitive principles of multimedia learning: The role of modality and contiguity. Journal of Educational Psychology, 91, 358–368.

Narayanan, N. H., & Hegarty, M. (1998). On designing comprehensible interactive hypermedia manuals. International Journal of Human-Computer Studies 48, 267–301.

Narayanan, N. H., & Hegarty, M. (2002). Multimedia design for communication of dynamic information. International Journal of Human-Computer Studies, 57, 279–315.

Parrish, P. (1999, June). Instructional illustrations for meteorology education and training. Paper presented at the 4th International Conference on Computer-Aided and Distance Learning in Meteorology (CALMet), Helsinki, Finland.

Schnotz, W., & Bannert, M. (2003). Construction and interference in learning from multiple representation. *Learning and Instruction, 13*, 141–156.

Trafton, J. G., Marshall, S., Mintz, F., & Trickett, S. B. (2002). Extracting explicit and implicit information from complex visualizations. In H. Narayanan (Ed.), *Diagramatic representation and inference* (pp. 206–220). Berlin: Springer-Verlag.

Trafton, J. G., Trickett, S. B., & Mintz, F. E. (in press). Connecting internal and external representations: Spatial representations of scientific visualisations. *Foundations of science*.

CHAPTER 28

Multimedia Learning About Physical Systems

Mary Hegarty

University of California, Santa Barbara

Abstract

This chapter examines how people understand diagrams, animations, and multimedia presentations in order to learn about physical systems. Comprehension of these representations is analyzed within an information-processing framework that specifies the cognitive processes involved in understanding external displays, including attention, encoding, inference, and integration of different representations. The chapter first reviews the literature on comprehension of physical systems from diagrams (both static and animated) alone and then reviews how people understand physical systems from multimedia presentations in which diagrams are augmented by verbal instruction. The picture that emerges is that diagram comprehension is an active process of knowledge construction, rather than a passive process of internalizing the information presented in an external display. Because multimedia understanding depends on active information processing, it can be influenced considerably by the abilities, skills, and knowledge of the student. What is learned from a multimedia display is jointly determined by aspects of the display and aspects of the learner.

Introduction

Diagrams accompanied by text have been a common means of representing and communicating information throughout history (Ferguson, 1992). In recent years, with advances in graphic technologies, innovations such as animations and interactive visualizations have made diagrammatic representations even more prevalent in scientific and technical discourse and in everyday life. These new media, and graphical displays in general, are believed to have enormous potential for education and training. But in order to realize this potential, we need basic research on how people comprehend and make inferences from diagrams and multimedia displays. The goal of this chapter is to review the literature on comprehension of static diagrams, animated diagrams, and multimedia (combining diagrams and verbal representations) from an information-processing perspective.

The chapter examines the representations and cognitive processes involved in understanding media, the abilities and skills on which this understanding depends, and the effectiveness of different media for communicating different types of content.

The chapter focuses on how people understand and learn about complex physical systems from different media. Physical systems include man-made mechanical systems and biological systems such as organs and organisms, that are made up of physical, visible subsystems that interact to accomplish some function, for example, stopping your car (in the case of car brakes) or pumping blood (in the case of the human heart). Most of the examples in this paper come from the domain of mechanics, specifically how mechanical devices work. However, I also briefly consider some other domains such as anatomy and geology.

Understanding a physical system involves several types of knowledge (Chi, de Leeuw, Chiu, & LaVancer, 1994; Hegarty & Just, 1993; Narayanan & Hegarty, 1998). First, it involves knowledge of the parts of the system, what they are made of, and how they are connected and configured in space, that is, the *configuration* of the machine. This knowledge corresponds to a static mental model of the machine. Second, it includes knowledge of how the components move and affect each other's motions, that is, the *behavior* of the machine. Central to this is knowledge of the causal chain or chains of events in the machine's behavior. It includes both kinematic understanding of how the different machine components move in space and affect each other's movements, and dynamic understanding of the forces that bring about these movements. This knowledge corresponds to a dynamic mental model of the machine. Finally it involves understanding the *function* of the machine, that is, what it is designed to do, and how the structure and behavior achieve this function.

In the first section of this chapter I present a theoretical framework that specifies the cognitive processes involved in understanding and learning about physical systems from multimedia presentations. In the second section, I discuss the different types of external representations (diagrams, animations, texts, etc.) that are used to represent physical systems in multimedia presentations. The third section addresses how and to what extent people can understand systems from diagrams (both static and animated) alone. Finally in the fourth section, I consider how people understand physical systems from multimedia presentations, that is, how they understand verbal information, in conjunction with static and animated diagrams, in order to construct mental models.

A Theoretical Framework for Understanding Multimedia Comprehension

Figure 28.1 represents the situation when someone has to understand a mechanical system from a single medium or multimedia display. The display is made up of text, diagrams, and so forth that are *external representations* of some system. The goal of comprehension is to construct an *internal representation* of that system, which can also be called a *mental model*. The information in the external display is perceived by the senses – vision (for text, diagrams, and animations) or audition (for commentaries). The user is not passive in this process, but actively attends to information in different locations in the display or in different modalities to encode the information at that location or in that modality. These basic attentional, perceptual, and encoding processes result in an internal representation of at least some of the information presented in the multimedia display.

In addition, to these basic perceptual, attentional, and encoding processes the user must integrate the information presented at different locations in the display and in different media and modalities to construct an internal representation or mental model of the referent of the text. This may include translating information from a verbal to a spatial code, or vice versa (e.g., to integrate

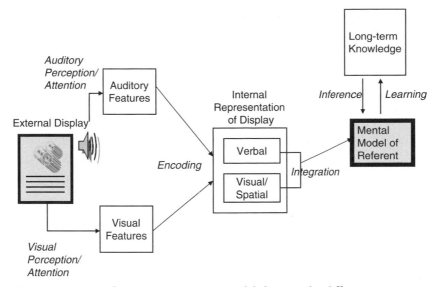

Figure 28.1. An information-processing model showing the different representations (external and internal) and cognitive processes involved in the comprehension of multimedia.

information in a text and diagram). In constructing this mental model, the user might also make some inferences from the information presented in the display, based on his or her prior knowledge or other inference mechanisms (e.g., visualizing how some object moves). These inference processes involve going "beyond the information given," that is constructing new knowledge, rather than merely making an internal copy of the information that is presented externally in the multimedia display. If inference processes occur, the resulting internal representation will contain information that is not presented explicitly in the external display.

The comprehension of a display therefore depends not just on qualities of the display itself (e.g., what information it contains and how this information is represented externally), but also on the quality of the comprehension processes that operate on the external representation, including perception, attention, encoding, integration, and inference. For example, if the user does not attend to all of the relevant information, his or her internal representation may contain less information than the external display. If he or she has limited working memory capacity, this might affect his or her ability to integrate

information that is presented in different locations or at different times. If he or she has a great deal of background knowledge about the topic of the display, he or she may draw inferences from the information presented that would not be part of the comprehension of a less knowledgeable user. Thus, the internal representation that results from comprehension might be quite different in content and format than the external representation that gave rise to this representation.

Representations of Physical Systems in Different Media

We now consider the main types of external representations used to communicate about physical systems, and the characteristics of these types of representations. A representation is something that stands for something else and can exist either in the world as an external representation, or in the mind of a person as an internal representation. The representations included in multimedia displays include various types of diagrams and verbal materials. To understand the nature of these representations, we must specify the nature of the object represented (i.e., the referent), the representational medium, the correspondence between these two, and the cognitive processes that operate on the representation (Markman, 1999; Palmer, 1978). Because diagrams and verbal materials are fundamentally different types of representations, they depend on different comprehension processes, and may be optimally suited to conveying different types of information.

Static Diagrams

Diagrams are spatial representations, that is, visual-spatial arrays, in which information is communicated by spatial properties such as shape, location, and adjacency of parts. Physical systems are also essentially spatial entities because their operation depends on the shape, connectivity, and movement of their components. Although spatial representations can represent both spatial and nonspatial information (e.g., graphs represent number), in the mechanical domain they typically represent spatial properties (Hegarty, 2004). Thus, most diagrams of physical systems are *iconic*, in the sense that spatial relations between objects in the representation correspond to, or are *isomorphic* to the spatial relations between the objects that they represent. Figures 28.2, 28.3, and 28.4 present examples of some types of diagrams that are typically used to communicate about machines. Note that an iconic diagram does not necessarily represent all of the visual features of its referent. For example, in Figure 28.1, pulleys are represented by circles, thus omitting a great deal of the visual detail of what a pulley looks like. This demonstrates another important characteristic of representations, which is that they can be schematic, in the sense that they represent some aspects of the referent but not others. Typically in instructional materials about machines, the important spatial relations between the parts of the machine are preserved in the diagram.

Static diagrams by definition do not move. However movement is an essential property of mechanical systems. Therefore understanding how a machine works from a static diagram involves the ability to infer the motion of the device from the information

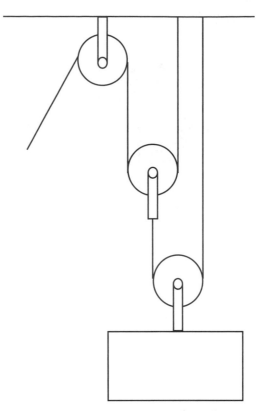

Figure 28.2. Schematic diagram of a pulley system.

given in the static diagram. In this chapter, I refer to the process of inferring motion from static displays as *mental animation* (Hegarty, 1992).

Engineers and graphic designers have developed several different graphic conventions to convey information about movement in static diagrams (Ferguson, 1992). Two common conventions are to annotate

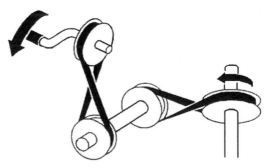

Figure 28.3. Diagram of a belt and pulley system, annotated by arrows. An example of a spatial mechanism in which the mechanical interactions are in different planes.

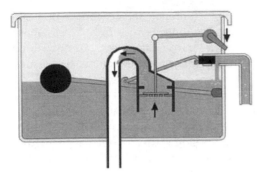

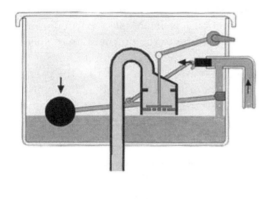

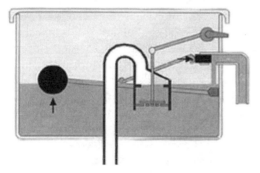

Figure 28.4. Three phase diagrams depicting different stages in the operation of a flushing cistern mechanism (this mechanism is often used to flush toilets) used by Hegarty et al. (2003) (Figure reprinted by permission of Lawrence Erlbaum Associates).

diagrams with arrows, (as in Figure 28.3) and to present a series of phase diagrams or "small multiples" (Tufte 1997), showing the configurations of the components of a mechanical device at different phases of its operation (as in Figure 28.4). When static diagrams are used to convey motion in this way, the information about how the machine moves is not directly represented in the diagram. In these situations, developing a mental model of the movement of the machine still involves some type of inference, such as inferring what movement causes the state shown in one phase diagram to be transformed into the state shown in another phase diagram, or interpreting arrows to imagine how the parts of a machine move to achieve its function.

Animated Diagrams

The animated diagram is a relatively recent graphic invention. An animation is essentially a sequence of static images, that when played at a relatively rapid rate, produces the effect of apparent motion. Animations allow us to represent the motion of a mechanical system directly (rather than through the more indirect means of arrows and phase diagrams). In this sense we can think of them as more *realistic* representations, that is, more isomorphic to the reality that they represent. Comprehension of how a machine moves from an animation depends on the ability to perceive the motion of the system (rather than to infer this motion).

Like static diagrams, animated diagrams can be more or less isomorphic to reality. They can show processes in real time, in slow motion, or speeded up (e.g., animations can take a few seconds to show geological phenomena that occur over millennia). Animations can also slow down critical phases of a process (that occur very quickly in reality) while speeding up others. In these cases, animations depart somewhat from reality. Animations can vary in their interactivity, that is, the extent to which the user has control over the speed and sequence of frames. A common method of adding interactivity to an animated diagram is to use a "slider bar," which allows users to move forward and backward through the animation at their own pace and in any order.

Finally, in addition to depicting motion, another common use of animated diagrams is to show the structure of a mechanical or biological system that cannot be easily depicted in a single two-dimensional diagram. Mechanical systems can be classified as *planar* or *spatial* mechanisms (Dar,

Joskowicz, & Rivlin, 1999). Planar mechanisms are those in which the mechanical interactions take place in a single plane (e.g., the pulley system shown in Figure 28.2 and the flushing cistern shown in Figure 28.4). Spatial mechanisms are those in which the mechanical interactions occur in three dimensions (e.g., the belt and pulley system shown in Figure 28.3). Biological structures, such as ball-and-socket joints, the heart, and lungs are spatial mechanisms. In spatial mechanisms it is not always possible to show all of the important mechanical interactions in a two-dimensional diagram. In these cases, an animation that shows the mechanism rotating in place can be used to show the three-dimensional structure of the device. Understanding such an animation involves the ability to integrate the sequence of two-dimensional views from different spatial locations to construct an internal representation of the three-dimensional structure of the device.

Verbal Materials

Verbal materials are descriptive representations, which express facts or assertions about their referents, depend on arbitrary symbols (i.e., words), and have a linear structure. Unlike diagrams, verbal representations are not isomorphic to the reality that they represent. For example, consider the following text describing the pulley system shown in Figure 28.2 (Hegarty & Just, 1993).

> The system consists of three pulleys, two ropes and one weight. The upper pulley is attached to the ceiling. The other pulleys are free to move up and down. The upper rope is attached to the ceiling at one end, goes under the middle pulley and over the upper pulley and is free at the other end.....
> (p. 721)

Understanding this text involves understanding the meaning of words such as *pulley* and *rope*, as well as using knowledge of the syntax and semantics of English to construct an internal representation of the configural relations between the parts of the device. In contrast to diagrams, verbal information has a linear structure, such that the order of words in a sentence and sentences in a discourse communicate meaning. In this sense it might be particularly suited to describing information that has a linear structure, such as a sequence of events.

Verbal information can be presented either as visual text or as an aural commentary. These involve some inherent differences. For example, reading text is self-paced in that text is static on the printed page, and the reader can slow down, speed up, or reread as often as he or she wishes in order to understand the text. In contrast, an aural commentary is heard at a particular rate, corresponding to the normal rate of speech. It is possible to make an aural commentary somewhat interactive, such that the user can replay sections, and so forth. However one cannot arbitrarily slow down or speed up the rate of speech and maintain comprehension.

Relations Between Diagrams and Verbal Instruction

Multimedia displays present information in both verbal and visual-spatial codes. The verbal and visual-spatial information can occur in different relations to each other. In terms of content, verbal and spatial information can be redundant (e.g., when a text describes the structure of an object that is also depicted in a diagram). Verbal and spatial information can also be complementary (e.g., in the case where a diagram shows the static structure of a mechanical system and a text describes how parts of the machine are free to move). In addition to these semantic relations, verbal and spatial information can have different relations as they are presented. For example, with printed media, the text can be either separate from the diagram, or integrated with the diagram and with animated media. A verbal commentary can occur either simultaneously with the animation that it explains or before or after this animation.

Finally, in addition to diagrams and verbal information, there are several other sources of information that may occur in multimedia displays, such as nonverbal sound effects (Moreno and Mayer, 2000) and haptic feedback. These are beyond the scope of this chapter, which will focus on static and animated diagrams and verbal materials presented in the visual and auditory modalities.

Understanding and Learning from Diagrams

In this section we will review how people learn about the structure and functioning of physical systems from diagrams alone, including static and animated diagrams. One might wonder why we should focus on comprehension of diagrams alone in a handbook of multimedia. That is, why should we examine comprehension of diagrams alone, without accompanying verbal instruction, when it has often been shown that people learn more from diagrams that are accompanied by explanatory text or verbal commentaries (e.g., Hegarty & Just, 1993; Mayer & Anderson, 1991; Mayer & Gallini, 1990). However, if our goal is a scientific account of how multimedia presentations are understood, it is important to specify the cognitive processes and comprehension outcomes that result from exposure to the individual media that make up multimedia presentations. This scientific account, in turn, can be the basis of a set of principles for the design of multimedia presentations (cf. Narayanan & Hegarty, 1998; 2002), for example by specifying when and how diagrammatic materials should be augmented by text.

Understanding Static Structure from Static Diagrams

An internal representation of the configuration of a physical system, (i.e., its static structure) is an important component of a mental model. Multimedia presentations typically include iconic diagrams to show the structure or configuration of parts of a system, including the shapes of components, how they are configured in space and how they are connected. In terms of the information-processing analysis in Figure 28.1, understanding the structure of a mechanical system from a static iconic diagram is essen-

tially a process of encoding the information in the external representation. Some studies have shown that people are quite good at this process. For example, Hegarty and Just (1993) found that showing people a static diagram (without accompanying text) was sufficient for understanding the structure of a pulley system. Similarly, when Heiser and Tversky (2002) presented students with static diagrams of different mechanical systems and asked them to describe the diagrams, their participants spontaneously described the structure of the systems.

However, even iconic static diagrams can be highly conventionalized, so that constructing a mental model of the structure of a system from a static diagram is not necessarily a trivial comprehension task. Two types of diagrams that have been shown to present problems for students are schematic diagrams and two-dimensional diagrams that depict three-dimensional objects.

SCHEMATIC DIAGRAMS

Highly schematic diagrams, which omit visual details of the appearance of their referents, can sometimes be misunderstood. Ferguson and Hegarty (1995) examined how students reasoned about pulley systems based on static diagrams or three-dimensional models (made up of actual pulleys and ropes). Like the example in Figure 28.2, the diagrams were highly schematized, for example, they used circles to represent pulleys and lines to represent ropes. Ferguson and Hegarty found no effect of instruction medium (schematic diagrams vs. real models) on how well students could learn to compare the efficiency of different pulley systems. However, when asked to apply their knowledge to novel tasks, students who learned from real models had superior performance. Furthermore, students' drawings indicated that those who learned from schematic diagrams did not understand the structure of the systems (i.e., the spatial relations between the ropes and pulleys). Schwartz (1995) also found differences in the types of mechanical reasoning afforded by realistic and schematic diagrams, such that more realistic diagrams induced students to simulate how the mechanical systems moved and more schematic diagrams were associated with more analytic strategies. These studies indicate that understanding the structure of a physical system from a diagram is not always a trivial comprehension task, and that more and less schematic diagrams may naturally evoke different inference processes.

DIAGRAMS OF THREE-DIMENSIONAL OBJECTS

Diagrams of three-dimensional objects can also cause comprehension difficulties. Because the printed page and computer screen are essentially two-dimensional entities, it is impossible to directly represent a three-dimensional object in these media. Any diagram of three-dimensional objects must involve some projection of three dimensions onto the two-dimensional plane. Graphic designers over the centuries have invented a number of graphic conventions to display three-dimensional structure in two-dimensional media, such as perspective views, multiple orthographic views, and cross-sections. Constructing a static mental model from these types of diagrams involves such processes as integrating different two-dimensional representations into a single three-dimensional internal representation, or visualizing the internal structure of an object. Students, particularly those with low spatial abilities, have difficulty both producing and comprehending such diagrams (Cohen, Hegarty, Keehner, & Montello, 2003; Eley, 1983; Kali and Orion, 1996).

Understanding Structure from Animated Diagrams

A recent solution to displaying three-dimensional structure in two-dimensional displays is to show the object rotating in depth on a computer screen. In this type of display, time is used to show the third dimension of space and the display exploits movement-based depth cues such as motion parallax to give a strong impression of a three-dimensional object in a two-dimensional display. Many educators believe that these types of displays may be particularly effective in overcoming students' limitations in understanding three-dimensional structures from two-dimensional displays. However, empirical research on use of animations to teach anatomical structures suggests that comprehension of these displays may be even more dependent on spatial abilities. In a study where multiple views of three-dimensional anatomy were presented to medical students using a rotating computer model, a subsequent test of anatomical knowledge showed a significant disadvantage to individuals with poor spatial abilities (Garg, Norman, Spero, & Maheshwari, 1999). For these students, learning was effective only if the display was restricted to a simple depiction entailing just two cardinal views, suggesting that complex three-dimensional computer visualizations may actually impair spatial understanding for low spatial individuals. The effects of spatial ability, however, can be moderated by the characteristics of the computer simulation. The performance of low spatial medical students has been enhanced, for example, by allowing them to direct the rotation of the model, suggesting that learner control contributes significantly to the successful integration of complex spatial information (Garg, Norman, & Sperotable, 2001). Other variables that might potentially enhance or diminish understanding include the complexity of the image, the depth cues available, and the type of interface used to interact with the animation. In order to guide the future evolution of three-dimensional visualizations, these factors need to be explored and the optimum combination of features established.

Understanding Dynamic Events from Static Diagrams

Understanding physical systems such as machines includes an understanding of how the parts move and constrain each other's movements to achieve the function of the system. Achieving this type of understanding from a static diagram depends on "mental animation," that is, the inference of kinematics (how objects move) from their static structure. There is little evidence that people do this spontaneously when they view a static diagram. For example, people have poor comprehension of the kinematics of a device after they study a static diagram (Hegarty and Just, 1993) and when asked to describe a static diagram of a mechanical system, they do not spontaneously describe how the parts move (Heiser & Tversky, 2002). In other words, viewing a static diagram of a mechanical system alone does not induce people to think about the kinematics of the device.

But can people mentally animate static diagrams when a cognitive task demands it? There is considerable evidence that they can, to some extent. Hegarty (1992) presented students with static diagrams of pulley systems, such as the one presented in Figure 28.2, and asked them to verify sentences such as "when the rope is pulled, the middle pulley turns clockwise." Many participants were readily able to make this inference. Similarly Schwartz and Black (1996a) found that people could accurately infer the direction of rotation of gears in a gear chain and further research on mental animation has generalized these results to the inference of motion in a variety of mechanical systems (Hegarty & Kozhevnikov, 1999; Hegarty & Steinhoff, 1997).

Research on mental animation has provided important insights into the nature of people's internal representations of mechanical systems. Although mechanical systems in motion involve continuous motion over time, people think of these systems in terms of a causal sequence of events. Hegarty (1992) measured errors, reaction times, and eye fixations as people inferred the motion of different components in a mechanical system. I found that reaction time increased and accuracy decreased when people inferred the motion of components later in the causal chain of events compared to components earlier in the chain of events. When asked to verify the motion of a component, say the middle pulley in Figure 28.2, people looked at that component, and components earlier in the causal chain of events (i.e., the up-

per rope and pulley), but not components later in that chain of events. These data indicate that people infer the motion of components piecemeal, beginning by imagining the rope being pulled, and working through the causal chain of events in the motion of the system.

Research on mental animation has also provided evidence for spatial imagery as a strategy in mental animation (Hegarty, 2004). For example, Schwartz and Black (1996b) found that when people inferred the rate of rotation of two interlocking gears (whether a knob on one gear would mesh with a groove on a second gear), response time was proportional to the angle of rotation, as in studies of mental rotation, suggesting that people were using an analog imagery strategy to infer how the gears would rotate. However, this does not mean that mental animation is a process of inspecting a holistic detailed visual image in the "mind's eye." As we have seen, mental animation involves imagining the motion of mechanical systems one component at a time (in order of the causal chain of events), and although this is sometimes an analog imagery process, the inference can also be based on verbally coded knowledge, for example, "every other gear in a gear chain turns in the same direction" (Schwartz & Black, 1996a).

Finally, although a useful strategy in understanding dynamic systems from static images, mental animation ability is limited. The research on naïve physics (Kaiser, Proffitt, Whelan, & Hecht, 1992; McCloskey, 1983) has revealed several systematic errors in people's inference of motion from static diagrams, for example the classic naïve intuition that a ball shot through a curved tube will emerge in a curved path (McCloskey, 1983). Furthermore low spatial-ability individuals are less accurate in inferring how mechanical systems move from static diagrams (Hegarty & Kozhevnikov, 1999; Hegarty & Sims, 1994; Hegarty & Steinhoff, 1997). The research on mental animation has therefore revealed that people have some ability to infer how a machine moves from a single static diagram, but that this ability is limited, especially for people with low spatial ability.

GRAPHIC DEVICES FOR COMMUNICATING
DYNAMIC EVENTS

As shown in Figures 28.3 and 28.4 graphic designers often communicate motion in static diagrams by annotating parts of the diagrams with arrows, or by presenting a series of phase diagrams showing the configuration of parts of a system at different phases of its motion. There have been relatively few studies that assessed the effectiveness of these graphic devices. Heiser and Tversky (2002) found that when people were asked to describe static mechanical diagrams that included arrows showing the motion of system parts, they spontaneously provided functional descriptions of how the system worked. In contrast, if the diagrams did not include arrows, people described only the structure of the system. Hegarty, Kriz, and Cate (2003) examined people's comprehension of a flushing cistern after they viewed the three static diagrams shown in Figure 28.4. People who viewed these phase diagrams had better understanding of the mechanical system compared to those who viewed a single static diagram. These studies indicate that arrows and phase diagrams are promising ways of communicating the kinematics of a device. Because these diagrams are static, understanding kinematics from these diagrams still depends on mental animation. However, arrows and phase diagrams may be useful ways of aiding this mental animation process, especially for low spatial-ability students and when explaining relatively complex mechanical systems.

Understanding Dynamic Events from Animated Diagrams

On an intuitive level, animations seem like an obvious way to communicate dynamic events, such as how a machine works. Animations portray the temporal changes in the operation of a machine explicitly so that the external display (i.e., the animation) can be isomorphic in both space and time to the dynamic process that it is intended to represent. In terms of the information-processing analysis presented in Figure 28.1, learning how a complex physical system works from an animation relies on the ability to *perceive* the motions of components, whereas learning from static diagrams depends on the ability to *infer* these motions.

It is therefore initially surprising to most people that there has been very little (if any) evidence that animations are more effective than static diagrams for communicating about dynamic processes. For example, in the study by Hegarty et al. (2003) students learned how a mechanical system (i.e., a flushing cistern) worked from either a single static diagram, the three phases diagrams shown in Figure 28.4, or an animation. We found that although the three phases diagram group and animation group had a better understanding than those who viewed a single diagram, there was no significant difference in comprehension between the three phases diagram group and the animation group. It appears, therefore, that participants were able to interpolate between the three phases shown in the static diagrams (i.e., 3 of the 140 frames included in the animation) to mentally animate their internal representations of the device, and this enabled them to understand the device as well as people who actually viewed all 140 frames of the animation.

It might be tempting to conclude that the animation used by Hegarty et al. (2003) was not a good one, or that the flushing cistern is a particularly difficult device to learn about from an animation. However, Narayanan and Hegarty (2002) found similar results when we used stimuli from the award-winning *The Way Things Work* book and CD-ROM (Macaulay, 1988, 1998). Furthermore, in a review of over 20 studies that compared learning from static and animated graphics in a variety of domains (e.g., Hegarty et al., 2002; Hegarty, Quilici, Narayanan, Holmquist, & Moreno, 1999; Narayanan & Hegarty, 2002; Palmiter & Elkerton, 1993; Palmiter, Elkerton, & Baggett, 1991; Pane, Corbett, & John, 1996; Rieber, 1989; Rieber & Hannafin, 1988) Tversky, Morrison, and Betrancourt (2002) concluded that there was no advantage of animations over static graphics. Although a small number of studies (e.g., Park & Gittelman, 1992;

Rieber, 1990, 1991) seemed to show such an advantage, on closer inspection, Tversky et al. (2002) found that in these studies the animations presented more information than the static diagrams, so that the two media were not informationally equivalent (cf. Larkin & Simon, 1987).

ARE ANIMATIONS MORE EFFECTIVE FOR LOW-SPATIAL STUDENTS?

One plausible hypothesis is that viewing animations might be more effective than static diagrams in the case of individuals with low spatial abilities, because these individuals have less ability to mentally animate static diagrams. If this is true, an animation might function as a type of cognitive "prosthetic" for those with low spatial ability. However, in a review of research that examined the effects of spatial ability on multimedia, Hegarty (2004) found no evidence for this hypothesis. In contrast, the literature indicated that in some cases (Hegarty et al., 2003; Narayanan & Hegarty, 2002) there was no aptitude treatment interaction (ATI) between spatial ability and format of diagrams (static versus animated) whereas in other cases, high spatial-ability individuals were better able to perceive and learn from animations (Garg et al., 1999; Isaak & Just, 1995; Mayer & Sims, 1994).

WHY ARE ANIMATIONS NOT MORE EFFECTIVE?

How can we explain why animations are not more effective than static diagrams in instructing people about dynamic processes. There are several plausible reasons. First, an important characteristic of animations is their transience (Ainsworth & Van Labeke, 2004; Stenning, 1998). In all of the experiments discussed in the preceding text the animations were computer controlled and played at a constant rate. When one views such an animation, one frame is seen at a time, and once the animation or video has advanced beyond a given frame, that frame is no longer available to the viewer. There is a question, therefore, of whether perception and comprehension of an animation can keep up with the pace at which the anima-

tion is presented, especially when different components of motion of the same object (e.g., rotation and translation), or the motions of different objects must be mentally integrated to understand the process being conveyed (cf. Isaak & Just, 1995). In contrast, viewing of static diagrams is self-paced and interactive in the sense that one can view a diagram for as long as one wishes or look back and forth between different phase diagrams as often as necessary to understand the dynamic process.

Second, visual attention might limit what is learned from an animation. In complex machines, several components move at once. For example, in the case of the flushing cistern, there are two chains of events that overlap in time; one that flushes water out of the cistern and the other that refills the cistern. To understand an animation of a complex machine, people need to attend to and relate changes that occur simultaneously in different regions of space. However, as recent research on change blindness has made clear, when our visual attention is focused on one location in a display, we are likely to be "blind" to changes in other regions of the display (Rensink, 2002). This will be particularly true when the most salient motions in the animation are not those that are most thematically relevant (Lowe, 1999, 2003).

Third, learning from animations might be less effective because viewing an animation is a passive process. In contrast, inferring how a system moves from a static diagram or series of phase diagrams (i.e., mental animation) is a more active cognitive process. Phenomena such as the self-generation effect (Slamecka & Graf, 1978) and the self-explanation effect (Chi et al., 1994) suggest that people learn more effectively if they are more active in the learning process, and generate ideas or explanations.

Fourth, there may be a mismatch between the format of an animation and the format of internal mental models of how machines work. When a machine is in motion, many of its components move at once, so a realistic animation of a machine shows these simultaneous motions. In contrast, when people attempt to understand how a machine works, or answer questions about how it works, they infer the motion of components one by one, in order of a causal chain of events (Baggett & Graesser, 1995; Hegarty, 1992; Hegarty & Sims, 1994, Narayanan, Suwa, & Motoda, 1994). That is, they represent a sequence of events (cf. Zacks & Tversky, 2001) rather than continuous motion.

CAN WE MAKE ANIMATIONS MORE EFFECTIVE?

Can understanding the limitations of animation comprehension help us design more effective animations? Tversky et al., proposed two principles for the design of effective instructional materials, the *apprehension principle* and the *resemblance principle*. The apprehension principle is that external representations should be designed such that they can be "readily and accurately perceived and comprehended" (p. 258). For example, a violation of this principle is to present animations so fast that that perception and comprehension processes cannot keep up with the speed of the animation. The resemblance principle is that animations should be designed to correspond to the type of internal representation that one wishes to foster.

With respect to the apprehension principle, many researchers are currently exploring the use of interactive animations to communicate how physical systems work (e.g., Lowe, 1999; 2003; Schwan & Riempp, 2004). In interactive animations, viewers can speed up or slow down the display to match their comprehension speed, and can view and review parts of the animation in any sequence, skipping over parts that they understand while slowing down when they get to more difficult sections. Thus, the learner can tailor the instruction to his or her own needs. Furthermore, when interacting with dynamic displays, viewers are much more active in learning.

Interactivity raises its own difficulties for comprehension, however. First, interactive animations must have an interface, and using an interface can take the viewer's attention away from the task of understanding and learning from the animation. Second, to be effective, interactive displays assume a learner who is not just motivated, but who has the metacognitive skills to use the interactivity effectively and the domain knowledge necessary to identify the most relevant aspects of the display. This is not always true in the case of novices. For example, Lowe examined how students interacted with an animation that displayed changes in weather conditions across the Australian continent over a seven-day period. In one study (Lowe, 1999) they were required to generate a verbal description of the animation, whereas in another (Lowe, 2004) they were asked to apply what they learned to predicting how weather conditions in another map would change over a 24-hour period. In both studies, students tended to pay attention to perceptually salient changes in the display and often ignored changes that were highly relevant to the meteorological tasks, but less conspicuous in the displays. Studies such as this indicate that interactive displays may not always be more effective than static displays especially for low knowledge students. Consistent with this view, Kriz and Hegarty (in press) found that students with low prior knowledge (humanities graduate students) were unable to construct accurate models of how a novel device works using interactive animations, whereas students with high domain knowledge (engineering graduate students) were able to construct the correct model.

There have been fewer studies addressing Tversky et al.'s (2002) apprehension principle, suggesting that animations should be designed to correspond to the type of internal representation that one wishes to foster. In this regard, studies of mental animation suggest that the internal representation of a dynamic physical system is of a causal chain of events, rather than a continuous animation (Hegarty, 1992). Therefore in accordance with Tversky et al.'s *resemblance principle*, it might be more effective to communicate how a machine works using a sequence of static phase diagrams that show the beginning and end points of the important causal events, and preliminary findings (Hegarty et al., 2003) are consistent with this prediction.

Understanding and Learning from Multimedia Presentations

In the final section of this chapter, I consider learning from truly multimedia presentations, that is, those that include both diagrammatic representations (static or animated) and verbal instruction. We have seen that although diagrams can be very effective in communicating about dynamic causal systems, they also have limitations, especially for learners with poor spatial ability and low domain knowledge. For example, the studies reviewed in the preceding text indicate that these individuals have difficulty understanding highly schematized diagrams, understanding the three-dimensional structure of an object from two-dimensional representations and mentally animating static diagrams. It is not surprising, therefore, that several studies have shown that people learn more from diagrammatic representations if they are accompanied by verbal instruction (e.g., Hegarty & Just, 1993; Mayer & Anderson, 1991; Mayer & Gallini, 1990). To better understand these results, I now consider the possible relations between verbal and diagrammatic representations in multimedia presentations, including content relations and format relations, and how these affect comprehension.

Content Relations Between Diagrams and Verbal Instruction

The content of verbal instruction can be redundant with the information in a static or animated diagram, or can augment or complement this information in a variety of ways. First, a verbal description provides information in a verbal code, in addition to the visual-spatial code provided by static or animated diagrams. According to dual-code theory, information represented in two codes is more memorable than information represented in a single code (Paivio, 1986). A verbal code may also enable the user to access prior knowledge about an item presented in a diagram. For example, a person may not recognize a rectangle in a highly schematic diagram as representing a cylinder

or a circle as representing a pulley. If these are labeled in the diagram or referred to by their names in the text, this might enable the user to access prior knowledge about what these components are typically made of and their typical functions (Narayanan & Hegarty, 1998).

Second, verbal instruction can direct processing of diagrams. Hegarty and Just (1993) monitored students' eye fixations while they read text accompanied by diagrams describing how pulley systems work. We examined where people switched between reading the text and viewing the diagram in the course of comprehension, and what they looked at in the diagram each time they switched. We found that people tended to switch from reading the text to viewing the diagram at the end of a clause of text, and when they switched to the diagram, they looked at the parts of the diagram that depicted the objects they had just read about in the text. The eye fixations indicated that the text was directing their processing of the diagram. Verbal direction may be particularly effective in drawing attention to areas of a diagram that are not visually salient or phases of an animation that occur quickly or involve small movements so they are unlikely to be noticed by viewing visual instruction alone (Hegarty et al., 2003; Lowe, 1999, 2003).

Verbal instruction might also be particularly important for communicating sequential information, such as the causal chain of events in a mechanical system. In complex physical systems, several objects typically move at once and there is no natural constraint on the order in which objects are fixated in a static diagram or animation of such a system. However, language has a linear structure so that language comprehension imposes a natural sequential order on information processing. This can be exploited to communicate information that has a linear structure, such as a causal chain of events.

Finally, a verbal text or commentary can provide information that is not easily communicated in static or animated diagrams. Although diagrams can provide information about the structure of a device, and its kinematics, (i.e., the geometry of movement in a mechanical system), they are less suited to communicating about nonvisible entities such as forces (Oestermeier & Hesse, 2000). In contrast, language can express all of these types of information. Consistent with this view, when Hegarty et al. (2003) examined comprehension of static and diagrams alone and those that were accompanied by text, they found that verbal instruction was most effective in enhancing understanding of mechanisms such as a siphon, which depend on an appreciation of forces rather than kinematics alone.

In summary, verbal information can clearly augment what is learned from static and animated diagrams in a multimedia display. It may be particularly effective in drawing students' attention to information that is not perceptually salient in diagrams, communicating sequential information, and providing information about nonvisible entities, such as forces, that cannot be depicted directly in a visual-spatial display.

Format Relations Between Diagrams and Verbal Instruction

We now turn to a consideration of how the format of multimedia instruction affects learning. There are two important aspects of instructional format that must be considered and that have received considerable attention in the literature. The first concerns issues of contiguity between verbal instructions and diagrams. The second concerns the media and modalities used to deliver instruction.

CONTIGUITY

As shown in Figure 28.1, an important process in understanding multimedia is that of integrating the information presented in the text and diagrams, because the goal of comprehension is a mental model of the referent of the multimedia presentation, which is usually based on information from both media. An important step in this process is that of resolving coreference between noun phrases in the text (e.g., "the upper pulley") and diagrammatic units (e.g., a circle) that refer to the same object, in order to construct

a mental model of that referent. To accomplish this step, the verbal and diagrammatic representations must be in working memory at the same time. People sometimes ensure this by frequently interrupting their reading of a text to inspect parts of the diagram that refer to the same objects, as found by Hegarty and Just (1993). However they can also benefit significantly if verbal and diagrammatic information is presented contiguously in the multimedia display. Thus, people learn better from text and diagrams if related visual and verbal information is presented as close as possible in space rather than in separate text and diagram representations (e.g., Mayer & Gallini, 1990), and people learn more effectively from animations if they are accompanied by simultaneous commentaries rather than commentaries that are heard either before or after animations representing the same events (Mayer & Sims, 1994; Moreno & Mayer, 1999). Similarly, Faraday and Sutcliffe (1997a, 1997b) have shown that students learn more effectively from movies accompanied by commentaries if visual cues such as arrows and highlighting draw their attention to the relevant parts of the display as they are described in the commentary. Contiguity and highlighting in a display can enhance the probability that spatial and verbal information will be in working memory at the same time, so that this information can be integrated to construct a mental model of their common referent.

MEDIA AND MODALITIES

As illustrated in Figure 28.1, multimedia instruction, including diagrams and verbal instruction, can be delivered in different media and using different modalities. For example an explanation of how a machine works can be presented on a computer screen or on paper, and verbal instruction can be presented either as visual text or as an auditory commentary. To what extent do the media and modalities used to present information affect comprehension and learning? In researching this question, it is important to compare multimedia displays that are as informationally equivalent as possible (cf. Larkin & Simon, 1987), such that they present the same information and follow the same design guidelines.

This approach was taken in a recent study by Narayanan and Hegarty (2002). They created multimedia presentations to explain two types of content, how a machine works and how specific computer algorithms work. In different presentations, they varied whether the information was presented on a computer screen and included animations, auditory commentaries and hyperlinks; or whether they were presented as printed text and diagrams. The verbal instruction in the computer and paper presentations was informationally equivalent, in that the auditory commentary presented in the computer-based instruction had the exact same words as the text in the paper-based instruction. With respect to the diagrammatic information, the computer-based instruction presented more information in that it presented a complete animation whereas the paper-based materials presented only selected frames of the animation. We examined students' comprehension of the materials and their abilities to apply this knowledge to solve novel problems. The overwhelming result was that comprehension measures were not affected by whether information was presented on a computer including animations, auditory commentaries, and hyperlinks, or on paper using traditional printed text and diagrams.

Mental Animation and Comprehension of Multimedia Displays

The fact that students have equivalent comprehension of animated and static diagrams in the context of multimedia displays again suggests that they may be able to mentally animate static displays. In the printed displays used by Narayanan and Hegarty (2002), diagrams presented the static structure of the systems while verbal instruction described the dynamic interaction between the parts. In this situation verbal instruction can augment people's natural but limited ability to mentally animate static displays by describing motions of system components that people may not be able to infer for themselves.

Mental animation may be an inherent part of the text comprehension process, as it involves converting a representation of the static structure of the device (encoded from the external diagram) to a dynamic mental model that includes a representation of how the parts of the system move to achieve its function. Consistent with this account, Hegarty and Just (1993) found that after people read a section of text describing the motion of a simple mechanical system (a pulley system), they spent several seconds inspecting a static diagram of the system that accompanied the text. Because the diagram provided no information about motion in the system, the people could not have been encoding information about motion from this diagram. The most likely interpretation of the eye-fixation behavior is that students were mentally animating the diagram to imagine the motions that they had just read about in the text. Text may be particularly effective for communicating how a system moves, because the linear structure of text can be used to guide learners through the causal chain of events that is an essential element in understanding how the system works (Narayanan & Hegarty, 1998).

Finally, asking people to mentally animate a system can enhance what they learn from multimedia. Previous research suggests that people often learn more effectively if they are more active in the learning process, and generate ideas or explanations (Chi et al., 1994; Slamecka & Graf, 1978) or first participate in activities that activate their knowledge relevant to the topic of the presentation (Britton & Graesser, 1996; Kintsch et al., 1993; McNamara, Kintsch, Songer & Kintsch, 1996). In recent studies, Hegarty et al. (2002; 2003) presented students with static diagrams of a device (a flushing cistern) and asked them to infer how the device worked (i.e. mentally animate the diagrams) before they learned about the device from multimedia presentations. Other groups of students in the same experiments learned from the multimedia presentations without this mental animation manipulation. We found that the mental animation phase enhanced learning from multimedia such that those who engaged in mental animation were better able to describe how the system works. One interpretation of this result is that attempting to mentally animate the device allowed learners to discover what they did not understand about the device, so that they could focus on this information when viewing the multimedia displays. Consistent with this account, Rosenblit and Keil (2002) found that people overestimated their understanding of how everyday mechanical devices worked and learned more effectively when this "illusion" of understanding was shattered.

Summary and Conclusions

In summary, this chapter considers the comprehension of diagrams, animations, and multimedia presentations from an information-processing perspective. An analysis of different types of external representations revealed that these representations vary in realism or isomorphism between the representation and its referent. For example, if the referent is a dynamic process, an animation is more realistic than a series of static diagrams and if the referent is the static structure of a system, an iconic diagram is more realistic than a verbal description. More and less realistic media depend on different processes for their comprehension. For example, if the external representation of a system is more isomorphic to reality, understanding the system depends more on perceptual processes, whereas if it is more abstracted from reality, understanding the system may depend more on cognitive processes such as inference. The picture that emerges from this review is that multimedia comprehension is often an active process of knowledge construction, rather than merely a passive process of internalizing the information presented in an external display.

Because multimedia understanding depends on active information processing, including inference and integration of different representations, it can also be influenced considerably by the abilities, skills, and knowledge of the student. We have seen that students with little domain knowledge or low spatial abilities often have difficulties with comprehension of multimedia displays. Thus what is understood from a multimedia display is jointly determined by aspects of the display and qualities of the student of a multimedia display.

The basic understanding of multimedia comprehension provided by this review can inform the design of multimedia by providing information about the effectiveness of different media for communicating different types of content. In general we have seen that iconic static diagrams can be effective for communicating the static structure of a system and also the basis for mental animation. However, comprehension of both static structure and more dynamic events can be enhanced when static diagrams are accompanied by verbal instruction, which can serve to direct readers' attention to the most relevant aspects of a diagram, guide the process of mental animation, and provide information about nonvisible entities, such as force, that cannot be represented directly in diagrammatic representations. Contrary to intuition, the literature reviewed provides no evidence that more realistic representations (e.g., animated diagrams showing movement) are more effective than more abstract representations (e.g., a series of static displays showing motion) of static displays. In contrast, traditional print media, that is, static diagrams accompanied by text, can provide highly effective external representations to aid the development of mental models of dynamic systems.

Glossary

External representation: A representation of some object, printed on paper or displayed on a computer monitor, that can be perceived by an individual.

Internal representation: A representation of some object in the mind of an individual.

Mental animation: The process of inferring how an object or physical system moves from a static display.

Mental model: The internal representation of a physical system. In other contexts, the term *mental model* has been used to denote a representation that is isomorphic to the physical situation that it represents. Although mental models of physical systems may be isomorphic to their referents, this chapter does not make a strong claim that this is always true.

Note

This research was supported by grant N00014-03-1-0119 from the Office of Naval Research and grant EIA-0313237 from the National Science Foundation.

References

Ainsworth, S., & Van Labeke, N. (2004). Multiple forms of dynamic representation. *Learning and Instruction, 14*, 241–255.

Baggett, W. B., & Graesser, A. C. (1995). Question answering in the context of illustrated expository text. *Proceedings of the 17th Annual Conference of the Cognitive Science Society* (pp. 334–339). Mahwah, NJ: Lawrence Erlbaum Associates.

Britton, B. K., & Graesser, A. C. (Eds.). (1996). *Models of understanding text.* Mahwah, NJ: Lawrence Erlbaum Associates.

Chi, M. T. H., de Leeuw, N., Chiu, M., & LaVancher, C. (1994). Eliciting self-explanations improves learning. *Cognitive Science, 18*, 439–478.

Cohen, C. A., Hegarty, M., Keehner, M., & Montello, D. R. (2003). Spatial abilities in the representation of cross sections. *Proceedings of the 25th Annual Meeting of the Cognitive Science Society.* Mahwah, NJ: Erlbaum.

Dar, T., Joskowicz, L., & Rivlin, E. (1999). Understanding mechanical motion: From images to behaviors. *Artificial Intelligence, 112*, 147–179.

Eley, M. (1983). Representing the cross-sectional shapes of contour-mapped landforms. *Human Learning, 2*, 279–294.

Faraday, P., & Sutcliffe, A. (1997a). An empirical study of attending and comprehending multimedia presentations. In *Proceedings of the ACM Multimedia Conference* (265–275). New York: ACM Press.

Faraday, P., & Sutcliffe, A. (1997b). Designing effective multimedia presentations. In *Proceedings of the ACM Conference on Human Factors in Computing Systems, CHI'97* (272–278). New York: ACM Press.

Ferguson, E. S. (1992). *Engineering and the Mind's Eye.* Cambridge, MA: MIT Press.

Ferguson, E. L., & Hegarty, M. (1995). Learning with real machines or diagrams: Application of knowledge to real-world problems. *Cognition and Instruction, 13*, 129–160.

Garg, A. X., Norman, G., & Sperotable, L. (2001). How medical students learn spatial anatomy. *The Lancet, 357*, 363–364.

Garg, A. X., Norman, G. R., Spero, L., & Maheshwari, P. (1999). Do virtual computer models hinder anatomy learning. *Academic Medicine, 74*, 87–89.

Hegarty, M., (1992). Mental animation: Inferring motion from static diagrams of mechanical systems. *Journal of Experimental Psychology: Learning, Memory, and Cognition, 18*, 1084–1102.

Hegarty, M. (2004). Mechanical reasoning as mental simulation. *TRENDS in Cognitive Sciences, 8*, 280–285.

Hegarty, M., & Just, M. A. (1993). Constructing mental models of machines from text and diagrams. *Journal of Memory and Language, 32*, 717–742.

Hegarty, M., Kriz, S., & Cate, C. (2003). The roles of mental animations and external animations in understanding mechanical systems. *Cognition & Instruction, 21*, 325–360.

Hegarty, M., & Kozhevnikov, M. (1999). Spatial abilities, working memory and mechanical reasoning. In J. Gero & B. Tversky (Eds.), *Visual and spatial reasoning in design* (pp. 221–239). Sydney, Australia: Key Centre of Design and Cognition.

Hegarty, M., Narayanan, N. H., & Freitas, P. (2002). Understanding machine from multimedia and hypermedia presentations. In J. Otero, A. C. Graesser, & J. Leon (Eds.),

The psychology of science text comprehension (pp. 357–384). Mahwah, NJ: Lawrence Erlbaum Associates.

Hegarty, M., Quillici, J., Narayanan, N. H., Holmquist, S., & Moreno, R. (1999). Multimedia instruction: Lessons from evaluation of a theory-based design. *Journal of Educational Multimedia and Hypermedia, 8,* 119–150.

Hegarty, M., & Sims, V. K. (1994). Individual differences in mental animation during mechanical reasoning. *Memory and Cognition, 22,* 411–430.

Hegarty, M., & Steinhoff, K. (1997). Use of diagrams as external memory in a mechanical reasoning task. *Learning and Individual Differences, 9,* 19–42.

Heiser, J., & Tversky, B. (2002). Diagrams and descriptions in acquiring complex systems. *Proceedings of the 24th Annual Conference of the Cognitive Science Society.* Mahwah, NJ: Lawrence Erlbaum Associates.

Isaak, M. I., & Just, M. A. (1995). Constraints on the processing of rolling motion: The curtate cycloid illusion. *Journal of Experimental Psychology: Human Perception & Performance, 21* (6): 1391–1408.

Kaiser, M. K., Proffitt, D. R., Whelan, S. M., & Hecht, H. (1992). Influence of animation on dynamical judgments. *Journal of Experimental Psychology: Human Perception and Performance, 18,* 669–690.

Kali, Y., & Orion, N. (1996). Spatial abilities of high school students in the perception of geologic structures. *Journal of Research in Science Teaching, 33,* 369–391.

Kintsch, W., Britton, B. K., Fletcher, C. R., Mannes, S. M., & Nathan, M. J. (1993). A comprehension-based approach to learning and understanding. In D. L. Medin (Ed.), *The psychology of learning and motivation* (Vol. 30, pp. 165–214). New York: Academic Press.

Kriz, S., & Hegarty, M. (2004). Constructing and revising mental models of a mechanical system: The role of domain knowledge in understanding external visualizations. In K. Forbus, D. Gentner, & T. Regier (Eds.), *Proceedings of the 26th Annual Conference of the Cognitive Science Society.* Mahwah, NJ: Lawrence Erlbaum Associates.

Larkin, J. H., & Simon, H. A. (1987). Why a diagram is (sometimes) worth ten thousand words. *Cognitive Science, 11,* 65–100.

Lowe, R. K. (1999). Extracting information from an animation during complex visual learning. *European Journal of Psychology of Education, 14,* 225–244.

Lowe, R. (2003). Animation and learning: Selective processing of information in dynamic graphics. *Learning and Instruction, 13,* 157–176.

Markman, A. B. (1999). *Knowledge representation.* Mahwah, NJ: Lawrence Erlbaum Associates.

Mayer, R. E., & Anderson, R. B. (1991). Animations need narrations: An experimental test of the dual-code hypothesis. *Journal of Educational Psychology, 83,* 484–490.

Mayer, R. E., & Gallini, J. (1990). When is an illustration worth ten thousand words? *Journal of Educational Psychology, 82,* 715–726.

Mayer, R. E., & Sims, V. K. (1994). For whom is a picture worth a thousand words? Extensions of a dual-coding theory of multimedia learning. *Journal of Educational Psychology, 86,* 389–401.

Macaulay, D. (1988). *The way things work.* Boston: Houghton Mifflin Company.

Macaulay, D. (1998). *The New Way Things Work* [CD-ROM]. New York: DK Interactive Learning.

McCloskey, M. (1983). Naïve theories of motion. In D. Gentner & A. Stevens (Eds.), *Mental models* (pp. 229–324). Mahwah, NJ: Erlbaum.

McNamara, D. S., Kintsch, E., Songer, N. B., & Kintsch, W. (1996). Are good texts always better? Interactions of text coherence, background knowledge and levels of understanding in learning from text. *Cognition and Instruction, 14,* 1–43.

Moreno, R., & Mayer, R. E. (1999). Cognitive principles of multimedia learning: The role of modality and contiguity. *Journal of Educational Psychology, 91,* 358–368.

Moreno, R., & Mayer, R. E. (2000). A coherence effect in multimedia learning: The case for minimizing irrelevant sounds in the design of multimedia instructional messages. *Journal of Educational Psychology, 92,* 117–125.

Narayanan, N. H., & Hegarty, M. (1998). On designing comprehensible hypermedia manuals. *International Journal of Human-Computer Studies, 48,* 267–301.

Narayanan, N. H., & Hegarty, M. (2002). Multimedia design for communication of dynamic information. *International Journal of Human-Computer Studies, 57,* 279–315.

Narayanan, N. H., Suwa, M., & Motoda, H. (1994). A study of diagrammatic reasoning from verbal and gestural data. *Proceedings of the 16th Annual Conference of the Cognitive Science Society* (pp. 652–657). Mahwah, NJ: Lawrence Erlbaum Associates.

Oestermeier, U., & Hesse, F. W. (2000). Verbal and visual causal arguments. *Cognition, 75*, 65–104.

Paivio, A. (1986). *Mental representations: A dual-coding approach*. New York: Oxford University Press.

Palmer, S. E. (1978). Fundamental aspects of cognitive representation. In E. E. Rosch & B. B. Lloyd (Eds.), *Cognition and Categorization* (pp. 259–303) Mahwah, NJ: Lawrence Erlbaum Associates.

Palmiter, S. L., & Elkerton, J., (1993). Animated demonstrations for learning procedural computer-based tasks. *Human-Computer Interaction, 8*, 193–216.

Palmiter, S. L., Elkerton, J., & Baggett, P. (1991). Animated demonstrations vs. written instructions for learning procedural tasks: A preliminary investigation. *International Journal of Man-Machine Studies, 34*, 687–701.

Pane, J. F., Corbett, A. T., & John, B. E. (1996). Assessing dynamics in computer-based instruction. In M. J. Tauber (Ed.), *Proceedings of the ACM Conference on Human Factors in Computing Systems* (pp. 797–804). New York: ACM.

Park, O. C., & Gittelman, S. S. (1992). Selective use of animation and feedback in computer based instruction. *Educational Technology, Research and Development, 40*, 125–167.

Rensink, R. (2002). Change detection. *Annual Review of Psychology, 53*, 245–277.

Rieber, L. P. (1989). The effects of computer animated elaboration strategies and practice on factual and application learning in an elementary science lesson. *Journal of Educational Computing Research, 5*, 431–444.

Rieber, L. P. (1990). Using computer animated graphics with science instruction with children. *Journal of Educational Psychology, 83*, 135–140.

Rieber, L. P. (1991). Animation, incidental learning, and continuing education. *Journal of Educational Psychology, 83*, 318–328.

Rieber, L. P., & Hannafin, M. J. (1988). Effects of textual and animated orienting activ-

ities and practice on learning from computer-based instruction. *Computers in the Schools, 5*, 77–89.

Rozenblit, L. G., & Keil, F. C. (2002). The misunderstood limits of folk science: An illusion of explanatory depth. *Cognitive Science, 26*, 521–562.

Scaife, M., & Rogers, Y. (1996). External cognition: How do graphical representations work? *International Journal of Human-Computer Studies, 45*, 185–213.

Schwan, S., & Riempp, R. (2004). The cognitive benefits of interactive videos. Learning to tie nautical knots. *Learning and Instruction, 14*, 275–291.

Schwartz. D. L. (1995). Reasoning about the referent of a picture versus reasoning about the picture as the referent: An effect of visual realism. *Memory and Cognition, 23*, 709–722.

Schwartz, D. L., and Black, J. B. (1996a). Shuttling between depictive models and abstract rules: Induction and fall-back. *Cognitive Science 20*, 457–497.

Schwartz, D. L., and Black, J. B. (1996b). Analog imagery in mental model reasoning: Depictive models. *Cognitive Psychology 30*, 154–219.

Slamecka, N. J., & Graf, P. (1978). The generation effect: Delineation of a phenomenon. *Journal of Experimental Psychology: Human Learning and Memory, 4*, 592–604.

Stenning, K. (1998). Distinguishing semantic from processing explanations of usability of representations: Applying expressiveness analysis to animation. In J. Lee (Ed.), *Intelligence and multimodality in multimedia interfaces: Research and applications*. Cambridge, MA: AAAI Press.

Tufte, E. R. (1997). *Visual explanations: Images and quantities, evidence and narrative*. Cheshire, CT: Graphics Press.

Tversky, B., Morrison, J. B., & Betrancourt, M. (2002). Animation: Can it facilitate? *International Journal of Human-Computer Studies, 57*, 247–262.

Zacks, J. M., & Tversky, B. (2001). Event structure in perception and conception. *Psychological Bulletin, 27*, 3–21.

CHAPTER 29

Multimedia Learning in Second Language Acquisition

Jan L. Plass

New York University

Linda C. Jones

University of Arkansas

Abstract

In this chapter, we discuss research on second-language acquisition with multimedia. We propose a model of cognitive processing in second-language acquisition that is based on interactionist models and on a cognitive theory of multimedia learning (CTML). For each of the major phases in this model, we discuss the cognitive processing involved, describe how multimedia can be used to support these processes, and report what the research says about the effectiveness of such multimedia support. We discuss limitations of existing research, derive implications for cognitive theory as well as for designers of instructional multimedia materials for second-language acquisition, and suggest directions for future research.

What Is Second-Language Acquisition with Multimedia?

Introduction

The use of a language – whether first or second – has as its goal the communication of ideas, maintenance of social relations, and creation of discourse, all of which require the development of several core competencies. These include input competencies, such as listening and reading, and output competencies, such as speaking and writing, and entail the process of receiving (input), attending to (interaction), and assigning meaning (output) to verbal (aural or written) and/or visual stimuli. They also include competencies in communicating in the target language, which includes an understanding of the cultural and situational context of such communication.

The goal of learning a language is ultimately to develop these core competencies. However, the approaches taken to the teaching and learning of a second language have changed considerably over the past 40 years, loosely mirroring the development of psychological theories and models of teaching and learning. A brief overview of some of the most important approaches might be helpful in defining what constitutes second-language learning and acquisition with multimedia (Kern & Warschauer, 2000).

The *structural approach*, advocated early in the 20th century, focused on the system of structures that defines a language and viewed language learning as the formation of habits. Following the influence of behavioral psychologists such as John Watson and B. F. Skinner, language competencies were thought to be best attained by drills of dialogues and language patterns based on linguistic categories, and with an emphasis on grammatically correct responses to linguistic stimuli. These drills, including, for example, audiolingualism, where grammar and vocabulary are taught orally, were designed without consideration of the cognitive or social processes involved in these competencies.

Advocates of what has come to be known as the *cognitive approach* to learning challenged the behaviorist view in the late 1950s and early 1960s by emphasizing the importance of considering the mental processes involved in learning. In language learning, Noam Chomsky proposed that language development was facilitated by innate cognitive structures, not by behavioral reinforcement (Chomsky, 1957). With this approach, second-language teaching began to focus on developing learners' use of cognitive strategies to improve competence in the language and incorporated learning materials that were based on an understanding of learners' cognitive processing of the information (Bacon, 1992; Chamot, 1995; Chamot, & Küpper, 1989; Long, 1989; O'Malley, Chamot, & Walker, 1987; Plass, Chun, Mayer, & Leutner, 1998; Postovsky, 1981; Rost, 1990). With the spread of the cognitive approach, the process of language learning was no longer restricted to passive, drill-and-practice, grammar-based activities but instead emphasized the development of linguistic competencies based on prior knowledge, linguistic knowledge, and interaction with and understanding of the text (Fischer & Farris, 1995; Joiner, 1986, 1997; Lynch, 1995; Pusack & Otto, 1997).

Somewhat parallel to the increase in popularity of the cognitive approach to second-language learning, a *constructivist perspective* was introduced that placed the agency of the learning process on the learner as an active constructor of meaning. Instead of insisting on a model of transferring the correct structure from the teacher to the student, the acquisition of a second language was now viewed as an individualized psycholinguistic process that, based on input that was comprehensible and natural, allowed learners to develop their own linguistic competence and, in the process, construct their own grammar of the language (Krashen, 1982).

The notion of active learning emphasized by this constructivist perspective could not be realized without introducing a social component into the learning process. The *sociocognitive perspective* focuses on the interaction of and communication among learners, redefining language competence by extending its linguistic focus to include sociolinguistic and communicative competence (Atkinson, 2003; Hymes, 1972). In this approach, the development of language competencies is seen as embedded in the particular sociocultural context that emphasizes both the learners' development of cognitive structures and the social component of discourse and activity (Canale & Swain, 1980).

In current views, a language is *acquired* in the process of natural communication, as compared to the conscious process of *learning* the language as emphasized by the structural approach (Krashen, 1988). For the purpose of this chapter, we will therefore adopt the term *second-language acquisition* to describe the meaningful interaction in the target language where the focus is on communication, and the acquisition of the language incidental, and the term *second-language learning* when the focus is on formal instruction about the language.

Second-Language Acquisition with Multimedia

Multimedia can be defined as the use of words and pictures to present material (Mayer, 2001). In this context, *words* are verbal materials that can be presented in printed or in spoken form. *Pictures* are either static materials, such as diagrams, graphs, photos, or maps, or dynamic materials, such as animation or video. The use of multimedia to acquire or learn a second language can be defined in the context of any of the approaches to language learning described previously. For the purpose of this chapter, we will focus on second-language acquisition with multimedia, that is, the use of words and pictures to provide meaningful input, facilitate meaningful interaction with the target language, and elicit meaningful output. In the following section, we will review the research literature that describes what we know about the use of multimedia for second-language acquisition based on the cognitive and constructivist/sociocognitive approaches. First, however, we will provide an example of second-language acquisition with multimedia.

An Example of Second-Language Acquisition with Multimedia

Consider the following language learning scenario: Students read a literary passage in a multimedia environment. In a traditional print-based scenario, students would read the material and consult their dictionary as needed to access translations of more difficult words. Alternatively, presented in a multimedia environment, students are first introduced to a prereading advance organizer, for example a video, that helps them activate their prior knowledge of the material to come, allows them to reflect upon the topic at hand, and enables them to better process the input once they begin to read. After viewing the advance organizer, students next access the text and read through it in a somewhat linear fashion. However, hyperlinks related to particular words and phrases within the text are available on each screen and provide helpful information in the form of translations, descriptive sentences, background information, pronunciation guides, images, or video. See Figure 29.1 for an example of such an environment (Chun & Plass, 1998).

Students have control over their learning environment. They can access helpful material as needed, and can review the text as preferred. Upon completion of work with the multimedia materials, students engage in a series of activities in the target language with the literary passage serving as a starting point for discussion, argumentation, and negotiation of meaning. In relation to the multimedia activity, students write a criticism of the material reviewed, develop a video that presents their interpretation of what they have read, or give a group presentation to their peers in the classroom environment. They post questions about the text and read other students' responses on a shared discussion list that is used by readers all over the world to exchange their thoughts.

What Do We Know About Second-Language Acquisition with Multimedia?

Research that examines second-language acquisition with multimedia runs the gamut from studies of instructional strategies for second-language acquisition that involve multimedia to those that focus on multimedia learning theories based in cognitive psychology. For the purpose of this chapter, we will use the interactionist perspective of second-language acquisition (Chapelle, 1997, 1998; Gass, 1997; Long, 1985; Pica, 1994), which defines three functions that are deemed crucial to language acquisition and learning: comprehensible input (Krashen, 1982), interaction (Long, 1985), and comprehensible output (Swain, 1985; Swain & Lapkin, 1995). In the terms of this approach, second-language acquisition with multimedia is the use of words and pictures designed to support the comprehensible input that the learner is exposed to and interacts with, and to elicit and negotiate comprehensible output. As shown in Figure 29.2, Chapelle (1998) describes a simplified model of interactionist components of the second-language acquisition process in research.

Figure 29.1. Picture annotation in the second-language acquisition multimedia learning environment *Ciberteca* (Chun & Plass, 1998).

In Figure 29.2, *Input* describes the wealth of linguistic material that the learner is presented with. Yet, only input that is *apperceived* can potentially be acquired (Chapelle, 1998). Therefore, in order to help students more richly apperceive incoming information, and eventually produce comprehensible output, *interaction* in the form of information links that provide simplification, elaboration, clarification, definitional support, or redundancy is needed (Chapelle, 1997, 1998; Larsen-Freeman & Long, 1991), suggesting that we should "provide learners with comprehensible input rather than just input" (Chapelle, 1998, p. 9). Thus, the interaction that occurs is two-way – directed toward the support of input and directed toward the support of output.

The *comprehension* of the semantic content of the apperceived input can be accomplished with or without an understanding of the syntax. *Intake* is comprehended input that can be *integrated* into the learner's linguistic system. *Comprehensible output*,

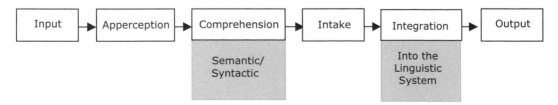

Figure 29.2. Interactionist model of basic components in the second-language acquisition process adopted from Chapelle (1998).

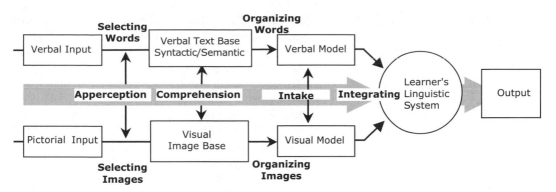

Figure 29.3. Integrated model of second-language acquisition with multimedia.

in which students identify their errors and adjust to correct these errors, is the observable result of comprehensible input and interaction. This output can be seen through communicative and noncommunicative goal-oriented tasks, such as problem solving, communication of ideas, vocabulary identification, and so on (Chapelle, 1998).

These same strategies can be well adapted to multimedia environments with the computer acting as a partner in the learning process. Therefore, the question of what we know about second-language acquisition with multimedia can be further specified to ask: In what way can multimedia support second-language acquisition by providing comprehensible input, facilitating meaningful interaction, and eliciting comprehensible output?

There are few research studies that use both second-language acquisition theory and multimedia learning theory as their foundation. One reason for this might be that there are no models of second-language acquisition that incorporate elements of multimedia learning (CTML). As a case in point, the interactionist model of second-language acquisition shown in Figure 29.2 does not incorporate any explicit references to the presentation mode of the linguistic input. The components and processes described by this model, however, are of a generative nature that has parallels to Mayer's (2001) Cognitive Theory of Multimedia Learning (see chapter 3). We therefore propose an integrated model that incorporates elements of Ellis's (1997) model of second-language

acquisition, elements of an interactionist perspective of second-language acquisition (Chapelle, 1997; 1998), and elements of the cognitive theory of multimedia learning (Figure 29.3).

In the following sections, we will, for each of the major phases in this integrated model, describe the cognitive processes involved, outline strategies of supporting these processes using multimedia, and discuss the results of research on the effectiveness of these strategies for second-language acquisition with multimedia.

Comprehensible Input: Selecting/Apperception

Before multimedia information can be processed, words and pictures need to be selected from what is presented, that is, learners need to direct their attention to a specific portion of the wealth of the linguistic and nonlinguistic information they receive that they deem relevant. Verbal information that is selected is internally represented in a text base, whereas selected pictorial information is internally represented in a visual image base. In the interactionist model of second-language acquisition, this process is described as *apperception*, and the process of focusing attention on certain aspects of the target language is often referred to as *noticing* (Schmidt, 1990). Influenced by Vygotsky's (1996) concept of the zone of proximal development (ZPD), second-language acquisition theory suggests that learners acquire language best by reading or listening to material that is just beyond their current levels of competence (Krashen, 1982). Krashen calls linguistic material *comprehensible input* when it is one step (i + 1) above students' current levels of competence (i), in which case more aspects of the input can be noticed, and, as a result, the acquisition of the language is more likely (Doughty, 1991).

In order to facilitate the acquisition of a second language, multimedia can be used to enhance the input and increase the likelihood of noticing. Strategies involving multimedia that have been used for the support of noticing include highlighting or otherwise marking words, sentences, and linguistic features, often in conjunction with providing comprehension aids in the form of multimedia annotations and pairing words with images. Input enhancers for aural input that use multimedia include the use of captioned text, nonverbal cues (e.g., supplemental video images), instant feedback to listening tasks, and repetitions of the audio input.

Early research on vocabulary learning with text and pictures has consistently found an input enhancement effect that resulted in better retention of vocabulary words when they were paired with pictures, a finding that led to the development of the dual-coding theory (Deno, 1968; Paivio, Clark, & Lambert, 1988; Paivio & Desrochers, 1979). In some cases, retention was increased when the pictorial presentation of the word was displayed before the written presentation (Brown, 1993).

For written input in reading comprehension, enhancement has been provided in the form of annotations for vocabulary items in the text. In order to show that annotations are available, words or sentences are often marked or highlighted. Although simple highlighting may not necessarily result in better vocabulary acquisition (De Ridder, 2002), the highlighting of words in conjunction with multimedia glosses has facilitated both vocabulary acquisition and reading comprehension (Chun & Plass, 1996a, 1996b; Laufer & Hill, 2000; Liu & Reed, 1995; Lyman-Hager, Davis, Burnett, & Chennault, 1993; Omaggio, 1979; Plass

et al., 1998), although in one case students appeared to prefer to look up the English translations instead of using multimedia annotations (Davis & Lyman-Hager, 1997).

Aural input in listening comprehension can be enhanced through dynamic visual information. Research has found, for example, that video is able to support the processing of linguistic information and facilitate language comprehension (Neuman & Koskinen, 1992; Sharp, Bransford, Goldman, & Risko, 1995) as well as vocabulary acquisition (Duquette & Painchaud, 1996). Hernandez (2004) conducted a systematic study of different presentation modes for comprehensible input in listening comprehension. In this research with students of English second language (ESL), scenes from a feature movie were presented either as audio (narration) only, as audio with captions, audio with video, or audio with video and captions. No differences were found among the four groups in vocabulary acquisition. However, groups receiving video (audio with video, or audio with video and captions) comprehended the narration better than those who did not, an effect that was stronger for learners with high-spatial ability than for those with low-spatial ability. The results of this study emphasize the importance of considering presentation modes other than text for providing and enhancing input. Other research has found that providing instant feedback to comprehension test items during listening tasks (Brett, 1997) and exact repetitions of the auditory input (Jensen & Vinther, 2003) can also serve as input enhancers.

Interactive Processing: Organizing/Comprehension

Once visual and verbal material has been selected or noticed, it needs to be organized into visual mental representations and verbal mental representations. Part of this process is to connect words to form a verbal model and to connect images to form a pictorial model. In second-language acquisition, these processes focus on understanding the semantic content of the input and forming a verbal model that also may include syntactic information, and developing a pictorial model that includes linguistic as well as nonlinguistic pictorial information.

Interactive processing theory (Kim, 2002; Samuels & Kamil, 1984; Silberstein, 1987; Swaffar, Arens, & Byrnes, 1991) is a popular approach to describe the process of organizing in the context of reading and listening comprehension. Interactive processing includes lower-level (bottom-up) strategies that emphasize words, structures and sounds, and higher-level (top-down) strategies that promote visualization or inferential strategies. Beginning second-language learners, for example, focus primarily on word identification or bottom-up processing in listening and reading activities. More proficient second-language learners use the available textual clues to confirm but also predict information about the text (Fischer & Farris, 1995). Within interactive processing, meaningful interaction with the material is essential in order to help students construct meaning, especially when learners' prior knowledge of a text is low (Faerch and Kaspar, 1986). Multimedia-based strategies to facilitate such interaction include providing multimedia annotations for vocabulary words and providing learners with a degree of control over the environment that allows them to meaningfully interact with the material according to their needs and styles.

As part of the interaction and meaning-making process, learners who are engaged in input processes such as reading and listening learn vocabulary incidentally, or as a by-product of their goal to comprehend the input (Hulstijn, 1992; Hulstijn, Hollander, & Greidenhaus, 1996; Yoshii & Flaitz, 2002). However, if the input is too challenging, learners may incidentally learn words incorrectly (Hulstijn, 1992; Yoshii & Flaitz, 2002). In order to prevent this, researchers have examined the use of various interactive strategies, such as providing marginal glosses, to assist learners in vocabulary acquisition as they read a paper-based text (Hulstijn et al., 1996; Kost, Fost, & Lenzini, 1999; Watanabe, 1997).

The use of annotations, or glosses, as an interactive processing strategy has more recently been applied to multimedia learning environments, and research on their effectiveness is one of the most widely studied topics in the context of second-language acquisition with multimedia. Several of our own studies (Chun & Plass, 1996a, 1996b; Jones, 2001; Jones & Plass, 2002; Plass et al., 1998; Plass, Chun, Mayer, & Leutner, 2003) have explored the use of annotations in second-language multimedia environments for reading and listening comprehension. These studies investigated how the availability of visual and verbal annotations for vocabulary items in the text facilitates vocabulary acquisition as well as the comprehension of a foreign language literary text. We found that especially the availability of picture annotations facilitated vocabulary acquisition, and that vocabulary words learned with picture annotations were better retained than those learned with textual annotations (Chun & Plass, 1996a). Our research showed in addition that incidental vocabulary acquisition and text comprehension was best for words where learners looked up both picture and text annotations (Plass et al., 1998).

Other researchers have replicated these studies and extended them to other learners, settings, and languages. Al-Seghayer (2001) compared the effect of glosses that contained text and pictures with glosses that contained text and video and found that the words annotated with glosses that included video were retained better. Yoshii & Flaitz (2002) examined the effects of different annotation types in the form of text, pictures, and a combination of the two in a multimedia-based reading comprehension activity on ESL students' vocabulary learning. Their results of both immediate and delayed tests showed that definitions for keywords in the form of both text and pictorial annotations led to better vocabulary learning than did the single annotations. However, pictorial annotations led to greater results on pictorial and written vocabulary recognition tests than did text annotations while text annotations lead to greater results on the production test than did pictorial annotations.

Jones and Plass (2002) investigated similar questions in the context of listening comprehension by providing students with a choice of pictorial and written verbal annotations for vocabulary in a listening text. They found that students recalled more vocabulary and remembered more ideas from the text when they chose both verbal and visual annotations for unknown words. However, results of delayed vocabulary and comprehension tests showed that, over time, the effect of visual annotations decayed much less than the effect of verbal annotations, emphasizing the importance of visual input in listening comprehension.

A controversial question related to providing annotations in a second-language text is whether or not these annotations should include translations in the learner's first language. Advocates of a communicative approach reject any such translations (Krashen, 1982, 1988; Underwood, 1984), citing that the need to infer meaning from context promotes a higher investment of mental effort, deeper processing, and, thus, deeper learning (Craik & Lockhart, 1972). Grace (1998) empirically examined this question in the context of French vocabulary acquisition in a multimedia environment with dialogues from a French comic books series. In addition to providing images, sound, and text annotations to all learners, one group received sentence-level translations of the dialogue, whereas the control group did not. Grace found in both immediate and delayed tests that interaction with these multimedia components resulted in increased vocabulary knowledge for both groups. Further, learners who received translations remembered significantly more words than learners who did not. These results, obtained with beginning-level students, indicate that, especially for novices, translations may be helpful as input enhancers.

Another issue that is relevant for interactive processing is the level of control over the order and pace as well as choice of materials that learners are afforded in a multimedia environment. A study by Yeh and Lehman (2001) provided students of English foreign language (EFL) with a range

of 7–10 years of previous English instruction with identical reading materials about historical events in the Middle East in two treatment groups. In the learner-controlled condition, students were able to review and access helpful material as needed. In the program-controlled condition, students had a predefined pace and sequence of the instruction. Results showed that students who could freely interact with the material and access information as desired recalled more ideas from the text than learners who did not have control over pace and order. In addition, learners with less-efficient English-learning strategies performed significantly worse in the program-controlled condition than in the learner-controlled condition, whereas learners with more efficient strategies did not differ. Yeh and Lehman (2001) argue that learner control provides students with the opportunity to interact with the materials to construct meaning, and that this interaction is especially necessary for students with less efficient learning strategies. However, learner control research has received much criticism (Reeves, 1993), and the preceding findings should be further investigated as they are in contrast to research conducted in other areas, where results have shown that low prior-knowledge learners need guidance and structure in multimedia learning environments and that only advanced users are able to navigate such systems without such guidance (Lawless & Brown, 1997).

We investigated a similar issue in our own research where we conducted two studies on the use of annotations while reading a German text. In one study, learners had the choice of selecting visual and/or verbal annotations for unknown vocabulary (Plass et al., 1998). In another study, learners were assigned to treatment conditions in which they had to view visual annotations, verbal annotations, or visual and verbal annotations. The control group received no annotations (Plass et al., 2003). Our research showed that learning environments that provide a choice of visual and verbal annotations equally supported visualizers and verbalizers in their different learning preferences. We found that these two types of learners did not differ in their overall vocabulary acquisition, but that they used different types of annotations during the reading process, and corresponding different cues to retrieve the translations for vocabulary words during the test (Plass et al., 1998). However, when instead of giving them a choice, learners were assigned to use either visual or verbal annotations or both, learners with low-verbal or low spatial ability who had to learn from visual annotations experienced higher cognitive load and remembered fewer words than learners with high verbal ability or high spatial ability. Independent of their abilities, learners assigned to receive only visual annotations comprehended the text less well (Plass et al., 2003). These results indicate that annotations meant to enhance the linguistic input need to be designed with care and suggest that learners should have control over the learning environment, with the option to view annotations rather than have them displayed by default.

A different type of interaction takes place between the individual, his or her prior knowledge, and the text. Pica, Doughty, and Young (1986) and Doughty (1991) suggest that the interactive nature of multimedia, when under a learner's control, mimics real-life interaction, in particular when one requests clarification, checks for comprehension, or strives to confirm or understand the topic at hand. This interaction will be reviewed next, when we discuss the process of integrating information.

Intake/Integration

Once incoming information has been organized into verbal and pictorial mental models, referential connections between these models need to be established, that is, the verbal and pictorial mental representations need to be integrated. Although all of the processes described in this model require cognitive resources, the integration of the representations into a coherent mental model is the most demanding process because it also involves the retrieval and processing of prior knowledge with which

the incoming information is integrated (Mayer, 2001).

In the acquisition of a language, the comprehension of the linguistic input, involving both semantic and syntactic processing, has as its result what is often referred to as *intake*, that is, "comprehended language that holds the potential for developing the learners' linguistic system" (Chapelle, 1998, p. 23). The process of integration involves the development of the linguistic system based on the intake, which, in the case of multimedia learning, is comprised of verbal and pictorial components.

Multimedia-based approaches employed to support the integration of newly acquired information with prior knowledge include the use of advance organizers (Ausubel, 1968). Providing introductory material in advance of the learning materials, and thereby activating existing prior knowledge, enables students to more successfully comprehend the input they receive in a reading or a listening environment. For second-language acquisition, studies have consistently found that advance organizers in the form of questions, statements, images, brainstorming, or video have helped students to grasp the concepts presented in the material that followed (Hanley & Cole, 1995; Herron, 1994, 1995; Herron, Hanley, & Cole, 1995; Herron, York, Cole, & Linden, 1998; Teichert, 1996). For example, Herron (1994) found that asking students to watch a video without providing precursor information was not sufficient for comprehending a second-language video. Instead, advance organizer information in the form of several short sentences, written in French, that summarized the principle scenes of the video greatly helped students to process a video and many associated concepts found throughout each scene of the video. Herron et al. (1998) further examined advance organizers in the form of declarative and interrogative phrases. Prior to reviewing the video, separate treatment groups heard either declarative phrases that represented information within the video or heard interrogative forms of these same declarative phrases. No significant differences were found between those who received either form of advance organizers. However, when no advance organizer information was provided, learning was less likely.

In their study of reading comprehension in a multimedia environment, Plass et al. (1998) provided learners with an advance organizer in the form of a two-minute video. Some of the propositions in the text were included in this video while others were not. Propositions that were depicted in the video were recalled significantly better than those that were not. In addition, visualizers recalled significantly fewer propositions that were not illustrated in the video than verbalizers. However, their recall for propositions that were included in the video did not differ.

Other research with learners of English as a foreign language (EFL) has found that students who received an advance organizer in the form of a text paragraph better comprehended the input they received from an interactive videodisc application than students who did not, regardless of their level of efficiency of English learning strategies and their level of program control (Yeh & Lehman, 2001). Additional research has shown that when advance organizers include pictures and text, students acquire more from the materials that follow than when they only include text (Herron et al., 1995).

Comprehensible Output

Comprehensible output (Swain, 1985) is a concept unique to second-language acquisition that describes the need for use of language in meaningful contexts to develop the learners' communicative competency. Thus, understanding of input is not enough; learners must also be given the opportunity to produce comprehensible output, such as conversational exchanges, that extend "the linguistic repertoire of the learner as he or she attempts to create precisely and appropriately the meaning desired" (Swain, 1985, p. 252). Swain's view is that comprehensible output is meant "to provide opportunities for contextualized, meaningful use, to test out hypotheses about the target language,

and to move the learner from a purely semantic analysis of the language to a syntactic analysis of it" (p. 252). Swain and Lapkin (1995) extend this argument by stating that learners will become more aware of linguistic problems brought to their attention by some form of external feedback and that this notification of a problem will "push" learners to modify their output. Noticing the gap leads them to produce modified output and to integrate their new knowledge into their current knowledge. Thus, meaningful interaction with output can enhance second-language acquisition just as much as input can.

Numerous researchers have examined how learners can modify their comprehensible output to make it more understandable and accurate for the listener (e.g., Lyster & Ranta, 1997; Pica, 1988, 1994; Swain, 1997; Van de Branden, 1997). Negotiation of meaning was found to be particularly important to help students modify their output because it allows for corrective feedback that encourages self-correction, which then leads to more precise output rather than just simple comprehension. Numerous studies, in fact, have shown that when students are asked to clarify incomprehensible remarks by native speakers, they self-correct their errors and thus attain a higher level of accuracy in their comprehensible output (e.g., Nobuyoshi & Ellis, 1993; Pica, 1988). Shehadeh (1999) further explored this issue by examining students' abilities to modify their comprehensible output using different types of communicative tools such as picture-dictation tasks and opinion-exchange tasks and clarification prompts by native versus nonnative speakers. Shehadeh found that the picture-dictation task provided for a greater proportion of modified comprehensible input than did the opinion-exchange task. He also found that the frequency of modified comprehensible output supported the importance of including this type of output as a part of second-langauge acquisition.

Multimedia can be used to provide such a meaningful context, that is to facilitate communication, and to act as a partner in this communication (Chapelle, 1998) by helping students notice their errors, revise their output to correct these errors, and by engaging them in a conversation in order to achieve a stated goal. Second-language educators have been using video, online communication, Web-based authentic materials in the target language, and speech recognition to elicit meaningful output with much success in the classroom (Bernstein, Najimi, & Ehsani, 1999; Chun, 2001; Herron, Dubreil, Cole, & Corrie, 2000; Lee, 1998; Nelson, & Oliver, 1999). However, few studies have investigated the issue of comprehensible output empirically within a multimedia environment, and these studies did not fully implement the communicative approach discussed in the preceding text. In her study of the effectiveness of annotations in listening comprehension, Jones (2004) used different types of vocabulary tests to examine students' vocabulary acquisition. One vocabulary test subscale employed test items based on recognition of words and recognition of pictures, another employed test items consisting of recall of words. The results of this research showed that the teaching mode (visual or verbal annotation available) did not affect performance on either the pictorial or written recognition subscale, but that on the verbal recall subscale, learners who had received pictorial annotations did not perform as well as learners who had received verbal annotations or both types of annotations. These results suggest that in multimedia learning environments, teaching modes and test modes should be compatible, and that testing should not be conducted using textual items only when the instruction involved pictures.

Borras and Lafayette (1994) examined students' abilities to produce comprehensible output when exposed to a French video with subtitles. They found that when subtitles were provided with the video, students not only comprehended the input better than when subtitles were absent but also produced superior comprehensible communicative output than did those without the helpful text aid.

Nikolova (2002) conducted a study to test elements of Channell's (1988) theory that second-language learners will acquire more vocabulary when they are engaged in developing lexical associations as they encounter new vocabulary. She examined the output of learners as a result of either learning from a computerized text that contained sound, text, and images as annotations, or of being asked to develop their own multimedia annotations. Nikolova found that students who developed their own annotations recalled words from the text better when time on task was not considered than groups that received premade annotations. However, when time on task was included in the analysis, group differences disappeared. She concluded that, although students' vocabulary acquisition benefited from the development of their own multimedia materials, additional time is required because of the creative activity itself.

Limitations of Existing Research on Second-Language Acquisition with Multimedia

Over the past decade, research on second-language acquisition with multimedia has significantly expanded our knowledge of how multimedia can enhance students' second-language development. Despite this progress, limitations exist in the present research that stem from problems with the research design and implementation and from limitations within the areas of second-language acquisition that have been investigated.

With regard to the design of empirical studies, researchers in second-language acquisition with multimedia are faced with the challenging task of conducting their investigations in authentic settings in which the language is acquired in natural communication, while at the same time employing rigorous research designs that can provide results that are meaningful and relevant. The study of language acquisition during natural communication does not readily allow for the use of rigorous quantitative designs, and studies that did try to employ quantitative methods in unaltered natural settings tended to be forced to employ suboptimal designs that led to a limited validity of the findings. Research design problems observed in this context reveal that some studies did not include useful control groups, did not assign participants to treatment groups randomly, did not control for confounding variables, used outcome measures with limited reliability and validity, and employed sample sizes that were too low for meaningful analysis of the results. In order to avoid these problems, researchers must either conduct studies of a more experimental nature in less authentic settings, or employ research methodologies that are more appropriate to the study of language acquisition in situ.

The problem with specifying meaningful control groups is related to another research design issue we encountered repeatedly. Many studies of second-language acquisition with multimedia employed a media comparison approach, examining, for example, the effects of multimedia instruction versus standard classroom instruction. While such a research design might be useful in some very limited cases, any attempt to meaningfully compare the effectiveness of different media in a "horse race" is bound to encounter such a significant number of variables that cannot be controlled for that the findings from such a comparison are all but meaningless (Clark, 1983). It appears to be far more useful to compare different treatment conditions within a particular medium.

Another area for improvement concerns the use of learning outcome measures. The typical measures used, such as recall protocols, cloze exercises, and production or recognition tests of vocabulary, represent what Myers (1990) refers to as *off-line measures* of the product of comprehension. Better examples can be found in studies that used measures such as think-aloud protocols and other language output strategies to assess learning, as done, for example, by Chun (2001), Lomicka (1998), and Wade, Buxton, and Kelly (1999). In addition, researchers have employed user-tracking software that, embedded in the learning environment, provides detailed information about students' actual behavior during the learning task that can be used to supplement performance data obtained using learning outcome measures (Leutner & Plass, 1998).

Problems related to the design of empirical inquiries can often be addressed by using a theoretical foundation from which to derive the research questions of the study. If such a framework is not articulated, or if frameworks are used that only focus on the second-language acquisition aspect of the materials and do not include multimedia learning theory, research designs often lack rigor in the missing area. We have therefore proposed the integrated model shown in Figure 29.3, which combines an second-language acquisition approach and a cognitive approach to multimedia learning. Based on this model, research questions can be derived that incorporate both aspects of second-language acquisition and multimedia learning and advance insights in both areas.

With regard to other limitations for existing research, we found that certain areas in second-language acquisition have received less attention by empirical researchers than others. One example is the study of listening comprehension in a multimedia environment, which has received very little attention to date (Brett, 1995, 1997; Hernandez, 2004; Jones, 2004; Jones & Plass, 2002). Because listening comprehension is considered to be the foundation of language learning that leads to more productive reading, writing, and speaking skills (Feyten, 1991; Joiner, 1986), this area of second-language development should be more closely examined in a multimedia environment.

Another area that lacks investigation is that of comprehensible output. Typical research studies in second-language acquisition with multimedia assess output of language competence obtained after interaction with an second-language acquisition multimedia environment, but do not provide students with an opportunity to adjust their output based on interaction and feedback. This is very much counter to Chapelle's (1997) argument that interaction is crucial to supporting both comprehensible input and comprehensible output. If, for example, students were allowed to recheck their knowledge after additional interaction with the material as suggested by feedback, the study of the original and the revised output could be very useful for understanding the processes of language acquisition indeed.

A further issue is related to the materials used for empirical studies. Existing research has primarily been conducted with materials solely designed for language teaching, leaving open the question as to whether the findings obtained with these materials transfer to materials that were not specifically designed for learners of the language, such as target culture Web sites and videos that provide authentic language experiences to students. Although Kern's (1995) hallmark study on computer-mediated communication has established that collaboration and interaction in the second-language learning environment can promote language acquisition, little to no empirical research has been conducted to examine the learning in more authentic settings, such as multimedia-mediated communication or video conferencing, that engage students in direct communication.

A final limitation is that we have yet to see the results of the studies described so far implemented into large-scale multimedia and Web-based applications. There are, however, exceptions to this, including the multimedia-based materials published with some language textbooks (e.g., Amon, Muyskens, & Omaggio Hadley, 2000; Heining-Boynton, Cowell, & Torres-Quiñones, 1999) and, most notably, the development of the Web-based French language program *Français Interactif* (University of Texas, 2004). However, although anecdotal evidence rates these materials very high, no systematic research has been conducted to examine their effectiveness.

Implications of the Research for Cognitive Theory

The study of language and its acquisition has long been an important source for the development of cognitive theory (e.g., Johnson-Laird, 1988; Just & Carpenter, 1992; Kintsch, 1998). The study of second-language acquisition, however, introduces several variables, such as communication with other learners and authenticity of the language input. Most of the research that included these variables employed research designs that are less suited for the advancement of cognitive theory. In addition, the absence of models or theories combining second-language acquisition theory and cognitive theories of multimedia learning makes it even more difficult to find studies that incorporate both approaches. The implications for cognitive theory that we can derive from the research we reviewed in this chapter are therefore modest.

Predictions from the Cognitive Theory of Multimedia Learning (Mayer, 2001) that have been tested in the area of second-language acquisition are the *multimedia principle* and *individual differences principle*. For the multimedia principle, although some studies have shown the visual mode to be stronger than the verbal mode (Jones & Plass, 2002; Kellogg & Howe, 1971; Terrell, 1986), it is the combination of both visual and verbal presentations of information that has most strongly and consistently supported listening and reading comprehension and vocabulary acquisition (Chun & Plass, 1996a, 1996b; Jones, 2001; Jones & Plass, 2002; Plass et al., 1998). For the individual differences principle, second-language acquisition research with multimedia has found indications that by providing learners with the choice of using visual versus verbal annotations in support of a reading text, vocabulary acquisition can be equally supported for visualizers and verbalizers (Plass et al., 1998). When learners were assigned to treatment conditions with specific types of annotations, vocabulary acquisition was worse for learners with low verbal ability and low spatial ability compared to learners with high spatial ability and high verbal ability when they received visual annotations. Vocabulary recall did not differ for learners with different levels of verbal or spatial ability when they received verbal annotations (Plass et al., 2003).

However, it may be interesting to observe that some of the other multimedia learning principles that were found in the context of science learning are not likely to extend to the area of second-language acquisition without modification. For example, the *coherence principle* suggests that unneeded or irrelevant words reduce learning of scientific content and should therefore be removed from the text. This principle does not extend easily to second-language acquisition, where any meaningful linguistic input has potential value for the acquisition of the language, and where the relevancy of words cannot be as clearly established as for texts that describe scientific systems and their causal relations. Similar arguments can be made for the *redundancy principle* and the *modality principle* – reading and listening are two competencies that both need to be developed, and in many cases one is used as input enhancement for the other.

Implications of the Research for Instruction Design

The research described in this chapter offers a set of principles and recommendations for the design of instructional multimedia materials for second-language acquisition. These principles and recommendations are not meant to be prescriptions. They should be used with the context in which they were obtained in mind and with an eye on the specific characteristics of the materials and learners for whom materials will be designed.

Principles

Principles are research findings that are in line with research in other areas or existing principles (Mayer, 2001) and that have been found to apply in the context of second-language acquisition with multimedia.

MULTIMEDIA PRINCIPLE

Students acquire language better from input enhanced by text and pictures than by text alone.

The availability of text and pictures allows learners to construct verbal and visual mental models of the input and build connections between them. These connections provide learners with two types of cues for the retrieval of the learned material as compared to only one when they learn with text only.

Several research studies have consistently shown that performance is enhanced when visual and verbal annotations are provided rather than verbal annotations only (Chun & Plass, 1996a, 1996b; Jones, 2004; Jones & Plass, 2002; Plass et al., 1998). These studies show that vocabulary acquisition and comprehension were improved when aural or written input was enhanced by visual and verbal annotations.

INDIVIDUAL DIFFERENCES PRINCIPLE

Students acquire language better when they have the choice of visual versus verbal annotations than when they do not have this choice. The availability of materials in different presentation modes allows learners to choose those modes that correspond to their preferred learning style (e.g., visualizers/verbalizers). With additional information only displayed upon request, learners can manage the level of cognitive load they experience. In comparison, displaying additional information by default requires learners to process it to evaluate its relevancy for the comprehension of the materials, potentially causing higher cognitive load. To support the different learning styles and cognitive abilities in learners (Reinert, 1976), giving students opportunities to choose the processing mode (visual or verbal) in which they access supportive information may be the most effective strategy of learner support to employ in a multimedia environment (Jones & Plass, 2002; Plass et al., 1998). Research has shown that visualizers and verbalizers prefer to use different types of annotations and that they use different cues to retrieve learned material (Plass et al., 1998). Studies in which learners were not given a choice resulted in higher cognitive load, especially for learners with low verbal ability and low spatial ability, when they were assigned to view additional information in a visual format.

ADVANCE ORGANIZER PRINCIPLE

Students acquire language better when they view an advance organizer before receiving input in reading or listening activities. Advance organizers presented in visual and verbal modes are more effective than those presented in only the verbal mode. Advance organizers, presenting higher-level conceptual information and summaries as a prereading or a prelistening activity, allow learners to activate relevant prior knowledge and therefore to more easily integrate the new information into their linguistic system. Several research studies have consistently shown that any form of advance organizer will improve comprehension of a listening or reading activity (Herron, 1994, 1995; Herron et al., 1995, 1998, 2000). They also show that advance organizers presented using text and pictures are more effective than when they are presented in text format only (Herron et al., 1995).

Recommendations

Recommendations are research results that have not been replicated in more than a few studies and that do not extend findings from other areas to second-language acquisition with multimedia. Additional research is needed to show whether these recommendations can be replicated as principles that are specific to second-language acquisition.

LEARNER CONTROL

There is indication that students acquire language better when they have control over the order, pace, and choice of multimedia materials than when the order, pace, and choice are controlled by the computer (Yeh & Lehman, 2001). Providing learners with a choice of the order in which they proceed through a multimedia environment may allow them to manage the cognitive load they experience and the amount and sequence of input they process at any given time. This may be a finding specific to second-language acquisition where, unlike in science learning, the materials are not necessarily presented in an order that needs to be followed to assure comprehension. Giving learners, especially those with low language proficiency or less-efficient language-learning strategies, the choice to modify the input they receive, potentially making it easier to comprehend, may indeed facilitate the acquisition of the language. For example, learners may clarify more difficult passages by clicking on keywords to access translations and or pictorial representations. Instructional designers should consider the task requirements of the learning environment and learner characteristics such as language proficiency and efficiency of language-learning strategies when making a decision as to how much learner control to provide.

COMPREHENSIBLE OUTPUT

There is considerable research evidence that learners acquire language better when they are engaged in communicating in language, that is, in producing output, and especially when they are asked to monitor and analyze their own output and, if necessary, correct it (e.g., Lyster & Ranta, 1997; Pica, 1988, 1994; Swain, 1985, 1997; Swain & Lapkin, 1995; Van de Branden, 1997). When provided with appropriate feedback, for example, students can check their responses, seek further clarification and then present newly formed output that demonstrates their enhanced competence. However, research investigating how this interaction with learners' output can be facilitated in a second-language multimedia-learning environment is lacking.

APPROPRIATE TESTING

In addition to principles and recommendations related to the effect of multimedia on second-language acquisition, there is also evidence that the testing mode used should coincide with the mode of the annotations accessed in a multimedia environment (Chun & Plass, 1996a; Jones, 2004). This is particularly true when students are asked to produce in writing the translations of key vocabulary words. Recognition of vocabulary usually involves multiple-choice testing whereby learners guess or select the correct response from the list of words provided. On the other hand, recall or production tests demand the retrieval of vocabulary from memory. Such a strategy is more difficult because students are not provided with cues to retrieve the correct response from long-term memory (Cariana & Lee, 2001; Glover, 1989; McDaniel & Mason, 1985). When the multimedia-based annotated information provided does not coincide with the testing mode used in a production test, output of knowledge is hindered, which is not the case when the mode of the test items and that of the annotated information provided coincide.

Future Directions for Research

Our discussion of research on second-language acquisition with multimedia learning and the implications for cognitive theory and instructional design we provided in this chapter cannot be concluded without outlining some directions that future research can and should take. These recommendations fall into three principal areas. One area is concerned with finding better ways to exploit the potential of multimedia in second-language acquisition, for enhancing comprehensible input, facilitating meaningful interaction, and eliciting comprehensible output. A second area is related to measures used to assess language competence. The third area is concerned with the need for a stronger integration of second-language acquisition research with cognitive theories of multimedia learning and the investigation of principles found in fields such as the comprehension of scientific materials in the context of second-language acquisition (see parts 2 and 3 in this handbook).

Enhancement of Second-Language Acquisition Materials Through Multimedia

If published research is any indication of the kind of multimedia materials second-

language educators use in the classroom, then we must conclude there is still more promise than actual delivery of the potential of multimedia to enhance the second-language acquisition experience. In many cases where innovative uses of technology have been developed, the research necessary to understand the success of such uses has been lagging behind. There are several unanswered questions related to the use of multimedia to make input more comprehensible, elicit meaningful output, and facilitate learners' interaction with the input and output. Chapelle (1998) discussed some of these questions in the form of hypotheses for the development of computer-assisted language learning materials for second-language acquisition. Most of these hypotheses, published several years ago, have to date not been empirically investigated. For future research, an adaptation of her questions, related to the enhancement of second-language acquisition materials through the use of multimedia, can be summarized as follows:

Comprehensible Input
- How can multimedia be used to enhance noticing of relevant linguistic features of the input?
- How can multimedia help learners in comprehending the semantic and syntactic aspects of the input?

Comprehensible Output
- How can multimedia enhance learners' opportunities to produce output in the target language?
- How can multimedia help learners notice errors in their output and correct them?

Interaction
- What kind of multimedia-based second-language acquisition tasks can be provided that engage learners in interaction with language input and output?
- How can multimedia help learners modify the structure of the target language input to make it more comprehensible?

There are several areas of second-language acquisition where only little research has been conducted on the use of multimedia in general. For example, listening comprehension has only been investigated in few studies, and the production of meaningful output, although well-developed conceptually lacks empirical research in the context of multimedia learning.

Language Competence Assessment

Language educators are already using a diverse set of methods to assess language proficiency, and researchers should incorporate more of these measures into their studies. In addition to recognition tests or cloze tests for vocabulary and recall protocols for comprehension, researchers would gain deeper insights into the second-language acquisition process, if students' abilities to utilize newly acquired vocabulary were examined in communicative contexts and natural settings, as think-alouds and other authentic output. In addition, performance data should be enriched by observing learners' behavior during the learning process (Leutner & Plass, 1998).

Integration of Second-Language Acquisition and Cognitive Theories of Multimedia Learning

A final area for future research is the integration of second-language acquisition theory and cognitive theories of multimedia learning. For example, when designing multimedia materials for comprehensible input, the level of cognitive load induced by the input enhancement and the role this load may play in the acquisition of vocabulary and construction of meaning needs to be taken into consideration. We have proposed a model (Figure 29.3) that combines elements of second-language acquisition theory with elements from Mayer's (2001) cognitive theory of multimedia learning. Future research needs to investigate the specifics of this model and, in particular, to what extent effects and principles that were found in the context of science learning can be applied to second-language acquisition.

Glossary

Advance organizer: Introductory materials provided in advance of learning that are intended to activate or provide prior knowledge relevant to the learning material.

Annotations: Visual or verbal supplementary items, such as a translation or visual representations, that provide additional information for selected keywords present within the text.

Apperception: The process of selecting words and pictures to support interaction and thus attain comprehension of the material.

Authentic materials: Materials created for a native language audience, that have not been pedagogically designed for second-language learners.

Comprehensible input: Input that is made more understandable for students through the use of interaction with the target material.

Comprehensible output: Output that is modifiable for learners through identification of their errors and allowance for adjustments to previously submitted responses.

Incidental vocabulary learning: A process whereby students learn vocabulary as an aside as they engage in reading and listening.

Input: The process of receiving information, either verbally or visually.

Interaction: Use of any number of helping aids such as annotations, images, elaboration, simplification, clarification, definitional support, or redundancy to assist learners' comprehension of input or presentation of output.

Interactionist perspective: A language learning strategy that defines three functions that are deemed crucial to language acquisition, comprehensible input, interaction, and comprehensible output.

Interactive processing theory: A theory that refers to the interaction between the individual, his or her prior knowledge, and the input.

L1: The typical reference for the native or first language of an individual, sample or population.

L2: The typical reference for the second language of an individual, sample or population.

Language acquisition: The result of meaningful interaction in the target language where the focus is on communication and the acquisition of the language is incidental.

Language learning: The result of instruction about the target language.

Noticing: The process of focusing attention on input.

Output: The process of assigning meaning to visual or verbal input.

Propositions: Individual idea units present in a reading or a listening passage.

Spatial ability: A cognitive strength that is a relatively stable indicator of how well individuals can process visual stimuli. Learners with high spatial ability can process visual information better than those with low spatial ability.

Verbal ability: A cognitive strength that is a relatively stable indicator of how well individuals can process verbal information. Learners with high verbal ability can process verbal information better than can those with low verbal ability.

References

Al-Seghayer, K. (2001). The effect of multimedia annotation modes on L2 vocabulary acquisition: A comparative study. *Language Learning and Technology*, 5(1), 202–232.

Amon, E., Muyskens, J. A., & Omaggio Hadley, A. C. (2000). *Vis à Vis*, (2nd ed.) [Computer software, CD-ROM]. Boston: McGraw-Hill.

Atkinson, D. (2003). Toward a sociocognitive approach to second language acquisition. *The Modern Language Journal*, 86, 525–545.

Ausubel, D. (1968). *Educational psychology: A cognitive view*. New York: Holt, Rinehart, & Winston.

Bacon, S. (1992). Authentic listening in Spanish: How learners adjust their strategies to the difficulty of the input. *Hispania*, 75, 398–411.

Bernstein, J., Najimi, A., & Ehsani, F. (1999). Subarashii: Encounters in Japanese Spoken Language Education. *CALICO Journal*, 17, 361–384.

Borras, I., & Lafayette, R. C. (1994). Effects of multimedia courseware subtitling on the speaking performance of college students of French. *The Modern Language Journal*, 78(1), 61–75.

Brett, P. (1995). Multimedia for listening comprehension: The design of a multimedia-based resource for developing listening skills. *System*, 23, 77–85.

Brett, P. (1997). A comparative study of the effects of the use of multimedia on listening comprehension. *System*, 25, 39–53.

Brown, C. (1993). Factors affecting the acquisition of vocabulary: Frequency and saliency of words. In T. Huckin, M. Haynes, & J. Coady (Eds.), *Second language reading and vocabulary learning* (pp. 263–286). Norwood, NJ: Ablex.

Canale, M., & Swain, M. (1980). Theoretical bases of communicative approaches to second language teaching and testing. *Applied Linguistics*, 1(1), 1–47.

Cariana, R. B., & Lee, D. (2001). The effects of recognition and recall study tasks with feedback in a computer-based vocabulary lesson. *Educational Technology Research and Development*, 49(3), 23–36.

Chamot, A. (1995). Learning strategies and listening comprehension. In D. J. Mendelsohn & J. Rubin, (Eds.), *A guide for the teaching of second language listening* (pp. 13–30). San Diego: Dominie Press.

Chamot, A., & Küpper, L. (1989). Learning strategies in foreign language instruction. *Foreign Language Annals*, 22, 13–24.

Channell, J. (1988). Psycholinguistic considerations in the study of L2 vocabulary acquisition. In R. Carter & M. McCarthy (Eds.), *Vocabulary and language teaching* (pp. 83–96). New York: Longman.

Chapelle, C. (1997). CALL in the year 2000: Still in search of research paradigms? *Language Learning and Technology*, 1(1), 19–43.

Chapelle, C. (1998). Multimedia call: Lessons to be learned from research on instructed SLA. *Language Learning and Technology, 2*(1), 22–34.

Chomsky, N. (1957). *Syntactic structures*. The Hague, The Netherlands: Mouton.

Chun, D. M. (2001). L2 reading on the web: Strategies for accessing information in hypermedia. *Computer Assisted Language Learning, 14*(5), 367–403.

Chun, D. M., & Plass, J. L. (1996a). Effects of multimedia annotations on vocabulary acquisition. *The Modern Language Journal, 80,* 183–198.

Chun, D. M., & Plass, J. L. (1996b). Facilitating reading comprehension with multimedia. *System, 24,* 503–519.

Chun, D. M., & Plass, J. L. (1998). Ciberteca [Computer software, CD ROM]. New York: St. Martin's Press.

Clark, R. E. (1983). Reconsidering Research on Learning from Media. *Review of Educational Research, 53,* 445–459.

Craik, F., & Lockhart, R. (1972). Levels of processing: A framework for memory research. *Journal of Verbal Learning and Verbal Behavior, 11,* 671–684.

Davis, J. N., & Lyman-Hager, M. A. (1997). Computers and L2 reading: Student performance, Student attitudes. *Foreign Language Annals, 30*(1), 58–72.

Deno, S. L. (1968). Effects of words and pictures as stimuli in learning language equivalents. *Journal of Educational Psychology, 59*(3), 202–206.

De Ridder, I. (2002). Visible or invisible links: Does the highlighting of hyperlinks affect incidental vocabulary learning, text comprehension, and the reading process? *Language Learning and Technology, 6*(1), 123–146.

Doughty, C. (1991). Second language instruction does make a difference: Evidence from an empirical study of SL relativization. *Studies in Second Language Acquisition, 13,* 431–469.

Duquette, L., & Painchaud, G. (1996). A Comparison of vocabulary acquisition in audio and video contexts. *The Canadian Modern Language Review, 54*(1), 143–172.

Ellis, R. (1997). *SLA research and language teaching*. Oxford, England: Oxford University Press.

Faerch, C., & Kaspar, G. (1986). The role of comprehension in second-language learning. *Applied Linguistics, 7,* 257–274.

Feyten, C. (1991). The power of listening ability: An overlooked dimension in language acquisition. *The Modern Language Journal, 75,* 174–180.

Fischer, R., & Farris, M. (1995). Instructional basis of Libra. *IALL Journal of Language Learning Technologies, 28*(1), 29–90.

Gass, S. (1997). *Input, interaction, and the second language learner*. Mahwah, NJ: Lawrence Erlbaum Associates Publishers.

Glover, J. A. (1989). The "testing" phenomenon: Not gone but nearly forgotten. *Journal of Educational Psychology, 81*(3), 392–399.

Grace, C. (1998). Retention of word meanings inferred from context and sentence-level translations: Implications for the design of beginning-level CALL software. *The Modern Language Journal, 82*(4), 533–544.

Hanley, J. E., & Cole, S. P. (1995). A comparison study of two advance organizers for introducing beginning foreign language students to video. *The Modern Language Journal, 79*(3), 387–395.

Heining-Boynton, A. L., Cowell, G. S., & Torres-Quiñones, S. S. (1999). *¡Atrévete!* [Computer software, CD-ROM]. Fort Worth, TX: Harcourt.

Hernandez, S. S. (2004). *The effects of video and captioned text and the influence of verbal and spatial abilities on second language listening comprehension in a multimedia environment*. Unpublished doctoral dissertation, New York University.

Herron, C. (1994). An investigation of the effectiveness of using an advance organizer to introduce video in the foreign language classroom. *The Modern Language Journal, 78*(2), 190–198.

Herron, C. (1995). A comparison study of the effects of video-based versus text-based instruction in the foreign language classroom. *The French Review, 68*(5), 775–795.

Herron, C., Dubreil, S., Cole, S., & Corrie, C. (2000). Using instructional video to teach culture to beginning foreign language students. *CALICO Journal, 17,* 395–429.

Herron, C. A., Hanley, J. E. B., & Cole, S. P. (1995). A comparison study of two advance organizers for introducing beginning foreign language students to video. *The Modern Language Journal, 79*(3), 387–395.

Herron, C. A., York, H., & Cole, S. P., & Linden, P. (1998). A comparison study of student retention of foreign language video: Declarative versus interrogative advance organizer. *The Modern Language Journal, 82*(2), 237–247.

Hulstijn, J. (1992). Retention of inferred and given word meanings: Experiments in incidental vocabulary learning. In P. J. Arnaud & H. Bejoint (Eds.), *Vocabulary and applied linguistics* (pp. 113–125). London: Macmillan.

Hulstijn, J., Hollander, M., & Greidanus, T. (1996). Incidental vocabulary learning by advanced foreign language students: The influence of marginal glosses, dictionary use, and reoccurrence of words. *The Modern Language Journal*, 80(3), 327–339.

Hymes, D. (1972). On communicative competence. In J. B. Pride & J. Holmes (Eds.), *Sociolinguistics: Selected readings* (pp. 269–293). Harmondsworth, England: Penguin.

Jensen, E. D., & Vinther, T. (2003). Exact repetition as input enhancement in second language acquisition. *Language Learning*, 53(3), 373–428.

Johnson-Laird, P. N. (1988). *The computer and the mind*. Cambridge, MA: Harvard University Press.

Joiner, E. (1986). Listening in the foreign language. In Barbara Wing (Ed.), *Northeast Conference reports: Northeast Conference on the Teaching of Foreign Languages* (pp. 43–70). Carlisle, PA: Northeastern Conference.

Joiner, E. (1997). Teaching listening: How technology can help. In M. Bush & R. Terry (Eds.), *Technology-enhanced language learning* (pp. 77–120). Lincolnwood, IL: National Textbook Company.

Jones, L. C. (2001). Listening comprehension in multimedia learning: An extension of the generative theory of multimedia learning. *Dissertation Abstracts International Section A: Humanities and Social Sciences*, 62(2-A), 538.

Jones, L. C. (2004). Testing L2 vocabulary recognition and recall using pictorial and written test items. *Language Learning and Technology*, 8(3), 122–143.

Jones, L. C., & Plass, J. L. (2002). Supporting listening comprehension and vocabulary acquisition in French with multimedia annotations. *The Modern Language Journal*, 86(4), 546–561.

Just, M. A., & Carpenter, P. A. (1992). A capacity theory of comprehension: Individual differences in working memory. *Psychological Review*, 99, 122–149.

Kellogg, G. S., & Howe, M. J. (1971). Using words and pictures in foreign language learning. *Alberta Journal of Educational Research*, 17(2), 89–94.

Kern, R. (1995). Restructuring classroom interaction with networked computers: Effects on quantity and characteristics of language production. *The Modern Language Journal*, 79(4), 457–476.

Kern, R., & Warschauer, M. (2000). Theory and practice of network-based language teaching. In M. Warschauer, & R. Kern (Eds.), *Networked-based language teaching: Concepts and Practice* (pp. 1–19). New York: Cambridge University Press.

Kim, M. (2002). The use of the computer in developing L2 reading comprehension: Literature review and its implications. (ERIC Document Reproduction Service No. ED472671).

Kintsch, W. (1998). *Comprehension. A paradigm for cognition*. Cambridge, UK: Cambridge University Press.

Kost, C. R., Foss, P., & Lenzini, J. J. (1999). Textual and pictorial glosses: Effectiveness on incidental vocabulary growth when reading in a foreign language. *Foreign Language Annals*, 32, 89–113.

Krashen, S. (1982). *Principles and practice in second language acquisition*. New York: Pergamon.

Krashen, S. (1988). *Second language acquisition and second language learning*. New York: Prentice Hall.

Larsen-Freeman, D., & Long, M. (1991). *An introduction to second language acquisition research*. London: Longman.

Laufer, B., & Hill, M. (2000). What lexical information do L2 learners select in a CALL dictionary and how does it affect word retention? *Language Learning & Technology*, 3(2), 58–76.

Lawless, K. A., & Brown, S. W. (1997). Multimedia learning environments: Issues of learner control and navigation. *Instructional Science*, 25(2), 117–131.

Lee, L. (1998). Going beyond classroom learning: Acquiring cultural knowledge via on-line newspapers and intercultural exchanges via on-line chatrooms. *CALICO Journal*, 16, 101–121.

Leutner, D., & Plass, J. L. (1998). Measuring learning styles with questionnaires versus direct observation of preferential choice behavior in authentic learning situations: The Visualizer/Verbalizer Behavior Observation Scale (VV–BOS). *Computers in Human Behavior*, 14, 543–557.

Liu, M., & Reed, W. M. (1995). The effect of hypermedia assisted instruction on second language learning. *Journal of Educational Computing Research*, 12(2), 159–175.

Lomicka, L. L. (1998). "To gloss or not to gloss": An investigation of reading comprehension online. *Language Learning and Technology*, 1(2), 41–50.

Long, M. H. (1985). Input and second language acquisition theory. In S. M. Gass & C. G. Madden (Eds.), *Input in second language acquisition* (pp. 377–393). Rowley, MA: Newbury House Publishers.

Long, D. (1989). Second language listening comprehension: A schema theoretic perspective. *The Modern Language Journal*, 73, 22–30.

Lyman-Hager, M., Davis, J. N., Burnett, J., & Chennault, R. (1993). Une Vie de Boy: Interactive reading in French. In F. L. Borchardt & E. M. T. Johnson (Eds.), *Proceedings of the CALICO 1993 Annual Symposium on Assessment* (pp. 93–97). Durham, NC: Duke University.

Lynch, T. (1995). The development of interactive listening strategies in second language academic settings. In D. J. Mendelsohn & J. Rubin, (Eds.), *A guide for the teaching of second language listening* (pp.166–185). San Diego: Dominie Press.

Lyster, R., & Ranta, L. (1997). Corrective feedback and learner uptake: Negotiation of form in communicative classrooms. *Studies in Second Language Acquisition*, 19, 37–66.

Mayer, R. (2001). *Multimedia learning*. New York: Cambridge University Press.

McDaniel, M. A., & Mason, M. E. J. (1985). Altering memory representations through retrieval. *Journal of experimental psychology. Learning, Memory, and Cognition*, 11, 371–385.

Myers, J. L. (1990). Causal relatedness and text comprehension. In D. A. Balota, G. F. d'Arcais, & K. Rayner (Eds.), *Comprehension processes in reading* (pp. 361–375). Hillsdale, NJ: Erlbaum.

Nelson, T., & Oliver, W. (1999). Murder on the Internet. *CALICO Journal*, 17, 101–114.

Neuman, B., & Koskinen, P. (1992). Captioned television as comprehensible input: Effects of incidental word learning from context for language minority students. *Reading Research Quarterly*, 27(1), 95–106.

Nikolova, O. R. (2002). Effects of students' participation in authoring of multimedia materials on student acquisition of vocabulary. *Language Learning and Technology*, 6(1), 100–122.

Nobuyoshi, J., & Ellis, R. (1993). Focused communication tasks and second language acquisition. *ELT Journal*, 47, 203–210.

Omaggio, C. (1979). Picture and second language comprehension: Do they help? *Foreign Language Annals*, 12(2), 107–116.

O'Malley, J. M., Chamot, A., & Walker, C. (1987). Some applications of cognitive theory to second language acquisition. *Studies in Second Language Acquisition*, 9, 287–306.

Paivio, A., Clark, J. M., & Lambert, W. E. (1988). Bilingual dual-coding theory and semantic repetition effects on recall. *Journal of Experimental Psychology: Learning, Memory, and Cognition*, 14, 163–172.

Paivio, A., & Desrochers, A. (1979). Effects of an imagery mnemonic on second language recall and comprehension. *Canadian Journal of Psychology*, 33, 17–28.

Pica, T. (1988). Interlanguage adjustments as an outcome of NS-NNS negotiated interaction. *Language Learning*, 28(1), 45–73.

Pica, T. (1994). Research on negotiation: What does it reveal about second-language learning conditions, processes, and outcomes? *Language Learning*, 44(3), 493–527.

Pica, T., Doughty, C., & Young, R. (1986). Making input comprehensible: Do interactional modifications help? *International Review of Applied Linguistics*, 72, 1–25.

Plass, J. L., Chun, D. M., Mayer, R. E., & Leutner, D. (1998). Supporting visual and verbal learning preferences in a second-language multimedia learning environment. *Journal of Educational Psychology*, 90(1), 25–36.

Plass, J. L., Chun, D. M., Mayer, R. E., & Leutner, D. (2003). Cognitive load in reading a foreign language text with multimedia aids and the influence of verbal and spatial abilities. *Computers in Human Behavior*, 19(2), 221–243.

Postovsky, V. A. (1981). The priority of aural comprehension in the language acquisition process. In H. Wintz (Ed.), *The comprehension approach to foreign language instruction* (pp. 170–186). Cambridge, UK: Newbury House publishers.

Pusack, J., & Otto, S. (1997). Taking control of multimedia. In M. Bush & R. Terry (Eds.), *Technology-enhanced language learning* (pp. 1–46). Lincolnwood, IL: National Textbook Company.

Reeves, T. C. (1993). Pseudoscience in computer-based instruction: The case of learner control research. *Journal of Computer-Based Instruction*, 20(2), 39–46.

Reinert, H. (1976). One picture is worth a thousand words? Not necessarily. *The Modern Language Journal*, 60(4), 160–168.

Rost, M. (1990). *Listening in language learning.* New York: Longman Group.

Samuels, S. J., & Kamil, M. L. (1984). Models of the reading process. In P. D. Pearson, R. Barr, M. L. Kamil, & P. Mosenthal (Eds.), *Handbook of reading research* (Vol. 1, pp. 185–224). New York: Longman.

Schmidt, R. (1990). The role of consciousness in second language learning. *Applied Linguistics*, 11, 129–158.

Sharp, D. L. M., Bransford, J. D., Goldman, S. R., & Risko, V. (1995). Dynamic visual support for story comprehension and mental model building by young, at-risk children. *Educational Technology Research and Development*, 43(4), 25–42.

Shehadeh, A. (1999). Non-native speakers' production of modified comprehensible output and second language learning. *Language Learning*, 49(4), 627–675.

Silberstein, S. (1987). Let's take another look at reading: Twenty-five years of reading instruction. *English Teaching Forum*, 25, 28–35.

Swaffar, J., Arens, K., & Byrnes, H. (1991). *Reading for meaning: An integrated approach to language learning.* Englewood Cliffs, NJ: Prentice Hall.

Swain, M. (1985). Communicative competence: Some roles of comprehensible input and comprehensible output in its development. In S. M. Gass, & C. G. Madden (Eds.), *Input in second language acquisition* (pp. 235–253). Rowley, MA: Newbury House Publishers.

Swain, M. (1997). Collaborative dialogue: Its contribution to second language learning. *Revista Canaria de Estudios Ingleses*, 34, 115–132.

Swain, M., & Lapkin, S. (1995). Problems in output and the cognitive processes they generate: A step towards second language learning. *Applied Linguistics*, 16, 371–391.

Teichert, H. U. (1996). A comparative study using illustrations, brainstorming, and questions as advance organizers in intermediate college German conversations classes. *The Modern Language Journal*, 80(4), 509–517.

Terrell, T. (1986). Acquisition in the natural approach: The binding/access framework. *The Modern Language Journal*, 70, 213–227.

Underwood, J. (1984). *Linguistics, computers and the language teacher.* Rowley, MA: Newbury House.

University of Texas. (2004). *Français interactif.* Retrieved April 7, 2004 from http://www.laits.utexas.edu/fi.

Van den Branden, K. (1997). Effects of negotiation on language learners' output. *Language Learning*, 47, 589–636.

Vygotsky, L. (1996). *Thought and language.* (Alex Kozulin, Ed.). Cambridge, MA: MIT Press.

Wade, S. E., Buxton, W. M., & Kelly, M. (1999). Using think-alouds to examine reader-text interest. *Reading Research Quarterly*, 34(2), 194–216.

Watanabe, Y. (1997). Input, intake, and retention: Effects of increased processing on incidental learning of foreign language vocabulary. *Studies in Second Language Acquisition*, 19, 287–307.

Yeh, S., & Lehman, J. D. (2001). Effects of learner control and learning strategies on English as a foreign language (EFL) learning from interactive hypermedia lessons. *Journal of Educational Multimedia and Hypermedia*, 10(2), 141–159.

Yoshii, M., & Flaitz, J. (2002). Second language incidental vocabulary retention: The effect of picture and annotation types. *CALICO Journal*, 20(1), 33.

CHAPTER 30

Multimedia Learning of Cognitive Skills

Susanne P. Lajoie
Carlos Nakamura
McGill University

Abstract

Examples of multimedia learning situations using technology are described from the perspective of enhancing cognition. Implications for instructional designers are provided along with some future directions for this field of research. We see a need for multimedia research to foster higher degrees of interactivity with more varied types of media. More importantly, such research requires the inclusion of more scaffolding of learners, more attention to assisting learners in self-regulation, and perhaps media that serves in a pedagogical manner through coaching, pedagogical agents, and realistic environments that may include virtual reality dimensions. This new generation of multimedia will focus more on active knowledge construction through performing or doing some task with guidance.

Introduction to Multimedia Learning of Cognitive Skills

In examining the mores of today's society one cannot help but notice that higher demands are placed on an individuals' processing capability. In fact, daily expectations exist for people to attend and respond to multiple forms of information efficiently. Multimedia learning refers to the ability to learn from multiple representations, in particular, verbal and visual representations that are used to present an instructional message (Mayer, 2003). Verbal representations are defined as text, spoken or written, and visual representations as pictures, static or dynamic. Other researchers have extended this definition to include descriptions of the different functions multiple representations play in learning, that is, complementing or constraining learning, or helping learners to construct new knowledge (Ainsworth, 1999).

This chapter addresses multimedia in the context of learning situations using computer technology. There are several theoretical themes that we discuss. Most relevant to the argument is the dual-coding perspective and the need to consider broader explanations of why multiple representations support cognition. A spectrum rather than a dichotomy can be used as an alternate explanation from a semiotics perspective. Mental model building is described with respect to the relationships between multiple representations and how complex systems operate. Learning is discussed in terms of observing and interacting with media. Research limitations are described in an attempt to guide theory development in this area for future studies.

What Is Multimedia Learning of Cognitive Skills?

The design of computer-based learning situations in schools and in the real world has changed as rapidly as the technology itself. In parallel, theories of learning and cognition have evolved along with these technological advances. These transformations in technology and theory have led to changes in the descriptions of multimedia learning of cognitive skills. The early use of computers in education was somewhat stilted by the power of technology, where sophisticated animations and imagery tended to slow down an instructional system to the point of being nonproductive. Now, however, such issues are rarely a problem because the increasing speed of Internet connections allows people to see animations in close to real time. The seamlessness of computer advances have made the use of computers less daunting, to the point where many consider computers as cognitive tools that can be used in personal, school, and work-related activities.

Cognitive science has experienced a theoretical shift. Early work in the area of information-processing theory focused on the acquisition of knowledge, through the transmission of information. This approach has moved toward a constructivist approach where learners act upon information to construct their own meaning (Mayer, 1997). Similarly, early multimedia studies examined how learners acquired information through observing information through two modalities with the intent of learning more through two channels than through one. Now, however, the emphasis in multime-

dia research is with regard to how learners interact with information in different modalities and actively construct knowledge through performing actions rather than observing them. The interactive aspects of multimedia have been studied under specific labels such as *hypermedia* (Azevedo, Cromley, & Seibert, 2004; Linn, 1992; Salomon, 1998) or *interactive media* or *multimedia* (Hedberg, Harper, & Wright, 1997; Kumar & Altschuld, 1999). Our research falls into the latter category, where multimedia includes a variety of representations with which to interact and learn.

The Effects of Multimedia from a Dual-Coding Perspective

Mayer (1997, 2001, chapter 3) describes three underlying cognitive assumptions responsible for multimedia learning from an information-processing perspective: Dual-channel processing, limited memory capacity, and active learning. Dual-coding theory refers to dual channels for processing and storing visual and verbal information (Clark & Paivio, 1991). The assumption is that text is processed and encoded in verbal systems and pictures are processed both in the visual and verbal systems. Pictures may be remembered better than text because they are coded twice (Paivio, 1986). However there are limits to the amount of processing that can be done in each channel (Baddeley, 1992). Meaningful learning occurs when learners have to actively process information, that is, when they integrate both words and pictures into a meaningful construction (Wittrock, 1989). Thus, in addition to learning through two modalities an integrated frame of reference is created when working with information (Reimann, 2003).

Mayer (2001, 2003) found that under appropriate conditions multimedia learning enhances understanding and leads to transfer of knowledge to new situations. Good instructional methods work across media when they are based on theories of learning. Mayer found multimedia presentations are more effective than single medium presentations, in particular, words and pictures together are more effective instructional messages than either medium alone. These assumptions were tested with two mediums, words and pictures, and narrations and animations and the effects were found for both. Additionally, learning occurs more deeply from words and pictures than from words or pictures alone when certain multimedia effects were present. He refers to these multimedia effects as coherence, spatial contiguity, and personalization effects. In the coherence effect, placing irrelevant information into the text dilutes the instructional message and interferes with learning (Harp & Mayer, 1998). Perhaps coherence and complementary information serve a similar function. According to Ainsworth (1999) one function of multimedia representations should be to present complementary information and support complementary cognitive processes. Evidence of the spatial contiguity effect shows greater learning when words and pictures are closer together than farther apart, and that there is coherence between types of material presented. Finally, the personalization effect refers to learning more deeply when explanations are presented in a conversational rather then a formal style (Moreno & Mayer, 2000).

For the purpose of this paper, we are interested in multimedia environments that are computer based rather than book based.

Example Learning Situations

One theme that most exemplifies our approach to the study of cognition using technology is that of *cognitive tools* (Jonassen & Reeves, 1996; Lajoie, 2000, in press; Lajoie & Derry, 1993; Pea, 1985; Perkins, 1985; Salomon, Perkins, & Globerson, 1991). Cognitive theories drive the design of such tools in order to promote specific cognitive skills. Cognitive tools aid cognition through interactive technologies that help students during thinking, problem solving, or learning by providing them with opportunities to practice applying their knowledge in the con-

text of complex meaningful activities rather than in isolation of their ultimate use. Examples of theory-driven design from our research perspective are described in the following text.

Learning in Real-World Contexts: Externalizing Plans, Goals, and Actions

Before promoting problem solving through the use of technology one must first understand the problem-solving domain as well as individual differences in how problem solving occurs in specific contexts. The expertise literature helps guide the development of cognitive tools for learning in several ways. Expertise can be fostered by making the expertise trajectory visible to learners through modeling expertise, that is, through feedback or examples that promote the active transfer of knowledge and self-monitoring (Lajoie, 2003). Expert models of problem solving promote awareness, and realistic problem-solving activities can be designed based on detailed analysis of expert performance in the field. An example is provided in the following text.

A computer-based learning environment, SICUN, was designed for surgical intensive care unit (SICU) nurses by first examining how experts differed from novices in conducting patient assessments (Lajoie, Azevedo, & Fleiszer, 1998). A cognitive task analysis was conducted. Extensive interviews with three head nurses from an SICU unit revealed the most difficult aspects of their job performance. Patient cases were designed that incorporated these curriculum issues into the SICUN. Nurses were presented with these cases and structured think-alouds were collected that elicited the cognitive components underlying their decisions. These interviews were audiotaped, coded, and analyzed based on elements of clinical decision making. All nurses arrived at the same solution but there was variability in how they made their decisions. Frequency differences were noted in such things as hypothesis generation, planning of medical interventions, actions performed, interpretation of evidence, and overall solution paths.

Based on the empirical results of the task analysis, cognitive tools were designed so that trainees could be monitored on such characteristics in the context of on-line problem solving and presented with alternative perspectives for problem solving. Nurses interacted with SICUN by posting their goals before conducting patient assessments, performing actions, and specifying the outcomes of their assessments. SICUN used multiple forms of representations. First, tools for planning and goal posting were designed within the context of a real patient-assessment problem. Second, visual decision trees were dynamically generated when nurses wanted to compare their plans and actions with those of an expert. These visual representations (that included verbal descriptions) served to externalize models of expertise that foster metacognition and self-regulation within the SICU environment.

A formative evaluation of SICUN was conducted to validate the tutor with subject-matter experts and to test novice nurses. Data included problem-solving traces of nurses while solving the case as well as pre-post tests on trauma patients requiring assessment. Preliminary results reveal that from pre- to post-test nurses became more systematic in their patient assessments, indicating that making mental processes explicit to learners serves as an aid for reflection in ongoing knowledge development. However, more data are needed to make any global statements as to the effectiveness of the tutor. Other learning situations are provided throughout the remainder of the paper.

What Are the Limitations of Research on Multimedia Learning of Cognitive Skills?

In reviewing the literature on multimedia many of the studies focus on a common domain: physical systems. Multiple representations are commonly used to explain such aspects of physical systems, such as chemical reactions (Kozma, 2003; Wu, Krajcik, and Soloway, 2001) acceleration and braking (Mayer, 1989, 2001, 2003; Mayer & Gallini, 1990), and how lightning is created (Mayer, 2001; Mayer, Bove, Bryman, Mars, & Tapangco, 1996; Mayer & Moreno, 1998). Here, *system* denotes an "interacting or interdependent group of items forming a unified whole" as "a group of interacting bodies under the influence of related forces" (Merriam-Webster, 2004). According to this definition, a representation of a system is only complete when both elements and relationships between these elements are represented.

In an instructional situation, if a given representation fails to convey the system in its entirety, learning can be compromised. Mayer and Gallini (1990) found significant differences between a treatment and control group when representations describing how brakes work were presented. Findings supported group differences when both steps and parts were presented but not when steps or parts were presented alone. It appears that in addition to having more then one type of representation, the completeness of a set of representations is central to learning.

Kozma's (2003) studies of chemistry students and expert chemists also corroborate the systematization assumption. Expert chemists envision a system of representations where each representation can complement each other according to specific goals and tasks. Consequently, expert chemists do not have difficulty moving between representations and can easily select and construct representations that are the most appropriate to the task. On the other hand, chemistry students have difficulties in converting one type of representation into another. Kozma's studies show that the development of scientific proficiency greatly depends on the systematic understanding of all underlying elements and processes. It is not just the representations that are assisting higher-order thinking but the emphasis on how systems work that may foster the development of mental model building.

In addition to positive multimedia effects on learning there are situations that may hinder learning (Lowe, 2003; Schnotz & Bannert, 2003). Schnotz and Bannert (2003) state that pictures can affect the structure of the mental model inappropriately if they are difficult to interpret. Similarly, Lowe (2003) found novices might have more difficulty selecting relevant information from an animation because they do not have a strong mental model in which to anchor such information. Perceptually conspicuous information may take precedence over other material. Even when learners could control the speed of the animation they did not always grasp the salient information (Lowe, 2003). Dynamic visuals are not necessarily superior to static visuals with regard to recall and only slightly superior with regard to comprehension (Lewalter, 2003). Reimann (2003) cautions that animations used in instructional designs must be carefully constructed and aligned so that irrelevant visual cues do not distract novices from the main conceptual messages and that instructional support may be needed when using animations.

Technology provides a variety of multimodal presentations where the effects have yet to be determined regarding learner comprehension. It is time for research to extend beyond the text versus narration and pictures versus animations studies and move toward more complex embedded designs that present opportunities for examining learning processes within interactive problem-solving environments. The Internet supports such mechanisms but environments must be carefully designed to determine what is enough and what is too much information in these contexts. As multimedia tools become more commonplace, learners are doing more with multimedia presentations than simply observing them. Some learners are designing their own multimedia presentations, or interacting with the presentations to learn something through performing (Reimann, 2003). Researchers are coming from different paradigms (namely the information-processing and situated-learning perspectives) to instantiate different instructional designs for multimedia studies (Reimann, 2003). Reimann describes the cognitivist approach as one where external representations are transformed into internal ones (i.e., propositional networks, mental models, etc.). He describes the situated approach as less focused on cognitive residues of multi-

media and more interested in how the tools provide opportunities to construct their own external representations and perhaps use them as problem-solving tools. In the following section we explore the emergence of these two paradigms in the implications for further research.

What Are the Implications of the Research for Cognitive Theory?

Multiple Representations: Beyond the Dual-Coding Theory

A special issue of *Learning and Instruction* (2003) on the current state of academic research on multimedia highlights the magnitiude of Paivio's (1986) dual-coding theory, directly and indirectly, in explaining the effects of multimedia representations on cognitive processes. Many researchers (Mayer, 2003; Rieber, 2000; Schnotz & Bannert, 2003; Wu et al., 2001) have developed models that relate external to internal (mental) representations depicting a symmetrical relationship between text and pictures. According to these models, text and pictures are associated only when they have been converted to internal representations (see Figure 30.1).

In many instances, however, it is not easy to trace clear-cut differences between how

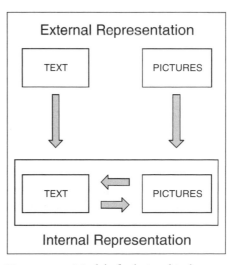

Figure 30.1. Model of relationship between external and internal representations.

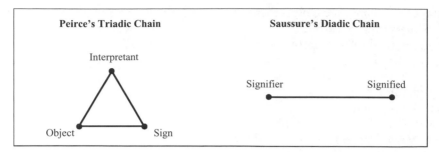

Figure 30.2. Triadic and dyadic models of signs.

people read text and pictures (or verbal and nonverbal signs). The study of multimedia and multiple representations can certainly benefit from a deeper investigation of the differences between verbal and nonverbal reading. One promising theoretical perspective that provides analytical tools for understanding multiple representations is Peirce's (1955, 1991) theory of semiotics. Peirce proposes that a triadic chain exists between a sign (or representation), an object, and an interpretant rather than a dyadic chain (Saussure, 1966) between the signifier and the signified (see Figure 30.2).

Peirce's triadic chain provides us with a more efficient tool to understand the differences between verbal and nonverbal communication (Moriarty, 1994). Peirce (1991) distinguishes between three types of signs: icons, indexes, and symbols. An icon resembles its object by mimicking some of its characteristics (e.g., a photograph). An index is a sign that is physically or causally connected to its object (e.g., footprints on the ground). A symbol is an arbitrary sign that only relates to its object by convention (e.g., the letters of the alphabet). From a semiotics perspective, verbal signs are symbols – arbitrary signs whose meanings are agreed upon convention. Pictorial signs are icons – "motivated" signs that resemble their object in some way (Moriarty, 1994).

Because the relation between a symbol and its object is conventionalized, the interpretant vertex of the triadic chain is attenuated. In verbal communication the association between the word *tree* and the entity tree should be immediate. On the other hand, the relation between an icon and its object is possible but not mandatory. A picture does not hold an unavoidable relation with the entity it depicts. Consequently, icons emphasize the relative weight of the interpretant vertex.

These arguments summarize the rationale of verbal and nonverbal communication from a semiotics perspective and are in harmony with most assumptions made in studies on multimedia and multiple representations. However, these postulates assume certain homogeneity in verbal and nonverbal communication that does not correspond to how people actually communicate. One can find many examples where pictorial signs operate symbolically as well as examples of verbal language being used in an iconic manner. Are the pictograms of a man or a woman on the doors of public restrooms icons? Are these pictograms supposed to convey a direct and unmistakable message? These signs, like words, have assumed conventionalized meanings. They are not supposed to incite subjective interpretation as, for instance, a painting in a museum. Their functional aspects demand a single and immediate interpretation. The same can be said about traffic signs. Despite their iconic nature, traffic signs convey very specific and conventionalized messages. So much so that no one is allowed to have a driver's license without having memorized these meanings (see Figure 30.3).

Conversely, verbal signs can often acquire iconic attributes that become more significant than their symbolic attribute. Metaphors are icons that hold a relation with their objects based on parallelism (Peirce, 1955). Hiraga (1994) elaborates on this idea

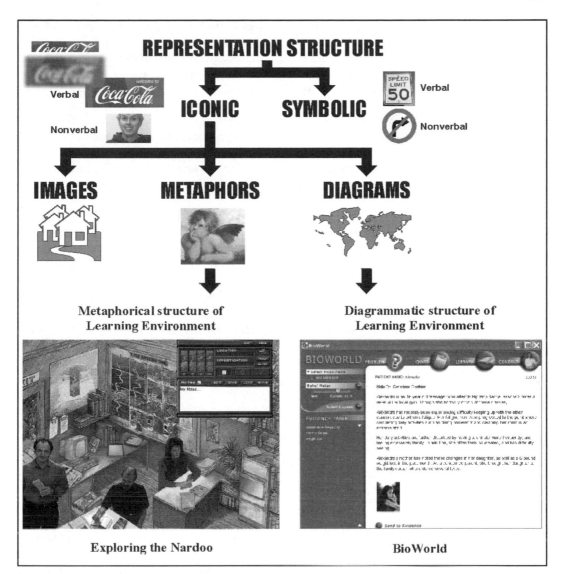

Figure 30.3. Semiotic perspective on representation structures.

with the following example: "Metaphors represent a parallelism in something else. A metaphorical icon (e.g., 'My love is a rose') signifies its object (e.g., 'my love') by pointing to a parallelism between the object (e.g., 'my love') and something else (e.g., 'a rose')." Logotypes also display how the iconic character of a word overshadows its symbolic character. Logotypes are designed to promote instant recognition, even in circumstances where the verbal message is compromised. For example, people are able to recognize the Coca-Cola logotype even when it is partially hidden or when they see

it from such a distance that they cannot actually read the letters (see Figure 30.3).

The above examples demonstrate that there is often contamination between verbal and nonverbal reading already at the perceptual level. In other words, we are constantly extracting verbal and nonverbal meanings from both texts and images. Consequently, a more adequate model of the interface between external and internal representations should take into consideration the permeability of verbal and nonverbal meanings (see Figure 30.4A). Alternatively, one may also propose a model where instead of a dichotomy between verbal and nonverbal signs, there actually exists a spectrum in which purely verbal and purely nonverbal signs are at the opposite ends. In this scenario, translations between external and internal representations may be traced at any angle between the two extremes (see Figure 30.4B).

Pierce further divides icons into three subtypes; images, diagrams, and metaphors (see Figure 30.3). Images reproduce some of the qualities of their objects (mimesis); diagrams reproduce the abstract structure of their object (analogy); and metaphors represent a parallel association between their objects and something else (parallelism). Although studies that focus on issues of multiple representations tend to take into consideration only images, the concepts of diagrams and metaphors are equally fundamental for understanding the role of representations in learning. Harper, Hedberg, Corderoy, and Wright (2000) argue for the strategic role of metaphors in learning environments in *Exploring the Nardoo* (see Figure 30.3). Their rationale is that students can roam through the multimedia resources, creating their own meanings and understandings of the phenomena they encounter. Information rich metaphorical landscapes provide different ways of viewing the multimedia experience where students interact with representations to conduct their own investigations.

Harper, Hedberg, Corderoy, and Wright (2000) tested these assumptions by providing two types of experiences for grade 9 students working with the learning environment *Exploring the Nardoo*. Students were divided into a structured problem group ($n = 10$) and an ill-structured problem group ($n = 12$). Using the environment, students in the first group were asked to investigate the causes of a weed infestation in the Nardoo River and then offer a solution. Students in the second group were asked to select a part of the river, identify a problem, and then offer a solution. Data consisted of daily student paper journals and electronic notes where they annotated their progress and future plans. The authors con-

cluded that, in general, the group of students responsible for the ill-structured task produced more complex and complete solutions. Students given the structured task did not try to find alternative explanations or identify other pertinent issues to the investigation.

Information-rich landscapes can help students understand the intrinsic structure of the domain and can be exemplified by diagrammatic icons as well as metaphors. The different sections or tools of a learning environment can be represented diagrammatically or metaphorically. BioWorld's "evidence table" (Figure 30.3) is an example of a cognitive tool that is largely diagrammatic (Lajoie, Lavigne, Guerrera, & Munsie, 2001). The evidence table is dynamically generated as students decide what information is important to attend to in the context of solving a patient case. The table is similar to an annotation tool in that students paste information from different sources (patient history, online library, laboratorial tests) into it. These postings help students self-regulate while trying to solve problems proposed by the learning environment. The evidence table has a verbal component (the title) and a nonverbal component (the rectangle that confines its field). The evidence table is nonverbal and iconic in a strictly diagrammatic way – it is a graphic representation but not a pictorial representation. BioWorld's interface is iconic in diagrammatic (e.g., page layout) and metaphorical ways (e.g., the picture of a book representing the online library), but the structure of the learning environment is communicated diagrammatically, not metaphorically. Moreover, representations that are at the same time nonverbal and nonpictorial (such as the rectangle in the evidence table) often can only exist within their own representation system. It only has a meaning and a function within the context of BioWorld's window. The way verbal and nonverbal codes operate in the evidence table example defies the boundaries of the dual-coding theory. Unlike the obvious relation that exists between, say, the word tree and the picture of a tree, there are no natural bonds to the nonverbal elements of

A   B

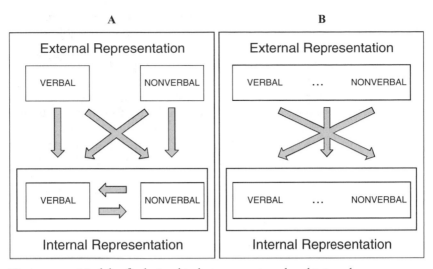

Figure 30.4. Models of relationship between external and internal representations.

page layout. Hence, we have to either accept that both verbal and nonverbal messages are being processed together or, if they are being processed through different channels, that a third message that connects the verbal and nonverbal messages must also be processed.

The dual-coding approach may not account for all nonverbal communication in learning environments. Studies of multiple representations need to further explore the notion of nonverbal representation. Computer icons and tools are different from conventional symbols[1] because icons and tools afford opportunities for direct action (Allen, Otto, & Hoffman, 2004). Allen et al. suggest that symbols within computer-based learning environments go beyond communicating or representing ideas, rather they are a means of carrying out activities. They suggest that graphical interfaces go beyond language communication toward interactive tools for pointing, dragging, pushing, and adjusting materials. Once again, the notion of representations pushing beyond visual and verbal representations toward actions with representations is supported.

The effectiveness of BioWorld has been tested in high school biology classrooms (Lajoie et al., 2001) as well as in comparable classrooms designed for students with learning disabilities (Guerrera, 2002) and recently

with medical students (Faremo, 2004). One focus of our analysis has been to examine which features of BioWorld are most conducive to learning. The features (i.e., patient scenario, online library, patient chart, evidence palette, and argumentation palette) embedded within BioWorld provide users with different learning opportunities. The patient scenario provides students with information that can be used as evidence to support a diagnosis. The depth of students' initial problem representations can be determined by examining the patient symptoms students select in the context of their hypothesis. The online library supports the acquisition of declarative knowledge by providing access to information about diseases, medical terms, and diagnostic tests. The patient chart supports procedural skill by allowing students to order diagnostic tests that can confirm or disconfirm their hypothesis. The evidence palette stores information students collect. The argumentation palette supports the posting of a scientific argument.

Our prediction was that students would become more expertlike in their use of information within each BioWorld feature. This prediction was tested in one study with 40 ninth-grade biology students (Lajoie et al., 2001). Student computer actions were dynamically stored in BioWorld. The dependent variables included frequency of symptoms collected, library entries made after making a diagnosis, evidence collected, diagnostic tests ordered, diagnostic accuracy, and the evidence contained in the first and final arguments. Teachers and physicians created indicators of competence for each BioWorld learning situation and student actions were compared to these benchmarks of performance (see Lajoie et al., 1995). Proportion of overlap of student actions with a predetermined benchmark (i.e., based on the types of plans and actions experts would take in specific problems) was computed for each of the variables in question.

A Pearson correlational analysis was performed to examine the relationship between students and expert actions for each feature. A significant correlation was found between proportion of expert symptoms collected during problem representation and overall evidence collected that was expertlike ($r = 0.59$, $p = 0.002$). The declarative knowledge acquired in the library was positively correlated with the proportion of expertlike diagnostic tests ordered ($r = 0.42$, $p = 0.04$). Hence, declarative and procedural knowledge as defined in this study were correlated. Furthermore, those who scored high on collecting expert evidence also scored highly on expertlike diagnostic tests ordered ($r = 0.49$, $p = 0.02$). These findings suggest that (a) initial problem representation, as identified by symptoms that students select as relevant to their current hypothesis, is related to the amount of expertlike evidence collected overall, (b) information collected in the library is related to whether or not appropriate diagnostic tests are taken, (c) the ability to select relevant from irrelevant information is indicated by the proportion of expertlike evidence collected as it relates to total number of symptoms entered, and (d) final arguments were examined in terms of expertlike evidence selected. Student dialogues during interactions support the computer trace data in that groups do use information from the disease library to form and revise their hypotheses about a patient's disease.

What Are the Implications of Research for Instructional Design?

There are specific issues that must be confronted when prescribing recommendations for instruction. Most importantly, multimedia and multiple representations must be considered in relation to the specific nature of the task being represented. For example, what combinations of representations best represent the task in question in the most complete and systematic manner? Instructors need to decide if the task would be more effective if students observed the phenomenon or interacted with the multimedia representations. Furthermore it is not simply the number of representations that increase learning but rather the completeness and coherence of the objects or systems being represented.

The purpose of the multimedia research might fall into three categories: problem representation, representation tool, and other cognitive tools. The problem-representation approach refers to studies in which the author examines the effects of combined forms of representation on the subjects' recall and/or problem-solving skills. Examples of this approach include Mayer's studies of multiple representations of the functioning of pumps and brakes (Mayer, 1989; Mayer & Gallini, 1990), the development of lightning storms (Mayer et al., 1996; Mayer & Moreno, 1998), and geographic time zones (Schnotz & Bannert, 2003).

The representation-tools approach refers to studies in which the author examines how experts and/or novices in different domains make use of multiple representations as tools to communicate with their peers and solve problems. Examples of this approach include studies on the differences between chemistry students and expert chemists in the use of multiple representations in science laboratories (Kozma, 2003).

The cognitive-tools approach refers to studies that examine the effectiveness of specific cognitive tools designed to support higher-order thinking within computer-based learning environments. The interactive and dynamic aspects of these tools are examined in terms of how such representations support learning (Reimann, 2003).

Regardless of which of the three approaches are utilized, consideration must be given to the nature of the relationship between multiple representations. Are representations designed to complement each other, constrain the knowledge building, or help learners construct deeper knowledge? What directions are multimedia tools designed to support? For instance, are they designed to support learners' internal representations by externalizing them? An example of this would be playing back the learners plans, goals, and actions in some form of decision tree. Or, is the goal of the multimedia to demonstrate external representations that will facilitate learners' internal knowledge building, as is the case when demonstrating how lightning is formed? Educators should be concerned about supporting both internal and external directionality. From a pedagogical perspective, the translation of internal to external representations and vice versa is what will foster the development of metacognitive skills specific to the domain in question.

Our bias is toward cognitive tools that will foster this bidirectionality. Tool representations can help externalize students' internal representations with the purpose of allowing them to assess their reasoning and problem-solving skills in contrast to an expert's representation. This comparison process can foster the internalization of more sophisticated mental models. By presenting learner's representations in contrast to an expert's solution, we can foster a trajectory of learning (Lajoie, 2003). Norman (1993) suggests that key elements of human cognition go beyond memory and ability to reason, and points to our ability to construct external artifacts and use them to compensate for our memory capacity. Another mechanism for learning in such environments is simply interacting in simulated real-world settings through interactions with the technology. Iconic and diagrammatic representations can be used to convey the structure of the entity they are representing. Such representations can promote an active learning situation through interaction as well as help in the construction of deeper understanding (Ainsworth, 1999). Metacognitive representation tools can be designed to induce students to reflect on their own reasoning by externalizing their internal representations. The importance of self-regulation in multimedia environments is beginning to be explored in systematic ways (Azevedo, 2002; Winne 2001; Winne & Hadwin, 1998).

Future Directions for Research

Given the complexity of the multimedia literature, as with all the literature on the effectiveness of technology in education, there are mixed results supporting and detracting from optimistic expectations. Finer attention must be paid to the approach supported by specific multimedia researchers in order to make appropriate comparisons of contentions and results in this area. Goldman (2003) suggested first- and second-generation uses of multimedia and we suggest a possible third generation.

The first generation of multimedia served to enhance learning through demonstrating the complexity of dynamic relations. Mayer's research specifically looked at the conditions that supported learning through the arrangements of verbal and visual information that highlight important relationships coherently, and manage information so that working memory was not overloaded. There are times that people fail to learn in multimedia situations and occasionally cognitive overload occurred when connections between representations were not made clear to the learners (Goldman, 2003).

The second generation has moved toward media-enabled affordances that support active processing of knowledge construction and reasoning. For instance, Kozma (2003) examines how multiple representations used by expert and novice chemists foster science understanding. He found that representational systems should have features that explicitly correspond to entities and processes underlying physical phenomenon. Whereas experts had no difficulty moving between representations novices had difficulty making the appropriate connections and identifying relevant information. A clear outcome of this type of research is the need for future research to more formally recognize individual differences when discussing the effectiveness of multimedia. Not all learners have the same amount of prior knowledge and hence have difficulty selecting the relevant from irrelevant information in these multiple external representations. Sometimes learners have difficulty in translating between representations (Ainsworth, 1999; Kozma, 2003). Whereas experts have the ability to benefit and use multiple representations to learn and express their understanding, novice learners often are lost due to their fragmented knowledge. Multimedia, in such cases, must have the appropriate scaffolds available to help new learners connect new knowledge to old knowledge, making the appropriate interconnections that will guide their personal theories within a specific domain of knowledge (Glaser, Lesgold, & Lajoie, 1987). Novices may have more difficulty with the nonlinearity of hypertext environments because their knowledge is fragmented and they may have difficulty making the necessary interconnections (Charney, 1987).

We see a need for a third generation of multimedia research that fosters higher degrees of interactivity with more varied types of media. This generation will require more scaffolding of learners, more attention to assisting learners in self-regulation, and perhaps media that serves in a pedagogical manner through coaching, pedagogical agents, and realistic environments that may include virtual reality dimensions. This new generation will focus more on active knowledge construction through performing or doing some thing with guidance. We believe that interactive multimedia and those that include immersive technologies are interesting directions for research (Reimann, 2003) but they are likely to place higher demands on learners to make important connections with their prior knowledge. Hence, greater scaffolding and self-regulation will be demanded (Azevedo, 2002; Winne & Hadwin, 1998). A special research issue on this topic is currently in preparation in *Instructional Science*. One future development for multimedia research is to examine the effectiveness of pedagogical agents. These agents come in different media forms that can be presented visually, either as a talking head, a virtual reality avatar, or cartoon, whose purpose is to guide the learning process (Clark & Mayer, 2003; chapter 31). They can also be represented verbally through machine-simulated voice, human-recorded voice or printed text. Pedagogical agents can be described in the context of a medium and a mediator. The medium refers to a channel of mediation whereas the mediator refers to an agent of mediation. In essence, a pedagogical agent is not generic; rather it lives within an instructional medium or context. Pedagogical agents are mediators because they have their own agency and act by scaffolding the learner when assistance is needed. There is evidence of success with this approach but still a need for future research (Greer et al., 2001; Moreno, Mayer, Spires, & Lester, 2001; Rickel & Johnson, 2000).

A related issue that needs to be developed is using sensory modalities in more creative ways to promote learning in multimedia environments. Eisner (1993), during his AERA presidential address, gave a most unusual multimedia presentation, using the poem Ulysses (Tennyson, 1870) as his anchor. Instead of just text and visual diagrams or animations, he used words, text, sound, music, and videos in contrasting contexts that had each individual in the room constructing their own understanding of the instructional message. What he did was bring an episodic and emotional perspective to learning, because each individual could connect to their own life and values associated with what they viewed in the message. Although this was not an empirical study this type of interaction with multimedia is personal and has the potential to both motivate and enhance one's memory for the message. Empirical research in this area is needed to determine how motivation and conative processes with cognitive processes might be realized through multimedia (Lepper, 1988; Snow, 1989).

Finally, virtual reality research has the potential to move multimedia research into a kinesthetic dimension. With the use of virtual reality gloves individuals can get a sense of manipulating objects, be they knobs on doors or using surgical tools to operate on a patient. How will using this modality transfer to learning in the real world? Research can also be conducted around issues of movement using technology. Consider how physical rehabilitation and sports training could benefit from technology that helps individuals reflect on their movement in a specific context, be it learning to walk again after an accident or learning to improve a golf swing. The power of technology has yet to be exploited in terms of externalizing an individual's physical actions by displaying them back to them through visual representations that document weaknesses or help them improve their skills by comparing their skills to more appropriate strategies. It is predicted that using such representations could positively improve physical skills by fostering cognitive reflection on physical abilities. Research in these areas is preliminary but the domains of sports medicine, kinesiology and sports psychology are beginning to address these questions.

Computer simulations also provide unique contributions to education. Simulation environments can eliminate risks to the learner or others in areas such as medical diagnosis or flight navigation. Simulations provide faithful reproductions of real situations and opportunities to practice decision making and problem solving in a safe venue (see chapter 33).

In conclusion, there are many untapped uses for multimedia and researchers have many exciting directions to pursue in terms of examining learning through and with multiple representations.

Glossary

Cognitive tool: Cognitive tools aid cognition through interactive technologies that help students during thinking, problem solving, or learning by providing them with opportunities to practice applying their knowledge in the context of complex meaningful activities rather than in isolation of their ultimate use. Cognitive theories drive the design of such tools in order to promote specific cognitive skills.

Dual-coding theory: Dual-coding theory refers to dual channels for processing and storing visual and verbal information (Clark & Paivio, 1991). The assumption is that text is processed and encoded in verbal systems and pictures are processed both in the image and verbal systems. Pictures may be remembered better than text because they are coded twice (Paivio, 1986).

Hypermedia: The combination of different types of media (e.g., text, images, sound, video) with hyperlinks. *Hypermedia* is also used to refer to multimedia environments containing interactive features.

Icon: Semiotics distinguishes between three types of signs: *icons*, *indexes*, and *symbols*. An *icon* resembles its object by mimicking some of its characteristics (e.g., a photograph). Icons can be further divided into *images*, *metaphors*, and *diagrams*. *Images* reproduce some of the qualities of their objects (mimesis); *diagrams* reproduce the abstract structure of their object (analogy); and *metaphors* represent a parallel association between their objects and something else (parallelism). (See also *sign*, *index*, and *symbol*.)

Index: Semiotics distinguishes between three types of signs: *icons*, *indexes*, and *symbols*. An *index* is a sign that is physically or causally connected to its object (e.g., footprints on the ground). (See also *sign*, *icon*, and *symbol*.)

Proposition: A proposition is the smallest unit of meaning that can be judged as either true or false.

Propositional network: Propositional networks are network-like graphic representations of propositions. Cognitive studies use propositional networks to represent declarative knowledge. In 1983 John R. Anderson proposed a cognitive architecture relating declarative and procedural knowledge through the use of propositional networks combined with production rules. (See also *proposition*.)

Semiotics: Semiotics is one of the normative sciences of the philosophical system proposed by Charles Sanders Peirce. It is commonly referred to as the science of signs. It concerns the study of all kinds of languages, verbal and nonverbal. Semiotics differs from Saussurean semiology in its conception of the basic structure of the communication process. While semiology is based on a dyadic chain of signifier and signified, semiotics is based on a triadic chain of sign, object, and interpretant. (See also *sign*.)

Sign: In semiotics, a *sign* is the representation of something by and/or for someone. The object of representation is called, what else, *object*. The logic that determines the relation between the *sign* and its *object* is called *interpretant*. Peirce's first classification of *signs* distinguishes between three basic types of signs: *icons*, *indexes*, and *symbols*. (See also *semiotics*, *icon*, *index*, and *symbol*.)

Symbol: Semiotics distinguishes between three types of signs: *icons*, *indexes*, and *symbols*. A *symbol* is an arbitrary sign that only relates to its object by convention (e.g., the letters of the alphabet). In semiology, the term *symbol* is the equivalent to the term *sign* in semiotics, see also *sign*, *icon*, and *index*.

Note

The authors would like to acknowledge the helpful input of Gloria Berdugo, Sonia Faremo, Nancy Lavigne, and Thomas Patrick.

Footnote

1. Allen et al. use the word *symbol* according to Saussure, which is equivalent to *sign* in Peirce.

References

Ainsworth, S. (1999). The functions of multiple representations. *Computers and Education, 33*, 131–152.

Allen, B. S., Otto, R. G., & Hoffman, B. (2004). Media as lived environments: The ecological perspective of educational technology. In D. H. Jonassen (Ed.), *Handbook of research on educational communication and technology, 2nd edition* (pp. 215–242). Mahwah, NJ: Lawrence Erlbaum associates.

Azevedo, R. (2002). Beyond intelligent tutoring systems: Computers as metacognitive tools to enhance learning? *Instructional Science, 30(1)*, 31–45.

Azevedo, R., Cromley, J. G., & Seibert, D. (2004). Does adaptive scaffolding facilitate students' ability to regulate their learning with hypermedia? *Contemporary Educational Psychology, 29(3)*, 344–370.

Baddeley, A. D. (1992). Working memory. *Science, 225*, 556–559.

Charney, D. (1987). Comprehending non-linear text: The role of discourse cues and reading strategies. *Proceedings of Hypertext '87* (pp. 109–120). Chapel Hill, NC: ACM.

Clark, J. M., & Paivio, A. (1991). Dual coding theory and education. *Educational Psychology Review, 3(3)*, 149–170.

Clark, R. C., & Mayer, R. E. (2003). *E-Learning and the science of instruction: Proven guidelines for consumers and designers of multimedia*. San Francisco: Jossey-Bass/Pfeiffer.

Eisner, E. (1993). Forms of understanding and the future of educational research. *Educational Researcher, 22(7)*, 5–11.

Faremo, S. (2004). Medical problem solving and post-problem reflection in BioWorld. Unpublished doctoral thesis, McGill University, Montreal, Quebec, Canada.

Glaser, R., Lesgold, A., & Lajoie, S. P. (1987). Toward a cognitive theory for the measurement of achievement. In R. Ronning, J. Glover, J. C. Conoley, & J. C. Witt (Eds.), *The influence of cognitive psychology on testing, Buros/Nebraska symposium on measurement, Volume 3* (pp. 41–85). Hillsdale, NJ: Lawrence Erlbaum Associates.

Goldman, S. R. (2003). Learning in complex domains. When and why do multiple representations help? *Learning and Instruction, 13(2)*, 239–244.

Greer, J., McCalla, G., Vassileva, J., Deters, R., Bull, S., & Kettel, L. (2001). Lessons learned in deploying a multi-agent learning support system: The I-help experience. *Proceedings of AIED'2001*, 410–421.

Guerrera, C. (2002). Testing the effectiveness of problem-based learning with learning disabled high school biology students. Unpublished dissertation thesis, McGill University, Montreal, Quebec, Canada.

Harp, S. F., & Mayer, R. E. (1998). How seductive details do their damage: A theory of cognitive interest in science learning. *Journal of Educational Psychology*, 90(3), 414–434.

Harper, B., Hedberg, J., Corderoy, R., and Wright, R. (2000). Employing cognitive tools within interactive multimedia applications. In S. P. Lajoie (Ed.), *Computers as cognitive tools, Volume 2: No more walls*. Mahwah, NJ: Erlbaum.

Hedberg, J., Harper, B., & Wright, R. (1997). Employing cognitive tools within interactive multimedia applications. In M. R. Simonson, N. Maushak, & K. Abu-Omar, (Eds.), *19th annual proceedings of selected research and development presentations* (pp. 67–75). Ames: Iowa State University.

Hiraga, M. K. (1994). Diagrams and metaphors: Iconic aspects in language. *Journal of Pragmatics*, 22, 5–21.

Jonassen, D. H., & Reeves, T. C. (1996). Learning with technology: Using computers as cognitive tools. In D. H. Jonassen (Ed.), *Handbook of research on educational communications and technology* (pp. 693–719). New York: Macmillan.

Jonassen, D. H. (2000). *Computers as mindtools for schools: Engaging critical thinking*. Upper Saddle River, NJ: Merrill.

Kozma, R. (2003). The material features of multiple representations and their cognitive and social affordances for science understanding. *Learning and Instruction*, 13(2), 205–226.

Kumar, D., & Altschuld, J. (1999). Evaluation of interactive media in science education. *Journal of Science Education and Technology*, 8(1), 55–65.

Lajoie, S. P. (2003). Transitions and trajectories for studies of expertise. *Educational Researcher*, 32(8), 21–25.

Lajoie, S. P. (Ed.). (2000). *Computers as cognitive tools (vol. 2): No more walls* (pp. 1–430). Mahwah, NJ: Lawrence Erlbaum Associates.

Lajoie, S. P., Azevedo, R., & Fleiszer, D. (1998). Cognitive tools for assessment and learning in a high information flow environment. *Journal of Educational Computing Research*, 18(3), 205–235.

Lajoie, S. P., & Derry, S. J. (Eds.). (1993). *Computers as cognitive tools*. Hillsdale, NJ: Lawrence Erlbaum Associates.

Lajoie, S. P., Lavigne, N. C., Guerrera, C., & Munsie, S. (2001). Constructing knowledge in the context of BioWorld. *Instructional Science*, 29(2), 155–186.

Lepper, M. (1988). Motivational considerations in the study of instruction. *Cognition and Instruction*, 5(4), 289–309.

Lewalter, D. (2003). Cognitive strategies for learning from static and dynamic visuals. *Learning and Instruction*, 13(2), 177–189.

Linn, M. C. (1992). How can hypermedia tools help teach programming? *Learning and Instruction*, 2(2), 119–139.

Lowe, K. K. (2003). Animation and learning: Selective processing of information in dynamic graphics. *Learning and Instruction*, 13(2), 157–176.

Mayer, R. E. (1989). Systematic thinking fostered by illustrations in scientific text. *Journal of Educational Psychology*, 81(2), 240–246.

Mayer, R. E. (1997). Learners as information processors: Legacies and limitations of educational psychologies second metaphor. *Educational Psychologist*, 31(3/4), 151–161.

Mayer, R. E. (2001). *Multimedia learning*. Cambridge, UK: Cambridge University Press.

Mayer, R. E. (2003). The promise of multimedia learning: Using the same instructional design methods across different media. *Learning and Instruction*, 13(2), 125–139.

Mayer, R. E., Bove, W., Bryman, A., Mars, R., & Tapangco, L. (1996). When less is more: Meaningful learning from visual and verbal summaries of science textbook lessons. *Journal of Educational Psychology*, 88(1), 64–73.

Mayer, R. E., & Gallini, J. K. (1990). When is an illustration worth ten thousand words? *Journal of Educational Psychology*, 82(4), 715–726.

Mayer R. E., & Moreno R. (1998). A split-attention effect in multimedia learning: Evidence for dual-processing systems in working memory. *Journal of Educational Psychology*, 90(2), 312–320.

Merriam-Webster. (2004). System. In *Merriam-Webster Online Dictionary*. http://www.m-w.com. (Retrieved on 08/15/2004).

Moreno, R., & Mayer, R. E. (2000). A coherence effect in multimedia learning: The case for minimizing irrelevant sounds in the design of multimedia instructional messages. *Journal of Educational Psychology, 92 (1)*, 117–125.

Moreno, R. Mayer, R. E., Spires, H., & Lester, J. (2001). The case for social agency in computer-based teaching: Do students learn more deeply when they interact with animated pedagogical agents? *Cognition and Instruction, 19*, 177–214.

Moriarty, S. (1994). Visual communication as a primary system. *Journal of Visual Literacy, 14(2)*, 11–21.

Norman, D. A. (1993). *Things that make us smart*. Reading, MA: Addison-Wesley.

Paivio, A. (1986). *Mental representations: A dual coding approach*. New York: Oxford University Press.

Pea, R. D. (1985). Beyond amplification: Using the computer to reorganise mental functioning. *Educational Psychologist, 20(4)*, 167–182.

Peirce, C. S. (1955). Logic and semiotic: Theory of signs. In J. Buchler (Ed.), *Philosophical writings* (pp. 98–119). New York: Dover.

Peirce, C. S. (1991). *Peirce on signs: Writings on semiotics by Charles Sanders Peirce* (J. Hoopes, Ed.). Chapel Hill and London: The University of North Carolina Press.

Perkins, D. (1985). The Fingertip effect: How information processing technology shapes thinking. *Educational Researcher, 14*, 11–17.

Reimann, P. (2003). Multimedia learning: Beyond modality. *Learning and Instruction, 13 (2)*, 245–252.

Rickel, J., & Johnson, W. L. (2000). Task-oriented collaboration with embodied agents in virtual worlds. In J. Cassell, J. Sullivan, S. Prevost, & E. Churchill. (Eds.), *Embodied conversational agents*. Boston: MIT Press.

Rieber, L. P. (2000). *Computers, graphics, and learning*. Madison, WI: Brown & Benchmark.

Salomon, G. (1998). Novel constructivist learning environments and novel technologies: Some issues to be concerned with. *Learning and Instruction, 8 (1)*, 3–12.

Salomon, G., Perkins, D., & Globerson, T. (1991). Partners in cognition: Extending human intelligence with intelligent technologies. *Educational Researcher, 20(4)*, 2–9.

Saussure, D. (1966). *Course in general linguistics* (C. Bally & A. Sechehaye, Eds.; W. Baskin, Trans.). New York, Toronto: McGraw Hill.

Schnotz, W., & Bannert, M. (2003). Construction and interference in learning from multiple representation. *Learning and Instruction, 13 (2)*, 141–156.

Snow, R. E. (1989). Toward assessment of cognitive and cognitive structures in learning. *Educational Researcher, 18(9)*, 8–14.

Tennyson, A. (1870). *The poetical works of Alfred Tennyson*. New York: Harper.

Winne, P. H. (2001). Self-regulated learning viewed from models of information processing. In B. Zimmerman & D. Schunk (Eds.), *Self-regulated learning and academic achievement: Theoretical perspectives* (pp. 153–189). Mahwah, NJ: Lawrence Erlbaum associates.

Winne, P. H., & Hadwin, A. F. (1998). Studying self-regulated learning. In D. J. Hacker, J. Dunlosky, & A. Graesser (Eds.), *Metacognition in educational theory and practice* (pp. 227–304). Hillsdale, NJ: Lawrence Erlbaum Associates.

Wittrock, M. C. (1989). Generative processes of comprehension. *Educational Psychologist, 24*, 325–344.

Wu, H.-K., Krajcik, J. S., & Soloway, E. (2001). Promoting understanding of chemical representations: Students' use of a visualization tool in the classroom. *Journal of Research in Science Teaching, 38(7)*, 821–842.

Part V

MULTIMEDIA LEARNING IN ADVANCED COMPUTER-BASED CONTEXTS

CHAPTER 31

Multimedia Learning with Animated Pedagogical Agents

Roxana Moreno

University of New Mexico

Abstract

In this chapter, I review the theoretical and empirical work on the use of animated pedagogical agents (APAs) in multimedia learning. After defining APAs and reviewing some of the existing applications, I present a cognitive theory of multimedia learning (CTML) from which predictions for APA design are derived. More specifically, I contrast the potential beneficial and detrimental effects for using APAs in interactive multimedia environments. Then, I provide a critical analysis of the literature summarizing what we know about APAs and discuss the implications of this research for instructional design. Finally, I explore future directions for advancing our understanding about the role of APAs in multimedia learning.

Introduction

The goal of this chapter is to review the theoretical and empirical work on the use of animated software pedagogical agents (APAs) in multimedia environments and to propose directions for future research based on a cognitive theory of multimedia learning (CTML). Multimedia instructional environments are widely recognized to hold great potential for improving the way that people learn (Mayer, 2001). Examples of multimedia environments for science and math learning are abundant and usually combine a description of a complex system or procedure in written or spoken words along with corresponding illustrations or animations depicting the system. This format of instruction, when made concise and coherent, has been shown to be effective in fostering student understanding as indicated by performance on solving problem-solving transfer questions (Mayer & Moreno, 2003). However, more and more frequently do we see that effective multimedia programs include highly visible APAs.

What Is Multimedia Learning with Animated Pedagogical Agents?

APAs are a kind of software agent, an entity that functions continuously and autonomously on behalf of the user in a virtual (computer-based) environment (Bradshaw, 1997; Laurel, 1997). This definition provides us with a number of possible functions that software agent mediation might entail, such as searching for information in distributed networks, acting as intelligent user interface managers, and helping users in their transactions (Brenner, Zarnekow, & Wittig, 1998). Most software agents tend to function behind the scenes, that is, they lack a physical presence or embodiment in the computer environment and, as a consequence, are impossible to distinguish from mere computer programs. Yet, in recent years, the trend has been to visually represent various types of personal assistants in the computer interface (Maes, 1991). APAs fall within this last type of software agents as they are highly visible personal agents designed to facilitate learning in computer-based environments (Baylor, 1999; Bradshaw, 1997; Craig, Gholson, & Driscoll, 2002; Johnson, Rickel, & Lester, 2000). The most sophisticated APAs are two- or three-dimensional anthropomorphic (i.e., humanlike) characters that advise and provide feedback to students (Towns, FitzGerald, & Lester, 1998) and even adapt intelligently to learner input by having their speech and behavior be contingent on the actions a learner takes (Clarebout, Elen, Johnson, & Shaw, 2002).

In reviewing research and development on APAs, it is useful to distinguish between their internal and external properties. Internal APA properties include those that determine the actions or instructional methods that the agent may carry out during its interaction with a student to facilitate or enable learning such as reducing the cognitive load from interactive multimedia environments (Moreno, 2004), expanding students' effective working memories (Moreno & Mayer, 1999), providing students with feedback, modeling, and guidance (Moreno, Mayer, Spires, & Lester, 2001), or increasing active learning (Moreno & Mayer, 2000). On the other hand, external APA properties include the visual and auditory presence of the agent, which are social features that are hypothesized to affect learning by making the learning experience more interesting, believ-

able, or natural. Agents with external properties are also referred to as embodied, interface, or personified agents and the potential learning effects corresponding to their visual and auditory presence has been called the *persona effect* (Lester, Towns, & Fitzgerald, 1999), *personal agent effect* (Moreno et al., 2001), or *embodied agent effect* (Atkinson, 2002). However, a more specific terminology distinguishes between the visual and auditory effects of agents by using the terms *image effect* and *modality effect*, respectively (Moreno et al., 2001). APA development clearly varies in the type of internal and external properties embedded in the agents. However, all APA applications share the fact of having a strong visual presence in a learning computer environment and the purpose of enhancing learning.

What Are Some Examples of Multimedia Learning with Animated Pedagogical Agents?

Efforts to create APAs spread widely in a number of organizations around 1990. These included the Jack project at the University of Pennsylvania (Badler, Phillips, & Webber, 1993); the Oz project at Carnegie-Mellon University (Bates, 1994); the work of Takeuchi and Nagao (1993) at Sony Computer Science Laboratory; the Autonomous Agents Group at the MIT Media Laboratory (Maes, 1991); and the CAIT project at Stanford (Hayes-Roth, Sinkoff, Brownston, Huard, & Lent, 1995). Most of these development efforts were geared toward representing intelligent assistants that could be viewed as believable lifelike characters possessing emotional and intentional states (Bradshaw, 1997), a design that was argued to support learning by increasing the credibility and appeal of the computer system (Mitrovic & Suraweera, 2000).

The effort to develop APAs is still present. Some recent examples are *Adele*, a two-dimensional female character who provides advice, coaches, and tests students as they work through medical case studies (Ganeshan, Johnson, Shaw, & Wood, 2000; Shaw, Effken, Fajen, Garrett, & Morris,

1997); *Steve*, a three-dimensional male character who demonstrates procedural skills in virtual environments, monitors learners' actions and reacts accordingly (Johnson et al., 2000); *Cosmo*, a three-dimensional anthropomorphized robot who uses adaptive coaching to teach Internet packet routing (Lester et al., 1999); *WhizLow*, a childish-looking three-dimensional human who teaches programming skills by monitoring learners' misconceptions and providing relevant advice (Grégoire, Zettlemoyer, & Lester, 1999); *AutoTutor*, a talking head designed to assist college students in learning an introductory computer literacy course (Graesser, Wiemer-Hastings, Wiemer-Hastings, & Kreuz, 1999); *PPPersona*, an animated agent who draws students' attention to Web-based materials by using deictic gestures (André, Rist, & Muller, 1999); *Herman-the-Bug*, a two-dimensional fictional lifelike animated character that teaches students about botany (Lester, Stone, & Stelling, 1999); *SmartEgg*, a SQL, cartoonlike tutor that gives feedback on student actions (Mitrovic & Suraweera, 2000); and *Dr. Phyz*, a three-dimensional animated character that explains how electromagnetic forces and electric currents work in an interactive virtual learning environment (Towns, Callaway, & Lester, 1998).

What Is the Role of Animated Pedagogical Agents in Multimedia Learning?

An analysis of the literature reveals that the most widely spread rationale underlying APA development is that of anthropomorphism: the fact that people unconsciously ascribe mental states to computers and are quite adept at relating to and communicating with other people. Based on the finding that interaction with computers can evoke human social responses (Reeves & Nass, 1996), agent developers feel that highly visible lifelike characters draw their strength from "the naturalness of the living-organism metaphor" (Laurel, 1997, p. 68). Based on APAs' external traits, learners can predict how a character is likely to think and feel and therefore communicate more

effectively. According to advocates of APAs, the naturalness of such agents, coupled with the enhanced motivation resulting from the higher degree of "entertainingness," should also support cognitive functions such as problem solving, understanding, and learning (Dehn & van Mulken, 2000).

In contrast, opponents of using APAs argue that humanizing pedagogical agents might hamper learning by inducing false mental models of the system (Norman, 1994; Shneiderman & Maes, 1997; Wilson, 1997). For instance, the social cues represented in an APA may lead students to believe that the agent resembles human beings in other cognitive and emotional aspects that APAs may not possess, thus leading to wrong expectations about their behavior (Shneiderman, 1997). A further argument put forward by opponents of APAs relies on the extra cognitive resources required to attend to the additional visual representation of the agent, which is a potential source of distraction (Walker, Sproull, & Subramani, 1994). Moreover, because people tend to treat the computer as a social agent even when no human representation exists, there seems to be no need to engage in the costly development of APAs (Nass, Moon, Fogg, Reeves & Dryer, 1995). In sum, most arguments in favor of presenting APAs have been centered around the potential motivational and cognitive benefits that the external properties of these agents entail, properties that opponents view not only as unnecessary, but as potential sources of distraction and interference with the learning task. In the next section I present a CTML to help understand these two opposing views.

What Does a Cognitive Theory of Multimedia Learning Predict About Animated Pedagogical Agent Design?

A useful framework to derive predictions about the design and potential effects of APAs resides in (Moreno, 2003; Moreno & Mayer, 2002a). CTML is based on the following three assumptions suggested by cognitive research: (1) dual-channel assumption – the idea that humans have separate channels for processing visual-pictorial representations and auditory-verbal representations (Baddeley, 1992; Paivio, 1986), (2) limited-capacity assumption – the idea that only a few pieces of information can be actively processed at any one time in each channel (Baddeley, 1992; Sweller, 1999), and (3) active processing assumption – the idea that meaningful learning occurs when the learner engages in cognitive processes such as selecting relevant material, organizing it into a coherent representation, and integrating it with existing knowledge (Mayer & Moreno, 2003).

Figure 31.1 summarizes the process of multimedia learning with an APA according to CTML. As you can see, the agent's explanations during learning may enter through the ears or the eyes, depending if the agent communicates with spoken or written words, respectively. Learners then need to select some of the words for further processing in the verbal channel, organize the words into a cause-and-effect chain, and integrate this verbal model with the corresponding visual materials and their prior knowledge. Simultaneously, the visual image of the agent and the other visual materials presented on the computer screen enter through the eyes, so learners select some of the images for further processing in the visual channel, organize the images into a cause-and-effect chain, and integrate this visual model with the corresponding verbal material and their prior knowledge.

By taking into consideration the dual-channel, limited-capacity, and active-processing assumptions, we can now draw the following five predictions about APA design from CTML. First, agents that communicate with the learner using spoken words are more likely to lead to meaningful learning than those that communicate with the learner using on-screen text. By using the auditory channel to process the verbal information, effective working memory is expanded because students are not forced to split their limited visual working memories between the on-screen text, computer graphics, and agent image (Moreno & Mayer, 1999). This I call the *modality hy-pothesis* for APA design. Second, a correlate to the prior hypothesis is that agents should communicate with the learner using spoken words alone rather than with redundant narration and on-screen text because the presentation of text, pictures, and APA image will overload students' limited cognitive resources (Moreno & Mayer, 2002b). This I call the *redundancy hypothesis* for APA design. Third, agents that are highly visible and animated are less likely to lead to meaningful learning than agents that are invisible or static because the image of APAs competes for students' limited visual working memories while they try to select relevant visual materials that may be necessary to make the lesson intelligible (Moreno & Mayer, 1999; Moreno et al., 2001). This I call the *split-attention hypothesis* for APA design. Fourth, active processing of the materials is most likely to occur when the APA is endowed with internal properties (i.e., instructional methods) that promote students' engagements in the cognitive processes of selection, organization, and integration of the materials (Moreno & Mayer, 2000). For example, effective APAs encourage students to make rather than take meaning from the multimedia materials. This I call the *active-learning hypothesis* for APA design. Fifth, students' invested efforts in processing the materials is most likely to increase when APAs make the learning task more interesting or motivating either through their internal or external properties (Moreno et al., 2001). This I call the *interest hypothesis* for APA design. In sum, according to CTML, some conditions for effective APA design include spoken explanations, images that do not distract students from processing relevant visual explanations, instructional methods that promote active engagement, and interfaces that stimulate students' interests. As can be seen, some of these predictions are consistent with the anthropomorphism approach – such as the interest hypothesis for APA design, whereas other predictions are consistent with anthropomorphism opponents – such as the split-attention hypothesis for APA design.

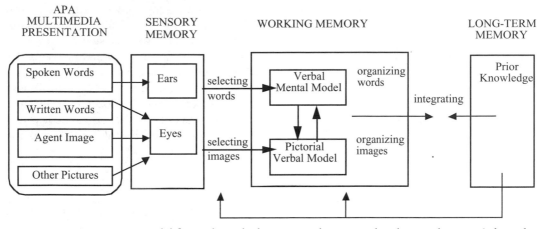

Figure 31.1. A cognitive model for multimedia learning with animated pedagogical agents (adapted from Mayer & Moreno, 2003).

What Do We Know About Multimedia Learning with Animated Pedagogical Agents?

Although APAs figure prominently in multimedia learning environments, there is no comparable research on their effectiveness and adequate design (Clarebout et al., 2002). Most studies on embodied agents have not focused on learning, but rather investigated other user effects (see Dehn & van Mulken, 2000, for a review) such as participant cooperation (Parise, Kiesler, Sproull, & Waters, 1999), agent persuasion (Fogg & Tseng, 1999), credibility (Burgoon et al., 2000), and believability (Okonkwo & Vassileva, 2001). However, because the focus of this chapter is on the role of APAs in multimedia learning, the following review only summarizes past research that includes at least one learning measure in its design.

THE PERSONA EFFECT

Several studies have investigated the affective impact of APAs on student learning by testing the *interest hypothesis* for APA design. This line of work examines the potential *persona effect*: the finding that the presence of an APA in an interactive learning environment has a positive effect on student's perceptions of their learning experience, which in turn, promotes learning (Lester et al., 1999;

Mitrovic & Suraweera, 2000). For example, Lester and colleagues (1999) asked middle school students to learn about plant design by interacting with one of five versions of the APA *Herman-the-Bug*. The five learning conditions presented different types of explanatory agent behaviors: (a) principle-based animation and voice advice plus task-specific advice; (b) principle-based animation and voice advice alone; (c) principle-based voice advice alone; (d) task-specific advice; and (e) no advice. Students were given pre- and posttests to assess learning and an 18-item questionnaire to assess students' perceptions about the computer program. Results showed that students in all conditions had higher posttest than pretest mean scores, with versions (a), (b), and (c), showing the largest difference. In addition, the researchers reported significant differences between question ratings for all groups, with the higher affective ratings corresponding to the credibility, concern, usefulness, and entertainingness of the agent. Students in condition (a) gave significantly higher scores on the usefulness of the advice and encouragement of the APA than those in all other conditions. Based on the authors' interpretation that affective scores were overall high and that all conditions showed increase on posttest performance, it was concluded that *Herman-the-Bug* produced a persona effect. However, to test the persona effect, a control group with no agent should have been used. In conclusion, the present study is inconclusive regarding the *interest hypothesis* for APA design.

In two experiments, Moreno and colleagues (2001) examined the personal agent (PA) or *persona* effect by having college students (Experiment 1) and seventh-grade students (Experiment 2) learn about environmental science through a multimedia lesson that either included an APA who spoke to them (group PA) or received identical graphics and explanations as on-screen text without the presence of an APA (group no-PA). The findings were that group PA outperformed group no-PA on transfer tests and interest ratings but not on retention tests, supporting the *interest hypothesis* for APA design on deeper learning. However, because the PA and no-PA learning conditions differed in more than one factor (image of the APA, voice of the APA, and student–agent interaction), the authors warned against this conclusion and conducted three follow-up experiments to investigate further the basis for the *persona* effect (see next two sections).

Moundridou and Virvou (2002) studied the impact of a three-dimensional APA who provided students with spoken feedback and guidance to solve mathematical word problems through the construction of algebraic equations. The study compared the behaviors, perceptions, and learning outcomes of an agent (image and voice) and a no-agent (no-image and no-voice) learning condition. Agent and no-agent groups spent comparable time on task and had no significant differences on pretest to posttest learning gains, although participants in the agent condition reported higher enjoyment levels and perceived the experience as less difficult than those in the no-agent condition. The results suggest that the persona effect may be limited to students' perceptions of the learning experience alone. However, because image and voice of the agent were confounded, the cause of affective differences and lack of learning differences between groups is unclear. Similarly, Bosseler and Massaro (2003) tested the learning effectiveness of *Baldi*, a three-dimensional animated talking head, on vocabulary and language learning in children with autism using a within subject design. Although children showed significant vocabulary learning both in immediate and delayed retention tests, because the computer lesson consisted of images of the vocabulary items and icon-based feedback in addition to the APA, it is not clear whether the learning effects were caused by the presence of the APA or not.

THE IMAGE EFFECT

A few studies have examined the role of APAs image alone on learning. For example, the *PPPersona* research team examined the cognitive and affective consequence of having college students learn about technical and nontechnical topics either with or without the animated *PPPersona* agent (van Mulken, André, & Muller, 1998). In the agent condition, *PPPersona* used his arm to point to the multimedia materials and gave narrated explanations. To make agent and no-agent conditions equivalent in their internal properties, the no-agent condition included an arrow that served the same function of guiding students' attention as the APA's arm and had identical narrated explanations. Results showed that the visual presence of the APA made no difference in recall or comprehension. However, participants found it easier and more entertaining to learn when the APA image was present but only for technical materials. Because agent image did not help or hurt learning, the authors speculated that the motivation and distraction originated by the APA image may have acted as antagonistic factors, with the benefits of the first factor being outweighed by the drawbacks of the second factor. In sum, the *interest* and *split-attention* hypothesis were not supported.

Mitrovic and Suraweera (2000) developed and evaluated SQL-Tutor, a computer-based system that helps students learn SQL with a tutor on the Internet. College students learned either with or without the image of *SmartEgg*, a cartoonlike character that gives written feedback on student actions. The goal of this study was to test the hypothesis that the visual presence of the APA would increase students' motivations and result in more favorable perceptions of the system and understanding of the content. Students took a three question posttest and were asked to rate the program on a questionnaire. Students presented with the agent image gave higher ratings of enjoyment and usefulness than the students in the control group but, due to the small number of participants taking the posttest, comparisons between groups on learning were not feasable. Consequently, the *interest hypothesis* for APA design remained untested.

Craig and colleagues (2002) explored the image effect by asking college students to learn about the process of lightning formation with a static agent, an agent who used deictic gestures, or no agent. Additionally, the picture features representing the scientific system in each of the three conditions were varied. Some students learned with sudden onset highlighting around key elements of the system, others learned with animations, and others learned with static pictures. Similar to van Mulken and colleagues (1998), the authors were interested in comparing the agent's deictic gestures to similar attention-drawing techniques not embedded in the APA (i.e., the sudden onset highlighting and animation). The results failed to support the *interest* and *split-attention hypotheses* for APA design as no differences were found between the different agent representations on students' perceptions of the learning experience or their learning outcomes. On the other hand, differences were found with regard to picture features, showing that both attention-drawing techniques led to the best learning outcomes.

DISTINGUISHING BETWEEN IMAGE
AND MODALITY EFFECTS

To better understand the relative contribution of the visual and auditory components of an APA's persona, Moreno and colleagues (2001) conducted two experiments where the image of the APA and modality of the APA's words (auditory versus visual) were manipulated separately. Students learned in one of the following four APA

conditions: image and voice, image and text, no image and voice, and no image and text. Both with the fictional agent *Herman-the-Bug* (Experiment 4) and a video of a human face (Experiment 5), students performed better on tests of retention and problem-solving transfer when words were presented as speech rather than on-screen text but the visual presence of the agent did not affect test performance. In addition, students who learned with spoken words gave significantly higher interest ratings (Experiment 4) and lower difficulty ratings (Experiment 5) than their counterparts. Based on these results, it was concluded that the visual presence of an agent does not necessarily provide any cognitive or motivational advantage for students' learning. Conversely, and similar to modality effects found on nonagent-based multimedia explanations, the findings suggest that spoken agent explanations help learning by expanding effective working memory through using both visual and auditory channels to process the multimedia materials (Moreno & Mayer, 1999).

Moreno and Mayer (2002a) continued this line of research by examining if the modality hypothesis for APA design would also hold for immersive virtual environments. To this end, they asked college students to interact with an APA who spoke to them or gave identical explanations as on-screen text on the same multimedia game used by Moreno et al. (2001). Students explored the environment in a desktop condition, a head-mounted display condition, or a head-mounted display and walking condition. Performance on tests of retention and problem-solving transfer and program ratings were higher when words were presented as speech rather than on-screen text, lending support to the *modality hypothesis* for APA design across the three media conditions.

Atkinson (2002) extended the work of Moreno and colleagues on APA modality and image effects by using a different learning environment and APA, namely, *Peedy*, an animated, anthropomorphized parrot. In Experiment 1, undergraduate students learned how to solve word problems with worked examples in one of five conditions: voice-plus-agent, text plus agent, voice only, text only, or control (i.e., no agent or instruction). The voice-plus-agent condition reported lower levels of difficulty and produced higher near- and far-transfer test scores than their counterparts in the control condition. In addition, participants who received narrated explanations reported lower levels of difficulty and produced higher near-transfer test scores than those who received textual explanations, lending support to the *modality hypothesis* for APA design. A second experiment was conducted to overcome some limitations of the first study (i.e., small number of subjects and few items in the learning assessments). Participants were assigned to three conditions: voice plus agent, voice only, or text only. Participants in the voice-plus-agent group outperformed the text-only group on near-transfer tests and had higher far-transfer scores and affective measures than both text-only and voice-only groups. Although on the surface this research seems to demonstrate a persona effect, a closer look at the internal properties of the agent warns us against this conclusion. In the words of Atkinson "the agent appeared to function as a visual indicator . . . by using gesture and gaze to guide learners' attention to the relevant material" (p. 426). Unlike other studies (Craig et al., 2002; van Mulken et al., 1998), because the APA's image confounded internal and external agent properties (i.e., guiding students' attention and representing the agent, respectively), it is not possible to conclude that the mere image of the agent was responsible for the reported positive effects.

Finally, Mayer, Dow, and Mayer (2003) examined the role of APAs auditory and visual presence by comparing the learning outcomes of college students who learned about how an electric motor works from the two-dimensional APA *Dr. Phyz*. Students performed better on a problem-solving transfer test when explanations were narrated rather than written (Experiment 1), but deleting the APA's image from the screen did not affect performance (Experiment 4). Similar to other studies, the results support the *modality hypothesis* for APA design and fail to support the *split-attention hypothesis* for APA design. A difference with past APA image research (Moreno & Mayer, 2002a; Moreno et al., 2001; van Mulken et al., 1998) is that this work did not include students' affective measures. Therefore, the *interest hypothesis* for APA design was not tested.

DISTINGUISHING BETWEEN IMAGE AND ANIMATION EFFECTS

Baylor and Ryu (2003) tested the role of APA's image and animation on preservice teachers' perceptions of agent characteristics and performance. Participants used a computer-based environment to design a study plan for a case study with the assistance of *Chris*, a three-dimensional personal agent who gives spoken and written information upon request. The agent's image was varied to compare the effects of three different conditions: animated, static, and no-image. Compared to the no-image group, image groups led to higher credibility ratings and more advisement requests than no-image conditions. Conversely, no overall difference was found on participants' ratings of how engaging and personlike the agent was, despite the fact that the animated group gave higher ratings than the static group on these measures. Another contrasting result was that whereas participants in the image groups reported more often how valuable the agent's information was, participants in the no-agent group reported less often how unlikable the agent was. Finally, no difference was found on the performance test across conditions. Although the results regarding perceptions about the agent are mixed and difficult to interpret, the learning effects are clear. Similar to other studies on image effects (Craig et al., 2002; Moreno et al., 2001; van Mulken et al., 1998), there were no learning benefits or disadvantages from interacting with a visible pedagogical agent, failing to support both the *interest* and *split-attention hypotheses*. Interestingly, the findings showed that even when students seek more help from a visible than from a nonvisible agent, an image effect on learning is not found.

THE REDUNDANCY EFFECT

Craig and colleagues (2002, Experiment 2) tested the *redundancy hypothesis* in agent-based multimedia. According to the redundancy hypothesis, presenting words as text and speech is worse than presenting words solely as speech (Mayer, Heiser, & Lonn, 2001; Moreno & Mayer, 2002b). Students learned with a static agent in one of three conditions: with written, spoken, or written and spoken words. Similar to past multimedia research in nonagent-based environments, the narration-alone group outperformed the other two conditions (Moreno & Mayer, 2002b), supporting both, the *redundancy* and *modality hypotheses* for APA design.

THE INTERACTIVITY EFFECT

One of the goals of the research program conducted by Moreno and colleagues (2001) was to vary the degree of student–agent interaction (Experiment 3) to examine the role of interactivity in APA design. Students who were allowed to participate in the process of knowledge construction by generating answers before listening to the APA explanations outperformed those who learned with identical materials but without participation. No differences between groups were found on affective ratings. Similarly, in a set of two experiments (Mayer et al., 2003, Experiments 2a and 2b), it was found that students who learn by asking questions to an APA outperform those who receive identical information as a noninteractive multimedia message on problem-solving transfer tests. Taken together, these findings support the *interactivity hypothesis* by showing that a potential role of APAs is to facilitate interactivity during learning.

THE PERSONALIZATION EFFECT

In an effort to extend past research on strategies to increase text comprehension, Moreno and Mayer (2000) tested the hypothesis that personalized messages in an agent-based multimedia environment can promote deep learning by actively engaging students in the elaboration of the materials. Students played an agent-based environmental science game (Experiments 3, 4, and 5) where instructional messages were presented either in a personalized style – receiving spoken or written explanations in the first and second person, or neutral style – receiving spoken or written explanations in the third person. The agent image was not present in the game. As predicted by the researchers, personalized rather than neutral messages produced better retention and problem-solving transfer performance across all experiments. No differences between groups were found on students' affective ratings of the program. Similarly, a more recent study (Moreno & Mayer, 2004) using the same multimedia game presented using a desktop computer (low immersion) or head-mounted display (high immersion), revealed that students who received personalized agent messages performed better on retention and problem-solving transfer tests across the two media and gave higher program ratings than those in nonpersonalized conditions. These findings support the *active-learning hypothesis* for APA design.

THE GUIDANCE EFFECT

To explore yet another potential role that APAs may have in multimedia learning, Moreno (2004) examined the *guided feedback hypothesis* according to which, discovery learning environments that use explanatory feedback (EF) to guide novice students in the process of meaning making promote deeper learning than those that present identical materials using corrective feedback (CF) alone. In two experiments, the EF group produced higher transfer scores and rated the computer game as more helpful than the CF group. Mental load rating scales provided evidence in both experiments that EF was effective due to reductions in cognitive load. Results support the *active learning hypothesis* for APA design by showing that novice students are most likely to learn from discovery multimedia when agents facilitate the cognitive processes of selection, organization, and integration of the materials using EF (Moreno & Mayer, 2000).

factor outweigh the drawbacks of the second factor, learning is not affected. Alternative explanations may be that students become familiarized with the agent on the computer screen and eventually process the APA image only marginally, or that students ignore the APA image altogether. More research is needed to understand the attentional demands of APAs' image and animations during learning.

What Are the Implications of the Research for Instructional Design?

The present review of the empirical work on APAs reveals many principles that should be embraced in the development of agent-based multimedia.

MODALITY PRINCIPLE

Software pedagogical agents should communicate with the learner with spoken words. The reviewed studies provide consistent evidence that students are better able to understand multimedia explanations when words are presented as speech rather than on-screen text, and replicate a similar modality effect reported for nonagent learning environments (Moreno & Mayer, 1999; Mousavi, Low, & Sweller, 1995).

REDUNDANCY PRINCIPLE

Software pedagogical agents should communicate with the learner with spoken words *alone*. The study from Craig et al. (2002, Experiment 2) demonstrated that adding on-screen text to an agent's spoken explanation hurt student learning. This finding replicates a similar redundancy effect reported for nonagent learning environments (Mayer et al., 2001; Moreno & Mayer, 2002b).

ACTIVE-LEARNING PRINCIPLE

The reviewed research has pinpointed some conditions under which agent-based multimedia learning can lead to substantial improvements in problem-solving transfer through increased behavioral or cognitive activity such as interactivity, personalization, guidance, and reflection.

INTERACTIVITY PRINCIPLE

Software pedagogical agents should be designed to promote students' interactions and manipulation of the learning materials by mixed, agent–student initiative designs that allow students to select answers before receiving explanations or to ask questions during learning (Lester et al., 1999).

PERSONALIZATION PRINCIPLE

Software pedagogical agents should communicate with the learner with personalized rather than monologue-style messages. Similar to other personalization effects, agent-based multimedia can result in broader learning if the communication model is centered around shared environments where the student is addressed as a participant rather than as an observer (Symons & Johnson, 1997).

GUIDANCE PRINCIPLE

Software pedagogical agents should provide principle-based explanations during learning. This is particularly important in the case of novice learners, who lack proper schemas to guide them in the selection of relevant new information (Tuovinen & Sweller, 1999).

REFLECTION PRINCIPLE

Software pedagogical agents should provide students with ample opportunities to reflect while engaged in the process of knowledge construction, such as thinking about key concepts before or during the computer lesson. According to CTML, reflection is a condition for ensuring the active processing of the multimedia materials (Mayer & Moreno, 2003).

COST-EFFICIENT PRINCIPLE

Finally, an important practical implication of this chapter is that there is no need to waste costly resources on developing highly visible APAs if the agent's image and behavior does not directly serve the educational objective of the lesson. Although none of the published APA studies report the relative cost and benefit of agent and nonagent treatments, their design is presumably more expensive than lower technology alternatives (Clark, 2003).

What Are Some Productive Future Directions for Research?

Based on the encountered limitations of past research on APAs, in the present section I will propose some productive future directions for research. For example, a common shortcoming of APA empirical work is the failure to adequately distinguish between the internal and external properties of the agent. Therefore, a first general recommendation is to design studies where learning benefits or drawbacks can be clearly attributed to either aspect of this medium and, therefore, to conduct more research where each aspect is manipulated separately with adequate control conditions.

Second, many existing studies have either focused on affective measures or learning measures alone. Although examining students' subjective perceptions of the learning experience may help determine the motivational role of APAs, it is crucial to determine if the beneficial effects that may be found on affective measures are accompanied by similar benefits on learning measures. Similarly, when investigating the effects of APA's external properties, affective measures (especially open ended) are necessary to fully understand how the representation chosen by the experimenter might affect students' motivation and interest. Moreover, further work is also needed to develop consensus definitions and valid and reliable subjective measures, especially in the areas of motivation, interest, and cognitive load (Brunken, Plass, & Leutner, 2003; Pintrich & Schunk, 2002).

Third, it is important to distinguish between superficial, transient learning benefits that may reflect a novelty effect from using this new medium and deeper, longer-lasting learning benefits. All studies reviewed in the present chapter consisted of very brief agent-based multimedia presentations where students were tested immediately after interacting with the computer program. Further research examining the role of agents' presence in longer learning conditions is needed to determine if any agent effect or lack of effect in the immediacy of the intervention subsides or remains with repeated exposures to the APA.

Fourth, most studies have been conducted with undergraduate students and only a few have included middle school learners. Because the main argument favoring the use of APAs has resided in their motivational potential, it is important to test the affective consequences of using APAs for other developmental stages. Two promising understudied groups are those of elementary children and nontraditional, older students.

Fifth, all reviewed studies have arbitrarily designed and assigned an APA to the participants. Because the role of choice has proven to be motivational and positively correlated with learning (Ryan & Deci, 2000), more research is needed to determine if the lack of persona and image effects from past studies remain when students are given the opportunity to design or choose an APA of their interest.

Lastly, in closing this chapter, I would like to invoke the classical distinction between method and media to bring a final reflection on the potential role of APAs in educational technology (Clark, 1999). In the past, printed books transformed education by allowing students to preserve and share information. Computer-based learning is also unique in that it provides dynamic displays and opportunities to construct understandings with interactive methods and individualized feedback. What are the attributes that make APAs a unique instructional medium? Are there other media that would yield similar learning gains? In answering these questions, it is possible to propose the study of APAs on roles that are yet to be explored and may be distinctive for this media. For example, as part of their literature review, Clarebout and colleagues (2002) propose five different roles that APAs may play in supporting learning: supplanting/scaffolding, demonstrating, modeling, coaching, and testing. Clearly, in three of these roles the visual presence of APAs is not necessary and, consequently, the agent's auditory presence combined with signaling is all that is needed to facilitate the respective pedagogies (i.e., scaffolding, coaching, and testing). On the other hand, when the role of the APA is to demonstrate or model a procedure, the agent's visual presence is an essential part of the instructional method and, therefore, should be carefully designed to provide all the visual information necessary for observational learning to occur. Therefore, in the future, it might be useful to extend APA research to nontraditional procedural domains such as physical education, dance, or technical training.

Glossary

Agent: Someone that acts on behalf of someone else to carry out a particular task.

Animated: Being endowed with movement to give the impression of being alive.

Anthropomorphic: Having the appearance and/or traits of humans.

Deictic gestures: An APA's use of hand gestures and locomotion to direct students' attention to visual stimuli on the computer screen.

Embodied: Having a body or visual presence on the computer screen.

Immersive: The sense of presence in a virtual environment or psychological perception of "being there."

Lifelike: Giving the illusion of being animated or alive.

Modalities: Each one of the sensory processing channels of information, such as the visual, auditory, or haptic modalities.

Modes: Also known as *codes*. Each one of two knowledge representation systems (verbal and nonverbal) according to Paivio's (1996) dual-coding theory.

Multimedia: A combination of words (i.e., text or narration) and pictures (i.e., static or dynamic graphics) to represent knowledge in a learning environment.

Software agent: A computer-enacted character that acts on behalf of a user to carry out a particular task.

Three-dimensional (3-D): Being represented by three dimensions on a real or virtual space.

Two-dimensional (2-D): Being represented by two dimensions on a real or virtual space.

Virtual environment: A computer simulation of a real environment.

Note

This research was supported by the ROLE grant 0231774 and CAREER grant 0238385 from the National Science Foundation. Any opinions, findings, and conclusions or recommendations expressed in this material are those of the author and do not necessarily reflect the views of the National Science Foundation. Correspondence concerning this article may be sent to the author at the following mailing address: 123 Simpson Hall, Educational Psychology Program, University of New Mexico, Albuquerque, NM 87131. E-mail may be sent to Roxana Moreno at *moreno@unm.edu*.

References

André, E., Rist, T., & Muller, J. (1999). Employing AI methods to control the behavior of animated interface agents. *Applied Artificial Intelligence*, 13, 415–448.

Atkinson, R. K. (2002). Optimizing learning from examples using pedagogical agents. *Journal of Educational Psychology*, 94(2), 416–427.

Baddeley, A. (1992). Working memory. *Science*, 255, 556–559.

Badler, N., Phillips, C. B., & Webber, B. L. (1993). *Simulating humans: Computer graphics, animation, and control*. Oxford, England: Oxford University Press.

Bates, J. (1994). The role of emotion in believable agents. *Communications of the ACM*, 37, 122–125.

Baylor, A. L. (1999). Intelligent agents as cognitive tools for education. *Educational Technology*, 39(2), 36–40.

Baylor, A. L., & Ryu, J. (2003). Does the presence of image and animation enhance pedagogical agent persona? *Journal of Educational Computing Research*, 28(4), 373–395.

Bosseler, A., & Massaro, D. (2003). Development and evaluation of a computer-animated tutor for vocabulary and language learning in children with autism. *Journal of Autism and Developmental Disorders*, 33(6), 653–672.

Bradshaw, J. M. (Ed.). (1997). *Software agents*. Menlo Park, CA: AAAI Press/MIT Press.

Brenner, W., Zarnekow, R., & Wittig, H. (1998). *Intelligent Software Agents*. Berlin: Springer-Verlag.

Brunken, R., Plass, J. L., & Leutner, D. (2003). Direct measurement of cognitive load in multimedia learning. *Educational Psychologist*, 38, 53–61.

Burgoon, J. K., Bonito, J. A., Bengtsson, B., Cederberg, C., Lundeberg, M., & Allspach, L. (2000). Interactivity in human-computer interaction: A study of credibility, understanding, and influence. *Computers in Human Behavior*, 16, 553–574.

Cassell, J., & Thorisson, K. R. (1999). The power of a nod and a glance: Envelope vs. emotional feedback in animated conversational agents. *Applied Artificial Intelligence*, 13, 519–538.

Chi, M. T. H. (2000). Self-explaining: The dual processes of generating inference and repairing mental models. In R. Glaser (Ed.), *Advances in instructional psychology: Vol 5. Educational design and cognitive science* (pp. 161–238). Mahwah, NJ: Erlbaum.

Clarebout, G., Elen, J., Johnson, W. L., & Shaw, E. (2002). Animated pedagogical agents: An opportunity to be grasped? *Journal of Educational Multimedia and Hypermedia*, 11(3), 267–286.

Clark, R. C. (1999). *Developing technical training* (2nd ed). Washington, DC: International Society for Performance Improvement.

Clark, R. E. (2003). Research on web-based learning: A half-full glass. In R. Brunings, C. A. Horn, & L. M. Pytlik Zillig (Eds.), *Web-based learning: What do we know? Where do we go?* (pp. 1–22). Greenwich, CT: Information Age Publishing.

Craig, S. D., Gholson, B., & Driscoll, D. M. (2002). Animated pedagogical agents in multimedia educational environments: Effects of agent properties, picture features, and redundancy. *Journal of Educational Psychology*, 94(2), 428–434.

Dehn, D. M., & van Mulken, S. (2000). The impact of animated interface agents: A review of empirical research. *International Journal of Human-Computer Studies*, 52, 1–22.

Doctorow, M., Wittrock, M. C., and Marks, C. (1978). Generative processes in reading comprehension. *Journal of Educational Psychology*, 70, 109–118.

Fogg, B. J., & Tseng, H. (1999). The elements of computer credibility. In *Proceedings of the CHI 99 Conference on Human Factors in Computing Systems* (pp. 80–87). New York: ACM Press.

Ganeshan, R., Johnson, W. L., Shaw, E., & Wood, B. (2000). Tutoring diagnostic problem solving. In G. Gauthier, C. Frasson, & K. van Lehn (Eds.), *Proceedings of the Fifth International Conference on Intelligent Tutoring Systems*. Berlin: Springer-Verlag.

Grégoire, J. P., Zettlemoyer, L. S., & Lester, J. C. (1999). Detecting and correcting misconceptions with lifelike avatars in 3D environments. In *Proceedings of the Ninth World Conference on Artificial Intelligence in Education* (pp. 586–593). Le Mans, France: AE-ED-Society.

Graesser, A. C., Wiemer-Hastings, K., Wiemer-Hastings, P., & Kreuz, R. (1999). AutoTutor: A simulation of a human tutor. *Journal of Cognitive Systems Research*, 1, 35–51.

Hayes-Roth, B., Sinkoff, E., Brownston, L., Huard, R., & Lent, B. (1995). Directed improvisation with animated puppets. In *CHI'95 Conference Companion*, 79–80. New York: ACM Press.

Johnson, W. L., Rickel, J. W., & Lester, J. (2000). Animated pedagogical agents: Face-to-face interaction in interactive learning environments. *International Journal of Artificial Intelligence in Education*, 11, 47–78.

Laurel, B. (1997). Interface agents: Metaphors with character. In Bradshaw, J. M. (Ed.), *Software agents*. Cambridge, MA: MIT Press.

Lester, J. C., Stone, B., & Stelling, G. (1999). Lifelike pedagogical agents for mixed-initiative problem solving in constructivist learning environments. *User Modeling and User-Adapted Interaction*, 9, 1–44.

Lester, J. C., Towns, S. G., & Fitzgerald, P. J. (1999). Achieving affective impact: Visual emotive communication in lifelike pedagogical agents. *International Journal of Artificial Intelligence in Education, 1 0*(3–4), 278–291.

Maes, P. (Ed.). (1991). *Designing autonomous agents.* Cambridge, MA: MIT Press.

Mayer, R. E. (2001). *Multimedia learning.* New York: Cambridge University Press.

Mayer, R. E., Dow, G. T., & Mayer, S. (2003). Multimedia learning in an interactive self-explaining environment: What works in the design of agent-based microworlds? *Journal of Educational Psychology, 95*(4), 806–812.

Mayer, R. E., Heiser, J., & Lonn, S. (2001). Cognitive constraints on multimedia learning: When presenting more material results in less understanding. *Journal of Educational Psychology, 93,* 187–198.

Mayer, R. E., & Moreno, R. (1998). A split-attention effect in multimedia learning: Evidence for dual processing systems in working memory. *Journal of Educational Psychology, 90,* 312–320.

Mayer, R. E., & Moreno, R. (2003). Nine ways to reduce cognitive load in multimedia learning. *Educational Psychologist, 38,* 43–52.

Mitrovic, A., & Suraweera, P. (2000) Evaluating an animated pedagogical agent. *Lecture Notes in Computer Science, 1 839,* 73–82.

Moreno, R. (2004). Decreasing cognitive load for novice students: Effects of explanatory versus corrective feedback in discovery-based multimedia. *Instructional Science, 32,* 99–113.

Moreno, R., & Durán, R. (2004). Do multiple representations need explanations? The role of verbal guidance and individual differences in multimedia mathematics learning. *Journal of Educational Psychology, 96,* 492–503.

Moreno, R., & Mayer, R. E. (in press). Balancing discovery and guidance in an agent-based multimedia game: Role of interactivity and reflection. *Journal of Educational Psychology.*

Moreno, R., & Mayer, R. E. (1999). Cognitive principles of multimedia learning: The role of modality and contiguity. *Journal of Educational Psychology, 91,* 358–368.

Moreno, R., & Mayer, R. E. (2000). Engaging students in active learning: The case for personalized multimedia messages. *Journal of Educational Psychology, 92,* 724–733.

Moreno, R., & Mayer, R. E. (2002a). Learning science in virtual reality multimedia environments: Role of methods and media. *Journal of Educational Psychology, 94,* 598–610.

Moreno, R., & Mayer, R. E. (2002b). Verbal redundancy in multimedia learning: When reading helps listening. *Journal of Educational Psychology, 94,* 156–163.

Moreno, R., & Mayer, R. E. (2004). Personalized messages that promote science learning in virtual environments. *Journal of Educational Psychology, 96,* 165–173.

Moreno, R., Mayer, R. E., Spires, A. H., & Lester, J. C. (2001). The case for social agency in computer-based teaching: Do students learn more deeply when they interact with animated pedagogical agents? *Cognition and Instruction, 1 9*(2), 177–213.

Moundridou, M., & Virvou, M. (2002). Evaluating the personal effect of an interface agent in a tutoring system. *Journal of Computer Assisted Learning, 1 8,* 253–261.

Mousavi, S. Y., Low, R., & Sweller, J. (1995). Reducing cognitive load by mixing auditory and visual presentation modes. *Journal of Educational Psychology, 87,* 319–334.

Nass, C., Moon, Y., Fogg, B. J., Reeves, B., & Dryer, C. (1995). Can computer personalities be human personalities? *International Journal of Human-Computer Studies, 43,* 223–239.

Norman, D. A. (1994). How might people interact with agents? *Communications of the ACM, 37,* 68–71.

Okonkwo, C., & Vassileva, J. (2001) Affective pedagogical agents and user persuasion. In C. Stephanidis (Ed.), *Proceedings of the 9th International Conference on Human-Computer Interaction* (pp. 397–401). New Orleans: AACE.

Paivio, A. (1986). *Mental representations: A dual coding approach.* Oxford, England: Oxford University Press.

Parise, S., Kiesler, S., Sproull, L., & Waters, K. (1999). Cooperating with life-like interface agents. *Computers in Human Behavior, 1 5,* 123–142.

Pintrich, P. R., & Schunk, D. H. (2002). Motivation in education; *Theory, research, and applications* (2nd ed.). Colombus, OH: Merrill-Prentice Hall.

Reeves, B., & Nass, C. (1996). *The media equation: How people treat computers, television, and new media like real people and places.* Stanford, CA: CSLI Publications.

Ryan, R. L., & Deci, E. M. (2000). Self-determination theory and the facilitation of intrinsic motivation, social development, and well being. *American Psychologist, 55*, 68–78.

Shaw, R., Effken, J. A., Fajen, B., Garrett, S. R., & Morris, A. (1997). An ecological approach to the on-line assessment of problem-solving paths: Principles and applications. *Instructional Science, 25*, 151–166.

Shneiderman, B. (1997). Direct manipulation versus agents: Paths to predictable, controllable, and comprehensible interfaces. In J. M. Bradshaw (Ed.), *Software agents*. Menlo Park, CA: AAAI Press/MIT Press.

Shneiderman, B., & Maes, P. (1997). Direct manipulations vs. interface agents: Excerpts from debates at IUI'97 and CHI'97. *Interactions, 4*, 42–61.

Symons, C. S., & Johnson, B. T. (1997). The self-reference effect in memory: A meta-analysis. *Psychological Bulletin, 121*, 371–394.

Sweller, J. (1999). *Instructional design in technical areas*. Camberwell, Australia: ACER Press.

Takeuchi, A., & Nagao, K. (1993). Communicative facial displays as a new conversational modality. In *INTERCHI'93 Conference Proceedings* (pp. 187–193). New York: ACM Press.

Towns, S., Callaway, C., & Lester, J. (1998). Generating coordinated natural language and 3D animations for complete spatial explanations. In C. Rich & J. Mostow (Eds.), *Proceedings of the Fifteenth Conference on Artificial Intelligence* (pp. 112–119). Cambridge, MA: MIT Press.

Towns, S., FitzGerald, P., & Lester, J. (1998). Visual emotive communication in lifelike pedagogical agents. In B. Goettl, H. Half, C. Redfield, & V. Shute (Eds.) *Proceedings of the Fourth International Conference on Intelligent Tutoring Systems*, (pp. 474–483), San Antonio: Springer-Verlag.

Tuovinen, J. E., and Sweller, J. (1999). A comparison of cognitive load associated with discovery learning and worked examples. *Journal of Educational Psychology, 91*, 334–341.

van Mulken, S., André, E., & Muller, J. (1998). The persona effect: How substantial is it? In H. Johnson, L. Nigay, & C. Roast (Eds.), *People and computers XIII: Proceedings of HCI'98* (pp. 53–66). Berlin: Springer.

Walker, J. H., Sproull, L., & Subramani, R. (1994). Using a human face in an interface. In B. Adelson, S. Dumais, & J. Olson (Eds.), *Human factors in computing systems: CHI'94 conference proceedings*, (pp. 85–91). New York: ACM Press.

Wilson, M. (1997). Metaphor to personality: The role of animation in intelligent interface agents. In *Proceedings of the IJCAI-97 workshop on animated interface agents: Making them intelligent*. Nagoya, Japan: Morgan Kauffman.

CHAPTER 32

Multimedia Learning in Virtual Reality

Sue Cobb
University of Nottingham

Danaë Stanton Fraser
University of Bath

Abstract

This chapter reviews the use of virtual reality to aid learning. First we give a description of virtual reality technology and the diverse ways in which it can be viewed and interacted with. Virtual reality has been used to support different types of learning in a variety of application areas including medical training, mainstream and special needs education, and rehabilitation. An overview of exemplary research in these areas is presented. Limitations of current research knowledge are discussed and recommendations for further work are made.

Introduction to Multimedia Learning in Virtual Reality

There are no single concise or generally accepted definitions of virtual reality and virtual environments. This is partly due to the continual state of evolution of the many technologies involved and also the terms being used in a variety of contexts. The Cambridge online dictionary defines *virtual* as; "something that can be done or seen using a computer and therefore without going anywhere or talking to anyone." It defines *virtual reality* as "a set of images and sounds produced by a computer, which seem to represent a place or a situation that a person can experience or take part in" (http://dictionary.cambridge.org). The definition used in this chapter is that virtual reality describes the combination of systems comprising computer processing (PC-based or higher), a building platform for creating three-dimensional environments, and peripherals such as visual display and interaction devices that are used to create and maintain virtual environments. Virtual environments refer to the three-dimensional environments created. The simulation may be of real or imaginary environments. The first defining feature of virtual environments is that they can be explored in real time with similar freedom to real-world exploration. The second defining feature is that the user may interact with objects and events in the simulation.

These virtual environments are used for many different applications including military, industrial, and medical training;

architectural modelling, industrial design and visualisation, and plant layout; mainstream and special needs education; and rehabilitation. When used specifically for educational purposes they have been described as virtual learning environments. (VLEs). Whilst some research fields tend to define VLEs as text-only systems, such as threaded chat and e-mail support for learning, here we are using the terminology to explore the use and evaluation of three-dimensional environments for learning.

Virtual Environment Technology

SOFTWARE

The first step toward building a virtual environment is to create three-dimensional models of all the objects to be placed in the virtual environment. These are constructed using three-dimensional modelling programs such as; 3D Studio (www.3dmax.com), Maya (www.alias.com/eng/index_flash.shtml), and Lightwave (www.newtek.com). These models are then imported into a virtual environment developer toolkit such as Superscape® (www.superscape.com), WorldToolkit (www.sense8.com), or Virtools™ (www.virtools.com). The virtual environment developer constructs the architecture for the virtual environment, positions objects within the virtual environment and assigns behaviours to the objects. The developer also determines the type of interactions the user will be able to make and the consequence of interactions upon the virtual environment. Methods for defining virtual-environment design and content are described by Eastgate (2001), Griffiths (2001), and Wilson, Eastgate, and D'Cruz (2002).

HARDWARE

One of the distinguishing features of virtual reality is that the user can be totally or partially immersed in the virtual environment. This can be achieved psychologically, in a similar way to being immersed in a good novel, or perceptually, using wearable or wraparound displays. Immersion in a virtual environment is measured by the ex-

perience of presence described by the user. Some researchers argue that presence is necessary to support effective use of a virtual environment, although there is much debate on this issue. A review of presence in VLEs and its importance for supporting conceptual learning is given by Waterworth and Waterworth (2000). Display hardware can potentially be applied to any virtual environment and may be interchangeable, although in practice virtual-environment applications tend to be constructed for a specific display type and interaction method. Different display-interaction configurations provide different types of user experience and are used for varying application requirements. D'Cruz (1999) makes a distinction between different types of virtual-reality system configurations: Desktop virtual-reality systems are usually the cheapest system, comprising standard PC and interaction devices (mouse or joystick), as shown in Figure 32.1, and projected virtual-reality systems in which the virtual environment is projected onto a large display on a single surface or multiple projection CAVE (cave automation virtual environment). These systems require high-end graphics workstations. Many people can view the display but only one can control interaction using a hand-held interaction device (e.g., joystick). Augmented reality systems are those in which transparent glasses worn by the user have virtual information (data, diagrams, animation, or video) projected on to them. The participant views this information whilst also looking at the real world. These systems are often used to support maintenance operations. Headset systems are those in which the user wears a head-mounted display/device to receive visual and auditory information from the virtual environment. They are completely immersed physically and cannot see the real world while wearing the head-mounted display/device. The user interacts with the virtual environment using a hand-held interaction device (e.g., wand, joystick, or dataglove) and trackers on the head-mounted display monitor user movement to control navigation through the virtual environment (see Figure 32.2).

Figure 32.1. A desktop VR setup. Reprinted with permission from the University of Nottingham © 1996.

USER PARTICIPATION

User participation defines how users access the virtual environment. In addition to the interaction methods already described, a distinction can be made between systems in terms of how many users can access and interact with a virtual environment at any one time. There are two main types of participation: single user and collaborative virtual environments. Single-user virtual environments (SVEs) are environments where one person controls the interaction. SVEs are the easiest to develop and have been most widely used for education applications (see Figure 32.3). One of the reasons is that they can be displayed on standard desktop PC systems and do not require additional expensive equipment. Collaborative virtual environments (CVEs) allow more than one individual to inhabit the environment at any

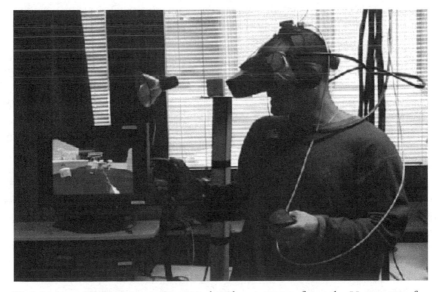

Figure 32.2. HMD system. Reprinted with permission from the University of Nottingham © 2001.

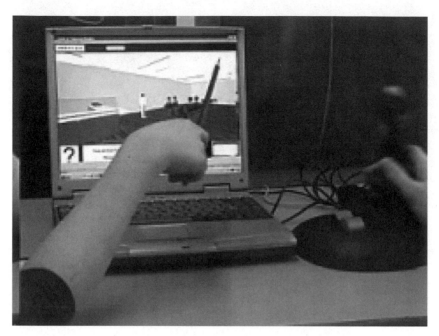

Figure 32.3. A student interacts with an Single-user virtual environment (SVE) using a joystick, receiving prompts from a teacher seated. Reprinted with permission from the University of Nottingham © 2001.

one time. Users need not be in the same location and can interact with each other and the VE through navigation of their virtual avatar and direct verbal communication using headset microphones (see Figure 32.4). This offers opportunities for social skills rehearsal (Cobb, Beardon et al., 2002), communication, and collaboration between distributed research groups (Koleva, Schadelbach, Benford, & Greenhalgh, 2001).

How Can Virtual Environments Be Used for Learning?

Virtual reality systems were originally created for use by the military, space, and aviation industries to enhance simulator systems used for training (Baum, 1992). However as virtual-reality technology became cheaper, more advanced, and widely available, applications were developed in a diverse number of fields including those supporting learning in medicine and rehabilitation; way-finding, and social skills training, mainstream and special needs education.

The application of virtual-reality technology to these areas has not always included theoretical consideration of learning theory. In the first instance, many research questions have focused on usability and interface design and the virtual-reality developer community has been interested in whether or not it is technically feasible to construct VLEs. In the case of special needs education, the basis for using virtual environments has been to provide alternative tools to complement the existing teaching methods used. Virtual reality was seen as an attractive media that may motivate some individuals who did not respond to other media. Medical and rehabilitation applications have generally been developed within projects aimed at supporting learning of a specific activity or skill. Evaluation of application success is based on evidence of cognitive or motor co-ordination training for individuals. Rizzo et al. (2000, 2001) list the range and types of cognitive training that can be supported using virtual environments.

It is in mainstream education that researchers have attempted to understand the learning theory underlying the effectiveness of VLEs. As a relatively new research field, there is no single consensus view, although constructivism has been most widely reported (see review by Youngblut, 1998). Virtual environments provide the facility for experiential learning by allowing the student to explore the virtual environment at their own pace and interact with the virtual environment in real time (Bricken, 1991; Dede, 1995; Winn, 1993). These features of virtual environments go some way to supporting learning according to a constructivist perspective (Neale, Brown, Cobb, & Wilson, 1999).

It is generally agreed that there are several characteristics or attributes that set virtual reality apart from other types of media and reasons why it lends itself to being a unique and potentially very useful educational technology. Salzman, Dede, Bowen Loftin, and Chen (1999) present a model in which they describe how characteristics of virtual-reality technology, individual characteristics of learners, and the interaction between the two affect learning experience and outcomes in mainstream education. They suggest that three-dimensional immersive virtual-reality technology can be more motivating than two-dimensional non-immersive equivalents and have the added advantage

that they can make use of multisensory cues to direct student attention to specific aspects within the virtual environment as required. Individual user characteristics including spatial ability and computer experience may influence effective use of virtual environments for cognitive learning.

Crosier (2001) presents a simplified version of Salzman et al.'s model and suggest that the virtual-reality attributes form a subset of the virtual-environment attributes (see Figure 32.5). This indicates that the virtual-environment attributes are those characteristics that can only be affected by the virtual environment. The virtual-reality attributes can be affected both by virtual reality in general features (e.g., the type of system used, input devices) and specific characteristics of the virtual environment (e.g., what is presented in the three-dimensional environment).

How Virtual Environments Have Been Used to Support Learning

Mainstream Education/Domain-Specific Knowledge

Perhaps one of the reasons why it is difficult to define a single learning theory underlying

Figure 32.4. A student interacts with a CVE, receiving prompts from a teacher through headset microphones. Reprinted with permission from the University of Nottingham © 2001.

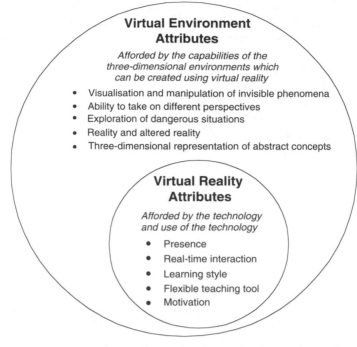

Figure 32.5. Attributes of virtual reality technology and virtual environments that are suitable for learning (Crosier, 2001). Reprinted with permission from the University of Nottingham © 2001.

design and use of virtual environments is that the technology is so versatile that it is used in many different ways. Moshell and Hughes (2002) distinguish between three types of learning activity supported by virtual environments: constructivist learning through the exploration of prebuilt virtual worlds; constructionist learning through students creating or modifying virtual worlds; and situated learning through interactive role play in shared or collaborative virtual environments.

VLEs developed in the first category have largely been developed as three-dimensional models to allow visualisation and exploration of complex or abstract scientific concepts (e.g., the molecules in a compound [Byrne & Furness, 1994], chemical reaction engineering [Bell & Fogler, 1995], The Virtual Cell [McClean, Saini-Eidukat, Schwert, Slater, & White, 2001], Virtual RadLab [Crosier, Cobb, & Wilson, 1999; 2001], shown in Figure 32.6, the Virtual Water Project [Trindade, Fiolhais, & Almeida, 2002], CyberMath [Taxén &

Naeve, 2002], MAT – super 3 D [Pasqualotti & Freitas, 2002], Virtual Solar System [Hay, Elliot, & Kim, 2002], Touch the sky and Touch the Universe projects [Yair, Mintz, & Litvak, 2001]).

The ScienceSpace project (Dede, Salzman, & Loftin 1996; Dede, Salzman, Loftin, & Ash, 2000; Salzman, Dede, McGlynn, & Loftin, 1996; Salzman et al., 1999) comprised a series of microworlds for teaching science relating to physics (Newton World), electrical fields (Maxwell World), and chemistry (PaulingWorld). This research took an holistic approach to evaluation of these virtual environments in order to inform the model of virtual-reality features and learner characteristics described previously. Difference measures were used to evaluate each virtual environment from a range of methods including survey of educator opinions, student performance on pre- and post–virtual-environment subject tests, observations of student interactions, and pre- and postsymptoms reported on the Simulator Sickness Questionnaire (SSQ) (Kennedy and Fowlkes, 1992). Experimental results on the subject knowledge tests indicated that learning in three-dimensional immersive Maxwell World was significantly better than with traditional or two-dimensional nonimmersive representations. The Virtual Chemistry Lab (Martínez-Jiménez, Pontes-Pedraja, Polo, & Climent-Bellido, 2003) was designed to help students to gain a better understanding of the techniques and basic concepts used in lab work. This was found to be particularly helpful for students of lower ability, a result also found by Crosier et al. (1999; 2001). The Virtual Water Project (Trindade et al., 2002) found an increased conceptual understanding of phase transitions in students with high spatial abilities. The curricular modules project (Wollensak, 2002) uses virtual reality to illustrate six scientific principles selected as concepts that are considered difficult to learn from textbooks and would benefit from presentation using a visual, interactive media. Early results demonstrate student enthusiasm for the virtual environments but no data has yet been collected assessing the experimental results for learning.

Examples of constructionist VLEs include the virtual reality roving vehicle (VRRV) project (Winn et al., 1999). Children aged 12–14 were assigned to one of three groups to learn about wetland cycles. Those groups had to design and build a virtual environment to represent the wetland cycle using information obtained from the library, Internet, or CD-ROM; traditional instruction on the wetland cycle using a study textbook, or with no instruction. Knowledge was assessed by asking the students to draw a concept map of the wetland cycle and answers to multiple-choice questions. The results found knowledge learning gain for both the virtual environment and traditional teaching methods and not for the no-instruction control group.

There are relatively few examples of multi-user collaborative virtual environments for mainstream education. In their review, Moshell and Hughes (2002) cite the Round Earth Project (Johnson, Mohler, Ohlsson, & Gillingham, 1999) and their own ExploreNet 2D collaborative improvisational drama simulation (Moshell and Hughes, 1996).

Special Needs Education and Rehabilitation

Early speculation about the potential uses for virtual-reality technologies outlined particular suitability for special needs education (Middleton, 1992; Powers & Darrow,

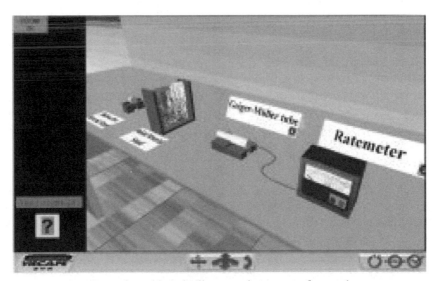

Figure 32.6. A virtual workbench allows students to perform radioactivity experiments (Crosier, 2001). Reprinted with permission from the University of Nottingham © 2001.

1994). Virtual-reality systems and virtual environments have subsequently been developed for users with physical and learning disabilities, and vision and hearing impairments. For example, virtual environments have been used to assess individual abilities and cognitive processes (Pugnetti et al., 1998), and to provide functional training, allowing the practice of daily living skills (reviewed by Rizzo, Buckwalter, & van der Zaag, 2002). For a review of virtual environments for rehabilitation see Riva, Wiederhold, and Molinari (1998). Additionally, the specialist biannual conference, the International Conference for Disability, Virtual Reality and Associated Technologies (www.cyber.rdg.ac.uk/ISRG/icdvrat/) reflects the research community interest in the application and evaluation of virtual-reality technology in these areas. This chapter cannot do justice to this growing community of research; so here we focus on three particular application areas of current significance: spatial cognition, life skills rehearsal, and social skills training.

Spatial Cognition

Spatial learning has received more experimental attention than other applications where virtual environments are being used as a medium to investigate spatial cognition (e.g., Foreman, Stanton, Wilson, & Duffy, 2003; Stanton, Foreman, Wilson, & Duffy, 2002, Stanton, Wilson, & Foreman 2003; Tlauka & Wilson, 1994; Wilson, Foreman, & Tlauka, 1997). Positive effects of the exploration of virtual environments on spatial skills have been reported (Stanton et al., 1996) and transfer of these skills to specific real-world situations have been demonstrated (Foreman et al., 2003). Here we summarise experimental work examining the way that people encode spatial information through exploration of virtual environments. This includes work exploring novel paradigms for configural knowledge, transfer of spatial information from virtual environments to the real world, and the importance of repeated exposure for transfer of training.

Alongside investigations of transfer of training through virtual environments, environments have been used to assess skills where the real-world evaluation of tasks would be difficult to carry out. For example, Tlauka and Wilson (1994) used virtual environments to examine the role of landmarks in learning a route, while Brooks et al. (2002) used virtual environments to assess the ability of stroke patients on a prospective memory task. In spatial studies, virtual environments have been used effectively as novel paradigms for the investigation of configural learning. Three-dimensional environments have been developed to recreate traditional animal paradigms examining spatial orientation and these have been subsequently used to test humans on the tasks, for example, Morris water maze (Astur, Taylor, Mamelak, Philpott, & Sutherland, 2002) and shortcut tasks (Stanton et al., 2003). The ability to take shortcuts demonstrates the formation of an effective internal representation of space. In a series of studies the experimental environment used by Chapuis, Durup, and Thinus-Blanc (1987) was created as a three-dimensional simulation and was used to test human participants (see Stanton et al., 2003). The environment consisted of five pathways connecting four rooms that appeared identical from the outside (see Figure 32.7).

Participants were required to explore the space and then take novel shortcuts to destinations within the environment. For example, they were asked to explore the route between rooms A and B (all other pathways were blocked by no-entry barriers). They were then asked to explore the path between rooms C and D, and then the path between rooms A and D. In the testing phase all the barriers were removed and participants were placed in room C and asked to find room B by the shortest route available. If the participants had formed an effective internal cognitive map of the environment it was hypothesised that they would be more effective at completing shortcuts within the test phase.

Twenty-four participants with a mean age of 22 years took part in the study. An experimental group explored three of the outer

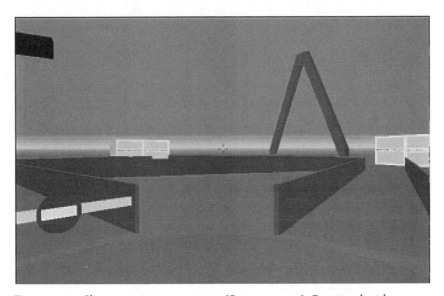

Figure 32.7. Shortcut test environment (Stanton, 1997). Reprinted with permission from the University of Leicester © 1997.

pathways on a route that was predetermined by the experimenter. The control group only explored two of the outer pathways. The pathway not explored and the inner pathway served as shortcuts for the test. The experimental group performed significantly better than the control group on both shortcut tests. These results demonstrate the advantage gained by exploring the pathway that links the two areas and demonstrate that the paradigm was an effective measure of the creation of an internal map and was a successful adaption of Chapuis et al.'s test environment (Stanton et al., 2003).

This environment was subsequently used to examine the development of internal spatial representations in children with physical disabilities, grouped according to their history of mobility. Twenty-four able-bodied children with a mean age of 13.6 years and 34 physically disabled children, with a mean age of 14.1 years, were divided into two subgroups: more mobile when they were younger or less mobile when they were younger. They environment and procedure were identical to the previous study except that all the children explored the three outer pathways. Children who were more mobile when they were younger were found to be significantly better at the shortcut task back-

ing up the argument that early independent exploration is crucial in the development of cognitive mapping skills (Stanton et al., 2002).

A series of studies was carried out to examine whether repeated exploration of several virtual environments promotes better encoding of virtual environments in general (Stanton et al., 1996, Stanton, Foreman, & Wilson, 1998). Children explored three virtual environments at fortnightly intervals. Each environment consisted of three rooms connected by a T-shaped corridor. The rooms were partitioned and each room contained two objects. Participants explored the environments and then carried out spatial tasks such as locating an object from the start point and pointing to objects from a number of test locations from which the objects could not be seen. A series of these studies, including one experiment comparing exposure to two-dimensional or three-dimensional environments between exploring the test environments, demonstrated that the skills disabled children acquired using virtual environments improved with exposure to successive environments, and that it was the three-dimensional nature of the environments that was crucial (Stanton et al., 1998).

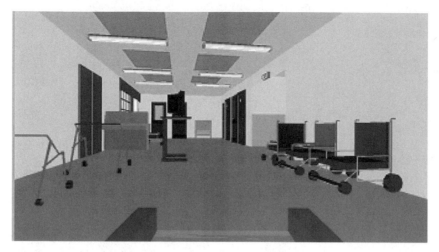

Figure 32.8. A wheelchair viewpoint within AshField school (Stanton, 1997). Reprinted with permission from the University of Leicester © 1997.

However, as it is essential that people can make practical use of virtual-environment training in a real-life situation, researchers have examined transfer of training from the virtual world to the real world. In these types of studies real-world environments are simulated with buildings developed to-scale from architect plans. Studies have shown transfer of spatial knowledge from a virtual environment to the equivalent real-world environment in a range of user groups including adults (Ruddle, Payne, & Jones, 1997; Wilson et al., 1997; Witmer, Bailey, & Knerr, 1995), children with physical disabilities (Foreman et al., 2003; Stanton, Wilson, & Foreman, 1998), and the elderly (Foreman, in press).

For example, one study examined transfer of virtual-environment knowledge to real-life training in physically disabled children. The experimental group consisted of seven physically disabled children with a mean age of 12.3 years. The control group consisted of seven undergraduate students with a mean age of 25.6 years. The primary section of a school in Leicester was created to scale (see Figure 32.8). The environment consisted of an entrance door with a corridor leading into a central area and nine rooms. The experimental group examined the virtual environment in four half-hour sessions over a week. Following this exposure, both the experimental and control groups were taken

to the real school. Pointing accuracy was measured from two relative locations from which the children had completed computer pointing tasks in the simulation, along with a third untrained location. Children were asked to estimate the direction of target objects from each of these locations using a hand-operated pointing device. The children were more accurate than the control group in pointing to landmarks that were not directly visible from three separate testing sites. They not only completed the tasks previously trained in the virtual school, but they also completed spatial tests that had not been trained in the virtual environment equally well. A follow-up study compared the virtual-environment training with that of a model of the school and found that the virtual environment was superior in enabling children to carry out spatial skills within the equivalent real environment (see Foreman et al., 2003).

While we are accumulating evidence of the positive effect of exploration of virtual environments on spatial navigational skills, further work is needed to examine whether skills learned in virtual environments transfer effectively to real-world environments. However, the challenge is not only to examine transfer from a simulation to a real-world equivalent, but also to examine more generally whether spatial skills in the real world improve after practice and experience using a virtual-environment.

Training of Everyday Life Skills

The Virtual City project was developed by the Virtual Reality Applications Research Team to support children with learning disabilities in learning life skills toward a degree of independent living (Brown, Kerr, & Bayon, 1998; Brown, Neale, Cobb, & Reynolds, 1999). The VLE consisted of a house, supermarket, and café, all of which were linked together by a virtual transport system. The integrated structure of the Virtual City allows a user to carry out many daily activities in a logical sequence. The participant is encouraged to make choices and carry out procedural tasks associated with dressing, washing, cooking, shopping, catching the bus, ordering food in a café, and dealing with emergency situations (see Figures 32.9 and 32.10). Evaluation of the project assessed usability and access as well as skill learning and transfer to the real world. A test–retest experimental design method was used to compare user performance in real-world tasks with the same tasks presented in the VLE. Individuals differed in the amount of support required to use the input devices and achieve task objectives in the VLE. Expert and user review methods indicated that the VLEs are seen to be representative of real-world tasks and that users are able to learn some basic skills (Cobb, Neale, & Reynolds, 1998).

An experimental study was conducted to investigate whether there was any evidence of the transfer of skills from a VLE to the real world using an early version of the Virtual Supermarket. Results showed that students who had previously practised shopping skills using a VLE could complete these tasks more quickly and more accurately in the real world compared with a control group (Brown, Standen, & Cobb, 1998; Cromby, Standen, & Brown, 1996).

The use of virtual environments for contextually based training of people with learning disabilities has since been further explored and more extensively tested by other research groups. Mendozzi et al. (2000) developed and extensively tested a virtual training environment that simulates the work environment at the warehouse, workshop, and office. The virtual environments

Figure 32.9. Doing the laundry in a virtual kitchen. Reprinted with permission from the University of Nottingham © 1998.

Figure 32.10. Learning how to use a pedestrian crossing. Reprinted with permission from the University of Nottingham © 1998.

built were flexible and allowed task complexity to be increased. Improvements in input device use and a decrease in anxiety were recorded over time. Evidence of skill transfer was found, as tasks that had been practised in the virtual environment were carried out faster and more accurately in the real world after a period of training. Rose et al. (Rose, Brooks, & Attree, 2000) have also examined the effects of training using virtual environments. They used a programme to teach vocational training to students with learning disabilities. This environment facilitated the practise of food preparation and cooking tasks to train for the catering NVQ level 1. Pre- and post-tests were carried out in a real kitchen and tasks were assigned a score (out of 20) for each "item" or task. Three 15-minute sessions of virtual-environment training over two to three weeks improved ability at both preparation tasks and hazard recognition. However, no significant difference was found between virtual-environment training and real training.

SOCIAL SKILLS TRAINING

The AS Interactive project evaluated the use of virtual environments for social skills training amongst children and adults with Autistics Spectrum Disorder (ASD), including Asperger's Syndrome (AS), (Cobb et al., 2002; Parsons et al., 2000). The project explored two types of VLE for this application (Cobb, Kerr, & Glover, 2001; Kerr, in press): SVEs and CVEs. In the SVE the user was guided through a social interaction task and invited to make choices about what to do and what to say in specific situations. Two scenarios were developed: a virtual café and a virtual bus. In each scenario the user was required to queue and then find a place to sit (see Figures 32.11 and 32.12). In the CVE several users, positioned at different PCs, simultaneously shared the same virtual environment representing a virtual café or an interview scenario. The intention of this VLE was that a teacher or training advisor could support the user by taking the role of one of the characters within the CVE and providing guidance using virtual social interaction.

Observations of how teachers used the VLE to support teaching of these specific skills in the classroom showed that they used the VLE as a visual prompt to promote discussion about what is happening in the social scenario and why characters behave as they do (Neale, Cobb, Kerr, & Leonard, 2002).

Figure 32.11. Find somewhere to sit in a busy café (Kerr, in preparation). Reprinted with permission from the University of Nottingham © 2004.

Teachers found that the VLE helped students to talk about their anxieties or worries in dealing with these situations. Case studies showed that rehearsing with the VLE gave students confidence to do things independently in the real world (Wiederhold & Wiederhold, in press). Experimental studies conducted to assess use and understanding of the SVEs found that people with ASDs can use virtual environments and have a basic understanding of their representational nature (Parsons and Mitchell, 2001, 2003). The virtual environmental was interpreted non-literally, imbuing avatars with "people-like" behaviour, but poor understanding of personal space was displayed (Parsons, 2001).

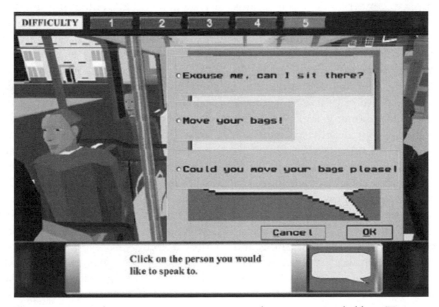

Figure 32.12. Ask appropriate questions to sit down on a crowded bus (Kerr, in preparation). Reprinted with permission from the University of Nottingham © 2004.

Students used a virtual café to find a place to sit and learned appropriate strategies for doing this. This social understanding was transferred to interview responses when questioned about a video recording of a real social situation (Leonard, Mitchell, & Parsons, 2002).

The CVEs were less successful, largely because of the complexity of the technical setup, which was not easy to do within the classroom, and also because the users required a greater amount of scaffolding of learning to encourage them to participate in virtual social interaction (Rutten et al., 2003).

Limitations of Research in Multimedia Learning in Virtual Reality

A workshop held at the Human Interface Technology Laboratory, University of Washington, discussed the added value of three-dimensional immersive virtual environments for student understanding of complex topics in science (Winn, 1997). Whilst it was recognised that virtual environments can provide students with the opportunity to learn by interacting and experimenting at their own pace, concern was raised regarding how well students could use the virtual environment to construct an understanding of the target learning objectives. It was concluded that allowing students freedom to explore a virtual environment is not sufficient – learning requires guidance, feedback to actions, and collaboration (social negotiation). Just because virtual environments offer a motivating learning space, this on its own does not ensure that they will learn. Students also need to understand how the virtual environment relates to the real world and apply their learning.

Salzman et al. (1999) point out that interactivity does not ensure learning and highlight the importance of effective virtual environment and interface design to support learning, rather than interfere with it. In their research studies in use of virtual environments for special needs educa-tion, Standen, Brown, and Cromby (2001) have also observed that effective use of the technology for learning requires guided interaction. They are currently conducting research comparing the effectiveness of human and software tutoring (Standen, Brown, Proctor & Horan, 2002). Moreno and Mayer (2004) found that immersion per se does not enhance learning; guidance through the learning activity is required.

It is essential to find the optimum way to present information in a virtual environment. Many studies have shown that self-directed activity is important. Standen and Low (1996) have found that virtual environments actually promote self-directed learning, but is it necessary for the subject to actively explore, or is it sufficient to actively direct another individual or purely watch another in order to gain spatial information? This is an important consideration, as many physically disabled children, if they are not equipped with appropriate input devices, may at present only be able to passively use virtual environments (i.e., they may require others to move their viewpoint using the keys or joystick). Péruch, Vercher, & Gauthier (1995) found that participants performed better on spatial tasks when active rather than passive. However, Wilson, Foreman, Gillett, and Stanton (1997) found that both active and passive participants gained similar levels of spatial knowledge from virtual environments, whereas Attree et al. (1996) found that active participation enhanced memory for spatial layout whereas passive observation enhanced object memory. Williams and Wickens (1993) found that active involvement or control within the virtual environment proved important in retaining a skill.

Many of the studies report successes in terms of motivation and interest from the students but comment that this could represent a novelty value. Several researchers report usability problems with virtual-reality systems. It is generally concluded that there is little agreement on how to design effective virtual environments for learning. Design should be directed by pedagogy, not technology. Virtual environments should be constructed with a clear view of how they support learning and ensure that learning requirements are foremost (Moshell & Hughes, 2002). The early studies have provided a basis for evaluation of virtual-environment effectiveness and some methods for design and evaluation. Further work is needed to consolidate this information and begin to develop guidelines for VLE designers.

Designing Virtual Learning Environments

The development of VLEs has often included a user-centred or participatory design approach and there is some debate concerning which is the most appropriate. The choice often depends upon the user group and the nature of the application being developed. It seems that the few studies that do include children in the development of VLEs involve them either as users, testers, and sometimes informants (Druin, 2002). Iterative development and redevelopment of the VLE usually takes place following a stage of formative evaluation, however there is little evidence of the active involvement of representative users in the development of VLEs. The Kahun project (Mitchell & Economou, 1999) did attempt to involve learners as active participants in the design of the technology, but faced a number of difficulties in getting them to come up with designs that would fully explore the potential of virtual-reality and virtual-environment technology. New projects are advocating the use of participatory learning environments (PLEs), particularly for mainstream applications (see Barab, Hay, Barnett, & Squire, 2001).

Design Methods

User-centred design (UCD) involves a range of stakeholders in the design process. Virtual-environment developers, virtual environment designers, human factors professionals, and psychologists work together with teachers and/or training professionals to define the design specification, virtual-environment content and presentation, interactive features, cues to learning, and embedded information. Different stakeholders may be involved at different stages of the design process and will contribute to different aspects of design (Neale, Cobb, & Kerr, 2003). End users may be included in the UCD process but their role is usually to review prototypes and comment on design aspects (see Cobb, Neale, Crosier, & Wilson, 2002). Meakin et al. (1998) give an example of how users were involved in the development of the Virtual City project.

Participatory design involves end users directly as design partners. This approach has been used successfully for development of new technology for children's storytelling (Druin et al., 2000). However, there is some debate over the ability of children to contribute to early design specification of virtual environments aimed at teaching of mainstream curriculum subjects as children don't know what they need to learn (Scaife & Rogers, 2001; Mitchell & Economou, 1999).

Participatory learning environments (PLEs) allow learners to build an understanding through collaborative construction of an artefact or shareable product (Barab et al., 2001). The constructionist VLEs take this approach where the goal is to establish rich environments that encourage explanation and discovery, nurture reflection, and support collaborative learning through shared activity.

Guidelines for Instructional Design

As a relatively new medium for learning, there are still few guidelines to help designers and virtual-environment developers know how best to construct VLEs to support learning. Cobb et al. (2002) detail the design process for developing VLEs and the model developed by Salzman et al. (1999) defines the considerations that need to be taken into account when designing VLEs. However, much more work is needed to explore the design and utility of VLEs before we are ready to produce definitive design guidelines.

Conclusions and Future Directions for Research

This chapter has presented many examples of how virtual environments have been applied to learning. Much of the evaluation of VLEs has concentrated on the success of the virtual-environment design (i.e., assessing student and teacher acceptance of the technology, attitudes toward it as a learning medium, and usability of the virtual-environment interface). Where possible, learning of the intended knowledge or skill has been assessed. However, due to the broad range of learning contexts to which the technology has been applied, there is still no clear understanding of how well virtual environments support learning and when they should be applied.

One of the issues that arises from these studies is that care should be taken to apply VLEs appropriately. For example, when using VLEs to replicate some aspect of real life, with the intention of supporting learning of important life skills, project developers should be aware of the limitations of the technology. Virtual environments differ from real environments in a variety of ways. The user is not fully immersed when using a desktop system and can be distracted by real-world stimuli. The field of view in the virtual environment is only as wide as the screen it is displayed on, typically with a maximum of 100 degrees. Due to the limited field of view there is a lack of peripheral vision that may be of importance when building up a representation of the environment. With a desktop system, movements are controlled by an abstract interface, such as a keyboard, mouse, or spaceball (Ruddle & Jones, 2001). Eye movement is not normally used, thus to glance over your shoulder involves rotating your entire viewpoint.

There is also the problem of time delays. When a large amount of detail is built into a virtual environment there will be delays in movement as the computer updates the viewpoint for the user's position within the environment. Wickens and Baker (1995) provide a discussion of the limitations of virtual reality as a navigational aid. When de-signing a virtual environment a balance between realism, computer memory and cognitive load must be maintained (e.g., high levels of visual reality increase time lags in updating the visual display, and thus they may increase effort and the necessary concentration span of the user).

Another important consideration is that some skills may be easier to support using VLEs than others. For example, in spatial virtual reality research, orientation has been more easily trained than distance judgments (Ruddle, Payne, & Jones, 1997) and in some cases virtual environments have been effective for spatial navigation but not spatial rotation (Stanton et al., 1996). Recent empirical studies suggest that there is some degree of vertical asymmetry in spatial memory (Wilson, Foreman, Stanton, & Duffy, 2003) that needs to be considered when using multilevel virtual environments for training.

Individual differences between learners may also contribute to the effectiveness of VLEs (Salzman et al., 1999). There is some indication that, depending upon the type of learning required, individual attitude, ability, and aptitude may affect learning outcome (Crosier et al., 2001; Trindade et al., 2002). Interaction with the VLE may also have an influence (Attree et al., 1996; Williams & Wickens, 1993) as can the amount and type of tutoring through the VLE (Moreno and Mayer, 2004; Standen et al., 2002). Due to the potential diversity of individual user needs, and the wide range of users and applications for which VLEs have been developed, it is not yet possible to define generic guidelines for design and presentation of VLEs. In the short term the solution is to construct VLEs to support individualised learning using tailored interfaces, with individualised methods for scaffolding learning built in (Kerr, in press). Despite the increasing number of VLEs being created, there is still insufficient experimental evidence of successful learning gain. One of the reasons for this is the wide variety of applications, user types, and learning contexts to which the technology is being applied. In addition, the diversity and flexibility of this relatively new technology means that research is still focused on the design process. In many cases evaluation studies tend to concentrate on user attitudes toward the technology and usability issues rather than learning outcome. There is a need now to begin to generate hypotheses of how the technology can support learning and conduct large-scale experimental studies to test these. One problem is that, for the very reasons that we may wish to use VLEs (e.g., visualisation of abstract concepts), it may not be possible to capture learning gain using traditional measures of knowledge acquisition (as we cannot measure understanding of abstract concepts). Measurement of learning gain is much easier for skills training applications because learning should be evident in changes to real-world activity and behaviour. However, studies have generally failed to demonstrate transfer of training, largely due to small sample sizes and short research time scales.

Much more work is needed before definitive comment can be made upon the value of VLEs for learning. Research studies generally report positive attitudes toward this technology; something about virtual reality is attractive to learners and educators alike. What is not known yet is whether this is just due to novelty or whether it really does offer a stimulating and motivating medium for learning. Further work is needed to follow up on the studies that have been reported in this chapter to determine the true impact of VLEs for learning. Education researchers need to conduct controlled evaluation studies to determine the learning potential of VLEs as compared with other teaching media.

Technology developers need to be mindful of the needs of learners in a range of settings, in mainstream and special schools, as well as in other sectors of the community. Working together with educationalists, they need to be realistic about what virtual reality and virtual environments can and cannot provide. We need to ensure proper steps toward implementation to ensure that teachers are aware of how VLEs can be utilised within an education programme and to provide them with adequate training and resources.

Note

The authors would like to thank colleagues from VIRART and the MRL at the University of Nottingham. Thanks to Paul Wilson from the University of Hull and Nigel Foreman from the University of Middlesex who were involved in some of the work described in this chapter. Projects described were funded from the National Lottery Charities Board (1997–1998), the ESPRIT i3 Research Programme, Experimental Schools Environments (1998–2001), the Shirley Foundation (2000–2003), BT and Community (1994–2003) and SCOPE (1999–2003).

Glossary

Avatar: A computer-generated character within a virtual environment representing a user. The user controls his/her avatar movement around the virtual environment and interactions with objects and/or other avatars in the virtual environment.

Collaborative virtual environments: Networked spaces in which multiple participants can access a shared primarily three-dimensional, world. Nonetheless, the term has been increasingly used over the past few years to indicate a broader range of text-based systems such as chatrooms and MUDs (Multi-User Dimensions), which have some notion of shared space but are not as concerned with its graphical presentation.

Virtual environment: Computer-generated three-dimensional spaces presented to users from a first-person perspective, which can be explored in real time.

Virtual learning environment: The use of the term *virtual learning environment* is as diverse as the number of technical systems designed to support learning activities, including text and two-dimensional graphical environments. In this chapter, we primarily focus on VLEs as three-dimensional environments for learning.

Virtual reality: According to commonly held current definitions, virtual reality encompasses both virtual environments (i.e., three-dimensional worlds), along with the means to access them (i.e., hardware such as displays, tracking, and other input and output devices).

Transfer of training: Experiments have shown that knowledge and skills acquired in simulated environments can be applied in corresponding real-world situations. Transfer of training occurs when learning in one situation affects learning in a different situation.

References

Astur, R. S., Taylor, L. B., Mamelak, A. N. Philpott, L., & Sutherland, R. J. (2002). Humans with hippocampus damage display severe spatial memory impairments in a virtual Morris water task. *Behavioural Brain Research*, 132, 77–84.

Attree, E. A., Brooks, B. M., Rose, F. D., Andrews, T. K., Leadbetter, A. G., & Clifford, B. R. (1996). Memory processes and virtual environments: I can't remember what was there, but I can remember how I got there. Implications for people with disabilities. In Paul M. Sharkey (Ed.), *Proceedings of the 1st European Conference on Disability, Virtual Reality and Associated Technologies* (pp. 117–123). Maidenhead, England.

Barab, S. A., Hay, K. E., Barnett, M., & Squire, K. (2001). Constructing virtual worlds: Tracing the historical development of learner practices. *Cognition and Instruction*, 19(1), 47–94.

Baum, D. R. (1992). Virtual training devices: illusion or reality? *Proceedings of the 14th Annual Interservice/Industry Training Systems and Education Conference*.

Bell, J. T. & Fogler, H. S. (1995, June). The Investigation and application of virtual reality as an educational tool. *Proceedings of the American Society for Engineering Education*.

1995 annual conference, session number 2513, Anaheim, CA.

Bricken, M. (1991). Virtual reality learning environments: Potentials and challenges. *Computer Graphics*, 25(3) 178–184.

Brooks, B. M., Rose, F. D., Potter, J., Attree, E. A., Jayawardena, S., & Morling, A. (2002). Assessing stroke patients' ability to remember to perform actions in the future using virtual reality. In P. Sharkey, C. S. Lányi & P. Standen (Eds.), *Proceedings of the 4th International Conference on Disability, Virtual Reality and Associated Technologies, Hungary*, 239–245.

Brooks, B. M., Rose, F. D., Potter, J., Jayawardena, S., & Morling, A. (in press). Assessing stroke patients' prospective memory using virtual reality. *Brain Injury*.

Brown, D. J., Kerr, S. J., & Bayon, V. (1988, September). The development of the virtual city. In P. Sharkey, D. Rose, & J. I. Lindstrom (Eds.), *The 2nd European Conference on Disability, Virtual Reality and Associated Technologies* (pp. 89–98). Skovde, Sweden.

Brown, D. J., Neale, H. R., Cobb, S. V. G., & Reynolds, H. R. (1999). Development and evaluation of the virtual city. *The International Journal of Virtual Reality*. Special disability issue.

Brown, D. J., Standen, P. J., & Cobb, S. V. (1998). Virtual environments, special needs and evaluative methods. In G. Riva, B. K. Wiederhold, & E. Molinari (Eds.), *Virtual environments in clinical psychology: scientific and technological challenges in advanced patient-therapist interaction* (pp. 91–103). Amsterdam: IOS Press.

Byrne, C., & Furness, T. (1994). Virtual reality and education. *IFIP Transactions, Computer Science and Technology*, 58, 181–189.

Campos, J., Svejda, M., Campos, R., & Bertenthal, B. (1982). The emergence of self-produced locomotion: Its importance for psychological development in infancy. In D. Bricker (Ed.), *Intervention with at-risk and handicapped infants*. Baltimore: University Park Press.

Chapuis, N., Durup, M., & Thinus-Blanc, C. (1987). The role of exploratory experience in a shortcut task by golden hamsters. *Animal Learning and Behaviour*, 15(2), 174–178.

Cobb, S., Beardon, L., Eastgate, R., Glover, T., Kerr, S., Neale, H., Parsons, S., Benford, S., Hopkins, E., Mitchell, P., Reynard, G., & Wilson, J. R. (2002). Applied virtual environments to support learning of social interaction skills in users with Asperger's Syndrome. *Digital Creativity*, 13(1), 11–22.

Cobb, S., Kerr, S., & Glover, T. (2001, September). *The AS interactive project: Developing virtual environments for social skills training in users with Asperger's Syndrome*. Paper presented at *Workshop on Robotic and Virtual Interaction Systems in Autism Therapy*, University of Hertfordshire, Hatfield.

Cobb, S., Neale, H., Crosier, J., & Wilson, J. R. (2002). Development and evaluation of virtual environments for education. In K. Stanney (Ed.), *Virtual environment handbook* (pp. 911–936). Mahwah, N.J: Lawrence Erlbaum Associates.

Cobb, S. V. G., Neale, H. R., & Reynolds, H. (1998, September). Evaluation of virtual learning environments. In P. Sharkey, D. Rose, J. I. Lindstrom (Eds.), *The 2nd European conference on disability, virtual reality and associated technologies* (pp. 17–23). Skovde, Sweden.

Cromby, J. J., Standen, P. J., & Brown, D. J. (1996). The potentials of virtual environments in the education and training of people with learning disabilities. *Journal of Intellectual Disability Research*, 40(6), 489–501.

Crosier, J. (2001). *Virtual environments in secondary science education*. Unpublished doctoral dissertation, University of Nottingham, England.

Crosier, J. K., Cobb, S., & Wilson, J. R. (1999, March). *Virtual reality in secondary science education – establishing teachers' priorities*. Paper presented at *CAL'99*, London.

Crosier, J., Cobb, S., & Wilson, J. R. (2001). Key Lessons for the Design and Integration of Virtual Environments in Secondary Science, *Computers and Education*, 38, 77–94.

D'Cruz, M. D. (1999). *Structured evaluation of training in virtual environments*. Unpublished doctoral dissertation, University of Nottingham, England.

Dede, C. (1995). The evolution of constructivist learning environments: Immersion in distributed, virtual worlds. *Educational Technology*, 35(5), 46–52.

Dede, C., Salzman, M., & Bower Loftin, R. B. (1996). ScienceSpace: Virtual realities for learning complex and abstract scientific concepts. *Proceedings of VRAIS'96*, 246–253.

Dede, C., Salzman, M., Loftin, R. B., & Ash, K. (2000). The design of immersive virtual learning environments: Fostering deep understandings of complex scientific knowledge. In M. Jacobson & R. Kozma (Eds.), *Innovations in science and mathematics education: Advanced designs for technologies of learning* (pp. 361–413). Mahwah, NJ: Lawrence Erlbaum Associates.

Druin, A. (2002). The role of children in the design of new technology. *Behaviour and Information Technology*, 21(1), 1–25.

Druin, A., Alborzi, H., Boltman, A., Cobb, S., Montemayor, J., Neale, H., Platner, M., Porteous, J., Sherman, L., Simsarian, K., Stanton, D., Sundblad, Y., & Taxen, G. (2000). Participatory design with children: Techniques, challenges, and successes. Proceedings of *The Participatory Design Conference PDC 2000*. New York: ACM Press.

Eastgate, R. M. (2001). *The structured development of virtual environments: Enhancing functionality and interactivity*. Unpublished doctoral dissertation, University of Nottingham, England.

Foreman, N., Stanton, D., Wilson, P., & Duffy H. (2003). Successful transfer of spatial knowledge from a virtual to a real school environment in physically disabled children. *Journal of Experimental Psychology: Applied*, 9(2), 67–74.

Foreman, N., Stanton, D., Wilson, P., Duffy, H., & Parnell, R. (in press). Transfer of spatial knowledge to a 2-level shopping mall in older people following virtual exploration. *Environment and Behaviour*.

Gibson, J. J. (1979). *The ecological approach to visual perception*. Boston: Houghton Mifflin.

Gibson, J. J. (1966). *The senses considered as perceptual systems*. Boston: Houghton Mifflin.

Griffiths, G. D. (2001). *Virtual environment usability and user competence: The Nottingham Assessment of Interaction within Virtual Environments (NAÏVE) Tool*. Unpublished doctoral dissertation, University of Nottingham, England.

Hay, K. E., Elliott, D. M., & Kim, B. (2002). Collaborative network-based virtual reality: The past, the present and the future of the Virtual Solar System Project. *Proceedings of Computer Supported Collaborative Learning*, Boulder, Colorado, 519–520.

Johnson, A., Mohler, T., Ohlsson, S., & Gillingham, M. (1999). The Round Earth Project: Deep learning in a collaborative virtual world. In B. Loftin & L. Hodges (Eds.), *Proceedings of the IEEEVR '99 Conference*. Houston, TX: IEEE Press, 164–171.

Kalawsky, R. S. (1993). *The science of virtual reality and virtual environments*. Addison Wesley: Wokingham, Berks.

Kalawsky, R. S. (1996). Exploiting virtual reality techniques in education and training: Technological issues. *SIMA*.

Kennedy, R. S., & Fowlkes, J. E. (1992) Simulator sickness in polygenic and polysymptomatic: Implications for research. *The International Journal of Aviation Psychology*, 2(1), 23–38.

Kerr, S. J. (in press). Individualised scaffolded learning in desktop VR. *The Virtual Reality Society Journal*.

Kerr, S. J. (in preparation). *Scaffolded learning in virtual environments*. Unpublished doctoral dissertation, University of Nottingham, England.

Koleva, B., Schadelbach, H., Benford, S., & Greenhalgh, C. (2001, September–October). Experiencing a presentation through a mixed reality boundary. *Proceedings of Group 01* (pp. 71–80). Colorado: ACM.

Leonard, A., Mitchell, P., & Parsons, S. (2002, September). Finding a place to sit: A preliminary investigation into the effectiveness of virtual environments for social skills training for people with Autistic Spectrum Disorders. P. Shaskey, C. S. Lányi & P. Standen (Eds.), *Proceedings of 4th ICDVRAT*. Veszprem, Hungary. 249–257.

Martínez-Jiménez, P., Pontes-Pedraja, A., Polo, J., & Climent-Bellido, M. S. (2003). Learning in chemistry with virtual laboratories. *Journal of Chemical Education*, 80, 346–352.

Meakin, L., Wilkins, L., Gent, C., Brown, S., Moreledge, D., Gretton, C., Carlisle, M., McClean, C., Scott, J., Constance, J., & Mallett, A. (1998). *User group involvement in the development of a virtual city*. Paper presented at the 2nd European Conference on Disability, Virtual Reality and Associated Technologies, Skovde, Sweden.

Mendozzi, L., Attree, E. A., Pugnetti, L., Barbieri, E., Rose, F. D., Moro, W., Loconte, A., Corrales, B., Maj, L., Elliott-Square, A., Massara, A. & Cutelli, E. (2000, September). *The VIRT-Factory Trainer Project: A generic productive process to train persons with learning disabilities. The International Conference on Disability, Virtual Reality and Associated Technologies* – ICDVRAT2000, Sassari, Sardinia, Italy.

McClean, P., Saini-Eidukat, B., Schwert, D. P., Slator, B. M., & White, A. (2001). Virtual worlds in large enrollment science classes significantly improve authentic learning. In Jack A. Chambers (Ed)., *Selected papers from the 12th International Conference on College Teaching and Learning* (pp. 111–118), Jacksonville, FL.

Middleton, T. (1992). Advanced technologies for enhancing education. *Journal of Microcomputer applications*, 1, 1–7.

Mitchell, W. L., & Economou, D. (1999). Understanding context and medium in the development of educational VEs. In S. Smith and M. Harrison (Eds.), Proceedings of the workshop on *User centred design and implementation of virtual environments* (pp. 109–115). University of York.

Mohl, R. (1981). *Cognitive space in the interactive movie map: An investigation of spatial learning in virtual environments*. Unpublished doctoral dissertation, the Cybernetics Technology Division of the Defence Advanced Research Projects Agency.

Moreno, R., & Mayer, R. E. (2004). Personalized messages that promote science learning in virtual environments. *Journal of Educational Psychology*, 96(1), 165–173.

Moshell, J. M., & Hughes, C. E. (1996). The virtual academy: A simulated environment for constructionist learning. *International Journal of Human-Computer Interaction*, 8(1), 95–110.

Moshell, J. M., & Hughes, C. E. (2002). Virtual environments as a tool for academic learning. In K. Stanney (Ed.), *Handbook of virtual environments, design, implementation and applications* (pp. 893–910). Mahwah, NJ: Lawrence Erlbaum Associates.

Neale, H. R., Brown, D. J., Cobb, S. V. G., & Wilson, J. R. (1999). Structured evaluation of virtual learning environments for special needs education. *Presence: Teleoperators and Virtual Environments*, 8(3), 264–282.

Neale, H., Cobb, S., & Kerr, S. (2003, March). An inclusive design toolbox for development of educational virtual environments. Paper presented at *Include 2003*, Royal College of Art, London.

Neale, H. R., Cobb, S. V. Kerr, S., & Leonard, A. (2002, September). Exploring the role of virtual environments in the special needs classroom. P. Sharkey, C. S. Lányi and P. Standen (Eds.), *Proceedings of the 4th International Conference on Disability, Virtual Reality and Associated Technologies (ICDVRAT)* (pp. 259–266). Veszprem, Hungary.

Parsons, S. (2001, September) *Social conventions in virtual environments: Investigating understanding of personal space amongst people with autistic spectrum disorders. Workshop on Robotic and Virtual Interactive Systems in Autism Therapy*, University of Hertfordshire, Hatfield, England.

Parsons, S., Beardon, L., Neale, H. R., Reynard, G., Eastgate, R., Wilson, J. R., Cobb, S. V., Benford, S., Mitchell, P., & Hopkins, E. (2000, September). Development of social skills amongst adults with Asperger's Syndrome using virtual environments: The AS Interactive project. *Proceedings of the International Conference on Disability, Virtual Reality, and Associated Technologies*, Sardinia.

Parsons, S., & Mitchell, P. (2001, April). Virtual reality and people with autistic spectrum disorders: Informal observations from the AS Interactive Project. *Proceedings of the 12th Annual Durham International Conference on Autism.*

Parsons, S., & Mitchell, P. (2003). The potential of virtual reality in social skills training for people with autistic spectrum disorders. *Journal of Intellectual Disability Research, 46*(5), 430–443.

Pasqualotti, A., & Freitas, C.M.D.S. (2002). MAT – super (3D): A virtual reality modelling language environment for the teaching and learning of mathematics. *Cyberpsychology and Behaviour, 5*(5), 409–422.

Péruch, P., Vercher, J. L., & Gauthier, G. M. (1995). Acquisition of spatial knowledge through visual exploration of simulated environments. *Ecological Psychology, 7*(1), 1–20.

Péruch, P., Belingard, L., and Thinus-Blanc, C. (2000). Transfer of spatial knowledge from virtual to real environments. In C. Freksa, W. Brauer, C. Habel, & K. F. Wender (Eds.), *Spatial cognition II*, LNAI 1849 (pp. 253–264). Berlin and Heidelberg: Springer-Verlag.

Powers, D., & Darrow, M. (1994). Special education and virtual reality: Challenges and possibilities. *Journal of Research on Computing in Education, 27*(1), 111–121.

Pugnetti, L., Mendozzi, L., Attree, E. A., Barbieri, E., Brooks, B. M., Cazzulo, C. L., Motta, A., & Rose, F. D. (1998). Probing memory and executive functions with VR: Past and present studies. *Cyberpsychology and Behaviour, 1*, 151–162.

Regian, J. W., Shebilske, W. L., & Monk, J. M. (1992). Virtual reality: An instructional medium for visuo-spatial tasks. *Journal of Communication, 4*, 136–149.

Riva, G., Wiederhold, B. K., & Molinari, E. (1998). *Virtual environments in clinical psychology: Scientific and technological challenges in advanced patient-therapist interaction.* Amsterdam: IOS Press.

Rizzo, A., Buckwalter, J. G., Bowerly, T., Van Rooyen, A., McGee, J., Van der Zaag, C., Neumann, U., Thiebaux, M., Kim, L., & Chua, C. (2000, September). Virtual reality applications for the assessment and rehabilitation of attention and visuospatial cognitive processes: An update. In Sharkey P., Cesarani A., Pugnetti L., & Rizzo A. (Eds.), *Proceedings of the 3rd International Conference on Disability, Virtual Reality, and Associated Technology.* Alghero, Sardinia, Italy.

Rizzo, A. A., Buckwalter, J. G., McGee, J. S., Bowerly, T., van der Zaag, C., Neumann, U., Thiebaux, M., Kim, L., Pair, J. & Chua, C. (2001). VEs for assessing and rehabilitating cognitive/functional performance. *Presence, 10*(4), 359–374.

Rizzo, A. A., Buckwalter, J. G., and van der Zaag, C. (2002). Virtual environment applications in clinical neuropsychology. In K. Stanney (Ed.), *Virtual environment handbook.* (pp. 1027–1064). Mahwah, NJ: Lawrence Erlbaum Associates.

Rose, F. D., Brooks, B. M., & Attree, E. A. (2000, September). Virtual reality in vocational training of people with learning disabilities. *The International Conference on Disability, Virtual Reality and Associated Technologies – ICDVRAT2000*, Sassari, Sardinia, Italy.

Ruddle, R. A., & Jones, D. M. (2001). Manual and virtual rotation of a three-dimensional object. *Journal of Experimental Psychology: Applied, 7*, 286–296.

Ruddle, R. A., Payne, S. J., & Jones, D. M. (1997). Navigating buildings in desk-top virtual environments: Experimental investigations using extended navigational experience. *Journal of Experimental Psychology, 3*(2) 143–159.

Ruddle, R. A., & Péruch, P. (2004). Effects of proprioceptive feedback and environmental characteristics on spatial learning in virtual environments. *International Journal Human-Computer Studies, 60*, 299–326.

Rutten, A., Cobb, S., Neale, H., Kerr, S., Leonard, A., Parsons, S., & Mitchell, P. (2003), The AS interactive project: Single-user and collaborative virtual environments for people with high-functioning autistic spectrum disorders. *Journal of Visualization and Computer Animation, 14*, 233–241.

Salzman, M. C., Dede, C., Bowen Loftin, R., & Chen, J. (1999). A model for how VR aids complex conceptual learning. *Presence, 8*(3), 293–316.

Salzman, M. C., Dede, C., McGlynn, D., & Loftin, R. B. (1996). ScienceSpace: Lessons for designing immersive virtual realities. *Proceedings of ACM CHI'96: ACM Conference on Human Factors in Computing Systems.*

Scaife, M., & Rogers, Y. (2001). Informing the design of a virtual environment to support learning in children. *International Journal of Human-Computer Studies, 55*, 115–143.

Standen, P. J., Brown, D. J., & Cromby, J. J. (2001). The effective use of VEs in the education and rehabilitation of students with intellectual disabilities. *British Journal of Educational Technology, 32*(3), 289–299.

Standen, P. J., & Low, H. L. (1996). Do virtual environments promote self-directed activity? A study of students with severe learning difficulties learning Makaton sign language. Paul M. Sharkey (Ed.), *Proceedings of the 1st European Conference on Disability, Virtual Reality and Associated Technologies* (pp. 123–129). Maidenhead, England.

Standen, P. J., Brown, D. J., Proctor, T., & Horan, M. (2002). How tutors assist adults with learning disabilities to use virtual environments. Disability and rehabilitation. 24, 11–12, pp. 570–577.

Stanton, D. (1997). *Spatial cognition and virtual environments.* Unpublished doctoral dissertation. University of Leicester, England.

Stanton, D., Foreman, N., & Wilson, P. N. (1998). Uses of virtual reality in training: Developing the spatial skills of children with mobility impairments. In G. Riva, B. K. Wiederhold & E. Molinari (Eds.), *Virtual environments in clinical psychology: Scientific and technological challenges in advanced patient-therapist interaction. Vol. 58* (pp. 219–233). Amsterdam: IOS Press.

Stanton, D., Foreman, N., Wilson, P., & Duffy, H. (2002). Use of virtual environments to acquire spatial understanding of real world multi-level environments. *4th International Conference on Disability, Virtual Reality and Associated Technologies* 2002. pp. 13–19 Vesprem, Hungary.

Stanton, D., Wilson, P., & Foreman, N. (1996, July). Using virtual reality environments to aid spatial awareness in disabled children. *The 1st European Conference on Disability, Virtual Reality and Associated Technologies* (pp. 93–101). Maidenhead, Berkshire, England.

Stanton, D., Wilson, P., & Foreman, N. (2002). Effects of early mobility on shortcut performance in a simulated maze. *Behavioural Brain Research, 136*, 61–66.

Stanton, D., Wilson, P., and Foreman, N. (2003). Human shortcut performance in a computer-simulated maze: A comparative study. *Spatial Cognition and Computation, 3*, 315–329.

Taxén, G., & Naeve, A. (2002). A system for exploring open issues in VR-based education. *Computers and Graphics, 26*, 593–598.

Tlauka, M., & Wilson, P. N. (1994). The effect of landmarks on route-learning in a computer-simulated environment. *Journal of Environmental Psychology, 14*, 305–313.

Trindade, J., Fiolhais, C., & Almeida, L. (2002). Science learning in virtual environments: A descriptive study. *British Journal of Educational Technology, 33*(4), 471–488.

Waterworth, J. A., & Waterworth, E. L. (2000). Presence and absence in educational virtual reality: The role of perceptual seduction in conceptual learning. *Themes in Education, 1* (1), 7–38.

Wickens, C., & Baker, P. (1995). Cognitive issues in virtual reality. In W. Barfield and T. A. Furness (Eds.), *Virtual environments and advanced interface design* (pp. 514–541). New York: Oxford University Press.

Wiederhold, B. K., Wiederhold, M. D. (in press). *Virtual healing: Human stories of success.* San Diego: Interactive Media Institute.

Williams, H. P., & Wickens, C. D. (1993). *A comparison of methods for promoting geographic knowledge in simulated aircraft navigation.* (Report No. ARL-93-9/NASA-93-3). Savoy, IL: Aviation Research Laboratory.

Wilson, J. R., Eastgate, R. M., & D'Cruz, M. (2002). Structured development of virtual environments. In K. Stanney (Ed.), *Virtual environment handbook,* (pp. 353–378). Mahwah, NJ: Lawrence Erlbaum Associates.

Wilson, P. N., Foreman, N., Gillett, R., and Stanton, D. (1997). Active versus passive processing of spatial information in a computer simulated environment. *Ecological Psychology, 9*(3), 207–222.

Wilson, P., Foreman, N., Stanton, D., & Duffy, H. (2004). Memory for targets in a multi-level simulated-environment: Evidence for vertical asymmetry in spatial memory. *Memory and Cognition, 32*(2), 283–297.

Wilson, P., Foreman, N., Stanton, D., and Duffy, H. (in press). Memory for targets in a multi-level simulated-environment: A comparison between able-bodied and physically disabled children. *British Journal of Psychology.*

Wilson, P. N., Foreman, N., & Stanton, D. (1997). Virtual reality, disability and rehabilitation. *Disability and Rehabilitation*, 19(6), 213–220.

Wilson, P. N., Foreman, N., & Tlauka, M. (1996). Transfer of spatial information from a virtual to a real environment in able-bodied adults and disabled children. *Disability and Rehabilitation*, 18(12), 633–637.

Wilson, P. N., Foreman, N., & Tlauka, M. (1997). Transfer of spatial information from a virtual to a real environment. *Human Factors*, 39, 526–531.

Winn, W. (1993). A conceptual basis for educational applications of VR. (*Technical Report TR 93–9*). University of Washington.

Winn, W. (1997, May). The impact of three-dimensional immersive virtual environments on modern pedagogy *(HITL Technical Report R-97-15)*. Discussion paper for NSF workshop. Seattle, WA: University of Washington, Human Interface Technology Laboratory.

Winn, W., Hoffman, H., Hollander, A., Osberg, K., Rose, H., and Char, P. (1999). Student-built VEs. *Presence*, 8(3), 283–292.

Witmer, B. G., Bailey, J. H., & Knerr, B. W. (1995). *Training dismounted soldiers in virtual environments: Route learning and transfer*. Alexandria, VA: U.S. Army Research Institute for the Behavioral and Social Sciences.

Wollensak, A. (2002). Curricular modules: 3D and immersive visualization tools for learning. *Computers and Graphics*, 26, 599–602.

Yair, Y., Mintz, R., & Litvak, S. (2001). 3D VR in science education: an implication for astronomy teaching. *Journal Computers in Mathematics and Science Teaching*, 20(3), 293–305.

Youngblut, C. (1998) Educational uses of virtual reality technology (Tech. Rep. No D-2128). Alexandria, VA: Institute for Defense Analysis.

CHAPTER 33

Multimedia Learning in Games, Simulations, and Microworlds

Lloyd P. Rieber
The University of Georgia

Abstract

This chapter reviews and critiques the scientific evidence and research methods studying the use of games, simulations, and microworlds as multimedia learning tools. This chapter focuses on interactive educational multimedia, which is distinguished from scripted forms of educational multimedia by the degree to which users participate in and control the multimedia software. This chapter also uses the distinction between explanation and experience to understand the unique design opportunities of interactive educational multimedia. The strongest empirical evidence comes from the simulation literature, especially that related to questions about how to design a simulation's interface to provide feedback and questions about students engaged in discovery learning activities. Microworld research is less empirically rigorous with evidence continuing to remain largely anecdotal based on implementation reports. Research on gaming is the most transitory, ranging from early research on learning from playing games to learning from designing games. Current debates among educational researchers about what constitutes scientific research are particularly relevant to anyone interested in research about interactive multimedia due to the increased use of qualitative research methodologies and the newly emerging trend toward design experiments.

What Is Multimedia Learning in Games, Simulations, and Microworlds?

The purpose of this chapter is to review the scientific evidence on the use of games, simulations, and microworlds as multimedia learning tools. This is a tall order. All three have very distinctive design and research pedigrees resulting in many cases from very distinctive philosophies about education. Despite these differences, there are advantages to considering all three in discussions of interactive multimedia because each has strengths and ideas that help mitigate weaknesses or gaps often found in the other two (see Rieber, 1992, 2003 for detailed discussions).

This chapter is written to consider games, simulations, and microworlds within the broad organizational framework of educational multimedia. Most of the educational multimedia studied by researchers is not interactive or experiential, but instead is used as part of instructional texts that explain content to students. For that reason, it is useful to consider the distinction between explanation and experience when trying to understand the design and use of educational multimedia. Multimedia that emphasizes explanation uses multimedia elements (e.g., text, static graphics, animation, and audio) in "scripted" ways. By scripted, I mean multimedia that is designed to be read or viewed in one particular way, similar to an encyclopedia article. Consider a multimedia article about aerodynamics, such as that available at HowStuffWorks.com. One section of the article involves text accompanied by an animation of the three-dimensional movements of a plane in flight. The text and animation work together as coordinated elements of the explanation – one textual and one visual (i.e., animated).

In contrast, games, simulations, and microworlds are examples of interactive multimedia. The emphasis here is on experience made possible by dynamic elements that are under the user's control. Rather than read about flight, a flight simulator gives the user control over an animated plane with increasing levels of challenge. If goals are included, especially ones that encourage the user to take on another identity, such as a military pilot on an important mission, the simulation also becomes a game. Interestingly, text and static graphics may also be involved, such as providing the user (i.e., pilot) "just in time" information, such as weather forecasts, instructions for the mission, or directions from a simulated traffic controller. The difference is that learning is based on the experience of flying the plane, rather than explanations about planes and flight. Of course, both explanation and experience are important in education, but advocates of games, simulations, and microworlds put experience first with explanations serving a supporting role.

The distinction between explanation and experience also highlights differences between different instructional and constructivist perspectives of education. Although an examination of the epistemological differences between these perspectives is outside the scope of this chapter, this distinction is important because it serves as the basis for very different multimedia software designs. Microworlds were born out of constructivist thinking (Rieber, 2003), whereas simulation and gaming have long been aligned with more traditional instructional uses of educational software (Gredler, 1996, 2003). However, except for the most radical interpretations, constructivist perspectives do not ignore the role of instruction, but instead place greater emphasis on a person's interaction in a content area and the relationship of that interaction to that person's prior knowledge about the content (Jonassen, 1991). Learning is believed to be achieved through active engagement in which the teacher provides support, resources, and encouragement. A constructivist perspective also places much emphasis on the social context of learning.

Current evidence suggests that technology has had little impact on education, despite the amount of money spent on it (Cuban, 2001; Cuban, Kirkpatrick, & Peck, 2001; Zhao & Frank, 2003). In contrast, technology has had its most profound impact on learning outside of schools. Perhaps the closest relative to educational computing, due to its involvement of almost all children of school age, is video games (Gee, 2003). It is interesting how the computer software business has competed for the opportunity to have children use their products in the education and gaming markets. In education, the marketing is aimed at educators whereas in gaming the marketing is directly aimed at the children. The amount of money spent on computer games is staggering, outpacing even that of the film industry (Poole, 2000). Many adults, usually consisting of those who have never actually played a computer game, are quick to criticize the culture of computer gaming. Computer gaming is largely viewed as a waste of time at best and an evil influence at worst, leading many to blame it as a significant cause of childhood violence. The reality is far more complicated, and far more interesting, even from strictly an educational point of view. Nevertheless, anyone wishing to understand the role of the computer within both educational and societal contexts must take interactive multimedia into account.

I write this chapter from the point of view of an educational technologist, not a psychologist. Despite this book's goal of presenting "just the facts" as revealed by empirical research, I fear I am less confident than many of my coauthors about the robustness of the research evidence, especially when we move from the laboratory to the field. The standards of scientific research in education has been the focus of much debate recently, especially since the release of the report *Scientific Research in Education* by the National Research Council (2002) (see Berliner, 2002; Erickson & Gutierrez, 2002; Feuer, Towne, & Shavelson, 2002, for examples of the debate). Generalization of the results from educational multimedia research to the "real world" of learning and performing in schools and the workplace should be viewed with considerable caution. Researchers have just begun to seriously study educational multimedia, so the time is ripe to question not only the results so far, but also the methods we have used.

What Is an Example of Multimedia in Games, Simulations, and Microworlds?

I begin by presenting two software examples to show the similarities and differences between games, simulations, and microworlds. Both are examples that have been the basis of much research. The first is a simple simulation that I designed for use in some of my own simulation research (see Rieber & Noah, 1997; Rieber, Noah, & Nolan, 1998). It also includes a simple gaming feature. The second example is a microworld called ThinkerTools (White, 1993; White &

Frederiksen, 1998). The class of software referred to as microworlds is very diverse, so it is difficult to capture it with one example. For example, many microworlds can be thought of as programming languages, such as Logo (Papert, 1980b) and Boxer (diSessa, 1997; diSessa, Abelson, & Ploger, 1991). However, ThinkerTools largely uses a graphical user interface allowing point-and-click methods to programming the computer. Both ThinkerTools and the software I designed are designed to learn about simple mechanics, namely Newton's laws of motion. ThinkerTools also has interesting parallels to simulation and gaming, hence it is a good candidate to begin understanding how microworlds relate to them.

Figure 33.1 shows an example of a simple simulation of Newton's laws of motion, specifically the relationship between acceleration and velocity. It also includes a gaming component. If you are not familiar with the physics of acceleration and velocity, it's important to know that each is a quantity specified by a magnitude and a direction (such quantities are known as *vectors*). *Velocity* is defined as the change in an object's position over time; it consists of the speed *and* direction of an object. *Acceleration* is defined as the change of the object's velocity over time, implying again that the direction in which this change is occurring is important. These two attributes, though very simple, often lead novices to confusion because their everyday encounters with the terms *acceleration* and *velocity* usually omit the idea of direction. Most people understand and agree that a driver who guns the accelerator pedal accelerates the car. But most nonphysicists have a hard time understanding that when slamming on the brakes the driver also accelerates *in the opposite direction that the car is moving* to bring the car to a quick stop. In this simulation, the user has direct control over the acceleration of a single object in the simulation – a ball. The simulation begins with the ball moving at a constant speed from left to right. Because the speed is constant, the acceleration is therefore zero. If the user clicks once on the right arrow button, the ball experiences a small but continuous acceleration to the right, similar to holding down the gas pedal a wee bit and keeping it there. Hence the ball's speed to the right increases at a constant rate – the ball goes faster and faster. If the user clicks on the right arrow again, the acceleration is increased and the ball's speed increases at a slightly greater rate. If the user then clicks on the left arrow twice, returning acceleration to zero, the ball's motion returns to a constant speed, albeit increased over its initial speed, to the right. If the user next clicks on the left arrow button, the acceleration of the object is to the left a slight amount. What does acceleration to the left mean when the ball is moving to the right? Simply that the ball slows down at a constant rate. An interesting thing happens if the user does nothing further: the ball slows down as it moves from left to right, eventually comes to a stop for just an instant, then starts moving right to left, slowly at first but then speeding up at the same rate that it slowed down. This changing of directions is called a *flip flop* in this simulation, clearly a nontechnical term, but highly descriptive for the nonphysicists using the software.

As this example demonstrates, every computer simulation has an underlying mathematical model programmed into it that dictates how the simulation behaves. The underlying model of this one happens to be based on Newton's laws of motion. However, a simulation can be based on any quantitative model that can be programmed into the computer to an acceptable degree. Scientific models are popular examples (e.g., physics, chemistry, biology, genetics) because the underlying models are more precisely defined than phenomena from other domains (e.g., sociology). When used for educational purposes, the students interact with the simulation to understand how this underlying model works. Whether the underlying model is taught before, during, or after experiencing the simulation is a key design question for both instructional designers and educational researchers.

Much of my own research has explored some of the many decisions about how to design the simulation's interface to help convey the underlying model to the user. These are the decisions most relevant to the design of interactive multimedia. For example, as shown in Figure 33.1, this simulation encourages the user to imagine that the ball is moving on a very long board that can be tilted in either direction. This helps to contextualize the simulation for the user by providing a model case designed to help to make the essential concepts and principles underlying the simulation more salient. For example, when the ball is moving at a constant rate it is equivalent to the board being flat (although this requires the user to understand and accept the idea that there is no friction generated between the ball and board that would slow the ball down). The example described in the preceding text of the ball moving from left to right with the user then choosing to accelerate it to the left is equivalent to tilting the board downward to the left. The idea of a "tilting board" is conveyed by presenting a dynamic "side-view" graphic, which shows the tilt of the board when viewed on its side (as compared to the "top-view" graphic). The goal of this tilting board model case is to help concretize the physics relationships at work here for users by tapping into their prior knowledge.

It's important to recognize that unless the instructor gives a student explicit directions or guidance, there appears to be no real purpose or goal to the simulation other than to explore it. The ability of students to *discover* the underlying model through free exploration is a question explored by much research (e.g., de Jong & van Joolingen, 1998). But how can the software be designed to provide an explicit goal to the student? Typical school-based approaches include giving the student a question to answer or a problem to solve using the simulation as their "laboratory." Another way to accomplish this is with gaming. The simulation shown in Figure 33.1 takes advantage of the flip-flop concept mentioned previously to create a little game. The goal of the game is to make the ball do a flip flop anywhere inside the small yellow box. When the student is successful, they get a point. The yellow box then moves to another random location on the screen. Obviously, the wider the yellow box, the

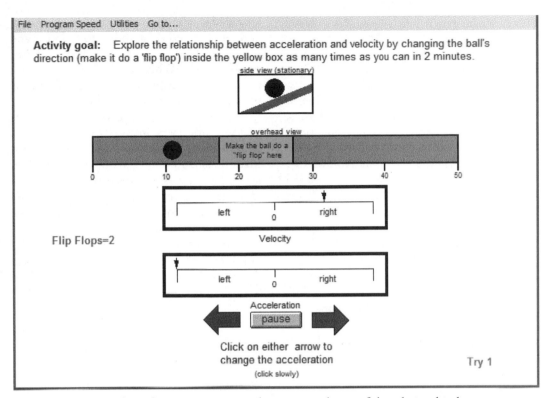

Figure 33.1. A snapshot of a computer screen during a simulation of the relationship between velocity and acceleration. A user manipulates the ball's acceleration by clicking on either large arrow. This simulation also contains a game in which the user tries to change the direction of the ball while it is inside a yellow box (marked "make the ball do a 'flip flop' here").

easier the task. This points to a fundamental design characteristic of games – the challenge of the game should be proportional to the skill level of the user. It is easy to program a computer game to increase the challenge as the user builds expertise. In this case, the expertise can be measured by the time interval between scoring points.

Is a game such as this an effective way to teach physics? Games are often touted for their motivational qualities. If a game increases a participant's enjoyment in the activity, they are likely to want to engage in and persist at the activity. But, what other influences might the game have on learning? From a cognitive processing perspective, a well-designed game might help focus a participant's attention on critical aspects of the content or help the participant organize incoming information due to the presence of game goals and outcomes. These questions were studied using the "flip flop in the yel-

low box" game described previously (Rieber & Noah, 1997). Interestingly, the use of the game did have an effect on learning – a negative one. Participants who were given the game actually scored significantly lower on the physics posttest than participants who were not given the game. However, all participants were also asked after each simulation trial to rate their overall enjoyment on a scale of 0 to 8 where 0 was "no enjoyment" and 8 was "extreme enjoyment." Participants who were given the game reported much greater levels of enjoyment than those who were not. The quantitative phase of this study points to some interesting antagonism between negative effects of a game on learning and positive effects of the game on participants' motivation. But, the quantitative results could not answer why this was so. In a follow-up qualitative phase of the study, we learned that participants became obsessive with the game. In the parlance of gamers, they went into "twitch" mode and focused exclusively on improving their score in the game. Due to this, they did not engage in reflection of their learning of physics. Experience without reflection is detrimental to learning. When engaged by the researcher to talk about the game's relationship to physics, participants were able to make connections that aided their learning.

In contrast to the simulation/game shown in Figure 33.1 there is a microworld called ThinkerTools shown in Figure 33.2. With the ThinkerTools software, students can either build their own physical models of motion, or they can interact and modify prebuilt models that come with the software. Unlike a simulation, the ThinkerTools microworld is best thought of as a "physics playground" offering literally unlimited ways to construct a physics model. In this microworld, the user can add any number of objects, called *dots*, that obey Newton's laws of motion. However, the user can control the value of a large collection of parameters, such as each dot's initial mass, elasticity (fragile or bouncy), and velocity. Users can also determine other forces acting on the model, such as gravity. Barriers and targets can be added to the model to add game-like designs. The user can decide whether to directly control other forces on the dots, such as with the keyboard or a joystick, similar to a video game, or to just run the model to see what happens over time.

What distinguishes ThinkerTools from the simulation described previously in this section is the amount of control the user has over the computer within the software. It closely resembles computer programming, albeit confined within the boundaries of physics. Users are limited only by their own creativity in determining what the Thinker-Tools software is for or what it can do. However, like other microworlds, ThinkerTools is also designed based on definite philosophical assumptions and ideals about learning. The best uses of the tool, according to its designers, is to support an inquiry and modeling curriculum to empower students to develop metacognitive "knowledge about the nature of scientific laws and models, their

knowledge about the process of modeling and inquiry, and their ability to monitor and reflect on these processes so they can improve them" (White & Frederiksen, 2000, p. 327). Simulations and games can also be used in inquiry approaches, but they, unlike microworlds, usually mirror the intentions of their designers instead of the students who use them. The use and role of simulations and microworlds in education can also be distinguished, respectively, in terms of *model using* versus *model building* (Penner, 2000–2001). Model using is where a student uses a model built by someone else, usually the teacher, in a learning activity. Model building is where students are given access to the modeling or programming tool to build their own models.

What Do We Know About the Multimedia Learning in Games, Simulations, and Microworlds?

Not surprisingly, the research on games, simulations, and microworlds is diverse, being based or motivated by very different pedagogical and philosophical approaches. The research methodologies are equally diverse and include quantitative experimental designs, qualitative designs, and the newly emerging methods of design experiments. In the following three sections, I examine some of the research on the educational use of simulations, microworlds, and games, respectively.

Simulations

This section reviews research related to the model-using role of simulations in education – learning from a simulation designed by someone else. Two areas of research are discussed here. The first deals with how characteristics of the simulation designed to represent the underlying model are perceived and used by students while interacting with the simulation. Much of this research asks questions similar to other multimedia research efforts, such as the role, influence, or effects

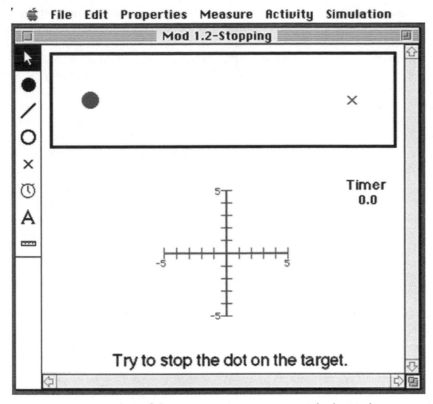

File Edit Properties Measure Activity Simulation

Mod 1.2-Stopping

Timer
0.0

Try to stop the dot on the target.

Figure 33.2. A snapshot of the computer screen running ThinkerTools, a microworld of Newtonian mechanics. In this activity, the user controls the ball by pressing the left or right arrow keys. Unlike a simulation, users can program their own activities and run their own experiments.

of different representational elements of the simulation on learning. An example would be examining the use of graphics or text for key elements of the simulation's interface, such as how the simulation provides feedback based on user actions or choices while operating the simulation. The second area of research examines students' scientific discovery learning with a simulation. This research concerns the degree to which students are able to discover and understand the simulation's underlying model on their own versus the degree to which they need varying levels of instructional support or guidance.

A good example of research investigating how different representations influence learning from simulations is a series of studies I conducted with colleagues (Rieber, 1990, 1991, 1996a; Rieber, Boyce, & Assad, 1990; Rieber & Kini, 1995; Rieber, Luke, & Smith, 1998; Rieber & Noah, 1997; Rieber

& Parmley, 1995; Rieber et al., 1996; Rieber, Tzeng, & Tribble, 2004). In this research, we examined the role of computer animation as graphical feedback during a simulation. When interacting with a simulation, a user must first be able to tell the difference between their goals and intentions, then be able to judge whether or not their intentions have been met. Norman (2002) refers to the differences in these two states as the gulfs of execution and evaluation, core principles of interface design. The typical method we used in this research was to design three versions of a physics simulation (similar to that shown in Figure 33.1) that varied in the way feedback was presented to users as they interacted with the simulation: animated graphical feedback, textual feedback, or a combination of both graphical and textual feedback. Similar to a video game, if the user wanted an object to move to the left, he or she would press a screen button that applied force to the object in the left-hand direction. An example of a simulation designed only with textual feedback is shown in Figure 33.3. Feedback is presented solely through the use of numeric readouts that depict the current position of the object being manipulated and, in the case of Figure 33.3, the position of a target that participants are trying to hit with their object. Both the graphical and text-based simulations use exactly the same underlying model. The only difference is the way the feedback is presented to students. We evaluated learning in both explicit and implicit ways. Explicit learning was measured using a traditional multiple-choice test of physics understanding, whereas implicit learning was measured by the ability of students to complete a game-like activity similar to the simulation. In most of our research, we used a scientific discovery approach, that is, we deliberately did not include physics instruction to accompany the simulation. We wanted to be sure that all learning occurred solely through interaction with the simulation.

As it turns out, this type of learning is very difficult for students who are novices in physics. One prediction is that animated graphical feedback would be a better way to represent information and relationships for Newtonian mechanics – animated balls are close analogs to actual moving balls. However, such representations may not make the relationships explicit, that is, learning might remain implicit in the simulation activity unless the person makes a deliberate effort to "translate" the relationship into the verbal terms needed to answer the posttest questions. A person given the textual feedback who is successful at the simulation would have to work hard to make such a translation, thus leading to the prediction that textual feedback would lead to more explicit learning, especially when measured with verbally stated multiple-choice questions.

When participants used the simulation in a discovery-oriented way, that is, without any accompanying instruction, results sometimes, but not always, favored the use of graphical feedback over textual feedback or graphical plus textual feedback on tests of explicit learning, such as traditional text-based questions (Rieber, 1996a; Rieber et al., 1996). In contrast, graphical feedback led to superior performance on tests of implicit learning (computer-game-like tasks). In other words, graphical feedback was more beneficial than textual feedback for implicit, or near-transfer, tasks. Yet, on explicit, or far-transfer, tasks requiring students to translate graphical symbols into verbal symbols, the difference was not as compelling.

What is needed to further help students explicitly learn the physics principles well enough to answer verbally presented problems? In follow-up qualitative studies where we interviewed participants as they used the simulation, we noticed that few people discovered the "secrets" of the laws of motion without some help or guidance by the interviewer. The guidance was not complex or time consuming – just pointing out some critical features to the participant based on their experiences or simple questions that helped them to focus on key physical principles. The guidance did not even interrupt their interactions with the simulation, but instead seemed to give them insights for their subsequent attempts. What was needed was guiding information – an explanation – to be given at just the right time.

In a follow-up research study we included the use of short, embedded multimedia explanations (with both text and animation) of the physics principles and showed them to participants *during the simulation* (Rieber et al., 2004). Providing these short explanations made a huge difference. Participants given graphical feedback far outperformed those given textual feedback, but only when accompanied by the short explanations. We think providing the explanations intermittently while using the simulation helps students to organize their experiences with the simulation, helping them to construct appropriate mental representations of the physics content. In contrast to full-blown tutorials that divide explanation and experience, the short explanations provide just the right amount of explanation at just the right time. Another interesting result

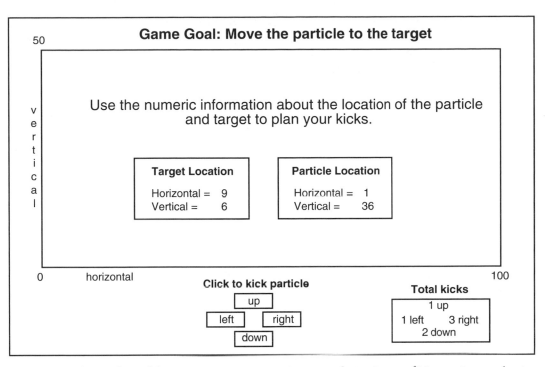

Figure 33.3. A snapshot of the computer screen running a simulation/game of Newtonian mechanics where all feedback is given to the user in numeric form.

emerged from our qualitative research on these simulations. Those participants who did master the simulation shifted their preference from the graphical feedback to the textual feedback. They did so for several reasons. The first was motivational – they were looking for a greater challenge. The second was tactical – as they began to develop strategies based on emerging mental models of the physics principles, textual feedback became more aligned with those strategies. For example, an implication of Newton's second law is the idea that when forces acting on an object in one dimension are balanced from either direction, the object stops moving in that direction. When participants understood this principle and began using it as one of their strategies for controlling the motion of the ball, it became easier for participants to use textual feedback that displayed the total accumulated force in numerical terms.

We also measured the frustration levels of participants by asking students throughout the research (right after each simulation trial) to report their current level of frustra-tion on a scale of 0 to 8 where 0 was "no frustration" and 8 was "extreme frustration." Participants given only textual feedback consistently reported much greater frustration than those given graphical feedback. This is not surprising because the mental effort in converting the numerical feedback into a spatial position on the screen is hard work.

The second area of simulation research reviewed here is that dealing with scientific discovery learning. The purpose of this research is to understand the process students go through to understand a simulation's underlying model in the absence of explicit instruction about the model. This research focuses on inquiry learning by students, as they use scientific reasoning to solve problems with the simulation. One of the most thorough reviews of this research is provided by de Jong and van Joolingen (1998). Their review demonstrates how difficult it is for students to use simulations in this way. For example, students are often prone to *confirmation bias*, the tendency to design experiments that will lead them to confirm early formed hypotheses. Students find it difficult to discard hypotheses, even when faced with contradicting data. Similarly, students find it difficult to construct hypotheses that can be easily tested with experiments. Students have difficulty in setting up an appropriate experiment to test even a well-stated hypothesis. Of the many conclusions offered by de Jong and van Joolingen, one is similar to that already discussed: information, guidance, or instructional support needs to be provided while students are using the simulation, as compared to extensive instructional treatments prior to using the simulation.

Another conclusion is that students benefit from simulations that progressively become more difficult and complex, doing so only as students gain expertise with earlier and simpler skills. De Jong and van Joolingen (1998) refer to this as the technique of *model progression*. A good example of this technique is research by Rieber and Parmley (1995). In this study, adult participants were given either a structured simulation on the laws of motion based on the model progression technique, or the full simulation. The structured simulation consisted of four activities, each of which included a controlled number of new subskills. Each successive activity incorporated the subskills from the preceding activity. In addition, half of the participants were given an explanative tutorial of this content and half were not. Results showed that participants given the structured simulation without the tutorial learned as much as other participants given the tutorial. In other words, explanations were not necessary when participants were given a carefully structured experiential approach. Interestingly, participants given the structured simulation without the tutorial reported less confidence about their answers to the posttest questions than participants who were given only the tutorial – learning without formal instruction was outside of their comfort zone. The purpose of this kind of research is not to advocate withholding instruction from students, but rather to gain a better understanding of when instruction is either unnecessary or most needed.

Microworlds

A microworld is an example of an *exploratory learning environment* (diSessa, Hoyles, Noss, & Edwards, 1995). The most well-known and studied microworlds include Logo (Papert, 1980b), StarLogo (Resnick, 1994), Boxer (diSessa & Abelson, 1986; diSessa et al., 1991), ThinkerTools (White, 1993; White & Horowitz, 1987), SimCalc (Roschelle, Kaput, & Stroup, 2000), Geometer's Sketchpad (Olive, 1998), and GenScope (Horwitz, 1999). Although different conceptions of microworlds exist, three goals are common to all. First, they offer a way for more people, starting at a younger age, to understand and explore concepts and principles underlying complex systems. Second, microworlds focus primarily on qualitative understanding based on building and using concrete models. Third, there is a deliberate attempt to reduce the distinction between learning science and doing science. Indeed, the goal is to have students use technology in ways similar to those of a scientist. Although the concept of a computer-based microworld can be traced back at least as far as Seymour Papert (1980a), a contemporary definition comes from Andy diSessa (2000):

> A *microworld* is a genre of computational document aimed at embedding important ideas in a form that students can readily explore. The best microworlds have an easy-to-understand set of operations that students can use to engage tasks of value to them, and in doing so, they come to understand powerful underlying principles. You might come to understand ecology, for example, by building your own little creatures that compete with and are dependent on each other. (p. 47)

Microworlds can be described by both their structural and functional affordances. Structurally, microworlds consist of the following (Edwards, 1995): (a) a collection of computational objects that model the mathematical or physical properties of the domain; (b) links to multiple representations of the underlying model; (c) opportunities or means to combine the computational objects in complex ways; and (d) inherent activities or challenges for the student to explore or solve in the domain. A functional analysis of a microworld focuses on the interaction between the student, the software, and the setting in which it is used. Students must be able to know how to use a microworld and *want* to use it. In other words, a microworld needs to match both the cognitive and affective states of the user. Students learn about a domain through exploration with the microworld.

Research on microworlds in education has been contentious. Early research in the 1980s was focused on studying the effects of Logo on children's learning (e.g., Clements & Gullo, 1984; Pea & Kurland, 1984). However, Papert (1987) felt such research studies missed the point:

> Consider for a moment some questions that are "obviously" absurd. Does wood produce good houses? If I built a house out of wood and it fell down, would this show that wood does not produce good houses? Do hammers and saws produce good furniture? These betray themselves as technocentric questions by ignoring people and the elements only people can introduce: skill, design, aesthetics. (p. 24)

Papert took the view that Logo would be used by children to explore and learn mathematics as naturally as they learned language. However, several interesting research programs that began in the 1980s began to show the need for some imposed structure and designed activities in order for students to learn with microworlds. The work of Barbara White is a good example, beginning with her dissertation on dynaturtles (White, 1984) that led to the development of the ThinkerTools software and curriculum (White, 1992, 1993; White & Frederiksen, 1998, 2000; White & Horowitz, 1987; White & Schwarz, 1999). Although White's early research and others (e.g., Harel & Papert, 1990, 1991) used traditional quantitative and qualitative methodologies, others have used a methodology now best known as *design experiments* (Brown, 1992; Cobb, Confrey, diSessa, Lehrer, & Schauble, 2003;

Collins, 1999; Newman, 1990; Richey & Nelson, 1996). A good example of this is research done with the SimCalc Project, an effort designed to give children opportunities to learn about the mathematics of change and variation, such as calculus (Roschelle & Jackiw, 2000; Roschelle et al., 2000).

A design experiment couples formative evaluation's aim of successively improving an innovation's design by studying its use in practice (see Dick, Carey, & Carey, 2001) with the scientific aims of theory building and theory testing (Cobb et al., 2003). A design experiment sets a specific pedagogical goal at the beginning and then seeks to determine the necessary organization, strategies, and technological support necessary to reach the goal (Brown, 1992; Collins, 1999; Newman, 1990, 1992). Such experiments involve an iterative and self-correcting process that resolves problems as they occur. The process is documented to show what path was taken to achieve the goal, what problems were encountered, and how they were handled. Unlike traditional experimental or case-based research, design experiments offer the ability for a researcher to show the evolution of an innovation's design, implementation, and use, rather than just focus on the results that come at the end of the design cycle.

Gaming

Similar to model using versus model building, using games in education as a route to learning can be conceptualized two ways: playing educational games designed by others or designing your own game. The research literature focusing on whether playing games leads to learning (i.e., gains in achievement) is mixed (Kirriemuir & McFarlane, 2004). When games are compared to traditional classroom instruction (the most common research method), few differences in learning are reported (Dempsey, Lucassen, Gilley, & Rasmussen, 1993–1994; Gredler, 2003; Randel, Morris, Wetzel, & Whitehill, 1992).

Another approach to studying gaming is what can students learn from designing their own games. A good example of this research on gaming comes from the work of Yasmin Kafai and colleagues (1994, 1995; Kafai & Harel, 1991). Their research has focused on student motivation and learning while building multimedia projects. In these "children as designers" studies, elementary school students are typically given the task of designing an educational game for a younger audience (i.e., fifth graders designing for third graders). In one example (Kafai, Ching, & Marshall, 1997), qualitative results showed how students used the design activity as an opportunity to engage in content-related discussions. Quantitative results also demonstrated increased learning of astronomy concepts by students.

For almost a decade I and many of my graduate students have spent time with elementary and middle school students designing and developing educational computer games (Rieber et al., 1998). The motivation for starting the project was based on a simple question: Would children be able to take advantage of the opportunity to engage in game design when properly supported to do so? The purpose of our research was to observe the social dynamics of children working collaboratively in teams. Besides the qualitative data produced from our observations, our other primary measure was whether or not the children produced a working game. If so, the game became an artifact for research by giving us insights into how children find ways to put subject matter they were learning in school to use in a context that they value (i.e., games). The children designed the games' goals, rules, characters, and graphics.

One research study (Rieber, Davis, Matzko, & Grant, 2001) focused on the following questions: (1) would children, *other* then those who designed the game, find these games motivating to play; and (2) based on the children's own play behavior, what features of these noncommercial games do children report as exemplary and noteworthy? To answer these questions, we gave students in two classrooms (30 students in all) the opportunity to play games designed by other students over a period of three weeks. As students chose to play the games, the computer also logged data about the children's playing behavior (which game they played, how often, and for how long). The children were also asked to rate the games throughout the three-week period. We tracked the students' rating patterns over the course of the study. These quantitative data, in combination with follow-up interviews with 12 of the 30 participants, yielded interesting outcomes. First, the children's ratings consistently matched their game-playing behavior. That is, the games they chose to play most frequently and for the longest periods were also the games they rated most favorably. The children's ratings were also stable and consistent over time. They came to form opinions about the games quickly and their opinions did not change much over time. Three game characteristics favored by children included: (1) the quality of the game's storyline, (2) competition, and (3) appropriate challenge. These characteristics are consistent with much of the game-design literature. However, unlike the game-design literature, two other game characteristics did not matter much to the children: (1) the game's production values and (2) the integration of the educational content with the game.

What Are the Limitations of Research on Multimedia Learning in Games, Simulations, and Microworlds?

Research on multimedia learning in games, simulations, and microworlds has used a diverse collection of research methods with equally divergent results. There is no one "right" approach. As any student of educational research knows, quantitative experimental research generally has strong internal validity, but weak external validity, whereas it is just the opposite for qualitative research. Experimental research based on randomized trials is often touted as the "gold standard" of scientific research (National Research Council, 2002). The strength of an experimental design is the ability to study one variable at a time while controlling all others in order to understand how much influence the variable has on learning. However, experimental research comes with the inherent criticism that the results reflect little on how learning actually occurs in the messy world of classrooms and homes. In contrast, qualitative designs yield interesting glimpses into particular cases, but run the risk of leading researchers astray if the small sample sizes are not representative of the target audience. Furthermore, qualitative research poses a constant risk that a researcher's bias for or against the innovative might "leak into" their interpretation.

For these reasons, the best advice is to advocate for mixed methods when studying interactive multimedia (see Johnson & Onwuegbuzie, 2004). Quantitative designs yielding answers to "what?" and "when?" research questions using data from large numbers of participants can be balanced with the strength of qualitative designs focusing on "why?" questions with small numbers of participants. A good example of the value of mixed methods is the study by Rieber and Noah (1997). The quantitative results showed no differences in the use of a visual metaphor in learning physics. However, in the qualitative stage of the research where we sat down and observed participants individually as they used the simulation, it was clear that participants used and processed the visual metaphor in very productive ways. They tried to understand the metaphor and, most importantly, tried to use it as a cognitive tool for understanding the physics. Why did our quantitative results not reveal something? It's most likely the quantitative instruments (e.g., multiple-choice post-test) were not sensitive to the kinds of cognitive processing actually triggered by the visual metaphor.

The study of interactive multimedia presents unusual problems and opportunities for researchers. Multimedia research is prone to many sources of confounding, one of the most significant is the nature of the innovation used in the research. A simulation, game, or microworld that is poorly designed or implemented leads to erroneous results that many researchers may find difficult to notice. Interactive multimedia cannot

be viewed merely as part of the "apparatus" of psychological research. Instead, they are believed to work with people as "partners" in the learning process (Salomon, Perkins, & Globerson, 1991) by acting as "cognitive tools" (Lajoie, 2000; Lajoie & Derry, 1993). As a result, research designs must be creative in understanding this partnership, especially because the design of the innovation is usually in a state of flux. As previously mentioned, one of the most promising research methodologies for the study of interactive multimedia is the design experiment.

What Are Some of the Implications of the Research for Cognitive Theory?

Given the richness of interactive software such as simulations, microworlds, and games, there are many theoretical perspectives one can use in trying to understand their role in learning and cognition. Only two will be reviewed here: dual-coding theory and mental models. Other relevant theories include activity theory (Barab, Evans, & Baek, 2003; Jonassen & Rohrer-Murphy, 1999) and play theory (Pellegrini, 1995; Rieber, 1996b; Sutton-Smith, 1997).

When viewed from the point of view of message design, the focus is on the way in which information is represented. Paivio's dual-coding theory has been used extensively to demonstrate the well-known picture superiority effect for memory tasks (Paivio, 1990, 1991; Sadoski & Paivio, 2001). Although adaptations of dual-coding theory exist (e.g., Mayer, 2001), dual-coding theory remains well suited to explain learning from multimedia. In my own work, I've tried to extend dual-coding theory to include a user's dynamic interactions with a simulation. A brief overview of the theory is in order.

Dual-coding theory divides cognition into two processing systems, one verbal (or semantic) and the other nonverbal. For the purpose of this discussion, the nonverbal system is best understood as a visual system. Dual-coding theory predicts three levels of processing within the verbal and visual systems – representational, associative, and referential. *Representational processing* describes the connections between incoming messages from the environment and either the verbal or visual system. For example, hearing the word tree, a verbal message, would trigger the verbal system whereas looking at a picture of a tree would trigger the visual system. *Associative processing* is when informational units within either of the systems are activated. Dual-coding theory predicts different hierarchical organizations within each system. The verbal system is considered as sequential or linear, whereas processing in the visual system is considered synchronous. For example, the memorization of a poem is stored within the verbal system such that one cannot easily scan memory to the third line; one would have to start from the beginning to get to the desired line of the poem in memory. In contrast, a person who has stored the image of a familiar place, such as one's work place, can easily imagine the place from any point and then mentally scan left or right. The final type of processing, *referential*, builds connections *between* the verbal and visual system. Simply put, this is defined as an image stored in the visual system being linked to a linguistic unit in the verbal system. A person who looks at a picture of a parent (visual system) can quickly state the parent's first name (verbal system) because the two bits of information are linked.

In general, then, we should be interested in how to dually code information because there are obvious advantages to having two routes to retrieving information from memory. But interactive software goes beyond mere recall of stored information in long-term memory. Learning with a simulation focuses much attention on identifying and using relationships being modeled in the simulation. The distinction between explanations and experience again is useful here. One can use dual-coding theory to predict that the verbal system is more apt to store explanatory accounts of conceptual relationships, whereas the visual system should be more suited to handle the experiential. When designed well, a user has many opportunities to build strong referential connections between both explanatory and experiential representations of the concepts and principles being modeled in the simulation. Two essential ingredients for forming these relationships are time to reflect on the relationships and guidance to test one's understanding.

The second theoretical framework – mental models – is particularly useful for explaining learning with simulations and microworlds. A mental model is one's "personal theory" of some domain or environment (Gentner & Stevens, 1983; Jih & Reeves, 1992; Mayer, 1989). The word *theory* may be too strong here in that a mental model is believed to be loosely organized and open to continual refinement. Everyone forms mental models to help predict the systems we confront in our environment, such as our home heating systems, refrigerators, or automobiles. For example, I grew up without whole-house air conditioning. When I was a young boy, I always wondered why we just didn't leave our refrigerator door open to cool the house. My mental model of a refrigerator was that of a device that "created" cold air. It wasn't until I got older that I developed a more refined mental model of the refrigerator transferring heat from the inside to the outside, thus making it clearer how important it was for the refrigerator's door to be closed. Of course, a physicist has a much more sophisticated mental model based on the laws of thermodynamics.

Working with a computer is another good mental model example to explore, although here we have an example of where the manufacturer tries to help us by *giving* us a mental model, that of a desktop. Of course, there really aren't little yellow folders stored in our computers, but this model helps us to predict how the computer system operates so we can use it. A desktop is a good example of a design device called a *conceptual model* (Norman, 2002). Simulations can obviously be built with similar conceptual models to help users understand what the simulation is modeling. Microworlds go one step further by allowing a user to build their own models, thus their creations become external artifacts of one's mental models.

What Are the Implications of the Research for Instructional Design?

Among the most important conclusions I draw from the research with simulations is the complex relationship between experience (during a simulation) and the nature and timing of explanations. As already discussed, it is very difficult learning from simulations in a discovery-oriented design, even though the potential for deeper levels of processing continue to make this an attractive area for design. Constructivist perspectives generally favor more open-ended learning environments over instruction-directed environments, yet the research consistently points to the need to give students some structure. Is there a way to provide structure without subverting the exploration and discovery process? The question of whether the teacher should coach, counsel, or teach will likely remain contentious for some time. The study by (Rieber et al. 2004) suggests an appropriate role for how explanations should be situated in a simulation. Although explanations were embedded directly into the simulation, one would predict a teacher or more capable peer should be able to offer much richer and more meaningful explanations than the few studied in this research. But the point deserves restating that short explanations seem to work best when offered at the right time *during* the simulation experience. Another promising strategy is to design the simulation to become progressively more difficult *only* after the learner masters earlier skills (i.e., model progression).

What Are Some Productive Future Directions for Research?

Much of the experimental quantitative research on interactive multimedia has been conducted over very short intervals. The average duration that participants interact with a simulation in my own research is about 90 minutes. Other simulation and gaming experimental research have participants interact with the materials for several sessions and several weeks. For a controlled experiment, the more time the research takes, the greater the likelihood that confounding factors will increase. In contrast, researchers of microworlds tend to also be the developers. They spend significant time with participants, such as elementary, middle, or high school students and their teachers over many months. But, the research that is generated is open to much criticism; it is largely anecdotal based on observation that is not held to rigorous qualitative methods. There are exceptions, such as the ThinkerTools research and other isolated examples (e.g., Harel & Papert, 1991).

I believe the most productive future direction of research in interactive multimedia will come from the combination of mixed methods and design research approaches. Design research is in a very formative period. Much of what is offered as design research now lacks scientific rigor and is instead based on anecdotal observations, often times heavily biased toward the innovation. However, design research based on strong and rigorous data collection methods and theory generation offers great promise in explicating those features of interactive multimedia most effective for learning based on a series of design iterations. In other words, rather than giving the results of a study, design research tells the complete story of what revisions were needed, what revisions were made, and how those revisions collectively related to learning. Interestingly, design research is not necessarily aligned with either quantitative or qualitative methods, but draws well upon both. Design research lends itself to research teams, which should increase the likelihood of involving researchers with methodological skills encompassing both qualitative and quantitative areas.

Glossary

Educational game: Competitive rule-based activities involving one or more players with an expressed goal of performing or meeting a goal at a superior

Paivio, A. (1990). *Mental representations: A dual coding approach* (2nd ed.). New York: Oxford University Press.

Paivio, A. (1991). Dual coding theory: Retrospect and current status. *Canadian Journal of Psychology*, *45*, 255–287.

Papert, S. (1980a). Computer-based microworlds as incubators for powerful ideas. In R. Taylor (Ed.), *The computer in the school: Tutor, tool, tutee* (pp. 203–210). New York: Teacher's College Press.

Papert, S. (1980b). *Mindstorms: Children, computers, and powerful ideas*. New York: BasicBooks.

Papert, S. (1987). Computer criticism vs. technocentric thinking. *Educational Researcher, 16*(1), 22–30.

Pea, R., & Kurland, M. (1984). On the cognitive effects of learning computer programming. *New Ideas in Psychology*, *2*, 1137–1168.

Pellegrini, A. D. (Ed.). (1995). *The future of play theory: A multidisciplinary inquiry into the contributions of Brian Sutton-Smith*. Albany, NY: State University of New York Press.

Penner, D. E. (2000–2001). Cognition, computers, and synthetic science: Building knowledge and meaning through modeling. *Review of Research in Education, 25*, 1–35.

Poole, S. (2000). *Trigger happy: Videogames and the entertainment revolution*. New York: Arcade.

Randel, J. M., Morris, B. A., Wetzel, C. D., & Whitehill, B. V. (1992). The effectiveness of games for educational purposes: A review of recent research. *Simulation and gaming, 23*, 261–276.

Resnick, M. (1994). *Turtles, termites, and traffic jams*. Cambridge, MA: MIT Press.

Richey, R. C., & Nelson, W. A. (1996). Developmental research. In D. Jonassen (Ed.), *Handbook of research for educational communications and technology* (pp. 1213–1245). Washington, DC: Association for Educational Communications and Technology.

Rieber, L. P. (1990). Using computer animated graphics in science instruction with children. *Journal of Educational Psychology, 82*, 135–140.

Rieber, L. P. (1991). Animation, incidental learning, and continuing motivation. *Journal of Educational Psychology, 83*, 318–328.

Rieber, L. P. (1992). Computer-based microworlds: A bridge between constructivism and direct instruction. *Educational Technology Research and Development, 40*(1), 93–106.

Rieber, L. P. (1996a). Animation as feedback in a computer-based simulation: Representation matters. *Educational Technology Research and Development, 44*(1), 5–22.

Rieber, L. P. (1996b). Seriously considering play: Designing interactive learning environments based on the blending of microworlds, simulations, and games. *Educational Technology Research and Development, 44*(2), 43–58.

Rieber, L. P. (2003). Microworlds. In D. Jonassen (Ed.), *Handbook of research for educational communications and technology* (2nd ed., pp. 583–603). Mahwah, NJ: Lawrence Erlbaum Associates.

Rieber, L. P., Boyce, M., & Assad, C. (1990). The effects of computer animation on adult learning and retrieval tasks. *Journal of Computer-Based Instruction, 17*(2), 46–52.

Rieber, L. P., Davis, J., Matzko, M., & Grant, M. (2001, April). *Children as multimedia critics: Middle school students' motivation for and critical analysis of educational multimedia designed by other children*. Paper presented at the annual meeting of the American Educational Research Association, Seattle, WA.

Rieber, L. P., & Kini, A. (1995). Using computer simulations in inductive learning strategies with children in science. *International Journal of Instructional Media, 22*(2), 135–144.

Rieber, L. P., Luke, N., & Smith, J. (1998). Project KID DESIGNER: Constructivism at work through play. *Meridian: Middle School Computer Technology Journal 1* (1). Retrieved May 19, 2004 from http://www.ncsu.edu/meridian/archive_of_meridian/jan98/index.html

Rieber, L. P., & Noah, D. (1997, March). *Effect of gaming and graphical metaphors on reflective cognition within computer-based simulations*. Paper presented at the annual meeting of the American Educational Research Association, Chicago, IL.

Rieber, L. P., Noah, D., & Nolan, M. (1998, April). *Metaphors as Graphical Representations within Open-Ended Computer-Based Simulations*. Paper presented at the annual meeting of the American Educational Research Association, San Diego, CA.

Rieber, L. P., & Parmley, M. W. (1995). To teach or not to teach? Comparing the use of computer-based simulations in deductive versus inductive approaches to learning with adults in science. *Journal of Educational Computing Research, 13*(4), 359–374.

Rieber, L. P., Smith, M., Al-Ghafry, S., Strickland, W., Chu, G., & Spahi, F. (1996). The role of meaning in interpreting graphical and textual feedback during a computer-based simulation. *Computers and Education, 27*(1), 45–58.

Rieber, L. P., Tzeng, S., & Tribble, K. (2004). Discovery learning, representation, and explanation within a computer-based simulation: Finding the right mix. *Learning and Instruction, 14*, 307–323.

Roschelle, J., & Jackiw, N. (2000). Technology design as educational research: Interweaving imagination, inquiry and impact. In A. Kelley & R. Lesh (Eds.), *Handbook of research design in mathematics and science education* (pp. 777–797). Mahwah, NJ: Lawrence Erlbaum Associates.

Roschelle, J., Kaput, J., & Stroup, W. (2000). SimCalc: Accelerating student engagement with the mathematics of change. In M. J. Jacobson & R. B. Kozma (Eds.), *Learning the sciences of the 21st century: Research, design, and implementing advanced technology learning environments* (pp. 47–75). Hillsdale, NJ: Lawrence Erlbaum Associates.

Sadoski, M., & Paivio, A. (2001). *Imagery and text: A dual coding theory of reading and writing.* Mahwah, NJ: Lawrence Erlbaum Associates.

Salomon, G., Perkins, D. N., & Globerson, T. (1991). Partners in cognition: Extending human intelligence with intelligent technologies. *Educational Researcher, 20*(3), 2–9.

Sutton-Smith, B. (1997). *The ambiguity of play.* Cambridge, MA: Harvard University Press.

White, B. Y. (1984). Designing computer games to help physics students understand Newton's laws of motion. *Cognition and Instruction, 1* (1), 69–108.

White, B. Y. (1992). A microworld-based approach to science education. In E. Scanlon & T. O'Shea (Eds.), *New directions in educational technology* (pp. 227–242). New York: Springer-Verlag.

White, B. Y. (1993). ThinkerTools: Causal models, conceptual change, and science education. *Cognition and Instruction, 10*(1), 1–100.

White, B. Y., & Frederiksen, J. R. (1998). Inquiry, modeling, and metacognition: Making science accessible to all students. *Cognition and Instruction, 16*(1), 3–118.

White, B. Y., & Frederiksen, J. R. (2000). Technological tools and instructional approaches for making scientific inquiry accessible to all. In M. J. Jacobson & R. B. Kozma (Eds.), *Learning the sciences of the 21st century: Research, design, and implementing advanced technology learning environments* (pp. 321–359). Hillsdale, NJ: Lawrence Erlbaum Associates.

White, B. Y., & Horowitz, P. (1987). *ThinkerTools: Enabling children to understand physical laws* (No. 6470). Cambridge, MA: Bolt, Beranek, and Newman.

White, B. Y., & Schwarz, C. V. (1999). Alternative approaches to using modeling and simulation tools for teaching science. In W. Feurzcig & N. Roberts (Eds.), *Modeling and simulation in science and mathematics education* (pp. 226–256). New York: Springer-Verlag.

Zhao, Y., & Frank, K. A. (2003). Factors affecting technology uses in schools: An ecological perspective. *American Educational Research Journal, 40*(4), 807–840.

CHAPTER 34

Multimedia Learning with Hypermedia

Andrew Dillon
Jennifer Jobst
University of Texas

Abstract

Hypermedia proponents suggest that its ability to make information available in a multitude of formats, provide individual control, engage the learner, and cater to various learning styles and needs makes it the harbinger of a new learning revolution. However, despite nearly two decades of research on hypermedia in education, researchers have not yet solved some of the basic issues raised by this technology. In this chapter, we review empirical studies performed since Dillon and Gabbard's (1998) landmark review in an attempt to analyze and draw conclusions from this diverse and extensive literature.

Introduction

Since Vannevar Bush's ground-breaking article *As We May Think* (Bush, 1945), the idea of using technology to link the world's information resources in new ways has been heralded by some as a revolutionary opportunity to design new instructional media. The term *hypermedia* is commonly used to refer to this type of information resources and is based on the term *hypertext*, coined by Ted Nelson around 1965 to refer to "nonsequential" or "nonlinear" text where authors and readers were free to explore and to link information in ways that made personal sense for them (Nelson, 1965). In general usage, the terms are often used interchangeably but to be strictly accurate, *hypermedia* consists of more than linked texts; it includes other forms of media as well, such as images, video, and sound.

Because of the diverse forms of media that can constitute a hypermedia document, hypermedia learning tools became *multimedia* in nature. By multimedia we mean that learning material is presented in both words and pictures, and may also include sound. Regardless of the term, this technology is based on nodes or chunks of information that are linked together and that a user or learner can explore by following links they deem relevant. Abstract as this sounds, the most obvious example of such an information space is the World Wide Web, wherein the linked structure provides a practically never-ending opportunity for a user to explore multiple documents and to follow paths of exploration as they fancy.

As with many new forms of media, hypermedia was initially touted as the harbinger of a new learning revolution (Fabos, 2001). As discussed in Dillon and Gabbard (1998), proponents tout its ability to provide nonlinear access to information, explore information on demand, provide self-paced instruction, and engage the learner. Hypermedia also caters to various learning styles and individual learning needs by providing information in a multitude of media formats. Debates still exist as to the pedagogical value of many hypermedia applications and, despite multiple experiments, researchers have failed to resolve many of the basic issues concerning the use of this technology for instruction. In the present chapter we review the most recent empirical work in the area in order to help readers make sense of this complicated and ever-expanding literature.

Theories of Hypermedia Learning

Its advocates see hypermedia as a natural form of information representation that supports the native tendencies of learners to explore and relate concepts. However, as noted by Dillon and Gabbard (1998), there has been limited theoretical analysis underlying much of the work on hypermedia learning, and the situation has not changed noticeably since then. Early discussions of this technology (the period up to 1995, approximately) tended to adopt a naïve associationist view of cognition and emphasized the similarities between linked information nodes and the presumed architecture of human cognition. While a more critical view of hypermedia and cognition has since evolved, formal theories of hypermedia learning have not developed in any substantial way. Instead, existing theoretical models from education and psychology have been applied to certain aspects of hypermedia design and use. The general tension between constructivist and information-processing views of learning is mirrored in the hypermedia literature, with behaviorist theories finding little application in this domain.

Hypermedia learning studies frequently make intuitive appeals to certain cognitive theories, such as the dual-coding theory (Pavio, 1986) or the cognitive flexibility theory (Spiro, Feltovich, Jacobson, & Coulson, 1991). By virtue of the media mix (implying an exploitation of dual coding for cognition) and the ability to restructure information in real time (enhancing flexibility), any number of studies have adopted a weak theoretical stance without formally testing or extending the broader implications of either perspective.

Currently, there is only one dedicated theory of multimedia learning that explicitly aims at guiding our analysis and understanding of learning in hypermedia environments: Mayer and colleagues' *generative theory of multimedia learning* (Mayer, 2001). Building on cognitive psychological theories, Mayer and colleagues assume that learners are limited-capacity dual encoders who actively process information in order to integrate it meaningfully with their existing knowledge (Mayer, 2001). By examining the impact of various hypermedia features on the learner's cognitive processes, the theory points to specific advantages that may be yielded by combinations of modalities (e.g., images with sound) designed to support the integration by the user without overloading limited cognitive resources. The value of this approach can be seen in recent work (Moreno & Mayer, 2000a; Plass, Chun, Mayer, & Leutner, 1998) that has led to the derivation of specific instructional principles for hypermedia learning, for example, the modality principle, which states that students learn better when visual or verbal information is presented in a congruent format (e.g., verbal information as sound rather than text). This work holds promise for solid theoretical advances in our understanding of multimedia design along the lines of classic cognitive engineering approaches to human-computer interaction.

Alternative theoretical approaches from constructivism tend to deal at a higher level of abstraction, concerned more with the context of learning, task relevance, and ability of, or opportunity for, learners to apply the material to be learned. The work of Spiro and colleagues (Spiro et al., 1991) examines how people can reconstruct information into meaningfully organized wholes to suit a task. Under this theory, less focus is given to determining appropriate modalities and forms of information within a hypermedia and more emphasis is placed on how the tool can facilitate multiple representations for a learner to explore. Indeed, it is an assumption of the cognitive flexibility theory that hypermedia is uniquely suited to learning complex or ill-structured material.

While theoretical developments have been limited, the empirical study of hypermedia has continued to grow and there is no shortage of papers that report how a given group of users perform with a specific design. The present chapter extends earlier reviews and attempts to bring up to the present date a summary of what has been observed.

Reviewing the Reviews

Over the last 15 years several attempts at reviewing the growing literature on hypermedia and learning have been made. Nielsen's (1989) review of 30 hypertext studies compared the effects of various user aspects of hypertext interaction and pointed to the large individual differences that exist in user response to the technology, a finding that has remained remarkably consistent to the present.

Chen and Rada's (1996) meta-analysis of 23 studies on the use of hypertext for a range of information tasks also concluded that the benefits for this technology were mixed. While pointing to the real advantages for hypermedia lying in what they termed *closed tasks*, those where the user is seeking specific information, these authors also noted that spatial ability was an important factor in determining user response to hypermedia documents.

All reviewers agree that firm conclusions are difficult to draw from available literature. However, several authors have also been highly critical of the quality of research in this area. Landauer (1995) noted in his review that he could identify only nine studies that were scientifically acceptable. Three years later, Dillon and Gabbard (1998) produced an extensive review of the quantitative, empirical findings on learning outcome from hypermedia. They also noted poor experimental design and flawed analysis in many studies, but drew three basic conclusions that serve as a useful starting point here:

- Hypermedia is generally advantageous for tasks that require rapid searching through large or multiple documents.
- Increased control over access to information is not equally beneficial to all users and may even be detrimental for low ability learners.
- Particular interface designs are best suited to certain learner styles.

Since then the literature on this topic has grown but the results continue to be mixed. Liao (1998), Parlangeli, Marchigiani, Bagnara (1999), and others have compared hypermedia with other forms of instruction and failed to show real benefit for any instructional form. However, the multiple variables that shape learning outcome are being teased out, albeit slowly, and researchers are beginning to pay more attention (although still insufficient amounts) to longitudinal examinations at learning outcome as a result of multimedia use. For example, Yildirim, Ozden, and Aksu (2001) tested 39 ninth-grade biology students receiving either traditional instruction or hypermedia on three different outcome measures: declarative, conditional, and procedural knowledge. Although the first posttest showed that there were no significant differences for the three types of knowledge, as is typical of many studies, on a retention test given one month after initial treatment, there was a significant difference in favor of the hypermedia group on all three types of knowledge. These results were found not to be dependent on prior knowledge. Such work requires us to view with caution strong claims based on single trial experiments or tests.

While most of the early reviews compared hypermedia with some other form of instruction, more recent work has compared varieties of hypermedia in order to determine which aspects of the technology have greatest influence on use. In part this may mark a more refined approach to the problem, a reflection of growing maturity in the research effort, but it also may reflect the generally ubiquitous status of hypermedia applications in learning situations nowadays. In the following sections we summarize what these last few years of research have taught us about hypermedia-based instruction. As in Dillon and Gabbard (1998), we emphasize only studies that meet minimal levels of control, and that have assessed learning outcome in some measurable fashion. It is perhaps, by now, not surprising that such literature does not form the majority of writings on this topic. We have divided the literature into three themes:

- Design, which covers the various forms of structure and interface features used to implement the hypermedia;
- Cognition, which covers the all-important psychological and individual differences research into learner response; and
- Context, which covers work examining the learning situation and its impact on hypermedia use.

Design Issues

The essence of hypermedia is linked nodes of data, which may include text, video, audio, or graphics. Understandably, the freedom to create new information forms of this kind has resulted in multiple versions of hypermedia instructional materials and, consequently, a major research initiative has evolved that attempts to identify the various forms and features that work best for users. While much literature exists on interface design for hypermedia (e.g., Dillon, 2004),

this section is concerned only with design manipulations where learning outcome was studied.

Information Structure

In this discussion, the term *structure* is used to describe how the information in a hypermedia is organized – in other words, how the *nodes* are physically connected together using *links*. The simplest structure is *linear* in format, meaning that the user must progress sequentially from one chunk of information to the next, rather like a book, where one page precedes another. *Hierarchical* structures have a "top" node from which all information stems in increasing levels of detail. Information can be linked in a *strictly hierarchical* format, where each node is only connected to nodes on the levels directly above and below it in the hierarchy. Alternatively, each node can also be linked to other nodes at the same level, or links can even skip levels. There is no agreement on what this type of hierarchical cross-referential linking structure should be called. For example, McDonald and Stevenson (1998), and Calisir and Gurel (2003) call this a *mixed* structure but it has also been called *referential* (Lin, 2003) or *hierarchical with partial linearity* (Nimwegen, Pouw, & van Oostendorp, 1999).

Regardless of terminology, typical studies of structural issues compare various topologies and measure navigation patterns and learning outcome success. For example, Melara's (1996) study using a hypermedia tool on the shortest path algorithm (an algorithm for calculating the shortest path between two vertices on a connected graph) on 40 undergraduates found that although structure (hierarchical vs. network) did not affect post-test scores, learners spent significantly more time using the hierarchical structure than the network structure, indicating that structure certainly impacts process of use. Shapiro (1998) compared linear, strictly hierarchical, and hierarchical with no navigational cues (which she termed *unstructured*) on 72 undergraduate students using a historical hypermedia document, "The

Gilded Age of America." When comparing the learning outcome between the linear and strictly hierarchical structures, those using strictly hierarchical hypertext showed significantly more factual knowledge acquisition based on the number of concept-map nodes drawn, but no significant differences were found on link familiarity, short-answer questions, or the essay. No process measures were studied. Shapiro is reticent of reading too much into the concept-map measure, but on the whole, these results support the general impression that structure is not a leading cause of learning outcome.

Many other studies support these findings. Spruijt and Jansen (1999), de Vries and de Jong (1997), and McDonald and Stevenson (1996) all reported that while structure affected process measures such as number of navigation problems, experience of disorientation, or time spent performing the task, in none of these studies was a significant learning outcome difference reported. Nimwegen et al. (1999) asked 80 subjects of different ages and from different departments from the University of Utrecht to answer 24 questions using a hypermedia guide to the city of Utrecht. The structure employed was either a strictly hierarchical or a mixed hierarchical structure. They concluded that users with the strictly hierarchical hypermedia were significantly faster, made significantly fewer deviations or views of superfluous pages, and had a significantly more positive opinion about their insight into the underlying structure of the hypermedia. Schoon and Cafolla (2002) compared the effects of using linear, star, hierarchical, and random structures on 261 undergraduates. Users had significantly better "navigational action efficiency" scores (a process measurement developed by the authors) when using a star or hierarchical structure than a linear or random structure, but there was no significant difference between the scores of star and hierarchical structure users. Learning outcome was not studied.

The literature is not completely consistent, however. Paolucci (1998) compared conventional, branching, and strictly hierarchical structures on 115 fifth-grade students' use of a hypermedia lesson on ecology. Paolucci measured levels of linkage, with conventional being the most interlinked and hierarchical being the least interlinked, and equated this with levels of freedom for the users. The data show that the number of links and the linkage pattern affects outcome as measured by posttest scores, with users of the branching pattern performing the best, followed by hierarchical and conventional. Logical reasoning, as determined by assessing structural knowledge using questions on analogies, associations, relationship proximity judgments, and semantic relationships, was also affected, with the branching group again performing significantly better than the conventional group, but not the hierarchical group. However, because the branching and conventional structures Paolucci used are unique to this study it is difficult to compare these findings to others. In general, it seems that structure will affect learning by influencing how well or how fast a learner can move through a hypermedia document, and despite the possibilities afforded by the technology to structure information in unique ways, hierarchies have real value for many users.

Advance Organizers

The provision of advance organizers can be seen as means of rendering structure explicit to users. While such devices tend to be standardized in print media (e.g., contents pages, chapter headings, abstracts), the endless possibilities for design within hypermedia means that such representations could take multiple forms thereby complicating any recommendation on their use. While an overview is likely to be beneficial for navigation purposes if it contains direct links to information, its layout and form provide a structure that may not always be optimal for learning purposes or for certain users. McDonald and Stevenson (1999) performed two experiments on low prior-knowledge learners to explore the differences between the use of spatial maps (which show the underlying informational structure), text-based content lists, conceptual maps (which show information grouped by concept), and no aid when using a hypertext on "The Nature of Human Learning." In the first experiment, spatial map users were able to navigate more efficiently (in terms of the time taken to locate a node and the number of additional nodes opened) than contents list users, but there was no significant difference in learning outcome although the no-aid group performed worst on both navigation and learning measures. In the second experiment, the spatial map appeared to help navigation the most whereas the conceptual map improved learning the most. Subjects with no aid navigated poorly, but, somewhat surprisingly, learned more than those in the spatial map group, suggesting that having to form linkages and structures for oneself may encourage active processing of the text, which could enhance learning.

This active-processing effect was observed in Brinkerhoff, Klein, Koroghlanian (2001). They studied the effects of overview mode on attitude, post-test scores, and instructional time. Participants (n = 79) either had no overview, a structured overview, or an unstructured overview. Although posttest scores were not affected by mode, having an overview of either type seemed to encourage learners to spend more time on instruction and resulted in a more positive attitude. Yeh and Lehman (2001) also report a beneficial effect for advance organizers. They tested 150 Taiwanese English as a Foreign Language (EFL) university students to see whether the presence or absence of an advance organizer (in the form of a short overview) affected posttest scores when studying a hypermedia about the creation of the state of Israel. Their results indicate that having an advance organizer did improve posttest performance. These experiments suggest a trend that learners perform better on several levels with advance organizers (regardless of type) than without.

Shapiro performed two experiments (1999, 2000) that considered the use of interactive overviews and learning goals in a hypermedia on fictitious animals by students with a low prior knowledge of biology. The overviews were organized by animal family or by ecosystem. The 1999 experiment (n = 46) showed no significant effect of overview type on acquiring explicit knowledge, but those who had an ecosystem overview performed significantly better on the ecosystem post-test. However, having an animal family overview did not seem to affect posttest scores on the animal family posttest. Shapiro speculates that this discrepancy may be due to the pretest selection procedure, which may have favored individuals who had prior knowledge about animal families. The 2000 (n = 44) experiment found no effect of overview condition on the total number of responses on a cued-association task, where students were asked to write three topics that came to mind when the name of an animal discussed in the hypermedia was presented. However, the overview condition did significantly affect the type of associations students made. Students with the animal family overview made significantly more animal family associations, and those with the ecosystem overview made significantly more ecosystem associations. On a sorting post-test, where students sorted cards into animal families or ecosystems, significantly more students in the animal family group sorted by animal family, whereas in the ecosystem group only slightly more students sorted by ecosystem than by animal family. However, this was a marked change from the pretest sorting strategy, where the majority of students sorted by animal family. Thus, Shapiro concluded that overview type can affect strategy, regardless of initial biases, although how far these results extend beyond sorting tasks is an open question.

Other studies compared different types of advanced organizers without the benefit of a control group, but manipulating a user variable such as cognitive style or knowledge level to assess possible interactions. For example, Chou and Lin (1998) studied 121 university students to see if map type and cognitive style (according to Witkin's Group Embedded Figures Test, or GEFT) affected searching, cognitive map development, or attitude. The results suggested that global maps, which showed the entire hierarchical knowledge structure, were more helpful than local maps, which showed smaller chunks of the hierarchical structure according to main headings. However, the authors hypothesize that global maps might be too unwieldy for efficient use on a larger-scale learning tool. No interaction on any measure was found between cognitive style and map type. Similarly, Hofman and van Oostendorp (1999) tested 40 first-year university students to see whether structural overviews or lists were more useful in a relatively short hypermedia on ultraviolet radiation. Structural overviews appeared to hinder less knowledgeable users, which the authors speculate may result from drawing the learner's attention to the macrostructure of the text at the expense of attention to the microstructure.

Deriving an overview style is left to the imagination of the experimenter in most cases. Hsu and Schwen (2003) examined 54 university students' use of one of three types of "metaphorical" designs, that is, hypermedia structures built around different forms of organization: a book metaphor, a combination book and folder metaphor, or no metaphor. The participants searched for answers to questions in a lengthy hypermedia on 19th-century American history. Metaphorical cues helped learners find a significantly greater number of correct answers. However, overview metaphor had no significant effect on time spent on task, navigation patterns, or satisfaction. We should note, of course, that unless the experiment explicitly forces it, provision of an overview is no guarantee of its use. Niederhauser, Reynolds, Salmen, and Skolmoski (2000) showed that students tended to examine the topic map either at the beginning or end of a session rather than during use. Given such usage patterns, any topic map may serve as either an overview or a summary.

Mixed Media

Perhaps the greatest promise of hypermedia learning tools is the ability to include multiple media, including text, pictures, sound, and video in a unified, easily accessible learning space. Interestingly, many of the studies reviewed made use of *hypertext* only, often citing the limited knowledge about how other media affect the learning process as a reason for using text. Only a few researchers have looked at the effects of media other than text, despite the importance of understanding how such media may benefit learning. Mixed media brings with it many new potential problems, such as appropriate combinations (e.g., is sound a complement to animation or should text and sound be avoided in certain contexts?). This would appear to be a topical area for new research.

Empirical data on the effects of sound in multimedia learning is limited. Kalyuga, Chandler, and Sweller (1999) tested 34 trade apprentices to find ways of circumventing possible split-attention effects. They found that when working with diagrammatic material to determine the proper type of solder for a specific task, the apprentices performed significantly better on posttests and reviewed the information fewer times when the information accompanying the diagram was read aloud instead of being presented in a textual format (i.e., a caption) on the screen. However, duplicating information by presenting it both visually and aurally – that is, having on-screen text *and* having the same text read aloud – was detrimental to learning.

It seems plausible that sound could be particularly useful if used appropriately, because potentially it adds more information to the learning context, which may complement visual stimuli. Mayer and Moreno (1998) showed that when working with an animation of natural or mechanical processes, providing university students with concurrent narration (i.e., coupling the spoken works to appropriate points in the animation sequence) was more beneficial than providing students with concurrent explanatory text. Presumably the text adds to the visual-processing load whereas the sound exploits the dual-processing capability of learner (see e.g., Wickens, 1992 for an information design model based on resource processing). Two further experiments by Moreno and Mayer (2000a) used the same two animations with concurrent auditory narration, but added irrelevant music, environmental sounds, or both to determine how irrelevant auditory material affected performance. In both experiments, groups receiving additional auditory material performed worse than the group that did not, demonstrating that irrelevant auditory material was detrimental to learning, serving as a distracter rather than an enhancer.

The use of graphics and video or animation in conjunction with text would seem to be an important area of study for multimedia although there are few formal experiments in the literature yet. Kalyuga et al. (1998) tested three instructional formats (integrated diagram and text, separate diagram and text, and diagram only) on trade apprentices with different levels of prior knowledge to determine how different types of instruction affect learning. In a series of three experiments on electric circuits, they found that low knowledge-level apprentices preferred diagrams with text, while more knowledgeable apprentices found integrated textual explanations redundant and thus preferred diagram-only instruction.

In two similar experiments, Kalyuga et al. (2000) tested trade apprentices on their understanding of how to determine RPMs needed for a cutting speed nomogram. Apprentices used a diagram with visual text, a diagram with auditory text, a diagram with both auditory and visual text, or a diagram only. Although the apprentices initially performed best on the posttest using the diagram with auditory text, after two training sessions, the diagram-only format performed just as well. In the second experiment, the diagram-only and diagram with auditory text formats were compared. The authors found that more experienced learners performed better on the posttest with the diagram-only format. These results suggest that learner experience and competence are important because preferences for one type of material over another may shift as experience is gained and competency improves. However, the success of diagram-only formats as witnessed by Kalyuga et al. is probably highly context dependent.

Learner Control Mechanisms

Proponents of hypermedia learning have argued that one of its greatest benefits is that the learner can control the learning situation and this factor was deemed generally significant in Dillon and Gabbard's (1998) review, although there is no consensus on what constitutes control in such learning situations. Jacobson, Maouri, Mishra, and Kolar (1996) provided different levels of learner control to 69 university students by either having the computer provide case-specific information or allowing the learner to select information as deemed necessary. The results suggest that providing learners with flexible control leads to improved learning on short answer and certain types of essays. Yeh and Lehman's (2001) study of students learning EFL manipulated control by allowing either students or the computer to set the pace of material presented. Students who controlled the pace and sequence of the hypermedia had significantly improved recall scores, although it is worth noting that this form of learner control had no effect on satisfaction.

Elements of learner control are also associated with generative activities, requirements, or opportunities for learners to take notes, summarize, or otherwise perform an activity while learning. Astleitner (1997) experimented with the benefits of using a memo pad, with mixed results. Thirty-eight high school students used a hypermedia on solar energy, and half were encouraged to use memo pads during interaction, but were not allowed to refer to their notes during the posttest. He found that action-oriented learners as determined by the action control subscale (Kuhl, 1985) acquired significantly more intentional (goal-based) knowledge when they were *not* using a memo pad, whereas non-action-oriented learners acquired significantly more intentional knowledge when they *did* use a memo pad. On the other hand, using a memo pad led to significantly more incidental (non-goal-based) knowledge acquisition, regardless of whether or not the learner was action oriented. Barab, Young, and Wang (1999) reported no effect for such generative activities however.

Conclusions

Issues of interface design for hypermedia learning contexts will likely remain at the forefront of research for some time. While the various structural forms that can be exploited have not been fully explored, it is clear that structure impacts the process of use in a significant manner, with hierarchical structures having some advantages in many instances. It remains to be seen if innovative structural forms may evolve to yield greater benefits. Mixing media remains an area of enquiry that sorely needs greater empirical study. As technology enables radically new designs of instructional materials, the possibilities offered by hypermedia are tremendously exciting, but exploiting these possibilities requires significant work to determine how the combination of media, in particular, can work to the advantage of humans in learning situations.

Individual Differences in Cognition

Studies of hypermedia designs represent a more recent trend in the literature as researchers seek to uncover the impact of particular aspects of hypermedia interfaces on information gain and learning. There still remains, however, broad interest in the effects of hypermedia on types of learner, an effect that has been shown to influence performance repeatedly. In the present section we report on the latest work in individual differences where researchers seek to understand what characteristics of the learner influence how learning occurs with this technology.

Domain and Prior Knowledge

There is mounting evidence that users' prior domain knowledge has a significant impact on their pattern of interaction with hypermedia in learning situations. Low prior-knowledge subjects either seem to experience more difficulty (Lawless & Kulikowich, 1996; McDonald & Stevenson, 1998) or have lower post-test scores (Kraus, Reed, & Fitzgerald, 2001; Niederhauser et al., 2000; Potelle & Rouet, 2003) than high prior-knowledge users when interacting with hypermedia learning tools. It has been suggested that those who are less familiar with

the subject matter cannot easily create new content representations, a problem that is exacerbated by the node-and-link structure of hypermedia. There is an unfortunate irony to this because hypermedia has long been advocated as a way of "leveling the playing field" and allowing all learners to proceed in a manner that suits their unique learning process.

As discussed in the design section, while it is no simple matter to determine the effects of structure across multimedia learning activities, it would appear that certain structural variables interact with specific learner types. Calisir and Gurel (2003) reported an interaction between structure and reading comprehension scores (the outcome measurement) for nonknowledgeable students, indicating that a hierarchical topology may be more beneficial for such learners. A similar manipulation by Potelle and Rouet (2003) tested 47 university students with either high or low prior knowledge in social psychology to see if concept-map type (which were based on linear, strictly hierarchical, and mixed hierarchical structures) affected learning. Their results suggested that, for low prior-knowledge users, a hierarchical map and underlying hierarchical structure improves learning outcomes at the macrostructural (e.g., categorical relationship), but not the microstructural (e.g., factual) level.

McDonald and Stevenson (1998) examined students (n = 30) with different levels of knowledge interacting with strictly hierarchical, mixed hierarchical, and network (i.e., nonlinear) hypermedia structures. They found that, regardless of knowledge level, structure directly influenced processes such as browsing and navigation, in terms of the number of nodes opened, number of nodes repeatedly opened, time taken to answer questions, and number of additional nodes opened. A mixed hierarchical structure produced the best performance, followed by a strictly hierarchical topology and finally a network topology. In general, knowledgeable participants performed better than nonknowledgeable participants. McDonald and Stevenson suggest that prior conceptual understanding of the information may reduce disorientation problems for the knowledgeable users.

However, both of Howard-Jones and Martin's (2002) studies on preservice teachers using a hypermedia on cutting and joining materials indicate that teachers who scored lower on the pretest scored higher on the posttest. In other words, the low prior-knowledge teachers learned more from the treatments. A study by Yildirim et al. (2001) also found that prior knowledge does not affect learning outcome. They considered prior knowledge as a factor when comparing the short- and long-term effectiveness of traditional and hypermedia instructional techniques on 39 ninth-grade biology students. No significant difference was found between the two groups on a short-term post-test, and all of the mean differences in test scores were attributable to prior knowledge. However, the group that received hypermedia instruction performed significantly better on a long-term retention test administered one month after the initial experiment, although prior knowledge was not found to be a factor in these differences. No explanation was offered for the lack of influence of prior knowledge, however these data suggest that certain hypermedia features may significantly affect the rate of learning, and this is an area that clearly warrants more detailed examination.

Spatial Ability

Bacause many users describe feeling lost or disoriented in hyperspace, helping people navigate has been one of the primary concerns of hypermedia developers over the years. Spatial metaphors (e.g., a house, desktop, or street) are sometimes used to mitigate this problem, on the theory that users will relate to familiar situations in the physical world (for a thorough discussion on the spatiality of hyperspace, see Boechler [2001]). A study by Padovani and Lansdale (2003) supports this argument. They tested 230 university students using two different hypermedia systems, one of which was based on a spatial metaphor and the other of which was based on a nonspatial metaphor. The spatial metaphor produced higher perfor-

mance (in terms of task completion times) under all conditions. Thus, it is clear that the spatiality of the virtual world is an important aspect of designing usable hypermedia learning tools. Consequently, it follows that a user's spatial skills may also be important in dealing with hyperspace.

Spatial skills are typically determined using a standardized test, for example in Nilsson and Mayer (2002), where they used the paper-folding test and Baddeley's three-minute intelligence test. Although the primary goal of their experiment was to test the cognitive load theory, spatial skills were also considered. Learners who had high scores on the paper-folding test were able to navigate more efficiently than those with lower scores, and learners who did well on the three-minute intelligence test were also marginally more efficient at navigating ($p < 0.07$). Nilsson and Mayer concluded that these two individual differences determined navigation efficiency for the experiment, although learning outcome was not studied.

The effect of skills such as spatial ability can be complicated to untangle. The study by Plass et al. (2003) mentioned previously used the Card Rotation Test from the *Kit of Factor-Referenced Cognitive Tests* (Ekstrom, French, & Harman, 1976) to assess the spatial ability of 152 English-speaking university students taking a second-year German course. Their study examined whether the use of either visual (i.e., pictures) or verbal (i.e., textual) annotations helped users with different levels of spatial skills and verbal skills when reading a hypermedia story in German. When students had visual annotations for vocabulary words, the high verbal and high spatial-ability students outperformed low ability students on recall of word translations. However, there was no difference between the two groups when the students had verbal annotations. Visual annotations produced the worst text comprehension for all learners. As hypothesized, the results were correctly predicted by Mayer's (2001) generative theory of multimedia, which states that visual information requires spatial-processing skills, thereby giving high spatial-ability students an advantage in a visual environment.

Cognitive Style/Learning Style

The long-standing interest in cognitive style among educators is based on the view that processing differences among learners need to be accommodated in the design of instructional contexts and technologies. The most common cognitive or learning style tests that have been used in hypermedia evaluations are Kolb's Learning Style Inventory (LSI) (1984) and Witkin's GEFT (1971). The LSI divides people into varying levels of convergers/divergers or accommodators/assimilators. Convergers tend to bring together pieces of knowledge into a single topic to deduce an answer, whereas divergers rely on brainstorming and idea generation to solve problems. Assimilators supposedly solve problems by inductive reasoning, while accommodators plan and experiment (Kolb, 1984). Individual learning styles are a mix of these four modes, although the converger/diverger and accommodator/assimilator scales are continuous, so an individual can be more or less strongly inclined toward one mode or another. The GEFT requires subjects to identify a simple figure within a more complex pattern. People who are good at finding the simple figures are said to be more *field independent*, which is defined by Witkin, Moore, Goodenough, and Cox (1977) as "the extent to which a person perceives part of a field as discrete from the surrounding field as a whole, rather than embedded in the field." Those who find it difficult to extract the pattern from the field are classified as *field dependent*, and are generally considered to be more sensitive to contextual effects.

Since Dillon and Gabbard (1998) reported that individual differences in information processing were an important part of the puzzle in explaining hypermedia's effects on learning, there has been a steady stream of further work exploring cognitive style. Rasmussen and Davidson-Shivers (1998), for example, used the LSI to test learning style and studied learner control based on hypermedia structure to determine the effect on both immediate and delayed test performance. Active (accommodative) learners, who tend to experiment during the learning process, scored best when using the hierarchical structure in both the immediate and delayed post-tests. These findings are somewhat contrary to previous studies that suggested that active learners perform best when high levels of learner control are available, and the authors speculate that for this study, active learners may have preferred the efficiency of the strictly hierarchical structure. On the other hand, reflexive (assimilative) learners performed best when using a strictly hierarchy structure that also included the ability to link together (i.e., associate) individual nodes. The authors suggest that the hierarchical structure provided these learners with the necessary structure to suit their learning style, but also with the opportunity to add their own interpretations of the information through the linking capability.

Kettanurak, Ramamurthy, and Haseman (2001) studied 154 undergraduate students to determine the effects of the LSI and three interaction modes on learning: no interactivity (a linear hypermedia), low interactivity, (a linear hypermedia that enabled learners to control information presentation order, and pacing, and provided the ability to review information), and high interactivity, (where, in addition to the features in the low interaction mode, the program kept track of the learner's location, provided feedback from questions at the end of each section, and had an index feature). Modes of interaction were found to have a significant effect on attitude, regardless of learning style, with students preferring high levels of interaction, although it should be noted that the no interaction condition was preferred to low interaction as employed here.

Two studies reviewed used the GEFT to determine cognitive style. Chou and Lin (1998) studied 121 Taiwanese university students using a hypermedia "Introduction to Computer Networks" to see if cognitive style affected searching, cognitive map development, or attitude. Results showed no main effect for cognitive style on the number of search steps learners used, their search efficiency, the ability to complete a search task, or attitude toward the experience. However, when judging the number of nodes in the hypermedia (estimation accuracy), cognitive style approached significance ($p < 0.052$). Here, field-independent students scored significantly better on the cognitive map test, which tested students' abilities to reconstruct the relationships among nodes in the hypermedia.

Cognitive style seems to mediate hypermedia-based learner performance in a complicated manner. For example, Palmquist and Kim (2000) tested 48 university students performing information searches of a university Web site. They reported a significant effect for field dependency but found its importance tended to be minimized as users gained experience. Field-independent and field-dependent students with high online experience spent almost the same amount of time on task, but field-dependent students with little online experience tended to spend far more time and visit more nodes than the field-independent students with the same amount of online experience. This may point to the impact of practice and once again, the need to study users over longer time slices than a single trial.

Plass et al. (1998) tested the potential effects of the verbalizer or visualizer learning preference, based on the Visualizer/Verbalizer Questionnaire by Kirby, Moore, and Schofield (1988) and the Edmonds Learning Style Identification Exercise (Reinert, 1976). One hundred and three university students used a hypermedia on German literature, and they were allowed to select which type of annotation they wanted to use (none, verbal, visual, or both verbal and visual) when they encountered an unfamiliar German word. The results indicated that visualizers performed better on vocabulary that had visual-only connotations, whereas verbalizers performed better on vocabulary that had verbal-only connotations. These findings demonstrate the importance of matching learning style with instructional material, at least in the case of visualizers and verbalizers. Ford and Chen (2001)

came to a similar conclusion, that matching cognitive style to learning experience was important. They had 73 postgraduate students create HTML pages using instructional hypermedia that was either matched or mismatched to their cognitive styles, as determined by Riding's Cognitive Styles Analysis. The overall gain for students in matched conditions was significantly higher than for those in mismatched conditions.

Conclusions

Individual differences remain a major concern in the educational literature on learning and it is clear that for hypermedia, such differences can significantly impact the experience and performance of learners. Given the myriad cognitive-style dimensions that have emerged over the last century of research into learning, it is important to identify the most likely candidates for empirical work and to determine how these differences manifest themselves in specific tasks or may be accommodated within specific designs. Domain knowledge is an obvious distinguisher of the type of learning environment required, but it would now appear that spatial ability is a reasonable predictor of user response on certain measures, such as navigation performance. Field dependence/independence is a most popular style dimension and seems to mediate the performance of inexperienced users. Tracing such differences over time remains a research problem in need of far more study.

Context Issues

Hypermedia learning situations can vary tremendously – learners may have different goals, may be working with different-sized documents, may be in different learning situations, and so forth. Instructional content and presentation formats vary widely as well. Because the majority of the studies reviewed in this paper do not make use of real-world hypermedia learning tools being used in an actual educational situation, it is important to consider context factors in experimental hypermedia, especially if we intend to generalize findings to a real-world setting.

Types of Study Employed in This Literature

More than 80% of the studies reviewed in this chapter used university students (including undergraduates and graduates) as experimental subjects. Three studies used high school students, and two used fifth-grade students. Only one study was performed on older adults. While it is clear that university education is an important location for the exploitation of hypermedia technologies, it is certainly not the only place where learning occurs and there is a very real opportunity for new studies to explore other contexts of use.

Typically, in studies of hypermedia, learners are asked to perform a reading-for-comprehension task, where they were told to take as much time as necessary to use a hypermedia document before being tested. Fully one-quarter of these studies also asked learners to perform a search-and-retrieval task, where learners were given questions for which they were to use the hypermedia to locate answers. We noted eight studies that used only search-and-retrieval as the experimental task.

Descriptive details of the hypermedia documents used in these studies are not always provided. Because it is likely that dealing with a large, multipage document structured with multiple links and a map will feel different than interacting with a four- or five-node document, it would help all of us to gain a better sense of the learning context if authors provided such details consistently. Our synthesis of these details indicates that most of the research is conducted on documents consisting of no more than 60 nodes. Only 11 studies used hypermedia with more than 60 nodes and only 6 of those had more than 100 nodes. While "node count" is an ambiguous measure, half the studies where details were provided reveal test documents with less than 2,000 words. Apparently we are not yet in the multimedia age, because over half of the studies that reported these

details used text-only documents as test materials. Only eight of the studies used more than three types of media (including text, graphics, audio, video, or animation). Overall, we are seeing research results from a very narrow range of hypermedia instantiations.

Only three studies required the learner to use the hypermedia in an active, applied manner (creating Web sites and designing a children's playscape). An additional three studies focused on comprehending a foreign language and four studies looked at learning mechanical procedures. Factual knowledge gain, measured by a post-task test, was by far the most common evaluation of outcome conducted. Analyzing navigation patterns, tracking time on task, having the learner draw concept maps, and writing short essays were also used regularly.

The subtle effects of contextual issues can be observed in a study by Moreno and Mayer (2000b). They reported the results of five experiments on the use of personalized messages in hypermedia learning. Messages were either written in a personal style, from the first- or second-person perspective, or in a neutral third-person point of view. In Experiments 1 and 2, students used a hypermedia on lightening formation, and in Experiments 3, 4, and 5, they played a game about environmental science. Experiments 1, 3, and 5 provided spoken (auditory) messages, while Experiments 2 and 4 provided on-screen textual messages. Across the five experiments, students who received personalized messages performed significantly better on problem-solving transfer tests and retention tests than students who received neutral messages. The authors suggest that these results indicate that students in a multimedia-learning environment should be addressed as participants rather than subjects for optimal learning outcome.

Gender

Gender is typically not the primary focus of studies on hypermedia learning, however several studies considered it as a variable. In fact, only the study by Leong and Hawamdeh (1999) focused specifically on whether or not gender is a factor in hypermedia use. They studied the attitude toward hypermedia instruction of 40 fifth graders in Singapore (17 boys and 23 girls) but the lack of statistical analysis by the authors led them to conclude only that there may be a difference in attitude between boys and girls.

Reed and Oughton (1997) tested 18 graduate students to determine whether prior computing experience or gender affected navigation style. There was no significant effect between gender and the number of linear or nonlinear steps taken, suggesting that, despite popular belief, gender is not a factor in navigation patterns, at least in hypermedia (although see Ford & Chen [2000] for a contradictory finding on use of indices, where females demonstrated greater use than males). Beccue, Vila, and Whitley (2001) came to similar conclusions in their study of the effects on audio in hypermedia on 86 university students. They found no significant difference in performance on either the labs or posttest scores between men and women either with or without audio.

While performance may not be directly affected, Ford and Chen (2000) found that women made fewer requests for guidance than did men. Schoon and Cafolla (2002) had somewhat mixed results when they considered whether gender was a factor when using different hypermedia structures. Although it took women fewer steps to find a specific node in the system, women had more restarts (i.e., jumps back to the home page, a common user behavior when lost or disoriented) than did men for the linear, star, and random Web sites.

Task and Goal Effects for Hypermedia Learning

Several authors have suggested that different forms of hypermedia best meet different learning goals. For example, Curry et al. (1999) studied 50 university students using a hypermedia on Lyme disease to see how learning goals affected both general knowledge recall and concept-map construction. The experimental group was given a scenario about a person with Lyme disease and asked to determine whether the individual had a clear understanding of the facts about the disease. They authors found that although there was no significant difference between the two groups on general knowledge recall, students with general learning goals tended to construct hierarchical maps (with the main idea and subordinate concepts listed below), whereas participants with specific learning goals were more likely to construct relational concept maps (with conceptual links between concepts that were not a part of the original hypermedia). This suggests that learners who have a specific goal in mind make their own connections amongst concepts presented in a hypermedia, and the technology may have different benefits or might best be designed differently, when applied in such learning tasks.

Dee-Lucas and Larkin (1999) tested hypertext segmented on different levels (more or less segmentation) combined with goal type (problem solving or information finding) on 64 university students to see if different levels of informational segmentation might be appropriate in different task situations. The results suggested that less-segmented hypertext may be more appropriate for goals where learners need to become familiar with a wide range of content, whereas more segmented hypertext may be better for narrowly defined goals such as locating specific or target information. Zumbach and Reimann (2002) studied 60 adults to see how different types of goals affected learning outcome. Participants were divided into three groups based on goals: (1) the *strategy* group, which received pretreatment training in asking questions before using the hypertext so that users could formulate their own goals; (2) the *goal-based scenario* group, which was given an authentic task to complete while using the hypertext; or (3) the *control* group, which had no specific goal and received identical information to that provided in the hypertext, but in a tutorial format with question/answer sessions after each module. Zumbach and Reimann concluded that while learners in the *goal-based scenarios* group were significantly more motivated and gained significantly more structural knowledge of the information, learners in the *control* group using the tutorial format actually gained significantly more factual knowledge than either of the other two groups. Such results are a salutary reminder that newer forms of presentation are not always pedagogically better than traditional forms.

Conclusions

The variability we can see across hypermedia studies has tended to be viewed as a source of difficulty for extracting general findings. In fact, while it is true that no two test systems are identical, the real source of variability lies neither in the applications nor the learners studied. The types of hypermedia used also tend to be fairly restricted and most test subjects are college students. There is a typical learning task, at least in this literature, and it most likely involves reading to learn, or at least to be able to pass some form of comprehension or memory test afterward. Because the learning goal seems to drive much of learner behavior, this variable really needs more systematic manipulation in future research for us to determine what hypermedia may really offer us.

Future research might also usefully consider extending the tasks and outcome tests used to capture data on a greater range of learning situations. Perhaps more importantly, studies of users with a variety of educational backgrounds and ages would add useful information to the current literature.

Discussion and Conclusions

Despite nearly two decades of research on hypertext and hypermedia learning tools, we are still a long way from knowing how best to exploit the power of this technology to support learning. It is clear that large individual differences exist among learners and that the freedom to jump and move at one's own pace through material is not equally beneficial to all. Despite these and other limitations, research is making progress on explaining the relevant phenomena.

Simple comparisons across media are really not terribly informative. Learning is complex and influenced by multiple factors. Certainly there is no one hypermedia application that can be considered truly representative of the technology in a cross-media comparison, but more importantly, gross media comparisons tend to hide the primary effects of key variables and render most differences nonsignificant. Over the last decade these lessons seem to have been learned and much of the recent empirical work in this area has sought to compare forms or types of hypermedia to identify the variables that matter. This is progress of a sort.

The ultimate question that we ask here is whether or not hypermedia is a real step forward for learning. The answer is the caveat-laden "it might be," if the appropriate factors are considered. In the interests of brevity, we provide a highly simplified set of guidelines that seem warranted from the empirical literature reviewed in this chapter:

- Not all learning tasks are equally well supported by hypermedia – determining how learners are to experience and use the material is crucial to designing effective interfaces to information.
- Individual differences, such as domain and prior knowledge, spatial skills, learning styles, and so forth, should be considered in designing and implementing any hypermedia.
- Providing advance organizers can aid navigation and perception of structure.
- Unless the information to be presented demands otherwise (through convention, genre, etc.), hierarchical structures seem to provide a suitable layout for the majority of users.
- Congruency of format for visual and verbal information presentation can assist cognitive processing for most users.

Future research must attempt to broaden the learner population studied so as to include older adults, children, and learners who have not had the advantages of college education. Similarly, there is great potential for task analysis to help determine where linked structures and specific media combinations might have the most applicability. Although it is a problem for all studies of human-computer interaction, there is a real need here for extended evaluations of learners over time because it is clear that single-task performance measures are not simply extended to predict long-term learning with interactive media.

The educational literature could learn lessons from the broader design literature of human factors, applied psychology, and information design. While there is no silver bullet to be found in these literatures, all have concerns with understanding user behavior with interactive systems. As McKnight, Dillon, and Richardson (1991) predicted, hypermedia has become an interface standard, and it is increasingly true that the differences between a learning tool and any other digital information space are difficult to draw firmly. Given this, the literature on user navigation, search performance, reading speed, scanning ability, and so forth can all provide some relevant insight into the actions of learners in hypermedia spaces.

As always, the best step forward will be made when an appropriate theoretical articulation is provided that can explain human performance and cognition in such environments. Perhaps the clearest sign of progress being made in this area is the emergence of Mayer's (2001) generative theory, which shows potential to unify the range of cognitive perspectives that have informed much work on user cognition. Its emergence within the educational field is surely a pointer for new work here but it is our view that it could also be of value in related fields such as Web design for nonlearning activities. Such an argument could not be convincingly made a decade ago, and thus it is one indicator of genuine progress within this field. The next decade may prove the most fruitful yet for educational hypermedia research.

Acknowledgment

This work was funded through the Digital Libraries Phase II program, with support from the National Science Foundation and the National Endowment of the Humanities (Award #9909068).

Glossary

Advance organizer: A means of rendering structure explicitly to users. Common advance organizers include site maps and textual overviews or summaries.

Generative activity: When learners must perform an activity, such as note taking, summarizing, answering questions, and so forth while learning.

Generative theory of multimedia learning: Learners are limited-capacity dual encoders who actively process information in order to integrate it meaningfully with their existing knowledge. Developed by Mayer and colleagues.

Group Embedded Figures Test: Developed by Witkin to determine learning style, it groups people based on their ability to identify simple figures within a more complex pattern. Those who are good at finding the simple figures are said to be more field independent and are less subject to contextual effects, while those who are more field dependent are more greatly affected by context.

Hypermedia: Consists of more than linked texts. It includes other forms of media as well, such as images, video, and sound. Often used interchangeably (although technically incorrectly) with hypertext.

Hypertext: Coined by Ted Nelson around 1965 to refer to "nonsequential" or "nonlinear" text where authors and readers were free to explore and to link information in ways that made personal sense for them.

Learner control mechanism: A technology that enables the learner to control the learning situation.

Learning Style Inventory (LSI): Developed by Kolb to determine learning styles based on varying levels of convergers/divergers or accommodators/

assimilators. Convergers tend to bring together pieces of knowledge into a single topic to deduce an answer, whereas divergers rely on brainstorming and idea generation to solve problems. Assimilators supposedly solve problems by inductive reasoning, while accommodators plan and experiment. Individual learning styles are a mix of these four modes, although the converger/diverger accommodator/assimilator scales are continuous, so an individual can be more or less strongly inclined toward one mode or another.

Multimedia: Material is presented in both words and pictures, and may also include sound.

Structure: In the context of this chapter, how information, chunked into *nodes*, is connected together using *links*.

Topology: The way in which information *nodes* are connected together using links. Can be used interchangeably with *structure*.

References

Astleitner, H. (1997). Effects of external learning aids on learning with ill-structured hypertext. *Journal of Educational Computing Research*, 17(1), 1–18.

Barab, S. A., Young, M. F., & Wang, J. (1999). The effects of navigational and generative activities in hypertext learning on problem solving and comprehension. *International Journal of Instructional Media*, 26(3), 283–309.

Beccue, B., Vila, J., & Whitley, L. K. (2001). The effects of adding audio instructions to a multimedia compter based training environment. *Journal of Educational Multimedia and Hypermedia*, 10(1), 47–67.

Boechler, P. M. (2001). How spatial is hyperspace? Interacting with hypertext documents: Cognitive processes and concepts. *Cyber Psychology and Behavior*, 4(1), 23–46.

Brinkerhoff, J. D., Klein, J. D., & Koroghlanian, C. M. (2001). Effects of overviews and computer experience on learning from hypertext. *Journal of Educational Computing Research*, 25(4), 427–440.

Bush, V. (1945). As we may think. *The Atlantic Monthly*, 176(1), 101–108.

Calisir, F., & Gurel, Z. (2003). Influence of text structure and prior knowledge of the learner on reading comprehension, browsing and perceived control. *Computers in Human Behavior*, 19, 135–145.

Chen, C., & Rada, R. (1996). Interacting with hypertext: A meta-analysis of experimental studies. *Human-Computer Interaction*, 11, 125–156.

Chou, C., & Lin, H. (1998). The effect of navigation map types and cognitive styles on learners' performance in a computer-networked hypertext learning system. *Journal of Educational Multimedia and Hypermedia*, 7(2/3), 151–176.

Curry, J., Haderlie, S., Ku, T., Lawless, K. A., Lemon, M., & Wood, R. (1999). Specified learning goals and their effect on learners' representations of a hypertext reading environment. *International Journal of Instructional Media*, 26(1), 43–52.

Dee-Lucas, D., & Larkin, J. H. (1999). Hypertext segmentation and goal compatibility: Effects on study strategies and learning. *Journal of Educational Multimedia and Hypermedia*, 8(3), 279–313.

de Vries, E., & de Jong, T. (1997). Using information systems while performing complex tasks: An example from architectural design. *International Journal of Human-Computer Studies*, 46, 31–54.

Dillon, A. (2004). *Designing usable electronic text* (2nd ed.). London: CRC Press.

Dillon, A., & Gabbard, R. (1998). Hypermedia as an educational technology: A review of the quantitative research literature on learner comprehension, control, and style. *Review of Educational Research*, 68(3), 322–349.

Ekstrom, R. B., French, J. W., & Harman, H. H. (1976). *Manual for kit of factor-referenced cognitive tests*. Princeton, NJ: Educational Testing Service.

Fabos, B. (2001). *Media in the classroom: An alternative history*. Paper presented at the Proceedings of the American Educators Research Association, Seattle, WA.

Ford, N., & Chen, S. Y. (2000). Individual differences, hypermedia navigation, and learning: An empirical study. *Journal of Educational Multimedia and Hypermedia*, 9, 281–312.

Ford, N., & Chen, S. Y. (2001). Matching/mismatching revisited: An empirical study of learning and teaching styles. *British Journal of Educational Technology, 32* (1), 5–22.

Hofman, R., & van Oostendorp, H. (1999). Cognitive effects of a structural overview in a hypertext. *British Journal of Educational Technology, 30*(2), 129–140.

Howard-Jones, P. A., & Martin, R. J. (2002). The effect of questioning on concept learning within a hypertext system. *Journal of Computer Assisted Learning, 18*, 10–20.

Hsu, Y., & Schwen, T. M. (2003). The effects of structural cues from multiple metaphors on computer users' information search performance. *International Journal of Human-Computer Studies, 58*, 39–55.

Jacobson, M. J., Maouri, C., Mishra, P., & Kolar, C. (1996). Learning with hypertext learning environments: Theory, design, and research. *Journal of Educational Multimedia and Hypermedia, 5*(3/4), 239–281.

Kalyuga, S., Chandler, P., & Sweller, J. (1998). Levels of expertise and instructional design. *Human Factors, 40*(1), 1–18.

Kalyuga, S., Chandler, P., & Sweller, J. (1999). Managing split-attention and redundancy in multimedia instruction. *Applied Cognitive Psychology, 13*, 351–371.

Kalyuga, S., Chandler, P., & Sweller, J. (2000). Incorporating learner experience into the design of multimedia instruction. *Journal of Educational Psychology, 92* (1), 126–136.

Kettanurak, V., Ramamurthy, K., & Haseman, W. D. (2001). User attitude as a mediator of learning performance improvement in an interactive multimedia environment: An empirical investigation of the degree of interactivity and learning styles. *International Journal of Human-Computer Studies, 54*, 541–583.

Kirby, J. R., Moore, P. J., & Schofield, N. J. (1988). Verbal and visual learning styles. *Contemporary Educational Psychology, 13*, 169–184.

Kolb, D. A. (1984). *Experiential learning: Experience as the source of learning and development.* Englewood Cliffs, NJ: Prentice-Hall, Inc.

Kraus, L. A., Reed, W. M., & Fitzgerald, G. E. (2001). The effects of learning style and hypermedia prior experience on behavioral disorders knowledge and time on task: A case-based hypermedia environment. *Computers in Human Behavior, 17*, 125–140.

Kuhl, J. (1985). Volitional mediators of cognition-behavior consistency. Self-regulatory processes and action versus state orientation. In J. Kuhl,

J. Beckman (Eds.), *Action control. From cognition to behavior* (pp. 101–128). Berlin: Springer.

Landauer, T. (1995). *The trouble with computers.* Cambridge, MA: MIT Press.

Lawless, K. A., & Kulikowich, J. M. (1996). Understanding hypertext navigation through cluster analysis. *Journal of Educational Computing Research, 14*(4), 385–399.

Leong, S. C., & Hawamdeh, S. (1999). Gender and learning attitudes in using Web-based science lessons. *Information Research, 5* (1).

Liao, Y. C. (1998). Effects of hypermedia versus traditional instruction on students' achievement: A meta-analysis. *Journal of Research on Computing in Education, 30*(4), 341–359.

Lin, D. M. (2003). Hypertext for the aged: Effects of text topologies. *Computers in Human Behavior, 19*, 201–209.

Mayer, R. E. (2001). *Multimedia learning.* New York: Cambridge University Press.

Mayer, R. E., & Moreno, R. (1998). A split-attention effect in multimedia learning: Evidence for dual processing systems in working memory. *Journal of Educational Psychology, 90*(2), 312–320.

McDonald, S., & Stevenson, R. J. (1996). Disorientation in hypertext: The effects of three text structures on navigation performance. *Applied Ergonomics, 27*(1), 61–68.

McDonald, S., & Stevenson, R. J. (1998). Effects of text structure and prior knowledge of the learner on navigation in hypertext. *Human Factors, 40*(1), 18–28.

McDonald, S., & Stevenson, R. J. (1999). Spatial versus conceptual maps as learning tools in hypertext. *Journal of Educational Multimedia and Hypermedia, 8*(1), 43–64.

McKnight, C., Dillon, A., & Richardson, J. (1991). *Hypertext in context.* New York: Cambridge University Press.

Melara, G. (1996). Investigating learning styles on different hypertext environments: Hierarchical-like and network-like structures. *Journal of Educational Computing Research, 14*(4), 313–328.

Moreno, R., & Mayer, R. E. (2000a). A coherence effect in multimedia learning: The case for minimizing irrelevant sounds in the design of multimedia instructional messages. *Journal of Educational Psychology, 92* (1), 117–125.

Moreno, R., & Mayer, R. E. (2000b). Engaging students in active learning: The case for personalized multimedia messages. *Journal of Educational Psychology*, 92(4), 724–733.

Nelson, T. (1965). *The hypertext*. Paper presented at the Word Documentation Federation Conference, Washington, DC.

Niederhauser, D. S., Reynolds, R. E., Salmen, D. J., & Skolmoski, P. (2000). The influence of cognitive load on learning from hypertext. *Journal of Educational Computing Research*, 23(3), 237–255.

Nielsen, J. (1989). *The matters that really matter for hypertext usability*. Paper presented at the Hypertext '89, Second ACM Conference on Hypertext, Pittsburgh, PA.

Nilsson, R. M., & Mayer, R. E. (2002). The effects of graphic organizers giving cues to the structure of a hypertext document on users' navigation strategies and performance. *International Journal of Human Computer Studies*, 57, 1–26.

Nimwegen, C. V., Pouw, M., and van Oostendorp, H. (1999). The influence of structure and reading-manipulation on usability of hypertexts. *Interacting with Computers*, 12, 7–21.

Padovani, S., and Lansdale, M. (2003). Balancing search and retrieval in hypertext: Context-specific trade-offs in navigational tool use. *International Journal of Human-Computer Studies*, 58, 125–149.

Palmquist, R. A., and Kim, K.-S. (2000). Cognitive style and on-line database search experience as predictors of Web search performance. *Journal of the American Society for Information Science*, 51(6), 558–566.

Paolucci, R. (1998). The effects of cognitive style and knowledge structure on performance using a hypermedia learning system. *Journal of Educational Multimedia and Hypermedia*, 7(2/3), 123–150.

Parlangeli, O., Marchigiani, E., & Bagnara, S. (1999). Multimedia systems in distance education: Effects of usability on learning. *Interacting with Computers*, 12, 37–49.

Pavio, A. (1986). *Mental representations: A dual coding approach*. New York: Oxford University Press.

Plass, J., Chun, D., Mayer, R., & Leutner, D. (1998). Supporting visual and verbal learning preferences in a second-language multimedia learning environment. *Journal of Educational Psychology*, 90(1), 25–36.

Plass, J. L., Chun, D. M., Mayer, R. E., and Leutner, D. (2003). Cognitive load in reading a foreign language text with multimedia aids and the influence of verbal and spatial abilities. *Computers in Human Behavior*, 19, 221–243.

Potelle, H., & Rouet, J. (2003). Effects of content representation and readers' prior knowledge on the comprehension of hypertext. *International Journal of Human-Computer Studies*, 58, 327–345.

Rasmussen, K., & Davidson-Shivers, G. (1998). Hypermedia and learning styles: Can performance be influenced? *Journal of Educational Multimedia and Hypermedia*, 7(4), 291–308.

Reed, W. M., & Oughton, J. M. (1997). Computer experience and interval-based hypermedia navigation. *Journal of Research on Computing in Education*, 30(1), 38–52.

Reinert, H. (1976). Identifying student learning styles. *The Modern Language Journal*, 60(4), 156–163.

Schoon, P., & Cafolla, R. (2002). World Wide Web hypertext linkage patterns. *Journal of Educational Multimedia and Hypermedia*, 11(2), 117–139.

Shapiro, A. (1998). Promoting active learning: The role of system structure in learning from hypertext. *Human-Computer Interaction*, 13, 1–35.

Shapiro, A. (1999). The relationship between prior knowledge and interactive overviews during hypermedia-aided learning. *Journal of Educational Computing Research*, 20(2), 143–167.

Shapiro, A. (2000). The effect of interactive overviews on the development of conceptual structure in novices learning from hypertext. *Journal of Educational Multimedia and Hypermedia*, 9(1), 57–78.

Spiro, R. J., Feltovich, P. J., Jacobson, M. J., & Coulson, R. L. (1991). Knowledge representation, content specification, and the development of skill in situation-specific knowledge assembly: Some constructivist issues as they relate to cognitive flexibility theory and hypertext. *Educational Technology*, 31(9), 22–25.

Spruijt, S., & Jansen, C. (1999). The influence of task and format on reading results with an online text. *IEEE Transactions on Professional Communication*, 42(2), 92–99.

van Nimwegen, C., Pouw, M., & van Oostendorp, H. (1999). The influence of structure and reading-manipulation on usability of hypertexts. *Interacting with Computers*, 12, 7–21.

Wickens, C. (1992). *Engineering psychology and human performance* (2nd ed.). New York: Harper Collins.

Witkin, H. A., Moore, C. A., Goodenough, D. R., & Cox, P. W. (1977). Field-dependent and field-independent cognitive styles and their educational research. *Review of Educational Research*, 47(1), 1–64.

Witkin, H. A., Oltman, P. T., Raskin, E., & Karp, S. A. (1971). *Group embedded figures test manual*. Palo Alto, CA: Consulting Psychologists Press.

Yeh, S., & Lehman, J. D. (2001). Effects of learner control and learning strategies on English as a foreign language (EFL) learning from interactive hypermedia lessons. *Journal of Educational Multimedia and Hypermedia*, 10(2), 141–159.

Yildirim, Z., Ozden, Y., & Aksu, M. (2001). Comparison of hypermedia learning and traditional instruction on knowledge acquisition and retention. *The Journal of Educational Research*, 94(4), 207–214.

Zumbach, J., & Reimann, P. (2002). Enhancing learning from hypertext by inducing a goal orientation: Comparing different approaches. *Instructional Science*, 30, 243–267.

CHAPTER 35
Multimedia Learning in e-Courses

Ruth Colvin Clark
Clark Training and Consulting

Abstract

E-learning is on the rise in both the public and private sectors. However, learning outcomes are either flat or remain unknown. Therefore, it is important to ground e-learning design, development, and selection on the basis of credible evidence. Research on multimedia instruction in the last two decades has moved beyond "Which media is best?" studies to more productive questions regarding the best use of instructional methods that support cognitive learning processes. This chapter reviews research evidence on what we know about how best to use three unique media features that together distinguish e-learning from other delivery media: audio modality, animations, and simulations. In each case, evidence suggests that practitioners exploit unique media capabilities by applying guidelines for their use that accommodate the strengths and limits of human cognitive processes.

Introduction to E-Learning

Although still a distant second to classroom instruction, e-learning is steadily increasing in media market share as an instructional delivery alternative for learners from 5 to 85. Sixteen percent of instruction in business and industry was delivered by computer in 2003 – up from 12% the previous year (Galvin, 2003) Almost 90% of all universities with more than 10,000 students offer some form of distance learning – nearly all of which use the Internet (Svetcov, 2000). Public education has also invested heavily in information technology with multimedia computer ratios dropping from 21 students per computer in 1997 to fewer than 10 in 2000 (Cuban, 2001).

The primary motivator behind the growth of e-learning among adult learners is economics. In the United States the private business sector makes an annual investment in training of between 50 and 60 billion dollars (Galvin, 2003). For these organizations e-learning is seen as a route to cost savings – primarily by decreasing travel costs and secondarily by reducing instructional time. The metric of e-learning success reported at Intel Corporation is ROS – return on savings. It is calculated by subtracting the costs associated with development and deployment of an e-learning course with those associated with the same course delivered in a classroom environment. The e-business training division of Intel recorded a savings of $10.3 million dollars over a four-year period during which time they deployed over 750 e-courses (Nguyen, personal communication). Whereas the business sector has looked to e-learning for cost savings, universities have generated revenue by expanding student enrollments and tuition fees for distance learning.

Evidenced-Based E-Learning

Increased classroom availability of technology and higher proportions of courses delivered by computer do not necessarily mean that computers are *either used* or are *used effectively* for instructional purposes. In a recent study of computer use in schools in the Silicon Valley, Cuban (2001) reports that "less than 10% of teachers who used computers in their classrooms were serious users (defined as using computers in class at least once a week); between 20 and 30% were occasional to rare users (once a month); well over half of the teachers were nonusers" (p. 133). In a similar vein, Roberts (2003) reports that faculty at a Scottish university use the Internet to keep up to date or to direct students to useful sites. Only about 15% constructed learning activities around Internet resources and about 7% used the Web interactively for either exercises or discussions.

Studies on the effects of computers on academic achievement concede that in the public education sector, there have been few effects (Cuban, 2001; Maddux, 2003). In a discussion of the impact of information technology on education Maddux concludes, "In fact, in a field marked by one fantastic development after another, the most fantastic of all may be that anything so ubiquitous and so powerful as information technology has had so little impact on teachers, students, and schools" (p. 36).

In the private business sector, the learning and transfer outcomes of training are rarely measured. Therefore the effectiveness of e-learning is unknown. Surveys of evaluation practices indicate that only a small proportion of courseware is evaluated beyond subjective learner ratings. Because of the extra investment in time and expertise needed to measure learning outcomes, it is unlikely that such measurements will increase in the near future in the private sector – especially given the cost-reduction motives behind computer delivery of corporate training programs. Cuban (2001) observes that in public education, although access to technology has increased, academic achievement has not benefited due to either nonuse by teachers or to uses that "largely maintain existing classroom practices" (p. 171). In summary, in spite of greater market share, achievement outcomes from the use of computers to deliver instruction are either flat or are unknown.

In both the private and public sector, it's important that e-learning design and selection of e-learning courseware be based on credible research evidence of instructional features that lead to learning. In the United States, the No Child Left Behind Act emphasizes educational reform that reflects *scientifically based research* defined in Section 9190 as "the application of rigorous, systematic, and objective procedures to obtain reliable and valid knowledge relevant to education activities and programs" (Mageau, 2004). What empirical evidence do we have about e-learning effectiveness? What research evidence can practitioners use to guide the development or selection of e-courses? Those are the main questions of this chapter. But first, I need to

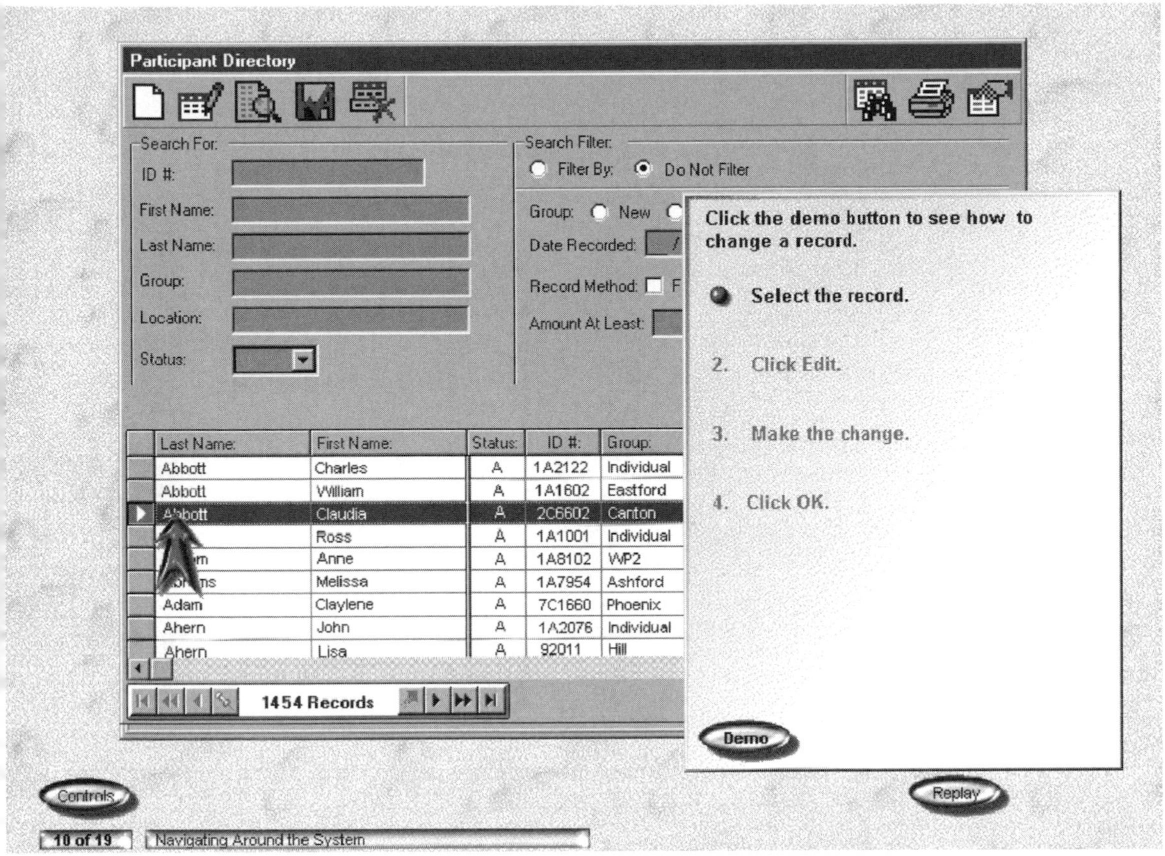

Figure 35.1. A screen from an e-learning tutorial designed for individual learning. Source: Clark & Lyons, 2004; credit: Mark A. Palmer.

consider a more fundamental question: What is e-learning?

What Is E-Learning?

E-learning is instruction delivered on a computer that is designed to achieve specific learning goals. Beyond this general definition, a closer look at individual e-learning courses reveals a kaleidoscope of examples. We've known for some time that it does not make sense to generalize about e-learning any more than it makes sense to generalize about book learning or classroom learning. Rather than treat e-learning as a unified type of instruction, we need to look closer to distinguish among different types of e-learning

and within those types, to identify ways that specific instructional methods can best be used to promote learning.

Synchronous Versus Asynchronous E-Learning: Solo or Collaborative

E-learning was historically designed for individual self-study. Figure 35.1 illustrates one screen from a tutorial designed for solo use. With the advent of online communication facilities, more recent courseware can accommodate interactions among learners and instructors in synchronous and/or asynchronous modes. Asynchronous e-learning is designed to be taken by individuals at any time and in any location. Asynchronous tutorials may be strictly for self-paced

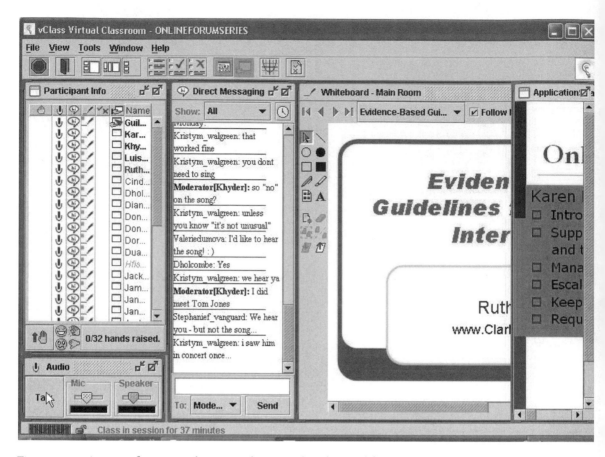

Figure 35.2. A screen from a synchronous e-learning class designed for group learning.

solo learning or they may incorporate asynchronous collaboration through discussion boards or e-mail. In contrast, in synchronous e-learning participants in remote locations participate in a learning event at the same time. The screen shown in Figure 35.2 is from a synchronous lesson delivered by the author to over 200 learners online at the same time. Virtual classroom software, such as Elluminate™ used in this example, offers facilities that allow the instructor and participants to dynamically interact through a combination of audio, text, and interface such as the whiteboard, chat window, polling options, or icons such as the happy face.

In 2003 21% of commercial organizations report frequent use of virtual classrooms such as that shown in Figure 35.2 while 44%

report frequent use of asynchronous self-study Web-based training formats shown in Figure 35.1 (Galvin, 2003). The majority of controlled research studies published to date focus on asynchronous e-learning tutorials designed for individual self-study. Therefore, many of the guidelines in this chapter apply most directly to that type of e-learning. However, because these guidelines are anchored in human cognitive processes, we should be able to apply them to synchronous environments. In addition, virtual collaboration is currently an active area of investigation and a growing body of research findings will soon lead to evidence-based guidelines for the most effective ways to use online communication facilities in both synchronous and asynchronous e-learning formats.

Figure 35.3. A receptive e-learning reference on human evolution. Source: TerraIncognita for ASU.

Receptive, Directive, and Guided Discovery E-Learning Designs

Both synchronous and asynchronous forms of e-learning can embody diverse instructional strategies. Clark (2000, 2003) and Clark and Mayer (2003) have summarized three different approaches to the design of e-learning, each one reflecting different learning assumptions. These are receptive, directive, and guided discovery. Receptive e-learning such as the human evolution course shown in Figure 35.3 is based on a transmission model of instruction. The goal of this type of e-learning is to inform, that is to provide a source of information. Receptive courses are characterized primarily by a lack of external interaction opportunities other than navigating to various resources made available by the site. Learners are presented with content and it is assumed that they convert that content into useful new knowledge and/or skills. Typically the main goal of receptive courseware is to present information, motivate, and/or to communicate basic knowledge. In contrast, both directive and guided discovery e-learning are designed to build skills. Directive lessons such as the one shown in Figure 35.1 use a deductive instructional approach based on behavioral learning theory. They present small chunks of content, examples or demonstrations, followed by practice with feedback. Most directive e-learning is designed to build procedural or near-transfer skills. Lessons designed to teach soft skills or routine tasks, such as taking a customer order or using a spreadsheet, are commonly designed in a directive fashion.

In contrast, guided discovery courses offer a more inductive learning environment and many use simulation to present an environment in which learners complete a series of job or goal-related tasks. Guided discovery courses are often designed to teach far-transfer skills that require learners to build flexible mental models that can be applied to a variety of situations. In many guided discovery courses the learning goal is as much to build problem-solving or inquiry skills in the domain as it is to acquire a specific body of knowledge and skills. Figure 35.4 is a screen from a simulation designed to help middle and high school students acquire basic principles of generic inheritance. By making a series of guided changes to specific genes on specific chromosomes and observing the changes in dragon features, learners build a mental model of genetic inheritance rules.

Beyond the Media Silver Bullet

A number of years of media comparison research conclude that asking about the effectiveness of any given media such as e-learning is not a productive question (Mayer, 1997). Not only do e-learning courses assume many diverse forms, but also the effectiveness of any one e-learning lesson is shaped by the context in which it is deployed. Thus a given lesson that is effective for novice learners who need to build specific procedural skills will be less effective for more experienced learners who need to build mental models that they can apply to diverse situations. While at one time we hoped for some silver bullets – some instructional approaches that were universally effective, the interactions among the instruction, the learner, and the desired instructional goal or content leave us with a more qualified set of instructional prescriptions. The most robust instructional principles are those based on a model of human psychological learning processes. By understanding

not only what works but also why it works, we are enabled to adjust the instructional method based on its psychological functions.

Instructional Media versus Instructional Methods

Richard Clark (1983, 1994) has extensively summarized media comparison research and concluded that instructional effectiveness was never a function of delivery media but rather depends on the instructional methods used. More recent meta-analyses summarizing dozens of media comparison studies continue to support his thesis by reporting no significant differences in learning (Dillon and Gabbard, 1998). Whether delivered in a classroom or on a computer, the same lesson invariably results in more or less the same learning. For example, Mayer, Mathias, and Wetzell (2002) obtained the same learning from a paper and an online version of a lesson teaching how hydraulic brakes worked. Both versions included the same visuals and words. I define an *instructional method* as a feature of an instructional environment that interacts in predictable ways with human psychological processes. The multimedia principles described in this handbook all provide the basis for specific instructional methods. Some examples include using relevant visuals (multimedia principle), using audio to describe complex visuals (modality principle), and avoidance of related but irrelevant words and graphics in lessons (coherence principle). Any given instructional method will be effective or ineffective depending on the extent to which it supports or disrupts basic-learning psychological processes regardless of the delivery media.

Instructional Methods and Psychological Learning Processes

From the definition and examples of instructional methods in the previous paragraph, we see that any given instructional method is context sensitive. Thus depending on the learner and the instructional content, the same instructional method may be more

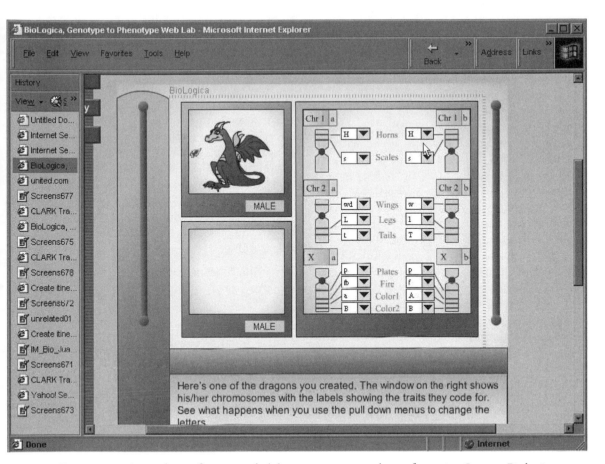

Figure 35.4. A simulation from a guided discovery course on laws of genetics. Source: Biologica Project.

or less effective. The reason is that human learning requirements will vary as a function of specific psychological features of the learner and the instructional goal. Because much of the modern research on instructional methods is based on a cognitive model of learning, it's relevant to quickly summarize the psychological features and processes that underlie human learning.

Working Memory Versus Long-Term Memory

Learning is predicated heavily on the architecture and consequent requirements of the two main memory systems involved in learning: working memory and long-term memory. These two memory siblings are quite disparate in their features and yet they work together in complementary ways. Working memory is the more active partner. It is responsible for all conscious processing including learning. Long-term memory is a relatively passive repository of all knowledge and skills stored in structures called *schemas*. Although long-term memory has a large storage capacity, working memory is much more limited in the amount of information it can manage at any one time. For example, imagine looking at a chessboard containing 24 pieces laid out in a midgame formation. How many times would you need to refer to this midplay chessboard in order to accurately reassemble all of the pieces from memory? In a now-famous experiment, Chase and Simon (1973) compared the number of times expert and novice chess players needed to refer back to a midplay chessboard in order to construct it. Not surprisingly, novice players needed to look back many more times. To demonstrate that the superior memory performance of the expert players reflected their prior knowledge and experience rather than any superior innate memory ability, Chase and Simon repeated the experiment using chess pieces randomly placed on the board. Faced with a random board, novices actually required *fewer referrals* to reconstruct the board than did experts. The reason? A board of 24 pieces represents 24 chunks of information to a novice no matter how the pieces are placed. However, for an experienced player, a 24-piece midplay chessboard includes as few as four chunks of information because experts represent the pieces as play clusters rather than as individual pieces. When placed randomly, attempts by experts to represent these pieces as familiar play clusters were so disrupted that overall memory performance was debilitated.

Therefore, because George Miller's (1956) characterization of working memory limits as *7 plus or minus 2 chunks* we have learned that chunks are not equivalent. Chunk sizes and thus working-memory virtual capacity depends on prior knowledge stored in long-term memory. The proficiency of experts is based on their ability to represent a great deal of complex information efficiently in working memory as a result of patterns experts impose on incoming data by preexisting schema stored in long-term memory.

These interactions between working memory and long-term memory help us understand the opposite effects of the same instructional methods on novice versus experienced learners. For example, instructional methods that reduce cognitive load such as replacing some practice exercises with worked examples are effective for novices but are ineffective for more experienced learners (Kalyuga, Chandler, Tuoviner, & Sweller, 2001; Sweller and Cooper, 1985). The adverse effect of many instructional methods that are beneficial for novice learners when used in lessons intended for more experienced learners has been widely

documented as the *expertise reversal effect* (Kalyuga, Ayres, Chandler, & Sweller, 2003).

Seven Learning Processes

The goal of instruction regardless of delivery media is to help learners encode new lesson content into existing schemas in long-term memory in a way that supports retrieval back into working memory when needed at a future time and situation. Clark (2003) and Clark and Lyons (2004) update Gagne's (1985) seven events of instruction based on recent cognitive learning models to include the following processes that require support during learning:

- Attention to important aspects of the instruction;
- Activation of appropriate prior knowledge in long-term memory;
- Management of cognitive load;
- Integration of new content with itself and with activated prior knowledge resulting in encoding of new skills into long-term memory;
- Retrieval of new knowledge and skills later when needed;
- Monitoring and management of these processes by metacognition; and
- Motivation to initiate and persist in a learning event.

Instructional Methods and Psychological Process Trade-Offs

Effective instructional methods promote one or more of these processes while ineffective methods ignore or disrupt one or more of these processes. Sometimes an instructional method used in the service of one psychological event disrupts a different event and thus ends in a zero sum or even a negative learning outcome. For example, it's common practice to include thematic story lines with supporting visuals to increase the motivational appeal of e-learning. However research by Harp and Mayer (1997, 1998) showed that the inclusion of such seductive details whether in the form of text, audio, or visuals severely depresses learning

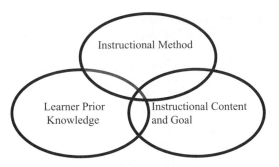

Figure 35.5. Three factors that shape the learning landscape.

outcomes compared to lesson versions that omit these embellishments. In a series of experiments Harp and Mayer (1998) used various countermeasures to offset the negative effects of seductive information. Only a countermeasure in which seductive elements were sequenced at the end of a lesson restored the effectiveness of the lesson to a level close to that of versions lacking seductive content. Harp and Mayer (1998) conclude that seductive details in various forms that appear early in a lesson depress learning by activating inappropriate prior knowledge from long-term memory. Thus an attempt to support learner motivation backfired by interfering with the critical process of prior-knowledge activation that is requisite to successful learning.

Three Factors That Shape the Learning Landscape

As mentioned previously, no one instructional method is effective for all learners and for all content. The virtual capacity of working memory for any given content is much greater for individuals with prior experience with that content. Chess masters, for example, require fewer referrals back to a midplay chessboard as a result of the schema stored in long-term memory allowing them to group individual pieces into larger chunks. Figure 35.5 summarizes the three most important factors that shape the learning landscape: learner prior knowledge, instructional content and goal, and instructional methods. First, learner differences, prior knowledge being the most important,

make up one major variable that will interact with instructional methods. Second, the instructional goal (near or far transfer) and associated content also determine the effectiveness of various instructional methods. For example, content that includes several items that must interact (high element interactivity) to achieve a given instructional goal will require more working memory capacity than content that can be meaningfully processed in isolation (Chandler & Sweller, 1996; Leahy, Chandler, & Sweller, 2003). The third factor is the instructional method that will interact with individual learner differences and with the instructional outcome goals. For example, when the instructional goal requires novices to learn content of high element interactivity, instructional methods that manage cognitive load are much more relevant than training aimed at more experienced learners and/or lessons that incorporate content of low complexity.

What Makes E-Learning Unique?

Although there is a general consensus that learning is a product of instructional methods more than of the media that deliver those methods, each medium has unique capabilities to carry specific instructional methods. For example, in comparing a course delivered by paper to one delivered by computer, the computer version has the following unique capabilities:

- *Dual modalities*: Ability to deliver content in both visual and auditory modes.
- *Movement*: Ability to deliver visual content in dynamic formats such as animation or video.
- *Simulation*: Ability to display environments that respond in dynamic and rule-based ways to user responses.

In the next sections I summarize research on how these three capabilities can be used in e-learning to promote one or more of the psychological learning events described previously.

Modalities in E-Learning

E-learning can present content in visual and/or auditory modes. For example a visual such as the screen capture shown in Figure 35.1 could be explained by words presented in text (visual–visual modes) or by words presented in narration (visual–auditory modes) or by both (visual/visual–auditory modes). Lessons can also include background music and/or environmental noises such as the lung or heart sounds of a patient. In the recent past, e-learning intended for Internet delivery has avoided the use of auditory modes in order to keep file sizes low and thus accommodate limited bandwidths. However as high-speed Internet and intranet connections are becoming more the rule than the exception, the opportunities for wider use of audio are expanding. What do we know about how best to use audio in e-learning? Does the dual-modality capability of e-learning argue for its potential greater effectiveness as a delivery media compared to a single modality medium such as paper?

Auditory and Visual Centers in Working Memory

As summarized previously, working memory has a very limited capacity of only a few chunks of information. More recent research on working memory shows that it has two subcomponents: one for visual content, such as diagrams and text, and one for auditory content, such as narration and music. When presented with two tasks that involve stimuli presented in two different modalities, such as a visual task combined with an auditory task, subjects have only a slight performance decline when doing both tasks compared to doing one task alone (Baddeley & Logie, 1999). For example, if asked to perform a visual task such as tracking a light beam at the same time as recalling a list of numbers read aloud, the numbers are recalled about as well as when they are recalled without the secondary visual assignment. In contrast, when asked to perform two tasks that simultaneously require the

same modalities such as recalling two different sets of information – each read simultaneously into the left and right ear – performance on both declines dramatically. When the instructional goal involves content that is complex and thus requires considerable working memory capacity and the learners are novice, cognitive load is likely to be high. One way to manage high load is to maximize working memory capacity by dividing the content between the visual and the auditory centers of working memory.

The Modality Principle

Several studies that compared learning from visuals explained by audio narration with visuals explained by text have shown an advantage to audio explanations – an effect known as the *modality principle* (Mayer, 2001; Tindall-Ford, Chandler, & Sweller, 1997). However the modality principle applies to situations in which working memory is subject to overload as a result of the complexity of the content and/or the complexity of the visual display. Sweller, van Merriënboer, and Paas (1998) define content complexity as a function of the number of elements that must be processed simultaneously in working memory to achieve the instructional goal. For example, a task that requires the coordination of several rules such as construction of a sentence in a foreign language would have greater element interactivity than a vocabulary task that requires the learner to recall the meaning of each word independently of other words.

Guideline 1 : Minimize Cognitive Load by Explaining Complex Visual Content With Audio Narration

Mayer and his colleagues compared the effects of words presented in text and words presented in audio narration to explain animated visuals that illustrated a scientific process such as how lightning forms. In six different studies, the narrated version resulted in better learning on problem-solving transfer tests with an average effect size of 1.17 (Mayer & Moreno, 1998, Moreno & Mayer, 1999; Moreno, Mayer, Spires, &

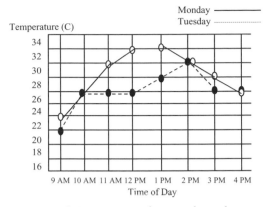

Figure 35.6. Temperature line graph used in research study summarized in figure 35.7. Adapted from Leahy et al. (2003).

Lester, 2001). In these studies the visual display was complex because it was presented in the form of an animation that ran independently of learner control. In addition, the content and instructional goals were complex in that the learner needed to integrate several stages of a scientific process to form a coherent mental model as the basis for solving problems on the transfer test.

Leahy et al. (2003) used the interpretation of the line graph shown in Figure 35.6 as a learning goal and compared a lesson version that presented the content visually with a lesson version in which the same content was presented in an audio-visual format. The all-visual version used text to explain and provide worked examples of how to interpret the graph while the audio-visual format used audio narration to present the same words as the all-visual version. Learners were tested with a series of questions: five of low complexity and nine of high complexity. As shown in Figure 35.7, there were no differences on low-complexity test items. However the audio-visual version yielded significantly better outcomes on questions of higher complexity that required learners to integrate several aspects of the graphs simultaneously. To achieve the instructional goal in this experiment, the learner needed access to both the diagram and the words describing the diagram to achieve the instructional goal. Neither the words nor the diagram were self-explanatory.

In summary, the best way to use audio in e-learning is to narrate words that explain high complex visual content that is not self-explanatory. If either the words or the visuals can stand on their own, adding audio becomes an extraneous input for working memory and both slows down the learning process and depresses the outcomes.

Guideline 2 : Minimize Cognitive Load by Omitting Extraneous Audio

In this section I describe three situations in which audio can be considered extraneous: the inclusion of environmental sounds with

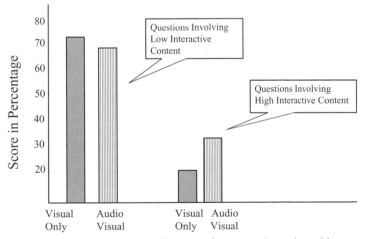

Figure 35.7. A comparison of learning from visuals explained by words in text and words in audio. Adapted from Leahy et al. (2003).

Transfer Test Results: Lesson on Brakes

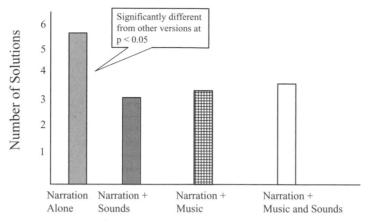

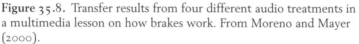

Figure 35.8. Transfer results from four different audio treatments in a multimedia lesson on how brakes work. From Moreno and Mayer (2000).

AUDIO AS SOUND AND MUSIC

Moreno and Mayer (2000) evaluated learning from two multimedia lessons that incorporated environmental sounds and music. One lesson was a 3-minute narrated animated explanation of how lightning forms and the other was a 45-second explanation of how car brakes work. To the base versions they added: (1) soft background music that did not obscure the narration and/or (2) environmental sounds related to the topics such as wind, crackling, and thunder for the lightning lesson and movement of pistons and grinding sounds of brake shoes against the brake pad for the brakes lesson. Learners were tested for recall of major points and for ability to transfer new mental models to solve problems such as, *What could you do to decrease the intensity of lightning?* or *What could be done to make brakes more effective?* The results are summarized in Figure 35.8. In both lessons, the versions with music and sound combined yielded the least learning while the versions with just the narration yielded the best learning. In the lightning lesson, environmental sounds alone did not depress learning where as in the brakes lesson they did. The authors conclude that "the major result is that adding sufficient amounts of entertaining but irrelevant auditory material to a multimedia instructional message was detrimental to student learning" (p. 123). The authors attribute the negative effects of extraneous audio on learning to overloading auditory working memory.

In some situations, environmental sounds are directly relevant to learning. For example, a medical case study presented in multimedia resulted in deeper discussion among the learning team than the same case presented in a text format. In this learning situation, the audio added cues that were relevant to the instructional goal. For example, a sample of dialog from the learning discussion shown in Figure 35.9, showed deliberate processing of the auditory material in a way that could not have occurred with a case presented in text only (Kamin, O'Sullivan, Deterding, & Younger, 2003).

AUDIO AND TEXT TO DESCRIBE VISUALS

A third situation in which audio is extraneous is the addition of audio narration to visuals explained by on-screen text. In these

Student 1: "No, because he is doing the things that, I mean he looked like he was trying to struggle and he looked like he had good tone. I mean when you put him back his feet went up."

Student 2: "He's more tending toward the lethargic rather than the irritable."

Student 3: "He was still trying to wiggle around."

Student 4: "He wasn't crying."

Student 1: "He wasn't crying, wasn't pissed off, wasn't interacting, was sort of protesting."

Figure 35.9. Sample of student discussion after viewing medical case presented in video. From Kamin et al. (2003).

situations the visual modality is self-explanatory and the addition of narration adds redundant information that becomes a source of overload. Mayer, Heiser, and Lonn (2001) compared learning of the lightning scientific processes described previously from e-learning courses that included animations described by audio alone with animations described by text and audio narration. In three different studies the versions that omitted the text resulted in better transfer learning with an effect size of 0.69 (Mayer, 2001; Mayer et al., 2001).

Leahy et al. (2003) attribute the negative effects of redundancy to overload of working memory because they found that learning was *more diminished* by redundant explanations of *high-interactivity content* than by redundant explanations of *low-interactivity content*. In a follow-up experiment to the study on interpretation of the graph shown in Figure 35.6, the research team made the diagram self-explanatory by embedding relevant text into the diagram. They then evaluated the learning benefits of the diagram explained by text against a version that included the diagram explained by both text and audio narration. The text/diagram-only group took an average study time of 62.3 seconds compared to the 135 seconds needed to play the audio version. In spite of using approximately half of the study time, the group studying the diagram with words presented in text resulted in better learning. Because the version that described the diagram with

words in text was already self-explanatory, adding audio to provide a redundant explanation lengthened the study time and resulted in less learning. Although the version that explained the diagram with audio narration resulted in better learning overall, the difference was most pronounced with high-complexity content. This interaction shows that the redundancy effect most likely reflects a negative effect of redundant content on working-memory capacity.

To summarize, research comparing e-learning that used the audio modality in the form of environmental sounds, background music, or narration of visuals explained with text found that when audio is extraneous to the instructional goal, it depresses learning by adding unnecessary load to working memory. Based on research to date, for novice learners faced with instructional goals and/or content that is complex, learning from multimedia presentations is best when words are presented in audio narration and when other audio inputs such as irrelevant sounds or music are omitted. When environment sounds are related to the instructional goal, such as sounds associated with normal breathing or equipment functions, audio becomes relevant and should be included.

Because audio is transient, any content that the learner will need for reference purposes during the instruction should be presented in text. Directions for exercises are one good example. Likewise, because audio is transient, audio segments should be kept brief.

Animation in E-Learning

Unlike lessons presented on paper, computers can display motion visuals in the form of animations. Mayer and Moreno (2002) define animation as "a simulated motion picture depicting movement of drawn (or simulated) objects" (p. 88). Animations are generally more expensive to construct than static visuals and require more bandwidth when delivered over the Internet. Does the capability of e-learning to display motion visuals argue for its potentially greater effectiveness as a delivery medium? In multimedia learning, animations are often used to focus attention as in a marquee-style pulsing dashed line surrounding a portion of a complex visual display. Animations are also used to present content such as procedures and processes that involve movement. Figure 35.1 shows one screen from an animated sequence demonstrating steps to complete an online procedure. Figure 35.10 shows two screens from a multimedia program that uses narrated animations to illustrate how components of hydraulic brakes work. Finally animations can be used to illustrate intangible principles such as an increase in molecular movement with increases in temperature. In this section of the chapter I review research on the value of animations to teach procedures or build mental models related to equipment operations.

Guideline 3: Consider Visual Alternatives to Animations

Clark and Lyons (2004) define a transformational visual as one that depicts changes in time or space. Some examples include animations as described in the previous paragraph as well as video, line drawings with arrows, or several line drawings showing different stages of movement explained by text. Several studies indicate that at least for simple procedures or processes, transformational graphics of diverse surface features, for example, animation versus static graphics, will result in similar learning outcomes. For example, Michas and Berry (2000) in two separate experiments evaluated the effects of various transformational visuals on learning a simple bandaging procedure. In both experiments participants could study the materials for as long as they wished and outcomes were assessed by a performance test as well as a written test. The first experiment compared learning from five representations of the steps: (1) text only, (2) line drawings, (3) text plus line drawings, (4) video without narration, and (5) several still frames from the video. There were no significant differences in study time among

the five groups, which lasted from 3 to 4 minutes. On the performance test, the video and text-plus-line-drawing treatments resulted in significantly better outcomes than the other three treatments, which did not differ from each other. In a second experiment, Michas and Berry focused on various techniques to communicate action information. They compared learning of the bandaging procedure from five different versions of line drawings as follows: (1) a simple line drawing, (2) the same line drawing with addition of motion indicators in the form of arrows, (3) the line drawing accompanied by text that described the motion involved, (4) the line drawing accompanied by text that did not describe the motion involved, and (5) the line drawing accompanied by arrows and text that described motion. Again there were no significant differences in study time. All treatments that included motion indicators (2, 3, and 5) resulted in significantly better learning than those lacking such indicators. Taken together, these studies suggest that treatments that can illustrate motion effectively whether they be video or line drawings accompanied by motion indicators can effectively support learning of a simple procedure. The authors conclude, "These findings suggest that technically simple methods can be very effective when training people to perform simple procedural tasks, and that it is not always necessary to use advanced technology for such purposes" (p. 571).

Two studies that focused on building a mental model of how equipment works likewise suggest that treatments that convey motion in ways that support psychological learning processes can be effective whether presented in a paper medium or using animations on computer. Mayer, Mathias et al. (2002) and Hegarty, Narayanan, and Freitas (2002) developed lessons that were built according to a cognitive model of learning and were presented on paper or on computer with animations. Mayer, Mathias et al. found that when learning how a mechanical system such as a hydraulic braking system works from a narrated animation, better

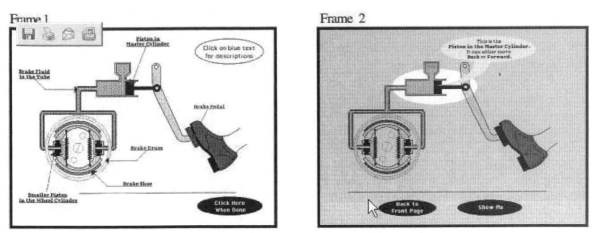

Figure 35.10. Two frames from multimedia lesson on how brakes work. From Mayer, Mathias et al. (2002).

learning occurs when pretraining orients the learner to the parts and functions of individual components of the system. Pretraining versions either displayed diagrams explained with text callouts on paper or presented diagrams explained by text and animation on computer (as shown in Figure 35.10). Both versions, supported better transfer learning compared to participants who studied the narrated animation without pretraining.

Hegarty et al. (2002) compared several lesson versions that explained how a toilet tank flushes. They found that a four-step instructional model based on cognitive learning requirements resulted in similar learning whether presented as diagrams explained by text on paper or as animations in hypermedia. The four steps included (1) initial study of subcomponents of the system, (2) questions that required learners to reason about interactions among components, (3) an animation (or multiple still diagrams) that showed successive flushing stages, and (4) a section that explained the physics principles of a siphon that underlies the behavior of the toilet tank. In these experiments, the hypermedia versions took longer to study as a result of the fixed time required to view the animated sequences compared to reviewing static diagrams with descriptive text. The authors conclude that "[a] particularly notable result of our experiments was the fact

that the provision of an animation did not lead to better understanding of the system than viewing a static diagram" (p. 380).

Although we need more evidence about the best use of animations, these studies provide preliminary evidence that at least for relatively simple procedures and processes, nonanimated treatments that communicate motion such as line drawings with motion indicators can result in learning equivalent to that resulting from animations.

Guideline 4: Manage Cognitive Load When Using Animations

It would not be surprising to find that animations impose greater cognitive load than displays that use a series of static diagrams. First an animated diagram includes a large amount of visual information often viewed in a relatively short time frame. Second, often animations run under program control so that the learner is exposed to the entire sequence at once. Third, animations are transient in nature. That is, the different stages disappear as the animation progresses in contrast to a series of line drawings that remain visible for inspection. Research points to four methods you can use to support learning from animations: pretraining/chunking, audio narration, allowing learner control over the display of the animation, and providing visual cues to direct attention to important elements of the display.

SEQUENCE RELATED CONCEPTS FIRST

Mayer, Mathias et al. (2002) found that pretraining in a lesson on how brakes work that presented the names of subcomponents of the full system as well as how each subcomponent could move resulted in better learning from a subsequent complete animated lesson. In a similar manner, the research described previously by Hegarty et al. (2002) involving a lesson on how a toilet tank flushes started with a section on the subcomponents of the system. In both cases, presenting the subcomponents before presenting the entire system manages cognitive load by presenting the related concepts associated with the entire process before showing the full process.

ALLOW LEARNER CONTROL OVER DISPLAY OF ANIMATIONS

Mayer and Chandler (2001) found that learners who received pretraining in the form of short animated segments that could be stopped and started as desired learned more from a subsequent complete animation than those who did not have the pretraining. In this research, the pretraining presented under learner control allowed learners to manage their own rate and pacing of content.

EXPLAIN ANIMATIONS WITH AUDIO NARRATIONS

Because animations require a great deal of visual working memory capacity, explain the animations with audio narration rather than with on-screen text. The advantage of audio narration to describe animations has been demonstrated in a number of studies and is a compelling example of the modality principle (Leahy et al., 2003, Mayer & Anderson, 1991; Mayer & Moreno, 2002).

USE CUES WHEN VISUAL SEARCH IS HIGH

When the animation involves narration of visuals that are sufficiently complex to de-

mand a high degree of visual search, direct attention to the relevant portion of the visual with a cueing device such as an arrow or colored circle defining the area being described. Jeung, Chandler, and Sweller (1997) found that when geometry problems that included complex diagrams were described by words in audio narration (applying the modality principle), learning was better than an all visual treatment only when the relevant portions of the diagram were cued visually by flashing to direct learner attention to the relevant portion of the graphic. For example, in the animated demonstration shown in Figure 35.1, the designer has used a red arrow to draw attention to the portion of the screen being described in narration.

In summary, when using animations to build mental models, manage cognitive load by presenting pretraining that focuses on individual components in the entire system, allowing the learner to control the rate of presentation of the animated segments, explaining the animation with audio narration, and providing cueing to direct attention to relevant portions of the animation being described.

Are Animations Effective?

Evidence regarding the best use of animations is not sufficient at this point to provide firm guidelines for its use. Given that animations can be expensive to produce, increase bandwidth requirements, and can require longer study times than simpler treatments that convey movement, I see no current basis for claiming a greater effectiveness of e-learning over other media because it can display movement. We will need more research to help define the learning goals that best profit from animated treatments as well as how animations can best be used to meet the requirements of our cognitive processing systems.

In the previous sections, I have discussed several evidence-based guidelines for best use of the unique modality options offered by computers including audio and animations. In the next section, I will look at the use of the programmable properties of computers to provide another unique instructional method: multimedia simulations.

Multimedia Simulations

Of all of the instructional methods that can be delivered by computers, simulations of various types generate the greatest "gee whiz" response. Simulations are often resource intensive both regarding bandwidth and design/development time and costs. Powell (2001) quotes euphoric hopes for simulations as "the ultimate promise of e-learning" (p. 40) and cites development times of one or more years at costs topping $1 million. Both the high expectations and the high costs suggest the need for practitioners to design and use simulations on the basis of evidence.

What Are Simulations?

Similar to e-learning, simulations also have a variety of incarnations. De Jong and van Joolingen (1998) define a computer simulation as a "program that contains a model of a system (natural or artificial; e.g., equipment) or a process" (p. 180). There are two main types of simulations: operational and conceptual. Operational simulations are designed primarily to teach procedural skills whereas conceptual simulations focus on learning of domain-specific principles or processes as well as problem-solving heuristics. In business and industry, operational simulations are primarily used to teach the use of computer systems. For example, the screen shown in Figure 35.1 is demonstrating the steps to complete an online task. This screen is followed by a similar screen on which the learner practices the steps on a simulated version of the system that responds to some degree like the actual system. About 10% of respondents to an annual industry survey report using computer-based simulations often (Galvin, 2003).

In contrast, conceptual simulations are primarily designed to build far-transfer mental models of a specific domain as well as associated problem-solving skills. Educational simulations of this type have been designed to teach scientific principles. For example in Figure 35.4, a genetics simulation called GenScope allows learners to manipulate genes on chromosomes and immediately see the effects on the dragon. An evaluation of a curriculum that incorporated GenScope in high school computer-lab classes reported substantial gains in genetics reasoning ability in all but 1 of 17 classes in one implementation and even higher gains in a follow-up study in which students used the simulation in a lap-top equipped classroom (Hickey, Kindfield, Horowitz, & Christie, 2003).

Conceptual simulations in the commercial sector have been used to power domain-specific whole authentic work environments for learning of far-transfer tasks such as assessing a commercial loan applicant, developing a battle plan, designing a computer security system, and preparing and delivering a legal plea. For example, Figure 35.11 is a screen from a course designed to teach commercial loan analysis to bank agents. From the virtual office the learner can access many resources to collect client data such as a credit report from the fax machine, industry information from the bookshelf, and client references from the telephone.

How effective are operational and conceptual simulations as vehicles to support learning? A variety of studies that compared achievement from scientific simulations with achievement from traditional tutorials have in general shown that "there is no clear and univocal outcome in favor of simulations" (de Jong and van Joolingen, 1998, p. 181). The value of a simulation will be a function of how the simulation is designed and used as part of the instructional environment. Therefore, more productive questions are: What features in the design of a simulation are linked to learning? What kinds of learning goals best profit from simulations versus less costly tutorial approaches?

Benefits of Simulations

In this section I review some benefits of computer simulations based on research evidence. These include the ability to build

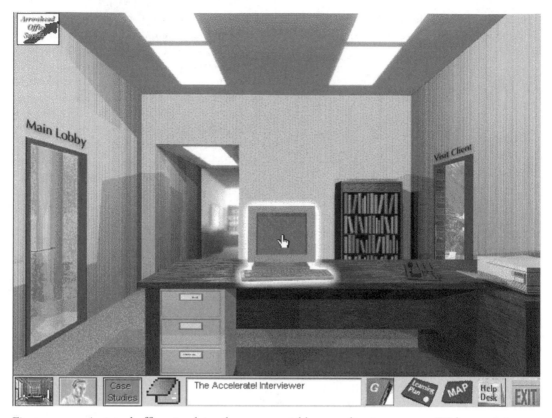

Figure 35.11. A virtual office simulates the commercial loan application process. With permission from Moody Financial Services.

procedural skills through practice in domains that involve high risk or safety consequences, and capability to accelerate expertise in domains of high cognitive complexity.

SIMULATIONS CAN BE EFFECTIVE FOR HIGH-CONSEQUENCE TASKS

Flying an aircraft, aircraft traffic control, and nuclear power control operations are examples of tasks with high adverse consequences of error. Physical simulators have been used for a number of years to provide practice for tasks such as these that would not be safe or do not often occur in actual operations. The emergence of virtual reality has expanded opportunities for operational computer simulations that build psychomotor skills. Grantcharov et al. (2003) compared the speed, error rate, and economy of movement between two groups of surgical trainees, one of which received laparoscopic skills training on a virtual-reality surgical trainer. Sixteen surgical trainees were

evaluated as they performed a laparoscopic cholecystectomy under supervision in the operating room. Half of these were randomly assigned to sessions on the trainer where they practiced ten repetitions of six tasks simulating the techniques used during the cholecystectomy. The other half received no additional training. Surgeons who received virtual-reality (VR) training performed laparoscopic cholescytectomy significantly faster than the control group. They also showed greater improvement in error rates and economy of movement scores. The authors conclude, "surgical simulation is therefore a valid tool for training of laparoscopic psychomotor skills and could be incorporated into surgical training programmes" (p. 146).

SIMULATIONS CAN ACCELERATE EXPERTISE FOR LOW-INCIDENCE TASKS

In many fields, opportunities to practice in the workplace are limited by the scarcity

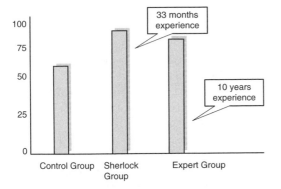

Figure 35.12. Troubleshooting performance compared among Sherlock learners, untrained participants, and expert technicians. Adapted from Gott and Lesgold (2000).

of available cases. For example, medical students are meeting fewer and fewer real patients because most routine patient cases are handled outside university clinics and rotations through medical departments are brief. As a result, medical educators have looked for alternative case-based learning methods. In some situations they have used human actors called *interactive simulated patients*. Simulated cases presented through multimedia offer yet another alternative for independent case practice. For example, Bergin and Fors (2003) describe development and field tests of multimedia case environments that offer opportunities for medical students to take a patient history through a simulated interview, conduct a physical examination, and select specific laboratory tests prior to submitting a diagnosis.

Another domain that offers few on-the-job opportunities to build a full range of skills is troubleshooting. Specific equipment failures are infrequent and do not follow optimal sequences for learning. Furthermore, real-world diagnosis and repair can consume hours or days. Gott and Lesgold (2000) summarize the results of a 12-year effort that resulted in a multimedia intelligent coached-practice environment called Sherlock that incorporates a simulation of the authentic troubleshooting tasks. The focus of Sherlock is to teach avionics troubleshooting of F15 test stations. They compared the proficiency of 41 apprentice and journeyman air force technicians randomly

assigned to either Sherlock or a normal work environment. The learners used Sherlock for an average of 25 hours in sessions lasting 1 to 1.5 hours over 15 days. They were then tested on troubleshooting both on the F15 test station, as well as on different system called Frankenstation, to evaluate transfer of learning. Test results from the Sherlock and no-training group were compared with test results from master avionics technicians with ten or more years of experience. Figures 35.12 and 35.13 show that the tutored technicians outperformed the control group with effect sizes ranging from 0.76 to 1.27. Gott and Lesgold (2000) conclude that "a learning by doing, situated instructional environment can both accelerate troubleshooting skill development and promote transferable skills among novice technicians. Posttest performance shows tutored airmen having 33 months experience on average outperform master technicians with 124 months on troubleshooting work sample tests" (p. 300).

The Sherlock instructional environment was built on the basis of a lengthy cognitive task analysis and incorporated a simulation of the work environment, an expert coach, and opportunities to reflect after completion of a troubleshooting case followed by a critique of their solution steps by the electronic coach.

In summary, we have evidence from medical and electronics domains that relatively brief exposures to instructional

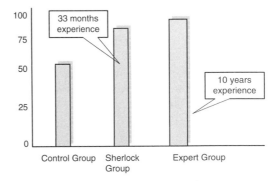

Figure 35.13. Troubleshooting performance on Frankenstation compared among Sherlock learners, untrained participants, and expert technicians. Adapted from Gott and Lesgold (2000).

environments that incorporate simulations can improve skills compared to equivalent learners who are not provided the training. The skill acquisition can be considerable as shown in the Sherlock study. However, in neither the surgical simulation nor the Sherlock study was learning from the simulated instructional environment compared to a group that was trained using a more traditional tutorial instructional design. Therefore we cannot assess the relative effectiveness of a simulated learning environment compared to a well-designed traditional tutorial lesson. In the next section I summarize some evidence-based guidelines about what we do know about how to effectively use simulations for learning.

Guideline 5: Provide Appropriate Scaffolding to Optimize Learning From Simulations

Mayer (2004) has summarized evidence from three decades of research demonstrating that pure discovery learning environments are ineffective. In many cases learners who are presented with pure discovery learning environments fail to learn the intended principles or concepts. This may be due to cognitive overload caused by a complex environment as well as a lack of metacognitive skills on the part of the learner to systematically exploit and learn from the environment. The challenge to designers of instructional simulations is to surround the simulation with sufficient support so that learners can acquire the intended skills or principles. This is the goal of a guided discovery environment that provides a problem to solve or tasks to accomplish with instructional support elements such as worked examples, coaching, feedback, process worksheets, expert advice, and reference sources. The general term for these kinds of supports is *scaffolding*.

We still have much to learn about what kind of scaffolding works best for specific learners and instructional goals. For example, in a geology simulation game Mayer, Mautone, and Prothero (2002) compared the effectiveness of a visual scaffold and a textual scaffold with no scaffold. The game required learners to make inferences about various topographic features on a new planet such as an island in the ocean or a trench on land that were not directly visible. To succeed, the learner needed to collect and interpret surface data from the planet. The visual scaffold was a sketch of each of the possible geological features. The textual scaffold suggested strategies for selecting data samples from the planet's surface. They found that the pictorial scaffold helped learners solve problems involving the same planet as the game with an effect size of 0.45 as well as from a different environment with an effect size of 0.83. In contrast, the strategic text scaffolding did not aid performance. The authors conclude that "[a]n important pattern in our results is that pictorial scaffolding – which is predominantly visual – had a strong positive effect, but various forms of modeling – which are predominantly verbal – did not. This pattern is consistent with the idea that authentic geology problems require visuo-spatial thinking, so the visually based scaffolding is particularly relevant" (p. 180–181).

We are still learning how to design and develop effective scaffolding to help learners maximize benefit from educational simulations. What we can conclude from evidence to date is that learner engagements with simulation environments in which they are left on their own to learn in a discovery mode are not effective.

Guideline 6: Limit the Simulation Fidelity and Scope Appropriate to the Instructional Goal

Previously I summarized research that showed that a virtual-reality surgical simulation did improve operating skills. How important is a highly realistic environment such as one provided by computer-modeled interactive graphics or virtual reality? Moreno and Mayer (2002) compared learning from a computer-simulation botany game in which they created higher and lower immersive virtual-reality versions. They found no learning benefits to the more immersive versions compared to learning from the same game in a much lower fidelity environment. Unlike the surgical simulation, which was focusing primarily on operational skills, the botany game was primarily designed to teach concepts and principles and did not benefit from highly realistic visual treatments.

In a summary of 12 years of experience building Sherlock, an intelligent coached-practice environment designed to teach troubleshooting of electronic equipment, Gott and Lesgold (2000) recommend that the designer only simulate what is needed to achieve the instructional goal. In the electronic-troubleshooting environment, most problems emerge in the course of routine work. Because the routine work was not the focus of the learning, they supplied only the interface for the switches that would be manipulated at each step of the routine task and used canned displays to indicate the results of the steps. When the learner did encounter an anomalous event that was the focus of the learning, they simulated only those portions of the equipment involved in that event. Thus they only had to simulate the circuit path as configured for the failed part as well as the circuitry that configured that circuit path. On occasion they also included simulations for "off path" actions that were identified as common errors during the task analysis phases. However, they stress that a fully faithful simulation of the entire system is not necessary to achieve instructional goals.

In summary, we have evidence that simulations can be used effectively to build both operational and conceptual skills. We also know that simulations are not effective when used in a pure discovery learning environment. Instead, various forms of scaffolding must be incorporated to ensure the learner does construct the intended mental models. In addition, it is not necessary to construct simulations that emulate all features of the actual environment. On a pragmatic level, the time and expense needed to develop a simulation seems justified to accelerate expertise in arenas that preclude learners from engaging with real-world tasks such as high safety-consequence tasks or tasks that are not readily available in the workplace. However, we need more research to provide guidelines about when a simulation provides an advantage in either learning or motivation to a traditional directive tutorial environment.

Is E-Learning a Better Learning Medium?

Because computers have greater flexibility than other delivery alternatives such as paper or video to offer instructional alternatives such as dual-modality instruction, animations, and simulations, can we infer that e-learning has greater instructional potential compared to other delivery media? Based on evidence discussed in this chapter, I offer the following conclusions:

(1) When used appropriately, the capability to present content in dual modalities, that is, relevant visuals described by concise related audio, is advantageous when learners are novices and the context is complex. Dividing related content between the visual and the phonetic centers of working memory will reduce cognitive load. In addition, in some situations, auditory discrimination is an important part of the instructional goal and the ability to provide audio opens computer-delivered instruction to a broader range of instructional requirements.

(2) The capability to display movement through animations is not greatly advantageous because alternative means to display motion may be just as efficient, at least for simple procedures and processes. As summarized in this review, comparison of the instructional effects of static visuals with motion indicators to animation has shown no significant differences in learning of simple procedures and processes. We need more research to define the instructional situations that benefit from animations.

(3) Both operational and conceptual simulations lead to effective learning when appropriately scaffolded. We have evidence that relatively short instructional periods on

a well-designed simulated system can accelerate expertise by exposing the participant to many authentic work situations in a compressed time period. We do not yet have definite prescriptions for the best kinds of scaffolds for all guided discovery environments that use simulations. Nor do we know under what circumstances a simulation lesson offers advantages over well-designed directive tutorials. Situations that allow learners to engage with tasks that cannot be practiced in real-world settings recommend the use of well-designed simulations. The cost benefit will depend, in part, on the criticality of the task, for example, life or death situations, or its alignment with important organizational operational objectives, for example, acceleration of expertise in commercial loan analysis. Another factor influencing cost benefit is the stability of the rules governing the behavior of the simulation. If the business process or variables are highly volatile, the amount of maintenance required may mitigate against use of a simulation.

Future Research Directions

We have seen in this review that research of the 1990s has abandoned less productive media comparison questions and focused instead on evaluation of instructional modes and methods that best promote cognitive learning processes. In this final section, I summarize some research questions that are relevant to both theory and practical applications.

How Generalizable Are the Multimedia Principles?

Many of the lessons that have led to multimedia principles such as modality and contiguity are of relatively short duration and focus primarily on scientific processes or technical procedures. For example, some of the studies used to establish the modality effect used the following treatments: a lesson on how lightning works lasting 180 seconds (Moreno and Mayer, 1999) or 140 seconds

(Mayer and Moreno, 1998), a lesson on how a bicycle pump works lasting 30 to 45 seconds, learning from four geometry problems ranging from 85 to 224 seconds of study time for each problem (Mousavi, Low, & Sweller, 1995), a lesson on how to use a voltmeter to conduct electrical tests with a study period of 5 minutes in one experiment and 10 minutes in another (Tindall-Ford et al., 1997), learning how to interpret the temperature line graph shown in Figure 35.7 involved a lesson of 185 seconds (Leahy et al., 2003), and a pretraining lesson on how brakes worked lasted 2 minutes followed by a 45-second animation (Mayer, Mathias et al., 2002). To what extent will these effects apply to longer lessons or to a series of short lessons? Likewise, will similar effects be realized with topics that are less technical in nature such as history, customer service, and supervisory skills? Because practice adds costs to any training environment, knowing how practice interacts with the other multimedia principles will have important implications for practitioners.

How Will Multimedia Principles Apply When Practice Is Included?

Several studies have shown interactions among multimedia principles such as modality or multimedia and the complexity of the content (Leahy et al., 2003) or the background knowledge of the learner (Kalyuga et al., 2003). Most of the lessons demonstrating these principles do not include opportunities for practice. For example, in the study involving interpretation of a line graph reported by Leahy, Chandler, and Sweller, learners had 185 seconds to study the explanation followed by a test. No practice opportunity was provided. Likewise, lessons on how hydraulic brakes function presented pretraining illustrating the parts of the system (on paper or multimedia) followed by animation of how system worked (Mayer, Mathias et al., 2002). No practice was incorporated prior to the test. An exception is found in a study described by Hegarty et al. (2002) on how a toilet tank flushes.

In one experiment some lesson versions required subjects to interact with the content by explaining how the system worked. The flushing system was displayed with either a static diagram or with animations. Learners who viewed the animation wrote more complete descriptions of the system than learners who did not view the animation. Those who practiced also wrote more complete descriptions. The effects of these two treatments were additive so that those who practiced and viewed the animation had the best performance. Research that compares the effects of the various multimedia principles in situations that incorporate practice and feedback will be useful to determine whether practice reduces the positive effects of load-reduction techniques, such as the modality principle, exerts an additive effect as in the Hegarty study, or has no effect on learning.

How Important are Cosmetic Features of E-Learning Displays?

In many instances, considerable time and money is invested in commercial e-learning programs to achieve a glossy look and feel. Graphic artists are employed to design aesthetically pleasing visuals and interfaces. In contrast, many lessons used for research purposes employ fairly simple treatments that include line drawings and that pay little attention to cosmetic elements of the program. How generalizable are the results generated from simple treatments to those that are produced with a more polished look and feel? Secondly, how do programs with greater effort invested in the surface features affect learning and learner motivation compared to more basic treatments lacking such embellishments? For example, the multimedia principle has established that including relevant graphics leads to better learning than presenting the same content with text only. Would different visual renderings of the same graphic significantly influence the outcomes? Does an investment in more polished treatments benefit either learning or motivation?

Under What Conditions Do Animations Support Learning?

I reviewed some evidence that indicated at least simple processes and procedures may be learned as effectively from simple line drawings with visual indicators, such as arrows, as from more complex animated versions. In some cases, animations may actually lead to overload and thus be counterproductive. Further research is needed to address more complex procedures and processes as well as other types of content that might profit from animated displays. Furthermore, animations may be more effective for high or for low spatial-ability learners. Therefore, a question for future research is: For what kinds of instructional goals and learners are animations most productive?

How Can Simulations Maximize Learning?

Simulations, when used in a guided discovery environment that includes appropriate scaffolding, can accelerate learning. However, there are few comparisons between simulated learning environments and directive tutorials designed to achieve the same learning outcomes. It would be useful to know the differences in learning, transfer, and motivation in simulation learning environments compared to well-designed traditional tutorial lessons. I reviewed evidence that scaffolds are needed to help learners best exploit simulations. But much more understanding is needed regarding the types of scaffolds that are most productive for specific instructional goals and learners.

How Can Synchronous E-Learning Formats Be Used Effectively?

Most research to date has focused on e-learning delivered in the form of asynchronous self-study tutorials. However, there is a rapidly growing use of synchronous forms of e-learning such as the lesson illustrated in Figure 35.2. Just as each new evolution of e-learning has opened new opportunities for use of different instructional methods, instructors and instructional designers need guidance on the best ways to exploit the combination of features available in these environments. For example, in the interface shown in Figure 35.2, the number of options for presentation of content and learner engagement could easily lead to overload if not well managed. We need to know how the multimedia principles discussed in this handbook can be adapted to synchronous e-learning formats. Practitioners also need guidelines on how to best design productive learning interfaces for synchronous e-learning.

How Can Virtual Collaborative Learning Facilities Be Used Most Effectively?

Recent Internet-delivered instruction opens opportunities for collaborative learning in synchronous and asynchronous modes. A number of years of classroom research have demonstrated conditions under which face-to-face collaborative learning environments can improve learning. How do these guidelines transfer to virtual collaboration? How can communication vehicles such as chat and discussion boards be used most effectively? How can interfaces be designed to maximize the learning potential of these communication options?

Translating Research Into Practice

"Educational research is not very influential, useful, or well funded" (p. 3). So begins a recent article by Burkhardt and Schoenfeld (2003) recommending improved processes and practices that will help practitioners use research to make better-informed, less-speculative decisions. It is very difficult for practitioners to find, translate, and apply the research findings published and presented in diverse academic journals and conferences. Likewise, many researchers do not have the resources to translate laboratory findings into useable guidelines through field trials and wide-scale implementations. A complete treatment of this issue is beyond the scope of this chapter. Perhaps in concluding, however, readers from both academic and practitioner communities can consider ways their respective communities can work together to more effectively bridge the gap from the laboratory to the learner to promote evidence-based e-learning decisions.

Glossary

Animation: A series of images that simulate motion.

Asynchronous e-learning: Instructional programs delivered by computer designed to be taken by learners in a self-paced mode at any time or any place. May or may not include opportunities for virtual collaboration.

Cognitive load: The amount of mental work imposed on working memory.

Coherence principle: Adding extraneous information in the form of audio, seductive graphics and stories, or lengthy text can depress learning.

Conceptual simulation: A model of a system or process designed to build understanding of domain-specific principles as well as problem-solving skills.

Deductive learning: An instructional approach in which learners build skills by being told rules or definitions followed by examples and application practice. The instruction encourages learners to build skills by exposure to general principles, rules, and their application. Often associated with directive learning environments.

Directive e-learning: Instruction delivered by computer designed to build skills using a deductive instructional approach in which learners are provided with rules, examples, and application practice. These courses are built primarily on a behavioral model of learning and are most often used for training of procedural skills. Contrast with *guided discovery* and *receptive e-learning*.

Dual modalities: The capability to deliver content in both visual and auditory modes.

E-learning: Instruction delivered on a computer that is designed to achieve specific learning goals. See also *asynchronous, synchronous, directive, guided discovery*, and *receptive e-learning*.

Element interactivity: A feature of instructional content referring to the number of content elements that needs to be held or processed in working memory at the same time.

Expertise reversal effect: Many instructional strategies that benefit novice learners are counterproductive for learning of individuals with greater prior knowledge.

Far transfer: Instructional goals that require learners to apply what they have learned to a novel problem or situation. Contrast with *near transfer*.

Guided discovery e-learning: Instruction delivered by computer designed to build skills using an inductive approach in which learners are provided an environment (which may include a simulation) through which they derive rules and concepts through interaction. These courses are built primarily on a constructivist model of learning and are most often used for training of far-transfer or principle-based skills. Contrast with *directive* and *receptive e-learning*.

Inductive learning: An instructional approach in which learners derive rules or inferences from examples or simulated experiences. The instruction encourages learners to form generalizations by exposure to specific instances. Often associated with guided discovery learning environments.

Instructional methods: Any instructional strategy used to promote learning efficiency or effectiveness. Useful instructional methods support human cognitive information processes associated with learning and include the use of techniques such as worked examples, audio narration of complex visuals, and practice exercises.

Learner control: Allowing the learner to select presentation elements in the lesson such as the pacing, topics, and instructional elements such as practice or examples.

Long-term memory: Part of the cognitive system that stores memories in a permanent form. Has a large capacity but cannot process information. A repository of knowledge and skills.

Media: A vehicle or mechanism for delivery of instruction such as books, computers, and instructors.

Methods: Any feature of an instructional environment that interacts in predictable ways with human psychological processes. For example, use of audio to describe complex visuals (modality principle).

Modality: The sensory format in which information is displayed; typically refers to either visual or auditory.

Modality principle: Describing a complex visual with words presented in audio can increase learning compared to presenting words in text.

Multimedia principle: Adding a relevant visual to text can increase learning.

Near transfer: Instructional goals that require learners to apply what they have learned to a problem or situation similar to that used in the training. Procedural tasks are near transfer for the most part. Contrast with *far transfer*.

Operational simulation: A model of a real system designed to teach procedures. They typically incorporate a realistic work interface and response. These are especially useful in situations where practice on actual equipment is dangerous and/or costly.

Receptive e-learning: Instruction delivered by computer designed to provide information or build awareness. Typically these programs do not include skill-building interactions in the form of practice. These courses are built primarily on a transmission model of learning. Contrast with *directive* and *guided discovery e-learning*.

Redundancy principle: Avoid explaining a complex visual display with words presented in both text and audio narration.

Scaffolding: An instructional technique placed in instructional environments that provide sufficient support to ensure the achievement of the intended instructional outcome. Scaffolds assume a variety of formats including worked examples, learning agents, or visual aids. Scaffolds are especially needed in guided discovery instructional environments.

Schema: A knowledge structure contained in long-term memory that is the basis for expertise. Also called *mental models*.

Seductive details: Visuals and/or text placed in instructional materials to add interest. They are generally related to the lesson topic but extraneous to the instructional goal. Seductive details have been shown to reduce learning.

Simulation: An interactive environment in which features in the environment behave similarly to real-world events. See also *operational* and *conceptual simulations*.

Simulation fidelity: The extent to which a simulated instructional environment appears and behaves like a real system.

Synchronous e-learning: Instructional programs delivered by computer designed to be taken by learners at the same time in any location. Usually provides opportunities for virtual collaboration.

Transformation visual: A graphic designed to show changes in time or space. May be displayed using animation or a series of static illustrations.

Virtual collaboration: The use of online communication tools such as chat and discussion boards to promote learning

Working memory: Part of the cognitive system in which the learner actively (consciously) processes incoming information from the environment and retrieved information from long-term memory. Working memory has two subcomponents (visual and auditory) and is limited in capacity.

References

Baddeley, A. D., & Logie, R. H. (1999). Working memory: The multiple component model. In Mikyake, A., and Shah, P. (Eds.), *Models of working memory: Mechanisms of active maintenance and executive control*. New York: Cambridge University Press.

Bergin, R. A., & Fors, U. G. H. (2003). Interactive simulated patient: An advanced tool for student-activated learning in medicine and healthcare. *Computers and Education, 40*, 361–376.

Burkhardt, H., & Schoenfeld, A. H. (2003). Improving educational research: Toward a more useful, more influential, and better-funded enterprise. *Educational Researcher, 32*(9), 3–14.

Chandler, P., & Sweller, J. (1996). Cognitive load while learning to use a computer program. *Applied Cognitive Psychology, 10*, 151–170.

Chase, W. G., & Simon, H. A. (1973). Perception in chess. *Cognitive Psychology, 4*, 55–81.

Clark, R. C. (2000). Four architectures of learning. *Performance Improvement, 39*(10), 31–37.

Clark, R. C. (2003). *Building expertise*. Silver Spring, MD: International Society for Performance Improvement.

Clark, R., & Lyons, C. (2004). *Graphics for learning*. San Francisco: Pfeiffer.

Clark, R. C., & Mayer, R. E. (2003). *E-learning and the science of instruction*. San Francisco: Pfeiffer.

Clark, R. C., & Mayer, R. E. (in press). Using rich media wisely. In J. Dempsy and R. Reiser (Eds.), *Trends and issues in instructional design and technology*. Upper Saddle River, NJ: Prentice Hall.

Clark, R. E. (1983). Reconsidering research on learning from media. *Review of Educational Research, 53*(2), 445–459.

Clark, R. E. (1994). Media will never influence learning. *Educational Technology Research and Development, 42*, 21–30.

Cuban, L. (2001). *Oversold and underused: Computers in the classroom*. Cambridge, MA: Harvard University Press.

De Jong, T., & van Joolingen, W. R. (1998). Scientific discovery learning with computer simulations of conceptual domains. *Review of Educational Research*, 68(2), 179–201.

Dillon, A., & Gabbard, R. (1998). Hypermedia as an educational technology: A review of the quantitative research literature on learner comprehension, control, and style. *Review of Educational Research*, 58(3), 322–349.

Gagne, R. M. (1985). *The conditions of learning and theory of instruction* (4th Ed.). Forth Worth, TX: Holt, Rinehart & Winston.

Galvin, T. (2003). 2003 Industry Report. *Training Magazine*, 40(9), 19–45.

Gott, S. P., & Lesgold, A. M. (2000). Competence in the workplace: How cognitive performance models and situated instruction can accelerate skill acquisition. In R. Glaser, (Ed.), *Advances in instructional psychology*, 5. Mahwah, NJ: Lawrence Erlbaum Associates.

Grantcharov, T. P., Kristiansen, V. B., Bendix, J., Bardram, L., Rosenberg, J., & Funch-Jensen, P. (2003). Randomized clinical trial of virtual reality simulation for laparosopic skills training. *British Journal of Surgery*, 91, 146–150.

Harp, S. F., & Mayer, R. E. (1997). The role of interest in learning from scientific text and illustrations: On the distinction between emotional interest and cognitive interest. *Journal of Educational Psychology*, 89, 92–102.

Harp, S. F., & Mayer, R. E. (1998). How seductive details do their damage: A theory of cognitive interest in science learning. *Journal of Educational Psychology*, 90, 414–434.

Hegarty, M., Narayanan, N. H., & Freitas, P. (2002). Understanding machines from multimedia and hypermedia presentations. In J. Otero, J. A. Leon, & A. C. Graesser (Eds.), *The psychology of science text comprehension*. Mahwah, NJ: Lawrence Erlbaum Associates.

Hickey, D. T., Kindfield, A. C. H., Horowitz, P., & Christie, M. A. T. (2003). Integrating curriculum, instruction, assessment, and evaluation in a technology-supported genetics learning environment. *American Educational Research Journal*, 40(2), 495–538.

Jeung, H., Chandler, P., & Sweller, J. (1997). The role of visual indicators in dual sensory mode instruction. *Educational Psychology*, 17(3), 329–343.

Kalyuga, S., Ayres, P., Chandler, P., & Sweller, J. (2003). The expertise reversal effect. *Educational Psychologist*, 38(1), 23–31.

Kalyuga, S., Chandler, P., Tuovinen, J., & Sweller, J. (2001). When problem solving is superior to studying worked examples. *Journal of Educational Psychology*, 93(3), 579–588.

Kamin, C., O'Sullivan, P., Deterding, R., & Younger, M. (2003). A comparison of critical thinking in groups of third-year medical students in text, video, and virtual PBL case modalities. *Academic Medicine*, 78(2), 204–211.

Leahy, W., Chandler, P., & Sweller, J. (2003). When auditory presentations should and should not be a component of multimedia instruction. *Applied Cognitive Psychology*, 17, 401–418.

Maddux, C. D. (2003). Twenty years of research in information technology in education: Assessing our progress. *Computers in the Schools*, 20(1/2), 35–48.

Mageau, T. (2004). A closer look at scientifically based research: What the words mean. *T.H.E. Journal*, 31, 26–30.

Mayer, R. E., (1997). Multimedia learning: Are we asking the right questions? *Educational Psychologist*, 32(1), 1–19.

Mayer, R. E. (2001). *Multimedia learning*. New York: Cambridge University Press.

Mayer, R. E. (2004). Should there be a three-strikes rule against pure discovery learning? *American Psychologist*, 59(1), 14–19.

Mayer, R. E., & Anderson, R. B. (1991). Animations need narrations: An experimental test of a dual-coding hypothesis. *Journal of Educational Psychology*, 81(4), 484–490.

Mayer, R. E., & Chandler, P. (2001). When learning is just a click away: Does simple user interaction foster deeper understanding of multimedia messages? *Journal of Educational Psychology*, 93, 390–397.

Mayer, R. E., Heiser, J., and Lonn, S. (2001). Cognitive constraints on multimedia learning: When presenting more material results in less understanding. *Journal of Educational Psychology*, 93, 187–198.

Mayer, R. E., Mathias, A., & Wetzell, K. (2002). Fostering understanding of multimedia messages through pre-training: Evidence for a two-stage theory of mental model construction. *Journal of Experimental Psychology: Applied*, 8(3), 147–154.

Mayer, R. E., Mautone, P., & Prothero, W. (2002). Pictorial aids for learning by doing in a multimedia geology simulation game. *Journal of Educational Psychology*, 94(1), 171–185.

Mayer, R. E., & Moreno, R. (1998). A split-attention effect in multimedia learning: Evidence for dual processing systems in working memory. *Journal of Educational Psychology, 90,* 312–320.

Mayer, R. E., & Moreno, R. (2002). Animation as an aid to multimedia learning. *Educational Psychology Review, 14*(1), 87–99.

Michas I. C., & Berry, D. C. (2000). Learning a procedural task: Effectiveness of multimedia presentations. *Applied Cognitive Psychology, 14,* 555–575.

Miller, G. A. (1956). The magical number seven, plus or minus two: Some limits on our capacity for processing information. *Psychological Review, 63,* 81–97.

Moreno, R., & Mayer, R. E. (1999). Cognitive principles of multimedia learning: The role of modality and contiguity. *Journal of Educational Psychology, 91,* 358–368.

Moreno, R., & Mayer, R. E. (2000). A coherence effect in multimedia learning: The case for minimizing irrelevant sounds in he design of multimedia instructional messages. *Journal of Educational Psychology, 92*(1), 117–125.

Moreno, R., & Mayer, R. E. (2002). Learning science in virtual reality multimedia environments: Role of methods and media. *Journal of Educational Psychology, 94*(3), 598–610.

Moreno, R., Mayer, R. E., Spires, H., & Lester, J. (2001). The case for social agency in computer-based teaching: Do students learn more deeply when they interact with animated pedagogical agents? *Cognition and Instruction, 19,* 177–214.

Mousavi, S. Y., Low, R., & Sweller, J. (1995). *Journal of Educational Psychology, 87*(2), 319–334.

Nadolski, R. J., Kirschner, PlA., van Merrienboer, J. G., & Hummel, H. G. K. (2001). A model for optimizing step size of learning tasks in competency-based multimedia practicals. *Educational Technology Research and Development, 49*(3), 87–103.

Powell, W. (2001). Like life? *Training and Development, 56*(2), 32–40.

Roberts, G. (2003). Teaching using the web: Conceptions and approaches from a phenomenographic perspective. *Instructional Science, 31,* 127–150.

Svetcov, D. (2000). The virtual classroom vs. the real one. *Forbes, 166,* 50–54.

Sweller, J., & Cooper, G. A. (1985). The use of worked examples as a substitute for problem solving in learning algebra. *Cognition and Instruction, 2*(1), 59–89.

Sweller, J., van Merriënboer, J. J. G., & Paas, F. G. W. C (1998). Cognitive architecture and instructional design. *Educational Psychology Review, 10*(3), 251–296.

Tindall-Ford, S., Chandler, P., & Sweller, J. (1997). When two sensory modes are better than one. *Journal of Experimental Psychology: Applied, 3*(4), 257–287.

Author Index

Subject Index